NEW TESTAMENT COMMENTARY

NEW TESTAMENT COMMENTARY

By

WILLIAM HENDRIKSEN

Exposition

of the

Gospel According to Luke

BAKER BOOK HOUSE

GRAND RAPIDS, MICHIGAN

Library of Congress Catalog Card Number: 78–58717

ISBN: 0-8010-4191-0

Fifth printing, January 1987

Printed in the United States of America

THIS BOOK IS DEDICATED TO
MY WIFE
RETA

who typed the entire final draft of the manuscript and without whose constant help in ever
so many other ways I could not have written it.

FOREWORD

This book completes my series of Commentaries on the four Gospels. The features to which the readers of my previous commentaries have become accustomed—such as my own translation, repetition of the text before each exegetical unit, summaries, conservative theology, Select and General Bibliographies, references to works and journal articles in several languages, differentiation between you (s.) and y o u (pl.)— are continued in the present volume.

Additional features are the following:

1. Discussion of Critical Theories, begun in N.T.C. on Matthew, pp. 54-76, is continued here, with a description and evaluation of the Redaction Theory. Though something was said about this also in N.T.C. on Mark, the present volume contains a more basic and lengthy discussion and criticism.

2. Separation of the treatment of Greek words, phrases, and constructions from the general explanation of the text. Otherwise, in a commentary of the Gospel by *versatile* Luke some pages would have become crowded with too many notes. The advantages of this change are: (a) the student of Greek, with his Greek New Testament before him, can study a section consecutively; and (b) the reader who is unacquainted with Greek is not bothered by constant intrusions of a language he cannot read.

3. Special Introduction to Luke's Central Section (9:51—18:14), since this part of the evangelist's beautiful book has given rise to doubts and problems.

4. "Practical Lessons" at the close of indicated sections have been added to the other homiletical material included in the explanation. In each case the "Practical Lessons" section is immediately followed by the discussion of "Greek Words, Phrases, and Constructions."

5. Since Luke's Gospel is famous for its many beautiful parables, more so than any other Gospel, two special studies have been added: (a) the suggestion of an easy method of *locating* these parables (pp. 545-549); (b) a study of the principles and methods of *parable interpretation* (pp. 551-555).

6. In answer to several requests a *Subject Index* of the Synoptics will be found on the closing pages.

It is my prayer that the same kind reception will be given to the present volume that was accorded to those that have preceded it.

William Hendriksen

TABLE OF CONTENTS

**Summaries are found at the close of the chapters.
Exception: for 9:51—18:14 see Summary of and
Introduction to Luke's Central Section (9:51—18:14).**

LIST OF MAPS

LIST OF ABBREVIATIONS

The letters in book abbreviations are followed by periods. Those in periodical abbreviations omit the periods and are in italics. Thus one can see at a glance whether the abbreviation refers to a book or to a periodical.

A. *Book Abbreviations*

A.R.V.	American Standard Revised Version
A.V.	Authorized Version (King James)
Gram. N.T.	A. T. Robertson, *Grammar of the Greek New Testament in the Light of Historical Research*
Gram. N.T. (Bl.-Debr.)	F. Blass and A. DeBrunner, *A Greek Grammar of the New Testament and Other Early Christian Literature*
Grk. N.T. (A-B-M-W)	*The Greek New Testament,* edited by Kurt Aland, Matthew Black, Bruce M. Metzger, and Allen Wikgren
I.S.B.E.	*International Standard Bible Encyclopedia*
L.N.T. (Th.)	Thayer's *Greek-English Lexicon of the New Testament*
L.N.T. (A. and G.)	W. F. Arndt and F. W. Gingrich, *A Greek-English Lexicon of the New Testament and Other Early Christian Literature*
M.M.	*The Vocabulary of the Greek New Testament Illustrated from the Papyri and Other Non-Literary Sources,* by James Hope Moulton and George Milligan
N.A.S. (N.T.)	New American Standard Bible (New Testament)
N.B.D.	*The New Bible Dictionary,* edited by J. D. Douglas and others
N.E.B.	New English Bible

N.I.V.	New International Version of The New Testament
N.T.C.	W. Hendriksen, *New Testament Commentary*
R.S.V.	Revised Standard Version
S.BK.	Strack and Billerbeck, *Kommentar zum Neuen Testament aus Talmud und Midrasch*
S.H.E.R.K.	*The New Schaff-Herzog Encyclopedia of Religious Knowledge*
Th.D.N.T.	*Theological Dictionary of the New Testament*, edited by G. Kittel and G. Friedrich, and translated from the German by G. W. Bromiley
W.D.B.	*Westminster Dictionary of the Bible*
W.H.A.B.	*Westminster Historical Atlas to the Bible*

B. *Periodical Abbreviations*

AJT	*American Journal of Theology*
BA	*Biblical Archaeologist*
BibZ	*Biblische Zeitschrift*
BS	*Bibliotheca Sacra*
BW	*Biblical World*
CTM	*Concordia Theological Monthly*
EQ	*Evangelical Quarterly*
ET	*Expository Times*
Eunt	*Euntes Docete*
Exp	*The Expositor*
GTT	*Gereformeerd theologisch tijdschrift*
HJ	*Hibbert Journal*
Interp	*Interpretation; a Journal of Bible and Theology*
JBL	*Journal of Biblical Literature*
JQR	*Jewish Quarterly Review*
JR	*Journal of Religion*
JTS	*Journal of Theological Studies*
MTZ	*Münchener theologische Zeitschrift*
NedTT	*Nederlands theologisch tijdschrift*
NT	*Novum Testamentum; an International Quarterly for New Testament and Related Studies*
NTSt	*New Testament Studies*
RHPR	*Revue d'histoire et de philosophie religieuses*
RIDA	*Revue des Sciences Religieuses*
SBibT	*Studia Biblica et Theologica*
Th	*Theology; a Journal of Historic Christianity*
ThG	*Theologie und Glaube*
ThZ	*Theologische Zeitschrift*
TSK	*Theologische Studien und Kritiken*

TT	*Theologisch tijdschrift*
ZNW	*Zeitschrift für die neutestamentliche Wissenschaft*

Please Note

In order to differentiate between the second person plural (see Luke 12:57: "Why do y o u not judge... ?") and the second person singular (the next verse: "... when you are going"), the letters in "y o u pl." are spaced, those in "you sing." are not.

Introduction

to

The Gospel According to Luke

I. Who Wrote This Gospel?

A. Luke Did.

Though not all agree, the traditional ascription of the Third Gospel to Luke, called by Paul "the beloved physician" (Col. 4:14), has the weight of evidence in its favor.

In Greek his name was *Loukas* (Latin *Lucas*). It may have been an abbreviation of *Loukanos* (Latin *Lucanus*). Abbreviation from *Loukianos* or from *Loukios* (Latin respectively *Lucianus, Lucius*) has also been suggested. Nevertheless, there is no good reason for some to identify the Luke who wrote the Third Gospel with the Lucius of Acts 13:1 or with the one of Rom. 16:21.

Name abbreviations—so that the abbreviation becomes a name in its own right—were, and have remained, popular; e.g., Antipas for Antipatros, Demas for Demetrius; and today: Dave for David, Don for Donald, Ed for Edward or for Edwin, Reta (or Rita) for Margaret, etc.

Now it must be granted at once that absolute proof for the traditional position, namely, that the Luke mentioned in Col. 4:14 was the author of the Third Gospel, is not available. Some even maintain that "There is nothing in the simple mention of the name Luke, or of Luke the physician in the epistles of Paul, to indicate the slightest connection with Luke the Evangelist."[1]

Nevertheless, when one compares the arguments pro and con, it becomes apparent that the negative position is weak, and that a high degree of probability attaches to the traditional view. The arguments in favor of the belief that it was indeed Luke, the beloved physician, who wrote the Third Gospel can be summarized as follows:

1. The name *Luke* occurs only three times in the New Testament (Col. 4:14; II Tim. 4:11; Philem. 24). In Col. 4:14 he is distinguished by Paul from those "of the circumcision" (see verse 11). This is in line with the fact that the language of Luke-Acts appears to be that of an educated Greek. More on this later. See point V A.

2. A comparison of Luke 1:1–4 with Acts 1:1, 2 ("The first account I composed, Theophilus," etc.) clearly indicates that whoever it was that wrote Acts also wrote the Third Gospel. Therefore, once we discover the identity of the author of Acts our problem is solved.

---

1. So, for example, P. C. Sense, *A Critical and Historical Enquiry into the Origin of the Third Gospel*, Oxford, 1901, p. 5. In the much more recent book by F. W. Danker, *Jesus and the New Age*, St. Louis, 1972, pp. xii, xiii, the anonymity of *Luke-Acts* is defended.

3. From the three passages mentioned under point 1 it is clear that Luke was Paul's loyal companion in travel. He was in Rome during both Paul's first Roman imprisonment (Col. 4:14; Philem. 24) and his second (II Tim. 4:11). Each time Paul mentions him by name. From the "we" and "us" sections in *the book of Acts*—more on these in point I B 6—we gather that the author of that book was in the apostle's vicinity during the latter's first Roman imprisonment. Yet the author of Luke-Acts never identifies himself. In Acts he mentions other fellow-laborers and fellow-travelers but never himself. Neither does he mention himself in the Third Gospel. This very fact may well point to Luke as the author, for also in none of the other three Gospels does the author ever identify himself. The Fourth Gospel refers to "the disciple whom Jesus loved" (13:23; 19:26; 20:2; 21:7, 20), without mentioning him by name. Mark (in 14:51, 52) may be referring to himself, but "the young man" remains anonymous. The same holds even with respect to the Gospel According to Matthew, for though the publican's name is mentioned in 9:9; 10:3, he does not call himself the author.

Now it is true that there is also another fellow-worker and (at times) fellow-traveler (of Paul) who is never mentioned by name in the book of Acts, though implied in Acts 15:2; cf. Gal. 2:3. We refer to Titus. See N.T.C. on Galatians, pp. 76–80, and on I and II Timothy and Titus, pp. 36, 37. There are those who, on the basis of II Cor. 8:18; 12:18, have arrived at the conclusion that Titus was Luke's literal brother, and that it is for this reason that the author of Luke-Acts never mentions him by name. However, on this question see the fine discussion by P. E. Hughes in his commentary on *Paul's Second Epistle to the Corinthians (New International)*, Grand Rapids, 1962, pp. 312–316. Even though these Corinthian passages may well refer to *Luke* as "the brother," the theory that *Paul* refers here to a literal blood-brother of Titus lacks proof. On the other hand if, as held by many prominent exegetes, past and present, "the brother"—in *Christ!*—is, nevertheless, Luke, the real point, namely, that *the author of the Third Gospel-Acts* never mentions himself by name, still remains. No completely satisfactory answer has been given to the question why *Titus,* mentioned so frequently by Paul—no less than thirteen times, mostly in II Corinthians—is never mentioned by name in Acts.

There is, however, another reason that points away from Titus to Luke as the author of Luke-Acts:

4. According to Col. 4:14 Luke—not Titus—was a medical doctor. Paul calls him "the beloved physician." W. K. Hobart, in his book, *The Medical Language of St. Luke,* Dublin, 1882 (reprint Grand Rapids, 1954) endeavored to prove that the language used by the author of Luke-Acts is that of a physician. H. J. Cadbury—author (among other works) of *The Style and Literary Method of Luke*—made an attempt to overthrow Hobart's theory. He calls it "an immense fallacy," and tries to show that the style of Luke-Acts is simply that of an educated person, not necessarily that of a physician. It is doubtful, though, whether this challenge has been completely successful.

The balanced view is probably that held by ever so many scholars—including Berkhof, Harnack, Plummer, Ramsay, Robertson, Zahn—and summarized by G. T. Purves in his article on *Luke* (W.D.B., pp. 364–366). His position is as follows: Given the fact that Luke was indeed a physician (Col. 4:14), certain passages in the Third Gospel (and in Acts) coincide with this description. To see this clearly these passages should be compared with their parallels in Matthew and/or Mark:

Accordingly, compare Luke 4:38 with Matt. 8:14 and Mark 1:30 (the nature or degree of Peter's mother-in-law's fever); Luke 5:12 with Matt. 8:2 and Mark 1:40 (leprosy); and Luke 8:43 with Mark 5:26 (the woman and the doctors). Other little touches can easily be added. So, for example, it is Luke alone who states that it was the *right* hand that was withered (6:6, cf. Matt. 12:10; Mark 3:1), *and among the synoptists* it is Luke alone who mentions that it was the *right* ear of the highpriest's servant that was severed (22:50; cf. Matt. 26:51 and Mark 14:47). Also compare Luke 5:18, 24 with Matt. 9:2, 6 and Mark 2:3, 5, 9; and cf. Luke 18:25 with Matt. 19:24 and Mark 10:25. Besides, though it is true that all four Gospels portray Christ as the Sympathetic Physician for soul and body, and in doing so reveal that their authors, too, were men of tender compassion, nowhere is this trait more abundantly evident than in the Third Gospel. See point V D.

5. Among the three Synoptics it is especially the third that breathes the spirit of Paul. Note the following points of resemblance:

a. *Salvation is universal, yet particular.* According to Paul's teaching, salvation, including *justification,* is a gift of God, imparted by his sovereign grace to men regardless of nationality, race, sex, age, or social position. In that sense salvation is *universal.* Nevertheless it is also *particular,* for none but believers inherit it. See Rom. 3:21–24; 10:11–13; II Cor. 5:18–21; Gal. 3:9, 14, 29; Eph. 2:8, 13, 14, 18; Col. 3:11.

Now the Third Gospel, too, stresses this *universalism-particularism.* See 2:30–32; 4:18, 19, 25–27; 6:17–19; 7:19, 22, 23, 36–50; 8:21; 9:48, 60; 10:1, 10–15, 30–37; 13:29; 14:23; 15:7, 10, 11–32; 17:11–19; 19:10; 24:47. It, too, places great emphasis on the necessity of *faith.* Study 1:45; 7:9, 50; 8:25, 48; 12:28; 17:5, 6, 19; 18:8, 42; 20:5; 22:32. And it even speaks of *justification* in the forensic sense; if not in 10:29; 16:15, at least in 18:14.

b. Along with Paul's emphasis on faith goes that on *prayer.* Note, for example, his own beautiful prayer recorded in Eph. 3:14–19, and that rich and oft quoted passage, Phil. 4:6, 7. See also Rom. 1:9; 12:12; 15:30; I Cor. 7:5; Eph. 1:16; Phil. 1:4, 9, 19; Col. 1:3, 9; 4:12; I Thess. 1:2, 3; 5:17, 25; II Thess. 1:11; 3:1; I Tim. 2:8; 4:5; Philem. 4, 22.

Luke, too, more than any other evangelist, stresses prayer. See 1:10, 13; 2:37; 3:21; 5:16; 6:12, 28; 9:28, 29; 10:2; 11:1–13; 18:1–8, 9–14; 19:46; 21:36; 22:32, 40–46.

c. Paul throughout his epistles emphasizes the truth that Jesus Christ is *Lord.* See Rom. 1:4; 10:9; 13:14; I Cor. 1:2; 2:8; 12:3; Gal. 6:14; and especially Phil. 2:11.

Now though in connection with Jesus the designation *Lord (kurios)* is found in all the Synoptics—yes, also in Mark—and Jesus even applies it to himself (Matt. 7:21, 22; 22:45; Mark 11:3), nowhere among the three does it occur as frequently as in the Third Gospel (2:11; 5:8; 6:5, 46; 7:13; 10:1; etc.).

d. The doctrine of the Holy Spirit receives much attention in the epistles of Paul (Rom. 8:1–16, 23, 26, 27; II Cor. 13:14; Gal. 5:16–18, 22; etc.).

This also holds for the Gospel which by tradition has been ascribed to Luke (1:15, 35, 41, 67; 2:25–27; 3:22; 4:1, 14, 18; etc.).

e. It is a well-known fact that although Paul endured many afflictions, including imprisonments (II Cor. 11:23–33), he was a *joyful* believer, filled with praise and gratitude even while a prisoner. In fact, the theme of joy, praise, and thanksgiving sings its way through Philippians, one of the prison epistles.

This same characteristic marks the Third Gospel (1:14, 46–55, 58, 68–79; 2:10, 14, 28; 4:18, 19; 6:23; 10:20, 21; 13:17; 24:52).

f. There is also a striking resemblance between Luke's account of the institution of the Lord's Supper and that of Paul. Cf. Luke 22:19, 20 with I Cor. 11:23–25. Did Luke obtain this report from Paul? Did both make use of the same source?

This remarkable six-item (from points a. to f.) similarity between Paul's epistles and Luke's Gospel—to which a seventh could easily be added; see point V D—confirms the position that it was indeed Luke, Paul's companion in travel, who wrote the Third Gospel.

A word of caution is in order, nevertheless. Though the relation between Paul and Luke was very close, and there are many words and phrases that are peculiar to them, exaggeration should be avoided. The statement of Irenaeus that Luke wrote what Paul preached is too simplistic. And perhaps even farther from the truth is the saying of Athanasius that Luke's Gospel was dictated by Paul.

Though Luke's writings resemble Paul's in several respects, there are also marked differences. By and large one can say that Luke narrates; Paul reasons, exhorts, doxologizes. Paul's personality stands out in his writings much more than does Luke's in his. Moreover, the Third Gospel's historical scene is earlier than is that of Paul's epistles. Besides, the style of deeply emotional, effervescent Paul is characterized by a greater number of breaks in grammatical structure (anacolutha of various kinds) than is Luke's generally more calm manner of writing. Most of all, the Preface to the Third Gospel (1:1–4) clearly shows that its author has gathered his material from many sources, not only from Paul. Therefore, the conclusion must be that in writing their respective Gospels Luke was not nearly as dependent upon Paul as was Mark on Peter.

When all this is taken into consideration, it is safe to reaffirm that the relation between Luke and Paul was close. And the evidence presented in points 1 through 5 adds further weight to *the strong tradition* in support of the belief that it was "the beloved physician," Paul's companion, who wrote Luke-Acts.

But is *the tradition* of the church indeed so consistent and emphatic? This introduces us to the next point.

6. About the year A.D. 400 Jerome wrote: "Luke, a medical man from Antioch, was not ignorant of the Greek language. He was a follower of Paul and a companion in all his travels and he wrote the Gospel" (*De Viris Illustribus* VIII).

A little earlier—that is, at the beginning of the fourth century—Eusebius, the church historian, wrote: "Luke, by race an Antiochian, and a physician by profession, had long been a companion of Paul, and had more than a casual acquaintance with the rest of the apostles. In two God-breathed books, namely, the Gospel and the Acts, he left us examples of the art of soul-healing which he had learned from them" (*Ecclesiastical History* III.iv.6; see also III.xxiv.15).

Before him Origen (fl. 210–250) stated, ". . . and thirdly the Gospel According to Luke [was written]. He wrote for those who from the Gentiles [had come to believe] the gospel that was praised by Paul" (quoted by Eusebius, *op. cit.*, IV.xxv.3–6).

Going back still a little farther, note the statement of Tertullian (fl. 193–216): "Of the apostles, therefore, John and Matthew first instil faith in us, while the apostolic men, Luke and Mark, renew it afterward" (*Against Marcion* IV.ii). Note "apostolic men."

At about the same time Clement of Alexandria (fl. 190–200) writes: ". . . it is written in the Gospel According to Luke, as follows, '. . . Jesus was coming to his baptism, being about thirty years of age.'" The burden of proof rests on those who doubt that this Luke was "the apostolic man" to whom Tertullian refers.

Note also the testimony contained in *The Muratorian Fragment*. This is an incomplete list of New Testament books, written in poor Latin and deriving its name from Cardinal L. A. Muratori (1672–1750), who discovered it in the Ambrosian Library at Milan. It may be assigned to the period 180–200. With respect to the present subject it reads as follows:

"The third book of the gospel [is that] according to Luke. Luke, the well-known physician, wrote it in his own name; according to the [general] belief, after the ascension of Christ, when Paul had associated him [with himself] as one zealous for correctness. Though he had not seen the Lord in the flesh, yet, having ascertained the facts, he was able to begin his narrative with the nativity of John."

This brings us to Irenaeus (fl. about 182–188), in whose writings there are numerous quotations from the Third Gospel. He was a pupil of Polycarp, who had known the apostle John. He writes, "Luke also, the companion of Paul, recorded in a book the gospel preached by him"

(*Against Heresies* III.i.1. See also in the same work III.xiv.1). This testimony, coming from a pupil of a pupil of the apostle John, is important. Moreover, because of his many travels and intimate acquaintance with almost the entire church of his day, what this witness says about the authorship of the Third Gospel must be considered of great significance.

Next, there is the testimony of The Anti-Marcionite Prologue (about 160–180): "Luke, an Antiochian of Syria, a physician by profession, was a disciple of the apostles. At a later date he accompanied Paul, until the latter's martyrdom. He served the Lord blamelessly. Having neither wife nor children, at the age of eighty-four he fell asleep in Boeotia, full of the Holy Spirit. While there were already Gospels in existence—that according to Matthew written in Judea and that according to Mark in Italy—Luke, under the impulse of the Holy Spirit, composed his entire Gospel in the region of Achaia. In his prologue he makes very clear the fact that other Gospels had been written before his, and that it was necessary to present to believers converted from the Gentile world an accurate account of the plan ('economy') of salvation, so that these people would not be led astray by Jewish fables, nor be deceived by heretical and futile fancies, and thus wander away from the truth. And so right at the beginning he relates for us the nativity of John, a most essential matter, for John is the beginning of the gospel. He was the Lord's forerunner and companion both in the preparation of the gospel and in the administration of baptism and the fellowship of the Spirit. This ministry [of John] had been mentioned by one of the Twelve Prophets [Malachi]. And afterward this same Luke wrote the Acts of the Apostles."

But we can go back even farther than this, for probably as early as A.D. 125 the four Gospels were assembled into a collection for use in the churches and were given titles. "According to Luke" was the title of—or superscription above—the longest of the four. That this "Luke" was someone other than the companion of Paul would have to be proved by those who affirm it.

This still leaves over half a century—from the moment when the Third Gospel was completed until A.D. 125—for which there is no written evidence naming Luke as the author. However, this is not strange. Why not? First, travel and communication were much slower then than they are today. Secondly, the Third Gospel and the Acts were, after all, in the first instance *private documents,* sent by *one* person, the composer, to *one* other person, Theophilus (Luke 1:3; Acts 1:1). And thirdly, even when these books finally began to be copied, circulated, and quoted—for example, in the writings of the apostolic fathers—these very early witnesses were not in the habit of mentioning the names of the authors whose works they quoted, probably deeming this to be unnecessary, since their authors were then still well known. For these several reasons this very early silence is not a sound basis for the contention that Luke, "the beloved physician" and Paul's companion in travel, did not write the Third Gospel and the book of Acts. As has been shown, the cumulative evidence in favor of Luke's authorship is as strong as anyone can reasonably expect it to be.[2]

B. *Who, Then, Was Luke? He Was:*

1. *A man from Antioch in Syria, with close ties—later residence perhaps?—in Philippi.*

His interest in Antioch is clear from the many references to that city (Acts 11:19-27; 13:1-3; 14:26; 15:22, 35; 18:22). And as to Philippi, if it became his "adopted" city, the manner in which he speaks of it in Acts 16:12 becomes easy to understand. Besides, as will be shown, Philippi was the place where Luke remained when Paul traveled on, and the place where Paul picked him up again.

2. *A convert from the Gentile world, probably a Greek.*

Though there are those who deny it, yet the most reasonable interpretation of Col. 4:14—contrast 4:10, 11, and on both see N.T.C. on Colossians, pp. 186-193—is that Luke was not a Jew. We have no means of knowing when his conversion to the Christian religion took place (but see Acts

---

2. Up to the time when Rationalism started to assail the books of the Bible, the view that it was Luke, "the beloved physician" and companion of the apostle Paul, who wrote the Third Gospel, was generally accepted. F. C. Baur and the Tübingen school maintained that the Gospel of Marcion, whom Polycarp, if we can rely upon the testimony of Irenaeus, addressed as "the first-born of Satan," and who began to teach at Rome about the year A.D. 140, was the original of our Third Gospel. When the influence of the Tübingen school started to decline, the opinion began to prevail that Marcion's Gospel, the only one he recognized, is a mutilation of Luke's. Accordingly, there was a return to the traditional view regarding the authorship of the Third Gospel.

In recent years, however, there has been a renewed attack upon this view. Leaders in this attack are the men who belong to the so-called Bultmann school, and in particular also P. Vielhauer. Their contention is that the author of Luke-Acts could not have been "Luke, the beloved physician," a close friend and companion of the apostle Paul, for between the epistles of Paul, on the one hand, and Luke-Acts there is a radical difference in theology; for example:

1. According to Acts the Gentiles in their ignorance are still worshiping God (17:23). They even live in him (17:25). According to Paul, however, "knowing God, they do not glorify him" (Rom. 1:21).

Answer: Luke-Acts does not place the unconverted Gentiles any closer to God than does Paul, for also according to Luke-Acts their ignorance is something for which they themselves are responsible and for which forgiveness is necessary (Luke 23:34). See also Dan. 5:23b. Such ignorance amounts to an unwillingness to acknowledge God as God.

2. Paul taught freedom from the law, and accordingly opposed circumcision (Gal. 5:1, 2). Luke-Acts reveals no such attitude; rather the opposite; see Acts 16:3; 21:17-26.

Answer: During the period of transition Paul was not opposed to circumcision for the Jews. He insisted, however, that circumcision never be regarded as a condition of salvation, and that circumcision should not be required of the Gentiles who turn to the Lord—a stand also endorsed by the Jerusalem Synod (Acts 15:19, 24-29).

3. Paul's emphasis on the doctrine of the cross (Gal. 6:14) is missing in Luke-Acts.

Answer: Not so; see Luke 22:19, 20; Acts 20:28.

At the conclusion of his valuable discussion of the modern attack on the traditional view regarding the authorship of Luke-Acts E. E. Ellis affirms that, with the exception of the major Pauline letters, the authorship of no section of the New Testament is as well supported as that of Luke-Acts by Luke the physician and Paul's companion. See Ellis' book, *The Gospel of Luke (The Century Bible)*, London and Edinburgh, 1966, pp. 40-52.

9

11:19–24), nor do we know whether or not before he became a Christian he had first been a proselyte to the Jewish faith.

According to the voice of tradition Luke was a Greek. The accuracy, breadth, and beauty of his Greek style—see point V A—are in line with this belief.

A. T. Robertson, in his book *Luke the Historian in the Light of Research*, New York, 1923, p. 18, uses, as another argument to prove that Luke was a Greek, the fact that the writer of Acts calls the inhabitants of Malta "barbarians" (Acts 28:2, 4). But even though the term *barbarians* can mean "non-Greeks"—whether by reason of descent or culture or both (cf. Rom. 1:14)—does this necessarily mean that the one who so describes them must be a Greek? Note the wide connotation given to the term *barbarian* in I Cor. 14:11.

On p. 21 of the same book Robertson uses still another argument to show that Luke must have been a Greek. His reasoning implies the syllogism:

a. Titus was a Greek (Gal. 2:3).

b. Luke was a *brother* of Titus (II Cor. 8:18; 12:18).

c. Therefore, Luke, too, must have been a Greek.

But it has already been indicated that this interpretation of the word *brother* in the Corinthians passages is not the only possible one, and perhaps not even the best.

Many fanciful tales have been concocted around Luke, a person about whom we really know very little. For example, it has been surmised that Luke had been a slave of Theophilus. The latter, recognizing the slave's extraordinary brightness and goodness of heart, set him free. He even enrolled Luke in the famous medical school that was part of the University of Tarsus. At this university Luke met "Saul of Tarsus." The two became and ever afterward remained close friends. Saul's—that is, Paul's—conversion led to Luke's conversion. Luke, in turn, stirred up the interest of Theophilus in the Christian religion. Etc., etc. R. Lloyd has even written a very interesting book bearing the title *The Private Letters of Luke*, New York, 1958.

But all this aside, the best cumulative evidence for the belief that Luke was probably a Greek could still be: Col. 4:10, 11, 14; the Greek of the Preface (Luke 1:1–4); and the voice of tradition.

3. *A medical doctor.*

This point has already been made clear. We are not carrying our imagination too far when we theorize that as such Luke must have been a real help to Paul in all his afflictions, some of them physical.

Did Luke practice his healing art on the island of Malta? There are those who defend this theory, on the basis of the following: (a) he was definitely in Paul's company when the shipwrecked passengers, etc., came ashore on that island (in Acts 28 note "us" in verses 2, 7, 10, and "we" in verses 10, 11); (b) he was a physician (Col. 4:14); and (c) he shared in the honors bestowed

10

by those who had been cured of their illnesses (note "who honored *us*"). Though this possibility must be granted, the fact that not Luke but Paul is said to have placed his hands on the father of Publius and to have been instrumental in healing him must not be overlooked. But it is safe, nevertheless, to affirm that whenever Luke was able to make use of his medical skill he did so gladly and without showing any partiality.

We should never forget, however, that Luke was a physician not only for the body but also for the soul. He, as well as Paul, was "a preacher," a "proclaimer of the way of salvation," Paul's "fellow-worker." See Acts 16:10, 13, 17; Philem. 24. Accordingly, Luke was an "evangelist" in a twofold sense: (a) he wrote a Gospel (an "evangel"); and (b) he preached the gospel. "Preached it," but even more: showed its force in his own life. It is not strange that Paul called him "the beloved physician."

Accordingly, Luke was actually

A medical missionary.

As such he was the forerunner of all the medical missionaries whereby the church and mankind have since been abundantly enriched!

4. *A kind and sympathetic person.* It is not without reason that Paul and Luke were warm friends. Their hearts were drawn together by the spirit of active, sympathetic benevolence. It is not strange, therefore, that Luke's Gospel abounds with stories which reveal Christ's kindness toward the less privileged. See under Point V D.

5. *A painter?*

A very old legend so describes him. For more on this legend see A. Plummer, *The Gospel According to St. Luke (The International Critical Commentary),* New York, 1910, pp. xxi, xxii. Whether or not it is based on fact can no longer be determined. Fanciful deductions should be avoided. Roger Van der Weyden (1400–1464) portrayed "St. Luke Painting the Virgin," the latter holding the babe Jesus!

It is true that in his books (both Gospel and Acts) Luke pictures scenes so vividly that artists have used many of his themes. The chart below, although incomplete, lists various artists who have depicted passages from Luke.

6. *Paul's travel companion.* It is not true that Luke accompanied Paul "in all his travels." At times he is with the apostle; at other times he is not. In describing Paul's journeys Luke frequently uses the pronoun *he* with reference to the apostle. At times, however, without any change in the style of the account[3] there is a transition from "he" to "we" and from "him" to "us."

---

3. This very fact—the continuation, in abundant supply, of Lucan language characteristics in the "we" sections—was one of the chief factors in changing Harnack from an opponent into an advocate of the traditional position regarding the authorship of the Third Gospel. See his books: *Luke the Physician,* 1906 (Engl. tr. 1907); *The Acts of the Apostles,* 1908 (Engl. tr. 1909); and especially *The Date of the Acts and of the Synoptics,* 1911. See also N. B. Stonehouse, *The Witness of Luke to Christ,* Grand Rapids, 1951, p. 15.

Art and the Gospel of Luke

Artist	Subject	Passage in Luke
Hacker, Van Eyck, and Van der Weyden	The Annunciation	1:26–38
Rossetti	"Ecce Ancilla Domini"	1:38
Merson	The Arrival at Bethlehem	2:1–7
Plockhorst	Tidings of Great Joy	2:8–14
Lerolle	The Arrival of the Shepherds	2:15–17
Van der Goes	The Adoration of the Shepherds	2:15–17
Memling, Van der Weyden, Meire, Rubens, Rembrandt	The Presentation in the Temple	2:22–38
Clementz	The Boy Christ in the Temple	2:41–51
Von Gebhardt	Jesus and the Doctors	2:41–51
Seegar	"Mary Has Chosen the Better Part"	10:42
Plockhorst	The Good Shepherd	15:1–7 (cf. Matt. 18:12–14; John 10:11, 14)
Soord	The Lost Sheep	as above: 15:1–7, etc.
Burnand	Der Verlorene Sohn	15:11–32
Rembrandt	The Return of the Prodigal Son	15:17–24
Girardet	The Walk to Emmaus	24:13–29
Eichstaedt and Rembrandt	The Supper at Emmaus	24:30, 31
Biermann	The Ascension	24:50–53 (cf. Acts 1:6–11)
Mastroianni (sculptor)	The Ascending Christ	also 24:50–53, etc.

According to what is probably the best Greek text the first "we" section describes events that take place during Paul's second missionary journey (Acts 15:36—18:22). The date for the entire journey is probably A.D. 50/51-53/54. The first "we" section is Acts 16:10–17, which relates certain happenings that occur during the *outward-bound* part of that trip. We are told that Luke joins Paul at Troas. It is here that the apostle in a vision receives a call from a Macedonian, "Come over and help us." Paul heeds this call, being convinced that God is ordering him to do so. Therefore after crossing the sea into Europe the missionaries—Paul, Silas, Timothy, and Luke—perform their spiritual labors in Philippi. Here the nucleus of a most—perhaps *the* most—loyal and generous church (of that day) is formed. It very quickly becomes Paul's "joy and crown," as he describes it several years later. See Phil. 4:1, 15, 16. Here Lydia is converted, and so is the jailer. Any church that can count such people, including also Luke, among its members, and is willing to follow their example, is certainly blessed!

It would seem that when the rest of the missionaries depart from Philippi (Acts 16:40), Luke remains there. At Philippi, considerably later, he rejoins Paul (20:6). This was during the latter's third missionary journey (Acts 18:23—21:16). The date for that entire journey is probably A.D. 53/54-57/58. Included in it there is one "we" section: 20:5-15 (or: 20:6-16), and the beginning of another: 21:1-16.

It is during the *homeward* stretch of this journey that Luke is again seen in the company of Paul. On their way to Jerusalem Paul and his companions call on the church at Troas. It is here that Luke attends a worship service which goes on and on and on. When Paul "prolongs his speech until midnight," a young man named Eutychus, by this time sound asleep, falls to the ground from a third-story window and is picked up dead. By Paul he is miraculously restored to life. In view of this "revival" is it possible that even the most strict and wholehearted believer in the doctrine of divine providence—and we all should be such believers—with its implication that, strictly speaking, nothing ever happens "by chance," could ever forget this young man's name, *Eutychus* (that is, *Fortunate, Lucky*)?

The next stop is Miletus, located on the western shore of Asia Minor, south of Ephesus. It is here that the emotion-filled meeting with the elders of the Ephesian church takes place. Although the "we" section (20:5-15, or 20:6-16, if one prefers) does not include the account of this "Farewell" gathering, the graphic manner in which what takes place here is described (see verses 17-38) probably indicates that Luke himself is present; that is, that he, too, is among those who at the close of the meeting kneel down and pray.

In any event when chapter 21 opens—and with it the second "we" section pertaining to Paul's *third* missionary journey (the third "we" section in all)—Luke is again, or is "still," with Paul. The company spends seven days at Tyre. After another touching "Farewell" (21:5), the party boards the ship and, after a brief stop at Ptolemais, spends some time at Caesarea. Luke is present when Agabus in a symbolic manner predicts Paul's imminent loss of liberty. The beloved physician is among those who accompany the apostle to Jerusalem. And with the arrival in that city, the third missionary journey, and also the "we" section *as far as it belongs to that journey*, end.

The next stage in the story deals with Paul's experiences in Jerusalem and Caesarea (Acts 21:17—26:32). A better way of putting this would be to say that what is here offered represents another stage in the work which Christ, from his exalted throne in heaven, is doing through the labors of Paul and those associated with him. See the phraseology used in Acts 1:1. It is Jesus himself who, through the agency of human beings, is "doing" and "teaching."

That the "we" section begun in 21:1-16 overflows into this new section is clear from the use of "we"—"us"—"us" in 21:17, 18. Moreover, the thought connection between these "we" passages and that which immediately follows in verses 19 ff. is so close that, in spite of the further absence of these pronouns until chapter 27 is reached, many authorities include most or all of chapter 21 in one "we" section. If this conclusion is correct, as it well may be, Luke is a witness of the events that transpire in Jerusalem: the conference with James, the inflammatory troubles experienced by Paul when he is manhandled in the temple, and his rescue from the mob and formal arrest by the military tribune.

Acts 22 reports Paul's address to the people from the stairs of the fortress of Antonia; chapter 23, the apostle's defense before the Sanhedrin. A plot of the Jews to kill Paul is frustrated by his nephew. Under strong guard Paul is sent to Caesarea where Felix, the procurator, has his residence. Hearings before Felix accomplish nothing, and Paul is left in prison in Caesarea until Festus succeeds Felix (Acts 24). Then, in order that he may not be taken to Jerusalem for trial Paul, making use of his right as a Roman citizen, appeals to Caesar (Acts 25:11). Accordingly, after a hearing before Herod Agrippa II, Festus also being present (Acts 26), Paul sails for Rome (Acts 27).

Where is Luke during Paul's Caesarean imprisonment? We hear nothing about him. Is it possible that during these two years he was doing research work? Was he gathering materials for his Gospel?

What we definitely know is that when the apostle, as a prisoner, starts out for Rome, Luke is at his side. We know this because another "we" section, the final one, starts at 27:1.

Throughout the voyage to Rome, on all the three ships (27:2; 27:6; 28:11) Luke is with Paul. The pronouns *we* and *us* are interspersed liberally all the way from Acts 27:1 to 28:16. As some writers see it 28:16 marks the end of this final "we" section. In a sense they are correct. But in view of the fact that (a) the rest of chapter 28 is closely connected in material content with that which immediately precedes, and (b) Paul himself informs us that Luke is with him as a highly appreciated fellow-worker and friend (Col. 4:14; Philem. 24), other interpreters include all of chapter 28 in this final "we" section.

In Rome "the beloved physician" must have visited the prisoner very regularly and must have helped him in many ways. That such visits were possible is clear from 28:30.

Intelligence, wisdom, skill, warmth of heart and mind, loyalty to Christ, to his cause, and to his followers, including especially Paul, such were the qualities that made Luke unforgettable.

As was indicated earlier, Luke—he *alone*—was with Paul also during the latter's second Roman imprisonment, the one that led to death.

"Having neither wife nor children, at the age of eighty-four Luke fell asleep in Boeotia." So, as we have seen, reads The Anti-Marcionite Prologue.

7. *The Author of the Third Gospel.*

This has been established.

II. Why Did He Write It?

Luke's purpose is clearly stated in 1:4, and receives further amplification from the very contents of his book. That purpose may be viewed as having been threefold:

A. *Immediate purpose:* To place in the hands of a person highly regarded by the writer, namely, Theophilus—meaning "loved by God"—an accurate account of the matters touching Jesus, matters in which the addressee had already received some instruction, and to do this in the interest of that person's spiritual well-being.

It is clear that the evangelist is a friend of the person whom he addresses, and regards him highly. Was Theophilus even now a believer in the Lord Jesus Christ? If so, Luke writes in order to strengthen that faith. On the other hand, has the addressee advanced no farther than being a deeply interested enquirer? If so, Luke writes in order to bring him to a decision, so that with heart, mind, and will he may surrender himself to Christ as his Lord and Savior. One thing seems certain: Theophilus, assailed from every direction by stories, rumors, and counter-rumors regarding Jesus (see Acts 28:22b), needs a fully reliable and systematically organized report with respect to the events centering in Jesus. For more on Theophilus see the explanation of Luke 1:1–4.

The idea has been suggested that Luke's Gospel is *a defense brief* or *apologia,* and that the evangelist as it were "dedicated" it to Theophilus in order to prove to him that in no respect was there any conflict between the Christian religion and the interests of Rome.

There may be an element of truth in this. Did not Josephus dedicate some of his writings to a certain Epaphroditus?

Some venture out farther, and suggest that the Third Gospel and Acts were written with the purpose of securing *Paul's* acquittal and release.[4]

Now it can be readily admitted that defense of the Christian religion against attack and misrepresentation, whether by Jew or Gentile, was in-

---

4. See, for example, H. Sahlin, *Der Messias und das Gottesvolk,* Uppsala, 1945, pp. 34 ff.

cluded in Luke's purpose. This may well be implied in the chronological note (3:1, 2), the genealogy of Jesus (3:23-38), the record of Pilate's repeated affirmation of Jesus' innocence (23:4, 14, 15, 22), the report of the centurion's testimony (23:47), etc. It is also true that whatever may have been Luke's purpose in writing Acts, the second part of that book (chapters 13-28; especially 15:36—28:31) loudly proclaims the greatness of God as revealed in the labors of Paul, a man who was proud of his *Roman citizenship* (Acts 22:28) and humbly thankful for his citizenship in the kingdom of heaven (Phil. 3:20). Nevertheless, when the evangelist himself states his purpose in writing the Gospel (Luke 1:4), he mentions none of these things. To the extent in which they are present, they remain in the background. Moreover, undue emphasis on the idea that Gospel-Acts was intended to be *an apologia in behalf of Paul* fails to answer the question why, if this be true, so much material irrelevant to the attainment of that particular goal was included.

Basing our answer, first of all, on Luke 1:1-4, it becomes clear that Luke's primary or *immediate* concern was *the spiritual well-being of Theophilus*, in the sense already indicated.

B. *Intermediate purpose:* To enlighten earnest enquirers and to strengthen the faith of believers, especially those who had been or were being gathered from the Greek-speaking Roman world, the converts from heathendom. Origen held that Luke's Gospel was composed "for the sake of Gentile converts."

Luke must have regarded Theophilus as a representative of that large company of contemporaries who either had already become committed to Christ or were seriously considering doing so. Both earnest enquirers and beginning believers were included in his purview.

There must have been many people who had recently entered the church, as well as many who were preparing themselves for this step. Such people, like Theophilus, needed further instruction in the story of redemption, and in Christian doctrine and ethics.

Even while Jesus was still on earth there were people who, when they came face to face with Jesus, when they saw his deeds and heard his words, were "astonished." Yes, astonished, but not fully assured; surprised, but not fully surrendered. There were those—at times including Christ's immediate followers—who asked questions (Luke 5:33-39; 7:19-23) and made suggestions, sometimes foolish and sinful (9:12, 13, 51-56). They revealed their ignorance (9:45, 49, 50), and were guilty of distorted evaluations (10:17-20). And, of course, to a certain extent these conditions continued even after Christ's resurrection. See Acts 1:6; 13:15; 18:24-26; 19:1-5. The Third Gospel was written for the sake of correcting the erroneous views of enquirers and strengthening the faith of believers, perhaps especially of those recently brought to Christ.

C. *Ultimate purpose:* To reach *all* the nations—including even the Samaritans—for the Triune God as revealed in Christ. See Luke 2:32; 3:6; 4:25-27; 9:51-56; 10:25-37; 17:11-19; 24:47.

III. What Were His Sources?[5]

A. *Material Contents of Luke's Gospel in Relation to the Other Gospels*

1. *New or "L" Material*

Having studied Mark's Gospel and Matthew's, and proceeding from there to a study of the Gospel According to Luke, we are immediately struck by the latter's unique character. Mark, it will be recalled, begins with a paragraph introducing The Ministry of John the Baptist (1:1–8). This is followed by one on The Baptism of Jesus (1:9–11). And that, in turn, by one on The Temptation of Jesus in the Wilderness (1:12, 13). With variations all this material is also found in Matthew and Luke (even to some extent in John); however, it is not found at the very beginning of those books. Nevertheless, Matthew, after only 48 verses (chapters 1 and 2) of material which to a large extent is peculiar to that Gospel, falls in line with Mark and describes The Ministry of John the Baptist.

But Luke introduces us into a new universe. To be sure, there is nothing that clashes with Mark and Matthew. Nevertheless, beginning at 1:1 and continuing through 2:52 the new (or at least mainly new) material covers 132 verses, that is, the entire first chapter—one of the longest in Scripture, 80 verses!—plus the entire second chapter, 52 verses. In fact, even chapter 3—minus verses 3, 4, 7–9, 16, 17, 21, 22—should be added, making in all 161 verses of new *or largely* new material (from 1:1 through 3:38, with the exceptions already indicated). This amounts to almost one-seventh of the total contents of Luke's Gospel.[6] And this is only the beginning of all that is new in Luke.

---

5. Among the many articles and works consulted on this subject were the following:

Barrett, C. K., *Luke the Historian in Recent Study*, London, 1961.

Bavinck, H., *Gereformeerde Dogmatiek*, four volumes, 3rd edition, Kampen, 1918, especially Vol. I, pp. 406–476.

Ellis, E. E., *op. cit.*, pp. 21–30.

Geldenhuys, N., *Commentary on the Gospel of Luke*, Grand Rapids, 1951, pp. 23–29.

Greijdanus, S., *Het Heilig Evangelie naar de Beschrijving van Lucas (Kommentaar op het Nieuwe Testament)*, two volumes, Amsterdam, 1940, 1941; especially Vol. II, pp. 1223–1230.

Harnack, A., *Luke the Physician*, 1906 (Engl. tr. 1907).

———, *Sayings of Jesus*, London, 1908.

Harrington, W. J., *The Gospel According to St. Luke*, London, 1968, pp. 8–14.

Hawkins, J. C., *Horae Synopticae*, Oxford, 1911, pp. 107–113.

Manson, W., *The Gospel of Luke*, London, 1948, pp. xiii–xx; 19–21.

Morgenthaler, R., *Die Lukanische Geschichtsschreibung als Zeugnis*, two volumes, Zürich, 1949.

Plummer, A., *op. cit.*, pp. xxiii–xxviii.

Robertson, A. T., "Luke, the Gospel of," I.S.B.E., Vol. III, pp. 1938–1940.

———, *Word Pictures in the New Testament*, Vol. II, Nashville, 1930.

———, *Luke the Historian in the Light of Research*, pp. 61–75.

Stonehouse, N. B., *The Witness of Luke to Christ*, pp. 22, 23.

Taylor, V., *Behind the Third Gospel*, Oxford, 1926.

———, *The First Draft of St. Luke's Gospel*, London, 1927.

Weiss, C. P. B., *Die Quellen des Lukas-Evangeliums*, Stuttgart, 1907.

6. The genealogy of Jesus, as presented by Luke, must be included in the "new" material, for although Matt. 1:1–17 also contains a genealogy of our Lord, the two, though not in conflict, are not truly parallel.

The following list shows where this *new* or "L" (for Luke) material can be found. However, the indicated references do not imply that within the listed passage everything is new. It may be, but need not be. The letter *m* following a reference means that although the passage is peculiar to Luke in a degree sufficient to be included in the list, it is of a *m*ixed character. Some of its content is not peculiar to Luke. That part may be non-Marcan Matthew-Luke material (e.g., Luke 3:1–20 in part) or may even be reflected in both of the other Synoptics, as is frequently true. Parallels in Mark 16:9–20 have not been included, since, as has been demonstrated in N.T.C. on Mark, there is no solid evidence to show that Mark's "long ending" is part of Scripture. Also, in this Commentary no parallel is listed in connection with Luke 3:23–38. Reason? See footnote 6. And no parallel is here suggested in connection with Luke 14:15–24, for Luke's parable of The Rejected (or Slighted) Invitation must not be confused with that of The Royal Marriage (Matt. 22:1–14). Similarly, Luke 19:11–27 (parable of The Pounds) has no real parallel, for the parable found in Matt. 25:14–30 is that of The Talents, which is indeed "a different story."

There are several passages not here listed which contain words, phrases, and sometimes entire clauses that are peculiar to Luke. See, for example, N.T.C. on Matthew, pp. 18, 19. The references given in the following "L" list are intended only to serve as an aid to the understanding of the general situation in connection with the contents of Luke as compared with the other Synoptics.

New Material in Luke

Reference	Subject Matter
1:1–4	Preface or Prologue
1:5–25	Promise of the Baptist's Birth
1:26–38	The *Annunciation* (Promise to Mary regarding the Savior's Birth)
1:39–45	Mary's Visit to Elizabeth
1:46–56	The *Magnificat* (Mary's Song of Praise)
1:57–66	The Birth of John the Baptist
1:67–80	The *Benedictus* (Zechariah's Prophecy)
2:1–7[m]	The *Birth* of Jesus
2:8–21	The Announcement to Shepherds of the Savior's Birth "Glory to God in the Highest" The Visit of the Shepherds The *Naming* of Jesus
2:22–38	The *Presentation* of Jesus in the Temple Simeon's *Nunc Dimittis* Anna's Thanksgiving

(continued)

New Material in Luke (continued)

Reference	Subject Matter
2:39, 40	The Return to Nazareth
2:41–52	The Boy Jesus in the Temple
3:1–20ᵐ	The Ministry of John the Baptist
3:23–38	The Genealogy of Jesus
4:14, 15ᵐ	The Beginning of The Great Galilean Ministry
4:16–30ᵐ	The Rejection of Jesus at Nazareth
5:1–11ᵐ	A Miraculous Catch
7:11–17	The Raising of the Widow's Son at Nain
7:36–50	Jesus Anointed by a Sinful Woman Cancellation: The Parable of The Two Debtors
8:1–3	Ministering Women
9:51–56	A Samaritan Village Refuses to Welcome Jesus
10:1–12	The Charge to The Seventy (or Seventy-two)
10:17–20	The Return of the Seventy (or Seventy-two)
10:25–37	The Parable of The Samaritan Who Cared
10:38–42	Mary of Bethany Makes the Right Choice
11:1–4ᵐ	"Teach Us to Pray" The Lord's Prayer
11:5–13	The Parable of The Troubled (or Embarrassed) Host
11:27, 28	True Blessedness
11:37–54ᵐ	Jesus Invited to Eat at a Pharisee's Home Pharisees and Law-Experts Denounced
12:13–21	The Parable of The Rich Fool
12:32–34ᵐ	"Do Not Fear" "Sell Y o u r Possessions and Give Alms"
12:35–40ᵐ	The Parable of The Watchful Servants
12:49, 50ᵐ	Fire and Baptism
13:1–5	Be Converted or Perish
13:6–9	The Parable of The Barren Fig Tree and The Magnanimous Vineyard-Keeper
13:10–17	The Healing of a Crippled Woman on the Sabbath

(*continued*)

New Material in Luke (continued)

Reference	Subject Matter
13:22-30	The Narrow Door
13:31-33	The Departure from Galilee
14:1-6ᵐ	The Healing of the Man Afflicted with Dropsy
14:7-14	A Lesson for Guests: The Parable of The Reserved Seats, and a Lesson for the Host
14:15-24	The Parable of The Rejected Invitation
14:25-33	The Cost of Discipleship The Parable of The Rash Builder The Parable of The Reasonable King
15:1-7ᵐ	The Parable of The Lost Sheep
15:8-10	The Parable of The Lost Coin
15:11-32	The Parable of The Lost Son
16:1-13	The Parable of The Shrewd Manager
16:14, 15	Pharisaic Self-righteousness Rebuked
16:19-31	The Parable of The Show-off (A Rich Man) and The Beggar (Lazarus)
17:5, 6ᵐ	"Increase Our Faith"
17:7-10	The Parable of the Coldly Calculating (or Unprofitable) Servant
17:11-19	The Cleansing of Ten Lepers, Only One of Whom Returned to Give Thanks
17:20-37ᵐ	The Coming of The Kingdom
18:1-8	The Parable of The Widow Who Persevered
18:9-14	The Parable of The Pharisee and The Tax-Collector
19:1-10	Jesus and Zacchaeus
19:11-27	The Parable of The Pounds
19:39, 40	"If These Were Silent, the Very Stones Would Cry Out"
19:41-44	"When He Saw the City He Wept Over It"
21:20-24ᵐ	Prediction of Jerusalem's Destruction
21:25-28ᵐ	The Coming of The Son of Man
21:34-36	Watch and Pray, with a View to The Son of Man's Return
21:37, 38	Summary of Jesus' Final Teaching in the Temple
22:3-6ᵐ	Satan Enters the Heart of Judas
22:14-23ᵐ	The Institution of The Lord's Supper

(continued)

New Material in Luke (continued)

Reference	Subject Matter
22:24-30	The Dispute About Greatness
22:31-34^m	Christ's Prayer for Peter
22:35-38	"Did Y o u Lack Anything?"
22:39-46^m	Jesus on the Mount of Olives
22:47-53^m	The Betrayal and Arrest An Ear Severed and Restored "This is Y o u r Hour"
22:54-62^m	Peter's Denial of Jesus
22:63-65^m	The Mocking and Beating of Jesus
22:66-71^m	Jesus Condemned by the Sanhedrin
23:1-5^m	Jesus Before Pilate
23:6-12	Jesus Before Herod
23:13-25^m	Jesus Sentenced to Die
23:26-43^m	Simon of Cyrene Jerusalem's Weeping Daughters Jesus Crucified Between Two Criminals The First Two Words from the Cross
23:44-49^m	The Death of Jesus
23:50-56^m	The Burial of Jesus
24:1-12^m	The Resurrection of Jesus
24:13-35	Christ's Appearance to the Men from Emmaus
24:36-49^m	Christ's Appearance to the Disciples
24:50-53	Christ's Ascension

2. Material Found Also in Mark

Nevertheless, not nearly everything in Luke is "new" or even "mainly new." A considerable portion of Luke's Gospel reminds one of Mark. This introduces us to the Synoptic Problem. Since this subject has already been treated in some detail,[7] only a reference to it will be necessary now.

For the purpose of *the study of sources* Luke's Gospel may be divided into the following three Parts or Sections:[8]

---

7. See N.T.C. on Matthew, pp. 6-54.
8. Note capital "S" to distinguish this from the smaller sections (small "s"), such as 1:1-4; 1:5-25, etc.

Divisions in the Gospel of Luke

Section I	Luke 1:1–9:50	about 8⅚ chapters, 58 sections
Section II	Luke 9:51–18:14	about 8⅜ chapters, 46 sections
Section III	Luke 18:15–24:53	about 6⅙ chapters, 42 sections
Entire Third Gospel		24 chapters, 146 sections

In Section I, 34 of the 58 sections are paralleled, to a greater or lesser extent, in Mark, as is shown in this Commentary in connection with the captions above each of these small sections.

In Section II—Luke's very interesting Central Part; for more on it see pp. 556–821—only 6 (or at most 8) of the 46 sections are similarly paralleled in Mark.

In Section III, 33 of the 42 sections are paralleled in Mark; sometimes generously, often sparingly. In the Passion account Luke retains only 27 percent of Mark's words, and at times (as elsewhere) departs from Mark's sequence in recording events.[9]

All in all one-half of Luke's small sections are, to some extent, paralleled in Mark. But since in many cases the parallel is only partial, it remains true that fully two-thirds of Luke's Gospel contains no Marcan material.

In almost every case in which Luke's Gospel is reflected in Mark it also has a parallel in Matthew. Exceptions: Luke 4:31–37; 4:42–44; 9:49, 50; 21:1–4.

3. "Q" Material

So far we have considered (a) material peculiar to Luke, and (b) Lucan material that is found also in Mark, at least to some extent. The words *is found also* do not mean "in that exact form." Each evangelist has his own style.

There is a third group of individual *passages* and at times *sections* (as a whole or in part): those that are found in Matthew and in Luke but not in Mark. Such material is indicated by the symbol *Q*, on which see N.T.C. on Matthew, pp. 21, 35, 47–49 (including footnote 50). To a large extent this "Q" indicates a *sayings* source.

Sometimes the resemblance between the passage in Matthew and its echo in Luke is so close that the two remind us of identical twins. A few examples from among many are here listed. Since this is a commentary on Luke, the right-hand (Luke) column is basic. That Gospel's sequence is followed. Matthew's column is placed on the left because that Gospel was in all probability composed before Luke.

9. See G. B. Caird, *Saint Luke (Pelican Gospel Commentaries)*, 1963, p. 25.

INTRODUCTION TO THE GOSPEL

Examples of Close Resemblances Between Matthew and Luke

Matthew	*The Passage Briefly Introduced*	Luke
3:7–10	Y o u offspring of vipers	3:7–9
12:43–45	Swept clean and put in order	11:24–26
24:45–51	Who is the faithful servant?	12:42–46
23:37, 38	Jerusalem, Jerusalem!	13:34, 35
6:24	No one can serve two masters	16:13

Note the difference in sequence between Matthew and Luke. Does it not seem more probable that Luke is here using Matthew's *notes* rather than the latter's Gospel? What is written on notes or scraps can be inserted wherever needed.

There are also many passages which reveal a lesser degree of resemblance. Sometimes, in fact, the resemblance is so remote that authors will differ as to whether such passages should be regarded as "Q" material. It is for this reason that according to some there are 200, according to others 250 non-Marcan verses common to Matthew and Luke.

Resemblance in varying degrees can be detected in the *sections* listed in the chart below. The list is not complete. Here, too, the *right-hand* column is basic:

Examples of Resemblance Between Matthew and Luke

Matthew	*Brief Indication of Contents*	Luke
4:23–25	Christ's Preaching, Teaching, and Healing	6:17–19
5:1–12	Beatitudes (Matt. & Luke) and Woes (Luke)	6:20–26
5:38–48	Love y o u r enemies	6:27–36
7:1–5	Do not pass judgment	6:37–42
7:17–20	No good tree bears corrupt fruit	6:43–45
7:24–27	The Two Builders	6:46–49
8:5–13	The Healing of a Centurion's Servant	7:1–10
11:2–19	Are you the Coming One?	7:18–35
8:19–22	I will follow you wherever you go	9:57–62
11:20–24	Woe to you, Chorazin!	10:13–16
11:25–27; 13:16, 17	I praise thee, Father—Blessed are the eyes, etc.	10:21–24
6:9–15; 7:7–11	The Lord's Prayer—Ask, seek, knock!	11:1–13

(*continued*)

Examples of Resemblance Between Matthew and Luke (continued)

Matthew	*Brief Indication of Contents*	Luke
10:28–31	Sparrows Two for a cent (Matthew); five for two cents (Luke)	12:4–7
10:32, 33; 12:32; 10:19, 20	Confessing versus denying Christ, etc.	12:8–12
6:21, 25–34	Where y o u r [your: Matt.] treasure is there will y o u r [your: Matt.] heart be also	12:22–34
10:34–36	No peace but division [a sword: Matt.]	12:49–53
5:25, 26	Settle with your opponent	12:57–59
7:13, 14, 21–23	The Narrow Door	13:22–30
24:17, 18, 23– 28, 37–41	As were the days of Noah	17:20–37

All the "Q" material is found in Sections I and II of Luke's Gospel. "Q" has no Passion account and no Resurrection narrative. It is not a Gospel or Message of Good News. As has been shown in N.T.C. on Matthew, there is no valid reason to believe that an actual document "Q" ever existed.

4. *Verbal Parallels Between Luke and John*

F. L. Cribbs, "St. Luke and the Johannine Tradition," *JBL,* 90 (Dec. 1971), pp. 422–450, and earlier G. W. Broomfield, J. V. Bartlet, J. A. Findlay, and others, have pointed out verbal parallels between Luke and John. See also E. E. Ellis, *op. cit.,* p. 28. Thus Annas, the highpriest, is mentioned only by Luke (3:2; cf. Acts 4:6) and by John (18:13, 24). The same is true with respect to Martha and Mary (Luke 10:38–41; John 11:1, 5, 19–21, 24, 30). Though it is a fact that the story of the anointing of Jesus by Mary of Bethany, the sister of Martha, is found not only in John 12:1 ff., but also in Matt. 26:6–13 and Mark 14:3–9,[10] her *name,* in connection with that incident, is mentioned only in John (12:3).

Another possible link between Luke and John is the fact that in no other Gospel do Samaria and the Samaritans figure as prominently as in Luke (9:51–55; 10:25–37; 17:11–19; cf. Acts 1:8; 8:1, 14, 25; 9:31; 15:3) and John (4:1–42). Moreover, only in these two Gospels is mention made of the fact that Satan entered (the heart of) Judas (Luke 22:3; John 13:27); that it was the *right* ear of the highpriest's servant that was struck (Luke 22:50; John 18:10); that Pilate no less than three times declared Jesus to be innocent (Luke 23:4, 14, 22; John 18:38; 19:4, 6); that Joseph's tomb was "new,"

---

10. Definitely *not* in Luke 7:37–39!

i.e., had never been used (Luke 23:53; John 19:41); that two angels were seen in the tomb of the resurrected Christ (Luke 24:4; John 20:12); and that after his resurrection Jesus appeared to his disciples in Jerusalem (Luke 24:33, 36 ff.; John 20:19–31). The visit of Peter to the tomb is reported in Luke 24:12, 24, and more fully in John 20:1–10, not in Matthew and Mark. Both Luke (5:1–11) and John (21:1–14) report a miraculous catch of fishes, but that reported by the latter occurred much later than. that described by the former. In fact, the miracle related so interestingly by "the disciple whom Jesus loved" is ascribed to Christ risen from the dead.

B. *The Sources of Luke's Gospel*

1. *The "L" Material*

That "L" ever existed as *an actual and distinct written document* is very doubtful. We have already seen that this can be said also with respect to "Q." Therefore the same unsubstantial character must be ascribed to "Proto-Luke," an imaginary combination of "Q" and "L" (minus the nativity account). Take away "Q" and "L," viewed as actually existing documents, or remove "Q" *or* "L," and Proto-Luke, viewed as Luke's first Gospel draft, to which he supposedly later added the nativity account and parts of Mark, also evaporates. This does not cancel the fact that if "L" and "Q" are viewed as being no more than symbols, so that the former indicates all the new material in Luke's Gospel—that is, material that cannot be found either in Matthew or Mark—and the latter refers to all non-Marcan Matthew-Luke material, these symbols, if used carefully, are unobjectionable and even useful.

It seems probable that at least some of the "L" material was derived from Semitic sources, probably both written and oral. The reason for this inference is that the language and style not only of the infancy narratives but also of several other "L" passages bear this linguistic characteristic. Luke specifically states that he had consulted the "eyewitnesses." Their everyday language was probably predominantly Aramaic, a Semitic language. At least some of them must have been acquainted with another and closely related Semitic tongue, namely, Hebrew. See further on 6. *Oral Sources.* And on Luke's language and style see below, heading V.

The fact that so much of the "L" material—no less than 34 sections as a whole or in part—is found in 9:51—18:14, and that it breathes the cosmopolitan spirit and strongly condemns all narrow exclusivism (see 10:25–37; 14:5–24; ch. 15; 17:11–19; 18:9–14) has caused some to ascribe "L" to the influence of Paul upon Luke. For Paul's "gospel for the world" emphasis see such passages as Rom. 3:21–24; I Cor. 7:19; Gal. 3:9, 29; Eph. 2:14, 18; Col. 3:11. Others, with equal justification, call such material "Johannine." See John 1:29; 3:16; 4:42; 10:16, etc.

We must not forget, however, that basically this so-called cosmopolitan spirit is evident throughout the Third Gospel (see above: point I A 5 a), and was that of Jesus Christ. He himself, by means of his oral teaching, was the primary "Source" of "L," as well as of the entire Third Gospel; yes, of the Good News everywhere: the message of salvation full and free, by God's sovereign grace granted to all believers, whether Jews or Gentiles.

And as to secondary "sources," we have no right to limit their number too rigidly. Luke 1:1 f. leaves the impression that the evangelist had a good many sources, both oral and written. Today it would be entirely impossible to trace them all.

2. *The Marcan Material*

It has already been shown—see N.T.C. on Matthew, pp. 36–47—that in all probability it was Luke who used Mark's Gospel, not vice versa. In fact, both Matthew and Luke probably had Mark as one of their sources. But the manner in which they used Mark differed. It would seem that Matthew was never able to forget Mark. He appears to be filling in the Marcan outline. Luke's Gospel, on the other hand, consists of alternating Marcan and non-Marcan blocks. See N.T.C. on Matthew, pp. 25–31 ("the three rivers"). It should also be remembered that Luke was personally acquainted with Mark (Col. 4:10, 14; Philem. 24).

3. *The "Q" Material*

This material found in the Gospels of Matthew and Luke but absent from Mark may, as remarked earlier, have been derived in part from notes and fragments written by early witnesses, especially by Matthew.

A problem presents itself at this point. There are those who claim that in Luke these passages and/or sections appear in a context different from that in Matthew. Thorough investigation, verse by verse, section by section, soon reveals that the problem is not nearly as serious as it is often represented to be. It is true, for example, that in Luke the sermon that includes the Beatitudes was delivered when Jesus stood on "a level place," while Matthew mentions "the mountain." But the seeming contradiction disappears by supposing that Jesus delivered his discourse on a mountain-plain. For another possible solution see N.T.C. on Matthew, p. 260.

Another seeming contradiction is that between Luke 11:1–4 and Matt. 6:9–15. Matthew includes the Lord's Prayer in the Sermon on the Mount; Luke, as some see it, ascribes the teaching of that prayer to a considerably later period of Christ's ministry. Here again the "contradiction" is in the mind of those who are looking for contradictions. More than one possible solution has been suggested: (a) In Matt. 5–7 Matthew includes sayings that belong to a later period; (b) Luke is simply recording what had happened earlier; (c) The Twelve, often forgetful (Matt. 16:9, 10), were in need of having this prayer repeated to them; (d) the disciple who asked, "Lord, teach us to pray" (Luke 11:1) was not one of The Twelve; so for him the prayer was new. Whichever of these solutions is adopted—see the comments on 11:1–4—a real contradiction cannot be proved. And so it is in every case.

To the itinerant preacher—minister, evangelist, missionary, theological student—who has used the same sermon in different places, it should cause no difficulty to believe that our Lord repeated his marvelous sayings. For example, the one recorded in Matt. 16:25; Mark 8:35; Luke 9:24; 17:33; John 12:25 may have been used several times. Was he not fully aware of the fact that the (by nature) selfish human heart needed to hear the demand of total self-surrender again and again, and in every age? Cf. Rom. 15:4.

Besides, the very fact that "history repeats itself" (though never precisely) adds weight to the need of constant repetition and reassertion of basic truths and principles. Parallel events abound in history and in the life of every individual. For that very reason illustrations of *déjà vu* (the illusion that one has previously experienced something similar) are plentiful.

In the United States of America, beginning with the year 1840, when Pres. W. H. Harrison was elected to office, every twentieth year (1840, 1860, 1880, 1900, 1920, 1940, 1960) marked the election (or re-election) of a president who died in office, whether because of illness or because of assassination. And in how many particulars did not the incidents which we associate with World War I recur in World War II? Besides, who would deny Luke the right to link a dominical saying spoken earlier with one uttered later, when he saw a connection in thought? See especially 9:51—18:14.

4. *The Johannine Material*

How shall we account for the similarities between Luke and John? Before writing his own Gospel had John seen Luke's and does this account for the similarities? L. Morris answers this question negatively. Clement of Alexandria (fl. 190–200), on the other hand, writes, "Last of all John, *perceiving that the external facts had been made plain in the Gospels,* being urged by his friends and inspired by the Spirit, composed a spiritual Gospel." Note the words I have placed in italics. This very early witness, therefore, must have thought that John was acquainted with the contents of the Synoptics. L. Berkhof's opinion is given in these words, "John may have read the Synoptics before he composed his work, but he did not use them as sources from which he drew a part of his material."[11] For passages in John's Gospel which, according to several interpreters, seem to indicate that John, in writing his Gospel, presupposed that its readers were already acquainted with the Synoptics see N.T.C. on John, Vol. I, p. 32.

On one fact all serious students of the four Gospels agree, namely, that there must have been a very rich common tradition, especially oral, from

---

11. For Morris see his *Studies in the Fourth Gospel,* Grand Rapids, 1969, p. 38. For Clement of Alexandria see Eusebius, *Ecclesiastical History* VI.xiv.7. For Berkhof see his *New Testament Introduction,* Grand Rapids, 1915, p. 114.

which both Luke and John were able to draw. That, more than anything else, may well account for the similarities between the Third and the Fourth Gospels,

5. *Overlapping Sources*

The various sources which Luke consulted were probably not so artificially separated that without qualification one would be able to say, "For the 'L' material Luke drew on *this* source, for 'Q' on *that*." Frequently the material contents of the sources must have overlapped. This holds too for written sources as distinguished from oral.

6. *Oral Sources*

We must be careful not to make Luke dependent upon *written* sources only. We know that the author of the Third Gospel, who was Paul's companion, was living at a time when many eye-and-ear witnesses had not yet died (I Cor. 15:6). In Caesarea Luke, bound for Jerusalem on Paul's third missionary journey, spent some time with Philip the evangelist (Acts 21:8 ff.). This was the very Philip who previously had been enabled by the Lord to perform a very successful ministry in Samaria (Acts 8:5-8). Can it be that the prominence of Samaria material in Luke's Gospel was due, in part, to this meeting of Luke with Philip?

Having arrived in Jerusalem, Luke spent some time in that city (Acts 21:17). Moreover, during the years A.D. 58-60, while Paul was kept in Caesarean imprisonment, Luke may have consulted several early witnesses. Could one of these have been Mary, the mother of Jesus? Or, perhaps, some of her close friends or relatives, to whom she had entrusted the facts pertaining to Christ's conception and birth?

It is considered possible that Joanna, the wife of Chuza, manager of *Herod's* household, gave Luke information with respect to matters touching Herod (Luke 8:2, 3; 23:56—24:10). This Joanna is mentioned only by Luke. He may have known and contacted her. Does this perhaps account for the fact that the story of Christ's appearance before Herod is found only in Luke's Gospel (23:6-12)?

Luke's close association with Paul, which began before the Third Gospel was written, must not be passed by in silence. Both before and after his conversion Paul had been in touch with the early witnesses (Acts 9:1 ff.; I Cor. 15:1-8; Gal. 1:18; 2:9).

7. *One Final Fact, the Most Important of All*

The fact I am about to state is generally left unspoken and unwritten in the treatment of this subject. Yet, without it, the treatment of sources is at best *deistic*. That fact is this, that with respect to the authors of Scripture the impulse to write, the investigation of the facts, and the actual writing took place under the guidance of the Holy Spirit (II Peter 1:21; cf. II Tim. 3:16, 17).

As a result of the operation of that same Spirit the reader, *at the very outset,* accepts the inspired record as being nothing less than the Word of God. "Protestants are bound to pay homage to a strict theory of inspiration, for if this falls by the wayside, everything falls" (H. Bavinck).

Very instructive are the words of S. Greijdanus. At an unusual place, namely, the *close* of his very thorough two-volume Commentary on the Gospel According to Luke, he writes a *Postscript* (Dutch *Naschrift*), which is actually an *Introduction* to the Third Gospel![12] His opening sentence on *Sources* (Dutch *Bronnen*) is as follows (my translation): "The search for sources, in order in connection with them to judge the historicity of that which Luke imparts to us in his Gospel, can be called both improper and thoroughly useless." He continues: "The truth of the position that the Lord Jesus is the Son of God, that according to his human nature he was conceived by the Holy Spirit, that he performed the miracles and spoke the words reported by Luke, and that he rose from the dead and ascended to heaven, cannot by means of source investigation be established by anybody. He who makes the recognition of these truths dependent on such research starts out with their rejection, at least with the assumption that they are debatable.... That he then reaches a negative result is not surprising. In the final analysis one either believes or rejects what Luke says about such matters."

If one reads these words of the Dutch scholar carefully, it will become clear that Greijdanus is not summarily denying the value of tracing sources. On the contrary, what he warns against is the process of carrying on such a study *without being properly motivated.* In all candor, are we not driven to admit that a good deal of negative criticism is tainted with this evil? Even when the Greek text is undisputed, the critic insists on digging deeper until he imagines that he has discovered why "the early church" (marvelously creative!) or even the evangelist himself modified or "edited" a saying of Jesus or a report of an event so as to produce the present text.

In a choice between, on the one hand, what the best Greek text actually says in the light of its own inspired context, and on the other hand, the frequently speculative product of quasi-research, let us adhere to the former!

IV. When and Where Was This Gospel Written?

A. *When?*

It would amount to a waste of space and time to discuss all the various views. Basic to much of the argumentation are the words of Jesus recorded in Luke 19:41–44; 21:20 f.:

---

12. *Kommentaar op het Nieuwe Testament,* Vol. II, pp. 1209 ff.

"The days will come upon you when your enemies will throw up a palisade [or: siegeworks] against you and encircle you and hem you in from all directions. . . . When y o u see Jerusalem surrounded by armies, y o u will know that its desolation is near. . . ."

Conservatives interpret these words as an actual prophecy of Jerusalem's fall. Since this fall occurred in the year A.D. 70, they date Luke-Acts[13] earlier than that year.

Liberals, on the other hand, regard these words to be a description, in the form of a prophecy to be sure, but actually written after Jerusalem's fall. They base this conclusion on the vividness and—as they see it—detailed character of the description. It follows that they assign to Luke-Acts a date after A.D. 70.

However, that the Jews were already rebellious during Christ's sojourn on earth is clear from John 6:15. That this attitude, unless checked in time, might well lead to the destruction of Jerusalem could be foreseen. Cf. John 11:48. For the rest, instead of considering the quoted words to be too detailed to have been spoken before the city was overwhelmed by the terrible catastrophe, would it not be appropriate to say in the spirit of Judg. 14:18:

> (When the enemy intends to take a city)
> What is more natural than siegeworks,
> And what more effective than a besieging army?

In other words, if the "description" had been written afterward, would it not have been more detailed? It is exactly the lack of detail that should have made it rather easy to believe that these words were spoken *before* Jerusalem's fall, and that Luke-Acts antedates A.D. 70. I hasten to add, however, that he who by God's sovereign grace has been led to regard Christ's claims as being true does not hesitate to believe that this Exalted Person was able to utter even minutely detailed prophecies (Matt. 17:27; 21:2; Mark 10:32–34). Could the *real* reason for the late-dating of Luke 19:41–44; 21:10 f., and consequently for the late-dating of Luke-Acts, be disbelief in the possibility of genuine predictive prophecy?

Among several other arguments advanced by those who accept a late date for Luke-Acts is one which is too interesting to pass by in silence. Josephus, in his work *Jewish Antiquities* (XX.97–99), states that during the period when Fadus was procurator of Judea a certain false prophet, named Theudas, caused a large crowd to believe that at his command the Jordan River would be parted. When Fadus heard about this, he sent a squadron of cavalry who slew many of the impostor's followers, made slaves of others, and caused Theudas to be beheaded. Several lines farther along Josephus makes mention of a certain rebel against the Roman government, named

---

13. *Considered as a single work,* in view of Luke 1:1–4; cf. Acts 1:1. For the single work theory see also N. B. Stonehouse, *The Witness of Luke to Christ,* pp. 12–14.

Judas (XX.102), *whose sons* were brought up for trial and crucified. Now in Acts 5:35–39 these same two names occur, and in that same sequence: Theudas and Judas. Luke records the words of Gamaliel, a famous Pharisee and member of the Sanhedrin. By means of an eloquent address this influential leader restrained his fellow councilmen from taking precipitous action against Peter and the rest of the apostles. In his speech Gamaliel relates how Theudas and Judas had perished. Accordingly, there are those who maintain that Luke must have derived his account about Theudas and Judas from Josephus, and that since *Jewish Antiquities* was not published until the year 93, the Third Gospel and Acts must be dated even later, perhaps around the turn of the century.[14]

Now it must be admitted that the identity of names is indeed striking. However, this argument for the late-dating of Luke-Acts fails for the following reasons:

a. The false prophets to whom Gamaliel refers lived at a date considerably earlier than did the two men mentioned by Josephus. The revolt to which *Antiquities* refers occurred in A.D. 45–46. When Gamaliel delivered his speech, some time before the year 37, the Theudas and Judas to whom he refers had already perished.

b. According to the speech of Gamaliel "about four hundred men" had joined Theudas. Neither Gamaliel nor Luke could have derived this detail from Josephus, for he does not mention it.

c. Josephus states that *the sons* of Judas were crucified; Gamaliel reports that *Judas himself* perished.

It is clear, therefore, that the two reports cannot refer to the same incident.

On the positive side it can be stated that for the book of Acts we have "an earliest probable date" (*terminus a quo*, if one prefers the Latin expression) and "a latest probable date" (*terminus ad quem*). The *earliest* probable date is A.D. 62. Reason: it can be established with a high degree of probability that Paul reached Rome in or about the year 60.[15] Since the book of Acts covers the life of Paul until the time when he had spent two years in Roman imprisonment (Acts 28:30), Luke cannot have finished it before the year 62. As to the *latest* probable date, here we must be very careful. It is sometimes said that since Paul must have been released about A.D. 63 or soon afterward and Acts ends with Paul still in prison, the book must have been written not later than the year 63, for if Luke had known about Paul's release he would probably have mentioned it.

This argument is rather weak, however. For, first of all, it must be borne in mind that Luke is not writing Paul's biography but the story of the

---

14. For the names of some of the defenders of this theory and the titles of their books see the editorial remarks appended to the passage in Loeb Library, Josephus, Vol. IX (Book XX), p. 441.

15. See the author's *Survey of the Bible*, pp. 66–68, 74.

Christ-controlled progress of the gospel from Jerusalem to Rome, and thus, in a sense, to the uttermost parts of the earth. See Acts 1:1-8. Besides, there are those who think that the expression "And he lived two whole years in his own rented dwelling" or "at his own expense" *may* have a *legal* meaning, namely, he waited *the two full years* (the limit established by law?) during which the accusers had the opportunity to press their charge. No one appearing (does Acts 28:21 point in that direction?), the trial ended by default, and Paul was released, the legal requirement of two years having been fulfilled.[16] So interpreted, Acts 28:30 would imply Paul's' release. Whether or not this interpretation is correct has not been established. It has become clear, however, that one can do very little with Acts 28:30, 31 in attempting to fix the latest probable date for Acts. Note, however, the following:

In the night between the 18th and the 19th of July of the year 64 a fearful conflagration broke out in Rome. It turned ten of that city's fourteen districts into a shapeless mass of ruins. Who or what caused that fire? An accusing finger was pointed at Nero. In order to divert attention from himself he, in turn, cast the blame on the Christians. Result: a fiendishly cruel persecution of believers, a bloodbath in Rome, bitter hostility toward Christianity on the part of the Roman government.

Not only is no mention of this horror made anywhere in the book of Acts, but the entire spirit of the book makes it almost impossible to believe that it could have been written during or after the middle of the year A.D. 64.

Luke constantly emphasizes the relative fairness, at times even the friendliness and helpfulness, of the Roman authorities. Rescued by the military tribune out of the hands of the murderous mob at Jerusalem, Paul is permitted to make his defense, first before the people, then before the Jewish council (Acts 21:31—23:9). By the tribune he is rescued once more, this time out of the hands of quarreling Pharisees and Sadducees (Acts 23:10); and even a third time, now from a band of more than forty oath-bound Jews. He is brought to Caesarea. Claudius Lysias writes a letter in his favor (Acts 23:12-35), addressing it to the governor Felix. The latter also permits Paul to make his defense, but desiring to do the Jews a favor, leaves him in prison. When Festus succeeds Felix, the apostle appeals to Caesar. Festus tells King Agrippa that Paul had done nothing worthy of death, and permits him to make his defense before the king. On board a ship on his way to Rome, the apostle is treated kindly by the Roman centurion, Julius (Acts 27:3), who also subsequently saves his life (Acts 27:43). After the storm and the shipwreck, having first been hospitably entertained by the chief of the island of Malta (Acts 28:7), and having afterward covered the final leg of the journey, he reaches Rome, where he is permitted to stay by himself with a soldier to guard him (Acts 28:16). Though he is a prisoner

---

16. See L. Pherigo, "Paul's Life After the Close of Acts," *JBL* LXX (December, 1951), pp. 277-284. See also the doctoral dissertation of N. G. Veldhoen, *Het Process van den Apostel Paulus*, Leiden, 1924. And see *GTT*, Vol. 55, No. 2, 3 (1955), pp. 60, 61.

awaiting trial, he is allowed considerable personal liberty as well as opportunity to preach the gospel (Acts 28:30, 31).

Conclusion: the book of Acts was probably written before the middle of the year 64. A reasonable guess would be A.D. 63. And since Luke-Acts is really a single work, the date when Theophilus received the Third Gospel cannot have been much earlier—probably "sometime during the period A.D. 61–63."

B. *Where?*

As has been indicated, the Anti-Marcionite Prologue states that Luke wrote his Gospel in Achaia, a province of ancient Greece. We know, however, that Luke reached Rome in the company of Paul, and that he was still—or again—in Rome when during this same first Roman imprisonment Paul wrote Colossians (see 4:14) and Philemon (see verse 24). Did Luke leave Paul for a while, in order to write his Gospel in Achaia, and did he then return to Rome? It is hard to imagine that Luke would have done this. The reference to Achaia, as the place where Luke wrote his Gospel, may be merely an inference from the fact that the beloved physician was completely "at home" in the Greek world, wrote excellent Greek, "was probably a Greek" (A. T. Robertson), and wanted his Gospel to be read by the entire Greek-speaking world of his day.

Of all the other guesses—namely, Ephesus, Corinth, Caesarea, Rome—the last seems to be the most reasonable. It would harmonize best with the facts already stated under point A. As already indicated, much of the preparatory work—gathering and sifting data and organizing them—may have been done in Caesarea and elsewhere.

Commenting on the date and place of *Acts*, A. T. Robertson writes, "On the whole, the early date has the best of it. We, therefore, date the Acts about A.D. 63 and in Rome."[17]

And F. F. Bruce points out that the exact date of Luke-Acts must remain uncertain and that it is an unimportant question in comparison with the authorship and historical character of the work.[18]

I can find no fault with either of these statements.

V. What Are Its Characteristics?

A. *Its Style Is Multi-Faceted*[19]

Luke's style is anything but uniform. That of the preface is classical; that of 1:5—2:52 Semitic; and that of the rest of his Gospel similar to the Greek

---

17. *Luke the Historian in the Light of Research,* p. 37.

18. *Commentary on the Book of Acts (New International Commentary on the New Testament),* Grand Rapids, 1964, p. 23.

19. See H. J. Cadbury, *The Style and Literary Method of Luke,* Cambridge, 1920.

of the Septuagint, but with wide variation. Sometimes it approaches classical Greek very closely; then again it is tinged with Semitisms.

Aside from the fact that the beloved physician was a very versatile person, there is no certainty as to what may have been the reason for this extraordinary variety of style. Worthy of consideration is the following: Luke uses classical Greek for the preface because it is natural for him to do so, especially when he is not using sources, and because he wishes to indicate at the very outset that his Gospel is meant for the entire Greek-speaking world. He expresses himself in Semitic style because wherever he does this—especially in the nativity account—he is making use of very early source material, perhaps written as well as oral. He adopts the style of the Septuagint in order to show that the story of Jesus is a true fulfilment of the Old Testament prophecies. These prophecies were read by many and were generally quoted by Luke as they had been translated in the Septuagint.

Luke uses no less than 266 words (not counting proper names) that are not found in the rest of the New Testament. This compares with less than half as many for Matthew, and less than one-third as many for Mark.

Even where Luke makes use of Mark's Gospel, he changes the style, so that where Mark co-ordinates clauses (and . . . and . . . and) Luke often subordinates. For the details see N.T.C. on Matthew, p. 39, footnote 37. Luke also omits Mark's Aramaic words. See N.T.C. on Matthew, p. 42. For "Cananaean" (Mark 3:18) Luke substitutes "zealot" (6:15); for "Rabbi" (Mark 9:5), "Master" (9:33); for "Rabboni" (Mark 10:51), "Lord" (18:41); and for "Golgotha" (Mark 15:22), "Skull" (23:33). And cf. Mark 5:41 with Luke 8:54.

It should be borne in mind, however, that the type of Greek used by each evangelist answers his purpose best. In this respect Mark's vernacular is not any worse than Luke's more polished style. All three Synoptics—in fact, all four Gospels—must be considered the product of divine inspiration. But inspiration, though indeed plenary, is organic. It makes use of evangelists with different backgrounds and qualifications, and equips each for his specific task.

B. *It Covers a Longer Span of History Than Do the Other Synoptics and More Often Relates Its Narratives to Contemporaneous Events*

Luke-Acts covers the history of redemption all the way from the prediction of the birth of John the Baptist (Luke 1:5-23) to the implantation and propagation of the gospel in Rome (Acts 28:16-31). Even Luke's first book surpasses the other Synoptics in point of completeness, for it traces the genealogy of Jesus all the way back to Adam (3:38) and ends with the record of Christ's ascension from the Mount of Olives (24:50-53). In fact, the Third Gospel even contains an allusion to the realization of the Father's promise, namely, the coming of the Holy Spirit. See Luke 24:49; cf. Acts 1:4, 8. To Luke, Jesus was one of our race. *The Son of God was also the perfect or ideal man.*

Again and again Luke relates his narrative to contemporaneous historical events. He informs us that it was during the days of Herod—the one often described as "Herod the Great"—that "a certain priest named Zacharias" received the promise of the birth of a son, who was to be called John (1:5); that it was "while Quirinius was governor of Syria" that the census took place and Jesus was born (2:1, 2, 7); and that it was "in the fifteenth year of the reign of Tiberius Caesar," etc., that "the word of God came to John," and that he accordingly began his ministry. Other chronological references can be found in the following passages: 1:36, 56, 59; 2:42; 3:23; 9:28, 37, 51; 22:1, 7, 66; 23:44, 54; 24:1, 13, 29, 33. On the other hand, at times Luke can be very indefinite: "Now it happened while he [Jesus] was in one of the towns" (5:12); "on one of those days" (5:17); "on another sabbath" (6:6); etc.

C. Its Geography and History Are Reliable.
This Thesis Defended Against Redaction Criticism

Today, perhaps more than ever, this reliability must be stressed. By no means all who have read and commented on Luke's writings have admitted their reliability. There is Gospel Criticism, and there are Gospel critics: those who do not believe that whatever is written by the four recognized evangelists is true.

In N.T.C. on Matthew several pages (54–76) were devoted to a brief summary of the views of these men, beginning with Harnack (1851–1930). It was made clear that each succeeding critic, while rendering a service by exposing the weak points in the theory of his predecessor, came up with a system of his own . . . which, in turn, was (at least to some extent) blasted by the next critic.

The last to be discussed was Bultmann, with his theory of single Gospel units and with his demythologization advice. He established what may be termed a "school" of disciples, many of whom today occupy influential chairs in various institutions of higher education on both sides of the Atlantic and elsewhere. His theories, however, have by no means escaped searching criticism. And the critics, in turn, while deserving praise for what they have accomplished in the way of criticism and sometimes even in other respects, are airing views which, in some cases, are also in need of demolition or at least serious modification.

Today "Redaction Criticism" is riding high. What is Redaction Criticism? A book bearing this very title was written by Norman Perrin.[20] The author of that book is himself an enthusiastic advocate of that ism. In his favor it must be said that in clear language he has given us a comprehensive view of this relatively new development in the study of the Gospels. I strongly urge the reader to study his treatise. Apart from a Foreword, a Glossary, and a Bibliography, the book has only 79 pages of reading material. It would be

---

20. *What Is Redaction Criticism?*, Philadelphia, 1969.

unfair to Perrin to depend entirely on what someone says about the contents of his writing. The book itself deserves to be read.

Briefly, then, Redaction Criticism, as outlined in the book to which reference was made, may perhaps be described as a discipline which regards the various Gospel units as being not accurate historical narratives, etc., but rather products of redaction, that is, of the revision and editing of miscellaneous traditions. The evangelists, instead of necessarily reproducing the facts as they actually occurred, gather, modify, and even create traditions. Often, therefore, the material found in the Gospels must be ascribed to the theological motivation of the evangelist or of this or that editor. See pp. 40, 42, 66, 69. The Gospel writers offer us information about the theology of the early church, rather than about the teaching of the historical Jesus.

To support this thesis Perrin refers, among other things, to the incident that occurred at Caesarea Philippi (Mark 8:27—9:1; cf. Matt. 16:13-28; Luke 9:18-27). It will be recalled that here Jesus asked his disciples, "Who do people say I am?" Upon receiving their answer, he asked, "But y o u, who do y o u say I am?" Peter answered, "Thou art the Christ," etc. Jesus then began to teach them that the Son of man must suffer many things . . . Peter took him aside and began to rebuke him . . . Jesus rebuked Peter. . . . Mark 8:34, 35 reads, "And having called the people to him along with his disciples, he said to them, 'If anyone wishes to come behind me, let him deny himself, take up his cross, and follow me. For whoever would save his life shall lose it, but whoever loses his life for my sake and the gospel's shall save it." It will also be recalled that Matthew's main addition to the Marcan account of this incident is found in 16:17-19: "Blessed are you, Simon Bar-Jonah," etc.

Perrin's argument to show that here we have instances of redaction includes the following:

a. The insertion, in Matt. 16, of verses 17-19, is a piece of tradition not paralleled in Mark or Luke. See Perrin, pp. 58, 59.

b. The words (here in italics) *"take up his cross"* and "for my sake *and the gospel's"* (Mark 8:34, 35) represent language that suits the situation in the early church, not any situation in the ministry of Jesus, p. 42.

c. The three passion predictions (Mark 8:31 f.; 9:31 f.; 10:33 f. and parallels) reveal a constant editorial pattern of prediction—misunderstanding—teaching, p. 45.

It is unnecessary for me to reflect on (a), since I have already done this in my N.T.C. on Matthew, p. 645. There is a very reasonable explanation for the omission of this passage from Mark and Luke.

As to (b), though it is true that Jesus had not as yet been crucified, this can be no objection against very early use of the phrase *take up his cross,* since crucifixion was not at all unusual in those days. The disciples of Jesus may very well have seen a man taking up his cross and being led away by soldiers for execution. They were therefore well able to understand that the act of deliberately taking up one's cross symbolized self-denial.

This holds too with respect to the phrase "for my sake *and the gospel's.*" Already in pre-Christian times the word *gospel* was used in the sense of "good news."[21]

And as to (c), this objection is certainly strange. Is not history full of repetitions and coincidences? Besides, was it not rather natural for these men, who until they began to associate with Jesus had probably never heard about a Suffering Messiah, to react negatively to these passion predictions, and to do so more than once? Do we actually need editorial redaction to account for this repetition?

If a historian should report that a soldier, upon entering a building, met a group of men carrying out a fatally wounded President of the United States; and that again, years later, this same soldier, now Secretary of War, upon entering a building, met a group of men carrying out a fatally wounded President of the United States; and that for the third time, years later, this same individual, upon entering a building met a group of men carrying out a fatally wounded President of the United States,[22] would there not seem to be far more reason to shout "editorial redaction"? The pattern would indeed be very arresting, for in the case of the passion predictions the negative reactions, though similar, were not nearly as similar as were the three above-mentioned experiences encountered by Robert Lincoln.

Redaction Criticism, in order to prove its point, will have to come up with something far better than it has presented thus far.

As to redaction critics and their books, note also the following:

J. Rhode, *Rediscovering the Teaching of the Evangelists,* Philadelphia, 1969.

G. Bornkamm, G. Barth, and H. J. Held, *Tradition and Interpretation in Matthew,* Philadelphia, 1963.

W. Marxsen, *Der Evangelist Markus,* Göttingen, 1959.

On p. 28 of his book Perrin calls Hans Conzelmann the most important of the true redaction critics. We shall therefore now turn our attention to him. His book, to which reference is going to be made, bears the title *Die Mitte Der Zeit,* Tübingen, 1954. The subtitle of the book is *Studien zur Theologie des Lukas.* Based on this subtitle is the title of the English translation, *The Theology of St. Luke,* New York, Evanston, San Francisco, London, 1957.

Without any disparagement of the translation which, it would seem to me, is good, it still remains a fact that it is always best to read the author's own words in the very language in which he wrote them. But there may be some readers of this commentary who are unable to follow the German. To accommodate everyone, the references given below are first of all to the German original (marked G.), then to the English translation (marked E.).

---

21. See A. Deissmann's *Light from the Ancient East,* New York, 1927, p. 366.

22. This interesting historical item is repeated here, in slightly abbreviated form, from *The Ft. Lauderdale News,* Sept. 6, 1975. For other striking historical coincidences see above, point III B 3.

Conzelmann believes that the Gospel writers were real authors, not simply men who gathered and strung together previously unconnected Gospel units. Take Luke as an example. He was not merely an author; he was a theologian. As he saw it the heart and *center*[23] of the good tidings is Jesus Christ himself. Great is the emphasis which Conzelmann places on this fact. And as for Christ's archenemy, Satan, that strong Adversary lacks every bit of independent authority. He must always serve God's purpose.[24] So far, so good.

There are, however, also other statements. With some of the views of Conzelmann many readers will not be able to agree, and rightly so. To provide a background for these very controversial positions note the following two passages from the Third Gospel:

"And when the devil had finished every temptation, he departed from him until an opportune time" (4:13).

"Then Satan entered Judas, called Iscariot, being of the number of the twelve" (22:3).

According to Conzelmann these two Lucan passages divide salvation history into three stages: (a) the Age of Israel, closing with 4:13; (b) the Age of Jesus, extending from 4:13 to 22:3; and (c) the Age of the Church, from 22:3 to the end.[25] As he sees it, the lines of demarcation cannot be too sharply drawn. The Central Age, moreover, that of Jesus, is protected from every activity of Satan.[26]

What Conzelmann means when he describes Luke as being a theologian has now become clear. To be sure, the evangelist is also interested in geography and history, but only to the extent in which they serve theology. In fact, as Conzelmann sees it, Luke's geographical interest is very strong; yet his geographical references must not be interpreted literally but symbolically, theologically; e.g., the Jordan is simply the sphere in which John the Baptist carries out his ministry. Conzelmann's interpretation of Luke 17:11 shows that he accepts the probability that Luke is frequently ignorant of the actual geographical situation.

Again and again Conzelmann casts doubt on the accuracy of the evangelist's knowledge about the exact place or territory where the events he writes about took place.[27]

And as to history, "There seems to be implicit in his [Conzelmann's] approach the traditional (and erroneous) view that the Gospel is intended to be a running chronological account of Jesus' ministry."[28]

---

23. Note German title of Conzelmann's book, meaning *The Center of Time.*
24. G. p. 135; E. p. 156.
25. G. p. 129 f.; E. p. 149 f.
26. G. p. 146; E. p. 170.
27. See the following pages:
G. 56, 57, 58, 60, 69, 78, 79.
E. 69, 70, 71, 73, 83, 93, 94.
28. E. E. Ellis, *op. cit.*, p. 147.

The objections to Conzelmann's position are as follows:

a. That it was Luke's intention to divide the history of salvation into *these* three stages is a mere assumption. Neither the text nor the context points in that direction. If three stages are required, why not the far more natural and scriptural: Adam to Christ's First Coming; Christ's First Coming to his Return to Judge; Gehenna and its opposite: The New Heaven and Earth? See such passages as the following: Matt. 25:46; Luke 3:23-38; 12:35-40; 16:16; 17:22-37; 21:25-28; 24:27; Gal. 4:4; Rev. 12:1-5; 20:14, 15; 21:1 ff.

b. Most of Luke's passages with respect to Satanic activity are found in the "Central Section," the very one which, says Conzelmann—G. p. 135; E. p. 156—is exempt from such activity.[29]

c. Ignorance or carelessness on the part of Luke with respect to geography and history has never been proved. Rather, the very opposite.

There was a time when William Ramsay also harbored doubts with respect to Luke's knowledge of geography and related subjects. Diligent research cured him.[30] Partly through Ramsay's (and Hobart's) influence did not Harnack reverse his position in connection with the authorship of Luke-Acts? Did not Goodspeed experience a somewhat similar change of mind with respect to the authorship of Matthew?

Frank Morison, convinced that resurrection from the dead was an impossibility, planned a book bearing the title *Jesus, the Last Phase.* By God's grace the study of the facts as reported in the Gospels caused him to change his mind. He did indeed write a book, with contents the very opposite of what had been his original plan.[31] So, let us hope and pray that in time Conzelmann, too, will change his mind with respect to Luke's ignorance and/or lack of accuracy.

When one reads what Conzelmann says, and even more often implies, with respect to Luke's carelessness about geography and history, the question arises, "Must the old battle be fought all over again?" Have not the works of Ramsay and of Robertson, the inscriptions and other archaeological discoveries, proved beyond possibility of reasonable doubt that Luke was a thoroughly reliable writer?

The following questions *used to be* answered with a thunderous "No":

Luke 2:1, 2. Was there a census when Quirinius was governor of Syria, one that took place before the census mentioned in Acts 5:37?

Luke 2:3, 4. To satisfy the requirements of this early census, did people have to return to their ancestral homes?

Luke 3:1, 2. Did John the Baptist begin his ministry "in the fifteenth year of Tiberius Caesar . . . when Lysanius was tetrarch of Abilene?"

---

29. For this item of criticism see also Schuyler Brown, *Apostasy and Perseverance in the Theology of Luke,* Rome, 1969, p. 6.

30. See his many books along this line; in the present connection especially *The Bearing of Recent Discovery on the Trustworthiness of the New Testament,* reprint Grand Rapids, 1953; and *Was Christ Born at Bethlehem?,* 1898. See also A. T. Robertson, *Luke the Historian;* and M. F. Unger, *Archaeology and the New Testament,* Grand Rapids, 1962.

31. Title of the book: *Who Moved the Stone?,* New York, London, 1930.

Luke 9:51; 13:22; 17:11. Does Luke's account of Jesus' journey to Jerusalem make sense?

Acts 13:7. When Paul proclaimed the word of God in Cyprus, did that island have a proconsul?

Acts 17:6, 8. Were the rulers of the city of Thessalonica called "politarchs"?

Acts 18:12. When Paul, on his second missionary journey, performed his ministry at Corinth, was Gallio proconsul of Achaia?

By this time, however, we know that *wherever it has been possible to check Luke's statements,* his impeccable reliability as a historian has come to light. In not a single case has it been established that he was wrong. It must be granted that not every problem with respect to the census mentioned in Luke 2:1-4 has as yet been solved; also, that commentators have not as yet reached unanimity in their interpretation of Luke 9:51; 13:22; 17:11. But the evidence in Luke's favor is overwhelming, as books and articles continue to testify.[32]

As to the solution of the difficulties mentioned above:

On Luke 2:1, 2 (Quirinius) see the treatment of this passage in the present Commentary; also the author's *Survey of the Bible,* pp. 139, 400.

On Luke 2:3, 4 (census) see on that passage.

On Luke 3:1, 2 (fifteenth year of Tiberius) see on that passage; also *Survey of the Bible,* pp. 66, 400.

On Luke 9:51; 13:22; 17:11, in the present Commentary see *Summary of and Introduction to Luke's Central Section;* especially under point B, pp. 541-545.

On Acts 13:7 (proconsul at Cyprus) and on Acts 17:6, 8 (politarchs at Thessalonica) see *Survey of the Bible,* p. 401.

On Acts 18:12 (Gallio) see *Survey of the Bible,* p. 67; also A. T. Robertson, *Luke the Historian,* pp. 175, 176.

What is, indeed, very striking is the remarkable correspondence between the Third Gospel and other sources as to the location of towns, villages, etc. The great majority of these geographical units present no formidable problem at all. That is true with respect to Nazareth (1:26; 2:39, 51, etc.); Capernaum (4:23, 31; 7:1, 2; 10:15); Nain (7:11); Jerusalem (2:22, 41; 4:9, etc.); the Lake of Gennesaret (5:1); Zarephath in the region of Sidon (4:26); the district of the Garasenes (8:26); Bethphage and Bethany at the hill called the Mount of Olives (19:37); Jericho (on the way

---

32. See, for example, F. F. Bruce's *Commentary on the Book of Acts.* Bruce furnishes an abundance of archaeological evidence in support and elucidation of such passages in Acts which at one time or another were used by the critics to show that Luke was not a trustworthy historian. See p. 344 on "politarchs," and p. 374 on Gallio. E. E. Ellis, *op. cit.,* writes that investigation has confirmed the conviction that Luke was "a careful historian" (p. 9). See also the excellent articles by H. W. Hoehner ("Chronological Aspects of the Life of Christ") that appeared in *BS* Vol. 130, No. 520 (Oct.-Dec. 1973), pp. 338-351; and Vol. 131, No. 521 (Jan.-March 1974), pp. 41-54. These articles answer many questions that arise in connection with Luke 2:1-4 and 3:1, 2.

toward Jerusalem from the northeast, 18:31, 35; 19:1); etc. As to Bethsaida (9:10; 10:13) see N.T.C. on John, Vol. I, pp. 216, 217; and on Emmaus see on Luke 24:13 in the present Commentary. Indeed, the Third Gospel's seemingly incidental remarks, relating to geography and history, to the extent in which comparison with other sources is possible, are in full agreement with what is known about the Palestinian and surrounding scene.[33]

What is true with respect to *geography* and *history* holds also for the *customs* prevailing in the days described in Luke's Gospel. All of them correspond with information available from other sources, sacred and secular. To mention but a few of these usual practices: temple liturgy and priestly duties (1:5–10, 21, 23; 6:4); customs pertaining to the birth and naming of a child (1:57–63); circumcision (1:59; 2:21); purification and presentation (2: 22); Passover attendance and preparation for the Bar Mitzvah ceremony (2:41, 42); the custom of "publicans" to exact more than their due (3:13); winnowing, gathering of wheat, burning of chaff (3:17); synagogue liturgy (4:16–21); the washing of nets (5:2). So one could continue.

With respect to Acts the story is no different:

1:8: "Jerusalem, Judea, Samaria, ends of the earth." From Jerusalem as starting point this division of terrain for successive missionary activity is logical.

1:11: The designation *men of Galilee* is accurate.

1:12: Mt. Olivet is indeed "about a sabbath day's journey"—circa 3000 feet—from Jerusalem.

1:19: Luke knows that the burial place which the chief priests purchased with Judas' tainted money came to be called "the Field of Blood."

2:9–11: The series of nations represented at Jerusalem on the day of Pentecost follows a natural pattern, as can be seen by tracing them on a map.

8:26: The designation *desert road* suits the one from Jerusalem to Gaza.

9:11: For "Straight Street" in Damascus see L. H. Grollenberg, *op. cit.*, Plates 387–390, p. 133.

9:32–38: Lydda (O.T. "Lod") is indeed "near to" (about 10 miles southeast of) Joppa (modern Jaffa) on the Mediterranean Coast. That the news with respect to the cure of Aeneas at Lydda would spread throughout the Plain of Sharon was to be expected.

10:1: That Caesarea, in the Plain of Sharon, should be mentioned next, is again very natural.

10:6: It was natural for a tanner to live outside the city, near the seaside. Think of the unpleasant odors connected with his trade, and the need of easy access to a body of water for washing the skins.

---

33. In this connection see L. H. Grollenberg, *Atlas of the Bible*, New York, etc., 1956, p. 132.

12:4–10: Note: prison, squads of four soldiers each, chains, sentries, iron gate. Luke has detailed knowledge of the prison.

12:12–17: He also knows exactly where the disciples were gathered; in fact, even knows the name of Mary's servant girl.

12:19–23: Luke is thoroughly acquainted with the *where, when, why,* and *how* of the death of Herod Agrippa I. Cf. Josephus, *Antiquities* XIX.343–350.

21:40: Again the evangelist shows his thorough knowledge of Jerusalem and its temple. The fortress of Antonia, northwest of the temple, was connected with the temple's outer court by means of two flights of steps.

One of the most dramatic, definitely exciting, chapters of Acts is the twenty-third. First we see Paul before the Sanhedrin. The apostle's claim that he had lived in harmony with the dictates of his conscience corresponds with what we find in Acts 24:16 and Phil. 3:6. The action of the highpriest, Ananias, a man despised even by the Jews because of his greed, was both legally and morally irresponsible. Therefore, Paul's reaction is at least understandable. The apostle's excusable failure to discern the identity of the man who had issued the order to strike him across the mouth shows how very "human" he was. The story of the plot against Paul's life, how it was discovered and how it was foiled, is presented in a most dramatic and true-to-life fashion. Note also the Roman tribune's kind attitude toward Paul's nephew, his letter, and his forceful action in behalf of the apostle. Then try to visualize the midnight ride from Jerusalem to Antipatris (about 35 miles), the trip from Antipatris to Caesarea (27 additional miles), and the arrival at the headquarters of Governor Felix in Caesarea. All is vivid, clear, manifestly accurate.

We are trying to be fair to "redaction criticism." What is good about it has been mentioned. Its errors have also been exposed. We shall have occasion to refer to it again; see pp. 553; 555; 991. See also earlier remarks (N.T.C. on Matthew, pp. 21, 22; and on Mark, pp. 599, 600). Our main criticism is that, having—whether explicitly or implicitly—cast aside the fact that the words of II Tim. 3:16, 17; II Peter 1:21 also apply to the first four books of the New Testament, redaction criticism frequently pays too little attention to what is written in the sacred text. At times instead of exegesis it offers fantasies. Not always, to be sure, but in many instances.

If this criticism seems too harsh, let the reader take note of the book review by Quentin Quesnell. See *JBL*, Vol. 93, No. 4 (Dec. 1974), pp. 614, 615. It deals with this very subject of *Redaction Criticism.* It warns that if this kind of criticism begins to exempt exegetes from adhering to the text it may already have outlived its usefulness. It correctly points out that the real question should always be, "What did the author of this text intend?" It shows that the wrong method of handling the material presented to us in the Gospels leads to "fantasy and foible." Exactly! Isa. 40:8!

D. *If Possible, Even More Than Do the Other Synoptics, Luke's Gospel Emphasizes Christ's Tender Love, His Far-Reaching Sympathy*

In each Gospel Jesus is pictured as the long-awaited Messiah, sent by the Father and anointed by the Spirit to be his people's Great Prophet, Sympathetic Highpriest, and Eternal King. It has already been indicated that it is the prophetic office that comes into the foreground in Matthew (see N.T.C. on Matthew, pp. 82, 83), and the kingly in Mark (N.T.C. on Mark, pp. 14, 17, 18).

Are we in danger of arbitrarily concluding, by a process of elimination, that Christ's highpriestly office is emphasized in Luke?

Answer: In describing the heavenly Highpriest Heb. 4:15 states, "We do not have a highpriest who is unable to sympathize with our weaknesses." This is clearly a litotes for "We definitely have a Highpriest who is able to sympathize—and does sympathize—with our weaknesses." His heart goes out to us to the extent that he offered himself for our sins (7:27). More even: He is constantly making intercession for us . . .; rather, *he ever lives to make intercession for us* (7:25), which is even more comforting and meaningful. In view of this sympathy, deep, tender, wide-embracing, the Savior rightly bears the title *Our Sympathetic Highpriest. And it is especially Luke who so describes him!*

Luke's book abounds in stories, parables, and sayings, in which our Lord's lovingkindness toward the less privileged, the weak, and the rejected comes to expression. His love in action is revealed to the poor and the social outcasts; to children, shepherds, and tax-collectors; to the sick, the handicapped, and lepers; to Samaritans and Gentiles (2:7, 8, 24; 4:18; 6:20; 7:2, 6, 9; 8:42, 55; 14:13, 23; 17:11–19; etc.). See, however, also on 2:39.

The beloved physician's book has been called The Gospel of Womanhood, for the Savior's tender and profound regard for women comes to the fore in this Gospel more clearly than in any other. Note, for example, the prominence accorded to Mary, the mother of Jesus, and to Elizabeth (chapters 1 and 2). Remember also that Anna, the prophetess, and Joanna, the loyal follower, are mentioned only in this Gospel (2:36–38; 8:3; 24:10). The beautiful story in which Mary (sister of Martha and of Lazarus) makes the right choice is told only here (10:38–42). This holds too for the stirring reports about Christ's kindness bestowed upon the widow of Nain (7:11–18), and upon the sinful woman who anointed the Lord (7:36–50). Unforgettable, too, is the parable of *The Widow Who Persevered* (18:1–8). And see 11:27, 28; 13:10–17; 23:27 f.

The Savior's own sympathy for those in distress, regardless of race, is marvelously portrayed in the parable of *The Samaritan Who Cared* (chapter 10). The Father's pardoning grace is most exquisitely enshrined in the parables of *The Lost ("Prodigal") Son* (chapter 15) and *The Pharisee and The*

Tax Collector (chapter 18), illustrative stories found only in Luke's Gospel. And it is here alone that we read the meaningful words, "And all flesh shall see the salvation of God" (3:6). On this ("the wideness of God's mercy") see also above: point I A 5. Cf. Isa. 52:10; Titus 2:11.

It is hardly necessary to add that when Luke so portrays Christ, he is not merely telling an interesting story. On the contrary, by means of the story he is saying: (a) "Accept that Sympathetic Highpriest as y o u r [or your] Lord and Savior"; and (b) "By God's grace show forth his virtues in y o u r [or your] lives [life]."

As to the source of Luke's stress on this aspect of Christ's activity, it has been traced by several authors to the physician's intimate friend, the apostle Paul. And it is true that the virtues extolled by Luke, and ascribed by him to Jesus, are also the very ones extolled and exhibited by Paul. See, for example, Rom. 12:9–21; 13:10; 14:19; 15:1–13; I Cor. 13; II Cor. 2:8; Gal. 4:19, 20; 5:22–24; Phil. 4:8, 9; Col. 3:12–17; I Thess. 2:11; etc. It would, therefore, be possible to add a seventh resemblance between Luke and Paul to the six that were mentioned previously.

Nevertheless, we must be careful here. After all, Luke reported the words and works of *Another,* namely, Jesus. And in Paul's epistles *Christ's* spirit is reflected. Luke and Paul were drinking water from the same Rock, and that Rock was—and is—Christ. Luke describes *him.* Paul reminds the readers of *him* (II Cor. 8:9; Eph. 4:31—5:2).

One further word of caution. We have dwelt long on the mercy and tender compassion of Christ, as it reflects itself in Luke and in Paul . . . in fact, in all God's true emissaries. But no matter how tender, deep, and far-reaching we picture this compassion and eagerness to help those in need, we must not—as is generally done—stop here, as if Jesus were the embodiment merely of humility, pity, and forgiveness, and as if both Luke and Paul had no further message to deliver. Such a representation is definitely out of balance.

What happens when God's love is unrequited? Read about it in I Cor. 5:3–5; Gal. 1:6–9; 5:1–4; yes, but also in Luke 3:17; 9:5, 41; 10:13–15; 11:17–19, 29–32, 39–52; 12:1, 2, 13, 14, 45, 46, 49–53; 13:28; 16:15; 19:22–27. Luke, rather than Matthew, reports that when Jesus spoke the Beatitudes he also uttered four Woes (6:20–26)! To proclaim the kindness of God, and then to omit his sternness (Rom. 11:22) is to preach half the gospel, which ultimately amounts to no gospel at all. And does not even this sternness have as one of its purposes to lead men to repentance? Do not Paul and Luke—and basically Christ himself—teach this? See I Cor. 5:5b; cf. II Cor. 2:6–8; also Luke 11:32; 12:15; 13:24, 34.

VI. What Is Its Theme and How Can It Be Outlined?

One of the differences between the authors of the other Gospels and Luke is that the latter presents an extensive birth narrative. Matthew offers a Genealogy of Jesus Christ and devotes 8 very important verses to his conception and birth, and then continues as follows: "Now when Jesus was born in Bethlehem of Judea in the days of Herod the King, behold, wise men from the east came to Jerusalem," etc. Mark presents no birth narrative at all. John reaches all the way back to eternity, stating, "In the beginning was the Word, and the Word was face to face with God, and the Word was God" (1:1; cf. 8:58). He summarizes the birth and life as follows: "And the Word became flesh, and dwelt among us as in a tent, and we beheld his glory, a glory as of the only begotten from the Father, full of grace and truth" (1:14). In accordance with his purpose (20:30, 31) John selects from the life of Jesus on earth certain important events, and also presents a death and resurrection narrative. He views Jesus as the One who came from heaven, having been given and sent by the Father (3:16; 6:51, 57; 8:42; etc.). Again, no birth narrative.

But Luke's Gospel is different. It devotes no less than 100 verses to the birth of Jesus and of his forerunner (1:1—2:20), then 32 more verses to the events of the holy child's eighth and his fortieth day and to what happened when he was twelve years of age, ending with the summary of 2:52.

Nevertheless, the Third Gospel, as well as the others, clearly indicates that in one very important respect the birth of Jesus differs from all other births. Not only was he born; he *was sent*. He *came with a task to perform, assigned to him by the Father* (22:29). That task was "to seek and to save what was lost" (19:10). See also 12:50; 22:22. Accordingly, a good theme (see John 17:4b) for the story told in any or all of the Gospels is:

The Work Thou Gavest Him To Do

The broad divisions would be the same for the three Synoptics, namely, this work (or this task):

   I. Begun
  II. Continued
 III. Accomplished

Or, in slightly different phraseology:

   I. Its Beginning or Inauguration
  II. Its Progress or Continuation
 III. Its Climax or Consummation

For the subdivisions of Luke, under each of these main headings, see the Table of Contents and the Outlines at the opening of the chapters.

VII. What Light Does This Gospel Shed on Today's Problems?

Having just now finished this Commentary on Luke, I address myself to this question. The answer can be divided into four parts:

A. *This Gospel is a Book of Doctrine Showing Us What to Believe.*

Apart from God's special revelation man is living in *darkness.* He may say that what was good enough to be believed by former generations is not good enough today, but he forgets that man's basic needs are still the same. The ultimate question as man faces not only the problems of life but also of death is still, "How can a man be just before God?" (Job 9:2). What man needs, therefore, is doctrine. *True* doctrine! Luke's Gospel presents itself as a book of doctrine. Its opening words may be summarized as follows, "Theophilus, I am writing this book so that you may know what to believe." The ruler of the synagogue is told, "Only believe" (8:50). Satan's aim is to see to it that the sinner does not believe and, as a result, will not be saved (8:12).

What, then, are some of the doctrines man must believe? There is space to mention only a few:

1. What must I do to be saved? Answer: I must confess my sinfulness to God and implore him for his grace, his pity (Luke 18:13).

2. I must believe that mercy is bestowed on us through the work of Jesus Christ, God's Son, who, being both God and man, and completely sinless, is able to save to the uttermost all those who surrender themselves to him. That Savior was born of a human mother, Mary, and is therefore *man.* But this human mother was a virgin when she conceived Jesus, and her conception was brought about not by man but by God. Jesus is therefore *God,* and *without any sin,* the Holy Spirit having taken care that sin's pollution was not transmitted to him. It is especially Matthew (1:21–23) and Luke (1:34, 35) who teach the doctrine of the Virgin Birth.

3. In any age it is a comfort to know that "my life in all its perfect plan was ordered ere my days began." Luke's Gospel gives prominence to this doctrine (2:14; 12:32; 18:7, 31; 22:22; cf. Acts 2:23). As these passages also show, in no way is human responsibility canceled.

B. *It is a Book of Ethics Telling Us How to Live.*

Because of the entrance of sin man *lacks a sense of duty.* He may boast about his accomplishments. Has he not reached the moon? At the same time unrest of every description is intensifying. The reason is that apart from God's special revelation man does not know how to live. Along with the other Gospels, but at times even more emphatically than the others, Luke stresses the threefold duty of *Humility*—the mother of Gratitude—

Homage, and *Helpfulness.* As to Humility, see Luke 9:46-48; 22:24-30; as to Gratitude, 17:11-19. Homage, including such elements as humble petition, praise, etc., is emphasized in 10:38—11:13. Helpfulness is illustrated unforgettably in 10:25-37.

The Christ depicted by Luke entered a world filled with class distinctions and barriers: racial, national, social, sexual. He insisted that by means of the application of self-sacrificing love for everyone these barriers be broken down (4:25-27; 7:9, 36-50; 8:3; etc.). We must love even our enemies (6:35), must proclaim the gospel to all nations (24:47), and in our enthusiasm for the mission cause must not forget to strengthen the brothers (1:1-4). All this must be done "to God's glory" (2:14, 20; 5:25; 18:43; 24:53).

C. *It is a Book of Comfort Teaching Us Why to Rejoice.*

More emphatically than any of the other Gospels Luke's book underscores the necessity and privilege of rejoicing. Joy sings its way through this book, as it does also, for example, through Paul's letter to the Philippians. Well, Luke and Paul were friends. They could often be seen in each other's company.

Luke's Gospel *begins* with five songs (see the Commentary), and *ends* with "great joy" and with continual praises to God (24:52, 53). In the heart and center of the book (10:20, 21; 15:7, 10) God himself is rejoicing . . . in the saved sinner's joy. Now, is not that beautiful?

The world in which we are living is filled with *despair.* Many of the most popular songs are superficial and fail to satisfy.

D. *It is a Book of Prophecy Informing Us What to Expect.*

1. It distinctly reveals to us that the glorious prophecy of Isa. 53 was fulfilled in Christ, and that he is therefore indeed the promised Redeemer (read the Commentary on 22:37; 23:34; 23:50 f.).

2. It emphasizes the need for the study of prophecy, with a believing heart (24:25 f.).

3. It discloses certain things about the afterlife which otherwise we might not have known (12:47, 48).

4. It proclaims to us that in the life to come Jesus will bestow upon us honor and joy almost unbelievable (see Commentary on 12:37).

In a world of *confusion* with respect to the future, how relevant is Luke!

Commentary

on

The Gospel According to Luke

The Work Thou Gavest Him To Do

Its Beginning

or

Inauguration

Chapters 1:1—4:13

Outline of Chapter 1

Theme: *The Work Thou Gavest Him to Do*

CHAPTER I

LUKE 1:1

1 1 Since[34] many have undertaken to draw up a narrative concerning the things that have been fulfilled among us, 2 just as they who from the beginning were eyewitnesses and ministers[35] of the word handed them down to us, 3 it seemed fitting for me also, having traced the course of all things accurately from the beginning, to write an orderly account for you, most excellent[36] Theophilus, 4 in order that you may know[37] the exact truth[38] with respect to the matters concerning which you received instruction.

1:1–4 *Dedicatory Preface*

Beginning with this section (1:1–4) the notes on Greek words, phrases, and grammatical constructions will be found or indicated at the close of the section.

In order to retain something of the flavor of Luke's beautiful and balanced sentence, I have resisted the temptation of cutting it up into several short statements.[39]

In ancient times prologues of this general character were rather common. Thus, Josephus begins his work *Against Apion* (I.1–3) as follows:

"In my history of our *Antiquities,* most excellent Epaphroditus, I have, I believe, made sufficiently clear to any who may peruse that work the antiquity of our Jewish race.... However, since I notice that a considerable number of persons, influenced by the malicious slanders of certain individuals, discredit the statements in my history . . . I deem it my duty to devote a brief treatise to all these points; in order at once to convict our detractors . . . to correct the ignorance of others, and to instruct all who desire to know the truth concerning the antiquity of our race." Vol. II of the same work opens as follows: "In the first volume of this work [cf. Acts

---

34. Or: Inasmuch as; or: since by now.
35. Or: servants.
36. Or: most noble.
37. Or: may come to know.
38. Or: the certainty.
39. Verses 1–4 are *one sentence* also in A.V., A.R.V., R.S.V., Moffatt, Weymouth, Riverside, Berkeley, N.A.S., Williams, Jerusalem Bible, Dutch (both Statenvertaling and Nieuwe Vertaling), and the French, Frisian, German, South African, Spanish, and Swedish translations in my possession.

53

1:1], most esteemed Epaphroditus, I demonstrated the antiquity of our race.... I also challenged the statements of Manetho, Chaeremon, and some others. I shall now proceed to refute the remaining authors who have attacked us." See also that same historian's introduction to his *History of the Jewish War*.

Compare the prologues with which the following writers begin their accounts: Greek medical men such as Hippocrates, Dioscorides, and Galen; the historians Herodotus, Thucydides, and Polybius; and the biographer and miscellaneous writer Plutarch.[40]

But although it is true that Luke, as a highly cultured author, writing flawless and elegant Greek, adopts the type of introduction that was customary with writers of that day and age, his prologue is more beautifully balanced than any of the others and also kinder in tone than some of them. A quick comparison with the introductions by Josephus immediately causes this contrast to stand out sharply: Luke's foreword, correctly interpreted, contains no recriminatory remarks. It is the product of divine inspiration!

Luke's Preface deals with two matters: (a) Motivation, and (b) Purpose.

Motivation

So important are the events concerning Jesus that many people have already taken in hand to blend into a narrative the reports concerning these happenings (verse 1).

Eyewitnesses have handed down these reports to us (verse 2).

I [Luke] have thoroughly investigated all essential matters (verse 3).

Purpose

Thus equipped, I [Luke] write this Gospel in order that you, Theophilus—and others like you—may know the exact truth with respect to the matters concerning which you have already received some instruction (verse 4).

1. Since many have undertaken to draw up a narrative concerning the things that have been fulfilled among us ...

a. "Since many have undertaken... it seemed fitting for me also to write."

Does Luke mean, "Since others have done such a poor job, I will do better"? The church historian Eusebius (*op. cit.* III.xxiv.15) seems to have been of that opinion. He represents Luke as saying, in effect, "What others

40. For more on such introductory sentences—Luke 1:1-4, etc.—see H. J. Cadbury, *The Beginnings of Christianity* (5 volumes, edited by F. J. Foakes Jackson and K. Lake, London, 1920-1933), Vol. II, p. 490 f.; H. Mulder, *De Eerste Hoofdstukken van het Evangelie naar Lukas in hun Structurele Samenhang*, doctoral dissertation, Amsterdam-Delft, 1948, pp. 105, 106; N. B. Stonehouse, *The Witness of Luke to Christ*, Grand Rapids, 1951, pp. 24, 25; and J. Sneen, "An Exegesis of Luke 1:1-4 with Special Regard to Luke's Purpose as a Historian," *ET* Vol. 83, No. 2 (Nov. 1971), pp. 40-43.

have somewhat rashly attempted I will remedy. I will correct what those others have written."

However, unbiased reading of 1:1–4 immediately shows that Luke does not say, "I will do better than they," but rather, "I will *also* put my hand to writing a narrative concerning these things." Note verse 3: "it seemed fitting for me also," etc.

The next question might well be, "But if Luke is not finding fault with what others have already done, and perhaps even approves of it, then why does he also wish to write?" The answer may well be that though others had written, no one as yet had composed as complete an account as Luke envisioned. Note verse 3: "having traced the course of *all things* accurately *from the beginning.* . . ." For more on this see *Introduction,* point V B, and see on 1:3. In this connection it must not be overlooked that when the evangelist wrote these four verses he undoubtedly already had in mind the writing of Acts as well as the Third Gospel. The story beginning with the annunciation of the birth of John the Baptist and extending all the way to the spreading of the gospel from Rome as a center, through the labors of the apostle-prisoner Paul, had never as yet been presented in one beautifully arranged account!

Luke writes, "Many have undertaken to draw up a narrative." Who were those "many"? Was Matthew included? The possibility that Luke made use of Matthew's Gospel must not be denied. On this see N.T.C. on Matthew, p. 53. Nevertheless, it is possible so to interpret Luke 1:2 that here in 1:1 Luke *is excluding* works by eyewitnesses, like Matthew. Besides, as has become abundantly clear—see *Introduction,* points III A 2, and B 2—a considerable portion of Luke's Gospel reminds one of Mark. It has been shown—see N.T.C. on Matthew, pp. 36–47—that in all probability it was Luke who used Mark's Gospel, not vice versa. Therefore, here in 1:1 Luke may well have been thinking of Mark as one of the "many" who had undertaken to draw up a narrative. Moreover, since a Hebrew or Aramaic written account certainly underlies Luke's nativity narrative (1:5—2:52) and probably also some of the later sections, the beloved physician most likely also included the author(s) of such materials in his reference to the "many" who had undertaken to write. And since Luke says "many have undertaken to draw up a narrative," the possibility must be allowed that some of these "many" had failed to complete that which they had begun to do.

b. "to draw up a narrative concerning the things that have been fulfilled. . ." See footnote 48 on the meaning of the word *fulfilled.*

It is clear from Luke's entire Gospel that he regards history not as the sum total of chance occurrences, or as the result of a series of fortuitous circumstances, but as the fulfilment of the divine plan; hence also of prophecy. This is clear especially from 22:22, but see also 1:45, 54, 55, 69, 70; 2:38; 3:3–6; 4:21, 43; 5:32; 7:20; 9:22, 44; 12:50; 18:31–33; 19:41–44; ch. 21; 24:25–28, 44–49. And for Acts see in that book 2:23; 3:18; 4:28.

c. "among us." Although this pronoun is broad enough to embrace all those among whom John the Baptist and Jesus walked and even those who were in any way affected by the outpouring of the Holy Spirit—the eyewitnesses, those to whom their reports were transmitted, Luke himself, his contemporaries, believers, unbelievers—it surely refers *especially* to the believing recipients of God's grace in Christ. It was to them alone that the birth of the Baptist and that of Jesus had been announced, that Messiah's suffering and death had been predicted, that the risen Christ had appeared. Upon them, them alone, the Holy Spirit had been poured out, etc.

2. ... just as they who from the beginning were eyewitnesses and ministers of the word handed them down to us... Note that Luke does not include himself among the eyewitnesses but among those to whom these eyewitnesses handed down their reports and testimonies. That the term *eyewitnesses* includes earwitnesses is clear from I John 1:1. Among these early witnesses one must certainly include the apostles Peter (Matt. 16:13–20; Luke 24:34; John 1:40–42; 21:15–23; I Cor. 15:5; I Peter 5:1; II Peter 1:16), and John (John 21:24; I John 1:1); in fact The Twelve (John 15:27); also the brothers of Jesus, his mother and other women (Acts 1:14); furthermore Joseph called Barsabbas, Matthias (Acts 1:21–23), etc. See also *Introduction,* point III B 6.

Luke does not specify whether the reports were handed down in oral or in written form. He leaves room for both types of transmission.

These same people, the eyewitnesses, not only received, they also gave: whatever they had seen and heard they proclaimed and "handed down" to others of their own generation and later ones. They became "ministers" or "servants" of the word, that is, of the gospel. It was with a feeling of profound reverence and awe that they handled the messages they had received from the lips of the Savior and the facts about him. They did not place themselves above the word, using it merely as a self-serving tool, but beneath it, becoming its *servants*.

To the two reasons already mentioned (see verses 1 and 2) Luke now adds a third, showing what it was that motivated and qualified him to write: **3. ... it seemed fitting for me also, having traced the course of all things accurately from the beginning...** This shows that Luke wants his treatise to be not only complete but also accurate. Was it perhaps for this very reason that when he draws on Semitic sources (e.g., the nativity narratives) he leaves the phraseology and style virtually untouched, and at times seems to simply translate, almost word for word, from Semitic into Greek?

Continued: **to write an orderly account...** According to the sense of the word *orderly* used in the original, an orderly account is one in which one says *next* what should be said *next*. It is an account which is not confused or haphazard. By no means is it true that the evangelist here promises to write a Gospel in which every event will be related in precisely chronological sequence. Even today history books do not always follow that pattern. One historian, to be sure, in describing the administration of George

Washington, will report its important events, of whatever character—political, military, social, economic, etc.—year by year or even month by month, in exact chronological sequence. Another, having pictured the *political* events from beginning (1789) to end (1797) will then go back to describe what took place during this period in the *economic* sphere; for example, the invention of the cotton gin by Eli Whitney (1793).

By and large the sequence of events as reported by Luke is chronological. On the other hand, with respect to individual details this is by no means always the case. Study (a) Luke's account of the three temptations (4:3-13), comparing it with that of Matthew (4:3-11); (b) the early place where Luke describes Jesus' rejection at Nazareth (4:16-30), comparing it with the far later place in their respective Gospels where Matthew and Mark cover the same event (Matt. 13:54-58; Mark 6:1-6); (c) the problem posed by Luke 9:51; 13:22; 17:11 (three separate journeys to Jerusalem?); and (d) the question raised by Luke 22:19-23 (cf. John 13:30) as to whether Judas Iscariot partook of the Last Supper. However, these items will be discussed in connection with each of the Lucan passages. For Luke 9:51; 13:22; 17:11 see the special study in this commentary, entitled *Summary of and Introduction to Luke's Central Section (9:51—18:14)*, subheading B, pp. 541-545. It will become clear that Luke makes no mistakes. He has his good reasons for writing exactly as he does, as guided by the Spirit. To him a logical or topical connection is frequently more important than precise chronological sequence. Throughout he is writing a truly "orderly" account, as he promises here in 1:3.

Continued: **for you, most excellent Theophilus.**

Who was Theophilus? Even when we grant—as we should—that Theophilus was a real person, and not a symbol for anyone "loved by God," which is the meaning of the name, we still discover that there is a wide difference of opinion regarding the addressee. Here are some of the different views:

a. Theophilus was, or had been, a slave owner. One of his slaves had been Luke, who, having won his master's confidence and affection, was given his freedom and even an education.[41] See also above (*Introduction*, point I B 2, p. 10).

Comment. This is an interesting theory, but unsupported by any evidence.

b. He was Luke's "patron of letters." Since Theophilus was an influential person and a man of means, and besides a friend of Luke, the latter expected him to defray the expenses involved in the composition and distribution of Third Gospel-Acts.[42]

---

41. D. A. Hayes, *The Most Beautiful Book Ever Written*, New York, etc., 1913, pp. 46, 50, 51.

42. This is a widely held opinion. See F. Godet, *A Commentary on the Gospel of St. Luke*, Edinburgh, 1890, Vol. I, p. 31; W. J. Harrington, *op. cit.*, p. 33; E. E. Ellis, *op. cit.*, p. 64, to mention only a few.

General agreement, however, is lacking. H. Mulder, in his doctoral dissertation, *De Eerste Hoofdstukken*, rejects this theory, deeming it to be in conflict with Luke's purpose stated in 1:4.

Comment. If the "patron" theory is adopted, because it is believed to be in harmony with what was at that time a rather general practice, and if securing such a sponsor is regarded as being in any sense Luke's purpose, this purpose must be thought of as definitely subsidiary to his main objective, clearly stated in verse 4.

c. He was a "God-fearer"; that is, he belonged to that large group of Gentiles who had renounced polytheism, had embraced the ethical monotheism of Judaism, attended the synagogue, but had not promised to obey the entire Jewish law, including its circumcision requirement. The fact that Luke often mentions these "God-fearers" or semi-proselytes (Acts 13:43, 50; 16:14; 17:4, 17; 18:7) points to the conclusion that Theophilus too belonged to this group.[43]

For comment see point (d).

d. As pictured in Luke 1:4 Theophilus is still a Gentile, for before the third century A.D. the epithet *most excellent* was never used in connection with believers in Christ. However, since in Acts 1:1 the adjective *most excellent* is dropped and only the name *Theophilus* remains, the conclusion is warranted that by means of the reading of the Third Gospel Theophilus had become a Christian.[44]

Comment on theories (c) and (d). There is no solid evidence in support of either of these theories. As to (c), it is not clear that Theophilus had arrived at the knowledge of the Christian religion via Judaism. He may have, but we do not know. And as to (d), there may have been any number of possible reasons why Luke dropped the epithet in Acts 1:1. One reason may have been that he regarded Luke 1:1-4 as a preamble to both books, as he probably did, and therefore did not consider the repetition of "most excellent" to be necessary.

e. "It is impossible for us to ascertain whether Theophilus is here addressed as occupant of a high position in the government, as belonging to the equestrian order, or simply as a person worthy of high honor. Therefore we are unable to say whether the proper rendering [in Luke 1:3] is 'your excellency' (or something similar), or rather 'highly honored,' 'preeminent,' or 'most noble.' In headings or dedicatory introductions the epithet used by Luke occurs rather frequently, at times perhaps as an expression of courtesy."[45]

Comment. This view makes sense. It does not restrict the possibilities too narrowly. The opinion that Theophilus may have occupied an important position in the Roman government has in its favor that, if this be true, the epithet *most excellent* would have approximately the same meaning here which it has in Acts 23:26; 24:3; and also in 26:25, in which passages it is

---

43. This is H. Mulder's own theory, as described in several of his books, including *Hoofdlijnen van Lucas 2*, The Hague, 1959, pp. 9-12.

44. This is T. Zahn's theory, adopted by Lenski, *op. cit.*, p. 23.

45. S. Greijdanus, *Kommentaar*, Vol. I, p. 11.

applied respectively to the procurators Felix and Festus. But, as Greij-danus also indicates, Theophilus may simply have been "a person worthy of high honor," or, as F. F. Bruce states, "a representative member of the intelligent middle-class public at Rome."[46]

Though it cannot be proved that Theophilus was living in or near Rome when Luke—perhaps also now at Rome; see above, *Introduction*, point IV B, p. 33—addressed him, neither is this idea entirely speculative. In Acts 28:15 Luke makes mention of both The Three Taverns and The Market of Appius (Latin: *Tres Tabernae, Appii Forum*). He mentions these two places without any further elucidation as to where they were located (rather close to Rome, respectively 33 and 43 miles south of the city). On the other hand, Luke is frequently more specific when he mentions places located a long distance away from Rome (Luke 1:26; 4:31; 8:26). Therefore, it may not be too risky to infer that the reason for this degree of difference in supplying geographical detail could be that Theophilus was living in or near Rome and was therefore not in need of receiving a more circumstantial report about nearby places.[47]

Having stated the reasons which motivated and entitled him to write this Gospel, Luke now proceeds to mention his purpose: **4. in order that you may know** [or: **may come to know**] **the exact truth with respect to the matters concerning which you received instruction.**

It is clear that Theophilus had already received some—perhaps even considerable—information in Christian doctrine. To a certain extent the truth of the Christian religion had been dinned into his ears; that is, he had been "catechized." However, he is in need of a more thorough grounding in the truth, the *facts* concerning Jesus and his church. That Luke regards this "truth" as significant is clear from what he has already said (see especially verse 3). For Theophilus *to know* (or: come to know) *the exact truth* was very important. For this there were two reasons: (a) to keep him from falling into error. Think of the many attacks upon the truth constantly being made by both Jew and Gentile (Matt. 19:3-8; 27:63; John 6:42, 52; 7:40-49; 9:24; Acts 26:24; 28:22; I Cor. 1:23); and (b) to obtain salvation in full measure to the glory of God.

In connection with (b), the words "that you may know [or: come to know] the exact truth" remind us of the statement of Jesus, "You will know the truth, and the truth will set you free" (John 8:32). Other significant passages showing the great importance which Jesus and the New Testament writers attach to *knowing the truth* are John 16:13; 17:17, 19; Gal. 2:5; Eph. 1:13; 4:15; II Thess. 2:10, 12, 13; I Tim. 2:4; 3:15; II Tim. 2:15; II Peter 1:12. And for the Old Testament see especially Hos. 4:6, "My people are destroyed for lack of knowledge."

---

46. *Commentary on the Book of Acts*, p. 31.
47. See C. F. Keil, *Commentar über die Evangelien des Markus und Lucas*, Leipzig, 1879, p. 184; and H. Mulder, *Hoofdlijnen*, p. 10.

This brings up the interesting question: Just how are the various elements of Christian experience—the intellectual, emotional, and volitional—related to each other? Which, if any, is basic and which follows in importance? How do they interact? For the answer, as this commentator sees it, consult N.T.C. on John, Vol. II, pp. 10, 11. The concluding lines of the discussion as found there are as follows:

"The only logical conclusion, in view of these various and (at first glance) seemingly (though never *really*) conflicting representations, is this: When we speak of *knowledge, love, and obedience,* we are not thinking of three altogether separate experiences, but of one single, comprehensive experience in which the three are united in such a manner that each contributes its share, and all cooperate unto man's salvation and God's glory. This experience is *personal* in character. Hence, we can no longer speak of the primacy of the intellect or of the primacy of the emotions or of the primacy of the will, but of the primacy of the sovereign grace of God influencing and transforming the entire personality for the glory of God."

It was that result which Luke was striving, by God's grace and power, to bring about in the heart and life of Theophilus, and all those whom he represented.[48]

Practical Lessons Derived from Luke 1:1–4

Verse 1

"The things that have been fulfilled among us." It is comforting to know that history—including that of our own lives—is the fulfilment of God's plan. This does not cancel human responsibility. See Luke 22:22; Acts 2:23.

Verse 2

"Servants of the word." He who rides a hobby is placing himself above God's Word.

Verses 2, 3

"Eyewitnesses... having traced the course of all things accurately from the beginning." The Christian religion is not a matter of "cunningly devised myths" (II Peter 1:16), but rests on solid, historical fact. We should thank God for having qualified such men as Luke and the other evangelists, with their varied talents, to write the four Gospels.

Verse 3

"Most excellent" or "most noble." The Christian religion does not destroy courtesy or excuse rudeness.

---

48. Notes on Greek words, phrases, and constructions in 1:1–4 begin on page 61.

Verses 3 and 4

"To write . . . in order that you may know." The believer—in this case Luke—is deeply concerned about his fellow man and endeavors to bring him to the knowledge of the truth.

Verse 4

"The matters concerning which you received instruction." The church that neglects *catechetical* instruction has itself to blame for its waning strength.

Notes on Greek Words, Phrases, and Constructions in 1:1–4

Whenever a Greek word is followed by an asterisk, its New Testament occurrence is confined to the Third Gospel. In a book written by versatile Luke we expect many such words. When the word is followed by a double asterisk, its New Testament occurrence is confined to the Third Gospel and Acts.

Verse 1

ἐπειδήπερ* is a strengthened form of ἐπειδή. The meaning of ἐπειδήπερ is: inasmuch as, since; or, if the sense is both causal and temporal: since by now.

ἐπεχείρησαν, third per. pl. aor. indicat. of ἐπιχειρέω**, to put one's hand (χείρ) to, to undertake, seek, attempt. Cf. Acts 9:29; 19:13.

ἀνατάξασθαι, aor. infinitive of ἀνατάσσομαι*, to arrange in proper order, draw up, compose.

διήγησις*; cf. διηγέομαι; German *durchführen,* Dutch *doorvoeren;* the meaning of the noun is: account, narrative, with emphasis on a degree of fulness.

πεπληροφορημένων, gen. pl. perf. passive participle of πληροφορέω; from πλήρης, full, and φορέω, cf. φέρω, to bring; hence, to bring to fulness, *to fulfill,* accomplish in full. The verbal form is a synonym of πληρόω, which occurs frequently in connection with fulfilment of prophecy (cf. 4:21; 24:44; Matt. 1:22; 2:15, 17). This is probably also the meaning here in Luke 1:1. When πληροφορέω is used in connection with persons, it has the meaning: to fully convince, persuade; in the passive: to be fully convinced (Rom. 14:5). There are those who ascribe this meaning also to the word as used here in Luke 1:1, resulting in the meaning: "on which there is full conviction among us," or something similar. Some authors seem to waver between this and the meaning mentioned earlier. See A. T. Robertson's rendering in *A Translation of Luke's Gospel,* New York, 1923, p. 13; and cf. with his rendering in *Word Pictures,* Vol. II, p. 4. As I see it, because Luke in 1:1 is speaking about *things* and because of his emphasis on fulfilment of prophecy—see the references given in the text—the rendering "the things that have been fulfilled among us" deserves the preference.

Verse 2

παρέδοσαν, third per. pl. aor. act. of παραδίδωμι. The word has various meanings, to hand over, deliver, betray, commit, commend, allow. Here and in several other cases it is used with respect to tradition (whether written, oral, or both); hence, to hand down, pass on, transmit.

αὐτόπτης, eyewitness. Cf. *autopsy.* For synonym see II Peter 1:16.

ὑπηρέτης, from ὑπό, under, and ἐρέσσω, to row; hence basically under-rower; here servant, minister. Other New Testament meanings: officer, helper, assistant, attendant.

τοῦ λόγου, of the word; that is, of the gospel, the message of salvation centering in Jesus Christ and made possible by him. The phrase "of the word" modifies "ministers," not "eyewitnesses." At times the word λόγος has reference to that which proceeds directly from Jesus' lips. For still another meaning see on verse 4. There is no justification for confusing the meaning of λόγος in the Third Gospel with the Logos idea in John's Gospel, as if also in the Third Gospel λόγος would refer directly to the Son of God.

Verse 3

παρηκολουθηκότι, dat. s. m. perfect participle of παρακολουθέω, to follow, attend; here: to follow through mentally, to investigate, to trace the course of events (from beginning to end). The perfect tense shows that Luke had done this before he started to write. For a somewhat different meaning of the verb see N.T.C. on I Tim. 4:6; II Tim. 3:10.

ἄνωθεν, from the beginning; cf. Mark 15:38: "from top to bottom." In John 3:3, 7: from above, again.

καθεξῆς** = κατά and ἑξῆς. κατά in such cases is distributive in meaning; ἑξῆς—from ἔχω, fut. ἕξω—means having, being after or next to; hence καθεξῆς here in 1:3 means: one after another; in regular order. To write an account in regular order means to write an orderly account. Related meanings: next, soon afterward (Luke 8:1), place to place (Acts 18:23), point by point (Acts 11:4).

κράτιστε, voc. s. m. of κράτιστος**, the superlative of κρατύς.

Verse 4

ἵνα, here with full final sense: in order that. Luke is stating his *purpose* in writing to Theophilus.

ἐπιγνῷς, sec. per. s. aor. subjunctive of ἐπιγινώσκω. For this verb see N.T.C. on Matthew, p. 502, footnote 482. Also here in Luke 1:4 the question is whether the prefix ἐπί in ἐπιγνῷς has an intensive meaning. Commentators differ widely. A possibility is: that you may come to know, etc. See also R. E. Picirelli, "The Meaning of 'Epignosis,'" *EQ* XLVII, No. 2 (April–June, 1975), pp. 85–93; and R. Bultmann on γινώσκω and related words, in Th.D.N.T., Vol. I, pp. 689–719; especially pp. 703, 704. In the present case the idea *exact* or *thorough* knowledge is implied in the combination of the verb ἐπιγνῷς and its object ἀσφάλειαν.

κατηχήθης, sec. per. s. aor. indicat. passive of κατηχέω. Cf. *echo, catechize.* The truth of the gospel has been "sounded down upon" Theophilus. He had been "instructed" in it. Cf. Acts 18:25; Rom. 2:18; Gal. 6:6a.

ἀσφάλεια. The cognate verb σφάλλω means: to cause to totter or fall; hence, the noun means: that which cannot fall; here in 1:4 exact truth, certainty; in I Thess. 5:3 (cf. Acts 5:23) safety, security.

λόγος, here thing, matter; so also in Acts 8:21; 15:6. Cf. the double meaning of Hebrew *dābhār.*

5 In the days of Herod, king of Judea,[49] there was a priest named Zechariah, who belonged to the priestly division of Abijah. His wife was also a descendant of Aaron,[50] and her name was Elizabeth. 6 Both were righteous in the sight of God, observing all the commandments and requirements of the Lord, blameless. 7 However, they were childless, because Elizabeth was barren, and both were advanced in years.

8 Once while Zechariah was serving as priest before God, in the appointed order of his division, 9 according to the custom of the priesthood he was chosen by lot to burn incense after having gone into the sanctuary of the Lord. 10 At the hour of the burning of incense the entire assembled congregation was outside, engaged in prayer.

11 Then there appeared to him an angel of the Lord, standing at the right of the altar of incense. 12 Now when Zechariah saw him, he became troubled and overwhelmed with fear.[51] 13 But the angel said to him, "Do not be afraid,[52] Zechariah, for your petition has been heard. Your wife Elizabeth will bear you a son, and you shall give him the name John.
14 You will have joy and exultation,[53] and many will rejoice over his birth; 15 for he will be great in the sight of the Lord. Wine or strong drink he must never touch, and he will be filled with the Holy Spirit even from his mother's womb. 16 Many of the sons of Israel will he turn to the Lord their God. 17 And he will go before him in the spirit and power of Elijah, to turn the hearts of the fathers to the children, and the disobedient to the frame of mind of the righteous, in order to make ready for the Lord a people well-prepared."

18 Then Zechariah asked the angel, "How can I be sure of this? For I am an old man, and my wife is advanced in years."

19 "I am Gabriel," the angel answered. "I stand in the presence of God, and I was sent to speak to you, and to bring you this good news. 20 And now, mark well, because you did not believe my words, which will be fulfilled in their proper time, you will remain silent and not able to speak until the day when these things take place."

21 Meanwhile the people were waiting for Zechariah and wondering why he stayed away so long in the sanctuary. 22 And when he did come out, he was unable to speak to them. Then they realized that he had seen a vision in the sanctuary, for he kept making signs to them but remained unable to speak.

23 And when the days of his service were completed he went back to his home. 24 After these days his wife Elizabeth became pregnant. For five months she kept herself in seclusion, saying, 25 "This is the way the Lord has dealt with me in the days in which he looked (with favor) upon me, to remove my disgrace among the people."

1:5-25 *The Birth of John the Baptist Foretold*

Luke has promised an orderly account. In his first two chapters he already begins to fulfil this promise. Note the exquisite symmetry, the pleasing parallelism:

Two births are promised: that of the herald and that of the One whom that herald is going to introduce to the people. In each case it is the angel Gabriel who foretells the birth. He predicts it respectively to the herald's prospective father Zechariah, and to the Great One's mother-to-be Mary

---

49. Or: king of the country of the Jews.
50. Or: and his wife was of the daughters of Aaron.
51. Literally: and fear fell upon him.
52. Or: Stop being afraid.
53. Or: and exuberant gladness.

(1:5-38). When and how did *Joseph,* to whom Mary had been promised in marriage, become aware of her pregnancy? See Matt. 1:18-25. The two narratives—Matthew's and Luke's—supplement each other. At no point is there conflict.

Next in Luke's Gospel the two prospective mothers, Elizabeth and Mary, are seen together, for Mary is visiting her relative Elizabeth, who lives in a town in the hill country of Judah. As Mary enters, Elizabeth exclaims, "Blessed are you among women, and blessed is the fruit of your womb," etc. Mary, in turn, utters her Magnificat (1:39-56).

Recorded also are the two births: that of John, born to Elizabeth (1:57), and that of Jesus, born to Mary in Bethlehem of Judea, to which the couple—Joseph and Mary—traveled from their home in Nazareth (2:1-7).

In each case Luke relates the circumstances attending the birth, the circumcision and the naming of the child (1:58-66; 2:21). But now notice the contrast: in the case of John *the eighth day incidents* are followed by the song of his father Zechariah (1:67-79). In the case of Jesus, however, the song cannot even wait. *The universe-shaking birth itself* is *immediately* followed by an announcement to shepherds, the song of an angelic choir, and the resulting visit by the shepherds. These events, including the "Glory to God in the highest," etc. (2:8-20), *precede* the happenings on the eighth day. What a remarkable and meaningful arrangement!

The forerunner's life up to the time when he makes his public appearance is summarized in one verse (1:80). Very appropriately in the case of the chief figure, namely, Jesus himself, the evangelist goes into greater detail. We read about the presentation in the temple, Simeon's "Nunc Dimittis," Anna's thanksgiving and testimony, the return to Nazareth, and "the boy in the midst of the teachers" (2:22-52). And see also Matt. 2.

It is fitting that Mark, in describing the coming of our *Eternal King,* begins his Gospel by introducing the King's herald; and that Matthew, in fixing the attention upon our *Great Prophet,* already in the first chapter (verses 22, 23) and repeatedly afterward makes mention of the fulfilment of prophecy in him, and pictures him as being himself God's Messenger. Think of the Lord's six discourses recorded by Matthew, and of the many dominical sayings.[54] And so also it is appropriate that Luke, who in his Gospel—see *Introduction,* point V D—underscores the very qualities which Scripture also elsewhere associates with our *Sympathetic Highpriest* (Luke 4:16-27; cf. Heb. 4:14-16; 7:25), at the very outset pictures a *priest* who enters the sanctuary in order to burn incense. *Temple* passages peculiar to the Third Gospel are: 1:5-23; 2:22-35, 36-38, 41-51; 18:9-14; 21:37, 38; 24:53.

5. In the days of Herod, king of Judea, there was a priest named Zechariah, who belonged to the priestly division of Abijah.

The days of Herod! This is Herod I, often designated "Herod the

---

54. .6 per verse in Matthew; .51 in Luke; .49 in John; and .42 in Mark.

Great." The date of his birth seems to have been 74 B.C. The period during which he ruled over the Jews is generally dated 37–4 B.C.

He did not all at once become the actual ruler of all of Palestine. Rather, he had been nominated king of Judea by the Roman senate in the year 40 B.C. An army was given him. With this army—hence, "with his own sword"—he was to carve out a kingdom for himself. In this he gradually succeeded.

He is mentioned here (Luke 1:5) and also in Matt. 2:1–22, but nowhere else in the New Testament. He should not be confused with his son "Herod the tetrarch," as Luke sometimes calls that son (see also Matt. 14:1).

Herod the Great, the ruler to whom reference is made here in Luke 1:5, was capable, crafty, and cruel. He was the man who, in order that no one would be able to take away from him, from him *alone,* the designation *the king of the Jews,* and to appease his wrath, was going to order all the boy babies of Bethlehem and its surroundings to be murdered. For a further description of this terrible tyrant, see N.T.C. on Matthew, pp. 155–168; 176–193; and note his Family Tree on p. 189 of that volume.

In the appellation *king of Judea* the term *Judea* may well indicate "the land of the Jews in its entirety." See also on 4:44 and see Acts 26:20.

In the days, then, of this diabolical monster there lived a man who, together with his wife, exhibited the very opposite traits of character. Terrible tyrant—pious priest, what a contrast! The name of this priest was Zechariah (Greek and A.V. "Zecharias"). He must not be confused with any of the thirty other persons of (basically) that same name mentioned in Scripture. That a name meaning "Jehovah has remembered" should be popular is easily understood.

The Zechariah of Luke's story was a member of the priestly "course" or "division" of Abijah. During the reign of David the priests had been organized and divided into twenty-four divisions (I Chron. 24:1–6). These divisions were reaffirmed by David's son Solomon (II Chron. 8:14). The eighth division, the one to which Zechariah belonged, was that of Abijah (I Chron. 24:10). Only four divisions returned from Babylon (Ezra 2:36–39). But these four were redivided into twenty-four, and given the old names. Twice a year each division was on duty in the temple, and each time the period of service was one week. **His wife was also a descendant of Aaron, and her name was Elizabeth.** Her name, too, has a beautiful meaning, namely, "God [or: my God] is an oath," that is, is "the Absolutely Reliable One."

It was indeed a great blessing for a priest to marry a wife of priestly stock.[55] This was not required by the law, which stipulated only that the wife should be a virgin of his own people (Lev. 21:14). Between Zechariah and Elizabeth there was no danger of incompatibility. The fact that, with-

---

55. According to W. H. Gispen, *Het Boek Leviticus,* Kampen, 1950, p. 303, this happened frequently. See also S.BK., II, pp. 55–71.

out benefit of computer (!), this man had married a woman with whom he could live in peace and happiness is clear from Luke 1:60, 63; note the thorough agreement between husband and wife. It appears also in verse **6. Both were righteous in the sight of God, observing all the commandments and requirements of the Lord—blameless.**

What is meant by ". . . were righteous"? Apart from the sovereign grace of God revealed basically in the atoning death (the "blood") of Christ no one can ever be truly "righteous" (Exod. 12:13; Psalm 49:7; Isa. 53:4-6; Matt. 20:28; Mark 10:45; Luke 22:19, 20; Rom. 3:21-24; Eph. 1:7; Heb. 9:22; I Peter 2:24; Rev. 7:14). Another way of saying this is that basically there is no way in which a person can be truly "righteous before God," or "blameless," other than by imputation, so that the sinner's guilt is laid upon the Savior, and the Savior's righteousness upon the sinner. Nevertheless, Scripture itself justifies the terminology: *righteousness by imputation* and *righteousness by impartation*. To the latter the name *sanctification* is often given. Although these two should be distinguished, they should never be separated. Though it is true that good works have never saved anybody, it is also true that the person who is conscious of having been saved by grace through faith will put forth every effort to do good works. Eph. 2:8, 9 must never be separated from 2:10; nor Titus 2:11 from 2:14. The "forgiven trespass" and the "true heart" are twins:

> How blest is he whose trespass
> Has freely been forgiven,
> Whose sin is wholly covered
> Before the sight of heaven,
> Blest he to whom Jehovah
> Will not impute his sin,
> Who hath a guileless spirit,
> Whose heart is true within.

No. 55 (Psalm 32), first stanza, *Psalter Hymnal* of the Christian Reformed Church, Grand Rapids, 1958.

At times Scripture makes reference to these two kinds of righteousness almost in the same breath. Rom. 8:1 is a good example. Cf. "He breaks the *power of canceled* sin" (in *O For a Thousand Tongues*, by Charles Wesley). At times the emphasis is on righteousness by imputation (Rom. 3:24, 28; 5:1; Gal. 2:16; 3:11, 13); at times, as here in Luke 1:6, on righteousness by impartation. The best commentary on "righteous in the sight of God" is surely the text itself: "observing all the commandments and requirements of the Lord." It was in that sense that in the sight of God these two people were "blameless." Is it not true that with God honest intention is equal to action? See I Kings 8:18.

"Commandments and requirements." Cf. "commandments and statutes" (Deut. 4:1, 40; 6:2). A person who observes both the commandment and the statute is interested not only in the underlying principle but also in its application to concrete life situations. Not only in a very general way does he try to keep the first commandment, "You shall have no other gods before me" (Exod. 20:3), but he is also fully aware of its corollaries, one of them being, "The firstfruits of your soil you shall bring into the house of the Lord your God" (Exod. 23:19). He does the same with the sixth commandment, "You shall not kill" (Exod. 20:13); for example, "You shall not oppress a stranger" (Exod. 23:9); with the eighth, "You shall not steal" (Exod. 20:15); for example, "You shall not take a bribe" (Exod. 23:8); with the ninth, "You shall not bear false witness against your neighbor" (Exod. 20:16); implying, "You shall not take up a false report" (Exod. 23:1); and so with every commandment. In this connection see also Christ's own treatment of the commandments in the Sermon on the Mount (note especially Matt. 5:21–48).

Zechariah and Elizabeth, then, were people like Job (Job 1:1) and Simeon (Luke 2:25).

So far everything with respect to Zechariah and Elizabeth was wonderful. But now note:

7. However, they were childless, because Elizabeth was barren, and both were advanced in years. Barrenness was about the worst thing that could happen to a married woman. Across the many intervening centuries we can still hear Rachel saying to Jacob, "Give me children, or else I die" (Gen. 30:1). It still hurts to read how Hannah suffered because her rival Peninnah, instead of sympathizing with her, maliciously kept reminding her of the fact that the Lord had shut up her womb (I Sam. 1:6). Result: Hannah shed bitter tears.

Besides, was not fertility among the blessings of obedience God had promised to Israel? See Deut. 7:14; Psalm 113:9.

The trouble was that many people drew the wrong deduction from this promise, as if in any individual case barrenness was an infallible sign of God's disfavor. Unjustly, but all too often, the barren woman would be shunned, looked down upon, despised.

For many of these sorrowing wives, however, dreary days and sleepless nights were somewhat brightened by the hope that the situation might still change. But for Zechariah and Elizabeth even this flame of hope had begun to flicker. At last it was extinguished altogether, for by now both were "advanced in years" (lit. "in days").

And then a most unexpected event occurred: **8–10. Once while Zechariah was serving as priest before God, in the appointed order of his division, according to the custom of the priesthood he was chosen by lot to burn incense after having gone into the sanctuary of the Lord. At the hour of the burning of incense the entire assembled congregation was outside, engaged in prayer.**

Each day the various functions of the priesthood were apportioned by lot. The most solemn part of the entire liturgy was the burning of incense. It was then that the priest approached closest to the veil separating the

Holy Place from the Holy of Holies. In the economy of the old dispensation did not the Holy of Holies "have the golden altar of incense"? To be sure, for understandable practical reasons that altar actually *stood* in the Holy Place (Exod. 30:6, 10). But it *belonged* to the Holy of Holies (Heb. 9:4). On the Day of Atonement, once a year, was not the incense brought from this altar into the Holy of Holies, and was not the blood that had been sprinkled on the mercy-seat applied also to the altar of incense? See Lev. 16:15-19. Do not the shedding of blood and the rising cloud of incense belong together? Do not redemption and thanksgiving form a pair like cause and effect?

It is understandable that to be chosen by lot to burn incense was considered a unique privilege. Only once in a lifetime was a priest allowed to receive this honor. Ever afterward he was considered "rich and holy." Numerically speaking, to be chosen by lot to burn incense was a privilege shared by few.

Twice a day this incense was offered: in the morning and in mid-afternoon. Some[56] believe that what happened now occurred in the morning. Others,[57] basing their view on the fact that according to Luke 1:10 on this particular day a multitude of considerable magnitude had entered the temple courts, believe that the incident about to be related occurred in the afternoon. However this may have been, what took place may be introduced as follows:

Zechariah proceeds toward the golden altar. He is accompanied by two assistants. One of these men is carrying in a golden bowl burning coals from the altar of burnt-offering, and is spreading them out on the altar of incense. He then withdraws. The other assistant is carrying a golden censer filled with incense. He arranges the incense upon the altar.

And now profound silence ensues, for the most solemn action of the ritual is about to occur. A signal is given. The sacred moment has arrived for Zechariah to place the incense upon the coals, causing a cloud to arise, its fragrance rising and spreading. Together with the ascending aroma a fervent prayer, consisting of thanksgiving for blessings received and of supplication for peace upon Israel, now issues from the heart and lips of the priest. The people, gathered "outside" the sanctuary but "inside" its courts (Israel's Court, Women's Court, with priests and Levites in evidence especially in the Priests' Court; see map, N.T.C. on Mark, p. 488) are also praying, in a prostrate position and with outstretched hands. Then they wait for Zechariah to return from the altar of incense and to proceed eastward to the steps in the front of *the sanctuary* (Holy Place and Holy of Holies). On these steps Zechariah, accompanied by other priests, is ex-

---

56. For example, A. Fahling, *The Life of Christ,* St. Louis, 1936, p. 67. Very interesting is S.BK., II, p. 75.

57. For example, Greijdanus and Lenski in their respective commentaries on this passage.

pected to pronounce the Aaronic blessing on the people. This benediction will be followed by songs of praise, public offerings, etc.[58]

The people wait . . . and wait . . . and wait. But for minutes that must have seemed like hours nothing happens. Explanation: **11, 12. Then there appeared to him an angel of the Lord, standing at the right of the altar of incense. Now when Zechariah saw him, he became troubled and overwhelmed with fear.** Suddenly the angel is standing there at the right side of the altar; that is, just to the south of it, for directions are indicated from the point of view of a man facing east. The angel, then, would have the golden altar to his left, and the candelabrum to his right and somewhat to the front. See map, as above.

It is natural that the sudden, unexpected appearance of a strong, holy, dazzlingly brilliant angel causes a weak, sinful human being to tremble. Fear "fell upon" Zechariah. See also Judg. 6:22; 13:22; Dan. 10:5-9; Luke 1:29; 2:9; Acts 10:4; and cf. Isa. 6:1-5.

13. But the angel said to him, Do not be afraid, Zechariah, for your petition has been heard. Your wife Elizabeth will bear you a son, and you shall give him the name John. Note the following points:

a. "Do not be afraid." In other words, "Stop being frightened; cheer up." Is it not encouraging to note how very often in Scripture God or Jesus Christ tells his people not to be afraid but instead to take heart? A partial list of passages in which, in some form or other, this exhortation is found would be: Gen. 15:1; 26:24; 46:3; Exod. 14:13, 14; Josh. 1:9; 11:6; Judg. 6:23; II Kings 19:6, 7; I Chron. 28:20; II Chron. 20:15; 32:7; Neh. 4:14; Ps. 49:16; 91:5; Isa. 10:24; 37:6; 41:10, 13, 14; 43:1, 5; 44:2, 8; Dan. 10:19; Zech. 8:13; Matt. 14:27; 17:7; 28:10; Mark 5:36; Luke 1:30; 2:10; 5:10; 8:50; 12:4, 7, 32; John 14:1, 27; 16:33; Acts 18:9; 27:24; Heb. 13:6; I Peter 3:14; Rev. 1:17. And is not "Do not be afraid" another way of saying, "Have faith"? Truly salvation by grace through *faith* is not a Pauline invention. It is firmly rooted in Scripture throughout.

b. "Your petition has been heard." Which petition? The one which Zechariah had barely finished when the angel suddenly appeared; hence, the supplication that peace in its richest sense—salvation—might be bestowed upon Israel? Or was the angel referring to the request for a child, a petition that belonged to bygone days? In spite of what certain commentators say to the contrary, it simply is not true that this question can be decided on the basis of grammar (tense of verb). Those who favor the former alternative base their conclusion on the fact that Zechariah had hardly ceased praying for the peace of Israel when the angel appeared. But with at least equal right those who favor the latter alternative point to the very close connection between "Your petition has been heard" and "Your wife Elizabeth will bear you a son." As it were "in one breath" these two

---

58. For a more detailed account read A. Edersheim, *The Temple*, London, 1908, pp. 157-173.

statements were made by the angel. If a choice must be made between these two alternatives, this interpreter would choose the latter.

But is it absolutely necessary to make this choice? Is there not a very close relation between the two? Is it not true that the son to whom Elizabeth would give birth was destined to be the forerunner of the Messiah, through whom salvation would come for Israel; in fact, for all God's children, whether Jew or Gentile?

c. "Your wife Elizabeth." The very one whose barren condition was common knowledge would be delivered from her affliction. Through Elizabeth, and not through some other woman, Zechariah would become the father of a child.

d. "a son." The very sex of the child is already predicted!

e. "... and you shall give him the name John." See on verses 59, 63.

The angel continues: **14. You will have joy and exultation, and many will rejoice over his birth.** The heart of Zechariah will be filled with exuberant gladness. Many others will also rejoice because of the birth of this child. Not only will his very birth bring about instant jubilation (1:58) but, as the immediate context (see verses 16, 17) indicates, in the future too when this child has become a man, many people are going to thank the Lord for the fact that John was born. Through his ministry multitudes will be turned from darkness to light; others will at least exclaim, "John is—or was—a prophet" (Luke 7:29; cf. Matt. 21:26, 32).

Continued: **15. for he will be great in the sight of the Lord.** It was about him that Jesus was going to say, "Among those born of women there has not arisen anyone greater than John the Baptist" (Matt. 11:11). This would be true not only because John was going to be himself a prophet but also because he was going to be one whose arrival on the scene of history had been predicted. He was destined to become the herald of the Messiah. As such he was going to direct the attention of the people to the long expected One, concerning whom he was going to say, "Look, the Lamb of God who is taking away the sin of the world" (John 1:29). He was going to emphasize the necessity of true conversion as the only way for the sinner to enter Messiah's kingdom (Luke 1:76, 77; 3:3). And since it is the duty of the herald to recede to the background when the King arrives, so John was going to resist the temptation of calling attention to himself. Instead, in humility of spirit he was going to say, "He must increase, but I must decrease" (John 3:30). Now in view of the fact that Jesus himself, in describing the nature of true greatness, always links it with humility (Luke 7:6, 9; cf. Matt. 8:8, 10; Luke 9:46–48; cf. Matt. 18:1–5; Mark 9:33–37; and see also Matt. 15:27, 28), is it not altogether probable that this characteristic which was to mark John is also implied here in Luke 1:15? Without humility would it even be possible for anyone to be "great," especially "in the sight of the Lord"?

Continuing on this theme of greatness, the angel adds, **Wine or strong drink he must never touch, and he will be filled with the Holy Spirit even**

from his mother's womb. Not with wine but with the Holy Spirit will John be filled. This same implied contrast (filled with wine versus filled with the Holy Spirit) is found also in other passages (Acts 2:15–17; Eph. 5:18). John is not going to derive his strength or inspiration from earthly means but from the Holy Spirit.

"Filled with the Holy Spirit even from his mother's womb." Does this expression imply that something mysterious took place in the heart of John while he was still in his mother's womb? Or is it simply an expression indicating extent of time: from the very beginning to the end of his life John will be filled with the Holy Spirit? Since the chapter contains two more references to John as a babe in his mother's womb (see verses 41 and 44), the discussion of this subject will be postponed until verse 44 is reached.

Was John a Nazirite? For "the law of the Nazirite" read Numbers 6. Note especially these two regulations: (a) During the period governed by their vow Nazirites were to abstain from wine and other fermented beverages, and (b) no razor was to be used on their head. In connection with Samson both of these restrictions are mentioned (Judg. 13:7; 16:17). As to Samuel, we know that his mother Hannah vowed that as a symbol of lifelong consecration to the Lord no razor would ever touch his head (I Sam. 1:11). Abstention from intoxicating drinks is not mentioned in his case. With reference to John the opposite holds: He was to avoid wine and (other) fermented drinks, but nothing is said about a razor. Consequently, some argue that John was not a Nazirite,[59] others that he was.[60] In order to reach a conclusion with respect to John it may help us to take note of the fact that according to our present passage (verse 15) *during his entire life-span* the promised offspring must never drink wine or (other) fermented beverages. In John's case, therefore, this restriction was far more rigid than in the case of priests, who were forbidden the use of these drinks only during the period of their service ("when y o u go into the tent of meeting," Lev. 10:9), and was at least more severe than in the case of the Nazirites, for in their case the prohibition was in force only during the days covered by their vow (Num. 6:4, 5). Therefore, if John was a Nazirite, he must be considered a Nazirite *for life*. Does not careful reading of Luke 1:15 leave the impression that the idea of *total, lifelong consecration to special service for the Lord* is here emphasized?

After what has already been said in connection with verse 14 ("Many will rejoice over his birth") not much need be added with respect to verse **16. Many of the sons of Israel will he turn to the Lord their God.** Instead of "sons" one can also read "children" or "people." That this prophecy was fulfilled has been shown.

---

59. S. Greijdanus, *Lucas (Korte Verklaring)*, p. 26.
60. W. M. Christie, art. "Nazirite," I.S.B.E., Vol. IV, p. 2125; A. T. Robertson, *Word Pictures*, Vol. II, p. 10; A. Plummer, *op. cit.*, p. 14. And cf. S.BK., II, p. 80 f.

One important lesson must not be passed by, however. It concerns the very heart of God. Note that Israel is here pictured in its "unturned," that is, "unconverted," state. Nevertheless, the angel informs Zechariah that even now God considers himself *their* God. He is still deeply concerned about them. In this connection read also Psalm 78:1 ("*My* people give ear," etc.); Isa. 1:3 ("*My* people do not understand"); Ezek. 16:21 ("*my* children"). Having made a covenant with his people, the Lord has a special claim on them, and a unique interest in them! That holds even today, for Gen. 17:7 finds its echo in Acts 2:38, 39. And in this connection do not forget Luke 13:6–10.

The angel concludes his message by giving Zechariah this further description of the relation of the promised child to the Messiah, the effect of his ministry upon family life, and the final purpose of all this: **17. And he will go before him in the spirit and power of Elijah, to turn the hearts of the fathers to the children, and the disobedient to the frame of mind of the righteous, in order to make ready for the Lord a people well-prepared.** What we have here is Christ's own commentary on the words of Mal. 4:5, 6. John's public appearance to Israel would precede that of Jesus. But what the text (both in Malachi and here in Luke) offers is more than a chronological item, though that too is clearly implied. Not only will John precede Jesus in time; he will actually be his herald or forerunner. As such he will announce and introduce his Master to the people. Even more: by means of his ministry—calling people to conversion—he will be an instrument in God's hand in preparing the people for the reception of their Messiah. See Luke 3:4 f.

Note "in the spirit and power of Elijah." Does this mean that John was Elijah? The answer is both "No" and "Yes." *Not literally,* as is clear from the fact that when John was asked, "Are you Elijah?" he truthfully answered, "I am not" (John 1:21). *But figuratively,* so that Jesus even calls him Elijah (Matt. 11:13, 14; cf. 17:12; Mark 9:12, 13). The solution is given here in Luke 1:17:

The "spirit and power of Elijah" was going to be clearly displayed in John the Baptist. Cf. Elijah's boldness, "I have not troubled Israel but you [Ahab] have" (I Kings 18:18), with the Baptist's (Matt. 14:4), "It isn't right for you [Herod Antipas] to have her [your brother Philip's wife Herodias]." And see also Matt. 3:7; Luke 3:7, 19.

Of the words "to turn the hearts of the fathers to the children, and the disobedient to the frame of mind of the righteous" there are two contrasting interpretations:

a. The "fathers" are the patriarchs. The conversion of many people through John's ministry would cause the patriarchs—Abraham, Isaac, Jacob, etc.—from their heavenly abodes to look down with favor upon their formerly disobedient but now transformed children.

Support for this theory, according to which the souls of the departed are spectators who are constantly looking down upon the arena in which their struggling descendants are still living, is found by its proponents in Heb. 12:1 ("the cloud of witnesses").[61]

Comment. We can understand that this type of interpretation would appeal to those who indulge in fanciful speculations concerning the life hereafter. One author points out its weakness as follows:

"Some people think this refers to the contrast between a devout ancestry and an apostate posterity. As we see it, this view is incorrect, since on the basis of that interpretation it is impossible to understand how the heart of the fathers, who died long ago, can be turned back to the children." He correctly concludes: "We must think of the relation between parents and their children."[62]

And as to the similarly speculative interpretation of Heb. 12:1, for the correct view read F. F. Bruce, *The Epistle to the Hebrews (New International Commentary)*, Grand Rapids, 1964, pp. 345, 346.

b. True conversion results, among other things, in revival of harmonious and loving relationships in the home.

Comment. This interpretation fits the historical background in Malachi. As a result of mixed marriages (Mal. 2:11) and easy divorce (2:14) family relationships had become disrupted.

Conditions of this character continued into the new dispensation, as is clear from Christ's teaching on divorce and remarriage (Matt. 5:32; 19:9). Nevertheless, family life is of the utmost importance, and this not only for the well-being, both spiritual and physical, of parents and children, but also for the true prosperity of the nation, the church, and society in general. From a spiritual point of view the generation gap is often ruinous.

To reverse this situation was one of the purposes of Malachi's preaching during the old dispensation, and of John's preaching at the beginning of the new dispensation. Given believing parents and similarly right-minded children, domestic harmony results; consequently also effective witness-bearing.

The end result of this ministry of the way-preparer will therefore be the bringing about of "a people well-prepared," that is, "fit for the Master's use" (II Tim. 2:21).

As some see it, the explanation given above is in conflict with the statement of Jesus recorded in such passages as Matt. 10:34–37 (cf. Luke 12:51–53; 14:26): "Do not think that I came to bring peace on earth. I did not come to bring peace but a sword. For I came to set a man against his father, a daughter against her mother," etc. However, any suggestion of real conflict is baseless. It is, in fact, very easy to conceive of a twofold result of the preaching of the gospel, whether by the Baptist or by Jesus: (a) In

---

61. Those who favor theory (a) also at times appeal to Isa. 29:22 f. This is a difficult passage, of which there are various, sometimes widely different, translations and interpretations. For that very reason an appeal to it hardly seems justified.

62. J. Ridderbos, *De Kleine Profeten (Korte Verklaring)*, Kampen, 1935, Vol. III, p. 234.

many families there would be a sharp division, some siding with the truth, others opposing it. (b) In other families, however, those who had been opposed were going to be converted, so that parents and children would become united in spirit, all serving the Lord.

Zechariah's reaction to the cheering words of the angel was disappointing: **18. Then Zechariah asked the angel, How can I be sure of this? For I am an old man and my wife is advanced in years.** For this reaction there was no excuse. It was definitely the response of unbelief.

In order to lessen the seriousness of the priest's improper question it has been argued that Abraham, Gideon, and Hezekiah reacted similarly to astounding promises. Did not Abraham ask, "How am I to know" (Gen. 15:8)? Did not Gideon ask for a sign; in fact, for two signs (Judg. 6:36–40)? And did not even King Hezekiah ask for a sign to show that he would indeed be healed (II Kings 20:8–11)?

There are differences, however:

a. As is clear from Gen. 15:6, Abraham's response was definitely that of faith, not of unbelief. In the light of that passage Gen. 15:8 can perhaps best be interpreted as a request for a sign to strengthen his faith.

b. The same holds, perhaps, in the case of Gideon. Note also his words of awe and reverence, "Let not thy anger burn against me," etc.

c. Similarly the very phraseology employed by Hezekiah shows that he was not offering an objection but wanted very definitely to believe God's promise.

Over against all this stands Zechariah's response which *almost* amounted to, "I don't believe you, for people as old as we are do not become parents." Besides, what is often passed by in silence is the fact that Zechariah acted as he did *in spite of the fact* that he had before him all these examples: God's faithfulness to his promise in the case of Abraham, Gideon, Hezekiah, and very many others.

For other illustrations of sinful skepticism read Gen. 3:6; II Kings 2:16–18; Luke 24:37, 38; John 20:24, 25; Acts 12:12–15; II Peter 3:4.

19. I am Gabriel, the angel answered. I stand in the presence of God, and I was sent to speak to you, and to bring you this good news.

It is true that the angel's "I am Gabriel" follows Zechariah's "I am an old man." Nevertheless, the intended contrast is not thus indicated. The confrontation is rather that between the priest's cold skepticism and the angel's towering certainty, between the former's presumptuous doubt and the latter's profound conviction. Gabriel is conscious of having delivered God's good news, bound to be fulfilled when the appropriate season arrives (verse 20). And because Zechariah has called in question a wonderful *gospel* promise that sprang from the heart and mind of God himself he deserved to be punished.

"I am Gabriel." The name *Gabriel* has been interpreted variously as meaning: "man of God," "mighty one of God," "Mighty (is) God." Elsewhere Gabriel is also mentioned in Dan. 8:16, where he explains the vision of the ram and the he-goat; in Dan. 9:21 f., where he interprets the prophecy of the seventy weeks; and in Luke 1:26-38, where he promises that in a very mysterious manner Mary will become the mother of the long-awaited Messiah. The only other angel mentioned by name in Scripture is Michael (Dan. 10:13, 21; Jude 9; Rev. 12:7).

Note also the significant words "I stand in the presence of God." Partly because of this added qualification several more or less speculative theories have sprung up with respect to Gabriel:

a. that he is not a created being but the Holy Spirit;

b. that in distinction from the task assigned to Michael and the other angels, it is Gabriel's special function not only to bring but also to interpret God's messages to those human beings for whom they are intended; and

c. that Gabriel is one of "the seven angels" (Rev. 8:2)—not to be confused with "the seven Spirits" (Rev. 1:4)—who stand in the presence of God.[63]

There is nothing in the text or context that even remotely suggests theory (a). As to (b), it is doubtful whether this conclusion is supported by sufficient evidence. As to (c), this theory may well be correct. At least the correspondence between Luke 1:19 and Rev. 8:2 is striking. Both Gabriel and the seven angels are described as "standing before God." Absolute certainty is, however, unattainable. Because of Matt. 18:10 one might ask, "But do not all the angels stand in God's presence, beholding the face of the Father?"[64]

Has the priest asked for a sign? He will receive a sign, but not the one he had asked for. So Gabriel continues: **20. And now, mark well, because you did not believe my words, which will be fulfilled in their proper time, you will remain silent and not able to speak until the day when these things take place.**

For his manifestation of unbelief Zechariah is going to be punished. Because he has made wrong use of his tongue, that tongue will be silent. But note how justice is tempered with mercy: "You will not be able to speak . . . *until the day when these things take place." That* they will occur exactly when their proper time has arrived is certain. *When* they—the birth and

---

63. All three theories are discussed by A. Kuyper in his book *De Engelen Gods,* Kampen, 1923, pp. 176-179. He rejects (a) but accepts (b) and (c). See also S.BK., II, p. 90 f., and p. 97 f.

64. On the general subject *angel, angels,* see also the following passages and the N.T.C. on them, as far as published:

Summary of scriptural doctrine with respect to angels; see on Matt. 18:10.
Angels in relation to God's law (Gal. 3:19).
As objects of worship (Col. 2:18).
Archangels (I Thess. 4:16).
Guardian angels? (Matt. 18:10).
Angels and marriage (Mark 12:25).
Luke on angels (in addition to 1:11, 13, 18, 19 see also: 26-38; 2:9-21; 4:10; 9:26; 12:8, 9; 15:10; 16:22; 20:36; 24:23).
Function of angels in connection with Christ's return (Matt. 13:39; 25:31; Mark 8:38; 13:27; II Thess. 1:7).

God's Justice Tempered with Mercy

Sin, Punishment, or Threat of Punishment		Divine Mercy, Patience
	revealed in the case of	
Gen. 3:16, 19	Adam and Eve	Gen. 3:15
Gen. 4:7, 11, 12	Cain	Gen. 4:15
Gen. 6:7	The Antediluvians	Gen. 6:3b
Gen. 18:20, 21	Sodom	Gen. 18:26–32
Exod. 32:10	The People of Israel	Exod. 32:32; 33:14
I Kings 21:19	King Ahab	I Kings 21:29
Matt. 26:74	Peter	Mark 16:7 (". . . and Peter"); Luke 22:61a; 24:34; John 21:15–17
Luke 13:7	The Barren Fig Tree	Luke 13:8, 9
John 20:25	Thomas	John 20:27
Matt. 26:56	The Twelve	Matt. 28:16–20; John 17:8; 20:19
Rev. 2:22, 23	"Jezebel"	Rev. 2:21 ("time to repent")

naming of the child—take place Zechariah will receive his voice back again, for in spite of the priest's serious error God's love is still resting on him.

Luke now turns our attention to the worshipers. In the courts of the temple they were waiting for Zechariah to return to them: **21. Meanwhile the people were waiting for Zechariah and wondering why he stayed away so long in the sanctuary.** For background see above, on verses 8–10. The people were waiting for Zechariah, waiting and wondering why he tarried so long in "the sanctuary." As has been mentioned elsewhere, it is necessary in this case to distinguish between: (a) *temple* in the sense of the entire building complex, including all the courts, and (b) *sanctuary,* consisting of the Holy Place and Holy of Holies. Zechariah had gone into the Holy Place. The people were in the courts.

According to The Talmud it was customary for the priest whose duty it was to offer incense to leave the altar as quickly as possible, lest unwittingly he commit some act of profanation. Cf. Lev. 10:1 f.; II Sam. 6:6, 7. But in the present case, completely contrary to custom, the priest "took such a long time" (thus literally) before returning from the sanctuary. **22. And when he did come out, he was unable to speak to them. Then they realized that he had seen a vision in the sanctuary, for he kept making signs to them but remained unable to speak.** As predicted by Gabriel (verse 20), Zechariah was dumb, unable to speak. By means of signs he was trying to convey this information to the assembled multitude.

Though the text nowhere states that fear was staring from the priest's eyes, blanched his cheeks, and caused his limbs to tremble, something akin to this may well have been taking place. In any event, as a result of his sign language—perhaps nodding and gesturing—the people realized that Zechariah had seen a vision (cf. Luke 24:23; Acts 26:19; II Cor. 12:1), an awe-inspiring object or being, one generally invisible to human eyes.

There are those who, on the basis of verse 62—which states that some-time later people began to make signs to Zechariah; if he was not deaf why did they not simply *speak* to him?—conclude that Zechariah must have been not only dumb but also deaf. For remarks on that theory see on verse 62.

Concluded: **23–25. And when the days of his service were completed he went back to his home. After these days his wife Elizabeth became pregnant. For five months she kept herself in seclusion, saying, This is the way the Lord has dealt with me in the days in which he looked (with favor) upon me, to remove my disgrace among the people.**

There is a close connection between verses 23 and 24. So interpreted verse 23, stating that Zechariah went back to his home after completing his term of service, becomes more meaningful than it would be if viewed merely as the end of a little paragraph. Rather, Zechariah went home and Elizabeth became pregnant.

The conception of John reminds one of the conception of Isaac (Gen. 21:1, 2). It took a miracle to open Sarah's womb (Heb. 11:11, 12). This was also true in the case of Elizabeth (Luke 1:7, 18, 36, 37). Similarly, it took a miracle to enable Abraham, Sarah's husband, to deposit seed (Rom. 4:19). In view of Luke 1:7, 18, indicating that Zechariah was "an old man," was not also the restoration of his productive capacity the result of a miracle?

In the case of Mary and her son Jesus the miracle was even more astounding. In physical terms, her son Jesus had no human father at all. God was his Father, Mary his mother. For further comment see on Luke 1:35.

Elizabeth conceived, for God's promises never fail. Then she kept herself in seclusion five months. The reason for this is not given. Some say that this conduct on her part was "according to custom." It may well be better to explain her seclusion in the light of the following context. In connection with verse 7 it was shown that by many people barrenness was considered a sign of God's disfavor. The thought occurs therefore (especially in connection with verse 25) that she decided not again to appear in public until the moment would draw near that people in general could see that the Lord had looked upon her with favor and had removed from her the (unjustifiable) "disgrace" of barrenness. That she was, indeed, a very devout woman is evident from the fact that she not only realizes but also openly confesses that her pregnancy was a divine blessing graciously bestowed upon her.[65]

---

65. Notes on Greek words, phrases, and constructions in 1:5-25 begin on page 79.

Practical Lessons Derived from Luke 1:5–25

Verse 5

"His wife was also a descendant of Aaron." Compatibility is essential to happiness in marriage.

Verse 6

"Righteous in the sight of God." Although "reputation" with men should never become a matter of indifference, "righteousness" in the sight of God matters most.

"Observing all the commandments and requirements of the Lord." God's moral law must be applied to actual life situations.

Verse 7

"However, they were childless." "Man's extremity is God's opportunity."

Verses 8–10

"Chosen to burn incense." Descending showers (of blessing) require ascending incense (of thanksgiving and prayer).

"The entire assembled congregation . . . engaged in prayer." Prayer is for the many, by the many. It must not become a monopoly.

Verses 11, 12

"Then there appeared to him an angel of the Lord." Though we generally do not see them, angels are there. They are interested in the establishment of God's kingdom on earth.

Verse 13

"Zechariah, . . . your petition has been heard." God's delays are not denials.
> "Ah nothing is too late
> Till the tired heart shall cease to palpitate."

(Longfellow)

Verse 14

"Many will rejoice over his birth." To weep with those who weep is good. Could it be that to rejoice with those who rejoice is at least just as good?

Verse 15

"He will be great in the sight of the Lord." The badge of true greatness is humility (cf. Luke 9:46–48).

"Filled with the Holy Spirit." Enthusiasm derived from intoxication leaves a bitter taste. Energy derived from transformation brings lasting reward.

Verse 16

"Many of the sons of Israel will he turn to the Lord their God." "He who winneth souls is wise."

Verse 17

"To turn the hearts of the fathers to the children."
Enter the love of God,
Exit the generation gap.
"To make ready for the Lord a people well-prepared." Salvation begins with God. It also ends with him.

Verses 18–20

"How can I be sure of this?" Skepticism with respect to God's promises is inexcusable.
"You will remain silent . . . until the day when these things take place." God's justice is tempered with mercy.

Verses 23–25

"This is the way the Lord has dealt with me." Blessings should not only be counted. They should be traced to the Giver, so that acknowledgment and thanksgiving may result.

Notes on Greek Words, Phrases, and Constructions in 1:5–25

Verse 5

ἐφημερία* = ἐπί ἡμέραν; hence basically a service limited to a prescribed number of *days;* here: a "division" or "course" of priests who performed this service. So also in verse 8.

Verse 6

A solemn sense of the Lord's active omnipresence, reminding one of Old Testament passages (Num. 3:4; Ps. 139, etc.), is indicated by such synonymous expressions as
ἐναντίον** τοῦ θεοῦ here in verse 6 (cf. 24:19);
ἔναντι** τοῦ θεοῦ in verse 8 (cf. Acts 8:21); and
ἐνώπιον τοῦ κυρίου in verse 15 (cf. 1:19).
Note here not the adverb *blamelessly,* as in I Thess. 2:10; 5:23, but the adjective *blameless,* without reproach, as in Phil. 2:15; 3:6; I Thess. 3:13.

Verse 7

στεῖρα, barren; cf. *sterile.*
προβεβηκότες . . . ἦσαν, periphrastic past perfect of προβαίνω; cf. the feminine participle in verse 18.

79

Verse 8

ἱερατεύειν, pres. infinitive of ἱερατεύω*, to serve as priest. With this compare in

Verse 9

ἱερατεία, priesthood, priestly office.

ἔλαχε, third per. s. aor. indicat. of λαγχάνω. Here the meaning is: to be chosen by lot. Cf. to obtain (by the will of God, II Peter 1:1); and: to cast lots (John 19:24). Note usual gen. construction after λαγχάνω. "Chosen by lot" connects grammatically with "to burn incense."

θυμιᾶσαι = aor. infinitive of θυμιάω*. Basic verb is θύω, to sacrifice. Cf. *fume*.

Verse 10

θυμίαμα, here: the burning of incense, the incense offering; elsewhere (verse 11; also Rev. 5:8; 8:3 f.; 18:13) incense. Related also is θυσιαστήριον (Luke 1:11). Note periphrastic imperfect ἦν προσευχόμενον: was engaged in prayer.

Verse 11

ἑστώς, perfect participle of ἵστημι, in the sense of the present: standing.

Verse 12

ἐταράχθη, third per. s. aor. indicat. pass. (probably ingressive) of ταράσσω. On this verb see N.T.C. on Mark, pp. 261, 262; and on John, Vol. II, pp. 262, 263.

Verse 13

Μὴ φοβοῦ, sec. per. s. pres. imperat. of φοβέω. This can also be rendered, "Stop being afraid."

Verse 14

ἀγαλλίασις = exultation. See also verse 44; Acts 2:46; Heb. 1:9; Jude 24. Cf. the cognate verb ἀγαλλιάω, to thrill (or leap) with (or for) joy (Luke 1:47; 10:21). The indicated joy is great, exuberant, unrestrained. See N.T.C. on Matthew, p. 280.

Verse 15

Note the strong negative οὐ μή, followed by the aor. subjunctive πίῃ: he shall in no wise drink; he must never touch.

πλησθήσεται, third per. s. fut. indicat. passive of πίμπλημι, in the New Testament almost confined to Luke's writings; but see also Matt. 22:10; 27:48.

ἐκ κοιλίας μητρὸς αὐτοῦ, probably another indication that Luke is here translating—or is at least strongly influenced by—a Semitic source. Cf. Num. 12:12; Judg. 16:17; Job 3:10; 31:18; Ps. 139:13; Eccles. 5:15.

Verse 17

αὐτός is not necessarily intensive: "he himself."

φρόνησις, frame of mind, disposition; in Eph. 1:8 insight. Cf. *phrenic, diaphragm*.

κατεσκευασμένον, acc. s. m. perf. passive participle of κατασκευάζω, to prepare, make ready; see also 7:27; cf. Matt. 11:10; Mark 1:2; but elsewhere: to construct, build (Heb. 3:3, 4; I Peter 3:20).

Verse 19

παρεστηκώς, perf. participle of παρίστημι, and like ἑστώς (in verse 11) with sense of the present; here: standing in the presence of; in 19:24 standing by; hence, assisting (Rom. 16:2).

Verse 20

ἰδού, used as a particle, has an acute accent, and is basically the aor. middle imperat. of εἶδον; hence means: see, behold, look; take note; in certain connections: listen, remember, mark well, there comes, suddenly, etc. The English equivalent— whenever the word must be translated, which is not necessarily always the case— depends on the context. The word is used to arouse the attention of the reader or hearer, especially when something new or striking is introduced. The frequent use of this particle (see also 1:31, 36, 38, 44, 48, etc.) is another reminder of the distinct probability that in this account the evangelist is making use of a Hebrew or Aramaic source. Cf. Hebrew ḥinnēh.

ἔσῃ σιωπῶν, sec. per. s. periphrastic fut. indicat. of σιωπάω; here: to remain silent.

The locative ᾗ, "on which," becomes ἧς, being attracted to the case of ἡμέρας. This is not at all unusual, especially in Luke. See Gram. N.T., pp. 715, 717.

ἀνθ' ὧν = because. The basic sense of ἀντί, in the place of, in return for, is clear also in this case. See my doctoral dissertation The Meaning of the Preposition ἀντί in the New Testament, Princeton, 1948, pp. 37, 40, 91, 92. The punishment suits the crime.

In distinction from χρόνος, καιρός views time from the aspect of the opportunity it provides, and not simply as a change from the past into the present into the future, not mere duration. See R. C. Trench, Synonyms of the New Testament, Grand Rapids, 1948, par. lvii.

Verse 22

ἐπέγνωσαν, third per. pl. aor. indicat. of ἐπιγινώσκω, here in the sense of to realize. See also on verse 4.

ἦν διανεύων, periphrastic imperfect of διανεύω*, to nod, to make signs.

κωφός, here: unable to speak, dumb; but in 7:22 unable to hear, deaf. See also N.T.C. on Mark, p. 302, footnote 346.

Verse 23

For ἐπλήσθησαν see the note on 2:6 on page 147, and the note on 4:28 on p. 261. λειτουργία = λαός and ἔργον, work for the people, a public service or office; here: service as priest. Cf. liturgy.

Verse 24

συνέλαβεν, third per. s. 2nd aor. indicat. act. of συλλαμβάνω. Meanings: (a) to seize, arrest (Luke 22:54; cf. Matt. 26:55; Mark 14:48; John 18:12; Acts 1:16; 12:3);

(b) to catch (Luke 5:9); (c) to take hold together; hence, to help, assist, aid (Luke 5:7; Phil. 4:3); and (d) to conceive, become pregnant (here in Luke 1:24; also in 1:31, 36; 2:21; and in a figurative sense in James 1:15).

It is not surprising that *Dr.* Luke uses several words to indicate the relation of women to pregnancy. In addition to the references already mentioned see Luke 1:7; 2:5; 20:28; 21:23.

περιέκρυβεν. It is not certain whether this is the 2nd aor. active indicat. of περικρύπτω*, or the imperfect indicat. of περικρύβω*. Note intensive or perfective περί, perhaps: she kept herself in seclusion "all around," that is, completely. However, such prefixes have a tendency to lose their intensive force. It is therefore frequently unnecessary to bring out this possible emphasis in the translation. Much depends on the context in any specific case.

Verse 25

ἐπεῖδεν, third per. s. of ἐπεῖδον**, used as 2nd aor. of ἐφοράω; here: to look upon with favor; in Acts 4:29 "with favor" drops out; hence there simply: to look upon, to consider.

ὄνειδος*, disgrace. For the cognate verb see 6:22.

---

26 In the sixth month the angel Gabriel was sent from God to Nazareth, a town of Galilee, 27 to a virgin pledged to be married to[66] a man named Joseph, of David's house. The name of the virgin (was) Mary. 28 Entering, he said to her, "Greetings, you highly favored one, the Lord is with you." 29 She was greatly troubled at his words and was wondering what kind of greeting this might be.
30 But the angel said to her, "Do not be afraid, Mary, for you have found favor with God. 31 And, behold, you will conceive in your womb and give birth to a son, and you shall give him the name Jesus. 32 He will be great and will be called the Son of the Most High. And the Lord God will give him the throne of his father David. 33 He will reign over the house of Jacob forever, and his kingdom will never end."
34 Mary said to the angel, "How can this be, since I am not living with a husband?"
35 The angel answered, "The Holy Spirit will come upon you, and the power of the Most High will overshadow you. Therefore also the holy offspring will be called the Son of God. 36 And look, Elizabeth, your relative, even she has conceived a son in her old age. This is, in fact, the sixth month for her who was said to be barren. 37 For with God nothing is ever impossible."
38 Mary said, "Behold, the handmaid of the Lord. May it be with me according to your word!" Then the angel left her.

1:26–38 *The Birth of Jesus Foretold*

From the prediction of the birth of the herald the author, in his "orderly account," now proceeds to the prediction of the birth of the One heralded:
26, 27. In the sixth month the angel Gabriel was sent from God to Nazareth, a town of Galilee, to a virgin pledged to be married to a man named Joseph, of David's house.
It was the sixth month of Elizabeth's pregnancy (verse 36). The same

---

66. Or: betrothed to.

angel, Gabriel, who had predicted the birth of John, is now sent to Nazareth, a town in Galilee.

This little town is situated picturesquely on one of the southernmost slopes of the Lebanon mountain range; or, to describe it differently, at the northern edge of the fertile Plain of Esdraelon. It is located near 35 degrees E. Longitude and, like Bagdad, Nagasaki, and Augusta (Georgia, U.S.A.), near 33 degrees N. Latitude. About 24 kilometers (15 miles) to the east of Nazareth is the southern tip of the Sea of Galilee, and 35 kilometers (22 miles) to the west of Nazareth is the Mediterranean Sea. Near—i.e. to the E.S.E. of—Nazareth is Mt. Tabor, a symmetrical cone, situated at the junction of the ancient territories of Naphtali, Zebulun, and Issachar.

It was to this little town in Galilee (see Isa. 9:1, 2; cf. Matt. 4:15, 16) that Gabriel was sent, for here lived Mary, a virgin pledged to be married to a man of the same town, namely, Joseph, who, like Mary herself, was of David's house.

Again and again, as the gospel story unfolds, Nazareth is going to be mentioned. In Luke see also 2:4, 39, 51; 4:16; elsewhere: Matt. 2:23; 4:13; 21:11; Mark 1:9; John 1:45, 46; Acts 10:38.

It was with serene dignity and commendable dispatch, such as one associates with angels, that Gabriel had carried out his mission to Zechariah. He had delivered a message of joy and gladness. Nevertheless the reception accorded him and his good news had not been altogether favorable. The reaction had been, "How can I be sure of this?" And now this same Gabriel is given another commission. From the point of view of earthly thinking the message he must deliver is even more unbelievable.

The great moment for which all preceding generations have been waiting has finally arrived. The Messiah is about to appear, and Gabriel has been ordered to announce his imminent arrival, an arrival by means of conception and birth.

This conception, moreover, will be unique, such as had never before occurred and will never again take place. It is to happen within the womb of *a virgin!* The mother-to-be, to whom the promise of the incarnation of the world's Savior (Matt. 1:21; John 4:42; I John 4:14), the King of kings and Lord of lords (Rev. 19:16; cf. 17:14), must be delivered, is living in . . . Rome certainly? No! In Jerusalem then? No! In Nazareth, a little Galilean town, by some lightly esteemed (John 1:46), never even mentioned in the Old Testament! And the womb that will carry this greatest of all treasures is that of . . . a princess? No! It is that of a virgin pledged to be married to the village carpenter! Cf. Isa. 55:8, 9.

Nevertheless, even though in comparison with the commission which Gabriel had carried out about six months earlier, this new one might be greeted with even colder skepticism, *Gabriel obeys immediately.*

Scripture everywhere stresses the holiness of the good angels, their unqualified surrender to God's will, as with solemn and rapturous adoration they stand in his awesome presence, instantly ready to carry out his orders

(Ps. 103:21; 148:2; Isa. 6:1-4). "Ready to do thy will, O Lord," is ever their motto.

As pictured by Ezekiel each cherub has four faces, and the throne-chariot "driven" by them has wheels within wheels. In other words, God's angelic messengers are ready and eager to move immediately in any direction their Sovereign desires. Does this not shed light on the third petition of the Lord's Prayer: "Thy will be done, *as in heaven* so on earth"?

Gabriel's message was to be delivered to "a virgin pledged to be married to a man named Joseph." For the concept *virgin* see the note on verse 27 on p. 91. Though this virgin has been "betrothed" to Joseph, that is, in the presence of witnesses had been solemnly promised to him, the marriage feast and the living together in the common relationship of marriage had not yet taken place. This was a matter for the future, according to the custom of that day and age. As already indicated, Joseph, the husband-to-be, who in an anticipatory sense could already be called "husband" (Matt. 1:19), was, like Mary, a descendant of David, as specifically stated by Luke, not only here but also in 2:4, and as shown in some detail by Matthew (1:1-17).

The name of the virgin (was) Mary. This Mary must be distinguished from the other women who bore that name: (a) the mother of John Mark (Acts 12:12); (b) Mary of Bethany (Luke 10:42; John 11:1); (c) the mother of James and Joses, who seems to have been the wife of Clopas (Matt. 27:61); and (d) Mary Magdalene (Luke 8:2).

In addition to what is said about Mary, the mother of Jesus, in the infancy narratives (Matt. 1:18, 23-25; 2:11, 14, 19-21; Luke 1:26-56; 2:1-20, 27, 33-35, 41-51) see also further references to her in Matt. 12:46-50; John 2:1-11; 19:25-27; Acts 1:12-14; and Gal. 4:4.

Before going into the details of verses 28-38, covering the meeting between Gabriel and Mary, it may be well to take a brief look at the whole. The following items are included:

a. The angel's gracious salutation (verse 28).

b. Mary's fear and perplexity (verse 29).

c. The angel's reassurance. His promise that Mary will conceive and give birth to a very special child (verses 30-33).

d. Mary's request for an explanation, since she is not living with a husband and accordingly does not understand how, in her present condition, she can conceive a child (verse 34).

e. The angel's comforting reply (verses 35-37).

f. Mary's courageous expression of wholehearted self-surrender, after which the angel leaves (verse 38).

How beautifully Mary's preliminary reactions—items (b) and (d)—are wedged in between the angel's words of encouragement and clarification! Gabriel's heart is in his work. He loves Mary. And he, in turn, is only doing what God had told him to do, and is only saying what God had ordered him to say. Therefore, rightly considered, the story reveals the wonderful love of God. The climax too, namely, Mary's expression of unqualified submission to God's will, is all one could desire.

Unless this bird's-eye view is taken first of all, and kept in mind throughout, one is likely to ignore the forest because of the trees.

28. Entering, he said to her, Greetings, you highly favored one, the Lord is with you. As appears from the expression *entering* (i.e., as a friend, relative, or neighbor would enter by the door) and the familiar word of salutation, namely, *Greetings,* from the very start the angel is trying to create an atmosphere of tranquility.

Gabriel continues, "you highly favored one." Here Jerome's Latin version (the Vulgate) reads *gratiae plena,* full of grace, not a bad rendering unless it is wrongly interpreted as if it meant, "Mary, you are filled with grace which is at your disposal to bestow on others." The true sense is, "You are full of grace which you have received . . . you are in a unique sense a divinely favored person." The immediately following context proves that this interpretation is correct, for the angel adds, "The Lord is with you."

29. She was greatly troubled at his words and was wondering what kind of greeting this might be. In spite of the angel's cordial entrance, Mary was startled. She experienced momentary fright. Why? In all probability because she, though being a young woman of excellent moral and spiritual character, was still a sinner, who was now unexpectedly face to face with a strong, brilliant, sinless being. It is true that the passage does not mention this cause of her alarm, but that is not a good reason to deny it (with some commentators). It surely was not necessary for Luke to state the altogether obvious.

Nevertheless, the evangelist calls attention to the fact that Mary was upset by *the words* of the angel. She knew that she was but a young woman of lowly social position—see verses 48, 52b—and therefore could not understand how it was possible for *her* to be addressed in such lofty terms. What? . . . *She* singled out by the Lord as the object of very special favor? The very thought shocked her.

Was Mary forgetting Ps. 138:6, "For though Jehovah is high, he has regard for the lowly"? And Isa. 57:15:

"For thus says the high and lofty One,
Who inhabits eternity, whose name is holy:
I dwell in the high and holy place,
With him also that is of a contrite and humble spirit,
To revive the spirit of the humble,
And to revive the heart of the contrite"?

30. But the angel said to her, Do not be afraid, Mary, for you have found favor with God. Also to Zechariah the angel had said, "Do not be afraid." As has been shown in connection with verse 13, this word of encouragement sings its way through Scripture. The next expression too—namely, "You have found favor with God"—is essentially a further explication of "You highly favored one, the Lord is with you." A very beautiful interpretive passage is Isa. 43:4, "I love you." Is not God's grace or favor his love toward the undeserving?

In the present case the contents or substance of this high favor is stated by the angel in verses

31–33. And behold, you will conceive in your womb and give birth to a son, and you shall give him the name Jesus.

He will be great and will be called the Son of the Most High. And the Lord God will give him the throne of his father David.

He will reign over the house of Jacob forever, and his kingdom will never end.

These thoughts, symmetrically arranged, constitute a climax; that is, in this little series of three lines the second adds meaning to the first, and the last fortifies the first and second. Briefly stated the three lines imply:

a. You, Mary, will have a son, Jesus (verse 31).

b. This son will be truly great, the Son of the Most High, and will receive the throne of his father David (verse 32).

c. His rule will never end (verse 33).

As to (a):

Note the similarity between this verse and Isa. 7:14. Here too, as generally, the word *Behold* introduces a surprising declaration: Mary, the *virgin*, is going to conceive and bear a son.

It is she who will name the child. In Matt. 1:21 it is Joseph. That spells perfect harmony, as was the case also with respect to Zechariah and Elizabeth (1:60, 63).

As to the name *Jesus,* not in Luke but in Matthew this name is explained: "for he will save his people from their sins." See N.T.C. on Matthew, pp. 108, 132, 133. The following passages shed further light on the meaning of the name *Jesus* and on the work which the Father gave him to do: Matt. 11:27–30; Luke 19:10; John 3:16; 14:6; Acts 4:12; 5:31; 13:23, 38; Rom. 5:1, 2; II Cor. 5:21; Heb. 7:25; Rev. 1:5.

As to (b):

Gabriel informs Mary that her son will be "great." Among the many passages in which this greatness is brought out are Isa. 6:3 (in the light of John 12:41); 9:6, 7; and 61:1–3 (see Luke 4:16–21). The Psalms too proclaim this fact prophetically (110:1, 2; 118:22, 23). The New Testament is full of corroborative evidence: Matt. 7:28, 29; 9:26, 33; 14:33; Luke 4:32, 36; 8:25, 49–56; John 20:30; Acts 4:12; Rom. 9:5; Eph. 1:20–23; Phil. 2:9–11; Col. 2:9; I Tim. 3:16; Hebrews 8:1, 2; Rev. 1:5–7; 17:14; 19:16.

In fact, this child will be called—that is, will actually be and will be acknowledged as being—"the Son of the Most High." In addition to Luke 1:32 the beloved physician uses this divine title in Luke 1:35, 76; 6:35; and Acts 7:48; also, in quotations from demoniacs in Luke 8:28 (cf. Mark 5:7); Acts 16:17.

The first use of the designation which stresses Jehovah's majesty and sovereignty is found in Gen. 14:18 ("And he was priest to *God Most High*"; Hebrew: 'ēl ᶜelyōn). Cf. Heb. 7:1. In the Old Testament this title, or simply *the Most High,* occurs frequently; see e.g., Deut. 32:8; II Sam. 22:14; Ps. 7:17; 9:2; 21:7; 46:4; 47:2; Lam. 3:35, 38; Dan. 4:17, 24; 5:18, 21; 7:18.

The "greatness" which in Luke 1:32 is prophetically ascribed to Mary's son, who is called "the Son of the Most High," is all the more pronounced because it is going to be combined with humility and the eagerness of this Exalted One to sacrifice himself for the salvation of sinners. Therefore, in listing passages that bear testimony to this greatness one should refer not only to Isa. 53:12a but also to 53:12b; not only to Matt. 11:27 but also to 11:28-30 and 12:17-21; not only to Matt. 28:18-20 but also to 20:28 (cf. Mark 10:45).

In fulfilment of prophecy (II Sam. 7:11b-13; see also Ps. 89:4, 29, 35-37; 132:11; Isa. 9:6, 7; 16:5; Jer. 23:5, 6; Rev. 5:5) the Lord God would give Jesus "the throne of *his father David.*" The prophecy found in II Sam. 7:11b-13 would find its ultimate fulfilment in Jesus. In this connection note that his descent from David, according to his human nature, is also here (in Luke 1:32) very definitely confirmed. Among the many other passages that prove this some have just now been mentioned (besides II Sam. 7:11b-13 especially Ps. 132:11; Jer. 23:5, 6; and Rev. 5:5); others are Mark 12:35; Luke 18:38; and Rom. 1:3. And see on Luke 1:69.

As to (c):

Not only will Mary have a son, and not only will this son be great, even the Son of the Most High, to whom God will give the throne of his father David, but thirdly, the rule of this Jesus will last forever: he will reign over the house of Jacob forever; his kingdom will never end.

It should be unnecessary to state that according to our Lord's own explanation it is not an earthly or political kingdom that is in view here, but rather the kingdom or rule of grace and truth established in the hearts and lives of all those who have the God of Jacob as their refuge (Ps. 46:7, 11). See Luke 17:21; John 6:15; 18:36, 37; Acts 1:6-8. In the words of the apostle Paul this kingdom is one of "righteousness and peace and joy in the Holy Spirit" (Rom. 14:17). Its ultimate outward manifestation will be "the new heaven and earth" and all the blessings that go with this gloriously renewed universe. See also N.T.C. on Matthew, pp. 249, 250.

Gabriel's statement, "and his kingdom will never end" (literally, "and of his kingdom there will be no end"), must be taken at face value:

> When we've been there ten thousand years,
> Bright shining as the sun,
> We've no less days to sing God's praise
> Than when we first begun.[67]
>
> John Newton

---

67. On the whole Lenski has given us an excellent explanation of Luke 1:30-33. However, on p. 45 he states that *time* conceived as "succession of moments" will end. One meets this thought frequently in Lenski's commentaries. Those who accept this view base it on Rev. 10:6. But this interpretation of that passage is erroneous, as I have shown in my book *The Bible on the Life Hereafter,* pp. 72-74.

Now Mary's second reaction:

34. Mary said to the angel, How can this be, since I am not living with a husband? It will be recalled that when Gabriel had told Zechariah that the latter's wife Elizabeth would have a son, the priest had answered, "How can I be sure of this?" His response amounted to "I can't believe it." Mary, on the other hand, is not guilty of lack of faith. She *believes* (see verse 45). But she is befuddled, bewildered, mystified. She has correctly interpreted the angel's message to mean that without the assistance of a husband she is about to conceive a child. So far so good. But *how* was this possible? Among humans conception without insemination was unheard of.

Though the answer Mary received still left certain questions unanswered, it contained all she needed to know at the moment:

35. The angel answered, The Holy Spirit will come upon you, and the power of the Most High will overshadow you. Thus the angel makes very clear to Mary that her conception will result from a *divine,* not a human, action.

The answer is cast in the form of synonymous parallelism, so that "The Holy Spirit" is paired with "the power of the Most High," and "will come upon you" with "will overshadow you." Resultant meaning: The personal Holy Spirit will bring about this wonder in Mary's womb by exerting his divine power.

The activity here described as "coming upon" or "overshadowing" is by most commentators brought into relation with the overarching Shekinah (cloud of light), by means of which Jehovah manifested his presence from a position above the ark of the covenant and between the cherubs (Exod. 25:22; cf. 40:34–38). See also Isa. 60:2; Matt. 17:5; Luke 2:9; Rom. 9:4. This reference is probably legitimate. Nevertheless, something must perhaps be added. The *overshadowing* or *covering* of which Luke speaks here is not static but active. It is creative, productive. It causes Mary to conceive a child. Our thoughts are therefore also—and perhaps especially—directed to the Spirit of God creatively hovering over the waters at the time of creation (Gen. 1:2). In this same connection see Ps. 104:30, expressed poetically in the line: "Thy Spirit O God makes life to abound." The overshadowing Spirit, therefore, not only protects but also creates. It brings about conception within Mary's womb.

The conclusion is very logical: **Therefore also the holy offspring will be called the Son of God.** Not of Joseph but of God!

Does this mean that Gabriel has now made everything "perfectly clear" to Mary? Of course not. As anyone who has ever taken a course in human embryology knows, even "ordinary" conception within the human womb is veiled in mystery. See Ps. 139:13–16. Therefore this unique conception, by means of which the pre-existing Word of God assumes the human nature, surpasses human comprehension all the more. Neither God nor Gabriel demands of Mary that she must understand everything. What is required of her is only this, that she *believes* and *willingly submits.*

In order to strengthen her faith the angel now directs Mary's attention to what may well be considered another "miracle," in order that from the acceptance of "the miraculous but not unique" (verse 36) her faith may advance (verse 35) to the acceptance of "the uniquely miraculous":

36. And look, Elizabeth, your relative, even she has conceived a son in her old age. This is, in fact, the sixth month for her who was said to be barren.

Note the following:

a. The conception of John was in a sense miraculous, as has been indicated. It was a miracle that this could happen to people well advanced in years. Nevertheless it was not unique. It could be compared with the conception of Isaac. On the other hand, the conception of Jesus was uniquely miraculous, for it took place without the assistance of any human male. If, then, the Almighty God is able to bring about the conception of Isaac and of John, will he not also be able to do that which is even more miraculous?

b. "Elizabeth your relative." Much has been written about this. Some, almost unbelievably, have drawn the conclusion that since Elizabeth was a descendant of Aaron, hence of Levi (verse 5), and since Mary was her relative (verse 36), it follows that Mary did not belong to the tribe of Judah! The next step is also usually taken: Jesus did not spring from Judah.

Comment. It has already been shown—see on verse 32—that according to the consistent teaching of Scripture Jesus, according to his human nature, was indeed a descendant of David and Judah. Besides, given two ancestors—Judah ancestor of Mary, Levi of Elizabeth—it is certainly conceivable that an anterior or a lateral relative of Mary, or of Elizabeth, had been married to a descendant of the other ancestor. The result would be that to some extent the tribes would become mixed, so that in the present case Mary, while certainly belonging to the tribe of Judah, and Elizabeth, while just as definitely being a descendant of Levi, could still be blood relatives. While this is being written the author is thinking of a certain retired minister of the gospel who is Caucasian on both his father's and his mother's side. Nevertheless, he has cousins, blood relatives, who, in addition to being part Caucasian, are also part Chinese, Malayan, and Ethiopian! Indeed, the fact that Mary was a descendant of David and Judah but her relative Elizabeth a descendant of Aaron and Levi presents no difficulty at all.

c. "even she has conceived in her old age. This is in fact the sixth month," etc. Since during that month the fetus is rapidly gaining in size and weight, Elizabeth's pregnant condition would soon become visible to everyone. See above, on verse 24. It has been suggested that Gabriel, in informing Mary about Elizabeth's condition, is hinting that she pay her relative a visit. By doing this she will see for herself that "Jehovah our God ... makes the barren woman to be ... a joyful mother" (Ps. 113:9).

37. For with God nothing is ever impossible. He is able to do whatever he wishes to do (Gen. 18:14; Ps. 115:3; Jer. 32:17; Dan. 4:35; Matt. 19:26;

Mark 10:27; Luke 18:27; Eph. 1:19; 3:20). Therefore he was able to give a child to Zechariah and Elizabeth though both had long given up hope of ever having one. And therefore he was also able to fulfil his promise to Mary, without any help from Joseph.

38. Mary said, Behold the handmaid of the Lord. May it be with me according to your word! Instead of "handmaid" some insist on the translation "slave." Most translators and commentators have concluded that in the present context that rendering would not be felicitous.[68]

This conclusion is based upon the fact that with the word *slave* we generally associate the ideas of forced subjection, involuntary service, and (frequently) harsh treatment. On the other hand, Mary's final reaction was the very opposite. "May it be with me according to your word" reminds one of the humble and fully surrendered attitude of the "Servant" in Isaiah's great "Servant" passages (42:1–9; 49:1–9a; 50:4–11; and 52:13—53:12). She is and is eager to be "the handmaid of the Lord," ready to do his will and to be used for carrying out his purpose.

In view of the story recorded in Matt. 1:18, 19 this was not easy. Mary knew that becoming pregnant at this particular time, before her marriage to Joseph had been consummated, would expose her to painful criticism and ridicule; perhaps to something even worse (see Deut. 22:23 f.). But she made a complete surrender. She placed herself, body and soul, at the disposal of the God who loved her and who, by means of this promised pregnancy and childbirth, was bestowing upon her an inestimable blessing.

Gabriel's mission had been fully accomplished. So we are not surprised to read: **Then the angel left her.**[69]

Practical Lessons Derived from Luke 1:26–38

Verses 26, 27

"Gabriel . . . sent from God to *Nazareth* . . . to a *virgin*." "Man looks at the outward appearance but the Lord looks at the heart" (I Sam. 16:7b).

Verses 28–30

"You highly favored one . . . you have found favor with God." From first to last our salvation is the work of God, the product of his grace or favor.

---

68. Among those who have *avoided* it are: A.V., A.R.V., R.S.V., Jerusalem Bible, Robertson, Amplified, Norlie, Riverside—all in favor of "handmaid" (sometimes "handmaiden"); Weymouth, in favor of "maidservant"; Berkeley, in favor of "servant girl"; Beck, N.E.B., N.I.V., in favor of "servant"; Dutch (both Statenvertaling and Nieuwe Vertaling), in favor of "dienstmaagd" = servant girl, handmaid, maidservant.

69. Notes on Greek words, phrases, and constructions in 1:26–38 begin on page 91.

Verse 31

"You shall give him the name Jesus."
"I know of a Name, a beautiful Name," etc.

Jean Perry

Verses 32, 33

"He will be great . . . and his kingdom will never end."
Crowns and thrones may perish, Kingdoms rise and wane,
But the Church of Jesus constant will remain.

Sabine Baring-Gould, third stanza of
"Onward Christian Soldiers"

Verse 35

"Holy offspring . . . Son of God." For man's salvation it was necessary that the Savior be: (a) man, (b) sinless, (c) God. This passage shows that Jesus was and is all three; hence, the perfect Savior.

Verses 36, 37

"Elizabeth . . . has conceived in her old age. . . . For with God nothing is ever impossible."

A mighty fortress is our God,
A bulwark never failing, *etc.*

Martin Luther

Verse 38

"Behold, the handmaid of the Lord," etc. Though Mary did not fully comprehend, she *believed!* Faith means committing one's way to the Lord, trusting him, knowing that he will do whatever is best (Ps. 37:5). For other descriptions of faith see N.T.C. on Mark, pp. 458, 459.

Notes on Greek Words, Phrases, and Constructions in 1:26–38

Verse 26

ἀπεστάλη, third per. s. 2nd aor. passive indicat. of ἀποστέλλω. Cf. *apostle.*

Verse 27

παρθένος. See N.T.C. on Matthew, pp. 133-144. The meaning is virgin. This—or unmarried girl, unmarried woman—has also been suggested as the English rendering for the Greek word παρθένος in I Cor. 7:25, 28, 34. With respect to I Cor. 7:36-38 translators and commentators are divided: some preferring "betrothed," "fiancée," "girl"; others "daughter," "single daughter," or something similar. The rendering "girl" will do in Matt. 25:1 f. Nowhere does the word refer to a married woman.

ἐμνηστευμένην, acc. s. f. present passive participle of μνηστεύω, to ask in marriage, to betroth; passive, to be betrothed, to be pledged in marriage. Cf. Luke 2:5; Matt. 1:18.

There is no good reason to connect "of David's house" with anything other than Ἰωσήφ. But see Lenski, *op. cit.*, p. 40.

Verse 28

κεχαριτωμένη, nom. s. f. perfect passive participle of χαριτόω, to favor; passive, to be visited with favor, to be (highly) favored. For this verb see also N.T.C. on Ephesians 1:6 (active voice there).

Verse 29

διεταράχθη (from διαταράσσω*), perfective of ἐταράχθη; see on 1:12.

διελογίζετο, third p. s. imperf. indicat. of διαλογίζομαι. On this verb see G. Schrenk's article in Th.D.N.T., Vol. II, pp. 93–98. In Luke see also 3:15; 5:21, 22; 12:17; 20:14. The verb also occurs in Matthew and (several times) in Mark. Cf. *dialog*.

εἴη, third per. s. pres. optative (in indirect question) of εἰμί.

Verse 30

εὗρες, sec. per. s. 2nd aor. indicat. of εὑρίσκω. Cf. *Eureka!* Luke is fond of this verb: he uses a form of it at least once in every chapter except chapters 3, 10, 14, 16, 20, and 21. Also in Acts this verb occurs often. It occurs frequently also in Matthew, Mark, John, and Revelation. Elsewhere its use is scattered. For χάρις see on 2:40.

Verse 31

συλλήμψῃ; sec. per. s. fut. (prophetic) indicat. middle of συλλαμβάνω, for which see on 1:24. Here in verse 31 ἐν γαστρί is added. Cf. synonymous expression ἐν γαστρὶ ἔχειν in Isa. 7:14; Matt. 1:18, 23; and see also Gen. 25:21.

γαστήρ, here *womb*. So also in Matt. 1:18, 23; 24:19; Mark 13:17; Luke 21:23; I Thess. 5:3; Rev. 12:2. In Titus 1:12, glutton. Basically γαστήρ means belly, stomach. Cf. *gastric*.

It stands to reason that τέξῃ and καλέσεις, co-ordinate with συλλήμψῃ, are also sec. per. s. fut. (prophetic) indicatives.

Verse 32

The divine title υἱὸς ὑψίστου needs no definite articles to make it definite.

Verse 34

οὐ γινώσκω, here of a woman; cf. Matt. 1:25, οὐκ ἐγίνωσκε, of a man. Meaning: (not) to have sexual relations with. Cf. Gen. 4:1, 17.

Verse 35

ἐπισκιάσει, third per. s. fut. (prophetic) indicat. of ἐπισκιάζω, to overshadow, cover, envelop. Cf. Luke 9:34; see also Matt. 17:5; Mark 9:7; Acts 5:15. Cf. *sky*. Related also is the Greek word σκότος (darkness).

γεννώμενον, nom. s. neut. present (probably futuristic) passive participle of γεν-νάω, to beget, to generate; hence literally "that which is [or: will be] begotten," and so: offspring (to be).

Verse 36

συγγενίς*, female relative.

γήρει, dat s. of γῆρας*, old age. Cf. *geriatrics*.

Verse 37

Note that, in accordance with the context in each case, in verse 37 ῥῆμα means "thing" (Hebrew usage), but in verse 38 it means (spoken) "word," here in the sense of prediction, prophecy.

Also note (literally) "Not will be impossible with God every thing," where we would say, "Nothing will be [or: is ever] impossible with God."

Verse 38

δούλη**, servant girl, handmaid. See also 1:48 and Acts 2:18. For further comments see the text.

γένοιτο, third per. s. aor. optative of γίνομαι.

---

39 At this time Mary hurried away to a town in the hill country of Judah,   40 where she entered the home of Zechariah and greeted Elizabeth.   41 When Elizabeth heard Mary's greeting, the baby leaped within her womb. Elizabeth was filled with the Holy Spirit,   42 and in a loud voice cried out:
Blessed are you among women,
And blessed is the fruit of your womb!
43 But how does this happen to me
That the mother of my Lord should come to me?
44 For as soon as the sound of your greeting reached my ears
The baby within my womb leaped for joy.
45 And blessed is she who believed,
Because there will be a fulfilment of the words
Spoken to her by the Lord.[70]

1:39-45 *Mary Visits Elizabeth*

39, 40. At this time Mary hurried away to a town in the hill country of Judah, where she entered the home of Zechariah and greeted Elizabeth. Undoubtedly Mary's decision to visit this dear older relative (see on verse 36) and to do this without delay was prompted by Gabriel's message regarding herself (verses 28–35) and regarding Elizabeth (verses 36, 37); yes, and also by the fact that even in her (Mary's) own case the predictions were already *beginning* to be fulfilled.

So she hurries to that part of the South Palestinian region which origi-

---

70. Or: ... she who believed that there will be, etc.

nally had been allotted to the tribe of the patriarch Judah.[71] The main city in this hilly country was Hebron. Neither here nor in verse 23 does the evangelist mention the name of the town where Zechariah and Elizabeth were living.

Having entered the home, Mary greets Elizabeth. What kind of greeting was this? There are those who believe that it was a very comprehensive salutation. They believe that Mary, having received from the angel Gabriel the announcement regarding the coming of the Messiah and of her own involvement in that coming (see especially verses 30-33, 35, 37), now in turn is passing on to Elizabeth this joy-imparting Messianic greeting.[72] In favor of this theory one might argue that it would have been natural for Mary to wish to impart to a dear relative of her own sex the tremendously important announcement she had received, one which was already beginning to be translated into historical reality, for Mary was already pregnant (see verses 42, 43). Besides, this theory as to the nature of the greeting addressed to Elizabeth would explain much that is otherwise mysterious; for example, that Elizabeth immediately calls Mary the most blessed woman in the world, and that she identifies the fruit of Mary's womb as the Messiah.

Nevertheless, the theory may be open to the objection that thus a broader meaning is assigned to the term *greeting* (between friends and relatives) than it generally carries. Besides, if any explanation must be given to the mystery of Elizabeth's exclamation (see especially verses 42, 43), does not Luke supply it in stating that she was "filled with the Holy Spirit"?

Having therefore paid to this theory the respect which it certainly deserves, but hesitating to endorse it, we will probably have to accept the more usual interpretation, namely, that the greeting to which reference is here made consisted of a warm embrace accompanied by a few genuinely loving words.

41. When Elizabeth heard Mary's greeting, the baby leaped within her womb. Elizabeth was filled with the Holy Spirit... At this stage of Elizabeth's pregnancy—note the expression *the sixth month* in verse 36—a ("quickening") movement of the fetus would generally not have been considered unusual. In this particular case, however, Elizabeth, illumined by the Holy Spirit, interpreted this action as an expression of the joy experienced by the unborn child. See on verse 44.

---

71. Just why it was that Luke writes "country of Judah" instead of simply "Judea" is not stated. Can it be that even this early in his account he wishes to direct the attention of the reader to the fact that Jesus, whose forerunner was John, was a descendant of Judah; in other words, that the evangelist is anticipating the idea more clearly expressed in 2:4 and 3:33? Improbable is the suggestion that the present "Judah" is really "Juttah," south of Hebron (Josh. 15:55; 21:16). That Luke's "Judah" here in 1:39 has the same meaning as it does in 3:33, where it clearly refers to a son of Jacob, must be regarded as probable.

72. See J. H. van Halsema, "De Groet van de engel en van Maria in Lukas 1," *NedTT*, 25 (April, 1971), pp. 186, 187.

Continued: **42. and in a loud voice cried out...** What Elizabeth loudly proclaimed is printed on p. 93. Note that it is there reproduced in the form of a poem. Indeed, it can truthfully be regarded as a Greek reproduction of a Semitic piece of poetry. The parallelistic structure of the lines, so characteristic of Hebrew and Aramaic poetry, the balanced form and contents of the neatly arranged clauses—note, for example:

> Blessed are . . .
> And blessed is . . .
> And blessed is . . .

mark them as being indeed a poem; or, if one prefers, a song, Elizabeth's Song. "Song" here means metrical composition. See p. 155.

This, then, is the first of five pieces of poetic literature centered about the nativity theme. In all five God is the object of *adoration* (1:43, 46–55, 68–73, 78, 79; 2:14, 30–32). This sentiment is at times accompanied by an expression of *astonishment*. The spirit of *humiliation* before such a great and wonderful Lord is also frequently in evidence (1:43, 48, 52, 77–79; 2:29).

When, with due consideration for what these poems have in common, the question is asked, "What is the outstanding feature that *distinguishes* each song from the others?" the answer is not easy. This is due to the fact that we find here a very pleasing intermingling of various attitudes of heart and mind. Nevertheless, the following attempt may be deserving of consideration:

Five Pieces of Poetic Literature in Luke

Name of Song	Textual Reference	Distinguishing Feature
The Song of Elizabeth	1:42b–45	L O V E
The Song of Mary	1:46–55	F A I T H
The Prophecy of Zechariah	1:68–79	H O P E
The Song of Angels	2:14	A D O R A T I O N
The Song of Simeon	2:29–32	R E S I G N A T I O N

The Song of Elizabeth

She cried out in a loud voice because her heart was filled with wonderment, thanksgiving, and, last but not least, love. She could not restrain herself; in fact, she did not even wish to hold back.

What she cried out was:

Blessed are you among women,
And blessed is the fruit of your womb!

"Blessed" means more than "Happy." "Happy" often indicates how a person feels; "Blessed" what he is. A person is blessed when God's favor rests upon him, when the Lord delights in him. See also N.T.C. on Matthew, p. 264.

"Blessed are you among women" is the Aramaic and Hebrew manner of expressing the superlative. The meaning, therefore, is, "Mary, among all women on earth you are the most blessed one!" See Gram. N.T., p. 660.

"And blessed is the fruit of your womb" shows that Mary is pregnant, and that not only Mary but also her son is the object of the Father's delight. The fact that throughout Christ's earthly ministry the Father took special delight in his Son is evident from such passages as Matt. 3:17 (cf. Mark 1:11; Luke 3:22); Matt. 17:5 (cf. Mark 9:7; Luke 9:35); Matt. 12:18; John 12:28; 17:24.

43. But how does this happen to me
That the mother of my Lord should come to me?

The fact that Mary went to visit her relative Elizabeth shows that these two had probably become acquainted at an earlier date. They may have been in each other's company for a while in connection with one or more of the great religious festivals. Cf. Luke 2:44. But the present passage shows that at this particular point of the story Elizabeth sees in Mary more than a relative or acquaintance. Zechariah's wife calls Mary "the mother of my Lord!"

How had Elizabeth discovered this fact? Had Mary already told her the big news? We have seen that in all probability the "greeting" as such does not necessarily imply this. Did the intra-uterine movement mentioned in verses 41 and 44 reveal this marvelous secret to Elizabeth? Yes, but not apart from the activity of the Holy Spirit, as Luke clearly indicates when he says, "The baby leaped within her womb. Elizabeth was filled with the Holy Spirit and . . . cried out," etc.

Note the significant expression *the mother of my Lord,* and compare Ps. 110:1 where David—again "in the Spirit" (Matt. 22:43, 44; Mark 12:36)— prophetically uses the title ("my Lord") to describe the coming Messiah. Cf. I Cor. 12:3.

Elizabeth continues:

44. For as soon as the sound of your greeting reached my ears
The baby within my womb leaped for joy.

Does this "leaping for joy" mean that *the child* in Elizabeth's womb had suddenly become cognizant of the nearby presence of the Messiah? There are those who defend this theory. The distinguished Dutch commentator S. Greijdanus, commenting on verse 44, wrote as follows: "The statement concerns an operation of the Holy Spirit which caused Elizabeth's child to feel, experience, and know that the mother of the Lord, and within her the Lord himself, was present here and now, and which caused that child to leap forward toward the Lord with a dance of joyful jubilation."[73] And

---

73. *Het Evangelie naar Lucas (Korte Verklaring der Heilige Schrift),* Kampen, 1941, Vol. I, p. 40. From here on whenever this book is indicated, its title will be abbreviated to *Korte Verklaring.*

again, "By means of this action Elizabeth's child also acknowledged his inferiority in relation to Mary's Child."[74]

But does Luke's account really say or imply all this? Rather it would seem that verse 44 (in connection with verses 40–43) states and implies only the following: (1) Mary greets Elizabeth. (2) Elizabeth hears the greeting. (3) The fetus within Elizabeth's womb leaps for joy. (4) Elizabeth, *filled with the Holy Spirit,* responds to the greeting. In her enthusiastic exclamation she calls Mary "the most blessed woman" and expresses surprised joy that the one whom she designates "the mother of my Lord" is honoring her with a visit. (5) She interprets the movement of the babe within her womb as being a sign of its joy, this very joy being the evidence *to her* of "the Lord's" presence in Mary's womb. See further on 1:67.

In our interpretation it is probably not safe to penetrate any deeper than this, or to accept the possibility of propositional religious knowledge on the part of a fetus of approximately six months. That at this stage of its development it already has all the nerves it will ever have and is normally able to react to stimuli is well known. In view of verse 15 it should be added that in some mysterious manner, incapable of further analysis, the Holy Spirit was already actively present in the soul of Elizabeth's child. Further than this we cannot go.[75] See also N.T.C. on John 1:31a.

Elizabeth adds,

45. And blessed is she who believed,
Because there will be a fulfilment of the words
Spoken to her by the Lord.

Although the rendering "And blessed is she who believed *that* there will be," etc., is also possible, the first translation has the following in its favor:

a. The positive assurance that God is going to fulfil his promises to Mary is a more solid ground, a more valid reason, for calling her "blessed" than her own subjective faith in the fulfilment of these promises.

b. "Blessed is she who believed" is a richer expression than "Blessed is she who believed that," etc. The first rendering more definitely than the second describes Mary as *a woman of faith.*

c. "Blessed is she who believed" is in line with "Blessed are those who, though not seeing, are yet believing" (John 20:29). See also Gen. 15:6 (cf. Rom. 4:3; Gal. 3:6, 9; James 2:23).

d. As to conciseness of phraseology, the beatitude "Blessed is she who

---

74. *Het Heilig Evangelie naar de Beschrijving van Lucas (Kommentaar op het Nieuwe Testament),* Amsterdam, 1940, p. 61. From here on whenever this book is indicated, its title will be abbreviated to *Kommentaar.*

75. Is not the interpreter who ascribes propositional religious knowledge to a fetus also in danger of erring in his conception of "innate ideas"? On this difficult subject see the comprehensive treatment by H. Bavinck, *Gereformeerde Dogmatiek,* third edition, Kampen, 1918, Vol. II, pp. 29–49; or, for those who cannot read Dutch, see my translation: H. Bavinck, *The Doctrine of God,* Grand Rapids, 1955, pp. 41–59.

believed" is also more in line with the familiar beatitudes of Luke 6:20 f., cf. Matt. 5:1 f.

e. Finally, the construction, "Blessed is she who believed," describes more adequately than does its alternative what had been Mary's reaction to Gabriel's message.

That reaction, it will be recalled, had been: first, alarm and astonishment (verse 29); then, an earnest request for an explanation (verse 34); and finally, the complete surrender that characterizes the person who lives by the rule, "Trust and obey" (verse 38). For the rest, see the note on verse 45 on p. 99.

As to . . . "there will be a fulfilment," etc., note the following: the words of the Lord (via Gabriel) recorded in 1:31a, 35a (unique conception) had already been fulfilled, and the promises contained in 31b, 32, 33, 35b (still largely unfulfilled) were going to be realized, as the rest of the Gospels, etc., abundantly prove.

What deserves special attention is this outstanding fact, namely, that in Elizabeth's entire exuberant exclamation (verses 41b–45) envy never raises its head. Elizabeth was, after all, much older than Mary (cf. 1:7, 18, 36 with 2:5). Yet this aged woman is deeply conscious of her own unworthiness and genuinely rejoices in the joy of her much younger relative!

How can this complete absence of the begrudging attitude be explained? The answer is found in I Cor. 13:4: "*Love* does not envy." Is not this a good reason for calling this poem "Elizabeth's Song of Love"?[76]

Practical Lessons Derived from Luke 1:39–45

Verses 39, 40

"Mary . . . hurried away to Elizabeth." God's grace spans the generation gap.

Verse 41

"Elizabeth was filled with the Holy Spirit." In this story note the following "fruits" of the Spirit's indwelling: knowledge, humility, gratitude, love.

Verse 42

"Blessed are you among women." In our legitimate opposition to Mary-worship we should guard against falling into the opposite extreme!

Verse 43

"My Lord." If Elizabeth so described Jesus when (according to his human nature) he was still a babe in Mary's womb, how much more should we not glorify the Christ who died for us and who lives evermore to intercede for us! See Heb. 7:25.

---

76. Notes on Greek words, phrases, and constructions in 1:39–45 begin on page 99.

Verse 44

"The baby within my womb leaped for joy." The fact that, in a manner mysterious beyond all explanation, the Holy Spirit can be actively present in the heart and life of a babe in the womb cannot be questioned. Cf. Luke 1:15.

Verse 45

"Blessed is she who believed!" Not only "he" (for example Abraham, Gen. 15:6) but also "she." Not just "happy" but "blessed." *When* did Mary believe? Not only when God's promise attained initial fulfilment, but even earlier. *What* did she believe? That what had never happened before—conception apart from any human father—would happen now; that the Hope of all the ages would be realized, in its initial stage, within the womb of a lowly Jewish virgin, namely, herself. *How* did she manifest her trust in God? By means of voluntary and complete surrender to his will. See 1:38. What a theme for a sermon!

"There will be a fulfilment." God is love (I John 4:8). Therefore, if his threats attain fulfilment, will not his promises?

Notes on Greek Words, Phrases, and Constructions in 1:39-45

Verse 39

ἀναστᾶσα, nom. s. 2nd aor. fem. participle of ἀνίστημι. This verb is very frequent in Luke; often, as probably also here, with weakened meaning, merely indicating the beginning of an action. In the present case it can even be omitted in the translation. Whether, in any particular instance, this participle can be considered redundant depends on the context. On this verb see also N.T.C. on Mark, p. 296, footnote 333; pp. 353, 354; and p. 406, footnote 495.

ὀρεινός, -ή, -όν*, hilly; hence, ἡ ὀρεινή (χώρα) = the hill country; cf. verse 65.

Verse 41

ἐσκίρτησεν, third per. s. aor. indicat. of σκιρτάω*, to leap for joy. See also verse 44 and 6:23. In Gen. 25:22 (LXX) the correct translation is probably *struggled*.

βρέφος, here and in verse 44, unborn babe; in I Peter 2:2 used in a figurative sense; in II Tim. 3:15 infancy, childhood; elsewhere baby, infant. Cf. *embryo*.

Verse 42

εὐλογημένη (f.) and εὐλογημένος (m.) are perfect passive participles, indicating what had become and continued to be a fact.

Verse 44

To depart from the more usual meaning of γάρ = "for" is probably unnecessary in the present connection. The sense may well be: "I (Elizabeth) suddenly perceived that you, Mary, are the mother of my Lord, *for* the motion of the babe within my womb made me aware of this." Translators who reject "for" substitute "Why," "I tell you," "Just think," etc. It must be admitted that γάρ can have these meanings. See also N.T.C. on Mark, p. 639, footnote 804.

For the noun ἀγαλλίασις and the verb ἀγαλλιάω (also in verse 47) see on verse 14. See also on verse 41.

Verse 45

Lenski's declaration (*op. cit.,* p. 53) that ὅτι, as used here, must mean *because,* and that A. T. Robertson is "quite alone" in judging that the meaning *that* is also possible is too strong. Either "because" or "that" makes good sense. The versions are rather evenly divided: "because" or "for" being favored, among others, by A.V., A.R.V., Williams, Norlie, and the Dutch (both Statenvertaling and Nieuwe Vertaling: "want"); and "that" by Moffatt, Berkeley, N.A.S., Jerusalem Bible, R.S.V., N.E.B., N.I.V., etc.

Those who favor "believed that," etc., can point to the fact that πιστεύειν followed by ὅτι in the sense of "that" (a) yields an intelligible meaning; and (b) is of rather frequent occurrence in the New Testament; especially in the writings of John (8:24; 11:27, 42; 13:19; 14:10; 16:27, 30; 17:8, 21; 20:31; I John 5:1, 5). Elsewhere it occurs occasionally (Matt. 9:28; Mark 11:23, 24; Rom. 6:8; I Thess. 4:14; Heb. 11:6); in all of Luke (Third Gospel and Acts) only in Acts 9:26 (and possibly here in Luke 1:45).

Nevertheless, while granting that "she who believed *that*" may be correct, I side with Lenski and others in my preference for "because." For my reasons see the explanation.

---

46 And Mary said,
"My soul magnifies the Lord,
47 And my spirit rejoices in God my Savior;
48 Because he has looked with favor upon his servant in her humble state.
For, indeed, from now on all generations will call me blessed.
49 Because the Mighty One has done great things for me:
Holy is his name.
50 And his mercy extends from generation to generation
To those who fear him.
51 He has performed mighty deeds with his arm;
He has scattered those who are proud in their inmost thoughts.
52 He has brought down rulers from (their) thrones,
But has lifted up the humble.
53 The hungry he has filled with good things,
But has sent the rich away empty.
54 He has helped Israel, his servant,
In remembrance of his mercy—
55 Even as he promised[77] our fathers—
(Mercy) to Abraham and to his seed forever."
56 Mary remained with Elizabeth about three months, and then returned to her home.

1:46–56 *Mary's Magnificat*

A few matters of an introductory character require attention:
1. This is Mary's famous "hymn of praise." It proceeded from her heart and lips when she visited Elizabeth. Its popular title, *The Magnificat,* is

---

77. Or: said to.

derived from the first word of the hymn in the Latin version: *Magnificat anima mea Dominum,* meaning, "My soul magnifies the Lord."

2. The theory according to which this song is ascribed to Elizabeth must be rejected, since the textual evidence for "Elizabeth" instead of "Mary" (in 1:46) is so meager that it can be dismissed.

3. It has been said that Mary's song is "saturated" with Hannah's Prayer (I Sam. 2:1-10). And it is true that there is a degree of resemblance between these two expressions of praise. This is not strange. Both authors were devout Jewish women. Hannah's son was born in answer to prayer; Mary's firstborn was conceived in realization of Gabriel's (hence God's) promise. Something wonderful was going to be written about the child Samuel (I Sam. 2:26). Almost the identical expression was going to be used with reference to the child Jesus (Luke 2:52).

One more fact must be borne in mind. The system of education in Israel was such that from early childhood children were taught "the sacred writings" (II Tim. 3:15). Parents and teachers were not, as a rule, afflicted with memorization-phobia. See N.T.C. on I and II Timothy and Titus, the special section on *Principles and Methods of Education in Israel,* pp. 296-300. It is very natural therefore that at a time of special joy Mary would express her exultation in biblical language and that, among other passages, phrases from Hannah's Song would have occurred to her. Resemblances are noted in the following chart:

Mary's Magnificat Compared with Hannah's Song

Mary's Magnificat *Luke 1:*	*Hannah's Song* *I Sam. 2:*
46, 47	1
"My soul magnifies the Lord," etc.	
49	2
"Holy is his name."	
51	4, 9, 10
"Who has scattered the proud."	
52	8
"He has lifted up the humble."	
53	5, 7
"The hungry he has filled with good things, But has sent the rich away empty."	

Upon close examination it becomes apparent, however, that the resemblances are rather few; also, that the similarity is seldom close. There is no such thing as "saturation." There is just enough resemblance to believe that Mary may well have been conscious of Hannah's Song.

If one is looking for precursors of the phraseology used in the Magnificat, he will find several in the Psalms; a few elsewhere. A number of these parallels are close, as examination of the following incomplete chart will show.

Mary's Magnificat Compared with Other Scripture Passages

Mary's Magnificat (Luke 1)	*The Psalms, etc.*
46, 47 "My soul magnifies the Lord, And my spirit rejoices in God my Savior."	Ps. 103:1
48 "Because he has looked with favor upon his servant in her humble state."	I Sam. *1*:11 (this is *not* part of Hannah's Song!); Ps. 25:18
49 "Holy is his name."	With slight variations this phrase is found in many of the Psalms: 22:3; 71:22; 89:18; 99:3; 103:1; etc.
50 "And his mercy extends from generation to generation to those who fear him."	Ps. 103:17
51 "He has performed mighty deeds with his arm."	Ps. 44:3; 98:1; Isa. 53:1
"He has scattered those who are proud."	Ps. 89:10; Job 12:19
52 "He has brought down rulers from their thrones."	II Sam. 22:28
"But has lifted up the humble."	II Sam. 22:18; Job 5:11
53 "The hungry he has filled with good things."	Ps. 103:5; 107:9
54 "He has helped Israel, his servant."	Ps. 98:3; 147:2, 19
"In remembrance of his mercy."	Ps. 25:6; 98:3; 136 (second part of each verse)
55 "—Even as he promised our fathers— (Mercy) to Abraham and to his seed forever."	Gen. 12:2, 3; 17:7; 22:15–18; Exod. 2:24; II Sam. 22:51; Ps. 105:6–10; Micah 7:20.

4. The Magnificat may be divided into four stanzas or strophes.[78] The arrangement is logical, and therefore easy to remember.

---

78. So also A. Plummer, *op. cit.*, p. 31, and others.

In the first strophe (verses 46-48) Mary extols God for what he had done for her, a maiden of lowly birth.

In the second (verses 49, 50) her thanksgiving and praise, having reached a climax ("Holy is his name"), begins, as it were, to take in more territory. Her spiritual horizon widens. From concentration on the manner in which God's mercy has affected *herself* she ascends to the contemplation of that divine lovingkindness as revealed "from generation to generation to those who fear him."

As the third strophe (verses 51-53) indicates, this *mercy* is all the more strikingly apparent when contrasted with God's *severity* toward those who do not fear him.

The conclusion (fourth strophe, verses 54, 55) of the Magnificat is indeed magnificent. It expresses a thought often neglected today even in conservative circles, namely, that the manifestation of God's mercy is the fulfilment of the covenant promise God made to the fathers, a promise of supreme value even today to believers and their seed (Gal. 3:9, 29).

We shall now discuss the Magnificat strophe by strophe:

The first strophe is as follows:

46-48. And Mary said,
  My soul magnifies the Lord,
  And my spirit rejoices in God my Savior;
  Because he has looked with favor upon his servant in her humble state.
  For, indeed, from now on all generations will call me blessed.

Her heart filled to overflowing with thanksgiving for that which God had done for her, Mary says, "My soul magnifies the Lord," that is, proclaims the greatness of Jehovah. Mary does this joyfully, enthusiastically, for she adds, "And my spirit rejoices in God my Savior."

It should be clear immediately that in these two parallel lines there can be no difference—and certainly no pronounced difference—between "soul" and "spirit." For more on this see N.T.C. on Mark, p. 315, footnote 370.

In what sense does Mary call God "my Savior"? No one, certainly, will wish to deny the fact that, in the Old Testament, words like *Savior, save, salvation* are not always used in a strictly spiritual sense. A person or a people may be saved or delivered not only from sin but also from sickness, death, an enemy, etc. See, for example, I Sam. 11:13; II Chron. 20:17; Ps. 22:21; 106:21; 116:8. Sometimes there seems to be a blending of physical and spiritual evil from which God's people are saved or delivered, so that God is their Savior in a double sense (Isa. 63:8, 9; etc.). There are also passages in which the terms in question refer either exclusively or at least predominantly to deliverance from sin and restoration to divine favor. See especially Ps. 51:12-14; and examine also Ps. 119:81 and Ezek. 37:23. And do not the following passages indicate that by divine operation a keen sense of sin and a deep desire to be delivered from it and to be restored to fellowship with God had been implanted in the hearts of God's people? See Isa. 1:18; 12:2, 3; chapter 53; Dan. 9:8, 9, 19; Mic. 7:19; Zech. 8:7, 8; 13:1.

What, then, does Mary mean by calling God her Savior? What does the context plus Old Testament background imply as to the probable answer? Is it sufficient to say that she was thinking solely of the fact that God had rescued her from the oblivion which otherwise would probably have been her lot? That something on this order must have been *included* in her reason for exuberant thanksgiving can be granted. Note the context which shows that she was conscious of her "humble state" and of the fact that the Lord had delivered her from it so that from now on all generations would call her blessed. But was she thinking of nothing else?

We must bear in mind that we are dealing here with a deeply spiritual and meditative child of God (Luke 2:19, 51; John 2:5); that, as has been shown, the "salvation" passages of the Old Testament by no means exclude deliverance from sin and enjoyment of fellowship with God; and, last but not least, that in another nativity passage (Matt. 1:21) God's angel declares, "You shall call his name Jesus, for he *will save* his people *from their sins.*" Do not these facts establish the answer that it was especially in the spiritual sense that Mary calls God "my Savior"?

Deeply conscious was Mary of the fact that she was a woman of "humble state," the "wife" (Matt. 1:20) of a village carpenter. In the eyes of many she was probably regarded as unlikely to become the object of God's special favor. Nevertheless, from now on not only Elizabeth (see verse 42) but all generations would call her blessed.

A "generation," in the sense in which the term is used here, means a number of people constituting any *one* rung of the ladder of descent, a group of contemporaries. Moreover, Mary does not say that all generations are going to consider her a *mediatrix,* and as such a legitimate object of *hyperdulia* (veneration of the Virgin Mary as holiest of creatures). What she means is that all generations are going to praise God because of the marvelous manner in which he has honored her.

The second strophe proves this:

49, 50. Because the Mighty One has done great things for me:
Holy is his name.
And his mercy extends from generation to generation
To those who fear him.

In the spirit of Ps. 71:19 Mary reflects on the great things God, here understandably called "the Mighty One," had done for her. Had he not lifted her from her humble state and bestowed on her the highest honor conceivable, namely, to be the mother of the Messiah, as far as his human nature was concerned? Had he not performed within her the miracle of parthenogenesis, conception without penetration of a passive female cell by an active male cell? How marvelous God's power!

But not only does Mary's Magnificat extol God's *power.* His *mercy*—call it "steadfast love" or even "lovingkindness" if you prefer—also elicits her praise. Using the phraseology of Ps. 103:17 she exclaims, "And his mercy extends from generation to generation to those that fear him."

104

As indicated earlier, here Mary's song ascends from the individual to the general, from what she herself had experienced to what was ever in store for one set of contemporaries after another throughout the course of history, being constantly repeated as the centuries roll along. Cf. Ps. 89:2; 90:2; Isa. 34:17.

Note, however, the qualifications: "to those that fear him," that is, to those who in heart and mind are filled with reverent regard for God; for the genuinely devout, the truly pious people.

Not as if the Lord had completely withdrawn his kindness from men in general. Study Gen. 17:20; 39:5; Ps. 36:6; 145:9, 15, 16; Matt. 5:42; Mark 8:2; Luke 6:35, 36; Acts 14:16, 17; Rom. 2:4; and I Tim. 4:10. Can anyone read the precious passage about God's tenderness toward the Ninevites, toward their little ones and even toward their cattle (Jonah 4:10, 11), without being overcome with emotion?

The denial of the manifestation of God's goodness to men in general—call it "common grace" if you wish, or invent a better name for it—is an extreme position. Yet, we must be careful not to endorse the opposite extreme. The present passage is only one among many that stress the favor of God bestowed *not* on everybody but on his people, on them, *on them alone.* Note: "his mercy . . . to those that fear him." See also Deut. 7:9; Ps. 25:10; 103:18; Isa. 55:3, 6; 57:15; Matt. 5:1–12; John 10:11, 15, 28; 11:25, 26. In fact, so very numerous are these limiting passages that it would be useless to try to cite them all. Mary, then, is thinking of the marvelous and never failing kindness which God is constantly causing to be felt and experienced by all needy ones who stand in awe of him and love him.

What is perhaps somewhat surprising is the fact that between these two statements about God, the first stressing his power, the second his mercy, stands the declaration "Holy is his name." At first glance these words may seem to be "out of context." One asks, perhaps, "But why did Mary insert this reference to God's holiness or sinlessness? What has that to do with the matter with reference to which she is lifting up her voice in sincere, eloquent, and enthusiastic praise?"

Some are of the opinion that in this connection Mary was thinking about her conception; and that, in view of the fact that so often among men sin is connected with bringing about conception, she is saying that in her case conception had been brought about by God's holy power, "utterly separated from the sin and sinfulness of man."[79]

But is not this interpretation of God's holiness too narrow? It should be borne in mind that Mary was a Jewess, instructed from childhood in the Jewish religion. Accordingly, her words and phrases must be understood in the light of the Old Testament. When this is done it soon becomes evident that her exclamation "Holy is his name"—that is, "Holy is God as he has revealed himself"—is definitely in place. To the Jew the adjective *qādōsh*

---

79. See Lenski, *op. cit.*, p. 57.

basically meant separate, set apart, exalted. To ascribe "holiness" to God meant to describe him as being lifted infinitely high above all creatures, hence also above all creaturely weaknesses including sin.[80] "Holiness, when ascribed to God, was not considered to be an attribute to be co-ordinated with the other attributes" (H. Bavinck). Perhaps the best way in which to gain a true idea of the *basic* meaning of the word *holy* as ascribed to God in the Old Testament would be to read and reread Isa. 6:1-5. Another helpful approach would be to sing that touching refrain, based on Ps. 148:

> Let them praises give Jehovah,
> For his name alone is high,
> And his glory is exalted,
> And his glory is exalted,
> And his glory is exalted,
> Far above the earth and sky.
>
> *Trinity Hymnal*, Philadelphia, 1961, No. 105.

Read also Isa. 57:15.

Applying all this to the Magnificat, we must conclude that Mary was so deeply impressed with the "great things" God had done for her, and to which she had just now referred (in the immediately preceding line of verse 49) that she cried out, "Holy [that is, *infinitely exalted*] is his name." And was it not also very natural that, reflecting on her own experience, she would apply this "holiness" or "incomparable greatness" of God not only to his *power* (the great things he did for me) but now also to his *mercy*? Hence, "Holy is his name, and his mercy," etc. When she reflected on the manner in which she had conceived, would not God's *power* stand out? When she thought of the honor God had bestowed on her, would not his *mercy* or tender compassion immediately occur to her? And since both of these qualities were marvelous in the highest degree, was it not after all very logical for Mary to express this fact by thus combining the two?

And now the third strophe:

51–53. He has performed mighty deeds with his arm;
He has scattered those who are proud in their inmost thoughts.
He has brought down rulers from (their) thrones.
But has lifted up the humble.
The hungry he has filled with good things,
But has sent the rich away empty.

Mary had said, "The Mighty One has done great things for me" (verse 49). She now elaborates on that theme and begins to praise God for the general manifestation of his power and mercy.

---

80. The fact that the Hebrew adjective, in a derived sense, in certain contexts indicates *set apart from sin, sinless and filled with virtue,* is not denied. We should begin, however, with what is *basic,* especially when the term applies to God. See also Brown, Driver, Briggs, *A Hebrew and English Lexicon of the Old Testament,* Boston and New York, 1906, p. 872.

She says that God has performed mighty deeds "with his arm." This is an ascription to God of something that pertains to man, namely, an arm. In other words, she is speaking anthropomorphically about the Highest. Such a figure of speech is rooted in the fact that God created man as his own image (Gen. 1:26, 27).

As was stated earlier, Mary is a Jewess, at home in the Old Testament, familiar with its phraseology. It mentions God's arm and hand (Deut. 4:34; Ps. 44:3; 89:13), his eyes and ears (Ps. 34:15), finger (Exod. 8:19; 31:18; Deut. 9:10); face (Ps. 27:8, 9; 143:7), and even nose (Exod. 15:8; Isa. 65:5).

These expressions must not be taken literally. The "arm" of God, mentioned here in verse 51, denotes his *power*. It can be used to deliver, to support, and to uphold. It can also be used to scatter, to bring down, and to drive out. In the present stanza God's "arm" does both.[81]

Mary now draws a contrast. Cf. I Cor. 1:26–29. In order to bring out sharply how deeply God's children are indebted to him she places the blessings they receive over against the punishments suffered by the wicked. On the one side she pictures the arrogant, mighty, and rich; on the other, the humble and hungry. In all probability she is thinking of only two categories of people: on the one hand, the rulers—proud, autocratic, and wealthy; on the other, God's children—lowly and poor.

With reference to the first group she says that God has *scattered*, that is, dispersed, broken up and chased in all directions (cf. Matt. 26:31 = Mark 14:27), those who were proud "in the imagination of their hearts."

According to Scripture the heart is the fulcrum of feeling and faith, the mainspring of drives, emotions, thoughts, words, and deeds. It is the very core of man's being, *his inner self.* See I Sam. 16:7; Prov. 4:23; Matt. 12:34; 15:19; 22:37; John 14:1; Rom. 10:10; I Tim. 1:5. The translation "proud in their inmost thoughts" is therefore excellent. What Mary is saying is that in the course of history God's mighty power has repeatedly punished these arrogant people. He has dispersed them, dethroned them, deprived them of their riches, and driven them away empty.

The *possibility* must be allowed that when Mary was saying this there occurred to her mind stories of rulers, both domestic and foreign, to whom exactly this had happened. Her "Bible" can have supplied her with abundant information along this line. She knew too that what had happened centuries ago was taking place today and was going to occur in the future. God's ways do not change (Mal. 3:6).

She was also deeply conscious of the fact that God was the One who "lifted up the humble." Had she not experienced this herself? See verses

---

81. Articles listed under the heading *Anthropomorphism* include the following: R. L. Dabney, *Systematic and Polemic Theology,* Richmond, 1927, pp. 34, 35; C. A. Beckwith, S.H.E.R.K., Vol. I, pp. 193, 194; J. Lindsay, I.S.B.E., Vol. I, pp. 152–154; and R. E. D. Clark, *The New International Dictionary of the Christian Church,* Grand Rapids, 1974, p. 46.

47, 48. In the following list, to which many items could easily be added, names of devout children of God who had received this help from above are found in the left column; the passage recording their humility and/or eagerness to serve, in the central column; and the manner in which God had "lifted them up" in the right one.

Help from Above

Person	Reference to Humility and/or Eagerness to Serve	How God Lifted Up
Moses	Exod. 3:11	Exod. 3:12
Joshua	Josh. 5:14	Josh. 1:5; 4:14
Gideon	Judg. 6:15	Judg. 6:14, 16
Ruth	Ruth 2:10	Ruth 2:11, 12
Hannah	I Sam. 1:11	I Sam. 1:17, 20, 27, 28
David	I Sam. 18:18	II Sam. 7:14–17
Abigail	I Sam. 25:24–31	I Sam. 25:32–35
Isaiah	Isa. 6:5	Isa. 6:6, 7
Jeremiah	Jer. 1:6	Jer. 1:7–10
Ebed-melech	Jer. 38:7–9	Jer. 38:10–13; 39:15–18

As to the statement, "The hungry he has filled with good things" (cf. Ps. 103:5; 107:9), note the following:

a. God's care for the *physically* hungry appears from such passages as I Sam. 21:1–6 (cf. Matt. 12:1–8); I Kings 17:1–16; 19:5–8; II Kings 4:42–44; Ps. 37:25.

b. Both the Old and the New Testament also recognize *spiritual* hunger (Isa. 55:1, 2; Amos 8:11; Matt. 5:6; John 6:35, 48). This too God satisfies for those who trust in him. This, as well as spiritual *thirst* (Ps. 42:1; Isa. 55:1; John 4:13, 14; 7:37; I Cor. 10:1–4; Rev. 22:17).

Whether Mary had any concrete examples of humility and hunger in mind when she sang her hymn of praise we do not know. What has been demonstrated, however, is that the Old Testament, her own experience, and what others had told her can have provided her with abundant material upon which to base the contents of verses 51–53.

The fourth or concluding strophe is:

54, 55. He has helped Israel, his servant,
In remembrance of his mercy—
Even as he promised our fathers—
(Mercy) to Abraham and to his seed forever.

Up to this point Mary has been praising God in song for his deeds. Now, in this closing stanza, she points out, still in song, what these deeds mean in relation to Israel and the promises made to the forefathers. "He has helped Israel." This had happened again and again in the past. The Old Testament records numerous instances in which God had taken sides with Israel against its enemies. See the beautiful summary in Isa. 63:9. Here "Israel" is looked upon as God's covenant people. Cf. Luke 1:16, 68; then also Exod. 4:22; Isa. 41:8-16; 44:1, 2, 21-23; 49:3. The modifier *his servant* strengthens this conclusion. The word *servant* here used is the more friendly of the two that could have been used to bring out the "servant" idea. In certain contexts this word is properly translated "child." See the notes on this word on pages 112, 113.

What Mary probably meant therefore was something along this line: Just as in the past God has so often helped Israel when it was in distress, so also he does now, in connection with the coming of the Messiah. Note also "in remembrance of his mercy." This is the "kindness toward those in misery" that extends "from generation to generation to those that fear him" (verse 50). It is not a mere kindly feeling or disposition but it is tender love in action, action that really helps . . . and saves!

This phrase "in remembrance of his mercy" is another instance of a human way of speaking about God (see above, on verse 51), since actually God never needs to be reminded of anything.

The parenthetical statement "Even as he said to [or promised] our fathers" takes us back in thought to Abraham. To him God had said, "In you all the families of the earth will be blessed." Sometimes "in your seed" is substituted for "in you," and "nations" for "families." The basic meaning remains the same. See Gen. 12:3; 18:18; 22:18.

That this blessing to Abraham remained in force for Isaac is clear from Gen. 26:3, 4, where not only the same message is repeated but it is even distinctly stated, "I will establish the oath which I swore to Abraham your father." In the time of Isaac's son Jacob this same covenant promise is still in effect (Gen. 28:14). It is even called a covenant "with Abraham and with Isaac and with Jacob" (Exod. 2:24). "I will be your God" holds, in fact, for Israel, viewed as God's covenant people (cf. Gen. 17:7 with Lev. 11:45; 26:12, 45). The Magnificat clearly shows that Mary views what was happening even now as a realization of the ancient promise to Abraham. The mercy she praised in song had reference "to Abraham and to his seed *to eternity*," that is, "forever." The promise was not annulled by the giving of the law (Gal. 3:17) or by the first coming of Christ (Gal. 3:9, 29).

That mercy still flows forth from the throne of grace. That covenant promise still holds. Cf. 1:72, 73. It is on the basis of this promise that believing parents have their children baptized (Acts 2:38, 39). The substance of the promise—"I will be your God"; hence, salvation full and free—is realized in the hearts of all those who by sovereign grace and through God-given *faith* embrace Christ as their Lord and Savior. See N.T.C. on Gal. 3:9, 16, 29.

Elizabeth had praised Mary's *faith* (verse 45). And is it not exactly Mary's faith that is expressed so touchingly in the Magnificat: faith in the Mighty and Merciful God, the Holy One, the Helper in the time of need, the God of the covenant, the One whom she calls "my Savior"? And is not this "profession of faith" which runs through these lines from beginning to end a good reason for calling her poem "Mary's Song of Faith"?

The song has ended. The visit, described from verse 39 on, was not exactly short. We read: **56. Mary remained with Elizabeth about three months, and then returned to her home.** So Mary must have stayed until—probably almost until—the day of John's birth. See verses 26, 36. Mary then "returned to her home," an expression almost the same as the one found in verse 23 with respect to Zechariah's departure from the temple to his home. We already know that to Mary "home" meant the place of her residence in Nazareth (verse 26). As to what happened there before Jesus was born see Matt. 1:18-24.

It was wise for Mary, in her condition, not to remain any longer with Elizabeth. Had she stayed any longer, Elizabeth's house would have been crowded with neighbors, etc., people who did not always use discretion in their talk (see verses 59, 61). Who knows what they might have said about Mary, or what at least they might have thought about her! Besides, a disagreeable confrontation between Mary and some of Elizabeth's neighbors might not have been pleasant for Elizabeth either . . . or even for Zechariah. Also, Mary must return to Joseph, who was a sincere child of God, a good man, and deeply in love with Mary. See N.T.C. on Matthew, pp. 130, 131.[82]

Practical Lessons Derived from Luke 1:46–56

Verses 46, 47

"My soul *magnifies* . . . my spirit *rejoices*." Though more than seventeen centuries passed by before The Shorter Catechism was adopted, note the striking resemblance between the answer to its first question ("to *glorify* God and to *enjoy* him forever") and Mary's Song.

Verse 48a

"He has looked with favor upon his servant." It is the favor (or blessing) of God that makes rich. See Prov. 10:22.

Verse 48b

"Will call me blessed." Not: "will invoke my blessing."

Verse 49

"Because the Mighty One has done great things *for me*." True religion is a very personal relationship between God and his child. It was this for David (Ps. 23, 27,

---

82. Notes on Greek words, phrases, and constructions in 1:46–56 begin on page 111.

51, 63), for the author of Ps. 42, for Asaph (Ps. 73), Isaiah (Isa. 6:5-8), Daniel (Dan. 9:18, 19), the "prodigal" son (Luke 15:17-21), the penitent publican (Luke 18:13), the man born blind (John 9:25), and Paul (Gal. 1:15, 16; 2:20; 6:14).

Verses 50, 54, 55

"From generation to generation . . . to Abraham and to his seed forever." Although salvation is a *personal* matter, it is also a *family* matter: as a rule God perpetuates his covenant in the line of the generations. This truth is definitely rooted in Scripture (Gen. 18:19; Ps. 105:6-10; Prov. 22:6; Acts 2:38, 39; II Tim. 1:5).

Verses 51, 52

"He has performed mighty deeds . . . has brought down rulers from (their) thrones." History books, newspapers, T.V., radio emphasize secondary causes. The Magnificat points to the Primary Cause, the God whose plan is being realized on earth in the interest of his people and for his own glory. See Rom. 8:28; Eph. 1:11.

Verse 53

"He . . . has sent the rich away empty." Even before the wicked rich are dispatched they are already "empty." See Isa. 48:22; 57:21.

Notes on Greek Words, Phrases, and Constructions in 1:46–56

Verses 46, 47

Literally the verb μεγαλύνω means: to make great, to enlarge (Matt. 23:5). Here in Luke 1:46 (cf. Acts 10:46) the sense is: to magnify, glorify, praise, extol; in Acts 5:13, to hold in high esteem, regard highly. And cf. Luke 1:58: "God had magnified his mercy," that is, "had been very kind."

In view of the fact that verse 47 closely parallels verse 46, Robertson is probably correct in calling ἠγαλλίασεν a timeless aorist, and in translating it as a present. See his book *A Translation of Luke's Gospel*, pp. 17 and 145. For the meaning of ἀγαλλιάω see the note on 1:14, page 80.

In the present case it would be wrong to posit any clear distinction between ψυχή and πνεῦμα. See N.T.C. on Mark, pp. 315, 316, footnote 370.

Verse 48

ἐπιβλέπω = (basically) to look at, into, or upon; here: to look upon with sympathy and favor (cf. 9:38); in James 2:3: to have regard for, pay special attention to. For words that have to do with *vision* see N.T.C. on Mark, p. 116, footnote 105; p. 322, footnote 378; p. 323, footnote 379; also N.T.C. on John, Vol. I, p. 85, footnote 33.

ταπείνωσις—cf. *tapis;* Dutch *tapijt* = carpet—low or humble state; in James 1:10, being made low, humiliation. "The body of our humiliation" = "our lowly body" (Phil. 3:21).

Verse 51

βραχίων, arm; cf. *bracelet.*

ὑπερήφανος = ὑπέρ, above, and φαίνομαι, to show oneself, make an appearance, make oneself appear; hence, a person who regards himself to be above or superior to others, a proud or arrogant person.

Verses 51–53

With respect to the nature of the six aorists in verses 51–53 there are, in the main, three opinions. They are (a) historical or narrative (R. C. H. Lenski, *op. cit.*, p. 58); (b) gnomic or timeless (A. T. Robertson, Gram. N.T., pp. 836, 837); (c) prophetic, describing what is going to happen in the Messianic Age as if it had already happened (A. Plummer, *op. cit.*, pp. 32, 33).

I can find no reason to accept (c). In the Magnificat Mary describes what "the Lord," "the Mighty One," etc., has done for her and also what he has done for others. When she wishes to call attention to what is still going to happen she uses the future tense (verse 48b).

Basically I agree with Lenski (historical or narrative aorist). Mary is clearly thinking of the marvelous manner in which God has been merciful to her (verses 48a, 49). In verse 50 she expands on this and shows that this mercy is still operating: it extends from generation to generation, etc. From verse 51 on she then proves her point by showing what the Lord, the unchangeable God, has done in times past to various groups of people.

But though basically these aorists are therefore historical, it is also a fact that they indicate actions that recur again and again. The very nature of God proves this. It is for that reason that I would call these aorists historical-gnomic. Lenski is right and so is Robertson.

Verse 52

δυνάστης, ruler, potentate, monarch. Cf. *dynasty.*

Verse 54

ἀντελάβετο, third per. s. 2nd aor. indicat. of ἀντιλαμβάνομαι. See my thesis, *The Meaning of the Preposition ἀντί in the New Testament*, pp. 83–86. Some insist that in this compound ἀντί means *facing.* Think of two men carrying a log, one at each end. They face and thus help each other. Others, in connection with this compound, make no mention of the idea of *oppositeness,* but in this case regard the basic meaning of ἀντί to be that of *substitution.* The resultant sense of the entire compound would then be: to take hold of *in turn.* Interpreted either way, the verb's meaning is *to help, to render assistance;* hence here in Luke 1:54, "He has helped Israel"; in Acts 20:35, "We must help the weak." See also N.T.C. on I Tim. 6:2. Very interesting is the double compound συναντιλαμβάνεται used in Rom. 8:26, "The Holy Spirit joins in to help us," thus correctly rendered in the Berkeley Version, and also in the Dutch Statenvertaling: "... komt onze zwakheden mede to hulp."

παιδός, gen. s. of παῖς. In Greek literature this word has various meanings; such as: child, boy, youth, servant, servant boy, etc. As this word is used in Luke's Gospel I suggest the following renderings, admitting that in some cases a different translation would do as well:

1:54 "He has helped Israel, his *servant.*"
1:69 "in the house of David, his *servant.*"
2:43 "the *boy* Jesus remained behind in Jerusalem."

7:7 (cf. Matt. 8:8) "Speak the word and my *boy* will be cured."

8:51 (cf. Mark 5:40) "the *child's* father and mother."

8:54 "my *child*, get up."

9:42 "Even while the *boy* was coming to him, the demon dashed him," etc.

12:45b (cf. Matt. 24:49) "and shall begin to beat up the men and women *servants*."

15:26 "having called one of the *servant boys* to him."

μνησθῆναι, aor. (reflexive) infinitive of μιμνῄσκω, to remind oneself of, to remember; here "in remembrance of his mercy."

Verse 55

τῷ 'Αβραάμ should not (with A.V.) be construed with ἐλάλησε, as if God spoke to Abraham forever. Besides, note change in grammatical construction: the acc. after πρός is replaced by the simple dative.

---

57 Now the time was fulfilled for Elizabeth to give birth, and she bore a son. 58 When her neighbors and relatives heard how kind the Lord had been to her,[83] they were rejoicing with her.

59 On the eighth day they came to circumcise the child, and they were going to call him[84] Zechariah, after the name of his father. 60 But the child's mother objected and said, "Definitely not; he must be called John!" 61 They said to her, "None of your relatives has that name." 62 So they began to make signs to his father (to discover) what he would wish the child to be called. 63 Having asked for a writing tablet, he wrote, "John is his name." And everybody was greatly surprised. 64 At once his mouth was opened, his tongue loosed, and he began to speak, praising God.

65 All those living around them were awestruck, and throughout the hill country of Judea people kept talking about all these things.[85] 66 And all who heard them laid them up in their hearts. They said, "What then will this child turn out to be?" For the hand of the Lord was with him.

1:57-66 *The Birth, Circumcision,*
and Naming of John the Baptist

The story now returns to Zechariah and Elizabeth.

57. Now the time was fulfilled for Elizabeth to give birth, and she bore a son. The usual period after conception having ended, Elizabeth gave birth to a child. It was a boy, as had been predicted by the angel Gabriel (verses 13, 19). **58. When her neighbors and relatives heard how kind the Lord had been to her, they were rejoicing with her.** In order to show their interest these neighbors and relatives came to visit Elizabeth.

Why are neighbors mentioned before relatives? Because the former were living closest, while the latter were spread in many directions, some living much farther away? Thus some interpret the order of the words in this sentence. But it is probably wrong to attach special significance to the

---

83. Literally: that the Lord had magnified his mercy toward her.

84. Or: and they tried to call him.

85. Literally: all these things continued to be talked back and forth.

sequence in which these two items—neighbors and relatives—are mentioned.

The visitors had heard "how kind [or merciful] the Lord had been" to Elizabeth. Literally, they had heard "that the Lord had magnified his mercy toward her."

This kind of language clearly shows that Luke is making use of Semitic—that is, Hebrew and/or Aramaic—sources. In the nativity account that is the rule, not the exception.[86]

Note also the emphasis, here as well as elsewhere (verses 50, 54, 55, 72, 78) on God's mercy or lovingkindness in action.

The theory that the rejoicing of these visitors was not in connection with the birth of the child (see verse 14) but only in connection with Elizabeth, because she had been relieved of her barrenness, is hard to accept. The clear meaning would seem to be: (a) Elizabeth rejoiced because, in fulfilment of Gabriel's prediction, this son had been born; and (b) the neighbors and relatives were rejoicing with her; that is, they joined in her joy. All were thankful and happy because of the birth of this child.

59. On the eighth day they came to circumcise the child . . . Probably a person specifically appointed for this purpose performed the rite, other visitors functioning as witnesses. In accordance with the law (Gen. 17:12; Lev. 12:3) circumcision took place on the eighth day.[87] Continued: **and they were going to call him Zechariah, after the name of his father.** In the old dispensation the naming of the child occurred in connection with its birth (Gen. 21:1-3; 25:24-26; etc.). The present passage (and cf. Luke 2:21) appears to be the earliest witness for the practice of connecting the naming of a child with circumcision.[88]

None of our sources show that it was a custom in Bible times to name a boy after his father. After a relative, probably, as may well be implied in verse 61, but not necessarily after the father. And certainly not even always after a relative. See on verse 61.

Nevertheless it is not difficult to suggest possible reasons why these visitors tried to persuade the parents to call the child after his father. Not only did the name have a beautiful meaning (see on verse 5), applicable also to the present situation, but the mysterious events that had occurred (the vision in the temple, etc.) may have fostered the desire that the boy be named after his now famous father.

---

86. All three languages—Hebrew, Aramaic, and Greek—were in use in Palestine, including even Judea, during the first and well into the second century A.D. See C. H. H. Scobie, *John the Baptist*, Philadelphia, 1964, pp. 51, 52; J. M. Grintz, "Hebrew as the Spoken and Written Language in the Last Days of the Second Temple," *JBL*, 79 (1960), pp. 32-47. See also the highly documented argument (in support of the theory that all three languages were used by Jews in first century Palestine) by R. H. Gundry, in his dissertation, *The Use of the Old Testament in St. Matthew's Gospel*, Leiden, 1967, pp. 174-177.

87. For the religious significance of circumcision see N.T.C. on Colossians, p. 116, footnote 85.

88. See S.BK., Vol. II, p. 107.

60. But the child's mother objected and said, Definitely not; he must be called John! Not for a moment did Elizabeth hesitate. She knew that through his angel God himself had ordered this child to be named John (verse 13). How did she know this? After all, Gabriel had not spoken to *her* but to her *husband*. And during the entire long period, between the appearance of the angel and the naming of the child, Zechariah had been deprived of the power of speech. Solution: Elizabeth's husband must have made good use of his writing tablet!

Not satisfied, the neighbors and relatives tried again: **61. They said to her, None of your relatives has that name.** This attempt also failed. No wonder, for what may have been a custom was by no means a hard and fast rule. See N.T.C. on Matthew, pp. 138, 139, footnote 146, showing how children's names were selected. Besides, Elizabeth knew what God had stipulated. **62. So they began to make signs to his father (to discover) what he would wish the child to be called.**

They began to make signs to him. But why? The man was not deaf . . . or was he? Before answering this question it should be pointed out that in Greek literature the word *kōphos* used at the end of Luke 1:22 and rendered "speechless" in A.V., "dumb" in R.S.V. and N.E.B., can have any one of three meanings, depending on the context in each specific case. The three are: deaf, dumb, deaf and dumb. The question is, What does this word mean in Luke 1:22? Opinions differ:

a. The very circumstance that in the present case these people were making signs—nodding, pointing with their hands, making motions with hands and eyes—proves that Zechariah was deaf as well as dumb. This made inquiry by means of signs necessary.[89]

Comment. Nowhere else *in the New Testament* does this one word *kōphos* have the double meaning "deaf and dumb." In Mark 9:25, where both meanings are combined, two words are used in the original to convey this thought. That passage reads, "You *dumb* and *deaf* spirit" (thus literally). Besides, in Luke 1:20, 22 the sentence pronounced on Zechariah is elucidated as follows: "You will remain silent and not able to speak until. . . . And when he did come out he was unable to speak to them," etc. These passages refer only to the priest's inability to speak. They do not make mention of any inability to hear. To this may be added verse 64, relating to Zechariah's cure, where again the reference is only to restoration of the power of *speech*, not hearing. Explanation (a) must be rejected.

b. In the popular mind there was a close connection between dumbness and deafness. It was for this reason that these people made signs to the father of the child.[90]

Comment. This explanation may well be the right one. It is at any rate better than answer (a).

---

89. Thus S. Greijdanus, *Korte Verklaring*, pp. 29, 47.
90. F. Danker, *op. cit.*, p. 17.

The possibility must also be granted that due to the excitement of the moment some people simply forgot that the priest was unable to speak but not unable to hear. We cannot be sure.

If, as has been pointed out (see verse 60), Elizabeth's answer was unequivocal, Zechariah's was, if possible, even more definite: **63. Having asked for a writing tablet, he wrote, John is his name.** The writing tablet was probably a little board covered with wax. With a stylus the words could be impressed upon it. By writing "John is his name," Zechariah is saying, "The child already has a name! That name is John." It was God who had named the child (verse 13).

The question may well be asked, however, "Why this name *John* in preference to some other name?" The basic reason for naming the child is, of course, "Because God so commanded." Is it possible to go beyond this and to point out the appropriateness of this name for this particular child?

Here we must exercise caution. The meaning of the name is "Jehovah is [or: has been] gracious." In connection with this meaning there are in the main two possibilities: (a) God ordered this name to be given to the child because he knew that the disposition or attitude of the parents was going to be: "The Lord has revealed his marvelous grace to us by giving us this child."

Is it not true that names often described *the giver* rather than the recipient? See N.T.C. on Matthew, p. 136. On the other hand, it is also true that in such cases in which the name describes the faith or feeling of the parents (often of the mother) that name is usually given by the mother herself or by the parents themselves; there was no divine command with respect to it.

It is accordingly reasonable to assume that in the present case, God himself having supplied the name, there is a close relation between the name and its *recipient* or *bearer*. See N.T.C. on Matthew, pp. 138, 139.

The objection may be raised, however, "But in that case how very inappropriate was this particular name. Is it not true that John the Baptist became a preacher of impending doom and judgment? Was not his preaching interspersed with the vocabulary of divine retribution; that is, with such words as 'offspring of vipers,' 'approaching wrath,' 'the axe laid at the root of the trees,' 'unquenchable fire'?"

To answer, with some, that Luke was not thinking about the etymology of the name *John* when he wrote the section about the naming of the child, is an attempt to rid oneself of the difficulty in too easy a manner. The basic question is not, "What was Luke thinking about?" but "Why did God insist that this child be named John?"

Besides, in the case of Mary's child too it was God who supplied the name, and that name was indeed descriptive of its bearer: "She will give birth to a son, and you shall call his name Jesus, for he will save his people from their sins" (Matt. 1:21). Must we assume then that in the case of Jesus' forerunner the name had no significance whatever? This would seem hardly possible.

In all probability the real and comforting solution lies in a different direction. (b) The name *John*—that is, Jehovah is gracious—was indeed suited to its purpose, for according to all of Scripture the warning of approaching judgment and doom unless true conversion takes place is a divinely selected means of urging men to turn away from the darkness of sin, to serve the Lord, and thus to enter into his kingdom of light. Among many passages that could be listed to prove this point are the following: Ps. 94:12; 119:67, 71; Prov. 13:24; Isa. 26:9b; Amos 4:9; Hag. 2:17; I Cor. 5:3-5; II Cor. 7:9, 10; Heb. 12:5 f.; Rev. 2:21; 3:19.

Thus viewed, the name *John* was apt indeed, for through him and his stern message many of the sons of Israel would be turned to the Lord their God (see on verse 16), and would experience that "Jehovah, indeed, is gracious."

And everybody was greatly surprised. Not because of the hearty agreement between Elizabeth and Zechariah but because of the total lack of doubt or hesitancy on the part of both.

64. At once his mouth was opened, his tongue loosed, and he began to speak, praising God. In accordance with Gabriel's promise (see 1:13, 20) Zechariah now immediately regains his power of speech. In typically Semitic style we are told that Zechariah's mouth was opened, his tongue loosed—see the note on this verse on page 120—and that he started to speak, "blessing," that is "praising" God.

Zechariah's song of praise is recorded in the following section (verses 67-80), though whether verse 64 already refers to this song cannot be established. There may have been a few praise exclamations that preceded the song. The main point is: his voice recovered, the first thing Zechariah did with this rewon blessing was to praise God!

Easy to visualize is the rustic scene pictured in verse **65. All those living around them were awestruck, and throughout the hill country of Judea people kept talking about all these things.** The Hebrew or Aramaic manner of writing continues. Literally we read, "And fear came on all them that dwelt round about them" (thus A.V.). The remarkable happenings filled the minds of the people with the conviction that God was present in their midst and was carrying out his plan on earth. They, as it were, trembled with holy awe because of his presence and deeds.

The events recorded in Luke 1:5-25, 39-64 remained for a long time one of the chief topics of conversation among the people living in the hill country of Judea. Many, indeed, were the strange and wonderful incidents that had taken place: Zechariah's vision in the temple, his inability to address the people who were awaiting his return from the altar of incense, Mary's visit, the birth of a child to parents well advanced in years, the fact that a boy had been predicted and a boy had been born, the unambiguous manner in which, contrary to the persistent urging of neighbors and relatives, both parents had insisted on naming the boy "John," the sudden opening of the aged priest's lips as an immediate reward of his obedience, and the sincere and enthusiastic manner in which he then praised God. All these matters continued for a long time to be tossed back and forth in country-style conversation.

That these things were taken very seriously appears from verse **66. And all who heard them laid them up in their hearts.** The people were evidently deeply impressed with these events and took their meaning to heart. Cf. I Sam. 21:12; Dan. 7:28; Luke 2:19, 51. They pondered their significance, wondering particularly what these incidents might indicate with respect to the character and future role of this child: **They said, What then will this child turn out to be?** Their hopes ran high.

Reflecting on all this in later years Luke, the evangelist and historian, writing under the guidance of the Holy Spirit, adds, **For the hand of the Lord was with him.** This is a typically Lucan expression. Cf. Acts 11:21; 13:11. See also Isa. 41:20, and above on verses 51–53.

What Luke is saying amounts to this: in entertaining such high expectations with respect to this child the people did not err. As later events proved, they were right, as is clear from the fact that as John grew up he was the object of God's tender care and guidance. See verse 80.[91]

Practical Lessons Derived from Luke 1:57–66

Verses 57, 58

"Elizabeth ... bore a son ... her neighbors and relatives ... were rejoicing with her." Rejoicing with the joyful is a Christian's joy.

Verses 59–63

"They were going to call him Zechariah. . . . John is his name." See also verse 13. God's plan cannot be frustrated. Cf. Dan. 4:35; Eph. 1:11.

Verses 60–63

"The child's mother objected . . . . His father . . . wrote, 'John is his name.' " Happy the home in which father and mother agree . . . to do God's will!

Verse 64

"At once his mouth was opened, his tongue loosed." It seems as if God could hardly wait to remove punishment and to reward obedience. Cf. Lam. 3:33; Ezek. 18:23, 32; 33:11; Hos. 11:8.

"He began to speak, praising God." The first use Zechariah made of his recov-

---

91. Notes on Greek words, phrases, and constructions in 1:57–66 begin on page 119.

ered speech was to praise God with it. By God's grace this man seems to have understood *the purpose* for which he had been chastened. God's message to all his children is:

Dutch Original	*Free Translation*
Drukt u mijn kruis,	Pressed by my cross,
Treft u mijn roe,	The rod I sent,
Vraag nooit *Waarom*	Don't seek *the cause*
Maar wel *Waartoe*.	But *the intent*.

Verse 65

"Throughout the hill country of Judea people kept talking about these things." Group discussion about *God's deeds* is far better than flippant gossip about *men's defects*.

Verse 66

"For the hand of the Lord was with him indeed." Suggestion for a series of sermons on the theme *The Hand of the Lord:* in addition to Luke 1:66b the "texts" could be Ps. 104:28; 145:16; Isa. 49:2; 50:2; 62:3; John 10:28; Rev. 1:17. See also Ps. 73:23-25.

Notes on Greek Words, Phrases, and Constructions in 1:57-66

Verse 58

ἐμεγάλυνεν. See on 1:46.

Verse 59

Note τὸ παιδίον ... αὐτό, and αὐτό again in verse 62: the child ... it ... it. In such cases English translators generally prefer the rendering: the child ... him ... him.
ἐκάλουν, third per. pl. imperf. act. indicat. of καλέω. The imperfect can be considered conative: they tried to, were going to, etc.

Verse 60

ἀποκριθεῖσα, nom. s. fem. aor. passive participle of ἀποκρίνομαι. This verb is often used even though no question has been asked. In such cases it indicates a *reaction* to a suggestion or situation. See also N.T.C. on Matthew, p. 84, footnote 89; and on Mark, p. 421, footnote 515.
οὐχί, an intensified negative.
Although the adversative particle ἀλλά can be rendered "but," "on the contrary," "rather," a literal translation by means of an English equivalent is not always necessary. The rendering, "Definitely not; he must be called John," already implies strong negation.

Verse 62

ἐνένευον, third per. pl. imperf. (here inchoative) of ἐννεύω*, to make signs. For the compound form see the note on 1:22, page 81. Note that τί ἂν θέλοι is preceded

119

by τό; hence treated as if it were a noun. The optative (third per. s. pres.) preceded by ἄν is proper in what may be considered the apodosis of a future less vivid conditional sentence. In the indirect question, as here, the optative with ἄν of the direct question is retained. The New Testament contains no example of a *complete* future less vivid conditional sentence. See Gram. N.T., p. 1020. Cf. Gram. N.T. (Bl.-Debr.), par. 386 on p. 195.

Verse 63

It is probably best to leave λέγων untranslated here, in order to avoid the interpretation—erroneous but nevertheless adopted by some—that the two actions, writing and speaking, occurred simultaneously. Verse 64 implies that Zechariah's mouth was opened immediately *after* he had written the words. In such cases λέγων is about the equivalent of our quotation marks, comma, colon, or "namely."

Verse 64

ἀνεῴχθη, third per. s. aor. indicat. pass. of ἀνοίγω, to open. Literally the first clause of this verse reads: "And opened was his mouth on the spot [or immediately, at once] and his tongue." But Luke has as much right as we have to make use of the figure of speech called *zeugma*, in which two nouns are construed with one verb, though only one of these nouns, generally the first, suits that verb. Another illustration would be "Milk I caused y o u to drink, not solid food" (I Cor. 3:2). Rightly considered is not zeugma really a branch of *abbreviated expression?* For this see N.T.C. on John, Vol. I, p. 206. In the present case we have a perfect right to adopt the rendering, "At once his mouth was opened, his tongue loosed." With respect to both the mouth and the tongue (really acting as one) the obstruction or impediment, of whatever nature, was removed. See L. Berkhof, *Principles of Biblical Interpretation*, Grand Rapids, 1950, p. 90.

εὐλογῶν, nom. s. masc. pres. active participle of εὐλογέω, to bless, etc. This verb is frequent in Luke's Gospel, though found also in Matthew, Mark, and once in John; further, in Acts, Hebrews, and once each in James and I Peter; in the Pauline epistles only in Romans, I Corinthians, and once each in Galatians and Ephesians. Verbal adjective (εὐλογητός), participial form of the verb (εὐλογήσας) and noun in dative (εὐλογίᾳ) occur together in Eph. 1:3. See N.T.C. on that passage.

The principal meanings of εὐλογέω are four:

a. to speak well of (note etymology: εὖ and λέγω; cf. λόγος); hence, to praise, extol, as here in Luke 1:64. Cf. *eulogy, eulogize.*

b. to impart benefits to (Acts 3:26).

c. to give thanks (as, for food). See N.T.C. on Matthew, pp. 595, 596.

d. to invoke God's blessing upon (Luke 24:50).

Verse 65

διελαλεῖτο, from διαλαλέω*, note διά and imperfect tense: they kept talking with one another, kept discussing back and forth. Cf. 6:11.

ῥήματα, pl. of ῥῆμα. The word ῥῆμα (cf. *rhetoric*) can mean *thing* as well as *word*. Cf. Hebrew *dābhār.*

Verse 66

ἔθεντο, third per. pl. sec. aor. middle indicat. of τίθημι, to set, put, lay.

---

67 Zechariah, his father, was filled with the Holy Spirit and prophesied, saying:
68 "Blessed (be) the Lord, the God of Israel,
Because he has looked after his people and brought about redemption for them,
69 And has raised up a horn of salvation for us
In the house of David, his servant,
70 As he spoke by the mouth of his holy prophets of old,
71 Salvation from our enemies and from the hand of all who hate us;
72 To deal mercifully with our fathers,
And to remember his holy covenant,
73 The oath he swore to Abraham, our father:
74 To grant us that we, having been delivered out of the hand of our enemies,
75 Should serve him without fear in holiness and righteousness
In his presence all our days.
76 "And you, (my) child, will be called a prophet of the Most High,
For you will go before the face of the Lord to make ready his ways,
77 To impart to his people knowledge of salvation
Through the forgiveness of their sins
78 Because of the merciful heart of our God,
With which the Rising Sun will visit us from on high,
79 To shine on those who sit in darkness and death's shadow,
To guide our feet into the path of peace."
80 And the child continued to grow and to become strong in spirit; and he was in the desert
regions until the day of his public appearance to Israel.

1:67–80 *Zechariah's Prophecy*

Zechariah's Song is a prophecy which was spoken under the illuminating guidance of the Holy Spirit. Note the words of introduction: **67. Zechariah, his father, was filled with the Holy Spirit, and prophesied, saying**. We must, accordingly, accept these two facts:

1. Zechariah was filled with the Holy Spirit. So, it will be recalled, was Elizabeth (verse 41). When Mary arrived, Elizabeth was so definitely guided, influenced, and illumined by the Holy Spirit that, in connection with the leaping of the babe within her womb, she suddenly knew (a) who Mary really was, namely, not just her relative but the most blessed of all women, the mother of her Lord, and (b) who the babe within Mary's womb was, namely, Elizabeth's Lord (1:41–43).

So now also this same illumination made it possible for Zechariah to see and to say things which otherwise he would not have been able to see and to say.

2. Zechariah's Song deserves the title *Zechariah's Prophecy;* note: "and prophesied." In which sense is this song a prophecy? Clearly in a double sense: (a) It is a proclamation of the truth, *a message from God to the people.* Taken in this sense, to prophesy means *to tell forth, to forthtell.* So interpreted

its contents may touch upon the past, the present, and/or the future. Whenever a servant of God faithfully proclaims God's message, whether that be a word of condemnation, reproof, command, admonition, consolation, prediction, or any combination of these, he prophesies. See also on verse 76. (b) It is also *a prediction.* Thus interpreted, to prophesy means *to foretell.* Though the element of prediction is already implied in the first part of this song (verses 68–75, note especially verses 74, 75), in the second part (verses 76–79) it predominates: "And you, (my) child, will be called ... For you will go before," and probably even "the Rising Sun will visit us."

Another name given to Zechariah's Prophecy is *The Benedictus,* in accordance with the first word of this hymn in the Latin version: *Benedictus esto Dominus Deus Israelis,* meaning, "Blessed be the Lord, the God of Israel."

The most simple way to divide Zechariah's Prophecy is into two parts, each consisting of one sentence (verses 68–75 and 76–79). In the first part Zechariah praises God for having provided salvation for his people, in fulfilment of prophecy and of "his holy covenant," "the oath he swore to Abraham." In the second part he, in harmony with Isa. 40:3; Mal. 3:1, summarizes his child's mission as way-preparer for the Messiah, whom he describes as "the Rising Sun," and with reference to whom he states that he will "shine on those who sit in darkness," etc.

The language of *The Benedictus* is again that of the Old Testament. Parallels or at least resemblances are noted on the following chart:

The Benedictus Compared with Old Testament Passages

Zechariah's Benedictus (Luke 1)	The Old Testament
68a "Blessed (be) the Lord, the God of Israel."	Ps. 41:13; 72:18; 106:48 = the conclusion of Books I, II, and IV of the Hebrew Psalter.
68b "Because he has ... brought about redemption for his people."	Exod. 4:31; Ps. 111:9
69 "And has raised up a horn," etc.	Ps. 18:2; 132:17
70 "As he spoke by the mouth of," etc.	Ezra 1:1; Jer. 1:9; Zech. 8:9
71 "Salvation from our enemies," etc.	Ps. 106:10
72a "To deal mercifully with our fathers"	Ps. 25:6; 98:3; 136 (second part of each verse)
72b, 73 "And to remember his holy covenant, The oath he swore to Abraham," etc.	Gen. 12:2, 3; 17:7; 22:15–18; Exod. 2:24; II Sam. 22:51; Ps. 105:6–10; Mic. 7:20

(*continued*)

The Benedictus Compared with Old Testament Passages (continued)

Zechariah's Benedictus (Luke 1)	The Old Testament
74, 75 "To grant us that we ... Should serve him," etc.	Exod. 19:6; Jer. 30:9, 10
76 "and you ... will go before," etc. See also Luke 1:17.	Isa. 40:3; Mal. 3:1
77 "In order to impart to his people the knowledge of salvation Through the forgiveness of their sins."	Ps. 103:11, 12; Isa. 1:18; 43:25; 53:5, 8, 10, 12; Jer. 31:34b; Mic. 7:19
78, 79 "Because of the tender compassion of our God, Whereby the Rising Sun will visit us ... To shine on those who sit in dark- ness," etc.	Ps. 107:10; Isa. 9:1; 42:7; 60:1-3; Mal. 4:2

First Part
Verses 68-75

68. Blessed (be) the Lord, the God of Israel,

Because he has looked after his people and brought about redemption for them ...

Zechariah begins with a doxology. He praises Jehovah, Israel's covenant God, for his concern about, and saving intervention in, the affairs of his people. He says that God has "looked after" them. Here he uses the same verb that occurs in Matt. 25:36, "I was sick, and y o u looked after me." See also the note on this verse on page 131.

He adds, "and brought about redemption for his people." Is this redemption political? Is it, for example, deliverance from bondage to a foreign oppressor? The decision will have to be made in the light of the context. Verse 71, taken by itself, affords little help, for the question remains, "Are these enemies and haters political or spiritual?" Verse 77, however, states, "to give his people the knowledge of salvation through the forgiveness of their sins." See also verses 74, 75: "that we ... should serve him without fear in holiness and righteousness," and verse 79, "to guide our feet into the path of peace." In such a context the "redemption" to which verse 68 refers would seem to be of a spiritual nature; at least to be basically and predominantly spiritual; probably redemption from Satan, sin, and all the consequences.

Another approach to the answer would be to ask, "What does the same word *redemption* (Greek *lutrōsis*) mean in the only other New Testament passages in which it occurs?" In Luke 2:38 we read, "Now coming up at that very hour, Anna was ... speaking to all those who were waiting for the *redemption* of Jerusalem." Must we believe that the emphasis of this aged and devout child of God and of those whom she addressed was on deliverance from the Roman yoke? Or from Herod's cruelties perhaps? Was it not rather on restoration to favor with God? And when the inspired author of the book of Hebrews states that Jesus "entered once for all into the holy place, having obtained *eternal redemption*" (9:12), did he not add "through his own blood"?

We can reach no other conclusion but that Zechariah had in mind salvation through Christ. If to some this explanation ascribes to Zechariah too high a Christology, the answer is that this priest was "filled with the Holy Spirit" as he spoke these words.

In line with this explanation is verse

69. And has raised up a horn of salvation for us
In the house of David, his servant...

As verses 71 and 74 indicate, this "horn" symbolizes power; in fact, destructive power. It does not refer to "the horn of plenty." The underlying figure is the horn of a ram, a wild ox, or a bull. See such passages as I Kings 22:11; Ps. 22:21; 75:5; Dan. 8:5-7. Nevertheless, by means of knocking out and scattering the enemy, the horn becomes "a horn of salvation" for the true Israel.

Note: "in the house of David, his servant." Not "in the house of Levi," though Zechariah himself belonged to that tribe. Zechariah was, accordingly, thinking of Jesus, the son of Mary according to his human nature. Was it not exactly Jesus who by means of his substitutionary suffering would destroy the power of Satan and would save his people? Not to be passed by in silence is the fact that here again the descent of Jesus via Mary from David receives confirmation. See above, on verse 32.

70. As he spoke by the mouth of his holy prophets of old... That the ancient prophets actually predicted the coming of the Offspring of David, the One who would destroy all his enemies and bring salvation to his people, is an undeniable fact. See Luke 24:27, 32, 44-47; Acts 10:43. Not that any prophet—with the possible exception of Isaiah (chapter 53)—told the entire story, but they told it collectively, one predicting this and the other that with respect to the coming Deliverer.

The Old Testament describes a fourfold preparation for the coming of the Messiah. That preparation was historical, typological, prophetical, and psychological. For elaboration with respect to these four lines see my *Survey of the Bible*, pp. 93, 94.

Limiting ourselves here to the prophetical preparation, it is clear that the persons listed in the chart below were among those who predicted the coming Lord and Savior.

Old Testament Prophets Who Predicted the Coming of the Lord

The Ancient Prophet	His Description of the Messiah As:
Moses	The prophet whom God would raise up (Deut. 18:15, 18; cf. Acts 3:22, 23; 7:37).
David	The One who would sit on God's right hand (Ps. 110:1; cf. Matt. 26:64; Heb. 1:3; 8:1; 10:12; 12:2; etc.). See also Ps. 16:10; cf. Acts 2:25-27.
Isaiah	Immanuel (7:14; 8:8), Wonderful, Counselor, etc. (9:6), the One wounded for our transgressions and bruised for our iniquities, etc. (ch. 53).
Jeremiah and Zechariah	The Branch (Jer. 33:15; Zech. 3:8; 6:12, 13; cf. Isa. 11:1).
Jeremiah	The Lord, our Righteousness (23:6).
Ezekiel and Zechariah	The Shepherd (Ezek. 34:23; Zech. 13:7; cf. Isa. 40:11; see also Matt. 26:31; Mark 14:27; Luke 19:10; John 10:11, 14-16, 26-28).
Daniel	A Son of man whose dominion is an everlasting dominion, etc. (7:13, 14; cf. Matt. 26:64; Mark 14:62).
Micah	Ruler in Israel, etc. (5:2; cf. Matt. 2:6).
Malachi	The Angel of the Covenant (3:1b).

In addition to all these see also Gen. 3:15; 49:10; Num. 21:8; Job 19:25; parts of Psalms 2, 8, 22, 31, 69, 72, 89, 118, etc.; Isa. 42:1-4; 61:1 f.; 63:9; Zech. 9:9; 13:1; etc.

Note, "He spoke by the mouth of his prophets...." The Speaker was God himself. The prophets were his mouthpieces.

71. Salvation from our enemies and from the hand of all who hate us. We now have a further definition of what was meant by "redemption" (verse 68).

Again and again Jesus Christ is pictured as the One who conquers Satan and his allies, sin, death, the grave, hell, all the hosts of evil (Gen. 3:15; John 12:31, 32; 16:11, 33; I John 3:8; Rev. 5:5; 12:5, 9, 10; 17:14; 19:11-16).

Hymnology has caught this truth: *A Mighty Fortress* ("and he must win the battle"), *See the Conqueror* ("Lord of battles, God of armies, He has gained the victory," etc.), *Battle Hymn of the Republic* ("Let the Hero born of woman crush the serpent," etc.).

What verse 71 implies is that when Christ conquers, his followers conquer with him (Rev. 17:14).

Note also: "salvation from the hand of all who hate us." Among those *who hate us* are also people. But the passage does not say that *we* should hate *them*. As to that, see Matt. 5:44; Luke 23:34.

72, 73. To deal mercifully with our fathers,
And to remember his holy covenant,
The oath he swore to Abraham our father.

When, through David's Offspring, God rescues his people from all their enemies and bestows salvation upon them, he is thereby showing kindness to the ancient fathers, with whom he established his covenant. He is keeping faith with them. For the rest, since verses 72, 73 are substantially identical in meaning with verses 54b, 55 of the Magnificat, see on those earlier verses.

Note, however, that now "his holy covenant" is distinctly mentioned; also even "the oath" he swore to Abraham our father. See Gen. 22:15–18. Note also in Heb. 6:13–18 the unforgettably comforting explanation and application of this covenant-promise and oath. Who, in reading these words, does not immediately think of the hymn *My Hope Is Built* (by E. Mote); specifically, of the words:

> His oath, his covenant, his blood
> Support me in the whelming flood?

So eager is God, as it were, to instil in the hearts of his children faith in his gracious promise that in order to confirm it he even takes an oath by himself!

74, 75. To grant us that we, having been delivered out of the hand of our enemies,
Should serve him without fear in holiness and righteousness
In his presence all our days.

The very wording shows that this purpose clause belongs to what was introduced in verses 68–71, so that the thought connection may be summarized as follows: The God of Israel brought about redemption for us, his people, with this purpose, namely, that we, having now been rescued from the hand of our enemies, should serve him, etc.

In the final analysis the goal of our salvation is the glory of God. The Lord redeems his people in order that out of gratitude they might worship him. According to our passage this worship or service should be:

a. without fear. That follows logically from the fact that we have been delivered out of the hand of our enemies. For corroborating evidence to show that those who were delivered should serve God without fear see Ps. 27:1 f.; 56:11; Rom. 8:31–39.

b. in holiness and righteousness. As some see it, the term *holiness* as here used indicates what should be the relation of the saved with respect to God; the term *righteousness* what should be their relation to men. Others, however, maintain that holiness means not doing what God forbids; righteousness, doing what he demands. Interpreted either way, however, it is clear that nothing less than perfection in the sight of God is what should be the aim of God's people.

c. in his presence. In the light of verses 15, 17, and 19, this phrase indicates that God's people should be deeply aware of the fact that they constitute "the priesthood of believers," and should therefore present their lives to God as a voluntary offering.

d. enduring. Note the expression *all our days*. Not just for a while. See Matt. 13:5, 6, 20, 21 and parallels.

The question now arises, "What, if any, is the relation between this child, namely, the future John the Baptist, and the divinely bestowed redemption for which the child's father has been praising God?" The answer is as follows:

Second Part
Verses 76–79

76. And you, (my) child, will be called a prophet of the Most High . . . What is so strikingly beautiful about this "prophecy" is the fact that Zechariah is not chiefly concerned about himself or even about his child but rather about the mighty work of grace which God is going to accomplish by means of "the horn of salvation" from the house of David. Of this great God, here again called "The Most High" (see on verse 32), Zechariah's child will be, and will be acknowledged as, "a prophet," that is, one who proclaims to the people whatever it is that his Sender wishes him to proclaim. We see the fulfilment of this prediction in such passages as Matt. 11:9 f. (Luke 7:26 f.); 14:5; 21:26 (Mark 11:32; Luke 20:6). Continued: **For you will go before the face of the Lord to make ready his ways.** See on verse 17. Cf. Isa. 40:3; Mal. 3:1; Matt. 3:3. The ways or paths of the Lord are those along which he proceeds in order to bestow his salvation. In the present connection we think especially of the divine call to conversion and to faith in Jesus as the Messiah.

A further elucidation of John's task follows in verse **77. To impart to his people knowledge of salvation through the forgiveness of their sins.** The sense is: "to make ready his ways, namely, to impart to his people," etc. That was all important, absolutely necessary, for it is through the knowledge of sin that salvation is attained; that is, consciousness of guilt and pollution precedes faith in Christ as complete and perfect Savior. See Rom. 7:24, 25.

It is God, God alone, who saves. John was God's chosen instrument to impart to the people the knowledge of salvation through forgiveness. He would be able to do this because of strength and wisdom given to him by God. Note: salvation through *forgiveness*, not through piling up merits. Cf. Ps. 32:1; 130:4; Dan. 9:9; Eph. 1:7; 4:32. The way of salvation is the same in Old and New Testament. It is the way of grace through faith (Gen. 15:6; Isa. 55:1; Eph. 2:6, 8).

It should be noted also that this salvation is a distinctly spiritual matter, though, to be sure, it affects all domains and aspects of life. It is not a

127

matter of deliverance from bondage to Rome. It is not a matter of gaining wealth, prestige, earthly glory, etc. It is a matter of reconciliation to God through the saving work of the promised Redeemer, whose forerunner John was appointed to be.

And if anyone should think that somehow, some way, the root or cause of salvation is after all to be found in man, the final passage of Zechariah's beautiful hymn should cure him completely: salvation through forgiveness of sins is on account of, or:

78, 79. Because of the merciful heart of our God,
With which the Rising Sun will visit us from on high,
To shine on those who sit in darkness and death's shadow,
To guide our feet into the path of peace.

Note the following:

a. "The merciful heart of our God" is literally "our God's entrails [or: bowels] of mercy." A discussion of this figure of speech can be found in N.T.C. on Philippians, p. 58, footnote 39.

b. "With which" = "equipped with this (merciful heart)."

c. "The Rising Sun" (some prefer "the Dawn" or simply "Dawn"), like "the horn of salvation" in verse 69, indicates and describes the Messiah. The point is that in and through him the Most High himself will in his tender mercy visit the people in order to help and save them.

Basically the Greek term used here (*anatolē*) means *rising* (cf. Matt. 2:2). It is but a small step from *rising* or *rise* to *sunrise,* and from there to *the Rising Sun.* Since we know that Zechariah, the author of this hymn, was deeply aware of the prophecies of Malachi (note resemblance between 1:17, 76 and Mal. 3:1), it is not difficult to believe that he is here echoing Mal. 4:2, the passage about the coming of "the sun of righteousness with healing in his wings."

d. There is considerable textual support for the reading "has visited us" instead of "will visit us." But the reading "will visit us" is at least equally strong. Besides, accepting the future tense here is favored by the fact that the passage occurs in a context of futures ("will be called," "will go before," verse 76). Also, Jesus was not yet born, so that "has visited" can be justified only if it be interpreted as a prophetic past. All in all it would seem that the future tense deserves the preference in this case.

e. The "visit" of this "Sun" has as its purpose: "to shine on those who sit in darkness and death's shadow" (verse 79). This phraseology is derived from Isa. 9:1, 2, which is also quoted in Matt. 4:16.

Sitting in *darkness* and death's shadow indicates a condition of danger, fear, and hopelessness, a pining away, with no human help in sight. In Scripture the designation *darkness,* when used figuratively, refers to one or more of the following features: delusion (blindness of mind and heart; cf. II Cor. 4:4, 6; Eph. 4:18); depravity (Acts 26:18); and despondency (Isa. 9:2; see its context, verse 3). Though all three qualities are probably in the picture here, yet the emphasis may well be on the last of the three (despondency, hopelessness).

The antonym of darkness is *light*, which, accordingly, refers to genuine learning (the true knowledge of God, Ps. 36:9), life to the glory of God (Eph. 4:15, 24; 5:8, 9, 14), and laughter (gladness, Ps. 97:11). All three may well be included, but here too the emphasis is perhaps on the last of the three.

The real meaning of the words, accordingly, is this, that Jesus Christ, by his presence, teaching, deeds of mercy and power, would fill the hearts of all his followers with the joy of salvation. No longer would they be pining away in gloom and despair. Whenever Jesus enters human hearts, the words of a popular hymn go into effect,

> The whole world was lost in the darkness of sin,
> The light of the world is Jesus.

f. "To guide our feet into the path of peace." Those who a moment ago were pictured as sitting down in despair are now standing on their feet; in fact, are walking. Their sadness has been turned into gladness. Note the connection: "to shine on those . . . to guide our feet." By means of shining, the Rising Sun guides our feet. All we, sinners, had gone astray and had turned to our own way (Isa. 53:6), not knowing "the way of peace" (Isa. 59:8, 9). Then the Sun rises, shines, directs our feet into the path of peace.

This peace is both objective and subjective. Objectively it amounts to reconciliation with God through "David's horn," "the Rising Sun," the Messiah (II Cor. 5:20). Subjectively it is the quiet and comforting assurance of forgiveness and adoption (Rom. 8:16 f.). It is the smile of God reflected in the reconciled sinner's heart, the shelter from the storm, the hiding-place in the shadow of his wings, the stream that issues from the fountain of grace. To that peace the Rising Sun directs our feet.

As this touchingly beautiful song draws to its close it seems as if already we hear the angels sing:

> Glory to God in the highest,
> *And on earth peace* among men he has graciously chosen.

We have studied "Elizabeth's Song of Love" and "Mary's Song of Faith." That we have every right to call the priest's prophecy "Zechariah's Song of Hope" can hardly be questioned. The very word *prophecy,* as here used, implies also the forward look, which, as has been shown, is the distinguishing trait of *this* song.

Luke's closing sentence is:

80. And the child continued to grow and to become strong in spirit; and he was in the desert regions until the day of his public appearance to Israel.

Like any normal child John grew up. Cf. Judg. 13:24, 25. Since his parents were already well advanced in years when he was conceived, the boy probably became an orphan early in life. But both physically and spiritually his development was very favorable. In fact, he became strong in spirit, filled with excellent mental, moral, and spiritual qualities.

He lived in desert regions. For more about this see on 3:2b. This lonely life lasted until the beginning of his public "appearance" or "presentation" to Israel. With this entire verse cf. what is said about the child Jesus in Luke 2:40.[92]

Practical Lessons Derived from Luke 1:67–80

Verse 68

"Blessed be . . ." Without doxology true religion is inconceivable.

Verse 69

"A horn of salvation for us in the house of David." There is nothing petty about Zechariah. Note how his thoughts and thanksgivings turn from his own child to that other Child, the One from the house of David.

Verse 70

"His holy prophets." The lower our view of inspiration, the smaller the blessing we receive and the capability of permitting the Word to be a blessing to others.

Verses 71, 74, 75

"Salvation from our enemies . . . that we . . . should serve him." When we are saved *from* something, we are at the same time saved *for* something, namely, to be of service to others, for God's glory. The latter is often forgotten.

Verse 72

"His holy covenant." Salvation never begins with us. It begins with God. It was he who established his holy covenant with Abraham, a covenant that is still in effect. Read Gal. 3:29; I John 4:19.

Verses 76, 77

"And you (my) child will . . . impart to God's people knowledge of salvation." The noblest aspiration parents can cherish for their children is that they become "channels of blessing."

Verse 78

"The merciful heart of God." What an encouraging phrase!

92. Notes on Greek words, phrases, and constructions in 1:67–80 begin on page 131.

Verses 78, 79

"The Rising Sun . . . to shine on those who sit in darkness." When he shines on them they too begin to shine . . . brighter and brighter until full day (Prov. 4:18). "To guide our feet into the path of peace." Being a channel of blessing brings peace.

Verse 80

"He was in the desert regions." Those who plan to influence multitudes should prepare themselves by being alone with God.

Notes on Greek Words, Phrases, and Constructions in 1:67–80

Verses 68 and 78

ἐπεσκέψατο (verse 68) is third per. s. aorist indicat. of ἐπισκέπτομαι; and ἐπισκέψεται (verse 78) is the third per. s. future indicat. of the same verb. See below, under verses 76–79. In Acts 6:3 this verb means *to look for, select.* The other New Testament passages in which a form of this verb is found are (in addition to Luke 1:68, 78) Matt. 25:36, 43; Luke 7:16; Acts 7:23; 15:14, 36; Heb. 2:6; and James 1:27. In all these ten remaining instances of its use the meaning is either: (a) to be concerned about, to look after; or (b) to visit. In several cases, however, translators and interpreters differ with respect to the question whether in a particular passage the verb falls under meaning (a) or meaning (b). The line of demarcation between the two connotations is at times almost invisible. In each case the context will have to decide.

Verse 73

ὅρκος, oath. Cf. *exorcise, exorcist;* see also Matt. 5:33; 14:7, 9 (= Mark 6:26); 26:72; Acts 2:30; Heb. 6:16, 17; James 5:12.

ὤμοσε, third per. s. aor. indicat. of ὀμνύω (another form of ὄμνυμι), especially frequent in Matthew and in Hebrews; to swear, to confirm by oath.

Verse 74

Though rather far removed from each other, the adverb ἀφόβως modifies the present infinitive λατρεύειν. Cf. *Mariolatry.*

Verses 76–79

κληθήσῃ and προπορεύσῃ are sec. per. s. fut. indicatives, respectively of καλέω and (cf. Acts 7:40) προπορεύομαι**. In verse 78 it is probably best, in line with these two verbs, to accept the reading ἐπισκέψεται ("will visit us"), another instance of the future tense, but now *third* per. s. The articular aor. infinitive τοῦ δοῦναι etc. (verse 77) is in apposition with ἑτοιμάσαι (verse 76). In verse 77 the phrase ἐν ἀφέσει, etc., goes best with σωτηρίας: the gateway to salvation full and free is forgiveness. And this forgiveness, in turn, is rooted in God's merciful heart; hence, so is the entire work of salvation. In verses 78, 79 ἐπιφᾶναι (see also Acts 27:20; Titus 2:11) modifies ἐπισκέψεται. The visiting has as its purpose to shine on those who sit in darkness. And this shining, in turn, is necessary "to guide our feet," etc.

Verse 80

In the opening of the sentence note the verbs in the imperfect tense. They do not merely state a fact; they picture it in the process of happening. Some interpret πνεύματι as referring to the Holy Spirit. In that case, however, would not Luke have used the fuller term, as in verses 15, 41, and 67? Besides, physical and spiritual growth form a pair.

The noun ἀνάδειξις* (here in the genitive ἀναδείξεως) occurs nowhere else in the New Testament. Basically it means holding something up for the purpose of exhibition; hence, public appearance, presentation.

Summary of Chapter 1

Dedicatory Preface (verses 1–4). Luke was moved to write because (a) the events centering in Jesus were so important that many people had already tried to draw up a narrative around them, (b) from reliable witnesses he had received information concerning these happenings, and (c) he himself had made a thorough investigation. His purpose was that his friend (sponsor?) Theophilus, a distinguished person, one who may have occupied a high position in the city of Rome, and who had already received some instruction in Christian doctrine, might get to know the truth concerning Jesus more fully. Undoubtedly the evangelist was trying to reach for Christ not only Theophilus but the entire Greek-speaking Roman world.

The Birth of John Foretold (verses 5–25). The angel Gabriel suddenly appeared to Zechariah, while this aged priest was performing his duties at the altar of incense in the Jerusalem sanctuary. Gabriel told the priest that his wife Elizabeth, also well along in years, would bear a son, to be named John, and that this son, when grown up, would "turn many of the children of Israel to the Lord their God." Zechariah did not believe it. As a result he was told that he would not be able to speak until the day of the prediction's fulfilment. When he came back to the waiting audience, the priest tried by means of signs to indicate what had occurred. After Zechariah returned to his home Elizabeth did indeed become pregnant.

The Birth of Jesus Foretold (verses 26–38). In a small Galilean village lived a virgin named Mary. By means of solemn ceremonies it had been arranged that she was to become the wife of Nazareth's carpenter, Joseph. He was a very kind man, who truly loved her. See Matt. 1:18, 19. Both Mary and Joseph were descendants of King David, and accordingly belonged to the tribe of Judah.

One day Gabriel, the very angel who had appeared to Zechariah, presented himself also to Mary. He told her that she had found favor with God, and would conceive and give birth to a son, to be named Jesus. He added that this child would be great, would be called "the Son of the Most

High," and would reign forever. When Mary wondered how, in her virgin state, this prediction could be realized, Gabriel answered that the Holy Spirit would overshadow her, bringing about conception. Result: her child would in reality be the Son of *God*. The angel added that because of God's almighty power even aged Elizabeth, her friend and relative, had conceived and was six months along in her pregnancy. Mary answered, "Behold, the handmaid of the Lord. May it be to me according to your word!" She was fully surrendered.

Mary Visits Elizabeth (verses 39–45). So Mary goes to the hill country of Judah to visit Elizabeth. The older woman, in addressing Mary, exclaims,

> Blessed are you among women,
> And blessed is the fruit of your womb!

The poem or hymn in which she showed how very happy she had been made by Mary's condition may be called "Elizabeth's Song of Love," for love does not envy (I Cor. 13:4).

Mary's Magnificat (verses 46–56). In this famous hymn, which may be called "Mary's Song of Faith," she gives evidence of her trust in the Mighty and Merciful God, the Holy One, the Helper in the time of need, the God of the covenant. The opening lines are:

> My soul magnifies the Lord,
> And my spirit rejoices in God my Savior.

The Birth and Naming of John the Baptist (verses 57–66). When Elizabeth's time of pregnancy had run its normal course she gave birth to a son, as had been predicted. On the eighth day, when the child was circumcised, the neighbors and relatives wanted to name him after his father, Zechariah. Elizabeth, however, insisted that he be called *John* ("Jehovah is gracious"). Asked about his own wishes in this matter, Zechariah wrote on a tablet, "John is his name." This act of obedience on his part was immediately rewarded by speech recovery. He began to speak, praising God. All of these wonderful events made a deep impression on the people living in the hill country of Judea.

Zechariah's Prophecy (verses 67–80). Another name would be "Zechariah's Song of Hope." It consists of two parts; in fact, of two long sentences (verses 68–75 and 76–79). In the first sentence Zechariah praises God for having provided salvation for his people, in fulfilment of prophecy and of his holy covenant with Abraham. In the second he, with firmly anchored hope, summarizes the child's mission as a way-preparer for the Messiah, whom he describes as "the Rising Sun" about to shine on "those who sit in darkness."

Luke's closing statement is: "And the child continued to grow and to become strong in spirit; and he was in the desert regions until the day of his public appearance to Israel."

Outline of Chapter 2

Theme: *The Work Thou Gavest Him to Do*

CHAPTER II

2 1 In those days a decree was issued by Caesar Augustus that a census should be taken of the entire [Roman] world. 2 This, the first census, took place while Quirinius was governor of[93] Syria.[94] 3 And all went on their way to be registered, each going to his own town. 4 So from Galilee, out of the town of Nazareth, Joseph too went up, into Judea, to the town of David, which is called Bethlehem. It was because he was of the house and family of David that he went there, 5 to be registered[95] with Mary, his betrothed, who was pregnant. 6 And while they were there the days were fulfilled[96] for her to give birth. 7 And she gave birth to her firstborn son. She wrapped him in strips of cloth and laid him down in a manger, because there was no room for them in the inn.

2:1-7 *The Birth of Jesus*
Cf. Matt. 1:18-25[97]

1. In those days a decree was issued by Caesar Augustus that a census should be taken of the entire [Roman] world.

Luke 1:5 made mention of Herod, the king; 2:1 refers to Augustus, the emperor. Malevolent Herod and Benevolent Augustus, to a certain extent how different they were! To be sure, they had in common that they were heathen, and men of superior ability, but that is about where the similarity ended. At the time of the census, mentioned here in Luke 2:1, 2, Herod the Great (or Herod I) was still alive. He must have died shortly afterward.

The census was ordered by the emperor. For at least twenty-three years (27-4 B.C.) the reigns of emperor and king overlapped, as shown in the diagram on the following page.

Now as to that census. But first something more must be said about the man who ordered it, Emperor Augustus. Getting acquainted with this renowned ruler may help us to understand Luke 2:1 f.

His original name was Gaius Octavius. For the earlier period of his life (i.e., for 63-27 B.C.) he is popularly known in the English-speaking world

---

93. Or: was in command of.
94. Or: This registration took place for the first time while Quirinius, etc.
95. Or: to get himself enrolled.
96. Or: completed.
97. Though these two narrative paragraphs harmonize, they are parallel only to a small extent.

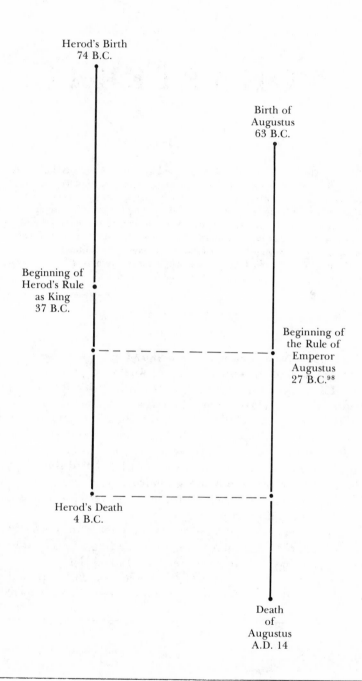

---

98. In reality the role of Octavian as sole ruler began a little earlier. Already in 29 B.C. he was declared Imperator; in 27, Augustus.

as Octavian. As shown on the diagram, he was Roman emperor from 27 B.C. (or a little earlier) until his death in A.D. 14. See what was said about him in N.T.C. on Matthew, pp. 158-160, 163, 164.

He was a grandnephew of Julius Caesar; that is, Octavian's mother Atia was a daughter of Julia, the sister of Julius Caesar:

Julius Caesar and his sister Julia

↓

Atia

↓

Octavian

His granduncle, Julius Caesar, thought highly of him and showered gifts and honors upon him. When the great Roman statesman and general was murdered (44 B.C.), Octavian learned that in his will he, the grandnephew, had been named Caesar's son and heir. He then changed his name to Gaius Julius Caesar.

A sister of Octavian was married to Antony, member of The Second Triumvirate (Lepidus, Antony, and Octavian). When Antony left his own wife behind and became infatuated with Egypt's bewitching Queen Cleopatra, and when, in addition, he began to show far greater concern for himself and Cleopatra than for the welfare of Rome, Octavian and the Romans understandably turned against him. In the naval battle of Actium (31 B.C.) Antony was defeated. Both he and Cleopatra shortly afterward committed suicide. Octavian conquered.

In the year 27 B.C. the Roman senate conferred on the former Octavian—now Gaius Julius Caesar—the title *Augustus* (= majestic, sublime, highly revered). From then on he was known as Caesar Augustus.

His character is hard to analyze. During his climb to power he was ruthless. Once in power, however, he mellowed. He became, in fact, a wise administrator and famous organizer, especially of his military forces and of his bodyguard. Cf. Phil. 1:13. By choosing his generals wisely he won many battles. He showed superb tact in dealing with his subjects, and allowed even the conquered provinces to retain a considerable measure of home rule. He respected their customs, religious convictions, and even their laws to the extent to which they did not interfere with Rome's. He caused an ordinance to be passed making adultery a crime. He stimulated the arts and encouraged cleaner literature. He was a great builder. He gave to the world a lengthy period of heretofore unknown peace. He has been called "a benevolent ruler," and even "the father of his country."

After fully 41 years of a predominantly successful rule he calmly passed away in the arms of his wife. Many of the reforms he instituted survived his death. By means of the census he unwittingly contributed to the fulfilment of the prophecy of Mic. 5:2.

In saying some good things about Augustus we are contrasting him with Herod I (often called "The Great"), who, in comparison with Augustus, was worse than a beast. By no means are we saying, "Augustus was just about a Christian." *Far from it!* That he was, after all, a heathen is clear not only from the ruthless manner in which he rose to power but also from various other facts: though by an act of law he made adultery a crime, as stated above, in his own personal life he certainly undermined the sanctity of marriage. When his first wife, Scribonia, failed to produce a son—she did give birth to a daughter, Julia—he divorced her and married Livia, with whom he had fallen madly in love. He also forced Livia's elder son (by her former marriage), Tiberius, who later became emperor, to divorce his wife and to marry Julia.

As to emperor-worship, because Augustus realized how unpopular his adoptive father, Julius Caesar, had made himself by accepting divine honors, he discouraged worship of himself. Nevertheless, he not only accepted for himself the title *Pontifex Maximus* or *Highest Priest,* i.e., head of all religious worship, but also insisted on the deification of the murdered Julius Caesar, even building a temple in his honor. Moreover, he did not discourage the erection of temples to "Rome and Augustus."

All in all, therefore, we are probably justified in saying this about Caesar Augustus: he was certainly better than most Roman emperors and than King Herod I. Yet he was far removed from measuring up to the Christian standard. Augustus was a heathen. Nevertheless by God, in his unsearchable wisdom, this heathen was used for the advancement of God's kingdom. It was the *Pax Romana* (Roman Peace), to which Augustus contributed liberally, that made it possible for the Christian religion to push forward until, in a very short time, it had spread across the entire Mediterranean world.[99]

Since, as has been indicated, Augustus was a methodical man and a good administrator, who had taken note of the confused state of affairs in the realm entrusted to his care, he ordered a census to be taken of the entire inhabited world, that is, the populated world as far as it was ruled by Rome. The census was ordered "in those days," a very indefinite expression, probably referring to "the days of Herod" (1:5).

Something can be said in favor of the interpretation that what the emperor actually ordered was not just *one* census but a regular system of censuses: a registration with a view to taxation that would occur at equal time intervals.

That such periodic enrolments actually occurred can no longer be denied. The very papers, indicating a registration every fourteen years, have

---

99. That Augustus was a self-worshiper appears also from his *Monumentum Ancyranum,* an obituary, written by himself, in which he recounts his own achievements. In his will he ordered this obituary to be engraved in bronze on two pillars in front of his mausoleum in Rome.

The *Cambridge Ancient History,* Vol. X, chapters 1–8 (1934), gives ample treatment to the life and times of Augustus and furnishes bibliographies. See also the article on *Augustus* in *Encyclopaedia Britannica,* Chicago, London, etc., 1969 edition, Vol. 2, pp. 758–761; and A. Hyma and J. F. Stach, *World History, A Christian Interpretation,* Grand Rapids, 1942, pp. 80, 86, 87.

been found; namely, those proving that a census must have been taken in the years A.D. 230, 216, 202, 188, 174, 160, 146, 132, 118, 104, 90, 62, 34. There are also indirect references to the censuses of A.D. 48 and 20.[100]

Subtracting 14 from A.D. 20 brings us back to A.D. 6, as having also been a census year. Indirect evidence for the correctness of this date is furnished by Josephus, *Antiquities* XVIII.26 (see also XVII.355; XVIII.1). He states that a census took place "in the 37th year of Caesar's defeat of Antony at Actium." Since we know that this battle occurred Sept. 2 of the year 31 B.C., this yields A.D. 6 as the date for the census that caused a great uprising among the Jews. See Acts 5:37; Josephus, *Jewish War* VII.253.

When we now once more subtract 14 years we arrive finally at the year 8 B.C., for the first census. But does this necessarily mean that in Herod's domain the census was completed in 8 B.C.? This introduces us to verse **2. This, the first census, took place while Quirinius was governor of Syria.** The sense is clearly that the system of periodic enrolments was put into operation for the first time when Quirinius was governor of Syria.[101]

At this point two difficulties arise, both relating to the date 8 B.C. The first concerns *8 B.C. and Quirinius;* the second, *8 B.C. and Jesus.*

As to the first difficulty, is it not true that according to Josephus (*Antiquities* XVIII.1) Quirinius was governor of Syria not in 8 B.C. but in A.D. 6, when he "arrived . . . to make an assessment," and when a certain Judas (cf. Acts 5:37) instigated a rebellion?

Answer: Inscriptions discovered by William Ramsay show that Quirinius was "governor" in Syria both before and after the birth of Jesus, though not necessarily in the same sense each time. For more details see the works of Ramsay and of Robertson mentioned earlier (on p. 39, footnote 30); especially Ramsay, *Was Christ Born at Bethlehem?*, p. 109; Robertson,

---

100. See W. M. Ramsay, *Was Christ Born in Bethlehem?*, pp. 129, 132, 170; *The Bearing of Recent Discovery*, pp. 246, 255–274; A. T. Robertson, *Luke the Historian*, p. 123.

101. By substituting the term *census* (or *enrolment* or *registration*) for *taxing*, A.V. (in Luke 2:2) is corrected to read, "And this census was first made when Cyrenius [better Quirinius] was governor of Syria," a good translation. Excellent also are the renderings found in Phillips, Berkeley, Beck, N.E.B., Amplified, and Dutch (Nieuwe Vertaling). Wrong is: "This was the first census that took place while Quirinius was governor of Syria," as if Luke is looking forward, and is saying: "Of the two censuses taken while Quirinius was governor of Syria this was the first; that mentioned in Acts 5:37 was the second." The very wording of the text, in the original, shows that Luke is not looking forward but back to a time when there was as yet no census. Thus also L.N.T. (A. and G.), p. 733.

Another questionable view is that according to which Luke would be saying, "This first census did not actually take place until [A.D. 6, when] Quirinius was governor of Syria." Though this eliminates the necessity of positing two censuses under Quirinius, it does not suit the immediately following context: "and all went on their way to be registered. . . . Joseph too went up . . . to Bethlehem . . . to be registered with Mary. . . . And while they were there she gave birth," etc. Besides, how this reconstruction can be reconciled with the actual wording of the Greek text is hard to see. That objection also holds with respect to the rendering by F. M. Heichelheim in *An Economic Survey of Ancient Rome,* edited by T. Frank, Vol. IV, Baltimore, 1938, p. 161, namely, "This census was the first before that under the prefectureship of Quirinius in Syria."

Luke the Historian, p. 128. In fact, with brief interruptions Quirinius functioned as military governor or commander-in-chief in Syria from 12 B.C. to A.D. 16.[102]

As to the second difficulty, if it be true that the census to which Luke 2:2 refers, and therefore also the birth of Jesus, took place in 8 B.C., then the beginning of Christ's ministry, when he was about thirty years of age (Luke 3:23), must be dated about the year A.D. 22, and the first cleansing of the temple (John 2:12 ff.) circa A.D. 23. But this brings us into conflict with John 2:20, according to which that structure, work on which was begun in 19 B.C., had been in the process of building for forty-six years. That forty-six year span brings us to the date A.D. 27 for the first cleansing of the temple, and to the date A.D. 26 for the beginning of Christ's ministry. The date late December of the year 5 B.C., for the birth of Jesus, is therefore not unreasonable. But 8 B.C. would be too early.

One reaches the same result by proceeding from the valid assumption that in all probability the birth of Jesus occurred shortly before the death of Herod I (see N.T.C. on Matthew, p. 181), on or before April 4, 4 B.C.[103]

How, then, must we account for the apparent discrepancy: census 8 B.C., birth probably 5 B.C., not earlier than 6 B.C.?

This remains a problem, though not a serious one. We may probably assume that in Herod's realm the carrying out of the decree was postponed. A few considerations point in this direction:

Ever since the events recorded in II Sam. 24 the Jews were afraid of a census. All the more were they opposed to one imposed upon them by a foreign power. This was going to become very clear from what happened in A.D. 6—hence, several years after Herod's death—in connection with the second census.

Herod's hesitancy to execute the emperor's decree is therefore understandable. He may have felt that a precipitous going ahead with the ordered census would mean trouble for him. So supposedly he obtained permission from the emperor to postpone the carrying out of the decree. It has been indicated that Augustus considered the desires of the subjugated nations. Let Herod therefore gradually prepare his people for the census. In his kingdom let the execution of the decree be postponed a while.

Postponement, however, does not mean annulment. Being a man of system, order, and determination, Augustus still insists on the census, and

---

102. F. W. Danker, *op. cit.,* p. 23.

Tertullian's statement (*Against Marcion,* Book IV, ch. 19) that in Judah the census was taken by Sentius Saturninus has little weight. He connects this census with the event related in Matt. 12:46–50, and is even inconsistent with himself, as elsewhere he gives an entirely different date for Christ's birth. See *The Ante-Nicene Fathers,* Grand Rapids, 1951, Vol. III, p. 378, footnote 3.

103. See also H. W. Hoehner, "Chronological Aspects of the Life of Christ," Part I: "The Date of Christ's Birth," *BS,* Vol. 130, No. 529 (Oct.–Dec. 1973), pp. 338–351. On p. 350 Hoehner states, "Late 5 B.C. or early 4 B.C. best satisfies the evidence." I agree.

this not only elsewhere—for example, in Egypt, which has yielded many evidences of a periodic census—but also in the kingdom of the Jews. Meanwhile, as has been indicated in N.T.C. on Matthew, pp. 158–166; 179–193, Herod's physical, mental, and especially moral condition is beginning to deteriorate, so that he becomes the murderer of those whom he should have loved most dearly. Once before, the emperor had written him, "Whereas formerly I treated you as a friend, I will now treat you as a subject." And now, having been informed about Herod's insensate and fiendish atrocities—he even caused some of his own sons to be killed!— Augustus remarks, "It is better to be Herod's swine (*hun*) than his son (*huion*)."[104] So the emperor now refuses to wait any longer. And thus it comes about that the census, originally ordered for 8 B.C., is finally carried out—or completed—in or about the year 5 B.C.

It should be stressed that this attempt to solve the problem *8 B.C. and Jesus* is conjectural. A more simple solution might be that the emperor from the beginning left the exact timing of the decree's execution to those immediately in charge. Or one might argue that especially in Herod's domain the taking of a census was time-consuming.

Whatever be the real solution, one fact stands out, as mentioned earlier (p. 40), namely, that wherever it has been possible to check Luke's statements, his impeccability as a historian has come to light. Nothing he says has been disproved.

It is nice to know this. More important, however, is the fact that the believer approaches Scripture in the firm conviction that it is true. He believes this without even waiting for so-called "confirmation" from outside sources.

3. And all went on their way to be registered, each going to his own town. In the land of the Jews, accordingly, the enrolment is "by households." This was also true in Egypt, as an edict of G. Vibius Maximus, governor of Egypt in A.D. 104, indicates.[105]

4, 5. So from Galilee, out of the town of Nazareth, Joseph too went up, into Judea, to the town of David, which is called Bethlehem. It was because he was of the house and family of David that he went there, to be registered with Mary, his betrothed, who was pregnant.

In N.T.C. on Matthew, p. 106, it was pointed out how important it was for the Jews to know their line of descent, their family tree. Joseph was "of the house and family of David," as is clear also from Matt. 1:6, 16. Note "house and family." "House" is here the more comprehensive word; otherwise "and family" would not have to be added.

---

104. The pun makes sense especially when one bears in mind that as king of the Jews, a ruler who tried to make his subjects believe that he worshiped their God and respected their laws, he was not supposed to eat pork! Pigs had nothing to fear from him, but his own sons did.

105. See A. Deissmann, *op. cit.,* pp. 270, 271, including figure 51. See also F. G. Kenyon and H. I. Bell, *Greek Papyri in the British Museum,* Vol. III, London, 1907, p. 125.

In I Sam. 20:6 Bethlehem is called "David's city." It was here that he was born. It was in the fields around this town that he tended the sheep (I Sam. 17:15). In fact, for a long time David and his relatives held a yearly sacrificial feast, a kind of sacred family reunion, in this place, as I Sam. 20:6 implies. See also II Sam. 23:15, 16. It may be assumed, therefore, that it was here that the family records were kept.

That Mary, who, as has been made clear, was also of the house of David (Luke 1:32, 69), was required by law to be present in person for the purpose of the registration has been denied. But from an enrolment form filled out and handed in by someone living in Egypt the conclusion can be drawn that in that country both husband and wife had to present themselves.[106] And do not the words "Joseph went up . . .to be registered with Mary" suggest that what was true for Egypt applied also to Herod's kingdom?

But whether her presence was required or not required, for Mary to remain in Nazareth was out of the question. She would in all likelihood have been exposed to slander. Joseph was too kind a person to allow this to happen. Besides, he wanted to be with her when her child was born. Also, the possibility that these two devout people, both of whom had received angelic messages concerning the One to be born (Matt. 1:20-23; Luke 1:26-37), were acquainted with the prophecy of Mic. 5:2 (cf. John 7:42) should not be ruled out.

The evangelist calls Mary "his [= Joseph's] betrothed." By this time Mary was Joseph's "wife," as is clear from Matt. 1:20, 24. But although the two were husband and wife, in one respect the betrothal relationship was continuing, as is clear from Matt. 1:24b, 25, ". . . he had no sexual relations with her until she had given birth to a son." That situation may well have been the reason for Luke's description of Mary as Joseph's "betrothed."

For Joseph the trip from Nazareth to Bethlehem may not have been too strenuous. But for Mary, in the final days of her pregnancy, to ride this considerable distance—about 90 miles, by the roundabout way of Trans-Jordan—must have been exhausting. And *if* this trip was made during the rainy season, a possibility we have no right to discount, the stress and strain would have been even greater.

Finally the two reached the valley from which they could see the rather steep ridge on which Bethlehem is located. Did they have time to think of David tending the sheep and/or playing the harp? Of Ruth gleaning in the fields of Boaz? But once they reached the town all such thoughts would have to make way for the pressing necessity of finding shelter.

6, 7. And while they were there the days were fulfilled for her to give birth. And she gave birth to her firstborn son. She wrapped him in strips of cloth and laid him down in a manger, because there was no room for them in the inn.

---

106. See G. J. D. Aalders, *Het Romeinsche Imperium En Het Nieuwe Testament,* Kampen, 1938, pp. 34, 35.

In connection with this simple yet all-important passage note the following:

a. The expression "While they were there the days were fulfilled [or: completed]" may mean that the two spent a few days in Bethlehem before the child was born. On the other hand, the words may simply place special stress on the fact that Jesus was indeed born in Bethlehem: the great event took place while they were *there*.

b. "The days were fulfilled." The birth occurred "in the fulness of time" (Gal. 4:4). In this particular case, however, the meaning may simply be that the birth took place when the normal period between conception and delivery had expired. Even though the conception itself was a miracle, the process of development within the womb was allowed to run its usual course.

c. "her firstborn son." Note: not "her only son," but "her firstborn son." The natural explanation is certainly this, that after Mary had given birth to Jesus she continued to bear children. The very names of Jesus' brothers are mentioned in the New Testament (Matt. 13:55). The fact that he had *brothers* is also clear from Matt. 12:46, 47 (cf. Mark 3:31, 32; Luke 8:19, 20); John 2:12; 7:3, 5, 10; Acts 1:14. And Matt. 13:56 makes reference to his *sisters*.

d. "She wrapped him in strips of cloth." Note: *she* wrapped him. Does this mean that Mary, having just given birth to her firstborn, now immediately with her own hands swaddled her babe? Not necessarily! No more than Herod's statement, "John I beheaded" (Luke 9:9), means that he in person had wielded the executioner's ax; and no more than Pilate's declaration, "I will therefore punish...him" (Luke 23:16), means that he intended to do this himself. If we assume that Mary gave the directions, and Joseph (or anyone else) carried them out, we have probably done full justice to the passage.

As to the manner in which a little one was swaddled see B. S. Easton's article "Swaddle, Swaddling-Band," I.S.B.E., Vol. V, p. 2874, though whether exactly this procedure was followed also in the present case may well be questioned. Let it suffice to say that with strips of cloth the baby was wrapped round and round tightly and securely. More about this in a moment.

e. "... and laid him down in a manger, because there was no room for them in the inn."

About this "inn" there are various, sometimes sharply contrasting,[107] interpretations. Note the following theories:

---

107. See especially Lenski, *op. cit.,* p. 80. This commentator, who has given his readers much worthwhile material, seems to lose his patience when he arrives at this part of the Christmas story. The idea that the New Testament would teach that Mary bore more children he calls "cheap exegesis," and the thought that Joseph and Mary would have stopped at an *inn,* particularly one as described by A. T. Robertson in *Word Pictures,* he describes as "ridiculous." All I can say is that in this case Lenski's own interpretation fails to measure up to his usual excellent standard.

(1) The inn or caravansary was built around the four sides of an inner court. It generally had two stories. On the second story, reached by a primitive staircase, the rooms for the travelers were located. Those who stopped at the inn carried along their own blanket and pillow. If a person had no blanket, he could wrap himself up in his robe. On the ground floor the animals were stabled. Here also the cargoes that were transported along the caravan route could be temporarily stored. And here the servants, in charge of the pack animals (donkeys, camels), found rest for the night. It was in such a "stable" that Joseph and Mary found lodging when there was no longer any room in the "inn" proper, the second story.[108]

(2) Akin to this is the explanation of A. T. Robertson, *Word Pictures,* p. 23, who, however, pictures the stables as being "on one side of the square, outside the wall." He is careful to point out that the manger in which the child was laid was either connected with the inn or was in a cave.

(3) The manger was in a cave, but that cave was definitely part of—or at least associated with—the inn.

(4) The inn was filled to overflowing: the upstairs was filled with weary guests. Even on the roof there was no room left. And downstairs the servants were crowding the courtyard, bedding down the animals for the night. At the suggestion of a villager Joseph and Mary then found shelter in a cave-stable.[109]

(5) The rendering *inn* is wrong. The right translation is "stopping place" (thus Lenski), or "upper room" (thus Christie, I.S.B.E., Vol. III, p. 1470, and several others).

Their reasoning is that the original (Greek) word here rendered "inn" means "upper room" in Mark 14:14 (= Luke 22:11); so, if it has that meaning there, why not here? As Lenski sees it, Joseph and Mary tried to find lodging with some relatives, but since all the extra space in their house proper had already been given away, these relatives put their guests up in an adjoining shed, where asses were kept.

Comment on theories (1) through (5).

Any of the first four theories may be correct. They have in common their support of the rendering *inn* in 2:7.

Why was there no room in the inn? Was it because Bethlehem was overcrowded with people that wanted to be registered? That is the reason often given. It may be right, but is probably wrong or at least incomplete. Deserving of consideration is the fact that the town just now was filled with men charged with the responsibility of taking the census: officials and soldiers of the Roman government. It is well known that since Augustus and those

---

108. See the very interesting description in H. Mulder, *Spoorzoeker in Bijbelse Landen,* Amsterdam, 1973, pp. 64–67.

109. G. E. Wright (editor), *Great People of the Bible and How They Lived,* Pleasantville, Montreal, etc., 1974, p. 320.

who carried out his decree were aware of the fact that the Jews, because of religious scruples, were terribly afraid of coming into contact with non-Jews, the census officials were to be quartered, as far as ever possible, *not* in private homes but in public places, in *inns* for example. It is not surprising, therefore, that it was exactly *the inn* in which there was no room for Joseph and Mary.

This also shows that the rendering *inn* is probably correct, and that theory (5) is probably defective. For more on this see the note on these verses on page 148.

The owner of the inn should not be charged with cruelty. Room was simply lacking, except in the inn-stable or cave-stable.

The belief that the travelers from Nazareth took up quarters "in a certain cave" dates all the way back to Justin Martyr (about A.D. 114–165). See his *Dialogue with Trypho,* ch. 78. A similar view was expressed by Origen, *Against Celsus* I.51.

Helena, the mother of Constantine, built a church on the presumed site of the nativity. The present church was built by Justinian. In its interior the steps on either side of the altar lead to a cave below, where the supposed birthplace of Jesus is indicated by a star. Did the stable in which the infant was born actually stand there? This can neither be proved nor disproved. It is not very important. One thing is certain: the glitter, splendor, and aroma of the present site do not truly represent the circumstances that obtained when this child was born. It cannot be emphasized too strongly that our Lord was born in a *stable* and was laid down in a *manger,* that is, a feeding trough for animals, possibly a niche carved out in the cave wall.

> "Greetings, you highly favored one, the Lord is with you."
> "There was no room for them in the inn."
> "He will be great and will be called the Son of the Most High."
> "She laid him down in a manger."

Why these contrasts? The answer is given in II Cor. 8:9: "For y o u know the grace of our Lord Jesus Christ, that though he was rich, yet for y o u r sake he became poor, that y o u through his poverty might become rich." See also John 3:16; Rom. 8:32.

It is not enough to be able to give a satisfactory interpretation of the nativity account, the Christmas story. We should be so deeply impressed with the love of God here revealed that we feel what the poet felt when he wrote:

> For me, dear Jesus, was thine incarnation,
> Thy mortal sorrow and thy life's oblation;
> Thy death of anguish and thy bitter passion,
> For my salvation.
>
> Johann Heermann
> Tr. Robert Bridges

The baby was born in a stable, not in a palace. It was laid in a feeding trough for animals, not in a pretty bassinet. All this spells poverty, deprivation.

And yet, and yet! There is another side to the story. *Love* shines through. *This* infant at least was securely wrapped in pieces of cloth. Not so the child mentioned in Ezek. 16:4. From the very start that little one was thoroughly rejected, left to die in the field if God had not intervened. Also, many children, even today, have no bed to sleep in. Here, on the contrary, it takes but little imagination to see Joseph putting some straw into that manger, so that the baby would be able to rest in comfort.

To be sure, as a grownup Jesus would be "a man of sorrows and acquainted with grief." Indescribable agonies would be his portion. Nevertheless, again and again during his ministry a voice would ring out from heaven, "Thou art my Son, my Beloved; with thee I am well pleased."

So here also this same love is revealed. And in a moment the angels are going to celebrate the infant's birth in song.[110]

Practical Lessons Derived from Luke 2:1–7

Verses 1, 2

"A decree was issued by Caesar Augustus." When the emperor sent out this order, little did he realize that God was using this decree for the realization of his own purpose with respect to the church. What a comforting passage is Rom. 8:28! Cf. Eph. 1:11.

Verses 4, 5

"So ... Joseph too went up ... to be registered with Mary." The One who was going to say, "What is due to Caesar render to Caesar, and what is due to God render to God" had not yet issued from Mary's womb, yet was already being obeyed: Joseph and Mary never thought of refusing to obey the emperor in a matter that was not contrary to the will of God.

Verse 7

"There was no room for them in the inn." This was not because the innkeeper was cruel or inhospitable, but because the inn was already overcrowded. So also there are hearts that never welcome Jesus, and this not because they definitely hate him but simply because these hearts are already so overcrowded with thoughts of riches, honor, prestige, pleasures, business affairs, etc., that they have no room for Jesus, no time to reflect on his will, no desire to go out of their way to do his pleasure.

---

110. Notes on Greek words, phrases, and constructions in 2:1-7 begin on page 147.

In this connection see the beautiful hymn by Emily E. S. Elliott, "Thou Didst Leave Thy Throne," ending with the stirring refrain,

> O come to my heart, Lord Jesus!
> There is room in my heart for thee.

Notes on Greek Words, Phrases, and Constructions in 2:1–7

Verse 1

δόγμα, decree, commandment, ordinance. Cf. *dogma* (authoritatively affirmed doctrine).

ἀπογράφεσθαι, present passive infinitive of ἀπογράφω: so also in verse 3: continued action indicated in both cases; here in verse 1 there may even be a reference to a regular system of censuses. Contrast this present infinitive with the aor. middle infinitive of the same verb in verse 5 (to get himself enrolled; hence, to be enrolled, a simple statement of fact there; no emphasis on the process).

Verse 2

ἀπογραφή**, basically a writing off, a transcript; here: enrolment or registration (name, address, occupation, marital status, income, etc.) mainly for the purpose of taxation; cf. Acts 5:37.

ἡγεμονεύοντος, gen. s. masc. pres. participle of ἡγεμονεύω*, a word with very wide meaning, to be in command, to govern. Cf. *hegemony*.

Verse 4

The fact that διὰ τὸ εἶναι αὐτόν modifies Ἀνέβη δὲ καὶ Ἰωσήφ should be clearly brought out in the translation. Even *listeners* in church must not get to hear that Bethlehem was the town of David because Joseph belonged to the house of David!

Verse 5

σὺν Μαριάμ. The point is not that Joseph went up with Mary, but that his purpose was to be registered with Mary.

τῇ ἐμνηστευμένῃ αὐτῷ, (with) the one betrothed to him; hence, his betrothed, dat. s. fem. perf. passive participle of μνηστεύω, to betroth.

ἐγκύῳ, dat. s. fem. of ἔγκυος*, pregnant.

Verses 6, 7

ἐπλήσθησαν, here and in verses 21, 22, third per. pl. aor. indicat. passive of πλήθω, alternate form of πίμπλημι; cf. 1:15, 23, etc., to fill; passive: to be filled, to be fulfilled or completed.

τοῦ τεκεῖν is the (articular) aor. infinitive; ἔτεκε, the third per. s. 2nd aor. active indicat.; and ἐτέχθη in verse 11, the third per. s. aor. passive indicat. of τίκτω, to bear, bring forth.

ἐσπαργάνωσεν, third per. s. aor. indicat. active of σπαργανόω, and in verse 12 ἐσπαργανωμένον is the acc. s. neuter perfect passive participle of this verb, meaning to swathe, swaddle, wrap tightly and securely. Cf. *spiral*.

φάτνη* in 2:7, 12, 16 means manger, feeding trough; perhaps even feeding place under the open sky; in 13:15 stall.

κατάλυμα (cf. *catalyst*) is related to the verb καταλύω, to loosen, unharness (the pack animals); hence, to rest, take lodging for the night. In Mark 14:14 (= Luke 22:11) the κατάλυμα is a guest-room. But this does not mean that in Luke 2:7 this word must also mean guest-room. The situations are entirely different. In Mark 14:14 and its parallel we are dealing with *a house*, the very word being mentioned in the text. In Luke 2:7, however, there is no mention of a house at all. In the first instance Jesus and his disciples wish to make use of a room in a house to celebrate the Passover, etc.; in Luke 2:7 Joseph and Mary are looking for a place to sleep, etc. Besides, as A. Edersheim already pointed out, the word κατάλυμα has several meanings (*The Life and Times of Jesus the Messiah*, two volumes, New York, 1897, Vol. I, p. 185, footnote 1). So, for example, in the Septuagint κατάλυμα is the Greek translation of no less than five different Hebrew words of widely different meanings. In Exod. 4:24 "inn" is the right translation: the Lord meets Moses in a lodging-place, an *inn;* so also the Dutch translations "herberg" (W. H. Gispen, *Exodus*—in *Korte Verklaring*—Kampen, 1932, p. 59), "nachtverblijf" (Nieuwe Vertaling). Any place that is adapted for rest is a κατάλυμα.

The possibility—it is no more than that—that there is a reference to an inn or lodging-place near Bethlehem even in the Old Testament (Jer. 41:17) cannot be excluded. The Hebrew word *gᵉruth*, when used as a common noun, does mean inn, lodging-place. Cf. *gēr*, sojourner.

---

8 Now there were shepherds in that region, living in the open fields and by turn keeping watch over their flock by night. 9 Suddenly an angel of the Lord stood by them, and the glory[111] of the Lord shone around them, and they were terribly frightened. 10 But the angel said to them, "Do not be frightened,[112] for, behold, I bring y o u good news of great joy that will be for all the people; 11 because to y o u is born this day in the town of David a Savior, who is Christ the Lord. 12 And this will be the sign for y o u: y o u will find a baby wrapped in strips of cloth and lying in a manger."

13 And suddenly there was with the angel a multitude of the heavenly host, praising God and saying:

14 "Glory to God in the highest,
And on earth peace among men of (his) good pleasure."[113]

15 After the angels had left them and had gone into heaven, the shepherds were saying to each other, "Without delay[114] let's go over to Bethlehem and see this thing that has taken place, which the Lord has made known to us." 16 So they hurried off and found Mary and Joseph, and lying in the manger the baby. 17 Having seen this, they made known what had been told them about this child. 18 And all who heard what the shepherds told them were amazed.[115] 19 But Mary continued to treasure up all these things, mulling them over in her

---

111. Or: splendor.
112. Or: Stop being frightened.
113. Or: on whom his favor rests; or: whom he has graciously chosen.
114. Or: Come on, etc.
115. Literally: And all the listeners were amazed about that which was spoken to them by the shepherds.

mind. 20 Then the shepherds returned, glorifying and praising God for all the things they had heard and seen, (which were) just as had been told them.

21 Now when eight days were completed for circumcising him, he was called Jesus, the name given him by the angel before his conception in the womb.

2:8-21 *Shepherds and Angels*
The Circumcision and Naming of Jesus

8. Now there were shepherds in that region, living in the open fields and by turn keeping watch over their flock by night.

During his public ministry Jesus once quoted the following words from Isa. 61:1 f.:

> The Spirit of the Lord (is) upon me,
> Because he has anointed me
> To proclaim good news to the poor;
> To set free the downtrodden,
> To proclaim the year of the Lord's favor.

It is certainly in harmony with this spirit that the very first proclamation of the fact that the Messiah had actually been born was made to poor and downtrodden shepherds.

They were indeed a despised class. Not only was it difficult for them, because of the very nature of their occupation, to observe all the regulations of the Mosaic law—and especially all the man-made rules superimposed upon that law!—but in addition they were suspected of confusing "thine" with "mine." For these reasons they were looked down upon, and were excluded from the company of those who were allowed to give testimony in the courts.[116]

Nevertheless, Luke's narrative makes abundantly clear that *these* shepherds, the ones to whom the first proclamation of the Savior's birth was made, were different. They were devout men, probably acquainted with Messianic prophecy, and like Simeon, "waiting for the consolation of Israel" (2:25). Proof: Note how the angel addresses them (2:10-12), and note also their exemplary reaction (verses 15, 17, 20).

They were encamped in the open, by turns keeping watch over their flock. Does the sing. "flock" mean that all these sheep were owned by one person, or does it mean that flocks of several owners had been brought together so as to form one flock? Suffice it to say that all the sheep under their care were regarded as one flock.

During the day these animals were out on the grass. In the evening they could, when necessary, be led into crude shelters, pens, or sheepfolds, to protect them against inclement weather, wild beasts, and thieves. Right near them, always watching, were the shepherds. Those men who needed

---

116. S.BK., Vol. II, p. 113.

sleep could retire to a hut made of branches. The actual work of keeping watch over the sheep was done "by turns," some resting while others watched.

Does the presence of these sheep in the fields mean that Jesus cannot have been born in the month of December? Before answering this question let it be definitely affirmed that it is impossible to ascertain in which month Jesus was born. The date December of the year 5 B.C.—even more precisely Dec. 25 of that year—can never be more than an assumption. But is it true that this date, interpreted even as being wholly tentative, a mere possibility, must be considered unreasonable, ridiculous, impossible?

Those who summarily reject it present the following arguments:

a. The sheep were at pasture.[117]

b. At this season of the year many roads in that region are impassable. No government would have forced people to travel *then* to the places where they must be registered.[118]

c. The decision that Christ's birth occurred on Dec. 25 was reached in the fourth century, i.e., during the reign of Constantine, the first Christian emperor (period of reign: A.D. 306–337). It was then that the date of the Savior's birth was made to coincide with Saturnalia, the orgiastic pagan festival celebrating the return of the sun after days of constantly increasing darkness. During that festival gifts were exchanged. Christians did not object to the giving of gifts, especially if they were in the form of donations to the poor. And as for rejoicing because of the sun's victory over the darkness, that too was no problem. According to Malachi's prophecy, reaffirmed by Zechariah (Mal. 4:2; cf. Luke 1:78, 79), is not Christ the Sun who illumines our darkness?

The third argument, then, amounts to this: since the determination of the date of Christ's birth was influenced by the Saturnalian Festival, since that date was not fixed until fully three centuries after the birth, and finally, since Christmas, as a festival, was not *generally* observed until the fourth or even fifth century,[119] therefore the selection of Dec. 25 as the date does not rest on a solid historical basis.

Those who believe that Christ's birth *may*, nevertheless, have occurred on or about Dec. 25 answer as follows:

With respect to (a). Jewish sources support the belief that sheep destined for sacrifices in the temple could be found in these fields even in the winter. Also today flocks of sheep are often seen in Shepherd Field at Christmas time. See N.T.C. on Matthew, p. 182.

With respect to (b). The author who on pp. 69, 70 of his book *Spoorzoeker*

---

117. E. E. Ellis, *op. cit.,* p. 78.
118. H. Mulder, *Spoorzoeker,* pp. 69, 70.
119. L. Dobler, *Customs and Holidays Around the World,* New York, 1962, p. 140.

uses this weather-and-roads argument to show that the date of Christ's birth was probably not Dec. 25, on p. 68 of that same book informs us that he and his wife traveled from Beirut to Jerusalem and to Bethlehem *during Christmas vacation!* In a personal letter (found in translation on p. 182 of N.T.C. on Matthew) he adds that the weather (in Jerusalem and Bethlehem) was beautiful. If we assume that the winter of the year when Jesus was born was mild, the rains not torrential, this argument against the possibility of Dec. 25 as the date of Christ's birth might no longer hold.

Besides, it is not at all certain that the people were ordered to do their traveling during the rainy season. According to A. Fahling[120] they were allowed to present themselves "any time during the year." Perhaps there were circumstances that prevented Joseph and Mary, traveling together from Nazareth to Bethlehem, from performing this duty in an earlier month. Luke 1:36, 39, 56 may shed light on this.

With respect to (c). It is true that during the reign of Constantine special enquiry was made with respect to the date of Christ's birth, and that Dec. 25 received official sanction. However, much earlier than this the attention of students was focused on this very date; for example, by Hippolytus.[121] He was a disciple of Irenaeus, who was a disciple of Polycarp, who was a disciple of the apostle John.[122]

For an ingenious method of arriving at the date Dec. 25 see A. Fahling, *op. cit.,* pp. 60, 732, 733. This is no endorsement of his theory.

Result: that Jesus was born on Dec. 25 can be neither proved or disproved. I fully agree, however, with Lenski's statement, "While Dec. 25 is only traditional . . . it is at least traditional."[123]

9. Suddenly an angel of the Lord stood by them, and the glory of the Lord shone around them, and they were terribly frightened.

It all happened with dramatic swiftness. One moment, except for the sounds always heard during the night, especially when shepherds are by turns watching their sheep, all was quiet. Then all of a sudden it happened: an angel of the Lord, holy, strong, brilliant, stood by them. They had not seen him come.

At the same time the glory of the Lord—heavenly brightness, rightly regarded as the manifestation of God's presence and power—flashed all around them. It is not surprising that the shepherds "feared with great fear," were terribly frightened. They were devout men; nevertheless, they were sinners, and what they now experienced had come upon them unexpectedly.

---

120. *Op. cit.,* p. 97.
121. See A. H. Newman's article "Christmas" in S.H.E.R.K., Vol. III, p. 47.
122. *Ante-Nicene Fathers,* Vol. V, p. 3, gives the birth-to-death date of Hippolytus as A.D. 170-236.
123. *Op. cit.,* p. 82.

10–12. But the angel said to them, Do not be frightened, for, behold, I bring y o u good news of great joy that will be for all the people; because to y o u is born this day in the town of David a Savior, who is Christ the Lord. And this will be the sign for y o u: y o u will find a baby wrapped in strips of cloth and lying in a manger.

Note the following:

a. The exhortation "Do not be frightened [or afraid]," or "Stop being frightened," here naturally in the plural, occurs also in 1:13 and in 1:30 (in both of these cases in the singular). For more on this and its implications see on 1:13.

b. "I bring y o u good news." The good news is that of the "evangel," the gospel. See also 1:19; 3:18; 4:18, 43; 7:22; 8:1; 9:6; 16:16; 20:1. Though the verb *to bring good news* was used first in the general sense of bringing good news of any kind, it was later going to be used especially to indicate the bringing of the good news of salvation through Christ (cf. to evangelize).

c. "of great joy." What greater joy could there be than the realization and wholehearted acceptance of the fact that God himself, through the sacrifice of his own and only Son, had brought about the solution of the world's greatest problem, that of sin? And was not the Son's incarnation the first step in this solution?

d. "for all the people," that is, *all* regardless of nationality, age, wealth, fame, social position, sex, education, etc. Even the shepherds are included; *all* God's people are included. The term *all the people* here in verse 10 is as wide as is the expression *men of his good pleasure* in verse 14.

The well-meant promise of salvation by grace through faith must be proclaimed throughout the world, but those who reject it cannot experience the "great joy" here mentioned. That marvelous blessing is only for those who believe. Cf. John 3:16. In view of the fact that the shepherds were believers, the message continued as follows:

e. "because to y o u is born this day in the town of David . . ." In the original the word *born* stands very close to the beginning of the sentence. Literally it reads ". . . because born to y o u this day," etc. As if to say, "long ago *promised,* promised, promised . . . now finally *born:* the promise has been fulfilled."

For "the town of David" see on verse 4.

f. "a Savior who is Christ the Lord." In order to place all the emphasis on the *saving* work of Jesus, the article is omitted in Greek; as if to say: above everything he is SAVIOR.

> Be my Example and my Guide,
> My Friend, yea everything beside,
> But first, last, best, whate'er betide,
> Be thou to me my SAVIOR.

Attention is at times called to the fact that in all the Synoptic Gospels this is the only place in which Jesus is called Savior. The fact as such is true.[124] In John's Gospel Jesus is called Savior in 4:42. Cf. also I John 4:14. For the rest, as a designation of Jesus, this term is found especially in the Pastoral Epistles and in II Peter. Also in Acts 13:23; Eph. 5:23; Phil. 3:20.

However, from this circumstance the deduction should not be drawn that the New Testament soft-pedals that precious name. Quite the contrary is the truth. Not only, as already indicated, does the angel, in addressing the shepherds, place great emphasis on it, but in other passages, too, *the saving work* of Jesus is stressed, and this both in the Fourth Gospel (see John 3:16, 17; 4:10, 14; 5:25; 6:50, 51; 7:37, 38, etc.) and even in the Synoptics. See Matt. 1:21; 4:15, 16; 12:21; 20:28 (= Mark 10:45); Luke 1:78, 79; 19:10; 22:19, 20.

This Savior, moreover, is here introduced as the *Christ,* that is, the *Messiah* or Anointed One. He is the One anointed by the Holy Spirit to be his people's Great Prophet, Sympathetic Highpriest, and Eternal King.

He is, moreover, *the Lord.* See on 20:41–44.

g. "And this will be the sign for y o u," etc. The angel did not tell the shepherds that they must go and see this child, no more than Gabriel had told Mary that she must visit Elizabeth (1:36). A mere hint sufficed in both cases.

Note *the* sign, not *a* sign, as the text is at times wrongly translated. Note also that the one sign is this, that the swaddled child is lying in a manger. There may well have been other newly born, swaddled babes in Bethlehem, but this was the only swaddled infant that was lying in a manger. The sign was therefore definite and helpful.

13, 14. And suddenly there was with the angel a multitude of the heavenly host,[125] praising God and saying:
> **Glory to God in the highest**
> **And on earth peace among men of (his) good pleasure.**

Surprise follows upon surprise. First one angel had descended and had taken his position in the immediate vicinity of the shepherds. Once he has made his announcement, all of a sudden an entire army of angels descends. These angels are now seen standing "with" the first angel, therefore also near the shepherds.

How considerate of God to arrange matters in such a way that the order was not reversed: first the army and then the one angel. Not until the shepherds have become somewhat used to the celestial brilliance that blazed around them, and had received from the *one* angel a message of cheer, did *the entire host* of angels descend. Cf. Ps. 103:14.

---

124. In Luke 1:47 the term *Sōtēr* (Savior) is applied to God, not specifically to Jesus. Cf. Jude 25.

125. Or: of the army of heaven.

Did the first Christmas resemble what nativity sets, paintings, exhibits, poetry, and popular fancy have made of it? In some respects it probably did. The humble surroundings of Joseph, Mary, and the child; the love and the tenderness mentioned earlier—see p. 146; the shepherds bowing in adoration, these are some of the items in the exhibits, etc., that probably approach reality.

If there were no legitimate place for art, why did God order the tabernacle and later on the temple to be made so beautiful? If poetry must be frowned upon, why did it please the Holy Spirit to fill Scripture with so many songs?

However, by no means everything actually was or happened as it has been popularly made to appear; for example, we may be sure that the wise men did not meet the shepherds in the stable!

This takes us back to these angels in the fields of Ephrathah (Mic. 5:2; Luke 2:8-14). Did they actually look and act as presented by famous artists? And did they really "sing" something that resembled the Aramaic version of the refrain in the Westminster Carol: "Glo..o..o..o..o..ria—in excelsis Deo"?[126] Or that resembled a Jewish chant, perhaps?

Does the text even say that they *sang* at all? Granted that the word *saying* at the end of verse 13 *may* include "singing," and also granted that the lines these angels uttered exhibit a pleasing parallelism: "glory" versus "peace," "God" versus "men," "in the highest" versus "and on earth," and that the *possibility* must be allowed that these words were sung or chanted, is this the best explanation? More about this in a moment.

How did these angels look? Art has pictured the scene. Take, as an example, Plockhorst's painting, "Tidings of Great Joy."[127] The sheep are huddled together in some kind of pen. Right near them are a few shepherds. Leaning against one of these sturdy men is the faithful shepherd's dog. One of the shepherds is peering into the sky. His eyes are focused upon a descending angel. That heavenly visitor resembles a kindly looking and very pretty young lady. Her hairdo is neat, fairly short, and with bangs! She is dressed in a lengthy white gown. Clutching her robe is a baby angel, and in the background one sees a few additional curly-headed angelets.

Looking at this pictorial representation, and then turning to Scripture and reading the words, "Do not be frightened," one cannot help asking himself, "Who was afraid of whom?" As far as the painting is concerned, does one not rather receive the impression that the robust shepherds are shouting to the nice young lady, "Come on down; don't be afraid of us; we'll not harm you"?

And as to the "song," did the angelets sing soprano, most of the big

---

126. No disparagement of that hymn is intended. It is beautiful!

127. See a copy of this painting in C. P. Maus, *Christ and the Fine Arts*, New York, 1959, p. 59.

angels tenor and alto, allowing the archangels to give body to the oft-repeated (?) refrain by supplying the bass notes? Was it a "chant"?

Is not the following a more scriptural interpretation?

These angels, having been associated with Christ in heaven before his incarnation, knew something about his glory, riches, and majesty. See Isa. 6:1-4; John 12:41. They had also become aware of man's fall. And they had been informed that God had provided a way of salvation for man. Gabriel's announcement to Joseph—"You shall call his name Jesus, for he will save his people from their sins" (Matt. 1:21)—clearly implies this. Did they also know that this work of saving man, while at the same time fully maintaining God's righteousness, meant that the Father would not spare his own Son; that the Son, though he was rich, for his people's sake would become poor, vicariously bearing the curse resting on those whom he came to save; and that the Holy Spirit would condescend to dwell in sinful hearts, applying to them the salvation merited by the Son? We can assume at least that the very birth of Christ in a condition of poverty and deprivation must have caused these angels to stand in awe of God's indescribably marvelous love. Was it not Paul who, when reflecting on this love, cried out, "Thanks be to God for his indescribable gift!" (II Cor. 8:9; 9:15)? And was not this very love probably included among "the things which angels desire to look into" (I Peter 1:12), but cannot fully comprehend?

Viewed in this light we begin to see that, whether literally song or not, the words of Luke 2:14 are above all else *an outpouring of adoration*. One might perhaps say that, having become informed about the Savior's birth, a birth under such circumstances and with such a self-sacrificing purpose, these angels never before had been so thrilled! No wonder, therefore, that from the bottom of their hearts they shout:

Glory to God in the Highest!

They desire that all creation shall praise God. They realize that this very Jesus, through the accomplishment of the task which the Father gave him to do, brings peace (John 14:27). That peace is: (a) reconciliation between God and man; (b) the believer's serene assurance that he has a share in this reconciliation. Cf. Rom. 5:1, 2; II Cor. 5:18-21. The more men sincerely praise God for the salvation he has brought about, the more also they possess this peace.

If the word *song* is used in its broadest meaning, not necessarily being a description of words set to music from the very start, but rather of words which because of their parallelistic structure can be adapted to music, then we may speak of "The Angels' Song of Adoration."

What did the angels exclaim or shout? In verse 14 did they use the word *eudokia* = good pleasure, good will? Or did they say *eudokias* (the same word with an additional sigma or "s")? The latter means *of good pleasure*. The Greek texts vary.

Some interpreters, having accepted the first reading as being genuine, adopt *the first view*, according to which the angels said:

> Glory to God in the highest,
> And on earth peace,
> Good will toward men.   (A.V.)

Others, having accepted the second reading, adopt *the second view*, according to which the angels said:

> Glory to God in the highest,
>   And on earth peace among men of (his) good pleasure.

The genitive simply means "of good pleasure." Whose good pleasure? Clearly God's. The angels are not glorying in man and his merits but in God and his grace. This is clear also from other references to this same concept (good pleasure). See especially Matt. 11:26; Luke 10:21; Eph. 1:4, 5, 9.[128]

Accordingly, when spelled out in full, the interpretation favored by the second view is this: "And on earth peace among men whom God has graciously chosen." His sovereign delight rests on them. With them he is well pleased.

Now even those who cannot read Greek but are sound in doctrine know that the second of the two views, rather than the first, is in line with biblical doctrine. True and lasting peace is the portion of those, and only of those, whom God has graciously chosen. See the following passages: Isa. 26:3, 12; 32:17; 48:22 (= 57:21); Hag. 2:9; Zech. 9:10; Luke 1:78, 79; John 14:27; 16:33; Rom. 5:1; Eph. 2:14, 17; Col. 1:20. The entire work of salvation, from start to finish, must be ascribed to him alone: Ps. 32:1; 89:33, 34; 115:1; Ezek. 20:14; Dan. 9:19; John 6:44; 15:16; Eph. 1:4; Rev. 5:9–14; 15:3, 4.

Greek students should also read the note on Luke 2:14 on page 161.

15. After the angels had left them and had gone into heaven, the shepherds were saying to each other, Without delay let's go over to Bethlehem and see this thing that has taken place, which the Lord has made known to us.

"After the angels had left them." That is always the critical time. What the shepherds should do had been clearly implied. Will they do it? The minister has delivered his sermon. Will the listeners (including himself) take it to heart? The doctor has prescribed medication. Will the patient follow his prescription?

By the use of the imperfect tense Luke shows very graphically that these

---

128. For more on this see N.T.C. on Matthew, p. 500; on Ephesians, pp. 74–81; on Philippians, p. 54; and on Colossians, p. 78, footnote 55.

devout men never hesitated. What about the care of the sheep? The shepherds must have found a solution. The angel had said, "Y o u will find," etc. So, they must go and search. And they were eager to do so.

At this point the original contains a couple words that require special attention. One of them is a little word of two letters. Frequently it means *indeed;* in the present context it can perhaps best be rendered "now" or "at once," or "without delay."

There is also the verbal form which basically means "Let us go through (to)," "Let us go over (to)."[129] This probably implies that these men had to cover an appreciable distance in order to reach Bethlehem. The place was not right next door.[130] Nevertheless, fully realizing that it was God himself who, through his angels, had spoken to them, they left immediately.

16, 17. So they hurried off and found Mary and Joseph, and lying in the manger the baby. Having seen this they made known what had been told them about this child. They felt constrained to relate their marvelous experience: how first one angel had addressed them, exactly what it was he had said about the child, and the sign he had given them; how that first angel had been followed by an entire army of angels, and what this heavenly host had joyfully proclaimed. These men hid nothing. They told their story to Mary and Joseph, and to many others besides (note in verse 18: "and *all* who heard what the shepherds told them," etc.).

So thoroughly convinced were these men of the truth of their story, and so sure were they of its importance, that they were willing to risk disbelief and even ridicule.

They remind us of the four lepers of Samaria. They too had made a marvelous discovery. They said:

"We are not doing right. This day is a day of good news; if we keep quiet and wait until morning light, punishment will overtake us. Come on, and let's go and tell the king's household" (II Kings 7:9).

"We've a story to tell to the nations," etc. See the hymn by H. E. Nichol. Also the versification of Psalm 78, containing the words:

> "The wonderful story our fathers made known
> To children succeeding by us must be shown."

And cf. Ps. 107:2; Mark 5:33.

18. And all who heard what the shepherds told them were amazed. This is not surprising. Just think of it: all those wonderful happenings—an imperial decree, angelic messages, divine directions—centering about . . .

---

129. It has that sense unless the prefix διά (in Διέλθωμεν) has lost its force. In that case, however, the simple verb would be more natural.

130. Therefore also the translation "in the nearby fields" (verse 8) is probably not the safest. Better and certainly closer to the original is "in that region" (so also R.S.V.) or "in the same region" (N.A.S.) or "in the same neighborhood" (Williams).

an infant lying in a manger, a child born in a stable! One can never appreciate this unless he is able to agree with the words of the poet:

> Veiled in flesh the Godhead see;
> Hail th'Incarnate Deity.
>
> Charles Wesley, lines in
> "Hark! the Herald Angels Sing"

Now *amazement* is fine, but it should lead to something better; as, for example, in the case of Mary:

19. But Mary continued to treasure up all these things, mulling them over in her mind. Cf. verse 51. Mary was treasuring, carefully storing away, all these things; such things as the following: what an angel had told Joseph, what Gabriel had told her, what her experience had been upon arriving in Bethlehem, what the shepherds had reported with respect to voices of angels, etc. "She was putting them all together in her heart" (thus literally), though in such a case as the present (because of "mulling over") English idiom would probably substitute "mind" for "heart."

Aside from the nativity narrative Scripture tells us little about Mary's development in faith. Nevertheless, such passages as John 2:5; Acts 1:14 show that she became a worshiper of the One to whom, with respect to his human nature, she had given birth. Her prayerful "putting together" of the things she had experienced, seen, and heard, was blessed by God and in course of time produced the result he had determined from eternity. To be sure, on Mary's part there were missteps along the way, but the end was victory.

And as to the shepherds? Their story too ends climactically:

20. Then the shepherds returned, glorifying and praising God for all the things they had heard and seen, (which were) just as had been told them. These men, upon returning, showed that they had not been offended by the low estate of Joseph and Mary. They did not shrink back from acknowledging the child in the manger as being indeed "a Savior, Christ the Lord." In fact, their faith was even strengthened when they reflected on the fact that they had found everything to be exactly as they had been told. Instead of complaining, they were constantly ascribing glory and praise to God.

Time marches on: **21. Now when eight days were completed for circumcising him, he was called Jesus, the name given him by the angel before his conception in the womb.** God had ordained that a son should be circumcised on the eighth day after his birth (Gen. 17:12; Lev. 12:3; cf. Luke 1:59). Therefore when the designated day had arrived the parents saw to it that Jesus received the sign and seal of circumcision.

This is not surprising. Was he not an Israelite; in fact, the one and only perfect Israelite, the one in whom Israel reached its climax? The question will be asked, however, "But does not the need for circumcision or excision symbolize that there was sin to be 'cut away'? Yet, this child was sinless. See

Isa. 53:9b; John 8:46; II Cor. 5:21. Is it not true then that he was exactly the one, the only one, who did not need 'a new heart'?" See Ezek. 36:26; Rom. 2:29.

The answer is: he had entered the world in order to remove the sins of his people. It was *their* guilt that rested on him. It was that sin which had to be removed. See Isa. 53:4-6, 8, 10-12; also N.T.C. on Gal. 3:13. The task of Jesus, as the last Adam, was to keep the law which the first Adam had failed to keep. He came into the world to bear the law's curse, thus delivering his people from it.

Besides, for Jesus too circumcision was, in a sense, a sign and seal of the righteousness of faith (Rom. 4:11). Perfect trust in his heavenly Father, and the obedience which that trust implies, was the pathway to victory for himself as Savior and for those whom the Father had given him, considered as those to be saved. It was thus that he was to accomplish fully the work which the Father had given him to do (John 17:4). In his willingness to submit to circumcision we see the Savior's passive obedience; in his insistence that he be baptized, his active obedience.

Nevertheless, Luke places the emphasis not on circumcision, which is merely implied, but on *the naming of the child.* The two, however, are closely connected. Submission to circumcision was an element in the Savior's required obedience, and without this obedience he could not be truly *Jesus,* that is, *Savior.* For further details on the significance of this name see N.T.C. on Matt. 1:1, 21; Luke 1:31. It was the name given to him by the angel before his conception in the womb. So important was this name that both Joseph (Matt. 1:21) and Mary (Luke 1:31) had been instructed to give it to him.[131]

Practical Lessons Derived from Luke 2:8-21

Verses 8-10

"Great joy." Gaiety, hilarity, festivity, mirth, laughter, in one measure or another these are found in many places throughout the world. But *great joy,* the "joy unspeakable and full of glory" (I Peter 1:8) is the portion of God's children, of them alone. This joy is deeply rooted. It satisfies, lasts, and even keeps on increasing, to God's glory.

Verse 11

"To y o u is born." Not to the emperor, the king, the highpriest, but to humble, devout shepherds. See Isa. 57:15; Matt. 12:20; Luke 4:18.

"A Savior, who is Christ the Lord." Without him, *so* regarded, there is no genuine commemoration of Jesus' birth, no real Christmas.

---

131. Notes on Greek words, phrases, and constructions in 2:8-21 begin on page 160.

Verse 14

"Glory to God ... peace among men of (his) good pleasure." God is always first; man comes next. That order must never be reversed.

Verse 16

"They hurried off and found...." The obedience of faith brings blessed results. Contrast what happens when skepticism asserts itself (Gen. 3:6, 8-21, 24; II Kings 2:15-18; Luke 1:20-22; John 20:24, 25, 29).

Verse 17

"Having seen this, they made known," etc. That is the lesson that has to be learned over and over again. See Matt. 5:14-16; John 15:27a; Acts 4:20. "Tell it out."

Verse 20

"Things... (which were) just as had been told them." The beauty of God's predictions and promises is that they are bound to be *completely* fulfilled.

Verse 21

"...when it was time for them to circumcise him." Not to abolish the law did Jesus come but to fulfil it.

"He was called Jesus." Jesus means Savior. He still bears that same name. For those who trust him this spells hope in every circumstance of life. Reflect on Jean Perry's hymn "That Beautiful Name."

Notes on Greek Words, Phrases, and Constructions in 2:8-21

Verses 8, 9

ἀγραυλοῦντες, nom. pl. masc. pres. participle of ἀγραυλέω*, to live or spend the time in the open fields; from ἀγρός, field, and αὐλή, place or court under the open sky (in one of its meanings); see N.T.C. on Mark 15:16, p. 642, footnote 808.

Note cognate accusatives φυλακάς after the pres. participle φυλάσσοντες, and φόβον after the ingressive aorist ἐφοβήθησαν. This is the kind of style one would expect if Luke is making use of a Semitic original. The plural φυλακάς probably indicates that the watching was by turns.

ἐπέστη, ingressive, aor. active indicative of ἐφίστημι, (suddenly) to stand by, come upon. For more see the note on 10:40 on p. 603.

Verse 10

Μὴ φοβεῖσθε, sec. per. pl. pres. middle imperat. of φοβέω. Either "Do not be afraid" or "Stop being afraid [or: frightened]" will do as a translation.

εὐαγγελίζομαι, I bring y o u good news. Cf. *evangelize.* This verb occurs with great frequency in the Third Gospel, Acts, and Pauline Epistles, once in Matthew (11:5), twice in Hebrews and in Revelation, and three times in I Peter. The noun εὐαγγέλιον occurs in every Pauline epistle except Titus; also in Matthew, Mark, and once each in I Peter and Revelation. As to the writings of Luke, this word does not occur at all in his Gospel; only twice in Acts. For contrary information as to Luke's use of the substantive see A. T. Robertson, *Word Pictures*, Vol. II, p. 24.

For ἐτέχθη see under verses 6, 7.

Verse 12

For Βρέφος, here and in verse 16, see the note on 1:41 on page 99; and for ἐσπαργανωμένον see the note on verse 7 above.

Verse 13

As to grammatical construction, note στρατιᾶς, gen. *sing.* followed by the *plural* present participle αἰνούντων. This, however, is not an error, since "host" or "army" is a collective noun which in Greek here takes a plural verbal form. This plural is "according to sense."

Verse 14

The genitive εὐδοκίας is to be preferred to the nominative εὐδοκία. Reasons: (a) From the point of view of external evidence the genitive has the edge, for the combination of B*ℵ* A W with D and the Old Latin outweighs E F G H, etc., several minuscules, the Syriac, Bohairic, and Georgian versions, Tatian and Eusebius. Besides, since the genitive case is, on the surface, harder to grasp, change to the nominative is understandable. The opposite process—changing from the nominative to the genitive—would be unnatural. Also, it must be borne in mind that Luke is making use of Semitic sources, and that in Hebrew the expression "men of [his, i.e. God's] good will" occurs frequently; see, for example, M. Burrows, *More Light on the Dead Sea Scrolls*, New York, 1958, p. 123.

For an excellent treatment of the question "In Luke 2:14 should we adopt the εὐδοκίας or the εὐδοκία reading?" see B. M. Metzger, *The Text of the New Testament*, Oxford, 1964, pp. 229, 230. For the opposite position see Lenski, *op. cit.*, pp. 85-87.

Verses 15-19

Διέλθωμεν, first per. pl. 2nd aor. subjunctive of διέρχομαι, to go through (to), go over (to). Bethlehem evidently was not next door. Note third per. s. fut. indicat. of the same verb in 2:35.

δή in the present connection probably means *now* or *at once, without delay.*

Note that in verses 15 and 19 the word ῥῆμα (pl. in verse 19) is used in the sense of *thing, matter;* in verse 17 in the sense of *word, message* ("what had been told them"). And see the note on 1:37 on page 93.

ἀνεῦρον, third per. pl. 2nd aor. indicat. of ἀνευρίσκω**, to find (after diligent search).

Verse 16 should be translated in such a fashion that even the listener does not get the impression that the entire family was lying in the manger.

συμβάλλουσα, nom. s. fem. pres. participle of συμβάλλω**, to throw or put together, revolve, ponder, mull (over). See also the note on 14:31 on page 740.

Verses 20, 21

ἐλαλήθη, third per. s. aor. indic. passive of λαλέω. For ἐπλήθησαν see the note on 2:6 on page 147. For συλλημφθῆναι, aor. passive infinitive of συλλαμβάνω, see the note on 1:24 on page 81.

---

22 And when the days for their purification according to the law of Moses had been completed, they [Joseph and Mary] brought him up to Jerusalem to present him to the Lord— 23 as it is written in the law of the Lord, "Every male that opens the womb shall be called holy[132] to the Lord"— 24 and to offer a sacrifice as prescribed in the law of the Lord: "a pair of turtledoves or two young pigeons."

25 And look, in Jerusalem there was a man named Simeon. This man was righteous and devout, waiting for[133] the consolation of Israel; and the Holy Spirit was upon him. 26 And it had been disclosed to him by the Holy Spirit that he would not see death before he had seen the Lord's Christ. 27 Guided by the Spirit[134] he came into the temple. And when the parents brought in the child Jesus to do for him what was customary according to the law, 28 Simeon took him in his arms, blessed God, and said:

29 "Now, Sovereign Master, thou art releasing thy servant,[135]
According to thy word, in peace,
30 Because my eyes have seen thy salvation
31 Which thou hast prepared in the sight of all the peoples,
32 A light for revelation to the Gentiles
And a glory for thy people Israel."

33 The child's father and his mother were amazed about the things that were being said about him. 34 And Simeon blessed them and said to Mary, the child's mother: "Mark well, this child is destined to cause the falling and rising of many in Israel and to be a sign[136] that is spoken against 35 —and a sword will pierce your own soul also—that the deliberations of many hearts[137] may be revealed."

36 There was also a prophetess, Anna, daughter of Phanuel, of the tribe of Asher. She was very old.[138] After her marriage[139] she had lived with her husband seven years, 37 and she had been a widow until she was now eighty-four.[140] She never departed from the temple, but continued to worship night and day with fastings and prayers. 38 Now coming up at that very hour, she was returning thanks to God and speaking about him [Jesus] to all those who were waiting for the redemption of Jerusalem.

---

132. Or: shall be consecrated.
133. Or: looking forward to. So also in verse 38.
134. Or: In the Spirit.
135. Or: thou art permitting thy servant to depart, etc.
136. Or: Mark well, this child is set for the falling and rising of many in Israel and for a sign, etc.
137. Or: minds.
138. Or: very advanced in years (literally: advanced in many days). Cf. 1:7, 18.
139. Literally: from her virginity.
140. Or: and she had now been a widow for no less than eighty-four years.

2:22-38 *The Presentation of Jesus in the Temple:*
Simeon's "Nunc Dimittis"
Anna's Thanksgiving and Testimony

**22-24. And when the days for their purification according to the law of
Moses had been completed, they [Joseph and Mary] brought him up to
Jerusalem to present him to the Lord—as it is written in the law of the
Lord, Every male that opens the womb shall be called holy to the Lord—
and to offer a sacrifice as prescribed in the law of the Lord: a pair of
turtledoves or two young pigeons.**

It is interesting to observe in how many different ways the wisdom of the
Mosaic legislation comes to light. S. E. McMillen, a Christian doctor, in his
book *None of These Diseases,* Westwood, N. J., 1963, has provided several
illustrations. One of them belongs to the general sphere of Purification. He
points out (pp. 15-18) how very, very slow medical science was in admitting
the fact that those who handle patients should have clean hands, and, by
way of contrast, how the scriptural method required not only washing in a
basin but repeated washings in running water, etc. Cf. Lev. 15:13; Num.
19:14-19.

In line with this were also the Mosaic regulations with respect to the
closely related subjects of menstruation and childbirth. As long as the
woman who had given birth was still discharging the ensuing impurities, in
general as long as her normal cycle had not fully returned, she was considered "ceremonially impure," and therefore not permitted to enter the
sanctuary. According to Lev. 12:1-4, after giving birth to a son, it was not
until the fortieth day that the time of her purification was completed.[141]
Then by means of offerings she was restored to full communion with the
worshiping multitude.

That fortieth day having arrived, Joseph and Mary go up to Jerusalem
from Bethlehem. Note "up to," even though on the average the altitude of
Jerusalem is somewhat lower than that of Bethlehem. But *God's house* (see
2:49) stood in Jerusalem. Hence "up to" is understandable.

For *their* purification! This has been explained in two ways: (a) Joseph too
was unclean, through contact with Mary (Plummer, *op. cit.,* p. 63); (b) as
head of the family Joseph had to provide the sacrifice and see to it that the
law was carried out (Lenski, *op. cit.,* p. 90). The second theory has in its
favor that the sacrifice which was brought was clearly for *one* person (Lev.
12:8), in the present case for Mary (Luke 2:24b).

In verses 22-24 mention is made not only of the mother's *purification* but
also of the child's *presentation.* The purification ended with a sacrifice (verse

---

141. I have not been able to find a satisfactory explanation of the rule that after the birth of a
girl the mother had to wait until the eightieth day. For strange theories see S.BK., Vol. II, p.
119.

24). The presentation, to which verses 22 and 25 f. refer, included *redemption*, the payment of a ransom fee.

On this fortieth day the Redeemer was himself redeemed! Strange as it may sound, the statement is true. Of course, he was not redeemed in the sense in which he was going to redeem his people, for he was, is, and ever will remain sinless, in fact the Fountain of all virtue. Yet, being his mother's firstborn son (Luke 2:7), and belonging to the tribe not of Levi but of Judah, he had to be exempted from official temple service by the payment of five shekels of silver (Exod. 13:1, 2, 11-15; Num. 3:11-13, 41, 44, 45, 47-51; 18:16).

If the shekel is considered the equivalent of $0.64, the redemption price would amount to $3.20 or (at the exchange rate when this was written) £1.40. This may not seem much, but at that particular time how many days would an ordinary laborer have to work to earn it? See N.T.C. on Matthew, p. 301, footnote 290.

The underlying idea of the redemption ritual was this: in the night of Israel's deliverance from "the house of bondage" all firstborn Egyptians were slain (Exod. 12:29). However, in God's holy sight not only the Egyptians but also the Israelites had forfeited their lives. In place of death God was willing to accept from the tribe of Levi lifelong service in the tabernacle or (later) temple, and from the firstborn of the other tribes five shekels, as a symbolic offering, a confession, as it were.

Jesus too was under the sentence of death. He was born "under the law" (Gal. 4:4), and this in the sense not only of being under personal obligation to keep the law but also of being duty-bound—with a duty to which he voluntarily obligated himself—*vicariously* to bear the law's penalty and to satisfy its demand of perfect obedience.

He had no personal guilt but had of his own free will taken upon himself the sin of the world (Isa. 53:4-6; John 1:29). Was the redemption fee paid at this time a symbol of the infinitely greater ransom to which the Savior was going to refer in saying, "The Son of man did not come to be served but to serve and to give his life a ransom for many" (Matt. 20:28; Mark 10:45)?

It was in connection with the payment of the redemption fee that Joseph and Mary publicly consecrated their child to God, as Samuel had once been similarly dedicated (I Sam. 1:11, 28).

On this same visit to the temple Joseph and Mary brought the purification sacrifice.

According to Lev. 12:6 f. this had to be "a lamb a year old for a burnt-offering, and a young pigeon or a turtledove for a sin-offering." However, that same law went on to stipulate, "If she cannot afford a lamb, then she shall take two turtledoves or two young pigeons, one for a burnt-offering and the other for a sin-offering" (verse 8). It was this poor person's offering that was brought in the present case.

From this it would be wrong to draw the conclusion that Joseph and

Mary were desperately poor. After all, Joseph was a carpenter. He must have had money to pay the redemption fee. On the way from Nazareth to Bethlehem he must also have been able to pay lodging fees and to defray other expenses. Besides, for forty days the little family had now been living in or near Bethlehem. Whether during this period Joseph found employment and earned wages we do not know. One fact is clear: the means at his disposal were insufficient to warrant purchase of the more expensive offering (lamb plus bird).

If by reason of the season of the year turtledoves were unavailable—being migratory birds they could be purchased only from spring to fall—there were always plenty of pigeons. One could purchase two birds for less than a tenth of the amount demanded for a lamb plus a bird.

25, 26. And look, in Jerusalem there was a man named Simeon. This man was righteous and devout, waiting for the consolation of Israel; and the Holy Spirit was upon him. And it had been disclosed to him by the Holy Spirit that he would not see death before he had seen the Lord's Christ.

Little is known about Simeon. The passage does not state that he was invested with any particular office; for example, that of priest. He was apparently what we today would call a "layman."

The church needs laymen as well as clergymen. Not only Moses and Joshua occupy an important place in the affairs of God's kingdom but so do Eldad and Medad (Num. 11:26-29).

Especially *such* laymen! Simeon is described as being *righteous*. So was Mary's husband Joseph (Matt. 1:19); so was Mary herself, and so were Zechariah and Elizabeth (Luke 1:6). And do not forget Joseph of Arimathea (23:50).

Simeon was "righteous *and devout*." For other instances of devout men see Acts 2:5; 8:2; 22:12. With utmost circumspection such men *take hold* of the duties God has assigned to them. They are conscientious in their planning, aiming always to advance their own and their neighbors' welfare, to the glory of God. The combination "righteous and devout" may well indicate that Simeon conducted himself in such a manner that his behavior both with respect to men (he was righteous) and God (he was devout) was the object of God's approval.

This man "was waiting for the consolation of Israel." To be sure, conditions were bad, very bad, in Israel at the time of Jesus' birth in Bethlehem. Think of loss of political independence, cruel King Herod, externalization of religion, legalistic scribes and Pharisees and their many followers, worldly-minded Sadducees, the silence of the voice of prophecy, etc. But in the midst of all this darkness, degradation, and despair there were men who were hopefully looking forward to, and earnestly expecting, "the consolation of Israel." There were such men . . . and *women* too! Already mentioned were Mary and Elizabeth. In a moment (see verses 36-38) Luke is going to add Anna to the list. That this group of devout men and women was considerable appears from the phrase "*all* those who were waiting for the redemption of Jerusalem" (2:38).

That these men and women were indeed justified in this hope is clear from prophecy. As an example study the many prophecies of Isaiah in which such blessings as comfort, peace, and joy are promised, and are associated with the Messianic Age (Isa. 7:14; 9:1-7; 11:1-10; 40:1-11; 49:8-13; 51:1-6, 12-16; 52:13—55:13; 60:1-3; ch. 61; 66:13).

Simeon had been endowed with a very rare and special blessing. In some manner, even now before Pentecost, the Holy Spirit rested abidingly upon him. He was being constantly influenced by that Spirit.

That same Comforter had revealed to him that he would not die before he had seen the Lord's Christ. For further light on the expression *the Lord's Christ* see Ps. 2:2; 45:7; 110:1; Isa. 61:1; Luke 4:18.

Some interpreters make a special point of emphasizing that this revelation does *not necessarily* mean that Simeon was an old man when the infant Jesus was being carried into the temple. That point must be granted. Nevertheless, are those commentators[142] entirely wrong who picture him as being an old man? Is it not rather natural to think of old age when we read such statements as, "It had been disclosed to him that he would not see death until" and "Now, Sovereign Master, thou art permitting thy servant to depart in peace," etc.? Was not Jacob also "an old man" when, speaking in similar vein, he said: "It is enough; Joseph my son is still alive; I will go and see him before I die" (Gen. 45:28)? Jacob was 130 years of age when he said this. He died at the age of 147 (Gen. 47:9, 28). I do not hesitate to picture Simeon as an old man, even though I admit that absolute proof for this position is lacking.

27-32. Guided by the Spirit he came into the temple. And when the parents brought in the child Jesus to do for him what was customary according to the law, Simeon took him in his arms, blessed God, and said:

Now, Sovereign Master, thou art releasing thy servant,
According to thy word, in peace,
Because my eyes have seen thy salvation
Which thou hast prepared in the sight of all the peoples,
A light for revelation to the Gentiles
And a glory for thy people Israel.

Note the following:

a. Literally the text reads, "In the Spirit he came into the temple." This "in the Spirit" is the same phrase that occurs in the Apocalypse (1:10; 4:2; 17:3; 21:10). In that book it indicates that the seer's soul seems for the moment to have been liberated from the shackles of time and space. In a high state of ecstasy it is, as it were, alone...with God.[143] Here in Luke, however, the meaning is slightly different. Simeon is thoroughly conscious

---

142. For example, S. Greijdanus, *Korte Verklaring*, p. 72.
143. For more on this see the author's book *More Than Conquerors*, Grand Rapids, 22nd edition, 1977.

of his surroundings. His soul is, however, flooded with thoughts of thanksgiving and praise. Moreover, he is—and is conscious of being—guided by the Spirit. The Spirit has taken care that at the precise moment when Joseph and Mary were walking into the temple, carrying the baby Jesus, to do for him what was customary according to the law (as has already been explained), Simeon also walked in.

b. "The *parents* brought in the child." This is no denial of the virgin birth (1:34, 35). In the legal sense Joseph and Mary were Jesus' parents. See also 2:48, "Your father and I."

c. "Simeon took him in his arms." Simeon did what Jesus himself was going to do later on (Mark 9:36; 10:16).

d. "He blessed God." When the Holy Spirit made clear to him that this very child was the Messiah, Simeon's heart was surcharged with gratitude to such an extent that before his Father's throne he poured out his ardent thanksgiving. As is clear from his *Nunc Dimittis,* he thanked God for what this child meant to him personally and for what it meant to the world of both Gentile and Jew.

e. Simeon's "Song" is the last of the five mentioned on p. 95. It is a hymn of Joyful Resignation.

f. The word *now* ("Now...thou art releasing") is not the weak transitional "now." It is definitely an adverb of time. What Simeon means is that he is *now* ready to die, since God is releasing him in peace, as he had promised to do. Simeon is holding in his arms and seeing with his eyes not just a little baby but "salvation," that is, the One through whom God would save his people. Since Simeon is a willing "servant," who joyfully acknowledges God's absolute right over him, he addresses God as "Sovereign Master." For other explanations see the footnote.[144] See also the note on verse 29 on page 176.

g. With reference to "thy salvation" Simeon continues:

---

144. Lenski (*op. cit.,* pp. 94, 95) rejects the idea that Simeon's "thou art releasing" has reference to death. My answer is that the expression *according to thy word* connects God's promise, namely, that Simeon would not *die* until he had seen the Lord's Christ, with Simeon's words of resignation.

A very popular view is the one according to which the noun *despotēs* (vocative *despota*) here (as well as in the Pastoral Epistles) indicates slave-master, and that *doulos* (accusative *doulon*) here (as well as in I Tim. 6:1 f.; Titus 2:9) means *slave.* The sense of the passage—at least the underlying figure—would then be, "Now, O *slave-master,* grant manumission, at least dismissal from further duty, to thy *slave.*" See E. E. Ellis, *op. cit.,* p. 82; Lenski, p. 94; Plummer, p. 68; Robertson, *Word Pictures,* p. 28, etc.

On the other hand, Danker, *op. cit.,* p. 32, aptly states that Simeon loves God, his Master, and would not seek manumission on any terms. Worthwhile also are Godet's remarks, Vol. I, p. 128. He writes that Simeon, by using the word *release* is asking to be relieved from his earthly duty and from the burden of life. Simeon is, as it were, a sentinel whom his master has placed in an elevated position and has charged to look for the appearance of a star. When that star appears Simeon must announce its appearance to the world. He sees it, proclaims its rising, and now asks to be relieved from the post he has occupied so long.

The idea of seeing in Jesus the expected "star" or "the Rising Sun" may find some support in Luke 1:78.

> Which thou hast prepared in the sight of all the peoples,
> A light for revelation to the Gentiles
> And a glory for thy people Israel.

There is nothing narrow about Simeon. He loudly proclaims the significance of Jesus not only for Israel but also for the Gentiles, the world outside of Israel. This is in line with such passages as Isa. 42:6, 7; Mic. 1:15; Matt. 28:19; John 3:16; 4:42; 10:11, 14, 16; Acts 13:47; Eph. 2:13, 14; Col. 1:27; Rev. 7:9–17.

The concept *thy salvation* is here defined as "light" and "glory." For the Gentiles salvation is *light:* the true knowledge of God, holiness and love, joy as never before experienced. Of course, it is also light for Israel, but the term is especially appropriate when applied to the Gentiles because their darkness was deepest.

For Israel salvation is *glory*. It is glory also for the Gentiles, but no one who knows his Bible will fail to understand why this description specifically suits Israel. It is with Israel that we associate the Shekinah, i.e., the "cloud" of light, a manifestation of Jehovah's presence (Exod. 40:34, 35; cf. I Sam. 4:21, 22). God had blessed Israel above all the nations (Ps. 147:19, 20; Amos 3:2a; Rom. 3:1, 2). Nevertheless, when we associate "glory" with Israel we are reminded especially of this unprecedented honor bestowed upon it, namely, that God chose it for the purpose of spreading the true religion among the nations of the world (Isa. 49:6; 60:1–3; Zech. 8:20–23). Even more specifically, that he selected it to bring forth the Christ according to his human nature (Rom. 9:5). And Christ is "the Light of the world" (John 8:12). *That,* more than anything else, was Israel's glory. It was because of this that Zion could be addressed as follows, "Thou shalt also be a crown of beauty in the hand of Jehovah, and a royal diadem in the hand of thy God" (Isa. 62:3; see context, verses 2, 12, and 60:3).

We have now finished consideration of the five "Hymns" that center about the birth of Christ. Nothing could excel the doxology of the angels. The glory of God is the chief end not only of men but also of the heavenly hosts. Omitting any further reference to that anthem of adoration, we are left with the series: Elizabeth's Song of Love, Mary's Song of Faith, Zechariah's Song of Hope, and Simeon's Song of Resignation; that is, of Joyful Self-Surrender.

These four form a kind of climax,[145] as follows:

Elizabeth's hymn centers about Mary. We would do her an injustice if we did not immediately add that she calls Mary "the mother of my Lord," and the one the fruit of whose womb is "blessed." But she begins with Mary (1:42) and ends with Mary (1:45). She breathes love.

---

145. So also H. Burton, *The Gospel According to St. Luke (The Expositor's Bible)*, Grand Rapids, 1943, Vol. V, pp. 16–18.

Mary reaches farther. She confesses her faith by magnifying Jehovah for his power, holiness, and mercy. She views him as *Israel's Helper* in time of need.

Zechariah is even more specific, approaches even more closely to the theme of Christmas. He speaks not only about "the Lord, the God of Israel," but with firmly entrenched hope looks forward and sees "the Horn of David," "the Rising Sun," that is, the Messiah.

Most world-embracing of all is Simeon. In lines filled with humble recognition of God's absolute sovereignty, with trustful resignation, and with the tenderness of heart with which he is holding the baby Jesus in his arms, he yields himself to the God who, in fulfilment of his promise, has allowed him to live long enough to be able to see the Messiah, and in him the realization of the plan of redemption for the world:

> A light for revelation to the Gentiles
> And a glory for thy people Israel.

Now Simeon has found peace. *Now* he is ready to depart from this life.

33-35. The child's father and his mother were amazed about the things that were being said about him. And Simeon blessed them and said to Mary, the child's mother: Mark well, this child is destined to cause the falling and rising of many in Israel, and to be a sign that is spoken against—and a sword will pierce your own soul also—that the deliberations of many hearts may be revealed.

What was it that amazed Joseph and Mary? Was it what some wish to call Simeon's clairvoyance, but can be more fittingly described as his Spirit-wrought profound insight into the future? The answer is that it was not Simeon himself but rather what Simeon said about the child that amazed them.

This is understandable. It is true that Gabriel too had said some wonderful things about the child (1:31-33), and so had the shepherds, in reporting to Joseph and Mary what an angel, and immediately afterward a host of angels, had proclaimed (2:8-14). But these earlier messages did not include anything specific about the significance of this child for both the Gentiles and Israel. Besides, the relevations which Joseph and Mary received about their child were all so wonderful that even a measure of repetition would not have curtailed their amazement. Even today Jesus Christ is so altogether marvelous and the salvation he has provided so bountiful that we love the song:

> Sing them *over again* to me,
> Wonderful words of life.
>
> P. B. Bliss

Simeon now invoked God's blessing on Joseph and Mary. Having done this, he addressed to Mary words that must have startled her. In substance he told her that her child would become the great divider; not, however, that events would simply turn out that way, but that in God's plan it had been so decided. Literally what he said was, "Mark well, this child is set for the falling and rising of many in Israel. . . ." In other words a person's relation or attitude toward Jesus would be absolutely decisive of his eternal destiny. Some would reject him; others would by sovereign grace accept him. The former would *fall;* that is, they would (unless they repented) be excluded from the kingdom. The latter would *rise;* that is, they would be welcomed to the kingdom and its wedding feast. See Luke 13:28, 29.

There is also another interpretation. According to it Simeon is speaking about *one* group: first the people belonging to this group fall, then they rise.

However, far more in line with two contrasting groups is what we read elsewhere not only in the nativity account—for example, in Mary's own Magnificat (1:50–53, note the contrasts)—but also in other parts of the Gospels. In Luke see also 6:20–23; 13:28, 29; 16:25; 18:9–14. With this can be compared the lengthy series of contrasts in Matthew: 7:24–27; 10:32, 33, 39; 11:25, 26; 13:11, 12; 18:5, 6; 21:28–32; 24:45–51; 25:1–13, 31–46. And to add one example from John's Gospel, see 3:18.

Not to be overlooked is the phrase *in Israel.* Even in Israel, in spite of all its advantages, there would be this sharp division between those who reject Jesus, the vast majority (John 1:11; 6:66), and those who welcome and embrace him (1:12, 13).

The child would be a "sign."[146] This means that he would point away from himself to his Sender, whose image he would reflect and whose works he would perform. In claiming this close relationship to his heavenly Father he would be "spoken against" or contradicted. That this is what actually happened is clear from Luke 4:28, 29; John 6:41, 52; 8:13, 31–59, to cite but a few references.

By means of their attitude to Jesus men would be constantly revealing the thoughts or deliberations of their hearts. They would show whether they were "for" or "against" him. Neutrality would be forever impossible (Luke 11:23; cf. Matt. 12:30).

In a parenthesis Simeon, in addressing Mary, states that a sword would pierce her soul; in fact, as the original indicates, a large and broad sword, the symbol of intense pain, of frightful and piercing anguish. For the fulfilment see John 19:25–27.

In this connection we are reminded of the poetic lines:

> Stabat mater dolorosa
> juxta crucem lacrimosa.

The English translation of these and the immediately following lines is:

---

146. See F. Stagg, "σημεῖον in the Fourth Gospel," unpublished dissertation submitted to the Faculty of Southern Baptist Theological Seminary, Louisville, Kentucky, 1943.

At the cross her station keeping
Stood the mournful mother weeping,
  Close to Jesus to the last;
Through her heart, his sorrow sharing,
All his bitter anguish bearing,
  Now at length the sword had passed.

The hymn might have been helpful, were it not for the fact that—aside from the questionable "to the last"—the doctrine here displayed is far from pure. Mary did not bear or share, and could not have borne or shared, *all* Christ's bitter anguish.

What Simeon said was true. But he did not see everything. He did not see that even in the midst of Mary's sorrow she would receive a measure of comfort. At the suggestion of the crucified Savior the disciple whom Jesus loved would take her to his home. Is it not possible that the very memory of Simeon's prophecy strengthened Mary in the moments of her deepest agony, proving to her that this too was included in God's plan and would therefore work together for good? Best of all, because of the resurrection on the third day Mary's sorrow would subsequently be changed to rejoicing and strengthening of faith.

If Simeon was remarkable, so by God's grace was Anna: **36–38. There was also a prophetess, Anna, daughter of Phanuel, of the tribe of Asher. She was very old. After her marriage she had lived with her husband seven years, and she had been a widow until she was now eighty-four. She never departed from the temple, but continued to worship night and day with fastings and prayers. Now coming up at that very hour, she was returning thanks to God and speaking about him [Jesus] to all those who were waiting for the redemption of Jerusalem.**

Anna
1. *Who was she?*

Her name means *Grace*. She was a widow, a daughter of *Phanuel*. This is the Greek transliteration of the more familiar Hebrew name *Penuel*, also spelled *Peniel*. It will be recalled that Jacob, returning to his homeland, was left alone at the river Jabbok. There he wrestled with the Angel, and his name was changed to Israel. In that connection we read, "And Jacob named that place Peniel; for (said he) 'I have seen God face to face, yet my life is preserved'" (Gen. 32:30).

Anna belonged to the tribe of Asher. Asher was the second son of Leah's handmaid Zilpah. He was named *Asher* (= *Happy*) because his birth made Leah happy. He was Jacob's eighth son. See Gen. 29:31—30:24; 35:16-20, 22-26 for the list of Jacob's children.

More important in the present connection are these two facts: (a) The very presence of a member of the tribe of Asher, a member who is living in Jerusalem, shows that the so-called "Lost Tribes" were not completely lost.

171

(b) The fact that Luke knows to which tribe Anna belongs indicates that the Jews were keeping their family registers or genealogies up to date. The reasons for this have been indicated in N.T.C. on Matthew, pp. 106, 107.

Anna was a prophetess. For many years the voice of prophecy had been silent. Now here suddenly there is this *prophetess!* She reminds us of the evangelist Philip's four unmarried daughters on whom similarly the gift of prophecy was going to be bestowed (Acts 21:9). A true prophet or prophetess is one who, having received revelations of the mind and will of God, declares to others what has been thus received. See Deut. 18:18. The apostle Paul regarded the gift of prophecy as being highly important (I Cor. 14:1).

2. *How old was she?*

She was indeed "very old"; literally "advanced in many days," or, as we might say, "very advanced in years." She had married, and had lived with her husband seven years. Up to this point there is no disagreement among commentators. What immediately follows, in verse 37a, is obscure, open to two interpretations. Literally the clause reads: "and she a widow up to eighty-four years." This can mean either:

a. "She had now been a widow for eighty-four years"

or

b. "She had now reached the age of eighty-four."

Which of these two theories is correct? Theory (a) is burdened with the consideration that if true this prophetess must have been a very, very old woman indeed. Even if she had been only 14 when she married—which is possible, for Jewish girls often married young—then she would now be (14+7+84=) 105 years of age! Theory (b) represents her as being now a woman of 84. As some see it, that is not "very old"; nevertheless Luke states that she was at this time "very old."[147]

For a good defense of theory (a) see Lenski, p. 99; Danker, p. 36; Greijdanus, *Korte Verklaring,* pp. 76, 77.

The arguments that have been advanced in favor of (a) are:

First of all, 84 years is not very old; 105 is indeed.

Secondly, Luke presents an addition: an indefinite number of years before Anna's marriage plus 7 years of marriage plus 84 years of widowhood. He places great emphasis on Anna's very advanced age.

Thirdly (Danker's argument): Luke may have been thinking of the parallel case of Judith; see the apocryphal book Judith 16:23.

---

147. Some commentators skip the entire problem. Some go in both directions; cf. A. T. Robertson, *Word Pictures,* Vol. II, p. 30, quoting Montefiore (106 years) without a word of dissent, with A. T. Robertson, *Translation,* pp. 24, 151 (84 years). Among those who give her age as 84 are A.V., N.A.S., Beck, R.S.V., Phillips, Jerusalem Bible. Among those who accept the opposite view are Lenski, Danker, Greijdanus, Stöger, Good News for Modern Man, The Living Bible. In several instances one view is presented without indication that the other is also possible. Among those who acknowledge that either theory may be correct are Plummer and N.E.B.

For a defense of theory (b) see E. J. Goodspeed, *Problems of New Testament Translation,* Chicago, 1945, pp. 74–81.

Brief summary of arguments that can be advanced in favor of (b):

First, in the light of Ps. 90:10 eighty-four years can indeed be called "very old."

Secondly, Luke's age-description is not at all necessarily an addition.

Thirdly, in the use of sources, as well as in composing, Luke was being guided by the Holy Spirit. There is no evidence whatever that he was being influenced by a book (Judith) filled with the most ridiculous and unhistorical nonsense.[148]

Conclusion: either view is certainly possible, though I, for one, favor theory (b). To the arguments already summarized I would add this one: not only is Anna described as being very old, she is also pictured as being still very active (verses 37, 38), which is more likely to have been the case at 84 than at 105.

3. *What kind of woman was she?*

"She never departed from the temple," etc. Unless Anna actually occupied quarters in the temple, so that she lived there, which is not impossible, this expression must be regarded as hyperbole. The meaning then would simply be: she attended very regularly, being present at both the public and the more private services. Even today when a person not only attends the services on Sunday but also the various "doings" in the church during the days of the week, he will at times be heard to say, "I live there." He is not afraid that anyone will take this literally.

"(She continued to worship) ... with fastings and prayers." This marks her as a woman who did not think highly of herself, was concerned about others, about God's kingdom, Israel's hope, etc., and remembered all these matters in prayer. On the general subject of fasting see N.T.C. on Matthew, pp. 340–343; and on prayer pp. 321–324.

4. *What was her attitude to Jesus?*

She was "coming up at that very hour" (or "moment"). We may picture her as being in one of the courts of the temple, perhaps "the court of women," when she sees Joseph and Mary with the infant Jesus. She carefully observes Simeon as he takes the baby into his arms. She listens to the words of his *Nunc Dimittis.* She distinctly hears every word for she has now "come up" and joined the little family. She is convinced that this child is indeed the Messiah.

Filled with gratitude she immediately returns thanks to God. Her prayer finished, she begins to speak to all like-minded people. Afterward this became a habit with her. She would speak to all who, being one in spirit

---

148. On Judith see B. M. Metzger, *An Introduction to the Apocrypha,* New York-Oxford, 1957, pp. 43–53.

with herself, were similarly looking forward to and eagerly expecting "Jerusalem's redemption," that is, "Israel's consolation" (see on verse 25), its deliverance from sin through the Savior, namely, Jesus. See above, on 1:68.

In view of the fact that the Gospels on ever so many pages are describing the wickedness and hardness of heart of Pharisees, scribes, and their many followers, it is certainly refreshing to know that, as it was in the days of Elijah (I Kings 19:18) and would be in the days of Paul (Rom. 11:5), so also now, in the days of the infant Jesus, there was "a remnant according to God's gracious election." Thus it will ever be.[149]

Practical Lessons Derived from Luke 2:22–38

Verses 22–24

"They brought him up to Jerusalem to present him to the Lord." It is the solemn duty and blessed privilege of parents to dedicate their children to the Lord.

Verse 25

"Waiting for the consolation of Israel." Evidently Simeon took prophecy seriously. Do we?

Verse 27

"Guided by the Spirit he came into the temple." If both preacher and parishioner entered the house of God thus equipped, would not blessings overflow? Cf. Eccles. 5:1.

Verse 29

"Sovereign Master." When God's sovereignty is recognized in every sphere there is consolation for life and death.

Verse 30

"My eyes have seen thy salvation." Simeon held in his arms and was looking at a baby...and saw in him *salvation*. Jesus looked at unstable Simon and saw a *Rock* (John 1:42). Jesus reflected on his approaching cross and saw *triumph* (John 12:32; 16:33b). Faith means vision...and victory!

Verses 30, 31

"Thy salvation... which thou hast prepared." Salvation is not a human achievement but a divine gift. Cf. Eph. 2:8.

---

149. Notes on Greek words, phrases, and constructions in 2:22–38 begin on page 175.

Verse 34

"This child is set for the falling and rising of many. . . ." Jesus is history's watershed, its dividing ridge: our relation to him is decisive for woe or weal, for bane or blessing.

Verses 36–38

"She was very old." There is work to do even for those who are far along in years. Anna spent her time in prayer, praise, and proclamation. What a blessed way to spend one's "declining" (?) years.

Notes on Greek Words, Phrases, and Constructions in 2:22–38

Verse 22

παραστῆναι, aor. infinitive of παρίστημι, to place beside; here: to present.

Verse 23

μήτρα, womb, should immediately remind one of μήτηρ, mother. Note similar resemblances between "mother" and "womb" in related languages: mater, matrix; mère, matrice; madre, matriz; mother, matrix; Mutter, Mutterleib; moeder, baar-moeder; etc.

Verse 24

εἰρημένον, (as) said, prescribed; acc. n. perfect passive participle of ἐρῶ. Cf. λέγω, ἐρῶ, εἶπον, εἴρηκα, etc. Cf. *rhetoric.*
ζεῦγος*, pair; in 14:19 yoke. Cf. *join.*
τρυγών*, turtledove.
νοσσός*, young. Cf. *new.*

Verse 25

εὐλαβής**, also in Acts 2:5; 8:2; 22:12; basically: taking hold of well; hence devout, pious.
προσδεχόμενος, pres. participle of προσδέχομαι, to wait for, look forward to; see also verse 38 and 12:36; 23:51; in 15:2 to welcome.
πνεῦμα ἦν ἅγιον. Because of the rather unexpected position of ἦν between πνεῦμα and ἅγιον some favor the rendering "an influence which was holy" or something similar. It is clear, however, from the following verse that Luke refers to the Holy Spirit. The omission of the articles in verse 25 may, however, place the emphasis on the *operation* of that Spirit, being indeed altogether *holy* in nature. For the rest, since "Holy Spirit" is a proper name, the term can be definite even without the use of articles. With Robertson and most translators and interpreters I, too, accept the rendering "the Holy Spirit" for verse 25. Cf. 1:15, 35, 41, 67.

Verse 26

ἦν κεχρηματισμένον, periphrastic pluperf. passive indicat. of χρηματίζω, to impart a revelation; in the passive: to receive a revelation or disclosure; to have something revealed to one; perhaps related to χρησμός, oracle. Here, as in classical Greek, πρίν is followed by aor. subjunctive ἂν ἴδῃ, before he would see; or: before he had seen.

Verse 27

εἰθισμένον, perf. passive participle of ἐθίζω*, to accustom; hence here: according to the custom of (i.e., as required by) τοῦ νόμου, the law. Cf. *ethics*.

Verse 28

ἀγκάλας, acc. pl. of ἀγκάλη*, arm (that is bent—hence, is at an angle—to receive something or someone). Cf. *angle*. See N.T.C. on Mark, p. 359, footnote 426; p. 384, footnote 461.

Verse 29

ἀπολύεις, sec. per. s. pres. active indicat. of ἀπολύω. The basic meaning of this verb is: to let go, to release. This meaning develops as follows:

a. to release a prisoner (Matt. 27:15-26),
b. to release a debtor, wiping out his debt (Matt. 18:27),
c. to forgive, pardon (Luke 6:37),
d. to dismiss a crowd (Luke 9:12), a person (Luke 8:38),
e. to divorce a marriage partner (Mark 10:2, 4),
f. to discharge a person from his earthly post, to let him depart in death. In this sense the verb occurs on gravestones; so also here in Simeon's *Nunc Dimittis*. And see also Num. 20:29 (LXX).

Verse 30

There is little, if any, distinction between τὸ σωτήριον and σωτηρία. Both indicate *salvation*, as is clear also from Luke 3:6; Acts 28:28; Eph. 6:17.

Verse 32

The concepts φῶς and δόξαν are in apposition with "salvation." On δόξα see N.T.C. on Philippians, pp. 62, 63, footnote 43.

Verse 34

κεῖται, third per. s. pres. passive indicat. of κεῖμαι, with sense of the perfect: to have been set, laid, or solemnly appointed.

πτῶσις, fall, falling; cf. πίπτω, to fall. In Matt. 7:27 the noun means: fall, collapse, crash.

ἀνάστασις, rise, rising, resurrection; for example, of Jesus from the dead (Rom. 1:4); of people: (a) of their souls (Rev. 20:4-6; cf. John 5:25); (b) of their bodies (John 11:24; cf. John 5:28, 29; Rev. 20:12-14).

Verse 35

ῥομφαία, the large and broad sword, here used in the figurative sense of piercing anguish of heart. In Rev. 6:4, 8 note contrast between μάχαιρα and ῥομφαία.

ἀποκαλυφθῶσι (preceded by ὅπως ἄν), third per. pl. aor. subjunct. passive (indicating purpose) of ἀποκαλύπτω, to reveal. Cf. *Apocalypse.*

διαλογισμός, deliberation, devising, thought, opinion, scheme. For more on this word see N.T.C. on Mark, pp. 282-289.

Verses 36-38

προφῆτις, a prophetess, as was "Jezebel" (Rev. 2:20), the only occurrences of this word in the New Testament; but that other prophetess was as godless as Anna was godly.

προβεβηκυῖα, as in 1:18; see the note on 1:7 on page 79.

παρθενία*, virginity.

ὀγδοήκοντα*, eighty; here and in 16:7.

ἀφίστατο, third per. s. imperf. middle indicat. of ἀφίστημι, to depart.

νηστεία, fast, fasting. Cf. νηστεύω, to fast; derived from the negative prefix νη- and ἐσθίω; hence, not to eat; and so, to fast.

ἀνθωμολογεῖτο, imperfect: was returning thanks, or: began to return thanks; from ἀνθομολογέομαι*. See my dissertation *The Meaning of the Preposition ἀντί in the New Testament*, pp. 82, 83. In this case the prefix ἀντί has been explained in three different ways: Anna was giving thanks: (a) *in return for* blessings received; (b) *in turn*, taking her turn as soon as Simeon was silent; or (c) in open *response;* hence publicly. Perhaps (a) is the best. Basically is not all thanksgiving making a return— and thus providing a substitute—for blessings received?

As to the base ὁμολογέω, by what process this verb, with root meaning *to say the same thing*, may have developed into various shades of meaning, including *to praise, give thanks* (to), has been indicated in N.T.C. on Matthew, pp. 497, 498, footnote 477.

Note also the fem. s. aor. participles ζήσασα (from ζάω) and ἐπιστᾶσα (from ἐφίστημι; see 2:9), and the present participle λατρεύουσα (from λατρεύω). For a discussion of the opening words of verse 37: "and she a widow up to eighty-four years" see the commentary.

---

39 And when they had accomplished everything required by the law of the Lord, they returned to Galilee, to their own town Nazareth.   40 And the child continued to grow and to become strong, being filled (day by day) with wisdom; and the favor of God was upon him.

2:39, 40 *The Return to Nazareth*
For Verse 39 cf. Matt. 2:19-23

39. And when they had accomplished everything required by the law of the Lord, they returned to Galilee, to their own town Nazareth.

Again, as in verses 22, 23, 24, 27, Luke stresses the fact that the conduct of Joseph and Mary was in harmony with God's law. Having accomplished everything required by the law they returned to Galilee. The evangelist does not say that after the events of the fortieth day the little family *immediately* made for the north. Room is left for Matthew's account of the coming of the wise men, the flight to Egypt, the slaughter of "the innocents," and the return of Joseph, Mary, and their child from Egypt; in other words, for the events reported in Matt. 2:1–21. At 2:22, 23 Matthew and Luke (2:39) are together again, with this difference, that Matthew states the reasons why the family did not settle in Judea but returned to Nazareth.

The question occurs, therefore, "How is it that Luke omits the material found in Matt. 2:1–21, particularly the visit of the wise men from the east and the temporary residence of Joseph, Mary, and Jesus in Egypt?"

Some are of the opinion that Luke omits it because he did not know about it. They argue that had he known about the magi he would have included their story in his book, for it would have harmonized beautifully with his emphasis on the universality of the gospel.[150]

According to others it is impossible to determine whether or not Luke knew anything about the incidents reported in Matt. 2:1–21.

But in this particular case it is probably unnecessary to give up so easily. One author[151] may well be pointing in the right direction when he states that Luke omitted this material because the plan for his book did not require its inclusion.

Probably we can go beyond this. While it must be admitted that certainty is impossible, there is a solution which at least merits careful consideration and may well be the right one. At the outset it should be stressed that the theory according to which Luke was, or may have been, totally ignorant about the visit of the wise men and about the flight into Egypt is very difficult to maintain. As appears clearly from such passages as Luke 2:19, 51—and see *Introduction,* Point III B 6—there must have been very close contact between Luke and Mary. Luke received information either directly from her mouth or else from the mouth of those close to her. Also the horrible massacre of Bethlehem's infants cannot have remained hidden. Luke must have heard about it.

Why, then, did he not include this material? The key to what may well be the solution has already been indicated: the inclusion of this material did not harmonize with his plan; that is, his plan for Luke-Acts.

It is true that in Luke's Gospel God's love even for Gentiles and Samaritans is clearly revealed and even emphasized. See p. 43. But this does not cancel another fact, namely, that to a very large extent the beloved physician reserved for inclusion in the book of Acts the narrative of the extension of God's kingdom among the Gentiles. In his "orderly account" (1:3) the *Gospel* describes Jesus' ministry in the land of the Jews, *Acts* his ministry (through the work of witnesses, but nevertheless *his* ministry, Acts 1:1) in and from Jerusalem into Samaria and to the ends of the earth (Acts 1:8b).

Was Jesus ever outside the land of the Jews? Matthew and Mark clearly answer "Yes." He was in Egypt (Matt. 2:13–15), in Syrophoenicia (Matt.

---

150. Plummer, *op. cit.*, p. 73.

151. S. Greijdanus, *Korte Verklaring*, p. 78. For a more detailed and excellent discussion see H. Mulder, *Spoorzoeker*, pp. 99–103.

15:21-28; Mark 7:24-30), and in Caesarea Philippi (Matt. 16:13 ff.; Mark 8:27 ff.). He was in the largely Gentile "country of the Gadarenes" (Matt. 8:28-34; Mark 5:1-17). And according to John's Gospel the Savior also carried on a fruitful ministry in Samaria (chapter 4).

But does *the Third Gospel* ever place Jesus anywhere outside of Jewish territory? The answer must be a definitely soft-pedaled "yes," a "yes" so small that it is almost transformed into a "no." Nothing at all is said in Luke about Christ's work in Syrophoenicia. Although Luke briefly mentions what happened in Caesarea, he does not indicate that region by name but simply states that once while Jesus was praying he asked his disciples, "Who do people say I am?" (9:18). The work of Jesus in the country of the Gadarenes, Gerasenes, or Gergesenes is by Luke immediately brought into relation with the more Jewish "Galilee" (8:26). And definitely Gentile Decapolis (Matt. 4:25; Mark 5:20; 7:31; see N.T.C. on Mark, pp. 198, 199) is not even mentioned by Luke.

All this is in harmony with Luke's already indicated plan. It is not surprising, therefore, that he also omits any reference to the wise men from "the east" and to the sojourn of the holy family in "Egypt." The omission of such material from his Gospel may well reveal Luke's laudable consistency.

40. And the child continued to grow and to become strong, being filled (day by day) with wisdom; and the favor of God was upon him.

This passage should be compared with somewhat similar ones in Judg. 13:24b; I Sam. 2:21b, 26; Luke 1:80; 2:52. With reference to the development of the child of Zechariah and Elizabeth Luke 1:80 states, "And the child continued to grow and to become strong in spirit." With the exception of "in spirit" exactly the same thing is said here about Mary's child. This indicates that the development of Jesus was:

a. *normal.* By and large it resembled the development of any other normal child. This brings to mind Heb. 4:15, "one who has been in every respect tempted as we are. . . ." (More about this passage a little later.)

The finite character of Christ's human nature is sometimes denied. For example, when it is suggested that even when he was a man there were certain things which, according to his human nature, Jesus did not know, some devout believers are shocked. Are they forgetting such clear passages as Matt. 24:36; Mark 5:32; 11:13; Luke 8:45? The present passage too shows very clearly that according to his human nature there were certain things which the child Jesus did not know from the start. He had to learn them. He had to grow up, and this not only physically but also mentally, etc. In a sense did not the process of learning continue throughout his life? See Heb. 5:8.

Those who deny this are in danger of acquiring the mentality that must have marked the authors of certain apocryphal writings. These picture Jesus as being, *even according to his human nature,* omniscient and almighty (or at least nearly so), and this from the very start. Lions and leopards worship him. The infant Jesus says to a palm, "Bend down and refresh my mother with your fruit," and it does so immediately. At five years of age Jesus models twelve sparrows out of soft clay. He claps his hands and the sparrows become alive and fly away, etc., etc.[152]

All this is clearly contrary to the pleasing reticence that marks Luke 2:40.

b. *physical.* Jesus "continued to grow and to become strong." It is encouraging to note that Luke does not belittle that which is physical. Is not the human body in its origin, composition, and development, a divine masterpiece? See especially Gen. 1:26; Ps. 139:15, 16; I Cor. 6:19, 20.[153]

A certain amount of physical strength was going to be required, and this not only to enable Jesus to wield the tools of a carpenter (Mark 6:3) but also to carry on his earthly ministry.

c. *spiritual.* Luke writes, "And the child continued to grow . . . being [or becoming] filled with wisdom." He uses the present tense of the participle, indicating that this development in wisdom was a gradual, day by day, process.

What is meant by wisdom? That it includes knowledge is clear. But it far surpasses knowledge. It implies the ability and the desire to use this knowledge to the best advantage. The truly wise man is reaching for the highest goal and uses the most effective means to achieve it.

> Behold, the fear of the Lord, that is wisdom;
> and to depart from evil is understanding."
>
> (Job 28:28; see also 28:18)

"But the wisdom (that comes) from above is first of all pure, then peace-loving, considerate, congenial, full of mercy and good fruit, impartial and unpretentious" (James 3:17).

The person who has these qualities is surely wise. It was in that wisdom that even as a child Jesus was constantly increasing.

d. *God-given.* "And the favor of God was upon him." In a marked and noticeable manner God manifested his favor and love to him. He guided him step by step and caused him to prosper.

Returning now to Heb. 4:15, note the very important qualification, "yet (he was) without sin." The *development* of this child was therefore perfect, and this along every line: physical, intellectual, moral, spiritual; for from beginning to end progress was unimpaired and unimpeded by sin, whether inherited or acquired. Between the child Jesus and his Father (see verse 49) there was perfect harmony, limitless love. This also introduces us to the next paragraph, in which the young boy Jesus reveals his closeness to his Father.[154]

---

152. See especially D. L. Dungan and D. R. Cartlidge, *Sourcebook of Texts for the Comparative Study of the Gospels,* Missoula, 1971.

153. Written in a style so simple that even children can enjoy it is Dr. A. I. Brown's book, *God and You: Wonders of the Human Body,* Findlay (no date).

154. Notes on Greek words, phrases, and constructions in 2:39, 40 begin on page 181.

Practical Lessons Derived from Luke 2:39, 40

Verse 39

"They returned . . . to their own town Nazareth." This was the village of which Nathaniel said, "Out of Nazareth can any good come?" (John 1:46). Yet, it was here that Jesus grew up. It was here that he spent much of his life.

Even today it is not the place that makes the man, but the man that makes the place (at least, that makes it go down in his history).

Verse 40

"Filled with wisdom. . . ." Wisdom and Truth are twins: "Die Weisheit ist nur in der Wahrheit" (Goethe).

Wisdom and Goodness are also twins: "Wisdom and goodness are twin-born" (Cowper).

"The favor of God was upon him." Blessings are not brought about by being born under a lucky star or attaching a horseshoe to the barndoor. On the contrary:

> Unless the Lord the house shall build,
> The weary builders toil in vain.
> Unless the Lord the city shield,
> The guards a useless watch maintain.
> *Psalter Hymnal* of the Christian Reformed Church,
> Grand Rapids, 1959, No. 269; see Ps. 127:1.

Old Dutch proverb: "Aan Gods zegen is alles gelegen" meaning: Everything is dependent on God's blessing.

Notes on Greek Words, Phrases, and Constructions in 2:39, 40

Verse 39

ἐτέλεσαν, third per. pl. aor. indicat. active of τελέω, to bring to an end, accomplish, finish, complete, fulfil. See also 12:50; 18:31; 22:37. Many sermons have been preached on τετέλεσται (John 19:30). Similar in form (to ἐτέλεσαν) is ἐπέστρεψαν from ἐπιστρέφω, to turn, return, turn back, turn around; also used in a spiritual sense, as in Luke 1:16, 17.

Verse 40

Note vivid imperfects ηὔξανεν and ἐκραταιοῦτο.

πληρούμενον, present participle. The process of being or becoming filled with wisdom was gradual.

χάρις. In the Synoptics the χάρις family of words is limited to Luke's Gospel. The noun χάρις is found in Luke 1:30; 2:40, 52; 4:22; 6:32, 33, 34; 17:9. The following shades of meaning are represented:

a. Basically the word means beauty, charm, attractiveness, graciousness. Thus 4:22 mentions "words of grace." Phillips renders the Greek: "beautiful words."

b. From "beauty" or "graciousness" to "grace" or "favor" is but a small step. Note 1:30, "You have found favor with God" (cf. 1:28, "You highly favored one"); also 2:40, "the favor of God," cf. 2:52. "Grace" and "favor" are used interchangeably in many translations. In such a passage as 2:40 either is correct. It is especially when χάρις acquires the meaning "unmerited favor bestowed on the unworthy" (Eph. 2:5, 8, etc.) that the rendering "grace" is generally used.

c. The next step is again a small one: "favor," regarded as a disposition, easily develops into "favor" viewed as a beneficence (kindly gift), benefit, reward, credit. Cf. "Do me a favor." Perhaps Luke 6:32-34, "What reward do y o u receive from this?" or "What credit is this to y o u?" belongs here.

d. Finally, the idea of a benevolent disposition and/or free gift suggests the response of thanks, thanksgiving, gratitude. Cf. "Thanks be to God for his inexpressibly precious gift" (II Cor. 9:15). In a far less emotional context "thanks" is also the meaning in Luke 17:9, "Does he give thanks to the servant?" See also the note on 7:47 on page 412.

---

41 Now his parents were in the habit of going to Jerusalem every year for the feast of the Passover. 42 So when he became twelve years of age they went up as usual according to the custom of the feast. 43 And after the days (of the feast) were over, while his parents were returning, the boy Jesus remained behind in Jerusalem, but they were unaware of it. 44 Supposing that he was in their company, they traveled on for a day. Then they began to search for him among their relatives and acquaintances. 45 When they did not find him they returned to Jerusalem, searching for him. 46 And after three days they found him in the temple, sitting in the midst of[155] the teachers, both listening to them and putting questions to them. 47 All who were listening to him were astonished at his insight and answers. 48 When his parents saw him, they were astounded. His mother said to him, "Son, why have you treated us like this? Indeed, your father and I have been anxiously looking for you." 49 He answered, "Why have y o u been looking for me? Didn't y o u know I had to be in my Father's house?" 50 But they did not understand the statement he made to them.

51 Then he went down with them, came to Nazareth, and rendered constant obedience to them. And his mother continued to treasure up all these things in her heart. 52 Meanwhile Jesus kept making progress in wisdom and in stature and in favor with God and men.

2:41-52 *The Boy in the Midst of the Teachers*

41. Now his parents were in the habit of going to Jerusalem every year for the feast of the Passover. For "his parents" see on 2:27. The law obligated all male Jews "of mature age" to go to Jerusalem thrice a year to attend the three great feasts: Passover, Pentecost, Tabernacles (Exod. 23:14-17; 34:22, 23; Deut. 16:6). The dispersion of the Jews made it impossible for them to comply literally with this commandment. And even after the return of a remnant to the land of the fathers, it was still very difficult for many who lived a long distance away from Jerusalem to go there three times a year. Therefore it became the custom of many to attend once a year. In the case of Joseph and Mary, as well as of many others, the feast selected was the Passover, which was held in commemoration of the deliverance of the Jews from Egyptian bondage.

---

155. Or: among.

The law did not require women to attend, though certain famous teachers (e.g., Hillel) strongly recommended this. But the divine commandment itself refers only to males. That Mary, nevertheless, also attended shows that we are dealing here with a very devout couple. Cf. Hannah (I Sam. 1:7; 2:19).

42-45. So when he became twelve years of age they went up as usual according to the custom of the feast. And after the days (of the feast) were over, while his parents were returning, the boy Jesus remained behind in Jerusalem, but they were unaware of it. Supposing that he was in their company, they traveled on for a day. Then they began to search for him among their relatives and acquaintances. When they did not find him they returned to Jerusalem, searching for him.

Jewish sources[156] reveal no unanimity with respect to the exact age when a boy became a "bar mitzvah" (son of the law), that is, when he attained the age of maturity and responsibility with respect to the keeping of God's commandments. The prevailing opinion may have been that at the age of 13 a boy should fully shoulder that responsibility but that in order to become prepared to do this it would be wise for the parents to take him along to the temple even earlier. We know at least that when Jesus became 12 years of age Joseph and Mary took him along to Jerusalem in order to attend the Passover festival. Though it is not stated in so many words that this was the first time he went along, is not this a reasonable inference?

What does "after the days (of the feast) were over" mean? According to the law the feast lasted fully seven days (Exod. 12:15, 16; 23:15; Lev. 23:6; Deut. 16:3). But since many considered a lengthy stay in Jerusalem a burden, such people would leave the city after attending one full day or at most two days. With respect to the question whether this procedure could be justified there was a difference of opinion among the religious authorities.[157]

The question arises, "Did Joseph and Mary stay on for the entire seven days or did they leave earlier?" The most natural explanation of "and after the days (of the feast) were over" would certainly seem to be that this devout couple and their son remained in Jerusalem for the entire period.[158] We assume that this conclusion is correct.

At the end of the feast, therefore, Joseph and Mary join the northward bound caravan. If the custom which can be verified for a later day prevailed even at this time, the women and children traveled in front, the men

---

156. Cf. Mishnah, Aboth 5:21; Niddah 5:6, with S.BK., Vol. II, p. 145.

157. S.BK., Vol. II, p. 147.

158. That is also the position taken by the following commentators, among others: Stöger, Greijdanus, Lenski, Danker, Godet, Geldenhuys, A. B. Bruce.

Others disagree. For example, H. Mulder, *Dienaren van de Koning*, Kampen, 1956, p. 92, is of the opinion that Joseph and Mary returned earlier, and that Jesus remained behind because he wanted to live in compliance with God's law. Objections: (a) The feast of Tabernacles also lasted seven days; yet Jesus arrived "in the midst of the feast" (John 7:2, 14); (b) if that had been the reason for Jesus' staying behind in the temple, would he not have indicated this?

and young men came on behind. At the age of 12 Jesus might fit into either category. However, he had not even joined the traveling party but had stayed behind in Jerusalem.

At first his parents did not miss him. Joseph may have thought, "He is in front with Mary." Mary may have reasoned, "He is in the rear with Joseph."

Generally the caravan was composed of people from the same town or from several small neighboring villages. On the evening of each day of travel the entire group would gather at a previously agreed rendezvous.

So, in the present case, when evening arrived and Jesus did not show up, his parents became worried. They searched "up and down" for him among their relatives and acquaintances. Unsuccessful, the next day they were on their way going back to Jerusalem. Thus the second day went by. Still no success. Then came the third day. As Robertson says, "One day out, one day back, one day finding him."

46, 47. And after three days they found him in the temple, sitting in the midst of the teachers, both listening to them and putting questions to them. All who were listening to him were astonished at his insight and answers.

The beautiful and very spacious "porches" of the temple provided ample opportunity for teaching. See Mark 12:41–44; Luke 19:47; John 10:23; also N.T.C. on Mark, p. 448 f. It was in one of these places that Joseph and Mary now found Jesus. He was sitting "in the midst of"[159] the teachers, listening to them, and at times directing questions to them.

Since these were the days immediately following the great feast, and since Jerusalem was the headquarters of the Jewish religion, we have a right to imagine that several famous Jewish teachers were still to be found in the temple, for teaching was not confined to the duration of the festivities. Here, then, was an opportunity for Jesus which Nazareth did not afford.

It was not at all unusual for students to ask and answer questions. In fact that was a favorite method of teaching among the Jews. The purpose was not to leave these questions unanswered but to arouse interest among the students and to arrive at definite answers. For more about this see the special section *Principles and Methods of Education in Israel*, N.T.C. on I and II Timothy and Titus, p. 296 f. And cf. S.BK., Vol. II, p. 150.

What was unusual in the present case was the kind of questions this boy, Jesus, asked, and the kind of answers he gave. Both questions and answers revealed such insight that all who were listening to him were astonished. Soon all eyes must have been riveted on him, so that in a very real sense whenever he spoke he became the center of attention: the boy in the midst of the teachers! Nevertheless, exaggeration must be avoided. Jesus was not yet the teacher. That would come later.

---

159. So also both Lenski and Robertson, though several translators and commentators prefer "among," a possibility that must be granted.

48. When his parents saw him, they were astounded. His mother said to him, Son, why have you treated us like this? Indeed, your father and I have been anxiously looking for you.

It was natural for Mary, the one who had given birth to this boy, to begin the conversation. Besides, Joseph is everywhere pictured as the quiet type, one who speaks little and acts when he is authoritatively told to act. See Matt. 1:18–24; 2:13, 19. Also, it should be constantly borne in mind that though Joseph could indeed be called the "father" of Jesus—as Mary does in this very passage—he was the father only in a legal sense.

Note the word expressive of strong emotion: When Joseph and Mary saw Jesus they were *astounded,* as it were "knocked out," "shocked." Mary's exclamation begins with the word *Son* or *Child.* It is not at all unnatural, in connection with deeply emotional occasions, that a mother even today will address her offspring by exclaiming "Child!" though that son or daughter may have reached the age of 12 or even 20.

The words, "Why have you treated us like this?" etc., reveal a medley of *surprise, reproach,* and *anguish.* Was Mary forgetting, for the moment, what Gabriel had told her about this child? If she had reflected on the words of Luke 1:30–35, would she have been so surprised and . . . almost indignant?

49. He answered, Why have y o u been looking for me? Didn't y o u know I had to be in my Father's house? Note the contrast, "your father" . . . .(the house of) "my Father." That contrast tells the whole story.

It is clear from this answer that Jesus even at the age of 12 was deeply conscious of the unique relation between himself and his Father in heaven. Later on he is going to refer to this marvelous theme again and again. It is he alone who thoroughly knows the Father, and the Father alone who thoroughly knows him (Luke 10:21, 22; cf. Matt. 11:25–27). He was conscious of having been sent by the Father, whose will he always obeys (John 6:37–40, 44, 57; 8:18, 28, 29, 38, 49, 54, 55). He is *one* with the Father (John 10:30, and read the intensely stirring chapter 17 of John's Gospel); and he finally commits his spirit to the Father (Luke 23:46).

"Didn't y o u [note the plural, obscured in most English renderings—Joseph and Mary] know that I had to be [must be] in my Father's house?" Although "about my Father's business" (A.V.) is possible, it is improbable. The entire question here is one of *whereness.* Joseph and Mary had been searching for Jesus, not knowing *where* he was. He answers, as it were, "In my Father's house, that's *where* I was, and had to be. Didn't y o u know that?" See also the note on 2:49 on page 188.

"I had to be" or "I must be." The fact that his entire life was controlled by the divine "must," a "must" which was in complete harmony with his own desire (Ps. 40:7; John 10:17, 18), dawned on the boy Jesus very early in life. The Gospels are full of this idea of *necessity, decree.* In Luke's Gospel note the following: Jesus *must* preach (4:43), suffer (9:22), go on his way (13:33), stay at the home of Zacchaeus (19:5), be delivered up, crucified, rise again (24:7), suffer these things and enter into his glory (22:37; 24:26), and fulfil all the Old Testament prophecies with reference to himself (24:44). The same truth is also emphasized in the other Gospels, particularly in John (3:14; 4:4; 9:4; 10:16; 20:9). Whatever happens to Jesus is the realization of God's eternal decree (Luke 22:22; cf. Acts 2:23).

50. But they did not understand the statement he made to them. Note the sharp contrast between verse 47, "All who were listening to him were astonished at his insight [or understanding]," and verse 50, "But they [Joseph and Mary] did not understand. . . ." One aspect of Jesus' suffering was exactly this, that men, including even his own relatives and his own disciples, failed to understand him: Matt. 16:22; Mark 9:10, 32 (= Luke 9:45); Luke 8:19-21; John 7:3-5. At times this failure took the form of their interpreting literally what was meant figuratively (Matt. 16:5-12; John 2:19, 20; 3:3, 4; 4:13-15; 6:51, 52; 11:11, 12).

When the two facts expressed in verses 49, 50—(a) Jesus' consciousness of being the Son of God in a unique sense, and (b) his awareness of the fact that Joseph and Mary did not understand him—are combined, the next statement becomes even more striking: **51a. Then he went down with them, came to Nazareth, and rendered constant obedience to them.** He did not ask to remain a while longer in his Father's house. *Unquestioningly* he went down to Nazareth with his "parents." Note "down," for whenever one leaves Jerusalem he goes *down,* no matter what the elevation of either place may be. To Joseph and Mary, moreover, with all their weaknesses and lack of understanding, he yielded continuing obedience.

51b. And his mother continued to treasure up all these things in her heart. She was doing what Jacob had done (Gen. 37:11), and Daniel (Dan. 7:28), and she herself twelve years earlier (Luke 2:19). That enabled her to tell the story to others, perhaps even to Luke himself.

52. Meanwhile Jesus kept making progress in wisdom and in stature and in favor with God and men. In wisdom, as already explained in connection with the similar verse 40; in stature, that is, in physical growth, not life-span (as in Matt. 6:27; Luke 12:25); and in favor with God and men. The last phrase means that he continued to experience increasingly the lovingkindness of his Father and also the friendliness of the people round about him. The words of Prov. 3:4 were fulfilled in him.

Between this description and what is said about Samuel (in I Sam. 2:21b, 26) there is a close resemblance. Note, however, in the case of Jesus the addition "in wisdom."

There is also a degree of resemblance between what is said about Jesus and what is said about John (1:80). But though John continued to grow and to become strong in spirit, it is only in connection with Samuel and Jesus that we have the addition, ". . . he kept making progress . . . in favor with God *and men.*" It should be borne in mind that early in life John separated himself from people, grew up in uninhabited regions, and when he did make an appearance before the public, must have impressed his audience as being rather stern, austere.

As to Mary's progress in faith, see John 2:5; Acts 1:14. As to Joseph, except for the mention of his name in the genealogy (Luke 3:23) there is no further reference to him in the Third Gospel. He may have died before Jesus began his public ministry.[160]

Practical Lessons Derived from Luke 2:41–52

Verse 42

Joseph and Mary took their son along with them to the temple "when he became twelve years of age." What can be done today to help children assume their covenant obligations?

Verse 43

"The boy Jesus remained behind in Jerusalem." What can be done today to make young people so enthralled with their religion that it captivates them and makes them active for Christ?

Verse 46

"Both listening to them and putting questions to them." Consider: "Within proper limits discussion, properly monitored, advances knowledge."

Verse 48

"Why have you treated us like this?" Mary forgets the implications of Gabriel's message. We all need the prayer of Ps. 86:11 and 119:125.

Verse 51

"Jesus rendered constant obedience to them." Are we kind to a child when we neglect to teach him the blessings of obedience? Are *freedom of expression* and *obedience* mutually exclusive?

"And his mother continued to treasure up all these things in her heart." Should an important place be assigned to the discipline of meditation?

Verse 52

". . . in favor with God and men." Granted that favor with God is by far the most important, is favor with men of any significance? Is the anti-social attitude Christian?

Notes on Greek Words, Phrases, and Constructions in 2:41–52

Verse 41

ἐπορεύοντο, imperfect of customary action.
ἔτος = Ϝέτος, year. Cf. *veteran*.

---

160. Notes on Greek words, phrases, and constructions in 2:41–52 begin on this page.

Verse 42

ἀναβαινόντων, gen. pl. masc. present participle of customary action. This is a gen. absolute. The entire event described in the following verses may be conceived of as taking place in connection with this "going up" to the feast.

Verse 43

τελειωσάντων, gen. pl. masc. aor. participle of τελειόω, to finish, complete. This is another gen. absolute.

παῖς, boy; no longer παιδίον (verse 40).

Verse 44

συνοδία* = σύν plus ὁδός ("along" with "road" or "journey"), a company traveling the same road, traveling party, caravan.

Verse 47

σύνεσις; cf. συνίημι, to put together; hence the noun indicates the ability to put things together in the mind, understanding, insight. Note third per. pl. aor. indicat. of *verb* (verse 50).

Verse 48

ἐξεπλάγησαν, third per. pl. 2nd aor. indicat. pass. of ἐκπλήσσω; see the note on 4:32 on page 267.

ὀδυνώμενοι, nom. pl. masc. pres. middle participle of ὀδυνάω**, to cause pain; in middle: to be in agony, anguish, pain, sorrow, distress; to agonize, be anxious. See also Luke 16:24, 25; Acts 20:38. Cf. ὀδύνη in Rom. 9:2, and see N.T.C. on I and II Timothy and Titus, p. 201 (on I Tim. 6:10). Cf. *anodyne*.

Verse 49

ἐν τοῖς τοῦ πατρός μου. Although the rendering "about my Father's business" (A.V. and Lenski) is possible, better is "in my Father's house." See L.N.T. (A. and G.), p. 554, sec. column, under 7; also E. J. Goodspeed, *Problems,* pp. 81–83; Plummer, *op. cit.,* p. 77; and see the explanation in the text of this commentary.

Verses 51, 52

ἦν ὑποτασσόμενος, periphrastic passive imperfect of ὑποτάσσω, to range under; in the middle or passive: to range oneself under, to be obedient.

διετήρει, imperfect of διατηρέω**; in the New Testament only here and in Acts 15:29. See also Gen. 37:11. A synonym is συντηρέω, verse 19, in one of its meanings. Another imperfect is προέκοπτεν, was chopping ahead or forward (as is done by pioneers), was advancing, making progress.

Summary of Chapter 2

The Birth of Jesus (verses 1–7). In the days of King Herod I an order was issued by Emperor Augustus that there should be a periodic census (registration for the purpose of taxation) of the entire Roman world. The first of these censuses took place while Quirinius was military governor of Syria. So everybody, women as well as men, went to be registered. In Herod's kingdom each person to be registered was traveling to his own town, that is, to the place where his family originated and his birth records were kept. For Joseph and Mary this meant traveling from Nazareth in Galilee to Bethlehem in Judea. While they were there the time for Mary to give birth arrived. However, in Bethlehem's inn there was "no vacancy," the men in charge of registration having probably occupied every available room. So it was in a nearby stable, perhaps a cave-stable, that Mary gave birth. The little boy was wrapped in strips of cloth and laid in a manger, a feeding trough for animals.

Shepherds and Angels; The Circumcision and Naming of Jesus (verses 8–21). This section consists of two very unequal parts:

Verses 8–20 take us to the fields of Ephrathah, where the darkness of night is suddenly pierced by an angel bathed in light. He brings to shepherds, who by turn were keeping watch over their flock, the good news that in the city of David (Bethlehem) there was born to them a Savior, Christ the Lord. To enable them to find him they receive the sign of a swaddled baby lying in a manger. Following hard upon this message was the "Glory to God" refrain by an entire host of angels.

The shepherds found everything exactly as it had been described to them. They related to Mary, Joseph, and others what the angel and the angels had proclaimed to them. Those who listened to their story were amazed. But Mary continued to treasure up all these things, mulling them over in her mind. The shepherds returned glorifying God.

Verse 21 states that on the eighth day the child was circumcised and named Jesus.

The Presentation of Jesus in the Temple; Simeon's "Nunc Dimittis"; Anna's Thanksgiving and Testimony (verses 22–38).

The Presentation (verses 22–24). On the fortieth day Joseph and Mary brought Jesus to the temple for the purpose of redemption (since he was the firstborn son; see Exod. 13:1, 2, 11–15) and presentation, public consecration of the child to God. Now too Mary's "purification" was climaxed by offerings which, since Joseph and Mary were rather poor, amounted to a pair of turtledoves or two young pigeons (Lev. 12:6–8).

Simeon's "Nunc Dimittis" (verses 25–35). Little is known about this devout man. He seems to have been a layman and perhaps well along in years. For a long time he had been patiently but ardently waiting for the Messiah to appear, bringing help and consolation to Israel. The Holy Spirit had revealed to Simeon that he would not die until he had seen the Messiah ("the Lord's Christ"). Guided by the Spirit he entered the temple. When Joseph and Mary brought in the child Jesus for the purpose already indicated the Spirit informed Simeon that this baby was indeed the Christ. So he took Jesus into his arms and uttered the words of wholehearted resignation,

"Now, Sovereign Master, thou art releasing thy servant, according to thy word in peace, because my eyes have seen thy salvation," etc. He described Jesus as "a light for revelation to the Gentiles and a glory for thy people Israel." He also declared that anyone's attitude toward Jesus would determine either his eternal weal or woe. Finally, he predicted that one day a "sword" (bitter anguish) would pierce Mary's soul. For fulfilment of this prediction read John 19:25-27.

Anna's Thanksgiving and Testimony (verses 36-38). One of the people who witnessed the scene of Simeon with the baby Jesus in his arms, and who heard the devout man's *Nunc Dimittis,* was Anna. She was indeed a very pious woman, one who never missed a service in the temple. She was very old. As some read verses 36, 37 she was 84; according to others she was about 105. She too became convinced that this child was the Messiah, and she made known her conviction to "all those who were waiting for 'the redemption of Jerusalem.' " (See commentary for explanation of this term.)

The Return to Nazareth (verses 39, 40). When Joseph and Mary had accomplished everything required by God's law they returned to Nazareth. As many see it, the events reported in Matt. 2:1-21 (arrival of the wise men, flight to Egypt, etc.) took place before the little family returned to their Galilean home. In Nazareth Jesus continued to grow physically and to become strong. With God's loving care resting upon him he also gradually increased in wisdom.

The Boy in the Midst of the Teachers (verses 41-52). Jesus' parents were in the habit of going to Jerusalem every year to attend the Passover. When their son became 12 years of age they took him along to the feast. The celebration ended, Joseph and Mary joined the returning caravan. Without their knowledge Jesus remained behind in Jerusalem. During the first day of travel the fact that his parents did not see him did not bother them. But afterward, when he still did not show up, they searched the caravan up and down. Not finding him they returned to Jerusalem. There, on the third day, they found him in the temple, sitting in the midst of (or among) famous teachers, listening to them and putting questions to them. His insight astonished everybody. Greatly surprised, Mary reproachfully said to him, "Son, why have you treated us like this? Indeed, your father and I have been anxiously looking for you." He answered, "Why have y o u been looking for me? Didn't y o u know I had to be in my Father's house?" They did not know what to make of this answer. They should have known! Nevertheless, he went down to Nazareth with them and obeyed them constantly. Mary continued to store up all these things in her memory and was in the habit of mulling them over in her mind. The story ends with the beautiful statement, "Meanwhile Jesus kept making progress in wisdom and in stature and in favor with God and men."

Outline of Chapter 3

Theme: *The Work Thou Gavest Him to Do*

CHAPTER III

3 1 In the fifteenth year of the reign of Tiberius Caesar—when Pontius Pilate was governor of Judea, Herod tetrarch of Galilee, his brother Philip tetrarch of the region of Iturea and Trachonitis, and Lysanius tetrarch of Abilene— 2 and during the high-priesthood of Annas and Caiaphas, the word of God came to Zechariah's son John, (while he was) in the wilderness. 3 He went into the whole Jordan neighborhood, proclaiming a baptism of conversion with a view to the forgiveness of sins; 4 as it is written in the book of the words of Isaiah the prophet:

A voice of one crying in the wilderness:
Make ready the way of the Lord,
Make straight his paths.
5 Every valley shall be filled up,
And every mountain and hill leveled down;
The crooked roads shall become straight,
And the rough ways smooth.
6 And all flesh shall see the salvation of God.

7 He [John] therefore was saying[161] to the crowds coming out to be baptized by him, "Y o u offspring of vipers! Who warned y o u to escape the approaching (outpouring of) wrath? 8 Bear fruit therefore in keeping with conversion; and do not begin to say to your-selves, 'We have Abraham as our father,' for I tell y o u that God is able to raise up children for Abraham out of these stones here. 9 And already the ax is laid at the root of the trees; every tree therefore that does not bear good fruit is cut down and thrown into the fire."

10 So the crowds kept asking him, "What then shall we do?"

11 He answered, "Let the one who has two shirts[162] share with the one who has none, and let the one who has food do likewise."

12 Tax-collectors too came to be baptized. They said to him, "Teacher, what shall we do?" 13 He told them, "Don't exact more than required."

14 Soldiers too were asking, "And we, what shall we do?" He replied, "Don't extort money by violence,[163] don't accuse people falsely, and be content with y o u r pay."

15 Now while the people were on tiptoe of expectation, and all were wondering in their hearts about John, whether he might be the Christ, 16 he expressly answered them all, "I on my part baptize y o u with water, but he who is mightier than I is coming—whose sandal straps I am not fit to untie—he will baptize y o u with the Holy Spirit and with fire. 17 His winnow-ing shovel is in his hand, and he will thoroughly clear his threshing floor. He will gather his grain into the granary, but the chaff he will consume with unquenchable fire."

18 Thus, continually exhorting with respect to many and different matters, John was preaching the gospel to the people.

---

161. Or: Then he [John] was saying.
162. Or: tunics.
163. More literally: "Do not shake people down."

19 But when Herod the tetrarch was repeatedly rebuked by John because of Herodias, Herod's brother's wife, and because of all the (other) evil deeds he had committed, 20 he added this to them all: he locked John up in prison.

3:1-20 *The Ministry of John the Baptist*
Cf. Matt. 3:1-12; 14:1-4; Mark 1:1-8; 6:14-18; John 1:19-28

By the grace of God resting upon him, Jesus, according to his human nature, was being gradually prepared for the task which the Father had assigned to him. His divine nature did not need any "preparation," was not even able to experience it, but the human nature was in need of it. This period of preparation (see especially 2:40, 52) was now about to end.

Accordingly between chapters 1 and 2, on the one hand, and chapter 3, on the other, there is a marked division. The "boy" of 12 (2:42) becomes the "man" of approximately 30 (3:23). The eighteen intervening years are passed by in silence.

But before Luke even narrates the events by means of which Jesus' public ministry was inaugurated he says something about the forerunner, John the Baptist, for the latter was about to do two things: first, he was to serve as God's instrument in preparing the hearts of the people for the reception of their Messiah (3:1-14); secondly, he must introduce the Messiah to the people (3:15-17; cf. John 1:29) and baptize him (3:21, 22).

As Luke does so often—see 1:5 f., 2:1 f., and *Introduction*, point V B—so here again he fits the history of redemption into the framework of the contemporary political situation. By means of six chronological items he indicates the time when John began his ministry.

One is prone to think that such a broad array of historical data, each a check on the other five, would leave no doubt in anyone's mind as to the exact year when the Baptist started his work. Nevertheless, it is precisely at this point that even today scholars reach diverging conclusions. Bypassing minor theories—there are several—the two main theories as to the date that marks the beginning of the forerunner's public introduction to Israel are these:

a. in A.D. 26. This is the traditional view; and

b. in A.D. 28-29. This theory, though not new by any means, has been refurbished in recent years and today enjoys a measure of popularity. In the course of the discussion the two theories will be designated as (a) and (b). At the very outset it should be made clear that the data supplied by Luke are insufficient to prove either theory *with finality*.[164] Great scholars have reached opposite verdicts. At the most one can reach probability, not absolute certainty.

In verse 1 Luke mentions various political regions into which the country

---

164. So also Geldenhuys, *op. cit.*, p. 42, footnote 1.

of the Jews had been divided and which existed when John began his public ministry. For their location see the map on p. 196.

1, 2. In the fifteenth year of the reign of Tiberius Caesar—when Pontius Pilate was governor of Judea, Herod tetrarch of Galilee, his brother Philip tetrarch of the region of Iturea and Trachonitis, and Lysanius tetrarch of Abilene—and during the highpriesthood of Annas and Caiaphas, the word of God came to Zechariah's son John, (while he was) in the wilderness.

The six chronological items mentioned by Luke will be discussed in the order 2, 3, 4, 5, 6, 1. This sequence will be followed because, as this author sees it, item 6 sheds light on the proper understanding of item 1.

2. The word of God came to Zechariah's son John "when Pontius Pilate was governor of Judea." See the chart on p. 136. What happened was this: Herod the Great had made a will which he revised several times. At his death (on or before April 4 of the year 4 B.C.) the Roman government allowed the final revision to be honored. Accordingly Archelaus, a son of Herod the Great by Malthace, was made ethnarch of Judea, Samaria, and Idumea. See chart of Herod's Family Tree on p. 189 of N.T.C. on Matthew. But because Archelaus was a cruel ruler—see N.T.C. on Matthew, pp. 187, 188 for details—he was deposed in A.D. 6. The emperor then appointed a "governor" to replace Archelaus, and made the triple region, which was now called the province of Judea, a division of the prefecture of Syria, so that to a certain extent the governor was subordinate to Syria's legate. However, in Judea itself the governor exercised unrestricted authority.

Governors followed each other in rapid succession. That was true also in the province of Judea. Pontius Pilate was the fifth of these "governors." In that capacity he ruled from A.D. 26 to 36. It is clear that both of the theories mentioned above—i.e., both (a) and (b)—can live with these dates.

3. "Herod tetrarch of Galilee." This man, usually known as "Herod Antipas," was a full brother of Archelaus. The same event that made Archelaus "ethnarch" made Herod Antipas "tetrarch," namely, of Galilee (and Perea). He continued in that position from 4 B.C. to A.D. 39, when he was banished to Lyons in Gaul. For the events that led to his banishment see N.T.C. on Matthew, p. 590. Sometime later the domain that had been taken away from him was added to the kingdom of Herod Agrippa I, who is the Herod referred to in Acts 12.

Herod Antipas is the "Herod" we meet in the Gospels (except Matt. 2:1–19 and Luke 1:5, where the reference is to his father, Herod I or Herod the Great). It is clear that the tetrarch's long reign leaves ample room for theory (a) and theory (b).

4. "His brother Philip tetrarch of the region of Iturea and Trachonitis." Philip was a son of Herod I by Cleopatra of Jerusalem (not to be confused with the Egyptian Cleopatra). Our information about him we owe largely to Josephus, *Antiquities* XVIII.106–108. It was he who enlarged and

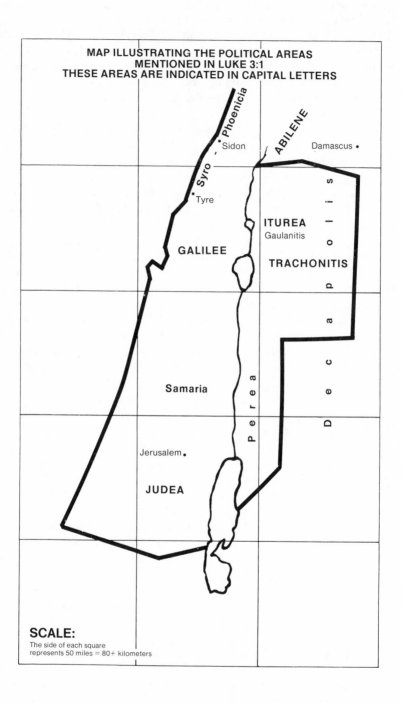

MAP ILLUSTRATING THE POLITICAL AREAS
MENTIONED IN LUKE 3:1
THESE AREAS ARE INDICATED IN CAPITAL LETTERS

SCALE:
The side of each square
represents 50 miles = 80+ kilometers

beautified the town of Paneas, located near the Jordan's source, and named it Caesarea. To distinguish that place from the Caesarea on the Mediterranean it began to be called "Caesarea Philippi" (Matt. 16:13). He also enlarged Bethsaida, that is, the Bethsaida located near the northern junction of the Lake of Galilee and the Jordan, and called it Bethsaida *Julias,* in honor of Julia, the daughter of Emperor Augustus, mentioned above (see p. 138). According to Josephus, this Philip was a man of excellent character, one who bestowed much personal care upon his people. He ruled from 4 B.C. until his death, A.D. 34. As far as his reign is concerned either theory (a) or (b) could again be right.

5. "And Lysanius tetrarch of Abilene." Luke's statement no longer stands alone, as it did for many years. It has been confirmed in an inscription on a rock west of Damascus.[165] This inscription states that Lysanius was indeed governor of this region, and at a time which again presents no problem for either theory (a) or (b).

6. "And during the highpriesthood of Annas and Caiaphas." Annas (or "Ananus" as Josephus calls him) had been appointed highpriest by Quirinius in the year A.D. 6, and was deposed by Valerius Gratus, about A.D. 15. But though deposed, he remained for a long time the ruling spirit of the Sanhedrin. Five sons and a grandson followed him in the highpriesthood; also a son-in-law, the very one mentioned by Luke, namely, Caiaphas. The latter held the highpriestly office from A.D. 18 to 36. The New Testament refers to Caiaphas in the following passages (in addition to Luke 3:2): Matt. 26:3, 57; John 11:49; 18:13, 14, 24, 28; and Acts 4:6; to Annas, also in John 18:13, 24; Acts 4:6.

It may seem strange that Luke assigns the beginning of the Baptist's ministry to the highpriesthood not only of Caiaphas but "of *Annas* and Caiaphas." Annas, after all, was deposed from that office in A.D. 15, long before John's ministry began, whether according to theory (a) or (b). That Luke assigns the beginning of John's ministry to the highpriesthood of Caiaphas (A.D. 18–36) we can understand, but why to that of Annas?

Nevertheless, Luke is correct. He is thinking of the *actual* situation, not the merely *formal* one. The actual situation was that both Annas and Caiaphas were "in the driver's seat" during the entire period of John's ministry and during the entire length of Christ's ministry; Annas as well as—perhaps even more than—Caiaphas. For more on these two men see N.T.C. on John, Vol. II, pp. 162–165, 385–388, 394–401. So here again either theory (a) or (b) may be correct.

1. We now turn to Luke's first chronological item, namely, "In the fifteenth year of the reign of Tiberius Caesar . . . the word of God came to Zechariah's son John. . . ."

There are those who argue that since John began his ministry "in the

---

165. L. H. Grollenberg, *op. cit.,* p. 136.

fifteenth year of Tiberius Caesar," and since Tiberius began to reign at the death of Emperor Augustus, Aug. 19 of the year A.D. 14, John's ministry must have started in the year A.D. 28 or perhaps even 29. For a defense of that theory (b) and our counter-arguments see the footnote.[166]

But the traditional view, theory (a), has by no means been overthrown. It rests on grounds such as the following:

First of all, "In Luke 3:1, 2 the analogy with the Annas-Caiaphas reference confirms the conclusion that Luke is thinking of the *actual* reign of Tiberius, which began with the latter's coregency, and that he is not thinking of Tiberius' sole rulership which began at the time of the death of Augustus."[167] A couple years before his formal assumption of sole em-

---

166. Arguments in favor of theory (b):

(1) The starting point for Luke's fifteenth year (Luke 3:1) must be A.D. 14, and not an earlier date, for "the princeps never dated his reign from the time when the great Augustus was still alive, nor do other sources for that era."

(2) The indirect threat of the Jews to appeal to Caesar against Pilate (John 19:12) would not have been likely before the fall of the anti-Semite Sejanus in October of the year A.D. 31. The pro-Jewish policy of Tiberius did not begin until after that date. Therefore A.D. 30 cannot be correct as the date of Christ's crucifixion; neither can A.D. 26 be correct as the date for the beginning of John's ministry. These dates are too early.

(3) Eusebius (*Chronicon* ii, ed. Migne, p. 535) states that Christ suffered "in the 19th year of the reign of Tiberius," i.e., in A.D. 33. This also makes the date for the beginning of John's ministry (and the date for the beginning of Christ's ministry) considerably later than A.D. 26.

This is only a summary. For the argument fully stated see P. L. Maier, *Pontius Pilate*, Garden City, N.Y., 1968, pp. 364, 365; also that author's article "Sejanus, Pilate, and the Date of the Crucifixion," *Church History* XXXVII (March, 1968), pp. 3–13.

Regardless of whether or not one is convinced by these arguments, it must be admitted that Maier's book on Pilate is very informative and interesting. The professor of Ancient History at Western Michigan University has already written much that is definitely worthwhile. Note, for example, his splendid article, "The Empty Tomb as History," *Christianity Today*, Vol. XIX, No. 13 (March 28, 1975). And as to Luke 3:1, 2, etc., the reader should by all means study what Maier himself says about it, and not depend solely on my attempt to summarize his views. Read also the fine article by H. H. Rowdon, "The Historical and Political Background and Chronology of the New Testament" in *A New Testament Commentary*, by C. D. Howley, F. F. Bruce, H. L. Ellison, eds., Grand Rapids, 1969, pp. 57–66. That article leans toward Maier's view, that is, in the direction of theory (b).

The following counter-arguments, however, deserve consideration:

Anent (1). "We get nowhere by considering how Tiberius himself counted the years of his reign or how these years were generally counted. What matters is how *Luke* counted them." Thus Greijdanus, who, as is pointed out in the text, believes that Luke was thinking of *actual*, not merely *formal*, years of reign, as his reference to Annas-Caiaphas clearly indicates.

Anent (2). In view of the well-known suspicious character of Tiberius, who did not refrain from putting to death anyone who was reported to be aiming to seize power, the argument with respect to the emperor's change of policy from anti-Jewish to pro-Jewish is rather weak. See the article on Tiberius in *Encyclopaedia Britannica*, 1969, Vol. 21, pp. 1105, 1106, and consult the works mentioned in the Bibliography at the close of that article.

Anent (3). There is in existence the much earlier testimony of Tertullian (*Against Marcion* I.xv), that "the Lord has been revealed since *the twelfth year* of Tiberius Caesar." This testimony, which, as generally interpreted, refers to Jesus' baptism and the beginning of his public ministry, when he was indeed "revealed" to the people, harmonizes beautifully with theory (a), but cannot be reconciled with theory (b).

167. S. Greijdanus, *Kommentaar*, Vol. I, p. 149. So also Lenski, *op. cit.*, p. 109; and see W. Manson, *op. cit.*, p. 24.

perorship the Roman Senate had conferred on Tiberius the authority to administer all the Roman provinces conjointly with Augustus.

Secondly, according to Josephus, *Antiquities* XV.380, Herod the Great began to build Jerusalem's temple in the eighteenth year of his reign (which began in 37 B.C.), hence in the year 19 B.C. According to the testimony of the Jews, as recorded in John 2:20, when Jesus attended the first Passover of his public ministry that temple had been in the process of building for forty-six years. This would make the date for that Passover A.D. 27. Therefore the beginning of Christ's ministry could well have been the latter part of A.D. 26, and the Baptist's first public appearance could have occurred a half year earlier.

Thirdly, it is agreed by several scholars that the events surrounding Christ's birth as described in Matt. 2 indicate that the birth itself occurred shortly before the death of Herod the Great. That king died on or before April 4 of the year 4 B.C. Therefore acceptance of late 5 B.C. as the date of Christ's birth is not unreasonable. If with this result we compare Luke 3:23—"Now Jesus himself was about thirty years old when he began his ministry," we again arrive at the close of A.D. 26 as the date of the beginning of that ministry, and at a date a half year earlier (see Luke 1:36) for the beginning of John's ministry. A. B. Bruce, though not taking a definite stand in this debate, points out that the date A.D. 26—rather than A.D. 28/29—"agrees with Luke 3:23."[168] It is true that Luke says, "when he was *about* thirty years" Jesus began to teach, but whether "about thirty years" can be stretched far enough to make it equal to "thirty-two" is open to question.

Though there are various ways in which the force of these arguments can be whittled down, and, as stated earlier, absolute certainty is impossible, I believe it has been shown that up to the present time the traditional view—that is, theory (a)—has not been annihilated.

Before leaving verses 1 and 2 there are two additional matters that require attention. First, the matter of political titles. Literally verse 1 reads, in part, "Pontius Pilate being governor of Judea, and Herod being tetrarch of Galilee, his brother Philip being tetrarch . . . and Lysanius being tetrarch," etc. The participle "being [or: ruling as] *tetrarch*" occurs three times in this verse. On p. 195 mention was made of the fact that at the death of "the *king*" (Herod the Great) Archelaus was made "*ethnarch*." So the question arises, "What is the difference between these three titles?"

The men so designated were rulers of semi-independent regions within the empire of Rome. In descending order of prestige the terms are king, ethnarch, tetrarch. If a ruler (a) was in control of a territory of considerable size and importance, (b) was able to maintain peace and order in his do-

---

168. *The Synoptic Gospels (The Expositor's Greek Testament,* Vol. I, the section on Luke, pp. 458–651 of that volume), Grand Rapids, no date, p. 480. Hereafter A. B. Bruce, *op. cit.,* indicates this particular work.

main, and (c) managed to collect large revenues for Rome's coffers, he was given the title *king*. If this did not happen to be the case, he had to be satisfied with the title *ethnarch* (literally "ruler of a people") or even *tetrarch* (originally, ruler of a fourth part), a kind of "petty prince." The terms were, however, flexible: any ruler of low rank might be called "tetrarch"; an ethnarch might be merely a "chief"; and even in the New Testament a "tetrarch" is sometimes loosely called a "king."

Nevertheless, how eager was the wife of a certain tetrarch to have her husband declared a "king"! See N.T.C. on Matthew, p. 590.

The second matter is the lofty, almost majestic, manner in which John, Messiah's herald, is now introduced. In phraseology that occurs nowhere else in the New Testament, but in one form or another frequently in the Old, we are told that "the word"—utterance or message—"of God came to Zechariah's son John, (while he was) in the wilderness." It came to him just as long ago it had come to Abraham (Gen. 15:1), Samuel (I Sam. 15:10), Nathan (II Sam. 7:4), Elijah (I Kings 17:2, 8; 18:1), and, to mention only one more, the closest parallel of all, Jeremiah (Jer. 1:1, 2). Did Luke perhaps deliberately select this Old Testament phraseology in order to impress upon Theophilus and others the fact that John was as genuine a prophet as those addressed by God during the old dispensation?

It was while John was "in the wilderness" (where Luke 1:80 left him) that he received the divine message ordering him (a) to awaken the people to the need of basic conversion, and (b) to introduce to them the Messiah (see verses 3, 8, 16). The term *wilderness* indicates the rolling badlands between the hill country of Judea to the west, and the Dead Sea and lower Jordan to the east, stretching northward to about the point where the Jabbok flows into the Jordan. It is indeed a desolation, a vast undulating expanse of barren chalky soil covered with pebbles, broken stones and rocks. Here and there a bit of brushwood appears, with snakes crawling underneath (see verse 7). It is clear, however, from verse 3 (cf. Matt. 3:5; John 1:28) that the terrain of John's activity extended even to the east bank of the Jordan.

3. He went into the whole Jordan neighborhood, proclaiming a baptism of conversion with a view to the forgiveness of sins. It is clear from the original that the terrain of John's activity included *the entire region around*—i.e., on both banks of this part of—*the Jordan*, "the whole Jordan neighborhood."

"Conversion" indicates nothing less than a radical change of mind and heart that leads to a complete turnabout of life. It includes both (a) *repentance,* that is, genuine sorrow for sin and an earnest resolution to break with the evil past, and (b) *fruit-bearing* (see verses 8, 9).

A man must already have experienced genuine basic conversion before he can be baptized. That is clearly implied in verses 7–14: there must be genuine sorrow for sin and a true determination to do away with the evil of the past before John is willing to baptize anyone. But it is also true that by means of baptism true conversion is powerfully stimulated. How could reflection on the meaning of the *cleansing* water of baptism, symbolizing and sealing the cleansing grace and power of God, his *forgiving* love, have any different effect? For the person who in that spirit receives baptism the outward sign and seal applied to the body, and the inward grace applied to heart and life, go together. "I will sprinkle clean water upon y o u, and y o u shall be clean . . . a new heart also will I give y o u, and a new spirit will I put within y o u" (Ezek. 36:25, 26); "buried with him through baptism . . . raised . . . so we might walk in newness of life" (Rom. 6:4).

Now baptism as such was not something altogether new. Historically proselyte baptism, the administration of this rite to those who from the Gentile world had been converted to the Jewish religion, preceded baptism as administered by John. The Jews regarded all Gentiles as being unclean, and therefore subjected them to baptism when they were won over to Judaism. What was new and startling for the Baptist's audience was that a basic transformation and its sign and seal were required even of the children of Abraham! They too were filthy! They too must acknowledge this openly!

Note that according to verse 3 John went into the whole Jordan neighborhood *proclaiming*—literally *heralding*—the need, even for the Jews, of "a baptism of conversion with a view to the forgiveness of sins." For "proclaiming" one may substitute "preaching," that is, just so it be understood that genuine preaching or heralding is lively, not dry; timely, not stale. It is the earnest proclamation of news initiated by God. It is not the abstract speculation of views excogitated by man.

And what can be more encouraging than the proclamation of conversion with a view to "the forgiveness of sins"? Such forgiveness means that these sins are sent away to a place from which they can never be recovered. God-fearing people in John's audience knew about the sin-laden goat that was sent into the wilderness *never to return* (Lev. 16:8, 20-22). They knew the promise of Ps. 103:12, "As far as the east is from the west, so far has he removed our transgressions from us," and they must have experienced the truth of Mic. 7:19, "Thou wilt cast all their sins into the depths of the sea."

In harmony with that which had already been hinted in verse 2 ("the word of God came to Zechariah's son John"), as explained previously, Luke now clearly indicates that in John prophecy was being fulfilled.

4-6. as it is written in the book of the words of Isaiah the prophet:
A voice of one crying in the wilderness:
Make ready the way of the Lord,
Make straight his paths.
Every valley shall be filled up,
And every mountain and hill leveled down;
The crooked roads shall become straight,
And the rough ways smooth.
And all flesh shall see the salvation of God.

The reference is, of course, to Isa. 40:3 f. Matthew (3:3) and Mark (1:3) quote only Isa. 40:3. Luke also quotes verse 4 and to a certain extent even reproduces part of verse 5. The last five lines, therefore, of Luke's quotation—hence, the lines beginning with "every valley" and ending with "the salvation of God"—are in the New Testament found only in Luke.

In addition to a minor difference (between the Greek text and the Hebrew original) in the beginning, for which see the footnote,[169] and a few other small differences farther on, the main variation concerns the close of the quotation. Here the Hebrew text (Isa. 40:5) has:

> and the glory of the Lord shall be revealed, and all flesh shall see it together; for the mouth of the Lord has spoken it.

The Septuagint has:

> and the glory of the Lord shall be seen [or: revealed], and all flesh shall see the salvation of God; for the Lord has spoken.

Luke (3:6) omits "and the glory of the Lord shall be revealed," but has retained "And all flesh shall see the salvation of God."

If it be borne in mind that God's, hence also Christ's, *glory* is revealed most marvelously in the work of *salvation* (John 12:23, 31, 32; 17:4, 5), it will be clear that there is no essential difference between these three representations.

Isa. 40:3-5 symbolically pictures the approach of Jehovah for the purpose of leading the procession of Jews who will be returning joyfully to their homeland after long years of captivity. In the Syrian desert, between Babylonia and Palestine, the way must be prepared for the Lord's coming. So, a herald cries out to the people,

> In the wilderness make ready the way of the Lord,
> Make straight in the desert a highway for our God.

This figure of the herald is in the Gospels applied to John, as Christ's herald. The Baptist, by saying, "I am the voice..." shows that he agrees with this interpretation (John 1:23). So does Jesus himself (Matt. 11:10). This shows that the deliverance granted to the Jews when, in the latter part of the sixth century B.C. and afterward, they returned to their own country was but a type of that far more glorious liberation in store for all who accept Christ as their Savior and Lord. In other words, Isaiah's prophecy regarding the voice that cried out lacked *total* fulfilment until both Messiah's forerunner and also the Lord himself had arrived on the scene.[170]

---

169. In the Gospels and in the Septuagint text the phrase "in the wilderness" modifies "of one crying," and not "make ready," as it does in the masoretic accentuation of the Hebrew text of Isa. 40:3, the latter construction being also supported by the parallelism: "in the wilderness make ready" and "make straight in the desert." However, this difference between the Gospels and the Hebrew text is unimportant, for it is natural to assume that the wilderness crier, as the mouthpiece of the One who sent him, wants a way to be cleared in the wilderness.

170. The fact that what is said of *Jehovah* in the Old Testament is referred to *Christ* in the New should cause no surprise. For similar instances of this transition from Jehovah to Christ see Exod. 13:21, cf. I Cor. 10:4; Ps. 68:18, cf. Eph. 4:8; Ps. 102:25-27, cf. Heb. 1:10-12; and Isa. 6:1, cf. John 12:41. It is in Immanuel that Jehovah comes to dwell with his people.

The appropriate application of Isa. 40:3 to John the Baptist is evident from the following: (a) John was preaching in the wilderness (Mark 1:3; Luke 3:4); and (b) the task assigned to him from the days of his infancy (Luke 1:76, 77), yes even earlier (Luke 1:17; Mal. 3:1), was exactly this, namely, to be Messiah's herald or way-preparer. He was to be the Lord's "voice" to the people, *all of* that but *not more than* that (cf. John 3:22–30). As such he must not only announce Christ's approach and presence but also urge the people *to prepare the way* of the Lord, that is, by God's grace and power to effect a complete change of mind and heart. This implies that they must *make straight his paths,* meaning that they must provide the Lord with a ready access into their hearts and lives. They must *make straight* whatever was crooked, *not in line with* God's holy will. They must clear away all the obstacles which they had thrown into his path; such obstructions as self-righteousness and smug complacency ("We have Abraham as our father," Matt. 3:9), greed, cruelty, slander, etc. (Luke 3:13, 14).

It is evident that both in Isaiah's and in John's preaching as recorded by the Gospel writers "the wilderness" through which a path must be made ready for the Lord is in the final analysis the people's heart, by nature inclined to all evil. Though the literal meaning is not absent, it is subsumed into the figurative. The underlying idea is indeed the actual wilderness. But the very sight of this dreary region must have impressed those who listened to John's preaching with the fact that they themselves were spiritually "wandering in a desert land where all the streams are dry."

It is always difficult to determine exactly to what extent Isaiah's language, as quoted here by Luke, is to be explained figuratively. A thorough-going symbolical interpretation is detailed in the chart below.

Symbolical Interpretation of Luke 3:4b–6

The Words of Luke 3:4b–6	*A Possible (?) Interpretation*
A voice of one crying in the wilderness:	The message of John the Baptist, shouting in the wilderness:
Make ready the way of the Lord, Make straight his paths.	By means of genuine conversion (Jer. 31:18) make it possible for the Lord to make a straight path to y o u r heart *with his salvation.*
Every valley shall be filled up, And every mountain and hill leveled down;	Every manifestation of feigned humility as well as every attitude of pride and arrogance will be and must be removed.
The crooked roads shall become straight,	Sly, perverse, deceitful habits must be and will be broken.
And the rough ways smooth.	Indifference, unconcern, and wayward-ness must and will make way for genuine interest and accessibility.

Symbolical Interpretation of Luke 3:4b–6 (continued)

The Words of Luke 3:4b–6	A Possible (?) Interpretation
And all flesh shall see the salvation of God.	Then people of every clime and nation, viewed in their weakness and need, will experience the salvation provided by God. Cf. Luke 2:32.

But it is also possible that such expressions as "every valley," "every mountain and hill," "the rough ways," etc., pertain only to the underlying figure of an approaching King, and have no further significance. The meaning then would simply be, "By God's grace remove every obstacle in the way of the entrance of the Lord into y o u r hearts and lives. Be converted." And is not that the central meaning in either case?

7–9. He [John] therefore was saying to the crowds coming out to be baptized by him, Y o u offspring of vipers! Who warned y o u to escape the approaching (outpouring of) wrath? Bear fruit therefore in keeping with conversion; and do not begin to say to yourselves, We have Abraham as our father, for I tell y o u that God is able to raise up children for Abraham out of these stones here. And already the ax is laid at the root of the trees; every tree therefore that does not bear good fruit is cut down and thrown into the fire.

There is very little difference between Luke 3:7–9 and Matt. 3:7–10.[171] Did Luke have before him a copy of Matthew's Gospel, or did both evangelists use a common source?

When we combine Matthew's opening sentence with that of Luke we conclude that large crowds, including a goodly number of Pharisees and Sadducees, were coming out to be baptized by John. The Baptist knew, however, that many of these candidates for baptism were insincere. It is in this light that we can understand his stern rebuke, "Y o u offspring of vipers." John was acquainted with these desert snakes. Though rather small in size they were very *deceptive*. At times it was easy to mistake them for dead branches. Suddenly, however, they would strike and cling (cf. Acts 28:3). The comparison was apt. Is not Satan, that deceiver (John 8:44), also called a *serpent* (Rev. 12:9, 20:2)? Are not these people his tools?

John adds, "Who warned you to escape the approaching (outpouring of) wrath?" In this connection the following ideas deserve attention:

---

171. The only variations are: (a) In verse 8 Luke uses the plural (fruits) where Matthew (also verse 8) has the singular (fruit); but unless the reference is distinctly to different kinds of fruit, which does not seem to be the case here, the English rendering "fruit" is correct in either case; (b) in verse 8 Luke has "and do not begin to say," while Matthew's parallel (verse 9) is "and do not presume to say"; (c) in verse 9 Luke's extra conjunction (*kai*) increases by a trifle the justification for beginning the translation of that sentence with "And" (Matt. 3:10 lacks this *kai*); and (d), the greatest difference of all, Luke writes, "He [John] therefore was saying to the crowds coming out to be baptized by him" (verse 7), while Matthew's parallel (verse 7) reads, "But when he saw many of the Pharisees and Sadducees coming for baptism he said to them. . . ."

First, this wrath, or settled indignation, rests upon unregenerate man by nature (Eph. 2:3). It pertains even to the present (John 3:18, 36; Rom. 1:18).

Secondly, the final outpouring of this wrath is reserved for the future (Eph. 5:6; Col. 3:6; II Thess. 1:8, 9; Rev. 14:10).

Thirdly, this final manifestation of wrath (Zeph. 1:15; 2:2) is connected with the (second) coming of the Messiah (Mal. 3:2, 3; 4:1, 5).

Fourthly, without genuine conversion man cannot escape it: "Who warned y o u to escape . . .?" This probably means, "Who deluded y o u into thinking that it is possible to evade God, and encouraged y o u to try it?" Cf. Ps. 139; Jonah 1:3.

Fifthly, for the true penitent there is indeed a way of escape: "Bear fruit therefore in keeping with conversion." Repentance, if it is to be genuine, must be accompanied by fruit-bearing. A merely outward confession of sin will never do. A mere desire to be baptized, as if this rite were a wonder-working charm, has no positive value. There must be that inward change which expresses itself outwardly in God-glorifying conduct, fruit-bearing *in keeping with* conversion. According to verses 10–14 this fruit-bearing must include such items as generosity, fairness, thoughtfulness, and contentment; according to Matt. 23:23, justice, mercy, and faith; and in view of the manner in which the Baptist descriptively addresses these people ("Y o u offspring of vipers"), there must be uprightness. On fruit-bearing see also Matt. 5:20–24; 7:16–19; 12:33; 13:8, 23; 16:6, 11, 12; ch. 23; Luke 13:6–9; John 15:1–16; Gal. 5:22, 23; Eph. 5:9; Phil. 1:22; 4:17; Col. 1:6; Heb. 12:11; 13:15; and James 3:18.

The deplorable lack of fruit-bearing on the part of the addressed is evident also from the words: "and do not begin to say to yourselves, 'We have Abraham as our father,' for I tell y o u that God is able to raise up children for Abraham out of these stones here." The reason why these people were headed for damnation was that for their eternal security they were relying on their descent from Abraham. Cf. Gal. 3:1–9 and see N.T.C. on those verses. John the Baptist was fully aware of the fact that physical descent from Abraham did not guarantee being a true son of Abraham. He also knew that entirely apart from such pedigree God could give sons to Abraham. The God who was able to create Adam out of the dust of the ground was also able to make true sons of Abraham out of the desert stones to which John probably pointed. Probable symbolical overtone: He can change hearts of stone into obedient hearts (Ezek. 36:26), entirely regardless of the nationality of these hearts of stone.

As far as salvation was concerned, the old distinctions were gradually disappearing. This does not mean that in the order in which this salvation was being proclaimed and in which the church was being gathered there was no distinction. The historical sequence, a reflection of God's plan from eternity, certainly was "to the Jew first and also to the Greek" (Rom. 1:16; cf. Acts 13:46; Rom. 3:1, 2; 9:1–5). But the beginning of a new day, a day in which there would be "no distinction between Jew and Greek," was dawning. See Matt. 2:1-12; 8:11, 12; 22:1-14; 28:19, 20; Acts 10:34-48; Rom. 9:7, 8; 10:12, 13; I Cor. 7:19; Gal. 3:7, 16, 17, 29; 4:21-31; 6:15, 16; Eph. 2:14-18; Phil 3:2, 3; Col. 3:11; and Rev. 7:9, 14, 15.

As to the impenitent, in verse 9 John the Baptist continues: "And already[172] the ax is laid at the root of the trees." Judgment is at hand. The ax lies right in front of (πρός) or, as we would say, "at" the root, with sinister intent, ready to hew down one tree after another. *Right now,* therefore, is the proper moment to repent and to believe. In this connection see also Ps. 95:7, 8; Isa. 55:6; Luke 13:7, 9; 17:32; John 15:6; Rom. 13:11; II Cor. 6:2; I John 2:18; Rev. 1:3. Continued: "every tree therefore that does not bear good fruit is cut down and thrown into the fire." The question might be asked, "But was the day of the final manifestation of God's wrath upon the wicked actually that close? Is it not true that many centuries have passed by since the Baptist spoke these words, and still the Lord has not returned for judgment?" The following facts should be borne in mind:

First, John reminds one of the Old Testament prophet who, in speaking about the last days or the Messianic age, would at times look upon the future as a traveler does on a distant mountain range. He fancies that one mountain top rises up right behind the other, when in reality the two are miles apart. The two comings of Christ are viewed as if they were one. Thus we read, "A shoot shall come forth out of the stock of Jesse . . . and he shall smite the earth" (Isa. 11:1-4). "Jehovah has anointed me to preach good tidings to the meek. He has sent me to bind up the broken-hearted, to proclaim liberty to the captives and . . . the day of vengeance of our God" (Isa. 61:1, 2). "I will pour out my Spirit upon all flesh, and y o u r sons and y o u r daughters shall prophesy, y o u r old men shall dream dreams, and y o u r young men shall see visions. . . . The sun shall be turned into darkness, and the moon into blood, before the great and terrible day of Jehovah arrives" (Joel 2:28-31). Cf. Mal. 3:1, 2. This has been called "prophetic foreshortening."

Secondly, Jerusalem's fall (A.D. 70) was drawing perilously near, and foreshadowed the final judgment.

Thirdly, impenitence has a tendency of hardening a person, so that often he is left in his present lost condition. Without genuine repentance death and the judgment are for him irrevocable and "at the door."

Fourthly, "one day is with the Lord as a thousand years, and a thousand years as one day" (II Peter 3:8).

Fifthly, John was by no means the only one who emphasized the imminence of the judgment and/or the need of becoming converted right now. Therefore, if on this score we find fault with the Baptist we would also have to blame the psalmists, the prophets, the apostles, and even the Lord himself! Surely, no true believer is ready to do this.

---

172. Note forward position of ἤδη.

Sixthly, all this does not necessarily mean that the Baptist himself always saw the present and the future in true perspective. See on 7:18 f. It only means that the Holy Spirit guided him so that in his actual preaching as here recorded he had a perfect right to say what he said.

The "fire" into which the unfruitful trees are cast is evidently a symbol of the final outpouring of God's wrath upon the wicked. See also Mal. 4:1; Matt. 13:40; John 15:6. Jesus spoke about "the Gehenna of fire" (Matt. 5:22, 29; 18:9; Mark 9:47). This fire is unquenchable (Matt. 3:12; 18:8; Mark 9:43; Luke 3:17). The point is not merely that there is always a fire burning in Gehenna but that God burns the wicked with unquenchable fire, the fire that has been prepared for them as well as for the devil and his angels (Matt. 3:12; 25:41).

After having given us this more or less general specimen of John's preaching, Luke reports three questions asked severally by three groups of individuals. Each group wanted to know how, in concrete life situations, they should reveal the genuine character of their conversion:

10–14. So the crowds kept asking him, What then shall[173] we do? —He answered, Let the one who has two shirts share with the one who has none, and let the one who has food do likewise.

Tax-collectors too came to be baptized. They said to him, Teacher, what shall we do? —He told them, Don't exact more than required.

Soldiers too were asking, And we, what shall we do? —He replied, Don't extort money by violence, don't accuse people falsely, and be content with y o u r pay.

The three groups consisted of: (a) people from the crowd, other than tax-collectors and soldiers; (b) tax-collectors; (c) soldiers. All three groups seem to have been oppressed by a sense of guilt. They realize that true conversion always implies sorrow for sin (repentance) and forsaking the old way of life.

Representatives of the first group ask, "What then shall we do?" John told them to share their clothes and food with those who were in need.

The "shirt" is really the "tunic," a garment which by both sexes was worn next to the skin, hence under the outer garment or robe. Either to protect oneself against the cold or to have a "spare" for future use, a person might own two or even more tunics. The Baptist exhorts those who have two to give one to the person who has none. With respect to food the same course is advocated.

Note, however, that John does not say that the state should step in and deprive the "rich" person of his property—though the state does indeed have a duty with respect to the poor and destitute—nor does he tell the man without a tunic that he must help himself to the property of his neighbor, nor does he in any way condone refusal to work in order to earn

---

173. Or: must; so also in verses 12 and 14.

money with which to purchase life's necessities. What he is advocating is *voluntary sharing.*

A very practical lesson indeed! When catastrophe overwhelms the people of any region, and food and clothing are urgently needed, are we at all living in harmony with this exhortation when we refuse to share? Think also of the millions upon millions who, even apart from natural disasters, are living in constant abject poverty. Must they not be assisted?[174]

Next, the "publicans" or "tax-collectors" are introduced. The tax-buyers or "farmers" had paid a fixed sum of money to the Roman government for the privilege of levying tolls upon exports and imports as well as upon whatever merchandise passed through the region. The main tax offices were located at Caesarea, Capernaum, and Jericho. The farmers would sublet their rights to "chief publicans" (Luke 19:2) who employed "publicans" to do the collecting. These charged what the traffic would bear, huge sums. So the "publican" had the reputation of being an extortionist. If he were a Jew, he was regarded by his fellows as being also a renegade or traitor, for he was in the service of the foreign oppressor.

The "publicans" who now address John probably belonged to the bottom rung of their profession. They knew that they had been fleecing the public, and, conscience-stricken, they now also ask, "Teacher, what shall we do?" They receive the curt reply, "Don't exact more than required" (literally: "...more than is appointed to y o u").

The reply is again very definite and uncompromising. There must be immediate, complete, wholehearted obedience. Dillydallying is deadly. Halfway measures work havoc. Sin, being a destructive force, must not be pampered. The right action must be substituted at once for the wrong. Cf. Matt. 5:29, 30; 18:8, 9; Rom. 12:21.

And now the third group: "those doing military service" (thus literally). In connection with registration with a view to taxation these people would often resort to torture, in order by this means to make slaves accuse their masters of understating their holdings. By maliciously informing against the rich and by the use of extortion they would obtain money, and this not only for the government but also for themselves. They were cruel, swaggering, disgruntled. By inhuman and dishonest methods they tried to supplement their earnings. But when these people were listening to the Baptist's awesome thunderings, his vivid descriptions of impending divine judgment, they too quailed. With fear and trembling they approached the preacher of doom with the question, "And we, what shall we do?"

He answered, "Do not shake people down" (thus literally). He adds, "and

---

174. In this connection much can be learned from W. and P. Paddock, *Hungry Nations,* Boston and Toronto, 1964. These authors, experienced in this field, point out that so-called "help" is often wasted because those charged with helping the hungry nations forget that the latter must be shown how to carry forward their own development based on their own resources.

don't be sycophants [slanderous accusers]." See the note on verse 14 on page 215. "Be satisfied with y o u r earnings."

In connection with the last two groups note that John does not say that being a tax-collector, even when this profession is practiced in the interest of a foreign government, is wrong as such; nor does he say that doing military service is wrong. What he says is that these occupations, if pursued, must be engaged in for good and not for evil.

While John's answer to the first group is couched in positive language, his reply to the second and third groups is stated in negative terms. Nevertheless, these negatives imply strong affirmatives. In fact, at bottom all three answers amount to this: "Show genuine love." According to both the Old and the New Testament such love is the fulfilment of the law (Lev. 19:18; Deut. 6:5; Matt. 19:19; 22:34-40; Mark 12:28-34; Luke 10:25-28; John 13:34; Rom. 13:8-10; I Cor. 13; Gal. 5:14).

Now apart from Christ and his Spirit the exercise of this love is impossible. Appropriately, therefore, Luke continues by describing John the Baptist in the act of preaching about Christ and his Spirit:

15-18. Now while the people were on tiptoe of expectation, and all were wondering in their hearts about John, whether he might be the Christ, he expressly answered them all, I on my part baptize y o u with water, but he who is mightier than I is coming—whose sandal straps I am not fit to untie—he will baptize y o u with the Holy Spirit and with fire. His winnowing shovel is in his hand, and he will thoroughly clear his threshing floor. He will gather his grain into the granary, but the chaff he will consume with unquenchable fire.

By and large this little paragraph is parallel to Matt. 3:11, 12; cf. Mark 1:7, 8. Peculiar to Luke, however, are the introductory words, "Now while the people were on tiptoe of expectation, and all were wondering in their hearts about John, whether he might be the Christ, he expressly answered them all. . . ."

That there was indeed a Messianic expectation is clear from such passages as Luke 1:76-79; 2:25, 26, 38. That this hope was not necessarily completely confined to the hearts and minds of devout Israelites but may even have glimmered among heathen who had been in touch with them must be granted.

Of late, however, this expectation had been intensified by the many stories that had been spreading, especially those about John. His sudden appearance, rigorous self-denial, stern call to conversion, all these had become matters of deliberation and discussion. But especially his baptizing. . . *of Abraham's children!* About this same time a committee was being sent to John with the question, "Who are you? . . . Then why are you baptizing if you are neither the Christ nor Elijah nor the prophet?" (John 1:19-25). According to John 1:26, 27 it was on this occasion that John uttered the words which, in almost identical form, are found also in Luke 3:16a. There is no reason to question the fact that words which, according to the Fourth

Gospel, were addressed to Pharisees were also, in amplified form, spoken to an entire multitude.

The people, then, were on tiptoe of expectation. They were wondering whether John, a man who spoke with such conviction and so forcefully, whose words found such a response in their own conscience, and especially, a man who started something new, namely, baptizing Jews, as if they too were unclean, might not himself be the Christ.

John now draws a contrast between what he is doing and what One mightier than he is about to do. He tells the people that the qualitative distance between himself and the Coming One, who is mightier than he, is so great that he, John, is not even worthy to untie (so also in Mark 1:7), remove and carry away (Matt. 3:11) that Coming One's sandals. To One so great the Baptist is not even worthy to render the services of a slave; of this he is convinced.

John baptizes with water; Jesus will baptize with the Spirit. He will cause his Spirit and the latter's gifts to come upon his followers (Acts 1:8), be poured out on them (Acts 2:17, 33), fall upon them (Acts 10:44; 11:15).

Now it is true that whenever a person is drawn out of the darkness into God's marvelous light he is being baptized with the Holy Spirit and with fire. Thus Calvin in his comments on Matt. 3:11 remarks that it is Christ who bestows the Spirit of regeneration, and that, like fire, this Spirit purifies us by removing our pollution. However, according to Christ's own words (Acts 1:5, 8), remembered by Peter (Acts 11:16), *in a special sense* this prediction was fulfilled on the day of Pentecost and during the era which it introduced. It was then that, through the coming of the Spirit, the minds of Christ's followers were enriched with unprecedented illumination (I John 2:20); their wills strengthened, as never before, with contagious animation (Acts 4:13, 19, 20, 33; 5:29); and their hearts flooded with warm affection to a degree previously unheard of (Acts 2:44-47; 3:6; 4:32).

The mention of *fire* ("He will baptize y o u with the Holy Spirit and with fire") fits this application to Pentecost, when "there appeared to them divided tongues of fire, resting on each one of them" (Acts 2:3). The flame illumines. Fire cleanses. The Spirit does both. Nevertheless, it would appear from the context (both before and after; see verses 9 and 17) and from Joel's Pentecost prophecy (Joel 2:30; cf. Acts 2:19), considered in *its* context (see Joel 2:31), that the ultimate fulfilment of the Baptist's words awaits Christ's glorious return to cleanse the earth with fire (II Peter 3:7, 12; cf. Mal. 3:2; II Thess. 1:8).

Often in Scripture fire symbolizes *wrath*. But fire is also indicative of the work of *grace* (Isa. 6:6, 7; Zech. 13:9; Mal. 3:3; I Peter 1:7). It is not strange, therefore, that this term can be used both in a favorable sense, to indicate the blessings of Pentecost and the new dispensation, and in an unfavorable sense, to indicate the terrors of the coming judgment day. It is Christ who both *purifies* the righteous and *purges* the earth of its dross, the wicked. Moreover, if the Old Testament prophets would often, by means of *prophetic foreshortening,* combine the events pertaining to Christ's first coming (taken in its comprehensive sense, including even Pentecost) with those of the second, why cannot that same feature be ascribed also to the style of John the Baptist, who resembled these prophets in so many ways? It is clear, therefore, that the case for the interpretation according to which the word *fire* here in 3:16 refers both to Pentecost and to the final judgment is strong.

The reasonable character of the explanation, according to which the baptism with fire includes a reference to the final judgment, is also evident from verse 17, which likewise refers to that great day: "His winnowing shovel is in his hand, and he will thoroughly clear his threshing floor." The underlying figure is that of a threshing floor where winnowing is taking place. Such a floor is either natural or artificial. If the former, it is the surface of a flat rock on top of a hill, exposed to the wind. If the latter, it is a similarly exposed area, about thirty to fifty feet in diameter, which has been prepared by clearing the soil of stones, wetting it down, and then packing it hard and smooth, causing it to slope slightly upward along the rim, and surrounding it with a border of stones to keep the grain inside. First, the sheaves of grain (barley or wheat) that have been spread out in this area are threshed by oxen pulling a sled the bottom of which is studded with stones whereby the kernels of grain are separated from the stalks. The chaff (whatever remains of the kernels' hard coat, dust, dirt, small pieces of straw) is, however, still clinging to the kernels. Now the winnowing, to which verse 17 refers, begins. Bunch by bunch the threshed grain is tossed into the air by means of a shovel equipped with two or more prongs; the afternoon breeze, generally sweeping in from the Mediterranean from May through September, blows away the chaff. The heavier grain kernels fall straight down upon the threshing floor. *Thus grain and chaff are separated.* The work of winnowing does not stop until the threshing floor has been thoroughly cleared.

Thus also Christ at his return will thoroughly clear the area where the judgment will take place. No one will escape detection. Even now he is fully equipped with all that is needed to perform the task of separating the good from the bad. "He will gather his grain into the granary, but the chaff he will consume with unquenchable fire."

The threshed and winnowed grain is brought to the granary; literally, *the place where things are put* (or: *stored*) *away*. It is *stored away* because it is regarded as being very valuable, very precious. From the underlying figure we proceed to the reality. Even *the death of believers* is described in Scripture in a very comforting manner. It is "precious in the sight of Jehovah" (Ps. 116:15); "a being carried away by the angels into Abraham's bosom" (Luke 16:22); "a going to Paradise" (Luke 23:43); a blessed departure (Phil. 1:23); "a being at home with the Lord" (II Cor. 5:8); "a gain" (Phil. 1:21); "better by far" (Phil. 1:23); and "a falling asleep in the Lord" (John 11:11; I Thess. 4:13). Then surely *the final stage* in the glorification of God's children, both body and soul now participating in this bliss, will be most precious: a going to "the house with many mansions" (John 14:2), a being welcomed to the very presence of Christ ("I will come again and will take y o u to be face to face with me, in order that where I am y o u may be also," John 14:3), a living forever in the new heaven and earth from which every stain of sin and every trace of the curse will have been removed; in which righteousness dwells (II Peter 3:13); in which "God will dwell with them, and they shall be his people, and he himself shall be with them and be their God, wiping away every tear from their eyes," etc. (Rev. 21:1-5); and in which the prophecy of Isa. 11:6-9 ("The wolf shall dwell with the lamb," etc.) and of Rev. 21:9—22:5 (the new Jerusalem) will reach its *ultimate* fulfilment.

Back to the underlying figure once more. From the grain we now turn to the chaff. This, having dropped down at a place, or places, away from the grain, is collected and burned. So also the wicked, having been separated from the good, will be cast into hell, the place of unquenchable fire. Their punishment is unending. Their worm never dies (Mark 9:48). Their shame is everlasting (Dan. 12:2). So are their bonds (Jude 6, 7). They will be tormented with fire and brimstone . . . and the smoke of their torment ascends forever and ever, so that they have no rest day or night (Rev. 14:9-11; cf. 19:3; 20:10).

In which sense is this "fire" to be understood? Answer: though the idea of a fire which in some sense is physical need not be excluded, yet according to Scripture the literal sense does not exhaust the meaning. Everlasting fire has been prepared "for the devil and his angels." Yet these are *spirits* and cannot be hurt by literal fire. Moreover, Scripture itself points the way to the symbolical meaning; i.e., to the divine *wrath* resting upon the impenitent and, consequently, to their anguish (Deut. 9:3; 32:22; Ps. 11:5, 6; 18:8; 21:9; 89:46; Isa. 5:24, 25; Jer. 4:4; Nah. 1:6; Mal. 3:2; Matt. 5:22; Heb. 10:27; 12:29; II Peter 3:7; Rev. 14:10, 11; 15:2).

The Baptist's warning, dire and dreadful though it may seem, is filled with mercy, for its purpose is that men may be converted.

Luke closes this paragraph by stating that he has given only a sample of John's preaching. He says: **Thus, continually exhorting with respect to many and different matters, John was preaching the gospel to the people.**

19, 20. But when Herod the tetrarch was repeatedly rebuked by John because of Herodias, Herod's brother's wife, and because of all the (other) evil deeds he had committed, he added this to them all: he locked John up in prison.

As is so often the case, Luke's account here is not chronological. John the Baptist probably began his ministry in the middle of the year A.D. 26, as has been shown in connection with the explanation of 3:1, 2. He may have been imprisoned at the close of the year A.D. 27, and put to death about the beginning of A.D. 29. This would mean that for about a year (late 26-late 27) the ministries of Jesus and of John were concurrent. Luke, not yet having told us anything about Jesus' ministry, already mentions John's imprisonment!

But though not always chronological, Luke's account is logical. He wishes to bring the story of John's ministry to a close, in order to write the story of Christ's ministry. There surely can be no objection to that.

This does not mean that Luke never mentions John again. There are references to the Baptist in 5:33; 9:7, 9, 19; 11:1; 16:16; 20:4, 6; and see especially 7:18–35. But the story of John's active ministry as a free man ends here.

Herodias, as shown on the chart (N.T.C. on Matthew, p. 189), was the daughter of Aristobulus, who was a son of Herod the Great by Mariamne I. Herodias had married her half-uncle (her father's half-brother) Herod Philip, a private citizen, son of Herod the Great by Mariamne II. Herod Philip must not be confused with his half-brother Philip the tetrarch.

Now Herod Antipas, another half-brother, on a visit to Herod Philip, became infatuated with Herodias. The two illicit lovers agreed to separate from their present marriage partners—Herodias from Herod Philip; Herod Antipas from the daughter of Aretas, king of the Nabatean Arabs—and to marry each other. This was done. When John the Baptist heard about this he rebuked Herod Antipas. He did this repeatedly. There was good reason for the rebuke, for such a marriage was incestuous (Lev. 18:16; 20:21). Was it not also adulterous (Rom. 7:2, 3)?

Of course, Herodias knew very well that whenever John rebuked the tetrarch he was also, by implication, denouncing her. So she insisted—by means of constant nagging perhaps?—that John be put to death. As to Herod Antipas himself, his attitude to the accuser was not entirely hateful. In fact there were certain qualities in John that he admired. See Mark 6:20. On the other hand, he had to "put up" with the woman whom he now considered his wife, and whose heart was seething with unmitigated, savage vengeance. Not at all to yield to her wishes seemed impossible. So he compromised. He arrested John, put him in chains, and shut him up in a terrible, deep, and hot dungeon that formed part of the castle-palace at Machaerus.

Note that Luke adds that Herod Antipas was also repeatedly rebuked "because of all the (other) evil deeds he had committed." What the evangelist is saying, then, is this, that of all the wicked deeds Herod Antipas ever perpetrated, this crime of imprisoning—in his mind did Luke add "and subsequently murdering"?—John the Baptist was the most revolting. It was disgusting, loathsome, for it was a crime against John, the gospel, the people, God![175]

Practical Lessons Derived from Luke 3:1–20

Verse 2

"The word of God came to ... John." Preachers can be effective only when they are truly "ministers of God's Word."

---

175. Notes on Greek words, phrases, and constructions in 3:1–20 begin on page 214.

Verse 3

"Conversion." A person is not saved by outward reformation. What he needs is inner transformation; that is, conversion.

Verses 4, 5

"Make straight his [the Lord's] paths." It is a terrible thing to cast obstacles into the path of God's approach to heart and life, or even to leave things as they are. Every impediment must be removed. See Ps. 86:11b.

Verse 6

"All flesh shall see the salvation of God." Rich man, poor man; black man, white man; highly educated, illiterate; male, female; old, young; there is one way for all. See Rom. 3:22–24.

Verse 7

"Offspring of vipers." John knew that the first step in being saved is always that I must know "how great my sins and misery are" (quoted from the Heidelberg Catechism). Cf. Rom. 7:24.

Verse 10

"What then shall we do?" In his answer the Baptist places great stress on human responsibility. That is as it should be; just so it is realized that only by the power and grace of God is man able to do what God demands of him.

Verse 16

"He who is mightier than I." John was truly great in God's sight . . . because he was truly small in his own sight.

Verses 19, 20

"Herod . . . locked John up in prison." And by doing this he was locking himself up in a far more terrible prison, one from which he was never going to escape. The word of God is ever mightier than the sword, even than the executioner's sword.

Notes on Greek Words, Phrases, and Constructions in 3:1–20

Verse 2

ῥῆμα θεοῦ, here probably a particular utterance of God, perhaps even in the sense of a command to proclaim God's message to the people. In our comments it is called "the divine message ordering John to awaken the people to the need of basic conversion."

Verse 5

φάραγξ*, a ravine, gulley, valley, chasm. Cf. *pharynx.*

πληρωθήσεται, third per. s. fut. passive indicat. of πληρόω, to fill. See also on 2:40.

βουνός* (cf. 23:30), hill. It can be associated with the familiar βάω, βαίνω, in the sense of *to ascend*, though etymological connection with that verb is uncertain.

ταπεινωθήσεται, another fut. passive indicat.; this one of ταπεινόω, to make low, humble. See the cognate noun in the note on 1:48 on page 111.

σκολιός, crooked. Cf. *scalene* (unequal).

τραχύς**, rough, uneven; cf. Acts 27:29. Cf. *trachea* (windpipe with its rough rings); also rugged *Trachonitis*.

λεῖος* (acc. fem. pl. λείας), smooth, plain; cf. *level*.

Verse 6

For τὸ σωτήριον see the note on 2:30 on page 176.

Verse 7

ἔχιδνα**, lizard, viper.

ὑπέδειξε, third per. s. aor. indicat. of ὑποδείκνυμι; literally: to show under; hence, to suggest. Cf. *indicate*.

Verse 10

ἐπηρώτων, imperfect, they kept asking.

ποιήσωμεν, deliberative first per. pl. aor. subjunctive. So also in verses 12 and 14.

Verse 12

τελώνης, tax-collector (= τέλος plus ὠνέομαι, to buy). Cf. *toll* and *vend*.

Verse 13

πράσσετε, sec. per. pl. active imperative of πράσσω. Cf. "Do not do them in"; that is, "Do not inflict great injury on them."

Verse 14

διασείσητε, sec. per. pl. aor. active subjunctive of διασείω*, to shake thoroughly, harass, extort, deceive.

συκοφαντήσητε, same construction as the preceding verb. The word is said to have been derived from σῦκον, fig, plus φαίνω, to show, to expose; hence συκοφαντέω* indicates the action of a person who shows up (informs against) anyone who exports figs out of Attica; and the meaning developed into: to accuse falsely, to slander, cheat. Whether this story of the origination of the verb and of the noun συκοφάντης (sycophant, defamer) is correct is uncertain.

ὀψώνιον, wages; from ὄψον, cooked food, plus ὠνέομαι, to buy; and so: ration, pay, soldier's pay; in I Cor. 9:7 a preacher's wages; in Rom. 6:23 sin's wages.

Verse 15

Note the two genitive absolutes.

μήποτε εἴη, third per. s. pres. optative of εἰμί: whether he might be, whether perhaps he were. In direct discourse the indicative would have been used.

Verse 17

πτύον, winnowing shovel.

διακαθάραι, cf. Matt. 3:12. The form used by Luke is the effective aor. infinitive of διακαθαίρω*, to cleanse or clear thoroughly. Cf. *catharsis*.

ἄσβεστος, unquenchable; cf. *asbestos* (with different meaning, however).

Verse 19

ἐλεγχόμενος, reproved, pres. passive participle of ἐλέγχω, to bring to light, expose, reprove, punish.

---

21 Now when all the people were baptized, and Jesus was also baptized and was praying, the heaven was opened,   22 and the Holy Spirit descended upon him in bodily form, as a dove. And a voice came out of heaven, "Thou art my Son, the Beloved; with thee I am well pleased."[176]

3:21, 22 *The Baptism of Jesus*
Cf. Matt. 3:13–17; Mark 1:9–11

21. Now when all the people were baptized, and Jesus was also baptized and was praying, the heaven was opened... When the question is asked, "Since Jesus was not stained by any sin, and since baptism indicates the washing away of sin, why then did he submit to baptism?" writers react in various ways. Some skip the problem entirely. That is the easy way out. Others answer that when Jesus saw people flocking to John to be baptized he joined the crowd, wishing to be identified with them. And still others give the enigmatic answer that Christ's baptism was his "priestly inauguration," and then leave this item unexplained.

There are, of course, also others who, in one form or another, have given the right answer. Thus S. Greijdanus states that "Baptism was the Lord's public assumption of his work as Messiah."[177]

If what we see here is a jigsaw puzzle, the various "pieces" can be fitted together so as to form a clear picture as follows:

a. The water of baptism signifies the necessity of being cleansed. In a certain sense that was true also in the case of Jesus. He himself was sinless (John 8:46; II Cor. 5:21; Heb. 4:15). *In* himself there was nothing that needed to be, or could be, cleansed. But *on* himself? See the next point:

b. According to Scripture's consistent teaching the Messiah took *on* himself his people's guilt, and *vicariously* bore (or: was to bear) its punishment (Isa. 53:5, 6, 8, 10, 12; Matt. 20:28; Mark 10:45; Luke 22:19, 20; Rom. 3:24, 25; 5:8; 8:1; II Cor. 5:21; Gal. 3:13; Rev. 1:5).

---

176. Or: in thee I take delight.
177. *Korte Verklaring*, p. 98. And did not even Turrettin say that Jesus took baptism "vicariously"? The quotation occurs in R. L. Dabney, *op. cit.*, p. 763.

c. In order to bring about this *vicarious* redemption, the Holy Spirit, with all his qualifying power (Isa. 11:2; 48:16; 61:1–3; Zech. 4:6; Luke 4:18, 19), descended on Jesus, qualifying him (according to his human nature) for *the task* he had taken upon himself.

d. For this symbolic public assumption of his *task,* that of *taking away* the sin of others, the Father caused his voice of love and approval to be heard from heaven (Matt. 3:16, 17; Mark 1:10, 11; Luke 3:22).

e. Shortly afterward the Baptist introduced Jesus to the crowd by saying, "Look, the Lamb of God, who is *taking away* the sin of the world" (John 1:29; see also verses 30–34).

When these "pieces" are thus fitted together, do they not produce a picture of the Christ in the act of publicly assuming his task: that of openly taking upon himself, atoning for, and carrying away "the sin of the world"?

As to what actually happened, we have noticed that in Luke 2:21 the emphasis was not on the circumcision but on the naming of the child. So here also the emphasis is not on Jesus' baptism but on what took place while he was praying, namely, the Spirit's descent upon him and the Father's approving voice.

What Luke writes is completely misconstrued when it is changed to something resembling the following: "Now after all the people had been baptized, Jesus was also baptized." Even today one actually hears sermons in which the text, so interpreted, is made the basis for a sermon on Christ's humility: he just stood there, stood there, stood there . . .patiently waiting until all the others were baptized. Only then did he also present himself for baptism! The words, "Now when all the people were baptized, and Jesus was also baptized," etc., simply imply that at the height of John's baptizing activity Jesus was also baptized. Note, however, that in this connection Luke does not even mention John's name, though it is clear from verses 2, 15, 16, 20, that it was indeed John who baptized Jesus. See also Mark 1:9; John 1:28–34. Matt. 3:13–15 even supplies further details, showing how John's hesitancy to baptize Jesus was overcome. The reason Luke omits the name of the man who baptized Jesus may well have been that this evangelist has now begun to tell us the story of *Christ's* ministry. He is no longer speaking about John the Baptist.

Note the significant words "and Jesus was also baptized *and was praying.*" Jesus attached great importance to prayer. He prayed not only in connection with his baptism, as shown here, but also when crowds were gathering (5:15, 16); just before choosing the twelve disciples (6:12); in connection with, and after, the miraculous feeding of the five thousand (Mark 6:41, 46; cf. Matt. 14:19, 23); when he was about to ask his disciples an important question (Luke 9:18); on the mountain where he was transfigured (Luke 9:28); just before extending the tender invitation, "Come to me all who are weary. . ." (Matt. 11:25–30; Luke 10:21); just before he taught the disciples the Lord's Prayer (Luke 11:1); at Lazarus' tomb (John 11:41, 42); for Peter, before the denial (Luke 22:32); during the night of the institution of the

Lord's Supper (John 17; cf. 14:16); in Gethsemane (Mark 14:32, 35, 36, 39; cf. Matt. 26:39, 42, 44; Luke 22:42); on the cross (Luke 23:34; Matt. 27:46; Mark 15:34; Luke 23:46); and after his resurrection (Luke 24:30). These references must be considered as being merely examples of a much more extensive life of prayer and thanksgiving. On the subject of Luke's own emphasis on prayer see *Introduction,* point I A 5 b.

If the meaning of Christ's baptism, as indicated in the preceding, is understood, it will not seem strange that Jesus, about to undertake a task so grievous, yet also so glorious, would feel the need of fellowship with his Father in heaven.

While Jesus was praying "the heaven was opened." **22 ... and the Holy Spirit descended upon him in bodily form, as a dove.** Suddenly heaven was as it were rent asunder, and with the symbolism of a dove the Third Person of the Trinity descended on Jesus.

What was seen physically was a bodily form resembling a dove. It was seen descending on Jesus. It is not clear just why God chose the form of a dove to represent the Holy Spirit. Some commentators point to the *purity* and the gentleness or *graciousness* of the dove, properties which, in an infinite degree, characterize the Spirit, and therefore also Christ (cf. Ps. 68:13; Song of Sol. 2:14; 5:2; Matt. 10:16). Thus equipped and qualified, he was able to carry out the very difficult task which the Father had given him to do. To save us from sin he himself needed to be *pure.* To endure torment, to pardon our iniquities, and to exercise patience with our weaknesses, he needed *gentleness, meekness, graciousness.* This, too, he possessed in an abundant measure, and he told his followers that, by the grace and power of God, they should acquire and exercise these same gifts (Matt. 11:29, 30; 12:19; 21:4, 5; Luke 23:34).

So far we have heard about *the Son's* baptism, thereby openly affirming his entire willingness to take upon himself "the sin of the world" (John 1:29); also about *the Spirit's* descent upon him, qualifying him for a task infinitely tremendous and sublime. It is therefore altogether fitting that the voice of *the Father's* wholehearted approval and delight be added, so that it may become clear that in the work of saving sinners, as in *every* divine work, the three are one. Note, therefore, the concluding words of this section: **And a voice came out of heaven, Thou art my Son, the Beloved; with thee I am well pleased [or: in thee I take delight].**

Whose voice was it? The Speaker is not named. Neither is this necessary, for the very phraseology ("my Son, the Beloved") identifies the Speaker as being, of course, the Father. Moreover, not only in his official Messianic capacity but also as Son by eternal generation, as the One who fully shares the divine essence together with the Father and the Spirit, Jesus is the Father's Beloved (John 1:14; 3:16; 10:17; 17:23). No higher love is possible than the love which the Father cherishes toward his Son. According to the verbal adjective (*beloved*) here used, this love is deep-seated, thorough-going, as great as is the heart of God itself. It is also as intelligent and purposeful as is the mind of God. It is tender, vast, infinite![178]

Not only that, but this love is also *eternal;* that is, it is timeless, raised far above all temporal boundaries. Though some disagree, the rendering "with thee I am well pleased" must be considered correct.[179] In the quiet recess of eternity the Son was the object of the Father's inexhaustible delight (cf. Prov. 8:30). The former's public affirmation, by means of baptism, of his purpose to shed his blood for a world lost in sin did nothing to diminish that love. That is what the Father is telling his Son. That is what he is also telling all of us.

How filled with comfort this paragraph, comfort not only for the Son and for John, but for every child of God, for it indicates that *not only the Son* loves his followers enough to suffer the pangs of hell in their stead, but that also the Spirit fully co-operates by strengthening him for this very task, and that the Father, instead of frowning upon the One who undertakes it, is so very pleased with him that he must needs rend asunder the very heavens, that his voice of delightful approval may be heard on earth![180] All three are equally interested in our salvation, and the three are One.[181]

Practical Lessons Derived from Luke 3:21, 22

Verse 21

"And was praying." It is especially Luke who emphasizes the fact that Jesus not only urged his disciples to pray, and even taught them to pray, but lived a life of prayer. When the teacher is himself seen doing the very things he tells others to do, his teaching is bound to be far more effective.

Verses 21, 22

Jesus was baptized . . . the Holy Spirit descended upon him . . . the Father caused his voice of love and approval to be heard. These three are always one. That is the secret of his people's salvation.

---

178. On the difference between ἀγαπάω and φιλέω, and their respective derivatives, see N.T.C. on John, Vol. II, pp. 494–500.

179. This is an excellent example of the timeless aorist. See Gram. N.T., p. 837; thus also in Matt. 3:17; 17:5; Mark 1:11.

180. On the entire subject of Christ's baptism read also the following: A. B. Bruce, "The Baptism of Jesus," *Exp*, 5th ser., 7 (1898), pp. 187–201; and W. E. Bundy, "The Meaning of Jesus' Baptism," *JR*, 7 (1927), pp. 56–71.

181. Notes on Greek words, phrases, and constructions in 3:21, 22 begin on page 220.

Notes on Greek Words, Phrases, and Constructions in 3:21, 22

Verse 21

ἐν τῷ βαπτισθῆναι, articular aor. infinitive of βαπτίζω. It does not mean that Jesus was baptized after everybody else had received this sacrament. There is no time element here. Wrong is the information given by Gram. N.T. (Bl.-Debr.), par. 404 (2) on p. 208. Correct is Gram. N.T., p. 1073; also *Word Pictures,* Vol. II, p. 43.

Verse 22

εὐδόκησα, timeless aorist.

23 Now Jesus himself, supposedly Joseph's son, was about thirty years old when he began (his ministry), being a son of Heli,
24 son of Matthat, son of Levi, son of Melchi, son of Jannai, son of Joseph,
25 son of Mattathias, son of Amos, son of Nahum, son of Esli, son of Naggai,
26 son of Maath, son of Mattathias, son of Semein, son of Josech, son of Joda,
27 son of Joanan, son of Rhesa, son of Zerubbabel, son of Shealtiel, son of Neri,
28 son of Melchi, son of Addi, son of Cosam, son of Elmadam, son of Er,
29 son of Joshua, son of Eliezer, son of Jorim, son of Matthat, son of Levi,
30 son of Simeon, son of Judah, son of Joseph, son of Jonam, son of Eliakim,
31 son of Melea, son of Menna, son of Mattatha, son of Nathan, son of David,
32 son of Jesse, son of Obed, son of Boaz, son of Salmon, son of Nahshon,
33 son of Amminadab, son of Aram, son of Hezron, son of Perez, son of Judah,
34 son of Jacob, son of Isaac, son of Abraham, son of Terah, son of Nahor,
35 son of Serug, son of Reu, son of Peleg, son of Eber, son of Shelah,
36 son of Cainan, son of Arphaxad, son of Shem, son of Noah, son of Lamech,
37 son of Methuselah, son of Enoch, son of Jared, son of Mahalaleel, son of Cainan,
38 son of Enos, son of Seth, son of Adam, son of God.

3:23–38 *The Genealogy of Jesus*[182]

23a. Now Jesus himself, supposedly Joseph's son, was about thirty years old when he began (his ministry)...

In our study of 3:1, 2 it has already been shown that the theory according to which Jesus "was about thirty years old" in or about the latter part of A.D. 26 agrees with other biblical data (Matt. 2; John 2:20). From Num. 4:47 we learn that thirty years was the age at which the Levites began their service. It was also at that age that Joseph became "prime minister" of Egypt (Gen. 41:46), and that David became king (II Sam. 5:4).[183] It is not strange, therefore, that Jesus began (implied, "his ministry") at that age.

What follows is a genealogy of Jesus:

**23b–38:... being a son of Heli,
son of Matthat, son of Levi, son of Melchi,
son of Jannai, son of Joseph,**

....

....

**son of Enos, son of Seth, son of Adam,
son of God.**

Similarities Between Matthew's List and Luke's

1. Matthew's first 14 names (Abraham to David) agree with Luke's.

2. Shealtiel and Zerubbabel are found in both lists. See Hendriksen's *Survey of the Bible,* Grand Rapids, 1976, p. 136, for one of the many theories showing how it was possible for the two lists to coincide at this point and then to part again.

These are two of the main similarities.

Differences

1. The great majority of the names in each list are absent from the other.

2. Matthew's list—Abraham to Jesus—is much shorter than Luke's—Jesus to Adam, son of God. See N.T.C. on Matthew, pp. 105–130.

3. Matthew skips more generations than does Luke. Between David and Shealtiel (inclusive) Matthew's genealogy contains 16 different names, Luke's 22. Between Shealtiel and Jesus (inclusive) Matthew mentions 13 names, Luke again 22.

4. Matthew presents three lists of 2 × 7 names each, though to arrive at that figure one name has to be repeated. There are those who think that

---

182. Though Matt. 1:1–17 also has a genealogy of Jesus, the two (Matthew's and Luke's) are "parallel" only in a loose sense and to a limited extent, as the explanation will indicate.

183. A. Stöger, *op. cit.,* p. 75, even adds that it was at the age of thirty that Ezekiel was called to be a prophet, but that interpretation of Ezek. 1:1 is questionable. And cf. S.BK., Vol. II, p. 155.

Luke is also operating with the figure 7. By including the names of Jesus, Joseph, and God a total of 77 (= 11 × 7) names results. Within this 77, other groupings of multiples of 7 are pointed out. It may be questioned, however, whether in the Third Gospel we should attach special significance to this phenomenon. Luke himself at least offers nothing that resembles Matt. 1:17.

5. Matthew presents a *descending* (from father to son) genealogy; Luke an *ascending* (from son to father) one.

6. It is not strange that Matthew, written to win the Jews for Christ, begins his list with Abraham, nor that Luke, whose horizon is world-wide, ends with Adam, son of God; for Jesus, the Messiah, has significance for the entire human race, and that race is derived from God himself. It has no animal origin!

Does Luke present the genealogy of Joseph or of Mary (more precisely: the genealogy of Jesus through Joseph or the genealogy of Jesus through Mary; for brevity's sake, however, the shorter designation will be used)?

To increase interest in this question we here present it in the form of a debate:

Resolved: That the Genealogy Presented by Luke Is That of Joseph
A. *Affirmative*[184]

Mr. Chairman, honorable judges, worthy opponent, and all other friends of biblical investigation:

I find it strange that the view according to which Luke presents a genealogy of Mary still finds defenders. Why, Mary's name is not even mentioned in the list! Is it at all reasonable to assume that a person would present a genealogy without even mentioning the name of the one person who—apart from Jesus himself—should be considered the most important of all?

Besides, the view that Luke presents Mary's genealogy was unknown in early times. It did not come into prominence until about the date of the discovery of America.[185] This should cause no surprise because the very language Luke uses clearly indicates that he is thinking not of Mary but of Joseph, whose name heads the list. Luke writes, "Jesus was . . . a son . . . of Joseph, son of Heli [or Eli]," etc. In all likelihood Joseph obtained this genealogy from a Jewish source. Jews were not in the habit of tracing the mother's genealogy, only the father's.

It is altogether natural to assume that Luke, having declared that Joseph was the reputed father of Jesus, would now proceed to trace Joseph's de-

---

184. Authors of commentaries favoring this position are, among others, A. B. Bruce, C. R. Erdman, W. J. Harrington, A. Plummer (for titles see Bibliography); exact references to the works of others will be given in the footnotes of this debate. In the commentaries consult the section on Matthew's genealogy and on Luke's.

185. For this argument see Howley, Bruce, Ellison, *op. cit.*, p. 142.

scent. In the eye of the law Jesus was, after all, the heir of Joseph, and that is what counted among the Jews.

If Luke were giving the genealogy of Mary, the word *son* would be used in a twofold sense: "Jesus, son, that is, *grandson* (through Mary) of Heli," who was "*son* of Matthat." That surely would be very confusing.

What is perhaps my strongest argument[186] is this, that in 1:27 Luke calls attention to the Davidic descent not of Mary but of Joseph. It is therefore natural to conclude that the genealogy he inserts in his book is also that of Joseph, not that of Mary.

B. *Negative*[187]

Mr. President, noble referees, friendly adversary, and all those interested in scriptural research:

If anything is clear, it is surely this, that *Matthew* intends his Gospel to be read especially by the Jews. For them indeed the descent of Joseph (Jesus' legal father) from David and from Abraham was most important. *Luke,* on the other hand, writes for Gentiles; one might say, for the whole world. What interested him and his readers was the meaning of Jesus for the human race. In presenting his genealogy he wanted to show that Jesus belonged indeed to that race. How? By being the offspring of Joseph? If there is anything Luke stresses it is surely this, that Jesus was not in any physical sense the offspring of Joseph. He was virgin born. This evangelist was not at all afraid, therefore, that his readers would understand him to mean that the genealogical tree he presents is that of Joseph. In 1:34, 35, and in fact throughout, had he not taken the definite position that, physically speaking, Jesus was solely the son of Mary, that Joseph had nothing whatever to do with the child's conception? And is it not true that it is Luke who tells the nativity story from the aspect of *Mary's* experiences?

To make this point doubly clear, even at the very beginning of the genealogy Luke states that only in the imagination of the people was Jesus the son of Joseph. He writes, "Jesus himself, supposedly Joseph's son." What he means is that people were wrong in regarding Joseph as the actual father of Jesus. Joseph was only Jesus' suppositional father; hence, in any physical sense not his father at all. That being granted, what sense would it make to append to that statement a lengthy genealogy of the man whom Luke has just now described as being only supposedly, but not at all really, the father of Jesus?

It is true that in showing why Joseph had to be registered in Bethlehem, Luke indicates that carpenter's descent from David. Does this prove that

---

186. See J. G. Machen, *The Virgin Birth of Christ,* New York and London, 1930, p. 204.

187. Authors of commentaries and related works in which the Mary theory is favored are, among others, R. C. Foster, N. Geldenhuys, F. Godet, S. Greijdanus, R. C. H. Lenski, A. T. Robertson (*Word Pictures*, Vol. II). Here also, see Bibliography for titles.

the genealogy is also necessarily Joseph's? Not at all. With more right—for the matter discussed is more pertinent to the issue—one could defend the Mary genealogy theory by pointing to Luke 1:32, 69, where Luke incorporates material in which *Mary's* descent from David is clearly implied.

Are the advocates of the Joseph genealogy forgetting that if their theory were true Joseph would have two fathers? According to Matt. 1:16 his father would be *Jacob;* according to Luke 3:23 *Heli.* It is really comical to see how proponents of the Joseph theory try to wriggle out of this difficulty: on this point there surely is no unanimity among them.

All difficulties, however, disappear when it is granted that, in harmony with the entire plan and purpose of each Gospel, Matthew gives us the genealogy of Joseph, Luke that of Mary.

C. *Rebuttal for the Affirmative*

Has it not become clear that my opponent's position is weak? He has left some of my arguments entirely untouched! We still do not know how he handles the objection that the Jews were used to tracing *the father's* family tree, not the mother's. Apparently he doesn't know how to answer that one.

Also, does he not realize, as I pointed out earlier, that if Luke is here presenting Mary's genealogy, he must be using the word *son* in a twofold sense? In that case Jesus must have been the *grandson* (through his mother Mary) of Heli, who was the *son* of Matthat, etc. What inconsistency!

There is another very important argument which my opponent must have found embarrassing; at least he conveniently forgot to say anything about it. It is the fact that the notion that this is Mary's genealogy was never heard of in early days.

I repeat, therefore, that the affirmative position is correct, namely, "that the genealogy presented by Luke is that of Joseph."

D. *Rebuttal for the Negative*

My friends, did y o u notice that my honored adversary has made himself guilty of the very error of which he accuses me? In not a single case did he himself, in what was supposed to be his "rebuttal," answer my arguments.

I will try to do better with respect to his latest observations:

First, then, it is precarious to state that tracing Mary's genealogy would have been impossible among the Jews. There are exceptions to almost every rule. When a father dies, his sons inherit the estate. Does this mean, then, that the daughters are absolutely excluded? Num. 27:8 warns us against taking that position. In the present case one is also dealing with a very special case, namely, with a child who, physically speaking, had no human father at all. In such a case "normal" or "usual" procedure simply stops.

Secondly, as to the use of the word *son* in more than one sense, that is true whether the list is Joseph's or Mary's. There are gaps in these genealogies no matter how they are intepreted. See N.T.C. on Matthew, pp. 119, 124. In several cases the "son" must have been "grandson" or even "great-grandson," for even Luke's list, *if* interpreted in the sense that in every case "son" must mean immediate male descendant, would be too short to reach all the way back from Jesus to Adam. Besides, in the item "Seth son of Adam, son of God," the word *son* cannot have the same meaning both times.

Thirdly, as to the objection that the theory that this is Mary's genealogy is of relatively recent origin, how does that harmonize with the fact that, even in the Talmud, Mary is called "the daughter of Heli," which is correct only if Luke's genealogy is interpreted as referring to Mary's—and not to Joseph's—family tree?[188] L. M. Sweet, in his article "Genealogy of Jesus Christ, The," I.S.B.E., Vol. II, p. 1198, speaks of "the early tradition of Mary's Davidic origin." The Sinaitic-Syriac MS. renders Luke 2:4 as follows: "They [both Joseph and Mary] were of the house and lineage of David."

Here ends the debate. All in all it would seem that it was won by the negative, in the sense that it is *not* true that the genealogy presented by Luke (3:23–38) is necessarily that of Joseph. On the contrary, it is probably that of Mary.[189]

Practical Lessons Derived from Luke 3:23–38

Verse 23

"Jesus . . . was about thirty years old when he began (his ministry)." This does not mean that Jesus did nothing before that time. On the contrary, see Luke 2:52. He was definitely already a blessing long before he reached the age of 30. But about the time when he reached that age he began his active ministry, his public task. The trouble with many people is that *they never actually begin* their ministry of exercising the priesthood of believers. They simply drift, are passive. Meanwhile the world is perishing! A passage which we should repeat to ourselves again and again is John 9:4, "While it is day we must work.... Night is approaching when no man can work."

Verses 23–38

"He [was] a son of Heli . . . son of Adam . . . son of God." Rightly considered, this genealogy not only teaches us how very close Jesus is to mankind but also how close, in a certain sense, mankind is to God. We refer to the closeness described in John 3:16, the passage that teaches the "God so loved the world" doctrine. The salvation promised in that passage is for "whoever believes in God's only-begotten Son." Salvation is for them *alone*. It is for them *all*.

---

188. See *Ḥaghigha* 77.4.
189. A note on the construction and translation of verse 23 appears on page 226.

Note on the Construction and Translation of Verse 23

The construction of this passage, as many see it, justifies the translation, "Jesus, when he began his ministry, was about thirty years of age, being the son (as was supposed) of Joseph, the son of Heli..." (R.S.V. and, with slight variations, many others).

This rendering has the merit of adhering closely to the order of the words in the original.

Objections

a. In all other cases the father's (grandfather's) name is preceded by τοῦ; this is not true with respect to the name *Joseph*. This fact is ignored in the translation.

b. This rendering also ignores the fact that Luke would be giving a lengthy genealogy of the very man whom he describes as only supposedly the father of Jesus; the expression *as was supposed* would make the entire genealogy a matter of conjecture.

c. It overlooks the fact that in his nativity account Luke not only teaches but strongly emphasizes Christ's virgin birth. On the other hand, if this is supposed to be Joseph's *legal* line of ascent, does it not, even at the very beginning, clash with the genealogy presented by Matthew?

In one way or another the following translations avoid these weaknesses:

"And he himself Jesus when beginning was about thirty years old, being a son (as was supposed of Joseph) of Heli..." (Lenski).

"And he himself, Jesus, when he began, was about thirty years old, being a son, as was supposed of Joseph, of Heli..." (Greijdanus).

"Jesus Himself, supposedly Joseph's son, began his ministry at about thirty, being a descendant of Heli..." (Berkeley Version).

"Now Jesus himself, supposedly Joseph's son, was about thirty years old when he began (his ministry), being a son of Heli..." (my rendering).

Summary of Chapter 3

The Ministry of John the Baptist (verses 1-20). In the fifteenth year of the reign of Tiberius Caesar and during the highpriesthood of Annas and Caiaphas, Zechariah's son John, at God's command, began to address great multitudes. They came to him in the wilderness of Judea. In fulfilment of the prophecy of Isa. 40:3 f. John courageously proclaimed the need of wholehearted conversion, so that the Lord, as King of glory, might ride triumphantly into their hearts and lives. Boldly he described the crowds as "offspring of vipers." He demanded that they, though Jews, should be baptized, thereby acknowledging their need of spiritual cleansing, and resolving by God's grace to live transformed lives. Too long had they been taking refuge in the slogan, "We are Abraham's children." John said, "I tell y o u that God is able to raise up children for Abraham out of these stones here." He urged them to bear good fruits, threatening that otherwise they would be cut down as a tree and thrown into the fire. When some asked him, "What shall we do?" he told them to start sharing their possessions with those in need. He admonished greedy tax-collectors to stop collecting more than the legal amount of tax, and ruthless soldiers to cease being cruel and to be content with their wages. In other words, he exhorted all to practice genuine love. In no uncertain terms he denied being the Christ. Instead he pointed to the real Savior, who, said he, "will baptize y o u with the Holy Spirit and with fire." He even rebuked the tetrarch Herod Antipas, who had run off with and married Herodias, his brother's wife. The result was that Herod locked John up in prison.

The Baptism of Jesus (verses 21, 22). At the height of John's preaching and baptizing activity he baptized Jesus, who, by submitting to this sacrament, publicly declared that he was taking upon himself the sin of the world (John 1:29). While *the Son* was being baptized (probably immediately afterward), *the Holy Spirit* descended upon him in the form of a dove, and *the Father* declared, "Thou art my Son, the Beloved; with thee I am well pleased."

The Genealogy of Jesus (verses 23–38). The family tree introduced by Luke at this point does not, as in Matthew, proceed from father to son, but from son to father, until it finally arrives at Adam, the son of God. It indicates that Jesus is, in a sense, the Savior of the world, his gracious invitation being extended to all, his grace being sufficient for all, and all who accept him by a genuine faith being actually saved. Is this the genealogy of Jesus through Mary, or through Joseph? For the answer see the debate on pp. 222–225.

Chapter 4:1–13

Theme: *The Work Thou Gavest Him to Do*

The Temptation of Jesus in the Wilderness

CHAPTER IV: 1-13

4 1 Filled with the Holy Spirit, Jesus returned from the Jordan, 2 and for forty days was led about by the Spirit in the wilderness, where he was being tempted by the devil.[190] He did not eat anything in those days, and when they were finished he was[191] hungry. 3 So the devil said to him, "Since you are God's Son, tell this stone to turn into bread." 4 Jesus answered, "It is written,
'It is not by bread alone that man shall live.' "
5 And he led him up (to a high place), and in an instant showed him all the kingdoms of the world. 6 The devil said to him, "To you I will give all their domain and splendor, for it has been handed over to me, and I give it to anyone I please. 7 So, if you'll worship me,[192] all will be yours." 8 Jesus said to him, "It is written,
'You shall worship the Lord your God,
And him only shall you serve.' "
9 And he led him to Jerusalem, and set him on the pinnacle of the temple, and said to him, "Since you are God's Son, throw yourself down from here, 10 for it is written,
'He will give his angels instructions concerning you, to guard you,'
11 and
'On their hands they will bear you up,
Lest you strike your foot against a stone.' "
12 Jesus answered, "It has been said,
'You shall not put the Lord your God to the test.' "
13 And when the devil had finished every temptation, he departed from him until an opportune time.

4:1-13 *The Temptation of Jesus in the Wilderness*
Cf. Matt. 4:1-11; Mark 1:12, 13

1, 2a. Filled with the Holy Spirit, Jesus returned from the Jordan, and for forty days was led about by the Spirit in the wilderness, where he was being tempted by the devil.

The Link Between What Precedes and What Follows

"Thou art my Son, the Beloved," the Father had said in connection with Jesus' baptism. So the devil is now going to tempt Jesus with respect to this very declaration. Not only once but, as Luke tells the story, twice Satan is

---

190. Literally: led about by the Spirit in the wilderness forty days being tempted by the devil.
191. Or: became.
192. Or: if you'll kneel before me.

going to introduce his temptations by saying, "Since you are God's Son [do this . . . do that]." See verses 3 and 9. The Spirit had descended upon Jesus, qualifying him for his task as our Great Prophet, Sympathetic Highpriest, and Eternal King. In the present account, as *Highpriest* he suffers being tempted (Heb. 2:18); as *Prophet* he thrice appeals to Scripture (verses 4, 8, 12); and as *King* he gives battle to his chief opponent and triumphs over him.

Man's fall was brought about when the first Adam, as mankind's representative, yielded to the temptation of the devil. Thus sin began. So now, as Jesus' public ministry was about to begin, it was proper that he, as the last Adam, the representative of all who trust in him, should resist the devil's temptation and render perfect obedience to God. Thus grace would receive an open door. Besides, is it not reasonable to believe that the Lord used these forty days *to prepare himself, by prayer and meditation, for the work which the Father had given him to do,* and which he, Jesus himself, had voluntarily taken upon himself? Was it not for this reason that the Spirit-filled Savior returned from the Jordan, in which he was baptized, and by the Spirit was led about in the wilderness? Think of Moses on Mount Horeb (Exod. 34:2, 28; Deut. 9:9, 18), of Elijah on his way to that same mountain (I Kings 19:8), and of Paul's retreat in Arabia (Gal. 1:17; see N.T.C. on Galatians, p. 56).

The Possibility of the Temptation

How was it possible for a sinless Jesus to be tempted? In our attempt to answer this question we should point out first of all that it was his human nature that was tempted. Jesus was not only God; he was also man. Moreover, his soul was not hard as a flint or cold as an icicle. It was a thoroughly human, deeply sensitive soul, affected and afflicted by suffering of every description. It was Christ who said, "I have a baptism to be baptized with, and how I agonize until it be accomplished" (Luke 12:50). Jesus was able to express affection (Matt. 19:13, 14), sympathy (23:37; John 11:35), compassion (Matt. 12:32), anger (17:17), gratitude (11:25), and a yearning for the salvation of sinners (11:28; 23:37; Luke 15; 19:10; John 7:37) to the glory of the Father (John 17:1–5). Being not only God but also *man,* he knew what it is to be weary (John 4:6) and thirsty (4:7; 19:28). Therefore, it should not really surprise us that, after a fast of forty days, he was very hungry, and that the proposal to turn stones into bread was a real temptation to him; and this all the more so because he knew that he was clothed with power to perform miracles! It remains true, nevertheless, that the possibility and reality of Christ's temptation surpasses our understanding. But is this not true with respect to every doctrine? And what do we really know even about ourselves, about our soul, and about the question how soul and body interact? Very, very little indeed! How then would it be possible for us to penetrate to the depths of *Christ's* soul and analyze it so thoroughly that we could furnish a completely satisfactory psychological explanation of his temptations?

Is Luke's Account of the Temptation in Conflict with Matthew's?

A good approach to this question might well be, "Is the New Testament infallible?" One might also ask, "Is the Bible infallible?" However, the answer to that question, though substantially the same as the answer to the first one, would require far more space. Besides, in the present connection it is unnecessary.

But what about the New Testament, is it infallible? Here one must be careful to define just what is meant and what is not meant by infallibility. There are those who keep clinging to an infallibility concept that is unreasonable. They insist that the King James—or any other version—from start to finish, including the rendering of every verse, and also including the particular Greek text on which that rendering is based, is without error.

We love these devout believers, and are sorry that we must disappoint them by stating that we cannot agree with them. Without realizing it, they are raising what is human to the level of the divine. Unbeknown to themselves, they are engaged in an activity which, though well-intentioned, is not exactly pious. *Translations* are human, therefore fallible. *Inasfar as* they truly reflect what God has said they are infallible, for God cannot commit error. And see II Tim. 3:16, 17; II Peter 1:21. But to the extent in which any translation fails to reflect what God has said, it is imperfect.

Besides, there is the matter of *the underlying Greek text.* By and large that text is uniform, in the sense that we need not fear that advances in textual criticism (essentially the study of the manuscripts on which the translations are based) will ever be able to overthrow any article of The Apostles' Creed. On the other hand, the very variety of the readings, one reading sometimes clashing with another, shows that they cannot all be correct at every point. They sometimes contradict each other. And this is where the need of calm reflection and comparison arises.

Now as to Luke 4:1, 2a, there are those who maintain that the only correct rendering of the last part of this passage is "in the desert where for forty days he was tempted by the devil," or, in similar vein, "in the desert for forty days, tempted all the while by the devil."

It must be granted that this or a similar rendering is indeed possible. The underlying Greek text will allow it. But it will also allow a different rendering. Goodspeed recognized this when he offered the following: "... led about in the desert for forty days by the Spirit, and was tempted by the devil"; similarly Phillips: "... led by the Spirit to spend forty days in the desert, where he was tempted by the devil." See also A.R.V. And note my rendering. Following the words, "Jesus returned from the Jordan," I suggest, "and for forty days was led about by the Spirit in the wilderness, where he was being tempted by the devil."

The difference is this: according to the first view Jesus was tempted by the devil *throughout the forty days;* according to the second, not necessarily: the constant temptation may have occurred *at the close of the forty day fast.* Which view deserves the preference?

Answer: probably the second. How do we know? Because the one and only detailed temptation account that is definitely arranged in chronological fashion, namely, Matthew's, clearly teaches that the temptation by Satan began at the close of Christ's forty day fast. See Matt. 4:2, 3: "After going without food for forty days and forty nights he was famished. The tempter came and said to him, 'Since you are God's Son, tell these stones to turn into bread,'" etc.

It is clear that with respect to this point Luke's account and Matthew's do not clash but are in beautiful harmony.

More important, undoubtedly, is the item that has been pinpointed for "bombing attacks" by those who reject the position that *Luke's* Gospel is divinely inspired in the same degree as are the others. That item is this: according to Matthew's Gospel the sequence in which the three temptations occurred is (a) change stones into bread, (b) throw yourself down (from the pinnacle of the temple), (c) worship me; but by Luke (b) and (c) are reversed. At synodical gatherings—i.e., gatherings of denominational assemblies—an appeal has been made to this difference, in an attempt to show that Scripture is not infallible.

The appeal is groundless. Here, too, we should again proceed from the basic position that it is Matthew's account alone that is *chronologically* arranged; note the adverbs: "then ... afterward ... then ... again ... then ... then" (Matt. 4:1-11). Matthew relates what occurred first, what followed, what came next, and how it all ended. *Luke has nothing of the kind.* See Luke 4:5, 9. His account is not arranged chronologically. He mentions the three temptations but does not indicate by even a single word that they occurred in that particular time sequence. Any mention of a possible clash or conflict between Matthew and Luke is therefore unreasonable.

"Why did Luke present these three temptations in a different order than Matthew?" A categorical answer is impossible. We simply do not know the reason. Nevertheless, the following approach may be worthy of consideration.

Luke is an artist. His arrangement is truly beautiful. He records the fact that in the first and in the third temptation—according to the order in which the beloved physician has arranged them—the devil starts out by saying, "Since you are God's Son." In the second or middle one the devil appeals to the eye rather than to the ear and, having shown the Redeemer all the kingdoms of the world in their splendor, blurts out, "To you I will give them if," etc.

Also—and this is very significant—Luke has so arranged his material that his *nativity account* is climaxed by a scene that takes place in the temple (2:41-52). His *entire book* also closes with a temple scene (24:53). So why should he not also end with a temple scene the first of the three large sections into which his Gospel can be divided? Luke, let it be borne in mind, more than any other Gospel writer, describes Jesus as "Our Sympathetic Highpriest." See *Introduction*, point V D. Priest and temple go together.

Luke's arrangement at this point (4:9–13) is, accordingly, in line with the spirit of his entire book. It harmonizes with his purpose.

The Temptation Step by Step
First Temptation

2b. He did not eat anything in those days, and when they were finished he was hungry. Luke shows that Christ's fast was complete, not partial. It is certainly not surprising that at the end of forty days of fasting Jesus was (or: became) hungry. The devil naturally selects this moment as his golden opportunity. The story continues: **3. So the devil said to him, Since you are God's Son, tell this stone to turn into bread.**

It must have been in the spirit of derision that the tempter uttered these words. He probably meant, "Since that is what the Father told you at your baptism [3:22], and what you believe, make use of your majestic dignity, and no longer be tortured by hunger. *Son of God . . . hungry.* How ridiculous! If, then, you are God's Son, tell this stone to turn into bread." The wilderness was full of stones. Matt. 4:3 has the plural of the words *stone* and *bread.* Luke uses the singular. Satan probably pointed to a single stone, "Tell this stone."

It was, of course, a wicked attempt (a) to cause "the last Adam" (I Cor. 15:45) to fail even as the first Adam had failed, in both cases in connection with food consumption. Was not one of the reasons why the Holy Spirit caused Jesus to be tested exactly this, that, as the Representative and Savior of all his people, he must in their stead triumph over temptation instead of succumbing to it as the first Adam had done? Moreover, on the part of the tempter this was a sinister endeavor (b) to destroy the Son's confidence in his Father's will and power to sustain him. What the tempter was asking Jesus to do was to distrust his Father, and to take matters entirely into his own hands.

Though, as has been pointed out, there are depths that we cannot fathom, it cannot be denied that this temptation was a very real one for Jesus. He knew that he was clothed with power to perform miracles. Also, there was an opportunity to use that power in his own behalf. He must have been very hungry by this time. The reality of the temptation and the severity of the trial may perhaps become even more clearly evident when *the last Adam's* situation is compared with that of *the first one.* Both were tempted by Satan. But the difference in the gravity of the test appears from the following threefold contrast:

a. Nowhere in Gen. 3:1–7 do we read that the Old Testament Adam had gone without food for any length of time. Jesus, on the contrary, had been fasting for forty days. He was famished.

b. Even had the father of the human race been hungry, he could have easily satisfied that hunger, for he had been told, "Of every tree of the garden you may freely eat" (Gen. 2:16). No such provision had been made for Christ.

c. Eve's husband, when tempted, had, as it were, everything in his favor, for he was living in *paradise*. Jesus, at the time of his temptation, was staying in this horrible wilderness!

Nevertheless, he withstood the temptation: **4. Jesus answered, It is written,**

It is not by bread alone that man shall live.

Note the expression, *It is written,* not only here in verse 4 but also in verses 8 and 10, every time with a reference to the same book, Deuteronomy, which, as is clear, Jesus regarded not as "a pious fraud" but as the very Word of God. Other passages that give expression to Christ's exalted view of Scripture are Luke 24:25–27, 44–47; John 5:39; and 10:35. For him the Old Testament Scriptures, as interpreted by himself, were evidently the ultimate touchstone of the truth for life and doctrine, the final court of appeal for the reason.

The first quotation is from Deut. 8:3. It pictures Moses reminding Israel of God's tender care for his people during the forty years of the wilderness journey. Particularly, it shows how the Lord had fed them with manna, heretofore completely unknown to them and their fathers, that he might teach them "that not by bread alone does man live but by everything proceeding out of the mouth of Jehovah does man live."

What Jesus means, therefore, may be paraphrased as follows: "Tempter, you are proceeding upon the false assumption that for a man, in order to appease hunger and keep alive, *bread* is absolutely necessary. Over against this erroneous idea I now declare that not bread but the creative, energizing, and sustaining power of my Father is the only indispensable source of my, and of man's, life and well-being." Luke, however, omits the last part of Deut. 8:3, "But by every word that comes," etc. Matt. 4:4 has these words. Luke frequently omits material, probably in order to have enough room in his Gospel for other topics.

On the part of Jesus this reply to Satan's advice was an expression of filial confidence in the Father's care. Certainly the One who, when there was no bread, had provided manna, and who quite recently had said, "Thou art my Son, the Beloved," would not fail his Beloved in this hour of trial!

Second Temptation (Matthew's Third)

5. And he led him up (to a high place), and in an instant showed him all the kingdoms of the world.

Just how we must conceive of this is not explained. Did the devil assume a physical body (Gen. 3:1; cf. John 8:44), and did the two—Jesus and the devil—walk side by side through the wilderness and reach a mountain from which Satan could show Jesus "all the kingdoms of the world"? In the vicinity of the Judean wilderness or of Jerusalem, which mountain would that be? Did they glide smoothly through the sky, the devil functioning as a kind of engine? Did they sail along together all the way to Mount Everest? But even then, would not some kind of miracle have been required to enable the devil from there to show Jesus *all* the kingdoms of the world, and this not just in dim outline, but very distinctly, so that "all their domain and splendor [or *glory*]" would be plainly visible; and again, not little by little during a lengthy period of time, but, as Luke here adds, "in a moment"?

This is not at all a question of believing Scripture or not believing it. It is simply a question of how best *to interpret* what we fully accept. The writer of this commentary has not been able anywhere to find a solution that satisfies him better than that of Calvin. In his Commentary Calvin remarks:

"It is asked, was he [Jesus] actually carried to this elevated spot, or was it done in a vision? . . . What is added, that *all the kingdoms of the world* were exposed to Christ's view . . . in one moment . . . agrees better with the idea of a vision than with any other theory. In a matter that is doubtful, and where ignorance brings no risk, I choose rather to suspend my judgment than to furnish contentious people with an excuse for a debate."

Calvin is being very careful. It is clear that he favors the vision idea. On the other hand, he does not wish to press it, leaving room for any other *reasonable* interpretation anyone might be able to offer. I only wish to add that Scripture contains two comparable passages in which we are told that someone is "set on" or "carried to" a high mountain. These two are Ezek. 40:2 and Rev. 21:10. Ezekiel plainly states that this happened "in the visions of God." To the seer of Patmos visions were shown while he was "in the Spirit" (Rev. 1:10). It was "in the Spirit" that he was carried away to a mountain great and high. Calvin's view, accordingly, is worthy of very serious consideration. The objection that if the temptations occurred to Jesus during visions they were not real is groundless. Was not Ezekiel's experience *real,* even though it occurred in a vision? Is John's description of Jerusalem the Golden bereft of value because it too came to him in a vision? Besides, if even a *dream* can be so vivid that there are said to be cases on record of people dying as a result, shall we then say that the reality of Christ's temptation experiences is diminished in any way because it was in *visions* that the tempter came to him and addressed him?

This view must not be confused with that according to which the temptations were of a merely subjective nature. No, even if it was in a vision that the devil came to Jesus, the great adversary was very real, and it was *he,* not the Lord, who said, "Tell this stone to turn into bread," "worship me," "throw yourself down." If it was in a vision that the Lord was urged to do these things, we may be sure that what occurred in the vision was as real to his mind as if there had been no vision at all, and everything had taken place with strict literality.

From the top of the very high place (whether or not it was in a vision makes no difference) the devil shows Jesus all the kingdoms of the world. All these are vividly displayed to Jesus in *just one* very significant moment! To gain some conception of what must have been included in the panorama that was spread out before the Lord, would it not be wise to read carefully the following three paragraphs: II Chron. 9:9-28; Eccles. 2:1-11; and Rev. 18:12, 13? All this wealth is by Satan offered to Christ, all for the price of just one genuflection! If Jesus will but *worship* the devil, he can have it all. He can have it in his possession and under his authority.

6, 7. The devil said to him, To you I will give all their domain and splendor, for it has been handed over to me, and I give it to anyone I please. So, if you'll worship me [or: if you'll kneel before me], all will be yours.

The question has been asked whether Satan was really the possessor of all these things, and whether he was actually in control of all of them to such an extent that he could offer them to anyone he wished. Often this question is answered in the affirmative, with an appeal to Eph. 2:2, where Satan is called "the prince of the domain of the air"; to 6:12, which speaks about "the spiritual forces of evil in the heavenly places"; to I John 5:19, which states that "the whole world lies in (the power of) the evil one"; and even to the present passage, in which the great adversary pictures himself as the rightful owner of, and ruler over, all. Further substantiation is found in the fact that Jesus in his answer (verse 8) did not in so many words dispute Satan's claim.

Do these passages really prove what those who appeal to them are trying to prove? I do not believe they do. The first three merely prove that Satan exercises a very powerful influence for evil over the lives of all those wicked people and spirits that acknowledge him as their master. But such references certainly do not prove that the devil is the ultimate owner and ruler of the nations, with the right and the might to dispose of them and of their wealth as he pleases, so that Christ himself, at least during the present dispensation, would have to take a back seat to him. The contrary is the truth, as is proved abundantly by such passages as Gen. 3:15; Ps. 2; Matt. 11:27; 28:18; Rom. 16:20; Eph. 1:20-23; Col. 2:15; and Rev. 12; 20:3, 4, 10. If it be argued that some of these passages refer to the power given to Christ in his exaltation, the answer is that even during Christ's humiliation Satan was able to do no more than Christ suffered him to do, as both Matt. 4:11 and also the Gospels in general testify (demon expulsions; Matt. 12:29; Luke 10:18; John 12:31). And as to Satan's boast here in Luke 4:6, it is too absurd to merit an answer. But if an answer of a sort be demanded, let it be John 8:44.

On the surface it may therefore seem as if this temptation was for Christ no temptation at all. Jesus knew that the devil was lying; that is, that the prince of evil had no enchanting kingdoms to give away. No doubt the Lord also knew that even if Satan had possessed them, he would not have fulfilled his promise. In what sense then can we say this attempt of Satan was also a real temptation for Christ? As I see it, only in this way that, although the particular form in which the proposal was made contained nothing that would recommend it to the mind and heart of the Savior, nevertheless the implied suggestion *to try to obtain the crown without enduring*

the cross was able to foment a bitter struggle within him. To be sure, it was
not a struggle that involved him in sin or could bring him to the point of
committing sin, but it was a state of agony, nevertheless. How else can we
explain the words uttered in Gethsemane, "My Father, if it be possible, let
this cup pass from me; nevertheless, not as I will, but as thou wilt" (Matt.
26:39)? Or, how can we explain Luke 12:50? It is clear, therefore, that for
Christ *this* temptation too was very real.

Satan received the answer he deserved: **8. Jesus said to him, It is written,**

> **You shall worship the Lord your God,**
> **And him only shall you serve.**

The answer reflects Deut. 6:13.[193] It also reveals the sharp contrast between Christ, who is ever doing what his Father wants him to do (John
5:30; 6:38), and Satan, whose purpose is the exact opposite (Gen. 2:17, cf.
3:4; Zech. 3:1, 2; John 8:44; I Thess. 2:18; I Peter 5:8; I John 3:8; Rev. 12;
20:8, 9).

Third Temptation (Matthew's Second)

**9-11. And he led him to Jerusalem, and set him on the pinnacle of the
temple, and said to him, Since you are God's Son, throw yourself down
from here, for it is written,**
He will give his angels instructions concerning you, to guard you,
and

> **On their hands they will bear you up,**
> **Lest you strike your foot against a stone.**

As has already been explained, worthy of serious consideration is the
theory according to which it was in a vision that Luke's third as well as his
second temptation—perhaps even all three temptations—occurred.

The present temptation, then, takes place in Jerusalem, to which the
devil has led Jesus. Satan has set the Savior on the very pinnacle (literally
wing) of the outer wall of the entire temple complex. The exact spot is not
given. It *may* have been the roof-edge of Herod's royal portico, overhanging the Kedron Valley, and looking down some four hundred fifty feet, a

---

193. Although the words of Jesus are not a precise rendering of any *single* passage either in
the original Hebrew or in the Septuagint, yet they are certainly in complete harmony with the
sense of both, for in both occur the following passages: "Jehovah your God you shall fear, and
him you shall serve..." (Deut. 6:13), followed by verse 14, "You shall not go after other
gods"; "You shall not *worship* them [i.e., graven images] or *serve* them; for I, Jehovah your
God, am a jealous God" (Deut. 5:9); to this may be added: "And from there you will seek
Jehovah your God and will find him if you search for him with all your heart and with all your
soul" (Deut. 4:29). Although the word *only* (of Luke 4:8) occurs in none of these passages, yet
in each case it is clearly implied: in the first two instances because of the context; in the last,
because of the phrase, "with all your heart and... soul." The word *only* does, however, occur
in I Sam. 7:3 ("Serve him only"). This too may have influenced Luke 4:8. Note the same
sequence *worship... serve* in Luke 4:8 as in Deut. 5:9. Besides, Christ's "You shall worship the
Lord your God" is a direct response to Satan's "Worship me."

"dizzy height," as Josephus points out (*Antiq.* XV.412). This spot was located southeast of the temple court, perhaps at or near the place from which, according to tradition, James, the Lord's brother, was hurled down. See the very interesting account in Eusebius, *Eccl. Hist.*, II.xxiii.

"Since you are the Son of God," says the tempter (exactly as in verse 3), "throw yourself down." His reasoning was probably along this line, "You will thus be able to prove your confidence in the Father's protection. Besides, if Scripture, which you so readily quote, is true, no harm can befall you, for it is written, 'He will give his angels instructions concerning you.' They will not merely *arrest* your fall. No, they will do more. *Very tenderly* they will bear you up on their hands, lest you, wearing only sandals, should hurt yourself by striking your foot against one of those sharp-edged stones present in abundance in the abyss below."

The passage quoted is from Ps. 91:11, 12. As rendered here in Luke 4:10, 11, it follows the Septuagint (Ps. 90:11, 12). As it is quoted by the devil, there is, however, an omission which some regard as being important, others not. According to the Hebrew, Ps. 91:11 ends with the words "to guard you in all your ways." Luke 4:10 merely has "to guard you." Hence the words "in all your ways" are left out. When these words are *included,* God promises to protect the righteous man in all his righteous ways; for these are the ways of the man who dwells in the secret place of the Most High, abides under the shadow of the Almighty and has found his refuge in Jehovah, upon whom he has set his love. They are, accordingly, the ways of the saint (Prov. 2:8), the good man (Prov. 2:20). It is to such a one that the words apply, "He will give his angels instructions concerning you, to guard you in all your ways." When these words "in all your ways" are *omitted,* does it not become easier to interpret the passage as if it were a promise of Jehovah to protect the righteous *no matter what he does?* So read, the passage would seem to correspond more closely with what the devil wants Jesus to do.

Nevertheless, this point is probably of minor importance, since what Satan omits amounts to far more than a few words in a quotation. He omits any reference to the scriptural truth that God does not condone but condemns and punishes rashness, a trifling with providence, an impetuous rushing into totally unwarranted danger (Gen. 13:10, 11; Esther 5:14; 7:9, 10; Ps. 19:13; Dan. 4:28–33; 5:22, 23; Rom. 1:30; II Peter 2:10).

Obedience to Satan's proposal was tempting, for Jesus knew that he possessed extraordinary powers. Besides, what man is there who, when asked to prove a point he has made, does not feel as if he should immediately comply, instead of first asking himself, "What right has my prompter to ask me to prove it?" Jesus, however, does not fall into this trap. He realizes that for him to do what Satan is urging upon him would amount to substituting presumption for faith, effrontery for submission to God's guidance. It would have meant nothing less than to risk self-destruction. The *false trust* in the Father which the devil demanded of Jesus in this temptation was not any better than the *distrust* he had proposed in the *first*. It would have amounted to *experimenting* on the Father.

A rabbinical tradition reads, "When the king, Messiah, reveals himself, then he comes and stands on the roof of the holy place."[194] On the basis of this tradition some commentators are of the opinion that the tempter was trying to suggest that Jesus, by casting himself from the temple's pinnacle, would establish himself as being indeed the Messiah, for, after a miraculous and safe landing, the crowd, having watched the descent with bated breath, would exclaim, "Look, he is unhurt. He must be the Messiah!" For Jesus, thus the argument continues, this would then be an easy way to success. The cross would be avoided, the crown obtained without struggle or agony.

It is an interesting theory. Nevertheless, there is nothing that would lend any further support to it. No spectators are even mentioned in the Gospel accounts. Moreover, Jesus, in his reply, does not refer to anything of the kind. I believe, therefore, that the entire idea should be dismissed. Luke 16:31 also argues against it.

The reason why Jesus peremptorily rejects the devil's proposal has already been given. It is clearly stated in verse **12. Jesus answered, It has been said,**

You shall not put the Lord your God to the test.

This is a quotation from Deut. 6:16, which reflects the situation of the Israelites described in Exod. 17:1-7, how at a place called Massah and Meribah they made trial of Jehovah and rebelled against Moses because of lack of water. They accused Moses of having cruelly brought them, their children, and their cattle, out of Egypt and into the desert, to destroy them all. They were almost ready to stone him and, instead of in a childlike manner "making all their wants and wishes known at the Father's throne," they insolently and provocatively challenged God, saying, "Is Jehovah among us or not?" Jesus knows that similar ill behavior on his part, by unnecessarily exposing himself to danger just to see what his Father's reaction might be, whether the latter would be with him or not, would amount to grievous transgression. He knows that the devil's proposal has nothing whatever to do with humbly trusting in the protecting care promised in Ps. 91. He therefore very appropriately answers the tempter by quoting Deut. 6:16.

Daily life all around us affords abundant illustrations of *false confidence*, similar to that which the devil urged Jesus to exercise. A person will earnestly beseech the Lord to bestow upon him the blessing of health; however, he neglects to observe the rules of health. Or, he will ask God to save his soul; however, he neglects to use the means of grace, such as the study of Scripture, church attendance, the sacraments, living a life for the benefit of others to the glory of God. Again, someone will plead with the Lord for

---

194. S.BK., Vol. I, p. 151.

the spiritual as well as physical welfare of his children, but he himself neglects to bring them up in the way of the Lord. A church member, admonished because at a circus he had eagerly rushed into a corrupt side show, defended himself by saying, "I cannot deny that I went there, but while I was there I was constantly praying, 'Turn away mine eyes from beholding vanity'" (Ps. 119:37 A.V.). "You shall not put the Lord your God to the test" is the answer to all of this.

13. And when the devil had finished every temptation, he departed from him until an opportune time. It was pointed out earlier (p. 39) that the position of Conzelmann, according to which the age or period of Jesus, extending from Luke 4:13 through 22:3, is protected from every activity of Satan, is contrary to the facts as reported in that Gospel. See 8:12, 13, 27 f.; 10:18; 11:4, 14 f. (especially 11:18); 13:16. What the present passage means, therefore, is not that Satan desisted for a long time from carrying out his sinister activities, but simply that "for the nonce" the prince of evil departed. He must have realized that he had been thoroughly defeated. This made him all the more angry. More than ever, therefore, he was determined to attack Jesus and his cause, and to do this at the very earliest opportunity.[195]

Practical Lessons Derived from Luke 4:1–13

Verses 1, 2a

"He was being tempted by the devil." Our Highpriest, having defeated the tempter, can help us in our temptations (Heb. 4:14 f.).

Verse 2b

"He was hungry." It was in the sphere of the appetite that man was first tempted. He lost (Gen. 3). The last Adam (I Cor. 15:45), as his people's representative, rendered the obedience which the first Adam, as mankind's representative, had failed to render.

Verses 4, 8, 12

"It is written" (bis), "It has been said." Resist Satan by appealing to Scripture, as Jesus did.

Verse 13

"The devil ... departed from him." In his battle against Jesus and his church Satan loses (Gen. 3:15; Job 1:6–12, 20–22; 2:1–10; 19:23–27; 42:10–17; John 10:28; 16:33; Rom. 8:31–39; 16:20; I Cor. 15: 55–57; Rev. 12:7 f.; 20:1–3, 10). What a comfort!

---

195. Notes on Greek words, phrases, and constructions in 4:1–13 begin on page 241.

The paragraph considered as a whole. There are those who believe that in these three temptations the devil holds out to Jesus three goals: those of becoming, respectively, a famous Food Supplier, an illustrious World Conqueror, and a Startling Magician. Textual support for this idea is lacking. Far more reasonable is the thought that throughout Satan was tempting Jesus by trying to show him how he could reach the crown without suffering the cross. See Luke 12:50; 22:42; Heb. 5:7, 8.

Jesus triumphed. Not for a moment did he leave the path of trust and obedience. He persevered in carrying out the task which the Father had given him to do. For us, too, the practical lesson is "Trust and obey."

Notes on Greek Words, Phrases, and Constructions in 4:1-13

Verses 1, 2a

In his *Translation,* p. 157, Robertson calls the position of ἡμέρας ambiguous. In *Word Pictures,* Vol. II, p. 48, he states that the expression *during the forty days* must be connected with "led," not with "tempted." I agree, for reasons stated in the comments.

Verse 2b

ἔφαγεν (οὐδέν), used as third per. s., 2nd aor. active of ἐσθίω, to eat.

συντελεσθεισῶν αὐτῶν, gen. absolute; fem. pl. because αὐτῶν represents ἡμερῶν.
The verb συντελέω has various meanings in the New Testament; such as, to finish, establish, round out, execute, accomplish, come to an end. The aor. active participle of this verb occurs in verse 13.

Verse 3

ἄρτος, according to Robertson, *Translation,* p. 30, "loaf of bread." But the English word *loaf* has a meaning that is foreign to the context here. The emphasis in the present connection is rather on the generic idea; that is, on the substance *bread,* to satisfy hunger. Even if a specific form of bread were meant, "bread-cake" would be preferable to "loaf of bread."

Verse 5

στιγμή*, point of time, moment. Cf. *stick.* The noun is related to στίζω, to prick.

Verses 7, 8

Verse 7 is a future more vivid (third class) conditional sentence. The protasis uses ἐάν with the sec. per. s. (ingressive) aor. subjunctive; the apodosis has the fut. indicative. Another form (sec. per. s. fut. indicat.) of the verb used in the protasis of verse 7 occurs in verse 8. The two forms are προσκυνήσῃς (verse 7), and προσκυνήσεις (verse 8).

Verse 9

πτερύγιον, pinnacle. The Greek word, in the New Testament occurring only here and in the parallel account (Matt. 4:5), is related to πέτομαι, to fly. Cf. *feather, pinion;* in fact, *pinnacle* itself is also related.

The words that embody Satan's third (according to Luke) temptation are in the form of a simple regular conditional sentence, with aor. imperat. in the apodosis.

Verse 10

ἐντελεῖται, third per. s. fut. indicat. of ἐντέλλομαι, to charge, order, command.
τοῦ διαφυλάξαι, articular aor. active infinitive of διαφυλάσσω*, to guard.

Verse 11

προσκόψῃς, sec. per. s. aor. subjunctive of προσκόπτω, to strike against.

Verse 12

εἴρηται, used as third per. s. perf. passive indicative of λέγω (past action with abiding result): it has been said and therefore stands. Cf. the parallel, Matt. 4:7, "it is written." And see John 19:22.
ἐκπειράσεις, sec. per. s. fut. indicative of ἐκπειράζω, to put to the test (to try out, sound out). See also Matt. 4:7; Luke 10:25; I Cor. 10:9.

Verse 13

ἄχρι καιροῦ, for a season; that is, until another favorable opportunity should present itself.

Summary of Chapter 4:1–13

Filled with the Holy Spirit, Jesus returned from the Jordan, where he had been baptized. For forty days he was led about by the Spirit in the wilderness. During these days he did not eat, so that when they were finished he was famished. So the devil said to him, "Since you are God's Son, tell this stone to turn into bread." The devil also led Jesus to a high place and in an instant showed him all the kingdoms of the world, promising that he would give them all to Jesus if the latter would worship him. The devil repeated the words (of the first temptation), "Since you are God's Son," when he set Jesus on the pinnacle of the temple, continuing, "throw yourself down from here." He strengthened (as he thought) his challenge by an appeal to Ps. 91:11a, 12.

In all three cases Jesus answered the tempter by using the Word as a weapon. He appealed to Deut. 8:3 in answer to the first temptation; to Deut. 6:13 in answer to the second; and to Deut. 6:16 in answer to the third (the terms *first, second,* and *third* here referring to Luke's arrangement, which is topical rather than strictly chronological).

By his voluntary submission to the rite of baptism and also by his equally voluntary obedience to the Father's will and the Spirit's direction when he was tempted by Satan, Jesus, as the last Adam, fulfilled the law which the first Adam had transgressed. By means of this obedience he was clearly indicating that he had taken upon himself and was taking away "the sin of the world." Cf. John 1:29. He was therefore ready to begin his ministry of teaching, preaching, healing, casting out demons, and overarching everything else, suffering and dying for all those lost "sheep" who would place their trust in him. See Isa. 53:6, 11; John 10:11, 14, 15, 27, 28.

The Work Thou Gavest Him To Do

Its Progress

or

Continuation

Chapters 4:14—19:27

Outline of Chapter 4:14-44

Theme: *The Work Thou Gavest Him to Do*
A. *The Great Galilean Ministry*

CHAPTER IV: 14–44

14 Jesus returned to Galilee in the power of the Spirit, and news about him spread through the entire surrounding region. 15 He[196] was teaching in their synagogues and being praised by everybody.

4:14, 15 *The Beginning of the Great Galilean Ministry*

Cf. Matt. 4:12, 17; 11:2; 14:3–5; Mark 1:14, 15;
Luke 3:19, 20; John 3:24; 4:1–3, 43, 44

A new section of Luke's Gospel begins here. A chapter division at this point would have been very proper. Luke does not indicate any chronological connection between 4:14, 15 and the preceding material: the account of Jesus' baptism and temptation (in this Gospel separated by a genealogy).

Between Luke 4:13 and 4:14, 15 there may well have been an interval of about a year, during which the events related in John 1:19—4:42 occurred. If so, the date when Jesus returned to Galilee, to begin his Great Galilean Ministry (Luke 4:14—9:17), was probably about December of the year A.D. 27 or a little later. See on 3:1, 2, 19, 20.

But though thus separated in time from the preceding events, yet what Luke is about to tell us is in material substance closely connected with that which precedes. The preparation for and inauguration of the work which the Father gave Jesus to do is ended. The beginning has been accomplished:

After an appropriate introduction (1:1–4) Luke has described (a) Jesus' forerunner, and (b) Jesus' birth. Luke's account, in both cases, is far more detailed than can be found anywhere else. He has even reproduced the accompanying "songs." He has related an incident that occurred when Jesus was 12 years of age, and has summarized his life in Nazareth. He has shown that by means of his baptism the Savior reaffirmed his decision to take upon himself the sin of the world. He has described Jesus' triumph over Satan in the desert of temptation. Nothing can now prevent the Christ from carrying forward his task as the Great Prophet, Eternal King, and Sympathetic Highpriest (with emphasis, in Luke, on the latter). He will re-

---

196. Or: He himself.

veal his sympathy not only to Jews but also to Gentiles, as is implied in Luke 4:16–30; for he is related, as the genealogy has shown, not only to David and Abraham but also to Adam, that is, to mankind in general. Nevertheless, as has been indicated, gospel work in Gentile *territory* is by Luke largely reserved for the book of Acts.

For the return to Galilee, mentioned here in 4:14, there were at least two reasons: (a) to avoid a premature crisis (see N.T.C. on Matthew, pp. 239–241); and (b) to fulfil prophecy by meeting Galilee's dire need (Isa. 9:1, 2; Matt. 4:15, 16).

As Luke here briefly summarizes the Great Galilean Ministry, particularly the teaching in which Jesus was then engaged, it had the following characteristics. It was:

a. *Spirit endowed:* Jesus performed his task as One who was filled with the Holy Spirit, who had descended upon him in connection with his baptism and had been his Guide in the wilderness (3:22; 4:1);

b. *widely advertised:* the news about it and about him was spreading throughout the entire surrounding region;

c. *synagogue-centered:* see Matt. 4:23a, and for the history and importance of the synagogue see N.T.C. on Mark, pp. 74–76; and

d. *popular.* Note the words, "and he was praised by everybody." For further confirming evidence showing how the people flocked to hear Jesus' teaching (both in the synagogue and elsewhere) see Luke 4:22a, 32; 5:1; cf. Matt. 7:28, 29; 9:35, 36; 13:1, 2, 54; Mark 1:21, 22; 2:13; 4:1; etc. It should be borne in mind, however, that this popularity was by no means unqualified. At times those who at first were filled with enthusiasm became adversely critical and even antagonistic as soon as they began to realize that Christ's teaching conflicted with their prejudices, as this very chapter shows.[197]

A Practical Lesson Derived from Luke 4:14, 15

What was it that made Jesus' teaching so popular? Answer: it was lively, authoritative, well-organized, practical, interesting, true. Cf. Matt. 7:28, 29. See also on Luke 4:31, 32. Does not this fact contain a hint that should be taken to heart by present-day preachers? And also a hint for parishioners, so that they may show appreciation to pastors who make this ideal their aim?

Notes on Greek Words, Phrases, and Constructions in 4:14, 15

Verse 14

φήμη, news, in the New Testament used only here and in Matt. 9:26. Cf. φημί, to say, affirm. The stem occurs in several English words; such as *prophecy, euphemism,*

---

197. Notes on Greek words, phrases, and constructions in 4:14, 15 begin on this page.

fable. Related also is *fame*, which in the present case, because of the favorable context, can even pass as a translation (see A.V., Weymouth, Berkeley).

Verse 15

Whether αὐτός has the intensive meaning "he himself" depends on the context. In the present case either meaning—"he" or "he himself" (as compared with "the news about him")—can be defended. The description is vivid, as is clear from the use of the imperfect "was teaching" and the similarly durative present passive participle "being praised."

---

16 He came to Nazareth, where he had been brought up; and, as was his custom, on the sabbath day entered the synagogue. He stood up to read. 17 The scroll of the prophet Isaiah was handed to him. Unrolling the scroll, he found the place where it was written:
18 "The Spirit of the Lord (is) upon me,
Because he has anointed me
To proclaim good news to the poor;
He has sent me to proclaim to the captives release;
And to the blind recovery of sight;
To set free the oppressed;
19 To proclaim the year of the Lord's favor."[198]
20 Then he rolled up the scroll, gave it back to the attendant, and sat down. The eyes of all in the synagogue were fixed on him. 21 He started out by saying to them, "Today, in y o u r very hearing, this passage of Scripture has been fulfilled."
22 All were speaking well of him and were amazed about the words of grace that were flowing from his lips.
They were asking, "Isn't this Joseph's son?"
23 Jesus said to them, "Undoubtedly y o u will quote to me this proverb, 'Physician, heal yourself: whatever we heard that was done in Capernaum, do also here, in your hometown.'"
24 He continued, "I solemnly assure y o u, no prophet is accepted in his hometown. 25 I tell y o u truthfully, during the days of Elijah, when the sky was shut for three years and six months, and there was a severe famine in the entire country, there were many widows in Israel; 26 yet Elijah was sent to none of them but to Zarephath in the region of Sidon, to a woman (who was) a widow. 27 And at the time of Elisha the prophet there were many lepers in Israel; yet none of them was cleansed; only Naaman the Syrian."
28 Now when they heard these things, all the people in the synagogue were filled with fury. 29 Arising, they drove him out of town and pushed him to the brow of the hill on which their town was built, intending to cast him down headlong. 30 But he walked right through their midst and went on his way.

4:16–30 *The Rejection of Jesus at Nazareth*
Cf. Matt. 13:53–58; Mark 6:1–6

A. *Introduction*

There is no agreement on the question why Luke departs from what was probably the historical sequence, and in his Gospel places the account of the rejection at Nazareth in the forefront of his coverage of the Great Galilean Ministry, while Matthew and Mark give a much later place to it. Some have suggested two rejections at Nazareth.

---

198. Or: the acceptable year of the Lord.

Reasons for accepting the theory that in all three cases the reference is to the same incident:

a. The general outline of the story is the same in all three: On a sabbath Jesus enters his hometown. He teaches in the synagogue. Result: astonishment, adverse criticism, rejection.

b. Essentially the same dominical saying occurs in all three accounts (Matt. 13:57; Mark 6:4; Luke 4:24).

c. The historical background creates no difficulty, since even according to Luke's account (see 4:23) Christ's rejection at Nazareth did not occur at the beginning of Christ's Galilean Ministry but much later.

The identification is made easier by the fact that, aside from what is implied in 4:23, there are no time references attached to Luke's account. It is clear from Matt. 13:53, 54 that the visit to Nazareth occurred sometime after Jesus spoke his kingdom parables, although how long afterward is nowhere indicated. Did this visit and rejection take place in late A.D. 28? This possibility must be granted.

Luke, in his rich coverage—15 verses compared to 6 for Matthew and 5½ for Mark—supplies the text and gist of Christ's sermon. In addition to telling us how it was received Luke gives us a much fuller account (than do Matthew and Mark) of the manner in which Jesus answered his critics and of their resulting hostile reaction.

But although we do not know why Luke places the rejection at Nazareth so early, the suggestion that he may have done this in order to indicate at once what would be the general trend with respect to the people's attitude to Jesus deserves consideration. That trend would be: first enthusiastic interest and amazement, then rejection.

Besides, it should be borne in mind that in chapters 1–3 Luke, in a manner more detailed and emphatic than any other synoptist, has held out bright hopes concerning Jesus (1:30–35, 42, 48, 78, 79; 2:10, 11, 14, 30–32, 34, 40, 52; 3:16–22). It should not surprise us, therefore, that now, without delay, he wishes to indicate that Jesus himself confirmed these expectations (verse 21).

And does not the inspired author of the Fourth Gospel also prefix a summarizing paragraph to his narrative about Jesus? See John 1:10–14.

B. *Jesus enters the synagogue*

16a. He came to Nazareth, where he had been brought up; and, as was his custom, on the sabbath day entered the synagogue. Even though Jesus was born in Bethlehem (Matt. 2:5, 6; Luke 2:4, 15; John 1:45; 7:42; cf. Mic. 5:2), and during a large part of his ministry had his headquarters in Capernaum (Matt. 4:13), he was and remained "Jesus of Nazareth" (Matt. 2:23; 21:11; 26:71; Mark 1:24; 10:47; 14:67; 16:6; Luke 18:37; etc.). Nazareth, as Luke reminds us (cf. 2:39, 40, 51, 52), was the place where Jesus had been brought up, his hometown.

Luke adds that on this particular sabbath day Jesus entered the synagogue. The fact that he attended the synagogue wherever he happened to be, particularly on the sabbath, is clear from several Gospel passages (Matt. 4:23; 9:35; 12:9; 13:54; Mark 1:21, 39; 3:1; 6:2; Luke 4:15, 16, 44; 6:6; 13:10; John 6:59; 18:20). However, here alone (Luke 4:16) note the significant addition "as was his custom."

Though even with respect to his human nature Jesus was far advanced in knowledge, wisdom, etc., above anyone else who imparted instruction in the synagogue, he did not stay away. The example set by Jesus should remind us of such passages as Deut. 12:5; Ps. 84:1-4; 95:2-7; 122:1-4; Isa. 37:1; Matt. 18:20; Luke 2:36, 37; 24:52, 53; Heb. 10:25.

It is true, nevertheless, that in nearly all of the Gospel references (the list given above, beginning with Matt. 4:23), we are told that Jesus himself did the teaching or preaching.

C. *He reads Scripture*

1. The material read

16b-19. He stood up to read. The scroll of the prophet Isaiah was handed to him. Unrolling the scroll, he found the place where it was written . . .

If sources later than New Testament times are applicable to the period of Christ's earthly sojourn, the sequence of liturgical elements in the synagogue service was probably about as follows:

a. Thanksgivings or "blessings" spoken in connection with (before and after) the *Sh͏ᵉmaʿ:* "Hear, O Israel, the Lord our God, the Lord is One, and you shall love the Lord your God with all your heart, and with all your soul, and with all your might."

b. Prayer, with response of "Amen" by the congregation.

c. Reading of a passage from the Pentateuch (in Hebrew, followed by translation into Aramaic).

d. Reading of a passage from the Prophets (similarly translated).

e. Sermon or word of exhortation.

f. The Benediction pronounced by a priest, to which the congregation responded with "Amen." When no priest was present a Closing Prayer was substituted for the Benediction.

"The freedom of the synagogue" implied that any person considered suitable by the ruler (or the rulers) of the synagogue was privileged and encouraged to deliver the sermon. Cf. Acts 13:15. It is easy to understand that this provision made it possible for Jesus, and also later on for Paul and other Christian leaders, to bring *the gospel* to the assembled congregation. Whether here in Nazareth Jesus had been asked to lead, or whether he simply knew that the people expected him to read and preach is not clear. Either is possible.

251

He stood up to read. By the attendant the scroll of the prophet Isaiah was handed to him. It seems to have been a separate scroll.[199]

Did the first lines of Isa. 61 constitute the *haphtara* (lesson from the Prophets) for that particular sabbath day, or did Jesus himself select these lines? The words, "Unrolling the scroll he found the place," etc., seem to point in the direction of the second alternative. We may perhaps also assume that it was Jesus himself who translated the Hebrew into Aramaic.

The quotation (Luke 4:18, 19) is from Isa. 61:1, 2a. The close resemblances, as well as the differences, become apparent in the chart below.

2. The explanation

The number at the beginning of each of the following paragraphs refers to the identically numbered passage in the three columns:

1. The Speaker throughout is evidently the Messiah himself. Luke 4:21 makes clear that this Messiah is Jesus. This shows that the fulfilment of Isaiah's prophecy, when Israel's remnant returned from the Babylonian captivity, was of a preliminary nature; and that the final fulfilment was ushered in by the incarnation, humiliation, and exaltation of Jesus Christ.

A Comparison of Isaiah 61:1, 2a with Luke 4:18, 19

Hebrew Isa. 61:1, 2a translated into English	*LXX (Greek Version) of Isa. 61:1, 2a translated into English*	*Luke 4:18, 19 translated into English*
1. The Spirit of the Lord God (is) upon me,	The Spirit of the Lord (is) upon me,	The Spirit of the Lord (is) upon me,
2. Because the Lord has anointed me to announce good news to the poor.	Because he has anointed me; He has sent me to proclaim good news to the poor,	Because he has anointed me to proclaim good news to the poor.
3. He has sent me to bind up the brokenhearted;	To heal the brokenhearted,	
4. To proclaim to the captives liberty;	To proclaim to the captives release;	He has sent me to proclaim to the captives release:
5. And to those bound opening of eyes;	And to the blind recovery of sight;	And to the blind recovery of sight;
6.		To set free the oppressed;
7. To proclaim the year of the Lord's favor.	To announce the year of the Lord's favor.	To proclaim the year of the Lord's favor.

199. S.BK., Vol. II, p. 156, indicates that the Major Prophets were written both on separate scrolls and combined on one scroll. The same reference indicates that the reader *stood* and the preacher *sat*.

It was upon him that, by an act of God the Father, the anointing Holy Spirit was caused to rest. See Luke 3:21, 22.

2. This anointing implied that the Savior had been set apart and qualified for a task. Part of that task was "to proclaim good news to the poor." The Greek word translated "poor" occurs also in the Beatitudes (Matt. 5:3; Luke 6:20). The Speaker in Isaiah was thinking of the destitute, those who know themselves to be such. Isa. 66:2 provides a good commentary, "But this is the man to whom I will look, he that is humble and crushed in spirit, and trembles at my word."

3. The words of the Messiah, found in the Isaiah passage, namely, "He has sent me to bind up the broken-hearted," reflected also in the LXX, "(He has sent me) to heal the broken-hearted," are omitted in Luke. Why? We can only guess. Possibilities: (a) Luke's intention was not to reproduce the entire *haphtara* (selection from the Prophets) but only the words used by Jesus as the text for his sermon; (b) correctly interpreted, the reference to "the poor" to whom the good news must be proclaimed made a further statement about "the broken-hearted" not absolutely necessary. There may be a better explanation.

4. The underlying figure—"captives"—is that of exiles, by the conqueror dragged away from their own homeland and transported into a foreign country where they endure many grievous hardships. This captivity symbolizes enslavement to sin and Satan. But Messiah was divinely commissioned to proclaim and to bring about release from this captivity. See John 8:36.

5. According to Luke's report—and compare the LXX Version—Jesus also read these words, "And (he has sent me to proclaim) to the blind recovery of sight." The parallel Isaiah passage is often rendered, "and the opening of the prison to them that are bound." It then becomes difficult to understand why the corresponding line in the LXX and in Luke speaks of "the recovery of sight." The transition from one idea—the opening of the prison—to the other—the recovery of sight—is then explained by pointing out that when men bound in dark dungeons are set free, they again see the light of day, and in that sense their eyes are opened. That explanation sounds reasonable. A quicker way to reach the same result is to adopt for the Isaiah passage the alternate rendering of the words in question, namely, "and to those bound opening of eyes."[200] One of the purposes for which the Messiah was sent into the world was indeed to open men's eyes, a right claimed by Jesus (John 9:39a).

6. "(He has sent me) to set free the oppressed." See also the note on 4:18 on page 260. Neither Isa. 61:1, 2a nor the LXX Version has anything that corresponds to item 6. It can perhaps be viewed as a *midrash* or *comment* on

---

200. See Brown-Driver-Briggs, *op. cit.*, p. 824.

the immediately preceding passage. The meaning then would be on this order, "When I said that the blind receive recovery of sight, I meant that this takes place when they are set free from the oppression they had been enduring in Satan's dark dungeon." Such a comment seems all the more natural at this point, in view of the fact that Isa. 58:6—a passage not far removed from the opening verses of Isa. 61—refers to the deliverance of those crushed or oppressed.

7. "(He has sent me) to proclaim the year of the Lord's favor," or "the acceptable year of the Lord" (A.V.). The underlying figure is the year of Jubilee, the fiftieth year, when, according to Lev. 25:8 f., the trumpet must be sounded, and "liberty throughout all the land" must be proclaimed. This is a symbol of the Messianic Age, for it is only by faith in Jesus Christ that true freedom is obtained: freedom from living in constant fear, from obligation to ever so many manmade ordinances, from guilt, pollution, Satan, sin and its results. "If therefore the Son will make y o u free, y o u will be free indeed" (John 8:36). This is freedom *plus*.

When an accused man is declared not guilty, he is free. Likewise when a slave has been emancipated, he is free. But the judge or the emancipator does not, as a rule, adopt the freed individual as his own son. But when the Son makes one free, he will be free indeed, rejoicing in the glorious freedom of sonship. And how does the Son make one free? Answer: see John 18:12; cf. Isa. 53:5; II Cor. 3:17; Gal. 4:6, 7.

If we bear in mind that when this Scripture passage was being read Jesus had already carried on an extensive ministry both in Judea and in Galilee, it becomes clear that to a considerable extent the mission here described had been performed. It was still being fulfilled and was going to be, until it had been accomplished. The poor received, are receiving, are going to receive good news (Luke 6:20; 12:32); captives (to sin and Satan), release (Luke 13:16; John 8:31 f.); the blind, recovery of sight (Luke 7:21, 22); the oppressed, freedom (Matt. 11:28 f.; John 7:37); while for all true believers "the acceptable year of the Lord" arrives (Luke 7:22; 10:24). In fact, to a certain degree even unbelievers are benefited by its arrival (Luke 17:17).[201]

Moreover, Jesus had come to save the entire man: body and soul. The promised blessings were both physical and spiritual. In every way, therefore, *the passage* read that day in the Nazareth synagogue was not only informative but also hortatory. The invitation to accept this great salvation is clearly implied.

---

201. Those who believe that Luke has reported the entire passage read by Jesus—a possibility that must be granted—face the question, "Why did Jesus not continue reading, that is, why did he not also read Isaiah's words, 'and the day of vengeance of our God'?" Whoever says, as is sometimes done, that the Master left off where he did because he wanted his message to be one of comfort is forgetting that the vengeance of which Isaiah speaks was meant not for Zion but for Zion's enemies. As to the question itself, so many possible answers suggest themselves that it is better not to speculate as to why Jesus stopped here.

D. *He begins his address*

20, 21. Then he rolled up the scroll, gave it back to the attendant, and sat down. The eyes of all in the synagogue were fixed on him. He started out by saying to them, Today, in y o u r very hearing, this passage of Scripture has been fulfilled.

A most interesting passage this! Here Jesus combines the natural and customary with the amazing and unexpected. Jesus rolls up the scroll, returns it to the attendant, and sits down to speak. In all this he did not depart from customary procedure. For a speaker to sit down when he was about to address an audience was natural (Matt. 5:1; Luke 5:3), though there were exceptions, as the easy-to-remember contrast between Acts 16:13 and 13:16 indicates.

But at this point the unexpected happens. Let us try to visualize the situation:

The atmosphere in the probably crowded synagogue is surcharged with curiosity. Everybody in the audience is wondering what their townsman, the former carpenter, about whom they have been hearing so much of late (see verse 23), is going to say in elucidation and application of the Scripture passage he has read a moment ago. He may have read more than Luke reports, but at least he has read that.

All is quiet, so quiet that one can hear a feather drop. Every eye is fixed on Jesus. He opens his mouth. He begins his address. Does he start out by reminding the audience of the golden days, now gone forever, when Jehovah stretched out his mighty arm and performed miracles on earth? He does not. Does he begin by entertaining his listeners with bright promises pertaining to the future? Not that either.

Instead, he speaks about *the here and now!* He assures the people with whom he had grown up that the golden age has actually arrived. *"Today,"* says he, "while y o u are listening to me, the passage I read to y o u has been and is being realized."

That was true, of course. Were not the blind gaining their sight, cripples walking, lepers being cleansed, deaf people having their hearing restored, and even some of the dead being raised back to life? Was not the good news being proclaimed to the poor? See Luke 7:22 . . . And who was "the Servant of the Lord" through whom all this was being accomplished? The implication is clear.

E. *The audience reacts*
with

1. amazement

22a. All were speaking well of him and were amazed about the words of grace that were flowing from his lips.

Jesus had spoken with such inner conviction, freshness, authority, and graciousness that his old acquaintances were struck with astonishment.

They were impressed by his wisdom and by the mighty works that were ascribed to him (Matt. 13:54; Mark 6:2).

2. doubt

22b. They were asking, Isn't this Joseph's son?

Mark's fuller account of this negative reaction is, "Isn't this the carpenter, the son of Mary, and brother of James and Joses and Jude and Simon? And aren't his sisters here with us? And they took offense at him" (6:3; cf. Matt. 13:55-57).

In order to understand what caused the initial favorable reaction to change into an unfavorable one, it should be borne in mind that Jesus had not only presented an encouraging message about *present* salvation, but by reading, "The Spirit of the Lord (is) upon *me*," and afterward explaining this to mean "Today, in y o u r very hearing this passage of Scripture has been fulfilled," he had also somehow linked himself with the bringing of this salvation. The people liked what he had said about the dawn of the Messianic kingdom, but they resented the implication that Jesus, the carpenter, who grew up among them, was himself instrumental in bringing this about. Familiarity brought contempt. The very fact that the people of Nazareth were so well acquainted with Jesus' family caused them to look down upon him. Who did he think he was anyway?[202] If he wanted them to believe his claims, he ought to prove his greatness by performing here in Nazareth—better still, right here in the synagogue?—a miracle similar to those he had reportedly worked elsewhere.

F. *Jesus resumes his address*

23-27. Jesus said to them, Undoubtedly y o u will quote to me this proverb, Physician, heal yourself: whatever we heard that was done in Capernaum, do also here, in your hometown—He continued, I solemnly assure y o u, no prophet is accepted in his hometown. I tell y o u truthfully, during the days of Elijah, when the sky was shut for three years and six months, and there was a severe famine in the entire country, there were many widows in Israel; yet Elijah was sent to none of them but to Zarephath in the region of Sidon, to a woman (who was) a widow. And at the time of Elisha the prophet there were many lepers in Israel; yet none of them was cleansed; only Naaman the Syrian.

With the exception of verse 24 this is material peculiar to Luke. He probably received it from an eyewitness.

It is evident that Jesus had read the thoughts of these people. So he told them, "Undoubtedly y o u will quote to me this parable," etc. The word *parable* used in the original has a wide range, and in this instance undoubt-

---

202. See N. B. Stonehouse, *The Witness of Luke*, p. 75.

edly means "proverbial saying." That saying was, "Physician, heal yourself." Among the ancients this proverb was well known. There can be no doubt about Jesus' meaning, for he immediately adds words that basically amount to, "Do in your hometown what you did elsewhere." The "yourself" of the proverb is expanded into "your hometown." Literally, however, Jesus represents his synagogue audience as thinking, "Whatever we heard that was done in *Capernaum* do also here, in your hometown."

To reason, as some do, that Jesus, by representing the Nazarenes as saying within themselves, "Whatever *we heard* that was done (by you)" instead of simply "whatever you did," implies that they doubted the reports they had received is unrealistic. That the people of Nazareth believed that Jesus had performed "mighty works" is clear from Matt. 13:54; Mark 6:2. Their "unbelief" (Matt. 13:58; Mark 6:6) did not touch that particular point. What they did not believe was that through the man whom they knew so well (as they thought), the tremendously significant and comprehensive prophecy of Isa. 61:1 f. was being realized! Even sin-hardened scribes and Pharisees accepted the fact that Jesus worked miracles (Luke 11:15; John 11:47). But that did not make them true believers in Jesus as the Christ, the fulfilment of Messianic prophecy.

Perceiving the basic unbelief of his synagogue audience, Jesus states, "I solemnly assure y o u, no prophet is accepted in his hometown." For parallels see Matt. 13:57; Mark 6:4; John 4:44. Meaning: "Wherever a prophet may be honored, he is certainly not honored in his hometown." It was a succinct expression of a general rule. Even today we say, "Familiarity breeds contempt." The source of this lack of honor is often envy. Cf. I Sam. 17:28.

With a deeply earnest "Amen" Jesus introduces this proverb. In Luke this "Amen" occurs here for the first time. In the entire Third Gospel it is found only six times, far less frequently than in any of the other Gospels. Wherever this word occurs it introduces a statement which not only expresses a truth or fact, but an *important* fact, a *solemn* truth, one that is generally in conflict with popular opinion or at least causes a measure of surprise or needs to be stressed. Hence, "I solemnly declare."

Next, Jesus refutes the people's mistaken opinion that Nazareth had a special claim on him since that was the place where he had been raised. They seemed to think that people living in other places should be treated as "outsiders." Their attitude was, "It has been reported to us that you have performed great works in *Capernaum,* but where do *we* come in?"

So Jesus now shows that "There's a wideness in God's mercy, like the wideness of the sea" (F. W. Faber). With emphasis, once more, on the veracity of his statements ("I tell y o u truthfully"), he selects two examples from the history of the old dispensation, to show that God's grace overleaps artificial, manmade barricades, not only those of village, city, and province, but even those of people and country:

a. During the days of Elijah... there were many widows in Israel; yet Elijah was sent to... a widow in Zarephath in the region of Sidon.[203]

Discrepancy hunters see a conflict between the historical account of this incident (I Kings 17:1–7; 18:1) and Luke 4:25: "when the sky was shut for three years and six months, and there was a severe famine in the entire country." But the Old Testament passages nowhere indicate the duration of the drought and famine; so there can be no conflict. The belief that the entire period spanned three and one-half years rested on a strong oral tradition, evidenced not only here (Luke 4:25) but also in James 5:17.

The widow in Zarephath trusted in the God of Israel (I Kings 17:12, 16, 18, 24) and was rewarded. By and large the situation in Israel was different (I Kings 19:10, 14). It was one of unbelief, though there were some favorable exceptions (I Kings 19:18).

b. Something similar occurred also during the days of Elisha. Though then, as always, there were many lepers in Israel, none of them was cleansed. That great blessing was bestowed only on the non-Israelite Naaman (II Kings 5:1–14). He too believed, though not immediately (II Kings 5:14).

This statement of Jesus was indeed very significant. It was a lesson needed by Christ's immediate audience here in Nazareth on this unforgettable sabbath. But it also served a wider purpose. It was a clear indication of the dawn of a new era in the history of redemption, an era both predicted and foreshadowed in the old dispensation, but not fully realized until the new; a long, long period, during which, beginning from Jerusalem, the door of salvation would be opened more and more widely to all true "comers" (Isa. 55:1; Matt. 11:28; John 6:37; 7:37; Rev. 22:17), regardless of race or nationality (Matt. 8:11, 12; 22:8, 9; Luke 24:47; John 3:16; 10:16; Acts 1:8; Rom. 10:12, 13; I Cor. 7:19; Gal. 3:9, 29; Eph. 2:14, 18; Col. 3:11; Rev. 7:9).

G. *The audience reacts*
with

3. murderous hatred

28, 29. Now when they heard these things, all the people in the synagogue were filled with fury. Arising, they drove him out of town and pushed him to the brow of the hill on which their town was built, intending to cast him down headlong.

The people of Nazareth are furious. To think that they are worse than Phoenician widows and Syrian lepers! Their wrath knows no bounds. The house of prayer and worship becomes a bedlam of confusion. They rush upon the speaker. Out of town they drive him. Is he not a false prophet?

---

203. Cf. Matt. 15:21–28; Mark 7:24–30 for another manifestation of God's mercy through Christ to be bestowed on a woman living in that general region.

And does not the law demand that such deceivers must be killed? See Deut. 13:1-5. To the hill on which their town was built—some say it was the cliff located on the southwest corner of the town, the one overhanging the Maronite convent—they push him, intending to hurl him down headlong to the rocks below.

H. *Jesus triumphs*

30. But he walked right through their midst and went on his way.

How must we account for this "escape"? Shall we say that Jesus' calm and majestic bearing, differing so sharply from their boisterous display of bitterness, made such a deep impression on these potential murderers that they froze on the spot? Cf. John 18:6. Whatever may be the explanation, it was *he* who triumphed![204]

Practical Lessons Derived from Luke 4:16–30

Verse 16

"As was his custom." Staying away from church prevents a man from securing a blessing for himself, for the congregation to which he belongs, and for the kingdom of God.

Verses 17–19

"He has anointed me to proclaim good news to the poor," etc. Is not a Christian "a partaker of Christ's anointing"? To a certain extent, therefore, these verses give expression to the believers' mandate. True Christianity is a doctrine, to be sure; even more precisely, it is a life based on this doctrine.

Verse 21

"*Today* . . . this passage of Scripture has been fulfilled." *Carpe diem* (Make the most of today's opportunities)! The past is gone forever. The future here on earth may never dawn for us. God has given us the present. Let us then snatch every opportunity to promote Christ's causes; such as outreach, benevolence, Christian education. Significant, in this connection, are also such passages as Ps. 95:7b (Heb. 3:7); John 9:4.

Verse 24

"No prophet is accepted in his hometown." That is the way it is, but not the way it should be. *Potential* elders, deacons, assistants (male or female), Sunday School teachers, soloists, leaders of boys' or girls' clubs, etc., are passed by, being considered unqualified. They move to another town or church and immediately become a great blessing because their talents are being recognized. Let us not be too sure that the church member with whom we grew up is unqualified!

---

204. Notes on Greek words, phrases, and constructions in 4:16–30 begin on page 260.

Verses 25-27

To a woman of Zarephath... to Naaman the Syrian. God's love is world-embracing. It is not limited to a single nationality, sex, age, or rung on the social ladder. It is as broad as are Isa. 45:22; John 3:16; 4:42; I Tim. 4:10; I John 4:14.

Notes on Greek Words, Phrases, and Constructions in 4:16-30

Verse 16

ἦν τεθραμμένος, pluperfect indicat. pass. (periphrastic) of τρέφω, to feed, nurse, nourish, rear, bring up. Cf. *atrophy*.

ἀνέστη, third per. s. 2nd aor. indicative of ἀνίστημι; see the note on 1:39 on page 99.

ἀναγνῶναι, 2nd aor. active infinitive of ἀναγινώσκω; literally: to recognize (the letters) again; hence, to read.

Verse 17

βιβλίον, book, scroll, certificate; here scroll. Paper was made from the stem of the βίβλος, papyrus plant; hence the name. Cf. *Bible*.

ἀναπτύξας, aor. act. nom. s. masc. participle of ἀναπτύσσω*, unroll. Cf. πτύξας, in verse 20, from πτύσσω*, to roll up.

Verse 18

οὗ εἵνεκεν, because. See L.N.T.(Th.), p. 215. So almost every translation. To insist on the rendering "therefore" raises the question, "Does it make sense to say, 'The Spirit of the Lord (is) upon me; *therefore* he has anointed me'?" Besides, the usual and, as I see it, in this case correct translation ("because") also brings Luke 4:18 into harmony with the Isaiah passage.

εὐαγγελίσασθαι, aor. middle infinitive of εὐαγγελίζω, as in 1:19. See the note on 2:10 on page 160.

αἰχμάλωτος* = αἰχμή and ἁλωτός; hence literally: one taken by the spear, a captive. But see also αἰχμαλωτίζω (Luke 21:24; Rom. 7:23; II Cor. 10:5; II Tim. 3:6), to make (or: take) captive, carry away as a captive, mislead, etc.

ἀποστεῖλαι, aor. active infinitive of ἀποστέλλω, to send away; with ἀφέσει, to send away into freedom, to set free.

ἄφεσις (cf. ἀφίημι, to send away, dismiss, let go), deliverance, freedom, release; also: debt cancellation, pardon, forgiveness (Matt. 26:28; Mark 1:4; 3:29; Luke 1:77; 3:3; 24:47; Eph. 1:7; Heb. 9:22; etc.).

τεθραυσμένους, acc. pl. masc. perfect passive participle of θραύω*, to break in pieces, shatter, crush, oppress; cf. *throe*.

Verse 19

δεκτός, here -όν, modifying ἐνιαυτόν; see also verse 24; Acts 10:35; II Cor. 6:2; Phil. 4:18, acceptable, favorable; cf. δέχομαι.

Verse 20

ἦσαν ἀτενίζοντες, third per. pl. periphrastic imperfect of ἀτενίζω, to look intently (at something or someone), gaze, be fastened or fixed upon. Cf. *tension, intently.*

Verse 22

ἐμαρτύρουν, third per. pl. imperfect of μαρτυρέω, to bear witness, testify; here: to testify favorably concerning, to speak well of.

οὐχί . . . ἐστιν. The expected answer is Ναί (Yes).

Verses 23, 24

παραβολή, word with wide range of meaning, in Luke used here for the first time. In Luke 15, and often, it refers to "an earthly story with a heavenly meaning," what even today we would call "a parable." Other related meanings: brief illustrative comparison (Mark 3:23), pithy saying, aphorism, mashal (Mark 7:17), a proverb (here in Luke 4:23).

Ἰατρέ, vocative of ἰατρός, physician. Cf. *psychiatry.*

θεράπευσον, sec. per. s. aor. imperative active of θεραπεύω, to serve (Acts 17:25), to heal, cure, restore (Matt. 4:24; 8:7, 16; also here in Luke 4:23, 40; 5:15; 6:7; etc.).

ποίησον, sec. per. s. aor. (ingressive) active imperative of ποιέω.

πατρίδι, dat. s. of πατρίς. See N.T.C. on John 4:44, where substantially the same saying is found, with this exception that there the word used in the original, namely *patris,* refers to the home*land,* i.e., Galilee, whereas here in Luke 4:23, 24 and its synoptic parallels it refers to the home*town,* as is clear from the context.

Verse 26

With γυναῖκα χήραν cf. our vernacular "widow woman."

Verse 28

ἐπλήθησαν, third per. pl. aor. passive indicat. of πλήθω; see πίμπλημι. Cf. the note on 2:6 on page 147. Same form here (4:28) and 2:6 as in 1:23; 2:21, 22; 5:26; 6:11; Acts 2:4; 3:10; 4:31; 5:17; 13:45. Luke is very fond of this verb. For other forms see Luke 1:15, 41, 57, 67; 5:7; 21:22; Acts 4:8; 9:17; 13:9; 19:29. Elsewhere in the New Testament this verb is found only in Matt. 22:10; 27:48.

θυμός, anger, fury, rage, passion. Luke uses this word only here and in Acts 19:28, both times with respect to human fury. Paul has it in II Cor. 12:20; Gal. 5:20; Eph. 4:31; and Col. 3:8, human anger in all these cases; and in Rom. 2:8, divine anger. It also occurs in Heb. 11:27 (the king's anger), and ten times in the book of Revelation. In seven of these ten the fury or anger is God's (14:10, 19; 15:1, 7; 16:1, 19; 19:15); in one case it is the devil's (12:12); and in two it is Babylon's (14:8; 18:3). When there is a distinction between θυμός and ὀργή, θυμός seems to indicate turbulent commotion, anger, fury, suddenly blazing up and quickly extinguished, like fire in straw, while ὀργή refers to settled indignation, wrath of a more abiding character. See R. C. Trench, *Synonyms,* par. xxxvii. See also F. Büchsel, article θυμός in Th.D.N.T., Vol. III, pp. 167–172. However, as was stated in N.T.C. on John, Vol. I, p. 151, "when applied to God it is probably wrong to press this distinction between the two words."

Verse 29

For ἀναστάντες, nom. pl. masc. sec. aor. participle of ἀνίστημι, see above, on verse 16.

ὀφρύς*, lit. eyebrow; here: brow of a hill.

ᾠκοδόμητο, third per. s. pluperfect passive indicative of οἰκοδομέω, to build. Cf. *domestic, dome.* The Greek word is derived from οἶκος, house, and δέμω, to build. Cf. *timber;* Dutch *timmeren* (to do carpenter's work); German *Zimmer* (room).

κατακρημνίσαι, aor. infinitive active of κατακρημνίζω* (= κατά, down, and κρημνός, precipice), to hurl down a precipice, to cast down headlong. Cf. *cremaster* (muscle).

---

31 He went down to Capernaum, a city of Galilee. And he was teaching the people on the sabbath. 32 They were astonished at his teaching because his message was (presented) with authority.

33 Now in the synagogue there was a man possessed by a demon, an unclean spirit.[205] In a loud voice he cried out, 34 "Ha! Why do you bother us, Jesus of Nazareth? Have you come to destroy us? I know who you are—the Holy One of God!"

35 But Jesus rebuked him, saying, "Be quiet and come out of him!" And when the demon had hurled him down into their midst, he came out of him, having done him no harm.

36 Amazement seized all, and they kept saying to each other, "What kind of message is this? For with authority and power he issues commands to the unclean spirits, and they come out."

37 And the news about him continued to[206] spread to every place of the surrounding region.

4:31–37 *The Healing of a Man with an Unclean Spirit*
Cf. Mark 1:21–28

At this point Luke's account begins to parallel Mark's more definitely. The present close parallel extends from here to the end of Luke's fourth chapter.

Luke 4:31–41 describes "A Busy Day in Capernaum." The first scene takes place in the synagogue, the second and third at Simon Peter's house.

31, 32. He went down to Capernaum, a city of Galilee. And he was teaching the people on the sabbath. They were astonished at his teaching because his message was (presented) with authority.

Luke does not indicate any time connection between the preceding story (Christ's rejection at Nazareth) and this one. He does not begin his paragraph with "Afterward" or even with "Then." He simply uses the word *kai,* which, in this instance, can either be left untranslated or rendered "And."

Luke has "he" where Mark has "they." Both are correct, for Luke's "he" refers to Jesus as the Leader of the group. From Mark's Gospel—1:16–20, 29—it is clear that this group consisted (at least) of Simon Peter and Andrew, James and John.

Note also "went down to Capernaum," *down* being appropriate because of the location of this place on the northwest shore of the Sea of Galilee,

---

205. Literally: a man with a spirit of an unclean demon.
206. Or: began to.

this sea itself being more than 200 meters (about 700 feet) below the level of the Mediterranean. The city has completely disappeared. The modern *Tell Hum* is by many regarded as its probable site. For more on Capernaum— why Jesus moved to this place from Nazareth, its strategic location, excavations, Jesus' prophecy (concerning this city) and its fulfilment—see on 10:15.

For the sake of Theophilus and other readers unacquainted with the detailed geography of the Holy Land Luke adds "a city of Galilee."

It was on *the sabbath* that Jesus was teaching (or: began to teach) the people. Luke's interest in the sabbath appears from the fact that he records no less than five healing miracles performed by the Savior on the day of rest and worship (4:31–37, 38–41; 6:6–11; 13:10–17; 14:1–6). We should add, however, that Luke, in turn, reveals Christ's own special concern about proper sabbath observance, in harmony with Isa. 58, and his stand in opposition to the legalistic views and practices advocated by the scribes and Pharisees and their followers.

Clearly this sabbath teaching took place *in the synagogue* (see verses 33, 38; also 15, 16; and cf. Mark 1:21). That those in charge would ask Jesus to read and to preach was to be expected.

So impressive was his presentation that the audience was "astonished." Cf. 4:22a. The people were dumbfounded, literally "struck out of themselves," that is, as it were, "out of their senses" in amazement and wonder. It was a state that did not leave them immediately but lasted for a while.

What were some of the reasons for this reaction on the part of the audience? One of them may well have been that he, a carpenter (Mark 6:3), revealed such wisdom. But especially there was this, that his "word" or "message" was presented "with authority." Cf. Matt. 7:28b, 29; Mark 1:22b. Consider the following points of contrast between Christ's teaching and that of the scribes:

a. *He* spoke the truth (John 14:6; 18:37). Corrupt and evasive reasoning marked the sermons of many of *the scribes* (Matt. 5:21 ff.).

b. *He* presented matters of great significance, matters of life, death, and eternity. *They* often wasted their time on trivialities (Matt. 23:23; Luke 11:42).

c. There was system in *his* preaching. As their Talmud proves, *they* often rambled on and on.

d. *He* excited curiosity by making generous use of illustrations (many of them reported in Luke's Gospel; see 5:36–39; 6:39–49; 7:31–35, 40–47; etc.). *Their* speeches were often dry as dust.

e. *He* spoke as the Lover of men, as One concerned with the everlasting welfare of his listeners, and pointed to the Father and his love. *Their* lack of love is clear from such passages as Luke 20:47.

f. Finally, and this is the most important, for it is specifically stated here, *he* spoke "with authority," for his message came straight from the very heart and mind of the Father (John 8:26), hence also from his own inner being, and from Scripture. *They* were constantly borrowing from fallible sources, one scribe quoting another scribe. They even prided themselves on never saying anything that was original! *They* were trying to draw water from broken cisterns. *He* drew from himself, being "the Fountain of living waters" (Jer. 2:13).

33, 34. Now in the synagogue there was a man possessed by a demon, an unclean spirit. In a loud voice he cried out, Ha! Why do you bother us, Jesus of Nazareth? Have you come to destroy us? I know who you are—the Holy One of God!

As is clear from Luke 4:40, 41; cf. Mark 1:32–34; 6:13, it is not true that the New Testament writers, in common with all primitive people, ascribed all physical illnesses and abnormalities to the presence and operation of evil spirits. It is contrary to fact that demon-possession is simply another name for insanity or for dissociation. The fact is that according to Scripture a *distinct* and *evil* being (here: "a spirit of an unclean demon"), foreign to the person possessed, has taken control of that individual. For more on the subject of demon-possession see N.T.C. on Matthew, pp. 436–438; Mark, pp. 64, 65.

Right here in the synagogue, at the top of his voice, the demon, making use of the wretched man's vocal organs, cried out, "Ha!" By means of this exclamation, found only here in the New Testament, the demon was giving expression to his surprise, disgust, and hostility. He continued, "Why do you bother us, Jesus of Nazareth?" Literally the question he asked was, "What (is there) to us and you," i.e., "What have we in common that you would want to have anything to do with us? Why not leave us alone?" See also Mark 1:24; 5:7; cf. Matt. 8:29. Note "with *us*." He seems to realize that what will happen to him is also going to happen to his fellow demons.

He calls the One who is about to expel him "Jesus of Nazareth," literally, "Jesus the Nazarene." Although being brought up in Nazareth spelled humble beginnings, and in the case of Jesus pointed to the Messiah's low estate (Matt. 2:23), and Nathanael by asking, "Out of Nazareth can any good come?" was either moved by town rivalry or more probably was thinking of good things in the Messianic category, yet calling Jesus "the Nazarene" does not always or necessarily imply disdain. In fact Jesus even uses the term with respect to himself (Acts 22:8).

That the form of address, "Jesus of Nazareth," used by the demon, was simply the designation by which Jesus was generally known, and not a title indicating disrespect, is clear also from the added words: "Have you come to destroy us? I know who you are—the Holy One of God." "Have you come" can hardly be taken to mean, "from Nazareth," for Jesus did not need to come from Nazareth to crush the power of Satan's emissaries. It is best taken to mean "Have you come from heaven into the world. . . ." The demon, accordingly, is asking whether the very One who had come *to seek and to save* the lost (Luke 19:10) had also come *to destroy* the demons, that is, now *already* (cf. Matt. 8:29) to hurl them into the abyss or dungeon where Satan is kept (Rev. 20:3).

When the demon declares, "I know," he is not telling a lie. There are certain things that are known to the prince of evil and his servants. Moreover, some of this knowledge causes them to tremble, to be frightened, to shudder (James 2:19). They know that for them there is no salvation, only dreadful punishment. The demon is thinking of this very fact, as he realizes that he is at this moment being confronted with his Great Opponent, the very One who came to destroy the works of the devil (I John 3:8), and whom he, again correctly, calls "the Holy One of God." He knows that holiness cannot brook sin. A demon . . . the Holy One of God, what a contrast! In connection with "Holy One" see also Mark 1:24; John 6:69; cf. Rev. 3:7. Jesus was "holy" not only in the sense of being sinless in himself, filled with virtue, and the cause of virtue in others, but specifically also in this sense, that he had been anointed, hence set apart and consecrated for the performance of the most exalted task (Isa. 61:1-3; Luke 4:18, 19; 19:10; John 3:16; 10:36; II Cor. 5:21).

When radicals deny Christ's deity they show less insight than the demons, for the latter are constantly acknowledging it. To be sure, they do not do this in the proper spirit. For reverence they substitute impudence; for joyfulness, bitterness; for gratitude, turpitude. But they do it all the same. They call Jesus "the Holy One of God" (here in Luke 4:34), "the Son of the Most High" (8:28), "the Son of God" (Matt. 8:29; Luke 4:41).

35. But Jesus rebuked him, saying, Be quiet and come out of him! —And when the demon had hurled him down into their midst, he came out of him, having done him no harm.

Jesus does not accept acknowledgment coming from a thoroughly corrupt demon. Besides, the demon had no right to interrupt the Lord's teaching. So Jesus issues the terse command, "Be quiet and come out."

The demon obeys immediately. But in leaving he, shrieking wildly, hurls the man into the midst of the assembled congregation, throwing him into convulsions (Mark 1:26). Luke, being a physician, in fact a "beloved one," must have asked his informant(s) whether the demoniac received any injuries as a result of the rough treatment to which he had been subjected. The answer was "No," which Luke reports.

We receive the impression that the expulsion of the evil spirit took but a few moments. The demon, moreover, did not win, not in any sense. Contrast all this with the exhausting, time-consuming ritual—and what happened to the priests?—as described in W. P. Blatty's *The Exorcist*.

36, 37. Amazement seized all, and they kept saying to each other, What kind of message is this? For with authority and power he issues commands to the unclean spirits, and they come out. —And the news about him continued to [or: began to] spread to every place of the surrounding region.

Characteristic of the early part of Christ's Great Galilean Ministry is what we read here about the spread of his fame. Not only were Capernaum's people astonished about his *teaching*, they were amazed about the *message* emanating from both his teaching and his demon-expulsion. Cf. Mark

1:27. What a contrast between *his* teaching and that of the scribes, and between *his* demon-expulsion and that claimed by the exorcists. He did both "with authority."

In fact, so astounding had been the events that transpired in the synagogue this sabbath that without delay one neighbor was telling another about it, and he still another, etc. The news was too good and too exciting to be confined to Capernaum. It began and continued to spread into every place of the surrounding region.[207]

Practical Lessons Derived from Luke 4:31-37

Verses 31, 32

"He was teaching.... They were astonished." Fine! But astonishment is not enough. Genuine faith is needed.

Verse 33

"In the synagogue ... a demon." The devil never misses a service. Therefore it is very necessary to heed the admonition of I Peter 5:8, 9a.

Verse 34

"I know who you are—the Holy One of God!" Who is the better theologian: the devil or the radical scholar?

Verses 35, 36

"Be quiet and come out of him ... he came out." How does Jesus reveal his greatness in this account? By his powerful preaching? By his ever successful, quick and thorough demon-expulsions? These seem to have been the manifestations of Christ's majesty that most deeply impressed the crowds. Were they forgetting about his tender love shown to the demoniac?

Verse 37

"The news about him continued to spread." Who were spreading it? Simon, Andrew, James, and John? They alone? Clearly, ever so many individuals who did not belong to the innermost circle of Jesus' disciples were also doing the broadcasting. And that is as it should be. See Matt. 5:14; Phil. 2:15.

Notes on Greek Words, Phrases, and Constructions in 4:31-37

Verse 31

ἦν διδάσκων, periphrastic imperfect.

---

207. Notes on Greek words, phrases, and constructions in 4:31-37 begin on this page.

Verse 32

ἐξεπλήσσοντο, third per. pl. imperf. indicat. pass. of ἐκπλήσσω, to strike out of (one's wits), to astound; passive, to be astonished or astounded, to be struck out (of one's senses). Cf. 2:48; 9:43, etc. Cf. πληγή, blow, stroke, wound; related is *plague*.

Verse 33

ἀκάθαρτος (-ον); here gen. (-ου), unclean, impure, vicious, evil. Cf. *cathartic* (purgative), *Catherine* (pure, virtuous).

Verse 34

ἔα*, ah!, ha!, exclamation showing surprise, disgust, hostility. On τί ἡμῖν καὶ σοί see M. Smith, "Notes on Goodspeed's 'Problems of New Testament Translation,'" *JBL,* 64 (1945), pp. 512, 513.
ἀπολέσαι, aor. active infinitive of ἀπόλλυμι, to destroy.

Verse 35

ἐπετίμησεν, third per. sing. aor. indicat. of ἐπιτιμάω. It has the sense *rebuke* in such passages as here in Luke 4:35, 39; also in Matt. 8:26; 16:22; 17:18; 19:13; Luke 9:42, 55; 17:3; 18:15; 19:39; 23:40; but at times means *warn* (Matt. 12:16; 16:20; Mark 3:12; Luke 9:21; 18:39).
φιμώθητι, sec. per. s. aor. passive imperative of φιμόω, to muzzle, to silence; passive, to be silent, still, quiet.
ῥῖψαν and βλάψαν, nom. s. neut. aor. act. participles, respectively of ῥίπτω, to hurl, and βλάπτω, to hurt.

Verse 36

θάμβος**, also in 5:9; Acts 3:10, amazement.
Is ὅτι, as here used, causal (because, for), declarative (that), consecutive (so that), recitative (" "), or can it be omitted in translation? A. T. Robertson seems to have changed his opinion. Cf. his *Translation,* pp. 33, 160, with his *Word Pictures,* Vol. II, p. 160. If it must be construed as recitative, it would be expected earlier in the sentence. It is perhaps best to regard it as causal, and to render it "for," as is done by most translators (A.V., R.S.V., A.R.V., Amplified, N.A.S., Williams, Berkeley, Weymouth, Goodspeed, Dutch [Nieuwe Vertaling, "want"], etc.). What we have here is probably an instance of abbreviated expression, discussed in N.T.C. on John, Vol. I, p. 206. Completely expressed, the meaning may well be, "What kind of person is this? [We have reason to be astonished] *for* with authority and power he issues commands to the unclean spirits and they come out."

Verse 37

ἦχος, also in 21:25; Acts 2:2; Heb. 12:19, sound, noise, rumor, news. Cf. *echo;* same base in κατηχήθης; see the note on 1:4 on page 62.

38 Jesus left[208] the synagogue and entered the home of Simon. Now Simon's mother-in-law was in the grip of a high fever,[209] and they asked Jesus to help her.[210] 39 Standing over her he rebuked the fever, and it left her. She got up at once and began to wait on them.

40 And when the sun was setting, all who had (dear ones) sick with diseases of various kinds brought them to him. He was laying his hands on them one by one and curing them. 41 Moreover, demons also were coming out of many, shrieking and saying, "You are the Son of God." But rebuking them he was not allowing them to speak, because they knew him to be the Christ.

4:38-41 *The Healing of Simon's Mother-in-law and of Many Others* Cf. Matt. 8:14-17; Mark 1:29-34

38, 39. Jesus left the synagogue and entered the home of Simon. Now Simon's mother-in-law was in the grip of a high fever, and they asked Jesus to help her. Standing over her he rebuked the fever, and it left her. She got up at once and began to wait on them.

From the synagogue Jesus seems to have gone directly to the home of Simon, that is, of Simon and Andrew, as Mark 1:29 informs us. That same evangelist also reports that James and John entered with Jesus. And from John (1:44) we learn that Simon and Andrew had come from Bethsaida.

Not only did Simon's mother-in-law have a fever, it was a "high fever," as "the beloved physician" (Col. 4:14) tells us. But no matter how "high" or "great" the fever, Christ's power and love were always greater.

Not only did "they"—evidently Simon and Andrew, who lived in this home—inform Jesus about her, but as Luke distinctly adds, they asked Jesus to come to her aid.

What must have struck Luke, as a doctor, was that Jesus now placed himself in the position so typical of a physician, namely, he *stood over her.*

How was the cure brought about? So few are the words devoted to it, so brief is the report, that one cannot help gaining the impression that those who were present when this miracle took place, and most of all the lady who experienced it, must have been overwhelmed by the Savior's majesty. All we read is, "he-rebuked the fever, and it-left her" (purposely so printed here, to show that in the original only six words are used). It all happened at once: a command to leave, and gone was the fever. The suggestion that the word *rebuked* implies a "personal" object, that is, that it was Satan or one of his servants who had caused the fever, is groundless. All we can safely infer is that Christ's power over disease is so great that at his word it must immediately cease to be.

Moreover, the cure was not only sudden, it was also complete. Simon's mother-in-law did not even say, "I'm rid of the fever, but completely

---

208. Or: And he arose and left.
209. Or: was suffering from a severe attack of fever.
210. Or: and they asked Jesus about her; or: and they made request to Jesus for her.

exhausted." Nothing of the kind. On the contrary, one moment, just before Jesus had taken her by the hand and had rebuked the fever, there were still those flushed cheeks, that burning hot skin, profuse sweating, dryness in the throat—or else, depending on the kind of fever, there may have been violent shivering—the next moment every fever symptom had vanished completely. Not only was the woman's temperature normal but such a surge of new strength was coursing through her entire being that she herself insisted on getting up. In fact, she actually got up and started to perform the duties of a busy hostess. She began to wait on all those present: Jesus, Peter, Andrew, James, John (Mark 1:29) and perhaps even on her daughter if she too was present, as is probable. Or, "mother" may have been ably assisting "daughter" in performing this act of hospitality.

40, 41. And when the sun was setting, all who had any (dear ones) sick with diseases of various kinds brought them to him. He was laying his hands on them one by one and curing them. Moreover, demons also were coming out of many, shrieking and saying, You are the Son of God. But rebuking them he was not allowing them to speak, because they knew him to be the Christ.

So quickly did the news of these two miracles—the expulsion of a demon (verses 31–37), and the cure of Simon's mother-in-law (verses 38, 39)—spread, that the people could hardly wait until the sabbath was over. At sunset they came, carrying their sick ones to Jesus. We may well believe that many of those who brought them were filled with genuine sympathy for their dear ones and hoped fervently that they might be healed.

So great was the crowd that Mark states, "And the whole town was gathered at the door [of Simon's house]." Note especially: "sick with diseases of various kinds," not just fever.

Luke, as we would expect of this doctor, pictures the procession of the sick being brought one by one to Jesus, who, paying due attention to, and lovingly placing his hands on, each in turn, healed them all. Mark, in harmony with Matthew and Luke, states that Jesus similarly cast out *many* demons. Matthew adds that it was "with a word," namely, the word of effective command, that the evil spirits were driven out (8:16).

Luke adds that in coming out the demons were screaming, "You are the Son of God." This reminds us of the synagogue scene (verse 34). But now, too, Jesus immediately rebukes the demons and he even forbids them to say anything further. Why? The answer may seem somewhat strange, ". . . because they knew him to be the Christ."

But how could this be a good reason to silence these demons? Many answers have been given.[211] Probably the most reasonable ones are the following:

a. The demons knew that Jesus was the Messiah. But if the people were

---

211. See especially, H. N. Ridderbos, *Zelfopenbaring en Zelfverberging*, Kampen, 1946, pp. 70–87.

to believe this and to act upon it, they might start a movement to make Jesus a king. Cf. John 6:15. And, of course, Jesus does not want this at all.

b. Closely connected with the first is the reasoning that, due to the expected opposition from the side of Jesus' enemies, any public acknowledgment (at this time) of Jesus as the Messiah would in all probability have brought about a premature crisis. Though it is true that Jesus "from his throne on high came into this world to die," he must not die immediately but at the appointed time.

c. During the period of Jesus' humiliation any proclamation of his identity as the Messiah would have been in conflict with the mandate he had to fulfil until the day of his resurrection. This is the position of H. N. Ridderbos, who offers as proof such passages as Mark 9:9, 30, 31.

Which of these three answers is the right one? Is there, perhaps, an element of truth in all three? Or is there still a better answer? Since Jesus himself never gave us any further explanation, it is probably well for us not to delve any more deeply into this subject.[212]

Practical Lessons Derived from Luke 4:38–41

Verse 38

"They asked Jesus to help her." Meaning: to help Simon's *mother-in-law.*

> Happy the home when God is there.
> And love fills every breast;
> When one their wish and one their prayer,
> And one their heav'nly rest.

Anonymous

Verse 40

"He was laying his hands on them one by one and curing them." Fitting and beautiful in this connection are hymns such as the following:
W. Hunter's "The Great Physician"
E. H. Plumptre's "Thine Arm, O Lord"
H. Twell's "At Even, When the Sun Was Set"
For titles of a painting, a drawing, and an etching illustrating this theme, see N.T.C. on Matthew, p. 253.
Christ's sympathy was—and is—deep, effective, personal. Is ours?

Verse 41

"Demons also were coming out of many."
Satan cannot be defeated by denying his existence. Our answer must be:

> And though this world, with devils filled
> Should threaten to undo us,

---

212. Notes on Greek words, phrases, and constructions in 4:38–41 begin on page 271.

We will not fear, for God has willed
His truth to triumph through us, *etc.*

From Luther's "A Mighty Fortress"

Notes on Greek Words, Phrases, and Constructions in 4:38–41

Verse 38

ἀναστάς, nom. sing. masc. 2nd aor. participle of ἀνίστημι. See the note on 1:39 on page 99. Either the word can be omitted in translation, or, if emphasis must be placed on the probability that Jesus had been seated (cf. 4:20), the rendering, "And he arose and left," may be adopted.

In verses 38, 39 expressions such as "a high fever," "standing over her," remind us of the fact that the author of this Gospel was himself a physician. For more on this see *Introduction*, point I A 4.

ἦν συνεχομένη, periphrastic passive imperfect of συνέχω. Basically the verb συνέχω means *to hold together*. It branches off into the following connotations: to hold in custody (Luke 22:63); to shut, stop (Acts 7:57); to press hard, crowd (Luke 8:45); middle and pass.: to be engrossed in (Acts 18:5), to be hard pressed (Phil. 1:23), and here (Luke 4:38) to be in the grip of, to be tormented by.

πυρετός, fever; cf. πῦρ, fire. Note *pyre*.

Verse 39

ἐπετίμησεν, see above, on verse 35.

ἀφῆκεν, third per. s. aor. indicat. of ἀφίημι, a word with a great variety of meanings; such as: to let go, utter, send away, divorce, pardon, release, forgive, stop, abandon, tolerate, permit, allow, and (here) leave. See also the note on 4:18 on page 260; and N.T.C. on Mark, footnote 830 on p. 664.

For ἀναστᾶσα, see the note on 1:39 on page 99.

διηκόνει, inchoative imperfect: she began to wait on them, began to serve. Cf. *deacon*.

Verses 40, 41

Note the gen. absolute which may be rendered "And when the sun was setting."

εἶχον, first per. s. and third per. pl. (here the latter) imperfect of ἔχω, to have, hold, etc.

ἀσθενοῦντας, acc. pl. masc. pres. participle of ἀσθενέω, to be infirm, weak, sick. Cf. *asthenia* (physical weakness), *calisthenics* (beauty and strength).

ἐπιτιθείς, nom. s. masc. present active participle (here iterative) of ἐπιτίθημι.

ἐθεράπευεν, third per. s. imperf. indicat. act. of θεραπεύω. See above, under 4:23.

Note the vividly descriptive style. A series of presents and imperfects, beginning with 4:40b, and continuing into verse 41, pictures what was happening: Jesus *was laying* (hands) on and *curing* (people). Demons *were coming out, shrieking* and *saying*, etc. They said, "You *are*," etc. He, *rebuking, was not allowing*, etc. They *were being aware* that he was (They knew him to be) the Christ.

εἴα, third per. s. imperfect of ἐάω, to allow, permit. Though ᾔδεισαν (from οἶδα) is pluperfect, it has the sense of an imperfect.

42 At daybreak he left and went to a lonely place. The crowds were looking for him; and when they came to where he was they tried to keep him from leaving them. 43 But he said to them, "Also to the other towns I must preach the good news of the kingdom of God, because for this purpose I was sent." 44 So he continued to preach in the synagogues of the country of the Jews.[213]

4:42-44 *Preaching the Good News to Other Towns Also*
Cf. Mark 1:35-39

42a. At daybreak he left and went to a lonely place. Had Jesus spent the night in Peter's home, and did that disciple upon arising discover that the Master had already left? This is possible but we do not know. What we do know is that according to Mark 1:35, "very early while it was still night," that is, still dark, and was just starting to get light (Luke 4:42), Jesus got up, left the house (whether his own or Peter's), and went off to a lonely or deserted spot, a quiet retreat. There, again according to Mark, he poured out his heart in prayer to his heavenly Father.

42b, 43. The crowds were looking for him; and when they came to where he was they tried to keep him from leaving them. But he said to them, Also to the other towns I must preach the good news of the kingdom of God, because for this purpose I was sent.

According to Mark 1:36 Simon and those who were with him went in search of Jesus. Luke mentions the crowds as the searching party. Did they perhaps come a little later and, having discovered where Simon had gone, did they then hurry to that same place? Something on this order may well have happened. There is no conflict between Mark and Luke, for even according to Mark (1:37) Simon, having found Jesus, told him, "*Everybody* is looking for you."

So happy were the people when the search ended successfully that they tried to keep Jesus from leaving them. They wanted to have him all for themselves!

But Jesus is not going to allow the people in general, or even his own disciples, to tell him what he should do or where he should go. Besides, in his great love he wishes to distribute his favors among the many. To be sure, Capernaum will see him again. It will remain for a while Christ's center of operations, his headquarters. But he does not wish to confine his labors to that one city. Therefore he says, "Also to the other towns I must preach." And what is it he must preach? Answer: the good news of the kingdom of God.

This is the first time the term *the kingdom of God* appears in Luke's Gospel (see, however, also 1:33). This evangelist uses that term at least thirty times (not counting its seven occurrences in the book of Acts); far more fre-

---

213. Literally: of Judea, but see the explanation. Another reading has: of Galilee.

quently, therefore, than Mark or John. Essentially the same concept occurs also with great frequency in the Gospel According to Matthew, but in slightly different form (generally "kingdom of heaven" instead of "kingdom of God"). See N.T.C. on Matthew, p. 87.

Luke speaks about preaching or proclaiming the kingdom of God (4:43; 8:1; 9:2, 60; 16:16), entering it (18:24, 25; 22:18), seeking it (12:31). It is "at hand" (10:9, 11; cf. 7:28; 17:20, 21); yet in another sense it belongs to the future (13:29; 21:31). It is essentially spiritual (17:20, 21; cf. Rom. 14:17), but embraces also the material realm (22:28–30). It is God's gift to his children (12:32).

Now all these traits become intelligible in the light of the following description:

In its broadest connotation the term *the kingdom of God* indicates "God's kingship, rule or sovereignty, recognized in the hearts and operative in the lives of his people, and effecting their complete salvation, their constitution as a church, and finally a redeemed universe." Note especially the four concepts:

a. God's kingship, rule, or recognized sovereignty. That is probably the meaning in Luke 17:21, "The Kingdom of God is within y o u" and in Matt. 6:10, "Thy kingdom come, thy will be done. ..."

b. Complete salvation, i.e., all the spiritual and material blessings—blessings for soul and body—which result when God is King in our hearts, recognized and obeyed as such. That is the meaning, according to the context, in Luke 18:24.

c. The church: the community of men in whose hearts God is recognized as King. Note the close connection between "Kingdom" and "church" in Acts 20:25, 28; cf. Matt. 16:18, 19.

d. The redeemed universe: the new heaven and earth with all their glory; something still future: the final realization of God's saving power. Thus in Luke 22:30; cf. Matt. 25:34, ". . . inherit the kingdom prepared for y o u. . . ."

These four concepts are not separate and unrelated. They all proceed from the central idea of the reign of God, his supremacy in the sphere of saving power. The "kingdom" or "kingship" (the Greek word has both meanings) of heaven is like a gradually developing mustard seed.

Jesus spoke of the work of salvation as the kingdom or reign of God or of heaven in order to indicate the supernatural character, origin, and purpose of our salvation. Our salvation begins in heaven and should redound to the glory of the Father in heaven. Hence, by using this term Christ defended the truth, so precious to all believers, that everything is subservient to God's glory.

Jesus, then, tells those who had gathered around him that he must proclaim this "good news" of the reign of God not only to Capernaum but also to the other cities. He adds, "because for this purpose I was sent."

In many passages Jesus, while on earth, emphasized that he had been

sent. In Luke see also 4:18; 9:48; 10:16; in John: 5:30; 6:38; 8:42; 9:4;
17:18, to mention only a few. This implies that whenever Jesus speaks he
does so with divine authority. Whoever accepts him accepts the Father;
whoever rejects him rejects the Father!

**44. So he continued to preach in the synagogues of the country of the
Jews.**

a. Jesus continued to preach. Proclaiming the glad tidings that the kingdom and all its blessings are God's free gift, and setting forth the responsibilities devolving upon the recipients were his joy.

Luke mentions only preaching. Mark also mentions casting out demons.
Though neither Mark nor Luke refers to healings, they may well be
suggested by demon-expulsions. But it must be borne in mind that *preaching* was, after all, the main thing. It was the *message* that must be accepted
unto salvation. So Luke mentions *that!* See Rom. 10:14, 15; and see N.T.C.
on II Tim. 4:1, 2.

b. He preached "in the synagogues." See N.T.C. on Mark, pp. 74–76.

c. Note "of the country of the Jews." Literally "of Judea." The parallel
passage (Mark 1:39; and cf. Matt. 4:23–25) pictures Jesus as going
"throughout all Galilee." Solution: the term *Judea* must be taken in the
broader sense as indicating the country inhabited by the Jews. The preaching tour probably covered a portion of *Galilee.* Note preceding context. On
this see also the note on 4:44 on page 275.

The prophecy of Isa. 9:1, 2 was being gloriously fulfilled![214]

Practical Lesson Derived from Luke 4:42–44

Verses 42–44

"They tried to keep him from leaving them. . . . Also to the other towns I must
preach. . . . So he continued to preach."

These people were of the opinion that in order to enjoy God's gifts they must
keep them all to themselves! They remind us of Jonah, who made himself comfortable "that he might see what would become of Nineveh" (Jonah 4:5). Note God's
answer in verses 10, 11.

Why is the Dead Sea dead, and why is the Sea of Galilee alive?

A good hymn in this connection is F. R. Havergal's "Tell It Out." As to relevant
Bible passages, see especially Gen. 22:18; Ps. 72:8; 87; Isa. 54:2, 3; 60:1–3; Matt.
16:25; 20:28; 28:19; John 3:16; 10:16; Acts 1:8.

Notes on Greek Words, Phrases, and Constructions in 4:42–44

Verse 42

The sentence begins with another gen. absolute (cf. the beginning of verse 40),
literally "Day having arrived," that is, "As day broke," or "At daybreak."

---

214. Notes on Greek words, phrases, and constructions in 4:42–44 begin on this page.

ἔρημος, deserted, lonely, solitary, desolate. Cf. *hermit.*

κατεῖχον, to keep or restrain. The redundant negative (μή) can be understood in the light of abbreviated expression: "They tried to restrain him so that he would *not* go away from them."

As to the word κατέχω itself, it is made up of κατά and ἔχω. Included in the meanings of the prefix are: *down, down on, against, toward.* The verb ἔχω means *to have, to hold.* It is with Greek as with English: we speak of "holding the tongue," that is, restraining it; of "holding down," that is, suppressing; of "holding toward," that is, making for; of "holdings," that is, possessions; and of "holding the line," that is, clinging to a course of action or conduct. The verb κατέχω has all these same meanings:

(a) to keep from, restrain (our present Luke 4:42; also II Thess. 2:6, 7); (b) to hold down or suppress (Rom. 1:18; cf. Rom. 7:6); (c) to hold toward or make for (Acts 27:40); (d) to take and keep, get possession of (Luke 14:9; Philem. 13: cf. I Cor. 7:30; II Cor. 6:10); (e) We should keep clinging to or holding on to that which we have (Luke 8:15; I Cor. 11:2; 15:2; I Thess. 5:21; Heb. 3:6, 14; 10:23).

Verse 43

καὶ ... θεοῦ; lit. "Also to the other towns it is necessary that the good news of the kingdom of God be proclaimed by me." With "I must preach" cf. John 4:4; 9:4; 10:16. It would seem that there is not a great difference between John and the Synoptics after all.

ἀπεστάλην, first per. s. 2nd aor. pass. indicat. of ἀποστέλλω. Cf. *apostle.*

Verse 44

ἦν κηρύσσων, third per. s. periphrastic imperfect.

τῆς Ἰουδαίας. Though this reading is probably correct, rather than τῆς Γαλιλαίας, here as in 1:5 (and cf. Acts 26:20) the wider meaning must be accepted, according to the context. It is definitely a day in Capernaum that is here described. See verses 31, 38, 42. Cf. L.N.T. (A. and G.), p. 379; A. T. Robertson, *Translation*, p. 162; Beck; N.E.B. footnote. Other passages in which the possibility should be considered that the term *Judea* may have the wider meaning—Palestine, the country of the Jews—are Luke 7:17; 23:5; Acts 10:37; 11:1, 29; I Thess. 2:14.

Summary of Chapter 4:14-44

The Beginning of The Great Galilean Ministry (verses 14, 15). Between Christ's baptism and temptation, on the one hand, and his arrival in Galilee, on the other, about a year may have elapsed, spent mostly in Judea. Then Jesus returned to Galilee, where he had spent most of his life. He began to teach the people. This teaching was:

a. Spirit-endowed, for so was the Teacher;

b. widely advertised;

c. synagogue-centered; and

d. popular ("he was being praised by everybody").

The Rejection of Jesus at Nazareth (verses 16–30). It is possible that Luke in his Gospel gives such an early place to this account because what happened here was typical of what was going to occur in general during Christ's work on earth: first, astonishment and approval; later, doubt and rejection.

In Nazareth's synagogue Jesus reads Isa. 61:1, 2a: "The Spirit of the Lord (is) upon me, because he has anointed me to proclaim good news to the poor . . . to the captives release," etc. Having rolled up the scroll and returned it to the attendant, he told the people, "Today, in y o u r very hearing, this passage of Scripture has been fulfilled." The audience reacted with amazement and approval. Upon further reflection, however, the people began to have their doubts. "Good news to the poor, to the captives release, to the blind recovery of sight," etc.—all this was fine. They liked it! But what did the speaker mean when he said that *in their very hearing* this passage of Scripture was being fulfilled? Did he actually mean that somehow the blessings of the Messianic Age were linked up with *him?* "Isn't this Joseph's son?" We know him. He grew up among us. Besides, why doesn't he do here, in our own presence, what he is reported to have done in Capernaum? Why doesn't he show us some of his miracles?

Jesus, in resuming his address, tells the audience that "hometown" and even "Jewish nationality" have nothing to do with the distribution of divine favors and privileges. God is sovereign. Whether the place happens to be Capernaum or Nazareth, the nationality Jewish or non-Jewish, is not at all the question. During the days of Elijah, when there was a severe famine, the prophet was sent to a widow of *Zarephath,* though there were many widows in Israel. And at the time of Elisha, Naaman *the Syrian* was cleansed, though there were many lepers in Israel.

On hearing this, the people in the synagogue became so angry that they drove Jesus out of town and pushed him to the brow of the hill on which their town was built. They intended to hurl him down headlong. But he walked right through their midst and went on his way.

The Healing of a Man with an Unclean Spirit (verses 31–37). In the synagogue at Capernaum Jesus teaches. The people are amazed at the content and the method of his teaching. In the synagogue that sabbath there was a man with an unclean spirit. "Ha! Why do you bother us?" asked the demon, making use of the man's vocal organs. "Have you come to destroy us?" The evil spirit seemed to fear that even now Jesus would hurl him and his fellow demons into the place where Satan is kept. Jesus commanded the demon to leave the man. Hurling him down into the midst of the people, the demon came out, without injuring the man. Reaction on the part of the synagogue audience to Christ's teaching and demon-expulsion in the synagogue: utter amazement. And the news about Jesus continued to spread.

The Healing of Simon's Mother-in-law and of Many Others (verses 38–41). Simon's mother-in-law, who lived in his home, was "in the grip of a high fever" (thus *Dr.* Luke). So, those in that home asked Jesus to come to the rescue. Jesus came and, as a doctor would do, he stood over her. Next, Jesus did something no doctor on earth could have done: he rebuked the fever and it left her. So completely restored was she that she even started to wait on all those who were gathered in Simon's home.

In view of what had already happened in the synagogue and in Simon's home it is not strange that at sunset—not before; it was the sabbath!—ever so many people brought their sick relatives, neighbors, and friends to Jesus. He healed all; not in the mass, however, but by bestowing personal attention on each in turn. He also expelled the demons. As they were leaving, they shrieked, "You are the Son of God." Jesus, for reasons of his own—but see comments on this—prevented them from saying anything further. *He* knew that *they* knew him to be the Messiah ("the Christ"). For good reasons, he did not want this fact to be published at this particular time, especially not by demons!

Preaching the Good News to Other Towns Also (verses 42–44). It is not surprising that after such a strenuous day Jesus felt the need of quiet communion with his Father (cf. Mark 1:35). Therefore at daybreak he left and went to a lonely place. The crowd—including Simon, perhaps preceded by him—went out to look for him. When they found him, they tried to prevent him from leaving them. But he said, "Also to the other towns I must preach the good news of the kingdom of God." He started to do just that.

Outline of Chapter 5

Theme: *The Work Thou Gavest Him to Do*

CHAPTER V

5 1 Once while the crowd was pressing upon him, listening to God's word, and Jesus was standing beside the Lake of Gennesaret, 2 he saw two boats lying at the edge of the lake,²¹⁵ but the fishermen had left them and were washing their nets. 3 Getting into one of the boats, the one belonging to Simon, Jesus asked him to push out a little from shore. Then he sat down and from the boat began to teach the people.

4 When he had finished speaking, he said to Simon, "Launch out into the deep and let down y o u r nets for a haul." 5 Simon answered, "Master, all through the night we toiled and caught nothing, but because you say so²¹⁶ I'll let down the nets."²¹⁷

6 Having done this, they enclosed such an enormous shoal of fish that their nets started to tear. 7 So they signaled their comrades²¹⁸ in the other boat to come and help them. They arrived and filled both boats, so that they began to sink.

8 When Simon Peter saw this, he fell at Jesus' knees and said, "Go away from me, for I'm a sinful man, Lord." 9 For, because of the haul of fish they had made, amazement had gripped him and all who were with him. 10 This was true also with respect to Zebedee's sons, James and John, who were Simon's partners.

Then Jesus said to Simon, "Have no fear; from now on you will be catching men."²¹⁹ 11 So, running their boats ashore, they left everything and followed him.

5:1-11 *A Miraculous Catch*

Again, as often, Luke is indefinite as to time. Note, however, the following: (a) we find Jesus still in Galilee; (b) the disciples are still being "called"—there were several steps in this calling (see N.T.C. on Matthew, p. 245); (c) it would seem that Levi (= Matthew) has not yet joined the group (Luke 5:27-32; cf. Mark 2:13-17); and (d) The Twelve, as a body, have not yet been chosen and charged (cf. Luke 6:12-16; 9:1-6; and see also Mark 3:13-19; 6:7-13; cf. Matt. 10:1-42). On the other hand, (e) "the calling of four fishermen" (Matt. 4:18-22; Mark 1:16-20) has already taken place.

---

215. Literally, standing beside the lake.
216. Literally, at your word.
217. Or: I'll have the nets lowered.
218. Or: partners (as in verse 10).
219. Literally: "catching men alive." This deserves consideration as a possible alternative rendering.

Taken as a unit, the story found here in Luke 5:1-11 is peculiar to Luke; it has no parallel.[220]

The incident is meaningful and even thrilling. It is all this because it shows what a wonderful Savior is Jesus. He stands revealed here in a fivefold aspect, each of the five little paragraphs setting forth one phase of his greatness; as follows:

A. *his practical wisdom*

1-3. Once while the crowd was pressing upon him, listening to God's word, and Jesus was standing beside the Lake of Gennesaret, he saw two boats lying at the edge of the lake, but the fishermen had left them and were washing their nets. Getting into one of the boats, the one belonging to Simon, Jesus asked him to push out a little from shore. Then he sat down and from the boat began to teach the people.

It will become clear that Jesus' practical wisdom is revealed in these first three verses. The situation was as follows. Jesus was standing on the shore of that body of water which Luke always calls a "lake," the other evangelists a "sea." In the present instance Luke adds "of Gennesaret" (according to some, meaning "princely garden"), the adjoining amazingly fertile plain (to the south of Capernaum) described in N.T.C. on Mark, p. 264. The Speaker, in his own captivating and authoritative manner, was bringing the *word* or *message* of God to his audience. That message was "the gospel of the kingdom," the reign of God in hearts, lives, and spheres. Cf. Mark 1:14, 15.

So huge was the assembled multitude that the One who addressed them was actually being crowded. The people were pressing closer and closer. Does not this remind us of Mark 4:1 and especially of Mark 3:9? Just then Jesus saw two fishermen's boats lying at the water's edge. They were empty, their occupants having stepped ashore to wash their nets, to ready them for another try. So, in order to solve his problem, Jesus stepped into one of these boats and asked its owner to push out a little from shore. Having arrived at a spot not too close to nor too far away from the land, the Lord sat down (the usual speaking position) and then began once more, or continued, to teach the people.

This was surely a very practical way of solving a problem. There was nothing stiff or inflexible about Jesus' method of reaching the people. Within reason almost anything could serve as his pulpit. Many a time he preached or taught at the regular synagogue service, as has already been shown (Luke 4:15, 16), and in Judea also in the temple (Matt. 26:55). But he did not limit himself to synagogue and temple. Sometimes he chose a

---

220. For the opposite view see A. T. Robertson, *Word Pictures,* Vol. II, p. 68. A. Plummer is not sure (*op. cit.,* pp. 141, 142). On this question see also N.T.C. on Matthew, p. 245; and Lenski, *op. cit.,* p. 176. Identification with the incident related in John 21:1-14, a post-resurrection occurrence, is impossible.

convenient spot on a mountain as his pulpit (Matt. 5:1), or a house (Luke 5:17 f.), or a desert (Mark 8:1, 4), or a cemetery (John 11:38). In the present instance speaking while seated in a fisherman's boat meant not only a more comfortable position but also a better view of the audience and even better acoustics.

However, in this case Jesus revealed his practical wisdom also in another way. The owner of the boat from which Jesus now addressed the people was Simon. It was to him that he addressed the request that, with his Master aboard, he push out a little from shore. Upon this very man, Simon, the Lord had already bestowed many a blessing. He had "called" him, and this not once but twice (John 1:42; then Mark 1:16–18). He had visited his home and had even healed this fisherman's mother-in-law (Luke 4:38, 39). But now he did the very opposite: he asked Simon to render a service to *him!* Today's preacher, teacher, etc., should take this practical lesson to heart. If you wish to see your church, class, or whatever, grow numerically and spiritually, not only do something for this group but also ask them to do something for the good cause. Get your people involved!

B. *his penetrating knowledge*

4, 5. When he had finished speaking, he said to Simon, Launch out into the deep and let down y o u r nets for a haul.
When Jesus was through speaking to the multitude, he told Simon to bring the boat to a place where the water was deep, and then, with the help of his men, to lower the nets for the purpose of catching fish. Note the change here from the singular to the plural. It took more than one individual to lower the nets.

The boat to which Luke refers was probably rather large, with room enough for Jesus and his disciples (cf. Mark 6:7, 30, 32). It is therefore reasonable to assume that also now, together with Jesus and Simon, there were others in this boat. One of them may have been Andrew (cf. Mark 1:16), though in this entire account he is never mentioned by name. The probability must also be granted that Simon and his partners (see verses 7 and 10) had employed a crew of hired men. Cf. Mark 1:20.

Humanly speaking, the order which Jesus issued—"Launch out into the deep," etc.—was strange. A carpenter telling an experienced fisherman how to catch fish! He was ordering him to fish at an unlikely place and time, that is, in deep water and in bright daylight. It must be borne in mind that Jesus had already twice addressed the people on the shore, each time presumably at some length (verses 1 and 3). By this time it may well have been around noon, therefore.

Accordingly, when Simon receives this order, faith and doubt, trust and misgiving, are battling it out. His fisherman's expertise raises a doubt and whispers to him that he must not obey Jesus. His conscience, illuminated by faith, tells him that he must obey. Faith conquers, though still tempered with some misgiving. **Simon answered, Master**—this is Luke's constant substitute for the term *Rabbi* of the other Gospels—**all through the night**[221] **we toiled and caught nothing, but because you say so I'll let down the nets.** This not, to be sure, all by himself but with the help of his men, so that the translation "I'll have the nets lowered" can be substituted.

Implied in Jesus' command is *at least* the fact that he *knew* that at the spot where Simon would lower the nets there would be an abundance of fish. How did he know this? Here we are confronted with a mystery. It cannot be denied that even during his sojourn on earth Jesus, according to his *divine* nature, was omniscient. That he actually knew the whereabouts of fishes is clear not only from our present passage but also from Matt. 17:27. He also knew where human individuals would be and what they would be doing at this or that particular moment (Mark 14:13; John 1:47–49). He was even aware of the contents and deliberations of hearts and minds (Luke 5:22; John 2:25). Yet, according to his *human* nature his knowledge was limited (Matt. 24:36; Mark 11:13; Luke 8:45, 46). How these two natures, each possessing certain characteristics in distinction from the other, could be inseparably united in one divine person is beyond human comprehension. The best we can do, when we contemplate this great mystery, is to derive comfort from our Savior's penetrating knowledge, so that with Simon Peter we cry out, "Lord, thou knowest all things; thou knowest that I love thee" (John 21:17b).

So far we have referred only to Christ's omniscience. But according to his divine nature he was not only omniscient but also omnipotent. Therefore we cannot rule out the possibility that he not only *knew* that at a certain moment this enormous shoal of fish would be at a certain definite place, but that he also actually *directed* them to that place! And if that is what happened, then he naturally *knew* where they would be.

When God created man he gave him "dominion over the fish of the sea." To an extent, at least, this dominion was lost when man fell. In Christ it is restored (Gen. 1:28; Matt. 11:27; 28:18; Heb. 2:5–8).

C. *his lavish generosity*

6, 7. Having done this, they enclosed such an enormous shoal of fish that their nets started to tear. So they signaled their comrades [or: partners] in the other boat to come and help them. They arrived and filled both boats, so that they began to sink.

So enormous was the quantity of fish caught that the nets started to tear. The meaning cannot be that they actually began to rip apart so that the fish could escape and swim away, but that noises were heard associated with the snapping of a little cord here, a little cord there. Because of this

---

221. I can see no good reason why the order of the words in the original, with emphasis on "all through the night," should not be retained in the translation.

emergency—the nets starting to tear, the boat's capacity inadequate—Simon and his men signaled their comrades in the other boat to come and help.

Note: they "signaled." Why did they not shout? It will be recalled that there were two boats (verse 2). One answer, then, might be that the second boat was either still lying ashore or was at least too far away from the first one to be reached by shouting. The first boat was "in deep water" (verse 4); the second may not have been. Another solution would be that, by reason of their very occupation, fishermen would communicate with each other not by shouts but by signals.

Who were those "comrades" in the other boat? Opinions are divided. According to Lenski (*op. cit.*, p. 180) they were "hired men"; while Plummer, too (*op. cit.*, p. 146), is not sure whether the signaled men of verse 7 and Zebedee's sons of verse 10 were the same people.[222] The position that they were the same in both cases, namely, Zebedee's sons, James and John, who were business associates of Simon, a view endorsed by many commentators including Greijdanus and Robertson, is in line with Matt. 4:18, 21; Mark 1:16, 19. It can be considered a reasonable assumption.

The summoned men arrived. The holds of both boats were now filled with fish. The result was that the two vessels became so heavy that they went down, down, down, reaching a level that was so near to the surface of the water that they were but barely kept afloat.

Here is an example of the lavish generosity of our Lord. When he gives he does not stint. "He giveth and giveth and giveth again." See Matt. 14:20, 21; 15:37, 38; also N.T.C. on John 1:16.

D. *his ineffable majesty*

8-10a. When Simon Peter saw this, he fell at Jesus' knees and said, Go away from me, for I'm a sinful man, Lord. —For, because of the haul of fish they had made, amazement had gripped him and all who were with him. This was true also with respect to Zebedee's sons, James and John, who were Simon's partners.

Note "Simon Peter," his name fully spelled out, as it is also in Matt. 16:16. In both cases this disciple pours out his heart in humble confession and adoration.

He fell at Jesus' knees. At this point some interpreters experience a difficulty. They cannot understand this posture and suggest that the meaning is probably that Simon fell on his knees before Jesus. The difficulty

---

222. Plummer on the same page states that the difference of words in the original—in verse 7 μέτοχοι and in verse 10 κοινωνοί—should be preserved in the translation. Two different words are used by Phillips, Goodspeed, Moffatt, Lenski, Dutch (Nieuwe Vertaling), etc.; while most of the other translators use the same word—generally "partners"—in both cases. A good argument can be presented for either alternative. If we accept the theory that the persons indicated in both verses were the same, namely, James and John, this point is rather insignificant. The difference in words may be simply stylistic. In both cases the Greek terms probably describe Zebedee's sons as Simon's "business partners."

disappears, however, when Jesus is pictured as sitting down. There was room for Simon to fall as well as there was room for Simon's men to walk around and do their work. The fish were in the hold.

When Simon now asks Jesus to depart from him, this must not be interpreted too literally, as if he were requesting Jesus to walk off the boat and into the lake. The words must be viewed as a sincere and humble expression of this disciple's recognition of his own unworthiness as contrasted with Christ's greatness and holiness. Peter stands in awe of his Master and confesses him to be his "Lord." Astonishment and fear had seized him, and not only him but also his men (see on verse 4) and his partners, James and John. They have become aware of the fact that Jesus is superhuman; in fact, that he is God! Again and again in the Septuagint (Greek translation of the Hebrew Old Testament) the title *Lord* is used as an equivalent of *God*. Instantaneously, under the impression of the astounding miracle, Simon Peter knew in his heart that his "Master" was at the same time his "Lord," truly worthy of worship and adoration. Over against this "Lord" Peter was nothing but a "sinful man."

In the presence of the holy God sinful man trembles. Other examples: Abraham (Gen. 18:27, 30, 32); Manoah and his wife (Judg. 13:20); Job (Job 42:5, 6); Isaiah (Isa. 6:5); the apostle John (Rev. 1:17). This applies even to groups: Israel (Exod. 20:19; Deut. 5:25); the nations (Isa. 64:2).

The question may be asked, "How is it that this confession fell from Simon's lips now and not before?" This, after all, was not the first miracle Simon had witnessed. In fact, Jesus had performed a supernatural healing act right in this disciple's own home (Luke 4:38, 39). The answer is probably that this particular miracle was performed in the very area which Simon regarded as his own, that is, in the sphere in which he considered himself a specialist, fishing!

When one is confronted with Jesus, it is impossible to remain neutral. His enemies react to his miracles with hatred and reviling; his true disciples, with homage and reverence. They stoop and worship.

E. *his profound mission-mindedness*

10b, 11. Then Jesus said to Simon, Have no fear; from now on you will be catching men. On "Have no fear" or "Do not be afraid" see the explanation of 1:13, including the note on that passage on page 80. Jesus, kind Shepherd that he is, has taken note of Peter's alarmed feeling. It is for this reason that he now puts his disciple's mind to rest. Next, he reveals to him that this is a critical moment, a turning point, in Peter's life. From this moment on the disciple's main vocation will change. Simon has been catching *fish*. He is going to be catching *men*. He has been catching in order *to kill*. He will be catching in order *to impart life*, that is, to be an instrument in God's hand in doing this. All this may well be implied in the words used in the original, which can also be rendered, "From now on you will be catching men alive," implying "and for life."

Once before Jesus had promised, "I will make y o u fishers of men" (Matt. 4:19; cf. Mark 1:17). But *this* time the words are more definite. It is clearly indicated that this altered stage in Peter's life—and he, of course, also represents the other disciples—begins here and now; and also that the effort will be crowned with a measure of success: "you will be catching men." Moreover, the continuity of the work is stressed: day by day, week after week, month upon month, etc., you will be engaged in this great and glorious task.

The reason Jesus wanted to catch men in his gospel net, and wanted his disciples to follow his example, was that this was a very important part of the task the Father had assigned to him. In order to accomplish this assignment he had come to earth (Luke 5:32). To bring about this result he was "sent" by the Father (4:18; 9:48; 10:16; cf. John 3:16, 17, 34, etc.; Gal. 4:4; I John 4:9, 10, 14). And he himself eagerly desired to rescue men from death and to impart life to them (Luke 10:2; cf. Matt. 9:36–38; John 4:34, 35), even though he fully realized what would be the cost to himself (Luke 12:50). O the depth of love! Yet his final aim did not center in man but in God, that *he* (God) might be glorified (Luke 17:18; cf. John 17:1, 4), and the ardent desire of the holy angels (Luke 2:14) might thus be fulfilled.

It is understandable, therefore, that in meditating on Jesus' promise to his disciples that from now on they would be catching men, we speak of his "profound mission-mindedness." For more on this general subject see on verse 32.

So, running their boats ashore, they left everything and followed him.
Note that *this* time Peter, James, and John leave *everything* behind to follow Jesus. Never before had they done this. There had been a call to accept Jesus of Nazareth as the Messiah (John 1:35–51); next, a call to become Christ's more steady companions, without bidding farewell to their occupation as fishermen (Matt. 4:18–22; Mark 1:16–20). But the present implied call meant that they must leave *all*.

As already mentioned, this call was *implied,* rather than expressed. It was implied in the promise, "From now on you will be catching men."

How great was the sacrifice these men were required to make? The answer becomes clear by studying a question raised by Peter sometime later, and especially by pondering Christ's answer to that question. See Luke 18:28–30 (cf. Matt. 19:27–30; Mark 10:28–31). To be specific: these men actually left their fish, boats, business, homes, families!

Note: *They* left everything, even though the promise had been made to Simon alone. The other disciples correctly understood that what Jesus had spoken to Peter concerned them also.

What became of the fish? Were they simply left to rot? Certainly not. He who was going to see to it that broken pieces of food were gathered (Matt. 14:20; 15:37) would never have allowed that to happen. If Zebedee himself was still alive, he could take charge. Besides, there were the hired men. The rich supply had been intended by the Lord, we may be sure, as food for many. A portion could be sold. Some could be given to the poor. The families of the fishermen could be supplied.

But why such an enormous provision? The thought occurs that God—Jesus, if one prefers—furnished such an immense quantity in order to rid the disciples of any worry about their families, as if to say, "Will not he who just now has blessed y o u so abundantly continue to care for y o u?" How great thou art![223]

Practical Lessons Derived from Luke 5:1–11

Many of the practical lessons are found in the explanation. For the rest, note the following:

Verse 1

"Pressing upon him, listening to God's word." For a successful service the preacher must proclaim God's word; the audience must listen eagerly.

Verse 4

"Launch out," figuratively speaking, by means of bearing witness by word of mouth, giving moral and financial support, being a living example.

Verse 5

"At your word I'll let down the nets." This is another way of saying, "I'll trust and obey." What a multitude of excuses we can offer to show why the business of spreading the gospel net should be left to others! These excuses will never convince God . . . or our conscience.

Verse 7

"They signaled their comrades . . . to come and help them." In unity there is strength. See Esther 4:16; Phil. 2:2.

Verse 8

"Depart from me." Is it not wonderful that the Lord did not grant this request? Sermon theme: "The Comfort of Rejected Petitions." Other examples: I Chron. 17:4; Mark 1:35–38; 5:19.

Verse 10

"You will be catching men." This promise still holds.

Verse 11

"They left everything and followed him." In order to catch men stay close to Jesus!

---

223. Notes on Greek words, phrases, and constructions in 5:1–11 begin on page 287.

Notes on Greek Words, Phrases, and Constructions in 5:1-11

Verse 1

ἐπικεῖσθαι, pres. infinitive of ἐπίκειμαι, to lie upon, press upon; in 23:23 in the sense of *insist*. Cf. John 11:38, a stone lying against the tomb; 21:9, a fish lying on a charcoal fire. See also Acts 27:20; I Cor. 9:16; Heb. 9:10.

αὐτός, unemphatic, "he." Luke has not prepared us for the conclusion (Lenski's) that καὶ αὐτός here means "he too."

ἦν ἑστώς, periphrastic imperfect, he was standing.

λίμνη, a body of water; specifically, the Lake of Gennesaret (Sea of Galilee). In chapters 19-21 of the book of Revelation mention is made of the λίμνη of fire = "the second death." The base of λίμνη is *li*; cf. *liquid*.

Verse 2

ἁλιεῖς, pl. of ἁλιεύς, fisherman; cf. ἅλς, salt, the sea.

ἔπλυνον, third per. pl. imperf. indicat. active of πλύνω, to wash. For synonyms and fine distinctions see N.T.C. on Mark, p. 272, footnote 309.

δίκτυα, acc. pl. of δίκτυον, net. This is the most general word for net. It can refer to any net whatever, even a hunting net or a net for catching birds. In the New Testament, however, it is confined to *fishing* nets of any description. The *sagene* is the *seine* or *dragnet*. And the *amphiblestron* is the casting-net.

Verse 3

ἐπαναγαγεῖν, 2nd aor. active infinitive of ἐπανάγω, lit., to bring or lead up or back (Matt. 21:18); here, in Luke 5:3, 4, to push off from shore, out to sea. Note also the sec. per. s. aor. active imperative in verse 4.

Verses 4, 5

χαλάσατε, sec. per. pl. aor. imperat. of χαλάω, to let down, to lower; cf. Mark 2:4 (a pallet); Acts 9:25 and II Cor. 11:33 (Paul); Acts 27:17 (an anchor); 27:30 (a boat). In verse 5 note the first per. s. fut. indicat. of this verb, perhaps causative here.

ἄγρα*, haul, catch (the act of catching); so probably also in verse 9, though it is difficult to separate the act of catching from its result: that which is caught.

ἐπιστάτα, voc. s. of ἐπιστάτης*, master; in Luke always in the vocative (cf. 8:24, 45; 9:33, 49; 17:13).

Verse 6

συνέκλεισαν, third per. pl. aor. active indicat. of συγκλείω, to enclose; cf. Rom. 11:32 and see N.T.C. on Gal. 3:22.

διερρήσσετο, third per. s. (*s.* because of neut. pl. δίκτυα) imperfect (inchoative) passive of διαρρήσσω (also spelled διαρήσσω), late form of the old verb διαρρήγνυμι, to break, rend, tear; in 8:29 to snap; elsewhere in the New Testament only in connection with a garment that is torn as a sign of grief or horror (whether real or feigned). See Matt. 26:65; Mark 14:63; Acts 14:14.

Verse 7

κατένευσαν (for synonym see 1:22), third per. pl. aor. active indicat. of κατανεύω*, to signal.

For the aor. middle infinitive συλλαβέσθαι see the note on 1:24 on page 81; and for ἔπλησαν see the note on 2:6 on page 147, and the note on 4:28 on page 261.

Something can be said in favor of the position that the difference between μέτοχοι here, and κοινωνοί (verse 10) should be preserved in the translation. But the point is not very important.

ὥστε is consecutive (indicates result), and is here followed by the present passive infinitive, to submerge, sink; hence here: to be submerged, to sink. See also N.T.C. on I Tim. 6:9. Cf. βυθός, bottom, deep sea; and cf. *abyss*.

Verse 9

περιέσχεν, third per. s. aor. active of περιέχω; lit. to hold all around, to encircle; and so here: to seize, grip. Cf. I Peter 2:6.

Verse 10

ἔσῃ ζωγρῶν, the latter from ζωός, alive, and ἀγρεύω, to catch; hence literally: to catch men alive. The periphrastic (continuative) future indicat. is used here: you will (constantly) be catching alive. The verb ζωγρέω occurs only here and in II Tim. 2:26. See N.T.C. on that passage. For the simple (uncompounded) ἀγρεύω see N.T.C. on Mark, footnote 578 on p. 480.

Verse 11

καταγαγόντες, nom. pl. masc. aor. participle of κατάγω. With this compare ἐπανάγω, to push out to sea (verses 3, 4). The verb used here in verse 11 means the opposite of the one in verses 3, 4. It means: to push away from the sea, to run (a boat) to shore. Both verbs are nautical terms.

---

12 While Jesus was in one of the towns, lo and behold, a man full of leprosy! When he saw Jesus, he fell on his face and implored him, "Lord, if you will, you can cleanse me." 13 So Jesus stretched out his hand, touched him, and said, "I will; be cleansed." And at once the leprosy left him. 14 And Jesus charged him to tell no one, "But [he said] go and show yourself to the priest, and for a testimony to them make an offering for your cleansing, as Moses commanded."

15 But all the more the news about Jesus continued to spread, and vast crowds were gathering to hear him and to be healed of their sicknesses. 16 And he[224] would go away to lonely places to pray.

5:12-16 *A Leper Cleansed*
Cf. Matt. 8:1-4; Mark 1:40-45

12. While Jesus was in one of the towns, lo and behold, a man full of leprosy! Jesus was "in one of the towns," perhaps on the outskirts, for lepers were not generally seen inside cities and towns.

---

224. Or: he himself.

The time and place are indefinite, both here and in the other Gospels. Most natural, however, is the theory according to which this meeting took place during the Galilean circuit to which the more chronologically arranged Gospel According to Mark has just referred (see Mark 1:39, 40). If so, the incident occurred shortly before the healing of the paralytic (Luke 5:17-26; cf. Mark 2:1-12), which, in turn, was followed by the call of Levi (Luke 5:27-32; cf. Mark 2:13-17). All this transpired sometime before the calling of The Twelve (to apostleship) and the preaching of the Sermon on the Mount (Luke 6:12-49; cf. Mark 3:13-19; and for the sermon cf. Matt. 5-7).

For a summary of the Bible's teaching on leprosy see N.T.C. on Matthew, pp. 388-391. And for a discussion of the question, "Was this leprosy?" see N.T.C. on Mark, p. 77.

"A man full of leprosy," and nevertheless approaching close enough to Jesus to be touched by him! It is not surprising, therefore, that Luke prefaces his description of the man by saying "lo and behold!" The closeness of this man's approach to Jesus is remarkable especially in view of Lev. 13:45, 46, ". . . Alone shall he dwell; outside the camp shall be his habitation." See also Num. 5:2-4; 12:14, 15; II Kings 7:3. With this compare "ten lepers who stood *at a distance*" (Luke 17:12). It is Luke, he alone, who describes this man as "full of leprosy," not simply "a leper." Of course, it is Luke, the beloved physician, who would have made inquiries concerning the exact physical condition of this individual. His leprosy must have reached a very advanced stage.

When he saw Jesus, he fell on his face and implored him, Lord, if you will, you can cleanse me. The man did not know whether the help he craved would be given to him. But there was nothing wrong in asking. He does this in a most humble manner. He drops to his knees (thus Mark), then lowers his face to the ground ("fell on his face," thus Luke), and implores or begs, "Lord," etc. By addressing Jesus in this manner he must have meant far more than "Sir." Otherwise, how could he have made the confession he actually made, namely, "You can cleanse me"? Of this *power* on the part of Jesus he is sure. Of Jesus' *willingness* to cleanse him he is not sure, as is indicated by the fact that he says, "*If* you will." But he submits himself to the Savior's sovereign disposition, hoping eagerly that he too may be the recipient of Christ's healing power and mercy.

13. So Jesus stretched out his hand, touched him, and said, I will; be cleansed. Repeatedly and in varying phraseology the Gospels speak of Christ's healing touch. To Luke 5:13 add 7:14; 22:51; cf. Matt. 8:3, 15; 9:29; 17:7; 20:34; Mark 1:41; 7:33. Sometimes, however, the sick touched Jesus (Luke 8:44-47; cf. Matt. 9:20, 21; Mark 3:10; 5:27-31; 6:56). Either way the afflicted ones were healed. Evidently in connection with such physical contact healing power issued from the Savior and was transmitted to the person in need of it (Mark 5:30; Luke 8:46). This, however, was no magic! The healing power did not originate in his fingers or his garment. It came straight from the divine and human Jesus, from his almighty will and infinitely sympathetic heart. There was healing power in that touch because he was, and is "touched with the feeling of our infirmities" (Heb. 4:15). It should not escape the reader that according to Mark 1:41 Jesus was "moved with compassion" when he stretched out his hand and touched the leper. The leper's need and faith found an immediate response in the Savior's eagerness to help. And in this readiness his power and his love embraced each other.

It is sometimes said that between the words of the leper and those of Jesus there is perfect correspondence. This is correct in the sense that the two statements do not clash but are in full harmony, revealing even a partial identity of phraseology. One could also say, however, that the words of the Lord excel mere "correspondence." To be sure, the leper's "you can cleanse me" is answered by Christ's "I can, indeed!" implied in his act of healing. But the leper's "*if* you will" is superseded by the Master's swift and splendid "I will." Here the *will* joins the *power,* and the subtraction of "if" conjoined with the addition of "be cleansed" transforms a condition of hideous disease into one of hardy health.

And at once the leprosy left him. One moment the man was "full of leprosy." The next moment not a speck of the disease was left.

The healings brought about by Jesus were complete and instantaneous. Peter's mother-in-law does not have to wait until the following day to be cured of her fever (Luke 4:38, 39). The paralytic immediately begins to walk away, carrying his little bed (5:17–26). The withered hand is restored at once (6:6–11). The demoniac, wild a moment earlier, all at once is fully cured (8:26–39). The same holds with respect to the woman who touched Christ's garment (8:43–48). Even the dead daughter of Jairus is in one moment restored to life, so that she arises and is given something to eat (8:40–42, 49–56). Let the healers of today imitate this! Let them cure every illness immediately. Yes, let them even raise the dead (7:11–17), for if their claim to be able to do what Jesus did and what he commanded his apostles to do is valid, they should certainly also raise the dead (Matt. 10:8). So far, however, they have not succeeded in doing this. In fact, they have not even succeeded in getting rid of death by denying its existence.

Continued: **14. And Jesus charged him to tell no one. But [he said] go and show yourself to the priest, and for a testimony to them make an offering for your cleansing, as Moses commanded.**

Exactly why the cured man was ordered to be silent has not been revealed. Was it in order to forestall a nationalistic movement centering in Jesus? Cf. John 6:15. Was it to prevent a premature crisis? To counteract the taking root of an erroneous conception of the Savior's character and identity, as if he were primarily a thaumaturgist (miracle-worker)? See also above, on 4:40, 41; and N.T.C. on Matt. 8:4 and on Mark 1:43, 44.

Hand in hand with the prohibition Jesus issued a positive command. The cleansed leper must present himself to the priest, so that he may be restored to full social and religious fellowship with his people. If he passes the inspection, so that the priest considers him cured, he must bring the required offering (Lev. 14:1-7). That offering consisted of two clean, living birds. One had to be killed. In its blood the other bird had to be dipped and then released. The blood of the slain bird was also sprinkled over the healed man; in fact, seven times. He was then pronounced cured. When the priests hear that it was Jesus who had so completely and instantly cured this man, they will have received an irrefutable testimony to Jesus' power and love. They will also know that even though Jesus condemns human traditions that make void God's holy law, he does not disobey that law.

It is clear from the entire context that the cleansed leper passed the test. Did he and others remain silent, as Jesus had ordered? The answer is given in verses **15, 16. But all the more the news about Jesus continued to spread, and vast crowds were gathering to hear him and to be healed of their sicknesses. And he would go away to lonely places to pray.**

The request of Jesus was ignored. What actually happened was the very opposite of that which Jesus had ordered. Instead of silence there were voices. Note "all the more." It was as if these voices were saying, "Now we'll advertise him more than ever." Moreover, according to Mark 1:45 it was the cleansed man himself who took the lead in this activity of disobedience.

The result was that vast crowds kept gathering for the twofold purpose of listening to the Master's teaching and being healed of their sicknesses; this probably implies, "and having their sick healed."

We can be sure of the fact that at least some of this enthusiasm was of an unhealthy nature.

So, again and again, Jesus would withdraw himself and steal away to lonely places. This withdrawal also had a positive purpose, namely, to pour out his heart in prayer in order that the reservoirs of his body and soul might be replenished from his Father's inexhaustible resources.

It was to be expected that Luke—the very evangelist who more than any other stresses the importance of prayer—would mention this. See *Introduction*, point I A 5 b.[225]

Practical Lessons Derived from Luke 5:12-16

Verse 13

"Jesus stretched out his hand and touched the leper." When Francis of Assisi reflected on the manner in which Jesus had treated the leper, a great wave of pity swept over him and changed his life. Should not Luke 5:12-16 and similar accounts have a sanctifying effect on us also?

Verses 15, 16

"Vast crowds were gathering... to be healed of their sicknesses.... And he would go away to lonely places to pray." Jesus gave us an example by not allowing anything to stand in the way of regular seasons of prayer.

---

224. Notes on Greek words, phrases, and constructions in 5:12-16 begin on page 292.

Notes on Greek Words, Phrases, and Constructions in 5:12-16

Verses 12-14

At the end of verse 12 note the future more vivid (third class) conditional sentence, with ἐάν followed by sec. per. s. pres. subjunctive in the protasis, and the sec. per. s. pres. indicat. in the apodosis. Note also the aor. active infinitive καθαρίσαι. For the verb καθαρίζω see the note on 4:33 on page 267 (a cognate adjective, negative). And see also the cognate noun (positive) καθαρισμός, cleansing, in 5:14 (there in the gen.); and the sec. per. s. aor. passive imperative καθαρίσθητι in 5:13.

At the end of verse 14 note αὐτοῖς, to *them*. Though no plural antecedent is expressed, it is implied in "the priest," for the latter represents the entire priesthood and probably even the people who adhered to its beliefs and instructions.

Verse 15

Note the two imperfects: the news was spreading (or: continued to spread) and the crowds were gathering (continued to gather).

For θεραπεύεσθαι, pres. passive infinitive of θεραπεύω, see the note on 4:23 on page 261.

With the gen. pl. ἀσθενειῶν cf. the cognate pres. participle in 4:40; see the note on that verse on page 271.

Verse 16

ἦν ὑποχωρῶν, periphrastic imperfect of ὑποχωρέω*. See also 9:10, to go (or steal) away, withdraw. Cf. *anchorite.*

---

17 On one of those days, as he was teaching, Pharisees and teachers of the law were sitting by. They had come from every village of Galilee and from Judea and Jerusalem. And the power of the Lord was with him for healing.

18 And look, some men were carrying on a bed a man who was paralyzed. They were trying to bring him in and to place him in front of Jesus. 19 Not finding a way to carry him in because of the crowd, they went up the roof and, together with his little bed, let him down through the tiles and into the midst (of the crowd), right in front of Jesus. 20 When he saw their faith he said, "Man, your sins are forgiven you."

21 But the scribes and the Pharisees began to reason, saying, "Who is this fellow that speaks blasphemies? Who but God alone is able to forgive sins?"

22 When Jesus perceived their (inward) reasonings, he said to them, "Why are y o u reasoning thus in y o u r hearts? 23 Which is easier: to say, 'Your sins are forgiven,' or to say, 'Get up and walk'? 24 But in order that y o u may know that the Son of man has authority on earth to forgive sins (he said to the paralytic), I say to you, get up, pick up your little bed and go home." 25 Instantly he stood up in front of them, picked up what he had been lying on, and went home, glorifying God.

26 Amazement gripped everyone,[226] and they glorified God. Filled with awe, they were saying, "We have seen incredible things today."

---

226. Or: All were seized with astonishment.

5:17–26 *The Healing of a Paralytic*
Cf. Matt. 9:1–8; Mark 2:1–12

Through constant repetition this story has become well known. Is it possible to renew interest in it? Perhaps. To this end we have tried a new approach, namely, in connection with the theme:

Jesus demonstrates his divine right to forgive sins

We have distributed the material contained in Luke 5:17–26 under the following five subheadings: a battle is brewing (between Jesus and his opponents), a challenge is flung (by Jesus, before his opponents), an attack is made (by the opponents), a victory is won (by Jesus), and a triumph is celebrated (by the onlookers). We believe that such a treatment is true to the meaning and purpose of the account, and preserves its unity.

A. *A battle is brewing*

17. On one of those days, as he was teaching, Pharisees and teachers of the law were sitting by. They had come from every village of Galilee and from Judea and Jerusalem. And the power of the Lord was with him for healing.

As often, Luke's reference to the time when this incident occurred is very indefinite: "on one of those days." But see also on 5:12. As to the place, from Mark's parallel account we learn that it was a house in Capernaum. Some think of Simon's house. But in that case would not Luke's reference to it have been more definite, as in 4:38? The possibility must be allowed that friends had provided Jesus with a house he could use while carrying on his ministry in and around Capernaum. That at this particular occasion the house was crowded is stated in so many words in Mark 2:2 and implied also in Luke 5:17, 19.

No doubt disciples and friends of Jesus were present, with genuine interest in the truth. Also, there must have been people who were merely burning with curiosity to see what Jesus would say and do. But Luke focuses our attention on still another group, consisting of straitlaced Pharisees and likeminded law-teachers.

In Luke's Gospel this is the first reference to the *Pharisees,* who are mentioned frequently in Matthew (beginning with 3:7) and in Mark (beginning with 2:16).

They were a relatively small sect of Separatists. They separated themselves not only from ceremonial impurity, from the heathen, publicans and "sinners," but even in a sense from the indifferent Jewish multitudes, whom they derisively dubbed "the people who do not know the law" (John 7:49).

The *scribes* were the men who studied, taught, interpreted, and transmitted the Mosaic law; that is, generally that law as explained by tradition. In fact, often the real law of God was in their teaching buried beneath tradition. See Matt. 15:6, and take note of the interesting example there given of this evil practice (15:1-5).

In the following passages Luke mentions the *scribes* in one breath with the *Pharisees* (5:21, 30; 6:7; 11:53; 15:2); and in the following the scribes are linked with the *chiefpriests* (9:22; 19:47; 20:1, 19; 22:2, 66; 23:10). In the present account (5:17-26) the combination "Pharisees and teachers of the law [= scribes]" is clear. For more on the scribes see N.T.C. on Matthew, pp. 382, 383; and on Mark, p. 96; for more on Pharisees and scribes, N.T.C. on Matthew, pp. 294, 295, 817 ff.; and on Mark, p. 100.

Now these Pharisees and these teachers of the law had come from *every* village of Galilee and from Judea and Jerusalem (probably hyperbole). It is clear from Luke's entire account that these men were anything but open-minded. They seem to have been filled with envy, probably deeply disturbed about the large crowds Jesus was attracting and about the content of his teaching.

Significantly Luke adds that the power of the Lord—that is, of Jehovah—was with Jesus "for healing," meaning: enabling him to heal. The "healing" described in the present story affected both soul and body, as will be shown.

Consider, then, these two groupings: on the one side Pharisees and teachers of the law, filled with a desire to destroy; on the other Jesus himself, overflowing with power to heal. Clearly a conflict is in the making, a battle is brewing.

B. *A challenge is flung*

18-20. And look, some men were carrying on a bed a man who was paralyzed. They were trying to bring him in and to place him in front of Jesus. Not finding a way to carry him in because of the crowd, they went up the roof and, together with his little bed, let him down through the tiles and into the midst (of the crowd), right in front of Jesus. When he saw their faith he said, Man, your sins are forgiven you.

Wretched indeed was this man. The disease that plagued him is characterized by extreme loss of power of motion, and is generally caused by inability of the muscles to function, due to injury in the motor areas of the brain and/or of the spinal cord. In addition to the parallels in Matthew and Mark see also Matt. 4:24; 8:5-13; Acts 8:7; 9:33. In the present case whatever may have been the parts of the body affected by paralysis and the point to which the sickness had progressed, one fact is clear: the stricken person was unable to move about. He had to be carried. *Four* men— relatives? friends?—performed this service for him, as Mark indicates.

The courage and resourcefulness of all five—the paralytic plus his four helpers—particularly also their faith in the success of their venture, hence ultimately their trust in Jesus, must be admired. If the house where the crowd had gathered had an outside stairway, then the four and their precious cargo reached the roof by means of that stairway. If that house did not have an outside stairway but the adjoining house did, then, having reached the top of that other house, they crossed over from roof to roof. In one way or another they reached the place directly above the spot where Jesus was addressing the people.

Now to get through the roof! This outside cover of a house was generally flat. It had beams with transverse rafters overlaid with brushwood, tree branches, etc., on top of which was a thick blanket of mud or clay mixed with chopped straw, beaten and rolled. Such a roof was not difficult to "unroof."

But Luke states that they lowered the man through the *tiles.* When the nature of these tiles is misconstrued and they are regarded as having been placed in a sturdy framework of very small squares, a difficulty is unnecessarily created. Besides, the roof opening did not have to be as long as the man was tall! By means of skillful manipulation of ropes even a sick man of average size could be gently lowered through a rather small opening. "Where there is a will, there is a way."

Much has been written about Luke's mention of "tiles." He has been accused of introducing non-Palestinian architecture into this passage,[227] since Palestinian roofs had no tiles. Or he has been described as accommodating himself to the intelligence of his Gentile readers.[228] Still another view is that proposed by G. C. D. Howley, F. F. Bruce, and H. L. Ellison, in their *New Testament Commentary,* p. 218, namely, that the term *tiles,* as used here, simply means "roof." That theory has the merit of absolving Luke from any error. However, even this solution may be unnecessary. N. Geldenhuys, *op. cit.,* p. 189, probably already pointed in the right direction when he asked the question, "With all the Gentile influence in Palestine at that time, why could not some Jewish homes have tiled roofs?" Recent discoveries have confirmed the fact that the tiled roof came into use before New Testament times and that Palestine was by no means excluded.[229]

Having made an opening in the roof, the four *lowered* the "little bed" on which the paralytic was lying. Since there were four men who lowered it, ropes had probably been attached to its four corners. Thus it was that the sick man landed right in front of Jesus. The latter, looking down, saw this patient; and glancing up, took notice of the four "friends in need" who were proving to be "friends indeed."

We do not read that the four, from their position on top of the roof, shouted anything to Jesus. Nor does any evangelist report that the sick man himself said anything to Jesus. As far as the paralytic is concerned, it is even

---

227. See *The Interpreter's Bible,* Vol. VIII, p. 106.
228. See R. H. Gundry, *A Survey of the New Testament,* Grand Rapids, 1970, p. 135.
229. See N.B.D., article "House."

possible that, due to his condition, he was unable to speak. But though the five did not talk, they trusted! And that was what really mattered.

The confidence of the five touched the very heart of Jesus, who now, in accents tender yet firm, said to the paralytic, "Man, your sins are forgiven you."

It was definitely the faith of the five that caused these words to flow from the Savior's lips. For corroborating passages, showing how very important Jesus regarded faith to be, see Luke 7:9, 10; 8:48, 50; 17:19; 18:42; and see also Heb. 11:32 f.

From the words of absolution spoken to this man some have concluded that Jesus traced the paralytic's sickness to his sin. This inference is, however, wholly unwarranted. Such passages as Luke 13:1–5 and John 9:1–3 clearly show that Jesus rejected the common Jewish error of thinking that a sorely afflicted individual must have sinned grievously (Job 4:7; 22:5–10; and for a similar belief among non-Jews see Acts 28:3, 4).

Jesus never took sin lightly. He never told people, "Do y o u have a sense of guilt? Forget about it." On the contrary, he regarded sin as inexcusable departure from God's holy law (Luke 10:25–28), as having a soul-choking effect (8:7, 14; cf. John 8:34), and as being a matter of the heart and not only of the outward deed (Luke 6:45; 8:15). But he also offered the only true solution. He was well aware of the fact that the advice, "Get rid of your guilt feelings; a little cruelty, promiscuity, infidelity is not so bad," creates more problems than it solves. He also knew that it was entirely impossible for a person to rid his soul of the sense of guilt by trying to offset his sins by good deeds. He knew that this philosophy would lead but to tragic failure and appalling despair. Instead, he had come to proclaim—no, not only *to proclaim* but first of all *to provide*—the one and only solution, namely *forgiveness*, and this on the basis of his own atonement for sin (22:20). Cf. John 1:29. When he therefore now says to the paralytic, "Forgiven are your sins," he is not only *conveying* to this man the news of God's forgiveness, as Nathan had done to penitent David (II Sam. 12:13); he is also in his own right *canceling* the paralytic's debt. He blots out his sins completely and forever. Cf. Ps. 103:12; Isa. 1:18; 55:6, 7; Jer. 31:34; Mic. 7:19; John 1:29. Moreover, such forgiveness never stands alone. It is ever "pardon *plus*." In Christ, God dispels the invalid's gloom *and* embraces him with the arms of his protecting and adopting love. Cf. Rom. 5:1.

By saying "Forgiven are your sins" (thus literally), Jesus had not only lifted a burden from the soul of this sin-burdened sufferer, but had also proclaimed that the cleansing of the soul was even more important than the healing of the body. He had done one more thing: he had claimed for himself the divine prerogative of pronouncing and actually bringing about freedom from guilt. To his opponents, therefore, he had thrown down the gauntlet. Will they take it up? If not openly, then at least in their hearts and minds?

C. *An attack is made*

21. But the scribes and the Pharisees began to reason, saying, Who is this fellow that speaks blasphemies? Who but God alone is able to forgive sins?

In the hearts of the scribes who had come here to find fault with Jesus there was no room for participation in the joy of this grievously stricken man who at this moment heard words of encouragement and cheer. In a highly derogatory manner these enemies are saying something decidedly unfavorable. However, they are not saying it out loud, only *within their hearts*. But hearts are very important. Are they not the mainsprings of dispositions as well as of feelings and thoughts? Does not a man's heart show what kind of a person he really is? See Mark 3:5; 6:52; 7:14–23; 8:17; 11:23; 12:30, 33; Eph. 1:18; 3:17; Phil. 1:7; I Tim. 1:5. Cf. Prov. 23:7 A.V.

In their hearts, then, the scribes are *attacking Jesus*. They are accusing him of speaking blasphemies. They are carrying on a *dialogue*, throwing thoughts back and forth. What they are saying is: "Who is this fellow that speaks blasphemies? Who but God alone is able to forgive sins?" Jesus is claiming for himself a prerogative that belongs to God alone.

The scribes were right in considering the remission of sins to be a divine prerogative (Exod. 34:6, 7a; Ps. 103:12; Isa. 1:18; 43:25; 44:22; 55:6, 7; Jer. 31:34; Mic. 7:19). To be sure, there is a sense in which we too forgive, namely, when we earnestly resolve not to take revenge but instead to love the one who has injured us, to promote his welfare, and never again to bring up the past (Matt. 6:12, 15; 18:21; Luke 6:37; Eph. 4:32; Col. 3:13). But *basically*, as described, it is God alone who forgives. It is he alone who is able to remove guilt and to declare that it has actually been removed.

But now the thinking of the scribes arrives at the fork in the road, and they make the wrong turn. Either: (a) Jesus is what by implication he claims to be, namely, God, or (b) he blasphemes in the sense that he unjustly claims the attributes and prerogatives of deity. The scribes accept (b).

Not only do they commit this tragic error, but, as the following context indicates, they compound it by reasoning somewhat as follows, "It is an easy thing for him to say, 'Your sins are forgiven,' for no one is able to disprove it, since no one can look into his neighbor's heart or enter the throne-room of the Almighty and discover his judicial decisions as to who is, and who is not, forgiven. On the other hand, to tell this man, 'Get up and walk' would be far more difficult, for if no cure results, as is probable, we are all here to witness his embarrassment." As they see it, therefore, Jesus is both blasphemous and flippant.

D. *A victory is won*

22–25. When Jesus perceived their (inward) reasonings, he said to them, Why are y o u reasoning thus in y o u r hearts? Which is easier: to

**say, Your sins are forgiven, or to say, Get up and walk? But in order that
y o u may know that the Son of man has authority on earth to forgive sins
(he said to the paralytic), I say to you, get up, pick up your little bed and
go home. —Instantly he stood up in front of them, picked up what he had
been lying on, and went home, glorifying God.**

Jesus perceived in his spirit what these scribes were thinking. Their inner
deliberations were not concealed from him. Cf. Matt. 17:25; John 1:45, 48;
2:25; 21:17. Had he not been God he would not have been able to penetrate so deeply into their "secret" cogitations (Ps. 139; Heb. 4:13). By means
of questioning these men—"Why are y o u reasoning thus?"—he sharply
reprimands them. Their "dialogue" was wicked (cf. Matt. 9:4), for they
were accusing him falsely. They themselves were the evil ones. Was it not in
order to find fault with Jesus that they had come here today, with the
ultimate purpose that they might destroy him (cf. Mark 3:6)? Let them then
examine their own hearts.

As to which was easier to say to the paralytic, "Your sins are forgiven," or
"Get up and walk," do not both in an equal measure require omnipotent
power? Jesus decides, however, that if, as the scribes reason, a miracle in
the physical sphere is required in order to prove to them his "authority"
(right plus power) in the spiritual realm, then let them see this miracle!

So to the paralytic he addresses the words, "I say to you, get up, pick up
your little bed and go home." Obedience to this command will prove that
he, the humble yet all-glorious "Son of man," has the divine authority on
earth—hence, before the door of grace is closed—to forgive sins.

Here for the first time in Luke, the term *Son of man* is found. In all it
occurs twenty-five times in this Gospel. It is Jesus' self-designation. As such
it emphasizes the fact that its bearer is not the nationalistic Messiah of
Jewish dreams but, in a sense, "the Savior of the world" (John 4:42; I John
4:14; cf. I Tim. 4:10). He himself is unique among men. He is *the* Son of
man. He is the man of sorrows, but this very path of sorrows leads to the
crown, to glory. Moreover, this glory is revealed not only when he comes
with the clouds (Dan. 7:13), but reaches back through his entire life on
earth and through every redemptive act. He is *always* the glorious Son of
man. For more on the title *Son of man* see N.T.C. on Matthew, pp. 403–407.

The glory of the Son of man is evident also in the present account. Jesus,
as Son of man, had commanded the paralytic to get up, pick up his little
bed, and go home. The man believed that he who had so ordered would
also enable him to obey the order. So, in full view of all the onlookers, he at
once got up, started to carry the very object on which he had been carried,
and went home. In fact, he went home in high spirits, "glorifying God,"
that is, Jehovah.

In heart and mind the scribes and Pharisees had made an attack on Jesus.
It had been a murderous assault, for inwardly they had accused him of
speaking blasphemy, and they knew very well that according to the law the
blasphemer must be put to death (Lev. 24:10–16). But by means of this

astounding miracle Jesus had demonstrated that he was clothed with divine authority and majesty. This being true, he also had the right and the power to forgive sins. His victory was therefore complete. O that everyone present would have taken it to heart!

E. *A triumph is celebrated*

26. Amazement gripped everyone, and they glorified God. Filled with awe, they were saying, We have seen incredible things today.

All three Synoptics report how jubilantly the onlookers reacted to what they had just now witnessed. Mark reports the people's astonishment. Never in all their past experience had they witnessed anything similar. According to Matthew the crowd was "awestruck." Luke here relates that amazement gripped everyone. This can also be rendered, "All were seized with astonishment." He adds, "Filled with awe, they were saying, 'We have seen incredible things today.'" Common to these three Gospel writers is the remark that the people glorified God: "all" (thus Mark and Luke) ascribed to God the honor and splendor due to him. This "all," as often, is very general, and does not mean that scornful and faultfinding scribes suddenly experienced a genuine change of heart and mind. That men of this type remained hostile and became more and more hardened is clear from Luke 5:30; 6:7, 11; 11:15, 53; 13:17; 15:1, 2; 19:47; etc. Nevertheless, the response of glorifying God was sufficiently general to warrant the use of the word *all*. And no doubt among the many who did exalt him there were those upon whom Christ's words and deeds had made a lasting and saving impression.

It is clear that Jesus had triumphed completely over his enemies. In the process of doing this he had imparted inestimable spiritual and physical blessings to a sorely afflicted man, and had cheered the four friends. Most of all, he had publicly demonstrated his divine right to forgive sin(s). He had proved himself to be The Savior.[230]

Practical Lessons Derived from Luke 5:17-26

Verse 17

"And the power of the Lord was with him for healing." If even Jesus, in his state of humiliation, was deeply conscious of the need of this power (John 5:19, 30), as was Paul (I Cor. 4:7; II Cor. 4:7; Phil. 4:13), should not we be also? Is not this an incentive to prayer?

Verse 19

"They went up the roof and . . . let him down through the tiles." Is not this our weakness, that so often we are willing to help the other man if this can be done without sacrifice and exertion? Contrast these four men. Even better: II Cor. 8:9.

---

230. Notes on Greek words, phrases, and constructions in 5:17-26 begin on page 300.

Verse 21

"Who is this fellow that speaks blasphemies?" If these critics had made a thorough and prayerful study of Isa. 35:5, 6; 42:8, 9; 61:1, 2, etc., they would have known better. This shows why earnest, systematic, prayerful Bible study is required.

Verses 25, 26

"He . . . they glorified God." If such ascription of glory to God is not merely a work of the lips but of the heart, it is exactly what is needed. I Cor. 10:31 should be our motto, as it was Paul's.

Notes on Greek Words, Phrases, and Constructions in 5:17–26

Verse 17

Hebraistic καὶ ἐγένετο can be translated "now it happened," or can be skipped in translation, it being implied.

αὐτός is unemphatic, simple "he," not "he himself." The immediately preceding καί (cf. Hebrew *waw* in such cases) may be rendered "that" or "as." Note also the periphrastic and vividly descriptive "he was teaching," and "they were sitting by." It is clear that Luke is not trying to be specific with respect to the time when this event took place. The word νομοδιδάσκαλος, pl. -οι, is confined to Christian writers. It refers to "teachers" or "doctors" of the (Mosaic) law. Cf. Acts 5:34; I Tim. 1:7. Synonyms are "scribe" (Luke 5:21) and "law-expert" (10:25).

ἦσαν ἐληλυθότες, periphrastic pluperfect. Does Luke mean that these men had come out of "every village of Galilee and Judea and Jerusalem"? See A. T. Robertson, *Word Pictures*, Vol. II, p. 74. Or even out of "every *city* of . . . Jerusalem"? See Robertson's *Translation*, p. 37. The question arises, "Did Jerusalem have villages and even cities?" Also grammatically possible is the rendering, "out of [or: from] every village of Galilee and (from) Judea and Jerusalem."

εἰς τὸ ἰᾶσθαι, to be healing or "for healing." The healing activity in which Jesus engaged was the result of the presence within him of Jehovah's power.

ἰᾶσθαι is the present infinitive of ἰάομαι. See the note on 4:23 on page 261 (Healer, Physician).

Verse 18

A κλίνη is a "bed" of any kind; in the present case (cf. Mark 2:4) a pallet, that is, a poor man's bed, perhaps a thin, straw-filled mattress or even a mat.

ἦν παραλελυμένος, periphrastic passive pluperfect. The man had been, and was still, paralyzed.

ἐζήτουν, third per. pl. conative imperfect active indicative of ζητέω: they were seeking or trying. Note the two aor. infinitives that follow this verb.

Verse 19

ποίας represents ποίας ὁδοῦ, literally "by what way," hence, "and not finding by what way they might carry him in."

κέραμος*, a tile. Cf. *ceramics*.

καθῆκαν, third per. pl. aor. active indicat. of καθίημι**, to *let* down (see also Acts

9:25; 10:11; 11:5), should not be confused with the verb κατέκειτο in verse 25, which is third per. s. imperfect indicat. of κατάκειμαι, to *lie* down, recline; see also 5:29; 7:37; elsewhere in the New Testament found in Mark, John, Acts, and I Cor. κλινίδιον* (also in verse 24), diminutive of κλίνη; hence, little bed.

Verses 20–23

In verses 20 and 23 note ἀφέωνται, third per. pl. Doric *perfect* passive indicat. of ἀφίημι, here in the sense of forgive, where the parallels in Matthew (9:2, 5) and Mark (2:5, 9) use the *present* passive. But whether one says "are forgiven" or "have been and remain forgiven," the result is the same: the man's sins are no longer reckoned against him. They "are forgiven." In verse 21 the aor. infinitive ἀφεῖναι stresses the fact of forgiveness as such, apart from any time reference. By contrast, the pres. active infinitive ἀφιέναι in verse 24 has reference to the continuing forgiving activity of the Son of man.

For the forms of the verb διαλογίζομαι, to reason, in verse 21 (pres. infinitive) and in verse 22 (sec. per. pl. pres. indicat.) and for the noun διαλογισμός (acc. pl. in verse 22), see the detailed discussion and chart in N.T.C. on Mark, pp. 283–289.

Verse 24

As to verse 24, does not the occurrence of very similar style, including even the mid-sentence parenthesis, in both Mark 2:10 and its parallels (Matt. 9:6; Luke 5:24), point in the direction of literary dependence? See the discussion of the Synoptic Problem in N.T.C. on Matthew, pp. 6–54. Literally the closing statement of verse 24 (Jesus' command to the paralytic) can be translated as follows, "I say to you, get up, and having picked up your little bed, go to your house."

Verse 26

For ἐπλήσθησαν see the note on 4:28 on page 261.

With ἔκστασις (amazement) cf. *ecstasy;* and with παράδοξα (incredible things) cf. *paradoxes.*

---

27 After this, Jesus went out and saw a tax-collector, named Levi, sitting at the tax-collector's booth; and he said to him, "Follow me." 28 So he left everything behind, got up and followed him.

29 Then, at his own house, Levi gave a big dinner[231] for him. There was a large crowd of tax-collectors and others who were reclining at table with them.

30 But the Pharisees and their scribes were grumbling against Jesus' disciples, saying, "Why are y o u eating and drinking with the tax-collectors and sinners?"

31 Jesus answered them, "It is not those who are healthy that need a doctor but those who are ill. 32 I have not come to call righteous people to conversion but sinners."

5:27–32 The Call of Levi
Cf. Matt. 9:9–13; Mark 2:13–17

As Matt. 9:9 indicates, the healing of the paralytic was followed closely by the call of Levi. That is the sequence reported in all three Synoptics. The

---

231. Or: reception, banquet.

present narrative may be conveniently divided into four paragraphs, in harmony with its four movements:

A. *Levi leaves everything behind and follows Jesus*

27, 28. After this, Jesus went out and saw a tax-collector, named Levi, sitting at the tax-collector's booth; and he said to him, Follow me. —So he left everything behind, got up and followed him.

Again, as before, when he had called the first four disciples, Jesus was walking along the Sea of Galilee (or "Lake of Tiberias," as Luke would call it). See Mark 1:16. It is not surprising that out of an uncomfortably crowded house the Master directed his steps to the refreshing breezes of the shore. As Mark 2:13, 14 indicates, it was in the vicinity of the seashore that Levi received the call to become one of Jesus' disciples.

Mark and Luke call this man Levi. For explanation of the name see Gen. 29:34. He calls himself Matthew (Matt. 9:9). Besides, in all the lists of the apostles he is called Matthew (Matt. 10:3; Mark 3:18; Luke 6:15; Acts 1:13).

When was his name changed from Levi to Matthew? Did Jesus give him this new name when the tax-collector became a disciple, as the Lord had also changed Simon's name to Cephas (= Peter) when the latter joined the group (Mark 3:16; John 1:42)? It is, however, possible that from the beginning the man here described as becoming a disciple had two names, as may also have been true with respect to Thomas (John 11:16) and Bartholomew (Matt. 10:3; Mark 3:18; Luke 6:14; Acts 1:13; cf. John 1:45–49; 21:2).

The identity of Levi and Matthew can hardly be questioned, as a comparison of the three Synoptic accounts of this event proves. Moreover, Luke calls Levi a "publican" (5:27), and in the list of The Twelve as recorded in Matt. 10:3 there is mention of "Matthew the publican."

Levi's father's name was Alphaeus, not to be confused (as is sometimes done) with the man by the same name who was the father of James the Less and of Joses (Mark 3:18; cf. 15:40). If Levi or Matthew had had a brother who was also one of The Twelve, this fact would probably have been mentioned, as it was in the case of Peter and Andrew, and of James and John.

When Jesus, proceeding along the shore, saw Levi, the latter was sitting at (i.e., in or near the entrance of) the tax-collector's booth, the place where the tariff was collected on any merchandise that passed along the international highway between Syria and Egypt.

Levi, then, was a tax-collector or "publican." See above, on 3:12. The low esteem in which publicans were held appears from passages such as the following: Luke 5:30; 7:34; 15:1; 19:7; cf. Matt. 9:10, 11; 11:19; 21:31, 32; Mark 2:15, 16. "Publicans" and "sinners" are at times mentioned in one breath. Yet it was to such a hated individual, such a *publican,* that Jesus now turned in order to make him one of his disciples. It was to him that the Master said, "Follow me."

When Jesus said, "Follow me," Levi immediately got up and followed him. In Matthew's own Gospel, as well as in Mark, the decisive and immediate obedience of the tax-collector is thus soberly reported. For more detail with emphasis on the greatness of the sacrifice, we must turn to our present passage, Luke 5:28. This informs us that Levi "left everything behind, got up and followed Jesus." He left his lucrative business and trusted that God would provide for his needs.

Accordingly, Levi's sacrifice was much greater than that made by the four earlier disciples (Simon and Andrew, James and John) as recorded in *Mark 1:18, 20*. Far more closely did it resemble what these men gave up a little later, as described in *Luke 5:11*. Besides, would it not have been easier for the fishermen to return to their fishing than for Levi to become re-employed as a collector of customs duties?

B. *At his home Levi gives a great reception for Jesus*

29. Then, at his own house, Levi gave a big dinner for him. There was a large crowd of tax-collectors and others who were reclining at table with them.

What is so wonderful about Levi is that surrendering everything made him "the happiest man in the world." So filled with deep, inner delight was he that he immediately arranged a feast in honor of the One whom he considered his Benefactor! The party was held at Levi's own home. Reclining at table with Jesus, his disciples, and Levi, were a good many tax-collectors and "others," people who were held in low esteem by the "better" citizens, by such worthies (?), for example, as the Pharisees and those scribes who belonged to their sect. It is not difficult to visualize Levi and all his guests reclining on mattresses, couches, or divans around low tables; each person resting on his left elbow, as was customary at least at festive occasions such as this one (see N.T.C. on John 13:23), and all enjoying the food and the fellowship.

That Levi would welcome *Jesus* we can understand. That the Master's *disciples* would not be barred is not strange, but why did Levi also welcome all those "shady" characters, those "publicans and sinners" (cf. verse 29 with verse 30; and see also Mark 2:15)? Is it sufficient to say that he would naturally invite tax-collectors because until this moment these people had been his associates, since he too was a tax-collector? Is not the real reason this, that Levi thought so highly of Jesus, who had become his Lord and Savior, that he wanted everybody—including by all means those with whom until this moment he had been on intimate terms—to know, trust, and love this wonderful Friend he had discovered; or rather, who had discovered him?

C. *Pharisees, etc., blame Jesus' disciples for partying with publicans, etc.*

30. But the Pharisees and their scribes were grumbling against Jesus' disciples, saying, Why are y o u eating and drinking with the tax-collectors and sinners?

Note: "the Pharisees and their scribes," thus phrased to distinguish between the scribes who were Pharisees (Mark 2:16) and those who were Sadducees. These men, then, were grumbling. They were not at all pleased with Levi's party. In all probability it was when the banquet had ended and the guests were departing that these Pharisees and their scribes approached Jesus' disciples with the reproachful question, "Why are y o u eating and drinking with the tax-collectors and sinners?"

As these hair-splitting legalists saw it, it would be impossible to remain ceremonially pure when one consented to dine with people whom they considered riffraff, scum. Did not the rabbis lay down this rule, "The disciples of the learned shall not recline at table in the company of the people of the soil (the rabble, the disreputable ones)"? Contamination must be avoided. Besides, did not eating and drinking with a person imply that one had entered into a covenant relationship with him? Was it not true that not only the rabbinical interpretation of God's law but even that divine law itself was being grossly violated by tax-collectors and their ilk? Were they not traitors and extortionists? Then why not stay clear of them?

Criticism of this nature was leveled against Jesus' disciples (thus Luke) and even against Jesus himself via his disciples (thus Matthew and Mark). This is no contradiction. It should be easy to understand that both Jesus and his disciples were the objects of Pharisaic disgust. See Matt. 10:25; Luke 6:40; 10:16.

> D. *Jesus defends his disciples' conduct and by implication his own*

31, 32. Jesus answered them, It is not those who are healthy that need a doctor but those who are ill.

The criticism of the scribes has been duly noted by Jesus. He himself, by means of what may have been a current proverb, flings back a clinching answer. When he associates on intimate terms with people of low reputation he does not do this as a hobnobber, a comrade in evil, "birds of a feather flocking together," but as a physician, one who, without in any way becoming contaminated with the diseases of his patients, must get very close to them *in order that he may heal them!* Moreover, it is especially the Pharisees who should be able to understand this. Are not they the very people who regard themselves as being healthy, and all others as being sick? See Luke 18:9. If, then, in the eyes of the Pharisees, publicans and sinners are so very sick, should they not be healed? Is it the business of the healer to heal the healthy or the sick? The sick, of course.

Jesus adds: **I have not come to call righteous people to conversion but sinners.** Substantially this is the reading also in Matthew and Mark, though in Matthew these words are preceded by a quotation from Hos. 6:6, and prefixed by "for"; while Luke here adds the phrase "to conversion," where most translators favor "to repentance."

The passage makes clear that the invitation to salvation, full and free, is extended not to "righteous people," that is, not to those who consider themselves worthy, but rather to those who are unworthy and in desperate need. It was sinners, the lost, the straying, the beggars, the burdened ones, the hungry and thirsty, whom Jesus came to save. See also Matt. 5:6; 11:28-30; 22:9, 10; Luke 14:21-23; ch. 15; 19:10; John 7:37, 38. This is in line with all of special revelation, both the Old Testament and the New (Isa. 1:18; 45:22; 55:1, 6, 7; Jer. 35:15; Ezek. 18:23; 33:11; Hos. 6:1; 11:8; II Cor. 5:20; I Tim. 1:15; Rev. 3:20; 22:17). It is a message full of comfort and "relevant" to every age!

As reported by Luke, Jesus adds that the call he had come to extend to sinners was "to conversion." Not only "repentance" or sorrow for sin is needed, but nothing less than complete transformation: change of mind, heart, will, conduct. For more material in defense of the rendering "conversion" instead of merely "repentance" see the note on Luke 5:32 on page 306.

Are we now finished with the explanation of Luke 5:27–32? Not entirely. Something must still be added. Otherwise the reader might conclude that the main purpose of the section is to show what a wonderful man Levi (= Matthew) was. He was, indeed, wonderful. Nothing should ever be said to detract from the value of his complete and immediate surrender to Jesus. However, that is not the legitimate point of emphasis. What is far more important is the fact that Jesus, who even at this early point in Luke's Gospel had performed so many miracles of mercy, added this to them all, namely, the exhibition of his power to bring about a radical and permanent change in the mind, heart, will, and life of . . . Matthew. So, whenever we read his beautiful Gospel let us think of the saving power of the Triune God as revealed through his Spirit in Christ.[232]

Practical Lessons Derived from Luke 5:27–32

Verses 27, 28

"Jesus said . . . 'Follow me.' . . . So Levi left everything and followed him." What a Magnet is Jesus. Cf. John 12:32. A magnet attracts; a repellent—think of water-repellent fabrics—rejects. What are we?

Verses 28, 29

"So he left everything behind . . . [and] gave a big dinner." What an example of joyful giving!

Verse 30

"But the Pharisees . . . were grumbling." Why? The answer is found in such passages as Mic. 6:8; Matt. 23:23. These passages also show how one may become filled with joy and cease to be a grumbling Pharisee.

Verse 32

"I have come to call . . . sinners to conversion." The importance of conversion is emphasized throughout Scripture. But how can it be achieved? See Jer. 31:18.

---

232. Notes on Greek words, phrases, and constructions in 5:27–32 begin on page 306.

Notes on Greek Words, Phrases, and Constructions in 5:27–32

Verse 27

ἐθεάσατο, third per. s. aor. indicat. of θεάομαι, to see, behold. For synonyms see N.T.C. on John, Vol. I, p. 85, footnote 33.

τελώνιον, tax-collector's booth (see Matt. 9:9; Mark 2:14); cf. *toll.*

Verses 29, 30

δοχή*; cf. δέχομαι, to receive; hence, reception, banquet, dinner; see also 14:13. Note graphic description: a periphrastic imperfect (verse 29b, "were reclining at table"), followed by a regular imperfect ("were grumbling"), and this, in turn, followed by two durative presents, "Why are y o u eating and drinking . . .?"

Verse 31

ὑγιαίνοντες, nom. pl. masc. pres. participle of ὑγιαίνω, to be in good health, whether literally, as here (with spiritual overtone), or figuratively, sound in doctrine (see I Tim. 1:10; 6:3; II Tim. 1:13; 4:3; Titus 1:9; 2:1). Cf. *hygiene.* See also on Luke 15:27.

οἱ κακῶς ἔχοντες; literally, "those having it badly," that is, "those who are ill." Cf. French *avoir mal.*

Verse 32

μετάνοια (here acc. -v). The rendering favored by almost all English translations, namely, "repentance," is too weak and one-sided. That translation emphasizes only the negative aspect of what is meant here. The word used in the original indicates a radical transformation. The Dutch rendering (both Statenvertaling and Nieuwe Vertaling) is correct: *bekering;* not merely *berouw.* The concept has two elements: (a) a definite sorrow for and turning from evil; (b) a resolute turning to God in faith and obedience. Only in such instances in which the emphasis is placed exclusively on sorrow for sin is the rendering "repentance" or (for the verb) "repent" justified. See, for example, Luke 10:13 (cf. Matt. 11:21). "They would have *repented* long ago, sitting in sackcloth and ashes." See further: the explanation of Luke 3:3 in this commentary; N.T.C. on Matthew, pp. 196, 197, including the footnotes on p. 197; and see also J. Behm on this word, Th.D.N.T., Vol. IV, pp. 999–1003. Note that on p. 1001 that author also endorses the rendering "conversion" for Luke 5:32.

---

33 They said to him, "John's disciples often fast and say prayers, and so do the disciples of the Pharisees, but yours keep on eating and drinking."

34 Jesus said to them, "So long as the bridegroom is with them, y o u cannot make the bridegroom's attendants fast, can y o u? 35 But days will arrive when the bridegroom will be taken away from them; then, during those days, they will fast."

36 He told them this parable: "No one tears a piece from a new garment and puts it on an old garment; otherwise he will tear the new, and the patch from the new will not match the old. 37 And no one pours new wine into old wineskins; otherwise the new wine will burst the skins and will be spilled, and the skins will be ruined. 38 But new wine must be poured into

fresh wineskins.   39 And no one, after drinking old (wine) wants new, for he says, 'The old is good.'"[233]

5:33-39 *The Question About Fasting*
Cf. Matt. 9:14-17; Mark 2:18-22

Neither Mark nor Luke informs us when this incident occurred. Matthew, however, establishes a clear chronological connection between this event and the shocking news Jesus received with reference to a ruler's daughter. That evangelist writes, "While Jesus was saying these things [regarding the question about fasting], a ruler came," etc. And the story about the resurrection of this child is, in turn, intertwined with that of the healing of the woman who touched Christ's garment. Both Mark and Luke leave the definite impression that these two miracles occurred after the preaching of The Sermon on the Mount and the commissioning of The Twelve. Cf. Mark 5:21-43 with 3:13 ff.; and Luke 8:40-56 with 6:12 ff. The probability is, therefore, that, while Matthew's call and the banquet at his home occurred before the sermon and the commissioning, the question about fasting—followed shortly by the double miracle—occurred afterward.

This would mean that there is probably no close chronological connection between the feasting in Matthew's house and the question about fasting; that is, between Luke 5:27-32 and 5:33-39. But there may well have been a logical or topical relationship. Fellowship with publicans and sinners, and this on more than one occasion (besides Luke 5:27-32 see also 7:34; 15:1, 2; 19:10; cf. Matt. 11:19), while the disciples of John and of the Pharisees abstained from such convivialities, and even practiced a measure of austerity, was sooner or later bound to lead to what is reported here in Luke 5:33-39.

The story readily divides itself into material for three subheadings:

A. *The question*

33. They said to him, John's disciples often fast and say prayers, and so do the disciples of the Pharisees, but yours keep on eating and drinking. As to "they," does this refer to "the Pharisees and their scribes" (see verse 30)? However, the parallel passage, Matt. 9:14, states that the questioners were "the disciples of John." The possibility must be granted that the pronoun *they* in Mark 2:18 ("They came and said") and here in Luke 5:33 ("They said") has no antecedent but simply means "some people." We shall have to be content, therefore, with identifying the questioners with "the disciples of John." But since not only they but also the Pharisees were actually fasting at this time (Mark 2:18), it is conceivable that the enquirers also included some Pharisees.

The law of God suggests only one fast in an entire year, namely, on the

---

233. Another reading is: the old is better.

day of atonement (Lev. 16:29-34; 23:26-32; Num. 29:7-11; cf. Acts 27:9). In course of time, however, fasts (not always total; see the text in each instance) began to multiply, so that we read about their occurrence at other times also: from sunrise to sunset (Judg. 20:26; I Sam. 14:24; II Sam. 1:12; 3:35); for seven days (I Sam. 31:13); three weeks (Dan. 10:3); forty days (Exod. 34:2, 28; Deut. 9:9, 18; I Kings 19:8); in the fifth and seventh month (Zech. 7:3-5); and even in the fourth, fifth, seventh, and tenth month (Zech. 8:19). The climax was the observance of a fast "twice a week," the boast of the Pharisee (Luke 18:12).

It is not surprising therefore that for some reason or other the Pharisees were once again keeping a fast. Their manner of fasting—looking glum, making their faces unsightly in order that everybody might see that they were fasting—was roundly condemned by Jesus (Matt. 6:16).

But why were the disciples of John also fasting? Various reasons have been suggested. John had probably made his first public appearance in the summer of the year A.D. 26. About the close of the year 27 he had been imprisoned. Jesus may have preached the Sermon on the Mount sometime during the spring to midsummer of the year 28. Not long afterward—perhaps near the beginning of the year 29—John was put to death. It is therefore not impossible that the fasting of John's disciples was essentially a mourning for their master.

It is not necessary to believe that the Pharisees and John's disciples were fasting for the same reason. But the opposite possibility—that both groups were indeed fasting for the same reason—must also be granted. It should be borne in mind that John was in a sense an ascetic (Matt. 11:18; Luke 7:33). He emphasized sin and the necessity of turning away from it. It is not inconceivable, therefore, that he may have encouraged fasting as an expression of mourning for sin, the very reason which the Pharisees probably also gave for much of their fasting (cf. Matt. 6:16).

With respect to those of whom it is predicated that they were now fasting, the reference to "John's disciples" presents no further important difficulty. Even after John's imprisonment his disciples continued as a separate group, one that distinguished itself from the followers of Jesus. There was, however, a relation of friendship and co-operation between the two groups, as is clear from such passages as Matt. 11:2, 3; 14:12, and probably even from the passage now under study, Luke 5:33. A difficulty arises, however, in connection with the phrase *the disciples of the Pharisees* (see also Mark 2:18). Considered as a group "Pharisees" were not technically teachers; hence they had no disciples. However, the difficulty may be more apparent than real. Luke, in writing "the disciples of the Pharisees," may well have had in mind disciples of "the scribes who were Pharisees," as in Mark 2:16. The main point is that John's disciples and presumably the disciples of these Pharisaic scribes were fasting, in harmony with the teaching and/or example of their leaders. Matt. 9:14 states that the Pharisees fasted "often." On the other hand, Christ's disciples did not join in observing these fasts, but kept on eating and drinking. This striking contrast gave rise to the question. In Matthew and Mark the question is expressed. In Luke it is implied.

In favor of these enquirers it must be said that they did not bypass Jesus but approached him directly and frankly. Also, their question, though perhaps not entirely free from a tinge of criticism, was probably an honest request for information rather than a veiled but bitter accusation.

In reality, however, there was no justification for this question. Had these men been better students of Scripture they would have known (a) that, as has been indicated, the only fast that could by any stretch of the imagination be derived from the law of God was the one on the day of atonement, and (b) that according to the teaching of Isa. 58:6, 7 and Zech. 7:1–10 it was not a literal fast but love, both vertical and horizontal, which God demanded.

B. *Jesus' answer*

34, 35. Jesus said to them, So long as the bridegroom is with them, y o u cannot make the bridegroom's attendants fast, can y o u?

In all three synoptics the question is so phrased that the answer must be "No." Jesus here compares his blessed presence on earth with a wedding feast. Again and again Scripture compares the relationship between Jehovah and his people, or between Christ and his church, with the bond of love between bridegroom and bride (Isa. 50:1 ff.; 54:1 ff.; 62:5; Jer. 2:32; 31:32; Hos. 2:1 ff.; Matt. 25:1 ff.; John 3:29; II Cor. 11:2; Eph. 5:32; Rev. 19:7; 21:9). Verse 34 speaks about "the sons of the bridal chamber" (thus literally), meaning "the bridegroom's attendants." These were friends of the groom. They stood close to him. They had been invited to the wedding, were in charge of arrangements, and were expected to do everything possible to promote the success of the festivities.

Bridegroom's attendants fasting while the feast is in progress! How absurd, suggests Jesus. Disciples of the Lord mourning while their Master is performing works of mercy and while words of life and beauty are dropping from his lips—how utterly incongruous!

Jesus adds, however, **but days will arrive when the bridegroom will be taken away from them; then, during those days, they will fast.** This is an early prediction of Christ's death on the cross. The prediction that the bridegroom, Christ, *will be taken away* is found also in the parallels (Matt. 9:15; Mark 2:20). It strongly reminds one of Isa. 53:8, "By oppression and judgment he was taken away."

It is remarkable how often in the Gospels *Jesus himself* quotes from (or at least alludes to passages from) Isaiah. Among the well-known are those found in Matt. 11:5 (cf. Isa. 35:5, 6); Luke 4:18, 19 (cf. Isa. 58:6; 61:1, 2); and 22:37 (cf. Isa. 53:12). In the Gospel According to Luke see also

Luke	Isaiah
6:21	61:3
7:22	35:5; 61:1
8:10	6:9, 10
10:15	14:13, 15
19:46	56:7
20:9	5:1
21:10	19:2
21:24	63:18
21:25	13:10; 24:19 (LXX)
21:35	24:17

The present passage, Luke 5:35, is not the only one containing at least an allusion to Isa. 53. See also Luke 23:9; cf. Isa. 53:7. Isaiah's expression "will be taken away," and this "by oppression and judgment," refers, of course, to a violent death; note context: "He was oppressed ... led to the slaughter ... cut off [cf. Dan. 9:26] out of the land of the living." It is natural to assume that here in Luke the meaning is similar.

With reference to "days will arrive," followed by Luke's "during those days," Jesus is saying that his approaching violent death will mean days of mourning for his disciples. Then, at that particular time, fasting as an expression of sorrow will be in order and will occur. That the mourning will not be of long duration is pointed out in John 16:16–22.

The important truth which Jesus here reveals and which makes the passage so practical and filled with comfort especially for today is that for those who acknowledge Christ as their Lord and Savior the proper attitude of heart and mind is not that of sadness but that of gladness. If it be true that "God *with* us" (Immanuel) spells joy for believers, should not "God *within* us" (the situation on and after Pentecost) awaken in every child of God joy unspeakable and full of glory? It was in order to bring such abounding joy that Jesus came on earth and that he, through his sacrificial death, brought salvation full and free. See Luke 2:10: "good tidings of great joy"; 24:52: "they ... returned to Jerusalem with great joy"; John 15:11: "that y o u r joy may be full"; 17:13: "that they may have my joy made full in themselves." The apostles learned that lesson (Rom. 5:11; 15:13; Gal. 5:22; Philippians, the entire epistle; I Peter 1:8; 4:13; I John 1:4; II John 12).

C. *Two illustrations in support of that answer*

36–39. He told them this parable: No one tears a piece from a new garment and puts it on an old garment; otherwise he will tear the new, and the patch from the new will not match the old. And no one pours new wine into old wineskins; otherwise the new wine will burst the skins and will be spilled, and the skins will be ruined. But new wine must be poured into fresh wineskins.

The first illustration is taken from the custom of patching clothes. If a piece torn from a new garment is used to patch an old one, both are ruined:

310

the new one because it has now been torn, the old one because it has received a patch that does not match it.

In Matthew and Mark the illustration is not exactly the same. There the patch of unshrunk cloth pulls to pieces the bordering cloth of the old, badly worn garment, so that a worse tear results. The difference between these two reports creates no real problem. As Jesus went from place to place he probably varied his illustrations. Is it not true that in either case (Matthew and Mark on the one hand, Luke on the other) the patch that was supposed to solve a problem creates a bigger one? The lesson is the same. Don't try to mix the new with the old; instead, accept the new, strong, vigorous, joy-imparting teaching of Jesus and the salvation brought by him. In the joy he and his teaching bring to those who by grace are transformed by it there is no room for Judaistic, legalistic fasting.

The second figure reinforces the first. It is taken from the use of wine-skins. The wineskin was usually made of the skin of a goat or a sheep. After being removed from the animal it was tanned, and after the hair had been cut close the skin was turned inside out. The neck opening became the mouth of the "bottle." The other openings, at the feet and the tail, were closed with cords.

What Jesus is saying is this: Old wineskins are no match for new, still fermenting wine. Such wine would burst the skins, resulting in the loss of both skins and wine. Similarly the new wine of rescue and riches for all who are willing to accept these blessings, even for publicans and sinners, must be poured into new, that is, fresh, strong wineskins of gratitude, freedom, and spontaneous service to the glory of God. Judaistic, legalistic, joyless fasting is out of line with the salvation Jesus is bringing.

And no one, after drinking old (wine) wants new, for he says, The old is good.

Verse 39 is a commentary on the ultraconservatism, the ingrained and inflexible traditionalism, of the Pharisees and their followers. They were constantly saying, "The old is good." So they rejected the "new," fresh, life-imparting teaching of Jesus.

Not that Jesus offered something that was entirely new, in the sense that it amounted to rebellion against the very essence of Old Testament teaching: "Love God above all... trust in him completely, exercise justice, mercy, and faithfulness." No, indeed! In that respect the teaching of Jesus was old in the best sense of the term. See, for example, Matt. 23:23; Luke 10:25–37. But the Pharisees had buried that law beneath their man-made "traditions." See Matt. 15:3. These traditional teachings had been passed on from generation to generation. It was to these (by this time) old rabbinical interpretations and applications of the law that the Pharisees of Jesus' day were clinging. They preferred stuffiness to fresh air. That was their downfall.[234]

---

234. Notes on Greek words, phrases, and constructions in 5:33–39 begin on page 312.

Practical Lessons Derived from 5:33–39

Verse 33

"John's disciples often fast . . . but yours," etc. Adherence to conventional forms is good *if* these forms are pervaded by the spirit of Jesus and his gospel. Don't cling to the old just because it happens to be old!

Verse 34

"So long as the bridegroom is with them, y o u cannot make the bridegroom's attendants fast." The religion of Jesus is one of "joy unspeakable and full of glory" (I Peter 1:8).

Verse 37

"No one pours new wine into old wineskins." Christian optimism and pessimism do not match. Salvation's joy and the habit of clinging to every detail of an old ceremony or liturgy, just because that detail was in vogue during the days of your great-grandmother, cannot dwell together peacefully in one and the same person.

Verse 39

"No one . . . wants new wine." By nature no one does. It takes grace to create within man's heart the desire for the new life in Christ and all this implies as to attitudes, deeds, and customs.

Notes on Greek Words, Phrases, and Constructions in 5:33–39

Verses 33–35

Note the durative (continuative, linear) present tenses in verse 33. Contrast (they) *fast,* present tense (verse 33), with (y o u cannot make the bridegroom's attendants) *fast* (verse 34). The latter is an aor. active infinitive. The aorist takes a snapshot; the present, a time exposure. It is sometimes stated that the aorist indicates a single act. Is this always the case? See John 2:20. Would not "a single *fact*" be the better wording?

For derivation of νηστεύω and its cognates see the note on Luke 2:37 on page 177.

Note pleonastic (Hebraistic) use of καί in verse 35.

Verses 36–39

For the term παραβολή see the note on 4:23 on page 261.

ἐπίβλημα, something put on, piece, patch.

σχίσας and σχίσει, respectively, nom. sing. masc. aor. active participle; and third per. s. fut. active indicat. of σχίζω, to tear. Cf. *schism.*

παλαιούς, acc. pl. of παλαιός, old; cf. *paleontology.*

συμφωνήσει, third per. s. future indicat. of συμφωνέω, to agree, to match; cf. *symphonize.*

Note the use of the word *new*. The original speaks of:
a. a new garment, new wineskins;
b. new wine.
Under (a) "new" (καινός, -ή, -όν) emphasizes quality and sometimes means "fresh"; under (b) "new" (νέος, -η, -ον) stresses age.

ἀσκός, wineskin.

ῥήξει, third per. s. fut. indicat. act. of ῥήγνυμι, to burst, tear, rend, break; cf. *wreck*.

ἐκχυθήσεται, third per. s. fut. indicat. pass. of ἐκχέω, to pour out, shed, spill; in pass., to be spilled. Cf. *chemist, gush, geyser, chyle, chyme;* German *ausgiessen;* Dutch *uitgieten.*

βλητέος*, verbal adjective or gerundive, meaning "must be put," or here "must be poured."

Summary of Chapter 5

A Miraculous Catch (verses 1–11). On the edge of Lake Gennesaret (= Sea of Galilee) Jesus, beleaguered by a vast listening crowd, climbs into Simon's (= Peter's) fishing boat, and asks him to push off a little from shore. Seated in this boat the Master then finishes his discourse.

That done, he gives Simon this surprising order, "Launch out into the deep and let down y o u r nets for a haul." Simon starts to protest, "All through the night we toiled and caught nothing." Then he quickly changes to, "But because you say so I'll have the nets lowered."

At once such a large quantity of fish is caught that the nets threaten to break. An S.O.S. is signaled to Simon's partners, James and John. They, in another boat, come rushing to the scene. Both boats are filled with fish. Even then, so enormous is the catch, the boats can hardly keep afloat.

Overwhelmed with awe, Simon Peter blurts out, "Go away from me, for I'm a sinful man, Lord."

Jesus answers, "Have no fear; from now on you will be catching men, alive and for life." Simon's partners correctly conclude that these words are meant also for *them.* So all leave behind everything—fish, boats, business, homes, families—and follow Jesus, this time "for keeps."

This story shows us Christ's practical wisdom, penetrating knowledge, lavish generosity, ineffable majesty, and profound mission-mindedness.

A Leper Cleansed (verses 12–16). Probably while Jesus was on the circuit to which Luke refers in 4:44 (see explanation of that verse), a Galilean tour according to Mark 1:39, a man full of leprosy came up to Jesus. In spite of Lev. 13:45, 46 he came close enough to be touched by the Master. Falling on his face he implored, "Lord, if you will, you can cleanse me." The Healer answered, "I will; be cleansed." At once the leprosy left him, so that he was completely cured. Not only that, but Jesus even saw to it that the man's standing among the public and in the religious life of Israel would be restored. For that purpose he sent him to the priest so that, having been pronounced cured by him and having brought the required offerings, he would be able to resume his place in society without being shunned by anyone. This very cure would bear testimony to Christ's greatness and obedience to the divine law. For reasons not stated Jesus charged the man not to broadcast what had happened to him: how and by whom he had been healed. Against the dark background of disobedience to this command—non-compliance in which, according to Mark 1:45, the cleansed man took a leading part—the mercy of Jesus stands out all the more conspicuously. Luke's story closes with these significant words, ". . . and vast crowds were gathering to hear him and to be healed of their sicknesses. And he would go away to lonely places to pray."

The Healing of a Paralytic (verses 17–26). Back in Capernaum Jesus is speaking the word in an overcrowded house (note verse 19; cf. Mark 2:2). Pharisees and teachers of the law, who had come from everywhere, are sitting by. By four men a paralytic is lowered through the roof-tiles, landing in front of Jesus. The Sympathetic Physician for both soul and body, deeply touched by the faith of the five and realizing that what bothered the sorely afflicted person most of all was his guilt in the sight of God, pronounces his pardon, full and free. The scribes and the Pharisees, bent on finding fault with their enemy, Jesus, in their hearts accuse him of blasphemy, for "who but God alone is able to forgive sins?" *Pronouncing* forgiveness is easy enough. Let him *do* something for the physically afflicted one. If he is unable to do this, his claim to bless the poor man's soul is false. So they reason. By means of instantly and completely delivering the paralytic of his illness "the Son of man" proves his claim, to the astonishment of everybody.

The Call of Levi (verses 27–32). After this Jesus goes out and sees a tax-collector, named Levi (= Matthew), sitting at his booth. He says to him, "Follow me." Immediately Levi obeys. Not only that but, having sacrificed his lucrative position to follow Jesus, he is so happy about it that he prepares a banquet or reception in honor of Jesus. Many tax-collectors ("publicans") and other people of low repute are also present. In answering the criticism of the Pharisees and their scribes, who were grumbling against Jesus' disciples and were saying, "Why are y o u eating and drinking with the tax-collectors and sinners?" Jesus reminds them that it was exactly to call sinners, not (self-)righteous people, that he had come.

The Question About Fasting (verses 33–39). One day some people (disciples of John, Matt. 9:14, and probably some Pharisees; see Mark 2:18) came to Jesus with an implied question, "John's disciples often fast and say prayers, and so do the disciples of the Pharisees, but yours keep on eating and drinking." They meant, "How do you explain this?" Jesus answers that in their capacity as "bridegroom's attendants" it would be improper and impossible for them to fast. By means of a double illustration—(a) a person does not place a piece of new cloth on an old and badly worn garment; otherwise he will tear the new, and the patch from the new will not match the old; and (b) new wine is not poured into old, stiff and rigid wineskins; otherwise the wine will be spilled, the skins ruined—Jesus drives home the lesson that the new message he is bringing requires a fresh reception, one of faith and freedom, not one of fear and fasting.

Outline of Chapter 6

Theme: *The Work Thou Gavest Him to Do*

CHAPTER VI

LUKE   6:1–2

6   1 Once on a sabbath, when Jesus happened to be passing through fields of standing grain, his disciples were picking and eating the heads of grain, rubbing them with their hands. 2 Some of the Pharisees asked, "Why are y o u doing what is not permitted on the sabbath?"

3 Jesus answered, "Have y o u not even read what David did when he and those with him were hungry: 4 how he entered the house of God, took and ate the consecrated bread which only the priests were allowed to eat, and gave some to those who were with him?" 5 And he said to them, "Lord of the sabbath is the Son of man!"

The Son of Man Asserting His Authority as Lord of the Sabbath
A. 6:1–5 *Picking, Rubbing, and Eating Grain on the Sabbath*
Cf. Matt. 12:1–8; Mark 2:23–28

One of the chief areas of conflict between Jesus and the Jewish leaders concerned the proper observance of the sabbath. It is not surprising, therefore, that Mark and Luke at this point report two sabbath controversies. Matthew also reports these two but not until much later in his Gospel.

In both Mark and Luke the story of these controversies follows Jesus' remarks about fasting. Nevertheless, there is probably no close chronological connection: the inquiry about fasting was made a little later, after the choosing of The Twelve and the preaching of The Sermon on the Mount. See above, p. 307. Worthy of consideration is the theory that three sabbath controversies (the first described in John's Gospel; the second and third in the Synoptics) took place in rather close succession during the spring to midsummer of the year A.D. 28. The three were: the argument about the healing at the pool ("Bethesda") at the time of the Passover (John 5:1–18); this was followed by the controversies concerning the picking of heads of grain (Luke 6:1–5 and parallels), and concerning the healing of the man with the "withered" hand (Luke 6:6–11 and parallels). The third of these three controversies seems to have been followed by the choosing of The Twelve and the preaching of The Sermon on the Mount (see Luke 6:12–49; cf. Mark 3:6, 13–19).

But although *no close chronological* connection between (a) Jesus' teaching on fasting and (b) the sabbath controversy reported here in Luke 6:1–5 is indicated, Mark and after him Luke may well have had in mind a *logical* connection. According to the teaching of Jesus, those who are living in close

317

fellowship with him, the Bridegroom, should be feasting instead of fasting; they must rejoice rather than mourn. And this manifestation of gladness instead of sadness must characterize even the manner in which the sabbath is kept. That is probably the connection and accounts for the order in which these events are here related.

For the slight differences in the manner in which this incident has been reported by the synoptists see N.T.C. on Mark, pp. 104, 105. Though there are these differences, there are no discrepancies or contradictions. From this point on we shall simply follow *Luke's* account, referring to the other Gospels only when necessary for elucidation.

The material here presented can be logically arranged under the following two subheadings:

1. *By implication the Pharisees accuse the disciples of sabbath desecration*

1, 2. Once on a sabbath, when Jesus happened to be passing through fields of standing grain, his disciples were picking and eating the heads of grain, rubbing them with their hands. Some of the Pharisees asked, Why are y o u doing what is not permitted on the sabbath?

Grain is evidently ripening. Jesus, accompanied by his disciples, is walking through the grain fields. The translation "fields of standing grain" is justified by the context. Literally the meaning is "that which was sown." It is the sabbath (verses 1, 6, 7, 9) and the disciples are hungry (Matt. 12:1). So they pick some heads or ears of grain. They rub them between the palms of their hands, and eat them. Did not the law (Deut. 23:25) clearly state that a person was permitted to do this? Yes, but . . . on the sabbath?

Suddenly some Pharisees arrive. Where they came from is not indicated. One moment they are absent; the next, there they are! Or had they been nearby all the while, spying "from around the corner" perhaps? The fact that this question is not answered makes the story the more dramatic. "Why are y o u doing what is not permitted on the sabbath?" they ask.

The underlying reasoning of the Pharisees was as follows: Was not work forbidden on the sabbath day (Exod. 20:8-11; 34:21; Deut. 5:12-15)? Had not the rabbis drawn up a catalogue of thirty-nine principal works, subsequently subdivided into six minor categories under each of these thirty-nine, all of which were forbidden on the sabbath? In accordance with this list was not plucking the heads of grain *reaping*?[235] And was not rubbing them with the hands *threshing*? Here were these disciples engaged in this forbidden activity, and Jesus was doing nothing about it! Obviously, what was happening was that Christ's enemies were burying the real law of God—which did not in any sense forbid what the disciples were now doing—under the mountain of their man-made, foolish traditions (Luke 11:37-52; 20:45-47; cf. Matt. 15:3, 6; 23:23, 24; Mark 7:8, 9, 12, 13; 12:38-40).

---

235. See Shabbath 7:2, 4; S.BK., Vol. I, pp. 615-618; and A. T. Robertson, *The Pharisees and Jesus,* New York, 1920, pp. 87, 88.

2. *Jesus defends them and asserts his authority as Lord of the sabbath*

**3-5. Jesus answered, Have y o u not even read what David did when he
and those with him were hungry: how he entered the house of God, took
and ate the consecrated bread which only the priests were allowed to eat,
and gave some to those who were with him?** "Have y o u not even read?"
As if to say, "Y o u pride yourselves in being the very people who uphold the
law, and y o u r scribes deem themselves to be so thoroughly versed in it as
to be able to teach others; yet are y o u yourselves unacquainted with the
fact that even this very law allowed its ceremonial restrictions to be ignored
in case of need?" See Mark 2:25: ". . . what David did when he was in
need?" "Have you not read about David and the showbread?" The reference is to consecrated bread, "bread of the Presence," in Hebrew *leḥem
happānîm* (Exod. 25:30). This showbread consisted of twelve loaves placed
on a table three feet in length, one and a half feet wide, two feet three
inches high. The table was overlaid with pure gold, surrounded by a mold-
ing of gold, and equipped with four rings of gold, a ring at each corner,
through which poles were passed, so that the table could be carried. The
description of this article of tabernacle furniture is found in Exod. 25:23,
24. In ancient times this table was standing in the Holy Place, not far away
from God's special dwelling-place: the Holy of Holies. The showbread was
laid on the table in two rows. The twelve loaves represented Israel's twelve
tribes and symbolized the constant fellowship of the people with their God.
The Israelites were, so to say, guests at his table, were consecrated to him,
and by means of the offering of these presentation loaves gratefully acknowledged their indebtedness to him.

Every sabbath the old bread was exchanged for fresh loaves (I Sam.
21:6). The old loaves were eaten by the priests. They were "for Aaron and
his sons," that is, for the priesthood, definitely *not* for everybody (Lev.
24:9). Yet when hungry David entered "the house of God," the court of the
sanctuary in Nob, which was the shrine where the ark was kept, he was
given this consecrated bread. See I Sam. 21:1-6; 22:9, 10. He took and
shared it with his equally hungry companions. They all ate of it, even
though by divine law it had been designated as food for the priests, for
them alone. The point is this: if David had a right to ignore a *divinely
ordained ceremonial provision* when necessity demanded it, then would not
David's exalted Antitype, namely, Jesus, God's Anointed in a far more
eminent sense, have a right, under similar conditions of need, to set aside *a
totally unwarranted, man-made sabbath regulation?* After all, to a considerable
extent the rabbinical sabbath regulations amounted to misapplications of
God's holy law. That was true also in the present case.

And he said to them, Lord of the sabbath is the Son of man! Since "all
authority" had been given to the Son (Matt. 11:27; 28:18), who is one with
the Father (John 10:30), with whom the Father is well pleased (Luke 3:22),
and who was sent into the world by the Father (cf. Luke 4:18, "he has sent
me"), it is clear that the Son of man is indeed Lord of the sabbath. As

sovereign Lord he possesses the authority to lay down principles governing that day. For "Son of man" see on Luke 5:24.[236]

Notes on Greek Words, Phrases, and Constructions in 6:1-5

Verse 1

With ἐγένετο δὲ . . . διαπορεύεσθαι αὐτόν (Once on a sabbath while he happened to be passing through—a rather free translation) compare the Hebrew *wayᵉhi* ("And it came to pass," etc.). In translation this can often be omitted. For the textual question, including the strange reading reflected in A.V., "on the second sabbath after the first," see Robertson, *Word Pictures*, Vol. II, p. 80.

ἔτιλλον, the sense of this imperfect may be either progressive (they were picking) or inchoative (they began to pick).

ψώχοντες, nom. pl. masc. pres. participle of ψώχω*, to rub. This verb may be related to others constructed on the ψα base, and indicating such activities as twitching the strings of a musical instrument. Cf. *psalm*.

Verse 3

οὐδέ, not even. An affirmative answer is expected when οὐ or οὐδε is used; yet, the implication is that they (the Pharisees) had not even read what David did. To bring out the full force of the question, one might render the original thus: "Y o u have surely read what David did, have y o u not?" See Gram. N.T., p. 1157; and Gram. N.T. (Bl.-Debr.), par. 427, p. 220.

ἀνέγνωτε, sec. per. pl. 2nd aor. indicat. of ἀναγινώσκω; for an analysis of this verb see the note on 4:16 on page 260.

Verse 5

Note emphatic position of Κύριος.

---

6 On another sabbath, when he entered the synagogue and was teaching,[237] a man whose right hand was shriveled[238] was present. 7 The scribes and the Pharisees, in order that they might find a charge against Jesus, were watching him closely (to see) whether he would heal on the sabbath. 8 But he knew their thoughts and said to the man with the shriveled hand, "Rise and stand here in front." So he got up and stood there.

9 Then Jesus said to them, "I am asking y o u, Is it right on the sabbath to do good or to do harm, to save life or to destroy it?" 10 Then he looked around at them all and said to the man, "Stretch out your hand." He did, and his hand was restored.[239]

11 They, however, were filled with senseless rage and began to discuss with one another what they might do to Jesus.

---

236. For Practical Lessons derived from 6:1-5 see p. 324.
237. Or: and began to teach.
238. Or: withered, wasted away, paralyzed.
239. Or: fully restored.

B. 6:6-11 *Healing a Shriveled Hand on the Sabbath*
Cf. Matt. 12:9-14; Mark 3:1-6

This is another illustration of the Son of man's assertion of authority in the sphere of sabbath observance. For a composite account, combining the records of the three Synoptics and indicating similarities and variations, see N.T.C. on Mark, pp. 113, 114.

1. A Tense Situation

6-8. On another sabbath, when he entered the synagogue and was teaching, a man whose right hand was shriveled was present. The scribes and the Pharisees, in order that they might find a charge against Jesus, were watching him closely (to see) whether he would heal on the sabbath.
As Luke tells the story, the conflict between Jesus and his opponents is beginning to intensify. In verses 1-5 it was against the disciples rather than against Jesus himself that the Pharisees launched their attack; in verses 6-11, however, their attention is riveted on Jesus himself. In the preceding section it is not entirely certain whether the religious authorities had arrived with the express purpose of finding fault. The possibility must be granted that they just happened to be on the scene when they caught the disciples in the act of transgressing sabbatical regulations. This time, however, they have come *in order to* find grounds for an accusation against Jesus.
It was "another"—not necessarily the next—sabbath.[240] Jesus has entered the synagogue, probably the one in Capernaum (with 6:6 cf. 7:1; with Matt. 12:9 cf. 11:23; with Mark 3:1 cf. 2:1). Here on this day there happened to be a man with a shriveled hand. The hand was paralyzed, due perhaps to muscular malfunction or atrophy. How this had come about is not made clear and it is useless to speculate. More important is the fact that it was the *right* hand, as Dr. Luke (Col. 4:14) informs us, that was thus affected.
The apocryphal Gospel According to the Hebrews states that the man was a stonemason who pleaded with Jesus to heal him that he might not have to spend his life as a beggar. Be that as it may, the point is that this is a sabbath, and though there may well have been a difference of opinion between the disciples of Shammai, with their stricter interpretation of sabbath observance, and those of Hillel, with their more lenient view—the more rigorous position prevailing in Jerusalem, the more lenient in Galilee—the rule that only in such cases in which a man's life was actually in danger would it be permissible to heal him on the sabbath was widely endorsed.[241] Would Jesus dare to oppose this rule, by the Pharisees regarded as a well-established and basic principle which must not be violated?

---

240. That it was indeed the sabbath is clear from all the synoptic accounts (Matt. 12:10, 11, 12; Mark 3:2, 4; Luke 6:6, 7, 9). In light of this fact Robertson's remark ("Only Luke notes that it was on a sabbath," *Word Pictures*, Vol. II, p. 81) may cause some difficulty.
241. See S.BK., Vol. I, pp. 622-629.

Very closely and insidiously do the scribes and Pharisees watch Jesus. By this time they had already become his enemies. As they saw it, had he not arrogated to himself the exclusively divine authority to forgive sins (Luke 5:20, 21; cf. John 5:18)? Did he not eat and drink with publicans and sinners (Luke 5:30–32)? Had he not previously transgressed the sabbath regulations held in honor by them (John 5:1–18; then Luke 6:1–5)? Besides, surely *this* case could wait. The man's life was not in danger. Here, then, so reason the scribes and the Pharisees, is their chance to build up a charge against Jesus.

But he knew their thoughts and said to the man with the shriveled hand, Rise and stand here in front. —So he got up and stood there.

In this tense situation the Lord takes the offensive. He knows their thoughts. See above, on 5:4, 5. He then tells the man to get up and stand where everybody can see him.

Jesus insisted on performing his miracles out in the open, so that every suspicion of deception and trickery would be excluded. Contrast with this the under-the-table, hidden-button, lights-out operations of later-day media! Besides, Jesus may also have wished to elicit the sympathy of the audience for this seriously handicapped man.

2. *An Astounding Miracle*

9, 10. Then Jesus said to them, I am asking y o u, Is it right on the sabbath to do good or to do harm, to save life or to destroy it? —Then he looked around at them all and said to the man, Stretch out your hand. —He did, and his hand was restored.

The question was reasonable and to the point. Were not the Pharisees and the scribes the very people who were always claiming that *they* knew what was "permitted," "lawful," and therefore "right"? Let them therefore give their expert opinion. Of course, the answer to Christ's question was so obvious that a child could have given it. If it is right *to do good*—for which see also Luke 6:33, 35; I Peter 2:14, 15, 20; 3:6, 17; 4:19; III John 11—on any ordinary day of the week, would it not be right to do good on the sabbath? Besides, in the Old Testament was it not exactly *doing good,* both with respect to God (loving, serving, and delighting oneself in him) and with respect to man (delivering him from bondage, feeding and clothing him), which God had required and even emphasized? And this in a context of fasting and sabbath observance? How strange that these adverse critics had not recalled the clear and definite teaching of Isa. 56:6; 58:6–14! The Lord had urged Israel to use the sabbath for the very purpose for which Jesus was here, now, and always using it. Nevertheless, it was with *him* that men who were supposed to be experts in the law were finding fault.

However, Jesus probed even more deeply. He exposed the perversity of the critics even more unequivocally; for not only did he ask whether it was permitted on the sabbath to do good and to save life, but he also added, "or to do harm and to destroy it?" Certainly, if it was improper to do harm and to destroy life on the other six days of the week, was it not very improper to engage in this sinister business on the day specifically set aside for honoring God and showing sympathy to man? Nevertheless this doing harm and destroying was exactly what these enemies were right now engaged in!

In which sense was it true that they were doing harm and destroying? Some answer that they were doing this by refusing to allow this man to be healed. Though that too may have been implied, is it not clear that something far worse was happening? The hearts and minds of these self-righteous scribes and Pharisees, who were finding fault with Jesus for wanting to deliver this man from his handicap, were engaged in killing the Messiah! For proof see verse 11; cf. Mark 3:6 ("how they might destroy him"). See also Matt. 5:21, 22; I John 3:15 ("Anyone who hates his brother is a murderer"). What Jesus is saying, therefore, amounts to this: "Is it right on the sabbath to do good and to save life, *as I am doing;* or to do harm and to destroy, *as you right now are doing?*" The confrontation was as sharp, dramatic, and bold as imaginable.

Then, looking around at them all (that is, at all these opponents), and "in anger, being deeply grieved at the hardening of their heart" (Mark 3:5), he said to the man, "Stretch out your hand."

The cure was instantaneous and complete. Cf. I Kings 13:6. In a manner too mysterious for any mortal to comprehend, the Savior had concentrated his mind on the plight of this poor man, and by means of his power and compassion, had willed and performed the cure; and this not "in a dark corner" but in the sight of everyone present.

3. *A Sad but Logical Reaction*

11. They, however, were filled with senseless rage and began to discuss with one another what they might do to Jesus.

Filled with madness were these scribes and Pharisees. They were boiling over, being beside themselves with fury. Jesus had given them a chance to answer his question: whether on the sabbath one should do good or inflict harm, save life or destroy it. Only one satisfactory answer was possible, but that answer would have exposed to ridicule their entire philosophy of life. So they had remained silent. Before the public they had been "shown up" for what they really were: leaders who set a higher value on their harsh, hairsplitting rules than on God's law of love, and were more concerned about their "traditions" than about the health and happiness of a tragically handicapped fellow man. And if their self-inflicted silence had already made them angry, the actual miracle Jesus performed made matters even worse for them. O that even now they had repented and confessed their wickedness! But no, they discuss back and forth, among themselves, what they might do to Jesus! Mark 3:6 indicates that they were trying to find a way to kill him, and chose as their co-plotters... of all people, the thoroughly unholy friends of Herod Antipas and his family. To such depths of degradation sin leads, unless grace intervenes.[242]

Practical Lessons Derived from Luke 6:1-11

Verses 2 and 11

"Why are y o u doing what is not permitted on the sabbath? . . . They, however, were filled with senseless rage." Illustration of a legalistic view of sabbath observance in later years: A sabbath in winter, snowdrifts blocking roads and highways. The only way in which a certain village pastor can get from his parsonage to the church is by skating over the frozen canal. This he does. Upon his arrival the consistory is not pleased. Was not what he had done tantamount to joyriding on the Lord's Day? After lengthy deliberation the decision is reached to demand of the pastor that he answer this question: "Did he enjoy his skating trip?" If the answer is "Yes," he must be censured; if "No," the case can be dropped, and the pastor's action can be charitably regarded as "a work of necessity."

Verses 5 and 9

"Lord of the sabbath is the Son of man. . . . Is it right on the sabbath to do good or to do harm, to save life or to destroy it?" On the sabbath Jesus, the Lord of the sabbath, regularly attended worship, taught, and performed works of mercy. See also Isa. 58:6-14. The lesson is clear.

Notes on Greek Words, Phrases, and Constructions in 6:6-11

Verse 6

ἐν ἑτέρῳ σαββάτῳ. This is indefinite (on another sabbath) and does not necessarily indicate the sabbath immediately following the one of 6:1.

Verse 7

παρετηροῦντο, third per. pl. middle imperf. indicat. of παρατηρέω (= παρά, cf. *parallel*, and τηρέω), to watch. The underlying picture is that of a person standing by the side of another, so that he can watch him closely. *To watch closely* is also the meaning in 14:1 and in 20:20.

Note εἰ in verse 7 ("whether," "if") and contrast with untranslatable εἰ in verse 9. The first εἰ is in an indirect question; the second, in a direct question.

ἵνα introduces purpose clause; εὕρωσιν, third per. pl. 2nd aor. active subjunct. of εὑρίσκω. Cf. *Eureka!*

κατηγορεῖν, present infinitive (durative) of κατηγορέω; cf. κατά, against, and ἀγορά, forum, assembly; ἀγορεύω, to speak, harangue; hence, to speak against in the assembly, in court; and thus, to accuse, denounce.

---

242. Notes on Greek words, phrases, and constructions in 6:6-11 begin on this page.

Verse 8

διαλογισμός, see the note on 2:35 on page 177, and the note on 5:22 on page 301. Derived from ἵστημι are στῆθι, sec. per. s. aor. imperative; and ἔστη, third per. s. 2nd aor. (ingressive) indicat.

Verse 9

ἐπερωτῶ = ἐπί and ἐρωτάω; literally, I put a question to (y o u), I am asking (y o u).
Note the four punctiliar aor. active infinitives: to do good, to do harm; to save, to destroy.

Verse 10

περιβλεψάμενος, aor. participle of περιβλέπομαι, to look around; elsewhere in the New Testament used only in Mark's Gospel. See N.T.C. on Mark, p. 116, footnote 105.
ἔκτεινον, sec. per. s. aor. act. imperat. of ἐκτείνω. ἀπεκατεστάθη, third per. s. aor. pass. (effective) indicat. of ἀποκαθίστημι, to set down again, to bring back, to restore; see also Matt. 12:13; 17:11; Mark 3:5; 8:25; 9:12. In Acts 3:21 ἀποκατάστασις means *restoration*.

Verse 11

Note emphatic αὐτοὶ δέ, "*They*, however. . . ."
For ἐπλήσθησαν see the note on 4:28 on page 261.
ἄνοια = ἀ plus νοῦς; literally "lack of understanding"; in the present context senseless fury, madness. The Dutch (Nieuwe Vertaling) reproduces the sense of the original beautifully: "Zij raakten volkomen hun verstand kwijt"; i.e., "They completely lost their mind (so angry they were)."
For διελάλουν see the note on 1:65 on page 120.
ποιήσαιεν, third per. pl. aor. optat. (here deliberative) of ποιέω. The deliberative optative of the direct question is retained in the indirect question.

---

12 Now it was during those days that he went out into the mountain to pray, and he spent the entire night in prayer to God. 13 When day came he called his disciples to him, and from among them he chose twelve, whom he also designated apostles:

14 Simon, whom he named Peter, and his brother Andrew, and James and John, and Philip and Bartholomew, 15 and Matthew and Thomas, and James the son of Alphaeus, and Simon who was called the Zealot, 16 and Judas the son of James, and Judas Iscariot, who became a traitor.

6:12–16 *The Choosing of The Twelve*
Cf. Matt. 5:1; 10:1–4; Mark 3:13–19

12. Now it was during those days that he went out into the mountain to pray, and he spent the entire night in prayer to God.
"During those days," "the mountain." Which days? Which mountain? Luke clearly is not the writer of a modern chronology. We are becoming

used to his indefinite time and place indications (1:5, 24, 39; 2:1; even 3:1–3 to a certain extent; 3:15; 4:1, 14, 16, 31; 5:1, 12, 17, 27; 6:6). So also here in 6:12. The favorable aspect of this peculiarity is the fact that any actual discrepancy or conflict between Luke's account and that of synoptic parallels, which at times are more definite, is thus avoided. But though the expression *during those days* is indefinite, it does say something. In the present instance the very broad interpretation "sometime during Christ's earthly ministry" is unwarranted. As has already been shown, the choosing of The Twelve probably occurred shortly after the sabbath controversies related in 6:1–11.

The definite article ("the" mountain, not just "a" mountain), unless the reference is to the mountain region in general ("the hills"), probably indicates that a well-known mountain is meant. Was it the *Horns of Hattin,* named thus because its peaks resemble two horns when seen from afar? This elevation is located about six and one-half kilometers west of the Sea of Galilee and about thirteen kilometers southwest of Capernaum. Or was it even closer to, and in the same direction from, Capernaum? If so, the reference could be to the gentle, grassy slope just west of Tabgha.[243]

Jesus went into the mountain "to pray." In fact, he spent the night in prayer to God. On the subject of Jesus' prayer habits and the prominence of prayer in Luke's Gospel see *Introduction,* point I A 5 b; 3:21; 5:16. If, as may be assumed, one of the items included in that prayer was the petition for wisdom in selecting a group of intimate followers, this would shed interesting light on the ways of God, especially when we bear in mind that the men who were selected were, at least mostly, run-of-the-mill individuals (cf. I Cor. 1:26). The group included even the man who was going to become a traitor, in order that, without in any way canceling human responsibility, God's counsel regarding the salvation of his people might be carried out. See Luke 22:22; Acts 2:23.

13. When day came he called his disciples to him, and from among them he chose twelve, whom he also designated apostles.

The connection between this account of the choosing of The Twelve and the preceding paragraphs is probably closer than may appear on the surface. It has become clear that the enemies of Jesus were increasing in numbers and in the intensity of their opposition (5:21, 30; 6:2, 7, 11). The idea of doing away with Jesus was already being discussed (Mark 3:6; John 5:18). Jesus knew this. He also knew that according to God's eternal decree the preaching of the gospel must continue, the gathering together of the elect must not cease. For that reason he was about to surround himself with a little band of witnesses, so that through their testimony this important task might be carried out after his own death and departure to heaven. He himself, the gloriously exalted Christ, through his Spirit, was going to

---

243. See Howard La Fay, "Where Jesus Walked," *National Geographic,* Vol. 132, No. 6 (Dec. 1967), p. 763.

continue to work and to teach by the agency of these followers. See Acts 1:1–8.

When day came he called "his disciples" to him. A disciple is a pupil, a learner. He is, however, more than a "bookworm," or even than a "student." Rather, he is an *adherent*, a *follower*. Between him and his Master there exists—at least should exist—a close personal fellowship. For more on the concept *disciple* see the note on this verse on page 333.

In the present case, as also in such passages as Luke 6:17; John 6:60, 66, the term *disciple* is used in the general sense of "follower." It refers to any member of a large circle of adherents. From this wider group Jesus selected twelve men. He called them to him, and they came.

Luke makes a special point of the fact that Jesus also designated these men "apostles." An apostle is a person who has been sent, commissioned. As such he represents his Sender, being clothed with authority, over life and doctrine, derived from him. In the New Testament the term *apostle* is used both in a looser and in a stricter sense. According to the broader application of the term such men as Barnabas, Epaphroditus, Apollos, Silvanus, and Timothy are all called "apostles." They all represent the cause of Christ. In doing so they may at times also represent certain definite churches whose "apostles" they are. See Acts 13:1, 2; II Cor. 8:23; Phil. 2:25. In the narrow and fuller sense, the term *apostle* is in the New Testament restricted to The Twelve and Paul. In the present context Paul is not yet in the picture. The reference is to the twelve men chosen at this time to be the constant followers of Jesus, the ones who, after having been *taught* by him, are going to be *sent out* on their important missions.

The idea, found in much present-day literature, according to which the "authority" of an apostle, *if any*, depends entirely on his charismatic gifts, lacks scriptural support. The authority is derived entirely from the Sender, and is real. See Matt. 10:1, 5, 14, 15, 20, 40; 16:19; John 20:21; Rom. 1:1; II Cor. 10:13; etc. The apostleship is an *office*, a divinely instituted *commission* with *authority* to carry it out.

The fact that Jesus appointed exactly twelve men, no more and no less, indicates that he had in mind the new Israel, for ancient Israel had twelve tribes and twelve patriarchs. The new Israel was going to be gathered from among all the nations, Jews and Gentiles alike (Matt. 8:10–12; 16:18; 28:19; Mark 12:9; 16:15, 16; Luke 4:25–27; John 3:16; 10:16; Rev. 21:12, 14). It was the continuation, in a new form, of the one and only "kingdom of God" that spans both the old and the new dispensation, as does "the church," represented at times by the twelve patriarchs (or "tribes") and the twelve apostles (Rev. 21:12, 14).

In the New Testament the names of The Twelve are listed four times (Matt. 10:2–4; Mark 3:16–19; Luke 6:14–16; Acts 1:13, 26). Acts 1:15–26 records the manner in which Judas Iscariot was replaced by Matthias. With that exception the twelve names undoubtedly indicate the same persons in each of the four lists.

Omitting the one given in Acts, the lists are as follows:

Lists of The Twelve in the Synoptics

Matthew	Mark	Luke
Simon, Andrew, James, John; Philip, Bartholomew, Thomas, Matthew; James (A), Thaddaeus, Simon (C), Judas Iscariot	Simon, James, John, Andrew; Philip, Bartholomew, Matthew, Thomas; James (A), Thaddaeus, Simon (C), Judas Iscariot	Simon, Andrew, James, John; Philip, Bartholomew, Matthew, Thomas; James (A), Simon (Z), Judas (J), Judas Iscariot

14-16. Simon, whom he named Peter, and his brother Andrew, and James and John, and Philip and Bartholomew, and Matthew and Thomas, and James the son of Alphaeus, and Simon who was called the Zealot, and Judas the son of James, and Judas Iscariot, who became a traitor.

Simon, whom he named Peter. He was a son of Jonas or John. By trade he was a fisherman, who with his brother Andrew first lived in Bethsaida (John 1:44), afterward in Capernaum (Mark 1:21, 29). Both Mark and Luke report that it was Jesus who gave Simon the new name *Peter.* For details of this event see John 1:42. This new name, meaning *rock,* was a description not of what Simon was when called, but of what by grace he was to become. At first, and for some time afterward, Simon was anything but a model of steadfastness or imperturbability. On the contrary, he was constantly swaying from one position to its opposite. He turned from trust to doubt (Matt. 14:28, 30); from open profession of Jesus as the Christ, to rebuking that very Christ (Matt. 16:16, 22); from a vehement declaration of loyalty, to base denial (Matt. 26:33-35, 69-75; Mark 14:29-31, 66-72; Luke 22:33, 54-62); from "By no means shalt thou wash my feet ever," to "Not my feet only but also my hands and my head" (John 13:8, 9). See also John 20:4, 6; Gal. 2:11, 12. Nevertheless, by the grace and power of the Lord this changeable Simon was transformed into a true Peter. In every list of the apostles Simon's name is always mentioned first. From here on *Luke* calls him Peter, no longer Simon; but see 22:31; 24:34. For his significance in the post-resurrection church see N.T.C. on Matt. 16:13-20. Accordingly, when Jesus at this early date—for Luke 6:14 reflects John 1:42—assigned to Simon his new name, that was an act of love, a love that was willing to overlook the present and even the near future, and to look far ahead. Wonderful and transforming grace of our loving Lord!

Two New Testament books are by tradition accredited to this apostle: I and II Peter. And even Mark's Gospel owes something to Peter, for Mark has not unjustly been called "Peter's interpreter."

His brother Andrew. It was he, also a fisherman, who brought Peter to Jesus (see N.T.C. on John 1:41, 42). For other references to Andrew see Mark 1:16, 17, 29; also study Mark 3:18; 13:3; John 6:8, 9; 12:22; Acts 1:13. See also below under Philip.

James and John. Luke mentions these two fishermen not only here and in 5:10 (see on that passage) but also later on (8:51; 9:28, 54; cf. Acts 1:13). There are also several references to them in the other Gospels. Probably because of their fiery nature Jesus called these two brothers Boanerges, "sons of thunder" (Mark 3:17). That the two did indeed have a fiery nature may perhaps be inferred from Luke 9:54-56. Cf. Mark 9:38. James was the first of The Twelve to wear the martyr's crown (Acts 12:2). While he was the first to arrive in heaven, his brother John was in all probability the last to remain on earth. On the life and character of John, considered by many (I believe correctly) as being "the disciple whom Jesus loved" (John 13:23; 19:26; 20:2; 21:7, 20), see N.T.C. on John, Vol. I, pp. 18-21. Five New Testament books have by tradition been assigned to John: his Gospel, three epistles (I, II, and III John), and the book of Revelation.

Philip was at least for a while a fellow townsman of Peter and Andrew, that is, he too was from Bethsaida. Having himself responded to the call of Jesus, he found Nathanael, and said to him, "The one about whom Moses wrote in the law and about whom the prophets wrote, we have found, Jesus, son of Joseph, the one from Nazareth" (John 1:45). When Jesus was about to feed the five thousand he asked Philip, "How are we to buy bread-cakes that these (people) may eat?" Philip answered, "Bread-cakes for two hundred denarii would not be sufficient for them so that each might get a little something" (John 6:5, 7). Philip apparently forgot that the power of Jesus surpassed any possibility of calculation. To deduce from this incident the conclusion that Philip was a coldly-calculating type of person, more so than the other apostles, would be basing too much on too little. In the Gospels Philip generally appears in a rather favorable light. Thus, when the Greeks approached him with the request, "Sir, we would see Jesus," he went and told Andrew, and these two, Andrew and Philip, brought the enquirers to Jesus (John 12:21, 22). It must be admitted that Philip did not always immediately understand the meaning of Christ's profound utterances—did the others?—but to his credit it must be said that with perfect candor he would reveal his ignorance and ask for further information, as is also clear from John 14:8, "Lord, show us the Father, and we shall be content." He received the beautiful and comforting answer, ". . . He who has seen me has seen the Father" (John 14:9).

Bartholomew (meaning: son of Tolmai) is clearly the *Nathanael* of John's Gospel (1:45-49; 21:2). It was he who said to Philip, "Out of Nazareth can any good come?" Philip answered, "Come and see." When Jesus saw Nathanael coming toward him he said, "Look, truly an Israelite in whom deceit does not exist." This disciple was one of the seven persons to whom the resurrected Christ appeared at the Sea of Tiberias. Of the other six only Simon Peter, Thomas, and the sons of Zebedee are mentioned.

Matthew. This disciple has already been discussed in some detail (see above on 5:27-32; also N.T.C. on Matthew, pp. 92-97; 421-426; and on Mark, p. 95).

Thomas. The various references to Thomas indicate that both despondency and devotion marked this man. He was ever afraid that he might lose his beloved Master. He expected evil, and it was hard for him to believe good tidings when they were brought to him. Yet when the risen Savior in all his tender, condescending love revealed himself to him it was he who exclaimed, "My Lord and my God!" For more information on Thomas see N.T.C. on John 11:16; 14:5; 20:24–28; 21:2. See also Acts 1:13.

James the son of Alphaeus. By Mark (15:40) he is also called "James the Less," which by some is interpreted as meaning "James the younger," but by others as "James small in stature." About him we have no further positive information. It is probable, however, that he is the same disciple who is referred to in Matt. 27:56; Mark 16:1; and Luke 24:10. If this be correct, his mother's name was Mary, one of the women who accompanied Jesus and stood near the cross. See N.T.C. on John 19:25. The Alphaeus who was the father of Matthew should probably not be identified with Alphaeus the father of James the Less.

Simon who was called the Zealot. Mark uses the expression *Simon the Cananaean,* this being an Aramaic surname which likewise means "enthusiast" or "zealot." In all probability this name is here given him because formerly he had belonged to the party of the Zealots, a party which in its hatred for the foreign ruler, who demanded tribute, did not shrink from fomenting rebellion against the Roman government. See Josephus *Jewish War* II.117, 118; *Antiquities* XVIII.1–10, 23. Cf. Acts 5:37.

Judas the son of James. He is called Thaddaeus in Matt. 10:3; Mark 3:18; and Lebbaeus in certain variants. He is in all probability "Judas not Iscariot" of John 14:22 (see on that passage); cf. Acts 1:13. From what is said about him in John 14 it would seem that he wanted Jesus to show himself to the world, probably meaning: to get into the limelight.

Judas Iscariot, who became a traitor. His name is generally interpreted as meaning "Judas the man from Kerioth," a place in southern Judea. (Some, however, prefer the interpretation, "the dagger-man.") The Gospels refer to him again and again (Matt. 26:14, 25, 47; 27:3; Mark 14:10, 43; Luke 22:3, 47, 48; John 6:71; 12:4; 13:2, 26, 29; 18:2–5). He is at times described as "Judas who betrayed him," "Judas one of the twelve," "the betrayer," "Judas the son of Simon Iscariot," "Judas Iscariot, Simon's son," or simply "Judas." This man, though thoroughly responsible for his own wicked deeds, was an instrument of the devil (John 6:70, 71). While other people, when they felt that they could no longer agree with or even tolerate Christ's teachings, would simply disassociate themselves from him (John 6:66), Judas remained, as if he were in full accord with him. Being a very selfish person he was unable—or shall we say "unwilling"?—to understand the unselfish and beautiful deed of Mary of Bethany, who anointed Jesus (John 12:1 ff.). He was unable and unwilling to see that the native language of love is lavishness. It was the devil who instigated Judas to betray Jesus, that is, to deliver him into the hands of the enemy. He was a thief; yet it was he who had been entrusted with the treasury of the little company, with the predictable result (John 12:6). When, in connection with the institution of the Lord's Supper, the dramatic moment arrived—forever commemorated in Scripture (Matt. 26:20–25; John 13:21–30) and emblazoned in art (Leonardo da Vinci, etc.)—in which Jesus startled The Twelve by saying, "One of y o u will betray me," Judas, though having already received from the chiefpriests the thirty pieces of silver as a reward for his promised deed (Matt. 26:14–16; Mark 14:10, 11) had the incredible audacity to say, "Surely not I, Rabbi?" Judas served as guide for the detachment of soldiers and the posse of temple police that arrested Jesus in the garden of Gethsemane. It was by means of perfidiously kissing his Master, as if he were still a loyal disciple, that this traitor pointed out Jesus to those who had come to seize him (Matt. 26:49, 50; Mark 14:43–45; Luke 22:47, 48). As to the manner of Judas' self-inflicted demise, see on Matt 27:3–5; cf. Acts 1:18.

What caused this privileged disciple to become Christ's betrayer? Was it injured pride, disappointed ambition, deeply entrenched greed, fear of being put out of the synagogue (John 9:22)? No doubt all of these were involved, but could not the most basic reason have been this, that between the utterly selfish heart of Judas and the infinitely unselfish and outgoing heart of Jesus there was a chasm so immense that either Judas had to implore the Lord to bestow upon him the grace of regeneration and complete renewal, a request which the traitor wickedly refused to make, or else he had to offer his help to get rid of Jesus? See also Luke 22:22; Acts 2:23; 4:28. One thing is certain: The shocking tragedy of Judas' life is proof not of Christ's impotence but of the traitor's impenitence! Woe to that man!

What points up the greatness of Jesus is that he took *such men as these,* and welded them into an amazingly influential community that would prove to be not only a worthy link with Israel's past but also a solid foundation for the church's future. Yes, he accomplished this multiple miracle with such men as these, with all their faults and foibles. Even when we leave out Judas Iscariot and concentrate only on the others, we cannot fail to be impressed with the majesty of the Savior, whose drawing power, incomparable wisdom, and matchless love were so astounding that he was able to gather around himself and to unite into *one* family men of entirely different, at times even opposite, backgrounds and temperaments. Included in this little band was Peter the optimist (Matt. 14:28; 26:33, 35), but also Thomas the pessimist (John 11:16; 20:24, 25); Simon the one-time Zealot, hating taxes and eager to overthrow the Roman government, but also Matthew, who had voluntarily offered his tax-collecting services to that same Roman government; Peter, John, and Matthew, destined to become renowned through their writings, but also James the Less, who remains obscure but must have fulfilled his mission.

Jesus drew them to himself with the cords of his tender, never-failing

331

compassion. He loved them to the uttermost (John 13:1), and in the night before he was betrayed and crucified commended them to his Father, saying:

"I have manifested thy name to the men whom thou gavest me out of the world; thine they were, and thou gavest them to me, and they have kept thy word. . . . Holy Father, keep them in thy name which thou hast given me, in order that they may be one, even as we are one. . . . I do not make request that thou shouldest take them out of the world, but that thou shouldest keep them from the evil one. They are not of the world, even as I am not of the world. Consecrate them in the truth; thy word is truth. Just as thou didst send me into the world, so have I also sent them into the world. And for thy sake I consecrate myself, in order that they also may be truly consecrated" (John 17:6–19, in part).[244]

Practical Lesson Derived from Luke 6:12–16

"He spent the entire night in prayer to God."

What an amazing power there is in earnest prayer. How tremendous are the results! After this All-Night Prayer Vigil Jesus accomplished the following:

1. By calling to himself his disciples and from among them choosing The Twelve so that they might become his apostles (verses 13–16) he

    a. organized the church in its New Testament manifestation, making it an institution for the good of mankind;

    b. laid the foundation for world-wide missionary enterprise, a work that is still continuing.

2. He also

    c. healed ever so many sick people (verses 17–19), thereby setting an example for all time of showing sympathy to and providing help for those in need; and

    d. preached an unforgettably beautiful sermon (verses 20–49), one that has been a source of blessing to many throughout the centuries and continues to hold its place among the most quoted portions of sacred literature.

All this to God's glory (Luke 2:14; cf. 17:18; 19:38; cf. Matt. 5:16; John 17:4).

Notes on Greek Words, Phrases, and Constructions in 6:12–16

Verse 12

προσεύξασθαι, aor. infinitive of προσεύχομαι, to pray, a verb occurring also in 1:10; 3:21; 5:16; 6:28; etc. Note cognate noun προσευχή (here dat. -ῃ). For synonyms see R. C. Trench, *Synonyms,* par. 51.

ἦν διανυκτερεύων, third per. s. periphrastic imperf. of διανυκτερεύω*, to pass or spend the night. English lacks a one-word equivalent. In 6:12 cf. Latin *pernoctaret.*

---

244. Notes on Greek words, phrases, and constructions in 6:12–16 begin on this page.

προσεφώνησεν, third per. s. aor. act. indicat. of προσφωνέω, to call to oneself (6:13; 13:12; Acts 22:2); to appeal to (23:20); to address, speak to, call out to (Matt. 11:16; Luke 7:32; Acts 22:2).

In the New Testament the term μαθητής is confined to the Gospels and Acts. In round figures it is found more than 70 times in Matthew, almost 50 times in Mark, almost 40 times in Luke, almost 80 times in John, and almost 30 times in Acts. Even when a few disputed occurrences are subtracted, it occurs about 260 times in the New Testament. At times it is used without reference to any specific master (Matt. 10:24, 25; Luke 6:40). Or the reference may be to the disciples of:

John the Baptist (Matt. 9:14a; 11:2; Luke 7:18, 19; John 3:25);
John and the Pharisees (Mark 2:18);
the Pharisees (Matt. 22:16);
Moses (John 9:28);
Paul (Acts 9:25).

In the great majority of cases the disciples of *Jesus* are indicated. Sometimes, as here in 6:13a, a large circle of followers or adherents is indicated. More often the reference is to The Twelve or to one or more men belonging to that inner group.

Basically a μαθητής is a learner. Cf. this noun with the verb *to learn*, μανθάνω. The root of such and similar words in Greek and related languages, including English, is MAN: to think. Has not *man* been called "a thinking animal"? Modifications of this same basic root are mind, mental, monition, monster, monument, medicine, mathematics, etc. Note also in the Greek New Testament ἀμαθής, ignorant; καταμανθάνω, to consider carefully; μαθητεύω, to make a disciple, to teach; μαθητεύομαι, to become a disciple; μαθήτρια, a woman-disciple; συνμαθητής, fellow-disciple.

It would be a mistake, however, to think that mere mental understanding or intelligence makes a person a true disciple of Jesus. It is part of the picture, an important part even, but only a part. The truth learned must be put into practice. It must enter into the very being of the person involved. *The true disciple lives in close fellowship with his Master.* This is true because the Master has chosen him, not vice versa (John 15:16). Jesus called him, and by God's grace this person has responded to that call. If he remains loyal to Jesus and his word, he is truly Christ's disciple (John 8:31).

On the meaning of the word *disciple* see also K. H. Renstorf's article on μανθάνω . . . μαθητής and related words (Th.D.N.T., Vol. IV, pp. 390-461).

ἐκλεξάμενος, nom. s. masc. aor. middle participle of ἐκλέγω, to pick out (for oneself), select, elect, choose. Cf. ἐκλογή, *election.*

ἀπόστολος, apostle, one who is sent, commissioned. See John 13:16; 20:21-23. In the Third Gospel this noun occurs 6 times (6:13; 9:10; 11:49; 17:5; 22:14; 24:10); in Acts 28 times (1:2, 26, etc.). In Matthew it is found only in 10:2; in Mark probably twice (3:14, if authentic; 6:30); in John once (13:16). It also occurs at least once in each of the remaining New Testament books, with the exception of II Thessalonians, Philemon, James, and the three epistles of John. On the term *apostle* see also N.T.C. on Gal. 1:1. In the Gospels the more usual name for the small group of constant followers—with whom Jesus surrounded himself, whom he taught and sent out to preach, to heal, to cast out demons, etc.—is *The Twelve.* See Matt. 10:5;

26:14, 47; Mark 4:10; 6:7; 9:35; 10:32; 11:11; 14:10, 17, 20, 43; Luke 8:1; 9:1, 12; 18:31; 22:3, 47; John 6:67, 70; 20:24.

Verse 16

προδότης (cf. προδίδωμι, to give before, to betray), betrayer, traitor. Judas *became* a traitor. He was not a traitor when Jesus called him.

---

17 Then he went down with them and stopped on a level place where there was a huge crowd of his disciples and a vast throng of people from all over Judea and Jerusalem and the coastal region of Tyre and Sidon. 18 They had come to listen to him and to be cured of their diseases. Those who were troubled by unclean spirits were being healed. 19 And all the people were trying to touch him, because power was going out from him and was curing everybody.

6:17–19 *Jesus' Power to Heal*
Cf. Matt. 5:1, 2

17, 18. Then he went down with them and stopped on a level place where there was a huge crowd of his disciples and a vast throng of people from all over Judea and Jerusalem and the coastal region of Tyre and Sidon. They had come to listen to him and to be cured of their diseases. Those who were troubled by unclean spirits were being healed.

According to Luke's account Jesus had gone into the mountain to pray and had chosen The Twelve. To this the evangelist now adds that together with this intimate band of followers the Master "went down" until he stood on "a level place." This may well have been a large level tract that coincides with the far larger gentle, grassy slope west of Tabgha, not far from Capernaum.

We see Jesus standing here surrounded by The Twelve, a huge crowd of other followers—"disciples" in the broader sense of the term (see on verse 13)—, and a vast throng of other people not only from the south (Judea, including Jerusalem) but even from the northwest, the coastal region of Tyre and Sidon. Is it not natural to see in this event a fulfilment, however partial, of Psalm 87:4 (LXX, 86:4)?

All these people had come to Jesus. Writing, no doubt, in general terms, Luke says that their purpose was twofold: (a) to listen to Jesus, and (b) to be cured of their diseases.

a. *to listen.*

Their desire for a message from his lips did not meet with disappointment, for it was to them and on this very occasion that Jesus addressed words that were bound to live forever, that is, to be repeated over and over again throughout the centuries and in ever so many languages and dialects all over the world.

Are we correct in regarding what is reported in Luke 6:20–49 as Luke's report of the same sermon recorded by Matthew in his chapters 5–7? But according to the Third Gospel this sermon was preached "on a level place," whereas according to Matt. 5:1, 2 it was proclaimed from a mountain. However, this surely is no discrepancy. The "problem," if it can even be considered such, disappears when we grant that "the level place" may well have been part of "the mountain." It was the elevation beyond which Jesus did not now descend. He "remained standing," or "stopped" here.[245]

Besides, as reported by Luke the sermon is introduced as follows, "Then he lifted up his eyes on his disciples and said. . . ." Compare this with Matthew's, "And he opened his mouth and began to teach them, saying. . . ." Luke's ending (7:1) reads, "After Jesus had concluded all his words in the hearing of the people. . . ." With this compare Matthew's, "Now when Jesus had finished these sayings. . . ." In addition, the train of thought is to a considerable extent the same in both Gospels: beatitudes, supremacy of love, the two builders.

It is admitted that the two reports are not identical. Matthew's coverage is more than three times as extensive as Luke's. This shows that the Gospel writers were not mere copyists. Each wrote in accordance with his own background, character, and endowment. Perhaps even more important: each wrote in harmony with his own specific purpose. Thus it is not surprising that Matthew includes various matters that were of special interest to his *Jewish* readers whom he was trying to reach for Christ (for example, 5:17-42; 6:1-6, 16-18). Since Luke was not primarily writing for Jews he omits such matters. On the other hand Luke's account contains material (e.g., 6:24-26, 38-40) not found in that identical form in Matthew, or not included by him in this sermon at all. It is not only possible but very probable that many of the sayings found in The Sermon on the Mount were repeated by the Lord as he traveled from place to place.

b. *to be cured.*

Note how carefully Luke distinguishes between the obviously "sick" who were cured of their diseases and the "troubled" who were delivered of "unclean," that is, evil, spirits. For demon possession and expulsion see on 4:33-37. In each classification there must have been a good many people who were healed at this time. Something similar had happened before (4:40, 41), and was to happen again (7:21, 22). Add to this the many healings that are separately reported in the Gospels (here in Luke see 4:38, 39; 5:12, 13, 24, 25; 7:10; 8:44, etc.). And do not forget John 21:25.

It should be borne in mind, moreover, that to the tenderly loving heart of Jesus people were not merely "cases." Each human being was the object of special treatment, such as was suitable for him, for him alone. Into each person's circumstances the Savior wholly entered with his sympathetic heart. See Luke 7:13; cf. Matt. 8:17; 9:36; 14:14; 20:34; Mark 1:41; 5:19; 6:34; John 11:35.

---

245. For another possible solution see N.T.C. on Matthew, p. 260.

19. And all the people were trying to touch him, because power was going out from him and was curing everybody.

In connection with 5:13 something was said about Christ's healing touch and about the people's desire to touch Christ. Obviously we are here concerned with the latter. All the people were trying to touch Jesus because healing power was constantly proceeding from him. That is clearly what the passage says, and we should not try to change it to something else. In fact, the truth here expressed is not confined to this single passage. The fact that our Lord at times sensed that healing power was proceeding from him is also expressed in Luke 8:46; cf. Mark 5:30. Probably with noble intentions—to guard against magical qualities being attributed to the garments or fingers of Jesus?—some prefer a different rendering for the last part of verse 19. They conceive of the words that follow the comma as constituting a compound clause, to be translated as follows, "because *power* was going out from him *and he* was curing everybody."[246] The vast majority of translators and commentators, however, have accepted the single clause rendering (power was going out from him and was curing) and this with good reason: (a) it harmonizes best with the passages cited earlier (Mark 5:30, see also verse 29; Luke 8:46); (b) if Luke had intended to introduce another clause into this short sentence, he would probably have done so without leaving any room for doubt. Since the evangelist states that the outgoing power was issuing from Jesus himself, making it clear that it was Jesus who was accomplishing the cure, there is no real difficulty.

It is not claimed that the "faith" of the people that caused them to rush toward Jesus so as to be able to touch him was necessarily free from all "foreign" elements. In many a case it may well have been mixed with superstition. But that is not *Luke's* emphasis. He wants us to rivet our attention on Jesus, whose *power* was enabling him to heal all, and whose *heart*, filled with sympathy, was impelling him to do just that![247]

Practical Lesson Derived from Luke 6:17-19

"They had come to listen to him and to be cured.... Power was going out from him and was curing everybody."

Jesus satisfies every need. See Fanny J. Crosby's "A Wonderful Savior Is Jesus My Lord" (also listed under "He Hideth My Soul").

---

246. Note: "and *he* was curing" (or "healing") or something similar is preferred by Phillips; by A. T. Robertson (*Translation*, p. 42); by S. Greijdanus, *Korte Verklaring*, pp. 155, 158; and cf. Dutch Bible (both Statenvertaling and Nieuwe Vertaling).

247. Notes on Greek words, phrases, and constructions in 6:17-19 begin on page 337.

Notes on Greek Words, Phrases, and Constructions in 6:17-19

Verse 17

ἔστη, third per. s. 2nd aor. indicat. of ἵστημι. Jesus *stopped*—or *remained standing*—here, did not descend any farther.

πεδινοῦ, gen. s. of πεδινός* (-ή, -όν), level, flat. Cf. πεδίον, a plain, a place convenient for travel by feet; cf. *pedestrian.*

παραλίου, gen. of παράλιος* (supply χώρα, the seacoast, coastal region), from παρά, by, and ἅλς, sea.

Note the ὄχλος series of words in verses 17, 18, 19, including ἐνοχλούμενοι, probably originally *crowded;* hence annoyed, troubled; pres. pass. participle of ἐνοχλέω; cf. Heb. 12:15.

Verses 18, 19

ἀκοῦσαι, aor. act. infinitive of ἀκούω, to hear, to listen to. When there is a distinction in meaning between this verb followed by the gen. and the same verb followed by the accusative, the former indicates hearing *sounds;* the latter, understanding *words.* See Gram. N.T., p. 506; also Acts 9:7; contrast Acts 22:9. But owing to the gradual intrusion of the accusative into the territories of the other cases, a process already apparent in the Koine, this rule is by no means inflexible. See also Robertson, *Word Pictures, Acts,* p. 118.

Note, in verses 18, 19, ἰαθῆναι . . . ἰᾶτο; the first being the aor. passive infinitive; the second, the third per. s. middle imperfect, of the verb ἰάομαι. There is little, if any difference in meaning between the two verbs for "healing" here used.

On ἐθεραπεύοντο, third per. pl. imperfect (progressive, descriptive) of θεραπεύω see also the note on 4:23 on page 261. In John's Gospel this verb is found once; in Mark 5 times; in Matthew 16 times, while Dr. Luke (in the Fourth Gospel and Acts) uses it 19 times. It is natural that the beloved physician took a deep interest in the therapeutics practiced by the Great Physician.

As presented by Luke, The Sermon on the Mount (see 6:12, 17; cf. Matt. 5:1), in which "the gospel of the kingdom" (6:20; cf. Matt. 4:23) is set forth, may be divided as follows:
  I. *Four Beatitudes and Four Woes*
       with reference, respectively, to those inside and those outside the kingdom (6:20-26)
 II. *The Standard of Life Demanded by the King* (6:27-45)
       A. The Light of Love He Commends (6:27-38)
       B. The Darkness of Sin He Condemns (6:39-45)
III. *Application: The Parable of The Two Builders* (6:46-49)
       Note resemblance between this Outline and the Sermon Summary found on pp. 262, 263 of N.T.C. on Matthew. In connection with this essential similarity note also the variety of presentation.

20 Then he lifted up his eyes on his disciples and said:
"Blessed (are) y o u poor,
for y o u r s is the kingdom of God.
21 Blessed (are) y o u who now are hungry,
for y o u shall be fully satisfied.
Blessed (are) y o u who now weep,
for y o u shall laugh.
22 Blessed are y o u when men hate y o u; when they exclude y o u, heap insults upon
y o u,[248] and spurn y o u r name as evil, on account of the Son of man.
23 Exult in that day and leap for joy,
for great, indeed, is y o u r reward in heaven; for in just the same way their fathers used to
treat the prophets."
24 "But woe to y o u who are rich,
for y o u have already received y o u r consolation in full.
25 Woe to y o u who now are well-fed,
for y o u shall go hungry.
Woe (to y o u) who now are laughing,
for y o u shall mourn and weep.
26 Woe (to y o u) when all men speak well of y o u,
for in just the same way their fathers used to treat the false prophets."

6:20-26   I. *Four Beatitudes and Four Woes*
For the Beatitudes cf. Matt. 5:1-12.

Our Lord's "Beatitudes" as Reported by Luke and by Matthew
Luke's Beatitude No. 1

Blessed (are) y o u poor,
for y o u r s is the kingdom of God.

Matthew's Corresponding Beatitude No. 1

Blessed (are) the poor in spirit,
for theirs is the kingdom of heaven.

Luke's Beatitude No. 2

Blessed (are) y o u who now are hungry,
for y o u shall be fully satisfied.

Matthew's Corresponding Beatitude No. 4

Blessed (are) those hungering and thirsting for righteousness,
for they shall be fully satisfied.

Luke's Beatitude No. 3

Blessed (are) y o u who now weep,
for y o u shall laugh.

---

248. Or: revile y o u.

Matthew's Corresponding Beatitude No. 2

Blessed (are) the mourners,
for they shall be comforted.

Luke's Beatitude No. 4

Blessed are y o u when men hate y o u, etc.
for great, indeed, is y o u r reward in heaven, etc.

Matthew's Corresponding Beatitude No. 8

Blessed (are) those persecuted for righteousness' sake,
for theirs is the kingdom of heaven, etc.

Thus, while, broadly speaking, Matthew has a beatitude corresponding
to each of Luke's, Luke has no parallel to Matthew's third, fifth, sixth, and
seventh (respectively concerning the meek, the merciful, the pure in heart,
and the peacemakers).

Correspondence between
Beatitudes and Woes
as reported by Luke

Beatitude No. 1

Blessed (are) y o u poor,
for y o u r s is the kingdom of God.

Woe No. 1

But woe to y o u who are rich,
for y o u have already received y o u r consolation in full.

Beatitude No. 2

Blessed (are) y o u who now are hungry,
for y o u shall be fully satisfied.

Woe No. 2

Woe to y o u who now are well-fed,
for y o u shall go hungry.

Beatitude No. 3

Blessed (are) y o u who now weep,
for y o u shall laugh.

Woe No. 3

Woe (to y o u) who now are laughing,
for y o u shall mourn and weep.

Beatitude No. 4

Blessed are y o u when men hate y o u

. . . .

for in just the same way their fathers used to treat the prophets.

Woe No. 4

Woe (to y o u) when all men speak well of y o u,
for in just the same way their fathers used to treat the false prophets.

Those who, comparing Matthew's report of this sermon with Luke's, see a contradiction, will find it difficult to prove this. In each case what has been preserved of this sermon is a summary. Would it not be unrealistic to believe that Jesus spoke less than fifty minutes? Nevertheless, it takes the average reader only about seven minutes to read Matt. 5:3—7:27, and only about two minutes to read Luke 6:20-49. As long as what each reporter has left us is what was actually said, main points being accurately reflected, there is no real problem, no conflict. In view of John 20:30, 31; 21:25 it is unreasonable to demand something corresponding to a complete tape recording of every spoken word. In the time it took Jesus to deliver this heart-searching address he had ample opportunity to utter the eight Beatitudes reported by Matthew and the four Beatitudes plus four Woes reported by Luke, all the more so when we bear in mind that with respect to the Beatitudes there is overlapping between the two reports.

For more introductory material on the Beatitudes see N.T.C. on Matthew, pp. 264-268.

A. 6:20-23 *Four Beatitudes*

20. Then he lifted up his eyes on his disciples and said:
Blessed (are) y o u poor,
for y o u r s is the kingdom of God.

Jesus looked meaningfully at his disciples. Who were these disciples? The word may indicate the wide circle of followers to which reference was made in verse 17. Even then, however, the words, "Blessed are y o u poor," were most suitable for The Twelve, whom the Master had chosen a little earlier this same day (verses 13-16), and who had given up everything to follow him (18:28).

Not that *the sermon* as a whole was meant only for Jesus' disciples. Verse 27 and the parable of The Two Builders (verses 47-49; cf. Matt. 7:24-27) show that this cannot have been true. Besides, the Woes of verses 24-26 were pronounced on the wicked, not on the followers of Jesus. But in the very nature of the case the *Beatitudes* suited the disciples, with implied warnings for everybody.

"Blessed (are) y o u poor" does not mean, "Blessed are all poor people," nor can it mean, "Blessed are y o u, my disciples, because y o u are poor in earthly goods." Physical poverty is not necessarily a blessing (Prov. 30:9b; Isa. 8:21). But Jesus was able to say, "Blessed (are) y o u poor," because, considered as a group, these men, poor with respect to earthly goods, had been made aware of their spiritual poverty and of their riches in God. See Ps. 40:17:

> Though I am poor and needy,
> The Lord thinks of me;
> My Help and my Deliverer art thou,
> O my God, delay not.

Thus interpreted, it is understandable that Jesus added, "for y o u r s is the kingdom of God." The sum total of blessings that result when God is acknowledged as King over heart and life belongs even now to the poor. This interpretation also brings Luke 6:20 in line with Matt. 5:3, "Blessed (are) the poor in spirit, for theirs is the kingdom of heaven."

21a. Blessed (are) y o u who now are hungry,
for y o u shall be fully satisfied.
In line with "Blessed (are) y o u poor," without the addition "in spirit," is Luke's Second Beatitude, "Blessed (are) y o u who now are hungry," without the addition "for righteousness" (as in Matt. 5:6). But here again what is expressed in Matthew is implied in Luke. In both cases the final reference is to spiritual hunger, hunger for righteousness.

In a parable reported only by Luke, that of *The Pharisee and The Tax-Collector*, Jesus has given us a touching illustration of this spiritual hunger. Note the words, "But the tax-collector, standing at a distance, did not even venture to lift up his eyes to heaven, but kept beating his breast, saying, 'O God, be merciful to me, the sinner' " (18:13). The hunger here meant is a yearning for mercy and forgiveness, for peace of mind and heart, purity and holiness, fellowship with God.

Full satisfaction is promised, as is the case also in the parable to which reference was made (see 18:14).

21b. Blessed (are) y o u who now weep,
for y o u shall laugh.
It is surely arbitrary to say, as is done by some, that Luke's third Beatitude has no equivalent in Matthew's Gospel. With most commentators[249] we see Luke's third reflected in Matthew's second. "Y o u who now weep" are "the mourners." And "for y o u shall laugh" has the same basic meaning as "for they shall be comforted."

The weeping to which reference is made here has its source in the tragedy of sin. It is not necessary, however, to limit this weeping to that

---

249. Including A. T. Robertson, *Word Pictures*, Vol. II, p. 88; R. C. H. Lenski, *op. cit.*, p. 222; S. M. Gilmour, *The Gospel According to St. Luke* (*The Interpreter's Bible*), New York, 1952, p. 118; F. Godet, *op. cit.*, Vol. I, p. 314.

which takes place because of a person's individual sins: those whereby he himself has grieved his God. That type of sorrow can be poignant indeed (Ps. 51:4). More, however, is undoubtedly included. The regenerated learn to love God to such an extent that they weep because of "all the deeds of ungodliness which the ungodly have committed in such an ungodly manner" (Jude 15). Their weeping is God-centered. They sigh and cry not only over their own sins, nor only over these plus the power of the wicked to oppress the righteous (Hab. 1:4; II Tim. 3:12), but over "all the abominations that are done in the midst of Jerusalem" (Ezek. 9:4). It grieves them that God, *their own* God whom they love, is being dishonored. Cf. Ps. 139:21. This type of grief "to the glory of God" is also strikingly expressed in Ps. 119:136, "Streams of water run down my eyes because *they* do not observe thy law." See also Ezra 10:6. In a most touching chapter Daniel, while weeping over and making confession of sin, combines his own personal sins and those of his people (Dan. 9:1-20; see especially verse 20). In doing so he pleads, "O Lord hear, O Lord forgive, O Lord hearken and do; defer not, for thine own sake, O my God, because thy city and thy people are called by thy name" (verse 19).

Nevertheless, these weepers, too, are pronounced "Blessed," the reason being, "for y o u shall laugh." The godly sorrow which now characterizes the devout listeners turns their souls to God. God, in turn, comforts them with the cheering news of his forgiving love. It is he who pardons, strengthens, delivers, reassures (Ps. 30:5; 50:15; Isa. 1:18; 55:6, 7; Mic. 7:18-20; Matt. 11:28-30). Thus tears, like raindrops, fall to the ground and come up in flowers (Ps. 126:5).

22, 23. Blessed are y o u when men hate y o u; when they exclude y o u, heap insults upon y o u, and spurn y o u r name as evil, on account of the Son of man.

Exult in that day and leap for joy,

for great, indeed, is y o u r reward in heaven; for in just the same way their fathers used to treat the prophets.

In a sense these words embody a prophecy. They describe what is going to happen to the followers of Jesus after his departure from this earth. However, it is not at all necessary to limit this description entirely to the future. Right at this very moment, while the Master is still with his disciples, this hatred is already manifesting itself. Otherwise how can we adequately account for such passages as Luke 6:27; cf. John 15:18, 19? Surely those who did not hesitate to address Jesus as follows, "Are we not correct in saying, You are a Samaritan and have a demon?" would not hesitate to show their hatred also to his disciples (John 15:20).

That this hatred implies exclusion, even expulsion from the synagogue, is clear from John 9:22, 34. Insults, too, were being, and were going to be, heaped upon believers (John 9:34). What was happening to the Savior (Matt. 27:29, 30, 39, 40 f.) would, in a sense, also befall his disciples (John 16:33; Acts 21:28; 24:5). Heaping scorn on a disciple's name, whether by

342

refusing to mention it at all, pronouncing it with disgust, slandering it, or expunging it from the synagogue membership roll, was another form of inflicting harm on the followers of the Man of Sorrows (Matt. 10:25; John 16:2; Acts 21:28; 24:5; 28:22). However, the very fact that these crimes were perpetrated "on account of the Son of man," that is, because of the disciples' connection with him and faith in him, guarantees the heavenly reward reserved for the Lord's loyal adherents (I Peter 4:13).

Let them therefore exult and leap for joy. Blessed, indeed, are they! Let them bear in mind that their reward is in proportion to, yet much greater than, their sacrifice (Rom. 8:18; II Cor. 4:17, 18). They, God's prophets, will receive a prophet's reward. Their very willingness to suffer on account of "the Son of man"—for this concept see on 5:24—proves that they are the true successors of the prophets. For the treatment the prophets received see N.T.C. on Matt. 5:11, 12, pp. 280–282.

B. 6:24–26 *Four Woes*

In each case the Beatitude and the Woe form a pair. For these corresponding or correlative pairs see p. 339. What holds with respect to the Beatitude is true also with respect to its complementary Woe: it comes as a surprise, for the thought expressed in it runs counter to worldly standards of evaluation. A worldly person believes that the poor man is to be pitied, the rich to be envied. Instead, Jesus says, "Blessed (are) y o u poor—Woe to y o u who are rich." And so throughout.

What is the nature of these Woes? There are those who maintain that they give expression to compassion, to nothing else. So interpreted, each Woe would have to be rendered "Alas!" or "Too bad!" Now it must be admitted that in the tenderly loving heart of the Master the element of sorrow with respect to the evaluations, words, and activities of unbelievers was real and strong. Cf. Ezek. 33:11; Matt. 23:37. Yet, this should not blind us to the equally important fact that what we have here, in both the Beatitude and the Woe, is *an authoritative declaration.* Just as for believers the Beatitudes are effective pronouncements of blessing, so also for impenitents the woes are effective pronouncements of the curse. The element of warning and threat must not be excluded from the Woe. It is exactly as Lenski observes, "'Woe' too is neither a wish nor a mere description, but the Lord's judgment, rendered now already."[250] See Ezek. 3:16–21; Matt. 23:38; also N.T.C. on Matthew, p. 826.

In each case, once the Beatitude is understood, the corresponding Woe follows so naturally that little need be said by way of further explanation.

24. But woe to y o u who are rich,
for y o u have already received y o u r consolation in full.

Jesus pronounces a Woe on the rich, that is, on those who trusted in riches (Mark 10:24). He does this because the attainment of earthly wealth,

---

250. *Op. cit.,* p. 225.

of whatever kind, was their sole ambition. It was their passionate, all-absorbing pursuit. Well, they had obtained what they were after. On a receipt they can write the words, "Received payment in full." That is their one and only "consolation." For their everlasting future they have provided . . . exactly nothing! They have nothing of real value to look forward to. See Luke 12:16–21; 16:25.

25a. Woe to y o u who now are well-fed,
for y o u shall go hungry.

On the threshold of eternity those who have placed their trust in earthly goods suddenly discover how desperately poor they are. Similarly, those who have set their hearts on earthly pleasures are going to discover in the end that they are stuffed so full that all desire is lost. Yet, having never shown any appreciation for the higher values of life, these gluttons, unless they are converted, face the never-ending future with a maddening ache that can never be assuaged, a burning thirst that can never be quenched, a ravening hunger that can never be alleviated.

25b. Woe (to y o u) who now are laughing,
for y o u shall mourn and weep.

The same holds too for those who now revel in silly merriment, while they reject God and his word and never weep about their sinful condition. In eternity their mourning will never cease. Their tears will never be wiped away.

26. Woe (to y o u) when all men speak well of y o u,
for in just the same way their fathers used to treat the false prophets.

What Jesus is saying amounts to this: "When everybody speaks well of y o u it must be that y o u are a deceitful, servile flatterer." Think of Absalom (II Sam. 15:2–6), who tried to ingratiate himself with everybody, but was insincere, seeking only his own honor and glory. He resembled a false prophet. To be sure, for a while these men basked in the favor of the crowds, the ancestors of those deceivers who were Christ's contemporaries.

The word of Jeremiah is ever applicable, "My people love to have it so." But this flattery is vacuous. When all men speak well of y o u there must be something wrong with y o u. Y o u are not taking a stand for the truth. Y o u are not being a blessing. And y o u are digging y o u r own grave.[251]

Practical Lessons Derived from Luke 6:20–26

Verses 20, 24

"Blessed (are) y o u poor. . . . But woe to y o u who are rich." Though Jesus never condemned wealth, he was aware of its dangers. If it makes people arrogant, self-centered, and cold-hearted, it becomes a curse. Prov. 30:7–9 should be taken to heart.

---

251. Notes on Greek words, phrases, and constructions in 6:20–26 begin on page 345.

Verse 22

"Blessed are y o u when men hate y o u . . . *on account of the Son of man.*" That final phrase must not be forgotten. If a person senses that he is unpopular, he should ask himself, "Is this because I am loyal to my Lord . . . or is it because I have failed to reveal a Christlike character?"

Verses 20–26

Verses 20–23, "Blessed"; Verses 24–26, "Woe." Some preachers are forever saying "Blessed." Others specialize in thundering "Woe." Jesus avoids both extremes. So should we. Cf. Isa. 3:10, 11.

Verse 26

"For in just the same way their fathers used to treat the false prophets." The study of history can be neglected only to a person's own hurt.

> Let children thus learn from history's light,
> To hope in our God and walk in his sight,
> The God of our fathers to fear and obey,
> And ne'er like their fathers to turn from his way.
>
> Lines from No. 149 (based on Ps. 78) of the
> *Psalter Hymnal* of the Christian Reformed Church
> (Centennial Edition), Grand Rapids, 1959.

Notes on Greek Words, Phrases, and Constructions in 6:20–26

Verse 20

ἐπάρας, nom. s. masc. aor. act. participle of ἐπαίρω, to lift up. The verb also has other, though related, meanings: to rise up, to raise (one's heel, voice, head). In the passive it is used in connection with Christ's ascension (Acts 1:9).

Verse 21

χορτασθήσεσθε, sec. per. pl. fut. passive indicat. of χορτάζω. This verb, though used at first with respect to the feeding and fattening of animals (there is an echo of this meaning in the clause: "all the birds *gorged themselves* with their flesh," Rev. 19:21), and applied to men chiefly by the Comic poets, was gradually losing its deprecatory sense and is here simply used as a synonym for *to have plenty, to be(come) fully satisfied.* Cf. Matt. 14:20; 15:33, 37; Mark 6:42; 7:27; 8:4, 8; Luke 9:17; 15:16; 16:21; John 6:26; Phil. 4:12; James 2:16.

γελάσετε, sec. per. pl. fut. indicat. of γελάω*, to laugh.

Verse 22

The four verbs which here have the meanings: to hate, exclude, revile (heap insults upon), and throw out (spurn), are all third per. pl. aor. subjunct. active forms.

The meaning of the basic form ὀνειδίζω is: to heap abuse or insults upon, rebuke, reproach, reprove, revile, chide, find fault with. See also the parallel (Matt. 27:44).

The meaning will become clear from the other New Testament passages in which this verb is used:

"Blessed are y o u whenever people heap insults upon y o u" (Matt. 5:11).

"Then he began to reproach the cities" (Matt. 11:20).

"And those crucified with him were also heaping insults on him" (Mark 15:32).

"He rebuked them for their lack of faith" (Mark 16:14).

"The reproaches of those approaching you fell upon me" (Rom. 15:3).

". . . who gives generously to all, without reproaching" (James 1:5).

"If y o u are reproached because of the name of Christ, blessed (are y o u)" (I Peter 4:14).

The suggested renderings are by no means the only good ones.

The root of the word seems to be *nid* (preceded by euphonic ὀ), but whether or not the Dutch word *nijdig* (angry), somewhat related in meaning, belongs to the same etymological family I do not know.

Verse 23

σκιρτήσατε, sec. per. pl. aor. imperat. of σκιρτάω. See also the note on 1:14 on page 80; and the note on 1:41, 44 on page 99.

Verse 24

ἀπέχετε, sec. per. pl. pres. indicat. active of ἀπέχω, to receive in full, so that one can hand out a receipt; so also in Matt. 6:2, 5, 16; and see N.T.C. on Phil. 4:18. Other related meanings: Mark 14:41, "It is enough"; Luke 7:6, "was (not far) from"; 15:20, "he was (still a long way) off"; and Philem. 15 "that you might have him back." In Acts 15:20, 29; I Thess. 4:3; 5:22; I Tim. 4:3; and I Peter 2:11 the sense is: to abstain from.

Verse 25

ἐμπεπλησμένοι, nom. pl. masc. perf. passive participle of ἐμπίπλημι, to fill, satisfy; in the passive, as here, to be well-fed, to have plenty to eat; in Rom. 15:24, to enjoy.

27 "But I say to y o u who are listening, love y o u r enemies, do good to those who hate y o u, 28 bless those who curse y o u, pray for those who mistreat y o u. 29 To the one who strikes you on the cheek offer also the other (cheek), and from the one who takes away your outer garment[252] do not withhold your undergarment.[253] 30 Give to everyone who asks you, and from the one who takes away what is yours do not exact reimbursement.[254] 31 And as y o u wish that men would do to y o u, so do to them.[255]

32 "If y o u are in the habit of loving those who love y o u, what credit is that to y o u? Why, even sinners[256] are in the habit of loving those who love them. 33 And if y o u are in the habit of doing good to those who do good to y o u,[257] what credit is that to y o u? Even sinners do

252. Or: cloak, coat, robe.

253. Or: tunic, shirt.

254. Or: do not ask that he give it back.

255. Or: And treat others as y o u would have them treat y o u.

256. I.e., notorious sinners, or those so regarded. So also in verses 33, 34.

257. Or: of treating those well who treat y o u well.

the same.   34 And if y o u lend to those from whom y o u are expecting to receive, what credit is that to y o u? Even sinners are in the habit of lending to sinners, that they may be repaid in full.

35 "But love y o u r enemies, and do good, and lend, without expecting to get anything back. Then y o u r reward will be great, and y o u will be sons of the Most High, because he is kind to the ungrateful and wicked.   36 Be merciful, just as y o u r Father is merciful.[258]

37 "Do not pass judgment (on others), and y o u will not have judgment passed on yourselves. Do not condemn, and y o u will not be condemned. Forgive, and y o u will be forgiven. 38 Give, and (gifts) will be given to y o u. A good measure, pressed down, shaken together, and running over will be poured into y o u r lap.[259] For in accordance with the measure with which y o u measure, it will be measured to y o u in return."[260]

6:27-45 II. *The Standard of Life Demanded by the King*
A. 6:27-38 *The Light of Love He Commends*
Cf. Matt. 5:38-48; 7:1, 2, 12a

That this entire section (verses 27-38) is really a unit is clear from the similarity in phraseology. Throughout, love for everybody, including even those who hate the listeners, is held up as the ideal to be cherished and cultivated. Note the following: "Love y o u r enemies, do good to those who hate y o u, bless those who curse y o u, pray for those who mistreat y o u; offer the other cheek; do not withhold; treat others as y o u would have them treat y o u; love y o u r enemies [again], and do good, and lend, without expecting anything back; be merciful, do not pass judgment, do not condemn; forgive, give."

Interspersed between these exhortations is the observation that anything less than this type of conduct is unworthy of a follower of Jesus: "If y o u are in the habit of loving those who love y o u, what credit is that to y o u?" etc. Not until verse 39 is reached does the style change and does a logically conceived new section begin: "He also told them this parable," etc.[261]

The Beatitudes and Woes have ended. The listeners are now told what kind of life they must live in order to prove that they have taken to heart the warnings implied in the Woes, and have a right, by grace, to claim the Blessings for themselves.

27, 28. But I say to y o u who are listening, love y o u r enemies, do good to those who hate y o u, bless those who curse y o u, pray for those who mistreat y o u.

"Love y o u r enemies" was not what the scribes were teaching the people. They were saying, "Love your neighbor and hate your enemy"

---

258. In both cases "compassionate" can be substituted for "merciful."

259. Or: into the fold of y o u r garment.

260. Or: For with the measure y o u use, it will be measured back to y o u.

261. See p. 337 for a summary of Luke's report of The Sermon on the Mount. In general, this is also the division favored by S. Greijdanus, *Korte Verklaring,* p. 161, and approaches that found in Lenski, *op. cit.,* p. 218. Accordingly, I depart here from the division into sections followed by Grk. N.T. (A-B-M-W) for 6:27-45.

(Matt. 5:43). By means of this addition—"and hate your enemy"—the emphasis was shifted away from the real intention of the law. The law placed all the emphasis on *love* over against *vengeance*. Note Lev. 19:18, "You shall not take vengeance, nor bear any grudge against the children of your people; you shall love your neighbor as yourself; I am Jehovah." The rabbinic misinterpretation soft-pedaled the word *love* and underscored "the children of your people," as if the meaning were, "the others you are allowed to hate to your heart's content." Human nature being what it is, it was but too easy for people who were chafing under the galling yoke of a foreign oppressor to yield to their malignant impulses. Thus a wall of separation was being built between Jew and Gentile; the former to be loved, the latter to be hated. But it was hard to stop here. Another barricade was erected between *good* Israelites, such as the scribes and Pharisees, and *bad* Israelites, such as those renegades, the publicans, and in general the entire rabble that did not know the law (John 7:49). In such an atmosphere it was impossible for hatred to starve. It had plenty to feed on.

It was in the midst of this intensely narrow-minded, exclusivistic, and intolerant environment that Jesus carried on his ministry. All around him were those walls and fences. He came for the very purpose of bursting those barriers, so that love—pure, warm, divine, infinite—would be able to flow straight down from the heart of God, hence from his own marvelous heart, into the hearts of men. His love overleaped all the boundaries of race, nationality, party, age, sex, etc.

When he said, "Love y o u r enemies," he must have startled his audience, for he was saying something that probably never before had been said so succinctly, positively, and forcefully. Thorough research of all the relevant sources resulted in the statement: "The conclusion remains that the first one who has taught mankind to see *the neighbor* in every human being, and therefore to encounter every human being in love was Jesus; see the parable of The Good (literally, the Compassionate) Samaritan."[262] Without in any way denying that statement one might add, Jesus taught the people that one should not even ask, "And who is my neighbor?" but should prove himself neighbor to the man in need, whoever that might be (see Luke 10:36).

Although in the form here expressed ("Love y o u r enemies") Christ's teaching was new, it did not contradict the law. Rather, it was the fruition of the seed planted earlier. As has been shown, the Old Testament forbade revenge. But it even went beyond that, teaching that whenever necessary one should render assistance to his enemy:

"If you happen upon your enemy's stray ox or donkey, you must bring it back to him. If you see the donkey of one who hates you lying (helpless) under its pack, you must refrain from leaving him with it. You must help him to lift it up" (Exod. 23:4, 5).

---

262. S.BK., Vol. I, p. 354.

From "Assist your enemy" to "Love him" was but a step. Jesus took that step. He added, "Do good to those who hate y o u." In other words, "Y o u r favorable disposition of heart and mind must reveal itself in deeds." The Master did not demand of his listeners that they approve of the evil perpetrated by their opponents. Neither did he reject the administration of law and justice (Matt. 5:25; Luke 20:25). What was wicked must be branded as such. But there must be no spirit of revenge; rather, the very opposite: the answer to a deed of cruelty must be a deed of kindness!

The exhortation, in fact, builds up to a climax: not only must there be love in the heart, love even for "enemies," plus, in general, good treatment, but even more specifically, "Bless those who curse y o u, pray for those who mistreat y o u," meaning at least this, "In all sincerity ask the Lord to bless those who curse y o u; be sure to show kindness to them and to intercede for them at the throne of grace."

Even more strikingly Jesus adds, **29a. To the one who strikes you on the cheek offer also the other (cheek).** What did he mean? That his words were not intended to be taken literally follows from his own reaction when he was struck in the face (John 18:22, 23). In fact, those who insist on interpreting every saying of Jesus literally get into difficulty again and again (Matt. 16:6–12; John 2:18–21; 3:3–5; 4:10–14; 6:51–58; 11:11–14).

What, then, did Jesus mean? When his words are read in the light of what immediately precedes in verses 27, 28, and when Matthew's parallel (5:39 f.) is read in the light of what follows in verses 43–48, it becomes clear that the key passage, identical in both Gospels, is, "Love y o u r enemies" (Matt. 5:44; Luke 6:27). In other words, Jesus condemns the spirit of lovelessness, hatred, yearning for revenge. He is saying, "Do not resist the evildoer with measures that arise from an unloving, unforgiving, unrelenting, vindictive disposition." Once this is understood it becomes clear that "turning the other cheek" means to show in attitude, word, and deed that one is not filled with the spirit of rancor but with the spirit of love. Rom. 12:19–21 presents an excellent commentary.

Jesus continues: **29b. . . . and from the one who takes away your outer garment do not withhold your undergarment.** Instead of being filled with bitterness and the lust for retaliation, show the very opposite attitude. Let him who deprives you of your robe take your tunic (worn next to the skin) also; and conversely (with Matt. 5:40), if anyone wishes to go to law with you and take your tunic (or shirt), let him take your robe also. Here again Rom. 12:19–21 shows what is meant.

30. Give to everyone who asks you, and from the one who takes away what is yours do not exact reimbursement.

The sentence has two parts. With respect to the first there is rather general agreement in interpretation. The "asking" or request is probably borne of poverty. Such interpretative passages as Deut. 15:7, 8; Ps. 37:26; Prov. 19:17; 21:26b come to mind immediately.

But how must we explain the second part? It is surprising how many commentators skip the problem one faces. Among those who have addressed themselves to it there is a division of opinion. According to some the person who "asks you" for a gift is also "the one who takes away what is yours." The petitioner and the taker are the same person. The meaning of the entire verse would then be: in cases of privation love demands that whatever is needed be freely given, without expecting any return.[263]

This interpretation may seem to have in its favor that the principle here expressed gains immediate assent. Who would not agree that a person who, through no fault of his, is too poor to make a return should be excused from doing so? On the other hand, the very naturalness of the interpretation may, in fact, make it less acceptable, since it is a known fact that The Sermon on the Mount is full of surprising—sometimes even shocking—statements.

According to the more widely accepted view, the *asker* of the first clause and the *taker* of the second clause are not the same person.[264]

I believe that this is the correct view and that the first interpretation is wrong, and this for the following reasons:

a. The one who has received a gift from you can hardly be described as taking away what still is yours.

b. In the original the phrase *from the one who takes away* occurs twice in that exact form, a fact obscured by most English translations. It is found first in verse 29b, then in verse 30. In verse 29b the reference is clearly to a forceful, unjust taking away. It is logical to believe that also in the immediately following verse the meaning is the same.

By accepting this interpretation have we not made matters more difficult for ourselves? Was Jesus really saying, then, that under no circumstances whatever should anyone ever make any effort to regain stolen property?

To answer this question it is necessary to re-emphasize that the sermon is full of startling statements, pronouncements which should not be interpreted in their strictly literal sense as being applicable to every situation in life. So, for example, the exhortation "Do not take any oath at all" (Matt. 5:34) cannot mean that in the entire realm of human relations there is never any room for the solemn invocation of the name of God in substantiation of an important affirmation or promise. For similar startling statements see Matt. 5:39, 40; 7:1; 23:3; Luke 6:29a, 37a. It is characteristic of Hebrew style that a startling statement is made in order to shake people, to arouse them from their lethargy. At times one startling statement seems to be a flat contradiction of another equally surprising one (cf. Prov. 26:5 with the immediately preceding verse). There is no real conflict, however. Each statement emphasizes one aspect of the total truth.

263. This interpretation is perhaps best represented by S. Greijdanus, *Korte Verklaring*, pp. 165, 166. He states, "Here naturally the reference is to a request borne of want or need, and an inability, due to poverty, to return what was given."

264. That is the position of the following, among others: A. Stöger, *Das Evangelium nach Lukas*, Eng. tr. *The Gospel According to St. Luke*, Dublin, 1969, Vol. I, p. 119; A. B. Bruce, *op. cit.*, Vol. I, p. 506; R. C. H. Lenski, *op. cit.*, p. 231; F. Godet, *op. cit.*, Vol. I, p. 323.

So it is also here in Luke 6:30b. That there are times when a person should stand up for his rights is clearly taught in such passages as John 18:22, 23; Acts 16:37-40. That the functioning of lawcourts is not infringed upon has been shown. What the present passage teaches is the very important truth that our personal attitude should never be one of taking revenge. In fact, at times the better course may well be to allow the thief to keep the stolen goods. We should be willing, if circumstances so demand, to forego our rights. In this connection read I Cor. 6:7; also study the example Jesus gave us, described so vividly in I Peter 2:21-24. Our disposition should ever be that of returning good for evil. So here, as in the case of Luke 6:29a and 29b, Rom. 12:19-21 offers the true explanation.

In order that a person may know at any moment how to conduct himself toward someone else, whether that other individual be man or woman, Jew or Gentile, bond or free, etc., Jesus now lays down a principle which, as it consists of measuring one's duty by one's self-love, is like a pocketknife or carpenter's rule, always immediately at hand, ready to be used. That principle is: **31. And as y o u wish that men would do to y o u, so do to them,** or rendered differently but expressing the same thought: **Treat others as y o u would have them treat y o u.**

In its negative form this principle is expressed in Tob. 4:15, "What you yourself hate do not do to anyone else." The great Jewish teacher Hillel stated similarly, "What is hateful to you, do not do to your neighbor." In one form or another the rule also appears in the writings of Plato, Aristotle, Isocrates, Seneca, etc.

There are those who contend that the difference between Christ's rule and that of others, for example, the one laid down by Confucius, consists in this, that the latter rule is merely negative, while Christ's rule is positive. Confucius said, "Do nothing to your neighbor which afterward you would not have your neighbor do to you" (*Mahabharata* XIII.5571). As I see it, however, the difference on this score has been exaggerated. To be sure, when the worst possible interpretation is given to the negative rule, as if it meant no more than, "Do not kill your neighbor and do not steal his marriage partner or his property, for you would not like to have him do this to you either; so, leave your neighbor strictly alone," then it must be admitted that in its positive form the rule is far better. However, even in its negative form this rule can be interpreted far more favorably. It can also mean, "Do not treat your neighbor with anything less than genuine love." Thus construed, the negative implies the positive. And must we not in fairness to Confucius grant that he had at least something of this positive implication in mind? Are not his words that were quoted preceded by the line, "This is the sum of all true righteousness. Treat others as you would yourself be treated"? That surely is positive.

Besides, is not the kernel of the Golden Rule already found in Lev. 19:18, "You shall love your neighbor as yourself"? This surely is a positive command, especially when the word *neighbor* is interpreted as infallibly as it is in Luke 10:25-37.

Similarly, Jesus teaches that the law with its *negative* commandments ("You shall not kill; you shall not commit adultery," etc.) is fulfilled in obedience to the *positive* rule, "You shall love your neighbor as yourself" (Matt. 5:21 ff.; 19:19; 22:39). Rom. 13:9 is conclusive on this point, "For this, 'You shall not commit adultery, You shall not kill, You shall not steal, You shall not covet,' and if (there be) any other commandment, is summed up in this one rule, 'You shall love your neighbor as yourself.'" Now it is true that in Christ's teaching the emphasis on love for the neighbor, not merely kind treatment, a love, moreover, that is bestowed even upon the enemy, receives greater stress than it does outside of Christianity. But it will not do to declare that a rule expressed negatively is, because of that very fact, necessarily inferior to one stated positively.

Nevertheless, there are important differences between Christ's truly Golden Rule and somewhat similar rules that have come to us from the non-Christian religions or are favored by religious liberals. These differences are as follows:

1. The non-Christian religious prophet views his rule as a requirement which man is able to fulfil in his own strength, or at best in the strength of someone or something other than the true God, who revealed himself in Jesus Christ. The Gospel of Luke emphatically denies that man by nature has this ability. He needs the Holy Spirit and the Father's drawing power (1:15; 11:13; 12:12; cf. John 6:44; Rom. 7:18, 24; Phil. 2:12, 13; II Thess. 2:13).

2. The religious liberal has a tendency to separate the rule of love for *man* from the commandment of love for *God*. He generally minimizes the latter's importance. According to his view the Golden Rule is the sum and substance of all ethics. The one important thing in life, as he sees it, is rendering service to fellow men. It is in support of this contention that an appeal is made to Christ's Golden Rule. But such an appeal is unjustified. According to the teaching of Jesus love for God and love for one's fellow man cannot be separated (Luke 10:25-28).

It should be noted that the Golden Rule does not read, "Treat others as they treat you," but "Treat others as y o u would have them treat y o u." Jesus wants his followers to be distinctive. This very thought receives added emphasis in

verses **32-34. If y o u are in the habit of loving those who love y o u, what credit is that to y o u? Why, even sinners are in the habit of loving those who love them. And if y o u are in the habit of doing good to those who do good to y o u, what credit is that to y o u? Even sinners do the same. And if y o u lend to those from whom y o u are expecting to receive, what credit is that to y o u? Even sinners are in the habit of lending to sinners, that they may be repaid in full.**

Sinners! They were "the irreligious," those who had no regard for God's law (cf. Ps. 1:1, 5); for example, the heathen (Matt. 26:45) and even those Israelites who, in the judgment of strict Jews, were guilty of reprehensible conduct. Undoubtedly some of these despised people were actually wicked. Prostitutes were generally regarded as "sinners." So were also "tax-collectors." On the other hand, the uncomplimentary term was even applied to those who lived in disregard of Pharisaic ceremonial prescriptions (Matt. 9:10, 11; Mark 2:15 f.; Luke 5:30). "Respectable" people did not want to be regarded as "sinners."

In the present little paragraph, consisting of just three verses, the term *sinners* is used three times, once in each verse. What Jesus is saying is that listeners who love merely those who love them, who do good only to those who do good to them, and who make only "safe" loans (such as they know will be returned, probably with interest), are not any better than the very "sinners" they are always looking down upon, for even those at the bottom of the social-religious scale love their own kind, do good to them, and lend to them, in the firm expectation that at some future time they, the givers and lenders, will be the recipients.

Accordingly, if those people who are now listening to this sermon do not rise above such self-centered ethics, they cannot expect God's special favor to rest on them. They are in a class with the very "riffraff" they so despise.

Over against the practices Jesus condemns he now places the very opposite, again mentioning the very same items to which he has just referred, and listing them in the same order, namely, loving, doing good, lending!

35. But love y o u r enemies, and do good, and lend,[265] **without expecting to get anything back.** In substance the exhortation of verse 27 is repeated here, and the admonition clearly implied in verse 34—that one should lend for the sheer joy of helping the person in need and not for any selfish reason—is here reaffirmed.

The admonition is striking, especially for the following reasons:

a. By nature a person does not love his "enemies," that is, those who hate him.

b. Many of those who were told to love, to do good, and *to lend* were poor (verse 20).

c. An earnest attempt to love enemies and even to do good to them might be regarded as possible, but even *to lend* to them when they are in need! Yet, this is what Jesus is urging.[266]

d. The addition "without expecting to get anything back" (cf. verse 30) makes this exhortation even more startling. For more on this addition see the note on this verse on page 359.

---

265. Meaning: But be in the habit of loving . . . and doing good and lending, etc.

266. Lenski (*op. cit.*, p. 235) disagrees, "for," says he, "enemies would not borrow from us." Yet both the immediate context ("Love y o u r enemies") and the similar passage (verse 27) support the conclusion that the entire closely connected series of commands (love, do good, lend) has as its object "y o u r enemies." Some even favor the translation, "But love y o u r enemies, do good to them, and lend to them." Whether this phrase *to them* should be inserted is a minor point. It is certainly implied, though strict adherence to the original favors its omission in the *translation*.

A great reward is promised to those who obey this command: **Then y o u r reward will be great....**

Jesus refers, of course, to the reward of grace, not to any wage won by human merit. The reward is in proportion to, yet always far greater than, the sacrifice (Rom. 8:18; II Cor. 4:17, 18). In this present life it consists of such things as the inner satisfaction of having been able to help others, hence rejoicing in their joy (Rom. 12:15), "the peace of God" and "the God of peace" within the heart (Phil. 4:7, 9). After this life there is the sum total of all the blessings of salvation throughout eternity (Matt. 16:27; 25:46). Of this God's children have a foretaste even now. In particular, there is the public acknowledgment by Jesus Christ himself at his glorious return (Matt. 25:34 f.).

What may well be the most glorious description of the reward is this: **and y o u will be sons of the Most High....** Not that unselfish love *makes* them sons, but it *proves* that they are sons. They are God's image bearers. For the transformation into that image see II Cor. 3:18; cf. I John 3:2. Note also the close relation between Christ, "the Son of the Most High" (Luke 1:32), and these "sons of the Most High." For the term *the Most High* see on 1:32.

Resemblance to God—always in a finite manner, as creatures; he alone, the Creator-Redeemer, is the Infinite—is demonstrated by the kindness, the active sympathy and helpfulness which the true followers of Jesus show even to those who are their enemies, that is, who hate them. In doing this the children of God reveal God's image, **because he is kind to the ungrateful and wicked.**

The ungrateful are those who do not from the heart thank God for the blessings he bestows on them. They are the "wicked," the "evil" ones. They fail to complete the circle; that is, when blessings drop down from heaven upon them, they do not make any return in the form of humble praises rising from earth to heaven.

A vivid illustration is provided by Luke 17:11-19. Ten lepers are cleansed, but only one responds by returning and glorifying God. Does this not prove that though there is what has been called "common grace" (see also Ps. 36:7; 145:9, 17; Acts 14:17; 17:25; I Tim. 4:10), there is no "common gratitude"?

What was definitely stated in verses 27–31, 35, and was implied in verses 32–34, is now summarized: **36. Be merciful, just as y o u r Father is merciful.** To be merciful means to be compassionate; that is, filled with the kind of sympathy that expresses itself in words and deeds. It is the concern the Father revealed when he sent—gave, *spared not*—his only-begotten Son to save us (John 3:16; Rom. 5:8; 8:32).

As we have already observed, *in a sense* even the ungrateful and wicked are the object of God's kindness (Luke 6:35). When Jesus walked on earth his heart went out to the throngs in their fatigued, forlorn condition (Matt. 9:36). He felt deeply for them and was eager to help them. See also Luke 7:13; cf. Matt. 8:17; 14:14; 15:32; 18:27; 20:34; Mark 1:41; 5:19; 6:34. It is comforting to realize that by means of this strong but deeply tender love, as well as by means of everything else, Jesus pictured the Father, so that he was able to say, "He who has seen me has seen the Father" (John 14:9).

When Jesus says, "Be merciful, just as y o u r Father is merciful," he is telling his audience to imitate the Father. Note how often Jesus, the apostles, etc., emphasized the oft neglected truth that men should strive to be imitators of God, of Christ, of God in Christ. In addition to Luke 6:35 and the somewhat similar Matt. 5:48 (see N.T.C. on that passage) see also Matt. 11:29; 16:24; John 13:15, 34; 15:12; Rom. 15:2, 3, 5, 7; I Cor. 11:1; II Cor. 8:7–9; 10:1; Eph. 4:32—5:2; 5:25; Phil. 2:3–8; Col. 3:13; Heb. 3:1 f.; 12:2; I Peter 2:21–24; I John 3:16; 4:10, 11. Of course, it takes special grace to obey this command. But the responsibility rests on all men.

Note "y o u r Father." When Jesus himself directly addresses the One who sent him, he says, "Father" (Luke 10:21, 22; 22:42; 23:34, 46) or "my Father" (Luke 2:49; 22:29; 24:49), showing that he was and is deeply conscious of his own unique relation to the Father, his own singular sonship.

In line with the command to be merciful is the tripartite exhortation, "Do not pass judgment... do not condemn... forgive," which now follows, beginning with **37. Do not pass judgment (on others)....**

Just what did the Lord mean when he said, "Do not pass judgment," or, as others prefer to translate, "Judge not"? Did he mean that all manner of judging is absolutely and without any qualification forbidden, so that with respect to the neighbor we are not allowed to form or express any opinion whatever, or at least that with respect to him we must never voice an adverse or unfavorable opinion? In the light of what Jesus himself says in this very chapter (verses 42, 45), where he implies that we must regard certain individuals as being hypocrites and evil, and of John 7:24; cf. I Cor. 5:12; 6:1–5; Gal. 1:8, 9; Phil. 3:2; I Thess. 2:14, 15; I Tim. 1:6, 7; Titus 3:2, 10; I John 4:1; II John 10; III John 9, and a good many other passages that could be added, it is clear that no such wholesale condemnation of forming an opinion about a person and expressing it can have been intended.

Jesus himself had arrived at certain conclusions regarding scribes and Pharisees, and he did not hesitate to express them (Luke 11:42–44; 20:46, 47). Though it is true that we, on our part, cannot read what is in our neighbor's heart, as Jesus was able to do (John 2:24, 25), so that *our* judgment must be more reserved and can never be final, there is nothing in the teaching either of Christ himself or of the apostles after him that relieves us of the obligation to form opinions about people and to act upon the basis of these opinions; this also implies that at times it will be our duty to express our judgments. Luke 6:37 has been used at times as an excuse for laxity in exercising church discipline, but in the light of its context, and also of Matt. 18:15–18 and John 20:23, such use of this passage is without any justification.

What, then, does Jesus mean? He means (see verses 41, 42) that it is wrong for anyone to concentrate his attention on the speck in his brother's eye and, while thus occupied, to ignore the beam in his own eye. The Lord is here condemning the spirit of censoriousness, judging harshly, self-righteously, without mercy, without love, as also the context (verses 35, 36) clearly indicates.

To be discriminating and critical is necessary; to be hypercritical is wrong. One should avoid saying what is untrue (Exod. 23:1), unnecessary (Prov. 11:13), and unkind (Prov. 18:8).

That the sin here condemned was very common is clear, for example, from the fact that David condemned to death the rich man who, so the king had been made to believe, had stolen and killed the poor man's little ewe lamb, not realizing that in thus condemning him he (David) was passing sentence on himself (II Sam. 12:1-7)!

This inclination to discover and severely condemn the faults, real or imaginary, of others, while passing lightly over one's own frequently even more lamentable violations of God's holy law, was common among the Jews (Rom. 2:1 f.), especially among the Pharisees (Luke 18:9; John 7:49), and is common always and everywhere. According to the words of Jesus here in Luke 6:37 . . . **and y o u will not have judgment passed on yourselves,** the habitual self-righteous faultfinder must remember that he himself can expect to be adversely criticized and condemned, and this not only by men but also and especially by God. See Matt. 6:14, 15; 18:23-35.

What Jesus forbids is brought out even more clearly by the explanatory addition: **Do not condemn, and y o u will not be condemned.**

The opposite of condemning is forgiving: **Forgive, and y o u will be forgiven.** On this see also Luke 11:4. The admonition is in line with Matt. 6:12, 14, 15; 18:21-35. As these passages indicate, the command is absolute. Neither here nor in Matthew are there any softening restrictions or qualifications ("Forgive unless . . ."; or "forgive if . . ."). The object of the ordered forgiveness is "men," not just "believers." And in order to receive the divine pardon it is necessary for a person to have within him, by God's grace, the disposition to forgive, a disposition that blossoms into action. "Do not pass judgment . . . do not condemn . . . forgive," an impressive climax!

The full climax has even now not been reached, however. We are told to go beyond forgiving wrongs; we should also bestow gifts, and this generously:

38. Give, and (gifts) will be given to y o u. A good measure, pressed down, shaken together, and running over will be poured into y o u r lap.

The underlying symbolism is that of the Near East grain market. But similar conditions are found all over the world. Anyone who has had anything to do with the sale of grains, fruits, or vegetables knows that a bushel loosely filled contains far less produce than one in which the grain or other agricultural products have been pressed down, shaken together, and added to until they run over the edge of the container.

The promise here given is that the person who gives generously will also receive back generously. The return gift or reward is pictured as being poured into his "lap," really into the pocket that is formed by his garment as it drops from the chest over the belt. Since one of the meanings of the English word *lap* is a garment's fold that serves as a repository, the rendering "into y o u r lap" is correct. That such a "pocket" could hold a considerable quantity of grain is clear from Ruth 3:15.[267]

The general principle with respect to rewards or returns is now stated: **For in accordance with the measure with which y o u measure, it will be measured to y o u in return.** For the same basic idea see II Cor. 9:6, "He who sows sparingly will also reap sparingly; and he who sows generously will also reap generously."

Examples of stingy giving—in some cases even complete refusal to do justice to the obligations one owes to God and/or to the other person—plus the sad results: Lot (Gen. 13:10, 11; 14:11, 12); Nabal (I Sam. 25:10, 11, 37, 38); the Israelites in the days of Haggai (Hag. 1:6, 9); and of Malachi (Mal. 1:6–8); the rich in the days of James (James 5:1–5). Examples of generous giving, plus reward: Abraham (Gen. 13:7–9; 15:1, 18–21; 17:1–8); Judah (Gen. 44:18–34; 49:8–10); Ruth (Ruth 1:16, 17; 4:13–22); Hannah (I Sam. 1:11, 19, 20; 3:19); David (II Sam. 7:1–3, 8–17); the woman of Shunem (II Kings 4:8–10, 36, 37; 8:1–6); Ebed-melech (Jer. 38:7–13; 39:15–18); Mary of Bethany (John 12:1–3; Matt. 26:6, 7, 10–13); The Twelve (Matt. 19:27–30); the apostle Paul (Phil. 3:7; II Tim. 4:8).[268]

Practical Lessons Derived from Luke 6:27–38

Verse 27

"Love y o u r enemies." Jesus did not say, *"Like* them, " but *"Love* them." One loves a person when he tries earnestly to promote that person's welfare.

Verse 29

"Offer also the other cheek." Cf. Rom. 12:21, "Overcome evil with good." This is the spirit of Acts 7:60; especially of Luke 23:34. To put this into practice requires (a) constant and diligent study of the example of Jesus as portrayed in the Gospels, (b) self-denial, and above all (c) prayer for the enabling grace of God.

Verse 31

"Treat others as you would have them treat you." This implies that one should always be strict with himself, lenient with the neighbor; for that is exactly the rule one wants the neighbor to obey.

Verse 34

"And if y o u lend to those from whom y o u are expecting to receive, what credit is that to y o u?" Here the basic assumption is, of course, that the person to whom

---

267. For other applications of the underlying figure see Ps. 79:12; Isa. 65:7; and Mark 4:24.
268. Notes on Greek words, phrases, and constructions in 6:27–38 begin on page 358.

one lends *is in need.* In no way does the passage forbid the practice of depositing money in a bank, with expectation of earning interest on it. See Matt. 25:27.

Verse 38

The reward is described as "a good measure, pressed down, shaken together, and running over." This is understandable when it is borne in mind that, in the final analysis, it is not man but God who recompenses. And God is far richer than man!

Notes on Greek Words, Phrases, and Constructions in 6:27-38

Verses 27-29

The imperatives *love, do good, bless, pray* (for), and *offer* are all second per. pl. presents; hence, "Continue to love," etc.

ἐπηρεαζόντων, gen. pl. masc. present participle of ἐπηρεάζω, to mistreat, abuse, speak maliciously (about); in the New Testament only here and in I Peter 3:16.

The basic meaning of σιαγών is jaw, jawbone (LXX Judg. 15:14-17). Nevertheless, the rendering "cheek" here in Luke 6:29 is not wrong. See LXX Isa. 50:6; also M.M., pp. 573, 574.

μὴ κωλύσῃς, sec. per. s. aor. subjunct. in a prohibition forbidding the action, viewed as a simple event; literally: "do not hinder [or stop] him (from taking). . . ."

Verse 30

Note present imperatives: continue to give; be in the habit of not asking him to return what he has taken away from you.

Verse 31

The two forms of the verb ποιέω are third per. pl. pres. (durative) subjunctive and sec. per. pl. active imperative.

Verse 32

Note the three forms of the verb ἀγαπάω: (a) sec. per. pl. pres. (durative) active indicat.; (b) pres. act. participle, pl. acc. (twice); and (c) third per. pl. pres. indicat. act. See also N.T.C. on John, Vol. II, pp. 494-500. For χάρις see the note on 2:40 on pages 181, 182.

Verse 33

ἐὰν ἀγαθοποιῆτε, sec. per. pl. pres. subjunct. (durative) in a future more vivid (third class) conditional sentence.

Verse 34

δανίσητε, sec. per. pl. aor. act. subjunct. of δανίζω, to lend, in a fut. more vivid (third class) conditional sentence. Matt. 5:42 uses the middle of this verb: "from him who wants *to borrow*," etc.

ἀπολάβωσιν, third per. pl. 2nd aor. active subjunctive of ἀπολαμβάνω, to receive in return, to get back, be repaid in full.

Verse 35

The expression μηδὲν ἀπελπίζοντες has been interpreted to mean "not without hope" or "not despairing" of getting back what y o u have loaned. See A. T. Robertson, *Translation,* pp. 44, 170. So interpreted, Jesus would here be recommending what he has censured just a moment ago (see verse 34). The real meaning must be, "without expecting to get anything back." It is a known fact that from the time of Chrysostom the expression has been so interpreted.

Verse 36

Γίνεσθε οἰκτίρμονες, second per. pl. durative or linear pres. imperative of γίνομαι, plus nom. pl. masc. adj.; hence, "Be and continue to be merciful [or: compassionate]." Cf. James 5:11.

Verse 37

κρίνετε, sec. per. pl. pres. act. imperative of κρίνω, "Do not continue to pass judgment (on others)." From the same verb is κριθῆτε (here preceded by οὐ μή). This form is sec. per. pl. 1st aor. pass. subjunct. Cf. *critic, criticism,* etc. Preceded by another double negative is καταδικασθῆτε "(Do not condemn and) y o u will not be condemned," that is, judgment will not be passed against (κατά) y o u, another sec. per. pl. 1st aor. pass. subjunctive. Though καταδικασθῆτε (aor. pass. subjunct.) is not actually an indicative, it does have *the force* of an emphatic fut. indicative (see Gram. N.T., p. 929).

ἀπολύετε, sec. per. pl. pres. act. imperat.; and ἀπολυθήσεσθε, sec. per. pl. fut. pass. indicat. of ἀπολύω, here used in the sense of *to pardon, to forgive.* For more on this verb see the note on 2:29 on page 176.

Verse 38

The verb δίδωμι, of which three forms appear in this one verse—(a) δίδοτε, sec. per. pl. pres. act. imperat.; (b) δοθήσεται, third per. s. fut. indicat. pass.; and (c) δώσουσιν, third per. pl. fut. indicat. act.—has many different meanings. In each case the correct translation into English depends on the context; that is, on *the thing* that is given. Examples: give, give up, give out, render, put, place, pour, pay, entrust. Instead of "they will pour into y o u r lap," the passive construction can be substituted: ". . . will be poured into y o u r lap."

Note the four modifiers of the word *measure:* good, pressed down, shaken together, running over; the first of these is an adjective; the second and third, perfect passive participles; the fourth, a present middle participle. Note particularly the last modifier, ὑπερεκχυννόμενον, with double prefix. The basic verb is ὑπερεκχύν-νομαι*. The return gift is represented as being so liberal that it is flowing *over* and *out of* its container.

In ἀντιμετρηθήσεται, third per. s. fut. indicat. pass. of ἀντιμετρέω, the prefix ἀντί has the meaning "in return." See my dissertation, *The Meaning of the Preposition ἀντί in the New Testament,* p. 81.

39 He also told them this parable: "A blind man cannot lead a blind man, can he? Will they not both fall into a pit? 40 A pupil does not outrank his teacher, but everyone who is fully trained will be like his teacher. 41 And why do you gaze at the speck in your brother's eye, while the beam that is in your own eye you do not (even) observe? 42 How can you say to your brother, 'Brother, let me take out the speck that is in your eye,' while you yourself do not (even) see the beam that is in your own eye? You hypocrite, first take the beam out of your own eye, and then you will see clearly (enough) to take the speck out of your brother's eye.

43 "For there is no healthy[269] tree that bears sickly[270] fruit; nor, on the other hand, does a sickly tree bear healthy fruit. 44 For every tree is known by its own fruit. Figs are not gathered from thorn-bushes, nor is a cluster of grapes picked from a bramble-bush. 45 The good man out of the good treasure stored in his heart produces what is good, and the evil man out of his evil storehouse produces what is evil. For out of the abundance of the heart his mouth speaks."

B. 6:39–45 *The Darkness of Sin He Condemns*
With 6:39 cf. Matt. 15:14
With 6:40 cf. Matt. 10:24
With 6:41, 42 cf. Matt. 7:3–5
With 6:43, 44 cf. Matt. 7:16–20
With 6:45 cf. Matt. 12:33–35

As Luke reports Christ's sermon, Jesus has been speaking about the light of love, love even for enemies, shining brightly in the hearts and lives of his followers. With this light of love the Master now contrasts the darkness of sin: self-delusion, a beam in the eye. Jesus closes the paragraph by picturing the good man producing what is good over against the wicked man producing what is wicked.

For the fact that these sayings are found also in Matthew (with variations) there are at least two reasons: (a) Luke 6:41–44 is part of The Sermon on the Mount, which is summarized also in Matthew (chapters 5–7); and (b) the few remaining sayings, those found in Luke 6:39, 40, 45, may very well have been used by Jesus on different occasions, and not always necessarily with identical application (see below, footnote 271).

39. He also told them this parable: A blind man cannot lead a blind man, can he? Will they not both fall into a pit?

Jesus makes a transition to a new subject. At first there may seem to be no connection at all with the preceding. Nevertheless there may well be one. The Master has been saying, "Blessed are y o u poor.... Woe to y o u who are rich.... Love y o u r enemies... lend without expecting to get anything back." All this was strange, startling, yet also thought-provoking. It was nourishing food for the soul. It contrasted sharply with the sickly, warmed-up stew that was being constantly ladled to them by their scribes. See Matt. 7:28; Mark 1:22. The people could not help noticing the dif-

269. Or: good (twice in this passage).
270. Or: bad (twice in this passage).

ference. So Jesus now explains this contrast: these scribes are blind. They cannot shed light because, to a considerable extent, they do not honor the light. They resemble a blind guide who is trying to lead a blind man, with the result that both fall into a pit.

In parabolic language Jesus asks, "A blind man cannot lead a blind man, can he?" The expected answer is, "No, indeed!" The next question is, "Will they not both fall into a pit?" The only logical answer is, "Yes, they will."

Palestine's rugged terrain was full of pits, holes into which people might fall and meet with very serious accidents. Note the many references to such pits in Scripture; Ps. 40:2; 57:6; Prov. 23:27; 26:27; 28:10; Eccles. 10:8; Matt. 12:11; Luke 14:5, etc. It is clear from these references that the term *pit* is frequently used in a figurative sense.

The implication is that people should not follow those blind guides. And is not another clear implication this, that The Twelve—and others too perhaps; cf. Luke 10:1—should replace these blind guides? To do this they must be trained for their task. They must be humble pupils of the Greatest Teacher of all.

So the Master continues: **40. A pupil does not outrank his teacher, but everyone who is fully trained will be like his teacher.**

On the part of The Twelve what may well have been the natural reaction to this suggestion? It should be borne in mind that most of them were men with very little education. They were "unschooled and untrained" (Acts 4:13a). How then would it ever be possible for them to take the place of these learned scribes, men drilled in the law and in tradition? Besides, if even the distance between The Twelve and the scribes was great, what about the immeasurably greater distance between these twelve men and their Teacher, Jesus?

Tenderly and lovingly the Master now assures them that although they will never be able to outrank or surpass him, yet thorough training under his direction will, if they accept it, cause them to become like their Teacher; that is, like him not in degree of knowledge or wisdom but in truly reflecting his image to the world, so that people instructed by them will begin to say, "We can notice that these men have been with Jesus" (see Acts 4:13b). For different explanations see footnote.[271]

---

271. Among several dissenting explanations there are two to which I wish to call special attention:

a. That of F. Godet, *op. cit.*, Vol. I, pp. 329, 330, namely, that Jesus here teaches what will happen to the people if they remain under the direction of the Pharisees. The further they advance in the school of such masters, the nearer they will come to . . . perdition.

Objection. The ring of the words, "Everyone who is fully trained will be like his master," is positive. It reminds one of II Tim. 3:16, and not of anything having to do with "perdition."

b. That of S. Greijdanus, *Korte Verklaring*, Vol. I, p. 170. He regards Luke 6:40 as similar in meaning to Matt. 10:24, 25. The sense then would be: a pupil must not expect to be treated better than his teacher. He will share his teacher's lot.

Objection. The contexts differ. Jesus at times used the same or a similar figure but with a different application. The treatment a teacher and his pupils can expect is stressed in Matt. 10:24, 25; thorough training under the direction of their Master whose image they will reflect is the point in Luke 6:40. In Luke 22:27 and John 13:16 the emphasis is on humility.

For a disciple to become an effective teacher and leader of men, and in fact for anyone to be an effective witness for God and his truth, *love* is necessary, a love that expresses itself in deeds of mercy and generosity. That is what Jesus has been saying in verses 27–38.

What is also necessary is *humility*, stressed here in verses **41, 42. And why do you gaze at the speck in your brother's eye, while the beam that is in your own eye you do not (even) observe? How can you say to your brother, Brother, let me take out the speck that is in your eye, while you yourself do not (even) see the beam that is in your own eye? You hypocrite, first take the beam out of your own eye, and then you will see clearly (enough) to take the speck out of your brother's eye.**

The beam is a heavy piece of timber fit to be used for the rafter or joist of a building. The "speck" or "mote" is a small piece of straw or of wood, a tiny chip from a beam, perhaps. Now in the figure which Jesus uses he asks the listener how it is that he is gazing at a mere speck in his brother's eye, and even requests permission to remove that speck, while at the same time he completely overlooks the incomparably larger beam in his own eye. Cf. John 8:7!

The question is: Who is this would-be eye-doctor? Answer: he is called a "hypocrite," a word which Jesus generally uses to characterize the scribes and Pharisees of his day (12:56; 13:15; cf. Matt. 6:2, 5, 16; 7:5; 15:7; 22:18; 23:13–15; 24:51; Mark 7:6), a class of individuals whom the Lord describes as "those who trusted in themselves that they were righteous and who despised all others" (Luke 18:9). Any person with a pharisaic disposition is meant, therefore. Since in the hearts of all, including even Christ's followers to the extent to which grace has not yet fully transformed them, there houses a Pharisee, the conclusion follows that this passage applies to all, in the sense that all need to examine themselves (I Cor. 11:28), lest without self-examination and self-discipline they find fault with and strive to correct someone else. A person may be ever so good in his own eyes (Cf. Luke 18:11, 12); yet, if he is not humble, then, as God sees him, there is a beam in his eye, the beam of self-righteousness. This makes him a blind eye-doctor who tries to perform an operation on someone else's eye! However grievous the other man's error may have seemed to the eye of the would-be corrector, was it not a mere "speck" compared with his own self-righteousness, a defect so glaring that in the sight of God it amounts to a beam in the critic's eye?

When by sovereign grace this beam has been removed, the former faultfinder will be able to see clearly enough to take the speck out of his brother's eye; that is, he will then be able to "restore such a person in the spirit of gentleness," and, examining himself in the light, let us say, of I Cor. 13, will look to himself lest he also be tempted (Gal. 6:1).

It is clear from the last clause, in which mention is made of removing the speck from the brother's eye, that it was not Christ's purpose to discourage mutual discipline. On the contrary, both self-discipline and mutual discipline are encouraged in this saying.

43, 44. For there is no healthy tree that bears sickly fruit; nor, on the other hand, does a sickly tree bear healthy fruit. For every tree is known by its own fruit. Figs are not gathered from thorn-bushes, nor is a cluster of grapes picked from a bramble-bush.

The little word *For* has given trouble to some. Now it is true that at times the Greek word on which it is based is better left untranslated. However, in the present case the rendering "For" makes excellent sense. The connection is close. Jesus is, as it were, saying, "Remove that beam of self-righteousness, *for* it is a very serious defect, showing that you are a spiritually sick person. You are not bearing good fruit." Good fruit shows that the tree from which it came is healthy; bad fruit indicates that the tree from which it fell is sickly. Every tree—the term *tree* as here used includes what we call a "shrub"—is known by its fruit.

The underlying figure *fruit* includes all the various ways in which a person expresses himself: his attitudes, words, deeds, etc. It includes his speech, confession, teaching. This is clear from verse 45b, "Out of the abundance of the heart his mouth speaks." See also Isa. 8:20; Matt. 15:9; Titus 1:9-12; Heb. 13:9; I John 4:1-3; II John 9-11. It also includes his deeds, general behavior; in fact, his entire life as it manifests itself: Luke 3:8-14; John 15:8-10; Gal. 5:22-24; Eph. 5:9-12; Phil. 1:11; Col. 1:10; James 3:17, 18.

The point Jesus drives home is that each tree yields the type of fruit for which it was planned by the Creator, a type not produced by any other tree or plant. Therefore from thorn-bushes one must not expect to gather figs, and from a bramble-bush one must not expect to pick a bunch of grapes. The same holds with respect to people; as Jesus now adds: **45. The good man out of the good treasure stored in his heart produces what is good, and the evil man out of his evil storehouse produces what is evil. For out of the abundance of the heart his mouth speaks.**

A person's heart is a reservoir, a storehouse, a *thesaurus.* (Compare Matt. 2:11 where the word is used to indicate a chest or box from which the wise men took gold, frankincense, and myrrh.) What a man produces from this inner storehouse, whether good or bad, depends on what he was carrying in it.

It is out of the *overflow* of the heart that the mouth speaks. As a teeming population will overflow into adjoining territory, and a too full cistern into an overflow pipe, so also the overplus of the heart will burst out into speech. If what is in the heart is good, this overflow will be good; if the contents of the inner being are bad, what spills out through the mouth will also be bad. Whatever a person has set his heart on will sooner or later be revealed in his speech. Therefore what is in his heart is very, very important.

This, however, does not provide any excuse for a fatalistic view of life. It does not make it right for a man to say, "Can I help what I have in my heart?" In Matthew the parallel passage is immediately followed by the words, "But I say to y o u that for every careless word that men shall speak

363

they shall render account on the day of judgment" (Matt. 12:36). The real solution is found in the prayer of Ps. 51:10.[272]

Practical Lessons Derived from Luke 6:39–45

Verse 42

"First take the beam out of your own eye." The basic requirement for the exercise of mutual discipline is self-discipline. Love toward man presupposes humility before God.

Verse 45

"Out of the abundance of the heart his mouth speaks." But what if there is no "abundance" of good things stored away in his heart and mind; such things as faith, hope, love, interest in the work of God in creation and redemption, eagerness to read edifying literature, desire to listen to uplifting music and song, zeal to win people for God and his kingdom, etc.? This shows how very important it is to take to heart Phil. 4:8, 9.

Notes on Greek Words, Phrases, and Constructions in 6:39–45

Verse 39

μήτι expects negative answer; οὐχί, affirmative.
βόθυνον, acc. s. of βόθυνος, pit.

Verse 40

For μαθητής see the note on 6:13 on page 333.
For διδάσκαλος, master, teacher, see N.T.C. on Mark, p. 177, footnote 172. Cf. *didactic*.
κατηρτισμένος, nom. s. masc. perf. passive participle of καταρτίζω, to restore, complete, mend, render fit, furnish or train completely. For a synonym see II Tim. 3:17.

Verse 41

The terms κάρφος, speck, chip, cinder; δοκός, beam, joist; and κατανοεῖς, sec. per. s. pres. act. indicat. of κατανοέω, to notice, detect, observe, perceive, are also found in Matt. 7:3–5.

Verse 42

ἄφες, sec. per. s., 2nd aor. imperat. of ἀφίημι. This verb has a wide range of meanings: let go, utter, send away, divorce, tolerate, permit, let, allow, pardon, forgive, leave off, leave behind, stop, abandon, etc. In 6:42 "let" is a good translation. See also, on this verb, N.T.C. on Mark, p. 664, footnote 830.

---

272. Notes on Greek words, phrases, and constructions in 6:39–45 begin on this page.

Verse 43

σαπρός, rotten, bad, decayed, sickly. Cf. *septic, saprophyte.*

Verse 44

Note the nouns ἄκανθα, thorn-bush; σῦκον, fig (cf. *sycamore*); βάτος, bramble-bush; and σταφυλή, a cluster of grapes.

τρυγῶσιν, third per. pl. pres. indicat. of τρυγάω. Cf. Rev. 14:18, 19. The characteristically Hebrew idiom "They do not gather figs from thorn-bushes" can be changed to "Figs are not gathered from thorn-bushes."

Verse 45

περισσεύματος, gen. s. of περίσσευμα, what is over and above, abundance.

---

46 "Now why do y o u call me 'Lord, Lord,' but do not put into practice what I say?
47 Everyone who comes to me and listens to my words and puts them into practice, I will show y o u whom he is like: 48 He is like a man building a house, who dug deep and laid a foundation on rock. Then, when a flood came, the torrent burst against that house but could not shake it, because it was well built.

49 "But he who listened and failed to put (my words) into practice is like a man who built a house upon the ground, without a foundation. The moment the torrent burst against it, it collapsed, and the crash of that house was tremendous."[273]

6:46–49 III. *Application: The Parable of The Two Builders*
Cf. Matt. 7:21, 24–27

As the sermon is about to be concluded, the necessity of bearing healthy fruit (see verses 43–45) is re-emphasized. Too many people fail to put their supposed religion into practice.[274] So Jesus continues by saying, **46. Now why do y o u call me Lord, Lord, but do not put into practice what I say?** When these people address Jesus as "Lord, Lord," the very least one can say is that they acknowledge the fact that they owe their allegiance to him. The suggestion that they even ascribed to him divine glory and majesty cannot be ruled out. In the Greek translation of the Old Testament—the rendering called the Septuagint (LXX)—the tetragrammaton (four consonant name YHWH) is reproduced by the Greek word *Kurios*, that is, *Lord.* But whatever may have been the degree of honor these people bestowed upon Jesus when they addressed him as "Lord, Lord," he stresses that they were dishonest; for, while confessing him to be their Lord, they failed to render obedience to him. So Jesus puts the question directly to them, "Why do y o u call me 'Lord, Lord'?"

---

273. Or: and the wreck of that house was complete.

274. Luke represents Jesus as directly addressing his audience, using the second person plural, where Matthew uses the third. Something similar occurs in connection with The Beatitudes. In a sermon of far greater length than either of these summaries, or of both put together, the Master may very well have used both the second and the third.

That, with a view to man's salvation, the actual doing of the Lord's will is of supreme importance is now set forth, namely, in the unforgettably impressive parable of The Two Builders. As already indicated, this parable is found also in Matthew (7:24-27). In both Gospels it forms the conclusion of the discourse, just as in both The Beatitudes constitute the beginning. The resemblances between the two reports of this parable are so many and so striking that it is generally admitted that we are dealing with the same story illustration.

Yet, there are also differences:

a. In Matthew's report the first builder is called "sensible," the second "foolish." Luke omits these designations. But is it not obvious that in Luke's view too the Master meant exactly that?

b. In Matthew's report the first builder constructed his house on rock, the second on sand. In Luke's the first builder, in constructing his house, "laid a foundation on rock," the second omitted any foundation. He simply built his house on the ground. But does not any impartial reader immediately understand that in connection with the first builder Luke, without in any way disagreeing with Matthew, adds something?

c. Matthew mentions both floods and winds; Luke makes no mention of winds. Why should he? Were not the raging floods, considered by themselves, sufficiently violent to prove the stability of the first house and the instability of the second?

It is clear that those who discover "discrepancies" here are "splitting hairs."[275]

47, 48. Everyone who comes to me and listens to my words and puts them into practice, I will show y o u whom he is like: He is like a man building a house, who dug deep and laid a foundation on rock. Then, when a flood came, the torrent burst against that house but could not shake it, because it was well built.

The words, "I will show y o u whom he is like [or: resembles]," indicate that Jesus wants everyone to listen carefully, for without his explanation the meaning would not be clear.

The first builder is a man with foresight, a cautious person. He realizes that fair, cloudless weather will not last. The rainy season is coming, bringing floods and washouts. So, deeper and deeper he digs, until at last he touches rock bottom. Upon this he constructs a foundation and builds his house.

In his explanation of the parable Jesus points out that the figurative meaning of what the first builder does is as follows. He represents everyone who comes to the Savior, listens to his words, and takes them to heart. He

---

275. Or, as the Dutch saying goes, "Zij zoeken spijkers op laag water," that is, they wait for the water to ebb in order to find nails!

puts into practice whatever Jesus commands, for he has placed his trust in him.

Such a man is truly building on the true foundation, the one that rests on the Rock, Christ (Isa. 28:16; cf. I Peter 2:6; see also Rom. 9:33; I Cor. 3:11; 10:4, etc.). In fact what is said about God as the believers' Rock (Deut. 32:15, 18; Ps. 18:2; 89:26; Isa. 17:10) is also applicable to Christ. See N.T.C. on Ephesians, p. 190.

The day of testing arrives. The rainy season begins. Rivulets start to descend from the hills. They combine and form a torrent, deep, swift, and furious. It dashes against the house of the first builder. However, the onrushing, swirling waters are not even able to shake it. It withstands the enormous force of the lashing, devastating flood. When the violence of the elements is completely spent, there stands that house, none the worse for all the punishment it has received. Reason: it was well built, its foundation resting on rock.

So also for everyone, including every hearer of the gospel, the test or crisis is coming. It comes in various forms and shapes: trial, temptation, bereavement, death, the final judgment. It often arrives with dramatic suddenness. That applies especially to the judgment day (Luke 17:24; cf. 21:27, 34b, 35; I Thess. 5:2). But as far as the first builder is concerned, what is the outcome? Never is he put to shame. He receives grace for every trial. Even the day of judgment is for him the day of triumph (I Thess. 2:19, 20; 3:13; 4:16; II Thess. 1:10; II Tim. 4:8; Titus 2:13, 14; Rev. 11:15–18; 17:14; 19:6–8).

49. But he who listened and failed to put (my words) into practice is like a man who built a house upon the ground, without a foundation. The moment the torrent burst against it, it collapsed, and the crash of that house was tremendous.

The second builder erects his house on loose gravel. A foundation of any kind he considers entirely unnecessary. He seems to think that bright and sunny days will never cease.

This represents the man who follows the promptings of his own sinful will. He listens to Christ's words, to be sure, but he does not place his trust in him. Therefore he fails completely to obey the Savior's commands.

It is understandable that it took hardly any effort for the angry torrent, sweeping down upon the second house, to undermine its walls and to carry away the very sand and gravel on which it had been erected. With a tremendous crash the foolish man's house fell into the water and was washed away, pieces of wreckage being strewn about everywhere. The ruin of this house was complete.

The ruin in store for those people who are building merely on ground or sand, and whose house lacks a foundation, is described at the very close of the sermon, probably all the more to impress upon the listeners and on those who afterward would be brought into contact with this earnest message that their reaction to the words of the Lord has significance for all eternity. In reality, therefore, the announcement of the unbelievers' tragic end is a manifestation of Christ's mercy, an implied serious invitation to repent, extended to all who are still living in the day of grace.[276]

Practical Lessons Derived from Luke 6:46–49

Taking this short paragraph as a unit, we note the following lessons:

1. Everyone is a builder, for to live means to build. According to this parable, it is especially every hearer of the gospel that is considered a builder.

2. There are only two kinds of builders, not three or more. There are wise builders and there are foolish builders.

3. The wise or sensible builder builds his house—that is, his life—on Christ, the solid Rock. He earnestly and prayerfully endeavors to regulate his life in harmony with the words of Jesus, as revealed in Scripture. The foolish builder goes his own way.

4. The hour of crisis is unavoidable. No one can escape it. The result is irrevocable. The wise builder's house is not even shaken by the downrushing torrent. The foolish builder's house immediately collapses. Application: build wisely.

> On Christ, the solid rock, I stand,
> All other ground is sinking sand.
>
> lines from Edward Mote's hymn,
> "My Hope Is Built"

Notes on Greek Words, Phrases, and Constructions in 6:46–49

Verse 46

Κύριε, vocat. s. of κύριος. For this word see N.T.C. on Mark, pp. 433–435.

Verses 48, 49

On the question whether ἔσκαψεν καὶ ἐβάθυνεν can be regarded as hendiadys there is a difference of opinion. Must we translate "he dug and went deep" or "he dug deep"? See A. T. Robertson, *Word Pictures*, Vol. II, p. 95, and same author, *Translation*, p. 171. Most translators accept the hendiadys, and even if the opposite view is accepted, the resultant difference is minor.

Note the genitive absolute, "a flood having arisen," i.e., "when a flood arose...." The word πλημμύρης, gen. s. of πλήμμυρα (cf. πλήθω, πίμπλημι), indicates a more than abundant amount of water, a flood.

Note προσέρηξεν twice, once in verse 48, once in verse 49. It is the third per. s. aor. indicat. of προσρήγνυμι, to break—or burst—against. Related to the basic verb

---

276. Notes on Greek words, phrases, and constructions in 6:46–49 begin on this page.

ῥήγνυμι is the noun ῥῆγμα, wreck, ruin, collapse, crash, in verse 49. Cf. *break, wreck, fracture, hemorrhage.*

Summary of Chapter 6

The Son of Man Asserting His Authority as Lord of the Sabbath (verses 1–11). Friends of the Bridegroom should be feasting instead of fasting (5:33–39). This attitude of gladness instead of sadness must also mark the manner in which the sabbath is observed. Once on a sabbath the disciples were picking and eating heads of grain, rubbing them with their hands. Criticized by the Pharisees for doing this, Jesus, with an appeal to what David did, as recorded in I Sam. 21:1–6; 22:9, 10, demolished the attack of the faultfinders and declared himself to be "Lord of the sabbath."

On another sabbath Jesus entered the synagogue and was teaching. He noticed a man with a shriveled hand. With murder in their hearts the scribes and Pharisees were watching, to see whether they could find a charge against Jesus for healing on the sabbath. He told the handicapped man to stand up in front of the entire audience. Then he asked the evil-minded spies, "Is it right on the sabbath to do good or to do harm, to save life or to destroy it?" When they remained silent, he told the man to stretch out his hand. It was completely restored. "They, however, were filled with senseless rage and began to discuss with one another what they might do to Jesus."

The Choosing of The Twelve (verses 12–16). Since the enemies of Jesus were planning his destruction and since gospel proclamation must continue even after his departure, Jesus, on a mountain and after an all-night prayer vigil, chose twelve men to be closely associated with himself and to be sent out to do his work. As listed by Luke their names are as follows (except that in the evangelist's account the names of Judas the Greater and Simon the Zealot are given in reversed order, James the Less is called "James the son of Alphaeus," and Judas the Greater is called "Judas the son of James"):

> Peter and Andrew, James and John,
> Philip and Bartholomew,
> Matthew next and Thomas too,
> James the Less and Judas the Greater,
> Simon the Zealot and Judas the Traitor.

Jesus' Power to Heal (verses 17–19). Having descended to a level place on this mountain, Jesus, surrounded by a vast throng from nearby and far-away places, healed their sick and demon-possessed.

The Sermon on the Mount (verses 20–49). For an expanded report of this sermon see Matt. 5–7. In this unforgettably beautiful sermon Jesus pronounced Blessings on his true followers, and Woes on the impenitents. From his lips there flowed such precious passages as, "Love y o u r enemies, do good to those who hate y o u, bless those who curse y o u, pray for those who mistreat y o u." He concluded the sermon by telling the parable of The Two Builders: the first digging deep and laying a foundation on rock; the second building his house upon the ground, without a foundation. Result: when the torrent struck those houses, the first was not even shaken; the second immediately collapsed. The first builder symbolizes the man who not only listens to Jesus but also puts his words into practice; the second listens . . . and then goes his own way.

Outline of Chapter 7

Theme: *The Work Thou Gavest Him to Do*

CHAPTER VII

7 1 After Jesus had concluded all his words in the hearing of the people, he entered Capernaum.

2 Now a certain centurion's servant, who was very dear to his master, was sick, at the point of death.[277] 3 The centurion, having heard about Jesus, sent to him elders of the Jews, asking him to come and heal his servant. 4 When they came to Jesus, they pleaded earnestly with him, saying, "He is worthy that you grant him this (favor), 5 for he loves our nation and he built the synagogue for us." 6 So Jesus went with them.

Now when Jesus was not far from the house, the centurion sent friends to say to him, "Do not trouble yourself, Lord, for I am not fit for you to come under my roof. 7 That is why I did not even consider myself worthy to come to you; but speak the word and my boy will be cured. 8 For I myself am a man set under authority, with soldiers under me, and I say to one, 'Go,' and he goes; to another, 'Come,' and he comes; and to my servant, 'Do this,' and he does it."

9 Now when Jesus heard this, he was amazed at him; and turning to the crowd following him, he said, "I tell y o u, not even in Israel have I found such great faith." 10 And when those who had been sent out returned to the house, they found the servant in good health.

7:1-10 *The Faith of a Centurion Rewarded by Jesus*
Cf. Matt. 8:5-13

A. *Introduction*

1. After Jesus had concluded all his words in the hearing of the people, he entered Capernaum.

Jesus' sermon, briefly summarized in Luke 6:20–49, has ended. Very properly a new chapter begins at this point. Nevertheless, between the final paragraph of Chapter 6 and the opening paragraph of Chapter 7 there is a close connection. In fact, that connection is threefold: (a) *geographical,* that is, if, as has been assumed, the distance between the locale of the sermon and Capernaum, which Jesus now enters, was not great; (b) *chronological,* for when Luke writes, "*After* Jesus had concluded all his words ... he entered Capernaum," he probably means "shortly afterward." Though it is true that the word here translated "after" is indefinite, and can indicate a longer or shorter period, in the present case there are no reasons to believe that the intervening period was substantial; besides, Capernaum was

---

277. Or: about to die.

nearby and was still in a sense Christ's headquarters. The connection is, however, also (c) *topical.*

This third item should be stressed, for, as is well known, topical or thematic connections abound in Luke's Gospel. In the final paragraph of Chapter 6 Jesus had, by means of a parable, driven home the lesson that *faith in himself should be unshakable,* like a house founded on rock. It should be *genuine,* so that the words of Jesus, having been heard, will not be ignored, but translated into action. In the opening paragraph of Chapter 7 the evangelist now exhibits *a prize example of such faith.*

B. *What the people—particularly "the elders of the Jews"—thought of a certain centurion: "He is worthy."*

2-6a. Now a certain centurion's servant, who was very dear to his master, was sick, at the point of death. The centurion, having heard about Jesus, sent to him elders of the Jews, asking him to come and heal his servant. When they came to Jesus, they pleaded earnestly with him, saying, He is worthy that you grant him this (favor), for he loves our nation and he built the synagogue for us. —So Jesus went with them.

The records of this miracle (Matt. 8:5-13; Luke 7:1-10) should not be confused with the story found in John 4:46-54. *That* story has to do with a royal officer's *son; this,* with a centurion's *servant.* John 4:46-54 places Jesus in *Cana;* in Luke 7:1 the Savior is entering *Capernaum.* The supplicant mentioned in John 4 could not immediately conceive of Jesus' power to heal at a distance; the centurion, on the other hand, took the initiative in declaring that Jesus had this power.

The centurion of Luke's (and Matthew's) story was an officer in the pay of Herod Antipas. Strictly speaking, as the very name implies, a *centurion* was a commander of a hundred soldiers. But then, as also today, military terms were flexible in meaning, so that a centurion might not actually be in charge of exactly one hundred men. We might say that his rank and authority ranged between that of a decurion (officer in command of ten soldiers) and that of a chiliarch (military commander of a thousand men). He was what we might call an army captain.

Centurions were generally men of good reputation. Scripture has many good things to say about them. At Calvary, after Jesus had breathed his last, a centurion exclaims, "Surely, this was God's Son" (Matt. 27:54; cf. Mark 15:39; Luke 23:47). The centurion also tells Pilate the truth about the body of Christ (that it was really dead, Mark 15:44, 45). Another centurion, Cornelius, is described as "devout and God-fearing, together with his entire family . . . held in high regard by all the Jews," etc. (see Acts 10:1, 2, 22, 33, 44-48). See also Acts 21:32; 22:25, 26; 23:17, 23; 24:23. Not many are the instances in which the New Testament records any flaw on the part of a centurion (Acts 10:25, 26). There is also Acts 27:11, but even that centurion, Julius, was well-disposed toward Paul (27:1, 3, 43).

But among all the fine things Scripture says about centurions highest praise is reserved for the one of our present account. This man had a servant—call him "slave" if you prefer, but see what follows—who was seriously ill. His physical condition was indeed desperate. According to Matt. 8:6 he was bedridden with paralysis, suffering terribly, fearfully tormented. Was this a case of progressive paralysis with muscular spasms dangerously affecting his respiratory system? Whatever it was, according to Luke's report the illness had brought the servant to the very portals of death.

Was there no hope for recovery? Yes, there was, for the centurion had heard about Jesus. In view of the fact that many of the mighty works of our Lord had been, were being, and were going to be performed in this very city, it is not surprising that the centurion, here stationed, had heard about Jesus.

Having heard about The Great Physician and what he had done for others, the centurion now pleads that the same mercy be shown to his own servant. The man's heart is in his plea, for so very dear (Luke 7:2) is the servant to his master that the latter calls him "my boy" (verse 7).[278]

According to Matthew it was the centurion himself who informed Jesus about the crisis that had arisen. On the other hand, Luke here states that the officer had sent some elders of the Jews to Jesus with the request, "Come and heal my servant." This involves no contradiction. He may have done both. On the other hand, more simple is the explanation that it was through the elders that the centurion's plea was made known to Jesus. Matthew may simply be abbreviating the story.

However, according to Luke's account (see verses 4, 5), the elders were more than mere transmitters of a message. As, through them, the centurion was interceding for his "boy," so the elders, in turn, were interceding for the centurion. They said, "He is worthy that you grant him this (favor), for he loves our nation and he built the synagogue for us." Note: *"He loves* our nation . . . and *he built* our synagogue" (a possible translation). This may imply that Capernaum at this time had only one synagogue, the very one whose construction had been financed by this centurion. If that inference should be correct, the relation between the Lord and this centurion becomes even closer, for it then appears that the construction of the very place of worship where Jesus had already revealed his miracle-working power (Luke 4:31-37; cf. Mark 1:21-28) had been financed by this officer. With respect to Capernaum and its synagogue see also on Luke 10:15.

Though this centurion was not a Jew (see verse 9) and may well have been a Roman, the very fact that he gave the Jews their synagogue probably indicates that he was rich, generous, and kind. Does it also show that he had

---

278. It is true that "boy" (Greek *pais*) for "slave" or "servant" (*doulos*) was not itself exceptional terminology. Yet, the present context—note the centurion's manifest concern in Matthew, and "was very dear to him" in Luke—shows that the appellation is here used in its most favorable sense, as a term of endearment.

said farewell to pagan polytheism and was inclined to favor—may even have adopted—Jewish monotheism? It will become clear, however, that by God's grace he had advanced much farther than this in the one and only true religion, namely, in his faith in Jesus, God's Son.

"He is worthy," said the Jewish elders. Worthy of what? Of receiving as a favor from Jesus the healing of this desperately ill servant? However well-meant this appraisal may have been, it smacks of the doctrine of human merits. It should be borne in mind that those who spoke thus were *Jewish elders!* The true doctrine is quite different. See Luke 18:13; Rom. 3:20, 23, 24; 7:18, 24; Eph. 2:8; Phil. 3:4-9.

"So Jesus went with them." A very short sentence indeed, but how full of meaning. According to Matt. 8:7, as Jesus started out on his way toward the home of the centurion he even said, "I will come and heal him." He did not refuse the fervent request. He did not say, "Why did this request not come earlier?" Nor, "Since the man who makes this request (whether directly or indirectly) is not even a Jew, and in fact represents the oppressor (the hated power of Rome), I will do nothing." Nor, "Since y o u, elders, seem to think that I owe him that favor because he built y o u r synagogue, I must turn down the request." Nothing of the kind. Without adding any "if's" or "but's" Jesus wends his way toward the house where his help is needed.

In reading this story the temptation is to concentrate our attention entirely upon the wonderful centurion. Well, by God's grace, he was indeed wonderful. But we should fix our attention especially on the "marvelous grace of our loving Lord."

> For the love of God is broader
>   Than the measure of man's mind;
> And the heart of the Eternal
>   Is most wonderfully kind.

F. W. Faber, lines taken from
"There's a Wideness in God's Mercy"

C. *What he (the centurion) thought of himself:* "I am not worthy."

6b-8. Now when Jesus was not far from the house, the centurion sent friends to say to him, Do not trouble yourself, Lord, for I am not fit for you to come under my roof. That is why I did not even consider myself worthy to come to you; but speak the word and my boy will be cured. For I myself am a man set under authority, with soldiers under me, and I say to one, Go, and he goes; to another, Come, and he comes; and to my servant, Do this, and he does it.

"He is worthy," the elders had said. But the centurion, on hearing that Jesus was on the way to his home, in fact was already nearby, becomes overwhelmed with the sense of his own unworthiness. After all, who is *he* in comparison with this Exalted One, this personal embodiment of majestic authority, all-embracing power, and condescending love, a love that bridges every chasm and overleaps every obstacle of race, nationality, class, and culture? Who is *he* to cause this kind Master to commit an act that would put him in conflict with the time-honored custom of his own people, according to which a Jew does not enter the house of a Gentile lest he be defiled (Acts 10:28; 11:2, 3; cf. John 18:28)?

As *Luke* makes clear, however, the difficulty with which the centurion struggled was not limited to his unwillingness to embarrass Jesus because of certain Jewish scruples or ritual taboos. If that had been all, the officer could have added, "But though I do not want you to ceremonially defile yourself by entering my home, I myself will go out to you. I will approach you, close enough so you can address me." Instead, what he adds is this, "I did not even consider myself worthy to come to you."

It is clear that this man is filled with a sense of *personal unworthiness*. He is deeply convinced of his own insignificance in comparison with Jesus. *Let Jesus therefore simply speak the word of healing!* That is all that will be necessary to bring about a complete recovery.

The centurion reasons: If, though I am but a military officer with very limited authority and power, an officer who must himself obey his superiors, even *my* orders are nevertheless immediately carried out by both soldier and servant, and this regardless of where I am when I issue them, then certainly *he,* this Great One, exercising independent authority and holding the universe in his all-powerful grasp, can command, and whatever it is that he desires will be done. When he says, "Go," sickness will go; when he says, "Come," health will arrive; and when he tells the body of "my boy," "Do this," it will immediately respond.

Here again, the fact that according to Luke this message was not addressed to Jesus directly but was on the Lord's approach conveyed to him by the centurion's friends, can, with Augustine and many after him, be explained as in the previous instance; see above, on verses 3-5. We are justified, perhaps, in assuming that the centurion, having gone outside, and having seen Jesus approaching, hurriedly sent his friends to him. The message was in any case the centurion's own answer to Jesus, which is what both Matthew and Luke are saying.[279]

The centurion is deeply convinced that the personal presence of Jesus is not required. All that is necessary is that he speak the word. He says, "I am not fit, not worthy." For more about this word *fit* or *worthy* see the note on 7:6 on pages 380, 381.

To return again to Jesus. At the beginning of the story the centurion had asked him to come (verse 3). But now that the Lord has almost arrived, the

---

279. Not only Matthew but also Luke here presents this view. See Luke 7:6 in the original; note the present participle *singular:* λέγων ("he saying").

officer says the very opposite, "Do not trouble yourself [to come]." It would seem, therefore, that the more, in the meantime, the centurion reflected on the greatness of Jesus, on his power, exalted majesty, holiness, and willingness to help, the more also he was ashamed of himself and impressed with the fact that his previous request had been unnecessary. So great is Christ!

D. *What Jesus thought of him: "Not even in Israel have I found such
great faith."*

9, 10. Now when Jesus heard this, he was amazed at him; and turning to the crowd following him, he said, I tell y o u, not even in Israel have I found such great faith. —And when those who had been sent out returned to the house, they found the servant in good health.

Jesus was astonished, and for a reason contrary to that mentioned in Mark 6:6. To make sure that his words would be understood he *turned* toward the crowd that was following him, including undoubtedly the centurion's friends (verse 6), and to them all he revealed that the faith of this officer of Gentile race surpassed in excellence anything he had found even among the Jews, in spite of their special privileges.

To be sure, also in Israel Jesus had found faith (Luke 5:5, 8–11; 6:20–23, 47, 48), but not a combination in one person of a love so affectionate, a considerateness so thoughtful, an insight so penetrating, a humility so outstanding, and a trust so unlimited. In many cases was not what Jesus had found *"little* faith"?

According to Matt. 8:13 Jesus now told the centurion—again by means of that officer's friends?—to re-enter his home. The Lord's message conveyed to him was, "Go home; as you believed, so let it be done for you." Matthew adds that from that very moment the boy was cured. Accordingly, when the friends whom the centurion had sent to Jesus returned to the officer's home, they found the servant in good health.

What lesson does Luke 7:1–10 teach? Is it this, that Luke was indeed a great historian, one who, once having announced his theme—the opening of the gospel door to non-Jew as well as Jew—never departs from it? That observation, made by many, is accurate. In addition to 7:1–10 see also 4:25–27; 10:33–37; 17:16; 24:45–47; Acts 10:28, 34, 35; 11:17, 18; 13:44–48, etc. Sometimes it is added that Luke's favorable mention of "the elders of the Jews," who thought very highly of a man who was a Gentile by birth and who showed a friendly and even reverential attitude to Jesus, was made in order to facilitate the entrance of non-Jews into church and kingdom.

But when we say no more than this have we not missed the *main* lesson? Do not these same passages, and many others besides, show us what a wonderful Savior is Jesus? Do they not point to him as the One who not only bids all men to embrace him by faith, to God's glory, but even praises them when they do so (Luke 7:9), even though he knows that this faith is not of their own making but is God's gift to them?

378

A wonderful Savior is Jesus my Lord,
A wonderful Savior to me, *etc.*

Fanny J. Crosby[280]

Practical Lessons Derived from Luke 7:1–10

Verses 3–6

"Elders of the Jews ... [said], 'He is worthy.' ... So Jesus went with them." The greatness of Jesus appears from the fact that: (a) though the centurion waited until it was almost too late (the servant was at the point of death), and (b) not being a Jew, belonged to a different ethnic group, and (c) though the ground on which the elders pleaded (he is worthy) was doctrinally unsound, nevertheless the Master started out at once to answer the call. What a comfort! But also: what an example for us to follow, to the extent to which by his power we are able to do so.

Verse 6

"I am not fit." Cf. "I am no longer worthy to be your son" (15:19); "O God, be merciful to me, the sinner" (18:13); and "sinners ... foremost of whom am I." What is the lesson?

> Let not conscience make you linger,
> Nor of fitness fondly dream;
> All the fitness he requireth
> Is to feel your need of him.
> This he gives you, this he gives you;
> 'Tis the Spirit's glimmering beam.
> Lines from "Come Ye Sinners," by Joseph Hart

Verse 9

"Not even in Israel have I found such great faith." Did the faith of this man consist only in this, that he was firmly convinced of the Master's power to heal a deathly sick servant from a distance? That this ingredient of his faith was indeed in the foreground is clear from the close connection between 7:6b–8 and verse 9. But was that the complete picture? Did not the centurion's faith also include warm affection for his "slave," generosity toward a conquered nation, and consciousness of his own unworthiness? And does not "great faith" always include a changed attitude to Christ, others, and self?

Notes on Greek Words, Phrases, and Constructions in 7:1–10

Verse 2

For κακῶς ἔχων see the note on 5:31 on page 306.

---

280. Notes on Greek words, phrases, and constructions in 7:1–10 begin on this page.

τελευτᾶν, pres. infinit. of τελευτάω, to die; cf. τέλος, end, limit, goal.

ἔντιμος, very dear, cf. held in honor, respected, esteemed. See also 14:8; cf. Phil. 2:29; I Peter 2:4, 6.

Verse 3

διασώσῃ, third per. s., aor. subj. act. of διασώζω, to restore to health, heal.

Verse 4

παραγενόμενοι, nom. pl. masc. 2nd aor. participle of παραγίνομαι, to be by the side of, to come, arrive.

παρέξῃ, sec. per. s. fut. middle of παρέχω, to grant, render, offer, confer.

Verses 4 and 7

The cognates ἄξιος (verse 4) and ἀξιόω (verse 7) are derived from the base ἄγω, to lead, bring, etc.; hence, to bring down the scale; that is, to be of sufficient weight; and so, to be worthy, deserving.

Though the idiomatic English equivalent of ἄξιος is not always "worthy," or even "deserving," nevertheless the meaning in any context can easily be traced to the basic concept of being worthy. This holds also for the verb ἀξιόω of which ἠξίωσα in verse 7 is the first per. s. aor. indicat. Limiting ourselves to Luke's writings, note the following examples of ἄξιος from *the Third Gospel:*

> fruits worthy of (i.e., in keeping with) conversion (Luke 3:8).
> He is worthy (7:4).
> The laborer is worthy of (deserves) his wages (10:7).
> things worthy of (things that called for) a beating (12:48).
> I am no longer worthy (15:19, 21).
> nothing worthy of (nothing that deserves) the death penalty (23:15).
> We are getting what we are worthy of (what we deserve, 23:41).

The same holds for the examples of ἄξιος in *Acts* (13:25, etc.).

This is also true with respect to the verb ἀξιόω:

> I did not even consider myself worthy (Luke 7:7).
> Paul did not consider it worthy (right, fitting, suitable) to take along, etc. (Acts 15:38).
> We consider worthy (We desire) to hear from you (Acts 28:22).

Verse 5

ἀγαπᾷ, here third per. s. pres. indicat. of ἀγαπάω. For the synonyms ἀγαπάω and φιλέω see N.T.C. on John, Vol. II, pp. 494–500, footnote 306.

Verse 6

For ἀπέχοντος see the note on 6:24 on page 346.

σκύλλου, sec. per. s. pres. imperat. middle of σκύλλω, to skin, flay, vex, trouble. Cf. *skin, Scylla* (and Charybdis).

ἱκανός. In the Gospels this word has the following meanings:

a. able, fit, worthy (Matt. 3:11; cf. Mark 1:7; Luke 3:16; also Matt. 8:8; cf. Luke 7:6).

b. large, considerable (Matt. 28:12, a large sum of money; Mark 10:46; Luke 7:11, 12).

c. long (with "time," Luke 8:27; 20:9; 23:8).

d. enough (Luke 22:38).

e. many (Luke 8:32; 23:9).

f. In combination with ποιεῖν the word ἱκανός acquires the meaning *to satisfy* (Mark 15:15. Cf. the Dutch *genoegdoening,* meaning *satisfaction;* literally *doing enough*).

In addition to the 10 occurrences in the Third Gospel Luke uses the word ἱκανός 18 times in Acts; therefore 28 times in all, more than twice as often as all other New Testament writers combined. In Acts, too, as well as in the Third Gospel, the meaning varies.

Verse 7

εἰπὲ λόγῳ, literally "speak with a word," where we would say, "speak the word." ἰαθήτω, third per. s. aor. imperat. passive of ἰάομαι. See also the note on 5:17 on page 300.

Verse 8

πορεύθητι, sec. per. s. aor. imperat. of πορεύομαι, to go.

Verse 10

ὑποστρέψαντες, nom. pl. masc. aor. participle of ὑποστρέφω, to turn back, return.

πεμφθέντες, nom. pl. masc. aor. pass. participle of πέμπω.

ὑγιαίνοντα; see the note on 5:31 on page 306.

---

11 Soon afterward Jesus went to a town called Nain. His disciples and a large crowd went along with him. 12 Now when he approached the gate of the town, look, a dead person was being carried out. He was his mother's only son, and she was a widow. A sizable crowd from the town was with her.

13 When the Lord saw her, his heart went out to her and he said, "Weep no more."

14 Then he came forward and touched the stretcher, and the men who were carrying it came to a halt. And he said, "Young man, I say to you, get up!" 15 Then the dead man sat up and began to talk, and Jesus gave him back to his mother.

16 Fear took hold of them all, and they glorified God, saying, "A great prophet has appeared among us, and God has come to look after his people." 17 And this report about Jesus spread throughout the country of the Jews[281] and the surrounding region.

7:11-17 *The Raising of the Widow's Son at Nain*

Our attention will be centered consecutively on God, the Widow, Jesus, and the Crowd.

---

281. Or: throughout Judea.

A. *God*

11, 12. Soon afterward Jesus went to a town called Nain. His disciples and a large crowd went along with him. Now when he approached the gate of the town, look, a dead person was being carried out. He was his mother's only son, and she was a widow. A sizable crowd from the town was with her.

Note connection with the immediately preceding account: (a) the miracle recorded here in 7:11–17 occurred "soon after" the healing of the centurion's servant (verses 1–10); and (b) that servant *was at the point of death* when Jesus healed him, but the widow's son *had actually died.*

Nowhere else in Scripture is *Nain* mentioned. It was probably the present *Nein*. The location is scenic. Picture it as situated ten kilometers southeast of Nazareth; i.e., forty kilometers southwest of Capernaum. To the north is Mt. Tabor, to the southeast Mt. Gilboa. Nain, then, was nestled on the northwest slope of the hill of Moreh, in a region that used to belong to the tribe of Issachar.

When Jesus drew near to this Galilean town he was by no means alone. Not only were his disciples with him but so were many others. Again and again the Gospels picture Jesus as surrounded or followed by crowds. This was true especially during the early part of his earthly ministry (John 6:66). The people wanted to hear him, for his messages were "different" (Matt. 7:28, 29). They wanted to see him, for his eyes were filled with deep earnestness and sympathy. They would bring their sick, handicapped, and demon-possessed to him, for he healed the troubled and oppressed. They wanted to be with him, for by his love he drew them. In the Gospel of Luke see also 4:42; 5:29; 6:17–19; 9:37; 14:25.

This time, *just as* Jesus approached Nain's gate something happened on which the evangelist, by writing "look," wishes to fix our special attention: a funeral procession was coming out; coming out of the gate because no burial was allowed inside a Jewish city.

Jesus *entering,* or about to enter; and simultaneously this procession *leaving:* was this "the hand of God" or a "mere coincidence"? Is not the Bible— and any person's life—full of facts and happenings that are often described as "mere coincidences"?

When Abraham needed a sacrifice as a substitute for Isaac, there, in the very neighborhood, was a ram (Gen. 22:13). Later, Abraham's most trusted servant is sent to Mesopotamia in order to bring back from there a wife for Isaac. Arriving in that strange country, the servant prays that God may direct him. Before his prayer is even finished there is Rebecca, the young lady he is looking for (Gen. 24:15).

Gideon needs courage in order to fight the Midianites. So, at God's direction, late in the day he and his servant sneak into the border of the enemy's camp. By the light of the campfires they are able to see. What they see is frightening: hostile forces "like locusts for multitude." But at that very moment Gideon hears a Midianite telling his dream to a comrade, the dream about the cake of barley-bread that tumbled into the camp, struck it, and overturned it. The dreamer's comrade interprets this as proof positive that Midian is about to be defeated by Gideon. Thus encouraged, Gideon and his three hundred triumph gloriously (Judg. 7:9–25).

Ruth, the Moabitess, starts out one morning for a field to gather some of the leavings of the harvest. "And she happened to come to the part of the field belonging to Boaz." That was exactly the right man . . . her future husband, although at the moment she did not know it (Ruth 2:3).

Jeremiah is cast into a cistern, where he is beginning to sink into the mire. Is there no one to rescue him? "When the need is highest, God is nighest." The prophet is rescued by an Ethiopian, who arrives just in time (Jer. 38:7; 39:1 ff.).

And it just so happens that when the Jews are very sure that their enemy, Paul, will not be able to escape them, so sure that more than forty of them even bind themselves with an oath not to eat or drink until they have murdered their enemy, Paul's nephew hears about the plot, and "Uncle Paul" is rescued (Acts 23:12–24). Was the intervention of "the eavesdropper" (?) the hand of God, or "mere coincidence"?

One day a minister, needing some time for relaxation after a heavy day's work, parks his car and strolls into a railroad depot. At that time travel by rail was still rather brisk. It is interesting to watch the trains come in, stop, unload their passengers, reload, and leave again. So it is also on this day. One of the many new arrivals, having entered the depot, looks around quizzically. Everyone in the huge crowd is a stranger to him. Suddenly he heads for the minister. Why just for him? "I'm looking for a Mr. A. [he mentions the name], but I have lost his address. Could you perhaps help me find it?" The minister answers, "Come along with me and step into my car. I'll be glad to take you to our good friend, that wonderful lay home missionary, whose work is being sponsored by two neighboring churches. I am the pastor of one of those churches." I will let the reader guess who that minister was.

So here also, at the very moment when the funeral procession is going out the city gate, Jesus is about to enter.

Are these strange concurrences actually "mere coincidences"? From a human point of view they are, for man did not so plan them. And even Scripture at times uses phraseology that is thoroughly human; for example, "*By chance* a priest was going by that road" (Luke 10:31). Nevertheless, from the divine point of view all these remarkable coincidences must be regarded as having been included in God's plan, and in such a manner that man's responsibility is never canceled.

The fact that these coincidences were indeed included in God's eternal, wise, all-comprehensive, immutable, efficacious plan is clearly taught in

Scripture (Ps. 31:15; 33:11; 39:4, 5; 119:89–91; 139:16; Prov. 16:4, 33;
19:21; Dan. 4:34, 35; Luke 22:22; Acts 2:23; 4:27, 28; 17:26; Rom. 8:28;
Eph. 1:4, 11). What a comfort!

> Ere into being I was brought
> Thine eye did see, and in thy thought
> My life in all its perfect plan
> Was ordered ere my days began.

Versification of Ps. 139:16. The poetic lines are part of No. 289 of the *Psalter Hymnal*, Centennial Edition, of the Christian Reformed Church, Grand Rapids, Mich., 1959.

B. *The Widow*

The dead person who was being carried out was his mother's *only* son,
and that woman was a widow. In this connection note also Luke's reference
to another *only* son (9:38), and to an *only* daughter (8:42).

With the death of this only son the woman's final source of support and
protection is gone and the hope of perpetuating the family line has vanished. Is this death, after the earlier death of her husband, also a severe
trial for her faith in a God who loves and cares? Though the text does not
indicate this, we must at least consider this possibility. Her condition is
indeed *tragic.*

It is true that both Old and New Testament place special stress on
everyone's obligation to show kindness to widows and to help them in their
distress. See N.T.C. on I and II Timothy and Titus, pp. 167, 168. But is it
not possible that the constant repetition of this admonition shows that
widows were sometimes being neglected? See on Luke 20:47.

On the other hand, we must not lose sight of the fact that the very
mention of "a sizable crowd" shows that this widow's distress was being
shared, namely, by those who knew her best ("a sizable crowd *from the
town*"). Cf. John 11:19.

But our attention should not be too exclusively fixed on this widow and
this only son. Instead, it should be concentrated on *God's* only Son. When *he*
steps into the picture, can the death of an earthly only son any longer be
considered hopeless?

C. *Jesus*

**13–15. When the Lord saw her, his heart went out to her and he said,
Weep no more.**

Note the title *the Lord.* That Luke recognized Jesus as Lord is clear also
from earlier passages (5:8, 12; 7:6). But there the evangelist introduces
other people who address Jesus as Lord. In 6:46 he quotes Jesus, who in
turn quotes others who call him "Lord, Lord." And in 6:5 "Lord of the
sabbath" is Christ's self-designation. The present passage (7:13) is the first
in which *the evangelist himself* uses the term *the Lord* to describe Jesus. He

384

does this also in 7:19; 10:1, 39, 41, etc. As to Mark's use of the term see
N.T.C. on Mark 11:3.

In all probability there was a special reason why Luke, in this particular
context, called Jesus "Lord," namely, that in the present instance the Savior
revealed himself as Lord and Master even over *death!*

First Jesus addressed the widow, who in all probability headed the funeral procession. His heart went out to her. This may well be one of the
best translations of the original. It was adopted by Phillips, N.E.B., N.I.V.
Another equally excellent rendering is, "His heart was moved with pity for
her" (Williams). See the note on 7:13 on page 390 for more on this.

Jesus was deeply touched by this woman's sorrow. Yet, it must have
sounded strange to all the listeners that at an occasion that generally called
for weeping, so that mourners were even hired, Jesus told the one person
who had more reason to weep than did anyone else, "Weep no more," or, as
the original can also be rendered, "Cease weeping." It would seem to be a
sensible command only if the One who spoke these words would remove
the cause of the widow's tears. But who can remove death?

What was very clear, however, was this comforting fact, namely, that the
heart of Jesus went out to this widow in her deep distress. Did Jesus'
sympathy resemble human sympathy in general? Was his compassion like
ours? That there is and was indeed a resemblance is clear from such passages as John 11:33, 35; Heb. 4:15. But is it not rather the difference or
contrast that stands out? Note the following items:

a. Among sinful men sympathy is often faked, not genuine. Think of the
people who take special pleasure in making lengthy visits to the sick, thinking, "Now he (she) is my captive. He (she) will have to listen to all the details
of my recent operation." On the other hand, when *Jesus* sympathized, he
really meant it. His compassion was genuine and deep. He was concerned
about the sick, the sorrowing, the bereaved. So concerned that of him it is
written:

> He has taken our infirmities upon himself
> And carried our diseases.   (Isa. 53:4; Matt. 8:17)

b. Merely human sympathy is often helpless. The *compassion* shown by
our Lord really helped. It was *effective.* In the present instance this is made
very clear:

**Then he came forward and touched the stretcher, and the men who
were carrying it came to a halt. And he said, Young man, I say to you, get
up! —Then the dead man sat up and began to talk, and Jesus gave him
back to his mother.**

No one asked the Lord to do anything. He acted on his own initiative.
What was there to ask? The man was dead, was he not? In connection with
fever (4:38), leprosy (5:12), and paralysis (7:3; cf. Matt. 8:6) there was
always a glimmer of hope, some reason to ask for help, but surely not when

385

death had entered. It is not surprising, therefore, that no one asked Jesus to restore to the mourning widow what she had lost. The case was regarded as absolutely hopeless. One is reminded of Luke 8:49.

And yet, for the Lord of life and death, the One who holds the keys of Death and Hades (Rev. 1:18), the situation even now was *not* hopeless. Cf. Luke 8:50. So Jesus touched the stretcher on which the enshrouded corpse was lying. But on the basis of Num. 19:11-22 (see especially verse 16) could it not be argued that touching a dead body or even the stretcher was defiling?

However, "to the pure all things are pure" (Titus 1:15). The One who was able to eat and drink with tax-collectors and sinners without becoming contaminated would not suffer pollution either by touching this frame. On the contrary, instead of becoming defiled he was now in the process of conquering death and defilement!

The "pallbearers" took the hint and stood still. Jesus then said, "Young man, I say to you, get up." In two other cases recorded in the Gospels the Lord also spoke to the dead (Luke 8:54; John 11:43). Cf. Ps. 33:6. Can we not assume that the very moment the Lord began to address the dead they revived? In a manner too mysterious for us to understand, his word of power spelled victory over death. In the present case the young man who had been dead sat up and began to talk, showing that he was really and fully alive.

The three restorations to life ascribed to Jesus—that of the widow's son, the ruler's daughter, and Lazarus—are unique. Nothing exactly similar had ever happened before or was going to happen during the period of Christ's earthly ministry. (The situation in connection with Matt. 27:52, 53 was different. See N.T.C. on Matthew, pp. 975, 976.) To be sure there are other revivification stories—for example, by Apollonius, by Joseph Smith, etc.—but the circumstances surrounding these "miracles" (?) render further discussion superfluous.

Different, though not in every respect, are also the resurrection accounts found in the Old Testament. (Since the story recorded in II Kings 13:20, 21 involves no living prophet, it does not engage our interest here.)

In some respects the five resurrections—two in the old dispensation, three in the new—are *similar:*

a. *God* was the Author of all. See I Kings 17:22; II Kings 4:33; implied also in Luke 8:50; John 11:40, 41; and acknowledged here in Luke 7:16.

b. In every case the bringing back to life of the individual is associated with *the restoration of family ties.* In the old dispensation the children who were raised from the dead are given back to their mothers. In the new, the command to give the ruler's daughter something to eat was probably directed to her parents; Lazarus is restored to loving fellowship with his sisters (cf. John 11:1 with 12:1, 2); and in our present account we read the beautiful words, "And Jesus gave him back to his mother" (Luke 7:15).

With this compare the almost exactly similar words of I Kings 17:23; and see also II Kings 4:36.

In other words, God loves the family. He is—let it be borne in mind always—the God *of the covenant,* that is, "of Abraham and his seed," not merely of Abraham. He wants the family to be a closely-knit unit. The children belong to him; they are his children, for he has a special claim on them. In his great love he tells them, "My son (daughter) give me your heart" (Prov. 23:26). The answer of each should be:

> Take my life and let it be
> Consecrated, Lord, to thee.
> Take my moments and my days;
> Let them flow in endless praise.
> Take my love; my God, I pour
> At thy feet its treasure store.
> Take myself, and I will be
> Ever, only, all for thee.

Stanzas from a hymn by
Frances R. Havergal.

For more on the biblical doctrine of the covenant of grace see Gen. 17:7; 18:19; Deut. 6:7; Josh. 24:15; Ps. 78:4; 103:17; 105:8; Ezek. 16:21; Acts 2:38, 39; I Cor. 7:14. See also the author's book, *The Covenant of Grace,* Grand Rapids, 1932. And read *What Jesus Did for the Family,* N.T.C. on Mark, p. 385.

But in one important respect what happened here at Nain and also what occurred in connection with the other two persons whom Jesus raised from the dead is *in sharp contrast* with the resurrections recorded in the Old Testament. Note the agonizing struggle of Elijah before the child's soul returns to its body: "He cried to the Lord . . . and he stretched himself upon the child three times . . . and cried to the Lord" (I Kings 17:20-22). More strenuous still and perhaps even longer is Elisha's struggle (II Kings 4:32–35). Compare all this with Luke 7:14b, 15a, "And Jesus said, 'Young man, I say to you, get up.' Then the dead man sat up," etc. There is no preliminary protracted conflict, no arduous wrestling. There is simply the word of majesty, and the young man is alive and talking! Reason: Jesus is God. Nothing less! His victory over death is immediate and complete.

D. *The Crowd*

16, 17. Fear took hold of them all, and they glorified God, saying, A great prophet has appeared among us, and God has come to look after his people. —And this report about Jesus spread throughout the country of the Jews and the surrounding region.

Those who witnessed this miracle were awestruck. They recognized that God alone can raise the dead. So they properly ascribed glory to God.

387

All this is understandable. Imagine that we ourselves should see a corpse suddenly come to life, get up, and start to talk. What would be our reaction? At first astonishment would probably prevent us from saying anything. Next, realizing that we had just now witnessed one of God's mighty doings, would we not exclaim, "How great thou art"?

The spectators saw more than God's *power*. They also bore testimony to his *loving concern*. They even understood that, by bringing this young man back to life so that he could be reunited with his mother, God was revealing his deep concern, his gracious help, to his people in general. Note their expression, "God has come to look after his people." Cf. Ruth 1:6; I Sam. 2:21; Luke 1:68, 78; cf. James 1:27.

As to their attitude toward Jesus, here we must be careful. The people were convinced that it was through Jesus that God had performed this unforgettable deed. By declaring, "A great prophet has appeared among us," they showed that, in their estimation, Jesus had acted as God's agent and representative. And is it not true that Jesus was, is, and ever will be God's Great Prophet? See Deut. 18:15; Luke 24:19; Acts 3:22, 23; 7:37.

Nevertheless, in the light of other passages—such as Matt. 16:13, 14; Mark 8:28; Luke 9:18, 19—it becomes clear that these crowds failed to see the true greatness of this Prophet. The very manner and degree in which this great deed surpassed in splendor all that had ever happened before, as has been shown, should have opened their eyes to the fact that standing in their midst was not just "one of the old prophets risen from the dead," not even merely "a great prophet," but the one and only Son of God himself, the long promised Messiah. But this they did not understand or acknowledge. They underestimated the majesty of Jesus. Cf. Isa. 53:4, 8; Luke 9:45; 18:34; John 1:11.

But Jesus performed his marvelous deeds of power and compassion not because of the recognition he received, but in spite of the fact that he failed to receive what was his due. This enhances his greatness. It causes his glory to shine forth even more brilliantly.

Nevertheless, even in the estimation of those who failed to accord him the full measure of honor he should have received from them, so striking had been the miracle that they began to spread the news. Result: without newspaper, radio, or TV the report concerning the miracle, and concerning him, circulated throughout the country of the Jews and the adjacent regions.

It is still circulating. It is performing its mission in the hearts and lives of all who take these inspired accounts seriously. It strengthens their faith and draws them closer to their Savior: a Prophet infinitely greater than any before him, a Highpriest exuding genuine and effective compassion, and a King who triumphs even over death. To him be the glory forever![282]

---

282. Notes on Greek words, phrases, and constructions in 7:11–17 begin on page 389.

Practical Lessons Derived from Luke 7:11–17

Verse 13

"His heart went out to her." There are various ways of showing kindness to widows, one of them being assigning to those who are physically able and mentally alert an important kingdom task. See N.T.C. on I Tim. 5:9, 10.

Verses 13, 15

"His heart went out to her. . . . He gave him back to his mother." What deep compassion!

Verse 13

"Weep no more." Thus Jesus promoted an atmosphere of calm. What infinite wisdom!

Verse 14

"He . . . touched the stretcher," thus ordering the procession to stop. "And he said, 'Young man . . . get up,'" thus commanding Death to surrender its prey. What limitless authority!

Verse 15

"Then the dead man sat up. . . . " Christ's word of command immediately restores the young man to life. What amazing power!

Deep compassion, infinite wisdom, limitless authority, amazing power! Hallelujah, what a Savior! On the Day of Resurrection it is he who will welcome his own. See Job 19:23–27; John 14:19; I Cor. 15:20; Phil. 3:20, 21. For by far the most of them the "Welcome Home!" will be experienced even earlier, namely, at the moment of death. See Luke 23:43; Acts 7:59; II Cor. 5:8; Phil. 1:23.

Notes on Greek Words, Phrases, and Constructions in 7:11–17

Verse 11

ἐν τῷ ἑξῆς**, supply χρόνῳ (according to what is probably the best text); literally, "in the following time period"; hence, "soon afterward." Even if the reading ἐν τῇ ἑξῆς (supply ἡμέρᾳ) should be correct, the difference in meaning would be small.

Verse 12

ἐξεκομίζετο, third per. s. imperf. indicat. pass. of ἐκκομίζω, to carry out.

τεθνηκώς, nom. s. perfect active participle of θνῄσκω, to die.

μονογενής = μόνος and γένος; hence, *only* son *born* (to his mother); hence *only*. In connection with Jesus cf. John 3:16, 18, "only begotten son" (A.V.).

389

Verse 13

ἐσπλαγχνίσθη, third per. s. aor. indicat. pass. of σπλαγχνίζομαι. See also N.T.C. on Philippians, p. 58, footnote 39. The heart of Jesus went out to the sorrowing widow.

Verse 14

ἥψατο, third per. s. aor. indicat. middle of ἅπτω, to touch, fasten. Cf. *aptitude, adapt.*

σορός, a portable frame on which a corpse is placed. The many attempts to find a suitable *modern* English equivalent have produced the following results:

a. *coffin.* However, archaeologists maintain that "coffins were unknown—at least unusual—in ancient Israel."

b. *open coffin.* This introduces us to the modern funeral parlor, where friends of the departed meet mourning relatives and view the body. This obviously cannot be the meaning here.

c. *litter.* This is technically correct. However, to many moderns is not a "litter" simply a number of puppies or of kittens born at the same time? Is the term *litter* in the sense of "stretcher," a meaning it certainly also has, still sufficiently familiar?

d. *hearse.* Does this suggest "a horse-drawn funeral carriage"? (At the time of our story the automobile had not yet been invented.) To be sure, the term has other meanings also, but would not the one just given be the first to suggest itself? But the portable frame of Luke 7:14 was moved by men, not by horses.

e. *bier.* This would be my second choice. It has been adopted by most translators and commentators. In its favor is the fact that the word has a wide meaning, indicating a frame of any kind on which either a corpse or a coffin is placed. It can therefore be considered technically correct. Nevertheless, as Williams implies (see the footnote in his translation), "bier" can hardly be considered an up-to-date English equivalent. Some even call it "archaic."

f. *stretcher.* When the object to which reference is made in 7:14 is described as "a frame consisting of two long poles connected crosswise by bands on which the corpse is laid"; and a *stretcher* is defined as "a frame, generally light, used for carrying injured, sick, or dead persons," the conclusion would seem to be justified that "stretcher" may well be the best rendering. It is my first choice. It should be borne in mind, however, that the portable frame of 7:14 may have been somewhat heavier in construction: perhaps a flat board equipped with staves and poles.

"A . . . striking peculiarity is that the dead person was not buried in a coffin. On the contrary, when the corpse had been shrouded it was carried out on a stretcher. That the reference is not to a coffin is clearly evident from the resurrection at Nain. The Savior touched the stretcher, and at his word 'the dead man sat up and began to talk.'" (A. Sizoo, *De Antieke Wereld en Het Nieuwe Testament*, Kampen, 1948, p. 48. The Dutch word for which I selected, and the dictionary allows, the English equivalent *stretcher,* can also be rendered "bier.")

See also M.M., p. 581; and J. Reiling and J. L. Swellengrebel, *A Translator's Handbook on the Gospel of Luke*, Leiden, 1971, p. 300. Little, if any, help can be derived from Josephus, *Antiquities* XVII.197, since the "bier" on which the body of King Herod the Great was borne to Herodeion "had a cover of purple over it," and differed therefore from the simple and obviously open stretcher to which reference is made here in Luke 7:14.

βαστάζοντες, nom. pl. masc. pres. active participle of βαστάζω. The verb βαστάζω occurs more than twenty-five times in the New Testament. It is especially
common in the Gospels and in Acts. It is used in connection with *carrying* a water-jar
(Mark 14:13; Luke 22:10), a stretcher (here in Luke 7:14), stones (John 10:31),
money (carrying it away, stealing it: John 12:6), a corpse (transferring it from one
place to another: John 20:15), a yoke (Acts 15:10), a man: Paul (Acts 21:35), and a
woman (Rev. 17:7). In Gal. 6:2 (and cf. Rom. 15:1) it can best be taken in the
figurative sense of "carrying" each other's burdens, lightening each other's loads *of
difficulty and grief*. For a slightly different metaphorical sense see Gal. 5:10 (bear
one's judgment, pay the penalty). We should not allow the exceptional sense which
the word has in Rev. 2:2 (tolerate, put up with) to determine the meaning elsewhere.

ἐγέρθητι, sec. per. aor. imperative passive (intransitive) of ἐγείρω, to arouse;
hence here *arise!, get up!* In verse 16 note third per. s. aor. passive of the same basic
verb. The form there used means "has appeared."

Verse 16

For ἐπεσκέψατο see the note on 1:68 and on 1:78 on page 131. "God has
visited his people" is perhaps a little too weak. Better is, "God has come to look
after his people," meaning: "has shown his concern for [or: interest in] them,"
has come to help (or rescue) them. Cf. Dutch (Nieuwe Vertaling), "God heeft naar
zijn volk omgezien."

Verse 17

For Ἰουδαία see the note on 4:44 on page 275.

---

18 John's disciples told him all these things. Summoning two of his disciples, 19 he sent
them to the Lord, to ask, "Are you the Coming One, or must we look for someone else?"
20 When the men came to Jesus, they said, "John the Baptist sent us to you to ask, 'Are you
the Coming One, or must we look for someone else?'"
21 Now at that very time Jesus cured many people of diseases, sicknesses, and evil spirits,
and on many blind persons he graciously bestowed sight. 22 So he gave this answer to the
messengers, "Go back and report to John the things y o u have seen and heard: (the) blind[283]
are gaining their sight, (the) cripples are walking, (the) lepers are being cleansed, and (the)
deaf are hearing, (the) dead are being raised, (the) poor are having good news preached to
them. 23 And blessed is he who is not repelled by me."
24 When John's messengers had left, Jesus began to say to the crowd concerning John:
"What is it y o u went out into the wilderness to look at? A reed swinging in the wind?
25 But what did y o u go out to see? A man dressed in soft garments? Surely those who are
gorgeously appareled and live in luxury are (to be found) in royal palaces. 26 But what did
y o u go out to see? A prophet? Yes, I tell y o u, even more than a prophet. 27 This is the one
of whom it is written:
'Behold, I send my messenger before thy face,
Who shall prepare thy way before thee.'
28 I tell y o u, Among those born of women there is no one greater than John; yet he who is
least in the kingdom of God is greater than he. 29 Now all the people, even the tax-
collectors, when they listened (to him), vindicated God's righteous requirements by submitting

---

283. Or: blind people . . . and so also for the other nouns in this series.

to John's baptism.[284]   30 But the Pharisees and the law-experts rejected God's purpose concerning them by refusing to be baptized by John.

31 "To what, therefore, shall I compare the people of this generation, and what are they like?   32 They are like children sitting in the market places and calling out to one another:
'We played the flute for y o u, and y o u did not dance;
We sang dirges, and y o u did not weep.'
33 For John the Baptist has come, neither eating bread nor drinking wine, and y o u say, 'He has a demon.'   34 The Son of man has come, eating and drinking, and y o u say, 'Look, a glutton and a drinker, a friend of tax-collectors and sinners.'   35 Yet wisdom is vindicated by all her children."

7:18-35 *The Doubt of John the Baptist*
and
The Manner in Which Jesus Dealt with It
The Parable of
Children Sitting in the Market Places
Cf. Matt. 11:2-19

A. *John's Doubt*

18-20. John's disciples told him all these things. Summoning two of his disciples, he sent them to the Lord, to ask, Are you the Coming One, or must we look for someone else?

When the men came to Jesus, they said, John the Baptist sent us to you to ask, Are you the Coming One, or must we look for someone else?

In the preceding paragraph Luke has related the story of the *raising* of the widow's son. In the present paragraph he quotes the words of Jesus, "Dead people are being *raised*." The connection is therefore clear. The news concerning the great miracle at Nain had spread far and wide, also reaching the prison where the Baptist was being kept. Result: the latter's question.

According to Luke 3:19, 20—see explanation of these verses—John the Baptist had been taken into custody by King Herod Antipas. He had been locked up in the gloomy fortress of Machaerus, modern Khirbet Mukâwer, located about eight kilometers east of the Dead Sea and twenty-four kilometers south of its northern tip. The prison was part of one of the Herodian palaces,[285] which explains the possibility of the action recorded in Mark 6:25-28. Though his imprisonment must have been a very grim ordeal, John was allowed to receive visitors, including his own disciples. From these he had learned about the activities of Jesus, the very One about whom the Baptist had said so many wonderful things (Matt. 3:11; Luke 3:16; John 1:15-18, 26, 27, 29-36; 3:28-30; 10:41; Acts 18:25; 19:4). So, the imprisoned herald may have been wondering, "If Jesus is that

---

284. Or: acknowledged, by submitting to John's baptism, that God's requirements were right.
285. Josephus, *Jewish War* VII.175; cf. *Antiquities* XVIII.119. See also L. H. Grollenberg, *op. cit.*, Plate 353 on p. 124, and map 34 on p. 116.

powerful, why does he not do something about my incarceration?" But especially: as John saw it, the gracious words that fell from the lips of the Savior and the miracles of mercy he performed did not harmonize with the manner in which he, the Baptist, had pictured him before the public. He had presented him as One who had come to punish and destroy (Matt. 3:7, 10; Luke 3:7, 9).

John's word had been true and inspired, the very "word of God" (Luke 1:76; 3:2). What Christ's herald missed, however, was this: he failed to discern that this prophecy of doom would go into fulfilment not now but at Christ's second coming. He had not seen the present and the future in true perspective.

John made a very wise decision when, instead of keeping his difficulty regarding Jesus to himself, or talking it over with others but not with the right person, he took it to Jesus. Owing to the fact that the Baptist was himself in prison, so that he was unable to go and see Jesus in person, he sent word by two of his (the Baptist's) disciples.

This does not mean, however, that the interpretation according to which it was not John himself who doubted but only his disciples who did, and that John now sends these men to Jesus so that the Savior may solve *their* problem, is correct. It is definitely incorrect. Why otherwise would Jesus have said, "Go and report to John" (verse 22)? There is no question about it: It was John himself who had a problem. It was he who wondered whether or not Jesus was "the Coming One."[286]

Due, perhaps, to the importance of the matter, the arrival of the two disciples is reported as is also John's question, in its exact original form.

B. *The Manner in Which Jesus Dealt with It*
1. *His message to John*

21-23. Now at that very time Jesus cured many people of diseases, sicknesses, and evil spirits, and on many blind persons he graciously bestowed sight. So he gave this answer to the messengers, Go back and report to John the things y o u have seen and heard: (the) blind are gaining their sight, (the) cripples are walking, (the) lepers are being cleansed, and (the) deaf are hearing, (the) dead are being raised, (the) poor are having good news preached to them.

The emissaries of John the Baptist arrived exactly at the right time, just when Jesus was demonstrating his healing love and power. Note the word *many:* Jesus cured "many" people . . . on "many" blind people he graciously bestowed sight. This was, accordingly, another season of multiple healings. Cf. 4:40, 41; 6:17-19.

First, mention is made of "diseases" or "illnesses," a term indicating any unhealthy condition of body or mind. This is followed by "sicknesses,"

---

286. Cf. J. Sickenberger, "Das in die Welt Kommende Licht," *ThG,* 33 (1941), pp. 129-134. See N.T.C. on the Gospel of John, Vol. I, pp. 78, 79.

literally "scourges," with emphasis on the painful nature of these afflictions. As to the expulsion of "evil spirits" (cf. 4:33, 34) see N.T.C. on
Matthew, pp. 436–438; on Mark, pp. 64, 65. The "blind" come in for
special mention. We see, therefore, that all three classes were the objects of
Christ's compassion and were affected by his healing power: the sick, the
demon-possessed, and the handicapped, the latter here represented by the
blind.

Again and again the Gospels make mention of blind people. In Luke see
4:18; 6:39; 14:13, 21; 18:35–43. There must have been many thus afflicted.
These were days when knowledge of the causes of blindness was about at
the zero level, when the importance of sanitary conditions was not as yet
appreciated, and when preventive measures had not as yet been discovered. All this indicates how great a Savior was, and is, Jesus. Just how he
cured all diseases, sicknesses, etc., we do not know. It cannot be explained
in terms of physical science. We joyfully accept it by faith.

So John's emissaries are told to go back and tell John what they themselves have witnessed (seen and heard): blind (people) are gaining their
sight, cripples are walking, etc. The very omission of the article causes all
the emphasis to rest on the tragic condition of these people.

"Dead (people) are raised" echoes what happened at Nain. This surely is
the climax; here the sentence must end, for there can be no greater work
than that of raising the dead. So we might reason. But the inspired
evangelist, who is reporting Christ's words, knows better. Raising the dead
is *not* the climax. There is something even greater, namely, "the poor are
having good news preached to them." That is the greatest work of all.

All these things must be reported to John, so that his doubts may vanish.
In which sense was this answer reassuring? Is it not true that John already
knew all this (verses 17, 18; cf. Matt. 11:2), and that the very fact that he
knew it had contributed substantially to his doubt? True indeed, but *the
wording* was new ... Or was it? It was "new" in the sense that friends who
had been reporting Christ's activities to John had not used this type of
formulation. On the other hand, the message *as phrased by Jesus* had a
familiar ring. It must have reminded John of certain prophetic predictions,
namely, Isa. 35:5, 6 and 61:1: "Then the eyes of the blind shall be opened,
and the ears of the deaf unstopped; then shall the crippled [or: lame] man
leap as a hart, and the tongue of the dumb shall sing for joy.... The spirit
of the Lord Jehovah is upon me, because Jehovah has anointed me to
preach good news to the poor [or: meek]." It is as if Jesus were tenderly
saying to John, *"Do you remember these prophecies? This, too, was predicted
concerning Messiah. And all this is being fulfilled today, namely, in me."*

In connection with these prophetic words and their fulfilment in Jesus
two additional facts should be noted: (a) Isaiah had referred both to miracles and preaching; Christ's message to John also contains a reference to
both; and (b) the fulfilment in Christ was even better than the prediction,

for in the latter not a word had even been whispered with reference to cleansing the leper and raising the dead.

The message addressed to John ends with the words: **And blessed is he who is not repelled by me.** How very gentle this rebuke. Jesus does not scold John for having asked, "Are you the Coming One, or must we look for someone else?" Instead, he reminds his wavering follower that a special blessing awaits him who does not fall into this trap but continues by God's grace to trust. For more on the word *repelled* see the note on verse 23 on page 403.

The Lord treats John as tenderly as he did the man born blind, the woman caught in adultery, Peter, Thomas, etc. In view of the fact that Jesus immediately proceeds to praise John publicly and to rebuke those who were finding fault both with this herald and with the One to whom he bore witness (verses 24-35), and also in view of such passages as Mal. 3:1; 4:5, 6; Luke 1:15-17, 76, 80; Phil. 1:6, it must be considered certain that the message of Jesus had the desired effect on John. But it is the wisdom and tenderness of Jesus that stand out in this message of reassurance addressed to John.

2. *His message to the people*

The tender love of Jesus is also shown in his defense of John, upholding his honor before the crowd. By now John's messengers have left, at least are going away (Matt. 11:7). Then Jesus asks the crowd a series of questions concerning their relation to John *in former days,* as compared to *now.* These questions have been correctly described as "quasi-satirical" (F. W. Danker, *op. cit.,* p. 97).

24-27. When John's messengers had left, Jesus began to say to the crowd concerning John:

What is it y o u went out into the wilderness to look at? A reed swaying in the wind? Here Jesus corrects the erroneous conclusion which some of the people were apt to draw with respect to John because of the question in which he had revealed his doubt concerning the very One whom he had formerly pointed out as the Messiah. The conclusion against which, by implication, Jesus warns is that the Baptist is a fickle, vacillating person. In the paragraph, taken as a whole, the Master is saying that it is wrong to condemn a person on the basis of one deviation from the straight course.

In order to form a true opinion about a man his entire life, past as well as present, must be taken into consideration. In the case of John that past had been glorious. The crowd should reflect on the tremendous impact the Baptist had made on them during his earlier appearance in the wilderness of Jordan. "What was it," says Jesus as it were, "that made y o u travel all the way from Galilee to the Judean wilderness? Was it perhaps to look at a man who resembled a reed swaying in [literally: being swayed by] the wind on the banks of the Jordan?" Of course, that could not have been the reason.

The person about whom everybody had been talking was like a sturdy oak, not like a trembling reed. Jesus takes for granted that the answer to the question voiced in verse 24 is "Indeed not. We definitely did not go out into the wilderness to look at a reed swaying in the wind." So he continues: **But what did y o u go out to see? A man dressed in soft garments?** Again the answer is a firm negative, as Jesus makes clear by continuing, **Surely those who are gorgeously appareled and live in luxury are (to be found) in royal palaces.** As to John's actual garments see Matt. 3:4. Those who wear "soft" garments are the people without backbone, sycophants who readily kowtow to those in authority and are rewarded with a high office in the king's palace, a position that enables them to be gorgeously appareled and to live luxuriously in harmony with the high station in life to which they have attained.

The people whom Jesus here addresses know very well that John is a totally different individual. Instead of flattering the king he had even rebuked him. So now, instead of enjoying gay palace life he was locked up in a horrid dungeon. Moreover, at the time when the Baptist was still free and preaching in the wilderness the people, by and large, had not even thought of finding fault with his stern message and rustic appearance. At that time John had been a popular hero (Luke 3:7, 15). No doubt even afterward many continued to hold him in high esteem (20:6). Yet opinions were beginning to change. What many formerly praised in John, his ascetic manner of life and unsparing warnings, they had now begun to criticize. It is for this reason that Jesus here takes them to task. Continued: **But what did y o u go out to see? A prophet?** The Lord answers his own question, and in doing so gives a true appraisal of John: **Yes, I tell y o u, even more than a prophet;** meaning, "Yes, y o u went out to see a prophet, and I assure y o u that he is even more than a prophet."

"More than a prophet" for John not only prophesied (see, for example, 3:9, 16, 17), but was himself also an object of prophecy. He was himself the predicted forerunner of the Messiah. Therefore Jesus continues: **This is the one of whom it is written:**

> **Behold, I send my messenger before thy face,**
> **Who shall prepare thy way before thee.**

That Mal. 3:1 refers indeed to John the Baptist as Messiah's herald is clear from the fact that this way-preparer is evidently "Elijah the prophet" of Mal. 4:5, who, in turn, is John the Baptist, according to Christ's own words as recorded in Matt. 11:14. We are justified in saying, therefore, that this is Christ's own interpretation of Mal. 3:1. Thus interpreted, the meaning, in brief, of Mal. 3:1 must be:

"Take note, I, Jehovah, send my messenger, John the Baptist, to be the forerunner of thee, the Messiah. The forerunner's task is to prepare everything—especially the hearts of the people [Mal. 4:6]—for thy coming." The meaning is "to pave the way" for Messiah's *first* coming, but in view of the fact that the first coming and the second coming are as it were two stages whereby God comes to his people in Immanuel, therefore also the way for his *second* coming. When applied in the latter sense the appellation *my messenger* attains a broader meaning, from which neither John the Baptist nor Christ's apostles nor their successors throughout the new dispensation can be excluded. Though it is true that the immediate context of Mal. 3:1 reaches forward to the final judgment (see especially verses 2 and 3), Luke very legitimately applies the prophecy especially to the first phase of the coming, or, to put it more simply, to the first coming.

It was in a marvelous manner that John the Baptist had fulfilled his task as herald. Hence Jesus is able to continue as follows: **28. I tell y o u, Among those born of women there is no one greater than John.**

As already indicated, John was greater because he was not only a prophet but one whose arrival upon the scene of history had been prophesied. It may well be questioned, however, whether this is all that Jesus meant when he made the tremendous statement found here in 7:28, introducing it with the formula, "I tell y o u." Is it not very probable that the Lord was thinking not only of the simple fact that John the Baptist, the herald, arrived in fulfilment of prophecy, but also of the marvelous manner in which this forerunner had fulfilled his task?

He had done exactly what a herald must do. First, he had very clearly announced the arrival of Messiah, directing the people's attention to that Great One: "Look, the Lamb of God who is taking away the sin of the world" (John 1:29). Secondly, he had emphasized the necessity of conversion (including repentance) as the only way for the sinner to enter Messiah's kingdom (Matt. 3:2 and parallels; see also Luke 1:76, 77). And thirdly, since it is the duty of the herald to recede to the background when the One whom he has introduced has fully arrived upon the scene, so John had resisted the temptation to call attention to himself. Instead, in humility of spirit he had said, "He must increase, but I must decrease" (John 3:30). Now in view of the fact that Jesus himself, in describing the nature of true greatness, always links it with humility (Matt. 8:8, 10, cf. Luke 7:6, 9; Matt. 18:1-5, cf. Mark 9:33-37 and Luke 9:46-48; Matt. 20:26, 27, cf. Mark 10:43-45; Matt. 23:11; and see also Matt. 15:27, 28), is it not altogether probable that he does this also in the present case? This humility, in turn, must be viewed as a gift which John had received from the Holy Spirit. Thus the word of the angel addressed to Zechariah, "He shall be great . . . and filled with the Holy Spirit from his mother's womb" (Luke 1:15), had been and was being fulfilled. Surely, *all* of this—(a) John not only "the prophet of the Highest" but himself the fulfilment of prophecy, (b) as such one who in a most humble manner fulfilled his task, (c) being filled with the Holy Spirit and this from his mother's womb—must be taken into consideration in order to do justice to the full meaning of Luke 7:28. When that is done it will be clear that the statement is not in any sense an exaggeration.

To this Jesus adds: **yet he who is least in the kingdom of God is greater than he.** This cannot mean that John, after all, was not a saved man. Perish the very thought! Rather, the statement must be explained in the light of 10:23, 24, "Blessed (are) the eyes that see what y o u are seeing! For I tell y o u that many prophets and kings wanted to see what y o u are seeing but did not see it, and to hear what y o u are hearing but did not hear it." The one least in the kingdom was greater than John in the sense that he was more highly privileged, for the Baptist in his prison was not in such close touch with Jesus as was this least one. And was it not this very circumstance which had also contributed to the herald's confusion with respect to whether or not Jesus was truly the Messiah?

As Luke has indicated (7:20, 21), at the very moment when the messengers sent by John submitted his question to Jesus, the latter was busily engaged in the act of healing and restoring. Is it not true that actually seeing all this happening before one's very eyes would be more likely to ring memory's bell, recalling to mind Isa. 35:5, 6; 61:1 ff., than would a dismal prison atmosphere, with no opportunity even to see, much less to speak to the One about whom the prisoner was thinking? Yes, in a sense the kingdom had already arrived: the afflicted ones were being delivered from their ills, the dead were being raised up, and the words of life and beauty were proceeding from the heart and lips of the Master. But in his sovereign providence, which no one has a right to question, John was not an immediate participant or even a direct witness. Also, he was not to see Calvary nor to experience Pentecost. However, he was not being forgotten or neglected. The message Jesus sent him (7:22, 23) was sufficient to reassure him.

It was thus that Jesus defended John in front of people who, as verses 24, 25, 33 clearly indicate, were beginning to find fault with the Baptist. Still thinking of these former days and the preaching of the Baptist, the Master continues:

29, 30. Now all the people, even the tax-collectors, when they listened (to him), vindicated God's righteous requirements by submitting to John's baptism. But the Pharisees and the law-experts rejected God's purpose concerning them by refusing to be baptized by John.

Probable meaning in the light of the context:

Jesus has shown that John was great indeed (verse 28). As God's voice to the people he had pressed upon them these divine requirements: they must turn from their evil ways and bear good fruit. In other words, they must be converted, must undergo a basic change. Repentance and faith are needed.

Now in those former days "all the people"—probably hyperbole for ever so many common people from "everywhere"—including even tax-collectors, having listened to John's preaching, acknowledged these divine requirements as being just ("righteous"). They showed this by turning to God and submitting to baptism.

Such a reaction was, of course, in line with God's saving *purpose*. See Isa. 1:18–20; 45:22; 55:1, 6, 7; Jer. 26:13; Amos 5:15; Acts 2:37, 38; 3:19; II Cor. 5:20; II Peter 3:9.

But the Pharisees and the law-experts—for details see above, on 5:17—though at first also standing in awe of John, some Pharisees even coming to his baptism (Matt. 3:7), in large numbers rejected God's saving purpose as far as they were concerned. Many common people, following their leaders, now also rejected what they had formerly accepted. Verse 31, "To what, therefore, shall I compare the [i.e., these fickle, changeable] people?" follows naturally.

There are those, however, who regard verses 29, 30 as a parenthesis inserted by Luke. Objections:

a. Nowhere else do we find such a Lucan parenthesis in the midst of a dominical discourse.

b. If verses 29, 30 are a Lucan parenthesis, then the words of Jesus found in verse 28, "Among those born of women there is no one greater than John," etc., would be followed by, "To what, therefore, shall I compare the people...?" An awkward connection.

c. What is perhaps the strongest argument against the "Lucan parenthesis" view is this: a thought similar to Luke 7:29, 30 is found in Matt. 21:31b, 32—see N.T.C. on Matthew, pp. 779, 780—*and is clearly ascribed to Jesus!* No Lucan parenthesis, therefore.

3. *His message to the people (continued):*
The Parable of Children Sitting in the Market Places

31–35. To what, therefore, shall I compare the people of this generation, and what are they like? They are like children sitting in the market places and calling out to one another:

We played the flute for y o u, and y o u did not dance;
We sang dirges, and y o u did not weep.

For John the Baptist has come, neither eating bread nor drinking wine, and y o u say, He has a demon. —The Son of man has come, eating and drinking, and y o u say, Look, a glutton and a drinker, a friend of tax-collectors and sinners.[287]

Note the majestic introduction, "To what, therefore... and what are they like?" which reminds one of Isaiah 40:18, 25; 46:5. On the lips of Jesus this kind of style, used when introducing a very serious subject, is certainly most appropriate.

It is clear that by means of this parable Jesus is accusing these critics of being childish. There is a difference between being childlike and being

---

287. The slight differences between Matthew's report and Luke's do not touch the essence. Each fully inspired author was allowed to use his own style. If Jesus actually said, "To what, therefore, shall I compare the people of this generation, and what are they like?" Matthew reproduces the essence in abbreviated form. So also Luke's "and y o u did not weep," and Matthew's "and y o u did not beat the breast" are synonymous. Both activities were usual in connection with funerals. Besides, Jesus may well have used both expressions. Matthew's "neither eating nor drinking" is more fully stated in Luke's "neither eating bread nor drinking wine," which is, of course, what Matthew also had in mind. And so for other slight variations. None in any way change the essence. Both accounts are fully inspired.

childish. The Lord recommends the first (Matt. 18:1–5 and parallel passages). He condemns the second. The picture he draws is that of children who on those days when no business is being transacted in the market gather in its ample spaces in order to play games. Today, however, nothing seems to succeed. Some children begin to play the flute, as an accompaniment not to mourning (Matt. 9:23) but to merriment (cf. Rev. 18:22). They want to play wedding. Others object. So the players put their flutes away and start to lament pitifully and/or moan a dirge, as they have heard their elders and the professional mourners do. That idea, too, does not go across. In a spirit of desperation they then scold their playmates for being so uncooperative, a complaint which the others return.

We can easily imagine something of this nature happening today. "Let's play wedding," says one child. Others chime in. "Let Mary be the bride, Ruth the maid of honor. I'll be the groom. Bert can be the best man, Peter the father of the bride, Jack will do very nicely for the preacher." "Yes, let's do that, " say some of the others, and they start whistling a wedding march. But many voices scream back in disgust, "Not that silly stuff. That's not for us." "Then let's play funeral," says the boy who had been the first to suggest playing wedding, and he adds, "I'll be the funeral director, the pállbearers are John, Bert, Peter, and Larry. Mike can be the corpse." Dolefully the speaker and some others begin to intone a funeral hymn. But their groaning is drowned out by loud protests: "Cut it out. We want none of this sad stuff." So a petty quarrel develops, in which those who had suggested the games are shouting to their playmates, "Y o u 're never satisfied. Y o u don't want to play wedding and y o u don't want to play funeral. What *do* y o u want to play?" The accused hurl back similar charges.[288] All are unhappy, disgruntled, sulky. Weddings are too silly, too glad; funerals, too gloomy, too sad. Not only are the children peevish and quarrelsome, they are also fickle, inconsistent: what they used to get all excited about they now look down upon.

Jesus, then, is saying, "That is the way y o u critics are behaving. Y o u are being childish. Y o u are frivolous and are acting irresponsibly, inconsistently. Y o u are never satisfied. Y o u used to be filled with enthusiasm about John; at least, y o u stood in awe of him and did not find fault with his austerity and call to repentance. But now y o u say, 'He is too harsh and unsociable; his message is too severe. Why, he must be possessed.' But y o u

---

288. Because of Luke 7:32, which clearly states that the children shouted "to one another," I cannot join those commentators who make a kind of allegory of this illustration, and, having divided the children into two groups, the complainers and those complained against, then proceed to identify the former (those who did "the piping and the wailing") with those who were *disappointed* with John the Baptist and Jesus; and the latter, with John the Baptist and Jesus. See, for example, Lenski, *op. cit.*, p. 429. I agree with R. V. G. Tasker, *The Gospel According to St. Matthew (Tyndale New Testament Commentaries)*, Grand Rapids, 1961, p. 116, when he states, "It is the general characteristics of children at play to which Jesus directs attention." So also H. N. Ridderbos, *Het Evangelie naar Mattheus (Korte Verklaring)*, Kampen, 1952, p. 22.

are also turning against me, the Son of man.[289] Y o u are pointing the finger at me and saying, 'Though he demands self-denial in others, he himself is a glutton and a drinker, a friend of tax-collectors and sinners. He is too sociable.' "

Jesus points out that in the end such thoroughly unfair and bitter criticism and intolerance will get nowhere. The victory is on the side of truth. He says, **Yet wisdom is vindicated by all her children.** The wisdom of John the Baptist, when he insisted on conversion, and of Jesus, when he held out the hope of salvation even to those with whom many in Israel would have nothing to do, was shown to have been fully justified by what it accomplished in the hearts and lives of "all her children"; that is, all those who allowed themselves to be guided by that wisdom.

John and Jesus each had his distinct mission to perform. Each carried out his assignment. By Jesus, who himself in person was and is "wisdom from God" (I Cor. 1:30), this assignment was carried out flawlessly; by John, by and large superbly. Wisdom's children, then, are all those who were wise enough to take to heart the message of John and of Jesus.

Between John and Jesus there was this similarity: both proclaimed the gospel. Even John's message was certainly not without hope (see especially John 1:29). Even when his emphasis was on repentance, his exhortation was hope-inspiring. See Luke 3:16, 18. Yet between John and Jesus there was also a contrast, not only the one pointed out here (7:33, 34), but also this, namely, that while John *proclaimed* the good news, Jesus not only proclaimed it but came into this world that there might be good news to proclaim!

Today we know that to a considerable degree wisdom's vindication has already arrived. For example, has not the designation that was originally intended as a disparaging nickname, "friend of tax-collectors and sinners," become one of the Savior's most hope-imparting and soul-stirring titles? Is this title not being "justified" by thousands upon thousands of lives that have taken it to heart and acted upon it? And will not the full and final vindication arrive on the day of the consummation of all things, and ever afterward?[290]

Practical Lessons Derived from Luke 7:18–35

Verse 19

"Or must we look for someone else?" Substitutes for Jesus: (a) the Jews still have no one. (b) Some substitute this or that earthly ruler (e.g., "F. D. Roosevelt is my God," exclaimed a man many years ago). Others substitute themselves. Cf. W. E. Henley's *Invictus* ("I am the master of my fate; I am the captain of my soul"). But

---

289. On this title see above, on 5:24.
290. Notes on Greek words, phrases, and constructions in 7:18–35 begin on page 402.

when his child, a beloved daughter, died, he found no comfort. Simon Peter had the true solution (John 6:67, 68).

Verse 26

"A prophet... even more than a prophet." Among the many admirable traits possessed by the Baptist two that stand out are his humility—reminding us of the centurion mentioned in Luke 7:6—and his courage, comparable to that of Nathan (II Sam. 12:7), Elijah (I Kings 18:18), and Amos (Amos, ch. 4; 7:14-17). For the lesson see N.T.C. on Matt. 11:12, pp. 488-490.

Verse 35

"Wisdom is vindicated by all her children," where Matthew (11:19) has "by her works [or deeds]." A conflict? Not at all. Wisdom is vindicated by what it *does* to *people* who by grace possess and exercise it. Thus Matthew and Luke are reconciled. For the lesson see I Cor. 1:30; James 3:17. The manifestation of true wisdom in the lives of human individuals brings peace and joy to their own hearts, is a blessing to others, and glorifies God. See Job 28:28; Prov. 3:13; 19:8.

Longfellow had the right idea:

> Lives of great men all remind us
> We can make our lives sublime,
> And departing leave behind us
> Footprints on the sands of time.
>
> *A Psalm of Life*

Notes on Greek Words, Phrases, and Constructions in 7:18-35

Verses 18 and 22

ἀπήγγειλαν, third per. pl. aor. indicat. of ἀπαγγέλλω. Cf. sec. per. pl. aor. active imperat. of same verb, in verse 22; to tell. See also the note on 8:20 on page 437.

Verse 19

προσδοκῶμεν, first per. pl. pres. indicat. of προσδοκάω, to look forward to, look for, expect.

Verse 20

For παραγενόμενοι (to come) see the note on 7:4 on page 380.

Verse 21

ἐθεράπευσεν, third per. s. aor. indicat. act. of θεραπεύω, to heal. See also the note on 4:23 on page 261.

A νόσος is a disease, illness. Some see a connection between νόσος and νεκρός, corpse, but this cannot be proved. A μάστιξ is basically a whip, scourge (cf. Acts 22:24; Heb. 11:36, scourging); then a sickness, calamity.

Verse 23

σκανδαλισθῇ, third per. s., aor. passive subjunct. of σκανδαλίζω. The σκάνδαλον is the bait-stick in a trap or snare. It is the crooked stick that springs the trap; hence, *snare, temptation to sin, enticement* (Matt. 18:7; Luke 17:1); also, object of revulsion, the stumbling-block of the cross (I Cor. 1:23; Gal. 5:11). Similarly the verb basically means *to ensnare, lure into sin, lead astray* (Matt. 5:29; 18:6; etc.). In the passive it may mean *to be repelled by* (Matt. 11:6; Mark 6:3; and here in Luke 7:23).

Verse 24

θεάσασθαι, aor. middle infinitive of θεάομαι, to look at, see. Cf. *theater*. See the note on 5:27 on page 306.

Verse 25

μαλακός, soft. Cf. *mellow, mild.*
For τρυφή (here dat.) see also II Peter 2:13: softness, indulgence, luxury, splendor. Cf. the root τερ, to rub; hence, by rubbing to render soft.

Verse 28

μικρότερος. Note that the comparative (ending in -τερος) is replacing the superlative. Cf. I Cor. 13:13 where a different kind of comparative replaces the superlative. See also the note on 7:42 on page 412.

Verses 29, 35

ἐδικαίωσαν, third per. pl. aor. indicat. active of δικαιόω, here in the sense of to vindicate, to acknowledge (God's) righteousness or righteous requirement(s). Note third per. aor. indicat. passive of the same verb in verse 35; there *gnomic* aorist, expressing what is usual.

Note "(by) being baptized with the baptism," thus literally, aor. passive participle with cognate accusative. This type of cognate construction, though certainly not absent from Greek literature, both classical and Koine, is even more frequent in Hebrew. For the Old Testament see Josh. 10:20; I Sam. 4:5; I Kings 1:40; Neh. 12:43; Isa. 66:10; Zeph. 3:17, to mention but a few examples. In the Greek of the New Testament see Matt. 2:10; Luke 2:8; John 7:24; Col. 2:19; I Tim. 1:18; 6:12; I Peter 3:14; I John 5:16; Rev. 17:6.

Verse 30

ἠθέτησαν, third per. pl. aor. indicat. of ἀθετέω, to set aside, reject. See also 10:16; cf. Mark 6:26; 7:9; John 12:48; I Cor. 1:19; Gal. 2:21, etc.
εἰς ἑαυτούς, for themselves.

Verse 32

For the verb προσφωνέω see the note on 6:13 on page 333. Here (in 7:32) dat. pl. masc. present participle.
ηὐλήσαμεν, first per. pl. aor. indicat. of αὐλέω; cf. αὐλός, a flute; also ἄω, αὔω, to blow. An αὐλή is an open-air place, court, sheepfold, etc. For more on this noun see the note on 22:55 on page 1000.

ὠϱχήσασθε, sec. per. pl. aor. indicat. of ὀϱχέομαι, to dance. Cf. *orchestra*.

ἐθϱηνήσαμεν, same construction as ηὐλήσαμεν. The verb θϱηνέω means: to sing dirges, to mourn, lament. See also 23:27; Matt. 11:17; John 16:20. Cf. *drone, threnody.*

Verses 33, 34

ἐλήλυθεν, in both verses, third per. s. 2nd perf. indicat. act. of ἔϱχομαι.

Verse 35

See above, under verses 29, 35.

---

36 Now one of the Pharisees invited Jesus to eat with him. So he entered the Pharisee's house and reclined at table.[291]   37 And look, there was a woman in town who was a sinner. When she learned that Jesus was having dinner in the Pharisee's house, she brought an alabaster jar of perfume,   38 and, continually weeping, took her stand behind his feet. She began to make his feet wet with her tears, and kept on wiping them with the hair of her head, kissing his feet, and anointing them with the perfume.

39 Now when the Pharisee who had invited him saw this, he said to himself, "If this man were a prophet, he would know who and what kind of person this woman is who is touching him, that she is a sinner."

40 Answering, Jesus said to him, "Simon, I must tell you something." He said, "Go ahead, Teacher."

41 "Two men were in debt to a certain moneylender. One owed (him) five hundred denarii, the other fifty.   42 Since they were unable to pay back what they owed, the moneylender graciously canceled the debt for both. Now, which of the two will love him most?"

43 Simon replied, "I take it that it was the one for whom he canceled most."

44 Jesus answered, "You have judged correctly." Then, turning toward the woman, Jesus said to Simon, "Do you see this woman? I entered your house. Water for my feet you did not provide. She, however, with her tears made my feet wet, and with her hair wiped them.   45 A kiss you did not give me, but she, from the moment I came in, has not stopped fervently kissing my feet.   46 With (ordinary) oil you did not anoint (even) my head, but she with perfume anointed my feet!   47 Therefore I tell you, her sins, many though they be, are forgiven, for she loved much; but the person to whom little is forgiven loves little."

48 Then he said to her, "Forgiven are your sins."

49 Those reclining at table with him began to say within themselves, "Who is this who even forgives sins?"

50 So, Jesus said to the woman, "Your faith has saved you. Go in peace."

7:36-50 *Jesus Anointed by a Penitent Woman*
The Parable of The Two Debtors

Must the woman of this story be identified with Mary of Bethany? In other words, does Luke 7:36-50 have a parallel in Matt. 26:6-13; Mark 14:3-9; John 12:1-8? The answer is *No*. For details see N.T.C. on John, Vol. II, pp. 174, 175. Neither is there any reason whatever for identifying her with Mary Magdalene. See on Luke 8:2.

---

291. Or: and took his place at the table.

A. *In the house of Simon the Pharisee Jesus is anointed by a Penitent Woman.*

36. Now one of the Pharisees invited Jesus to eat with him. So he entered the Pharisee's house and reclined at table.

Place and time are not indicated. Nevertheless, there is a connection with the preceding. In verse 30 Luke, quoting the words of Jesus, focused our attention upon self-righteous Pharisees, and in verse 34 on people of bad reputation, "sinners." An example of each is given in the present account.

One day a Pharisee, named Simon (verse 40)—not to be confused with "Simon Peter" nor with "Simon the Zealot," with "Simon the father of Judas Iscariot," with "Simon of Cyrene," with "Simon the tanner," nor even with "Simon the leper"—invited Jesus for dinner. Why did he extend this invitation? We are not told. Verses 44–46 clearly indicate, however, that he did not do so out of love or even high regard for Jesus. He may have been motivated by curiosity. Having heard that many people were calling the Master "a great prophet" (7:16), he may have invited Jesus in order to see whether there was any substance to this fame the so-called prophet was acquiring. Even the possibility that he wanted to have an opportunity to find a basis for formulating a charge against Jesus cannot be entirely excluded. Cf. 6:7.

Jesus accepts the invitation and enters the Pharisee's house. So broad is his sympathy that he eats not only with the tax-collector Levi (5:29) but also with the Pharisee Simon, and with other Pharisees when they invite him (11:37; 14:1). On "and reclined at table" see the next passage:

37, 38. And look, there was a woman in town who was a sinner. When she learned that Jesus was having dinner in the Pharisee's house, she brought an alabaster jar of perfume, and, continually weeping, took her stand behind his feet. She began to make his feet wet with her tears, and kept on wiping them with the hair of her head, kissing his feet, and anointing them with the perfume.

The exclamatory phrase, *And look,* indicates that Luke wishes to call our special attention to the strange incident that now occurred. In this particular town there happened to be a certain well-known woman of bad reputation. To say that she was probably a harlot is being unfair to her. A woman could be a "sinner" without being a harlot. Besides, it is clear from the present account that whatever she had been she was no longer. She must have heard the words of Jesus. And these words, spoken on previous occasions, must have been applied savingly to her. Also, even now there was present in her heart the beginning of a consciousness of having been divinely pardoned. Otherwise how can we explain the fact that, having learned that Jesus was in the house of the Pharisee, she not only came to this house but brought an alabaster jar of perfume? Such an alabaster jar was a vase of white (or perhaps delicately tinted) fine-grained gypsum. It had a long neck. To pour out its contents this neck had to be broken. It is clear that she felt the need of bringing an offering of thanksgiving to him who had been instrumental in changing her life.

That she was permitted to enter this home at all is, *in a way*, not so strange. It was not at all unusual for uninvited persons to enter a home in which a dinner was being given. They would generally seat themselves along the wall, observe everything that was happening and even engage some of the invited guests in conversation.[292] Nevertheless, that this particular woman, widely known as a "sinner," had the courage to enter the home of *a strict Pharisee,* that was something else again. The only way we can explain it is by assuming that the urge within her to express gratitude to Jesus was so irresistible that nothing could stop her from doing what she wanted to do.

Overwhelmed with genuine sorrow for her past sinful life, the woman stands at Jesus' feet. We assume, with the majority of translators and commentators, that those who partook of this meal were reclining on low couches arranged around a table. Each person, facing the table, would be lying slantwise, with his feet stretched out backward. He would be leaning on his left arm, in order to keep his right hand free to handle the food. It is therefore understandable that the woman was standing behind him, that is, at his extended feet.[293]

To anoint Jesus with perfume she has come today; note: with *perfume,* costly and fragrant (cf. Matt. 26:7, 12; Mark 14:3-5; John 11:2-5), not just with ordinary olive oil (see verse 46). Nothing is too good for Jesus! But as she stands there, she hesitates. In fact, she is overcome by emotion. Overwhelming sorrow for past sin is mingled with profound gratitude for the present sense of forgiveness. Her heart is filled to overflowing with love and reverence for the One who has opened her eyes and has brought about a radical change in her life. Result: she bursts into tears. This "heart water" (Luther) drops down on the feet of Jesus. Impulsively she does what in those days no woman was supposed to do in public: she loosens her tresses. Then, bending down with her hair thus let down, she, while continually

---

292. For archaeological aspects of this story (customs at meals, etc.) see especially A. Stöger, op. cit., Vol. I, pp. 142–146; A. Sizoo, *De Antieke Wereld,* pp. 49, 50; also indices of F. R. Cowell, *Everyday Life in Ancient Rome,* Edinburgh, 1961; and C. Guignebert, *The Jewish World in the Time of Jesus,* London, 1939.

293. Not all agree with this very generally accepted representation. On the basis of such Old Testament passages as Judg. 19:6; I Sam. 20:5; I Kings 13:20, all of which speak of *sitting* at table, and of his own observations in The Near East, where he lived and taught for several years, Dr. H. Mulder (*Spoorzoeker,* pp. 87–91) arrives at the conclusion that "just like the other guests so also Jesus *sat* in kneeled position, his feet extended backward with the underside turned upward." He calls attention to the fact that lying down to eat was a "western" (Greek and Roman) custom, and he states that this eating style had not been universally adopted in Palestine and the surrounding regions.

The matter is probably not as important as it may seem, for whether Jesus was reclining or sitting at the table, in either case his feet were in a position that made it possible for the woman to stand behind them.

weeping, keeps on wiping Jesus' feet, kissing them, and from the already broken jar pouring perfume upon them.

B. *He is criticized by Simon.*

39. Now when the Pharisee who had invited him saw this, he said to himself, If this man were a prophet, he would know who and what kind of person this woman is who is touching him, that she is a sinner.

Simon, a typical Pharisee, is deeply offended by what this woman is doing. Even more, his sense of propriety is wounded by the fact that Jesus tolerates such behavior on her part. Has Simon been wondering whether Jesus is really a prophet? If so, he wonders no longer. He is convinced that had Jesus been a prophet he would immediately have discerned the character of this base intruder, this "sinner." See explanation of 6:32–34; 7:34. He would have pushed away this infamous wretch.

Self-righteous Simon did not understand—or did not want to believe—that Jesus associated with sinners *in order that they might be converted and saved.* Cf. 5:31, 32; 15:1, 2; 18:14.

C. *By means of the parable of The Two Debtors Jesus makes his self-defense. He reassures the woman.*

40–42. Answering, Jesus said to him, Simon, I must tell you something. He said, Go ahead, Teacher. Two men were in debt to a certain moneylender. One owed him five hundred denarii, the other fifty. Since they were unable to pay back what they owed, the moneylender graciously canceled the debt for both. Now, which of the two will love him most?

In verses 40–48 Jesus exposes Simon's errors. He proves that:

1. he knows this woman, her past history and her present condition;

2. he even knows what Simon has been saying to himself;

3. he is, accordingly, a prophet; in fact a discerner of hearts and minds;

4. he is nothing less than the divine Savior, clothed with authority to forgive sins.

When Jesus says to Simon, "I must tell you something," the host is curious to know what that could be. So he answers, "Go ahead, Teacher." The parable of The Two Debtors follows. It requires very little in the way of explanation. Briefly the meaning is:

Once upon a time two men were in debt to a moneylender. One debtor owed him an amount equal to what a common laborer earns during a period of five hundred days (excluding sabbaths); the other, an amount for which such a laborer would have to work fifty days. However, neither was able to pay. Then what did the moneylender do? Instead of having these two deadbeats thrown in jail, he very generously canceled the debt for both. . . . Probably looking straight at Simon, Jesus asks him, "Now which of these two debtors will reveal greatest love toward the moneylender?"

43. Simon replied, I take it that it was the one for whom he canceled most.

In the spirit of indifference, real or feigned, Simon, ill at ease and wondering what Jesus is trying to prove, answers, "I take it [or I suppose, I presume] that it was the one with the larger, now canceled debt."

44–47. Jesus answered, You have judged correctly. —Then, turning toward the woman, Jesus said to Simon, Do you see this woman? I entered your house. Water for my feet you did not provide. She, however, with her tears made my feet wet, and with her hair wiped them. A kiss you did not give me, but she, from the moment I came in, has not stopped fervently kissing my feet. With (ordinary) oil you did not anoint (even) my head, but she with perfume anointed my feet! Therefore I tell you, her sins, many though they be, are forgiven, for she loved much; but the person to whom little is forgiven loves little.[294]

In his great patience Jesus limits his comment (on Simon's reply) to the statement that the Pharisee has judged correctly. Then, very dramatically, the Master directs Simon's attention to "this woman." Does Simon see her? Has he at all understood the significance of her actions? "I entered your house," Jesus continues, not even adding, as he might have, "at your own invitation." Next, the Master exposes before everybody the shabby treatment he had received from his host. The latter had omitted all the customary evidences of hospitality, all the amenities to which, as everyone knew, an honored and invited guest was entitled. Simon had not provided water to wash Jesus' feet (Gen. 18:4; Judg. 19:21), had not welcomed him by means of a kiss (Gen. 29:13; 45:15; Exod. 18:7), and had not anointed his guest's head, not even with cheap olive oil (Ps. 23:5; 141:5). The reception had been cold, patronizing, discourteous.

The Master shows that in all three respects he had received the very opposite treatment from the penitent woman. Instead of water for Jesus' feet, this woman had provided tears, indicative of repentance. Instead of a kiss upon the cheek, she had planted ever so many fervent kisses on the feet, symbols of humble gratitude. And instead of cheap olive oil for the head, she had poured precious and fragrant perfume on the feet!

Jesus adds, "Therefore I tell you, her sins, many though they be, are forgiven," etc. To bring out the full emphasis of the original the rendering would have to be expanded somewhat as follows: "Therefore I tell you,

---

294. When for verses 44b–46 (i.e., from "Water for my feet" to "she with perfume anointed my feet") one compares most translations with the one here offered, the difference will be apparent. Those readers who, above everything else, go for smooth style, will prefer the usual renderings. There certainly is a place for that. But there also is a place for the translation here presented. It has the advantage of bringing into sharper focus the contrasts and emphases of the original. Though the translation here offered is not exactly the same as any of the following four—Robertson, Weymouth, Lenski, Dutch (Nieuwe Vertaling), all of them excellent—in many respects it resembles them, resulting from a common aim, as already stated.

forgiven are her sins, many though they be. They are forgiven, as is clear from the fact that she, conscious of this forgiveness, has shown that she loves me so intensely. It is the person who is forgiven little who shows little love." What Jesus teaches is that *the outpouring of love results from the sense of having been forgiven.*

In other words, what he does is this: he turns the roles around. Simon regarded himself as righteous, forgiven (if he even felt the need of any forgiveness), and looked upon the woman as a sinner, unforgiven. Jesus shows that it is Simon who by his lack of love proves that he has not been forgiven—this inference mercifully attenuated to "has been forgiven little"—while the woman can rejoice in the freedom from guilt she has received as a gift of God's grace.

Love for Jesus—hence, for God—is, and must ever be, the result of forgiveness:

> Nothing to pay! yes, nothing to pay!
> Jesus has cleared all the debt away,
> Blotted it out with his bleeding hand!
> Free and forgiven and loved you stand.
>   Hear the voice of Jesus say,
> Verily thou hast nothing to pay!
> Paid is the debt, and the debtor free!
> Now I ask thee, Lovest thou me?

> Frances Ridley Havergal,
> lines from "Nothing to Pay!"

48–50. Then he said to her, Forgiven are your sins. —Those reclining at table with him began to say within themselves, Who is this who even forgives sins?

So, Jesus said to the woman, Your faith has saved you, Go in peace.

What the woman already knew in principle is now reaffirmed. In view of her past life in sin she probably needed this reassurance, so that what she already sensed to be true—hence, her great outpouring of love—might become even more firmly established in her heart, namely, that once for all and completely her sins had been and were now blotted out. And such forgiveness never stands alone. It is ever *pardon plus.* God, in Christ, embraces this penitent woman with the arms of his protecting and adopting love. Cf. Rom. 5:1. And for the entire statement ("Forgiven are your sins") see what was said in connection with 5:20.

This statement of Jesus provoked resentment within the hearts of those who were reclining at table with him, probably mostly Pharisees. They said within themselves, "Who is this who even forgives sins?" It must not be overlooked that when Jesus publicly declared, "Forgiven are your sins," he said this not only for the sake of the woman herself, that she might be doubly assured, but also for the sake of the other guests, that they might no longer regard her as "a sinner." Having heard Jesus make this declaration of absolution, they, however, are not satisfied. The scene of 5:21 is here being virtually repeated. Hence, see on that passage.

Jesus, however, ignores what is happening inside these self-righteous hearts. He does not ignore the woman, however. It is to her, as he dismisses her, that he addresses his marvelously comforting remark, "Your faith has saved you. Go in peace."

On the essence of faith see N.T.C. on Mark, pp. 458, 459. Briefly stated, this faith, ever the gift of God's grace (John 3:3-8; Eph. 2:8), is the woman's humble trust in Jesus, her act of committing herself entirely to him. For the expression, "Your faith has saved you," see also Matt. 9:22; Mark 5:34; 10:52; Luke 8:48; 17:19; 18:42. Is it not marvelous that Jesus, in addressing this woman, says nothing about his own power and love, the root cause of her present state of salvation, but makes mention of that which apart from him she would neither have possessed nor have been able to exercise? That our Lord attached great value to faith appears also from such other Lucan passages as 5:20; 7:9; 8:25; 12:28; 17:6; 18:8; 22:32; as well as from many a passage in the other Gospels (Matt. 9:29; 14:31; 15:28, etc.; Mark 2:5; 4:40, etc.; John 3:16, etc.).

"Go in peace," says Jesus, as he dismisses her. Certainly nothing less than what is implied in the Hebrew *Shalom,* prosperity for both soul and body, can be meant here. This peace is the smile of God reflected in the heart of the redeemed sinner, a shelter in the storm, a hiding-place in the cleft of the rock and under his wings. It is *the rainbow* around the throne whence issue flashes of lightning, rumblings, and peals of thunder (Rev. 4:3, 5).[295]

Practical Lessons Derived from Luke 7:36-50

Verse 36

"So he entered the Pharisee's house and reclined at table." Though Jesus knew that the Pharisees, as a group, were unfriendly to him, he did not shun them. See also 11:37; 14:1. This is a lesson for us all.

Verse 39

"If this man were a prophet, he would know ... that she is a sinner." Simon did not really *know* (understand) Jesus. As a result he did not really know this woman, neither did he know himself. For this lack of knowledge there was no excuse (Luke 13:34; Rom. 1:28).

Verses 44-46

"Water for my feet you did not provide.... A kiss you did not give me," etc. The practice of Christianity does not exclude social graces (hospitality, kindness, etc.).

---

295. Notes on Greek words, phrases, and constructions in 7:36-50 begin on page 411.

Though this is not directly taught here, it is certainly implied. Professing believers can at times be very rude.

Verse 47

"Her sins, many though they be, are forgiven, for she loved much," meaning, "as is clear from the fact that she was very generous in showing how much she loved me. If she had not loved me so much, she would not have done what she did just now." Forgiven, she loved. Is it true that showing love, in turn, also increases the assurance of having been forgiven?

Verse 50

"Your faith has saved you. Go in peace." Does this section (7:36–50) show us how we should deal with fallen ones? With penitents? If so, in which way?

Notes on Greek Words, Phrases, and Constructions in 7:36–50

Verse 36

Ἠρώτα, third per. s. imperf. indicat. act. of ἐρωτάω, to ask; here, to invite.

ἵνα φάγῃ, third per. s. 2nd aor. subjunct. of ἐσθίω, in a sub-final clause, to eat, to have a meal (with him).

κατεκλίθη, third per. s. aor. indicat. pass. of κατακλίνω*, to recline at table. See also 9:14, 15; 14:8; 24:30.

Verses 37, 38

As shown in the explanation, this ἰδού is certainly understandable: what the woman did was indeed remarkable.

Note the three nom. s. fem. aor. participles: ἐπιγνοῦσα, on which see the notes on 1:4 on page 62, and on 1:22 on page 81; κομίσασα, of κομίζω, to bring; and στᾶσα, of ἵστημι, to set, place, etc. These aorists are followed by the nom. s. fem. *present* participle κλαίουσα, of κλαίω, to weep, cry. Note how the difference between aorist and present can be brought out in the translation.

κατάκειμαι, to lie down: (a) because of illness (Mark 1:30; Luke 5:25); (b) in order to eat, as here in Luke 7:37; hence, to recline at table, to dine, to eat. Here the present tense is retained in indirect discourse, "is having dinner," where we would say, "was having dinner."

Verses 38, 44–46

As to βρέχειν, in verse 38, pres. infinit. after ἤρξατο, and cf. ἔβρεξεν (verse 44), third per. s. aor. act., these forms are derived from βρέχω, to wet, to cause to rain, send rain, to rain. Cf. βροχή, rain (Matt. 7:25, 27: "Down came the rain"). Cf. *brook, embrocation.*

In verse 38 note the imperfects: she kept on drying, kissing, and anointing. In the summarizing statement of verses 44–46 observe the aorists: she made them wet and wiped and did not stop (kissing and anointing).

411

With respect to κατεφίλει (verse 38) see N.T.C. on Matt. 26:49, pp. 923, 924; especially footnote 851.

Verse 39

The statement "Jesus is a prophet and therefore knows," etc., *is contrary to fact,* not actually but *in the mind of Simon the Pharisee.* That accounts for the second class, or contrary to fact, conditional formulation, "If this man were," etc.

Verse 40

The nom. s. masc. aor. participle ἀποκριθείς here, as often, is not a reply to a question asked by Simon, but a reaction or response to that Pharisee's presupposition that Jesus was not a prophet and that this woman was not a worthy object of attention.

Verse 41

A χρεοφειλέτης* (from χρέος, debt, and ὀφείλω, to owe), mentioned also in 16:5, is a debtor. A δανειστής* is a creditor or moneylender. For the related verb see the note on 6:34 on page 358.

Verses 42, 43

ἐχαρίσατο (twice), third per. s. aor. indicat. of χαρίζομαι, to give graciously, freely; here: to forgive, cancel, remit.

Note that the superlative form of πολύς, πολλή, πολύ (namely, the form πλεῖστος, -η, -ον) is being replaced by the comparative form πλείων, here πλεῖον. Cf. μείζων in the sense of a superlative ("greatest") in Matt. 18:1, 4; 23:11; Mark 9:34; Luke 9:46; 22:24, 26; I Cor. 13:13. Exception II Peter 1:4, where the superlative form (in the elative sense) is retained. See also above, the note on 7:28 on page 403, and N.T.C. on Matthew, p. 686, footnote 638.

Verses 44–46

Note forward position for emphasis on the demonstrative pronoun αὕτη in each of these three verses. And in the clause preceding each of these αὕτη clauses note forward position of the three objects—(respectively) water, kiss, oil. For more on verses 44–46 see above, in connection with verses 38, 44–46.

Verses 47–49

οὗ χάριν; here χάριν is the acc. of χάρις. It occurs here as a preposition. English has a similar idiom: "thanks to this or that" often means "on account of this or that," and so "therefore."

Note different forms of ἀφίημι in these verses: in verses 47 and 48 ἀφέωνται, third per. pl. (Doric) perf. passive indicat.; in verse 47 ἀφίεται, third per. s. pres. *passive* indicat.; and in verse 49 ἀφίησιν, third per. s. pres. *active* indicat.

Summary of Chapter 7

In the closing paragraph of The Sermon on the Mount Jesus had driven home the lesson that true faith implies that one is not only a hearer but also a doer of the word. So now, in the section on "The Faith of a Centurion Rewarded by Jesus" (7:1–10) Luke exhibits a prize example of such genuine faith. The centurion had a servant of whom he thought very highly. This servant, however, became very sick, was at the point of death when the help of Jesus was requested. The centurion, who by means of the elders of the Jews made this request, was so humble that he felt unworthy to receive Jesus into his home or even to go out and meet the Savior personally. At the same time he believed that the Master was fully able to heal the "boy" from a distance. "Speak the word and my boy will be cured," he said. And that was exactly what happened. "Not even in Israel have I found such great faith," said Jesus.

The centurion's servant was *at the point of death* when Jesus healed him. The widow's son (at Nain) *had actually died.* Jesus brought him back to life (verses 11–17). We are shown: (a) God's all-inclusive plan, which so regulated all the circumstances that Jesus reached Nain's gate just when the funeral procession was leaving; (b) the widow's overwhelming sorrow: first her husband had died, and now her only son; (c) Jesus' deep compassion, infinite wisdom, unlimited authority, and amazing power, all of these clearly evident in the manner in which he comforted the widow and gave her son back to her, alive and well; and (d) the crowd's reaction, outwardly favorable ("they glorified God, saying, A great prophet has appeared among us"), but inwardly not all it should have been. See Luke 9:18–20; cf. Matt. 16:13–16.

John the Baptist heard about the words and deeds of Jesus. Though this herald and forerunner had spoken with profound conviction about Jesus, there came a moment when he began to have his doubts (verses 18–35). So he sent two of his disciples to Jesus with the question, "Are you the Coming One, or must we look for someone else?" Probable reasons for his doubt: (a) He was in a grim and gloomy prison and was not being rescued; (b) The activities of Jesus, reported to the Baptist, did not seem to harmonize with the manner in which John had described the Messiah.

John had pictured impending judgment (the axe already at the root of the trees), but words of grace were falling from Jesus' lips, and works of mercy were being performed by him. Yet what John had said was correct, based on prophecy. However, he had not been able to distinguish between the first and the second coming. So he expected first-coming fulfilments of second-coming predictions. Jesus dealt very kindly with him. He directed his attention to that aspect of Old Testament prophecy—promises of healing, deliverance, and restoration—which pertained to the first coming, and he reassured him by showing that right now these good tidings were being gloriously fulfilled. At the same time he defended John before the public,

413

speaking with distinct approval of the work he had done as a herald. Not a reed swayed by every gust of wind was John, nor a flatterer. Had he been a flatterer he would right now have been in the king's *palace* instead of in the king's *dungeon*. The people therefore should take to heart John's preaching. They should not be like children in the market place, quickly condemning what they formerly applauded, whether in John or in the Son of man.

Did the common people regard Jesus as "a great prophet"? Simon the Pharisee was going to see about that. At least this may have been his motive in inviting Jesus over for dinner (verses 36–50). While Jesus was reclining at table in the Pharisee's house, a woman who had been a great sinner but had repented (in all probability after hearing Jesus), took her stand behind him, made his feet wet with her tears, and continued to wipe them with her hair, to kiss them, and to anoint them with perfume. She did all this because she sensed that she had been forgiven. In his heart Simon condemned Jesus for permitting this woman, whom he, this self-righteous Pharisee, regarded as still "a sinner," to do all this. By means of the parable of "The Two Debtors" Jesus defended himself and this woman. He then reassured her that her sins were forgiven, and told her, "Your faith has saved you. Go in peace."

Outline of Chapter 8

Theme: *The Work Thou Gavest Him to Do*

CHAPTER VIII

8 1 Soon afterward Jesus was traveling from town to town and from village to village, preaching and bringing the good news of the kingdom of God. The twelve (were) with him, 2 as (were) also some women who had been cured of evil spirits and diseases: Mary called Magdalene, from whom seven demons had been expelled,[296] 3 and Joanna wife of Chuza, the manager of Herod's household;[297] Susanna, and many others. Out of their own resources these women were helping to support him.

8:1-3 *Ministering Women*

It will be recalled that after ministering to large multitudes (Luke 6:17-19) Jesus preached what is generally known as "The Sermon on the Mount" (6:20-49). He climaxed his sermon by demanding unshakable faith in himself, a faith that would demonstrate its genuine character by means of actions (6:46-49). This faith was exemplified by the centurion whose servant was *"at the point of death"* when Jesus healed him (7:1-10). *"Already dead,"* however, was the son of the widow of Nain, but Jesus brought him back to life (7:11-17). He performed many other deeds in which not only his power but also and emphatically his *sympathy* was revealed (7:22).

John the Baptist, however, had predicted the fast approaching outpouring of *wrath* (3:7). He had pictured the Messiah as the One "whose winnowing shovel is in his hand" and who would "thoroughly cleanse his threshing floor" (3:17). It is entirely possible that hearing about Jesus' deeds of *mercy* had something to do with the question John now asked, "Are you the Coming One, or must we look for someone else?" (7:18-20). How Jesus dealt with him is related in 7:21-35. By this time the Master had gained the reputation of being indeed "a great prophet" (7:16).

But was he, indeed, what he was reputed to be? It may well have been in order to discover the answer to this question that a certain Pharisee, named Simon, now invited Jesus to dinner. In connection with that dinner the Great Physician of soul and body, the Merciful Highpriest, was anointed by a penitent woman. He pronounced her pardon, and (partly) by means of a parable administered a rebuke to self-righteous Simon (7:36-50).

---

296. Or: from whom seven demons had gone out.
297. Or: Herod's steward.

417

The story of this *woman,* who had become a follower of Jesus, connects easily with that of other women who likewise had been befriended by him and had surrendered their lives to him (8:1-3).

All the material that has been briefly summarized here (i.e., Luke 6:17—8:3) is lacking in Mark's Gospel. Beginning with the parable of The Sower (8:4) Luke returns to Mark.

1. Soon afterward Jesus was traveling from town to town and from village to village, preaching and bringing the good news of the kingdom of God.

As often, Luke is indefinite about time and place. He merely says (a) "Soon afterward," that is, soon after the incident related at the close of the previous chapter; and (b) "from town to town and from village to village," evidently in Galilee. When the trip to *Jerusalem* is about to take place, Luke will make specific mention of this (9:51).

It is true that this time, in contrast with 4:15, Luke makes no mention of synagogues. Does this mean, then, that, due to the opposition of the Jewish leaders, the opportunity to preach in the synagogue had been taken away from Jesus, so that he was now forced to do his speaking under the open sky? In view of several passages—especially John 18:20—this would seem to be an unwarranted conclusion. Not everything has to be spelled out. Wherever possible Jesus availed himself of the opportunity offered by "the freedom of the synagogue." Besides John 18:20 see also Matt. 12:9-14; 13:54-58; Mark 6:1-6; Luke 4:15-30, 31-37; 6:6-11. But he was not limited to this means of communication.

What is important is the fact that wherever it was that Jesus spoke, in whatever town or village, whether in a house, a synagogue, or outside, he was with enthusiasm and earnestness proclaiming the good news of "the kingdom of God"—for this concept see on 4:43. Over against the yoke of bondage to all kinds of man-made regulations, he was heralding the realm of grace in which God is King, and salvation is his free gift to all who trust in him.

The twelve (were) with him ... This time mention is made not only of Simon (Peter), as in 4:38; 5:3-5, 8; or of Simon, James and John, as in 5:7-10; of Levi (= Matthew), as in 5:27-29, but of *all twelve,* as in 6:13-16.

The question is often asked, "How were the physical needs of these thirteen men—Jesus and The Twelve—supplied?" Shall we answer: "Peter and Andrew, James and John, being fishermen, must have had some means of support; and Matthew, having been a tax-collector (publican), was probably well-to-do"? But does this answer do justice to such passages as Luke 5:11, 28? Perhaps their families (see especially Mark 1:20) continued to provide for them? The only real answers we have are contained in such passages as Matt. 10:10; Luke 10:7 ("The worker is entitled to his support, his wages"), and here in:

2, 3. (The twelve were with him) **as (were) also some women who had been cured of evil spirits and diseases: Mary called Magdalene, from**

whom seven demons had been expelled, and Joanna wife of Chuza, the manager of Herod's household; Susanna, and many others. Out of their own resources these women were helping to support them.

These women, then, had been the objects of Christ's special care. Jesus had cured them of (a) evil spirits and (b) diseases. Note how carefully Dr. Luke distinguishes between the two, and see further on 4:33, 34. See also N.T.C. on Matt., pp. 436–438; and on Mark, pp. 64, 65.

It is important to observe that while Socrates, Aristotle, Demosthenes, the rabbis, and the men of the Qumran community held women in low esteem, Jesus, in harmony with the teaching of the Old Testament, assigns a place of high honor to them. Moreover, it is especially in the Gospel According to Luke that the Savior's tender and profound regard for women is emphasized. See *Introduction,* point V D.

First among the women here mentioned is *Mary called Magdalene;* that is, Mary of Magdala (meaning The Tower) located on the western shore of the Sea of Galilee and south of Capernaum. She figures very prominently in all the four Passion accounts. She was one of the women who later: (a) watched the crucifixion (Matt. 27:55, 56; Mark 15:40; John 19:25); (b) saw where Christ's body was laid (Matt. 27:61; Mark 15:47; Luke 23:55); and (c) very early Sunday morning started out from their homes in order to anoint the body of the Lord (Matt. 28:1; Mark 16:1; Luke 24:10). Besides, she was going to be the first person to whom the Risen Christ would appear (John 20:1–18; see also Mark's disputed ending, 16:9).

The item about the seven demons that had been expelled from Mary Magdalene has led to the wholly unjustifiable conclusion that she was at one time a very bad woman, a terribly immoral person. But there is not even an inkling of proof for the supposition that demon-possession and immorality go hand in hand. Weird and pitiable mental and/or physical behavior are, indeed, often associated with demon-possession (Luke 4:33, 34; 8:27–29; 9:37–43, and parallels), not immorality.

As to Joanna wife of Chuza, manager of Herod's household, she, too, was among the women who were to hear the glad tidings, "He is not here, but is risen" (Luke 24:6, 10). The significance of Luke's reference to her has already been pointed out. See *Introduction,* points III B 6 and V D. It is Luke alone who refers to her (8:3; 24:10).

About Susanna, mentioned only here in Luke 8:3, nothing further is known. Her name should not be forgotten, however. Her deeds of kindness toward her Lord and his disciples were pure and fragrant and accordingly resemble a beautiful "lily" (the meaning of her name).

We are happy to read that in addition to the three women here mentioned "there were many others." What we have here, therefore, is a genuine Ladies' Aid.

The New Testament records the attitudes and deeds of certain foolish and sometimes even wicked girls and women, real or imagined (Matt. 10:34, 35; 14:1–12; 25:2, 3; Acts 5:1, 2, 7–11; Rom. 1:26; II Tim. 3:6, 7;

Rev. 2:20–23), so that the statement sometimes made, namely, that females never took a stand against Jesus or his cause is in need of careful circumscription. Nevertheless, it is a fact that, with very few exceptions, the girls and women mentioned or referred to in the New Testament were on the side of the Lord. By and large it is true that though Peter denied Christ, and Judas betrayed him, and Herod mocked him, and Pilate condemned him, *the women* honored him and ministered to his and to his disciples' needs. To the extent to which they did this, the comforting words of Matt. 25:34–40 are certainly applicable to them.[298]

Practical Lessons Derived from Luke 8:1-3

In general the following three applications are immediately apparent:

1. Mention of "Joanna, wife of Chuza, the manager of Herod's household," teaches us that the gospel should be brought to the manor as well as to the market place, to those in high positions as well as to those who perform menial tasks. Cf. Eph. 6:5–9; Phil. 4:22.

2. Scripture assigns a vital role to women, namely to be helpers, to serve (Acts 9:36; 16:14, 15, 40; 18:26; Rom. 16:1, 2; Phil. 4:2, 3; II Tim. 1:5. See also N.T.C. on I and II Timothy and Titus, pp. 105–114, 132, 133, 172–179). To overestimate the value of a properly functioning Ladies' Aid (or "Women's Guild") is almost impossible.

3. "Women who had been cured . . . were helping to support" the little group consisting of Jesus and The Twelve. Just as the rain that descends upon the earth to bless it leaps up again through the action of the sun and forms the clouds, so also the spiritual cycle—the one mentioned in Ps. 50:15; cf. 116:3-6, 12–14—must be kept going. Blessings that descend from heaven must be returned in the form of sincere and humble thanksgiving!

Notes on Greek Words, Phrases, and Constructions in 8:1-3

Verse 1

καθεξῆς, see the note on 1:3 on page 62.
διώδευεν, third per. s. imperf. of διοδεύω**, to travel through.
κατά, distributive use, as also in verse 4.

Verse 2

ἦσαν τεθεραπευμέναι, third per. pl. perf. pass. periphrastic of θεραπεύω, on which see the note on 4:23 on page 261. The participle, considered by itself, is nom. pl. fem.
ἐξεληλύθει, third per. s. pluperf. of ἐξέρχομαι.

---

298. Notes on Greek words, phrases, and constructions in 8:1-3 begin on this page.

Verse 3

An ἐπίτροπος (cf. the verb ἐπιτρέπω) is someone to whom a responsibility or task has been *turned over* or *entrusted;* hence, depending on the context, a manager, steward, foreman, or guardian. See also Matt. 20:8; Gal. 4:2.

διηκόνουν, third per. pl. imperf. indicat. act. (here progressive) of διακονέω, to serve, wait on, care for; here, help to support; sometimes: serve as a *deacon* (I Tim. 3:10). See the note on 4:39 on page 271. Cf. Rom. 15:25; Heb. 6:10.

Note partitive use of ἐκ, followed by a noun in the genitive. Since the verb ὑπάρχω (see also verse 41) means *to be, to be present, to be available* or *at one's disposal,* it is not strange that τὰ ὑπάρχοντα would indicate that which is at someone's disposal; hence, his goods, property, possessions. Moreover, those who speak about *sub*stance or economic *under*pinnings should experience no difficulty with the word ὑπάρχοντα = ὑπό and ἄρχω. In the Third Gospel see also 11:21; 12:15, 33, 44; 14:33; 16:1; 19:8; cf. Acts 4:32; elsewhere in the New Testament see Matt. 19:21; 24:47; 25:14; I Cor. 13:3; Heb. 10:34.

---

4 Now when a large throng was gathering and people from town after town[299] were coming to Jesus, he said by way of parable:
5 "The sower went out to sow his seed. As he was sowing, some (seed) fell by the side of the path. It was trodden under foot, and the birds of the air gobbled it up. 6 Some fell on rock. As soon as it sprang up, it withered away because it had no moisture. 7 Some fell in the midst of the thorns. They shot up along with it and choked it off. 8 And some fell into good soil, grew up, and bore fruit, a hundredfold."
While saying these things, he was crying out,[300] "He who has ears to hear, let him hear."

8:4-8 The Parable of The Sower
Cf. Matt. 13:1-9; Mark 4:1-9

Women had placed their trust in Jesus and his cause (8:1-3). In their case the Master's message had evoked the response of gratitude. One might say, "The seed sown had fallen into good soil." But could this be truly affirmed with respect to *everyone* who listened to Jesus as he spoke the words of life and beauty? In 8:4-8 the evangelist shows how Jesus himself answered that question.

The paragraph before us shows how plenary, organic, verbal inspiration operates. On the one hand it produces a beautiful and understandable report, free from all error and in thorough harmony with its parallels in Matthew and Mark. On the other hand it permits the human author to use his own style, in harmony with his own mental and spiritual equipment and purpose. Though throughout there is not even an inkling of real conflict between the three accounts (Matt. 13:1-9; Mark 4:1-9; Luke 8:4-8), yet in not a single case does a verse in Luke *exactly* duplicate the corresponding verse in either of the other Gospels.

---

299. Or: was gathering, namely, of those who from town after town, etc.
300. Or: he was repeatedly crying out.

Thus in verse 4 Luke omits the place where this parable was spoken (from a boat near the shore, according to Matthew and Mark). In this same verse, for "in [or: by means of] parables" Luke substitutes "by way of parable." In verse 5 it is Luke alone who omits the introductory interjection *Behold* (thus literally), and at the end of that sentence adds "his seed." In the next line of that same verse it is Luke alone who quotes the Master as telling the audience that the seed which fell along the path "was trodden under foot," and that the birds *of the air* (not merely "the birds") gobbled it up. In verse 6 the beloved physician represents Jesus as saying that the seed which fell on rock withered away "for lack of moisture," and in verse 7 that the thorns there mentioned shot up "along with the seed." Finally, in verse 8 Luke mentions only the "hundredfold" yield. He omits any reference to smaller yields. There is no contradiction: Luke does not quote the Master as saying that *all* of that seed yielded a hundredfold! As happens repeatedly throughout this Gospel, the author abbreviates.

4. Now when a large throng was gathering and people from town after town were coming to Jesus . . . Again a large crowd. Cf. 4:40, 42; 5:1, 3, 15, 19; 6:17–19; 7:11. In view of the Master's unique style of preaching and in view of his miracles, including even the raising of the dead, the gathering of this huge crowd is understandable. The people had come from "town after town." Today we would probably say, "from ever so many places." Continued: **he said by way of parable . . .** From a boat near the shore Jesus, making use of parables, addresses the vast multitude.

This was not the first time Jesus made use of "an earthly story with a heavenly meaning." Luke 6:47–49 is also a parable. For parables and parabolic sayings see also 4:23; 5:10, 31, 34–39; 6:38, 39, 41–45; 7:24, 25, 31–35. The words of our Lord were always sparkling with figures of speech, proverbs, similes, metaphors, etc. But this time the parabolic form began to predominate; see Matt. 13:34; Mark 4:34.

As Matthew 13 indicates, Jesus at this particular occasion delivered a series of kingdom parables. See N.T.C. on Matthew, pp. 21–25, for their number, character, and classification. First, basic, and probably most important of all was the parable of *The Sower*, also called that of *The Four Kinds of Soil.*

5. The sower went out to sow his seed. As he was sowing, some (seed) fell by the side of the path. It was trodden under foot, and the birds of the air gobbled it up. The scene must have been familiar to most of the people in the audience, perhaps to all. It was customary for wheat, barley, etc., to be sown by hand. But it made all the difference in the world how that seed was received. As this man was sowing, it was unavoidable that a portion of his seed would fall on or along the path which he was treading. Human footsteps had hardened this part of the ground, so that it was impossible for the seed to enter "into" the soil. It had no chance at all. It was trodden *down,* and a little later *down* (see the original) it went into the alimentary canals of the air's feathered creatures.

6. Some fell on rock. As soon as it sprang up, it withered away because it had no moisture. It is typical of Palestine—now Israel and its surroundings—that a considerable portion of its tillable soil is found on top of layers of rock. Often the rocky layer reaches up so near the surface that the soil above it has hardly any depth. In such a situation the seed, in the process of sprouting, has only one way to go, namely, up. So, instead of becoming firmly rooted, it springs up immediately. However, not having roots to draw water from the soil, and the soil itself being very inadequate, the little plant soon withers away for lack of moisture. This process of withering is hastened by the sun's scorching rays (Matt. 13:6; Mark 4:6).

7. Some fell in the midst of the thorns. They shot up along with it and choked it off. Since each patch of ground had room for only a definitely restricted amount of plant life, and nothing grows faster than that which is not wanted, soon the thorns outgrew the noble grain and choked it to death.

Not all was lost, however. **8a. And some fell into good soil, grew up, and bore fruit, a hundredfold.** There was also some—perhaps even a considerable amount of—good soil; that is, soil not hardened by human footsteps, nor lacking in depth, nor infested with weeds, but wholly suitable for healthy plant growth. Here the seed yielded an abundant crop. Matthew (13:8) and Mark (4:8) make mention of thirtyfold and sixtyfold (as well as hundredfold) yields. Luke, bypassing these smaller results, refers only to the maximum yield, namely, a hundredfold, one grain of seed producing a hundred grains. Cf. Gen. 26:12.

8b. While saying these things, he was crying out, He who has ears to hear, let him hear. Loudly—perhaps even again and again—Jesus cried out these words. Ears must be used to hear, that is, to listen closely and take to heart. In all of Christ's teaching, both on earth and from heaven, it would be difficult to discover any exhortation that he repeated more often, in one form or another, than the one of verse 8b. See also 8:18 in both Mark and Luke; 13:9 in both Matthew and Revelation; further: Matt. 11:15; 13:43; Mark 4:23; Luke 14:35; Rev. 2:7, 11, 17, 29; 3:6, 13, 22. This repetition is not surprising. Is not lack of receptivity that which, if persisted in, leads directly to the unpardonable sin? The results of unwillingness to hear, or of hearing but not heeding, are set forth in Jesus' own explanation of the parable (verse 12–14).

For *Practical Lessons* and *Greek Words,* etc., see pp. 431–435.

---

9 His disciples were asking[301] him what this parable meant.   10 He said, "To y o u it has been granted to know the mysteries of the kingdom of God, but to the rest I speak in parables, that:

'seeing, they may not see;
and hearing, they may not understand.'"

---

301. Or: began to ask.

8:9, 10 *The Purpose of the Parables*
Cf. Matt. 13:10-17; Mark 4:10-12

9. His disciples were asking him what this parable meant. The connection is again almost unforgettable, for it is natural to assume that the disciples—The Twelve and those who happened to be with them (Mark 4:10)—would ask Jesus what the parable meant. Sowing and at a later time fruit-bearing presuppose a gradual and time-consuming process, one which the disciples, often impatient, may not have expected with respect to the kingdom.

10. He said, To y o u it has been granted to know the mysteries of the kingdom of God.

The word *mystery* is very interesting. Outside of Christendom, in the realm of paganism, it referred to a secret teaching, rite, or ceremony having something to do with religion but hidden from the masses, and known (or practiced) only by a group of initiates. In the LXX (Greek) translation of Daniel 2, where the word occurs no less than eight times (as a singular in verses 18, 19, 27, 30, and 47b; as a plural in verses 28, 29, and 47a), it refers to a "secret" that must be revealed, a riddle that must be interpreted. In the book of Revelation, where it occurs four times (1:20; 10:7; 17:5, 7), it is perhaps best explained as being "the symbolical meaning" of that which required explanation. The word occurs twenty-one times in Paul's epistles (Rom. 11:25; 16:25; I Cor. 2:1, 7; 4:1; 13:2; 14:2; 15:51; Eph. 1:9; 3:3, 4, 9; 5:32; 6:19; Col. 1:26, 27; 2:2; 4:3; II Thess. 2:7; I Tim. 3:9, 16). There it can be defined as *a person or a truth that would have remained unknown had not God revealed him or it.*

This same general definition of "mystery," namely that it is a divinely disclosed secret, fits very well into the context of the present passage of Luke's Gospel (8:10) and its parallels (Matt. 13:11; Mark 4:11), the only Gospel instances of its use. Here *the mystery* is the powerful manifestation of the reign ("kingdom," "kingship") of God in human hearts and lives; this reign, in connection with Christ's coming, was attended by mighty works in both the physical and the spiritual realms. Jesus declares that this mystery—that it was indeed God who was doing all these things, not Satan—had been "given," that is, "graciously disclosed" to those who were with him at this time; in fact, to all who had accepted him by genuine faith.

To the true followers of Jesus, then, the fact that he speaks in parables will not be hurtful. In fact, it will be helpful, for not only will the stories, etc., readily fix themselves in their minds but the Author is their Lord, Savior, and Friend, and will be glad to give them the needed explanations.

Continued: **but to the rest I speak in parables, that:**
    seeing, they may not see;
    and hearing, they may not understand.

The "rest" of the people are obviously those who had not accepted Jesus by genuine faith but had hardened themselves. Self-righteous scribes and

Pharisees had shown increasing hostility to Jesus. See Luke 5:21, 30; 6:2, 7, 11; 7:30, 44–46. They had many followers.

When Luke writes, "that seeing, they may not see," etc., he is reproducing the words of Isa. 6:9, 10 in greatly abbreviated form. One might also say, "Luke, having before him Mark's already abbreviated reproduction of Isaiah's words, abbreviates them still further." The most complete quotation is found in Matt. 13:13–15.

There is a difference, however, between Matthew's reproduction and that of Mark-Luke. Matthew states that Jesus made use of parables *because* the people's heart had become dull, their ears hard of hearing, etc. Mark-Luke changes this "because" or "for" into "that" or "in order that." Which report is right, Matthew's or Mark-Luke's?

The answer is: "Both are correct." It was *because* by their own choice these impenitent Pharisees and their followers had refused to see and hear, that, as a punishment for this refusal, they are now addressed in parables, "*that* [or *in order that*] seeing, they may not see; and hearing, they may not understand. They must "endure the blame of their own blindness and hardness" (Calvin on this passage). God had given these people a wonderful opportunity; but they had refused to avail themselves of it. Result: it is God's sovereign will to remove what man is unwilling to improve, to darken the heart that refuses to hearken. He hardens those that have hardened themselves. If God even surrenders to the lusts of their hearts the unenlightened heathen when they hold back the truth in unrighteousness (Rom. 1:18, 26), will he not punish more severely the impenitents before whom the Light of the world is constantly confirming the truthfulness of his message? And if he blesses those who accept the mysterious, will he not curse those who reject the obvious? It is evident, therefore, that Matt. 13:13 is in harmony with Mark 4:12 and Luke 8:10; in fact, the "because" of the former helps to explain the "that" or "in order that" of the latter. When, of their own accord and after repeated threats and promises, people reject the Lord and spurn his messages, then he hardens them, in order that those who were not willing to repent will not be able to repent and be forgiven.

For *Practical Lessons* and *Greek Words,* etc., see pp. 431–435.

---

11 "Now this is the (meaning of the) parable:

"The seed is the word[302] of God.   12 Those along the path are the ones who heard it; then the devil comes and snatches away the word from their hearts, that they may not believe and be saved.

13 "Those on rock are the ones who when they hear the word receive it with joy, but they have no root. For a while they believe, but in time of trial[303] they fall away.

14 "As for that which fell among the thorns, those are the ones who have heard, but they are being progressively choked by the cares, riches, and pleasures of life. So they never mature.

---

302. Or: message.
303. Or: testing.

15 "But as for that in good soil, those are the ones who, having heard the word with an honest and good heart, cling to it and by persevering produce a crop."

8:11–15 Explanation of the Parable of The Sower
Cf. Matt. 13:18–23; Mark 4:13–20

11. Now this is the (meaning of the) parable. Jesus now gives a more specific answer to the question asked by his followers (see verse 9). He says, **The seed is the word of God.** It is the message coming from God, in the present instance clearly by the mouth of Jesus. This also answers the question with respect to the identity of the sower. That sower is, of course, the Speaker, namely, Jesus. See also Matt. 13:37, "The one who sows the good seed is the Son of man," and anyone who truly represents him, any genuine Christian witness-bearer. See Luke 10:16.

What is meant by the soil? Clearly man's heart. This is definitely implied in verse 12, ". . . from their hearts." Cf. Matt. 13:19a.

In each of the four instances recorded in the parable the "ground" or "soil," that is, the "heart," hence the person, is different. One might speak of *the unresponsive heart* (Luke 8:12), *the impulsive heart* (verse 13), *the preoccupied heart* (verse 14), and *the good, responsive, or well-prepared heart* (verse 15). The "heart" indicates the "person" or "hearer" as he is in his inner being. The following is therefore correct: "What, then, is the lesson? The Savior has given us the answer in his own interpretation of the story. The seed is the word of God, or the word of the kingdom; and the soil is human hearts: so that, reduced to a general law, the teaching of the parable is, that the result of the hearing of the gospel always and everywhere depends on the condition of heart of those to whom it is addressed. The character of the hearer determines the effect of the word upon him."[304]

Unresponsive Hearts

Jesus continues: **12. Those along the path are the ones who heard it; then the devil comes and snatches away the word from their hearts, that they may not believe and be saved.**

Meaning: the people that are represented by seed sown along the path (see verse 5) are the kind that allow the devil, the great adversary, to snatch away the message that has been sown in them. By no means does Jesus excuse these people, as if only the devil and not they themselves were responsible for what happened to the divine message that had been spoken to them. Verse 12 does not cancel verse 8b or verse 18a! But here in verse 12 these frivolous hearers are being told that in treating the word of God so lightly they are co-operating with the prince of evil, whose purpose is to prevent them from believing and being saved!

These people do nothing with the message. They do not use it to good

---

304. W. M. Taylor, *The Parables of Our Savior, Expounded and Illustrated*, New York, 1886, p. 22.

advantage. "Immediately" after they have heard it, any favorable effect it might have had on them is annihilated. What accounts for their negative reaction? Perhaps it is ill will toward the messenger. Or perhaps hostility with respect to this particular message. Or they do not wish to be inconvenienced (Acts 24:25). The spirit of indifference may have crept into them, perhaps little by little until it was total, their hearts having become as hard as the path on which the seed of the parable was scattered.

The Lord, addressing Ezekiel, gave this description of the prophet's audience: "You are to them like a lovely song, sung with a beautiful voice, and played well on an instrument; for they hear your words, but refuse to practice them" (Ezek. 33:32). Cf. Luke 6:49. The following lines may also be appropriate in this connection:

> And I always came to his church before my Sally were dead,
> And I heard him a bumming away like a buzzard clock over my head;
> And I never knew what he meant, but I thought he had something to say,
> And I thought he said what he ought to have said, and I went away.

Impulsive Hearts

13. Those on rock are the ones who when they hear the word receive it with joy, but they have no root. For a while they believe, but in time of trial they fall away.

These are the emotional people. Now it is a good thing to be emotional. Did not the penitent woman described in 7:37-50 weep because of sorrow for her sins, and probably also because of gratitude for the salvation she had found in Christ? Did not Paul shed tears on more than one occasion? See Acts 20:19, 31; Phil. 3:18, and the section on "Paul's Deeply Emotional Nature," N.T.C. on Philippians, p. 181. See also Acts 20:37. Did not Jesus himself weep at the grave of Lazarus (John 11:35)? However, the trouble with the people symbolized by seed that fell on rock is that their emotions are superficial, not based on deep-seated convictions. These people "have no root."

They are impulsive. After the sermon—especially, perhaps, when it is delivered by a visiting pastor—they *rush* (note the word *immediately* in Matt. 13:20; Mark 4:16) toward the preacher to tell him how his message gripped them. They are "overwhelmed," moved to tears. In fact, they may even faint. The orator would do well, however, not to congratulate himself too readily. "She performs that little trick every once in a while; then goes back to her old sinful ways," was the way the conduct of a certain individual was described by those who knew her well.

In any given case, how does one know whether marked emotional behavior is the evidence of genuine faith? The answer is, "It *is*, *if* it can endure testing." See James 1:12. The people described in Luke 8:13 cannot. In time of trial they fall away. Of course, such people never really belonged to Christ's flock. I John 2:19 describes their situation exactly, "They left us, but they never really belonged to us; for if they had belonged to us, they would have stayed with us." See also John 10:27, 28; Phil. 1:6.

Preoccupied Hearts

14. As for that which fell among the thorns, those are the ones who have heard, but they are being progressively choked by the cares, riches, and pleasures of life. So they never mature.

This parable is truly striking. Each group of people differs from the one described before. Those belonging to the first category, represented by the seed that fell along the path, never respond in any way to the preaching of the word. They are and remain callous, insensitive. Those of the second group respond immediately and enthusiastically . . . and as quickly drop out. Those belonging to Class No. 3 also perish, but more gradually.

At the outset these individuals show some interest in the message of the kingdom. We think of Herod Antipas who actually "used to enjoy listening to John the Baptist and was greatly perplexed" (perhaps the best reading; another reading is ". . . and did many things"). However, his entanglements spelled his ruin. That characterizes the group: extraneous matters soon begin to crowd out whatever good plans or intentions these people may have had. See Mark 6:20.

As his message is summarized by Luke in verse 14 Jesus warns especially against three dangers:

First, the *cares* or *worries* of life. We speak of "corroding cares," that is, worries that eat away one's soul little by little. Worry not only breaks down resistance to disease and therefore shortens life, but also prevents one from concentrating on the blessings God is constantly providing. Jesus said many fine things on this subject (Luke 12:4-12, 22-34; cf. Matt. 6:25-34; 10:19, 20, 28-31).

The second danger to the development of spiritual life—one might say "the second thorn"—is *riches,* the craving for wealth and/or the inordinate yearning to cling to it, come what may. A good example is that of "the rich young ruler" (Luke 18:18-24). See also the unforgettable parables of that *notorious* character, The Rich Fool (Luke 12:13-21), and of The Show-off and The Beggar, i.e., The Rich Man and Lazarus (16:19-31).

Thirdly, there are *the pleasures of life.* These, too, if a person does not watch out, may become soul-ruining entanglements. They are of two kinds: (a) those that are wrong in themselves: drunkenness, drug addiction, gambling, sexual vice, etc.; (b) those that are wrong when a person over-indulges in them: games, sports, entertainments, etc.

Like a proliferating cancer gradually killing the body, or a destructive parasite little by little destroying its host, so also these "thorns" slowly but surely choke the souls of those people who extend a welcome to them. Such individuals never mature. They never produce fruit "for everlasting life" (John 4:36). "Demas has deserted me, because he fell in love with the present world" (II Tim. 4:10; cf. I John 2:16).

Nevertheless, not all the sowing had been in vain (Isa. 55:11):

Responsive Hearts

15. But as for that in good soil, those are the ones who, having heard the word with an honest and good heart, cling to it and by persevering produce a crop.

These people receive the message with an open, unprejudiced mind, as did the Bereans described in Acts 17:10-12. Their prayer is that of Ps. 119:18, "Open thou my eyes, that I may contemplate the wonders of thy law."

Moreover, they *keep clinging* to it. How do they do that? Of course, by *giving away* this precious message, proclaiming it everywhere, and this not only by means of their words but also, and most of all, by consecrated lives.

Finally, by means of their perseverance these people produce a crop; for example, love, joy, peace, longsuffering, kindness, goodness, faithfulness, meekness, self-control (Gal. 5:22, 23), unto their own inner joy, the conversion of souls, and God's glory.

The real lesson of the parable is not grasped unless its clear implication is understood. On the basis of 8:8, 18 (cf. Matt. 13:9; Mark 4:9), that lesson is, "Examine yourself to discover to which group you belong. If you belong to any one of the first three groups, be converted! Not, of course, by power residing in yourself but by God's sovereign grace! Even if you should belong to the fourth group, ask yourself the question, 'Am I sufficiently fruitful?'" The parable is therefore really *An Exhortation to Self-examination, leading either to Basic Conversion or else to further Sanctification.*

For *Practical Lessons* and *Greek Words*, etc., see pp. 431–435.

---

16 "No one lights a lamp and covers it with a vessel or puts it under a bed. On the contrary, he puts it on a lampstand in order that those who enter may see the light.   17 For there is nothing hidden that will not be disclosed, and nothing concealed that will not be known and brought to light.   18 Take care, therefore, how y o u listen. For whoever has, to him (more) will be given, but whoever does not have, even what he thinks he has will be taken away from him."

8:16-18 *Various Sayings of Jesus*
Cf. Mark 4:21-25
Also
For verse 16 cf. Matt. 5:15; Luke 11:33.
For verse 17 cf. Matt. 10:26; Luke 12:2.
For verse 18a cf. Matt. 11:15; 13:9, 43; Mark 4:9; Luke 14:35;
and see above: the explanation of Luke 8:8b.
For verse 18b cf. Matt. 13:12; 25:29; Luke 19:26.

Though the connection between the parable of The Sower (8:4-8, 11-15) and the present little paragraph, containing other sayings of Jesus, is not clear, it may have been as follows:

Soil must be productive; that is, hearts must be fertile. Now fertile hearts resemble shining lamps, witness-bearing, hence fruit-bearing. Cf. Matt.

5:16. The "word" or "message" of God is symbolized by a *seed* that is sown (Luke 8:11). It is also called a *lamp* (Ps. 119:105). It was that "seed" and that "lamp" which the rabbis were hiding under an elaborate load of human traditions and hypocritical actions. That seed must reveal its power once more. The lamp must shine forth again in all the pristine purity of its light, in order to be a blessing to men. So Jesus says:

16. No one lights a lamp and covers it with a vessel or puts it under a bed. On the contrary, he puts it on a lampstand in order that those who enter may see the light.

The bed, to which reference is made here, was a kind of mattress which, when not in use, was rolled up. No one, says Jesus, would think of first lighting a lamp and then covering it up with this or that vessel or placing it under a rolled-up mattress. A lit lamp belongs on the lampstand. Then only will it serve its purpose for those who enter the house.

As to the "lamp," it was often a terra cotta saucer-shaped object with a handle on one end; on the other end there was a nozzle-shaped extension with a hole for a wick. In the lamp's upper surface there were two holes, one for adding oil, the other for air. The "lampstand" was generally a very simple object. It might be a shelf extending from the pillar in the center of the room, or a single stone projecting inward from the wall, or even a piece of metal conspicuously placed and used for the same purpose.

The point is, of course, that believers, too, must let their light shine. Cf. Matt. 5:14–16; Phil. 2:15. They must permit the word of God to be in full control of their lives. It is God's intention that the mystery given to his children be disclosed. It is hidden only from those who continue to harden themselves against its appeal. Thus, while the teaching of 8:10b is not retracted, the emphasis is now on that which must happen *first of all:* the seed must be sown; the lamp must shine; the mystery must be disclosed, not concealed.

But whether revealed or concealed, whatever is done with it will not go unnoticed: **17. For there is nothing hidden that will not be disclosed, and nothing concealed that will not be known and brought to light.** Men may try to cover up things, but they will be unsuccessful, for God brings everything out into the open. One day whatever is now concealed will be revealed. See Eccles. 11:9; 12:14; Matt. 10:26; 12:36; 16:27; Mark 4:22; Luke 12:2; Rom. 2:6, 16; I Cor. 4:5; Col. 3:3, 4; Rev. 2:23; 20:12, 13. Men may think that they can get away with their evil thoughts, plans, words, and actions. God, however, will expose all this. It is therefore not surprising that, as reported by Luke, Jesus continues: **18. Take care, therefore, how y o u listen.**

With respect to men's responsibility in the matter of hearing or listening, three things are stressed in the Gospels:

a. *That* they should hear (Luke 8:8b), the emphasis being on hearing over against refusing to hear;

b. *What* they should hear (Mark 4:24), over against what not to hear; and

c. *How* they should hear (the present passage, Luke 8:18), attentively, judiciously, over against how not to hear.

As to "Take care," "Take heed," or "Be on y o u r guard," see also Luke 21:8.

Continued: **For whoever has, to him (more) will be given, but whoever does not have, even what he thinks he has will be taken away from him.**

In line with the preceding context (see especially verse 15), the meaning must be: whoever with due attention and a yearning for salvation listens to the message and by means of the exercise of faith obeys it, yielding fruit, will receive the blessings of salvation in an ever-increasing measure.

In matters spiritual, standing still is impossible. A person either gains or loses; he either advances or declines. Whoever has, to him will be given. The disciples (exception Judas Iscariot) had "accepted Jesus." With reference to them he was later on going to say to the Father, "They have kept thy word" (John 17:6) and "They are not of the world" (17:16). To be sure, this faith was accompanied by many a weakness, error, and flaw. But the beginning had been made. Therefore, according to heaven's rule, further progress was assured: an advance in knowledge, love, holiness, joy, etc., in all the blessings of the kingdom of heaven, for salvation is an ever deepening stream (Ezek. 47:1–5). Every blessing is a guarantee of further blessings to come (John 1:16). "He shall have abundantly." The theory according to which Jesus (or Luke) was referring only to an increase of knowledge or even insight is improbable. Such discernment is, to be sure, included, but there is nothing in the context that would limit so rigidly the blessing here promised.

On the other hand, whoever does not have, from him shall be taken away even that semblance of knowledge, that superficial acquaintance with matters spiritual, which he once had or thought he had. Is there not an analogy of this in the realm of knowledge on a level below the strictly spiritual? Is it not true that the person who has learned enough music to play a few simple melodies, but not really enough to be able to say, "I have mastered this or that instrument," and then stops practicing altogether, will soon discover that the little skill which he had at one time has vanished? The man who refuses to make proper use of his one talent loses even that (Matt. 25:24–30).[305]

Practical Lessons Derived from Luke 8:4–18

Verses 4–8, 11–15

"Some (seed) fell by the side of the path. . . . Some on rock. . . . Some in the midst of thorns . . . some into good soil." Let the preacher be encouraged by the fact that at least some of the seed (the message) falls into good soil (well-prepared hearts).

---

305. Notes on Greek words, phrases, and constructions in 8:4–18 begin on page 432.

Verse 10

"To y o u it has been granted to know the mystery of the kingdom of God." By no means has this mystery been revealed to all. That it was made known to us was pure grace. Hence, all the more we should, with gratitude to God, share what we have freely received. "Woe to me if I do not preach the gospel" (I Cor. 9:16).

Verse 16

"No one lights a lamp and covers it with a vessel or puts it under a bed," etc. Lighting a lamp and then deliberately covering it up is ridiculous. Becoming "enlightened" (Heb. 6:4) and then concealing this Light from others is ruinous.

Verse 18

"Take care, therefore, how y o u listen."
Some people listen hardly at all (Isa. 40:21).
Some listen merely to be entertained (Ezek. 33:31, 32).
Some listen in order to find fault (Mark 12:13; Luke 11:54).
Some listen in order to obtain true wisdom and to put it to good use (Acts 17:10, 11).

Notes on Greek Words, Phrases, and Constructions in 8:4–18

Verse 4

Does this verse present (a) two co-ordinate genitive absolutes: "Now a large throng gathering," and "people from town after town resorting to him [i.e., to Jesus]"? Or (b) should the translation be, "Now when a large throng was gathering, namely, of those who . . ."? Either is possible. If (a) is correct, then the "large throng" could be folks from nearby Capernaum, and the "people from town after town," those from the surrounding places. If (b) is chosen, we are simply being told that the crowd was large because many a town contributed its quota of individuals. For συνίοντος see the note on 9:18 on page 509.

Verse 5

Note the following four words, all based on the same stem:
σπείρων, sower; τοῦ σπεῖραι, articular aor. act. infinitive of purpose; τὸν σπόρον, cognate accusative (seed); and ἐν τῷ σπείρειν, articular pres. infinitive active, where we would probably expect a participle. But such an infinitive is not unusual, especially by reason of Hebrew or Aramaic influence. The basic verb is σπείρω.
Note also that ὃ μὲν (verse 5) is followed by καὶ ἕτερον in verses 6, 7, and 8. Some insist that ἕτερον, being neuter, cannot refer to σπόρος, which is masc. The question might well be asked, "To what then does it refer?" To an implied "portion" (μέρος, τό) perhaps? But even then, it would be a portion of the *seed* the sower was scattering. But the concord between words and their antecedents was not nearly as rigid as it is sometimes represented to have been. See N.T.C. on Ephesians, p. 123, footnote 61. The translation "some . . . some," etc.—L.N.T. (A. and G.), p. 315—is correct.

Verse 6

τὴν πέτραν should probably be interpreted generically; hence, not "the rock," but "rock."

φυέν, nom. s. neut. 2nd aor. pass. participle (ingressive) of φύω, to grow, germinate, spring up. Cf. *physical.*

ἐξηράνθη, third per. s. aor. indicat. pass. of ξηραίνω, to *dry* up, wither. Cf. *xerox,* a duplicating machine operating by means of a *dry* electric process.

ἰκμάδα, acc. s. of ἰκμάς, moisture.

Verse 7

συμφυεῖσαι, nom. pl. fem. aor. pass. participle (intransitive) of συμφύω, in the pass.: to grow up with. This is a compound of φύω (verse 6).

ἀπέπνιξαν, third per. pl. aor. (effective) act. of ἀποπνίγω*, to choke off. See also verse 33. Cf. *pneumonia.* See related form in verse 14.

Verse 8

ἐφώνει, third per. s. imperf. indicat. act. of φωνέω, to call, call out, cry out. Cf. *telephone, symphony.*

Verse 9

εἴη, third per. s. pres. optat. in an indirect question after a verb in the past (here imperf. indicat. act.) tense. In direct discourse the verb would have been ἐστιν.

Verse 10

δέδοται, third per. s. perf. indicat. pass. of δίδωμι, to give.

γνῶναι, aor. act. infinitive of γινώσκω. This verb refers to a knowledge by recognition, observation, or experience, as distinguished from οἶδα, which indicates a knowledge by intuition, reflection or insight.

ἵνα, *that,* or *in order that.* In the present case it expresses *purpose.* What follows ἵνα is clearly a quotation from Isa. 6:9, 10, which expresses purpose, as the context there plainly indicates; note: "lest they see with their eyes, and hear with their ears," etc., meaning, *"in order that* they may *not* see with their eyes," etc. The very fact that Jesus connects parabolic teaching with the citation from Isa. 6:9 ff. shows that he considers the arcane parables to be indeed a judgment on deliberate unbelief, stubborn hardness of heart.

Accordingly, assigning a weakened sense to ἵνα as here used—see, for example, H. Schürmann, *Das Lukasevangelium (Herders Theologischer Kommentar zum Neuen Testament),* Freiburg, etc., 1969, Vol. I, pp. 460, 461—is questionable. A. T. Robertson, in his *Translation,* pp. 52, 176, ascribes the consecutive sense to ἵνα as used here. But cf. his *Word Pictures,* Vol. II, pp. 112, 113.

Favoring the telic or purposive sense (*that,* in the sense of *in order that*) are also the following, among others: John Calvin, *Commentary on a Harmony of the Evangelists, Matthew, Mark, and Luke,* Grand Rapids, 1949 ff., Vol. II, p. 129; S. Greijdanus, *Korte Verklaring,* pp. 202, 203; A. Plummer, *op. cit.,* p. 220; R. C. H. Lenski, *op. cit.,* pp. 282, 283; C. R. Erdman, *An Exposition of the Gospel of Luke,* Philadelphia, 1929, p.

83; F. Godet, *op. cit.*, Vol. I, pp. 370, 371; N. Geldenhuys, *op. cit.*, p. 243; and E. E. Ellis, *op. cit.*, p. 128. See also on ἵνα, L.N.T. (A. and G.), p. 378.

Others, though accepting the theory that ἵνα, both here and in Mark 4:12, expresses purpose, are convinced that Jesus himself could never have taught this, and that the "error" (as they see it) must be ascribed to whoever was responsible for these Gospels in the form in which they have been transmitted to us. See, for example, S. M. Gilmour, *op. cit.*, pp. 148, 149. Cf. W. Manson, *op. cit.*, p. 90; and J. De Zwaan, *Het Evangelie van Lucas, Tekst en Uitleg*, Groningen, Den Haag, 1917, p. 84. But there is no reason whatever to doubt the genuine character of these words as ascribed to Jesus. They are in complete harmony with the Isaiah passage. For the rest, see the explanation in this commentary.

Verse 12

ἵνα μὴ . . . σωθῶσιν, telic again, ". . . that they may not (believe and) be saved." The verb is third per. pl. aor. subjunct. pass. of σώζω, to save.

Verse 13

ἀφίστανται, third per. pl. pres. middle of ἀφίστημι. Cf. *apostasy, apostatize.*

Verse 14

Note τὸ δὲ . . . πεσόν, οὗτοι εἰσιν: *that* which fell . . . these are. Not strictly grammatical? What matters is that the sense is clear: that which fell among the thorns represents those who, etc.

μέριμνα, that which divides (cf. μερίζω, to divide; μέρος, piece) the mind; that which makes one "go to *pieces*," care, worry. Hence ὑπὸ μεριμνῶν means "by the cares."

πλοῦτος, wealth, riches. Cf. *plutocrat.*

ἡδονή, pleasure. Cf. *hedonist.*

συμπνίγονται, third per. pl. pres. indicat. pass. of συμπνίγω. See also verse 42 and cf. Matt. 13:22; Mark 4:7, 19, to crowd together, press upon; by an easy transition the word develops (in the passive) into *to choke.*

For the construction of πορευόμενοι συμπνίγονται see the article by S. Zedda, "Poreuomenoi sympnigontai (Lc. 8, 14)," *Eunt.* Dec. 27 (1-2, 1974), pp. 92-108. Zedda argues convincingly that πορευόμενος is a descriptive participle, marking the transition from one action to another. In the LXX (by which Luke was influenced) such a construction indicates continuity and progression. Here the thought conveyed is that the seed that fell among the thorns represents those people who *are being progressively choked* by the cares, riches, and pleasures of life, until at last they are completely suffocated and perish.

τελεσφοροῦσιν, third per. pl. pres. indicat. act. of τελεσφορέω*, lit. to bring to maturity; here: to mature. Cf. τέλος, end, goal.

Verse 15

κατέχουσιν (= κατά and ἔχω), to hold down, hold fast, cling to. Cf. Rom. 1:18.

Verse 16

λύχνος, lamp; λυχνία, lampstand. Cf. *light, luminous.*
ἅψας, aor. participle of ἅπτω; in act., to light, kindle; in middle, to touch, take hold of, cling to. See on 7:14.

Verse 17

κρυπτός, hidden, concealed. Cf. *cryptic.*
ἀπόκρυφος, hidden away. Cf. *apocryphal* books. Those were the ones that were hidden away from—i.e., were not to be read to—the assembled congregation, because they were not considered authentic but spurious.
Note the emphatic negative οὐ μὴ preceding the third per. s. aor. subjunct. pass. (γνωσθῇ); i.e., everything will most certainly be made known.

Verse 18

ἀρθήσεται, third per. s. fut. indicat. pass. of αἴρω, to take up, pick up, lift up, take (snatch or sweep) away, take along, remove, destroy; here in passive: will be taken away. In John 10:24 (with τὴν ψυχὴν ἡμῶν) the meaning is *to keep (us) in suspense.*

---

19 And Jesus' mother and his brothers came to (see) him, but they could not get near him because of the crowd. 20 And it was told him, "Your mother and your brothers are standing outside, wishing to see you." 21 But he answered them, "Mother to me and brothers to me are those who are listening to the word of God and are putting it into practice."[306]

8:19-21 *The Mother and The Brothers of Jesus*
Cf. Matt. 12:46-50; Mark 3:31-35

Matthew and Mark place this incident *before* the parable of The Sower. Luke, without in any way indicating when it occurred, places it here, perhaps because it embodies a concrete illustration of that parable and its appended sayings. Note:
"But as for that in good soil, those are the ones who, having heard the word with an honest and good heart, cling to it and by persevering produce a crop" (Luke 8:15).
"Take care, therefore, how y o u listen" (8:18).
And now 8:21: "Mother to me and brothers to me are those who are listening to the word of God and are putting it into practice."
All these passages emphasize the fact that those, those alone, belong to Christ's true family, who not only hear the message but also live in accordance with it.
As happens so often, Luke here again abbreviates. Comparing his ac-

---

306. Or: and are doing it.

count with Mark's we notice that Luke omits any reference (a) to the person who was sent to Jesus to call him, (b) to the question Jesus asked ("Who is my mother and who are my brothers?"), and (c) to the fact that Jesus looked around at those who were sitting in a circle about him. Also, Matthew's item about Jesus stretching out his hand over his disciples (12:49) is not found in the Third Gospel.

19. And Jesus' mother and his brothers came to (see) him, but they could not get near him because of the crowd.

Just why the mother and the brothers of Jesus were trying to contact him has not been revealed. It is probable, however, that Mark 3:21, 22 sheds some light on this question. If so, then the most charitable and probably also the most natural explanation would be that disturbing remarks about Jesus—for example, that his opponents regarded him as being demon-possessed and that even his friends thought he was out of his mind—had induced Mary and Jesus' brothers, out of natural affection and concern, to try to remove him from the public eye and to provide for him a haven of rest and refreshment.

As to the identity of these "brothers," the evidence favors the position that Jesus and these men had issued from the same womb. For arguments in favor of this view see above: the explanation of 2:7.

In their attempt to reach Jesus these people encounter a difficulty: the huge crowd (cf. 8:4) makes direct access to him impossible.

20. And it was told him, Your mother and your brothers are standing outside, wishing to see you.

Mark 3:32 supplies the details which Luke omits. One can almost see and hear how the message is being passed from Jesus' mother and brothers to the special messenger, from him to the people sitting closest to the Master, and from them to Jesus himself. In a very natural and thoroughly human way Jesus has now received the information that his mother and brothers are looking for him and wish him to come out to them.

21. But he answered them, Mother to me and brothers to me are those who are listening to the word of God and are putting it into practice.

What Jesus means is that spiritual ties supersede physical ties. Not as if physical ties are unimportant. On the contrary, the relation between Jesus and his earthly mother was a close one, so close that even when he was suffering the agonies of hell on the cross he thought of and tenderly provided for her (John 19:25-27). In fact, subsequently both the mother and the brothers came to believe in him as their Savior (Acts 1:14). But what the Master so strikingly teaches at this time is that the will of his heavenly Father must be obeyed. The Son of man must do the work which the Father gave him to do (John 17:4). Interference cannot be tolerated.

Therefore, those who not only listen to the word of God but also actually obey it are to be considered Christ's mother and brothers. All who have taken to heart the messages of Jesus, and have translated them into lives rich in fruits to God's glory, belong to the spiritual family, a family far more important than any merely physical family could ever hope to be.[307]

Practical Lesson Derived from Luke 8:19-21

Verse 21

"Mother to me and brothers to me are those who are listening to the word of God and are putting it into practice."

Loyalty to one's spiritual family—see N.T.C. on Eph. 3:15—should transcend all other loyalties (cf. Luke 9:59-61; 14:26). Observing this rule is also the best service we can render to our earthly family.

The great importance which Jesus attached to listening to the word or message of God is also clear from this passage. Even more: the necessity of putting into practice what is heard.

Notes on Greek Words, Phrases, and Constructions in 8:19-21

Verse 19

παρεγένετο, third per. s. 2nd aor. indicat. of παραγίνομαι. It is sing. because of the closest noun in the compound subject. The plural of this verb is *implied* in connection with "and his brothers." See also the note on 7:4 on page 380.

συντυχεῖν, 2nd aor. infinitive of συντυγχάνω (= σύν plus τυγχάνω, to meet with), to get near, approach.

Verse 20

ἀπηγγέλη, third per. s. 2nd aor. indicat. pass. of ἀπαγγέλλω, to announce, declare, proclaim, tell (back); here in pass.: it was told (him). See also the note on 8:36 on page 453.

ἑστήκασιν, third per. pl. 2nd perf. indicat. of ἵστημι, they have taken their stand; hence, are (still) standing.

Verse 21

Though οὗτοι is the subject, note emphatic position of the predicate, which can be reflected in the translation.

---

22 Now it came about on one of those days that Jesus[308] got into a boat with his disciples; and he said to them, "Let us cross over to the other side of the lake." So they set out. 23 Now as they were sailing he fell asleep. Then a furious squall[309] descended upon the lake, and they began to be swamped and to be in danger.

---

307. Notes on Greek words, phrases, and constructions in 8:19-21 begin on this page.
308. Or simply: One day Jesus, etc.
309. Literally: a squall of wind.

24 So they came to him and woke him up, saying, "Master, Master, we're perishing!" He got up and rebuked the wind and the surge of the water. They subsided and there was a calm.

25 Then he said to them, "Where (is) y o u r faith?" Awestruck and filled with amazement they asked one another, "Who then is this, that he commands even the winds and the water, and they obey him?"

8:22-25 *A Tempest Stilled*
Cf. Matt. 8:23-27; Mark 4:35-41

A. *Departure by boat to the lake's eastern shore*

22. Now it came about on one of those days that Jesus got into a boat with his disciples; and he said to them, Let us cross over to the other side of the lake. —So they set out.

Mark 4:35 makes clear that this incident occurred during the evening of the day when Jesus addressed the multitudes by means of parables, including the one of The Sower. Luke, on the other hand, by writing, "on one of those days," shows that he is not interested in the exact time when this event took place. If he had been, he probably would not have placed this account right after the one concerning "the mother and the brothers of Jesus." See Matt. 12:46-50; Mark 3:31-35. In both of these places that story precedes the report concerning the kingdom parables (Matt. 13; Mark 4). All Luke is interested in is to show how Jesus revealed himself, his power and his love, during a violent storm.

For the relation between Luke's account and the somewhat more detailed coverage of this event in Matthew and Mark see N.T.C. on Matthew, pp. 409-413; and on Mark, p. 175.

It had been a very busy day for Jesus. From a boat offshore he had been speaking, probably somewhat at length. Afterward "at home" (or: in a house) he had been giving private instruction to his disciples. It is not surprising that when evening arrived he was tired and exhausted.

So back to the shore he went, and said to the disciples, "Let us cross over to the other side of the lake" (Luke calls this body of water a "lake," the others call it a "sea"). Since Jesus was not only thoroughly divine but also thoroughly human, he was in need of rest. He needed to get away from all those people: not only did they crowd the shore; they even surrounded him in boats, as Mark 4:36 shows.

Though Mark states that the disciples took Jesus along with them in the boat, it was he who took the initiative by issuing the order, "Let us cross over. . . ." But *they* were the boatsmen, the navigators. So "up" the sea they went.

We must not forget that divine guidance was operative here, as always: Jesus must be on these waters in order, by means of an astounding miracle, to strengthen the faith of his disciples. He must land on the eastern shore because there a demon-possessed man needs him (8:26-39). To what ex-

438

tent Jesus, according to his human nature, was aware of these matters is not revealed.

B. *A furious tempest*

23. Now as they were sailing he fell asleep. Do not these words create the impression that the Master fell asleep as soon as (or almost as soon as) the boat had left the shore? Soon he was sound asleep, showing how very tired he must have been; also showing that his trust in the heavenly Father—*his own* Father—was unfaltering.

Then a furious squall descended upon the lake, and they began to be swamped and to be in danger.

To describe this violent atmospheric disturbance Mark and Luke speak of a *lailaps,* that is a whirlwind (cf. Job 38:1; Jonah 1:4) or storm that breaks forth in furious gusts, a fearful squall or series of squalls. Matthew calls it "a great shaking" or "sea-quake." It must have been a very violent upheaval, a howling tempest. Suddenly this *lailaps* came down upon the lake.

What caused this storm? The opinion has been expressed that Satan had a hand in it.[310] In support of this theory the following arguments have been presented:

1. Job 1:12, 19 suggests that it was Satan who caused a great wind to come up from the desert.

2. In the present account it is made clear that in the region toward which the group was sailing there were many demons (see verse 30).

3. Verse 24 states that Jesus "rebuked" the wind, etc. Cf. Mark 4:39, "Be muzzled." These expressions imply that he was addressing an animate object.

However, this line of argumentation is rather weak, because:

1. According to Job 28:25 it is God, not Satan, who is in control of the winds. See also Ps. 48:7; 78:26; 104:3; 107:25; 135:7; 147:18; 148:8; Isa. 11:15; Jer. 10:13; Amos 4:13; Jonah 1:4; 4:8.

2. That these demons had anything to do with bringing on the storm is not stated.

3. See on verse 24.

Far more reasonable, therefore, is the theory according to which it was *God* who made use of physical forces he had himself brought into being, employing them for the realization of his own purpose. The so-called "laws of nature" are, after all, *his* laws. In this connection note the following:

The sea of Galilee is located in the north of the valley of the Jordan. It is about thirteen miles in length and seven and one-half miles in width. It lies approximately six hundred eighty feet below the level of the Mediterranean. Its bed is a depression surrounded by hills, especially on the east side with its precipitous cliffs. When cool currents rush down from Mt. Hermon

---

310. See S. Greijdanus, *Korte Verklaring,* p. 211, and many others.

439

(9,200 feet) or from elsewhere and through narrow passages between the steep hills collide with the heated air above the lake basin, this downrush is impetuous. The violent winds whip the water into a fury, causing high waves that splash over bow, side rails, etc., of any vessel that happens to be plying the water surface. In the present instance the fishing craft, swamped by towering billows, was becoming water-logged, the toy of the raging elements. When Luke says, "They began to be swamped," he means "Their boat did." From a human point of view the little group was certainly in great danger.

C. *A frantic outcry*

24. So they came to him and woke him up, saying, Master, Master, we're perishing!

The disciples were thoroughly frightened. This shows that the present storm must have been something out of the ordinary. After all, these veteran fishermen were used to this "lake" and its erratic behavior. They must have encountered many a storm. But this one was different. Probably never before had they experienced anything like it. Humanly speaking, the peril to which they were now exposed was formidable, the danger increasingly grave. So, in their state of alarm they woke up the still sleeping Master. It was to him they went for help. So far so good. Did not John the Baptist, when seized with doubt, also turn to Jesus for a solution?

On the other hand, in what spirit did the disciples approach the now awakened Savior? To be sure, with an earnest plea, an urgent entreaty, as Matt. 8:25 shows ("Lord, save us"), but alas, also with words of reproach, as Mark 4:38 indicates ("Master, don't you care that we're perishing?").

Luke omits both the plea and the implied rebuke. On the other hand, this evangelist, under the inspiration of the Holy Spirit, makes his own contribution. By doubling the word of address—hence, *"Master, Master, we're perishing"*—he in his own way gives expression to the frantic terror that had taken hold of these men.

Besides, before we begin to shout "Gospel discrepancy" we should bear in mind that in a situation of terrified distress one disciple would cry one thing, another something else.

D. *An astounding miracle*

He got up and rebuked the wind and the surge of the water. They subsided and there was a calm.

According to Matthew 8:26 Jesus stood up and *"rebuked* the winds and the sea." According to Mark 4:39 he *"rebuked* the wind, and said to the sea, Hush! Be still." Luke, too, uses the same verb *rebuked.* There are those who say that this verb implies an animate object. They maintain that this inference is strengthened by Mark 4:39, which is then translated, "Peace! Be muzzled!" But, to begin with the latter, a word does not always retain its

440

basic or primary connotation. "Hush! [or Peace!] Be still!" is the more usual and better rendering of Mark 4:39.

As to the expression, *He rebuked,* it should be borne in mind that Luke does not say, "Jesus rebuked the devil," or "the demons," or "the evil spirits that were in the wind." He simply says, "He rebuked the wind and the surge [or raging] of the water." It would seem, therefore, that this is simply a figurative or poetic manner of speaking (cf. Ps. 19:5; 98:8; 106:9; Isa. 55:12; etc.). So also in Luke 4:39, where we are told that Jesus "rebuked" the fever by which Peter's mother-in-law was being afflicted. The really important fact conveyed by the expression *He rebuked* is that in a very effective manner Jesus asserted his authority over the elements of nature, so that their fury subsided and all became calm.

What is very striking is that not only the winds immediately quiet down, but so do even the waves. Generally, as is well known, after the winds have perceptibly diminished, the billows will continue to roll for a while, surging and subsiding as if unwilling to follow the example of the now subdued air currents above them. But in *this* instance winds and waves synchronize in the sublime symphony of a solemn silence. Something comparable to an evening stillness of the starry heavens settles upon the waters. Suddenly the surface of the lake had become smooth as a mirror.

E. *A loving admonition*

25. Then he said to them, Where (is) y o u r faith?

As *Matthew* pictures it (8:25, 26), when Jesus was awakened from his sleep he did not immediately still the storm. On the contrary, while the tempest was still raging and the boat being tossed to and fro by the billows, the Master with perfect serenity and self-composure addressed his terrified disciples as follows, "Why are y o u frightened, O men of little faith?"

On the other hand, Luke, in the passage before us, makes it clear that not only before but also *after* the miracle the disciples were afraid and needed to be strengthened in their faith. They had been frightened by the storm. *Now* they were filled with fear because of the presence of One who had so suddenly, completely, and dramatically stilled the storm. For similar instances of awe induced by the consciousness of being in the presence of Majesty see Isa. 6:5; Ezek. 1:28; Luke 5:8; Rev. 1:17. Cf. Judg. 13:20, 22.

So Jesus asks them, "Where (is) y o u r faith?" As if to say, has not the stilling of the storm and the soothing of the waves taught y o u that this Master of y o u r s is not only very powerful but also very loving? Therefore, should not y o u r response be that of childlike trust?

It is also possible that by asking, "Where is y o u r faith?" Jesus is referring both to their recent and their present fear. If so, his question would mean, "With me as y o u r Lord and Protector, why *were* y o u so afraid of the storm, and why *are* y o u even now so afraid because I stilled it? Where is y o u r childlike trust?"

F. *A profound effect*

Awestruck and filled with amazement they asked one another, Who then is this, that he commands even the winds and the water, and they obey him?

Note both the awe and the amazement, the fear and the astonishment, of the disciples. As we would express it today, "They just couldn't get over it." Filled with deep reverence were they. They began to realize: Jesus is even greater than we had previously imagined. He exercises control not only over audiences (4:32), sicknesses (6:19), demons (4:35, 36), and death (7:11–17; cf. 7:22), but even over the elements of nature, the winds and the water.

Much that is wrong on earth can be corrected. There are mothers who dry tears, repairmen who fix machines, surgeons who remove diseased tissues, counselors who solve family problems, etc. But it takes deity to change the weather. It is Jesus who commands the elements of the weather, with the result that even the winds and the water obey him!

To be sure, in answer to prayer Elijah, in a sense, had caused a drought and afterward had brought down the rain (James 5:17, 18). But here was One who, *in his own right and by the exercise of his own power and authority,* had brought about a sudden and radical change in the weather. Who, then, is this?

The answer is not given. See, however, verse 28. Very appropriately the present narrative ends by fixing the attention upon the person of Jesus Christ, so that everyone who reads it may give his own answer, may profess his own faith, and add his own doxology.

To the extent to which The Twelve were filled with holy reverence they must be commended. But was there not also a sinful element in their "fear"? See *Practical Lessons* at the end of this section.[311]

Practical Lessons Derived from Luke 8:22–25

Verses 23, 24

"Now as they were sailing he fell asleep.... So they... woke him up." It is comforting to know that an outcry of human distress awakens the One whom a most violent storm cannot awaken.

Verse 25

"Then he said to them, 'Where (is) y o u r faith?'" First these men had been afraid of the storm. That is understandable, though not entirely excusable. Afterward they were filled with awe because of the presence of One who had suddenly and dramatically revealed his power and authority in stilling the storm. Up to a point

---

311. Notes on Greek words, phrases, and constructions in 8:22–25 begin on page 443.

such "awe" is good. Cf. Ps. 4:4; 15:4; 33:8; 119:161. The element of "holy reverence" is to be commended. On the other hand, the element of "panic" must be condemned. The disciples exhibited this hysterical fear. They were filled with it both while the storm was still raging and also afterward. They should have said, "Even though we walk through the valley of the shadow of death, we will fear no harm, for thou art with us" (Ps. 23:4; cf. Ps. 27:1; 46:1-3).

Notes on Greek Words, Phrases, and Constructions in 8:22-25

Verse 22

ἐνέβη, third per. s. 2nd aor. of ἐμβαίνω, to step or get into, embark. Note κατέβη in verse 23.

For διέλθωμεν see the note on 2:15 on page 161.

ἀνήχθησαν, third per. pl. aor. pass. of ἀνάγω. In Luke's writings this word occurs with great frequency; both in the sense of *to lead* or *bring up* (Luke 2:22; 4:5; Acts 9:39; 16:34) and as a nautical term (Luke 8:22; Acts 13:13; 16:11; 18:21; 20:3, 13, etc.), *to set sail, set out, put to sea*. The verb is also found in non-Lucan New Testament writings, but not in a nautical sense ("Jesus was led up by the Spirit into the wilderness," Matt. 4:1; and in connection with Christ's resurrection, his being brought up from the dead, Rom. 10:7; Heb. 13:20).

Verse 23

πλεόντων, gen. pl. masc. pres. participle of πλέω, to sail. Cf. *float, fleet*. Except for Rev. 18:17, in the New Testament this verb is peculiar to Luke (see also Acts 21:3; 27:2, 6, 24).

ἀφύπνωσεν, third per. s. aor. (ingressive); here: to go off to sleep, fall asleep. The form is derived from ἀφυπνόω*. Cf. *hypnotism*.

συνεπληροῦντο, third per. pl. imperf. indicat. pass. of συμπληρόω**, to fill up; here, "they began to be filled up (with water)"; i.e., "they [their boat] began to be swamped." In all three New Testament instances the verb occurs in the passive. When it is used in connection with a span or a point of time, the idea conveyed is that *according to God's plan* this span is running out (Luke 9:51) or this predetermined day has arrived (Acts 2:1). Accordingly, to bring out their full meaning these two passages would have to be translated after this fashion: "Now it came about that, as the predetermined days before his ascension were running out," etc. "And when, in fulfilment of God's plan, the day of Pentecost had come." See G. Delling on this verb, Th.D.N.T., Vol. VI, p. 308.

ἐκινδύνευον, third per. pl. imperf. indicat. of κινδυνεύω, to be in danger; so also in Acts 19:27, 40; I Cor. 15:30.

Verse 24

διήγειραν, third per. pl. aor. indicat. act. of διεγείρω, to awaken thoroughly, to arouse; see also Mark 4:39; John 6:18; II Peter 1:13; 3:1. From the same basic verb comes also διεγερθείς, nom. s. masc. participle, aor. pass.

ἐπιστάτα, voc. of ἐπιστάτης, one who stands over others, overseer, master. See also N.T.C. on Mark, p. 177, footnote 172.

ἀπολλύμεθα, third per. pl. pres. (durative) indicat. middle of ἀπόλλυμι, to destroy, kill; in the middle: to perish, be ruined, be lost. Forms of this verb abound in the New Testament, especially in the Gospels (8 times in Luke 15).

For ἐπετίμησεν see the note on 4:35 on page 267.

Verse 25

Note τίς ἄρα; here ἄρα is added to enliven the narrative; that is, to emphasize the question and to make it more vivid. It should not be skipped in translation.

---

26 They sailed on to the region of the Gergesenes,[312] which is opposite Galilee. 27 Now when Jesus stepped ashore, a certain demon-possessed man from the town met him. For a long time he had worn no clothes, and he was not living in a house but in the tombs. 28 Now when he saw Jesus he cried out and fell down before him, shouting at the top of his voice, "Why do you bother me, Jesus, Son of the Most High God? I beg you, don't torture me!" (29 For Jesus had commanded the unclean spirit to come out of the man. Because many a time it had seized him, and though he was bound with chains and shackles and kept under guard, he would snap his bonds and by the demon would be driven into solitary places.)

30 Jesus asked him, "What is your name?" "Legion," he replied, because many demons had gone into him. 31 And they begged Jesus again and again not to order them to go into the abyss.

32 Now a herd of many pigs was feeding there on the hillside. So the demons begged him to let them enter them; and he gave them permission. 33 When the demons came out of the man, they entered the pigs. And the herd rushed headlong down the cliff into the lake and were drowned.

34 When those in charge of the pigs saw what had happened, they fled and spread the news in town and countryside. 35 So the people came out to see what had happened. They came to see Jesus and found the man from whom the demons had gone out, sitting at Jesus' feet, clothed and in his right mind; and they were afraid.[313] 36 Those who had seen it told the people how the demon-possessed man had been cured. 37 Thereupon, because they were terribly frightened, the entire population of the region of the Gergesenes asked Jesus to leave them. So he stepped into a boat and returned.

38 Now the man from whom the demons had gone out kept begging to go with him. But Jesus sent him away, saying, 39 "Return home, and tell what great things God has done for you." So he went away, proclaiming all over town what great things Je s had done for him.

8:26-39 *In the Land of the Gergesenes:*
Helpfulness over against Heartlessness
Cf. Matt. 8:28-34; Mark 5:1-20

The connection between the preceding paragraph and this one is probably as follows: (a) *chronological.* The two events actually followed each other in historical sequence. Note "Let us cross over.... So they set out.... Now as they were sailing.... They sailed on to [implying: and arrived at] the region of the Gergesenes." Also (b) *topical* or *thematic.* Note the sharp contrast between, *on the one hand,* the howling tempest and hysterical disciples of verses 22-25; similarly, the screaming demoniac, clamoring demons,

---

312. Some manuscripts read *Gerasenes* (cf. Mark 5:1), others *Gadarenes* (cf. Matt. 8:28).
313. Or: became frightened.

terrified pigs, and frightened populace of verses 26–39; and, *on the other hand,* in both accounts, *Jesus,* endowed with majestic calm, as is clear from all his words and actions.

A. *Jesus asserts his authority over the demons*

26. They sailed on to the region of the Gergesenes, which is opposite Galilee.

The group, consisting of Jesus and The Twelve, had sailed "up" the lake from the shore (8:22), and then "down" toward the land. They now arrived there. According to the reading of the original, as represented here by Grk. N.T. (A-B-M-W), the region where they stepped ashore was that of the *Gergesenes.* However, in Matt. 8:28 the same source has *Gadarenes;* and in Mark 5:1 *Gerasenes.* In each case variant readings are recognized in the notes.

It was a region of tombs, some of them probably empty, chambers hewn into the cliffs arising from the eastern shore of the lake. The territory was located "over against" Galilee. A steep hill descended sharply to the very edge of the water (verse 33). The combined information given in the text suits *Khersa,* situated diagonally opposite Capernaum.[314]

27–29. Now when Jesus stepped ashore, a certain demon-possessed man from the town met him. For a long time he had worn no clothes, and he was not living in a house but in the tombs. Now when he saw Jesus he cried out and fell down before him, shouting at the top of his voice, Why do you bother me, Jesus, Son of the Most High God? I beg you, don't torture me! (For Jesus had commanded the unclean spirit to come out of the man. Because many a time it had seized him, and though he was bound with chains and shackles and kept under guard, he would snap his bonds and by the demon would be driven into solitary places.)

The confrontation between Jesus and this man took place right near the shore, the very moment the Master stepped out of the boat. Note that the man was "from the town." He had seen better days. There was a time when he lived among his fellows and wore clothes. Now he wore scarcely any; in fact, in view of such passages as Mark 5:5b, 15, probably none at all. He used to have a home (Luke 8:39), but no longer. For a long time he had been living where he was living now, in the tombs.[315] He was demon-possessed. For more on demon-possession see above, on 4:33 f. He was fierce (Matt. 8:29) and, as his loud screams show (verse 28; cf. Matt. 8:29; Mark 5:5), thoroughly unhappy. His fellow citizens regarded him as a public nuisance. They had never shown any interest in him, any desire to help him. To protect themselves from him they had again and again tied

---

314. See A. M. Ross, art., "Gadara, Gadarenes," *Zondervan Pictorial Bible Dictionary,* Grand Rapids, 1963, p. 293; and J. L. Hurlbut and J. H. Vincent, *A Bible Atlas,* New York, etc., 1940 ed., p. 101.

315. See S.BK., Vol. I, pp. 491 f.; Vol. IV, p. 516.

him up, hand and foot, but even though they kept close watch over him, so strong and ferocious was he that again and again he had snapped his bonds. Meanwhile, in the midst of his hideous screaming, the demoniac was making things worse for himself by gashing the flesh of his naked body with the sharp edges of broken stones (Mark 5:5).

The confrontation between Jesus and this fierce, dangerous, unhappy demoniac took the following course. As soon as the wild man notices that a boat with some men aboard is nearing the shore, he starts rushing down the hill for the attack (cf. Luke 8:33 with Mark 5:6). He—really the demon(s) within him—becomes aware of the identity of the little group's Leader. Awed by the latter's majestic presence, he prostrates himself before him. This "homage," however, is an act of fear rather than humble reverence. At the top of his voice he shouts, "Why do you bother me, Jesus, Son of the Most High God?" (see above, on 1:32). By thus addressing Jesus, does he not show that he, the demon, has the answer to the question the disciples were still asking? See verse 25.

It must have been at this time that Jesus issued his stern command, "Come out of the man" (indirect discourse in Luke, direct in Mark 5:8). Luke, in characteristic fashion, implies that the Lord was moved by pity for the wretched demon-possessed man, frequently seized by the demon who was in the habit of driving him into solitary places. Cf. Luke 11:24.

When the demon realizes that he is about to be expelled from this man over whom he has exercised control for such a long time, he is filled with alarm. He probably thinks, "I am about to be driven out of this man, but whither? To the bottomless pit perhaps, the place of torture?" So he says, "I beg you, don't torture me." For more on this see verse 31.

Without answering this plea Jesus now addresses himself directly to the grievously afflicted person, the demon-possessed man:

30. Jesus asked him, What is your name?

Jesus wishes to reveal to the demoniac the seriousness of his condition. In order to deliver him from it he wishes to calm him down and *to strengthen his consciousness of his real self.* He wants to "draw him out from under," that is, to tear him loose from his close association—almost identification—with the demon, or demons, that had so long a time exercised dominion over him.

Legion, he replied, because many demons had gone into him. The reply indicates the depth of the demoniac's misery. He is under the control not of just one demon, the spokesman, but of an entire host, a Legion![316] The word must not be taken literally, as if it meant that a force of at least 6000 demons were in control of the poor man. The meaning here is undoubtedly figurative: a very large number. It is also possible that the term *Legion* conjured up the vision of an army of occupation, cruelty, and destruction. We are not dealing here with a legion of protecting angels (cf. Matt. 26:53: "more than twelve legions of angels"). We are confronted here with Satan's

---

316. The Latin term *legio* had been absorbed by Hellenistic Greek and even by Aramaic.

army of terror and death. That more than one demon would at times occupy and enslave a person is clear also from other Scripture passages. See Luke 11:26 (cf. Matt. 12:45); Luke 8:2 (cf. Mark 16:9).

It having now been clearly established that the demon who addressed Jesus in verses 28 and 30 was the spokesman for many others, from this point on the plural ("demons," "they") is used instead of the singular ("demon," "he"). So the story continues:

31. And they begged Jesus again and again not to order them to go into the abyss.

Here the agonized request of verse 28b is amplified. See also Matt. 8:29, "Did you come here to torture us before the appointed time?" The demoniac world realizes that on the day of the final judgment its relative freedom to roam about on earth and in the sky must cease forever, and that its final and most terrible punishment is destined to begin at that time. They know that right now they are face to face with the One to whom the final judgment has been committed. They are afraid that even now, before the appointed time, Jesus might hurl them into "the abyss" or "dungeon," that is, into hell, the place where Satan is kept. But if not into the abyss, what then? The answer is given in verses

32, 33. Now a herd of many pigs was feeding there on the hillside. So the demons begged him to let them enter them; and he gave them permission. When the demons came out of the man, they entered the pigs. And the herd rushed headlong down the cliff into the lake and were drowned.

In the vicinity, on the hillside, a herd of pigs—about two thousand of them (Mark 5:13)—was feeding. So the demons ask permission to enter these pigs. Jesus gave them permission. The point should not escape us that without this permission the demons would not have been able to carry out their plan. The evangelist impresses upon the readers the fact that everything, even the realm of demons, is completely under Christ's control.

Jesus granted their wish. Shall we say that pigs—according to the law (Lev. 11:7; Deut. 14:8) unclean—were the proper place for unclean spirits? However that may be, the demons now release their vise-like grip on the man and enter the pigs. Result: all those pigs rush pell-mell down the cliff into the lake and are drowned.

Two questions demand consideration. First, "What ethical justification was there for Jesus to allow this to happen to these animals?" Is not Rom. 9:20, "Nay but, O man, who art thou that repliest against God?" (A.V. rendering), the real answer? Cf. Dan. 4:35.

That same answer will also do for the second question, namely, "Was it right for Jesus to deprive the owners of so large a proportion of their material possessions?" In addition, however, to the appeal to God's sovereignty, it should also be pointed out that by permitting this loss Jesus was actually *helping* these owners; that is, he was helping them if only they were willing to take the lesson to heart. These owners—and in general the people of this community—were selfish. In their scale of values the acquisition, retention, and multiplication of material possessions, such as pigs, ranked higher by far than the liberation and restoration to health and freedom of a man unfree, unhappy, unloved, and uncared for; yes, enslaved, wretched, hated, and abandoned. Hence they needed this lesson.

B. *He reveals his love to men*

34–36. When those in charge of the pigs saw what had happened, they fled and spread the news in town and countryside. So the people came out to see what had happened. They came to see Jesus and found the man from whom the demons had gone out, sitting at Jesus' feet, clothed and in his right mind; and they were afraid. Those who had seen it told the people how the demon-possessed man had been cured.

The men who had been tending the pigs must have witnessed the meeting between Jesus and the demoniac. They had also observed that the wildness of this man had left him and had, as it were, been transferred to the pigs, with the result that the entire herd had perished in the water. The swineherds drew the correct conclusion that it was Jesus who had ordered and allowed all this to happen. He had ordered the demons to leave, and had allowed them to enter the pigs. The loss of the pigs was therefore not the fault of those who had been tending them. The herdsmen, accordingly, ran back to where the people were living. They wanted the owners and everybody else, in town and countryside, in the little city and on the farms, to know who was and who was not to blame.

Luke pictures the people coming to see what had happened. This was probably the morning after the miracle had occurred. What did the people see? They saw Jesus. They also carefully observed the man who had been a demoniac. There was no doubt about it. It was the very man. Now, however, he was no longer rushing down the hill but sitting down, and right at the feet of Jesus, reminding us of Mary (Luke 10:39). No longer was he naked but clothed. And no longer was he acting like a madman but in his right mind (cf. II Cor. 5:13).

The power and majesty of Jesus who had brought all this about caused these people to become frightened, a reaction that was not lessened when right here, on the spot where it had all happened, the details of the story—"how the demoniac had been cured"—were rehearsed by the eyewitnesses: herdsmen and disciples.

What should have been the result? Initial sadness because of the loss of the pigs would have been natural. But should not the owners and all who were in any way affected by this loss have spoken somewhat as follows: "We see now that the loss of our property was a small price to pay for the lesson we have learned. These pigs, that property, meant everything to us. We were selfish. We never felt concerned about the needs of our fellow citizen, this poor, wretched man. Now we see things differently. We now understand that human values surpass material values by far"? Should they not have congratulated the man who was sitting there at Jesus' feet? Should they not have brought their sick and handicapped to Jesus to be healed? Surely, the people of this general region could not have been entirely ignorant about this great Benefactor! See Matt. 4:25. Should they not have tried to prevail upon Jesus to stay a while longer in their midst, in order to impart blessings for body and soul? Cf. John 4:40.

Their real reaction was quite different. It was in fact the very opposite. Jesus must leave, the sooner the better:

37. Thereupon, because they were terribly frightened, the entire population of the region of the Gergesenes asked Jesus to leave them. So he stepped into a boat and returned.

The people were frightened. Did they sense, perhaps, that a Power had been at work here over which they had no control; an action had taken place which they could not even understand? Whatever was the cause of their fear, it did not bring them close to Jesus. It was not the kind of fear described above, in verse 25. *That* fear was, at least to some extent, "a deep reverence" which had led to the question, "Who then is this...?" On the contrary, the fear of the probably largely heathen population described in the present account was in all likelihood superstitious in character. It was definitely sinful. Note that they show no interest whatever in the restoration of the demoniac. They seem never to have learned to rejoice with those who rejoice (Rom. 12:15). It should not escape us that this unconcern on their part was all the more reprehensible because their attention had just now been called to the cure of the demoniac! Note the context: "Those who had seen it told the people how the demon-possessed man had been cured. *Thereupon they... asked Jesus to leave them.*" Their hearts must have been very hard indeed. And there seem to have been no favorable exceptions among them: "the entire population of the region" made this request.

So Jesus left. He was not going to force the favor of his continued presence upon people who by word and deed were saying, "We do not want you." Does this mean, then, that his withdrawal was complete and absolute? It does not, as the touchingly beautiful climax will show:

38, 39. Now the man from whom the demons had gone out kept begging to go with him. But Jesus sent him away, saying, Return home, and tell what great things God has done for you. —So he went away, proclaiming all over town what great things Jesus had done for him.

Note the following:

a. The One who had granted the request of the demons, permitting them to enter the pigs, and of the people, that he leave their district, *refuses* to grant the request of a man who has become his own ardent follower. We learn from this that when God allows his people to get whatever it is they wish to have, this is not always an unmixed blessing. And when he refuses to say "Yes" in answer to their earnest petition, this is not necessarily a sign of his disfavor.

449

b. True missionary activity begins at home.

c. The man is ordered to tell his people what great things *God* has done for him. The words, "He went away, proclaiming . . . what great things *Jesus* had done for him," show that he is aware of the very close relation between God and Jesus.

d. What may well be considered the main lesson is that which concerns *the cause of missions.* Jesus is showing great kindness, and that not only to this man but to the entire community that had so shamefully rejected him. *They* had asked him to leave, but he, in his great love, cannot completely separate himself from them. So he sends them a missionary, in fact the best kind of missionary, one of their own people, a person who was able to speak from experience. "Return home," Jesus said to him. The cured man did even better than that, for, as Luke indicates, "he proclaimed *all over town* what great things Jesus had done for him." So filled with joy and gratitude was he! In fact, as Mark 5:20 shows, this man's missionary activity extended even far beyond his own town.

The cause of missions is indeed basic to the understanding of this story. What Jesus is represented as doing here is breaking down the power of Satan, so that the souls of men may be ready for the reception of the gospel.

Demon expulsion and *missionary activity* are related far more closely than is commonly realized. God's purpose is to turn men "from darkness to light and from the power of Satan to God" (Acts 26:18). This is by no means the only passage in which the destruction of the works of the devil is placed in close relation to the spread of the gospel. See also the following:

"Or how can one enter the strong man's house and carry off his goods unless he first *binds* the strong man?" (Matt. 12:29). Cf. Matt. 12:18, "And he shall proclaim justice to the Gentiles."

"The seventy-two [missionaries] returned with joy, saying, 'Lord, even the demons were subject to us in thy name!' He said to them, 'I was watching Satan fall from heaven like lightning' " (Luke 10:17, 18).

"Now is the judgment of this world. Now shall the prince of this world be cast out. And I, when I am lifted up from the earth, will draw all men to myself" (John 12:31, 32, in a context describing how some Greeks expressed the wish to see Jesus).

Undoubtedly these passages also shed light on the true interpretation of Rev. 20:1-3.

As was stated earlier—see above, on 2:39—the author of the Third Gospel hardly ever describes Jesus in the act of entering Gentile territory. Though even in his first book he repeatedly emphasizes the meaning of Christ for both Jew and Gentile, he reserves the actual *story* of the evangelization of the Gentiles for his second book, namely, Acts. Yet, here (Luke 8:26-39) for once he places Jesus in predominantly Gentile territory. To be sure, the period of the wide opening of the door of grace (multitudes of Gentiles entering in) had not yet arrived. But that door was standing ajar.

The message and the lesson are clear: Calvary has meaning for both Jew and Gentile. The wonderful story must be joyfully and earnestly proclaimed to both. Satan must be banished from hearts and lives, so that Christ may enter in. That is the central meaning of the present account.[317]

Practical Lessons Derived from Luke 8:26-39

Verse 27

"A certain demon-possessed man from the town met Jesus." The reality of Satan and his hosts is clearly demonstrated in this story. What is even more definitely emphasized is the fact that it is God—one can also say Jesus Christ—who is in control, not the demons. (See verses 28, 31, 32.) It is he who expels demons from human hearts in order that the truth of the gospel may enter in.

Verse 28

"Jesus, Son of the Most High God." That was and is correct. Nevertheless the demons are not saved. Why not? Cf. James 2:19, 20.

Verse 35

"They . . . found the man from whom the demons had gone out, sitting at Jesus' feet, clothed and in his right mind." True religion affects every department of life and every "faculty" of man's innermost being.

Verse 37

"The entire population . . . asked Jesus to leave them." A most terrible request. Contrast it with the request found in verse 41.

Verse 39

"Return home, and tell what great things God has done for you." Even though Jesus himself heeded the request of the people that he leave, he, in his goodness and wisdom, gave them a missionary, one of their own people, the very man whom the Master had healed. For other instances in which Jesus returned good for evil see Luke 7:19, cf. 27-29; 23:5, 18, 21, 23, 33, cf. 23:34; John 18:15-18, 25-27, cf. 21:15-17; and see also Luke 6:27-29.

Notes on Greek Words, Phrases, and Constructions in 8:26-39

Verse 26

κατέπλευσαν, third per. pl. aor. indicat. act. of καταπλέω*, to sail from "the high sea" toward the shore; the opposite of ἀνάγω, to put to sea (verse 22).
ἀντιπέρα*, opposite.

---

317. Notes on Greek words, phrases, and constructions in 8:26-39 begin on this page.

Verse 27

χρόνῳ ἱκανῷ, for a long time; see the note on 7:6 on page 380.

οὐκ ἐνεδύσατο ἱμάτιον, he had worn no clothing; aor. where we would normally use the pluperfect. See also verse 29, "For Jesus had commanded. . . ."

ἱμάτιον, here probably generic, clothing; cf. verse 35.

μνῆνα, literally: a memorial erected for the dead; hence, a tomb. Cf. μιμνήσκω, to remember.

Verse 28

For τί ἐμοὶ καὶ σοί see the note on 4:34 on page 267. On "the Most High God" see the explanation of 1:31-33.

μή με βασανίσῃς, sec. per. s. aor. subjunct. act. in a prohibition, "Don't torture me." βασανίζω, to torture. The noun βάσανος (cf. our English word *basanite*) indicates (a) basically, a *touchstone* to test gold and other metals; (b) *the instrument of torture* by which slaves were tortured; i.e., were forced to reveal the truth; and (c) *torment or acute pain*. See also footnote 288 on p. 260 of N.T.C. on Mark.

Verse 29

The manuscripts are divided between the aorist παρήγγειλε (where English would use the perfect; hence, "he had commanded") and the imperfect παρήγγελλεν ("he was commanding"). The difference is minor, though "he had commanded" seems more logical: for then the demon's plea, "Don't torture me," more naturally follows Christ's command, "Come out of the man."

πολλοῖς . . . χρόνοις can be regarded as locative: "on many occasions"; hence, oftentimes, many times.

συνηρπάκει, third per. s. pluperf. indicat. act. of συναρπάζω**, to seize. Cf. Acts 6:12; 19:29; 27:15.

ἐδεσμεύετο, third per. s. imperf. pass. of δεσμεύω, to bind. For ἁλύσεσιν καὶ πέδαις see footnote 181, N.T.C. on Mark, p. 189.

διαρρήσσων, nom. s. pres. act. participle of διαρρήσσω (cf. διαρρήγνυμι), to rend, break, snap. Cf. *break, wreck, fracture, hemorrhage.*

ἠλαύνετο, third per. s. imperf. passive of ἐλαύνω, to drive. Cf. *elastic*, which springs (is driven) back.

Verse 31

ἄβυσσος (= ἀ without, plus βυσσός or βυθός, depth, bottom), bottomless (pit or region), abyss.

Verses 32, 33

ἦν . . . βοσκομένη, periphrastic imperf. of βόσκω, to feed. Cf. *proboscis, botany.* Note also "those who were feeding," i.e., the herdsmen (verse 34), and cf. 15:15.

Luke's account is factual rather than emphatically descriptive: note all the aorists: the demons *begged* him . . . he *gave* them *permission*. Having gone out of the man, the demons *entered* the pigs. The herd rushed headlong down the cliff . . . and *were drowned* (where Mark has the descriptive imperfect: and *were drowning*). The verb ὁρμάω, *to rush headlong*, reminds us of *hormone;* the noun κρημνός, *cliff*, of the *cremaster* muscle.

Verses 34, 35

In both verses note τὸ γεγονός, 2nd perf. participle, neut. s. (here acc.) of γίνομαι. ἐφοβήθησαν, third per. pl. aor. indicat. pass. of φοβέω, they were afraid; or, if ingressive, they became frightened. See also the note on 2:9 on page 160.

Verse 36

ἀπήγγειλαν, third per. pl. aor. indicat. act. of ἀπαγγέλλω, to tell, announce, proclaim, declare. See also the note on 8:20 page 437. This verb occurs frequently in the Third Gospel (besides 8:20 also in 7:18, 22; 8:34, 36, 47; 9:36; 13:1; 14:21; 18:37; 24:9); and especially in Acts (16 times, beginning with 4:23). Matthew uses it 8 times; Mark (1:1—16:8) 3 times; John, in his Gospel, only once (16:25). In the rest of the New Testament it is found only in I Cor. 14:25; I Thess. 1:9; Heb. 2:12; and I John 1:2, 3.

Verse 37

συνείχοντο, third per. pl. imperf. pass. of συνέχω; literally, to hold together tightly, to hem in, seize; hence, they were held in the grip of, were seized with, great fear (instrumental); they were terribly frightened. See also the note on 4:38 on page 271. In 8:45 the meaning of the verb is: to crowd.

Verse 38

ἐδεῖτο, third per. s. imperf. middle of δέομαι; he kept begging. ἐξεληλύθει, third per. s. pluperf. act. of ἐξέρχομαι, to go out, depart. Cf. ἐξῆλθον (verse 35).

Verse 39

διηγοῦ, second per. s. pres. imperat. of διηγέομαι, to carry (a narrative) through from beginning to end, to declare, tell. The third pers. pl. aor. indicat. of this verb occurs in 9:10.

The preposition κατά (here καθ'), which in verses 1 and 4 was used distributively, is here used to indicate extension in space: "throughout the whole city," or "all over town."

---

40 Now on Jesus' return the crowd welcomed him, for they were all expecting him. 41 Just then a man named Jairus, a ruler of the synagogue, came, fell at Jesus' feet, and began to plead with him to come to his home, 42 because his only daughter, about twelve years old, was dying. But as he went, the crowds continued to press upon him.[318]
43 And a woman who had been subject to hemorrhages for a period of twelve years,[319] and could not be cured by anybody, 44 came from behind and touched the tassel of his garment. Instantly her hemorrhage stopped.
45 "Who was it that touched me?" Jesus asked. When they were all denying it, Peter said, "Master, the people are crowding and pressing against you." 46 But Jesus said, "Someone did touch me, for I was aware that power had gone out of me."

---

318. Or: almost crushed him.
319. The words, "having spent all she had on doctors," are of dubious textual validity. But see Mark 5:26.

47 Now when the woman realized that she had not escaped notice, she came trembling, fell at his feet, and declared in the presence of all the people the reason why she had touched him and how she had been instantly cured.

48 He said to her, "Daughter, your faith has made you well; go in peace."

49 While he was still speaking, someone came from the synagogue ruler's (house), saying, "Your daughter is dead; don't bother the Teacher any more." 50 But Jesus, hearing (this), said to Jairus, "Fear no longer; only believe, and she will be made well."

51 When he arrived at the house, he allowed no one to enter with him, except Peter and John and James and the child's father and mother.

52 The people, meanwhile, were all weeping and wailing[320] over her. Jesus said, "Stop weeping, for she is not dead but asleep." 53 But they were laughing in his face, for they knew that she was dead. 54 And having grasped her hand, he called out, "My child, get up!" 55 Her spirit returned and she got up at once. Then he directed that something be given her to eat. 56 Her parents were astonished, but he instructed them to tell no one what had happened.

Two Miracles
8:40–42a, 49–56 *The Restoration to Life of Jairus' Daughter*
and
8:42b–48 *The Healing of the Woman Who Touched Christ's Garment*
Cf. Matt. 9:18–26; Mark 5:21–43

The transition from the preceding section (verses 26–39) to this one (verses 40–56) is well-nigh unforgettable. From the request amounting to "please go away," the story advances to the earnest and moving petition, "Please come" (contrast verse 37 with verse 41). When Jesus was asked to leave, he left; that is, he recrossed the sea and landed at the Capernaum side, where a ruler of the synagogue was in sore need of help, for his little daughter was dying; in fact, before Jesus arrived at the home, she had died (verses 49, 53). So, from the story of the miraculous blessing bestowed on a man who had his dwelling in a locality associated with death (verse 27) we advance to that of triumph over death itself (verses 54, 55).

It would seem that when Jesus landed, the disciples of John the Baptist were waiting for him, with their question about fasting. See N.T.C. on Matt. 9:18 (cf. Luke 5:33–39). It was while he was still speaking with them that Jairus made his request.

The synagogue was ruled by a board of elders. One of its responsibilities was to maintain good order at the synagogue meetings. The man who came to Jesus was a member of such a board. Since he was probably living in Capernaum we may assume that he had heard about, and perhaps even witnessed, some of the miracles performed by Jesus.

The reports of the present double miracle vary: Matthew's is very brief, nine verses; Luke's covers seventeen verses; Mark's twenty-three.

Matthew omits the ruler's request (see Mark and Luke) that Jesus heal the very *sick* child. In fact, Matthew in his very brief summary leaves out

---

320. Or: weeping and beating (their) breasts.

several items mentioned by one or both of the other synoptists. However, it is he alone who relates that the ruler asks Jesus to lay his hand upon the dead girl, adding "and she will live" (9:18). Also, he alone mentions the flute-players in the house of mourning (9:23).

Several items are common to Mark and Luke, though not found in Matthew. Thus we are told that the name of the ruler was Jairus (Mark 5:22; Luke 8:41), that Jairus made his first request before the child had died (Mark 5:23; Luke 8:42), that she was about twelve years of age (Mark 5:42; Luke 8:42), that Peter, James, and John, and also the child's parents were with Jesus when he performed the miracle (Mark 5:37, 40; Luke 8:51), and that Jesus did not want the news of this miracle to spread (Mark 5:43; Luke 8:56).

It is Luke alone who reports that the daughter was an only child (8:42), and that Jesus did indeed hear the remark to which he paid no attention (8:50). For items peculiar to Mark see N.T.C. on Mark, p. 201.

In all the three accounts the story of the bringing back to life of the daughter of Jairus is interrupted by that of the healing of the woman who touched Christ's garment.

The material as here presented permits the following outline. Under the general theme that has already been indicated (Two Miracles, etc.) we arrive at these subdivisions or "points":

	Verses
The first miracle introduced	40–42
The first miracle interrupted	
by	
the second miracle	
faith concealed	43–44a
faith rewarded	44b
faith revealed	45–48
The first miracle performed	
a word of encouragement	49, 50
a word of revelation	51–53
a word of love and power	54–55a
a word of tender concern	55b–56

A. *The first miracle introduced*

40–42. Now on Jesus' return the crowd welcomed him, for they were all expecting him. Just then a man named Jairus, a ruler of the synagogue, came, fell at Jesus' feet, and began to plead with him to come to his home, because his only daughter, about twelve years old, was dying.

As Mark 5:21 shows, Jesus was again to be found "beside the sea," near Capernaum, with a large and "expectant" (cf. Luke 8:40) crowd assembled about him. It was then that Jairus fell prostrate at the Master's feet. Think of it: a "ruler of the synagogue," accordingly a man of high position and reputation, expressing his reverential respect for Jesus by means of this humble gesture! Jairus may well have seen and heard Jesus many a time, right here in Capernaum. It is not at all unlikely that he had witnessed previous miracles. And now his pleading is fervent and impassioned, for he loves his dying child. Is she not his *only* daughter? It is characteristic of Luke to call the reader's attention to such a fact (cf. 7:12; 9:38). She was twelve years old, but he calls her "my little daughter" (Mark 5:23).

Mark 5:24 states that Jesus responded to this urgent request ("he went with him"), and Matthew 9:19 adds that the disciples accompanied him. Luke *implies* as much; as to Jesus (verse 42b), as to his disciples (verses 45, 51). **But as he went, the crowds continued to press upon him.** This statement is closely connected with what precedes. It also introduces and sheds light on that which follows in verses 43–48. The fact that the people were almost crushing Jesus made progress toward the house of Jairus slow and difficult. It also explains the action of the woman whose story follows. She thought that because of the huge crowd she would be able to do what she wanted to do, and escape detection (verse 47).

B. *The first miracle interrupted by the second miracle*

1. *faith concealed*
43, 44a. And a woman who had been subject to hemorrhages for a period of twelve years, and could not be cured by anybody, came from behind and touched the tassel of his garment.
While Jesus is on his way to the home of Jairus suddenly there is an interruption. Again and again during his earthly ministry Jesus was interrupted; namely, in his speaking to a crowd (Luke 5:17–19), conversing with his disciples (12:12 ff.), sleeping (8:22–24), praying (Mark 1:35 ff.), and traveling (Mark 10:46 ff.). The fact that none of these intrusions floor him (not for a moment is he at a loss as to what to do or what to say), shows that we are dealing here with the Son of man who is also the Son of God! What *we* would call an "interruption" is for him a springboard or take-off point for the utterance of a great saying or, as here, for the performance of a marvelous deed, revealing his power, wisdom, and love. What for us would have been a painful exigency is to him a golden opportunity.

This time the interrupter is a woman. For twelve years she had been subject to hemorrhages; literally she had been "in (a condition of) flow of blood." There are those who believe that the drain was constant. Another view would be that throughout the twelve years an excessive loss of blood, occurring periodically, had made it impossible for her ever to feel strong and healthy, and that at this particular moment she was again suffering as a result of loss of blood.

Note the coincidence: the daughter of Jairus was twelve years of age. The woman had been sick twelve years.

Mark states, "She had suffered much at the hands of many physicians." Though this was true, it is not surprising that Luke, himself a physician

(Col. 4:14), brings out the fact that this woman's illness was, humanly speaking, and in the light of the therapeutics of that day, incurable.

Poor woman! She had lost her health, her wealth (Mark 5:26), and because of the nature of her illness, also her standing in society, particularly in the religious community. Her condition was such that it would make her ceremonially "unclean" (Lev. 15:19 ff.).

There was this last reason for hope: Jesus! What is so striking in this connection is that not only prominent people, such as Jairus, turned to Jesus in their distress, but so did also proletarians, like this poor woman. They seemed to have sensed that his power and his pity would respond to the needs of people from every social class.

Because of her condition the woman is afraid to come out into the open. She is not going to come into physical contact with Jesus himself. She will merely touch his garment, and even then only one of the four wool tassels which every Israelite was ordered to wear on the corners of his square outer robe (Num. 15:38; cf. Deut. 22:12) to remind him of the law of God. See also N.T.C. on Matt. 23:5.[321] Naturally the quickest and easiest way to bring oneself into physical contact with a garment without being noticed was to come from behind and touch the tuft swinging freely from the back of the robe. The wearer, so this woman thought, would never even notice what was happening. So, having heard the wonderful reports about Jesus, she came from behind and touched the tassel.

2. *faith rewarded*

44b. Instantly her hemorrhage stopped.

The greatness of this woman's faith consisted in this, that she believed that the power of Christ to heal was so amazing that even the mere touch of his clothes would result in an instant and complete cure. That this faith was, nevertheless, by no means perfect appears from the fact that she thought that such an actual touch was necessary and that Jesus would never notice it. But imperfect though her faith was, the Lord rewarded it. The recovery, moreover, was instant. In one brief moment the hemorrhage stopped completely. Health and vigor began to surge through every part of her body.

The reward affected not only her body, also her soul. Not only was her faith *rewarded*, it was also *improved*, brought to a higher stage of development, so that faith concealed became:

3. *faith revealed*

45a. Who was it that touched me? Jesus asked.

Jesus was not ignorant of the fact that someone had touched him, and this not accidentally but purposely, and not just with a finger but with faith. He knew that it was to that faith that the power within him and proceeding from him had responded.

---

321. Cf. S.BK., Vol. IV, p. 277.

What Jesus wants is that whoever it was that had thus meaningfully touched him shall now complete the circle indicated in many passages of Scripture, including, for example, Ps. 50:15:

> Call upon me in the day of trouble;
> I will deliver you,
> And you shall glorify me.

This woman, in her own way, had called upon Jesus. He had rescued her, but she had not as yet glorified him. Up to this point she was like the nine cleansed lepers of Luke 17:17, 18: "Then Jesus said, 'Were not ten cleansed? Where are the nine? Was no one found to return and give thanks to God except this foreigner?'" To be sure, she had "believed with her heart." But she had not as yet "confessed with her mouth" (Rom. 10:9). It was in order to bring about this favorable change that Jesus immediately turned around in the crowd and asked, "Who was it that touched me?" Interpreted: ". . . touched me meaningfully."

45b. When they were all denying it, Peter said, Master, the people are crowding and pressing against you.

At this point, as Luke shows, it was Peter who spoke up. That was typical of him. The other disciples joined in (Mark 5:31), but Peter, as often, took the lead. It was he who spoke most vociferously. When he said, "Master, the people are crowding and pressing against you," he committed the oft repeated error of interpreting Christ's words in the most starkly literal fashion, as if Jesus had been inquiring about a merely physical touch. The following passages are among those that show that the rule of literal interpretation is anything but safe unless it is presented with the proper qualifications: Mark 8:15, 16; John 2:19-22; 3:3-5; 4:10-15; 6:52; 8:56-58; 11:11-13. To be sure, Jesus was not denying the literal touch, but he meant something far more than this, the touch *in faith,* the very effective touch. It was a touch *with a purpose,* not a merely accidental touch.

Peter's remark revealed not only lack of insight but even lack of proper respect, the subdued reverence which this disciple should have shown to his Master. It was thoughtless and tasteless, crude and rude. It reminds one of Matt. 16:22.

46. But Jesus said, Someone did touch me, for I was aware that power had gone out of me.

Here Jesus shows how he knew that someone had indeed touched him, touched him in faith and with a purpose to be healed, and this not without cost to the Healer (Isa. 53:4-6; Matt. 8:17). He declares that he knew it because at the moment it happened healing power had gone out of him. For the explanation of the last clause see above, on 6:19. He insists, therefore, that the person who had touched him in this manner come out into the open. Why? There may have been several reasons: Confession (public testimony, witness-bearing) is good for the soul of the individual who makes it, as well as for those who hear it. If it is done in the proper spirit,

God is glorified by it. Besides, Jesus wants the people in general to know that the person involved is now no longer to be regarded as "unclean" and excluded from mingling socially and religiously (in synagogue and temple) with the rest of men. The cured individual must be welcomed back.

47. Now when the woman realized that she had not escaped notice, she came trembling, fell at his feet, and declared in the presence of all the people the reason why she had touched him and how she had been instantly cured.

The woman had already started to leave. This is clear from the words, *She came,* here evidently meaning "came back." She had heard Jesus say, "Who was it that touched me?" And again, "Someone did touch me," etc. She now realizes that her earlier plan, namely, to touch the tassel and then quickly slip away, could no longer be carried out. She must reveal herself. So she came. Her conscience told her to go and to speak.

Nevertheless, it was not easy for her to do what she felt she had to do. At that time and in that country for a woman to speak in public was generally considered improper. This all the more on a subject such as this, the particular physical scourge by which she had been afflicted. And would not even the fact that she, in that condition, deliberately had touched the Master add to the impropriety in the eyes of the bystanders? Yes, and even, perhaps, in the eyes of Jesus himself? Would he scold her perhaps?

We can understand, therefore, both why she confessed, and why she did this while "trembling." In the presence of all the people she declared: (a) the reason why she had touched him, and (b) how she had been instantly cured. See verses 43, 44.

48. He said to her, Daughter, your faith has made you well; go in peace.

Lovingly Jesus calls her "Daughter," even though she may not have been any younger than he was. But he speaks as a father to his child. Moreover, he praises her for her faith, even though that faith, as has been indicated, was by no means perfect; and even though, as Mark 5:27 ("after hearing about Jesus") indicates, it was he himself who, through his earlier marvelous words and deeds, had brought about that faith. Her faith, though not the basic cause of her cure, had been the channel through which the cure had been accomplished. It had been the instrument used by Christ's power and love to effect her recovery. Cf. Eph. 2:8. Is it not marvelous that Jesus, in speaking to this woman, says nothing about his own power and love, the root cause of her present state of well-being, but makes special mention of that which apart from him she would neither have possessed nor have been able to exercise? Moreover, by saying, "Your faith has made you well" (cf. 7:50), was he not also stressing the fact that it was his *personal response* to her *personal faith* in him that cured her, thereby removing from her mind any remnant, however small, of superstition, as if his clothes had contributed in any way to the cure?

As has already been indicated, by means of these cheering words Jesus also opened the way for the woman's complete reinstatement in the social

459

and religious life and fellowship of her people. Now she can go and continue to travel the rest of her life "in peace," that is, with the smile of God upon her and the joyful inner knowledge of this smile. Cf. Isa. 26:3; 43:1, 2; Rom. 5:1.

Probably even more is included in this encouraging command, "Go in peace." In view of the fact that in all probability Jesus spoke these words in the then current language of the Jews (Aramaic), have we not a right to conclude that nothing less than the full measure of the Hebrew *Shalom*, well-being for both soul and body, is here implied?

C. *The first miracle performed*

1. *a word of encouragement*

49. While he was still speaking, someone came from the synagogue ruler's (house), saying, Your daughter is dead; don't bother the Teacher any more.

The messenger may have been a relative of Jairus, or perhaps a friend. At any rate, he was not very diplomatic in conveying the alarming news. Rather bluntly he said, "Your daughter is dead." He adds, ". . . don't bother the Teacher any more." As this messenger (and others with him, Mark 5:35) saw it, there was not even the remotest possibility that Jesus would be able to restore a dead person. For a while there had been hope, namely, when the child was sick; very sick, to be sure, but Jesus was on the way. But then there had been that tragic interruption (verses 43–48). And now the blossoms of hope had withered away. However, note what happens:

50. But Jesus, hearing (this), said to Jairus, Fear no longer; only believe, and she will be made well.

Though Jesus hears the words of the messenger, he pays no attention to them (Mark 5:36). With majestic calmness he refuses completely to lend an ear to the herald of doom, the messenger of despair. He wants Jairus to do the same.

Jairus is afraid. Now it is not easy to drive out fear. There is only one way to do it, namely, by firmly believing in the presence, promises, pity, and power of God in Christ. It takes the positive to drive out the negative (Rom. 12:21). Jairus must by an *act* of faith accept Christ's promise that the child will be healed; that is, will be brought back from death. He must *continue* to believe this (Mark 5:36).

Throughout the history of redemption it has ever been thus. When it seemed that all was lost, believers placed their trust in God and were delivered (Ps. 22:4; Isa. 26:3, 4; 43:2). This was true with respect to Abraham (Gen. 22:2; James 2:21–23), Moses (Exod. 14:10 f.; 32:10, 30–32), David (I Sam. 17:44–47; Ps. 27), and Jehoshaphat (II Chron. 20:1, 2, 12), to mention but a few. When the need was highest help was nighest.

This was true also in the case of Jairus. *The word of encouragement* was not in vain. He took it to heart (Matt. 9:18) and was heard.

2. *a word of revelation*

51. When he arrived at the house, he allowed no one to enter with him, except Peter and John and James and the child's father and mother.

The crowd must have wondered what Jesus was going to do, now that the situation was hopeless. Before entering the house Jesus, with authority, dismissed the entire multitude, even the disciples, with the exception of Peter, James, and John.

Most of the events pertaining to Jesus' sojourn on earth could be safely witnessed by all the twelve disciples. There were others, however, that took place in the presence of only three of these men. Exactly why this was we can only guess. Did Jesus allow only three disciples to enter the room where the resurrection of the daughter of Jairus took place, because the presence of the entire group would not have been in accord with proper decorum and might have disturbed the child when she reopened her eyes? Was the Master's Gethsemane agony too sacred to be witnessed by more than three of the disciples (Matt. 26:37; Mark 14:33), and was it for this reason that even then it was "witnessed" by these three to only a very limited extent? And is it possible that the transfiguration could have only three disciples as eyewitnesses (Matt. 17:1; Mark 9:2; Luke 9:28), because otherwise the injunction mentioned in Matt. 17:9 would have been more difficult to enforce? Such may have been the reasons, but we do not know.

That Peter was among the three does not surprise us, in view of Matt. 16:16–19. It is entirely possible that John's spiritual affinity with his Master—he was "the disciple whom Jesus loved" (John 13:23; 19:26; 20:2; 21:7, 20)—accounted for his inclusion in this innermost circle. But what about James, John's brother? Was it not considerate of the Lord to grant to him, who was going to be the first of The Twelve to seal his testimony with his blood (Acts 12:2), the privilege of being included among the three most intimate witnesses?

These are considerations that may well be taken into account in attempting to answer the question, "Why these three?" Nevertheless, it must be frankly admitted that the answer to this question has not been revealed. It is easier to understand why there had to be witnesses at all, namely, so that, when the proper time arrived, they could testify to the church concerning the things they had seen and heard. Besides, see Deut. 19:15; Matt. 18:16; John 8:17; II Cor. 13:1; I Tim. 5:19.

52. The people, meanwhile, were all weeping and wailing over her. Jesus said, Stop weeping, for she is not dead but asleep.

A scene of confusion greeted Jesus and the three disciples as they entered the home of the synagogue ruler. Matt. 9:23 mentions the noise-making crowd; Mark and Luke, the noise or tumult, the loud weeping and wailing, basically (and perhaps here also) breast-beating. It was a thoroughly disorderly mob.

As, according to custom, burial followed soon after death, this was the crowd's only opportunity, and the professional mourners (cf. Jer. 9:17, 18) made the most of it, perhaps all the more because a ruler of the synagogue was a very important person! Here then was weeping and wailing, moaning

461

and groaning, at its loudest. There was howling without any attempt at restraint. And every once in a while, as Matt. 9:23 informs us, above the confused noises issuing from the throats of the mourners could be heard the shrill notes of the flute-players.

Jesus told these noisemakers to stop their clamor, "for," said he, "she is not dead but asleep." What the mourners were doing was completely out of place, and this for two reasons: (a) they—at least many of them—were insincere, as verse 53 shows; and (b) there was cause here not for lamentation but for jubilation, not for bewailing a death but for celebrating a near-at-hand triumph over death.

Of course, we cannot very well blame these people for not knowing that life was about to triumph over death. What was wrong, though, was (a) their insincerity, and (b) their unwillingness to accept the fact that what Jesus was saying about the child not being dead but sleeping was a *word of revelation,* deserving of solemn reflection, not scorn.

That Jesus cannot have meant that the child had merely fallen into a coma is clear from the following:

a. Luke 8:53 declares that the people knew that she was dead.

b. Luke 8:55 states that at the command of Jesus "her spirit returned." It is clear, therefore, that there had been a separation between spirit and body.

c. In John 11:11 we have something similar. Jesus tells his disciples, "Our friend Lazarus has fallen asleep." But in verse 14 he affirms, "Lazarus died."

In both instances the meaning is that death will not have the final say. Not death but life is going to triumph in the end. Also, just as natural sleep is followed by awakening, so this child is going to become awake, that is, is going to live again.

53. But they were laughing in his face ...

The identical statement is found also in Matt. 9:24 and Mark 5:40. The reference is probably to repeated bursts of derisive laughter aimed at humiliating Jesus. These mourners were endowed with the dubious talent of shifting suddenly from dismal moaning to uproarious mirth. But this very laughter confirms the fact that the child had really died. Hence Luke adds: **for they knew that she was dead.** Do not this ridicule and this conviction on their part also confirm the genuine nature of the child's restoration from death?

3. *a word of love and power*

54, 55a. And having grasped her hand, he called out, My child, get up! —Her spirit returned and she got up at once.

From *the house* Jesus has expelled the scornful noisemakers (Matt. 9:25; Mark 5:40). Then he enters *the room* where the dead child lies. With him in this room are only the child's parents and Peter, James, and John.

The ruler had asked Jesus to place his hands upon the child (Mark 5:23). However, the Master does even better, for with authority, power, and tenderness he takes hold of her hand, and as he does this he says, "My child, get up." As Mark 5:41 indicates, he addresses her in her own native tongue (cf. N.T.C. on John 20:16), using the very words by which her mother had probably often awakened her in the morning, namely, "Talitha koum." It has already been shown (see *Introduction,* point V A) that whereas Mark often retains Aramaic terms, Luke translates them into Greek. So also here.

At the word of Jesus death immediately surrendered its prey: the child's spirit returned. So complete was the restoration to life that she even started to walk around (Mark 5:42).

4. *a word of tender concern*

55b. Then he directed that something be given her to eat.

Jesus realizes that the little girl, who because of her fatal illness had probably not been able to eat for some time, is in need of food; and that the parents, in the ecstasy of their joy, might overlook this need. Hence, the command.

This is a very important point. It should not be lightly passed by. Cf. Isa. 57:15. One moment Jesus triumphs over death; the next moment he appeases hunger; rather, in all probability, prevents it from becoming a reality. His power cannot be fathomed; nor his compassion measured.

This is the same Savior who went out of his way to enhance the reputation of one doubter (Luke 7:18–35) and to accept the presumptuous terms of another (John 20:24–29), who defended widows (Luke 18:1–8; 21:1–4), helping them in their needs (7:11–17), took little children into his arms and blessed them (Mark 10:16; cf. Luke 18:15–17), wept over Jerusalem's recalcitrant inhabitants (Luke 13:34; 19:41), and showed kindness to the woman who had been a public sinner (7:36–50). In his own most bitter agony he provided a home for his mother (John 19:26, 27), entrance into paradise for a robber (Luke 23:43), and forgiveness for his torturers (23:34). Even after his resurrection he is the same tenderhearted Savior; witness his treatment of the man who had but recently disowned him (Mark 16:7; Luke 22:61; John 21:15–17). That is the context in which this very precious passage, Luke 8:55, should be read.

Jesus is, moreover, *the Hope of the hopeless.* He showed this to the man who could not be tamed (Luke 8:26–39); to the woman who could not be cured (verses 43–48); and to the father who was told that he could no longer be helped (verses 40–42; 49–56).

56. Her parents were astonished, but he instructed them to tell no one what had happened.

That the parents were not only overjoyed but, as stated here, "astonished," requires no further comment. But why this order that they tell no one what had happened?

The objection has been raised, "But how could this miracle remain hidden? Was not everybody able to see that this child, once dead, was now alive and in good health? Did not everybody know that this restoration to life had occurred after Jesus had entered the death-chamber?" The answer is: that is probably true, though with one rather important qualification. Those people, *if there were any,* who had given a literal interpretation to the words, "She is not dead but asleep," *and had believed this to be true,* would be able to say that no actual *resurrection* had taken place. As far as all the others were concerned, including even the professional mourners, who were sure that the child had died, the fact of the child's resurrection could not be concealed.

Nevertheless, Jesus does not want the parents to broadcast what has happened. Let them rather take care of the child. Let them glorify God. Talking to everybody about Jesus' miracle-working power is exactly what they should *not* do. For the probable reason why such an injunction was issued see above, on 5:14.

Again, the order Jesus issues may seem to be in conflict with verse 39, where Jesus commands the very thing to be done which he here (verse 56) forbids. But Decapolis (including the region of the Gergesenes), with its strongly Gentile atmosphere, was not Galilee. The latter, though far more under the influence of the Gentiles than Judea (see Matt. 4:15), was at the same time far more Jewish than Decapolis. And the present miracle has taken us back to Galilee, full of Pharisees, scribes, spies, etc. To be sure, Jesus came on earth to die, but he wished to die at his own predestined hour, not earlier. Therefore the parents, who (except for Peter, James, and John, and the child herself) knew best exactly what had happened to the one so dear to them, must remain silent. Even for the sake of the child the less publicity the better!

It is admitted that not all questions have thus been answered. Yet, in light of the facts already mentioned, to which may be added the contents of Matt. 17:9; Mark 9:9, 10; and Luke 9:36, Christ's prohibition no longer seems so strange.[322]

Practical Lessons Derived from Luke 8:40–56

Verse 40

"The crowd welcomed him." No wonder, for he was concerned about crowds (Luke 10:2; 13:34; cf. Matt. 9:36, 37; 23:37). But, as the present story teaches, he was also concerned about individuals: Jairus, the latter's daughter, a woman subject to hemorrhages, etc. This holds even today.

Verse 41

"Just then ... Jairus ... began to plead with him." The best refuge for any troubled heart is Jesus:

---

322. Notes on Greek words, phrases, and constructions in 8:40–56 begin on page 465.

From every stormy wind that blows,
From every rising tide of woes
There is a calm, a sweet retreat,
'Tis found beneath the mercy seat.

Thomas Hastings

Verse 42

"His only daughter, about twelve years old, was dying." Death does not respect age, neither old age nor youthfulness.

Verses 44–46

"She touched the tassel of his garment.... 'Who is it that touched me?'... 'Master, the people are crowding and pressing against you.'... But Jesus said, 'Someone did touch me.'" There are different ways of "touching" Jesus: (a) outwardly, or (b) inwardly (by faith). That makes all the difference in the world.

Verse 47

"The woman realized that she had not escaped notice." "God's eyes are open to all the ways of men" (Jer. 32:19; cf. Heb. 4:13).

"She ... declared in the presence of all the people," etc. Faith concealed must become faith revealed. The woman is impelled to bring her testimony: (a) for her own strengthening in the faith, (b) for the benefit of others, and (c) for the glory of God.

Verse 49

"Don't bother the Teacher any more." Whoever said this *intended* to be kind, but this kindness was mistaken, since it failed to figure with Christ's power. There is a lesson here.

Verse 50

"Fear no longer; only believe."

Only believe, only believe,
All things are possible, only believe.

Paul Rader

Verse 55

"Then he directed that something be given her to eat." The Lord who raises the dead is not insensitive to the needs of a child. See Isa. 57:15.

Notes on Greek Words, Phrases, and Constructions in 8:40–56

Verse 40

With ἐν the present infinitive is natural, though there are exceptions. See Gram. N.T., p. 891.

ἀπεδέξατο, third per. s. aor. indicat. act. of ἀποδέχομαι**, to receive with joy, welcome.

ἦσαν ... προσδοκῶντες, periphrastic imperf. act. of προσδοκάω. They "were looking *forward* to his coming," "were (eagerly) expecting him."

Verse 41

ὑπῆρχεν, third per. s. imperf. of ὑπάρχω. See also the note on 8:3 on page 421. *The New Testament in Modern Greek* has ἦτο.

Verse 42

For μονογενής see the note on 7:12 on page 389; there the reference is to a son; here to a daughter. See also 9:38 (son); John 1:18; 3:16: God's only (begotten) Son.

ἀπέθνῃσκεν, third per. s. imperf. of ἀποθνῄσκω, to die. The child "was dying." Literally, to die off; that is, to die and thus be *away from* this earthly realm. Cf. German *absterben;* Dutch *afsterven.*

συνέπνιγον, third per. pl. imperf. act. of συμπνίγω, to press upon. See the note on 8:14 on page 434.

Verse 43

ῥύσις αἵματος, flow of blood, hemorrhage.

As the textual apparatus, Grk. N.T. (A-B-M-W), indicates, the words translated "having spent all she had on doctors" have dubious validity.

Verse 44

The noun κράσπεδον can mean edge, hem, or tassel.

ἔστη, third per. s. 2nd aor. indicat. act. of ἵστημι. The hemorrhage stopped; the blood stopped flowing, stanched.

Verse 45

See 8:37 on συνέχουσιν, same construction as:

ἀποθλίβουσιν, third per. pl. pres. (progressive) indicat. act. of ἀποθλίβω*, to press from every side, press (hard) upon or against.

Verse 46

ἔγνων, first per. s. 2nd aor. indicat. act. of γινώσκω ("I was aware").

ἐξεληλυθυῖαν, fem. s. 2nd perf. act. participle of ἐξέρχομαι; here in indirect discourse.

Verse 47

ἔλαθεν, third per. s. 2nd aor. indicat. of λανθάνω, to escape notice or detection.

τρέμουσα, fem. nom. s. pres. participle of τρέμω, to tremble.

Verse 48

σέσωκεν, third per. s. perf. indicat. act. of σώζω, to save, restore to health. See also the explanation of 7:50. From the same verb is also σωθήσεται (third per. s. fut. indicat. pass.), verse 50.

Verse 49

τέθνηκεν, third per. s. perf. indicat. of θνῄσκω, to die. They said, "Your daughter has died [= is dead]."

μηκέτι σκύλλε, sec. per. s. pres. imperat. act. of σκύλλω, in a negative command. The original meaning of σκύλλω is to *skin, flay*. The modified and weaker connotation, as here, is *bother, trouble*. See also N.T.C. on Matt. 9:36; pp. 439, 440, including footnote 426.

Verse 52

ἐκόπτοντο, third per. pl. imperf. middle of κόπτω; here, to beat one's breast in mourning; hence, to wail or mourn (over) someone. Cf. 23:27.

Verse 53

κατεγέλων, third per. pl. imperf. of καταγελάω; lit. to laugh down; hence, to laugh in one's face, to ridicule.

Verse 55

Note the two infinitives: δοθῆναι, aor. pass. of δίδωμι; and φαγεῖν, 2nd aor. act. of ἐσθίω.

Verse 56

ἐξέστησαν, third per. pl. 2nd aor. indicat. of ἐξίστημι. Cf. 2:47. They "were knocked out of their senses," "were (thoroughly) astonished."

Summary of Chapter 8

Chapter 7 closed with a description of a penitent *woman* in the act of anointing Jesus. Chapter 8 begins by mentioning the names of other *women*. They rendered service by contributing to the material support of the little group consisting of Jesus and his disciples. The names of three of these women are mentioned: Mary Magdalene, Joanna, and Susanna. We are told that there were many others (verses 1–3).

We must not suppose, however, that all those who listened to Jesus responded with deeds of gratitude. Hearts differ. In this respect they resemble the various kinds of soil on or into which seed is sown. These kinds are: hard, rocky, thorn-infested, and good. Only the last of the four produces a harvest, at times yielding as much as a hundredfold (the parable of The Sower—verses 4–8).

Next, Jesus described the purpose of addressing the people by means of parables, that purpose being *to reveal* the mysteries of the kingdom to those who are willing to accept the truth, *and to conceal* them from those who have hardened their hearts against the truth (verses 9, 10).

At the request of his disciples Jesus then explained to them the parable of The Sower. He started out by saying, "The seed is the word of God." He continued by informing them that the four kinds of soil indicate respectively unresponsive, impulsive, preoccupied, and well-prepared hearts. It is the last kind of heart alone that is fertile (verses 11–15).

Fertile hearts resemble shining lamps. Both are a blessing. Now when a person lights a lamp, he does not hide it under a bed but places it on a stand. Similarly, hearts and lives must be outgoing. They must not be hid but must shine for Jesus and his kingdom. *The mystery* must be revealed.

But whether revealed or concealed, whatever is done with the mystery will not go unnoticed. There is nothing hidden that will not be disclosed. This shows how very important it is to listen carefully to whatever Jesus has to say: "Take care, therefore, how y o u listen." Whoever heeds the message will receive an ever-increasing blessing. Whoever hardens himself against it will lose even that which he thinks he already possesses (verses 16–18).

It may have been disturbing remarks about Jesus—that his opponents regarded him as being demon-possessed and that even some of his friends thought he was out of his mind—that caused his mother Mary and his brothers to make an attempt to contact him, with the intention, probably, to take him along with them, removing him from the public eye and providing for him a haven of rest and refreshment. But however well-intentioned this attempt, it amounted to sinful interference with Christ's own predesigned program of activities. Mary and his brothers must be made to understand that his comings and goings cannot be determined by earthly ties but only by the will of God. Hence, when Jesus is told that his mother and brothers are standing outside, wanting to see him, he answers, "Mother to me and brothers to me are those who are listening to the word of God and are putting it into practice" (verses 19–21).

Once Jesus stepped into a boat with his disciples and said to them, "Let us cross over to the other side of the lake." According to Mark 4:35 this incident occurred on the evening of the day Jesus addressed the crowds by means of parables. Almost as soon as the boat had left the shore Jesus fell into a deep sleep. He must have been very tired. A furious tempest arose, so that the boat was becoming water-logged. So the disciples, frantic with fear, awaken Jesus, crying, "Master, Master, we're perishing." He arises and with a word of command stills the winds and the waves. Addressing his disciples, he asks them, "Where (is) y o u r faith?" Awestruck and filled with amazement, they ask one another, "Who then is this, that he commands even the winds and the water, and they obey him?" (verses 22–25).

In the rest of chapter 8 Luke describes Jesus as the Hope of the hopeless. These closing sections move on to a gradual and exciting climax. They picture a demoniac who was hopelessly wild (verses 26–39), a woman who was hopelessly ill, and a father who became hopelessly bereaved (verses 40–56); *hopelessly* in each case "by human standards." But now notice the climax: *the people in general* (see verse 29) had reached the point where they were totally unable effectively to bind the demoniac; *no one* was able to cure the woman (verse 43); and, of course, *no power in the universe* was able to raise a child from the dead! Not even the Teacher? No, not even the Teacher . . . so everybody thought. Note the statement: "While he [Jesus] was still speaking, someone came from the synagogue ruler's (house), saying, 'Your daughter is dead; don't bother the Teacher any more.'"

Yet Christ, in his majesty, power, and compassion, triumphed over this hopelessness in all three cases: he dispelled the demons and transformed the demoniac into a missionary; he healed the woman and perfected her faith, changing it from faith concealed to faith revealed; and he not only, to the amazement of everybody, brought the child back to life, but even in his tenderness took care that she got something to eat!

What is especially important is the fact that not only the power but also the pity of Christ is revealed. His compassionate heart is laid bare. The lesson, therefore, is this: "Give your heart to the wonderful Savior." A second lesson is this:

"I have given y o u an example, in order that just as I did to y o u so also y o u should do" (John 13:15).

"Be therefore imitators of God, as beloved children, and walk in love, just as Christ loved y o u and gave himself up for us, an offering and a sacrifice to God, for a fragrant odor" (Eph. 5:1, 2).

Satan must be banished from hearts and lives, and the wonderful story must be told!

Outline of Chapter 9:1-17

Theme: *The Work Thou Gavest Him To Do*

CHAPTER IX:1-17

9 1 Jesus called the twelve together and gave them power and authority over all the demons and to cure diseases. 2 And he sent them out to preach the kingdom of God and to heal the sick. 3 He told them, "Take nothing for the journey: neither staff nor traveler's bag nor bread nor money nor (even) have two tunics. 4 And whatever house y o u enter, there remain and leave from there. 5 And wherever they do not welcome y o u, when y o u leave that town shake the dust from y o u r feet as a testimony against them." 6 They departed and went about from village to village preaching the gospel and healing everywhere.

9:1–6 *The Charge to The Twelve*
Cf. Matt. 10:5-15; Mark 6:7-13

1, 2. Jesus called the twelve together and gave them power and authority over all the demons and to cure diseases.

In Mark's Gospel the story about the double miracle (5:21–43; cf. Matt. 9:18-26; Luke 8:40-56) is followed by Christ's rejection at Nazareth (Mark 6:1-6a), which, in turn, is followed by the mention of *his* teaching tour (6:6b). There follows a brief account of the sending forth of *The Twelve* on a mission tour (6:7-13). The teaching tour and sending out of The Twelve are combined also in that same order in Matt. 9:35—10:4.

It will be recalled that the *appointment* of these men to be Christ's disciples and apostles had occurred a little earlier, namely, just previous to the preaching of The Sermon on the Mount. See Luke 6:12, 13, 17, 20. And now, somewhat later, during that same summer (of the year A.D. 28?) the Master sends out these men on a mission assignment.

These men were to be Christ's official ambassadors or "apostles," men clothed with authority to represent their Sender. That exactly twelve men, no more, no less, receive this assignment must mean that the Lord designated them to be the nucleus of the new Israel, for the Israel of the old dispensation had been represented by twelve patriarchs. Cf. Rev. 21:12, 14.

It is Mark alone who relates that the men were sent out two by two. Why were they sent out at this time? A good guess may well be that the Master knew that his Great Galilean Ministry was rapidly approaching its end.

Note that the Master equipped The Twelve with both power and authority; that is, with both the might and the right to carry out the mandate he assigned to them.

471

And he sent them out to preach the kingdom of God and to heal the sick.

In committing this task to them the Master called these men together (Luke 9:1) and to himself (Matt. 10:1; Mark 6:7).

The mandate given to them, according to Luke 9:1, 2, consisted in these two functions: healing and heralding. The healing comprised both the expulsion of demons and the cure of the sick. The Gospels sharply distinguish between demon-possession and physical illness (Luke 4:40, 41; Mark 1:32–34; 6:13).

As to "preaching," this has been described in connection with the explanation of 3:3. And the essence of "the kingdom of God" has been set forth in connection with 4:43. Preaching of the kingdom of God means therefore the lively proclamation of the reign of God in human hearts unto salvation full and free. For many of the listeners what they heard must have been surprising and heartening. They were now learning that people are saved not by means of strict adherence to hairsplitting rabbinical stipulations but by the entrance of the God of love and grace into their hearts and lives.

3. He told them, Take nothing for the journey: neither staff nor traveler's bag nor bread nor money nor (even) have two tunics.

Note these five items:

staff. In non-biblical Greek it refers at times to a *magic wand.* Other meanings are: *fishing rod, rodlike streak of light* from the sun, etc. In Ps. 23:4 (LXX 22:4) the word refers to *the shepherd's rod.* Cf. Mic. 7:14. In the New Testament the rod is at times an *instrument of punishment* (I Cor. 4:21), a meaning which easily connects with "the rod of iron" of Rev. 2:27; 12:5; 19:15. Then there is also *the ruler's scepter* (Heb. 1:8); *the rod that gives support* so that one can lean on it (Heb. 11:21); and *Aaron's rod* that budded (Heb. 9:4). But here in Luke 9:3 and its parallels it is *the traveler's staff* that is meant.

traveler's bag. This was a kind of knapsack, a bag "for the road" or "for traveling." It is a bag that, before leaving, a person would fill with supplies which he thinks he might need while traveling.

bread. Here and in Mark 6:8 the word is used generically.

money. Basically this word means "silver," but according to the context the reference must be to silver coins, small change.

two tunics. The tunic was an undershirt worn next to the skin. It reached almost to the feet and was equipped with arm holes. Cf. Matt. 5:40; 10:10; Mark 6:9; Luke 3:11; 6:29.

Luke does not even mention "sandals" (Matt. 10:10; Mark 6:9).

The Master, then, tells The Twelve that on *this* trip (contrast Luke 22:36) they must not take along more than is absolutely necessary.

In this connection there is a little problem. According to Mark 6:8 Jesus told his disciples to take along a staff, but according to Luke 9:3 he instructed them not to do this. For a possible solution of this problem see N.T.C. on Mark, p. 229. The conclusion there reached is that Jesus is saying: an *extra* tunic, *extra* pair of sandals, and *extra* staff must not be taken along.

4. And whatever house y o u enter, there remain and leave from there.
How the disciples must decide in which home to stay is answered in Matt. 10:11. It is the duty of the hearers to extend hospitality. All the more so when the travelers enrich the people with the pearl of great price. And the visitors themselves must show a co-operative spirit. They must not be so fastidious that whenever some small detail is not to their liking in one home, they immediately leave and enter another where the facilities seem to be more desirable and the food more palatable. The spread of the gospel has the priority over personal likes and dislikes. Hence the missionaries—not only traveling but also probably lodging two by two; see Mark 6:7—must remain in the home that is kind enough to extend hospitality to them. When they leave the town, they must leave from that home. A very practical lesson!

5. And wherever they do not welcome y o u, when y o u leave that town shake the dust from y o u r feet as a testimony against them.
After traveling through heathen territory Jews had the custom of shaking the dust off their sandals and clothes before re-entering the Holy Land.[323] They were afraid that otherwise in their own country levitically clean objects, as well as they themselves, might be rendered unclean. What Jesus is here saying, therefore, is that any place whatever—note "wherever"—be it a house, village, city, hamlet, that refuses to accept the gospel must be considered unclean and must be treated as such. The inhabitants of such a place must be looked upon as being not any better than Gentiles! Paul and Barnabas obeyed this commandment when a persecution was organized against them in the Jewish district of Antioch in Pisidia (Acts 13:50, 51). A heavy load of guilt rests on such a place. See Matt. 10:15.

The symbolic action—shaking the dust from the feet—is a public declaration of the divine displeasure that rests on a place that has refused the gospel. It amounts to a testimony "against" such a place and its people, its purpose being that they may repent. Cf. Rev. 16:9. It is a revelation of God's marked disapproval, for the spreaders of the good tidings are *his* ambassadors. They are bringing *his* word. By rejecting them, these wicked people are rejecting God, hence also Christ.

6. They departed and went about from village to village preaching the gospel and healing everywhere.
This passage indicates that the disciples must have covered a considerable territory in Galilee. They did as Jesus had told them to do (see verses 1, 2). They did the very kind of work Jesus too had been doing and was doing. See Luke 4:40, 43; 6:19; 8:1, etc. In fact, one might say that Jesus was carrying out his ministry through them. See Acts 1:1.

323. S.BK., Vol. I, p. 571.

For *Practical Lessons* and *Greek Words,* etc., see pp. 482–485.

---

7 Now Herod the tetrarch heard about all the things that were happening. And he was perplexed because by some it was said that John had risen from the dead, 8 by others that Elijah had appeared, and by still others that one of the ancient prophets had come back to life.

9 But Herod said, "John I beheaded. Who, then, is this man about whom I am hearing such things?" And he was trying[324] to see Jesus.

9:7–9 *Herod's Anxiety*
Cf. Matt. 14:1–12; Mark 6:14–29

7a. Now Herod the tetrarch heard about all the things that were happening.

Note that while Mark calls Herod Antipas a "king" (6:14, 22, 25–27), and Matthew designates him either as "king" (14:9) or "tetrarch" (14:1), and all three at times simply speak of "Herod" (Matt. 14:3, 6; Mark 6:16–22; 8:15; Luke 3:19b; 9:9; 13:31; 23:7, 8, 11, 12, 15; cf. Acts 4:27), Luke, whenever he ascribes a title to this ruler, calls him "tetrarch" (3:1, 19a; 9:7; Acts 13:1). In a sense both "king" and "tetrarch" are correct: "king" as popular title, "tetrarch" as official appellation. Officially or technically this man was not a king and was never going to become one. From 4 B.C.–A.D. 39 he was tetrarch over Galilee and Perea. For more on this see above, on 3:1, 2.

For the Family Tree of Herod The Great, the father of Herod Antipas (and others), see N.T.C. on Matthew, p. 189.

It is not strange that when at Christ's word even hopelessly sick people were suddenly and completely healed, lepers cleansed, storms hushed, demons expelled, and even the dead brought back to life (a widow's son, Jairus' daughter), as the preceding sections of Luke's Gospel have shown, the fame of the One who accomplished all this, and who now was even performing remarkable miracles through his apostles, was brought to the attention of the tetrarch. Herod did not know what to make of all this. He was puzzled, perplexed even. The explanatory reports that reached him were threefold:

7b, 8. And he was perplexed because by some it was said that John had risen from the dead, by others that Elijah had appeared, and by still others that one of the ancient prophets had come back to life.

a. Some people were convinced that Jesus was John the Baptist restored to life. This may seem somewhat odd, since Scripture nowhere ascribes any miracles to the Baptist. But it is probable that by this group John was held in such high esteem that the ability to perform miracles was attributed to him.

b. Another group said, "Elijah has appeared." Had not Elijah's return, as Messiah's forerunner, been predicted by Malachi (4:5)? Cf. Isa. 40:3; and see above, on Luke 1:76; 7:27 (cf. Mark 1:1–3).

---

324. Or: kept trying.

c. The third group, not wishing to be very definite, was convinced, nevertheless, that in the person of Jesus one of the ancient prophets had come back to life. See also on verses 18, 19.

9a. But Herod said, John I beheaded. Who, then, is this man about whom I am hearing such things?

Note that Luke does not report what the tetrarch thought of suggestions (b) and (c). Herod may have reflected on these answers briefly, and then dismissed them from his mind. It would seem that, after some hesitation, he was always coming back to suggestion (a).

"John I beheaded," that is, "John the Baptist I caused to be beheaded." The evangelist does not state how Herod answered the question, "Who, then, is this man . . .?" That answer is found, however, in Matt. 14:2 (cf. Mark 6:16). The ruler, a man with a terribly disturbed conscience, and filled with haunting superstitions and dark forebodings, arrived at the conclusion "Jesus is John risen from the dead." Though *Luke* does not say this, he surely leaves room for it.

9b. And he was trying to see Jesus. Probably to be confirmed in his belief and to satisfy his curiosity. When at last Herod's desire to see Jesus was fulfilled, he, the hardened sinner, mocked the Silent Sufferer (Luke 23:8–12).

For *Practical Lessons* and *Greek Words,* etc., see pp. 482–485.

---

10 The apostles came back and reported to Jesus all they had done. Then he took them with him and withdrew privately to a town called Bethsaida. 11 But the crowds learned about it and followed him. He welcomed them and began to speak to them about the kingdom of God, and to heal those in need of healing.

12 As the day began to decline, the twelve came up to him and said, "Send the people away that they may go to the villages and farms round about, get lodging, and find food, because here we are in a lonely place." 13 He said to them, "Y o u give them to eat!" They replied, "We have only five bread-cakes and two fishes, unless we go and buy provisions[325] for all these people." 14 For there were about five thousand men.

But he said to his disciples, "Have them recline in groups of about fifty each." 15 They did so and had them all recline. 16 He took the five bread-cakes and the two fishes, and looking up to heaven gave thanks for them,[326] broke them, and kept giving them to his disciples to set before the people. 17 They all ate and were filled.[327] And what they had left of the broken pieces was picked up, twelve baskets (full) of broken pieces.

9:10-17 *The Feeding of the Five Thousand*
Cf. Matt. 14:13-21; Mark 6:30-44; John 6:1-14

A. *Setting indicated*

10a. The apostles came back and reported to Jesus all they had done.
All four evangelists relate this event. The similarities and differences are summarized in N.T.C. on Mark, pp. 244-246.

---

325. Or: food.
326. Or: blessed them.
327. Or: were satisfied.

Having accomplished their mission tour (verses 1–6), The Twelve are gathered around Jesus. Here and also in 6:13; 17:5; 22:14; 24:10 Luke calls these men "apostles." They must be regarded as men through whom Jesus Christ himself is accomplishing his work on earth. They are his official ambassadors, having been commissioned by him to carry out certain specific tasks: preaching, healing, and casting out demons. He who rejects them rejects Christ himself (Matt. 10:40; Luke 10:16; John 13:20). It is in their capacity as "apostles" that they have been at work on the tour that is now ended.

The report these men brought back to Jesus must have been exciting: "They reported to Jesus all they had done."

Much had been happening during the last months: John had been cruelly murdered. His decapitated body had been buried. Jesus had been informed about this (Matt. 14:1–12; Mark 6:14–29). Herod Antipas had become greatly disturbed when he heard about the miracles performed by Jesus, whether directly or through his apostles. All kinds of rumors had been going the rounds as to the identity of Jesus. As a result the "tetrarch" had said, "John I beheaded. Who, then, is this man about whom I am hearing such things?" The disciples-apostles had been sent on their mission tour and had now returned.

All this had taken time. It is not strange, therefore, that the miracle of the feeding of the five thousand, described here in 9:10–17, took place when Passover, probably April of the year A.D. 29, was already approaching, as is clear from John 6:4. The Great Galilean Ministry, probably extending from about December of A.D. 27 to about April of A.D. 29, was drawing to its close.

B. *Rest needed*

10b. Then he took them with him and withdrew privately to a town called Bethsaida.

Working without resting, being busy without ever taking a vacation, performing all the arduous duties pertaining to ministerial or missionary activity and not making a retreat for relaxation, discussion, prayer, and meditation, will never do. Even Jesus, because of the heavy burden he had taken upon himself, needed periods of withdrawal (4:42). So did the disciples. It was for this reason that he invited them to come away with him to a remote place, where they would be able to rest up.

What made the need even more urgent, as Mark 6:31 indicates, was the fact that a boisterous and demanding crowd, with people constantly coming and going, was making even eating impossible. Result: "Privately," that is, "all by themselves," Jesus, The Twelve, *but no one else*, take off for Bethsaida Julias, located on the northeast shore of the Lake of Gennesaret (= Sea of Galilee). For the debate about its location see N.T.C. on John, Vol. I, pp. 216, 217. Actually, the little group was not headed for the town itself but for a quiet and secluded spot in its vicinity (see verse 12).

C. *Rest curtailed*

11a. But the crowds learned about it and followed him.

As soon as the people from the Capernaum side of the lake became aware of the fact that Jesus was leaving them and crossing over by boat to the opposite shore, they started to run around the northern edge of the water in order to be with Jesus again. Were they afraid, perhaps, that, due to the tetrarch's hostile attitude toward the true religion—he had already killed John the Baptist—their Great Teacher might never return to them?

The most natural interpretation of Matt. 14:13, 14; Luke 9:11; and John 6:3, 5 is that Jesus disembarked *before* the arrival of the crowd from the western shore. And it is impossible to prove that Mark 6:33 contradicts this conclusion. See N.T.C. on Mark, pp. 248–250.

The fact deserving special attention is this: the rest and relaxation which the Master and his disciples were seeking is to a large extent denied them. Not entirely, for Jesus and The Twelve seem to have been together for a little while (John 6:3), but this breathing-spell is considerably curtailed.

How does Jesus react to this interruption of his rest? The answer is found in:

D. *Compassion shown*

11b. He welcomed them and began to speak to them about the kingdom of God, and to heal those in need of healing.

Had Jesus been an ordinary human individual seeking rest and relaxation, he would probably have addressed the crowd as follows, "We came here to find peace and quiet; so please go home. We are tired; see us some other time." But Jesus was—and is—different. He actually welcomes those who had come to disturb his rest, for "his heart went out to them" (Mark 6:34). The needs of people, sick, ignorant, disconsolate, and also hungry (as they were soon to become, Luke 9:12, 13) meant far more to him than his own convenience and ease.

So he began to speak to them about *the kingdom of God*. See on 4:43. For people living under the oppressive yoke of Pharisaism and rabbinism the teaching of Jesus—according to which man's salvation *is not* basically a result of human effort and strict obedience to regulations but a product of God's gracious reign in human hearts—must have been truly startling.

For constant fear Jesus substituted fortitude (Luke 11:9–13); for put-on sadness, gladness (Matt. 6:16–18); for spiritual night, light (Matt. 4:16); for antipathy, sympathy (Luke 10:36, 37); for egoism, altruism (Luke 6:32–36); for pomposity, humility (Luke 18:9–14); and for the Pharisaic "You must," the truly Christian "I trust" (Mark 7:1–5; Luke 12:22–32). Once the "kingdom" or "kingship" of God is established in hearts and lives, everything undergoes a radical change. The world is "turned upside down" (Acts 17:6).

In line with this is the fact that the establishment of the kingdom of God affects not only the soul but also the body: ". . . and to heal those in need of healing." When anyone, conscious of the need of being healed, approached Jesus, the latter healed him.

It should not escape our attention that there is an exact correspondence between verse 11b and verse 2: whatever the Master had been doing through his disciples, he was also doing personally.

E. *Hunger anticipated*

12. As the day began to decline, the twelve came up to him and said, Send the people away that they may go to the villages and farms round about, get lodging, and find food, because here we are in a lonely place.

Christ's teaching and healing activity must have consumed a considerable amount of time. And now, though the sun has not yet set, it is already late in the afternoon: the day is drawing to a close. By means of his teaching and miracles of healing the Lord has so captivated the crowds that even now they are not departing. If they are to eat, they must leave; and if they are going to leave, they must be told to do so. Besides, the multitude is in need of lodging for the night. But as yet no one is even stirring.

It is at this point that the disciples, probably in a body, approach Jesus with the advice that he dismiss the people, so that they might find food and lodging in the surrounding villages and farms. They give as their reason, "because here we are in a lonely place." In other words, this is not a city, containing all kinds of bazaars within easy reach, where food may be bought; it is a desolate region. Also, to go to any of the surrounding villages or farms to buy food will take time, and "the day is already drawing to a close" (Mark 6:35).

F. *Orders issued*

13a. He said to them, *Y o u* give them to eat!

Such an order comes as a surprise to them. They are confused. They must have thought, "How can *we* provide food for all these people?"

What did Jesus mean by saying, "*Y o u* give them to eat"? It may be impossible to give a fully satisfactory answer to this question. A few things can be pointed out, however:

a. Jesus means that these men must not be so quick to shake off responsibility. As the Gospels picture them, they were often ready to do this very thing, and to say, "Send the people away" (here in verse 12); "Send her [the Syrophoenician woman] away" (Matt. 15:23). They even "rebuked" those who brought little children to Jesus that he might touch them (Luke 18:15). See also 9:49, 50. "Don't bother the Master and don't bother us," was too often their slogan. In the light of this evidence it is safe to say that Jesus wants to remind these men of the fact that simply trying to get rid of people in need is not the solution. It is certainly not God's way of doing things (Matt. 5:43–48; 11:25–30; Luke 6:27–38; John 3:16).

b. He wants them to ask, seek, and knock (Matt. 7:7, 8); in other words, to claim God's promise for themselves, and to go to him who is able to supply every need. He who, when there was a shortage, supplied wine (John 2:1-11), can he not also supply bread?

c. In view of the fact that "bread," as the term is used in this account (see verses 13, 16), while referring to be sure to that which supplies a physical need, is also symbolical of Jesus as the Bread of Life (John 6:35, 48), is he not also telling these "fishers of men" that they must be the means in God's hand to supply the *spiritual* needs of the people?

13b, 14a. They replied, We have only five bread-cakes and two fishes... According to John 6:8, 9, it is Andrew who conveys the information, "There is a lad here who has five barley-cakes and two fishes." However, in desperation he immediately adds, "But what are these for so many?" And as Andrew speaks so they all reason. All join in calling Christ's attention to what they consider the totally insufficient amount of presently available food: **unless we go and buy provisions for all these people.** The evangelist adds the explanatory remark: **For there were about five thousand men.**

As they see it, this suggested solution is entirely impracticable. Where would they get all that food? And where the money to buy such a huge quantity? Food for a crowd consisting of five thousand adult males, not even to mention the women and children who, after all, must also be fed (Matt. 14:21).

The trouble with these disciples was that they concentrated all their attention on the vast, hungry crowd. They were forgetting about Jesus, his power and love. This forgetfulness on their part was inexcusable:

a. Earlier in the day Jesus had already asked Philip, "How are we to buy bread-cakes that these people may eat?" Philip and the other disciples had had sufficient time to reflect on the ability of Jesus to supply whatever was needed. See John 6:5.

b. Jesus had this very day manifested his miracle-working power (see verse 11b).

Without even rebuking his disciples Jesus now provides the solution: **14b, 15. But he said to his disciples, Have them recline in groups of about fifty each. —They did so and had them all recline.**

Jesus issued this command to the disciples, and they in turn to the people. Mark 6:39 states that the crowd reclined "upon the green grass." There was, accordingly, this strikingly colorful arrangement of people dressed in their bright garments, reclining under the blue vault of heaven on the grassy slopes. While according to Mark they reclined "in hundreds and in fifties" (6:40), here in Luke they are said to have reclined "in groups of about fifty each." If they reclined in a hundred rows of fifty each, the two accounts would be in perfect harmony. Not only that, but the total of (about) "five thousand men" (women and children being left uncounted), a

479

figure mentioned in all four accounts (Matt. 14:21; Mark 6:44; Luke 9:14; John 6:10), would result. The grouping was very practical. It made distribution of bread and fish, and also counting, easier.

It has been suggested[328] that this grouping may be an echo of ancient practice in Israel. See Exod. 18:21; Deut. 1:15. And is not the true Israel of the old dispensation continued in the true church of the new? See Gal. 6:16. Cf. Ps. 125:5; II Cor. 6:16; Eph. 2:14-22.

G. *Miracle performed*

16, 17a. He took the five bread-cakes and the two fishes, and looking up to heaven gave thanks for them, broke them, and kept giving them to his disciples to set before the people. Jesus took the five bread-cakes and the two fishes. He looked up to heaven. For this lifting heavenward of the eyes in prayer see also Ps. 25:15; 121:1; 123:1, 2; 141:8; 145:15; John 11:41; 17:1; I Tim. 2:8.[329]

Looking up to heaven Jesus "blessed," thus literally. The same verb is also found in the Synoptic parallels (Matt. 14:19; Mark 6:41). John, on the other hand, has "having given thanks" (6:11). Solution: "blessed" in this instance means "gave thanks," and can be thus translated. When a person blesses or praises God is he not giving thanks to him? It was the custom of the Jews to thank God before starting a meal. However, since it is abundantly clear from the Gospels that our Lord never spoke as did the scribes, that is, that his words were always characterized by freshness and originality (cf. Matt. 7:29), we may well believe that this was true also on the present occasion.

Then from the bread-cakes Jesus began to break off fragments of edible size. He kept giving these to his disciples who carried them (in baskets collected here and there from the crowd?) to the people. With the fishes the procedure was somewhat similar. Mark says, "He . . . *divided* the two fishes among them all."

The striking beauty of the account is heightened by the fact that only a few simple words are used to relate the miracle of the multiplication of the fragments. One might even say that the miracle is implied rather than expressed. **They all ate and were filled.** Exactly when were the bread and the fish multiplied? "Under his hands"? Probably, but even this is not stated. All we really know is that there was plenty of bread and fish—in fact, plenty and to spare—for everybody. At some point of time between the breaking or dividing and the reception of the fragments by the people the miracle must have occurred. All ate and "were filled," that is, "had all they wanted," "were fully satisfied."

---

328. See F. W. Danker, *op. cit.,* p. 113.

329. The subject *Prayer Postures* is treated in some detail in N.T.C. on I and II Timothy and Titus, pp. 103, 104.

H. *Leftovers collected*

17b. And what they had left of the broken pieces was picked up, twelve baskets (full) of broken pieces.

Even though the Lord would have been able to supply food whenever needed, he did not want leftovers to go to waste. These, too, were to be regarded as "good gifts coming down from the Father of lights" (James 1:17; cf. I Tim. 4:3, 4). For today's world, in which some nations have an oversupply while others suffer scarcity, is there not a lesson here? Good use could be made of the twelve baskets full of broken pieces. There were many poor and hungry people.

In this story it is the *wonder-working power* of Jesus that stands out. He is the One whose ability to supply every need is unlimited. In the old dispensation he was foreshadowed (I Kings 17:16; II Kings 4:43, 44. See also Deut. 18:15–18; cf. John 6:14; and see John 6:32).

What, however, stands out just as clearly, if not even more so, is Christ's *tender compassion.* He was deeply concerned about the spiritual welfare of these people; so, he taught them. And about their physical needs; so, he fed them. It is Luke's Gospel that similarly (a) pictures a Savior whose heart goes out to Nain's grieving widow (7:13); (b) contains the parable of The Samaritan Who Cared, being an example to all (10:33, 37); and (c) in unforgettable language portrays the tender love of a father—symbol of the Heavenly Father—for his penitent, returning son (15:20)!

In close connection with the preceding, what the abundant leftovers proved was the Master's *regal lavishness,* his *uncalculating generosity.* Before performing this miracle did Jesus say to himself, "Exactly so much is needed to feed a multitude of this size. So I will give them exactly so much, but no more"? Not at all! Moreover, as John 14:9 makes clear, what is true of Jesus holds for God Triune.

With the account of The Miraculous Feeding of the Five Thousand Luke's coverage of The Great Galilean Ministry ends. Matt. 14:22–33; Mark 6:45–52; and John 6:15–21 contain the report of the return to the western shore. During the course of this crossing Jesus, who had sent The Twelve ahead and had himself remained behind to pray, surprised his disciples by his sudden appearance, walking toward them on the water during a violent storm.

In Matt. 14:34–36 and Mark 6:53–56 the story of the landing at and healings in Gennesaret follows. It is probable that from there Jesus and The Twelve proceeded to Capernaum, where he delivered the discourse on The Bread of Life (most of John 6). It may have been about the same time and place that the event described in Matt. 15:1–20 and Mark 7:1–23, namely, the clash between Jesus and the Pharisees regarding Ceremonial versus Real Defilement, took place.

481

See pp. 492, 493 for an answer to the question, "Why does Luke pass by what is found in Mark 6:45—8:26?"[330]

Practical Lessons Derived from 9:1–17

Verses 2, 11

"He sent them out to preach the kingdom of God.... He ... began to speak to them about the kingdom of God." Preaching the kingdom (or: kingship, rule) of God means no less than proclaiming God's absolute sovereignty in every sphere: heart, mind, life, family, village, city, state, nation, world; education, industry, commerce, art, science, politics, etc. Cf. I Cor. 10:31; II Cor. 10:5.

Verse 2

"And to heal the sick." A life in harmony with the rule "Trust and obey" produces blessings for both body and soul. We should thank God, both privately and publicly, not only for Christian pastors, missionaries, lay evangelists, but also for Christian doctors, nurses, etc.

Verse 6

"They ... went about from village to village." The Christian ministry must be carried out not only in cities but also in villages; not only in spacious auditoriums but also in chapels. Did not Spurgeon ascribe his conversion to a sermon preached (with God's blessing) in a small chapel by a layman? What is small in the eyes of man may be very important, indeed, in the eyes of God. See Mic. 5:2; Zech. 4:10; John 1:46; I Cor. 1:26–29.

Verse 7

"He was perplexed." In spite of wealth and prestige, Herod was a very unhappy man. Oppressed by a guilty conscience, he did not follow David's example. Therefore he did not prosper. See Ps. 32:5; Prov. 28:13.

Verse 9

"He was trying to see Jesus." Cf. 23:8. So was Simeon (2:26–30); and so were: the mother and brothers of Jesus (8:20), Zacchaeus (19:3, 4), and some Greeks (John 12:21). The results varied. Why? What is the lesson?

Verse 13a

"*Y o u* give them to eat!" In our constant emphasis on Christian *liberty,* are we forgetting Christian *responsibility?*

Verse 13b

"We have only five bread-cakes and two fishes." What were they forgetting?

---

330. Notes on Greek words, phrases, and constructions in 9:1–17 begin on page 483.

Verse 17

"They all ate and were filled." Examples of divine generosity: Gen. 22:15–18; I Kings 3:2–15; Ps. 81:10b; 91:14–16; 116:12; Isa. 1:18; 55:1–3, 6, 7; Mic. 7:18–20; Luke 6:38; 15:20–24; John 1:16; 3:16; Rom. 5:6–11, 16–19; 8:31–39; I Cor. 3:21–23.

Notes on Greek Words, Phrases, and Constructions in 9:1–17

Verse 1

For θεραπεύειν, pres. act. infinitive of θεραπεύω, to cure, heal, render service, see the note on 4:23 on page 261. Cf. *therapy, therapeutics.*

Verse 2

ἀπέστειλεν, third per. s. aor. indicat. act. of ἀποστέλλω, to send (someone or something), to commission, delegate. Note, as objects, after "he sent (them)," the infinitives of purpose: to preach and to heal. See the note on 5:17 on page 300; also N.T.C. on I and II Timothy and Titus, pp. 308–310.

Verse 3

The four words ῥάβδος, staff; πήρα, traveler's bag; ἄρτος, bread (generic sense), and χιτών, tunic, are also found in Mark 6:8, 9. For Mark's χαλκός, copper coin, Luke substitutes ἀργύριον, silver. In both cases the contextual meaning is *money, small change.*

ἔχειν, have. Greek at times uses the infinitive where we would use the imperative. In the present case this use is not difficult to understand. One might construe the original to mean, "He told them . . . not to have two tunics." In other cases, where such a word of saying or commanding is absent, the question whether such an infinitive with the sense of an imperative must be viewed as a case of ellipsis is in dispute. Cf. Gram. N.T., pp. 943, 944 with Gram. N.T. (Bl.-Debr.), pp. 196, 197 (par. 389).

Verse 5

δέχωνται, third per. pl. pres. subjunct. middle, after indefinite relative pronoun with ἄν and negative particle. The verb is derived from δέχομαι, to take, accept, receive, welcome. Cf. *toe, digit.*

κονιορτός, dust; cf. κόνις, κονία. Note *incinerate.* See also Matt. 10:14; Luke 10:11; Acts 13:51; 22:23.

ἀποτινάσσετε, sec. per. pl. pres. imperat. act. of ἀποτινάσσω**, to shake off. See also Acts 28:5.

Verse 6

ἐξερχόμενοι . . . διήρχοντο, departing, they went about (or: were going through). Note also the present durative modifiers.

Distributive use of κατά here, as in 8:1.

Verse 7

διηπόρει, third per. s. imperf. of διαπορέω** (= διά plus ἀπορέω), literally, to be thoroughly (διά) without (ἀ) a resource (πόρος, ford, means of crossing a river; hence, in general, a way, means, resource); and so: to be at a loss what to do, to be perplexed.

Verse 8

ἐφάνη, third per. s. 2nd aor. indicat. pass. of φαίνω, to shine, bring to light, appear. Cf. *phantom, phenomenon.*

Verse 9

Note emphasis: John I myself beheaded; or: As to John, I myself ordered him to be beheaded. The verb is the first per. s. aor. indicat. act. of ἀποκεφαλίζω (ἀπό plus κεφαλή).
ἀκούω, I am hearing, pres. progressive.

Verse 10

For διηγήσαντο see the note on 8:39 on page 453.
ἐποίησαν, they did, where we would say, "they had done."
ὑπεχώρησεν, third per. s. aor. indicat. of ὑποχωρέω*; see the note on 5:16 on page 292.

Verse 11

Besides its occurrence here in Luke 9:11, in the New Testament the noun θεραπεία, in the sense of *healing,* is found only in Rev. 22:2, where the "healing" is to be understood in a figurative sense: "and the leaves of the tree are for the healing of the nations." It is also found in Luke 12:42, but there it has the meaning οἰκετεία, *household,* or οἱ θεράποντες, *the servants.*
For ἰᾶτο see the note on 6:18, 19 on page 337.

Verse 12

ἤρξατε κλίνειν, began to decline; i.e., to wear away (A.V.). The sun was beginning to set. Cf. *recline, incline, decline.* Note also in verse 14 κατακλίνατε, have them recline; from κατακλίνω*; and note κλισία*, a (reclining) group.
ἀπόλυσον, sec. per. s. aor. imperat. act. of ἀπολύω, to release; here in the sense of to *send away,* to *dismiss.* See also the note on 2:29 on page 176.
In the New Testament the word κύκλος, ring, circle (cf. *cycle*), is not used as a noun but *adverbially:* sitting around (Mark 3:34); going around (Mark 6:6); so also in Rom. 15:19: Paul preached the gospel from Jerusalem "and round about even to Illyricum." On that passage see John Murray, *The Epistle to the Romans (International Commentary on the New Testament),* Grand Rapids, 1965, Vol. II, pp. 213, 214, including footnote 23.
Preceded by an article, the word is used *as an adjective* here in Luke 9:12, "to the villages and farms round about," or "to the surrounding villages and farms." Cf. Mark 6:36. Finally, it occurs *as a preposition* in Rev. 4:6; 5:11; 7:11, "around the throne."

καταλύσωσιν, third per. pl. aor. subjunct. act. of καταλύω, to loosen (cf. *catalyst, loose, analysis*), to unharness (the pack animals); hence, to rest, to take lodging for the night. The same verb also has other, closely related, meanings: to throw down (Luke 21:6, etc.), to destroy (Acts 6:14, etc.). For the cognate noun, κατάλυμα, lodging place, inn, guest-room, see the note on 2:7 on page 148.

ἐπισιτισμός*, acc. -ν, supplies, provisions, victuals, food. Cf. σῖτος, grain, wheat, flour, food (Luke 3:17; 12:18, etc.). Cf. *parasite*.

Verse 13

Δότε, sec. per. pl. aor. imperat. act. of δίδωμι. Cf. *donation*.
Note emphatic ὑμεῖς!
εἰ μήτι, unless; in the protasis of a fut. more vivid (third class) conditional sentence, followed by ἀγοράσωμεν, first per. pl. aor. subjunct. act. of ἀγοράζω, to buy; cf. ἀγορά, market place (Luke 7:32, etc.).

Verse 14

Note ἄνδρες, *men,* in distinction from *women;* Lat. *viri.* Cf. German *Mann,* not *Mensch;* Dutch *man,* not *mens.* In both of these languages, with numerals, the singular can be used for the plural.
For κατακλίνατε, from κατακλίνω*, and for κλισία (here acc. pl. -ας), see on 9:12.

Verse 16

ἐδίδου, vivid iterative imperfect, he kept giving them.
παραθεῖναι, 2nd aor. act. infinitive of παρατίθημι, to set before. Related meanings: to set before (or: to present) *in teaching* (Matt. 13:24, 31); to entrust, commit, with various shades of meaning, depending on the context in each case (Luke 12:48; 23:46; I Tim. 1:18; II Tim. 2:2, etc.).

Verse 17

For ἐχορτάσθησαν, third per. pl. aor. pass. of χορτάζω, see the note on 6:21 on page 345.

Summary of Chapter 9:1–17

Chapter 8 closed with an account of three astonishing miracles performed by Jesus: a (humanly speaking) hopeless demoniac was cured, a woman whom the physicians of that day regarded as incurable was instantly restored to health, and a dead child was brought back to life.

We can imagine how such happenings must have strengthened the disciples' power of witnessing. This was the proper time to send them out on a mission tour. Besides, the Master knew that his Great Galilean Ministry was rapidly approaching its close. If more was to be done, more territory to be covered, it must be done now. So Jesus sends out these men. He issues directives. They must take along no more than is absolutely necessary. God will provide. The Twelve must place their trust in him. To this may be added Matt. 10:10b: upon those who *hear* the gospel rests the obligation to provide for those who *bring* it (9:1-6). The result is twofold:

First, the tetrarch, Herod Antipas, hears what Jesus and The Twelve have been doing. His conscience is aroused, so that when he hears rumors, including the one according to which Jesus was actually John the Baptist risen from the dead, he exclaims, "John I beheaded. Who, then, is this man about whom I am hearing such things?" (verses 7-9).

Secondly, the disciples, having returned from their mission tour, are in need of rest. So, together with them, Jesus crosses the lake and withdraws to Bethsaida Julias on the northeastern shore. When the Galileans learn about this departure they hurry on foot around the upper part of the lake in order to be with Jesus again. Surveying this huge crowd, his heart goes out to them. He welcomes them and speaks to them about the kingdom of God. Those in need of healing he heals. When evening arrives, instead of dismissing the hungry crowd (as the disciples had requested), he performs the miracle of making five bread-cakes and two fishes do for five thousand adult males, not counting women and children. Twelve baskets full of leftovers are collected after everyone has had plenty to eat (verses 10-17).

Outline of Chapter 9:18-50

Theme: *The Work Thou Gavest Him to Do*

B. *The Retirement Ministry*

CHAPTER IX:18-50

18 Once while Jesus was praying in private—(only) his disciples were with him—he asked them, "Who do the people[331] say I am?" 19 They replied, "John the Baptist; and others (say) Elijah; and still others, that one of the ancient prophets has come back to life."[332]

20 He asked them, "But y o u, who do y o u say I am?" Peter answered, "The Christ of God."

9:18-20 *Peter's Confession*
Cf. Matt. 16:13-19; Mark 8:27-29

The theme of the Synoptics, including Luke, we may conceive to be *The Work Thou Gavest Him to Do*. The first division under this theme is *Its Beginning or Inauguration* (Luke 1:1—4:13). The second is *Its Progress or Continuation* (4:14—19:27). The first subdivision of this second part, namely, *The Great Galilean Ministry* (4:14—9:17), has now been completed. The second subdivision, *The Retirement plus Perean Ministries,* begins at this point (9:18) and continues through 19:27.

Reasons for this kind of outline, as also a brief description of the main contents of each division and subdivision, can be found on pp. 8-10 of N.T.C. on Matthew. *Tentative* dates (certainty is impossible) are as follows: Retirement Ministry A.D. 29, April to October; Perean Ministry A.D. 29, December, to A.D. 30, April. For the intervening Later Judean Ministry, October to December, see especially the Gospel According to John (7:2—10:39).

Luke 9:18-50 covers events that occurred during *The Retirement Ministry*. The shift to this ministry from the one that preceded it is not abrupt and radical but rather a matter of emphasis. For example, during the lengthy period which to a large extent Jesus had spent in Capernaum and vicinity (Luke 4:14—9:17) he was often surrounded by crowds. Now too (9:18-50) he does not escape those multitudes (9:37). But there is a difference in emphasis: generally he is now seen in the presence not of crowds but of his disciples. He is *teaching* them (9:18-27, 43b-50). He fully realizes that the cross cannot be far away. Accordingly, he is expounding to The Twelve the

---

331. Or: the crowds.
332. Or: has risen again.

lessons of the cross (9:22, 43b, 44). This continues even into the Perean Ministry (18:31, 32). In order to be able to impart this important information effectively Jesus is seeking places of seclusion, apart from the busy centers. A considerable amount of time is spent in predominantly Gentile territory.

If allowance is made for areas of relative uncertainty, the map (p. 491) showing Christ's Retirement Ministry (Luke 9:18-50, but reported more fully in Mark 7:24—9:50) may be helpful. There may, however, have been trips not reported in the Gospels. Cf. John 20:30, 31; 21:25. In the Gospel According to *Mark* fourteen sections cover events that occurred during this period of retirement.

It is suggested that the following paragraph be studied with the aid of the map on p. 491.

In *Mark's* Gospel we are shown that:

1. In the vicinity of Tyre the Syrophoenician woman's faith was rewarded (7:24-30).

2. In the Decapolis region a deaf-and-dumb man was healed (7:31-37), and

3. Four thousand people were fed (8:1-10).

4. At Dalmanutha the Pharisees, craving for signs, were rebuked (8:11-13).

5. While crossing over to Bethsaida Julias, Jesus told his disciples to be on guard against the yeast of the Pharisees and the yeast of Herod (8:14-21).

6. At Bethsaida Julias he healed a blind man who saw people as if they were trees walking around (8:22-26).

For all these six sections except the last there are parallels in Matthew. The striking fact is that *none of the six are clearly paralleled in Luke*.[333] In fact, as was pointed out on p. 481, *Luke's "omission" of Marcan material begins even earlier, namely, at Mark 6:45. Accordingly, Luke omits what is found in Mark 6:45—8:26.*

(Still following the map on p. 491) we note that Luke begins to parallel Mark again in connection with the story of

7. Peter's confession at Caesarea Philippi (Mark 8:27-30; cf. Luke 9:18-20).

Parallel and identical in sequence are also the accounts concerning:

8. The first prediction of the passion and the resurrection (Mark 8:31—9:1; cf. Luke 9:21-27).

9. Jesus' transfiguration (Mark 9:2-13; cf. Luke 9:28-36).

10. The healing of an epileptic boy (Mark 9:14-29; cf. Luke 9:37-43a).

11. The second prediction of the passion and the resurrection (Mark 9:30-32; cf. Luke 9:43b-45). Here, however, Luke omits any reference to *the resurrection.*

---

333. There is a vague resemblance between Mark 8:11-13 and Luke 11:29-32.

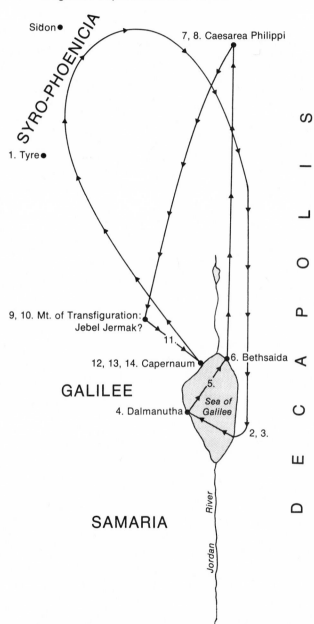

THE RETIREMENT MINISTRY
Begin at Capernaum and follow the arrows

12. Question and answer concerning "greatness" (Mark 9:33-37; cf. Luke 9:46-48).

13. Jesus' answer to John's implied question (Mark 9:38-41; cf. Luke 9:49, 50).

At this point Luke's story takes a sharp turn and ceases to follow the sequence of Mark; that is, Mark's

14. "And whoever causes one of these little ones who believe in me to sin," etc. (9:42-50), is *not* paralleled in Luke 9:51 f. but in 17:1, 2.

The question, then, is, "Why, after closely following Mark's sequence up to and including Mark 6:44, does Luke bypass the material found in Mark 6:45—8:26, resume his parallel account at Mark 8:27, and break it off again at Mark 9:41?"

Many answers have been given, including the following:

a. Luke has planned his Gospel in such a manner that, within the compass of a single papyrus roll, he will have room for the inclusion of much material—especially many strikingly beautiful parables—not found in the other Synoptics.

b. Having already reported several examples of Christ's teaching and healing during The Great Galilean Ministry, the beloved physician, guided by the Holy Spirit, decided that this sufficed for the attainment of his goal.

c. Specifically, having already reported one miraculous feeding, that of the five thousand (Luke 9:10-17; cf. Mark 6:30-44), Luke did not deem it necessary to report still another, that of the four thousand (Mark 8:1-10). Besides, that miracle took place in predominantly Gentile territory, and, as stated earlier (see on 2:39), on the whole Luke reserves for the book of Acts the account of work among the Gentiles.

d. Luke did not think that Mark's lengthy account concerning ceremonial versus real defilement, including a sharp denunciation of *the Pharisees* (Mark 7:1-23), was appropriate in a Gospel intended mainly for *Gentile* readers.

Unquestionably, these explanations are valid, but more should be added, for up to this point the last part of our question—namely, "Why does Luke resume his parallel account at Mark 8:27, and break it off again at Mark 9:41?" has not yet been answered.

It is exactly in connection with this question that the real beauty and importance of the Third Gospel becomes evident. There is nothing haphazard about Luke's inclusions and omissions. What we have here is a step-by-step answer to the question of Mark 8:27; Luke 9:18, "Who do the people say I am?" That is why at this particular point the evangelist resumes his policy of paralleling Mark. Stated even better: Luke is simply following his own plan. At 9:18-21 (cf. Mark 8:27-30) Luke is in the midst of a process of answering the question touching the identity of Jesus. Note the evangelist's own climactic arrangement:

a. Beginning at Luke 9:7-9 Herod asked, "Who, then, is this man about whom I am hearing such things?"

b. By means of the miraculous feeding of the five thousand (verses 10-17) Jesus starts to give an answer to the question of his identity. This is true especially in the light of such parallel passages as John 6:14, "This is really the Prophet who is to come into the world," and 6:35, 48, "I (myself) am the bread of life."

c. Next, Luke reports that the people were divided in their opinion about Jesus. Their answers were threefold: "(He is) John the Baptist... Elijah... one of the ancient prophets come back to life" (verses 18, 19).

d. Peter's answer is brief and striking, "(Thou art) the Christ of God" (verse 20). In this connection Jesus points out that being the Christ—that is, the long-awaited Messiah of prophecy—means the cross for himself, and in a sense even for all his true followers; some of whom, however, will not taste death until they see the kingdom of God (verses 21-27).

e. The climax is reached in the answer given by the Father, as recorded in the account of the transfiguration (verses 28-36). It is as follows, "This is my Son, my Chosen One; listen to him" (verse 35).

f. Once having reached this climax, and having again described the sense in which Jesus is the Messiah (verse 44) and who his true followers are, a group from which no one must be arbitrarily excluded (verses 46-50), Luke had, for the time being, accomplished his purpose. He could then concentrate his attention on those precious materials (parables, etc.) that are, to a large extent, not found in the other Gospels.

Truly Luke's Gospel is not a hodgepodge. It "stands on its own feet," evincing an organic beauty and unity of its own.

18. Once while Jesus was praying in private—(only) his disciples were with him—he asked them, Who do the people say I am?

As to both place and time when this incident occurred, Luke, in harmony with the plan of his Gospel (see p. 178), is very indefinite. From Matt. 16:13 and Mark 8:27 we learn that the place was the vicinity of Caesarea Philippi.

By Philip the tetrarch this place had been enlarged, beautified, and named in honor of Caesar Augustus. Near it was a sanctuary to the pagan god Pan, which gave rise to the name *Paneas* to mark the general site where Caesarea was subsequently located. The designation *Pan* is still reflected in *Bāniyās*, as it is called today. To distinguish this Caesarea from its namesake, the important seaport south of Mt. Carmel, and to indicate its founder, the more northern city was called Caesarea *Philippi*.

Situated near one of the sources of the Jordan River, with 9,232 feet high majestic Mt. Hermon, snow-covered throughout most of the year, in the immediate background, it was truly a landscape of unforgettable picturesqueness, a place exactly suited to the purpose for which Jesus wished to use it, namely, for private prayer, as here stated, and for imparting instruction to his disciples.

Having been strengthened through fellowship with his heavenly Father—cf. Luke 3:21; 5:16; 6:12—Jesus now asks his disciples, "Who do the people say I am?"

Already Jesus knew that at the appropriate moment, that is, after the disciples' reply, he would ask an even more important question, the one found in verse 20. What had been veiled heretofore must now come out into the open; not as yet for announcement to the general public, but so that the disciples may know who this Jesus really is and what is going to happen to him. Afterward, when the dramatic events do actually take place, these men will not remain as thoroughly perplexed as would have been the case had they not been preinformed about them. Cf. John 14:29; 16:1, 4, 33.

19. They replied, John the Baptist; and others (say) Elijah; and still others, that one of the ancient prophets has come back to life.

The answer, similar to the reports Herod the tetrarch had been hearing (verses 7, 8), was that some were of the opinion that Jesus was John the Baptist risen again. This seems to have been the most general opinion. But others held Jesus to be Elijah. These first two groups may have viewed Jesus as a forerunner of the Messiah. Finally, there were those who considered Jesus to be neither John the Baptist nor Elijah but simply one of the ancient prophets come back to life. Jeremiah perhaps? See Matt. 16:14.

Note that in this connection the opinion that Jesus might himself be the Messiah is here not even mentioned. See, however, John 6:14. But even if, as a result of the miracle of the feeding of the five thousand, the idea that Jesus was the Messiah had taken root in the minds of some, it was the earthly, political Messiah of Pharisaic hope whom they then imagined to see in him, as is clear from John 6:15.

20. He asked them, But y o u, who do y o u say I am?

In the original the pronoun *y o u* is very emphatic. Jesus wants his disciples to make an open confession of their faith. That, in turn, would enable him to purify that faith; that is, to tell them that he was not the Messiah of popular expectation but the One who, in harmony with Isa. 53, etc., would suffer, be rejected, killed even . . . and on the third day raised up. See verse 22.

Peter answered, The Christ of God.

Since the question had been put to all, that is, to The Twelve, and none objected to the answer, we may safely assume that here, as well as in the parallel passages (Matt. 16:16; Mark 8:29), Peter was the spokesman for all. He often acted in this capacity (Matt. 15:15, 16; 19:27, 28; 26:35, 40, 41; Mark 1:36; Luke 8:45; 9:32, 33; 12:41; 18:28; John 6:67–69; Acts 1:15; 2:14, 37, 38; 5:29).

Before leaving this subject, special attention should be called to the fact that the words of Jesus, "But y o u, who do y o u say I am?" convey a very important lesson, namely, that a true believer is one who is willing, whenever necessary, to fly in the face of popular opinion and openly to express a conviction that is contrary to that of the masses. In the best sense of the term, the believer is willing to stand up *boldly* in the interest of the truth.

Conformity with the world, compromise on basic issues, the unwilling-ness to be distinctive, is strongly condemned in Scripture (Rom. 12:2; II Cor. 6:14; I John 2:15-17). When "the sons of God" marry "the daugh-ters of men" (Gen. 6:1, 2), the result is the deluge. When Israel worships a golden calf, three thousand Israelites lose their lives (Exod. 32:28). When Israel, with the purpose of being like other nations, demands a king, the final result is shameful defeat in a battle in which that king commits suicide (I Sam. 31:4). When the compromiser Jeroboam institutes calf-worship at Bethel and Dan, he is leading the people into a path that finally results in shameful deportation into a pagan country (I Kings 12:26-30; 14:16, 19, 26, 31; II Kings 3:3; 10:29, 31, etc.).

Not being "of the world" (John 17:16), believers are shining lights in the midst of the world (Matt. 5:14; Phil. 2:15). They are spiritually different from the world, in order to be a blessing to the world. So also here in Luke 9:19, 20, while everybody else is saying that Jesus is but a man—whether John the Baptist, Elijah, or one of the (other) prophets, it makes no essen-tial difference, for all these were but men—the true follower of Jesus an-swers, "(Thou art) the Christ of God."

The importance of this momentous confession can hardly be exagger-ated. It implies that The Twelve here acknowledge Jesus to be no less than the long-awaited One, God's Anointed, the Messiah. For more on this see N.T.C. on Matthew 16:13-19, pp. 641-652.

What the confession does *not* imply, however, is that The Twelve, or even Peter himself, understood *in what sense* Jesus was the Christ. It would take these men a very long time to learn this.

For *Practical Lessons* and *Greek Words*, etc., see pp. 508-511.

---

21 But he warned and commanded them to tell this to no one. 22 And he said, "It is necessary that the Son of man suffer many things and be rejected by the elders and the chief priests and the scribes, and be killed, and on the third day be raised up."

23 Then he said to all: "If anyone wishes to come behind me, let him deny himself, take up his cross daily, and follow me. 24 For whoever would save his life shall lose it, but whoever loses his life for my sake, he shall save it. 25 For what good does it do a man to gain the whole world and yet lose or forfeit his life? 26 For whoever is ashamed of me and my words, of him shall the Son of man be ashamed when he comes in his glory and in that of the Father and of the holy angels. 27 Moreover, I tell y o u truly, there are some of those standing here who shall not taste death until they see the kingdom of God."

9:21-27 *The First Prediction of the Passion and the Resurrection*
Cf. Matt. 16:21-28; Mark 8:31—9:1

21. But he warned and commanded them to tell this to no one.
Possible reason for this strict order: The people would have interpreted the term *Messiah* = "Christ" in the political sense (cf. John 6:15). This might have fanned the flames of enthusiasm about him, as a potential Deliverer from the Roman yoke, to such an extent that the opposition and

envy roused by such widespread attention might have brought his public ministry to an untimely end. This must not happen. When an open announcement must finally be made to the Jewish religious authorities, Jesus himself will make it (Matt. 26:63, 64; cf. Luke 22:66–70). We should also bear in mind that it would not have been proper for Jesus, during the days of his humiliation, to encourage *public* acclaim. That must be postponed until after his death and resurrection (Matt. 17:9). See also on Luke 5:14. The very fact of this death, followed by resurrection and ascension, will shed light on the character of Jesus' messiahship (Acts 2:36; I Peter 1:3).

22. And he said, It is necessary that the Son of man suffer many things and be rejected by the elders and the chief priests and the scribes, and be killed, and on the third day be raised up.

Characteristically Jesus calls himself "the Son of man," a self-designation very fitting indeed, especially when the Master speaks about his coming suffering, death, and resurrection. See on 5:24. The present prediction is the first of three recorded in the Synoptics. For the second see Luke 9:43b–45 (cf. Matt. 17:22, 23; Mark 9:30–32); and for the third, Luke 18:31–34 (cf. Matt. 20:17–19; Mark 10:32–34).

The first prediction regarding Messiah's rejection, etc., has the following characteristics:

a. This prediction was *necessary*. When the disciples, by the mouth of Peter, had confessed Jesus to be "the Christ of God" (verse 20), Jesus, by not contradicting this statement, had obviously assented to it. And in view of the fact that messiahship was by many interpreted in an earthly and political sense, it was necessary that the disciples be taught what it meant to be the Christ.

b. It was *startling*. The Son of Man, the very Messiah, actually to suffer and die; yes, *to be killed*, it was almost unbelievable. Even more shocking was this announcement in view of the fact that Jesus reveals that he, the Messiah, *must* be subjected to suffering and *must* be killed. This was true because of the Father's will (John 3:16; Rom. 8:32), the Son's own promise (Ps. 40:7), prophecy (Isa. 53), and the demands of the law (Gen. 2:17; Rom. 5:12–21; II Cor. 5:21). He *must* do what he himself also *wanted* to do (John 10:11; II Cor. 8:9; Gal. 2:20). In this first prediction all the emphasis is on *necessity*.

However, note also: on the third day he *must* be raised up. See Isa. 53:10; Luke 24:26, 27. In view of Luke 18:34 (cf. Mark 9:32) it is very doubtful whether this optimistic climax was appreciated by those who heard it.

c. It was *revealing*. Elders, chief priests, and scribes, the men who were supposed to protect and promote the religious interests of the people, those from whose circles the Sanhedrin was chosen, are actually going to *kill* Israel's own Messiah!

Who, exactly, were these three groups?

As to *elders*, by this time the term had come to mean the lay members of the Sanhedrin. They were generally members of the highly privileged patrician families in Jerusalem.

The *chief priests* were members of the highpriestly families including the highpriest himself.

The *scribes* were the trained and ordained theologians of the day, the men versed in the Torah, the rabbis. Their task was to study, interpret, transmit, copy, and teach the law.

d. It was *kind and wise.* In order to spare the feelings of the men who were so dear to him, Jesus did not at this time convey to them the details of his gruesome approaching passion. Cf. John 16:12; Ps. 103:12-14.

e. It was *clear.* Earlier Messiah's suffering, death, etc., had been indicated prophetically (Ps. 22; 69; 118; Isa. 53; Zech. 9, 11) and figuratively (Luke 2:35). Jesus himself, too, had spoken about it in a veiled manner (Mark 2:20; John 2:19). Now, however, he speaks *plainly* (Mark 8:32).

There is a sense in which Christ's suffering and his death are unique. It is *alone* he pays the ransom for sin (Isa. 53; Matt. 20:28; Mark 10:45; II Cor. 5:20, 21; Gal. 3:13; Eph. 2:8-10; Phil. 3:7-9; Titus 3:4-7).

Over against every human claim to self-merit, be it the tiniest, this truth must be stressed and stressed and stressed.

> It was alone the Savior prayed
> In dark Gethsemane;
> Alone he drained the bitter cup
> And suffered there for me.
> Alone, alone, He bore it all alone;
> He gave himself to save his own,
> He suffered, bled and died alone, alone.
> Ben H. Price

Equally scriptural, however, is the truth that believers are sharers in Christ's suffering, as they are also in his glory. So closely-knit are Christ and his people that it is difficult to think of the one apart from the other. This unity in love and consequently also in grief and glory, pain and pleasure, reproach and rejoicing, is taught in such passages as Matt. 10:22, 24, 25; 25:40; Luke 10:16; John 16:33; 17:21-24; Acts 9:4; 22:7; 26:14; Rom. 8:17; II Cor. 1:5; Gal. 6:17; Phil. 3:10; II Tim. 2:12; I Peter 4:13, to mention only a few. It is also taught in the passage which immediately follows, beginning with the words:

23. Then he said to all ...

As Mark 8:34 shows, at this point Jesus calls to himself the multitude, for the earnest exhortation which follows is of significance to all; in fact, is for all a matter of life or death, of everlasting life versus everlasting death. Hence, *all*—not only The Twelve—must hear what follows.

Continued: **If anyone wishes to come behind me, let him deny himself, take up his cross daily, and follow me.**

To "come behind" means to attach oneself to Jesus as his disciple. The figure is based on the fact that Christ's "followers"—not only The Twelve but also many others—often accompanied the Master, and frequently literally *came on behind* him.

What, then, must a person do in order to be considered a true disciple? Well, if he wishes to come behind me, says Jesus, then *first,* he must deny himself; that is, he must once and for all say *No* to his old self, the self as it is apart from regenerating grace. A person who denies himself gives up all reliance on whatever he is by nature, and depends for salvation on God alone. He turns away in dismay not only from whatever thoughts and habits are patently sinful but even from reliance on "religious"—for example Pharisaic—thought patterns that cannot be harmonized with trust in Christ. See II Cor. 10:5. He must be willing to say with Paul, "Such things that once were gains to me these have I counted loss for Christ. . . ." See Phil. 3:7–11.

Secondly, he must take up his cross. The underlying figure is that of a condemned man who is forced to take up and carry his own cross to the place of execution. However, what the convict does under duress, the disciple of Christ does willingly. He voluntarily and decisively accepts the pain, shame, and persecution that is going to be *his* particular—note: *his,* not someone else's—lot because of his loyalty to Christ and his cause. Luke has even retained Jesus' insistence on making the taking up of one's cross a *daily* assignment.

Finally, he must begin to follow and must keep on following Jesus. Here following the Master means trusting him (John 3:16), walking in his footsteps (I Peter 2:21), and obeying his commands (John 15:14) out of gratitude for salvation in him (Eph. 4:32—5:2).

To summarize, verse 23 may be paraphrased as follows: "If anyone wishes to be counted as my adherent, he must once and for all say farewell to self, decisively accept pain, shame, and persecution for my sake and in my cause—day in, day out—and must then keep on following me as my disciple. He must subject himself to my discipline."

We must be careful not to conceive of this self-denial, etc., in a chronological fashion, as if the Lord were exhorting his hearers to practice self-denial for a while, then after a lapse of time to take up and carry the cross, and, once having shouldered that burden for another time period, to follow Jesus. The order is not chronological but logical. Together the three indicate *true conversion,* followed by lifelong *sanctification.*

A second error to be guarded against is the notion that a person would be able *in his own power* to deny himself, take up his cross, and follow the Savior. Conversion (as well as the process of sanctification that follows it), though certainly a human responsibility, is impossible without regeneration (John 3:3, 5), which is the work of the Holy Spirit in man's heart. Moreover, that Spirit does not leave man to his own resources once the latter has been reborn, but remains with him forever, enabling him to do what otherwise he would not be able to do. It is, nevertheless, human responsibility and activity upon which the emphasis falls here in verses 23 ff.

In the next three verses (24–26) the obligation to be converted, etc., and the reward that results are brought into sharp contrast with the loss experienced by those who refuse to deny themselves, to take up their cross, and to follow Jesus. Each of the three verses begins with "For."[334] These "For" sentences or verses may therefore be considered as presenting, in a way, the basis for the urgent command of verse 23. What we have here is a phenomenon often occurring in Scripture and also in daily conversation, namely, *abbreviated expression*.[335] Fully expressed, the meaning of verses 24-26 would be somewhat as follows, with implied words in parentheses: 24 (Let him not refuse) For whoever would save his life shall lose it, but whoever loses his life for my sake, he shall save it. 25 (Let him not follow the wrong course) For what good does it do a man to gain the whole world and yet lose or forfeit his life? 26 (Let him not refuse, therefore) For whoever is ashamed of me and my words, of him also shall the Son of man be ashamed when he comes in his glory and in that of the Father and of the holy angels.

Accordingly, with an implied "Let him not refuse," there follows in verse **24. For whoever would save his life shall lose it, but whoever loses his life for my sake, he shall save it.** Meaning: the individual who would—or "should wish to"—save his life shall lose it. Exactly what is it that he wishes to save? Answer: his life, that is, himself. Here, however, we must make a distinction. In the present case the "life," "soul" or "self" which this person presumably wishes to save is his own immaterial and invisible being considered apart from regenerating grace. This man clings to that sinful life of his, holding on to it tenaciously. He reminds us of the rich fool described in Luke 12:16-21. See also 16:19-31. He piles up material goods, thinking all the while of self, never of others. He imagines that material possessions, or else pleasure, prestige, fame, can bring him the inner peace and satisfaction he is looking for. But this selfish narrowing of his horizon makes his soul narrower and narrower. He loses it; that is, he loses whatever remnant of the higher, nobler life was left in him at the beginning.

On the other hand, whoever loses his life "for my sake," he shall save it. One "loses" his life in the present sense by devoting oneself completely to Christ, to the service of those in need, to the gospel. Cf. "for my sake and the gospel's" (Mark 8:35). Note that Christ lays claim to absolute devotion. This proves that he regards himself as Lord of all, and that the evangelist was fully aware of this! The person who offers this devotion saves his life, that is, his soul, or as we can also say, *himself.* The *self* here indicated is the inner being as influenced by divine grace. It is only by losing oneself— looking away from self in order to serve the Master and his "little ones" (cf. Matt. 25:40)—that one can ever be saved. The soul with wide horizons expands, becomes wonderfully enlarged. It overflows with peace, assur-

---

334. In the original γάρ is never found at the very beginning of a sentence. In the present case, as often, it is in each instance the second word. In English, however, γάρ is properly represented by the first word in the sentence. So also A.R.V., N.A.S., R.S.V., Williams, etc.
335. See N.T.C. on John, Vol. I, p. 206; and on γάρ as represented in Mark 8:35; Luke 9:24, see L.N.T. (A. and G.), p. 151.

ance, joy, etc. In helping others, it helps itself. In loving, it experiences love, that of others, especially that of God. Consequently, Jesus urges upon every person in his audience not to follow the wrong course, the course of turning inward upon oneself, in an attempt to hang on to all one's earthly "treasures." To do so would amount to stupendous and, if persisted in, incurable folly.

The importance of this saying is clear from the fact that, in one form or another, Jesus makes use of it on different occasions throughout his ministry; for example, in connection with (a) The Charge to The Twelve (Matt. 10:39); (b) The First Prediction of the Passion and Resurrection (Matt. 16:25; cf. Mark 8:35; Luke 9:24); (c) The Discourse on The Coming of the Kingdom (Luke 17:33); and (d) The Request of the Greeks to See Jesus (John 12:25). And since it is clear that by no means all the words and works of the Master were reported in the Gospels (John 20:30; 21:25), he may well have expressed this same thought on still other occasions. He repeated this important principle or slogan again and again because

a. it was rooted in his own Great Decision to leave the glories of heaven in order to accomplish the great work of redemption (II Cor. 8:9; cf. Matt. 20:28; Mark 10:45; Luke 22:24-27), and

b. for the sinner salvation is impossible apart from obedience to this rule.

Hymnology has been slow to incorporate this principle in its popular songs. Its basic idea is, however, nicely reproduced in George Mattheson's similarly paradoxical lines:

> Make me a captive, Lord,
> And then I shall be free;
> Force me to render up my sword,
> And I shall conqu'ror be.

And, of course, in substance it is also reflected in the prayer of Francis of Assisi:

> It is in giving that we receive;
> It is in pardoning that we are pardoned;
> And it is in dying that we are born to eternal life.

25. For what good does it do a man to gain the whole world and yet lose or forfeit his life? Imagine for a moment that a person should gain the whole world—all its hidden gems and resources, whatever good things grow on it, the cattle upon a thousand hills, all the world's splendor, prestige, pleasures and treasures—but in the process of doing this should lose or should forfeit—i.e., lose the right to possess—his own (higher) life or self, what good will this do him? Implied answer: no good whatever, only evil.

This becomes even clearer when attention is focused on the lot of the self-centered man in the hereafter. Let no one ignore this, **26. For whoever is ashamed of me and my words, of him shall the Son of man be ashamed when he comes in his glory and in that of the Father and of the holy angels.**

To be ashamed of Jesus means to be so proud that one wants to have nothing to do with him and with his words. Jesus is going to be ashamed of such people. Cf. Matt. 7:23; Luke 13:27. At his return he will reject and condemn them. Cf. Matt. 25:41–46a. Note Christ's self-designation, "the Son of man," as in verse 22; see on that verse and on 5:24.

The Son of man is the One who, coming from above and therefore intrinsically glorious throughout, here on earth suffers. But through his vicarious suffering he attains to a glory that is not only inward but also outward. He shall come in his own glory (John 17:1, 5, 24), and in that of the Father and of the holy angels, a threefold glory, therefore. Cf. Dan. 7:9–14; Matt. 25:31; II Thess. 1:7.

Jesus concludes the statement begun in verse 26, namely, about his and the kingdom's "coming," by adding:

27. Moreover, I tell y o u truly, there are some of those standing here who shall not taste death until they see the kingdom of God.

Clearly verses 26 and 27 belong together. If verse 26 has reference to a great happening in the history of redemption, namely, Christ's second coming, verse 27 cannot very well indicate an event entirely different in character. Jesus is speaking about the state of exaltation in store for himself and in a sense also for those who are not ashamed of him. Accordingly, to interpret this passage—whether verses 26, 27 in their entirety, or verse 27 taken by itself—as having reference to the fall of Jerusalem in the year A.D. 70[336] will not do.

In a statement both startling and significant—hence, "I tell y o u truly" (cf. 12:44 and 21:32)—Jesus regards the entire state of exaltation, from his resurrection to his second coming, as a unit. In verse 26 he refers to its final consummation; in verse 27, to its beginning. He is saying that some of those whom he is addressing (see verse 23) are going to be witnesses of that beginning. They are going to see "the kingdom of God"; that is, they are going to be witnesses of its powerful manifestation, its coming "with power" (Mark 9:1).

The reference is in all probability to Christ's glorious resurrection, an act of *power* (John 10:18b; Rom. 1:4; I Cor. 6:14), his return in the Spirit on the day of Pentecost, when Christ's followers would receive *power* (Acts 1:8), and in close connection with that event, Messiah's coronation in heaven, his

---

336. A. Plummer, *op. cit.*, pp. 249, 250; R. C. H. Lenski, *op. cit.*, p. 332; S. Greijdanus, *Korte Verklaring*, pp. 238, 239; N. Geldenhuys, *op. cit.*, p. 277. On the other hand, see A. B. Bruce, *op. cit.*, Vol. I, p. 531; F. W. Danker, *op. cit.*, p. 115; footnote on Luke 9:27 in Berkeley Version, p. 70; and N. B. Stonehouse, *The Witness of Luke to Christ*, pp. 155, 156.

exaltation to "the Father's right hand . . . far above every principality and authority and *power*" (Eph. 1:20, 21). See especially Luke 22:69.

Changes so vast would then begin to take place on earth that, as outsiders were going to remark, the world would be turned "upside down" (Acts 17:6). Momentous events would occur: the becoming of age of the church, its extension among the Gentiles, the conversion of people by the thousands, the presence and exercise of many charismatic gifts, etc. Jesus predicts that all this will begin to take place during the lifetime of some of those whom he is now addressing (see verse 23).

This prediction was literally fulfilled. By no means all who heard it, not even all of The Twelve, lived or were present to see its plenary fulfilment. Some "tasted death," that is, died, before it began to be fulfilled; for example, Judas Iscariot. Thomas was not present on Easter evening. James, the brother of John, saw only the beginning of this wonderful period (see Acts 12:1, 2). Some apostles were absent when certain other important events took place (John 21:2). But many others, both of the apostles and of other followers of the Lord (I Cor. 15:6), including undoubtedly "some of those standing here," did not taste death until they saw these events transpiring before their eyes.

The transfiguration (Luke 9:28-36), at which occasion "our Lord Jesus Christ . . . received from God the Father honor and glory" (II Peter 1:17), also "majesty" (verse 16), is by some[337] regarded as included in the prediction made here in Luke 9:27. It was witnessed by only three of Christ's apostles. But whether it be included or not, sufficient evidence has been given to show that Christ's prediction was literally and gloriously fulfilled.

For *Practical Lessons* and *Greek Words*, etc., see pp. 508-511.

---

28 Now about eight days after these sayings, Jesus took along Peter and John and James, and went up into the mountain to pray. 29 While he was praying, the appearance of his countenance changed, and his clothing was flashing like lightning, so bright. 30 Suddenly two men were talking with him. They were Moses and Elijah, 31 who, appearing in glorious splendor, were speaking about his departure, which he was about to accomplish at Jerusalem.

32 Now Peter and those with him were weighed down with sleep. But having suddenly become wide awake, they saw his glory and the two men who were standing with him. 33 And just as these men were starting to leave, Peter said to Jesus, "Master, how good it is for us to be here! Let us make three shelters, one for you, one for Moses, and one for Elijah"—not realizing what he was saying.

34 But while he was saying this, a cloud came and enveloped these men, and they [the disciples] grew alarmed as these men entered the cloud. 35 And a voice came out of the cloud, saying, "This is my Son, my Chosen One; listen to him!" 36 When the voice ceased, Jesus was found alone. They [the disciples] kept silent, and in those days told no one anything of what they had seen.

---

337. See E. E. Ellis, *op. cit.*, p. 141. In fact, C. R. Erdman, *op. cit.*, p. 97, is among those who regard Christ's transfiguration as *the* fulfilment of Luke 9:27. So does A. Stöger, *op. cit.*, Vol. I, pp. 176, 177.

9:28–36 *The Transfiguration of Jesus on the Mountain*
Cf. Matt. 17:1–8; Mark 9:2–8

The exaltation of Jesus, from resurrection to second coming, is foreshadowed in the transfiguration, recorded here in 9:28–36. This transfiguration served the twofold purpose of (a) preparing the Mediator to face with courage his bitter trial, by reminding him of the Father's constant love (9:35) and of the glory that would follow his suffering (Heb. 12:2); and (b) confirming the faith of Peter, James, and John—and indirectly of the entire church afterward—in the truth that had been revealed to and confessed by Simon Peter, as spokesman for The Twelve (9:20; cf. Matt. 16:16; Mark 8:29).

There is no reason whatever to accept the rationalistic theory (Wellhausen, Bultmann, etc.) that originally what is here presented was an account of an appearance of the risen Christ (cf. I Cor. 15:5–8). Not only the report itself but also the context, both preceding and following, militates against that view.

28. Now about eight days after these sayings Jesus took along Peter and John and James, and went up into the mountain to pray.

The expression *about eight days after these sayings* is not in conflict with "six days later" (Matt. 17:1; Mark 9:2). While Luke was probably using the inclusive method of time computation, including in his count both the day of Peter's confession and that of Christ's transfiguration, the other synoptists were likely referring only to the six intervening days. Besides, Luke does not even intend to be precise, for he says "*about* eight days."

It should be added, however, that by stating "about eight days after these sayings" the beloved physician is not only furnishing a chronological note, but also providing a logical link between the "sayings," on the one hand, and the Master's experience on the Mount of Transfiguration, on the other; that is, 9:31 is explained by and explains 9:22.

Why did Jesus take with him Peter and John and James when he ascended the Mount of Transfiguration? For a discussion of this question see above, on 8:51.

It is impossible with certainty to identify the "mountain" (Luke 9:28), or "high mountain" (Matt. 17:1; Mark 9:2), to which Jesus brought the three. Some say, "It was Mount Tabor." However, in view of the fact that there was at that time a city or fortress on top of that mountain it is not easy to see how the Lord and these three men could here have found the privacy they were seeking. Mount Hermon is favored by others. However, when Jesus (with the three) descends from the mountain he is met by "a great multitude," including scribes (Mark 9:14). This seems to indicate that "the Mount of Transfiguration," as it can safely be called, was not in the far north, populated mostly by Gentiles. A far more logical place is *Jebel Jermak* (or *Jermuk*) in Upper Galilee, the highest elevation in that entire region, rising 4,000 feet above the Mediterranean Sea, affording a beautiful view in all directions. From this mountain it was but a relatively short distance to Capernaum, which Jesus seems to have reached soon afterward (Matt. 17:24; Mark 9:28, 33). We are, of course, not certain that this was the mountain to which Luke refers, but at least it fills all the requirements.[338]

It is Luke alone who mentions that Jesus went up into the mountain *to pray*. It is exactly Luke who could be expected to report this purpose. See above, *Introduction,* point I A 5b. It is understandable that the Mediator would often pour out his heart to the Father in prayer, and that he would do this especially now, since he knew that before long he would be wending his way toward Jerusalem and the bitter agony that awaited him there.

29. While he was praying, the appearance of his countenance changed, and his clothing was flashing like lightning, so bright.

Suddenly the face of Jesus "shone like the sun" (Matt. 17:2). The brightness even affected his clothes, so that they "became white as the light" (thus Matthew); "whiter than any laundryman on earth could make them" (Mark 9:3). The source of this dazzling brightness is not indicated. But see also on verse 35.

30, 31. Suddenly two men were talking with him. They were Moses and Elijah, who, appearing in glorious splendor, were speaking about his departure, which he was about to accomplish at Jerusalem.

The expression *appearing in glorious splendor* probably indicates that the two were "surrounded with heavenly brightness." That "his departure [literally *exodus*] . . . at Jerusalem" refers to the Lord's bitter suffering and death on the cross needs no proof. But if any is needed, see II Peter 1:15, where one of the three who witnessed Christ's glory on the Mount of Transfiguration uses the same term with reference to his own death. Did this term, as used here in Luke 9:31, also include Christ's resurrection? In view of the fact that in all three predictions of these coming events (*a.* Luke 9:22, cf. Matt. 16:21, Mark 8:31; *b.* Matt. 17:22, 23, cf. Mark 9:31[339] *c.* Luke 18:31–33, cf. Matt. 20:17, Mark 10:32–34) humiliation is followed by exaltation, death by resurrection; and also in view of both Luke 9:35 and II Peter 1:16, 17, passages clearly showing that for Jesus the experience on the Mount of Transfiguration was one of comfort and strengthening, the answer must be in the affirmative. Besides, is it even conceivable that these heavenly messengers should speak with Jesus about his sufferings and death, but not about "the glory that should follow" (I Peter 1:11)?

---

338. This location is favored also by W. Ewing in his article "Transfiguration, Mount of," I.S.B.E., Vol. V, p. 3006; and by E. G. Kraeling, *Rand McNally Bible Atlas,* New York, etc., 1966. He mentions *Jebel Kan'an,* north of Capernaum, as another possibility.

339. Luke 9:44 abbreviates, omitting any reference to the third day. But, as Matthew and Mark clearly indicate, the fuller report in all three cases includes both the humiliation and the subsequent exaltation.

32, 33. Now Peter and those with him were weighed down with sleep. But having suddenly become wide awake, they saw his glory and the two men who were standing with him. And just as these men were starting to leave, Peter said to Jesus, Master, how good it is for us to be here! Let us make three shelters, one for you, one for Moses, and one for Elijah—not realizing what he was saying.

It would seem that the transfiguration and the arrival of the two visitors from heaven occurred while the three disciples were wrapped in deep slumber. At least, it was not until they had suddenly become wide awake that they clearly saw Jesus *in all his glory.* They also recognized Moses and Elijah, who were standing near him.

How did the disciples know that the two from the other world who suddenly appeared upon the scene were Moses and Elijah? Did these visitors introduce themselves? Did the disciples know this by intuition? Did they gather this information from the words spoken by each—Moses, Elijah—in his conversation with Jesus? Had the looks or personal appearance of the two heavenly visitors been transmitted to the disciples by tradition, whether oral or written, so that for this reason it was easy to recognize them and to tell them apart? Had the identification been divinely revealed to them? Or, last but not the least fanciful, was Moses carrying in his hand a copy of the law, and did Elijah descend from heaven to the mount in his fiery chariot? All we know, and need to know, is that in a manner not revealed to us the three disciples recognized the two visitors.

As to Moses, we know that he had died and had been buried (Deut. 34:5, 6). Had his body subsequently been disinterred and translated to heaven, and does Jude 9 indirectly support this theory? Or was his body still buried, and did God equip his soul with another body to be used just for this occasion? As to Elijah, we know that he never died, but was bodily translated to heaven (II Kings 2:11).

Why just these two? Leaving aside all useless speculation, the simplest and best answer is probably that Moses and Elijah represented respectively the law and the prophets, both of which Jesus had come to fulfil (Matt. 5:17; Luke 24:27, 44).

At the very moment when the two men had finished their conversation with Jesus and were beginning to take their departure, Peter addressed the Lord as follows, "Master, how good it is for us to be here! Let us make three shelters," etc.

The trouble with Peter was that too often he spoke first and did his thinking afterward, if at all. So also here. Still, we should not be too hard on him, for he had just been awakened out of a deep sleep and, as the text indicates, did not know what he was saying. Also, he certainly does not evince any selfishness: he wants to make *three* shelters, not four (including one for himself) or six (also one for James and one for John).

Nevertheless, his suggestion was foolish. As if Jesus and the two visitors

505

had no other means of protecting themselves against the weather and the environment. Besides, would branches and shrubbery—let us suppose that they were immediately available—provide sturdy protection, had it been needed?

It might be said in Peter's favor that he at least submits the suggestion to the Lord, so that the latter may decide. On the other hand, this apostle's very desire to prolong the glory-scene ("how good it is for us to be here!") shows that he had not yet fully taken to heart what Jesus had taught him (see on 9:22). From suffering, from the cross, whether for Jesus or for himself, he wishes to stay far removed.

Peter's question did not even receive an answer; either that, or else: the answer was included in the action reported in verse

34. But while he was saying this, a cloud came and enveloped these men, and they [the disciples] grew alarmed as these men entered the cloud.

In Scripture the presence of God is often indicated by the mention of a cloud. In several cases, as also here, it is a bright, white, or luminous cloud (cf. Exod. 13:21; 16:10; 40:35; I Kings 8:10, 11; Neh. 9:19; Ps. 78:14; Rev. 14:14–16).

The disciples grew alarmed. So much is clear. They became frightened because "these men" or "they" entered the cloud. The question is, "Who entered the cloud?" Here commentators divide into four groups:

a. those who skip the question.

b. those who say "Moses and Elijah did." So, for example, Greijdanus; also Williams ("they were frightened as the two visitors entered into the cloud").

c. those who regard as more natural that Jesus, Moses, and Elijah all entered the cloud (thus Godet, Knox, etc.).

d. those who say "certainly Jesus with Moses and Elijah, but just as certainly also the three disciples." Thus Schürmann.

Possible solution of this problem:

As Godet (*op. cit.,* Vol. I, pp. 429, 430) and others have pointed out, the voice coming *out of the cloud* (verse 35) "could scarcely be addressed to any but persons who were themselves outside the cloud." This would mean, therefore, that Peter, James, and John did not enter the cloud.

It is therefore reasonable to assume that the cloud served as a kind of chariot to remove Moses and Elijah from the earthly scene and to carry them back to their heavenly abode; for, as verse 36 makes clear, they are no longer present. Cf. Acts 1:9.

The question remains, "Where was Jesus? When Moses and Elijah had entered the cloud, had he momentarily entered with them?" Though this is not specifically stated, does it not seem natural to suppose that he had done exactly that, for from verses 30–33 we learn that he had been standing and conversing with the two visitors. If this conclusion is correct, it follows that the disciples, being themselves outside the cloud, had suddenly noticed that the enveloping formation of diffused light covered Jesus, Moses, and Elijah. Also, on the basis of this supposition the "alarmed" condition of the three disciples becomes all the more understandable: to be suddenly separated from their Master frightened them. See also the note on verses 33, 34 on page 511.

35. And a voice came out of the cloud, saying, This is my Son, my Chosen One; listen to him!

As already indicated, the Father's voice was addressed not to Jesus—though the latter also heard it and was comforted by it—but to the three disciples outside the cloud. Now if these men knew their Bible and interpreted it correctly, they realized that the voice—ending with "listen to him"—was a clear confirmation of Jesus' messiahship, for it reflected Deut. 18:15, a messianic passage (see Acts 3:22; 7:37) containing similar words ("to him y o u must listen").

This exhortation to listen was certainly necessary, for The Twelve did not always take to heart their Master's teachings. At times they thought their own knowledge and wisdom surpassed his (Luke 8:45). And did not the constant eagerness of these men to be "the greatest" (Luke 9:46; 22:24) prove how badly they needed to hear and to heed his advice? Peter had even descended to the level of flat, breath-taking contradiction (Matt. 16:22).

"Listen to *him*!" He is no less than what the Father here calls him: (a) "my Son," an echo of the messianic Ps. 2:7; (b) "my Chosen One," a reminder of the equally messianic Isa. 42:1.

The Father loves and delights in his Son; hence this voice and this glory. See II Peter 1:16–18; cf. John 1:14; I John 1:1. No wonder, for the Son, by his very recent refusal to fall into Satan's trap—an attempt to get Jesus to seek to win the crown without bearing the cross (Matt. 16:22, 23)—and by his present calm discussion of the "exodus" in Jerusalem (Luke 9:31), was reaffirming his desire and purpose to redeem his people, whatever the cost. For further elucidation of this passage see the comments on the largely similar words that were heard at Jesus' *baptism*, Luke 3:22.

What especially must not escape our attention is the infinitely tender nature of the Father's love as here revealed: love for his Son, his Chosen One; and, implied, love for his people; in a sense even love for "the world" (John 3:16; Rom. 8:32).

36. When the voice ceased, Jesus was found alone.

Upon hearing the voice, the disciples had fallen on their faces, for they were terribly frightened (Matt. 17:6). No better commentary on Luke 9:36 is possible than Matt. 17:7, 8, "Then Jesus approached, touched them, and said, 'Get up and do not be afraid.' And when they raised their eyes they saw no one but Jesus only."

Conclusion: **They [the disciples] kept silent, and in those days told no one anything of what they had seen.**

This silence was in obedience to the order issued by Jesus, as recorded in

Mark 9:9. Cf. Matt. 17:9. Jesus knew that the time for public disclosure of his glory had not yet arrived. When the first open announcement to the people, as represented by their leaders, must be made, he himself would make it (Matt. 26:64; Mark 14:62; Luke 22:69). After his resurrection the disciples would be free and even duty-bound to relate far and wide what they had seen, heard, and experienced on the Mount of Transfiguration. The very fact of Christ's death, followed by his resurrection and ascension, would illumine the transfiguration account, setting it in its proper perspective.[340]

Practical Lessons Derived from 9:18–36

Verses 18–20

"Who do the people say I am? . . . But y o u, who do y o u say I am?" Two lessons stand out very sharply here:

a. Ever so many people regard Jesus as being, at best, the equal of other "great" ones; such as Moses, Elijah, Isaiah, Jeremiah, John the Baptist, Buddha, Mohammed, Lincoln, Gandhi. Those who by grace are God's true children regard him as being unique, "the Christ of God." Cf. John 14:6; Acts 4:12.

b. Faith is a personal matter. The question is not what others *say;* it is what we *say and believe.* Cf. Isa. 55:7; Mark 9:23, 24; Luke 8:50; 15:17–19; 18:9–14; John 9:35–38; Rom. 10:9; Gal. 2:20; I Tim. 1:15–17; II Tim. 1:3–5, 12; 4:6–8.

Verse 23

"If anyone wishes to come behind me, let him deny himself, take up his cross daily, and follow me." To deny oneself, etc., means to substitute the discipline of Christ for the cravings of one's own sinful nature. This can be done only by the grace and power of God. Note the word *daily.* To be genuine, *basic* conversion must be followed by *daily* conversion.

Verse 24

"For whoever would save his life shall lose it, but whoever loses his life for my sake, he shall save it."

Contrast the river that runs through its deep and narrow channel without ever becoming a blessing to its desert environment, with the raging torrent that has a dam constructed across it, and thereby gives rise to a great inland lake, converting the surrounding barren soil to fertile fields.

What accounts for the fact that the Sea of Galilee teems with life, while the Dead Sea is, indeed, dead?

Verse 31

"His departure, which he was about to accomplish at Jerusalem." It is comforting to know that, in the final analysis, our salvation does not rest upon our own

---

340. Notes on Greek words, phrases, and constructions in 9:18–36 begin on page 509.

changeable and subjective spiritual condition, but upon God's eternal plan. See Ps. 2:7, 8; 40:7; 89:15-18, 24, 28, 33; 138:8; Eph. 1:3-14. That throughout his earthly ministry Jesus was deeply conscious of the fact that he had been "sent" to carry out or "accomplish" *the work which the Father had given him to do* is clear from ever so many dominical utterances. See, for example, Luke 4:18; 5:32; John 7:6; 13:1; 17:4; 19:30; and see also the many references to this same conviction in chapters 3-10 of John's Gospel. Those are right who sing:

> I sing the gracious, fixed decree
> Passed by the great eternal Three,
> The counsel made in heaven above,
> The Lord's predestinating love.

Verse 33

"Master, how good it is for us to be here! Let us make three shelters," etc. It seems that Peter had not taken to heart the Master's words recorded in Matt. 16:23. This is by no means the only injudicious remark issuing from this apostle's lips and recorded in the Gospels. See also Matt. 16:22; 26:33, 35, 69-74; Luke 8:45; John 21:21. Nevertheless, even this man was saved. He became a great witness-bearer. In fact, before the days of Paul, he was the most influential leader in the early Christian church. See N.T.C. on Matthew, pp. 648, 649. Explanation? See Luke 22:31, 32; John 21:15-17; Eph. 2:8.

Notice that here Jesus gives Peter the silent treatment. It is not always necessary to answer a foolish remark. Prov. 26:4. This, too, is a lesson we may well take to heart.

Verse 36

"When the voice ceased, Jesus was found alone." Love for his Father, for The Twelve, and for all those he came to save prevented him from accompanying Moses and Elijah on their way back to heaven. Hallelujah, what a Savior!

Notes on Greek Words, Phrases, and Constructions in 9:18-36

Verse 18

ἐν τῷ εἶναι αὐτὸν προσευχόμενον, articular periphrastic pres. infinitive of προσεύχομαι, to pray, the most comprehensive word among the entire group to which it belongs. For synonyms see R. C. Trench, *Synonyms*, par. 51; also N.T.C. on I and II Timothy and Titus, pp. 91-93. Cf. periphrastic imperfect in 1:10.

συνῆσαν, third per. pl. imperf. of σύνειμι**, from σύν and εἰμί; cf. Acts 22:11, to be with (someone); not to be confused with the form used in 8:4, where συνιόντος is gen. s. masc. pres. participle of σύνειμι*, from σύν and εἶμι, to come together.

Verse 22

Note emphatic position of δεῖ (it is *necessary*) at the very beginning of the quotation.

Verse 23

The words of Jesus here quoted form a simple or first class conditional sentence, with εἰ plus third per. s. pres. indicat., followed by pres. middle infinitive, in the protasis; and in the apodosis a series of three imperatives (the first two ingressive aorists; the third, present linear).

Verse 24

θέλῃ, third per. s. pres. subjunct. act. of θέλω, with indefinite relative pronoun *whoever*.

σῶσαι, aor. act. infinitive of σώζω, to save; see the note on 6:9 on page 325.

Note resumptive οὗτος. In order to retain the full flavor and emphasis of the original, this pronoun should be retained in translation; as is done by A.V., N.A.S., R.S.V., N.E.B., Berkeley, Amplified, Jerusalem Bible, Dutch (both Statenvertaling and Nieuwe Vertaling), etc.

Verse 25

ὠφελεῖται, third per. s. pres. indicat. pass. of ὠφελέω, to help, profit, benefit, do good (to). The *anopheles* mosquito is *not helpful*.

κερδήσας, nom. s. masc. aor. act. participle of κερδαίνω, to gain, profit, win. This participle is here used in the conditional sense: "if he gain" or "to gain."

ἀπολέσας, nom. s. masc. aor. act. participle of ἀπόλλυμι; see the note on 8:24 on page 444.

ζημιωθείς, nom. s. masc. aor. pass. participle of ζημιόω, to visit with loss; in the passive: to suffer loss, damage; to sustain injury, to forfeit, to lose the right to possess or receive something. Cf. *damage*.

Verse 26

ἐπαισχυνθῇ, third per. s. aor. subjunct. pass. (but with acc. με; hence, transitive) of ἐπαισχύνομαι, to be ashamed of. Note also ἐπαισχυνθήσεται, third per. s. fut. indicat. pass., with acc. pronoun τοῦτον.

ὅταν ἔλθῃ, third per. s. aor. subjunct., "when he comes."

Verse 27

ἑστηκότων, gen. pl. masc. perf. participle of ἵστημι, to set; here: they have set themselves; hence, are standing.

Note strong negative οὐ μή.

γεύσωνται, third per. pl. aor. subjunct. middle of γεύομαι, to taste. Cf. *gustatory*. Also cf. Latin: *de gustibus non disputandum est* (taste is not a matter for debate); or, as the Frenchman would say, *chacun à son goût* (each to his taste).

ἴδωσιν (after ἕως ἄν), third per. pl. 2nd aor. subjunct. act. of ὁράω, to see.

Verse 29

τῷ προσεύχεσθαι, articular pres. infinitive (in temporal sense) of προσεύχομαι, to pray.

ἐγένετο ... τὸ εἶδος τοῦ προσώπου αὐτοῦ ἕτερον; literally: the appearance of his countenance became different.

ἐξαστράπτων, nom. s. masc. pres. participle of ἐξαστράπτω*, to flash like lightning, to gleam, glisten.

Verse 31

ὀφθέντες, nom. pl. masc. aor. pass. participle of ὁράω, to see; in pass.: to be seen, to appear.

Verse 32

ἦσαν βεβαρημένοι, third per. pl. pluperfect pass. periphrastic of βαρέω, to be heavy, weighed down. Cf. *barometer,* an instrument that measures the *weight* of the air.

διαγρηγορήσαντες, nom. pl. masc. aor. participle, with perfective διά, of διαγρηγορέω*, to awaken thoroughly, to become wide awake. Cf. *Gregory* (watchful).

Verse 33

διαχωρίζεσθαι, pres. infinitive of διαχωρίζομαι, to separate oneself; hence, to depart, leave.

Note: Matt. 17:4 Κύριε, Lord; Mark 9:5 'Ραββί, Rabbi; Luke 9:33 Ἐπιστάτα, Master. Clearly, in the present passages these three terms must be considered synonyms. All aim to do justice to the exalted character of the Savior. Each evangelist offers his own translation of the Aramaic word Peter must have used.

ποιήσωμεν (so also Mark 9:5), first per. pl. aor. act. subjunct. (hortatory) of ποιέω, to make, form, construct, put up. Cf. this "let us make" with "I will make" (Matt. 17:4). Peter's idea seems to have been that under his own direction all three disciples would construct those shelters.

Verse 34

For the verb ἐπισκιάζω (the form here used is third per. s. imperf. indicat. active) see the note on 1:35 on page 92.

As to the fiercely debated meaning of αὐτούς, occurring twice in this verse, and once in verse 33, is not the best solution to interpret all three instances of its occurrence as having the same meaning, and referring in each case to the two men, Moses and Elijah, who were standing with Jesus (according to verse 32)? Whether, in this connection, one also directly includes Jesus in the meaning of the pronoun as used in verse 34, or by reason of the context concludes that he, too, must have entered the cloud (see the explanation), the result is the same: the disciples, seeing that the cloud of diffused light covered Jesus, Moses, and Elijah, became alarmed.

Verse 36

ἀπήγγειλαν, from ἀπαγγέλλω, same form as in 7:18; 8:34, 36; 18:37; 24:9; see the note on 7:18 on page 402.

---

37 On the next day, when they had come down from the mountain, a large crowd met him. 38 Suddenly a man from the crowd cried out, saying, "Teacher, I beg you to look upon my son, because he is my only child. 39 All at once a spirit seizes him and suddenly he screams. Then it throws him into convulsions so that he foams at the mouth, and while mauling him it will scarcely let him go. 40 I asked your disciples to cast it out, but they could not."

41 Jesus replied, "O faithless and perverted generation, how long shall I be with y o u? How long shall I put up with y o u? Bring your son here."

42 Even while he [the boy] was approaching, the demon dashed him to the ground and threw him into a convulsion. But Jesus rebuked the unclean spirit, healed the boy, and gave him back to his father. 43a. And they were all astonished at the majesty[341] of God.

9:37–43a *The Healing of an Epileptic Boy*
Cf. Matt. 17:14–20; Mark 9:14–29

Raphael's painting, *The Transfiguration,* on which that famous artist worked himself to death, dramatizes the contrast between that which had taken place on the summit of the mountain and what was happening in the plain below. Only, Raphael has united the two scenes that must have occurred at a considerable distance from each other and, as verse 37 shows, a day apart. But in bringing the two scenes together Raphael rendered a real service, emphasizing exactly what the synoptists also seem to stress, namely, the tremendous contrast between the glory above (represented by the upper half of Raphael's masterpiece) and the shame and confusion below (the lower half). Above is the light, below are the shadows.

Nevertheless, there is also similarity: on the summit the Father, in spoken words, had reaffirmed his love for his Son, his Chosen One; in the plain a father agonizingly intercedes in behalf of his only child, a son grievously afflicted. We are shown how the great, unique Only Son, in his infinite love, revealed his power and compassion to this other only son and to the latter's father.

Luke presents this happening in greatly abbreviated form. Mark's account is far more detailed. Luke says nothing about the discussion between Jesus and his disciples with reference to the coming of Elijah (Mark 9:11–13), about scribes who were arguing with the disciples (Mark 9:14), or about the lad's inability to speak (9:17). He also omits entirely that part of the conversation between the Master and the boy's father that took place immediately after the lad had been brought to Jesus (9:21–24), ending with the father's agonizing cry, "I do believe, help my unbelief." Luke reduces Mark's three-verse description (9:25–27) of the manner in which the cure was brought about to just one-half verse (Luke 9:42b). Finally, Luke omits entirely the subsequent conversation between Jesus and his disciples, during which the Lord told them, "This kind can come out only by prayer" (Mark 9:28, 29).

The question arises, therefore, since Matthew also presents this story in condensed form, is it possible that the beloved physician was following Matthew instead of Mark? However, a look at these two reports (Matthew's and Luke's) will convince one that the two, though not exposing any so-called "discrepancies," are too dissimilar to prove any marked dependence of one upon the other.

---

341. Or: greatness.

Clearly, though Luke here as well as elsewhere is certainly making use of sources, probably both written and oral, and though these sources may well have included both Mark and Matthew, he is following a plan of his own. In a very orderly manner he is relating four incidents in which the disciples' failings are brought out into the open; namely, their lack of:

a. faith (verses 40, 41)
b. understanding (verse 45)
c. humility (verse 46)
d. tolerance (verse 49).

In all but (b) Luke also shows how the Master responded to these failings.

Result: more than ever we are led to see how, at the end of The Retirement Ministry, and facing the way to Jerusalem and the cross, Jesus suffered, "alone," in a sense "*all* alone." This enhances the greatness of his sacrifice.

A. *Setting*

37. On the next day, when they had come down from the mountain, a large crowd met him.

It was the day after the transfiguration. Jesus, accompanied by Peter, James, and John, has completed the descent from the mountain. The four are met by a large crowd. In fact, so eager were the people when they saw Jesus that they came running up to him to welcome him (Mark 9:15). According to Mark 9:14 present were also some scribes who were arguing with the nine disciples who had been left behind when Jesus and the three ascended the mountain. But, as has already been indicated, Luke omits this part of the story.

B. *Double Tragedy*

The first part of this tragedy is described in verses **38, 39. Suddenly a man from the crowd cried out, saying, Teacher, I beg you to look upon my son, because he is my only child. All at once a spirit seizes him and suddenly he screams. Then it throws him into convulsions so that he foams at the mouth, and while mauling him it will scarcely let him go.**

From this huge crowd one man suddenly stepped up to Jesus. Respectfully he addresses Jesus as "Teacher" (so also in Mark), and as "Lord" (thus according to Matthew). In the course of his speech the man may have used either title, or else each evangelist is giving his own translation of an Aramaic form of address.

The man continues by calling upon Jesus to "look upon" his only child. He means "to look upon with favor and compassion"; hence, to help him.

With reference to this son Luke reveals the following items:

1. He was *an only child.* Naturally Luke would be the evangelist to emphasize this fact. Was not also Nain's young man, whose body was being carried outside the gate, a widow's *only* son? Cf. 7:12. And was not the child of Jairus an *only* daughter (8:42)?

513

2. He was probably *an epileptic*. The symptoms mentioned by Luke—especially seizures, convulsions, and foaming at the mouth—are characteristic of epilepsy. It is true that in Matt. 17:15 a word is used in the original which, transliterated, would make this demoniac a "lunatic," a translation actually adopted for that passage by A.V. and Phillips. But the rendering favored by most translators is "epileptic." A "lunatic" is an insane person, and there is nothing in the present context that indicates insanity.

3. He was *a demoniac* or *demon's captive,* and this to such an extent that when the evil spirit caused him to have a seizure, and in the process mauled him, it would scarcely let him go again.

4. He was *a deaf-mute* (Mark 9:17, 25).

The second part of the tragedy is found in verse

40. I asked your disciples to cast it out, but they could not.

Evidently the man's original intention had been to bring his grievously stricken boy to Jesus. But when he noticed that Jesus was not in the company of the nine disciples that had been left behind, he had asked them to heal the afflicted one. Did not demon expulsion and healing the sick belong to the task that had been assigned to The Twelve? And is it not true that they had experienced some success in doing it? See Luke 9:1, 6, 7, 10; cf. Mark 6:13. But in the present case the disciples had failed. Luke does not enter into this part of the story. See Matt. 17:20; Mark 9:29.

C. Light amid Darkness

1. The darkness of unbelief rebuked

41a. Jesus replied, O faithless and perverted generation, how long shall I be with y o u? How long shall I put up with y o u?

Cf. Deut. 32:5; Matt. 17:17. Jesus was deeply moved, as the word *O* indicates. By means of this exclamation Jesus expressed his pain and indignation. The fact that he directed his complaint to the "generation" shows that he cannot have been thinking only of the nine disciples who had failed in this emergency. He was evidently deeply dissatisfied with his contemporaries: with the father, who lacked sufficient faith in Christ's healing power (cf. Mark 9:22–24); with the scribes, who, instead of showing any pity, were in all probability gloating over the disciples' impotence (Mark 9:14); with the crowd in general, which is pictured in the Gospels as being generally far more concerned about itself than about others (John 6:26); and last but not least, with the nine disciples, because of their failure to exercise their faith by putting their whole heart into persevering prayer (Mark 9:29).

To a greater or lesser extent all were faithless, lacking in the exercise of true, warm, enduring faith, a faith operating effectively. When Jesus adds, "How long shall I be with y o u; how long shall I put up with y o u?" he shows that in view of his own trust in the heavenly Father, a confidence that was faultless, and in view of his own love which was infinite and tender, it was painful for him to "put up with" (the exact meaning of the original) those who lacked these qualities or who failed to exercise these virtues in a sufficient degree. His ministry had lasted almost three years by now. He was longing for the end.

Not only condemnation and crucifixion brought suffering to the Lord, but so did also the unbelief and wickedness of the people among whom he lived. Nevertheless, mercy always triumphed. So here also. Jesus does not reject the prayer of the agonizing father or ignore the plight of the sorely afflicted son:

2. *The light of an implied promise*

41b. Bring your son here.

When Jesus said this, he did not mean, "I will see whether I can heal him," but "I will heal him."

D. *Deliverance*

1. *The demon's final attack*

42a. Even while he [the boy] was approaching, the demon dashed him to the ground and threw him into a convulsion.

That this was not an *ordinary* case of epilepsy but one brought about and aggravated by a demon is clear from these facts: (a) the convulsion occurred at the very moment when the boy was approaching, and the demon saw Jesus (Mark 9:20); and (b) it was not a cerebral disorder operating by itself that produced the convulsion; no, it was the demon that dashed the boy to the ground and threw him into a convulsion.

At this point Mark 9:21–24 relates a brief but significant conversation between Jesus and the boy's father, ending with the latter's oft-quoted words, "I do believe, help my unbelief." Both Matthew and Luke omit this conversation and concentrate the reader's attention on the cure.

2. *The cure*

42b. But Jesus rebuked the unclean spirit, healed the boy, and gave him back to his father.

Just as previously Jesus had "rebuked" demons (4:35, 41), a fever (4:39), winds and waves (8:24), so here also in a very effective manner he asserted his authority over this unclean spirit. For more on this verb *rebuked* see on 8:24; also the note on 4:35 on page 267. Having been thus "rebuked," there was only one thing the spirit could do: it left. Thus the Master healed the boy.

Significant are the words *and gave him back to his father*. In connection with so many instances of cures effected by Jesus it becomes evident that he was far more than a miracle-worker. His *heart* was in his healings. These were manifestations not only of his amazing power but also of his tender love. Thus, for example, he not only heals the paralytic but also forgives him (5:17–24), not only cures the centurion's servant but also commends the centurion (7:2–10), not only restores to health the Gergesene demoniac but also makes him a missionary (8:26–39), not only heals but also comforts the woman who touched his garment (8:43–48), not only raises from the dead the daughter of Jairus but also sees to it that the child gets something to eat (8:40–42, 49–56). Along the same line what strikes us in the present incident is that just as the son of Nain's widow was not only raised from the dead but then also very tenderly returned to his *mother* (7:11–17), so this deaf-mute and epileptic demoniac, now restored to health, is, with equal compassion and concern, given back to his *father*. Cf. Isa. 53:4; Matt. 8:16, 17. Jesus stands revealed here as not only *a* Healer, but as *the* Healer, the Healer with a heart!

E. *Astonishment*

43a. And they were all astonished at the majesty of God.
This statement has both its plus and its minus. It was wonderful that when the people noticed that Jesus was able to do what his disciples could not do, and triumphed even over this utterly corrupt but powerful demon, they expressed their astonishment and recognized in this act of healing the majesty of God. On the other hand, however, it is clear that they did not acknowledge Jesus as the Messiah sent from God. They did not surrender their hearts to him. Astonishment is fine . . . but not enough!

For *Practical Lessons* and *Greek Words,* etc., see pp. 522–525.

43b Now while all were marveling at all the things Jesus was doing, he said to his disciples, 44 "Let these words sink into y o u r ears: the Son of man is about to be betrayed[342] into the hands of men." 45 But they did not know what to make of this statement. It had been hidden from them, that they should not grasp it. And they were afraid to ask him about this statement.

9:43b–45 *The Second Prediction of the Passion (and the Resurrection)*
Cf. Matt. 17:22, 23; Mark 9:30–32

43b,[343] 44. Now while all were marveling at all the things Jesus was doing, he said to his disciples, Let these words sink into y o u r ears: the Son of man is about to be betrayed into the hands of men.
Jesus did not allow himself to be diverted from his goal, namely, to accomplish his "exodus" in Jerusalem. Not even universal acclaim and astonishment because of the great miracle he had just now performed could cause him to deviate from the course he had chosen to follow. So, from the crowd he now turns to his disciples. Again, as once before (verses 21, 22), he speaks about his approaching death. In the first announcement, however, he had laid special stress on the *necessity* of the coming events; now he is going to emphasize their *certainty.* That is why he says, "Let these words sink into y o u r ears," that is, pay close attention to what I am about to tell y o u; listen very carefully; store it up in y o u r memory; roll it over in y o u r minds; take it to heart.

What Jesus tells them is that he, the Son of man—as in verse 22; see on

---

342. Or: delivered; or: handed over.
343. A new verse should have started here.

5:24—the all-glorious One of Dan. 7:13, 14, is about to be delivered into the hands of men, the very men already mentioned in the first prediction, namely, the elders and the chief priests and the scribes. We know that they, in turn, will deliver him to the Gentiles—think especially of Pilate—who will deliver him to the soldiers for scourging and crucifixion. But not all of this is as yet spelled out in detail; especially not in Luke's greatly abbreviated account. Mark's parallel passage, and also that of Matthew, mention the being killed and *the rising on the third day.* But our present passage speaks only of the fact that the Son of man is about to be betrayed, or delivered, into the hands of men.

45. But they did not know what to make of this statement. It had been hidden from them, that they should not grasp it.

Because of their own misconceptions and worldly expectations concerning Messiah and his kingdom, they were unable to make sense out of this prediction. Messiah ... delivered into the hands of men! How was this possible?

Up to this point there is general agreement. But now another element is introduced. There appears to have been an additional reason why The Twelve did not grasp what Jesus had said. "It had been hidden from them," etc. It seems, therefore, that their inability to understand was not due solely to their own obtuseness—cf. Luke 24:25; Acts 13:27—but also to someone or something else. "It had been concealed from them."

Commentators differ widely on the identity of "the Concealer." Who or what was he or it? Among the many answers given to this question the following four stand out:

a. the apostles' own preconceived ideas
b. the devil or "the forces of evil"
c. Jesus
d. God.

As to (a). The words *It had been hidden from them* clearly show that Luke was thinking of a principle, force, or person outside of the hearts and minds of the apostles.

As to (b). It has been said, "When you don't know whom to blame, blame the devil." That is the easy way out of the difficulty. That answer is, however, completely foreign to the present context.

As to (c). This contradicts verse 45c; see below on that line.

As to (d). This answer, adopted by many interpreters, is probably the best. It by no means excludes the element of human responsibility, error, and obtuseness. As in several other biblical passages, so here also, the overruling providence of God is recognized.

An illustration based on the Old Testament shows how human error and God's good and overruling providence may combine.[344] It is as follows:

"Rehoboam's absurd answer was 'the breath which kindled the dead

---

344. I present it here in abbreviated form. For the full text of the illustration see the author's *Survey of the Bible,* pp. 106, 107.

coals of wars.' Did not the representatives of the contending tribes realize that there is strength in union? ... How deplorable this disruption! Gone was the political unity, the strongly centralized government, the religious consolidation.... The throne had lost its luster. The glory had departed!

"That is one way of looking at it. While fully maintaining the true element in this appraisal, we must not forget the *divine* point of view, as stated in I Kings 11:12, 13; 12:15, 24b, and especially in 11:36. We read: *'I ... will rend ...; it was a thing brought about by Jehovah.... This thing is of me ...* that David my servant may have a lamp always before me in Jerusalem.'"

When the question is asked, "Why was it that God concealed from The Twelve the full meaning of the prediction found in verse 44?" it must be admitted that the answer has not been revealed. Could it be that previous to not only the death but also the resurrection, ascension, and coronation of the Lord, and the outpouring of the Holy Spirit, the disciples were not psychologically prepared to "bear" the contents of the words, "The Son of man is about to be betrayed into the hands of men"? In other words, does John 16:12, 13 possibly lead us to the answer?

And they were afraid to ask him about this statement. Had they only asked him, he might at least have spoken some word to comfort them. That he himself was the Concealer is not even hinted.

Why were they afraid to ask him for more light on the subject of his fast-approaching agony? We do not know. It has been suggested, however, that the mild rebuke they had received in answer to a previous question—see Matt. 17:19, 20—may have kept them from asking another one. This is possible, but we do not know.

For *Practical Lessons* and *Greek Words,* etc., see pp. 522–525.

---

46 Now there arose a dispute among them as to which of them might be the greatest. 47 But Jesus, aware of what they were thinking in their heart,[345] took a little child and had him stand by his side. 48 Then he said to them, "Whoever in my name welcomes this little child welcomes me, and whoever welcomes me welcomes him who sent me. For he who is least among y o u all, he is the one who is (truly) great!"

For comments on the somewhat larger accounts of this incident see N.T.C. on Matthew, pp. 683–689; and on Mark, pp. 354–360. On pp. 355, 356 of N.T.C. on Mark one can also find a discussion concerning the so-called "discrepancies" between the three accounts.

9:46–48 *Who Is the Greatest?*
Cf. Matt. 18:1–5; Mark 9:33–37

Jesus had said—and this very recently—"Let these words sink into y o u r ears: the Son of man is about to be betrayed into the hands of men" (9:44). The continuation is shocking: **46. Now there arose a dispute among them**

---

345. Or: knowing their thoughts.

as to which of them might be the greatest. On the one hand, marvelous self-sacrifice; on the other, base self-centeredness.

The historical background was as follows: Jesus and The Twelve had reached Capernaum (Matt. 17:24). On the way to "the house" an argument about rank develops among the disciples. Indoors Jesus asks them, "What were y o u discussing on the road?" But they keep quiet (Mark 9:33, 34). Were they ashamed of the fact that they had been discussing the question, "Who among us may be the greatest?"

47. But Jesus, aware of what they were thinking in their heart—a typically Semitic expression, where we would probably say, "But Jesus, knowing their thoughts"—**took a little child and had him stand by his side.**

How did Jesus know what these men had been arguing about and what they were now thinking? It is useless to try to comprehend the exact manner of Christ's acquisition of knowledge. At this particular occasion his divine nature may have imparted information to his human nature.

Was it, perhaps, when these men became convinced of the fact that Jesus already knew what they had been discussing that they finally decided to make a clean breast of it? They admitted that their question had been, and was even now, "Who among us may be the greatest?" (cf. Matt. 18:1).

In order to impress upon these men the lesson they needed so desperately, Jesus now takes a little child and has him stand by his side.

It is pleasing to note the frequency with which the presence of children around Jesus and/or his love for them is mentioned in the Gospels. See Matt. 9:18, 19, 23–26 (cf. Mark 5:21–24, 35–43; Luke 8:40–42, 49–56); 14:21; 15:38; 18:1–6 (cf. Mark 9:33–37; Luke 9:46–48); 19:13–15 (cf. Mark 10:13–16; Luke 18:15–17); 21:15 and in a sense even 23:37 (cf. Luke 13:34).

In this connection it should not escape us that when Jesus speaks about "children," he is thinking of them as characterized by such traits as unpretentiousness and humble trustfulness. So considered "the Lord's little ones" are not necessarily only those who happen to be young in age and small in physical stature, but all those who reveal the *spiritual* characteristics just mentioned. Hence, to the passages already mentioned, as illustrating Christ's attitude to "children," should be added also Matt. 11:25, 26 (cf. Luke 10:21).

48. Then he said to them, Whoever in my name welcomes this little child welcomes me, and whoever welcomes me welcomes him who sent me.

This dominical saying fits the present context as it does also that of Matt. 10:40; see N.T.C. on that passage.

Here in Luke 9:48 (cf. Mark 9:37) the logic is somewhat as follows: Jesus is telling his disciples to forget all about themselves, their rank and importance; and instead, to concentrate their attention on this child standing by the Master's side. They should not only "become like" this child (cf. Matt. 18:1–4), but should "welcome" it (cf. Matt. 18:5), and others like it.

Moreover, their welcome should be in Christ's *name*. The name of Christ is Christ himself viewed in his glorious self-revelation. Therefore, to truly welcome such a child means to treat it with all the love and consideration Jesus has told his followers to bestow upon it.

Since the relation between Jesus and this child—or any similar child—is very close, therefore whoever in Christ's name or "for his sake" welcomes the child, welcomes Christ. Finally, since the relation between Jesus and his Sender, the Father, is infinitely close (John 17:10, 21, 24-26), it follows that whoever welcomes Jesus also welcomes his Sender.

Now such an attitude of looking away from oneself in order to see what can be done for Christ's children presupposes humility. And such *humility, revealed in humble service to the Lord's little ones, is greatness;* or, as the Master himself phrases it: **For he who is least among y o u all, he is the one who is (truly) great.** With this compare Matt. 20:24-28; Mark 10:41-45; Phil. 2:5-11; I Peter 5:5. And do not forget Isa. 57:15.

For *Practical Lessons* and *Greek Words,* etc., see pp. 522-525.

---

49 "Master," John said, "we saw a man casting out demons in your name, and we tried to stop him because he is not following along with us."

50 But Jesus said to him, "Do not stop him, for he who is not against y o u is for y o u."

Here again Luke abbreviates. For the additional material in Mark 9:39b and 41 see N.T.C. on Mark, pp. 362, 363.

9:49, 50 *He Who Is Not Against Y o u Is for Y o u*
Cf. Mark 9:38-40

49. Master, John said, we saw a man casting out demons in your name . . .

On the surface it might seem that between the preceding paragraph (verses 46-48) and this one (verses 49, 50) there is no thought connection of any kind. It has been suggested that the apostle John, embarrassed by the implied reprimand which he and the rest of The Twelve had received, brought up this incident concerning an exorcist merely to change the subject. Others are of the opinion that the insertion of the present little paragraph, not found in Matthew but only in Mark and (abbreviated) here in Luke, was suggested by the phrase "in my [or your] name" which occurs both in verse 48 and in verse 49. However, another possibility must not be ignored. John's conscience may have been aroused by Christ's remarks of implied disapproval (verse 48), so that he now wondered whether he, John, and others had behaved properly toward a certain exorcist. Whether there is any truth in any of these guesses as to the nature of the connection or lack of connection cannot be ascertained.

The title *Teacher* or *Master* (as here in Luke 9:49), either being a good equivalent of the Aramaic word John must have used in addressing Jesus, was always very appropriate (John 13:13), and might seem all the more appropriate if Christ's teaching on humility had just now been completed.

What bothered John was that he and others—note "we"—had seen someone cast out demons in Christ's name, though that exorcist did not belong to The Twelve and perhaps not even to the broader circle of constant followers (Luke 6:13; 10:1).

What kind of man was John talking about? Not a would-be exorcist, like the seven sons of Sceva (Acts 19:13-16), for these were frauds. Nor was he an exorcist in the sense of those condemned in Matt. 7:22. No, this man was in all probability a true believer in Jesus. He may have been someone who, having listened to the Master and having given his heart to him, had not as yet established close relationships with the Master's other followers. All that we know for certain is that he had been casting out demons in Christ's name, and that John and others—perhaps other apostles—had strongly disapproved of his actions: **and we tried to stop him because he is not following along with us.**

Apparently the attempt to stop the man had not succeeded. He must have been fully convinced of the fact that what he was doing was right and proper. He had been doing it "in Christ's name," that is, as explained previously, in full accordance, as he saw it, with the mind and words of Jesus. With this man the phrase *in Christ's name* was not a magical formula; it was reality.

The reason given by John for the attempt to stop him was "because he is not following along with us." It is entirely possible that John had taken a leading part in the attempt to stop this man from doing what he was doing. If this seems strange, could the reason have been that it took some time before this "son of thunder" (Mark 3:17; cf. Luke 9:54) was changed into "the disciple whom Jesus loved"? See John 13:23; 19:26; 20:2; 21:7, 20. But is it not more likely that it was exactly love for his Master—misguided love—that caused John and others to try to stop that exorcist, who had not joined Christ and his steady followers?

50. But Jesus said to him, Do not stop him, for he who is not against y o u is for y o u.

Since it is a fact that once a person has been confronted with Christ neutrality is forever impossible, it stands to reason that whoever is not *against*—down on—him is *for*—in favor of—him; and similarly, that one who is *not against* Christ's intimate associates—here "y o u"—would be *for* them.

What kind of attitude is it against which Jesus warns in this little paragraph? Answer: that of intolerance, narrow exclusivism. It is the kind of mental state that was present already during the old dispensation. Eldad and Medad, who are very definitely children of God and true witnesses, for some reason or other have remained in the camp instead of going to the tent or tabernacle where they may have been expected. Perhaps they did not hear the call. But in the camp, among the people, they are prophesying.

Excitedly a young tattletale rushes to the authorities with the news. "Eldad and Medad are prophesying in the camp!" Even Joshua thinks that this is appalling. "My lord Moses, make them stop!" he exclaims. But Moses answers, "Are you jealous for my sake? Would that all Jehovah's people were prophets, that Jehovah would put his Spirit upon them!" (Num. 11:26–29).

Even today that spirit of narrow exclusivism is at times mistaken for loyalty to one's church or denomination. We hear people say, "*Our* denomination is the purest manifestation of the body of Christ on earth." As long as we are on this sinful earth, a terrain where hypocrisy in high places frequently corrupts not only political but even ecclesiastical life, would it not be better to leave such judgments to God? Let us not be more restrictive than was Moses. Let us not be less broad-minded than was Paul (Phil. 1:14–18). Let us follow the teaching of Jesus and, while maintaining what we ourselves regard as purity of doctrine, let us reach out the hand of brotherhood to all those who love the Lord Jesus Christ and build upon the firm foundation of his infallible Word. Doing this, let us pray that we may be instrumental in leading others to the way of salvation, to the glory of God (I Cor. 9:19, 22; 10:31, 33).[346]

Practical Lessons Derived from 9:37–50

Verse 39

"All at once a spirit seizes him... throws him into convulsions... and while mauling him it will scarcely let him go." Cf. John 3:16. What a contrast between the heart of God and that of the devil! To which of these two have we sworn allegiance?

Verse 40

"But they could not." Note the contrast between The Twelve (the three plus the nine), on the one hand; and Jesus, on the other: As to The Twelve, on the mountain we found the slumbering three (Luke 9:32a); and now, in the valley we see the bumbling nine. Meanwhile on the mountain Jesus was fully awake, steadfast, and loyal; and now, in the valley he is signally alert, strong, and loving. Let us therefore heed Heb. 4:14–16.

Verse 41

"How long shall I put up with y o u?... Bring your son here." When *we* are in deep distress, we are prone to lose interest in others. On the other hand, *Jesus,* even in his deepest sorrows—see also Luke 23:34, 43; John 19:26—still thinks of others, and even helps and saves them!

Verses 43a, 44

"And they were all astonished at the majesty of God.... 'The Son of man is about to be betrayed into the hands of men.'" What an act of voluntary humiliation is implied here! Cf. II Cor. 8:9.

346. Notes on Greek words, phrases, and constructions in 9:37–50 begin on page 523.

Verse 45

"But they did not know what to make of this statement. It had been hidden from them." The second statement "at least relieves the disciples to some extent of full responsibility for their ignorance about the death of Jesus" (A. T. Robertson, *Word Pictures, Luke,* p. 136). I agree. To be sure, they were guilty; see Luke 24:25–27. But there were mitigating circumstances, and so also in Luke 23:34. When someone errs grievously and/or inflicts injury, do we, too, always make allowance for mitigating circumstances?

Verses 47, 48

"Jesus . . . took a little child and . . . said . . . 'Whoever in my name welcomes this little child welcomes me.'" It is true that the Savior wants his followers to be childlike in humble trustfulness (see Matt. 18:1–4); yet, it is not so much *that* as *rendering humble service to the weak and needy* that is recommended here in Luke's passage. Cf. Matt. 25:31–40.

Verses 49, 50

"We tried to stop him because he is not following along with us" . . . "Do not stop him."

Denominational loyalty is good, but bigotry must be condemned.

Patriotism is fine, but chauvinism is horrible.

Granted that your denomination is the most pure in its confessions, is it possible that the other organized religious group is more biblical in its church government and perhaps even in faith, hope, and love?

Granted that our country is the most blessed of all the nations in the world, is it possible that in certain *areas* nations in other continents—for example, Europe, Asia, Africa—are ahead of us?

The exhortation found in Phil. 2:3 is needed by every individual and by every group. One should have very good reasons, indeed, before he looks down upon that which others are trying to achieve.

Notes on Greek Words, Phrases, and Constructions in 9:37–50

Verse 37

Note Luke's use of genitive absolutes; here "they having come down," and in verse 42 "even while he [the boy] was approaching."

τῇ ἑξῆς ἡμέρᾳ, on the next day. See the note on 7:11 on page 389.

Verses 38–40

Luke is fond of the verb δέομαι. He uses it 8 times in his Gospel, 7 times in Acts. In the rest of the Gospels it occurs only once (Matt. 9:38). Meaning: to ask, beg, implore, make request, pray. δέομαι (verse 38) is first per. s. pres. indicat., while ἐδεήθην (verse 40) is first per. s. aor. indicat. The verb also occurs in the following Lucan passages: Third Gospel 5:12; 8:28, 38; 10:2; 21:36; 22:32; and Acts 4:31; 8:22, 24, 34; 10:2; 21:39; 26:3. Paul uses it in Rom. 1:10; II Cor. 5:20; 8:4; 10:2; Gal. 4:12; I Thess. 3:10.

ἐπιβλέψαι, aor. act. infinitive of ἐπιβλέπω, to regard with compassion. See the note on 1:48 on page 111. In James 2:3 the sense is: to show special attention to.

ἐξαίφνης, suddenly. This is exactly the kind of word Luke, a doctor, would be using in connection with an epileptic attack. But he uses it also to picture the dramatic appearance of a heavenly host (2:13), and the unexpected flashing of a bright, encircling light (Acts 9:3; 22:6). In Mark 13:36 the word indicates the *sudden* arrival of "the owner of the house."

σπαράσσει, third per. s. pres. indicat. of σπαράσσω, here: to throw into convulsions. So also in Mark 1:26; 9:26. The verb is probably related to σπαίρω, to gasp, pant, quiver. Cf. *spasm.*

ἀφροῦ, gen. of ἀφρός*, froth, foam. Cf. *Aphrodite.* According to mythology she sprang from the *foam* of the sea. For the cognate *verb* ἀφρίζω see Mark 9:18, 20. Literally verse 39 (middle) reads, "Then it throws him into convulsions with foam," which means, "Then it throws him into convulsions so that he foams at the mouth."

μόγις*, with difficulty, scarcely, hardly. Cf. μόγος, labor, toil, drudgery, hardship. Cf. *"moil* and toil."

συντρῖβον, nom. s. neut. pres. active participle of συντρίβω (from σύν and τρίβω, to rub together), to bruise, maul. Cf. *tribulation.*

ἠδυνήθησαν, third per. pl. aor. indicat. (Attic form) of δύναμαι, to be able. δύναμις is power, might, ability. Cf. *dynamite.*

Verse 41

ἄπιστος, here: faithless; in Acts 26:8, unbelievable, incredible; a word of frequent occurrence in the New Testament; especially in I Cor. Often it has the sense of unbelieving persons, unbelievers.

διεστραμμένη, perverted; nom. s. fem. perf. pass. participle of διαστρέφω, to turn thoroughly, this way and that way; to twist, pervert, make crooked, mislead. Cf. strophe (originally the *turning* of the Greek chorus).

ἀνέξομαι, first per. fut. middle indicat. of ἀνέχομαι, to put up with, endure.

Verse 42

ἔρρηξεν, third per. s. aor. (effective) indicat. act. of ῥήσσω, alternate form of ῥήγνυμι, to rend; meaning here: to dash to the ground. Cf. *wreck, break, hemorrhage.* See also the note on 5:37 on page 313.

Verse 43

ἐξεπλήσσοντο, third per. pl. imperf. indicat. pass. of ἐκπλήσσω, to strike out: they were struck out of their wits, were overwhelmed, astonished. See the note on 4:32 on page 267.

μεγαλειότητι, dat. s. of μεγαλειότης, greatness, magnificence. Cf. *majesty,* which is also a good *translation.* The word occurs, too, in Acts 19:27 (in connection with Artemis) and in II Peter 1:16 (with reference to the transfiguration).

Verse 44

θέσθε, sec. per. pl. 2nd aor. imperat. middle of τίθημι, to set, lay, put; here: pay attention to, allow to sink into.

ὦτα, ears, nom. and acc. (here acc.) pl. of οὖς, ear. Cf. *parotid.*

γάϱ, explanatory use ("for, y o u see"). Little is lost by leaving it untranslated, as here used.

Verse 45

ἠγνόουν, third per. pl. imperf. indicat. of ἀγνοέω, not to understand, not to know what to make of. Cf. *agnostic.*

ἦν παϱακεκαλυμμένον, third per. s. periphrastic pluperf. pass. indicat. of παϱακαλύπτω*, to cover over, veil; the opposite of ἀποκαλύπτω, to unveil. Cf. *Apocalypse.*

αἴσθωνται (after ἵνα μή), third per. pl. 2nd aor. subjunct. middle of αἰσθάνομαι*, to perceive, grasp, understand. Cf. *aesthetics.*

Verses 46–48

διαλογισμός, deliberation; here: dispute, argument. Cf. *dialog.* See the note on 2:35 on page 177, and N.T.C. on Mark, pp. 282–289. The clause introduced by τό is an acc. of general reference.

ἄν εἴη, "(as to which) might be," is third per. s. pres. optat. of εἰμί. In the New Testament the optative with ἄν occurs only in Luke's writings. In the present instance we have what some consider and what may well be regarded as an indirect question. See E. D. Burton, *Syntax of the Moods and Tenses in New Testament Greek,* Chicago, 1923, p. 80, and A. T. Robertson, *Word Pictures, Luke,* p. 136. See, however, also Gram. N.T. (Bl.-Debr.), par. 386.

μείζων and μικρότερος are comparatives with sense of superlatives. See the note on 7:28 on page 403, and the note on 7:42 on page 412.

Verses 49, 50

ἐκωλύομεν, first per. pl. conative imperf. of κωλύω, to hinder, stop. Cf. *colytic.* Cf. the note on 6:29 on page 358. Derived from the same verb is also κωλύετε, sec. per. pl. pres. imperat. active.

Summary of Chapter 9:18–50 (The Retirement Ministry)

By means of the feeding of the five thousand (Luke 9:10–17) Jesus had revealed his greatness so strikingly that the crowds wanted to crown him king (John 6:15). It was time, accordingly, for Jesus to reveal to The Twelve (a) that he was indeed the long-awaited One, and (b) in which sense this was true.

In order to achieve the first purpose Jesus, being *alone* with the men he had chosen to be his constant followers, asked them, "Who do the people say I am?" They replied, "John the Baptist . . . Elijah . . . one of the ancient prophets." There follows, "But y o u, who do y o u say I am?" Speaking for all, Peter answers, "The Christ of God" (verses 18–20).

Jesus warns his disciples not to publicize this fact. Then, to these same men he makes the first clear prediction of his fast approaching passion and resurrection. This takes care of purpose (b) above.

To an audience consisting of The Twelve *plus many others* he now makes

525

clear that his true followers are partakers of his suffering, "If anyone wishes to come behind me, let him deny himself, take up his cross daily, and follow me," etc. It was also at this time that Jesus spoke those mysterious words, "Moreover, I tell y o u truly, that there are some of those standing here who shall not taste death until they see the kingdom of God" (verses 21–27).

About eight days afterward Jesus took along Peter and James and John and went up into the mountain to pray. While Jesus was thus engaged, the Father imparted glory and honor to him (II Peter 1:16, 17), by (a) enveloping his body, including even his clothes, with heavenly brilliance, (b) sending heavenly messengers (Moses and Elijah) to discuss with him his "exodus" at Jerusalem, and (c) causing him, as well as the others, to hear the heavenly voice, "This is my Son, my Chosen One; listen to him." Peter's suggestion to prolong the glory-scene did not even receive an answer. A cloud came and enveloped Moses and Elijah (probably also Jesus). When the two emissaries disappeared, and the voice (already mentioned) was no longer heard, Jesus was found alone. In obedience to an order issued by the Master (Mark 9:9), the disciples who had been with Jesus on the Mount of Transfiguration kept silent, and in those days told no one anything of what they had seen (verses 28–36).

What a contrast between the glory on top of the mountain, and the misery, shame, and confusion below; particularly the misery experienced by a demon-possessed only son, and by his father. The tragedy was twofold. Quoting the father: (a) "All at once a spirit seizes him and suddenly he screams. Then it throws him into convulsions so that he foams at the mouth, and while mauling him it will scarcely let him go"; and (b) "I asked your disciples to cast it out, but they could not."

When Jesus saw: (a) this father, who admitted lack of faith (Mark 9:22, 24), (b) the disciples who, because of a similar weakness, had not been able to cure this boy, (c) the crowd of curiosity seekers, and (d) the scribes gloating over the disciples' failure (Mark 9:14), he cried out, "O faithless and perverted generation, how long shall I be with y o u? How long shall I put up with y o u?" However, turning to the boy's father, the Master mercifully added, "Bring your son here." That very order spelled defeat for the demon. Though dashing the boy to the ground and throwing him into a convulsion, at the word of Jesus the evil spirit was expelled. Thus Jesus healed the boy and tenderly returned him to his father. "And they [the crowd of spectators] were all astonished at the majesty of God" (verses 37–43a).

The disciples had failed. They failed again in connection with Christ's second passion prediction, "the Son of man is about to be betrayed into the hands of men." Though in the light of Luke 24:25 this failure, too, was inexcusable, it must not be exaggerated, as the words, "It had been hidden from them," indicate (verses 43b–45).

A very serious failure on the part of these men is now reported. While

Jesus was thinking of his great sacrifice for them, as the passion (and resurrection) predictions show, *they* were asking, "Who among us is the greatest?" So Jesus took a little child and told his disciples, "Whoever in my name welcomes this little child welcomes me, and whoever welcomes me welcomes him who sent me." He meant that he, he alone, is truly great whose humility is expressed in deeds of love toward those who are weak and small, that is, toward the Master's "little ones" (verses 46–48).

The story of a climactic failure on the part of the disciples—specifically of John and those with him—closes this section. The incident is told in these words, "Master, . . . we saw a man casting out demons in your name, and we tried to stop him because he is not following along with us." Jesus answered, "Do not stop him, for he who is not against y o u is for y o u." From this answer it is clear that though Jesus surely commended loyalty, he took a firm stand against bigotry (verses 49, 50).

The disciples' failures point up Jesus' victories! *Their* pettiness fixes our attention on *his* greatness!

Luke's Central Section

The Perean Ministry
with
Episodes and Excerpts
from
Other Ministries

9:51—18:14

Outline of Chapters 9:51—19:27

Theme: *The Work Thou Gavest Him to Do*

C. *The Perean Ministry,* etc.

1. Luke's "Central Section": The Perean Ministry, with episodes and excerpts from other ministries, 9:51—18:14.
2. The Perean Ministry (continued), 18:15—19:27.

SUMMARY OF AND INTRODUCTION TO LUKE'S CENTRAL SECTION (9:51—18:14)

This portion of Luke's Gospel has always been considered one of the most precious parts of Scripture. It contains such oft-quoted passages as 9:51, 57, 58, 62; 12:4-7, 22-34; 15:7; such instructive stories as that of Christ's visit to the home of Martha and Mary (10:38–42) and that of the cleansing of ten lepers, only one of whom—and he a Samaritan!—returned to give glory to God (17:11-19); and no less than 21 of Luke's 27 parables! In fact, of the 18 parables that are peculiar to Luke's Gospel, this Central Section contains 16. Among these 16 are *The Samaritan Who Cared* (10:25-37) and *The Lost ("Prodigal") Son* (15:11-32).

Even apart from many parables much that is found here is without parallel. But there are also many paragraphs that are duplicated elsewhere, at least to some extent (9:57-62; 10:13-16, 21-24, etc.). The parallels are nearly always found in Matthew's Gospel, not nearly as often in Mark.

We are faced here with the peculiar phenomenon that the same evangelist who in the earlier part of his Gospel—that is, in chapters 4, 5, 6, 8, and 9 (partly)—seems to be following Mark, suddenly stops doing so. He has been adhering to Mark's outline so closely that once a person knows in which chapter of that Gospel—whether 1, 2, 3, 4, 5, or 6—certain material is found, in many cases all he has to do is add 3 or sometimes 4 to the number of the chapter in Mark in order to locate Luke's parallel. After the close of Luke's Central Section that author returns to Mark, so that now by adding 8 to the number of Mark's chapter, the Lucan chapter can generally be located. Not as if Luke is ever *merely* following Mark. He has a style and purpose of his own, adds certain passages and paragraphs—even entire (or large parts of) chapters (e.g., Luke 1, 2, 3, 7, 19, 24)—and omits certain Marcan materials. Nevertheless, for much of the earlier and some of the closing material of Luke's Gospel the parallel is clear. The two, Mark and

Luke, run side by side. Accordingly, once a person has made himself familiar with Mark's Gospel he is well on the way to finding his way also in the earlier and the later portions of Luke. In fact, he will now even be able to locate most of *Matthew's* materials. All this has been explained in N.T.C. on Matthew, pp. 12-16, 26-30, 387. See also on Mark 14:1, 2, and see *Introduction,* point III A 2.

But with respect to the Central Section of Luke (that is, 9:51—18:14) the situation is different. Here, to a large extent, Luke has turned away from Mark. In fact, for about half the paragraphs that belong to Luke's Central Section that evangelist has even turned away from Matthew. Since by and large this Central Section does not follow a pattern with which we have become familiar from the study of the other Gospels, it may not at first seem easy to store in mind the arrangement of its materials.

What adds to the difficulty is the fact that in several cases Luke leaves us in the dark with reference to the connection, if any, between one reported incident and the next, or expresses himself indefinitely.

Nevertheless, without at least a summary knowledge of the contents of any Bible book, so that a person is able immediately to find what he is looking for, progress in the study of that book will be slow and time will be wasted. It is hoped, therefore, that the following *three methods* of finding one's way through that which on the surface looks like the labyrinth of Luke 9:51—18:14 may be of some help.

The material under (A) at the same time serves as a series of *Summaries* of the various sections and chapters of Luke 9:51—18:14.

A. *Thought Transition*

Links between a passage and its predecessor may be divided into three groups: (a) those that present no problem but are immediately clear (for example, 10:12, 13; 10:20, 21; 11:26, 27; 11:36, 37; 12:21, 22; 13:30, 31; 14:14, 15); (b) those which, in the light of the context, gradually become clear (such as 13:5, 6, see verse 9; 15:7, 8, see verse 10); and (c) those with respect to which it is impossible with any degree of certainty to point out the thought connection with the preceding, *if* there even is any (study 10:25; 11:14; 12:54; 15:1). For the sake of memorization we can, however, in all three cases, *consider* links, or in the third instance *possible* links, with the definite understanding that what seems to us to be a possible connection may not have been the actual connection in the mind of Luke.

Ch. 9:51-62

1. The face of Jesus as revealed in 9:51 fills us with awe. His mind is fully made up. He is determined to go to Jerusalem in order to lay down his life for his own. High resolve to carry out the task which the Father has assigned to him, and love for his "sheep," make his step firm, his face radiant and stedfast. Nothing, not even the refusal of the Samaritans to lodge him, can cause him to swerve from his course. To *the cross* he must go. What sublime, *wholehearted devotion* (9:51-56)!

2. It was this devotion which, in one form or another, was lacking in the case of the would-be disciples described in the chapter's closing paragraph (9:57–62).

Ch. 10

1. With the cross so near and still so much to be done, it is not surprising that Jesus "appointed *seventy* (-*two*) others" and sent them ahead two by two into the harvest of souls. He issued specific directions and warned them that by many their message would be *rejected* (10:1–12). Note: Matt. *10:* Charge to the 12; Luke *10:* Charge to the 70 or 72.

2. Terrible punishments will be visited upon rejecters, such as Chorazin, Bethsaida, and Capernaum (10:13–16).

3. Upon their return the seventy (or seventy-two) exclaim, "Lord, even the demons were subject to us in thy name." Jesus purifies his disciples' emotions by telling them that their chief *rejoicing* should be over the fact that their names are *recorded in heaven* (10:17–20).

4. Jesus himself also rejoices and praises the Father. He assures his disciples that they have heard and seen *things far greater than* those which in former days had been revealed to kings and prophets (10:21–24).

5. The thought connection, if there is any, between this and the next paragraph is not clear. *If* Luke intended a connection, it *may* have been as follows: A certain law-expert was not pleased with the words Jesus had spoken to the disciples. He said to himself, "By assuring the seventy [or seventy-two] that their names are recorded in heaven and that they have received revelations far greater than those formerly granted to kings and prophets, he has told them that even now they have inherited life everlasting. But surely in order to obtain this great blessing far more is required than these men have accomplished." However that may have been, putting Jesus to the test he raises the question, "What must I do to inherit everlasting life?" Jesus responds by eliciting from the lips of this "lawyer" a summary of the law, namely, "You shall love the Lord your God with all your heart ... and your neighbor as yourself." In order to justify himself the lawyer asks, "And who is my neighbor?" By means of the beautiful parable of *The Samaritan Who Cared* (or *The Good Samaritan*) Jesus now indicates that a person should not even ask such a question but should *prove himself a neighbor* toward any needy person whom God places in his path (10:25–37).

6. The question may easily arise, however, "But does being a good neighbor, taken all by itself, assure salvation?" Indeed not, and lest anyone should judge differently Luke now, in the chapter-closing story about *Mary making the right choice*, turns the attention of the reader from the neighbor to the Lord. Active love toward the neighbor must result from and accompany *listening to and heeding* the words of the Master (10:38–42).

Ch. 11

1. However, this cannot mean that salvation is a merely human achievement, so that a person can say, "All I have to do is be a neighbor to man and

listen to God." The power even in principle to observe God's command-ments originates not in man but in God. It is he, he alone, who saves. This explains the importance of prayer directed to him. Hence, very appro-priately the paragraph containing *Christ's Teaching About Prayer* follows. To be sure, the immediate occasion of this teaching was the Master's own praying, followed at once by the request of one of his disciples, "Lord, teach us to pray." The evangelist is very indefinite about time and place. He says, "Now it so happened that as Jesus was praying in a certain place, when he ceased one of his disciples said to him, 'Lord, teach us to pray,'" etc. Whether a very brief span of time or a longer period intervened between 10:38–42 and 11:1 f., and which came first, we do not know. See also under (B), p. 544. The point, as has been shown, is this: the three things—being a good neighbor, listening to Christ, praying—belong together.

Appropriately, Luke's version of *The Lord's Prayer* is found in this para-graph, as is also the accompanying parable about *The Troubled*—or *Embarrassed*—*Host.* This illustrative story stresses the fact that if even on earth and under difficult circumstances a man will grant the request of a friend, we can certainly expect that the heavenly Father will in answer to prayer give his children the Holy Spirit and all this implies (11:1–13).

2. As was pointed out previously, no connection is indicated between *Christ's Teaching About Prayer* (11:1–13) and the next paragraph (11:14–23) dealing with the subject: *Christ's Miracles: Proof of Beelzebul's Dominion or of His Doom?* It would seem as if at this point Luke starts a new subject. He begins to relate the intensification of the struggle between Jesus and his enemies. To be sure, even in the preceding chapters collisions had been described (4:28–30; 5:21–24, 30–32; 6:2–5, 7–11; 7:39–46; 10:25). But now, after Jesus expels a demon, the conflict becomes far more severe and embittered. *Reacting unfavorably,* those who hate Jesus accuse him of *being in league with Satan.* They say, "It is by Beelzebul, the prince of the demons, that he casts out demons." In the present paragraph Luke describes how the Lord annihilated that false accusation.

But is there in fact no connection between the preceding paragraph and this one? Luke does not definitely indicate any. Nevertheless, it would be very difficult to forget the sequence: *prayer* (11:1–13), *demon-expulsion* (11:14–23). See Mark 9:29, "This kind can come out only by prayer." Does not this mighty miracle (a *double* one according to Luke 11:14; a *triple* one according to Matt. 12:22) prove that God is almighty; hence, is able, *in answer to our prayers,* to fulfil all our needs?

3. The connection between 11:14–23 and verses 24–26 is so close that one might almost consider the two accounts to belong to one and the same paragraph. Have the Pharisees accused Jesus of being in league with Satan? In 11:24–26—the parable of *The Return of the Unclean Spirit*—Jesus tells his adversaries that they themselves resemble a man who is repossessed, so that in their case the *one* evil spirit has now been replaced by *eight,* namely, by the original demon and seven others "more wicked than [the first demon] itself."

4. Also very close is the connection with the next little paragraph. Not everyone reacted unfavorably to that which Jesus had said and done. Not only were the crowds astonished (11:14), but one woman, *reacting favorably,* "lifted up her voice" and exclaimed, "Blessed is the womb that bore you, and the breasts at which you nursed." While not denying this, Jesus improves upon it by replying, "Yes, but better still, blessed are those who listen to the word of God and observe it" (11:27, 28).

5. The astonishment of the people and the praise Jesus received from this woman may well have been among the causes that aroused the ire of the Pharisees and their followers, so that, in order to discredit him, they asked him to perform a *sign* "from heaven" (cf. Matt. 12:38). Jesus answers that they will receive no sign except that of Jonah (see the book by that name 1:7; 2:10). The descent into the tomb and the triumphant resurrection of Jesus, dimly foreshadowed by the Old Testament prophet's experience, would spell the doom of all impenitent, sin-hardened enemies. In the final judgment the Ninevites will condemn "this generation," and so will the queen of Sheba (11:29–32).

6. The flagrant character of the sin of *rejecting* Jesus, as those who demanded a sign were doing, appears all the more clearly from the fact that the Father had sent the Son into the world to be its Light, a light not hidden but shining brightly (11:33–36).

7. It is not surprising that in the closing paragraph of this chapter Jesus pronounces six *woes* upon rejecters, that is, upon these impenitent, legalistic Pharisees, etc. Cf. Matt. 23.

A Pharisee who had invited Jesus to his home for a meal "was surprised"—probably "horrified"—because Jesus had not (ceremonially) "washed" before eating (11:37–54)!

Ch. 12

1. Entirely in line with these woes by means of which Jesus had just now exposed the insincerity and inconsistency of the Pharisees he now, as a new chapter (the twelfth) opens, warns The Twelve (and probably other followers also; cf. 6:13; 10:1) against them (12:1–3).

2. Warning is followed by encouragement. Jesus fully realizes that the wrath of the opponents will be poured out not only on himself but also on his followers. He therefore admonishes his friends not to be afraid of those who "kill the body and after that can do no more" (12:4). He concludes by repeating, in slightly varied form, phrases he had used also on another occasion, namely, in *The Charge to The Twelve.* Speaking about God's protecting care he says, "Are not five sparrows sold for two pennies? Yet not one of them is forgotten by God. Indeed, the very hairs of y o u r head are all numbered. Have no fear; y o u are of more value than any number of sparrows" (12:4–7; cf. Matt. 10:29–31).

3. Dwelling on the marvelous theme of the Father's care, is it any wonder that the Master now declares that what is true with respect to the present age holds also for the coming one, and what can be said about *the*

Father's love pertains also to *the Son's* and to *the Holy Spirit's?* Note (verses 8–12), "I say to y o u, Whoever shall confess me before men, the Son of man shall also confess him before angels of God. But he who shall deny me before men will be denied before the angels of God." Cf. Matt. 10:32, 33. Continued: "And everyone who shall speak a word against the Son of man, it shall be forgiven him; but anyone who blasphemes against the Holy Spirit shall not be forgiven." Cf. Matt. 12:32a. Finally, "when y o u are brought before synagogues, rulers and authorities, do not worry about how y o u will defend yourselves or what y o u will say, For the Holy Spirit will teach y o u at that time what y o u should say." Cf. Matt. 10:19, 20. "Do not worry but trust" in The Triune God is the substance of Christ's exhortation.

4. The transition from 12:4–12 to 12:13–21 is unforgettable, not because of its smoothness but because of its harshness. Jesus has been encouraging filial trust in the heavenly Father, who fulfils every need. So someone in the crowd says, "Teacher, tell my brother to share the inheritance with me." Has this man been sleeping? It is clear at any rate that the words of Jesus have had no effect on him whatever. In response to the impudent fellow's demand Jesus tells the parable of *The Rich Fool*. Note especially these words: "You fool! This very night your soul will be demanded of you, and the things you have prepared (for yourself) whose will they be?"

5. As abrupt as was the change from 12:4–12 to 12:13–21, so natural is the transition from the latter to 12:22–34, beginning with "Therefore I say to y o u, Do not be anxious about y o u r life, what y o u are going to eat; or about y o u r body, what y o u are going to wear.... Consider the ravens: that they do not sow ... the lilies, how they grow." This immediately reminds the reader of Matt. 6:25–34. Again, "For where y o u r treasure is there will y o u r heart be also" (Luke 12:34). Cf. this with Matt. 6:21, which has the singular "your treasure, your heart." Note also the strikingly touching line, "Fear not, little flock, for y o u r Father takes pleasure in giving y o u the kingdom" (verse 32).

6. The transition from the *notorious (The Rich Fool)* to the *noble* is easy to remember. So Luke now reports Christ's parable of *The Watchful Servants* (12:35–40). Whereas the notorious rich fool had his mind set on *earth*, these noble servants are watching for the coming of the Son of man from *heaven*. After Peter's question (verse 41) the same theme—the necessity of watchfulness with a view to the Lord's return—is continued in the parable of *The Faithful Versus The Unfaithful Servant* (12:42–46). The degree of punishment for unfaithfulness coincides with the extent to which any servant has known his Master's will (verses 47, 48).

7. Was it the relative separation just indicated (between those who knew and those who did not, verses 47, 48) that caused Jesus now to mention the far more radical division described in verses 49–53? Or is the thought transition as follows: The Master has been discussing the work and faithfulness of his disciples. This leads him now to discuss his own task—an

agonizing one indeed!—and its effect upon mankind, namely, division. Note his words: "Do y o u think that I have come to give peace on earth? No, I tell y o u, but rather division."

8. Commentators are not agreed as to whether or not there is any topical connection between the immediately preceding paragraph and verses 54–56. *If* any, it could be this: the very division which Jesus brings about and which becomes more and more sharply delineated is a sign of the times, a sign far more significant than any signs of approaching weather.

9. The saying of Jesus (verses 57–59) that closes this chapter begins as follows: "Why do y o u not judge for yourselves what is right?" Does "for yourselves" link with the immediately preceding, so that the meaning is "apart from any consideration based upon the seriousness of the times"? Or does it mean "apart from any advice others—e.g., I or even the Pharisees—might wish to give y o u"? Either way, the main point is this: "Be reconciled with God!" In other words, "Repent." This reconciliation is necessary here and now. The matter is very urgent, for an impenitent person will never escape (hell's) prison. Conversion includes repentance!

Ch. 13

1. The topical connection of 13:1–5 with the ending of ch. 12 is close: ". . . unless y o u are converted, y o u too will all perish" (13:5; cf. 12:59). There is also a *temporal* connection between the close of chapter 12 and the beginning of chapter 13, as the expression *at that very time* indicates. But for that and the story of "the Galileans whose blood Pilate had mixed with their sacrifices" see on 13:1.

2. In the parable of *The Barren Fig Tree and the Magnanimous Vineyard-keeper* (verses 6–9) Jesus teaches that it was because of God's marvelous generosity and patience that the impenitent had not as yet perished. Note the words of the man who took care of the vineyard, "Leave it alone this year also, while I dig around it and fertilize it." Continued *impenitence* will mean destruction. Doom comes at last: ". . . if it bears fruit next year [fine!], but if not, cut it down."

3. But even though Jesus strongly urged conversion, his opponents did not even repent, as is evident from the story of the healing of the crippled woman on the sabbath (verses 10–17).

4. Does this manifestation of impenitence mean that the kingdom would never be established? Not at all. Did not this healed woman become one of its citizens? One must have the correct understanding of the nature of the kingdom. Therefore Jesus tells the parables of *The Mustard Seed* and of *The Yeast* (verses 18–21; cf. Matt. 13:31–33; Mark 4:30–32).

5. *If* there is any thought connection between the preceding paragraph and this one (verses 22–30), it could well be this: Jesus had made very clear that the kingdom of God does not come all at once, but little by little. Now this one enters, then that one; sometimes several, sometimes very few. So

someone now asks the question, "Lord, will the saved be few in number?" Jesus answers that instead of being inquisitive about a matter such as this, one should strive to enter by the narrow door. It should be borne in mind that once the door is closed it will not be reopened (verses 22–30; cf. Matt. 7:13, 14, 21–23; 25:10–12).

6. But though Christ's exhortation was certainly earnest and well-meant, in the case of men with hardened hearts it fell on deaf ears. With the warning and threat, addressed to Jesus, "Get out and move on from here, because Herod wants to kill you," these sinister individuals tried to frighten Jesus and chase him into Judea, in order that there, where the hostility was the most bitter, he might be killed.

In the stirring *Lament over Jerusalem* Jesus clearly reveals that he knows that Jerusalem will kill him. The moving words of this lament, filled with tenderness, compassion, and grief, were spoken a little later, namely, during Passover Week. Cf. the present paragraph (verses 31–35, especially verses 34, 35) with Matt. 23:37–39.

Ch. 14

1. Were all Pharisees about equally hostile toward Jesus? Well, here is one who, as *host*, invited Jesus to be his *guest*. But among those present there were those who were filled with hatred for Jesus and with a sense of their own importance. Also present was a man suffering from dropsy. It was the sabbath. The Pharisees and lawyers (experts in the legal system of Judaism) were watching Jesus to see whether he would heal this man. He did exactly that. Moreover, by means of the illustration of a son or an ox that had fallen into a well but was rescued on the sabbath, he exposed the inconsistency of his opponents (verses 1–6).

2. The preceding paragraph blends nicely into the one found in verses 7–14. The new paragraph contains a lesson for *guests,* followed by one for the *host.* As to the first, having observed how the guests upon entering made for the best places, Jesus, in the parable of *The Reserved* (or *Chief*) *Seats* (seats set apart for honored guests), castigates this rude habit. Cf. Matt. 23:2, 6; Luke 11:43. Next, he said to his host, "When you give a luncheon or dinner, do not invite your friends . . . or your rich neighbors . . . rather invite the poor, the crippled, etc. . . . and you will be blessed."

3. Again the transition is an easy one. When a fellow guest remarked, "Blessed is the man who will partake of the feast [literally, who will eat bread] in the kingdom of God," Jesus, by means of the parable of *The Rejected* (or *Slighted*) *Invitation,* also known as *The Great Supper,* showed what will happen (a) to those who, by reason of their *mistaken priorities, slight,* and thus in essence *reject,* the invitation, and (b) to the house where the feast is held: that house will nevertheless be filled (verses 15–24).

4. "Mistaken priorities," that was the trouble with the people whose horrible mistake was exposed in the preceding paragraph. To them a recently acquired field, five yoke of oxen, or a bride meant more than the earnest invitation from the almighty and merciful God to attend his banquet!

That same subject is continued here in verses 25–33. A person must be ready to surrender *all* in order to follow Christ. And he should do so consciously, considering the cost. This thought leads naturally to the parable of *The Rash Builder* and to that of *The Reasonable King.*

5. Yes, a follower of Jesus must know what he is doing and must be willing to follow wholeheartedly. He must be genuine, "pure salt." Salt that has lost its flavor is useless (verses 34, 35).

Ch. 15

1, 2, 3. *The Father's Yearning Love for the Lost* is illustrated in the three unforgettably moving parables of *The Lost Sheep* (verses 1–7, summarized in Matt. 18:12–14), *The Lost Coin* (verses 8–10), and *The Lost Son* (verses 11–32).

Is there any topical connection between chapters 14 and 15? This has been denied. *If,* nevertheless, there is one, could it be the same as that between chapters 10 and 11, human responsibility being stressed in the former, divine sovereignty—here particularly God's sovereign *love*—in the latter? Note also the word *hear* both in 14:35 and 15:1. Publicans *heard* Jesus.

But instead of making an attempt to find a connection, though there probably is one, should we not rather place the emphasis on the fact that the immediate occasion for the telling of these parables is clearly stated in 15:1, 2? The Pharisees had said, "This man welcomes sinners and eats with them." By means of these parables Jesus proves that in associating with despised people he is following the example of his heavenly Father, the One who sent his Son into the world to seek and to save the lost. Note particularly the hostile attitude of the elder brother at the close of the chapter.

Ch. 16

1. This attitude, that of the elder brother, so typical of the Pharisees, is not only very sinful; it is also very foolish, for in the end such cold-hearted individuals will have no one to welcome them into heaven's everlasting habitations; in fact, they will not even enter there. In the parable of *The Shrewd Manager (The Steward with Foresight)* Jesus shows that worldly people are often more shrewd, more forward-looking, than are the people upon whom the light has been shining. Of course, none of this means that Jesus in any way whatever praises this "manager" for his dishonesty. The very opposite is true, as verses 10–13 (climaxed by "Y o u cannot serve God and mammon") clearly show.

2. It is not surprising that the Pharisees now sneered at Jesus, for they were the people who tried to serve God (outwardly) and mammon (inwardly). They were *lovers of money.* Jesus tells them how detestable they and all self-justifying people are in the eyes of God. They were far worse than the very people whom they were always condemning. Ever since the days of

John (the Baptist) those belonging to the latter group were pressing forward vigorously to enter the kingdom. Cf. Matt. 11:12. These were the very people who, following where Jesus led, interpreted the law according to its original meaning and intention. So viewed, not even the tiniest hook on a letter of the law would ever drop out. Cf. Matt. 5:18. The Pharisees, however, that is, those men who posed as the guardians of the law and condemned all who did not agree with them, were the people who trampled upon it, as is clearly evident from their position on marriage and divorce (verses 14-18).

3. Unless they *repent,* what is going to happen to these "lovers of money"? That is made very clear in the parable of *The Rich Man and Lazarus,* that is, *The Show-off and The Beggar* (verses 19-31).

Ch. 17

1. Not only are the Pharisees and their followers culpable by reason of their own impenitence; they are also deserving of condemnation because they lead others astray. Is this perhaps in the background of the admonition addressed specifically to Christ's disciples, namely, "For temptations must come, but woe to him through whom they come"? Cf. Matt. 18:7. Instead of causing people to sin, Christ's followers should be kind to them and forgive them. When the Master spoke these words, "the apostles" (note designation in verse 5 and compare with verse 1, "his disciples"), conscious of the fact that they needed this warning, replied, "Increase our faith." So, first of all, in the parable of *The Coldly Calculating* (or *Unprofitable*) *Servant*—also called *The Plowing Servant*—(verses 7-10), who did only what he was expressly told to do, Jesus teaches The Twelve that genuine faith never operates in that mechanical fashion but is prompted by love.

2. Such love is the result of gratitude, as beautifully illustrated in the story of the ten lepers who were cleansed, only one of whom returned to give thanks, and that one a Samaritan (verses 11-19).

3. It is such inner qualities as these—active faith prompted by love, a love resulting from gratitude—that are brought about by the reign, kingship or "kingdom" of God. "The kingdom of God is within y o u" says Jesus, in answer to a question asked by the Pharisees, who reappear upon the scene here.

This does not exclude an outward, visible manifestation of the kingdom at the close of the new dispensation. The Son of man will be seen by all. His arrival will be as sudden as was the coming of the deluge in the days of Noah. Those who are ready will then be taken; the others will be left. They will suffer the punishment merited by their selfishness and lack of genuine faith. In frequently recurring phraseology—see Matt. 10:39; 16:25; Mark 8:35; Luke 9:24; John 12:25—Jesus drives home this important principle: "Whoever tries to keep his life shall lose it, but whoever loses his life shall preserve it" (verses 20-37).

Ch. 18:1-14

1. What Jesus told his disciples about the necessity of manifesting genuine faith, a faith prompted by love and gratitude (17:5-19), and this especially in view of the sudden return of the Son of man (17:20-37), is very appropriately climaxed by his exhortation that they should persevere in prayer. Faith and prayer cannot be separated. Therefore the parable of *The Widow and the Judge* or *The Widow Who Persevered* (or *Persisted*) is definitely appropriate at this point (verses 1-8).

2. To be genuine, faith must not only persevere; it must also be the expression of a humble heart. If the heart is humble, so will be the prayer, as Jesus sets forth in the gripping parable of *The Pharisee and The Tax Collector,* climaxed by the memorable epigram, "For everyone who exalts himself will be humbled, but he who humbles himself will be exalted" (verses 9-14).

B. *Time and Place Connection*

Not long ago a good friend told the author of this commentary the following true story. A bright and promising young man was enrolled in one of the country's best seminaries. He was happy, studied diligently and seemed to be well on the way to becoming a very useful laborer in God's vineyard. Then, rather suddenly, a change came over him. When questioned, he revealed that the doctrine of inspiration bothered him. He lost interest in his studies and left school. Upon further investigation it was discovered that his difficulties with the Gospel According to Luke had contributed powerfully toward the deplorable situation.

It is especially the central section of Luke's Gospel that has disturbed many a reader. This is not surprising. From 9:51 he receives the impression that the evangelist is about to give us "a chronologically running account"[347] of a trip which Jesus made from north to south; that is, from Galilee to Jerusalem and its vicinity. According to 10:38-42 Jesus actually reaches the village of Martha and Mary, presumably Bethany, very close to Jerusalem. But according to 13:31 he is still in the domain of Herod Antipas; hence, has not arrived in Judea. In fact, he himself admits that he must still cover a considerable distance before he will have reached Jerusalem. And, to cap the climax, when we finally reach 17:11 we discover that the Master is still in the north, for he is described as "traveling along the border between Samaria and Galilee."

For many readers a summary of all the attempts to solve this problem might become wearisome.[348] In the main, commentators are divided into

---

347. See the article by G. Ogg, "The Central Section of the Gospel According to St. Luke," *NTSt*, Vol. 18, No. 1 (Oct. 1971), pp. 39-53.

348. Those who are nevertheless interested in such a summary should consult Ogg's fine article, pp. 39, 40.

three groups. Basic to their variant theories are the following three travel passages:

"Now it came about that, as the days before his ascension were running out, he resolutely set his face to go to Jerusalem" (9:51).

"Now he was traveling through cities and villages, teaching and making his way to Jerusalem" (13:22).

"Now it came about that, as Jesus was going on to Jerusalem, he was traveling along the border between Samaria and Galilee" (17:11).

First of all, then, there are those who believe that these three passages describe three separate trips which Jesus made from north to south during the last half year of his public ministry. One can find a vigorous defense of this view in A. T. Robertson's book, *A Harmony of The Gospels for Students of The Life of Christ*, New York, 1922, pp. 276-279. He refers to the problem before us as "the most perplexing question in harmonistic study." His solution is that Luke's three journeys must be identified with John's three, in such a manner that:

Luke 9:51 is parallel to John 7:2, and refers to Christ's journey to Jerusalem in order to attend the Feast of Tabernacles; Luke 13:22 corresponds to John 11:17, and deals with the Lord's trip to Bethany in order to raise Lazarus from the dead; and Luke 17:11 agrees with John 12:1, and describes Jesus' coming to Jerusalem (via Bethany) to attend the final Passover, to die, and to rise again.

Secondly, there are those who say, "We do not know." Thus, for example, S. Greijdanus, *Kommentaar*, Vol. II, p. 444, writes, "Even though in this part [of his Gospel] Luke refers three times to the Lord's journey to Jerusalem ... his account does not clearly inform us whether or not he is in each case referring to the same journey."[349]

Thirdly, there are those who favor the idea that all three references (Luke 9:51; 13:22; 17:11) indicate one and the same journey, namely, Christ's final journey from Capernaum via Perea and Jericho to Jerusalem and thus to the cross, resurrection, and ascension. Thus A. B. Bruce, *op. cit.*, p. 567, states, "It is always the same journey."[350]

The defense of the third and probably correct view is as follows:

a. Though John's Gospel shows that Jesus, during the final six months of his earthly journey previous to his crucifixion, made more than one trip to Jerusalem, there is nothing in the three Lucan passages (9:51; 13:22; 17:11) to show that all three correspond to the passages in John (respectively to John 7:2; 11:17; 12:1). Luke says nothing about a going to

---

349. N. Geldenhuys, *op. cit.*, p. 293, expresses himself similarly.

350. Among several others who in their commentaries—see Bibliography at the close of this volume for titles—defend the "one journey" view are Gilmour, Godet, and Harrington; also Ogg in the article to which reference was made. For excellent material see also A. Plummer, *op. cit.*, p. 261. He accepts the journeys to Jerusalem that are reported by John, and then correctly states, "But although there is room in Luke's narratives for what John tells, we do not know where to place it."

Jerusalem to attend the Feast of Tabernacles or to raise Lazarus from the dead.

b. Even the very first of Luke's three passages (9:51) has a tone of finality about it. It shows that at the very beginning of his trip Jesus was conscious of the nearness of his ascension. Does not this point to Christ's *final* journey?

c. Luke 9:51 closely resembles Mark 10:32, which has to do with Christ's *final* journey to Jerusalem. See N.T.C. on Mark 10:32.

d. If it be true that even the journey introduced in Luke 9:51 finally reaches Jerusalem, and there is no sign anywhere in Luke's central section that Jesus subsequently returned to Galilee, is it not logical to conclude that also 13:22 and 17:11 refer to the same final journey? In all three passages Jesus is described as traveling "to Jerusalem," never "to Galilee."

e. Parallelistic or synchronistic style—in which an author first states a fact, lays down a proposition, or tells a story, and then, for the purpose of amplification, clarification, or reminding, retraces his steps and returns to what he has already stated or narrated—abounds in Scripture. A few examples: Is not Gen. 2 to a certain extent a return to and amplification of the story of creation first told in Gen. 1? Does not II Kings 7:16-20 remind the reader of the events reported in verses 3-15? Do not the four "beasts" of Dan. 7 correspond to the parts of the king's dream image, described in Dan. 2? Does not Mark 6:17-29 repeat and clarify verses 14-16? And is not the structure of John's first epistle and of his book of Revelation definitely parallelistic?

Now if this parallelistic style is borne in mind, so that one is aware of the fact that in writing in this manner Luke is doing what many others before him had done and others were going to do, an obstacle to faith will have been removed. One will then begin to realize that it was entirely proper for Luke to decide on his starting-point (9:51) and then twice to return to it (13:22; 17:11).

Another stumbling block will have been removed when one realizes that very often this evangelist, in narrating incidents from Christ's life on earth, or in recording his sayings, omits all *definite* time and place references (9:57; 10:25, 38; 11:1, 14, 29, 37; 12:22, 54; 13:20; 14:1, 25, etc.). By means of these omissions he avoids conflicts with passages in the other Gospels. See the *Introduction,* point V B; also comments on 1:1-4; 4:1-13; 10:38.

The fact that, as was shown, Luke never planned to compose a strictly chronological account also means that in this Central Section he does not need to limit himself to that which took place during any one particular ministry of Christ, whether Great Galilean, Retirement, or Perean. Though it is true that The Perean Ministry is ever in the background and is basic, the evangelist allows himself the freedom any time the Spirit so guides him to include in his narrative incidents that occurred, or dominical sayings that were spoken, during The Great Galilean or The Retirement ministries. To him topical connection is often more important than chronological or geographical.

LUKE

The beauty and clarity of Luke's style and the warmth and tenderness of the Savior's love—revealed especially in such *parables* as are recorded in 10:29-37; 11:5-13; 13:1-9; chapter 15; 18:1-14; in such *miracles* as are related in 13:10-17; 14:1-6; 17:11-19; and in such *dominical sayings* as are found in 10:21; 12:6, 7, 22-32; 14:12-14—contribute their share in causing Luke 9:51—18:14 to stand out as one of the most faith-strengthening portions of Scripture.

Are there any time-and-place links between Luke's Central Section and Mark? Links that could serve as an aid to the memory, in addition to those mnemonics mentioned under the heads (A) and (B)?

From the study of Mark we learned that on his final journey to the south Jesus traveled to Jerusalem (Mark 10:32), by way of Jericho (10:46), and Bethany (11:1). It is interesting to observe that also in Luke's account Jerusalem, Jericho, and Bethany are indicated in that order (Luke 9:51; 10:30; 10:38-42). Is it possible that the parable about "the man who went down from Jerusalem to Jericho" was spoken when Jesus was in or near Jericho? This is only a conjecture. Nevertheless, when a person has mastered the summary of Mark, he may well discover that locating the well-known parable and the story describing how Mary made the right choice has become a little easier. Luke, however, does not indicate when *this* visit of Jesus to Bethany occurred. That it did not take place very close to the final Passover is clear from John 11:1, 2; 12:1.

Is it possible that with the map of The Retirement Ministry (see p. 491) before us we can conjecture another geographical-historical link between Mark's story and Luke's? Here, however, we must be very careful.

During that ministry Jesus first traveled from Capernaum to Syrophoenicia, where he wished to be in seclusion, probably for having more time to teach his disciples. Was it at this time that a disciple asked, "Lord, teach us to pray"? Cf. Mark 7:24 with Luke 11:1. From there Jesus traveled to Decapolis and then crossed the sea to Dalmanutha, where the Pharisees asked for a sign. Cf. Mark 8:11-13 with Luke 11:16, 29-32. A slight difficulty might be this: Luke 11:16, 29-32 clearly parallels Matt. 12:38-42, which, however, belongs to The Great Galilean Ministry. However this is a difficulty only for those who believe that Christ's adversaries asked only once for a sign. Asking for a sign was a habit with them. See I Cor. 1:22. The answer, too, could well be the same. Finally, while recrossing, but now in the direction of Bethsaida Julias, Jesus warned the disciples against "the leaven of the Pharisees." Cf. Matt. 16:5-12; Mark 8:14-21; Luke 12:1. *But* see on Luke 12:1. We should distinguish between identical and similar events!

The material presented under (A) and (B) and the careful reading of Luke 9:51—18:14 should: (a) enhance our appreciation of this beautiful portion of Holy Writ, and (b) enable us with some ease to locate its incidents and sayings, including the *parables*, to which we now turn. An attempt will be made to answer two important questions:

1. Is there an easy method to remember where they are located?
2. How should they be interpreted?

C. *Parable Location*

The sense in which the New Testament (on the basis of the Old) uses the Greek word *parabolē* is broader than that which we commonly associate with our English word *parable*. The *parabolē* need not be a story. It may simply be a "dark saying"; see Mark 7:15, 17. Or it may be a proverb; see Luke 4:23 ("Physician, heal yourself"). It can be an illustrative type or symbol; see Heb. 9:9. But often it is, indeed, "an illustrative story." Whenever this is true, the Greek *parabolē* has the same meaning as our "parable." Some of the clearest examples of *parabolē* = (English) "parable" are Luke 8:4, 9–11; 12:16; 15:3; 18:1, 9; 19:11; 20:9, 19; 21:29. When we now speak of parables, we are using the term in the latter, to us more familiar, sense.

In a parable an important truth is expressed by means of word pictures. What is constantly happening in the natural realm is vividly portrayed, in order to show what transpires in the spiritual realm. Or else, what is bound *not* to happen in connection with ordinary human relations is made the symbol of that which either (a) will even more certainly never take place in the kingdom of God; or (b), by contrast, always occurs in that heavenly realm.

Nature and grace resemble one another in ever so many ways, the reason being that God originated both. Nevertheless, at times, because of the entrance of sin, nature and grace form a striking contrast. See Isa. 49:15; cf. Matt. 20:8–10; Luke 18:6, 7.

Using the term *parables* in the more usual, the popular, sense, we can say that Luke's Central Section contains 21 of that Gospel's 27 parables. Of these 21 no less than 16 are peculiar to Luke. But how can we retain in the memory the place where they are found? Part of the answer has been given under heading (A). If more is needed, consider also the following easy method. The list contains the titles of these 16 parables found in 9:51— 18:14. For good measure the title of the parable found in 19:11–27 is also included; hence 17 parables (peculiar to Luke) in all, in this part of Luke's Gospel.

A few words about the titles in the middle column. Several of them are so familiar that no further comment is necessary. As to No. 1 (Luke 10), not only was this Samaritan "good," he revealed his goodness in *action,* proving himself to be *The Samaritan Who Cared.* The notes introducing Nos. 3 and 4 (ch. 12) indicate that we are dealing here with a contrast—notorious versus noble—these notes are no titles, yet are significant, as will become clear. As to No. 5 (ch. 13), Luke 13:8, 9 shows that we should fix our mind not only on the fig tree but also on the vineyard-keeper. Besides, the suggested double title reminds us—as the familiar title does not—that this fig tree had been planted *in a vineyard.*

"Rash Builder" and "Reasonable King" have been suggested for Nos. 8 and 9 (ch. 14). In connection with the Builder it is indeed rashness that is

LUKE

Seventeen Parables in Luke

No.	Chapter		Name of Parable	Other Names
1	10		**Th**e **S**amaritan Who Cared	The Good Samaritan
2	11		**Th**e **T**roubled (or Embarrassed) Host	The Friend at Midnight
3	12	**Th**e **N**otorious Individual:	The Rich Fool	
4	12	**Th**e **N**oble Individuals:	The Watchful Servants	
5	13		The Barren Fig Tree and **Th**e **M**agnanimous Vineyard-keeper	The Barren Fig Tree
6	14		**Th**e **R**eserved (or Chief) Seats	
7	14		**Th**e **R**ejected (or Slighted) Invitation	The Great Supper (or Banquet)
8	14		**Th**e **R**ash Builder	
9	14		**Th**e **R**easonable King	
10	15		**Th**e **L**ost Coin	
11	15		**Th**e **L**ost Son	The Prodigal Son
12	16		**Th**e **Sh**rewd Manager (or Steward)	The Unrighteous Steward
13	16		**Th**e **Sh**ow-off: A Rich Man; and The Beggar: Lazarus	The Rich Man and Lazarus
14	17		**Th**e **C**oldly Calculating (or Unprofitable) Servant	The Plowman
15	18		**Th**e **W**idow Who Persevered (or Persisted)	**Th**e **W**idow and the Judge
16	18		**Th**e **Ph**arisee and The Tax Collector (or Publican)	
17	19		**Th**e **P**ounds	

emphasized (verses 29, 30). But the King deliberates, reasons, is reasonable (verse 31).

Some readers may regard No. 11 (ch. 15) as unfamiliar. Actually it is not, for it occurs in several parable expositions. Besides, it is better than the older title. The designation *Parable of The Prodigal Son* destroys the intentional triad: *lost* sheep, *lost* coin, *lost* son. As to No. 12 (ch. 16), the title *The Unrighteous Steward* misses the main point of the parable: the man was shrewd, prudent. He had foresight. As to No. 13 (again ch. 16), do not verses 19, 20 fully justify this title? As to No. 14 (ch. 17), the old designation *The Ploughing Servant,* or *The Plowman,* says nothing about the real thrust of the parable. On the other hand, the title I suggest finds support in Luke 17:10. The title *The Widow and the Judge* for No. 15 (ch. 18) is probably a good one—and even suits our present purpose (how to locate the parables), as will become clear—but would not the appellation *The Widow Who Perse-vered (or Persisted)* be even better? See Luke 18:1, 5, 7.

After careful consideration it would seem, therefore, that all the titles as proposed in the middle column can be defended.

The question will be asked, "But how does this list help us to locate any specific parable?" The answer is simple. Memory experts[351] have pointed out that consonants can be represented by numerical figures. Thus, the letter "t," having *one* down-stroke, can be represented by the figure 1. Letters close to "t" in sound—namely, "d," and "th"—are also represented by 1. The letter "n" has *two* down-strokes and is therefore equivalent to 2. Similarly "m" = 3; "r" = 4 (note f o u *r*); "l" = 5 (cf. Roman numeral L = 50). The letter "j" somewhat resembles and is represented by 6. With "j" we should associate "sh," "ch," and soft "g," all of them being represented by the figure 6. For a similar reason "k," hard "g," hard "c," and "q" are represented by 7. The *cursive* "f"—that is, the "f" in Mr. Coffin's *signature*—resembles the figure 8, its numerical equivalent. To this "f" group, all of them represented by 8, belong also "ph," "v," and (I would add) "w." The letter "b" is an upside-down figure 9, its numerical equivalent. Naturally the letter "p" is also equivalent to 9. Finally, it is easy to remember that "z" represents zero; hence the "cipher" (0). With "z" are associated "s," and soft "c." The letters "h" and "y" and also the vowels have no numerical equivalents.

As already indicated, the author of this commentary has not created this system of "consonants and their numerical equivalents." His own contribution is merely this, that having slightly modified it, he has seen and has grasped the opportunity of applying it to the distinctly Lucan parables, as follows:

In the above chart of Parable Titles note the boldface letters. It now becomes clear that the parable entitled "**The S**amaritan Who Cared" is found in Luke 10 (Th = 1; S = 0). Similarly, "**The L**ost Coin" and "**The L**ost Son" are found in chapter 15; "**The Sh**rewd Manager" in chapter 16; and "**The P**ounds" in chapter 19. And so for all the others.

Now that we have indicated how easy it is to remember where, in the Central Section of Luke (plus ch. 19), the parables peculiar to Luke are found, what about the remainder of Luke's parables?

Aside from the seventeen already mentioned, Luke's Gospel has only one other parable that is peculiar to that book. Its theme is Cancellation of Debts, and it is found in the seventh chapter (hard "c" = 7). As for the name or title of that parable it is probably impossible to improve on *The Two Debtors* (7:40-50).

There are nine parables *common* to Matthew and Luke. Three of these nine can also be found in Mark. See N.T.C. on Matthew, p. 24. To discover where these nine are found the "letter = figure mnemonic" is not needed.

---

351. For example, B. Furst, *How to Remember*, 1948 (place of publication not indicated), p. 132; D. M. Roth, *The Famous Roth Memory Course*, Cleveland, 1934, p. 160.

It is well known that the names of the twelve apostles are given in Matt. 10, a chapter which contains Christ's *Charge to The Twelve*. Perhaps equally well known is the fact that these names are also found in Luke 6. In Matthew the account of the sending forth of The Twelve as "kingdom ambassadors" is followed in the next (the 11th) chapter by a report of Christ's tribute to "the herald of the kingdom," John the Baptist. See N.T.C. on Matthew, p. 28. The parable of *Children Sitting in the Market Places* (Matt. 11:16–19) belongs to this word of tribute. It is easy to remember, therefore, that also in Luke the chapter that contains the names of The Twelve (ch. 6) is followed by the one (ch. 7) which has the parable about the frivolous behavior of the children.

We have already taken note of the fact that the parable of *th*ose *n*oble people, namely, *The Watchful Servants*, is found in Luke 12. It is therefore easy to remember that the somewhat similar parable of *The Faithful Versus the Unfaithful Servant* is found in that same chapter; in fact, it immediately follows (respectively verses 35–40; 41–48). The same parable occurs also in Matt. 24. One naturally looks for the parable of *The Lost Sheep* in Luke 15; for, though not entirely peculiar to Luke (an abbreviation is found in Matt. 18), it belongs to the trio: Lost Sheep, Lost Coin, Lost Son. And if we bear in mind the rule that for the earlier chapters of Mark and of Luke one can frequently add 3 or 4 to the number of the chapter in Mark in order to locate some of its contents in Luke, it creates no surprise that the parable of *The Sower* (or *The Four Kinds of Soil*) occurs both in Mark 4 and in Luke 8. It is also the first of the seven kingdom parables found in Matt. 13.

If all this is easy, the rest is perhaps even easier. We assume that, assisted by N.T.C. on Matthew, pp. 26–30, and by the repeated reading of Matthew, one knows his way around in that beautiful book. All one has to do now is to remember that Luke's remaining five parables parallel Matthew exactly or almost exactly. In two cases the number of the chapter is the same for Luke and Matthew; in the other three subtract 1 from Matthew's number—after all, Luke has fewer chapters than Matthew—and find the number of Luke's chapter:

The Last Five Parables in Luke

Name of Parable	Ref. in Matt.	Ref. in Luke
The Mustard Seed	13:31, 32	13:18, 19; also in Mark 4
The Yeast (or Leaven)	13:33	13:20, 21
The Two Builders	7:24–27	6:47–49
The Return of the Unclean Spirit	12:43–45	11:24–26
The Wicked Sharecroppers (or Tenants)	21:33–41	20:9–16; also in Mark 12

The Entire List of Lucan Parables

Ref.	Those Peculiar to Luke	Those in Luke, etc.	Found Also in
6:47–49		The Two Builders	Matt. 7:24–27
7:31–35		Children Sitting in the Market Places	Matt. 11:16–19
7:40–50	(Cancellation) The Two Debtors		
8:4–15		The Sower or The Four Kinds of Soil	Matt. 13:3–9, 18–23; Mark 4:3–9, 14–20
10:29–37	**The S**amaritan Who Cared		
11:5–13	**The T**roubled (or Embarrassed) Host		
11:24–26		The Return of the Unclean Spirit	Matt. 12:43–45
12:13–21	(**The N**otorious One) The Rich Fool		
12:35–40	(**The N**oble Ones) The Watchful Servants		
12:41–48		The Faithful Versus The Unfaithful Servant	Matt. 24:45–51
13:1–9	The Barren Fig Tree and **The** Magnanimous Vineyard-keeper		
13:18, 19		The Mustard Seed	Matt. 13:31, 32; Mark 4:30–32
13:20, 21		The Yeast (or Leaven)	Matt. 13:33
14:7–11	**The R**eserved (or Chief) Seats		
14:15–24	**The R**ejected (or Slighted) Invitation		
14:28–30	**The R**ash Builder		
14:31–33	**The R**easonable King		
15:1–7		**The L**ost Sheep	Matt. 18:12–14
15:8–10	**The L**ost Coin		
15:11–32	**The L**ost Son		
16:1–13	**The Sh**rewd Manager (or Steward)		
16:19–31	**The Sh**ow-off: A Rich Man; and The Beggar: Lazarus		
17:7–10	**The C**oldly Calculating (or Unprofitable) Servant		
18:1–8	**The** Widow Who Persevered (or Persisted)		
18:9–14	**The Ph**arisee and The Tax Collector (or Publican)		
19:11–27	**The P**ounds		
20:9–16		The Wicked Sharecroppers (or Tenants)	Matt. 21:33–41; Mark 12:1–9

LUKE

D. *Parable Interpretation*

In a commentary one cannot expect to find a detailed history of parable interpretation. A summary must suffice. A sample of the many books and articles on this subject is given in the footnote, *to which frequent reference will be made.*[352] Also consult the commentaries.

352. Allis, O. T., "The Parable of the Leaven," *EQ*, 19 (1947), pp. 254-273.

Bailey, K. E., *The Cross and the Prodigal, the 15th Chapter of Luke, Seen Through the Eyes of Middle Eastern Peasants* [here called *The Cross*], St. Louis, London, 1973.

......., *Poet and Peasant* [here designated P. & P.], Grand Rapids, 1976.

Ballard, P. H., "The Parable of the Great Supper, Luke 14:14-24, esp. 14:18-20," *JTS*, 28 (1972), pp. 341-350.

Baverstock, A. H., "The Unjust Steward: An Interpretation," *Th*, 35 (1937), pp. 78-83.

Brouwer, A. M., *De Gelijkenissen*, Leiden, 1946.

Bruce, A. B., *The Parabolic Teaching of Christ*, New York, 1895.

Buttrick, G. A., *The Parables of Jesus*, New York, 1928.

Calvin, J., *Commentary on a Harmony of the Evangelists, Matthew, Mark, and Luke* (tr. of *Commentarius in Harmoniam Evangelicam, Opera Omnia*), Grand Rapids, 1949 ff.

Carlston, C. E., "Reminiscence and Redaction in Luke 15:11-32," *JBL*, 94 (1975), pp. 368-390.

Chappell, C. C., *Sermons from the Parables*, Nashville, 1933.

Childs, A. T., *Parables to the Point*, Philadelphia, 1963.

Coates, T., *The Parables for Today*, St. Louis, 1971.

Crossan, J. D., *In Parables*, New York, etc., 1973.

Derritt, J. D. M., "Fresh Light on St. Luke XVI," *NTSt*, 7 (1960-61), pp. 198-220, 364-380.

Dodd, C. H., *The Parables of the Kingdom*, London, 1953.

Donfried, K. P., "The Allegory of the Ten Virgins (Matt. 25:1-13), as a Summary of Matthean Theology," *JBL*, 93 (1974), pp. 415-428.

Finck, E., "Die Parabeln Christi über die Zöllner und Pharisäer, Luk. 15 und 16," *TSK*, 7 (1834), pp. 313-334.

Flood, E., *Parables of Jesus*, New York, 1971.

Fonck, L., *Die Parabeln des Herrn*, Innsbruck, 1902.

Funk, R. W., *Jesus As Precursor*, Philadelphia, 1975.

Glen, J. S., *The Parables of Conflict in Luke*, Philadelphia, 1962.

Goebel, S., "Die Gleichnisgruppe Luk 15 und 16, methodisch ausgelegt," *TSK*, 47 (1874), pp. 506-538; 48 (1875), pp. 656-707.

......., "Das Gleichnis Mark 4, 26-29," *TSK*, 51 (1878), pp. 565-582.

Gray, A., "The Parable of the Wicked Husbandmen," *HJ*, 19 (1920-21), pp. 42-52.

Harrington, W. J., *Parables Told by Jesus*, New York, 1974.

Hendriksen, W., "Preaching from the Parables," *The Banner* 86 (1951), pp. 295, 310, 327, 343, 359, 374.

Houseman, H. G., "The Parable of the Tares," *Th*, 3 (1921), pp. 31-55.

Hunter, A. M., *The Parables Then and Now*, Philadelphia, 1971.

Jeremias, J., *Rediscovering the Parables*, New York, 1966.

Jülicher, A., *Die Gleichnisreden Jesu*, Zweiter Teil, Darmstadt, 1963.

Kingsburg, J. D., "Parables of Jesus in Current Research," *Dialog* 11 (1972), pp. 101-107.

Knap, J., *Gelijkenissen des Heeren*, Nijkerk, 1921-1922.

Krämer, M., *Das Rätsel der parabel vom Ungerechten Verwalter*, Lk. 16, 1-13, Zurich, 1972.

Lang, G. H., *The Parabolic Teaching of Scripture*, Grand Rapids, 1955.

Martin, H., *The Parables of the Gospels*, London, 1962.

Morgan, G. C., *The Parables and Metaphors of Our Lord*, New York, London, 1943.

Piper, O. A., "The Understanding of the Synoptic Parables," *EQ*, 14 (1942), pp. 42-53.

......., "Parables of Jesus Christ," article in S.H.E.R.K., Extension Vol. 2, pp. 840-841.

Renkema, W., *De Gelijkenissen onzes Heeren Jezus Christus voor de Gemeente Verklaard*, Doesburg, 1905.

Schippers, R., *Gelijkenissen van Jezus*, Kampen, 1962.

Smith, B. I. D., *The Parables of the Synoptic Gospels*. Cambridge, England, 1937.

Swete, H. B., *The Parables of the Kingdom*, London, 1921.

In the early church the allegorical method of parable interpretation gained a measure of popularity. This method amounted to an attempt to discover a hidden meaning in every element of the story-illustration. There was nothing new about this. Greek philosophers, unable to "swallow" the many foolish myths about gods and goddesses, but also realizing that out-right rejection would make them the objects of public wrath and persecu-tion, resorted to the subterfuge of saying, as it were, "These tales that have been handed down to us from antiquity, though valuable, cannot be taken literally. Their outer form conceals an inner truth."

When in certain centers—Alexandria for one—Greek philosophy and gospel proclamation met head-on, the result was not only opposition but also compromise. There were those who were willing to accept the narra-tives about Jesus' works and words, including the parables, if they were permitted to indulge in their favorite pastime of allegorization. Even among the most prominent leaders of theological thought there were those who resorted to this practice. We think especially of the great Augustine, by God's grace a truly marvelous leader, one whose writings contain treasures of thought and expression suited to every age. Nevertheless, he was an allegorizer of the first rank. See, for example, his *Quaestiones Evangeliorum* II.19. To this group of over-interpreters belongs also Jerome, as will be shown. They had many followers both then and afterward, especially throughout the Middle Ages.

It is only fair to mention, however, that even during the early period the allegorizers did not have everything their own way. Among those who opposed and frequently warned against over-interpretation of parables was the great orator and uncompromising church reformer, John Chrysostom.

We now turn to the sixteenth century, that of The Reformation. Its emphasis on the Bible as the only source of redemptive truth brought about a renewed emphasis on sensible parable interpretation. Even today one can derive real benefit from John Calvin's warm and practical com-ments on the parable of The Sower. At the very beginning of the discussion he reveals the main lesson this parable teaches: "The general truth con-veyed is that the doctrine of the gospel, scattered like seed, is not everywhere fruitful, the reason being that it does not always meet with a fertile and well-cultivated soil." The rest of the explanation, too, is a mas-terpiece of succinct interpretation and application to life. And the manner in which, at the conclusion, Calvin annihilates the allegorizers is unforget-table. Commenting on the fertile soil, producing a hundredfold, sixtyfold,

Tannehill, R. C., *The Sword of His Mouth,* Philadelphia, 1975.
Taylor, W. M., *The Parables of Our Savior,* New York, 1886.
Te Selle, S. M., *Speaking in Parables,* Philadelphia, 1973.
Trench, R. C., *Notes on The Parables of Our Lord,* Philadelphia, 1878.
Van Wyk, W. P., *My Sermon Notes on Parables and Metaphors,* Grand Rapids, 1947.
Via, D. O., "Relationship of Form to Content in the Parables; The Wedding Feast," *Interp.* 25 (1971), pp. 171-184.

and thirtyfold (Matt. 13:8), he says, "These three gradations are tortured by Jerome in an absurd manner, as if [respectively] they indicated virgins, widows, and married persons" (Vol. II, pp. 112, 118).

It was especially the archbishop of Dublin, Ireland, namely, R. C. Trench (born 1807, died 1886), a man of saintly character and a great scholar, who tried to bring order into the chaos of interpretations. In the early pages of his book he carefully defines the concept "parable," contrasting it with "myth," "fable," "proverb," and "allegory." He even warns against falling into either of the two extremes: under-interpretation and over-interpretation or allegorization. But a little later he himself becomes guilty of adopting the latter extreme (pp. 247–253). In connection with the parable popularly known as that of The Good Samaritan he describes that good man as in reality being Jesus Christ. Also, as he sees it, the inn represents the church. And the robbed and grievously injured traveler, who after his encounter with highwaymen had been left "half-dead," pictures the sinner. Trench argues that, due to the fall, Adam's posterity was left spiritually "half-dead" . . . Eph. 2:1, 5 notwithstanding!

One of the most influential figures among British New Testament scholars who flourished during the middle of the twentieth century was C. H. Dodd (born 1884, died 1973). In his book he accepts many propositions with which every careful scholar can wholeheartedly agree; such as, that the typical parable presents a single point of comparison, while in an allegory each item has a separate meaning (pp. 18, 19); that there is a resemblance between the kingdom of God and the process of nature, so that illustrations can be drawn from the latter to describe the former (p. 22); that the terms *kingdom of God* and *kingdom of heaven* are synonyms (p. 34); and that the attempt to eliminate ethical precepts from the teaching of Jesus is unjustified (p. 104).

That which, however, distinguishes Dodd's presentation is the theory that has become known as "realized eschatology" (p. 51). Thus Dodds points out that in the parable of The Mustard Seed (Matt. 13:31, 32) *right now* the birds are finding shelter in the plant which has now become a tree. The harvest, pictured in John 4:35–38, is *now* (pp. 111, 179, etc.), not at some future moment of time. When the objection is raised that in a number of parables—see Matt. 24:45–51; 25:1–30; Luke 12:35–48—Jesus disclosed the future and even foretold a period of waiting between his death-and-resurrection, on the one hand, and his return in glory, on the other, Dodd's answer is that these parables never proceeded in that form from the lips of Jesus but were reinterpretations by the early church.

Objection: When the Gospels were first published, many people who had either heard Jesus personally or had learned about his sayings from the earliest witnesses were still living. Nevertheless, Dodd wants us to believe that the Gospel writers would put into the mouth of Jesus all kinds of parables which, in the form now presented, had never been spoken by him. Without offering any objection did everybody accept the new versions as if they represented what Jesus had actually taught? Is this at all credible?

Besides, in I Thess. 5:2, 3—"For y o u yourselves know very well that the day of the Lord comes like a thief in the night," etc.—the apostle is clearly speaking about Christ's second coming, and he does so in language borrowed from the Lord's own sayings (Matt. 24:43, 44; cf. Luke 12:39, 40). Did Paul then also naively accept a lie? The only possible conclusion is that there is no justification for Dodd's textual and literary criticism, nor for his "realized eschatology."

In this series of commentaries we have frequently referred to the theories of the redactionists. See N.T.C. on Matthew, pp. 21–23; on Mark, pp. 599, 600; and now on Luke, pp. 35–42. Unsurprisingly the parables, too, have not escaped their attention. What merits comment, however, is this, that there is little agreement among the proponents of this view. That which is solemnly affirmed by one higher critic is just as definitely rejected by another.

Very revealing and refreshing, in this connection, is the article by Carlston. He points out that (a) according to the redactionist J. Sanders, the parable popularly known as that of The Prodigal Son consisted originally only of Luke 15:11–24, thus omitting entirely verses 25–32 (about the elder son); (b) according to another critic Luke, not Jesus, invented this story-illustration; (c) still another assigned the entire parable to Jesus. By means of a series of linguistic arguments Carlston himself reaches the conclusion "that the parable probably originated with Jesus in substantially its present form." We are thankful for this conclusion, even though we cannot see any good reason for endorsing the qualifying words "that its original sharpness has been blunted and shifted slightly in transmission and redaction."

We heartily endorse Piper's statement (see his encyclopaedia article), "Recent scholarship has pointed out the typically Aramaic form of these narratives and their Palestinian background, which would make it impossible to ascribe them to any but the earliest period of the primitive church. . . . These considerations make it advisable, if not imperative, to regard Jesus as the author of all of them."

Thorough study of the original, both Aramaic and Greek, is necessary. Does this mean that sermon-books on the parables (see the footnote) can be dismissed? Not at all! The very fact that these parables do not deal with abstractions but with the day-to-day lives of men, women, and children proves that a truly practical sermon at times reaches the parable's depth of meaning more adequately than does abstract linguistic research. But both research and sermons are needed, sermons based on research and on life. Not only sermons in the English language, however, but also those in other languages. Besides, much can be learned from the best commentaries. And as to the books and articles mentioned in the footnote, it should be pointed out that even though one may not agree with every one of Bailey's conclusions, he has rendered a real service in teaching us in a most interesting way that if one wishes to understand a parable based on a Near East background, knowledge of the conditions and customs of that part of the world cannot be neglected.

On the other hand, increasing emphasis has been placed in recent years on the fact that one cannot penetrate to the depth of the parable as long as he neglects to see himself as the object of its teaching. In other words, we must put ourselves into the parable, so that it begins to grip us, to put us to shame, and by God's grace to bring us to the proper attitude of mind and heart; in fact, it must lead us to take the required *action*. In this respect Te Selle's book, and also Tannehill's (see pp. 202, 203), have been and are a real blessing.

In conclusion note the following points on parable interpretation:

Though not all agree—see R. W. Funk, p. 56—it is safe to assume that as a general rule a parable teaches a single lesson. It has *one* "third of comparison." Somewhere, whether in the body of the parable, in its introduction or opening sentence, or in its conclusion, this central thrust is made clear. Thus, the main lesson of the parable of The Two Builders (Matt. 7:24-27) is "Be a doer of the word, not merely a hearer" (see verse 24). Similarly, the parable of The Lost Son (Luke 15:11-32) teaches "God the Father warmly welcomes penitent sinners; so should we" (see verses 2, 7, 20b, 43).

It should not be taken for granted, however, that it is always possible to express this central lesson in one short and simple statement. The story of The Marriage Feast of the King's Son is really a threefold or three-in-one parable. The three easily recognizable parts are: (a) the rejected invitation (Matt. 22:1-7), (b) the filled wedding hall (verses 8-10), and (c) the missing wedding robe (verses 11-14). The lesson is, "Accept God's gracious invitation, lest while others enter glory you are lost; but bear in mind that membership in the visible church does not guarantee salvation. Basic and continual renewal—the putting on of Christ—is necessary."

One more question, perhaps the most difficult of all, deserves consideration. It is this, "What must be done about those various single items within the body of the parable, items which may or may not importantly touch the central thrust?"

Some items *very clearly* pertain merely to the story as such, having been added in order to make the illustration more vivid. They may be said to belong to the "fringes" of the parable. But there are also other items where this is not so clear. Here are three examples:

In the parable of The Lost Sheep (Luke 15:1-7) do the ninety-nine that are left behind have any figurative meaning, and if so, to whom do they refer? According to Taylor (see his excellent book, pp. 313, 314) they represent the angels who have kept their first estate. He is not entirely sure about this but favors this explanation.

In the parable of The Leaven (Matt. 13:33) what is meant by the leaven? The famous English congregationalist, author and lecturer, G. C. Morgan, who throughout his active life was a channel of blessing to ever so many, was of the opinion that the leaven represented something bad, namely, "the principle of disintegration" (p. 65).

And in the parable of The Five Foolish and the Five Sensible Girls (Matt. 25:1-13) what, if anything, is meant by "They all grew drowsy and (soon) were sleeping" (verse 5)? As Donfried, employing "the redaction-critical method" sees it, basing his argument partly on I Thess. 4:15–17, the reference is to those Christians who had died (p. 426).

Undoubtedly all of these three opinions—that of Taylor, that of Morgan, and that of Donfried—are questionable. As to Donfried's, how I Thess. 4:15–17 can serve as an aid to the interpretation of Matt. 25:5, which is totally different, is a mystery. As to the opinions of the other two authors, see below on Luke 15:1–7, especially on verses 4 and 7; and on Luke 13:21 (parallel to Matt. 13:33).

Of course, the various items in those parables which Jesus has himself interpreted for us do not present any *great* difficulty. See Matt. 13:18–23, 36–43. But how must we interpret the details of all the other parables? In many cases the task is rather easy. So, for example, in the parable of The Two Builders the man who built his house on rock is the person who not only hears but puts into practice the words of Jesus. The other builder represents the individual who hears the Master's words but does not put them into practice. So also in the parable of The Lost Son the younger boy in his return to his father represents the penitent sinner (see Luke 15:1, 2), while his older brother clearly symbolizes the self-righteous Pharisee (see 15:2, 28–30). The human father pictures the heavenly Father in his forgiving and yearning love.

Here and there, however, we are confronted with a problem. There are parables with respect to which, though the central lesson is clear, the separate items are not nearly as perspicuous. Do these details belong to the "fringes" of the story, necessary to make the total picture more graphic, but not to be figuratively interpreted? The answer may depend on the context, parallel passages, word usage, etc. Each case will have to be judged on its own merits.

The problem can, however, be exaggerated. In most cases it is perhaps not as serious as at first it may seem to be. Referring again to the parable of "The Ten Virgins" (to use the older title), its single lesson is clear enough. It is stated in Matt. 25:13, "Keep on the alert therefore, because y o u do not know the day or the hour." Several ancillary truths can easily be derived from this lesson. See N.T.C. on Matthew, pp. 878, 879. But what about the oil? Does it or does it not have a symbolical meaning? We can probably not be sure. However, we can always say, "*If* the oil does have symbolical significance, then, in line with the use of the word elsewhere and in keeping with the parable's central thrust, namely, 'Keep on the alert,' etc., does the oil perhaps represent the Holy Spirit, through whose transforming and enabling power and activity men are being spiritually prepared and kept on the alert to welcome the Bridegroom?" See Isa. 61:1; Zech. 4:1–6; II Thess. 2:13.

In connection with each parable the main lesson or third of comparison must be grasped. If, with respect to a marginal matter, absolute certainty cannot be obtained, what is wrong with saying, "I do not know"?

Outline of Chapter 9:51–62

Theme: *The Work Thou Gavest Him to Do*

CHAPTER IX:51-62

51 Now it came about that, as the predetermined days before his ascension were running out,[353] Jesus resolutely set out for[354] Jerusalem. 52 And he sent messengers on ahead.[355] They went and entered a village of the Samaritans to make preparations for him. 53 But the people (there) refused to welcome him, because he was headed for[356] Jerusalem. 54 Now when the disciples James and John saw this, they asked, "Lord, do you want us to bid fire to come down from heaven and consume them?"[357] 55 But he turned and rebuked them.[358] 56 And they went to another village.

9:51-56 *A Samaritan Village Refuses to Welcome Jesus*

51. Now it came about that, as the predetermined days before his ascension were running out, Jesus resolutely set out for Jerusalem.

As has been shown and is clear from the present passage and also from 9:53; 10:38; 13:22, 33, 34; 17:11; 18:31; 19:11, 28, 29, Jesus is starting out on his way to Jerusalem, the cross, etc. Verse 51 implies at least the following:

a. Everything in Christ's life, including this trip to Jerusalem, happened in accordance with the divine plan.

b. Jesus himself was fully conscious of this fact (9:22, 27, 31; 22:22).

c. Not only that, but his will was in harmony with it. Though the contemplation of the indescribable bitterness that lay ahead meant nameless agony for him (12:50), he was fully determined to accomplish "the work which the Father had given him to do" (John 17:4).

d. Luke, writing long after Calvary, etc., had become history, does not say "before his death" but "before his ascension." He realized that the cross was a steppingstone to the crown. Cf. Heb. 12:2.

---

353. Or: were being completed.
354. Literally: set his face to go to.
355. Literally: before his face.
356. Literally: his face was going toward.
357. There is insufficient evidence for the addition, "... as Elijah did."
358. Probably also unauthentic are the words added in some manuscripts: "And he said, 'Y o u do not know of what spirit y o u are, for the Son of man did not come to destroy men's lives but to save them."

52, 53. And he sent messengers on ahead. They went and entered a village of the Samaritans to make preparations for him. But the people (there) refused to welcome him, because he was headed for Jerusalem.

The reason for Jesus' action is clear. The unheralded arrival of a group of perhaps thirteen men—Jesus plus The Twelve—to be fed and lodged, would have caused hardship.

However, the Samaritans who received the news did not greet it with rejoicing or even with indifference. On the contrary, in essence they said, "Go away. We do not want y o u."

There had long been a feud between the Jews and the Samaritans, a mixed race (II Kings 17:24–41). Is it not true that toward the close of the sixth century B.C. the Jews had rejected the offer of the Samaritans to help in the rebuilding of Jerusalem's temple (Ezra 4:1–3)? Sometime later had not one of the Maccabean rulers, John Hyrcanus, destroyed the Samaritan temple on Mt. Gerizim? In order to gain an insight into the extent of the bitterness between Jews and Samaritans one should read Josephus, *Jewish War* II.232–246; *Antiquities* XX.118–126. Frequently, as Josephus informs us, Galilean Jews, on their way to Jerusalem to attend a religious festival, would pass through Samaria. So implacable was the resentment of Samaritans toward such Jewish pilgrims that, instead of showing hospitality, they would hinder the travelers in every way, even to the extent of actually murdering some of them. See also N.T.C. on John, Vol. I, pp. 159–161.

54. Now when the disciples James and John saw this, they asked, Lord, do you want us to bid fire to come down from heaven and consume them?

James and John, originally fishermen by trade, were sons of Zebedee (Luke 5:10). They were among Christ's earliest disciples (Matt. 4:21, 22; Mark 1:19, 20; see also N.T.C. on John, Vol. I, p. 106). They also figure in other narratives (Mark 5:37, cf. Luke 8:51; Matt. 17:1, cf. Mark 9:2 and Luke 9:28; Matt. 20:20–28, cf. Mark 10:35–45). Probably because of their fiery nature, of which they give evidence here in Luke 9:54, Jesus called them "sons of thunder" (Mark 3:17; for one of these two brothers, namely, John, see also Luke 9:49, 50).

These two disciples, then, asked the Lord whether he wanted them to call down fire from heaven to consume these inhospitable Samaritans. At this point some manuscripts (cf. A.V.) add the words *as Elijah did*. Although this addition is not supported by the best textual evidence, it must be considered possible that the two brothers, having recently seen Elijah on the Mount of Transfiguration, were reminded of the incident recorded in II Kings 1:10–12.

Viewed in the most favorable light, the question asked by James and John was a manifestation of loyalty to their Master. Also, their question demonstrated faith in God—or in Jesus—who, they firmly believed, would, in answer to their request, immediately bestow upon them the power to imitate Elijah's deed.

Nevertheless, they were sadly mistaken. What a vast contrast between their attitude and that of Jesus, who said, "For God sent his Son into the world, not to condemn the world, but in order that the world might be saved through him" (John 3:17); "I did not come in order to judge the world but in order to save the world" (John 12:47); and "For the Son of man came to seek and to save what was lost" (Luke 19:10).

What immediately follows requires no comment. **55. But he turned and rebuked them.** There is insufficient manuscript evidence for the addition, "And he said, Y o u do not know of what kind of spirit y o u are, for the Son of man did not come to destroy men's lives, but to save them." Nevertheless, these added words may very well express the essence of the rebuke.

56. And they went to another village, perhaps to a Jewish village near the Galilee-Samaria border.

For *Practical Lessons* and *Greek Words,* etc., see pp. 564–566.

---

57 As they were walking along the road, a man said to him, "I will follow you wherever you go." 58 Jesus replied, "The foxes have holes,[359] the birds of the air roosts, but the Son of man has nowhere to lay his head."

59 He said to another man, "Follow me." But he answered, "Lord, allow me first to go home and bury my father." 60 Jesus said to him, "Let the dead bury their own dead, but as for you, go and proclaim the kingdom of God."

61 Still another man said, "I will follow you, Lord, but first permit me to say good-bye to the folks at home." 62 Jesus replied, "No one who has just put his hand to a plow and (then) continues to look back is fit for the kingdom of God."

9:57–62 Would-Be Followers of Jesus
Cf. Matt. 8:19–22

Christ's firm determination to go to Jerusalem, there to die for all those who would place their trust in him, is here contrasted with the weak, conditional commitment (?) of three would-be followers. It is as if Jesus were saying, "My own determination to accomplish the task assigned to me, whatever the cost, must be an example to all my followers." The connection between verses 51–56 and verses 57–62 reminds us of that between verse 9:22 and verse 9:23 f. Thus viewed, the link between verses 51–56 and the paragraph about to be considered is topical rather than chronological.

57. As they were walking along the road, a man said to him, I will follow you wherever you go.

The opening words are very indefinite: place and time are not indicated and are of no importance in the present context. As was stated earlier, "Though it is true that the Perean Ministry is ever in the background and is basic, the evangelist allows himself the freedom any time the Spirit so guides him to include in the narrative incidents that occurred, or dominical

---

359. Or: lairs.

sayings that were spoken, during the Great Galilean or the Retirement ministries."

It is clear from Matt. 8:19-22 that at least the first two incidents—those recorded in Luke 9:57-60—occurred during the Great Galilean Ministry, more precisely just previous to Christ's departure by boat from Capernaum to the land of the Gadarenes or Gergesenes. See Matt. 8:19 f.; cf. Mark 4:35.

As to the first aspirant, what he says to Jesus is a remarkable declaration indeed, especially coming, as Matthew states, from *a scribe*. For a description of scribes and their functions see above, on Luke 9:22. As a group the scribes were generally hostile to Jesus (Luke 5:21, 30; 6:7; 9:22; 11:53, 54; 15:2; 19:47; 20:1, 2, 19, 46; 22:2, 66-71; 23:10). Moreover, the scribes were themselves teachers; yet this teacher acknowledges Jesus as *his* teacher and so addresses him. Finally, of his sincerity there can be no doubt. At the particular moment when he uttered his promise he actually meant it: he wanted to be a constant follower of Jesus.

There is something very attractive about the words, "I will follow you wherever you go." Who can read them without being immediately reminded of Ruth's glorious resolution, "Wherever you go, I will go..." (Ruth 1:16, 17)? Nevertheless, as Christ's answer clearly indicates, this man's intentions were not altogether honorable. He saw crowds, miracles, enthusiasm, etc. It seemed so good to be closely associated with the One who was in the very center of all this action. So, he wanted to be Christ's disciple, but he failed to understand the implications of discipleship, namely, self-denial, sacrifice, service, suffering! **58. Jesus replied, The foxes have holes, the birds of the air roosts, but the Son of man has nowhere to lay his head.** Foxes were plentiful in the country of Christ's travels (Judg. 15:4; Neh. 4:3; Ps. 63:10; Song of Sol. 2:15; Lam. 5:18; Ezek. 13:4). Their holes, dens, or lairs were often burrows in the ground. From these they would make their nightly raids, not only hunting frogs, rabbits, mice, poultry, and birds, but also devouring eggs, fruits, etc., and devastating the fields, orchards, and vineyards. The point Jesus emphasizes is, however, that these animals have their definite dwelling-places, their homes to which they return again and again. The same is true also with respect to birds. Ecological conditions (weather, food supply) permitting, they have their definite roosts, temporary lodging places, the place where they, as it were, pitch their tents. If "enemies" try to intrude, they drive them away if they can at all do so.

For "the Son of man" (see on 5:24), things are entirely different, however. In his wandering from place to place he, for whom there was no room in the inn, has no place on which he can figure to spend the night. As the story develops, Judea rejects him (John 5:18), Galilee casts him out (John 6:66), Gadara begs him to leave its district (Matt. 8:34), Samaria refuses him lodging (Luke 9:53), earth will not have him (Matt. 27:23), and finally even heaven forsakes him (Matt. 27:46). Therefore let the scribe figure the cost before he builds the tower. Let him consider that permanent disciple-ship implies struggle and warfare. It is said that at the time of the Civil War (U.S.) there were many volunteers who eagerly joined the ranks, as if going to war meant nothing more than taking part in parades, drills, and reviews, and receiving medals and honors! To be sure, there are glorious rewards for all true followers of the Lord, but it is ever the way of the cross that leads home (Matt. 10:24; Luke 14:26; John 16:33; II Tim. 3:12; Heb. 13:13). Whether this scribe ever became a steadfast follower is not re-corded. After all, that is not nearly as important as is the lesson itself.

As has been shown, the would-be follower mentioned in verses 57, 58 was *too ready* to become one of Christ's constant disciples. The next aspirant is *too unready:*

59. He said to another man, Follow me. —But he answered, Lord, allow me first to go home and bury my father.

While the first aspirant offered to follow Jesus, this man is asked by Jesus to follow. He evidently belonged to that large group of people that had been impressed by the words and works of Jesus. Frequently this aspirant was to be found in Christ's audience. When he reported his experiences to others, he spoke favorably and enthusiastically about Jesus. In the wider sense of the term he was therefore a disciple of Jesus. His desire is to become a disciple in the more narrow sense, a steady follower, one who belongs to the inner circle. However, he does not seem to be quite ready to take this step immediately. If he does not exactly impose his own terms for joining the group, he at least inquires about the possibility of making a time reservation. His father has just died. So this aspirant asks Jesus to allow him first to go home and bury his father.[360]

According to custom, burial generally took place very soon after death (John 11:1, 14, 17; Acts 5:5, 6, 10). In Israel giving an honorable burial to the dead was considered a duty and a *kindness* (Mic. 6:8) that ranked higher than any other service requiring attention. Filial piety obliged a son to attend to this bestowal of the final act of devotion. Cf. Gen. 25:9; 35:29; 49:28—50:3; 50:13, 14, 26; Josh. 24:29, 30; etc. According to the rabbis, providing a decent burial for one's dear one took precedence over almost everything else, including attending religious services, studying the law, etc.[361] It is not surprising therefore that Jesus was asked by this man for permission to *first* bury his father. On the surface the request for delay seemed to be reasonable.

At first glance the answer he received comes as somewhat of a surprise:

---

360. The suggestion that the father had not really died, and that what the disciple meant was this, "Let me stay home with my father until he dies and I provide for his funeral," does not impress me as being very valuable. In that case Jesus would be implying that at that future point of time those whose duty it would then be to provide for the funeral would still be spiritually dead, that also the father would have died in unbelief, etc. The words of Jesus clearly apply to a *present* situation.

361. Cf. S.BK., Vol. I, pp. 487–489.

60. Jesus said to him, Let the dead bury their own dead, but as for you, go and proclaim the kingdom of God. What Jesus means is clear enough, namely, "Let those who are spiritually dead tend to the funeral of one who belongs to their own company." The question might be asked, however, "Why did not Jesus consent to this request, especially since this aspirant, having performed his functions in connection with the funeral of his father, could then immediately return, to be with Jesus?" Various possibilities occur to the mind:

1. As customarily conducted, funeral ceremonies were not exactly conducive to spiritual growth and edification. They were noisy affairs, often characterized by excessive and hypocritical mourning. See Matt. 9:23, 24; Mark 5:38–40; Luke 8:52, 53: vociferous wailing suddenly changes into derisive laughter. Jesus wanted to spare the man this agony. He wanted him to receive a blessing for himself and to be a blessing to others by spending much time with the Savior, so that, thus strengthened in the faith, this "disciple" would be able to "proclaim the kingdom of God," as Jesus orders him to do.

2. As the parallel passage (Matt. 8:18) indicates, Jesus had already issued the order to leave and was about to embark. If this man wanted to be in Christ's immediate company he must therefore join right now. Others could attend to the funeral.

3. The fact that Jesus is sovereign Lord, and that following him means doing whatever he commands, without any qualification, condition, or reservation, must be deeply impressed upon the mind and heart of this man (cf. John 15:14). Jesus knew that the aspirant was the kind of individual who stood in special need of being reminded of this.

4. Jesus wishes to teach him that in the kingdom of heaven the ties pertaining to earthly family life are superseded by those that knit together the members of the heavenly or spiritual family (cf. Luke 8:19–21 and see N.T.C. on Eph. 3:14, 15).

Mentioning these four points does not mean endorsing them all! We do not know which and how many of the suggested answers were present in the mind of Christ when he said, "Follow me. . . ." There may even have been other reasons. I trust, however, that those suggested will have shown that the *mashal* (veiled and pointed remark) here uttered, far from being unreasonable, was filled with wisdom. As given, it suited this particular person, as, for example, Luke 18:22 answered the needs of "the rich young ruler." Occasions and personalities differ, and to conclude from the answer Jesus gave that believers must never help to provide for, or attend, funerals of unbelievers, including those of members of their own family, would be completely unwarranted. It would be just as unjustified as to declare that Matt. 5:34 (see on that passage) condemns every oath.

And now the third aspirant, the one whose case is described only in Luke:

61. Still another man said, I will follow you, Lord, but first permit me to say good-bye to the folks at home.

What could be wrong with that request? Was it not altogether reasonable? However, we have already taken note of the fact that also in connection with the second aspirant, *on the surface* the request seemed moderate, yet was rejected.

In order to arrive at a reasonable interpretation of these rejected requests we should take account of the fact that Jesus was able to see what *we* cannot see. He was able to search hearts and to read minds (Luke 5:20, 22; 6:8; John 1:47; 2:25; 21:17). He knew that for this particular person it would be dangerous first to go home. His priorities had not as yet been well established. He had not as yet reached the ideal mentioned in Col. 1:18, "that in all things he [Christ] might have the pre-eminence."

In a sense this man reminds us of the first aspirant, for in both cases the would-be follower volunteers his allegiance by saying, "I will follow you." Jesus knows, however, that this third aspirant, on reaching "the folks at home," would fall an easy prey to their fervent and emotional pleas to stay home and not to join Jesus and his company.

62. Jesus replied, No one who has just put his hand to a plow and (then) continues to look back is fit for the kingdom of God.

The fact that this proverb was not original with Jesus but can be traced back to Hesiod (fl. about 800 B.C.) does not make it any less appropriate. The man who puts his hand to a plow and starts plowing forward, but then immediately looks back and continues to do so, constantly trying to plow forward while he looks behind him, cannot run a straight furrow. It is entirely proper for him to stop his plow and then, while standing still, to view what he has done, in order to correct mistakes. But to plow in one direction while looking in the opposite direction will never do.

This man's heart was divided. He should stop following the example of the Israelites (I Kings 18:21), and instead should follow in Paul's footsteps (Phil. 3:13, 14). Then, by God's grace and power, he will be "fit" for the kingdom of God, "very useful to the Master" (II Tim. 2:21). He must learn to say, and to mean it:

> Teach me to love Thee as Thine angels love,
> One holy passion filling all my frame—
> The baptism of the heaven-descended Dove;
> My heart an altar, and Thy love the flame.
>
> —George Croly[362]

---

362. Notes on Greek words, phrases, and constructions in 9:51–62 begin on page 564.

Practical Lessons Derived from 9:51–62

Verse 51

"Jesus resolutely set out," etc. See also Dan. 1:8. What, if anything, is right; and what, if anything, is wrong with New Year's resolutions?

Verse 52

"And he sent messengers on ahead," etc. There is a very practical lesson here. What is it?

Verses 53, 54

"But the people (there) refused to welcome him," etc. "Lord, do you want us to bid fire to come down from heaven and consume them?"

It is clear that the disciples had not yet taken to heart the lesson of Exod. 23:4, 5; II Kings 6:21–23; Matt. 5:44 (cf. Rom. 12:19–21).

Verses 57–62

How would you distribute the following three failures among the three aspirants, assigning *one* failure to each?

a. failure to pay undivided attention to one's task.
b. failure to render to Christ the unselfish devotion of the heart.
c. failure to allow Christ to have the pre-eminence in one's life.

Notes on Greek Words, Phrases, and Constructions in 9:51–62

Verse 51

For συμπληροῦσθαι, pres. pass. (durative) infinitive of συμπληρόω see the note on 8:23 on page 443.

ἀνάλημψις* (here gen. -εως), ascension; cf. ἀναλαμβάνω, in the sense of: to take up (used of Christ's ascension in Acts 1:2, 11, 22; I Tim. 3:16).

The expression "he set his face to go to" and (verse 53) "his face was going to" (thus literally for both expressions) remind one of Ezek. 6:2; 13:17; 14:8; 15:7. In fact, the entire passage (verses 51–53) is strongly Semitic in style. See also II Sam. 17:11b.

ἐστήρισεν (alternate form of ἐστήριξεν), third per. s. aor. act. indicat. of στηρίζω, to set, set up, fix, make strong, strengthen. See also Luke 16:26; 22:32; Acts 18:23; used several times by Paul, beginning with Rom. 1:11; see also James 5:8; I Peter 5:10; II Peter 1:12; Rev. 3:2. The verb is derived from the very prolific Aryan root STA; cf. *establish*, which in several cases is also a good *translation*.

Note the various forms, used in verses 51–57, of the verb πορεύομαι: πορεύεσθαι, pres. middle infinitive; πορευθέντες, pl. aor. participle; ἦν πορευόμενον, periphrastic imperfect; ἐπορεύθησαν, aor. indicat.; and πορευομένων, gen. pl. pres. participle. The basic meaning of the verb is: to go, travel, proceed. Cf. *Bosporus, emporium*.

Verse 52

ὡς, here indicating purpose; hence, to, in order to.

ἑτοιμάσαι, aor. act. infinitive of ἑτοιμάζω, to prepare, make ready.

Verse 53

οὐκ ἐδέξαντο, they did not welcome, refused to receive or welcome; third per. pl. aor. indicat. act. of δέχομαι, a word of frequent occurrence in the New Testament, especially in Luke's writings.

Verse 54

θέλεις, sec. per. s. pres. indicat. of θέλω, to be willing, to wish, want, be disposed to.

εἴπωμεν, first per. pl. subjunct. (here deliberative) of εἶπον (used as 2nd aor. of λέγω, here in the sense of: to bid). Note that ἵνα is not needed between θέλεις and εἴπωμεν. For θέλω without ἵνα see also Mark 10:36, 51; 14:12. There is a tendency not only in Greek but in language generally to omit words that are not felt to be strictly necessary. Usually the longer and the shorter expression exist side by side for a while. Thus also in English "in order to" often becomes "to," and many a "that" is today simply omitted.

ἀναλῶσαι, aor. infinitive act. of ἀναλίσκω (ἀνά and ἁλίσκω; hence, to use up, destroy, consume). Cf. *analyze* in the sense of "to take apart."

Verse 55

στραφείς, nom. s. masc. 2nd aor. pass. (reflexive) participle of στρέφω; see also Luke 7:9, 44; 10:22, 23; 14:25; 22:61; 23:28, the identical form in each case.

For ἐπετίμησεν see the note on 4:35 on page 267.

Verse 57

ἀκολουθήσω, both here and in verse 61, first per. s. fut. indicat. of ἀκολουθέω; cf. ἀκολούθει in verse 59, sec. per. s. pres. (durative) imperat.: follow and keep on following. Cf. *acolyte, anacoluthon.*

ἀπέρχῃ (after ὅπου ἐάν), sec. per. s. pres. subjunct. of ἀπέρχομαι, to go away, to go.

Verse 58

ἀλώπεκες, nom. pl. of ἀλώπηξ, fox; see also 13:32 and Matt. 8:20. Cf. *vulpecula, vulpine.*

φωλεούς, acc. pl. of φωλεός, lair, hole, den; so also in Matt. 8:20.

κατασκηνώσεις, acc. pl. of κατασκήνωσις, a place where a bird can set *down* (κατά) its *tent* (σκηνή); hence, a roost.

Verses 59–61

ἐπίτρεψον, in verses 59 and 61, sec. per. s. aor. imperat. of ἐπιτρέπω, to turn to, entrust, permit, allow.

θάψαι, in verses 59 and 60, aor. act. infinitive of θάπτω, to bury. Cf. *epitaph*.

ἄφες, sec. per. s. 2nd aor. imperat. of ἀφίημι, let. See the note on 4:39 on page 271.

ἀποτάξασθαι, aor. infinitive of ἀποτάσσομαι, to take leave of, bid farewell (or: say good-bye) to; so also in Mark 6:46; Acts 18:18, 21; II Cor. 2:13; but in Luke 14:33, to give up, part with. Closely related to the latter meaning is also the sense of this same verb in Josephus, *Antiquities* XI.232, to refuse.

Verse 62

ἄροτρον*, plow. Cf. *arable*.

Note aor. (punctiliar) act. participle ἐπιβαλών, lit. having put (his hand) to, followed by the pres. act. (durative) participle βλέπων, continuing to look (back). Translation, "No one who has just put his hand to a plow and (then) continues to look," etc.

εὔθετος (from εὖ and θετός, from τίθημι), well placed, well adapted, fit. So also in 14:35; in Heb. 6:7: useful.

Summary of Chapter 9:51–62

See p. 532.

Outline of Chapter 10

Theme: *The Work Thou Gavest Him to Do*

CHAPTER X

10 1 After this the Lord appointed seventy-two[363] others and sent them on ahead of him, two by two, into every town and place where he himself was about to go. 2. He said to them, "The harvest (is) plentiful but the laborers (are) few. Pray therefore the Lord of the harvest to thrust laborers into his harvest. 3 Go! Listen! I am sending y o u out as lambs in the midst of wolves. 4 Carry no purse, no traveler's bag, no sandals, and do not greet anyone on the road. 5 With respect to whatever house you enter, first say, 'Peace (be) to this house!' 6 And if a lover of peace[364] is there, y o u r peace will rest on him; but if not, it will return to y o u. 7 Remain in that very house, eating and drinking whatever they give y o u, for the worker is entitled to his wages. Do not keep moving about from house to house. 8 And with respect to whatever town y o u enter and in which y o u are welcomed, eat what is set before y o u. 9 Heal the sick who are there and tell them, 'The kingdom of God has come near to y o u!'

10 "But whenever y o u enter a town and are not welcomed, go into its streets and say, 11 'Even the dust from y o u r town that sticks to our feet we wipe off against y o u. Nevertheless, know this, that the kingdom of God has come near.' 12 I tell y o u, it will be more tolerable for Sodom in that day than for that town."

10:1-12 *The Charge to the Seventy-two (or Seventy)*

After hearing about the three would-be followers (9:57-62) it is a delight to read about a large group of sincere and enthusiastic disciples of Jesus, men who offered no excuses when called to serve. Without reservation they answered the call and, to a considerable extent, were successful in their mission (see verse 17).

Chapter 10 is clearly divisible into two parts. In Part I (verses 1-24) we are told that Jesus sent out seventy or seventy-two men to announce and prepare the people for his own coming, and with that in view to proclaim the gospel of the kingdom of God (see verse 1b). As shown in the summary on p. 533, these twenty-four verses can be divided into four paragraphs, as follows: (a) the appointment of these men and the charge given to them (verses 1-12); (b) the punishment awaiting those who reject their and/or their Master's message (verses 13-16); (c) the report of the missionaries upon their return, a report filled with joyful enthusiasm (verses 17-20); and (d) Jesus' own rejoicing voiced in praise addressed to the Father, and

---

363. According to other manuscripts *seventy*.
364. Literally: a son of peace.

his assurance, given to the returned witnesses, that they had been privileged above "many prophets and kings" (verses 21–24).

1. After this the Lord appointed seventy-two [or seventy] others and sent them on ahead of him, two by two, into every town and place where he himself was about to go.

Note the following:

a. "After this." This probably means: after Jesus started on his journey to Jerusalem, as recorded in 9:51.

b. "The Lord." Elsewhere—see N.T.C. on Mark, p. 435—it has been shown that the title *Lord* was given to Jesus long before his bodily resurrection, and that not only Luke and John but also Matthew and Mark use this appellation with reference to him. It is true, nevertheless, that Luke calls Jesus by this name far more often than do any of the other evangelists. It ascribes to the Savior ownership, authority, majesty.

c. "... appointed seventy-two. ..." Textual evidence (both here and in verse 17) is insufficient to establish, beyond reasonable doubt, whether "seventy" or "seventy-two" is correct. Even aside from this, for every argument in favor of "seventy" there is a counter-argument in support of "seventy-two." The debate might run somewhat as follows:

Brown

Seventy is right, for it is clear that Jesus is here pictured as the Antitype of Moses, who, at God's command, appointed seventy elders to assist him. On these seventy the Spirit rested. See Num. 11:16–25.

Smith

You are forgetting Eldad and Medad, on whom God's Spirit also rested (Num. 11:26), making seventy-two in all.

Brown

But by entering Trans-Jordan Jesus and these missionaries, who were sent ahead to prepare the way for him, were coming into the largely non-Jewish "world." The people of that day believed that "the world" contained seventy nations; see the Hebrew text of Gen. 10. So Jesus appointed seventy missionaries, as it were one for each nation.

Smith

But the Septuagint, i.e., Greek, text of Gen. 10 has seventy-two names of ancestors who gave rise to nations. Luke, himself a Greek, must have been aware of the analogy between the seventy-two nations of Gen. 10 and the seventy-two men whom Jesus appointed as his ambassadors.

Brown

But the Jerusalem Sanhedrin had seventy members.

Why should this have influenced Jesus in deciding on the number of heralds he appointed at this time? Besides, exactly seventy Sanhedrin members is probably not even correct, for you are forgetting the presiding officer, who certainly was also a member.

So far the debate on this rather unimportant matter.

I, for one, do not have the answer, though I lean toward seventy-two. Jesus may well have chosen *twelve disciples* (Luke 6:13–16; 9:1) to continue the line of the twelve patriarchs and twelve tribes, thereby indicating that Israel was being continued in the church of the new dispensation. Thus conceived, the number *twelve* would have symbolical significance. In harmony with this is the fact that in the book of Revelation the heavenly Jerusalem is described as having twelve foundation stones and twelve gates made of twelve pearls. There were twelve angels at the gates. On the gates were written the names of the twelve tribes. And the city itself was 12,000 stadia in length, width, and height. See Rev. 21:12–21. As to multiples of 12 (in addition to "12,000") think of the 24 thrones on which 24 elders were sitting (Rev. 4:4, 10; 11:16; 19:4), of the 1260 days during which the two witnesses prophesy (11:3), and of the 144,000 sealed individuals (7:1–8).

Now seventy-two is the multiple of 12 and 6. The number *seventy-two* would therefore be in harmony with this entire scheme of twelves. It would proclaim that our Lord appointed not only twelve leaders but also 6 × 12 = 72 other ambassadors, so that the gospel might be published far and wide. Again, this is no proof. A good argument can also be advanced for seventy (= 7 × 10).

d. "... two by two. ..." It has been shown that Luke 9:51—18:14 stands by itself, in the sense that as a rule it no longer parallels Mark. Here, however, there is a tiny exception. (There are going to be a few more exceptions before we reach 18:14.) It is Mark—he alone—who relates that also when *The Twelve* were charged, they were sent out "two by two" (6:7).

When the question is asked, "Why two by two?" practical considerations such as: to help and encourage each other (cf. Eccles. 4:9); and to be valid witnesses (Num. 35:30; Deut. 19:15; Matt. 18:16; John 8:17; II Cor. 13:1; I Tim. 5:19; Heb. 10:28) occur to the mind immediately. The same practical considerations undoubtedly also explain why the seventy-two were sent out "two by two."

Did not also John the Baptist send two of his disciples to Jesus with an important question (Luke 7:19)? At a later time we notice that Peter and John bring their united testimony (Acts 3:1; 4:1, 13, 19); that Barnabas and Saul are sent out together on their missionary journey (Acts 13:1–3); and that afterward Paul and Silas are together "commended by the brothers to the grace of God" (15:40). And let us not forget Barnabas and Mark

(15:39), Judas and Silas (15:27), Timothy and Silas (17:14), and Timothy and Erastus (19:22).

e. "(He sent them on ahead of him) . . . into every town and place where he himself was about to go." Why *all* these heralds? Because the amount of work still to be accomplished was vast, the time during which it must be completed short, and the cause important beyond comprehension.

Besides, does not the mention of these seventy or seventy-two stress the fact that kingdom work is not limited to the few; for example, to Jesus and The Twelve, but that every believer should participate? Note: first there was Jesus; then also The Twelve, now also the seventy-two; and these, in turn, are told to pray that the Lord may send forth (still more) laborers into his harvest. "There is a task for everyone. There is a task for me." Finally, it is important to realize that when Jesus himself arrives, he must be welcomed properly! See Isa. 40:3; Mal. 3:1.

2. He said to them, The harvest (is) plentiful, but the laborers (are) few. Pray therefore the Lord of the harvest to thrust laborers into his harvest.

As Jesus had done when he called The Twelve (Matt. 9:37, 38), and at least on one other occasion (John 4:35), so also now he tells his disciples—in the present case the seventy or seventy-two—that the harvest is plentiful but the laborers are few. He exhorts them to beseech the Lord of the harvest to thrust laborers into his harvest. Note the following:

a. For more on God's well-meant, yes even urgent, offer of salvation see N.T.C. on Matthew, pp. 441, 442. The Savior's deep and tender concern for man's everlasting welfare, as this reveals itself in *Luke's* Gospel, is clear also from the following passages: 10:21, 33-37; 11:42; 12:7, 32; 13:6; 17:17-19; 19:10.

b. This tender concern is present even though the territory Jesus was about to enter contained many Gentiles. Christ's love was by no means limited to Jews. Samaritans and Gentiles were also the objects of his loving concern.

c. As it was then, so ever increasingly is it true today that the field is large—it is *the world!* (Matt. 13:38)—the laborers are few. Hence, *all the more* the present passage applies to present-day conditions. The need is there *always:* hence also *now! Especially* now!

d. Note the beautiful balance maintained here between divine sovereignty and human responsibility. It is God, he alone, who is able to endow men with the qualities necessary to carry out the mission mandate. It is God who sends out—sometimes almost forcefully, thrusts out, for not all are immediately willing (Exod. 4:10, 13; I Kings 18:7-16; Esther 4:9-17; Jer. 1:4-7—equips, qualifies, ordains. On the other hand, this by no means renders superfluous human prayer and exertion. The seventy or seventy-two must pray that it may please God to send out laborers.

e. *Laborers . . . not loafers.* Let every minister, evangelist, missionary, etc., take note!

f. These laborers must work in "his"—i.e. *God's*—harvest. Those people whom we try to win for the Lord do not belong to *us,* to do with as it may please *us;* they are *his* harvest. This must always be borne in mind.

3. Go! Listen! I am sending y o u out as lambs in the midst of wolves. Since Jesus is about to make a statement of a most startling character, he introduces it by saying "Go! Listen!" There follows the saying describing the situation of the men that are being sent out. They will not be resting on a bed of ease. On the contrary, they will be as *lambs*—in a somewhat similar context Matt. 10:16 reads "sheep"—in the midst of wolves. Does this not spell utter helplessness? Extreme danger? So it seems. But note the emphatic *I* in "I am sending y o u out." It is no one less than their Shepherd who is speaking. Apart from him, to be sure, they are, and will be, in a hopeless situation. But commissioned by *him,* as *his apostles,* the opposite is true. Will *he* not gather the lambs in his arms and carry them in his bosom? See Isa. 40:11. Let them then depend on him . . . entirely. So conceived the continuation is natural:

4. Carry no purse, no traveler's bag, no sandals, and do not greet anyone on the road.

No purse or money bag, no traveler's bag or knapsack (see on 9:3) will be needed. No sandals either; that is, as has been explained in N.T.C. on Matthew, pp. 457, 458, and on Mark, p. 229, no extra pair, just those they are wearing. "Place y o u r trust entirely in God. He will supply all y o u r needs," is what the Savior means.

Moreover, since the business of the King is urgent, no time must be wasted in (typically Eastern) time-consuming greetings along the way.

At this point critics have raised an objection. They have pointed out that this so-called *Charge to the Seventy-two,* which Luke, he *alone!,* reports, bears such a close resemblance to *The Charge to The Twelve,* recorded in Matt. 10 (see also 11:21–23), that it must be regarded as fiction, merely a product of Luke's mind, with no basis in fact. Note the following resemblances:

Luke	*Matthew*
10:3	10:16
10:4	10:9, 10
10:5–7	10:11–13
10:9a	10:8a
10:10–12	10:14, 15; 11:24
10:13–15	11:21–23
10:16a	10:40

The answer is: (a) Luke evidently regarded the two charges—the one to The Twelve and the one to The Seventy-two—as different, for he reports both (9:1 ff., 10:1 ff.); (b) it is entirely reasonable to believe that Jesus, confronted with a task so comprehensive and to be accomplished within such a short period of time, would appoint seventy-two additional missionaries; and that, since the nature of their work was the same in substance as that of the smaller group, there would also be a close resemblance between the instructions imparted to each of the two groups.

5, 6. With respect to whatever house y o u enter, first say, Peace (be) to this house! And if a lover of peace is there, y o u r peace will rest on him; but if not, it will return to y o u.

When the men enter any house they must first pronounce their greeting upon it. They must say, "Peace be to this house!" This reminds us of the familiar formula, "Peace to y o u," a customary greeting *then* (Gen. 43:23; Judg. 6:23; 19:20; I Sam. 25:6; I Chron. 12:18; Ps. 122:8; Dan. 4:1; 6:25; 10:19; Luke 24:36; John 20:19, 21, 26), as even *today*. Nevertheless it makes a difference who says it. In the mind of an unthinking person it may be no more than a conventional phrase. Among friends it was and is undoubtedly the expression of a sincere wish. In the present instance, however, "Peace be to this house" is far more than a wish. In the name of their Sender these "apostles" not only *wish* peace but actually *bring* it. Cf. Num. 6:24–26. Yet, there was nothing magical about this. The special blessing was for those who by grace were worthy to receive it, not for others. If the home is undeserving "y o u r peace . . . will return to y o u," says Jesus; that is, in that case no blessing will be bestowed.

7. Remain in that very house, eating and drinking whatever they give y o u, for the worker is entitled to his wages. Do not keep moving about from house to house.

Each missionary pair must remain in the house which had proved itself worthy by extending a warm, hearty welcome. Having entered such a home, the men must consider it their headquarters until they leave that town for another place. For a possible reason for this instruction see on 9:4, where the same rule is laid down for The Twelve. We might add that the missionaries would, of course, not wish to impose too heavy a burden on any *one* family by staying too long. When they leave, what then? Move to another home in the same place? No, indeed! The King's business is urgent. When the time to leave the home has arrived, the men must move . . . not to another home in the same place, but to another place! Cf. Mark 1:36–38; Luke 4:42, 43.

Now while staying at this home Christ's ambassadors do not need to have any compunctions of conscience about getting free lodging and eating free meals. Are they not doing this home a great favor? The worker, after all, is worthy of, entitled to, his wages.

The principle Jesus here announces is rooted in the Old Testament. See Deut. 25:4, quoted first in I Cor. 9:8–12, later in I Tim. 5:18:

"For the Scripture says, 'A threshing ox you shall not muzzle, and worthy of his pay (is) the worker.'"

To every worker, therefore, whether that worker be an ox, a common laborer, or a minister of the gospel, God has given the right to partake of the fruits of his work. For more on this see N.T.C. on I and II Timothy and Titus, pp. 179–182.

8, 9. And with respect to whatever town y o u enter and in which y o u are welcomed, eat what is set before y o u.

It must be borne in mind that the men who were being sent out on this mission—at least most of them, we may well assume—were Jews. But, as has been stated previously, as heralds of Jesus they were entering Trans-Jordan, a region where many Gentiles lived. That might create a problem with respect to food. So the Master tells these seventy-two men to go right ahead and eat whatever is placed before them, without asking any questions. Cf. I Cor. 10:25, 27. This directive was entirely in line with the rest of Christ's teaching about matters clean and unclean. See Mark 7:14, 15, 19, and N.T.C. on these passages.

Continued: **Heal the sick who are there** . . . Jesus instructed and empowered this large group of heralds to heal the sick. In other words, they were to be busy doing *his* work, the very activity in which he himself was constantly engaged (Matt. 4:24; 8:16; Mark 1:29–32; 6:53–56; Luke 4:40; 7:21–23), and which he had also assigned to The Twelve (Matt. 10:8; Luke 9:2). However, equally important—perhaps even more so—was the work that must constantly accompany the healing of the sick, namely, *preaching:* **. . . and tell them, The kingdom of God has come near to y o u.** As has been shown previously—see on 4:43—that kingdom is God's kingship, rule or sovereignty, recognized in the hearts and operative in the lives of his people, and effecting their complete salvation.

In verses 8, 9, Jesus has indicated the blessings that are in store for the town that welcomes his missionaries: the gospel will be proclaimed to its inhabitants and their sick will be healed. But what happens when the town refuses to welcome these men? For this we turn to verses

10–12. But whenever y o u enter a town and are not welcomed, go into its streets and say, Even the dust from y o u r town that sticks to our feet we wipe off against y o u. This symbolic action—shaking the dust from the feet—was a public declaration of the divine displeasure resting on any place that refused the gospel. For more on this see above, under 9:5. Continued: **Nevertheless, know this, that the kingdom of God has come near.** By means of these words the grievous character of rejecting the good tidings must be impressed upon the minds and hearts of the people. They must be told that in rejecting Christ's messengers they are rejecting him . . . in fact, they are shutting themselves out! The kingdom cannot be stopped. But rejecters will bring down upon themselves its curse. Let this be proclaimed to them loudly and clearly, in order that they may still repent.

Directly addressing the seventy or seventy-two Jesus concludes his charge by saying: **I tell y o u, it will be more tolerable for Sodom in that day than for that town.**

As there are degrees of glory (I Cor. 15:41, 42), so there are also degrees of punishment (Luke 12:47, 48). Sodom, to be sure, sinned grievously (Gen. 13:13; 19:9, 13; Isa. 3:9; Lam. 4:6; II Peter 2:6, 7; Jude 7); but the cities selected by the Lord Jesus Christ for receiving *the very special privilege* of having his personal representatives sent to them with a pleading and urgent appeal will have sinned even more grievously if they reject their golden opportunity. Therefore, in the day of the final judgment *their* sentence will be even more terrifying than that which will then be pronounced on Sodom.

What is often ignored, in this connection, is that the message Jesus orders the seventy or seventy-two men to deliver to these cities if they should refuse to welcome his ambassadors is really meant not only for the wicked rejecters but even for the missionaries themselves; namely, in this sense, that it underscores and enhances the importance of Christ's gracious invitation. The effect upon these men must surely have been that they became more thoroughly convinced than ever about *the significance of their mandate,* so that, as a result, they exerted themselves all the more to be their Master's loyal representatives.

For *Practical Lessons* and *Greek Words,* etc., see pp. 585–590.

---

13 "Woe to you Chorazin! woe to you Bethsaida! for if the mighty works done in y o u had been done in Tyre and Sidon, they would have repented long ago, sitting in sackcloth and ashes.   14 But for Tyre and Sidon it will be more tolerable in the judgment than for y o u. 15 And you Capernaum, will you be exalted to heaven? To Hades you shall be thrust down![365]

16 "He who listens to y o u listens to me; but he who rejects y o u rejects me; and he who rejects me rejects him who sent me."

10:13–16 *Woes Pronounced on Impenitent Cities*

These *Woes* on the impenitent cities were first pronounced during the middle or latter part of The Great Galilean Ministry. See N.T.C. on Matthew (11:20–24), p. 494. If their presence here in Luke is viewed as an indication that they were also included in Christ's Charge to the Seventy-two, as is probably correct (see on verse 21), then Jesus must have repeated these solemn words at this time. There can be no objection to that. Do today's speakers (including preachers!) never repeat themselves?

One thing is certain: the *topical* connection with the immediately preceding is clear. Having indicated what will be the result of possible future impenitence (verses 10–12), Jesus now directs the attention of those whom he is addressing to the destiny of people who have already hardened their hearts.

13. Woe to you Chorazin! woe to you Bethsaida! for if the mighty works done in y o u had been done in Tyre and Sidon, they would have repented long ago, sitting in sackcloth and ashes. It is probable that Chorazin and

---

365. Or (based on a different reading): you shall descend!

Bethsaida were situated very close to Capernaum, which is mentioned last of all, namely, in verse 15. The ruins of present-day Kerazeh, northwest of the Sea of Galilee, and two and one-half miles north of what used to be Capernaum, are all that is left of ancient Chorazin. The Bethsaida here mentioned could be either Bethsaida Julias, located just southeast of the point where the Jordan River, coming from the north, flows into the Sea of Galilee, or else another Bethsaida, situated closer to Capernaum.[366] In view of the mention of Chorazin and Capernaum in this very connection, the latter would seem to be probable. If so, it was the Bethsaida located in the plain of Gennesaret (Mark 6:53), which stretches northwest from the Sea of Galilee. It was the home town of Philip, the place where Andrew and Peter also originally came from (John 1:44). It is easily understood that since Capernaum was for a long time Christ's headquarters, his mighty deeds would have been performed not only inside this city but also in the nearby towns of Chorazin and Bethsaida. Jesus states that if the mighty works done in the two last-named cities had been done in Tyre and Sidon, these Phoenician cities, situated more northerly, along the eastern shore of the Mediterranean, would have repented long ago. Yet, from Isa. 23 and Ezek. 26–28 one receives the definite impression that the commercial seafarers and colonizers who inhabited these cities were proud, money-mad, and cruel. Amos denounced the Tyrians for selling Israelites into slavery to the Edomites (Amos 1:9). The Phoenicians also sold "the children of Judah and the children of Jerusalem" to the Greeks (Joel 3:6). In the description of pleasure-mad, arrogant, presumptuous "Babylon" of Rev. 17–19 there is much that brings back to mind the heathen center of wickedness and seduction, Tyre. The assertion, therefore, that had Tyre and Sidon been favored in a manner similar to Chorazin and Bethsaida, the people of these Phoenician cities would have repented long ago shows with what revulsion the Lord views *those who were far more highly privileged* but had remained impenitent. The "woe" pronounced upon them amounts to a curse.

Tyre and Sidon would have repented "in sackcloth and ashes," says Jesus. Since the material of which sackcloth was made was a coarse kind of cloth, dark in color ("black as sackcloth of hair," Rev. 6:12), it was especially appropriate as a symbol of mourning. The sackcloth worn by mourners was actually a kind of shirt, with openings for neck and arms, slit down the front, and cast about the loins. It could be worn over an undergarment (Jonah 3:6) or directly over the skin (I Kings 21:27; II Kings 6:30; Job 16:15; Isa. 32:11). This symbolic reference to sorrow is even strengthened by the addition of "and ashes." Continued: **14. But for Tyre and Sidon it will be more tolerable in the judgment than for y o u.** For explanation see on verse 12.

The Lord now turns to the very heart and center of his activity, namely,

---

366. For the arguments favoring two Bethsaidas see N.T.C. on John, Vol. I, pp. 216–218.

Capernaum: **15. And you Capernaum, will you be exalted to heaven? To Hades you shall be thrust down!**

Capernaum can mean *village of Nahum*. Even so, it is not at all certain that the place was named for the Old Testament prophet who predicted Nineveh's overthrow. Originally the reference may have been to some other Nahum. Or, since Nahum, in turn, means *compassionate,* the name may also be interpreted as "village of compassion" or "of consolation." No one knows. What is established, however, is that at one time Matthew, the author of the Gospel named after him, had his office at this place. He was a "publican," that is, a tax-collector or revenue officer.

It was in the vicinity of this town that Jesus had called his first disciples (John 1:35–42). For details (including geography) see N.T.C. on John, Vol. I, pp. 92, 93, 102–108. It was here also that Peter and Andrew, James and John were subsequently invited to become "fishers of men" (Matt. 4:18–22; Luke 5:10). Capernaum became the center of Christ's activities, his headquarters during The Great Galilean Ministry. It was here that Jesus performed many miracles (Luke 4:23, 31–37; 7:1–10; John 2:12), customarily attended the synagogue, and delivered several messages, including the address on The Bread of Life (John 6:24–65). Matthew even called Capernaum Christ's "own city" (9:1).

The ruins of a Capernaum synagogue have been unearthed. It has been partly restored. That structure dates back to the second or third century A.D. It is thought that an older house of worship, probably the very one that had been provided by the centurion who loved the Jewish nation (Luke 7:5, 6), and where Jesus taught, lies buried beneath the foundation of the one uncovered. It is evident that a detachment of soldiers was garrisoned at Capernaum. The story about the royal officer whose son Jesus healed (John 4:46–54) may indicate that Capernaum was also a center of political administration.

In the year 1905 excavations were started at Tell Hum on the northwestern shore of the Sea of Galilee. They were completed by the Franciscans, who supplied evidence to show that Tell Hum is the site of ancient Capernaum, situated about two-and-a-half miles west of the place where the Jordan River, coming from the north, enters the sea.

For Jesus and his disciples the location was strategic, for from this point in (what used to be) the Zebulun-Naphtali territory, most of the towns and villages of Galilee and surroundings were easily accessible. They could be reached either by land—for Capernaum was situated on the rather thickly populated shore and on the trade route that connected Damascus and the Mediterranean—or else by sea.

By and large the population of Capernaum had remained impenitent in spite of all the labor of love which Jesus had bestowed upon it. It is for this reason that he now addresses this center of his activity in terms that remind one of Isa. 14:13, 15, where the king of Babylon is pictured as boasting that he will ascend into heaven, and is then described as actually descending into Sheol's lowest depth. In a question full of dramatic emphasis Jesus, accordingly, asks, "And you Capernaum, will you be exalted to heaven?" In other words, "You don't really expect to be exalted to heaven, do you?" As far as the form is concerned, the question is so phrased as to expect a negative answer.[367] This is irony, for Capernaum expects to be thus exalted. Swift as an arrow from a bow comes the answer, "To Hades you shall be thrust down!" Note position of Hades (before the verb) in this answer, making this curse-filled prediction all the more emphatic, an emphasis that is lost in many of the renderings. Here (and in the parallel, Matt. 11:23), as probably everywhere in the *Gospels,* but not everywhere in the entire New Testament, Hades means "hell." Note how sharply it is contrasted with "heaven." Hades is here the place of torments and of the flame (Luke 16:23, 24). See also N.T.C. on Matt. 16:18.[368] And see below, on Luke 16:23, 24.

That the utter ruin here predicted for the people of Capernaum also implied the destruction of their city is clear. As to the destruction of the city itself, what occurred here was so shocking that for centuries even Capernaum's *site* was a matter of dispute. Similarly, the punishment which was visited upon the people of Sodom and Gomorrah included the loss of their city. Nevertheless, in both cases it is the curse upon the *people* that is primary. It is as a result of their sin that the city too is destroyed, not vice versa.

16. He who listens to y o u listens to me; but he who rejects y o u rejects me; and he who rejects me rejects him who sent me.

The importance of this dominical saying can hardly be exaggerated. Jesus assures these seventy-two men that when *they* speak, *he* speaks. When the people listen to *them,* they are listening to *him.* Not only that but, since he was sent by the Father and always faithfully represents him, it follows that those who, with a receptive heart and surrendered will, cup their ears to the message of Christ's ambassadors are paying attention to Christ's *Sender.*

However, the emphasis of the passage now before us falls rather on the counterpart of this truth, namely, on the fact that anyone who *rejects* those who are commissioned by the Savior is rejected by the latter's Sender. And what could be more serious than that?

Now all this places a heavy burden of responsibility on men; not only on all prospective listeners but also on the seventy-two missionaries. It is clear that if they do not in word and deed truly represent their Lord, the comforting assurance imparted in verse 16a no longer holds for them.

On the other hand, on the assumption that a prayerful, consistent, and vigorous effort is being made by any servant of Christ—whether he be a teacher, evangelist, minister, missionary, elder, deacon, or lay witness—to

---

367. Note μὴ . . . ὑψωθήσῃ; see Gram. N.T., p. 917.

368. See the more detailed discussion in my book *The Bible on the Life Hereafter,* Chapter 17, "What Is Meant by Sheol and Hades?" pp. 83–87.

impress the message of his Lord and Savior on the hearts and lives of people, on that assumption it is Christ himself who is speaking through that messenger. Moreover, it is not only Jesus who is being accepted or rejected but God Triune, who reveals himself in and through the Mediator.

A generation or so ago much was being said and written about *Christus Mysticus;* that is, "Christ and those who by sovereign grace are his own united by means of an invisible bond." What a comfort this Spirit-wrought, organic, vital, transforming, personal union, definitely presupposed in the present passage! We find its echo not only in one or two other passages— e.g., Matt. 10:40 and John 13:20—but also, whether completely or in part, in the following references: Zech. 2:8; Matt. 10:25; 18:5; 25:40; John 10:27–30; 15:5, 18–21; Acts 9:4, 5 (22:7, 8; 26:14, 15); Rom. 8:38, 39; II Cor. 1:5; 4:10; Gal. 1:16; 2:20; 6:17; Eph. 4:15, 16; 5:23–32; Col. 1:24, to which others could easily be added.

For *Practical Lessons* and *Greek Words*, etc., see pp. 585–590.

---

17 The seventy-two[369] returned with joy, saying, "Lord, even the demons were subject to us in thy name!" 18 He said to them, "I was watching Satan fall from heaven like lightning. 19 Look, I have given y o u authority to step on snakes and scorpions, and over all the power of the enemy, and nothing will in any way hurt y o u. 20 Nevertheless, it is not this in which y o u should rejoice, that the spirits submit to y o u, but this, that y o u r names are recorded in heaven."

10:17–20 *The Return of the Seventy-two (or Seventy)*

17. The seventy-two returned with joy, saying, Lord, even the demons were subject to us in thy name!

How long it took the seventy-two to accomplish their mission and at which place they returned to Jesus has not been revealed. What we do know is that they returned with joy and expressed their elation over the fact that even the demons had been subject to them in Christ's name. Evidently they had been successful in their mission: probably both in their preaching and in their healing and, what surprised them—because as far as we know it had not even been included in the task that had been assigned to them (see verse 9)—also in the matter of *demon-expulsion!*

18. He said to them, I was watching Satan fall from heaven like lightning.

Of this passage there have been several interpretations:

a. Jesus meant, "I saw Satan's original fall, his expulsion from heaven."

b. He meant, "In my victory over the devil during the wilderness temptation I saw his fall."

The trouble with both of these interpretations is that they are not contextual.

---

369. Some manuscripts read *seventy.*

The right view is undoubtedly that expressed by Godet (*op. cit.*, Vol. II, p. 24) in these words: "[Jesus meant] While y o u were expelling the subordinates [the demons] I was seeing the master [Satan] fall."

While in the present passage Jesus speaks about Satan's sudden (note "like lightning") *fall*—sudden and startling because the disciples had not expected this victory; perhaps even because the devil himself had not anticipated it—elsewhere the Master refers to the prince of evil's *ejection* (his *being cast out,* John 12:31, 32), and this in connection with Christ's own activity of drawing "all men" to himself. To this *falling* and *being cast out* should be added one more symbolic expression, that of *binding* "the strong man," Beelzebul (Matt. 12:27, 29). In the interpretation of Rev. 20:1–3 we should certainly give these passages their due. A good exegetical rule is always to allow Scripture to interpret Scripture!

One important item should be added to this interpretation: in all probability the Master's exalted language, "I was watching Satan fall from heaven like lightning," was not only a reference to this *one* event, namely, the success of the seventy-two, but rather to all similar events that would take place afterward. In other words, Jesus viewed the triumph of these seventy-two as being symptomatic of ever so many other victories over Satan throughout the course of the new dispensation, triumphs accomplished through the work of thousands of other missionaries. He was looking far into the future (cf. Matt. 24:14). He saw the ultimate discomfiture of the ugly dragon and all his minions.

Continued: **19. Look, I have given y o u authority to step on snakes and scorpions, and over all the power of the enemy, and nothing will in any way hurt y o u.**

These words have frequently been quoted in close connection with Mark 16:18. A literal interpretation is then given to both passages. At times Acts 28:3 is also cited. But Paul did not deliberately pick up a venomous snake nor did he step on it. As to the authenticity of Mark 16 (16:9–20) see N.T.C. on Mark, pp. 682–687. In the passage now under discussion, namely, Luke 10:19, the figurative explanation is almost certainly the correct one. Note the following:

a. Jesus often made use of figurative language, though such language was frequently interpreted literally (Matt. 16:6–12; Luke 8:52, 53; John 2:19–21; 3:3, 4; 4:13–15; 6:51, 52; 11:11–13, etc.).

b. In the immediately preceding passage (verse 18) the Lord had used symbolical language when he spoke of seeing Satan falling from heaven like lightning.

c. If elsewhere Satan is called "dragon" and "serpent" (Rev. 12:9; 20:2), why should it be strange if also here in Luke 10:19 the domain of the prince of evil is called that of snakes and scorpions? Is it not Satan's intention to *poison* the minds of men and to impart the *sting* of death to all who oppose him?

d. There is no record of any *literal* fulfilment of this statement.

e. The true interpretation is also supported by the explanatory expression "(I have given y o u authority over) . . . *all the power of the enemy.*" For explanation see Rom. 16:20, "The God of peace will soon crush Satan under y o u r feet."

As to the promise, "And nothing will in any way hurt y o u," see John 10:27, 28; Rom. 8:28–39.

Jesus took delight in the joy of the seventy-two. However, he did more than that: he purified that joy by telling them: **20. Nevertheless, it is not this in which y o u should rejoice, that the spirits submit to y o u, but this, that y o u r names are recorded in heaven.**

Jesus does not mean that these men erred in rejoicing over their God-given power over demons. Did not their ability to cast them out redound to God's glory? Did it not also result in delivering the enslaved from the powers of darkness? What the Master must have meant was that authority over demons was, after all, insignificant in comparison with having one's name recorded in heaven's book of life. Cf. Isa. 4:3; Dan. 12:1; Rev. 3:5; 20:12, 15.

Casting out demons ceases when life here on earth ends. But right standing with God, resulting in everlasting salvation to his glory, never ends. Besides, authority over demons does not guarantee salvation. It is entirely possible that even upon Judas had been bestowed the ability to cast out demons. See Luke 9:1. But that did not make him a saved man!

For *Practical Lessons* and *Greek Words,* etc., see pp. 585–590.

---

21 At that time Jesus rejoiced greatly in the Holy Spirit, and said, "I praise thee Father, Lord of heaven and earth, that thou didst hide these things from the wise and learned (people) and didst reveal them to babes; yes Father, for such was thy good pleasure. 22 All things have been handed over to me by my Father, and no one knows who the Son is except the Father, and no one knows who the Father is except the Son and anyone to whom the Son chooses to reveal him."

23 And turning to his disciples he said privately, "Blessed (are) the eyes that see what y o u are seeing! 24 For I tell y o u that many prophets and kings wanted to see what y o u are seeing, but did not see it, and to hear what y o u are hearing, but did not hear it."

10:21–24 *The Rejoicing of Jesus*
Cf. Matt. 11:25–27; 13:16, 17

The beginning of this paragraph so closely resembles what is found in Matthew's Gospel that the opinion of many, namely, that the same event is being described in Matt. 11:25 ff. as here in Luke 10:21 ff., may well be correct. That event was the return of the "seventy," or perhaps better, as has been indicated, the "seventy-two."

Verses 1–24 of Luke's tenth chapter are clearly a unit: the charge to the seventy-two (verses 1–12), the serious consequences of rejecting their (hence their Savior's) message (verses 13–16), their return and exuberant report (verses 17–20), and Jesus' own rejoicing coupled with the benediction he pronounced on the seventy-two (verses 21–24) belong together.

21. At that time Jesus rejoiced greatly in the Holy Spirit, and said, I praise thee Father, Lord of heaven and earth, that thou didst hide these things from the wise and learned (people) and didst reveal them to babes; yes Father, for such was thy good pleasure.

"At that time" here indicates "at the time of the return of the seventy-two and the report they brought." By mentioning the fact that Jesus rejoiced greatly "in the Holy Spirit" Luke means that this Spirit, by which the Savior had been anointed (4:18), was the cause and originator of his joy and thanksgiving. As was indicated in the *Introduction,* point I A 5 d, one of the many things which Luke and Paul have in common is their stress on the doctrine of the Holy Spirit.

Filled, then, with the Holy Spirit, and rejoicing because of the report brought by the seventy-two, Jesus lifts up his heart and voice to his Father, and says, "I praise thee Father," etc.

Jesus does not say "Our Father," the form of address he taught his disciples to use, but "Father," and in verse 22 "my Father," and this because the One who had sent him was and is his "Father" in a unique sense.

Altogether fitting is also the next title of address, *Lord of heaven and earth.* As such the Father is the sovereign Ruler, whose decisions must not be criticized.

The question may be asked, "But how could Jesus praise the Father not only for *revealing to some* matters touching salvation, but even for *concealing* them from others? Perhaps the context supplies the answer, at least as far as an answer is possible. Jesus says, "(I praise thee Father . . . that thou didst hide these things) *from the wise and learned people.*" The reference seems to be to those who were "wise in their own conceits" (Rom. 11:25; cf. 12:16). Is not he the One who resists the proud but imparts grace to the humble (James 4:6)? That the Lord actually is thinking about conceited people as contrasted with those who are humble seems to follow also from the words "and didst reveal them to babes."

In the spiritual sense "babes" are those who have no confidence in self but are conscious of their complete dependence on the might and mercy of the heavenly Father, in whom they have placed their trust:

"For thus says the high and lofty One who inhabits eternity, whose name is holy: I dwell in the high and holy place, with him also who is of a contrite and humble spirit, to revive the spirit of the humble, and to revive the heart of the contrite" (Isa. 57:15).

It is as if the Mediator wishes to linger for a moment on this comforting thought, for in reverence and adoration he now continues, "Yes Father, for such was thy good pleasure." Says H. Bavinck, "In a certain sense the fall, sin, and eternal punishment are included in God's decree and are willed by him. But this is true *in a certain sense* only, and not in the same sense as

583

grace and salvation. These are the objects of his delight; but God does not delight in sin, neither does he take pleasure in punishment."[370]

Whatever the sinner needs Jesus has at his disposal. He *has* all and *knows* all. **22. All things have been handed over to me by my Father, and no one knows who the Son is except the Father, and no one knows who the Father is except the Son and anyone to whom the Son chooses to reveal him.** This statement varies slightly, but not at all essentially, from its parallel in Matt. 11:27.

The Son *has* whatever the sinner needs. He has whatever is necessary for carrying out his mediatorial task. He was endowed with the Spirit of Jehovah, that is, with the Spirit of wisdom and understanding, counsel and might, knowledge and the fear of Jehovah (Isa. 11:1, 2). All these spiritual qualities and many more have been entrusted to the Mediator by the Father, in order that from him as the Fountain they might flow out to others. Can anything be lacking in the Son's saving power? No, indeed, for so inexhaustible are his resources that the Father alone knows the Son. It is the Father alone who is able to penetrate to the depths of the Son's essence, his infinite treasures of wisdom, grace, power, etc.

In order to be saved and to live to the glory of God Triune, does the sinner need to know the will of the Father? No one knows who the Father is except the Son... and now notice the significant and very comforting addition: "and anyone to whom the Son chooses to reveal him." Truly

> Thou, O Christ, art all I want;
> More than all in thee I find.
>
> —Charles Wesley

Up to this moment Jesus has been addressing the seventy-two, to be sure (see especially verses 18–20), but in the presence of other people. Now he turns definitely to the large group of returned missionaries, and away from whatever crowd may have been present. This little touch, graphic and interesting, shows that Luke must have received his information from eyewitnesses. How otherwise would he have known this? Of course, under the guidance of the Holy Spirit. We read:

23, 24. And turning to his disciples he said privately, Blessed (are) the eyes that see what y o u are seeing! For I tell y o u that many prophets and kings wanted to see what y o u are seeing, but did not see it, and to hear what y o u are hearing, but did not hear it.

In substance these words—with slight variation; for example, "righteous persons" instead of "kings" as here—had also been addressed to The Twelve. See Matt. 13:16, 17. But now they are being spoken to this far larger group of witnesses.

---

370. H. Bavinck, *Gereformeerde Dogmatiek,* Vol. II, 3rd edition, Kampen, 1918, "Het Dogma over God," p. 405; or, for those who cannot read Dutch, see my published translation (of this theological *locus*), which bears the title *The Doctrine of God,* Grand Rapids, 1955, p. 390.

What a difference between, *on the one hand,* many prophets and kings, namely those living on earth during the old dispensation; and even then not all the "kings" but such devout monarchs among them as David, Hezekiah, and Josiah; and, *on the other hand,* these seventy-two ambassadors! To be sure, even to the saints of the old dispensation glimpses of coming glory were given at times, even while these men were still living on earth. Thus, with the eyes of faith the *prophet* Isaiah in a *vision* saw Messiah's glory and spoke of him (John 12:41). *King* David in the Spirit ascribed to the coming Messiah the name *Lord* (Ps. 110:1; cf. Matt. 22:44; see also Mark 12:36; Luke 20:42, 43; Acts 2:34, 35; Heb. 1:13). But none of these prophets and kings, while still on earth, *saw* the incarnate Christ. None *heard* his words. None witnessed his miracles. They all "died in faith, not having received the fulfilment of the promises" (Heb. 11:13, cf. verse 39). That "better thing" (Heb. 11:40), the fulness of Messianic blessing, had been reserved for believers of the new day. And among all these believers The Twelve and the Seventy-two had been among those closest to Jesus. How blessed they were![371]

Practical Lessons Derived from 10:1–24

Verse 2a

"The harvest (is) plentiful." That was true then. How much more now!

Verse 2b

"Pray therefore the Lord of the harvest to thrust laborers into his harvest." Though all depends on God, he accomplishes his work by human means. Does this amount to saying, "God has no hands but our hands"?

Verse 5

"First say, 'Peace (be) to this house!'" Having entered the home, do not wait for those who live there to start the conversation. It is you who should start. And let your approach be positive, not negative.

Verse 7

"The worker is entitled to his wages." Congregations and denominations should take this to heart. Those who devote themselves entirely and wholeheartedly to religious work—ministers, missionaries, etc.—should not be regarded as objects of charity. The congregation or denomination *owes* them a living.

Verse 14

"But for Tyre and Sidon it will be more tolerable in the judgment than for y o u." Responsibility varies with opportunity, and over the course of the centuries how these opportunities have increased!

---

371. Notes on Greek words, phrases, and constructions in 10:1–24 begin on page 586.

Verse 16b

"He who rejects y o u rejects me; and he who rejects me rejects him who sent me."
What requirements must a minister satisfy before he has a right to believe that he
has been or is being unjustly rejected? What standards must a congregation meet
before it has the right to feel aggrieved because of its minister?

Verse 18

"I was watching Satan fall from heaven like lightning." The believer is comforted
by the assurance that by grace the victory belongs to him. It is his because it is
Christ's.

Verse 20

"Nevertheless, it is not this in which y o u should rejoice, that the spirits submit to
y o u, but this, that y o u r names are recorded in heaven." How often men rejoice
in earthly honors or accomplishments! How little in heavenly blessings, past, present, and future!

Verse 24

"Many prophets and kings wanted to see what y o u are seeing, but did not see it."
The poorest Christian is richer by far than the richest worldling!

Notes on Greek Words, Phrases, and Constructions in 10:1–24

Verse 1

The textual evidence is evenly balanced between "seventy" and "seventy-two."
Note distributive use of ἀνά; cf. 9:14.
πρὸ προσώπου, lit. "before his face" (A.V.), the word *face* again, as in 9:51–53,
used in Semitic sense.

Verse 2

The word θερισμός, harvest, occurs three times in this verse; nominative, genitive, and accusative; nowhere else in Luke. It is found also in Matthew, Mark, John,
and Revelation. At times this word refers to harvest-time and harvesting (Matt.
13:30). There, as also in Rev. 14:15, harvest-time indicates the final judgment. But
here in Luke 10:2 (cf. John 4:35) "the people" are viewed as a crop or field that is
ripe for the harvest. Cf. *thermometer*. Harvest-time generally comes during the latter
part of the "heat season" (θέρος).

Verse 3

ἄρνας, lambs, acc. pl., as if from ἀρνός, but the nominative was no longer in use.
See, however, ἀρήν; and in the New Testament ἀμνός (John 1:29, 36; Acts 8:32;
I Peter 1:19).

586

Verse 4

βαλλάντιον*, purse; πήραν, traveler's bag; ὑποδήματα, sandals; acc. forms of, respectively, βαλλάντιον, πήρα, and ὑπόδημα (ὑπό, under, plus δέω, to bind; hence, underbinding, a sole fastened to the foot with thongs).

ἀσπάσησθε, sec. per. pl. aor. middle subjunct. of ἀσπάζομαι, to greet.

Verse 6

υἱὸς εἰρήνης, son of peace, probably again a Hebraism, meaning only that it occurs with greater frequency in Hebrew than in Greek. It indicates that the person or thing so described stands in some relation to the object mentioned after "son of." That relation may be one of quality, resemblance, derivation, destiny, etc. See the diagram on p. 588. In Eccles. 12:4 notice even "daughters of music." "Musical sounds" perhaps? Or simply "songbirds"? See J. F. A. Sawyer, "The Ruined House in Ecclesiastes 12: A Reconstruction of the Original Parable," *JBL* 94 (1975), p. 530. See p. 588 for diagram.

ἐπαναπαήσεται, third per. s. fut. indicat. middle of ἐπαναπαύω, to rest upon; in Rom. 2:17, to rely upon. Cf. *pause.*

Note the two prefixes ἐπί and ἀνά; hence, as if "to lean *back upon.*"

ἀνακάμψει, third per. s. fut. indicat. act. of ἀνακάμπτω, basically: to bend back; in the New Testament (besides Luke 10:6 also Matt. 2:12; Acts 18:21; Heb. 11:15), to turn back, to return.

Verse 7

μεταβαίνετε, sec. per. pl. pres. (durative) imperative (here in a prohibition) of μεταβαίνω, to go or move from one place to another.

Verse 8

παρατιθέμενα, acc. pl. neut. pres. pass. participle of παρατίθημι, to set before. Cf. 9:16.

Verse 9

ἤγγικεν, third per. s. perf. indicat. act. of ἐγγίζω, to approach, come near; so here and in verse 11: has come near. Cf. ἐγγύς, near, as to relationship, place, or time.

Verse 10

πλατεία, wide avenue, street; from πλατύς, broad, wide. Cf. *place, plateau.*

Verse 11

κολληθέντα, acc. s. masc. aor. pass. participle of κολλάω, to stick, adhere to, unite with. Cf. *colloid.* There may even be a distant connection between this Greek word and *glue.*

ἀπομασσόμεθα, first per. pl. pres. indicat. middle of ἀπομάσσω*, to wipe off.

The Probably Hebraic Expression "son(s) of"

	Reference	Phrase *"son" or "sons" of*	Probable Meaning
1	I Sam. 14:52	*bravery*	brave men
2	II Sam. 3:34	*wickedness*	wicked people
3	II Sam. 7:10	*violence*	violent men
4 & 5	I Sam. 26:16; Psalm 79:11	*death*	men doomed to die or deserving to die
6	Matt. 23:15	*hell*	man worthy of and bound for hell
7	Mark 3:17	*thunder*	men of fierce disposition
8	Luke 10:6	*peace*	lovers of peace
9	Luke 16:8a	*this world*	worldly people
10	Luke 16:8b	*the light*	people who possess the "light" of wisdom, holiness, joy, etc.
11	John 17:12	*perdition*	man doomed to perish, utterly lost (Judas)
12	Acts 4:36	*exhortation* *(or encouragement)*	expert in imparting encouragement
13 & 14 15	Eph 2:2 & 5:6; Col. 3:6	*disobedience*	disobedient people
16	I Thess. 5:5	*light and of day*	same as No. 10 (Luke 16:8b)
17	II Thess. 2:3	*perdition*	same as No. 11 (John 17:12), but now with reference to the Antichrist.

Verse 12

ἀνεκτότερον, more tolerable (so also in verse 14), comparat. of ἀνεκτός, -ή, -όν. Cf. ἀνέχω, to hold up under, put up with, endure, bear, tolerate. See the note on 9:41 on page 524.

Verse 13

πάλαι, adverb indicating past time; here: long ago.

σποδῷ, dat. s. of σποδός, ashes.

μετενόησαν, third per. pl. aor. indicat. of μετανοέω, to undergo a basic change, to be converted; here, because of context—note "in sackcloth and ashes"—to repent. For more on this verb see N.T.C. on Matthew, pp. 196, 197; on Mark, pp. 57, 58.

Verse 15

καταβιβασθήσῃ, sec. per. s. fut. indicat. pass. of καταβιβάζω*, to cause to descend; hence, in pass.: to be made to descend, to be thrust down. However, the reading is in doubt. The variant καταβήσῃ (as in Matt. 11:23) may be correct also here in Luke 10:15. If so, the meaning would be, "To Hades you shall descend."

Verse 16

ἀθετῶν, nom. s. masc. pres. act. participle of ἀθετέω (ἀ and τίθημι), to set aside, reject. Note also the third per. s. ἀθετεῖ. Each form occurs twice in this verse.

Verse 18

Here ἐθεώρουν is first per. s. imperf. indicat. act. of θεωρέω, not third per. pl. though the form is the same. The meaning is: to observe, watch; hence here "I was watching." On this verb and its synonyms see also N.T.C. on John, Vol. I, p. 85, footnote 33.

ἀστραπή, lightning, but in Luke 11:36 shining brightness.

Verse 19

πατεῖν, pres. act. infinitive of πατέω, to tread. Cf. *path.* ὄφις, serpent; here gen. pl. ὄφεων. Cf. *ophidian.* Note also the strong negative, which may be rendered "nothing at all," "nothing in any way."

Verse 20

ἐγγέγραπται, third per. s. perf. indicat. pass. of ἐγγράφω, in the New Testament occurring only here and in II Cor. 3:2, 3, to record, write in. The names have been, and thus remain, recorded. Once written, they stand. Cf. *engrave.*

Verse 21

For ἠγαλλιάσατο (cf. 1:47), third per. s. aor. indicat. middle of ἀγαλλιάω, to leap or thrill with joy, to rejoice greatly, see the note on 1:14 on page 80.

ἐξομολογοῦμαι, first per. s. pres. indicat. middle of ἐξομολογέω, here and in Matt. 11:25 in the sense of: to praise, to give thanks. For more detailed discussion of this verb see N.T.C. on Matthew, footnote 477 on pp. 497, 498.

ἀπέκρυψας, sec. per. s. aor. indicat. act. of ἀποκρύπτω (= ἀπό and κρύπτω), to hide (away), conceal. Cf. *Apocrypha.*

συνετῶν, gen. pl. of συνετός; cf. συνίημι, to send together. The reference is to those who are able "to put two and two together," that is, to the intelligent or learned people. Note the last four words of verse 21; literally, "for so it was [or: became] good pleasure before thee," another marked Semitism.

εὐδοκία, good pleasure. Sometimes this noun is used with reference to human delight, good will, pleasure, or resolve (Rom. 10:1; Phil. 1:15; II Thess. 1:11). So it is also with the verb εὐδοκέω (Rom. 15:26, 27; II Cor. 5:8; I Thess. 2:8; 3:1; II Thess. 2:12). When the reference of the noun is to God's good pleasure or delight the contexts are as·follows: Those with whom God is delighted (literally: "men of [God's] good pleasure," Luke 2:14); God's delight in choosing a people for himself (Eph. 1:5, 9) and in the fact that, by means of the strength imparted by God, believers are working out their own salvation (Phil. 2:13). As to the verb, the action positively expressed, the references are to the Father's delight in the Son (Matt. 3:17; 12:18; 17:5; Mark 1:11; Luke 3:22; II Peter 1:17), to his good pleasure in (a) giving his children the kingdom (Luke 12:32), (b) the salvation of his people through the preaching of the gospel (I Cor. 1:21), (c) revealing his Son in Paul (Gal.

1:15), and (d) the decision that in Christ all the fulness should dwell (Col. 1:19). Negative references: God is *not* delighted with unbelievers (I Cor. 10:5), with burnt-offerings (Heb. 10:6, 8), and with those who shrink back (Heb. 10:38).

Verse 22

According to Lenski's *Interpretation of St. Luke*, p. 373, the aorist παρεδόθη ("handed over" or "entrusted") refers to the incarnation. The tense itself, however, says nothing whatever about the length of time in which the indicated action took place, nor does it tell us when it took place. In the immediately preceding context (verse 21), however, there was a reference to the Father's sovereign *good pleasure* (εὐδοκία) regarding the revelation of the matter of salvation to babes. This *good pleasure* (same word in the original), used in a similar connection, is by Paul linked with the election and foreordination "in Christ" that took place "before the foundation of the world" (Eph. 1:4, 5). What was decided from all eternity was realized in time (Eph. 1:7 ff.). It would seem, therefore, that also here in Luke 10:22 it is not necessary or even advisable to connect the action indicated by παρεδόθη with one particular moment in Christ's existence, for example, with the incarnation. The entire process—what happened in eternity, at the incarnation, at the baptism, and even later—may well be indicated by the verb. The use of the aorist is no obstacle. See also N.T.C. on John, Vol. I, p. 125, footnote 64.

βούληται, third per. s. pres. subjunct. of βούλομαι, with "the Son" as subject. The meaning of the verb is: to be willing.

---

25 And behold, a certain law-expert stood up to test him. "Teacher," he asked, "What must I do to inherit[372] everlasting life?" 26 He answered, "What is written in the law? How do you read (it)?" 27 He answered, "You shall love the Lord your God with all your heart, with all your soul, with all your strength, and with all your mind; and your neighbor as yourself." 28 Jesus replied, "You have answered correctly; keep on doing this, and you shall live." 29 But he, wishing to justify himself, said, "And who is my neighbor?" 30 Taking him up on this, Jesus said:

"A certain man was going down from Jerusalem to Jericho, and he fell among robbers. They stripped him, struck him blow upon blow, and went off, leaving him half dead. 31 Now a priest happened to be going[373] down that road, but when he saw him, passed by on the opposite side. 32 So too a Levite came to the place, and when he saw him passed by on the opposite side. 33 But a certain Samaritan, as he traveled, came down to him, and upon seeing him his heart went out to him. 34 So he approached him and bandaged his wounds, pouring on oil and wine. Then he mounted the man on his own beast, took him to an inn, and took care of him. 35 The next day he took out two denarii, gave them to the innkeeper and said, 'Take care of him, and whatever more you spend I myself will duly repay you when I return.' 36 Which of these three, do you think, proved to be a neighbor to the man who fell into (the hands of) the robbers?" 37 The law-expert replied, "The man who took pity on him." Jesus said to him, "Go and keep on doing likewise."

---

372. Or: to obtain possession of.
373. Or: by coincidence was going.

10:25-37 *The Parable of The Samaritan Who Cared*

A. *A preliminary conversation*
between
Jesus and a law-expert

The connection, if any, between the immediately preceding account (10:21-24) and the one here introduced is unclear. In the Summary (p. 533) a mere possibility has been suggested.

It is true that a digest of the law, similar to the one found here in verse 27, also occurs in Matt. 22:37; Mark 12:29-31, but the two accounts—Matthew-Mark's and Luke's—do not describe the same incident:

a. In Matthew-Mark it is Jesus himself who summarizes the law; in Luke the law-expert does this.

b. In Matthew-Mark the summary is given in answer to the question, "Which is the great commandment in the law?" In Luke it is given in response to, "What is written in the law? How do you read (it)?"

c. In Matthew-Mark Jesus has something good to say about the scribe. In Luke the description given with respect to the law-expert is not nearly as favorable.

d. The incident reported in Matthew-Mark occurred on Tuesday of Passion Week; the one related here in Luke occurred earlier.

25. And behold, a certain law-expert stood up to test him. Teacher, he asked, What must I do to inherit everlasting life?

Though certainty is lacking with respect to the precise circumstances that gave rise to this question, the following reconstruction is probably not wide of the mark:

Jesus has been teaching the people. Before he leaves, a law-expert rises. For a description of the group to which he belonged see on 5:17. Supposedly well-versed in the Pentateuch, this man attempts to embarrass Jesus. He tries to show him up before the public. It is clear both from verse 25 ("he stood up to test him") and verse 29 ("but he, wishing to justify himself") that this man's motives were far from honorable.

The question he asked must have sounded innocent, commendable even: "What must I do to inherit [or: obtain possession of] everlasting life?"

"Everlasting life," how beautiful the term, and how superlatively precious the essence indicated by it! It refers to the kind of life that is not only endless in duration but also priceless in quality. It embraces such treasures as "the love of God shed abroad in our hearts" (Rom. 5:5), "the peace of God that surpasses all understanding" (Phil. 4:7), "joy inexpressible and full of glory" (I Peter 1:8), and "fellowship with God the Father and with his Son" (John 17:3). It is not suggested that this law-expert was aware of the full significance of the term he used, but it must be admitted that he was making inquiries about a most important matter. On the other hand, does not the very fact that everlasting life is such a glorious commodity make a wrongly motivated question about it all the more reprehensible?

26. He answered, What is written in the law? How do you read (it)?
Note how marvelously Jesus parries the question. Instead of answering it, he asks the lawyer a counter-question. By implication he is also immediately informing the questioner that he, Jesus, is not teaching a new doctrine; he is adhering strictly to the basic principles of *God's holy law*. Cf. Matt. 5:17.

27. He answered, You shall love the Lord your God with all your heart, with all your soul, with all your strength, and with all your mind; and your neighbor as yourself.

The law-expert's answer was a correct restatement of Deut. 6:5 and Lev. 19:18. These passages imply that the very essence of all true religion is love, outgoingness; that this love must have both God and the neighbor as its objects; that in relation to God it must be exercised by all the faculties with which God has gifted man, and must be wholehearted—note the fourfold "with all"—and that with respect to the neighbor it must be neither less in extent than nor inferior in quality to the love for self.

28. Jesus replied, You have answered correctly; keep on doing this, and you shall live.

The answer is clear. If any human being would actually fulfil this law of love to perfection, he would indeed obtain everlasting life.

There was nothing wrong with this high requirement of the law: "The law is holy, and the commandment is holy and righteous and good" (Rom. 7:12). "The man who does these things will live by them" (Gal. 3:12). The trouble is not with the divine principle that perfect obedience results in everlasting life. What, then, is wrong? Paul answers in these words, "We know that the law is spiritual; *but I am carnal, sold under sin*" (Rom. 7:14). If only the law-expert will now admit this. If only he will cry out, "O God, be merciful to me, the sinner!" If he will do this, Jesus can supply the further answer to the lawyer's question, that answer being, "Come to *me* you who are weary and burdened, and I will give you rest." See Matt. 11:28. Cf. John 3:16, 36; 5:24; 6:51; 7:37; 10:27, 28; Rev. 22:17.

What the law-expert does, however, is the very opposite. He knows, of course, that he has by no means "arrived," has not at all reached the goal of perfection. So he tries to exculpate himself. He seems to be thinking, "The law is not very clear, especially in the matter of loving the neighbor. Who is my neighbor anyway? Let Jesus provide a definition, a precise description or formulation."

Undoubtedly the questioner, proud man that he probably is (cf. Luke 18:9), is already chuckling within, thinking, "I have you where I want you now. You will never be able to answer this difficult question." He is again trying to lure Jesus into committing a faux pas, a blunder. Simultaneously he is trying to absolve himself from any guilt: **29. But he, wishing to justify himself, said, And who is my neighbor?**

On this point there was a wide variety of opinion among the Jews.[374]

---

374. See S.BK., Vol. I, p. 353.

There were those who perverted the command of Lev. 19:18 into meaning: "You shall love your neighbor *and hate your enemy.*" Jesus refutes this interpretation in Matt. 5:43–48. A widely accepted view seems to have been, "Love your neighbor, *the Israelite.*" The Pharisees, however, narrowed this down even more, namely, to "Love your neighbor, *the Pharisee.*" They reasoned, "But this rabble that does not know the law, accursed are they" (John 7:49). And the Qumran people were declaring that anyone who did not belong to their little group was "a son of darkness" and should be hated.[375]

It is clear, therefore, that with the question, "And who is my neighbor?" the law-expert tried to quiet his own conscience and embarrass Jesus.

B. *The parable*

At this point in the conversation Jesus begins to tell his parable, a story that will live forever. By means of it he is going to show the law-expert that the latter's very approach, his very question, is wrong.

30. Taking him up on this, Jesus said: A certain man was going down from Jerusalem to Jericho, and he fell among robbers. They stripped him, struck him blow upon blow, and went off, leaving him half dead.

"A certain man," or simply "A man." Though Jesus does not say to what nationality this person belonged, the story itself makes it clear that the man in question was a Jew. If he had not been a Jew the Lord would have said so.

This man, then, was going down from Jerusalem, about .9 kil. (3000 ft.) above sea level, to Jericho, over .3 kil. (more than 1000 ft.) below the level of the Mediterranean Sea. Since the distance between Jerusalem and Jericho (to the east) is about 27+ kilometers (17 miles), it is immediately obvious that the decline is rather steep. As a photograph of part of this road (No. 351 on p. 123 of Grollenberg, *Atlas of the Bible*) shows, this road passes through mountainous territory. It is rugged and rocky, and during the days of Christ's sojourn on earth—and, in fact, until rather recently—dangerous for traveling, skirted, as it is, by many a cave or hollow, facilitating escape for robbers and other criminals.

According to the parable, then, this man, traveling all by himself, was attacked by highwaymen. Escape was impossible, for, according to the Greek original, the robbers surrounded him. They stripped him; and this, we may be sure, not only of his clothing but of whatever he had taken along with him. If up to this point he had been riding on a donkey, they took that. If he had any money on him, they did not allow him to keep that, etc. Quickly he was rendered helpless, for they struck him blow upon blow. In colloquial language we might say, "They beat him up, socking him again and again," until they left him lying along the side of the road, half dead.

Then they left. Will anyone come to the rescue? Or is he about to die?

---

375. See M. Burrows, *The Dead Sea Scrolls,* New York, 1956, p. 257.

31. Now a priest happened to be going down that road, but when he saw him, passed by on the opposite side. How unfeeling! And that for a *priest,* a holy man! In fact, one who only a little while ago had probably been engaged in sacred temple activities, and was now very likely on his way home, traveling from Jerusalem to Jericho, where many a priest and Levite lived.

This priest, a Jew of course, refuses to render assistance to a fellow Jew. He avoids his duty and, instead of "rescuing the perishing" who needs him very badly, he passes by on the opposite side of the road.

For such base neglect there is no excuse. The attempt to absolve him by theorizing that by coming into contact with a corpse he would incur ritual impurity, making it impossible for him to function in the temple, fails. For, first of all, he was not now on his way to the temple but homeward bound, and he might not have to return to the temple for some time. See on Luke 1:8, 23. And even more important is the fact that showing mercy to those in need is one of the most basic and imperative requirements of the law of God. See Mic. 6:8. If Israelites were required to show mercy even to strangers (Lev. 19:34) and enemies (Exod. 23:4, 5; II Kings 6:8–23), then surely to fellow Israelites! For the priest's sinful neglect there was no justification whatever. The man just did not want to "get involved." Does that phrase have a modern ring?

32. So too a Levite came to the place, and when he saw him passed by on the opposite side. The priest's helper is not any better than the priest. He, too, as soon as he sees the grievously wounded man, makes sure that he remains as far as possible away from him, passing by on the opposite side of the road.

Is the waylaid, robbed, and tortured Jew going to be left to die then? So it looks. For, as if all this were not trouble enough, there comes . . . a *Samaritan!*

33. But a certain Samaritan, as he traveled, came down to him. Now things are bound to get worse. Did not the Jews and the Samaritans hate each other? When the enemies of Jesus wanted to vent their spleen at him, did they not call him "a *Samaritan*" (John 8:48)? And did not the Samaritans return hatred for hatred (Luke 9:53)? Surely, now the last, faint glimmer of hope is about to vanish.

So it might well appear. But what happens?

Continued: . . . **and upon seeing him his heart went out to him.** As soon as the Samaritan saw the sorely afflicted one, his heart went out to him. This makes us think of Jesus himself (Matt. 9:36), though it would be wrong to say that the Samaritan represents or symbolizes Jesus. And can anyone who knows his Bible read this story and not be reminded of the similarly loving attitude and deed of other people, in the long ago, people who in a certain sense were countrymen of him whose eyes were now filled with genuine sympathy, and who was about to dismount and go into action? See II. Chron. 28:15.

34. So he approached him and bandaged his wounds, pouring on oil and wine. Having dismounted, the Samaritan crosses over to the side of the road where the half-dead man is lying. He immediately administers first aid by washing his wounds with wine (because of its alcoholic content being a disinfectant and antiseptic), and by pouring into them soothing oil, acting as a kind of salve. **Then he mounted the man on his own beast, took him to an inn, and took care of him.** What a marvelous picture: the Samaritan walking by the side of his donkey and giving support to the tragic figure on the way to the inn!

When they arrived there, the Samaritan did not say, "Here's where my responsibility ends. I've already spent too much time on this man. Now let others take over." No, he "took care of him" personally. Did he keep vigil "all through the night," rising every once in a while to see how his charge was doing?

The next day arrives. The Samaritan—was he a businessman perhaps?—must be on his way. Even now, however, he does not say, "I've done my full duty. From here on it's up to the innkeeper and the man himself." No, the text continues: **35. The next day he took out two denarii, gave them to the innkeeper and said, Take care of him, and whatever more you spend I myself will duly repay you when I return.**

Two denarii was an amount equal to two days' wages for the average laborer (cf. Matt. 20:9), a sum which, according to the prices charged at that time for "room and board," would amply suffice for several days. The Samaritan is careful to assure the innkeeper that the latter will not suffer any loss in taking good care of the Jew. He says, as it were, "On my return *I myself* will repay any additional expense you may incur. So charge it to me, not to him."

C. *The conversation resumed and concluded*

36. Which of these three, do you think, proved to be a neighbor to the man who fell into (the hands of) the robbers? The exact wording should be noted. The law-expert had asked, "And who is my neighbor?" Jesus now asks him, "Which of the three proved to be [or: was] a neighbor to the man . . .?" What Jesus is emphasizing, therefore, is this, "The question is not, 'Who is my neighbor?' but 'Am I being a neighbor to those needy ones whom the Lord places in my path?'" **37. The law-expert replied, The man who took pity on him.** The fact that he did not say, "The Samaritan," should not be counted against him, as if he hated the Samaritans so thoroughly that even now he did not want to mention them by name. On the contrary, since the answer given showed *what kind of a man* had come to the rescue, it was even better than the reply "the Samaritan" would have been.

Jesus said to him, Go and keep on doing likewise, meaning, That manner of life should from now on be yours.

It may be asked, "Does this answer of our Lord shed any light on the law-expert's original question, 'What must I do to inherit everlasting life?'" The answer would have to be, "Yes, it does." Not as if "being a good neighbor" would all by itself assure salvation. But proving oneself to be a neighbor, and doing this *to perfection,* and besides, loving God with a love that is also *perfect,* would indeed result in everlasting life.

We hasten to add, however, that such perfection is impossible on this sinful earth. Yet, the demand of God's law is not abrogated. The solution of this problem has been furnished by God himself. Jesus Christ, by the sub-stitutionary sacrifice of himself and by his life of *perfect* obedience, has done for us what we ourselves would never have been able to do. See Rom. 8:1–3; II Cor. 5:21; Gal. 3:13. Therefore:

a. We must sincerely confess that it is forever impossible for us, by our own action, to fulfil the demands of God's law: "By the works of the law shall no flesh be justified" (Gal. 2:16).

b. We must, by God's grace and the power of his Spirit, place our trust in Christ (John 3:16, 36).

c. *Out of gratitude* for the salvation which, because of Christ's merits, we have received as a free gift, we must now, guided and empowered by the Holy Spirit, live a life to the glory of God Triune. This means that even though while on earth we cannot love God and the neighbor perfectly, yet *in principle* we will begin to live in accordance with his law. The law of love has not been abrogated. See Rom. 13:8–10.

There are, accordingly, two songs we should sing. Both are right and both are beautiful. One is:

Free from the law, O happy condition,
Jesus hath bled, and there is remission.

P. P. Bliss

The other has this refrain:

O how love I thy law, O how love I thy law!
It is my meditation all the day.

From the Chorus of
"Most Perfect Is the Law of God,"
U. P. Psalter, 1916.

A closing thought: Does not the very fact that Jesus created and told this parable show: (a) what kind of Savior he is, and (b) what kind of people he wants us to be?

For *Practical Lessons* and *Greek Words,* etc., see pp. 600–604.

---

38 As they were traveling, Jesus came to a certain village where a woman named Martha welcomed him to her home. 39 She had a sister called Mary who, seated at the Lord's feet, was listening to his word. 40 But Martha was becoming distracted about all that had to be done. Suddenly she came to him and asked, "Lord, don't you care that my sister has left me to do the work all by myself? Tell her to take hold and help me."

41 "Martha, Martha," the Lord answered, "You are worried and upset about many things;
42 but only one thing is necessary. Mary has chosen that good portion, and it will not be taken
away from her."

10:38–42 *Mary of Bethany Makes the Right Choice*

The waylaid man of the parable (verses 25–37) was traveling from
Jerusalem to *Jericho*. Now Jesus has arrived at *Bethany*. But this visit must
not be confused with those that took place a little later, closer to Passover
(John 11:1, 2; 12:1 ff.).

Exactly when the incident now recorded occurred has not been revealed.
This creates no real problem. Once Jesus arrived in Judea several visits to
the hospitable home of true disciples and warm friends can have been
made. A series of passages points in this direction (Matt. 21:17; 26:6–13—
cf. Mark 14:3; John 12:1–8—Mark 11:11; John 11:3; and, as some see it,
even Luke 21:37).

But Luke is not mainly interested in chronology. As has been indicated
previously, his arrangement, though certainly logical, is often topical. Accordingly, the evangelist could not have chosen a better place to present the
present narrative than he did. Active love for the neighbor is wonderful,
but listening to and putting into practice the words of the Master are also
necessary. We might even say: while the parable of The Samaritan Who
Cared places the emphasis on the second table of the law, the present story
stresses the first. "Love your neighbor" is followed by "Give heed to the
word of God."

The story before us readily divides itself into three parts, as will be
indicated:

A. *A Scene of Serenity*

**38. As they were traveling, Jesus came to a certain village where a
woman named Martha welcomed him to her home.**

Jesus and The Twelve were traveling. Cf. 9:51. The name of the village
at which they arrived is not mentioned. However, Luke does state that
Martha and Mary lived here. Since John 11:1 and 12:1–3 mention these
same sisters, and also their brother Lazarus, and inform us that they lived
in Bethany, we know that also here in Luke 10:38 the "certain village" is
Bethany. Luke too was acquainted with this place (see 19:29; 24:50),
though, for some reason, he does not here name it.

Bethany was situated east of Jerusalem, and on the eastern slope of Mt.
Olivet. Its present name is *el-ʿAzarîyeh* (cf. Lazarus). The distance between
Jerusalem and Bethany is given as being eight stadia (John 11:18), that is,
three kilometers, slightly less than two miles.

Of the two sisters Martha is mentioned first, this not only here in Luke
10:38, 39 but also in John 11:19, 20; 12:2, 3; while in John 11:5 she is even
mentioned before "her sister and Lazarus." True, in John 11:1 Bethany is

called "the village of Mary and her sister Martha," but the order in which
the two sisters are mentioned there, with Mary first, can be explained by
the fact that the story continues, in verse 2, with a reference to the Lord's
anointing by Mary. Note also that here in Luke 10:38 we are told that it was
Martha who welcomed Jesus to *her* home. Is the conclusion, drawn by some,
warranted that Martha must have been the oldest—at least of the two
sisters, and perhaps even of the three siblings—and that the house belonged to her? To begin with the last, the expression *her home* probably
means "the home where she (as well as the other two) lived." As to the first,
this sounds more reasonable. She may indeed have been the oldest, but this
too is not certain.

We are on firmer ground when we state that of the two sisters, as pictured in Scripture, Martha is the one who generally takes the lead. Here in
Luke 10:38 it is she who takes the initiative in extending a warm welcome to
Jesus. Typical is also John 11:20, "Now when Martha heard that Jesus was
coming, she went and met him. But Mary continued to sit in the house."
Add to this John 11:21, 28; 12:2. Not inappropriately Martha has been
called "the hostess."

**39. She had a sister called Mary who, seated at the Lord's feet, was
listening to his word.**

Up to this point what a scene of serenity, tranquility. All is well in the
lovely home at Bethany. A moment ago Martha extended a hearty welcome
to Jesus. And now Mary, her sister, is already seated at his feet, those very
feet which at a later occasion she is going to anoint (John 12:3; cf. Matt.
26:6, 7; Mark 14:3). Here she is now sitting, eagerly listening to the words
of life that are issuing from the Savior's heart and lips. "All is well. All is
well."

B. *An Outburst of Irritability*

40. But Martha was becoming distracted about all that had to be done.
Poor woman! We sympathize with her, do we not? If bringing the story
up-to-date is permissible, so that a modern setting is provided for it, the
result might be somewhat as follows:

Martha's mind *is pulled in every direction.* "How will I ever be able to take
care of all the details of this elaborate meal: the appetizers, the salad, meat,
vegetables, relishes, rolls, dessert, arranging of the guests around the table,
etc.? And all of this for:

> Jesus and for Lazarus,
> Mary too and Martha, plus
> Peter and Andrew, James and John,
> Philip and Bartholomew,
> Matthew next and Thomas too,
> James the Less and Judas the Greater,
> Simon the Zealot and Judas (who was
>   to become) the traitor."

Even if the name of Lazarus is subtracted, since he is not mentioned in the present account and may have been elsewhere at the time, this would still leave fifteen.

However, someone may object that the report speaks only about Jesus, so that we must assume that the disciples were not with him. That *possibility* must, of course, be granted. The *probability*, however, is that they too were present. Reasons for believing this:

a. Verse 38 reads: *"They* were traveling." That this plural immediately changes to the singular *he* (in "he came," etc.) does not mean that The Twelve suddenly left Jesus. The singular is used because he naturally was the Leader of the group. For similar references to Jesus in the singular when the presence of his disciples is implied see, for example, Luke 6:1; 17:11.

b. The very first sentence of the account which immediately follows also shows that the disciples were with the Master: "one of his disciples said to him," etc. (11:1). Accordingly, the actual absence of the disciples in the intervening paragraph (10:38–42) would seem rather strange.

c. John 12:2 describes a similar scene. There we read, "They made *him* a supper," not "They made a supper for him and his disciples." Yet, verse 4 shows that the disciples too were present.

It is understandable, therefore, that A. B. Bruce comments, ". . . it is not implied that he was alone, though no mention is made of disciples in the narrative." Greijdanus, in his *Korte Verklaring,* commenting on these verses (Vol. I, p. 286), takes for granted that the disciples were probably with their Master.

Continued: **Suddenly she came to him and asked, Lord, don't you care that my sister has left me to do the work all by myself? Tell her to take hold and help me.**

All this work, and Mary just sits there . . . doing nothing! Martha explodes with anger. She is exasperated. She feels that she has good reason to be thoroughly annoyed. In her outburst she finds fault not only with Mary but also with Jesus for allowing Mary to just sit there . . . idly.

C. *The Voice of Authority*

41, 42. Martha, Martha, the Lord answered, You are worried and upset about many things; but only one thing is necessary. Mary has chosen that good portion, and it will not be taken away from her.

The expression *Martha, Martha* reveals marked disapproval, to be sure, but also tender affection and grave concern, for, as the Searcher of hearts knows, Martha was inwardly worried and outwardly upset. This was very clear from the way she looked, spoke, and acted. "About many things," as if to say, "Such an elaborate meal was not at all necessary. Besides, there are things which in excellence and importance far surpass eating."

"Only *one* thing," says Jesus, "is really necessary." Some have interpreted this saying to mean, "Only one dish would have been needed." But what immediately follows certainly favors the other and widely-held interpretation, namely, "The one thing necessary is the portion Mary has chosen, that is, listening to my words." Can there, in fact, be anything greater in value than wholehearted devotion to and adoration of the Lord Jesus Christ, the revelation of God Triune? That, and not something else—this or that dish of food, for example—is the portion that will never be removed from Mary, and, for that matter, from anyone who copies her example. See Ps. 89:28; John 10:28; Rom. 8:38, 39.

The question is asked at times, "But was not Jesus a bit unfair to Martha? After all, did she not have a case?" The following must be borne in mind:

a. Except for the finishing touches, the meal should have been ready when Jesus and his group arrived. We have every reason to believe that he had taken care that this hostess knew about his coming. Was he not always sending men ahead to announce his arrival? See Isa. 40:3-5; Mal. 3:1; Luke 9:52; 10:1; 22:8.

b. This also means that upon his arrival one of the sisters should have . . . shall we say "entertained"? . . . the honored guest. Rather, "should have been ready to sit at his feet in order to listen to his words." Not to do so would, even under ordinary conditions, have been impolite, contrary to good form, but in *this* case would have been most irreverent. Therefore Mary did exactly the right thing.

c. 10:40 "has left me," etc., probably implies that *at an earlier moment* Mary too had done her part in the preparation of the meal.

Martha learned her lesson. She knew that Jesus' words of reprimand had been spoken in love, for "Jesus was holding in loving esteem Martha and her sister and Lazarus" (John 11:5).

We are not surprised, therefore, that two of the most marvelous professions of faith found in Scripture were going to issue from the heart and lips of Martha:

"Lord, if thou hadst been here, my brother would not have died. And even now I know that whatever thou wilt ask of God, God will give thee" (John 11:21, 22).

"Yes, Lord, I have believed that thou art the Christ, the Son of God, the One coming into the world" (John 11:27).

The story, therefore, has a glorious ending. God was glorified, and this is always what matters most.[376]

Practical Lessons Derived from 10:25–42

Verse 30

"A certain man," etc. Teachers, preachers, etc., should make use of illustrations to drive home Scripture's precious truths.

---

376. Notes on Greek words, phrases, and constructions in 10:25–42 begin on page 601.

Verse 31

"A priest . . . passed by on the opposite side." Performing religious functions is one thing. Practicing religion is another.

Verse 37

"The law-expert replied, 'The man who took pity on him.' Jesus said to him, 'Go and keep on doing likewise.'" Don't become so involved in theology that you forget philanthropy.

Verses 38, 39

"A woman named Martha . . . a sister called Mary." This story and many others prove that on Christ's value scale there is no difference between male and female. He loved all equally.

Verse 42

"Mary *has chosen*," etc. Divine *selectivity* does not shut out human *activity*. But see I John 4:19.

"It will not be taken away from her." Divine preservation is taught here, as in many other passages. It does not exclude but definitely includes human perseverance.

Notes on Greek Words, Phrases, and Constructions in 10:25-42

Verse 25

For the pres. participle ἐκπειράζων, here expressing purpose, see the note on 4:12 on page 242.

Verse 27

πλησίον is derived from πλησίος, near, close by; hence ὁ πλησίος, used as a noun, means "the one nearby," "the neighbor." Similarly in English the "neighbor" is the "nigh boor."

Verse 29

δικαιῶσαι, aor. act. infinitive of δικαιόω, here used in the sense of "to vindicate." For the sense "to be accounted and pronounced righteous by God" see on 18:14; also N.T.C. on Galatians, pp. 96-100.

Verse 30

ὑπολαβών, nom. s. masc. 2nd aor. participle of ὑπολαμβάνω. The basic sense seems to be: to take up. Hence here: "Taking him up on this, Jesus replied." In the sense of "I take it (to be)," that is, "I assume," the verb occurs in 7:43; cf. Acts 2:15, "y o u assume." See also the more literal sense in Acts 1:9, "A cloud took him up from their sight," thus hiding him from view. Unsurprisingly there is also the meaning "to take up from under," that is, to support, brace up, undergird, show hospitality to (III John 8).

With respect to ληστᾱῖς, dat. pl. of ληστής, the meaning *robber, highwayman* (here: "among robbers") suits the present context. The word would seem to have that meaning also in verse 36; 19:46; Matt. 21:13; John 10:1, 8; II Cor. 11:26. In the following passages the alternative meaning "revolutionary," "insurrectionist," is at least deserving of consideration: Matt. 26:55; Mark 14:48; Luke 22:52; John 18:40. Either sense has its defenders in Matt. 27:38, 44; Mark 15:27, though Luke 23:33 may tip the scales toward "robber" in these passages. Cf. *lucre*.

ἡμιθανῆ, acc. s. masc. of ἡμιθανής*, cf. ἡμι, half; θάνατος, death; hence, half-dead.

Verses 31, 32

κατὰ συγκυρίαν*, σύν plus κυρέω, to happen together, fall in with; hence κατὰ σ. means "by chance," "by coincidence or *concurrence*"; and κατὰ συγκυρίαν . . . κατέβαινεν means: happened to be going down.

ἀντιπαρῆλθεν, third per. s. 2nd aor. indicat. of ἀντιπαρέρχομαι*, to pass by on the opposite (or: other) side. As I have shown in my dissertation, the verb belongs to that group of ἀντί-compounds in which ἀντί has the sense of local oppositeness. The same form occurs twice (verses 31 and 32).

Verse 33

ἐσπλαγχνίσθη, third per. s. aor. indicat. pass. of σπλαγχνίζομαι; same form as in 7:13. See the note on that verse on page 390.

Verses 34, 35

κατέδησεν, third per. s. aor. indicat. act. of καταδέω*, literally "to bind down," that is, "to bind securely, to bandage." Cf. *cata*clysm and dia*dem* (*down*-wash and something *bound* around the head). Where the Greek language says "bind down" our idiom is "bind up."

τραῦμα*, wound (here pl. -τα). In the sense of violently produced injury or emotional shock, English also speaks of a *trauma*.

ἐπιχέων, nom. s. masc. pres. participle of ἐπιχέω, to pour upon. Cf. *chemist, chyle, chyme;* perhaps even *gush.* See the note on 5:37 on page 313; see also the note on 11:50 on page 647.

ἐπιβιβάσας, nom. s. masc. aor. participle of ἐπιβιβάζω, to mount, set upon; see also 19:35 and Acts 23:24.

κτῆνος, possession, property (especially in animals), beast of burden, pack animal. The pl. in I Cor. 15:39 means "beasts"; in Rev. 18:13, "cattle."

The noun κτῆνος reminds one of κέκτημαι (perf. of κτάομαι), to possess.

πανδοχεῖον, inn; literally a place that receives everybody. πανδοχεῖ, dat. s. of πανδοχεύς, innkeeper.

προσδαπανήσῃς, sec. per. s. aor. subjunct. of προσδαπανάω* = "to spend [δαπανάω] in addition" (πρός).

ἐπανέρχεσθαι, pres. infinitive of ἐπανέρχομαι*, to come back, return. See also 19:15.

Verse 38

The idea of Lenski (*op. cit.*, pp. 384, 385) that αὐτός is here contrasted with αὐτούς, implying that Jesus *all by himself* enters Bethany, while the disciples go elsewhere, has not found much support. In the Greek of the New Testament this pronoun does not always carry that much weight. At another occasion (John 12:2) we are told "they made *him* (αὐτῷ) a supper." Nevertheless, the context clearly shows that the disciples too were present. See 12:4 and the parallel in Matt. 26:6–8; cf. Mark 14:3.

ὑπεδέξατο, third per. s. aor. indicat. of ὑποδέχομαι, to receive, welcome. Here Lenski offers "invited" as English equivalent. Though this rendering might help to solve a problem—for in that case we would know immediately that Martha *expected* this guest (or these guests, if the disciples were also present), and her subsequent outburst would therefore be even less excusable—it is probably incorrect. If Luke had intended to write "invited" why did he not use a form of the verb καλέω, as in 7:39; 14:7, etc.? Of course, this does not shut out the possibility that Martha may indeed have *invited* the group. It is reasonable to suppose that Martha knew that Jesus and his disciples were going to arrive. But the verb here used does not mean *invited*.

Verse 39

παρακαθεσθεῖσα, nom. s. fem. aor. participle of παρακαθέζομαι*, to sit beside. The immediately preceding καί is probably pleonastic, based on Hebrew usage; hence, best left untranslated.

Verse 40

περιεσπᾶτο, third per. s. imperf. pass. of περισπάω*; in the passive: to become distracted, agitated; literally, to be drawn or pulled in every direction.

ἐπιστᾶσα, nom. s. fem. 2nd aor. participle of ἐφίστημι; transitive: to place upon; intransitive, as here, to come suddenly upon (cf. Luke 2:9; 24:4); other meanings: to come near, come up, stand, confront, approach, be at hand, stand beside, be urgent, spring upon. See also the note on 2:9 on page 160.

συναντιλάβηται, third per. s. 2nd aor. subjunct. of συναντιλαμβάνομαι, to take hold of along with someone; here either: to take hold of "at her end" (Robertson) or "in turn." Either way, the resultant meaning is: to help.

Verses 41, 42

μεριμνᾷς, sec. per. s. pres. indicat. act. of μεριμνάω, to worry, be worried about. Note that μέρος, in one of its meanings, indicates "piece." Martha was "going to pieces over" all the things she imagined that she had to do.

θορυβάζῃ, sec. per. s. pres. pass. of θορυβάζομαι*, to be troubled, disturbed, upset.

A minor group of manuscripts reads "but few things are necessary." Another reading is "but few things are necessary or only one." All in all, the reading ἑνὸς δέ ἐστιν χρεία, though subject to considerable doubt, is probably the best. Not only does it have definite textual support, but "only one thing" also harmonizes best with "that good portion" in the next clause.

ἀφαιρεθήσεται, third per. s. fut. indicat. pass. of ἀφαιρέω, to take away, remove; so also in 1:25; 16:3. A related meaning is "to cut off" (22:50 and parallels).

Summary of Chapter 10

See p. 533.

Outline of Chapter 11

Theme: *The Work Thou Gavest Him to Do*

CHAPTER XI

11 1 Now it happened that while he was in a certain place, engaged in prayer, when he stopped, one of his disciples said to him, "Lord, teach us to pray, just as John taught his disciples." 2 He answered, "When y o u pray, say:

'Father,
Hallowed be thy name,
Thy kingdom come.
3 Give us each day our daily bread;
4 And forgive us our sins,
for we ourselves forgive every one who is indebted to us;
And lead us not into temptation.' "

5 Then he said to them,

"Who of y o u shall have a friend, and shall go to him at midnight and say, 'Friend, lend me three bread-cakes, 6 because a friend of mine, on a journey, has come to me,[377] and I have nothing to offer him'; 7 and he from inside shall answer, 'Don't bother me; the door is already locked, and my children and I are in bed; I can't get up and give you (anything)'?	"Suppose one of y o u has a friend, and goes to him at midnight, and says, 'Friend, lend me three bread-cakes, 6 because a friend of mine, on a journey, has come to me,[377] and I have nothing to offer him'; 7 then will the one inside answer, 'Don't bother me; the door is already locked, and my children and I are in bed; I can't get up and give you (anything)'?

8 "I tell y o u, even though he will not get up and give him (anything) because he is his friend,[378] yet, because of the man's persistence, he will get up and give him whatever he needs.

9 "So I say to y o u, Ask, and it shall be given to y o u; seek, and y o u shall find; knock, and it shall be opened to y o u. 10 For whoever asks receives, and the one who seeks finds, and to him who knocks, it shall be opened.[379]

11 "What father is there among y o u who, when his son asks him for a fish, will give him a serpent? 12 Or also (if the son) asks for an egg, will give him a scorpion? 13 If, therefore, y o u, evil though y o u are, know how to give good gifts to y o u r children, how much more will y o u r heavenly Father give the Holy Spirit to those who ask him!"

11:1-13 *Christ's Teaching on Prayer*

Loving the neighbor (10:25-37), listening to the Lord's words (10:38-42), and now praying (11:1-13), these clearly belong together.

The present section has two subdivisions: (a) The Lord's Prayer (verses 1-4) and (b) The Parable of The Troubled Host (verses 5-13).

---

377. Or: to my home.
378. Or: for friendship's sake.
379. According to another reading: it is opened.

A. *The Lord's Prayer*

1. Now it happened that while he was in a certain place, engaged in prayer, when he stopped, one of his disciples said to him, Lord, teach us to pray, just as John taught his disciples.

With respect to both place and time Luke is very indefinite. For a possibility see above, p.544. It is certain that at least one of Christ's disciples was so deeply impressed with the manner in which Jesus prayed that he said to him, "Lord, teach us to pray," and he added, "just as John taught his disciples."

Who this disciple was we do not know. It has been suggested that he may have been a member of that larger group of Christ's followers who did not belong to the company of The Twelve. The existence of this much larger group is clear from several passages, including Luke 6:13. He may even have been one of the seventy-two specially appointed missionaries (Luke 10:1-12, 17-20). On the other hand, the *possibility* that this disciple was one of The Twelve must not be excluded.

As to the manner in which "The Lord's Prayer," as recorded here in Luke 11:2-4, differs from the earlier one found in Matt. 6:9-13 (part of The Sermon on the Mount), this becomes clear when the two versions are placed side by side:

The Lord's Prayer in Matt. 6:9-13 and in Luke 11:2-4

	Matthew	*Luke*
Invocation	Our Father who art in heaven,	Father,
First Petition	Hallowed be thy name,	Hallowed be thy name,
Second Petition	Thy kingdom come,	Thy kingdom come.
Third Petition	Thy will be done as in heaven so on earth.	
Fourth Petition	Give us this day our daily bread;	Give us each day our daily bread;
Fifth Petition	And forgive us our debts as we also have forgiven our debtors,	And forgive us our sins, for we ourselves forgive every one who is indebted to us;
Sixth Petition	And lead us not into temptation, but deliver us from the evil one.	And lead us not into temptation.
Conclusion	[For thine is the kingdom, and the power, and the glory, forever. Amen.]	

It is clear that the prayer as recorded in Luke is shorter than the one included in The Sermon on the Mount. In the Third Gospel the invocation or address consists of just one word, *Father*. By the omission of the third petition ("Thy will be done," etc.) the number of petitions has been reduced from six to five. The reason for the omission is probably that Matthew's third petition is essentially included in the second, for how can the Father's kingdom be established in the hearts and lives of men unless his will is being obeyed? For a similar reason the second clause of Matthew's sixth petition ("but deliver us from the evil one") is omitted in Luke; for it, too, is implied in the immediately preceding line ("and lead us not into temptation"). In what in Matthew is the fifth petition the word *debts* has in Luke been changed to "sins," and the next clause ("as we also have forgiven our debtors") has been reworded, though not with any essential change in meaning. Finally, Luke's version has no conclusion or closing doxology.

This variety is pleasing. It teaches us that it was never Christ's intention to demand that time after time exactly the same words be spoken. Certainly the exhortation, **2. He answered, When y o u pray, say,** here in Luke, suggests that, for a start, these very words may be used. But in The Sermon on the Mount Jesus said, "This, then, is *how* y o u should pray." This shows that "The Lord's Prayer" is essentially *the model prayer*. It should serve as a *model* or *pattern* for our devotions.

As to the meaning of the prayer, see the full interpretation in N.T.C. on Matthew, pp. 324-340. Here, in the treatment of Luke 11:1-4, it is not necessary to repeat all this. A summary·should suffice.

Some writers are of the opinion that the prayer's primary reference is to matters that pertain to the end of the age; in other words, that the prayer is eschatological in character. Thus "Thy kingdom come" would mean, "May Israel be delivered from its enemies, and by a single divine act may this age be ended." Similarly "Lead us not into temptation" would mean, "Grant that we may be delivered from Satan's final onslaught."[380]

However, in the language used by Jesus, whether as recorded by Matthew or by Luke, there is nothing that suggests this unnatural meaning and application.

Briefly, then, the sense is as follows:

1. "Father." This shows that the prayer is for believers in the Lord Jesus Christ, apart from faith in whom no one can come to the Father (John 14:6). Accordingly, the believer begins his prayer in the humble and cheering consciousness that God is his Father, and that he, the suppliant, is that Father's child and heir (Rom. 8:15-17; Gal. 4:6, 7).

2. "Hallowed be thy name." The name represents the being; in this case God himself, viewed as he has revealed himself in his work of creation and redemption. By uttering this petition the person who by grace has been brought into fellowship with the Father calls upon everyone to share this experience with him and to exalt this glorious God. He is saying, as it were, "O magnify Jehovah with me, and let us exalt his name together" (Ps. 34:3).

3. "Thy kingdom come." Meaning: "May thy rule be established more

---

380. See R. E. Brown, *New Testament Essays*, Milwaukee, 1965, p. 253; W. J. Harrington, *op. cit.*, pp. 156-162. Though I disagree with these authors on this point, I hasten to add that their books contain much excellent material. By all means read them.

and more, both extensively and intensively, in order that thy will may be done on earth as it is in heaven."

4. "Give us each day our daily bread." Meaning: "Since we are in constant need, *continue* to supply us, day by day, with the portion needed for 'the day in being.'" Here "bread" indicates whatever is necessary to sustain physical life. Note *our* bread. Cf. Gal. 6:10.

5. "And forgive us our sins, for we ourselves forgive every one who is indebted to us." Meaning: not that our forgiving disposition earns God's pardon; rather, God's pardoning grace is based solely on Christ's merits graciously applied to us. Thus our sins are laid upon Christ, and his righteousness is imputed to us. See Isa. 54:4–6; Rom. 3:24; II Cor. 5:20, 21; Eph. 1:7; Rev. 7:14. But an unforgiving heart is not in a condition that can accept forgiveness.

6. "And lead us not into temptation." Meaning: "If it be thy will, do not permit us, weak as we are and prone to sin, to enter into situations which in the normal course of events would expose us to temptation and to a possible fall; but whatever be thy way with us, deliver us from the evil one. Grant that we may remain watchful at all times, and that at last we may triumph completely." See Eph. 5:15, 16; II Thess. 1:11, 12; I Tim. 6:11–16.

B. *The parable of The Troubled Host*

The structure of verses 5–7 presents a problem. All agree that Jesus starts out by asking a question, namely, "Who of y o u shall . . .?" However, as concerns the continuation, it has been stated that "the interrogation is lost in the prolongation of the sentence" (E. Plummer, *op. cit.,* p. 298). It is for this reason that many translators (N.A.S., Williams, N.E.B., N.I.V., Robertson, Moffatt) begin their translation with "Suppose," and omit the question mark entirely. That is one way of treating the problem. Others, again, favor a more literal rendering, beginning with "Which of you. . . ." They place a question mark at the end of verse 6. Thus A.V. and Weymouth. And still others regard verses 5–7 as a unit and as being *one* long rhetorical question. Accordingly, they place the question mark at the close of verse 7. Thus A.R.V., R.S.V., Beck, Lenski, Geldenhuys, Harrington, etc. Without implying that the first two methods are wrong, I, too, am following this last course. I do so because: (a) The unit is introduced as a question, with "Who of y o u . . ." placed at the beginning. (b) The question Jesus is asking, the situation he pictures, does not end with the last word of verse 6. It very definitely includes verse 7; in fact the emphasis is on that verse. (c) In verse 8 Jesus answers his own question, the question of verses 5–7. This too indicates that he viewed verses 5–7 as a unit, a single, indivisible question.

Even so, there are two possible renderings, one, the more literal, for which see the left column on p. 607; the other, less literal but perhaps somewhat easier to the ear, shown in the right column. From here on I shall follow the right column.

1. A man facing a midnight emergency

**5, 6. Then he said to them, Suppose one of y o u has a friend, and goes
to him at midnight, and says, Friend, lend me three bread-cakes, because
a friend of mine, on a journey, has come to me, and I have nothing to
offer him . . .**

It is late in the evening. Suddenly a friend appears at your door. He is
tired from the trip he has been making. In order to escape the heat of the
day he has been traveling at night. But now, tired and hungry, he stops at
your house. He expects hospitality: food and lodging. But there is no more
food in the house. "The cupboard is bare."

So in your predicament you go to another friend of yours. When you
arrive at his home it is midnight. You awaken him and say, "My friend,
kindly lend me three [flat, round] bread-cakes, because a friend of mine
stopped in and I have nothing to set before him."

2. Will his friend refuse to help him?

**7. then will the one inside answer, Don't bother me; the door is already
locked, and my children and I are in bed; I can't get up and give you
(anything)?**

The meaning is somewhat as follows: Will the man who, bedded in for
the night in this one-room house, and now suddenly awakened, then answer, "Stop pestering me. Don't you realize that my children are sound
asleep, lying here on their mats? If I get up, walk across the floor, and
remove the huge bolting bar from the door, the hubbub will scare them out
of their sleep. Sorry, but I just can't get up to give you anything." Jesus asks,
"Is that how the friend is going to react?"

3. Christ's answer

We can already anticipate Christ's answer to his own question. It will be
along this line, "The one inside will definitely not say . . . 'I can't get
up. . . .'" Or (shaping the answer in accordance with the question in the left
column on p. 613) the answer will be, "None of y o u will receive such a
refusal from a friend to whom y o u go for help."

All this is, of course, *implied*. But the *actual* answer Jesus gives is even
better, for it is phrased positively, as follows:

**8. I tell y o u, even though he will not get up and give him (anything)
because he is his friend, yet because of the man's persistence,[381] he will
get up and give him whatever he needs.**

Jesus says that the friend will certainly get up and give this person the
three bread-cakes for which he asked; in fact, he will give him "whatever he
needs."

As to the donor's motive, that's another question. Perhaps he gives be-

---

381. Or: Shamelessness.

cause he is a true and sympathetic friend. But if not, then he gives because the other man keeps on asking. Some people might be ashamed to repeat their request, but not this man.

The point is this: if even an earthly friend would certainly extend help, whatever be his motive, then will not the heavenly Father, about whose motivation there can be no question, generously answer our petitions?

4. *The parable's lesson*

9, 10. So I say to y o u, Ask, and it shall be given to y o u; seek, and y o u shall find; knock, and it shall be opened to y o u. For whoever asks receives, and the one who seeks finds, and to him who knocks, it shall be opened.

Jesus here continues to emphasize the effectiveness of prayer. Linked with this is another lesson, namely, the importance of perseverance in prayer. It is not surprising therefore that the words of Matt. 7:7, 8 are now repeated. A threefold *exhortation* accompanies a threefold *promise*. The threefold exhortation is as follows: ask, seek, knock. Note also the emphatic "So I say to y o u" which here in Luke begins the sentence.

First, then, the words of command or exhortation: "Ask, *seek*, **KNOCK**. Clearly the three are arranged in a rising scale of intensity.

Ask

Asking implies humility and a consciousness of need. The verb is used with respect to a petition which is addressed by an inferior to a superior. The Pharisee of the parable (Luke 18:10–13) asks nothing. He *tells* the Lord how good he is. The publican *asks*, that is, *pleads*, "God be merciful to me, the sinner." Asking also presupposes belief in a personal God with whom man can have fellowship. When one asks, he expects an answer. Hence, this implies faith in a God who can, does, and will answer, that is, faith in God the Father. Having such a faith makes the prayer warm and personal. Such a supplicant would not be able to say, "O God, if there be a God, save my soul if I have a soul."

Seek

Seeking is *asking plus acting*. It *implies* earnest petitioning, but that alone is not sufficient. A person must be active in endeavoring to obtain the fulfilment of his needs. For example, one should not only *pray* for a deep knowledge of the Bible but should also diligently *search* and *examine* the Scriptures (John 5:39; Acts 17:11), attend the services (Heb. 10:25), above all strive to *live* in harmony with God's will (see Matt. 7:21, 24, 25; cf. John 7:17).

Knock

Knocking is *asking plus acting plus persevering*. One knocks again and again until the door is opened. In reality, however, perseverance is probably already implied in all three imperatives, since all are in the present tense; hence, a possible rendering would be "continue to ask, to seek, to knock." This all the more in view of Luke 18:1, 7; cf. Rom. 12:12; Eph 5:20; 6:18; Col. 4:2; I Thess. 5:17. But what is probable for all three is a certainty with respect to the last, the very idea of biblical knocking already implying perseverance. One continues to knock at the door of the kingdom-palace until the King, who is at the same time the Father, opens the door and supplies whatever is needed.

As to *the promise* that is fulfilled when the command is obeyed, in each instance the correspondence between command and promise is exact: hence, *ask* is followed by *given; seek* by *find;* and *knock* by *opened.* Note that in verses 9 and 10 this promise, in one form or another, occurs no less than six times. The first three promises, those of verse 9, are virtually repeated in verse 10, and even strengthened by the introductory word *whoever,* the inclusiveness of which is re-emphasized by *the one who* and *to him who,* as if to say: of those who obey the command not a single one will be disappointed. An answer to the kind of prayer that is accompanied by seeking and knocking is promised to every sincere follower of the Lord.

The certainty that persevering prayer accompanied by the activity of faith will be rewarded is strengthened by an argument from the less to the greater.

Though in essence the argument as worded in Matthew is similar to that in Luke, the form differs somewhat, as follows:

Matt. 7:9-11	Luke 11:11-13
Or what man is there among y o u, who, when his son asks him for bread, will give him a stone? Or also (if the son) asks for a fish, will give him a serpent? If, therefore, y o u, evil though y o u are, know how to give good gifts to y o u r children, how much more will y o u r Father in heaven give good gifts to those who ask him!	**What father is there among y o u who, when his son asks him for a fish, will give him a serpent? Or also (if the son) asks for an egg, will give him a scorpion? If therefore, y o u, evil though y o u are, know how to give good gifts to y o u r children, how much more will y o u r heavenly Father give the Holy Spirit to those who ask him!**

For points of grammar, etc., see the notes on these verses on page 616.

If a son asks his father for a fish, the father will certainly not give him a snake! Or if the son asks for an egg, it is inconceivable that the father would instead give him a dreadful scorpion, with stinging tail that pricks its victim into insensibility. Now if even an earthly father, though by nature evil (Ps. 51:1-5; 130:3; Isa. 1:6; Jer. 17:9; John 3:3, 5; Rom. 3:10; Eph. 2:1), provides his children with nothing but good things, and not with things that could harm them, how much more will not the heavenly Father—lit. the Father from heaven—who is free from all evil and is, in fact, the source of all goodness, give . . . what? Here Matthew's version has "good gifts," while

Luke's has "the Holy Spirit." These two are in perfect accord, for is not the Holy Spirit the very Source of all that is good?

Significantly both Matthew and Luke end the sentence with "to those who ask him," thus beautifully re-emphasizing the main thrust of the entire passage, namely, "Ask, and it shall be given to y o u . . . whoever asks receives![382]

Practical Lessons Derived from 11:1–13

Verse 1

"Lord, teach us to pray." Which of the following is right? Or wrong?

a. Children should memorize a prayer and then pray it over and over again;

b. We should not assist children to pray, but allow them to pray their own prayers;

c. Any other suggestion?

Verse 2

"When y o u pray, say: 'Father, hallowed be thy name.'" The notable prayers recorded in Scripture have this in common, that in all of them God's glory is the ultimate aim. See, for example, the prayers of Solomon (I Kings 8:23–53), David (Ps. 51), Agur (Prov. 30:7–9), Daniel (Dan. 9:4–19), Paul (Eph. 3:14–21), and most of all, Jesus Christ himself (John 11:41, 42; John 17).

Verses 2–4

"The Lord's Prayer."
What gives this prayer its power?
It ne'er says *mine* but *our*.
Why does it grip me thus?
It ne'er says *me* but *us*.
What may its beauty be?
It ne'er says *I* but *we*.
It humbles me, but why?
It ne'er says *my* but *thy*."

Does the element of truth certainly embodied in these poetic lines need modification?

Verses 5–7

The parable. The lesson this parable teaches is so powerful and striking because with God it is never midnight; he never lacks anything; he is never "bothered" when any humble child approaches him; and he is never taken by surprise.

---

382. Notes on Greek words, phrases, and constructions in 11:1–13 begin on page 615.

Verse 13

"How much more will y o u r heavenly Father give the Holy Spirit." People some-times complain because God did not give them exactly what they asked. But did they ask for the Holy Spirit and the grace he imparts, grace sufficient to cause us to rejoice in the midst of our sorrows and afflictions?

Notes on Greek Words, Phrases, and Constructions in 11:1–13

Verses 1 and 2

ἐν τῷ εἶναι αὐτὸν... προσευχόμενον, periphrastic pres. (durative) infinitive ("while he was... engaged in prayer").

προσεύχεσθαι, pres. infinitive of προσεύχομαι, to pray.

προσεύχησθε, sec. per. pl. pres. subjunct. (after ὅταν).

ἁγιασθήτω, third per. s. aor. imperat. pass. of ἁγιάζω, to consecrate, sanctify, hallow, set apart to be revered. The aor. is timeless; this is true also with respect to ἐλθέτω, third per. s. 2nd aor. imperat. of ἔρχομαι.

Verse 3

For the meaning of ἐπιούσιον see N.T.C. on Matthew, pp. 332, 333.

Note δίδου, pres., hence request for *continued* giving, where Matthew has δός, aor., emphasis on giving as such.

Verse 4

ἄφες, sec. per. s. 2nd aor. imperat. of ἀφίημι; see the note on 6:42 on page 364.

εἰσενέγκῃς, sec. per. s. aor. act. subjunct. (in a prohibition) of εἰσφέρω. As is generally true, the exact meaning of the verb and its translation into English de-pend on the specific context in which it is used; in the case of εἰσφέρω the result will be about as follows:

  a. to lead, bring, or carry into (Matt. 6:13; Luke 11:4; I Tim. 6:7; Heb. 13:11).
  b. to bring to (our ears, Acts 17:20).
  c. to bring or carry in (Luke 5:18, 19).
  d. to drag in (Luke 12:11).

For the construction of verses 5–7 see p. 610.

ἕξει and πορεύσεται are deliberative future indicatives; and εἴπῃ (both here and in verse 7) is a deliberative aor. subjunctive.

χρῆσον, sec. per. s. aor. imperat. of κίχρημι*, to lend. However, the verb here used differs in meaning from δανείζω (Luke 6:34, 35), to lend money, generally in order to earn interest on it. Illustrations of the verb used here in Luke 11:5 are I Sam. 1:28 (LXX I Kings 1:28), where Hannah is said to have *lent* her child (Samuel) to the Lord; and Josephus, *Jewish War* III.359, "We will *lend* you a right hand and a sword."

Verse 6

πρός με, "to me," or "to my house."

Verse 7

Μή μοι κόπους πάρεχε; Don't bother me; literally: "Do not cause troubles [or difficulties] for me." The verb is sec. per. s. imperat. act. of παρέχω, to bring about, cause.

κέκλεισται, third per. s. perf. indicat. pass. of κλείω, to close, lock, shut. Cf. verse 52, where the acc. of κλείς, key, is used. Cf. *clef*.

Verse 8

ἀναίδειαν, acc. s. of ἀναίδεια. αἰδώς = a sense of shame; so ἀναίδεια means lack of a sense of shame, shamelessness; here: in making requests; and so, persistence, perseverance.

χρήζει, third per. s. pres. indicat. of χρήζω, to need, want; cf. χρηστός, useful, good, gracious. Note *chrestomathy* (a collection of passages *useful* for learning).

Verses 9, 10

κρούετε, sec. per. pl. pres. imperat. of κρούω, to knock (at a gate or door); κρούοντι, dat. s. masc. pres. participle. τῷ κρούοντι = to him who knocks.

For the verb ἀνοίγω see the note on 1:64 on page 120. Here in Luke 11:9 ἀνοιγήσεται is third per. s. 2nd fut. pass of ἀνοίγω, to open; and in verse 10 ἀνοίγεται is third per. pres. indicat. pass. of the same verb. It is possible, however, that in verse 10, as in verse 9, the reading ἀνοιγήσεται (cf. Matt. 7:7, 8) is correct.

Verses 11, 12

Note the anacoluthon: τὸν πατέρα is the object of "his son asks"; and the unmentioned but implied πατήρ is the subject of "will give him."

ᾠόν*, egg. Cf. *ovum, ovary*. The longer (three contrasts) reading, reflected in A.V., probably resulted from conflation with Matthew's text.

Verse 13

"The Father from heaven" is "the heavenly Father." Heaven is his dwelling place, and it is from there that he pours down his blessings.

---

14 And Jesus was expelling a demon who had deprived a man of the power of speech.[383] When the demon had gone out, the man who had been deprived of the power of speech spoke, and the crowds were amazed. 15 But some people said, "It is by Beelzebul, the prince of the demons, that he casts out demons." 16 Others, tempting (him), were demanding of him a sign from heaven. 17 But he, knowing their thoughts, said to them, "Any kingdom divided against itself is on the way to ruin, and a house divided against a house fails. 18 Moreover, if Satan is divided against himself, how shall his kingdom stand? (I say this) because y o u are asserting that I expel demons by Beelzebul. 19 Now if it is by Beelzebul that I cast out demons, by whom do y o u r sons cast them out? Therefore they shall be y o u r judges. 20 But if it is by the finger of God that I cast out demons, then the kingdom of God has come upon y o u.

21 "When a strong man, armed to the teeth, guards his own house, his possessions are

---

383. Literally: ... a demon, and it was mute.

secure. 22 But when someone (who is) stronger than he comes and overpowers him, he carries off the armor in which the man trusted, and distributes his goods as spoils.

23 "He who is not with me is against me, and he who does not gather with me scatters."

11:14-23 *Christ's Miracles: Proof of Beelzebul's Dominion or of His Doom?*
Cf. Matt. 12:22-30; Mark 3:22-27

14. And Jesus was expelling a demon who had deprived a man of the power of speech. When the demon had gone out, the man who had been deprived of the power of speech spoke, and the crowds were amazed.

Between the three previous accounts there is a very close connection: being a neighbor to those needy ones who by divine providence have been placed in our path (10:25-37), eagerly listening to the words of the Lord (10:38-42), and, in turn, addressing him in prayer (11:1-13), these three form an unbreakable chain. But now suddenly there seems to be a break. Enters Satan! See what has been said about this apparent lack of connection on p. 534. Perhaps Cowper's familiar lines will assist us in remembering the relation between *prayer* and *the evil one:*

> And Satan trembles when he sees
> The weakest saint upon his knees.

On demon possession and expulsion see what has been said previously (on 4:33).

Between the three accounts in which this demon-expulsion is related (see heading) there are no conflicts; that is, none of the three evangelists affirms what one or both of the others deny, or denies what is affirmed by the other(s). There are variations in reporting: Matthew relates that the demoniac had lost the power not only of speech but also of vision; Luke is indefinite about the identity of Christ's attackers ("some people"); Matthew calls them *Pharisees;* Mark, *scribes.* That these three designations are readily reconciled does not need to be demonstrated. For the rest, see N.T.C. on Mark, p. 134, footnote 128.

As is clear from the parallel accounts, the demon-expulsion here related occurred during The Great Galilean Ministry. A demoniac was brought to Jesus, who cured him instantly and completely, so that the man who had been grievously afflicted was now no longer demon-possessed. Also, he was able to talk. Unsurprisingly the crowds who witnessed this miracle were astonished. A feeling of amazement, coupled no doubt with a measure of fear in the presence of the One who had performed this miracle, took possession of them. Matthew even reports that the people were saying, "Surely, this cannot be the Son of David?"

However, not all was harmony: **15. But some people said, It is by Beelzebul, the prince of the demons, that he casts out demons.**

As Mark 3:22 shows, scribes had "come down" from Jerusalem. The

Great Sanhedrin, with its headquarters at that place, had become worried. It had become clear to that body that Jesus was able to expel demons and to perform other works of power. How was it that he had this power? By this time the Jewish authorities had become well aware of the fact that on some points which they regarded as important Jesus' teaching was not in line with theirs. So they must have drawn the conclusion that the mysterious powers exercised by "the prophet of Galilee" were anything but God-given; no doubt they were satanic. An investigation was certainly in order, so they thought. They seem not to have considered the possibility that they might be mistaken about the source of the Nazarene's power. Now they had come from Jerusalem to prove their theory, namely, that what was going on in Galilee was the work of Beelzebul. Soon after they arrived on the scene, they were pronouncing their verdict, "It is by Beelzebul, the prince of the demons, that he casts out demons."

But who was Beelzebul? To discover the answer we must go back to the Old Testament. It was as Baal-zebu*b* (II Kings 1:2, 3, 6) that Baal was worshiped at Ekron. King Ahaziah, who sent messengers to inquire of Baal-zebub whether he would recover from the results of his fall, was told that because of this disloyalty to Jehovah he would die. The New Testament passages substitute Beel[=Baal]zebu*l* for -zebu*b*. Beelzebul means "lord of the dwelling." The reason for the change in spelling is not clear. It may have amounted to no more than an accident of popular pronunciation. Another explanation is that there is here a play on words, for -*zebul* resembles *zebel:* dung. Thus, those who despised the Baal of Ekron were able, by means of a slight change in pronunciation, to heap scorn upon him by conveying the thought that he was nothing but a "lord of dung." But, however this may be, in New Testament usage Beelzebul is definitely "the prince of the demons," as Luke 11:15, 18 proves. Beelzebul is Satan.

What these men are saying, then, is this: "Not God but the devil has given Jesus the power to cast out demons." Mark's parallel account even adds a second charge, namely, "He has Beelzebul," that is, "He is possessed by Beelzebul, by Satan." Cf. John 7:20; 8:48, 52; 10:20.

It is indeed hard to understand how the very One who became incarnate in order to heal the oppressed (Acts 10:38), to seek and to save the lost (Luke 19:10), and who, in order to achieve his purpose, was willing to undergo agonies that are beyond human description and comprehension, was by these religious "experts" described as being possessed by Satan and as performing miracles, including that of expelling demons, *by Beelzebul's power.*

That this terrible hatred continued for some time among the Jews, especially among their leaders, is clear from an examination of the sources mentioned in the following footnote.[384]

---

384. Helpful literature on the relation between Jews and Christians during the early centuries A.D. is represented by the following books and articles:

In the brief summary here given, the books and articles to which reference is made are listed in the note.

Both Justin Martyr (ch. 117) and Eusebius (Book II, ch. 3) make mention of the phenomenal growth of the church during the apostolic and post-apostolic era. It is easy to understand that this fact did not please the Jews.

They did not deny the reality of the miracles Jesus had performed, but ascribed them to magic, sorcery, help furnished by Satan. See, for example, the Babylonian Talmud *Sanhedrin* 43a (Baraitha), and Justin Martyr, ch. 69. They regarded the fact that Jesus was crucified as proving that God had rejected him (Justin Martyr, ch. 32; cf. Matt. 27:43).

This hostile attitude of the Jews toward Jesus is also clear from their view of the *minim*, that is, those of their own race who had become Christians. (See *minim* titles in footnote.)

In this connection something should be said about the *Shemoneh Esreh*. The word means *eighteen*, in the present context referring to the eighteen-item prayer, according to tradition composed by the men of The Great Synagogue. It was intended to be prayed three times a day. It is a very impressive prayer, beginning and ending with "Blessed art thou, Lord." In this prayer the worshiper not only praises God for blessings received, but also asks for an increase in the knowledge of his "law," for forgiveness of sin, healing, peace, favor to be bestowed on proselytes, etc.

But what happened to this prayer? It was soon felt that it should contain an imprecation against the *minim*. The following formula was adopted, "May the Nazarenes and the *minim* perish and be exterminated in a moment." The inclusion of this item gave rise to the remark of Justin Martyr, "In y o u r synagogues y o u curse those who believe in Christ" (ch. 16; cf. ch. 96).

Dalman, G., *Christentum und Judentum*, Leipsic, 1898; English tr. *Christianity and Judaism*, Oxford, 1901.

Eusebius, *The Ecclesiastical History* (Loeb Classical Library), London, 1953.

Finkelstein, L., *The Jews, Their History, Culture, and Religion*, New York, 1949.

Hertzberg, A. (editor), *Judaism*, New York, 1962.

Justin Martyr, *Dialogue with Trypho*, especially chapters 9, 16, 32, 69, 117. This work—as also the works of the other fathers—has been published in several "sets," e.g., in *The Ante-Nicene Fathers*, Grand Rapids, various dates; *The Fathers of The Church*, New York, various dates, etc.

Lachs, S. T., "Rabbi Abbahu and the Minim," *JQR* 60 (1969–1970), esp. p. 198.

Mishna, The, Engl. tr. by H. Danby, London, 1933.

Montefiore, C. F., *Rabbinic Literature and Gospel Teaching*, New York, 1970.

Moore, G. F., *Judaism in the First Five Centuries of the Christian Era*, Cambridge, 1927–1930.

Mulder, H., *De Minim*, Kampen, 1971.

. . . ., *Geschiedenis van de Palestijnse Kerk*, Kampen, no date.

Origen, *Against Celsus*, in *The Ante-Nicene Fathers*, etc.

Pick, B., *The Talmud, What It Is*, New York, 1887.

Schürer, E., *Geschichte des jüdischen Volkes im Zeitalter Jesu Christi*, Leipzig, 1886–1890. Engl. tr.: *A History of the Jewish People in the Time of Jesus Christ*, Edinburgh, 1890, 1891.

Strack, H. L., *Jesus, die Häretiker und die Christen nach den ältesten jüdischen Angaben*, Munich, 1910.

S.BK., for title see The List of Abbreviations, p. xi.

Talmud, The Babylonian, Engl. tr. Boston, 1918; esp. *Sanhedrin* 43a (Baraitha).

Walker, T., *Jewish Views of Jesus*, New York, 1951.

So intense was this Jewish hostility toward Jesus and his followers that, while it was willing to overlook the error of the synagogue leader who, in reciting the *Shemoneh Esreh,* inadvertently skipped one or two petitions, it ruled that he who skipped the imprecation touching the *minim* must lose his position.

It is only fair to state that in the course of the centuries this terrible item was gradually modified, so that today no one surely can find fault with the petition, "May all wickedness vanish."

The terrible words, "It is by Beelzebul, the prince of the demons, that he casts out demons," show how intensely these critics hated Jesus. They despised him because of the crowds that were always gathering around him; because he claimed divine prerogatives; did not honor their traditions about the sabbath, fasts, and ablutions; associated with publicans and sinners; exerted what they considered a baneful influence upon the people; and was their opposite. To be sure, not all the Pharisees and scribes hated Jesus, but many did.

In their heart of hearts Christ's enemies must have realized that Jesus was infinitely better than they were. His humility (Luke 22:27) stood in sharp contrast with their pomposity (Matt. 23:5-7); his sincerity (John 8:46) with their hypocrisy (Mark 7:6); his sympathy (Luke 7:13) with their cruelty (Matt. 23:13).

16. Others, tempting (him), were demanding of him a sign from heaven. They demanded a sign, as if the double miracle—triple, according to Matt. 12:22—was insufficient evidence in support of the question asked by some of the people, "Could this be the Son of David?" (Matt. 12:23).

Who were these sign-seekers? Answer: "Some of the scribes and Pharisees" (Matt. 12:38).

What did they want? That he would cause fire to come down from heaven? Unwilling to acknowledge that God's great Sign (Luke 2:34; 11:29, 30) was standing in their very midst, they asked for a sign! In fact, they were *always* asking for signs (I Cor. 1:22) . . . and wondering how to destroy the Sign by God sent down from heaven to earth! Christ's answer to their demand is found in 11:29-32.

For the present Jesus annihilates their wicked assertion: "It is by Beelzebul, the prince of the demons, that he casts out demons." His refutation of their contention is found in verses 17-22. Luke's report of this answer begins as follows:

17-20. But he, knowing their thoughts, said to them, Any kingdom divided against itself is on the way to ruin, and a house divided against a house fails. Moreover, if Satan is divided against himself, how shall his kingdom stand? (I say this) because y o u are asserting that I expel demons by Beelzebul. Now if it is by Beelzebul that I cast out demons, by whom do y o u r sons cast them out? Therefore they shall be y o u r judges. But if it is by the finger of God that I cast out demons, then the kingdom of God has come upon y o u.

Jesus knew exactly what was going on in the minds of his critics. Cf. 5:22;

6:8; 9:47; John 2:25; 21:17. He then, in substance, answers them as follows:

a. If what y o u say were true, Satan would be destroying his own work. No kingdom divided against itself survives. No house or family either. (Was he thinking of his own family? See Matt. 12:46, 47; John 7:5. But see also Acts 1:14. Clearly the family of Jesus did not remain divided, mother against brothers, but became united at last.) Jesus' argument continues as follows:

b. It is inconsistent for y o u, my critics, on the one hand to approve of the work y o u r "sons"—probably "followers"—are doing when they presumably cast out demons, and, on the other hand, to condemn my demon-expulsions. Will not y o u r sons, sensing this inconsistency, be y o u r judges?

c. The very fact that the envoys of Satan, God's archenemy, are being expelled proves that it is *by God's finger*—his *power* (see Exod. 8:19)—that I am driving them out. It shows that God's royal dominion has reached y o u, that here and now the divine sovereignty is revealing itself in works of power and mercy.

The Savior's argument continues as follows:

21, 22. When a strong man, armed to the teeth, guards his own house, his possessions are secure. But when someone (who is) stronger than he comes and overpowers him, he carries off the armor in which the man trusted, and distributes his goods as spoils.

Here Jesus compares Satan to a fully-armed, strong man. As long as no one attacks this powerful tyrant he is secure in the possession of the souls and bodies of his demon-possessed victims. But when Someone who is stronger than he overpowers him, the Stronger One renders him powerless as far as his victims are concerned. The armor in which he had placed his trust is carried away by the victor.

The Stronger One is Jesus himself. See Matt. 3:11; Mark 1:7, 8; Luke 3:16. In the desert of temptation had he not proved himself to be indeed mightier than the tempter?

The Stronger One, having conquered, distributes "the goods"—formerly Satan's, but now Christ's—as "spoils." Here Ps. 68:18 (LXX 69:19) comes to our mind. That is the passage of which Paul, in Eph. 4:8–10, makes such excellent use. See N.T.C. on Ephesians, pp. 189–191.

The "spoils" are *distributed*. They become "gifts to men." A good illustration is found in Luke 8:38, 39 (cf. Mark 5:19, 20). That passage too, like verse 14 here in Luke, concerns a man who a little earlier was a demoniac. It reads as follows: "Now the man from whom the demons had gone out kept begging to go with him. But Jesus sent him away, saying, 'Return home, and tell what great things God has done for you.' So he went away, proclaiming all over town what great things Jesus had done for him." That man, previously numbered among Satan's "goods," became one of the "gifts" distributed by Christ.

The preceding has made very plain that Jesus and his critics are diametrically opposed. The critics are saying, "It is by Beelzebul, the prince of the demons, that he casts out demons." But there are other people in the audience who are wondering whether Jesus could perhaps be the Christ (Matt. 12:23). Are there also some who would like to be on the side of both Jesus and his critics? Or on neither side? Is neutrality possible? That question is answered with a strong negative in verse

23. He who is not with me is against me, and he who does not gather with me scatters.

In the struggle between Christ and Satan neutrality is impossible. See also Matt. 12:30; Mark 9:40. If a person is not on the side of Christ, he is *down on,* that is, *against* Christ.

Compromise fails. When "the sons of God" marry "the daughters of men," the result is the Flood (Gen. 6:1, 2, 13). When King Saul brings God an offering of partial obedience, he is rejected (I Sam. 15:1-23). By subordinating the true religion of Jehovah to selfish political interests Jeroboam brings a curse upon himself, his family, and his nation (I Kings 12:25-30; 13:4, 5; 14:6-16). And when Peter, in a moment of weakness, compromises the doctrine of "salvation solely by grace," he deserves the rebuke administered by Paul (Gal. 2:11-21). The policy of "fearing Jehovah and worshiping one's own gods" (II Kings 17:33) never succeeds.

Joshua knew this (Josh. 24:15), and so did Elijah (I Kings 18:21).

Moreover, the sinister policy of half-covenanting with the world, the attempt to compromise, confuses and therefore *scatters* the sheep (Matt. 9:36); while steadfast loyalty *gathers* them (Isa. 40:11; John 10:16).

For *Practical Lessons* and *Greek Words,* etc., see pp. 632-635.

---

24 "Now when the unclean spirit goes out of a man, it wanders through waterless places, seeking rest; and, finding none, it says, 'I will return to my house that I left.' 25 It goes and finds it swept clean and put in order. 26 Then it goes and fetches[385] seven other spirits more wicked than itself, and they come and live there. And the final condition of that person becomes worse than the former."

11:24-26 *The Parable of The Return of the Unclean Spirit*
Cf. Matt. 12:43-45

Verse 24 may seem to introduce an entirely new subject. More probable, however, is the theory according to which the entire rather lengthy section, beginning with verse 14 and extending at least through verse 36 and in a sense even to the end of the chapter, forms a unit. In verse 16 some people are asking for a sign; not until verse 29 does Jesus reflect on this request. Also Luke 11:14, 15 speaks about "a demon" and "demons," and verse 24 similarly about "the unclean spirit." Finally, in an almost exact parallel

---

385. Or: brings along.

(Matt. 12:43–45) and its context the expression *evil generation* occurs in both
verse 39 and verse 45 (cf. Luke 11:29).[386]

With this as background, we arrive at the conclusion that the gist of Luke
11:24–26, in its context, is this: Some people—Pharisees, scribes, and their
followers—have accused Jesus of being allied with Satan, even of being
demon-possessed (Mark 3:22; cf. John 7:20; 8:48, 52; 10:20). Jesus is now
stating that these enemies are themselves "repossessed," and not just by *one*
but by *eight* demons.

Religiously things had not always been as bad as they were now. There
had been a time when the positive note, "Be converted," sounded by John
the Baptist, had gained many followers (Matt. 3:5; Luke 3:7). A little later
the same admonition proceeding from the lips of Jesus (Matt. 4:17), together with his other very positive teaching, had been greeted with enthusiasm (John 3:26). It may have seemed for a while as if a demon had
been driven out of the Israel of that day. But under the influence of scribes
and Pharisees, envious men, the picture was even now rapidly changing. At
this very moment these wicked leaders are plotting Christ's destruction
(Matt. 12:14). And at last the Jewish people as represented in front of the
cross will cry out, "Crucify, crucify" (Matt. 27:20–23; Luke 23:21, 23). They
will do so prompted by their leaders (John 19:6, 15, 16). The *one* demon
was being replaced by *eight.*

Understood in this light, the illustration Jesus uses becomes clear. The
connection is seen to be *very close.*

**24, 25. Now when the unclean spirit goes out of a man, it wanders
through waterless places, seeking rest; and, finding none, it says, I will
return to my house that I left. It goes and finds it swept clean and put in
order.**

Questions arise; for example, "Why is this unclean spirit described as
wandering through 'waterless places'?"

Possible answer: If we are accustomed to associate the good angels with
places in which order, beauty, and fulness of life prevail, does it not seem
natural to link evil angels with regions where disorder, desolation, and
death dominate?

And what about the house that is left empty ("swept clean and put in
order")? That kind of condition may well describe Israel during the days of
the Baptist's active ministry and shortly thereafter. Many people seem to
have been scared of "the axe already lying at the root of the tree." They
were frightened sufficiently to accept baptism, and were perhaps even
willing to stop committing some of their gross sins. But harmlessness is not

---

386. The slight difference between Matthew's and Luke's version of this saying do not touch
the essence. Luke, as often, abbreviates. Thus, in addition to "swept clean and put in order"
Matthew has the word *unoccupied;* to "fetches" or "brings back" Matthew adds "with it"; and
Matthew's final sentence, "So it shall also be with this generation," is lacking in Luke; but see
Luke 11:29.

the same as holiness. *An empty house* is not *a warm, welcoming home.* Desisting from doing wrong differs by a whole heaven from being a blessing.

What Jesus demands is the entire devotion of the heart, so that it will render spontaneous thanksgiving to God and for his sake will be a blessing to the neighbor. Nothing less than this is required. The fig tree that produces nothing but leaves is cursed even though it produces no rotten fruit (Matt. 21:19). The man who buried his "pound" (Luke 19:22, 23) is rejected. Those who during the present life have done nothing for the hungry, thirsty, etc., never enter the halls of glory (Matt. 25:41–46). Cf. James 4:6.

It was for this very reason that there was bound to be a collision between Jesus and his critics. Kindness began to clash with coldness, broadmindedness with clannishness, outgoingness (love) with selfishness. Moreover, the Pharisees and scribes had their many followers among the people in general. Jesus too had many disciples. As his enemies saw it, that made matters worse. So they hated him even more. Their condition got to be like the one pictured in the parable: the once-*possessed* individual became *repossessed:*

26. Then it goes and fetches seven other spirits more wicked than itself, and they come and live there. And the final condition of that person becomes worse than the former.

Do these words seem rather harsh perhaps? In reality they are not. They reveal the truth. Besides, do we not detect a summons to conversion? See such passages in this chapter as verses 9–13, 20, 23, 28, 32, 35, 41, 42, and the implied warning in *this* very verse (26b).

For *Practical Lessons* and *Greek Words*, etc., see pp. 632–635.

---

27 Now when he was saying these things, a certain woman from the crowd lifted up her voice and said to him, "Blessed is the womb that bore you, and the breasts at which you nursed!" 28 But he said, "Yes, but better still, blessed are those who listen to the word of God and observe it!"

11:27, 28 *True Blessedness*

27. Now when he was saying these things, a certain woman from the crowd lifted up her voice and said to him, Blessed is the womb that bore you, and the breasts at which you nursed!

It is not surprising that it was Luke, he alone, who recorded this exclamation. One of the outstanding characteristics of his Gospel is that again and again it introduces incidents showing with what tenderness and love Jesus treated women, and also, as in the present case, how women responded to him. For details see *Introduction*, point V D.

It is clear that this lady was standing in the audience that had gathered around Jesus. She listened and listened. At last she became so deeply impressed and carried away by the force, truthfulness, and wisdom of his words that the thought struck her: "How truly blessed his mother must be!"

She could not restrain herself. Suddenly, in the hearing of all, she cried out, "Blessed is the womb that bore you," etc.

Of course, she was right. Had not Elizabeth, "filled with the Holy Spirit," pronounced a similar blessing on both Mary and "the fruit of her womb"? See 1:41, 42; cf. verse 48.

Yes, what she said was good. It was wonderful . . . but not complete, as Jesus is about to show:

28. But he said, Yes, but better still, blessed are those who listen to the word of God and observe it!

Jesus did not deny what this lady had said. In fact, he confirmed it. But he also broadened its scope and in that sense perfected it. He widened the sphere of true blessedness so as to include not only Mary but all genuine believers.

After all, Mary's personal blessedness did not consist exclusively or even primarily in the fact that she had given birth to the Messiah but in this, that she had listened carefully to the word of God and had surrendered herself to his will. Confronted with mystery, she had said to Gabriel, "Behold, the handmaid of the Lord. May it be with me according to your word!" Though she erred at times (2:49; John 2:3, 4), there can be no question of the fact that her faith conquered every obstacle (John 2:5; 19:25; Acts 1:14). And that, after all, is what counts, namely, listening to the word of God and observing it. Thus also Luke 6:47, 48; 8:21; cf. Matt. 7:24; 12:50.

For *Practical Lessons* and *Greek Words*, etc., see pp. 632–635.

On the basis of Matt. 12:23; Luke 11:14b–16, picture the composite

---

11:29–32 *The Craving for Signs Rebuked*
Note the almost verbal parallel, especially that between Matt. 12:42 and Luke 11:31; and that between Matt. 12:41 and Luke 11:32. Since this chart appears in a commentary on Luke, *its* sequence has been followed.

MATTHEW 12 (Also see Mark 8:12)	LUKE 11
Verse 38	*Verse 16*
Then some of the scribes and Pharisees answered him, saying, "Teacher, we wish to see a sign from you."	Others, tempting (him), were demanding of him a sign from heaven.
Verse 39	*Verse 29*
Answering, he said to them, "An evil and adulterous generation is looking for a sign, but no sign shall be given to it except that of Jonah the prophet.	Now as the crowds were increasing, he said, "This generation is a wicked generation. It seeks a sign, but no sign shall be given to it except that of Jonah.
Verse 40	*Verse 30*
For as Jonah was in the belly of the sea-monster three days and three nights so also shall the Son of man be in the heart of the earth three days and three nights.	For as Jonah became a sign for the Ninevites, so also shall the Son of man be for this generation.

Verse 42	*Verse 31*
The queen of the South shall arise in the judgment with this generation and shall condemn it, for she came from the end of the earth to listen to the wisdom of Solomon; and behold, something greater than Solomon is here.	The queen of the South shall arise in the judgment with the men of this generation and shall condemn them, for she came from the ends of the earth to listen to the wisdom of Solomon; and behold, something greater than Solomon is here.
Verse 41	*Verse 32*
Men of Nineveh shall stand up in the judgment with this generation, and shall condemn it, for they repented at the preaching of Jonah; but look, something greater than Jonah is here."	Men of Nineveh shall stand up in the judgment with this generation, and shall condemn it, for they repented at the preaching of Jonah; but look, something greater than Jonah is here."

scene: A large and constantly increasing crowd surrounds the Savior. Deeply impressed with his miracles, including the double one mentioned in Luke 11:14, some of the people wonder whether Jesus could be the Christ. Scribes and Pharisees, on the contrary, ascribe his miracle-working power to satanic influence. While some are trying their level best to convince the people that this is the solution to the problem of the remarkable things they have been witnessing and about which everybody is talking, others are already urging Jesus to bring about "a sign from heaven." And no doubt there were many curious onlookers, wondering what was going to happen next. Whatever it was, they did not wish to miss it. For the explanation of verse 16 see above, p. 620.

Then Jesus responded.

29. Now as the crowds were increasing he said, This generation is a wicked generation. It seeks a sign, but no sign shall be given to it except that of Jonah.

As to this sign, what the people wanted was something thrilling, exciting, sensational, a sign *from heaven*. Well, just what did they mean? Did they want Jesus to cause the heavenly constellations to change places in the zodiac? Did they want him to make the Bull (Taurus) catch up with the Giant Hunter (Orion)? Must he perhaps blaze his name across the sky in enormous letters of gold? Was he expected to produce in the sky above them a vision of Michael suddenly leaving his celestial abode and coming forth to deliver the Jews from the galling yoke of the Romans? Their demand was wicked, for in addition to being insulting and impudent it was also hypocritical, for they felt sure that what they had asked Jesus to do he could not do anyway.

Jesus begins by calling these sign-seekers "wicked." Matthew adds "adulterous," that is, unfaithful to Jehovah, Israel's "Husband." See Isa. 54:5; Jer. 3:8, 20, 21; 31:32; Ezek. 16:35 ff.; Hos. 2:1 ff., and cf. II Cor. 11:2.

"Wicked" or "evil" was not too strong a term, for it must be constantly borne in mind that this request for a sign was made (a) at the very moment when a multiple sign had just been performed; (b) in spite of the fact that all kinds of signs—miracles of healing, demon-expulsions, even the raising of the dead—had already occurred; and (c) all of this and much more—for example, those marvelous discourses—in clear fulfilment of prophecy!

It is not surprising therefore that Jesus refuses to give these enemies, the Pharisees and scribes and their adherents, the sign for which they are asking. He (and the Father in connection with him) will give them his own sign, a sign in which he will triumph completely over them, to their everlasting dismay, namely, the sign of Jonah the prophet, the latter's recovery from "the three days and three nights" in the belly of the sea-monster. The point is that as Jonah was swallowed up by the sea-monster, so Jesus will be swallowed up by the earth; and as Jonah was delivered from his imprisonment, so also Jonah's great Antitype will arise from the grave. Rescued Jonah and Resurrected Jesus are signs.

Luke, however, expresses himself very briefly. On p. 626 cf. Matt. 12:40 with Luke 11: **30. For as Jonah became a sign for the Ninevites, so also shall the Son of man be for this generation.**

The idea of some, namely, that the authentic preaching of the word of God, first by Jonah, later by Jesus, is what Luke has in mind when he speaks of a "sign," is clearly inadequate. This is true especially in view of the parallel passage, Matt. 12:40, which cannot be set aside, as if these two evangelists, Matthew and Luke, were referring to different matters.

For the Ninevites the "sign" was clearly the miraculous reappearance of the man thought to be dead. Had he not been cast into the sea during a raging storm, and even swallowed by a "great fish"? Yet, here he was, alive and well! For Christ's contemporaries the sign was going to be his glorious resurrection; see not only Matt. 12:40 but also John 2:18 (the request for a sign) and verse 19 (Christ's answer).

Though all this is true, there is perhaps an even better way of saying it; at least *another* way, one which, on the basis of Scripture, must receive recognition. It is this: *Jonah and Jesus are themselves signs.*

Take a good look at rescued Jonah. Does he not *signify* the amazing *power* of God, his ability to rescue a man who, in the normal course of events, should certainly have died? And does he not also signify the *grace*—or, if you prefer, *love*—of God, his willingness to use a man who, by going west when God had directed him to go east, and by his attempt to hide from God(!), as if that were possible, had stubbornly defied God's command?

And rivet your attention on Christ, resurrected from death! Is not he also a *sign*? Does he not *signify* in his very person the *might* of God? And also his *covenant faithfulness* to all those precious Messianic prophecies and promises? Read again what was said on p. 126 in explanation of Luke 1:72, 73.

Jesus Christ, crucified and then risen from the dead, himself God's Sign! Is not that also what Simeon said in so many words? He said, "Mark well, this child is destined ... to be a sign." Did not Jesus point away from himself, viewed separately, to The Triune God, his Sender? Or, if one prefers, to the Father, as representing the Trinity? Can one even think

The Scribes and Pharisees and The Queen of the South

Scribes and Pharisees and Their Followers:	The Queen of the South (See I Kings 10; II Chron. 9)
a. For them the truth is near at hand, within easy reach (Luke 22:53).	a. She braved the hardships of a lengthy journey over difficult terrain. She probably came from what today is Yemen, in the southwestern part of the Arabian peninsula, on the Asian shore of the Red Sea, opposite Ethiopia (Africa). Her trip must have covered about 2000 kilometers.
b. They have access to One wiser, better, and greater by far than Solomon.	b. She came from what was then considered "the ends of the earth," to listen to Solomon's wisdom, "in connection with the name of the Lord," even though the truth concerning God was but very imperfectly reflected in Solomon.
c. They *give nothing*, but are plotting *to take away* Christ's very life.	c. She *gave* Solomon of her treasures, an enormous present (I Kings 10:10).
d. They have enjoyed many religious advantages.	d. She had merely heard reports.
e. They have been invited, urged even, to accept Jesus, and the truth in him (Matt. 11:28-30; cf. 22:1-5; Luke 14:15-24).	e. It is not reported that she had received any invitation at all.

rightly about Jesus, crucified and risen again, without also thinking of God's faithfulness to his covenant promise?[387]

Jesus now continues what he began in verse 29, namely, to emphasize the wickedness of the people of his generation. He does this now by contrasting his own contemporaries with "the queen of the South." The reference is to the Queen of Sheba.

31. The queen of the South shall arise in the judgment with the men of this generation and shall condemn them, for she came from the ends of the earth to listen to the wisdom of Solomon; and behold, something greater than Solomon is here.

Jesus tells his audience that in the final judgment, when this queen will arise alongside the men of his generation who are rejecting him, she will condemn them. In the eyes of the Judge her case will be far more favorable than theirs.

Similar is the next contrast:

32. Men of Nineveh shall stand up in the judgment with this generation and shall condemn it, for they repented at the preaching of Jonah; but look, something greater than Jonah is here.

---

387. The idea here set forth, namely, that Jesus himself is "the sign" is also defended by S. F. H. J. Berkelbach van Der Sprenkel in his book *Het Evangelie van Lukas*, 'S-Gravenhage (The Hague), 1964, p. 212. Worthy of study is also Zech. 3:8, "Men that are a sign" (A.R.V.).

Comparison Between Those Whom Jesus Addresses, and Ninevites

Scribes and Pharisees and their followers:	*Ninevites:* See the book of Jonah
a. It is the Son of God himself, "one greater than Jonah," who addresses them again and again, and bids them to be converted (Luke 5:32; 13:3; etc.).	a. It was a minor prophet who preached to them.
b. This Christ is completely sinless (John 8:46), filled with wisdom and compassion (Matt. 11:27–30; 15:32; I Cor. 1:24).	b. This prophet was a sinful, foolish, and rebellious person (Jonah 1:3; 4:1–3, 9b).
c. He presents the message of grace and pardon, of salvation full and free (Luke 19:10; John 7:37).	c. His message was one of doom. Though a call to repentance and conversion was certainly implied, the emphasis was on "Yet forty days, and Nineveh shall be overthrown" (Jonah 3:4).
d. This message is being fortified by miracles in which prophecy is being fulfilled (Luke 4:16–21; cf. Isa. 35:5, 6; 61:1–3).	d. There were no miracles or other authenticating signs to confirm Jonah's message.
e. It is being brought to a people who have enjoyed ever so many spiritual advantages (Deut. 4, 7, 8; Ps. 147:19, 20; Isa. 5:1–4; Amos 3:2a; Rom. 3:1, 2; 9:4, 5).	e. Jonah's message was addressed to a people with none of the advantages that scribes, Pharisees, and their followers had enjoyed.

Yet Ninevites repented; most of the Israelites do not (John 1:11; 12:37). Less enlightened people obeyed less enlightened preaching, but more enlightened people refuse to obey the Light of the world. The question is asked, "But was this repentance of Ninevites genuine, that is, unto salvation?" The answer, often given, is that it was not, otherwise Nineveh would not have been destroyed. Objection: The destruction of this great city occurred about the year 612 B.C., that is, about a century and a half after Jonah's preaching. It is therefore unjust to charge Ninevites of Jonah's day with the sins of a much later generation.

Scripture nowhere claims that the repentance of *all* Ninevites was genuine, but neither does it leave the impression that none of them were saved; rather the opposite. That there were indeed genuine conversions in Nineveh, perhaps many of them, seems to be implied both in the prophetic book and here in Luke 11:32. The idea that the repentance of Ninevites was not genuine, that it was merely from vice to virtue, is open to objections: (a) in Luke 10:13–15 Nineveh is not included in the list of Old Testament impenitent cities; and (b) if the repentance referred to here in Luke 11:32 is not genuine it is hard to explain the statement, "Men of Nineveh *shall stand up in the judgment* with this generation and shall condemn it." It should be noted that concerning these "men of Nineveh" it does not say, as it does in the case of those of Sodom and Gomorrah, Tyre and Sidon, that in the judgment it will be "more tolerable" for them, but that, like the queen of the South (Luke 11:31), they shall stand up in the judgment and shall condemn "this" generation, that is, the generation of the scribes and Pharisees and their followers. Since it is the teaching of Scripture (Dan. 7:22; Matt. 19:28; I Cor. 6:2; Rev. 15:3, 4; 20:4) that God's children are going to participate in the final judgment (for example, by praising God in Christ for his judgments?), this statement of Jesus about the role of certain Ninevites in that Great Assize is understandable, especially if their repentance was genuine.

Again the Pharisees and scribes are reminded of the greatness of their sin in rejecting and blaspheming the Christ, the One far more exalted than Jonah.

For *Practical Lessons* and *Greek Words*, etc., see pp. 632–635.

---

33 "No one, after lighting a lamp, puts it in a cellar or under the peck-measure, but on the lampstand, in order that those who come in may see the light. 34 Your eye is your body's lamp. When your eye is sound, your whole body will be illumined; when it is in poor condition, your body will also be darkened. 35 Therefore watch out that the light within you may not be darkness. 36 So, if your whole body is full of light, no part of it being darkened, it will be entirely illumined, as when the lamp illumines you with its shining brightness."

11:33–36 *The Light of the Body*
Cf. Matt. 5:15; 6:22, 23

The resemblance between Luke 11:33 and 8:16 (see also Matt. 5:15; Mark 4:21) is apparent at once. But this should present no problem. Why should it be wrong for a speaker to use the same, or a similar, saying on more than one occasion? In the case of Luke 11:33 and its parallel in Matthew contextual study even shows that the two passages do not have the same purpose. In the Matthew context the meaning is, "Be witnesses." Here in Luke the basic sense is rather, "Permit the light to shine into your own hearts. Do not obstruct it." It is true that the broader purpose—to allow the light to illumine others—is also present. However, as the sequel clearly shows, that is not here the main thought.

Besides, a moment's study immediately reveals that the Lucan paragraph harmonizes beautifully with the preceding context. Christ's enemies have been slandering him. They have been saying, "It is by Beelzebul, the prince of the demons, that he casts out demons" (verse 15). Also they have been demanding "a sign from heaven" (verses 16, 29–32). What all this amounts to is that they have been saying, "It is *your* fault that we do not believe in you."

It is therefore most appropriate that Jesus now shows them that the actual situation is the other way around; to put it colloquially, that "the shoe is on the other foot." It is not Jesus who is at fault but his enemies are to blame. The Light is shining, but *they* are obstructing it! The Father had sent his Son into the world to be its Light, but these people are turning their backs on this great Gift!

33. No one, after lighting a lamp, puts it in a cellar or under the peck-measure, but on the lampstand, in order that those who come in may see the light. For "lamp" and "lampstand" see on 8:16. What Jesus means is this: "In the natural sphere no one would think of lighting a lamp and then hiding it in a cellar or under the peck-measure; yet that is exactly what y o u, my critics, are doing in the spiritual sphere. Instead of allowing my light to shine into y o u r hearts and lives ['on the lampstand,' where everyone who enters can see it], y o u are obscuring it." How were they doing this? See Matt. 15:3; 23:23.

Continued: **34. Your eye is your body's lamp. When your eye is sound, your whole body will be illumined; when it is in poor condition, your body also will be darkened.**

The figure is easy to understand. When a person's eyes (sing. "eye" here for pl.) are in good condition, the entire body "will be illumined," will know exactly what to do. The foot will know where to step. The hand will realize how to take hold, etc. The opposite is true when, through some illness, a person's eyes do not function properly. Such a person will be groping in the dark. Those bodily organs over which he would normally exercise conscious control will now refuse to function properly. They are, as it were, "in the dark" as to what to do.

So also when a person's inner disposition is right, having been sanctified by the Holy Spirit, his entire personality will be illumined. He will possess the true knowledge of God, will experience peace of mind that passes all understanding, and will be able to thank the Lord for joy unspeakable and full of glory. On the contrary, when his heart is not right with God, this lamentable condition will also affect his entire personality. Instead of spiritual progress there will be spiritual retardation and deterioration.

35. Therefore watch out that the light within you may not be darkness.

It is important to notice that while in verses 19, 20 Jesus was addressing his audience as a whole, using the plural y o u and y o u r, he now directs his attention to each person individually, and binds it on the conscience of each to ask himself whether the light of the gospel has brought about a genuine, deep, inner change in his heart and life; that is, whether he now truly loves God and the neighbor, so that the fruits of the Holy Spirit are evident in his life; or whether perhaps even that which he considers to be *light* is actually *darkness*. See also *Practical Lessons* on this verse.

36. So, if your whole body[388] **is full of light, no part of it being darkened, it will be entirely illumined, as when the lamp illumines you with its shining brightness.**

Though this sentence may at first appear to be an illustration of meaningless repetition, careful study of its parts proves that it is not. Note the emphasis on *completeness* in the condition: "no part of it being darkened." Then note the stress on *quality* in the conclusion: "as when the lamp il-

---

388. Or: person.

lumines you with its shining brightness." In other words, the meaning may be paraphrased as follows: "So, if your *entire* person is full of spiritual light [holiness, wisdom, spiritual rejoicing, etc.], it will be *really* illumined. In fact, it will be as bright as when the lamp is shining upon you with undiminished brilliance."[389]

Practical Lessons Derived from 11:14–36

Verse 15

"But some people said, 'It is by Beelzebul, the prince of the demons, that he casts out demons.'" Hatred is an enemy of straight thinking.

Verse 22

"Someone (who is) stronger than he ... overpowers him." Not only during the trials of life but surely also at the approach of death it is a great comfort to know that Christ, symbolized by "the strong man," has conquered Satan. Therefore Rom. 8:31–39 applies.

Verse 23

"He who is not with me is against me."
Ascribed to several different authors are the lines:

> In things essential unity;
> In doubtful things liberty;
> In all things charity.

In all *essential* matters—those touching the basics of the Christian faith—a firm and united stand is required. There must be no attempt at compromise.

Verse 25

"Swept clean." "I don't smoke; I don't drink; I don't swear. Hallelujah, I'm a Christian." If a telephone pole could talk, it might say the same thing. But a series of zeros does not make a Christian. A million negatives do not produce even one positive. We pity the man with an empty *mind*. But what about the person with an empty *heart* ... and an empty *life?*

Verse 26

"The final condition of that person becomes worse than the former." Not to advance means to retreat. There is no standing still.

Verses 27, 28

"Blessed is the womb that bore you." Better still, "Blessed are those who listen to the word of God and observe it." An emotional outburst, if rooted in truth, has its

---

389. Notes on Greek words, phrases, and constructions in 11:14–36 begin on page 633.

value. One must be careful, however, not to make primary that which is, after all, secondary. Note the careful manner in which Jesus corrects and completes this lady's statement. He does so without discouraging her . . . a lesson for us all.

Verse 32

"Men of Nineveh . . . repented." Did we? Greater privileges imply heavier responsibilities. *Carpe diem!*

Verse 35

"Therefore watch out that the light within you may not be darkness." There are two kinds of darkness: (a) that of ignorance, and (b) that of stubborn unbelief. The second kind, here in view, is by far the more dangerous. It was that kind of darkness which reigned in the hearts of those who hated Jesus. Once present, it is hard to dislodge. "Watch out, therefore."

Notes on Greek Words, Phrases, and Constructions in 11:14-36

Verse 14.

κωφός, -ή, -όν; here: unable to speak, dumb, as in 1:22; but see also N.T.C. on Mark, p. 302, footnote 346.

Verse 15

Note instrumental use of ἐν = by.

Verses 17, 18

διαμερισθεῖσα, nom. s. fem. aor. pass. participle of διαμερίζω. Another form of the same verb is διεμερίσθη, third per. s. aor. indicat. pass. Cf. μέρος, part. Hence, the verb means: to separate into parts, to divide; sometimes, to distribute (Acts 2:45); in the pass.: to be divided.

ἐρημοῦται (cf. ἔρημος, desert), third per. s. pres. indicat. pass. of ἐρημόω, to ruin, lay waste, depopulate; here, in the pass., to be on the way to ruin. Cf. *hermit.*

σταθήσεται, third per. s. fut. indicat. pass. of ἵστημι; in pass., to stand, a word of very frequent occurrence both in the New Testament and in Greek generally.

Verse 19

This is a present general or first class conditional sentence, a statement assumed to be true.

διά has here the meaning "I say this because." See N.T.C. on John, Vol. I, p. 206, for remarks on "abbreviated expression."

Verse 20

Note the instrumental case of δάκτυλος, finger; in the New Testament used only in the Gospels. Cf. *dactyl* (a metrical foot of three syllables, like the three joints of a finger). For δακτύλιος, ring, see 15:22; and for χρυσοδακτύλιος, gold-ringed, see James 2:2.

ἔφθασεν, third per. s. aor. indicat. act. of φθάνω.

The following contextual translations should be considered for the various forms of this verb:

"has come upon" (Matt. 12:28; Luke 11:20; I Thess. 2:16).

"have attained" (Phil. 3:16).

"has not attained" (Rom. 9:31).

"were the first to come" (II Cor. 10:14).

"shall have no advantage over" or "shall not precede" (I Thess. 4:15).

Verses 21, 22

With ὅταν (verse 21 and 34) compare ἐπάν (verse 22). When there is a distinction, as is true here, ὅταν is more general, "whenever," referring to actions that may, or may not, occur; ἐπάν, more particular, more definite: a very concrete incident is portrayed in verse 22.

καθωπλισμένος, nom. s. masc. perf. pass. participle of καθοπλίζω (= κατά in perfective sense: completely, to the teeth; plus ὁπλίζω, to arm, equip; cf. I Peter 4:1). Cf. τὰ ὅπλα, arms, weapons (John 18:3, etc.); *hoplite, panoply*. The very word πανοπλία, armor, appears in verse 22; also in Eph. 6:11, 13. For αὐλή (here acc. -ν) see on 22:55.

ἐπεποίθει, third per. s. 2nd pluperf. of πείθω, to convince, persuade, etc. The 2nd perf. has the meaning of a present: to trust, rely on; hence, the pluperf. as used here means "he trusted," "he was trusting."

σκῦλα, acc. pl. of σκῦλον, spoils, that which is captured from the slain body of the foe. Cf. σκύλλω, basic meaning: to skin.

διαδίδωσιν, third per. s. pres. indicat. act. of διαδίδωμι, to divide up, to distribute as spoils (so here in Luke 11:22), or simply: to distribute (18:22; John 6:11; pass. Acts 4:35).

Verse 23

σκορπίζει, third per. s. pres. indicat. act. of σκορπίζω, to scatter. Here and in Matt. 12:30; John 10:12; 16:32 this verb is used in an unfavorable sense; in II Cor. 9:9 in a favorable sense: to distribute lavishly.

Verse 25

σεσαρωμένον, acc. s. masc. perf. pass. participle of σαρόω, to sweep; hence here: "swept," or "swept clean." There is, however, considerable support for σχολάζοντα, empty, unoccupied (as in Matt. 12:44).

κεκοσμημένον (same construction as the Greek word for "swept"), from κοσμέω, to order, adorn. Cf. *cosmos,* both in Greek and in English, the ordered universe, adornment.

Verse 26

χείρονα, nom. pl. neut. of χείρων, comparative of κακός; hence, worse.

Verse 27

ἐπάρασα, nom. s. fem. aor. act. participle of ἐπαίρω, to lift up, raise; in II Cor. 10:5 "that sets itself up against."

ἐθήλασας, sec. per. s. aor. indicat. act. of θηλάζω, (of the mother) to suckle; (of the child) to suck, nurse at. Cf. θηλή, breast.

Verse 28

μενοῦν*, a particle that corrects, confirms, and emphasizes. To give the exact English equivalent would be difficult, if not impossible. Worthy of consideration are such attempts as: (a) rather; (b) yes, but better still. Of these two I prefer the latter.

Verse 29

ἐπαθροιζομένων, gen. pl. pres. middle participle of ἐπαθροίζω* (= ἐπί, perfective, plus ἀθροίζω, to gather, as in 24:33), to gather increasingly, to increase.

Verse 32

εἰς in εἰς τὸ κήρυγμα is interpreted variously. Perhaps "at" is sufficiently broad in meaning to suffice as English equivalent.

Verse 33

κρύπτη*, a cellar; cf. crypt. Cf. κρύπτω, to hide, conceal. A cellar is, in a sense, a hidden place.

Verses 34–36

ἁπλοῦς, -ῆ, -οῦν, basically: simple, uncomplicated, but here in the sense of sound, healthy, normal.

φωτεινόν (occurring once in verse 34, twice in verse 36), illumined, full of light. By contrast σκοτεινόν, in these same verses, means darkened, full of darkness.

The possibility that in verse 36 σῶμα, basically *body*, indicates the entire *person* or *personality* deserves consideration. It seems to have that meaning in Rom. 12:1 and in Phil. 1:20. The context seems to favor that meaning also here in Luke 11:36.

ἀστραπῇ, dat. (instrumental) s. of ἀστραπή, "shining brightness," see the note on 10:18 on page 589.

---

37 Now after he had finished speaking, a Pharisee invited him to eat at his home. So he went in and reclined at table. 38 When the Pharisee saw that he had not ceremonially washed before the meal, he was surprised. 39 The Lord said to him, "Now then, y o u Pharisees clean the outside of the cup and of the plate, but inside y o u are full of extortion and wickedness. 40 Y o u fools! Did not he who made the outside make the inside also? 41 But put y o u r inner self into the business of helping the poor, and everything will be clean for y o u.

42 "But woe to y o u Pharisees, because y o u tithe mint, rue, in fact every garden herb; but y o u bypass justice and the love of God. But these y o u should have practiced, without neglecting the others.

43 "Woe to y o u Pharisees, because y o u love the chief seat in the synagogues and the formal salutations in the market places.

44 "Woe to y o u, for y o u are like unmarked graves: the people are walking over them without being aware of it."

45 One of the law-experts said to him, "Teacher, by saying these things you are insulting us as well." 46 So he replied,

"Woe to y o u also, law-experts, because y o u burden the people with burdens that are hard to bear, but y o u yourselves do not even touch these burdens with one of y o u r fingers.

47 "Woe to y o u, because y o u are building the tombs of the prophets,[390] and y o u r fathers killed them. 48 So y o u are testifying that y o u approve of the deeds of y o u r fathers: they killed them, and y o u build (their tombs). 49 For this reason also the Wisdom of God said, 'I will send them prophets and apostles. Some of them they will kill (and others) they will persecute'; 50 that the blood of all the prophets shed since the founding of the world may be exacted[391] from this generation, 51 from the blood of Abel to the blood of Zechariah, who perished between the altar and the sanctuary; yes, I tell y o u, it will indeed be exacted from this generation.

52 "Woe to y o u law-experts, because y o u have taken away the key to knowledge. Y o u yourselves did not enter, and y o u hindered those who were entering."

53 When he left there, the scribes and the Pharisees began to be violently enraged against him, and to ply him with questions, 54 plotting, as if in ambush, to catch him with respect to something (that might fall) from his lips.

11:37–54 Six Woes
Cf. Matt. 23:1–36; Mark 12:38–40; Luke 20:45–47

An invitation to eat at the home of a Pharisee is the connecting link between the preceding paragraph and this one. But is there not also a topical connection? Did not the seriousness of the sin of Jesus' enemies, in rejecting the light (verses 33–36), make it very appropriate for him (whose heart was ever filled with yearning to save the lost) to reveal to them what would be the result of their continued hostility? He now does this by pronouncing "woes" upon them.

As to the nature of these woes, they must be regarded as "denunciations." Any softer way of describing them fails to do justice to the exclamation *Y o u fools* (verse 40), and to such passages as verses 42, 44, 52, etc. But they are also "expressions of sorrow." These two designations—denunciations and expressions of sorrow—are not necessarily self-contradictory. See I Sam. 3:15–18; 15:13–31; II Sam. 12:7–13.

The woes here pronounced remind us of the similar ones recorded in Matt. 23.

37. Now after he had finished speaking, a Pharisee invited him to eat at his home. So he went in and reclined at table.

The strained relations between Jesus and the Pharisees did not prevent the latter from extending invitations to him to eat with them. Cf. 7:36. So once, after speaking, Jesus receives an invitation to lunch at the home of a Pharisee. He accepts, so that presently he has taken his place at the Pharisee's table. It appears that the Pharisee has also invited several of his comrades, both Pharisees and scribes (verses 39, 46, 53). The Pharisee may have invited Jesus because he was desirous to find out more about the man who was the topic of conversation on the part of so many people, the object of both praise and criticism. And Jesus probably accepted the invitation because he had a message for the Pharisees and scribes.

---

390. Or: memorial tombs (or: monuments) for the prophets.
391. Or: required. So also in verse 51.

Similarities Between Luke 11 and Matthew 23

Luke 11		Matt. 23
verse(s)		verse(s)
39	"but inside full of . . ."	25
42	"y o u tithe mint," etc.	23
43	"y o u love the chief seat"	6, 7
46	"heavy burdens"	4
47, 48	"prophets' tombs"	29–32
49	"some they [y o u] shall kill"	34
50, 51	"the blood of Abel"	35, 36
52	"y o u not entering"	13

Differences Between Luke 11 and Matthew 23

a. Luke 11 records six woes; Matthew records seven.

b. Those reported by Luke were addressed to Pharisees (verses 42–44) and law-experts, scribes (46, 47, 52). Those reported by Matthew, though also directed to the scribes and Pharisees, were *addressed* "to the crowds and to Christ's disciples."

c. Those found in Luke were spoken somewhat earlier than those found in Matthew (the latter on Tuesday of Passion Week).

d. The six were pronounced in a home, the seven in the temple.

38. When the Pharisee saw that he had not ceremonially washed before the meal, he was surprised.

The Pharisees continued to advocate strict compliance with the rules laid down by the prominent rabbis of former days. These rules had been passed on from one generation to another. In fact, ever so many minute ceremonial regulations regarding hundreds of matters were being constantly handed down as if salvation itself depended on all-out obedience. See Mark 7:3, 4. Thus also the very manner in which the water was supposed to be poured over the hands had been prescribed.[392]

This was not a matter of hygiene. It had nothing to do with germs. It was a matter of fear of ceremonial defilement; for example, on the way home from the synagogue one might have touched a Gentile or an article he had held in his hand.

Also, although it is true that for "ceremonially washed" the original uses a form of the verb *to baptize,* it is clear that in the present context this verb

392. See *The Mishna: Yadaim* 1:1 ff.

cannot very well refer to the immersion of the entire body. It refers, of course, to the already indicated act of pouring water over the hands.

Although it is not reported that the Pharisee made any remark about this omission on the part of Jesus, the Master knew exactly what his host was thinking. The text does not state this, but it is certainly implied in verses **39–41. The Lord said to him, Now then, y o u Pharisees clean the outside of the cup and of the plate, but inside y o u are full of extortion and wickedness. Y o u fools! Did not he who made the outside make the inside also? But put y o u r inner self into the business of helping the poor, and everything will be clean for y o u.**

Note the following:

a. "Jesus declared that to wash the body while the heart is impure is as absurd as to clean the outside of an unclean cup or platter. He declared that God who made the body created the soul also, and that God is more concerned with the latter than with the former" (C. R. Erdman on this passage).

b. There is a list of Old Testament passages in which obedience to ceremonial ordinances is contrasted with obedience to "the more important requirements of the law: justice and mercy and faithfulness" (Matt. 23:23). The list includes such passages as Isa. 1:10–17; 58:4–8; Amos 5:21–24; Micah 6:6–8. Surely if obedience to *divinely ordained* ceremonial ordinances does not rank as high in the eyes of God as does "to do justly, and to love kindness, and to walk humbly with your God," then obedience to purely *man-made* ceremonial regulations, while "the inside" is "full of extortion and wickedness," is worthless.

c. In several of these Old Testament passages "putting one's inner self into the business of helping the poor" is essentially what (using different phraseology) is advocated. It is therefore very probable that Luke 11:39–41 must be interpreted in the light of these Old Testament references. Not as if anyone can earn salvation by helping the poor, but when one's "inner self" expresses itself in performing works of mercy and kindness, doing this out of gratitude for mercy received, the divine approval rests upon the person so engaged (Matt. 5:7; II Cor. 9:7).

Jesus now proceeds to pronounce the six woes. The first three are specifically addressed to the Pharisees; the last three, to the law-experts or "lawyers."

42. But woe to y o u Pharisees, because y o u tithe mint, rue, in fact every garden herb; but y o u bypass justice and the love of God. Such *p*iosity!

The men here addressed scrupulously observed the tithing ordinance of Lev. 27:30–33; Deut. 14:22–29. In fact, as was usual with them, they even overdid it, by giving to the Lord the tenth portion of the small aromatic herbs which they grew in their gardens, and requiring their followers to do likewise. As they saw it, the "sweet-smelling" mint, the strong-scented rue, in fact every garden herb must by all means be tithed! Now in the law of Moses not a word is said about tithing these. However, if a person had reminded these Pharisees and company of this fact, they would immediately have answered, "But does not the law definitely demand that 'all increase of your seed' be tithed?" To the mind of a Pharisee this would have amounted to an unanswerable argument in favor of his position. However, careful examination of *the context* shows that what the law really meant—at least emphasized—was that, as far as products of the field were concerned, the three "great" crops of the land, namely, grain, wine, and oil, should be tithed. Pharisees were always illegitimately overextending or overstretching the law. Was not that exactly what they also did with respect to fasting, hand-rinsing, sabbath-observance, etc.?

However, they committed even a far greater sin: their inflexible insistence on tithing small garden herbs was coupled with neglect of the more important requirements of the law, namely, justice and the love of God. They stressed human regulations at the expense of divine ordinances! It is upon this point that all the emphasis is placed here in verse 42.

We see immediately that by the combination *justice* and *the love of God* not only the duty a man owes to his neighbors is emphasized (for this see also Zech. 7:8–10; Col. 3:12, 13), but in the same breath also his obligation toward *God:* loving him above all else.

Jesus adds: **but these y o u should have practiced without neglecting the others.**

This addition has led to conflicting interpretations. Two extreme positions should be avoided. On the one hand we should not interpret this to mean that, after all, Jesus is here endorsing the tithing of every little garden herb. If he were saying this, would he not be defeating his very argument? On the other hand, it is not necessary to draw the conclusion that since these words seem to be out of line with Christ's doctrine of freedom and with his entire argument against the Pharisees, he cannot have uttered them; so that, consequently, they must be regarded as a marginal note which, without any justification, was by a legalistic scribe subsequently inserted into the text. What Jesus probably meant was this: "These, that is, God's ordinances with respect to tithing, y o u should have observed, without neglecting the weightier matters of the law: justice and the love of God." As long as the divinely enacted ceremonial ordinances had not been blotted out (Col. 2:14), that is, as long as Jesus had not as yet died on the cross, the law with respect to tithing was still valid. The reference here is to *God's* law, not to man-made overextensions of God's law. Such totally unwarranted misapplications and misuses of the law had, of course, never been justified.

When the question is asked, "What principles does the New Testament contain to guide the believer in the financial contributions toward kingdom causes which he feels impelled to make?" the answer would be as follows:

(a) he should give systematically and proportionately, that is, in proportion to his ability (I Cor. 16:2); and (b) he should give generously and cheerfully (II Cor. 9:7).

The second woe:

43. Woe to y o u, Pharisees, because y o u love the chief seat in the synagogues and the formal salutations in the market places. Such *h*aughty behavior!

The chief seat in the synagogue was the one in front, facing the congregation. Thus seated a person enjoyed the double advantage of (a) being near the person reading or leading in prayer, and (b) being able to see everybody. Besides, being ushered to such a seat was regarded as a mark of honor.

As to "the formal salutations in the market places," this indicates not a mere cheery "hello" but a demonstration of respect, an elaborate verbal recognition of the prominence of the person(s) addressed.

44. Woe to y o u, for y o u are like unmarked graves: the people are walking over them without being aware of it. Such *a*dverse influence on unsuspecting followers!

According to a Jewish custom, just before the arrival of vast caravans of people traveling to Jerusalem to attend the Passover, graves were whitewashed. The reason this was done was that they might be clearly visible, so that no one would ceremonially defile himself by walking over a grave. But at times some graves were inadvertently left unwashed, unmarked. What Jesus is saying then is this: just as by walking over such an unmarked grave a person would become *ceremonially* defiled, so by "walking" (conducting oneself) in accordance with the teaching of the Pharisees one would become *spiritually* defiled.

To the ears of the Pharisees, present at this meal, this "woe" must have seemed very harsh indeed, for they were the people "who trusted in themselves and looked down on everybody else" (18:9, cf. 10–12). Yet, a quick look at Matt. 15:1–6 proves that Jesus had good reason to say exactly what he said.

45. One of the law-experts said to him, Teacher, by saying these things you are insulting us as well.

In view of the incisive character of Christ's remarks we are rather surprised that not until now does someone finally raise an objection. Was it the marvelously calm and definite manner in which Jesus had spoken, and the voice of conscience telling these people that what he said was true, that caused all these fellow guests and even the host to listen quietly, without any exclamation of protest?

Finally, one of the law-experts is unable to remain quiet any longer. He is aware of the fact that up to this point Jesus has made mention only of "Pharisees." But was it not true that most of the men who were law-experts by *profession* were members of the *religious party* of the Pharisees? For this distinction see also on 5:17. This man asks Jesus, therefore, whether he does not realize that by thus assailing the Pharisees he is also "insulting" the law-experts. It is at this moment, therefore, that Jesus begins to pronounce his "woes" against the law-experts. In reality all six woes were meant for the Pharisees and the law-experts, but Nos. 4, 5, and 6 were more directly aimed at the men who had made the study of the law, in the light of tradition (!), their main field of interest.

46. So he replied, Woe to y o u also, law-experts, because y o u burden the people with burdens that are hard to bear, but y o u yourselves do not even touch these burdens with one of y o u r fingers. Such *l*ying conduct!

These burdens consisted of the many regulations by means of which the ancient rabbis, and the law-experts after them, had buried the law of God and deprived men of their liberty and peace of mind; ordaining, for example, that picking and eating heads of grain on the sabbath, and rubbing them with their hands (6:1), amounted to reaping and threshing; that healing a person on the sabbath was wrong unless that individual's life were in immediate danger (6:6–11); and that ceremonial washing (or rinsing) of the hands in connection with every meal was required of everybody (11:38). See also John 5:9, 10, 16, 18; 9:14, 16.

Jesus points out that these law-experts had themselves mastered the art of avoiding these very burdens. They did not permit themselves to be hamstrung by their own regulations, did not even touch these burdens with one of their fingers.[393] Cf. Matt. 23:3: "For they say (things) but do not do (them)."

47, 48. Woe to y o u, because y o u are building the tombs of the prophets and y o u r fathers killed them. So y o u are testifying that y o u approve of the deeds of y o u r fathers: they killed them, and y o u build (their tombs). Such *a*ffectation!

These men wanted the people to think that by building or rebuilding (and/or redecorating) the tombs of the prophets they were honoring the prophets! However, for Christ's contemporaries the only *real* way to honor the prophets was to regulate their lives according to the teaching of the prophets! This they were not doing at all. Therefore, by merely doing some masonry work they were proving that they were not any better than their fathers. They were simply finishing what their fathers began: the fathers had killed the prophets, and these descendants were constructing or re-modeling their tombs! They probably did this in order to impress the people. Such hypocrites! Never yet had they condemned their fathers' sin in killing the prophets.

---

393. I cannot accept the interpretation, favored by some, according to which the meaning is this: "the law-experts were unwilling to adjust the burdens they had placed on other people's shoulders." The very prominent and forward position of αὐτοί, stressing the contrast between burdened men, on the one hand, and the law-experts *themselves,* on the other, favors the interpretation given above. The expression "Y o u yourselves do not even touch these burdens with one of y o u r fingers" does not necessarily mean "in order to adjust them." It can mean "in order to carry them yourselves."

49-51. For this reason also the Wisdom of God said, I will send them prophets and apostles. Some of them they will kill (and others) they will persecute; that the blood of all the prophets shed since the founding of the world may be exacted from this generation, from the blood of Abel to the blood of Zechariah, who perished between the altar and the sanctuary; yes, I tell y o u, it will indeed be exacted from this generation.

Note the following:

a. *For this reason.* This phrase links verse 48 with what follows through verse 51. The meaning, therefore, is: since y o u r fathers were such prophet-killers, and y o u are in agreement with them, the blood of the murdered ones will be exacted from y o u.

b. *The Wisdom of God.* This is probably not the name of a book from which Jesus is about to make a quotation. No such book has been found. Besides, none of the usual quotation formulas occurring in the New Testament is here used. The meaning is therefore probably, "God in his wisdom has declared." Cf. 7:35.

The question arises, "But why make mention of this divine wisdom at all in the present connection?" Could it be because God's wisdom is "that divine quality or attribute which reconciles seeming irreconcilables"? In verses 49-51 Jesus speaks about the rejection of "this generation." But Paul makes clear—see Rom. 11:25-36—that the very rejection of carnal Israel, by means of several steps, which he enumerates, would result in the salvation of all God's true people. When that apostle meditates upon this he exclaims, "O the depth of the riches both of *the wisdom and the knowledge of God!*" There is that word *wisdom* again. It is true that in our present passage (Luke 11:49-51) that end result is not mentioned. However, an important link in the chain of causes is definitely in view here, namely, the rejection of carnal Israel ("so that the blood . . . may be exacted from this generation").

c. *I will send them prophets and apostles.* Matthew writes "prophets and wise men and scribes." This shows that the designations here used do not indicate separate groups of people. They simply view God's emissaries from different angles. God's ambassadors are *prophets* because they are God's mouthpieces who convey his message to the people. They are *apostles* because they are officially sent and commissioned.

d. *Some of them they will kill (and others) they will persecute.* It is remarkable how literally this prophecy was fulfilled. For the Old Testament prophets see N.T.C. on Matt. 5:12. And as to the New Testament prophets and apostles, think of what happened to James, the brother of John (Acts 12:1, 2), and to Peter (John 21:18, 19). Both were killed. Jesus, the greatest Prophet of all, was crucified. John was persecuted (Rev. 1:9). Paul and his helpers met with fierce opposition in Pisidian Antioch (Acts 13:45, 50), Iconium (14:2), Lystra (14:19), Thessalonica (17:5), Berea (17:13), Corinth (18:12; 20:3), Jerusalem (21:27; 23:12), and Caesarea (24:1-9).

e. *. . . so that the blood of all the prophets . . . may be exacted from this generation.*

The question is asked, "But was it fair to punish the Jews of Christ's time for the blood that had been unrighteously shed 'since the founding of the world'?" The biblical answer is that responsibility increases with the years. Every new generation that fails to take to heart the lessons of the preceding generation is adding to its own guilt and therefore also to the severity of its punishment. This is clear, for example, from such passages as Prov. 29:1; Jer. 7:16; Ezek. 14:14; Luke 13:34. And see especially Dan. 5:22.

f. *. . . from the blood of Abel to the blood of Zechariah . . . it will indeed be exacted from this generation.*

The reference is to Abel killed by his brother Cain (Gen. 4:8); and to Zechariah, whose courageous testimony and cruel death are recorded in II Chron. 24:20-22. The reason why Jesus says "from Abel to Zechariah" is that according to the arrangement of the books in the Hebrew Bible *Genesis* (hence "Abel") comes first; *Chronicles* (hence "Zechariah") last.

Note also that Matt. 23:35 calls Abel "righteous." That made the deed of Cain all the more terrible. Think also of the manner in which Cain had been admonished earnestly and tenderly (Gen. 4:6, 7). Nevertheless he went ahead and murdered his brother.

And consider the kindness that had been bestowed on Joash by Jehoiada, the father of Zechariah. In spite of this it was at the command of Joash that Zechariah, God's true and faithful servant, had been murdered. Moreover, this deed of cruelty had been committed in *the immediate vicinity of the sanctuary!*

Between Abel and Zechariah ever so many other righteous men had been murdered in cold blood. And even while Jesus was saying this, Israel, by and large, had not repented. In fact, as is clear from 11:53, 54, while Jesus was saying these things the hearts of the scribes and the Pharisees were filled with wrath, vengeance, murder, the murder of the very One who was addressing them!

Looking again at this entire passage (verses 49–51), one can hardly fail to be impressed by the marvelous manner in which the divine decree and human responsibility are intertwined here, each receiving its due. Cf. Luke 22:22; Acts 2:23.

52. Woe to y o u law-experts, because y o u have taken away the key to knowledge. Y o u yourselves did not enter, and y o u hindered those who were entering. Such *w*ickedness!

Think of it: the very men who are supposed to *un*lock the Scripture—is not that the essence of their profession?—are *locking* it! They are burying the law of God under a load of man-made "traditions." See Matt. 15:3, 6. For salvation by trust in God, hence in Jesus Christ whom he sent, they have substituted salvation by obedience to countless man-made regulations and hairsplitting stipulations. For the real key to the true knowledge of God as revealed in Scripture, hence also to the palace of salvation, see such passages as Matt. 3:2; 4:17; 11:28-30; John 3:16; Rom. 3:24; then also

Matt. 23:23; Luke 10:27; 11:42; I Cor. 10:31. But these men have substituted work-righteousness for salvation by grace through faith. By this method they are shutting out themselves and those who might otherwise have entered. See also John 14:6 and Hos. 4:6. Woe to them!

53, 54. When he left there, the scribes and the Pharisees began to be violently enraged against him, and to ply him with questions, plotting, as if in ambush, to catch him with respect to something (that might fall) from his lips.

It is clear that the Master's earnest warnings did not have the desired effect. The Pharisees and *scribes*—note this synonym for *law-experts*—begin a bitter campaign against Jesus. Being violently enraged against him, they ply him with questions, hoping by this method to draw out of him some unguarded utterance, an indiscreet statement, which they would then be able to use in framing a charge against him.

So intense is their hatred, so vicious their attack, that they are, as it were, lying in ambush in order to catch him. They are trying to hunt him down, as if he were a wild beast. Their curiosity about him has turned into deadly aversion.[394]

Practical Lessons Derived from 11:37–54

Verse 40

"Y o u fools." Whether, as English equivalent, we prefer "Y o u fools" or "Y o u foolish ones," either way, would a modern audience approve of being addressed in this manner? We should remember, however, that Christ's all-seeing "eyes" were able to do what today's ministers cannot do. Those eyes were able to penetrate to the very depths of human hearts. Accordingly, the passage cannot mean that any clergyman now has the right to call the members of his congregation "fools."

On the other hand, it is also true that there are times when a faithful minister will have to use language that is not exactly complimentary. The result? The following summarizes what actually happened in the case of a pastor who was bidding farewell to his congregation. A certain lady shook his hand very firmly and, with tear-filled eyes, remarked, "No minister has ever hurt me as much as you did. Thanks be to God. I needed it!"

Verse 41

"But put y o u r inner self into the business of helping the poor." No one has a right to say that Jesus neglected the social side of the gospel. See also such passages as 12:33; 14:12–14; 18:22; and Matt. 25:34–46.

Verse 42

"Y o u tithe mint, rue," etc. Is it possible that rigid insistence on such trivial matters was a cover for inner insecurity? Should not every Christian make the

---

394. Notes on Greek words, phrases, and constructions in 11:37–54 begin on page 645.

words of Ps. 139:23, 24 ("Search me, O God," etc.) his own, frequently making use of them in prayer?

Verse 53

"The scribes and the Pharisees began to be violently enraged against him." Why? For the answer see Luke 18:9, 11, 12. Jesus had exposed the depths of their sinful nature. When that happens, hearers frequently divide into two groups: (a) some would like to stone the minister; (b) others, by God's grace, cry out, "O God, be merciful to me, the sinner."

Notes on Greek Words, Phrases, and Constructions in 11:37–54

Verse 37

In connection with ἐν τῷ λαλῆσαι translators vary between "While he was speaking" and "When he was finished speaking." Grammatically either is possible. Use of the aor. infinitive does not rule out "While he was speaking." Nevertheless, is it not more natural to suppose that the Pharisee would delay his invitation until Jesus was through speaking? Good, too, is "Jesus had been speaking, when . . ." (Beck).

ἀριστήσῃ, third per. s. aor. subjunct. (after ὅπως) of ἀριστάω, to have a meal, to eat. Originally the ἄριστον was a light meal, probably breakfast; later, a more substantial meal, perhaps luncheon. See M.M., p. 77, on ἄριστον. See also below, on 14:12.

ἀνέπεσεν, third per. s. 2nd aor. indicat. act. of ἀναπίπτω, to fall backward, to recline for a meal. To a certain extent ἀναπίπτω, ἀνακλίνω, and κατακλίνω are synonyms. In the sense already indicated, Luke also uses ἀναπίπτω in 14:10; 17:7; 22:14. And see Matt. 15:35; Mark 6:40; 8:6. John also uses this verb (6:10; 13:12, but in 13:25; 21:20 in the sense of *to lean back* on Jesus' breast). In addition Luke uses ἀνακλίνω, but not always in the same sense. See 2:7; 12:37; 13:29. For this verb see also Matt. 8:11; 14:19; Mark 6:39. Luke alone uses κατακλίνω (7:36; 9:14, 15; 14:8; 24:30). For the exact shade of meaning the context should be examined in each individual case.

Verse 38

ἐβαπτίσθη, third per. s. aor. indicat. pass. of βαπτίζω; here: to wash ceremonially. The verb refers here to Jewish ritual washing.

Verse 39

πίνακος, gen. s. of πίναξ, plate, platter, dish. See also Matt. 14:8, 11; Mark 6:25, 28. Cf. *pine.*

ἁρπαγῆς, gen. s. of ἁρπαγή, extortion. Note ἁρπάζω, to rob, plunder. Cf. *harpy, rapacious.*

Verse 41

τὰ ἐνόντα, acc. pl. neut. pres. participle of ἔνειμι, to be within; hence, what is within; probably "the inner self."

ἐλεημοσύνην, acc. s. of ἐλεημοσύνη, almsgiving, the business of showing mercy to the poor. Cf. ἔλεος, mercy. Note also *eleemosynary* (philanthropic).

Verse 42

ἀποδεκατοῦτε (ἀπό plus δεκατόω), sec. per. pl. pres. indicat. act. of ἀποδεκατόω, to tithe.

ἡδύοσμον (=ἡδύς plus ὀσμή: pleasant smelling), mint.

πήγανον, rue.

λάχανον (cf. λαχαίνω, to dig; e.g., a garden), garden herb.

παρεῖναι, 2nd aor. infinitive of παρίημι, to leave undone, neglect, let go, drop, droop; cf. Heb. 12:12 "drooping hands."

Verse 43

πρωτοκαθεδρίαν, acc. s. of πρωτοκαθεδρία, elsewhere pl., chief seat.

ἀσπασμούς, acc. pl. of ἀσπασμός, greeting; here: formal salutation.

Verse 44

ἄδηλος (lit. not clear), unmarked; here pl. ἄδηλα, as modifying pl. noun, μνημεῖα, graves.

Verse 45

ὑβρίζεις, sec. per. s. pres. indicat. act. of ὑβρίζω, to scoff at, insult, abuse. In the New Testament this verb occurs in the following passages: Matt. 22:6; Luke 11:45; 18:32; Acts. 14:5; I Thess. 2:2. Cf. cognate noun ὕβρις, arrogance, insolence, outrage (as in Josephus, *Antiquities* VI.61, "outrage against God"), but in the New Testament ὕβρις is "insult" (II Cor. 12:10), and "loss," "damage" (Acts 27:10). It is not difficult to conceive of such loss as being the result of the "arrogance" of the elements of nature, such as a violent storm. A person described as a ὑβριστής is a wanton aggressor, bully, or tyrant (Rom. 1:30; I Tim. 1:13). The meaning of basic ὑπέρ in both verb and noun is easily grasped: *over*bearing people act *up*pishly.

Verse 46

Note the cognate accusative, which, in order to preserve the flavor of the original, is preserved in the translation, "y o u burden the people with burdens. . . ."

δυσβάστακτος (= δυς, hard, plus βαστάζω, to bear; hence), unbearable, hard to bear; here acc. pl. neut. δυσβάστακτα, modifying φορτία, burdens.

προσψαύετε, sec. per. pl. pres. indicat. act. of προσψαύω*, to touch (perhaps "lightly").

Verse 47

The possibility must be granted that μνημεῖα has here the meaning "memorial tombs" or "monuments." See also N.T.C. on Mark, p. 671, footnote 836.

Verse 48

συνευδοκεῖτε (= σύν, with; εὖ, well; and δοκεῖτε, from δοκέω, to think; hence), to think well of in agreement with; that is, to approve. The form of συνευδοκέω that is used here is sec. per. pl. pres. indicat. active. See also Acts 8:1; 22:20; Rom. 1:32; I Cor. 7:12, 13.

Verses 50, 51

ἐκζητηθῇ (verse 50), third per. s. aor. subjunct. pass. (after ἵνα); and ἐκ-ζητηθήσεται (verse 51), third per. s. fut. indicat. pass., are forms of ἐκζητέω, to seek intently or earnestly, to search after (Acts 15:17; Rom. 3:11; Heb. 11:6; 12:17; I Peter 1:10); but here in Luke 11:50, 51, to exact, require.

ἐκκεχυμένον, perf. pass. participle of ἐκχύννομαι (related to ἐκχέω), to pour out, shed. See the note on 5:37 on page 313; cf. ἐπιχέων (10:34).

Verse 53

δεινῶς, adv., in the New Testament used only here and in Matt. 8:6, terribly, vehemently, violently; cf. *dinosaur* (terrible reptile).

ἐνέχειν (pres. infinitive after ἤρξαντο), to be enraged; cf. English "to have it in (for someone)." See also Mark 6:19. Whether in this particular instance the verb ἤρξαντο should be left untranslated is hard to determine.

The meaning of ἀποστοματίζειν, another pres. infinitive, from ἀποστοματίζω*, is not entirely certain, but the context seems to justify the rendering "to ply [or besiege] with questions." They continued thus to assail Jesus.

Verse 54

ἐνεδρεύοντες, nom. pl. masc. pres. participle of ἐνεδρεύω*, to lie in ambush. An ἐνέδρα (ἐν, in, plus ἕδρα, sitting) is a sitting in, an ambush or lying in wait.

θηρεῦσαι, aor. infinitive of θηρεύω*, to hunt, catch. Cf. θήρ, wild beast; θήρα, hunting.

Summary of Chapter 11

See p. 533.

Outline of Chapter 12

Theme: *The Work Thou Gavest Him to Do*

CHAPTER XII

12 1 In the meantime, when a crowd of so many thousands had gathered that they were trampling on each other, he began to say first of all to his disciples: "Be on y o u r guard against the yeast of the Pharisees, which is hypocrisy. 2 Nothing is concealed that will not be revealed, or hidden that will not be made known. 3 Wherefore whatever y o u have said in the dark will be heard in the light, and whatever y o u have whispered[395] behind closed doors[396] will be proclaimed from the housetops."

12:1–3 *Pharisaism Exposed*
Cf. Matt. 10:26; 16:6; Mark 4:22; 8:15; Luke 8:17

In the previous chapter Jesus was speaking *to* Pharisees and scribes. He now speaks *about* them, *to* his "disciples" (see verses 1, 22) and *to* the crowds (see verse 54). He warns against *hypocrisy* and other evils.

The first part of the discourse, though delivered before a huge audience—the luncheon is over, and Jesus is outside again—is meant *especially* for the disciples, while the final part is directed *specifically* to the multitudes. For details see on verses 13, 14, 16, 22, 54.

It is probably best to consider the contents of the entire chapter as consisting of one connected discourse. With two exceptions it is Jesus who is speaking throughout. The two exceptions may be considered interruptions. Or they may have been words addressed to Jesus when he for the time being ceased speaking.

The first interruption was by a man from the crowd. He desired to have an inheritance dispute settled in his favor, and he took for granted that Jesus could bring about the desired result. The second interruption was by Peter. He wanted the Master to tell him whether the words he had just spoken were meant for the disciples or for everybody.

As indicated in the Outline, the chapter can be subdivided into nine parts. It contains some of the most often quoted sayings of Jesus (verses 6, 7, 22–28, 31, 32, 34, 47, 48); also three well-known parables.

1. In the meantime, when a crowd of so many thousands had gathered that they were trampling on each other, he began to say first of all to his

---

395. Literally: spoken in the ear.
396. Literally: in the inner (or: most private) rooms.

disciples: Be on y o u r guard against the yeast of the Pharisees, which is hypocrisy.

"In the meantime" is a very indefinite expression. The events of 11:14–36, relating to The Great Galilean Ministry, are no longer in view. With 11:37 ("Now—or Once—, after he had finished speaking, a Pharisee invited Jesus to eat at his home") time and place have changed. Even the warning against "the yeast of the Pharisees," recorded in Mark 8:15 (noted above this chapter merely for comparison), and referring to an incident that occurred during The Retirement Ministry, is not a true parallel to Luke 12:1–3; that is, it does not cover the same event. This becomes very clear when the two stories are placed side by side. What took place as related by Luke here in 12:1–3 probably occurred somewhat later, perhaps during The Perean Ministry. That ministry, let it be borne in mind, is the framework of Luke's Central Section, though the author frequently departs from it; namely, when he sees a good topical or logical connection with a happening that took place at another point of time during Christ's earthly sojourn.

The true situation, then, is as follows. This is a continuation of the story begun in Luke 11:37. Jesus and his disciples are no longer in the Pharisee's house. Outside, a huge crowd has gathered around the Master. Among the reasons for the size of this multitude ("many thousands," see the note on this verse on page 658) there may well have been these two: (a) interest in Jesus as spellbinder and miracle-worker; (b) curiosity aroused by the controversy between Jesus and his Pharisaic opponents (11:37–54). So, everybody wants to hear what the "Prophet" is now saying. Since modern equipment was not available, the only way for people to hear was to get near enough to the speaker. No wonder that "they were trampling on each other."

Jesus, then, directs his message first of all to his disciples. On this "first of all" see the note on this verse on pp. 658, 659. The word *disciple*, however, must not be taken in too narrow a sense. In addition to The Twelve, Jesus had many other followers (6:13; 10:1; 19:37; John 6:60, 66). Besides, he knew, of course, that his words would also be heard by the crowds in general, and that is what he wanted. But primarily he was now addressing his disciples.

He begins his message by issuing a warning against "the yeast of the Pharisees, which is hypocrisy." This warning is closely linked with that which the Master had said a moment before, while he was still in the house (see Luke 11:39–44, 46). Hypocrisy means play-acting. It refers to the evil habit of hiding one's real self behind a mask. It amounts to insincerity. *Hypocrisy* is *dishonesty, deception.*

Implied, of course, is the exhortation, *"Be sincere!"*

2. Nothing is concealed that will not be revealed, or hidden that will not be made known. Not only is hypocrisy dishonesty, it is also *folly.* As is stated over and over again in Scripture: the truth will come out, perhaps already in this life; but if not, then certainly on the day of the final judgment. See Eccles. 12:14; Matt. 10:26; Rom. 2:16; I Cor. 3:13; 4:5. The "books" will be opened (Rev. 20:12).

The Dutch have the following proverb:

> Al is de leugen nog zo snel,
> De waarheid achterhaalt haar wel.

The meaning is:

> E'en though the lie runs e'er so fast,
> The truth her overtakes at last.

Having stated the general truth, Jesus now applies it particularly to his disciples. He says:

3. Wherefore whatever y o u have said in the dark will be heard in the light, and whatever y o u have whispered behind closed doors will be proclaimed from the housetops.

Says the Psalmist:

"Even the darkness hides not from thee,

The night shines as the day;

The darkness and the light are both alike to thee" (Ps. 139:12).

Therefore the Revealer of "the secrets of men" (Rom. 2:16) will experience no difficulty in bringing out into the open whatever men, including the disciples of Jesus, have done or said in secret.

Are there certain things which have been whispered into the ear in "inner rooms"? The word *inner rooms,* used in the original, has reference to enclosures (generally within the homes of the well-to-do) where treasures were kept, and where at times "top secret" conferences were held.

Today the expression *whispered behind closed doors* is considered more idiomatic than "spoken in the ear in the inner chambers" (A.R.V.) or ". . . in closets" (A.V.). What Jesus is saying, then, is that whatever was at one time whispered behind closed doors will be publicly proclaimed. Since radio and TV had not yet been invented, and since the nearest thing to present-day broadcasting was at that time making something known by shouting it from the flat roof of a house, the latter figure is here used.

Implied in the lesson, "Hypocrisy is folly," is the command, *"Be wise!"*

For *Practical Lessons* and *Greek Words,* etc., see pp. 657–661.

---

4 "I tell y o u, my friends, do not be afraid of those who kill the body and after that have nothing more they can do. 5 But I will show y o u whom y o u should fear. Fear him who, after killing, has power to cast into hell; yes, I tell y o u, fear him!

6 "Are not five sparrows sold for two cents? Yet not one of them is forgotten in God's sight. 7 In fact, the very hairs of y o u r head are all numbered. Have no fear; y o u are of more value than any number of[397] sparrows."

---

397. Lit., than many.

12:4-7 *Fear Not*
God Cares
Cf. Matt. 10:28-31

We have seen that hypocrisy is dishonesty and folly. It also signifies *inability*, lack of power. Those who worship at its shrine are weaklings. **4. I tell y o u, my friends, do not be afraid of those who kill the body and after that have nothing more they can do.**

Note emphatic "I tell y o u": here and again in verse 8. Also note "my friends," used here alone in the Synoptics. However, does not John 15:14, 15 imply that Jesus made frequent use of this term? For its implications see N.T.C. on John, Vol. II, pp. 306, 307.

The disciples must take to heart the fact that the enemies are powerless. They are unable to inflict permanent injury. They cannot kill the soul. Killing the body is definitely all they can do. Their power to hurt God's children does not go beyond that.

For that reason Jesus urges his disciples not to be afraid of these bitter opponents. The implied directive is *"Be strong!"*

Jesus continues: **5. But I will show y o u whom y o u should fear.** To be sure, Jesus wants his disciples to fear, but the *object* of that fear must be God (definitely implied). And the *nature* of that fear? It amounts to a standing in awe of the majesty and holiness of God.

In our own day it is getting to be the custom of some to address God as if he were a "chum" or "pal" or "hail-fellow well met." Such surely was not the attitude of Isaiah when in a vision he saw "the Lord sitting upon a throne, high and lifted up" (Isa. 6:1-4). The prophet's response was, "Woe is me, for I am undone; because I am a man of unclean lips, and I dwell in the midst of a people of unclean lips: for my eyes have seen the King, Jehovah of hosts." Cf. Rev. 1:17.

It is those, those alone, who, by sovereign grace, have learned to pay such subdued, filial reverence to God, that can also enter into the sweetness of fellowship and friendship with him.

Those who are able to lift up their hearts to God and say:

> O God, how wonderful thou art,
> Thy majesty, how bright!
> How beautiful thy mercy-seat
> In depths of burning light!

> O how I fear thee, living God,
> With deepest, tenderest fears,
> And worship thee with trembling hope
> And penetential tears.

They have a right to add:

> Yet I may love thee too, O Lord,
> Almighty as thou art;

652

For thou hast stooped to ask of me
The love of my poor heart.
—F. W. Faber

Continued: **Fear him who, after killing, has power to cast into hell...**
The sense of the passage is this: the power to bring about momentary physical death is certainly not to be compared with the power to cast into never-ending punishment! Stand in awe, therefore, in the presence of him who is able to bring about this indescribably agonizing retribution. Note the repetition, adding emphasis: **yes, I tell y o u, fear him!** In other words, *"Be reverent!"*

The term rendered *hell* is *Gehenna.* It comes from Gē-Hinnōm, that is, the land of Hinnom, a valley belonging originally to Hinnom and later to his sons. One can find this valley on any good map of Jerusalem (just south of the city and curving toward the west). Originally, no doubt, this was a beautiful valley. But it did not remain so. It was in this valley that a high place was built. It was subsequently called *Tophet,* meaning, according to some, "place of spitting out" or "abhorrence"; according to others, "place of burning." Either interpretation would fit very well. It would seem that in the top of this high place there was a deep hole in which much wood was piled, and that this wood was ignited by a stream of brimstone (see Isaiah 30:33). The wicked kings Ahaz and Manasseh actually made their children pass through this terrible fire as offerings to the gruesome idol Moloch (II Chron. 28:3; 33:6; cf. Lev. 18:21; I Kings 11:7). Others copied their wicked example (Jer. 32:35). Jeremiah predicted that the divine judgment would strike Tophet; God would visit the terrible wickedness that occurred in Gē-Hinnōm with such mass destruction that the place would become known as "the valley of slaughter" (Jer. 7:31–34; 19:6; 32:35). God-fearing King Josiah defiled this idolatrous high place, and stopped its abominations (II Kings 23:10). Afterwards Jerusalem's rubbish was burnt here. Hence, whenever a person approached the valley, he would see those rubbish-burning flames.

Now by adding these various ideas represented by Gē-Hinnōm—namely, ever-burning fire, wickedness, abomination, divine judgment, slaughter— it is easily seen that this Gē-Hinnōm became a symbol for the everlasting abode of the wicked, namely, hell. Gē-Hinnōm becomes (in Greek) *Gehenna,* the place of never-ending torment.

The required awe and reverence do not amount to alarm, however. They must be combined with *trust,* for God is not only majestic and holy; he also loves and cares.

And so in this very heart and center of Luke's Gospel—how many verses precede and how many follow?—we turn now to the central passage concerning the heart of God. It begins thus:

6, 7. Are not five sparrows sold for two cents?
Sparrows and other small birds were caught, killed, skinned, roasted,

and consumed. They were considered delicacies, as is still the case in certain countries. They were (and are) an article of commerce. The price at the time when Jesus spoke these words was "two for an *as* [or *assarion*]" (Matt. 10:29), a Roman copper coin worth only about a sixteenth of a denarius. We might call the *as* a cent or penny; hence, "two for a penny." Our present passage shows that for the price of *two* pennies an extra sparrow was thrown in; hence, "five for two cents."

But even though sparrows were cheap in comparison with other articles, Jesus assures his disciples: **Yet not one of them is forgotten in God's sight.** Not even the most insignificant of God's creatures lies outside the sphere of his loving care. Jesus adds, **In fact, the very hairs of y o u r head are all numbered.** God knows how many there are and pays attention to each and to all. Does not each hair belong to one of his children? Jesus adds, **Have no fear; y o u are of more value [or: are worth more] than any number of sparrows.** The implication is *"Be fearless, trusting."*

Note these last words: "any number of sparrows." Literally the original reads "many sparrows." Several translators and commentators prefer this rendering, which is certainly correct. The same idea expressed somewhat more picturesquely would be "a flock of sparrows," "many flocks of sparrows," "hundreds of sparrows," "a great many sparrows." All of these renderings have been suggested, and there is merit in them all. I can see no valid objection to any of them.

Two other attempts are "sparrows" ("you are worth far more than sparrows," Moffatt) and "any number of sparrows"; see explanation in N.T.C. on Matthew, p. 473; also N.E.B. Why these last two? Probably to avoid a misunderstanding, as if Jesus were saying, "Y o u are worth more than *many*—but not worth more than *all*—sparrows." But all this is a minor matter. The main lesson is this: Jesus is assuring his disciples that God's tender love and care will never fail them, not even in the hour of death. Cf. Rom. 8:31–39.

For *Practical Lessons* and *Greek Words*, etc., see pp. 657–661.

---

8 "I tell y o u, whoever shall confess me before men, the Son of man will also confess him before the angels of God.   9 But he who denies me before men will be denied before the angels of God.   10 And everyone who speaks a word against the Son of man will be forgiven, but anyone who blasphemes against the Holy Spirit will not be forgiven.

11 "And when they are bringing y o u before[398] synagogues, rulers, and authorities, do not worry about how y o u will defend yourselves[399] or what y o u will say,   12 for in that very hour the Holy Spirit will teach y o u what y o u should say."

---

398. Or: . . . y o u are brought before.
399. Another reading has: how or what y o u will answer in defense.

12:8-12 *Fear Not*
The Son of Man Will Acknowledge Y o u; the Holy Spirit Will Help Y o u
Cf. Matt. 10:32, 33; 12:32; 10:19, 20

8, 9. I tell y o u, whoever shall confess me before men, the Son of man will also confess him before the angels of God. But he who denies me before men will be denied before the angels of God.

The disciples must not fear men. They must trust God. That was the essence of the exhortation found in verses 4-7. In close connection with this, verse 8 now indicates: (a) the reward of trust that reveals itself in confessing Christ; and (b) the punishment that will follow fear of men, a fear expressing itself in disowning Christ.

It is clear, therefore, that even though Jesus has uttered a similar saying previously (Matt. 10:32, 33), he may very well have repeated it here, in somewhat altered form. The saying, in whichever form, fits beautifully into either context.

Note that where Matthew has "I" (in "I will confess"), Luke writes "the Son of man," proving that the term *the Son of man* is Christ's self-designation. For "Son of man" see also on 5:24. Further, note that where Matthew has "before my Father who is in heaven" Luke has "before the angels of God." In view of Dan. 7:10; Matt. 16:27; 25:31, this presents no difficulty. Where the Father is, there are also his holy angels.

Jesus promises that he will confess or acknowledge before the angels of God those who confess him. This word *confess* or *acknowledge* shows that the message to be brought by the disciples must not be coldly objective, a mere recitation of memorized words. On the contrary, the hearts of these men must be in their message. Their preaching must be witness-bearing. It should *include* their personal testimony (Ps. 66:16). Jesus, then, promises that he himself will acknowledge those true witnesses to be his own. He will confess them before the angels of God. In this connection read especially Matt. 25:34-36, 40. The lesson is *"Be outspoken"* in the defense of the faith!

On the other hand, those who deny or disown him will be denied before these same angels. See Matt. 25:41-43, 45. In this case Jesus is not quoted as saying, "I will deny them." What we read is "they will be denied [or disowned]." This change was made, perhaps, to emphasize all the more strongly the sorrowful lot of those who will be thus rejected.

10. And everyone who speaks a word against the Son of man will be forgiven, but anyone who blasphemes against the Holy Spirit will not be forgiven.

Having spoken about the Father and his care, and about the Son of man and his public acknowledgment of those who are his own, it is but logical that Jesus should now also speak about the Holy Spirit.

First, in comparison with the Son, and then with respect to his relation to the disciples. Is not that a very logical order?

That those who sinned against the Son of man are, upon repentance, forgiven, is clear from many passages, including, for example, Matt. 27:44; cf. Luke 23:42, 43.

The question is, "How is it to be understood that blasphemy against the Holy Spirit is unpardonable?" As to other sins, no matter how grievous or gruesome, there is pardon for them. There is forgiveness for David's sin of adultery, dishonesty, and murder (II Sam. 12:13; Ps. 51; cf. Ps. 32); for the "many" sins of the woman of Luke 7; for the prodigal son's "riotous living" (Luke 15:13, 21–24); for Simon Peter's triple denial accompanied by profanity (Matt. 26:74, 75; Luke 22:31, 32; John 18:15–18, 25–27; 21:15–17); and for Paul's preconversion merciless persecution of Christians (Acts 9:1; 22:4; 26:9–11; I Cor. 15:9; Eph. 3:8; Phil. 3:6). But for the man who "speaks against the Holy Spirit" there is no pardon.

Why not? Here, as always when the text itself is not immediately clear, the historical context must be our guide. See Luke 11:15, 18; Mark 3:22; cf. John 7:20; 8:48, 52; 10:20. From it we learn that the bitter opponents of Jesus have been ascribing to Satan what the Holy Spirit, through Christ, was achieving. Moreover, they were doing this willfully, deliberately. In spite of all the evidences to the contrary they were still affirming that Jesus was expelling demons by the power of Beelzebul. Now to be forgiven implies that the sinner be truly penitent. Among the opponents such genuine sorrow for sin was totally lacking. For penitence they substituted hardening; for confession, plotting. Thus, by means of their own criminal and completely inexcusable callousness, they were dooming themselves. Their sin was unpardonable because they were unwilling to tread the path that leads to pardon. For a thief, an adulterer, and a murderer there is hope. The message of the gospel may cause him to cry out, "O God be merciful to me, the sinner." But when a man has become hardened, so that he has made up his mind not to pay any attention to the promptings of the Spirit, not even to listen to his pleading and warning voice, he has placed himself on the road that leads to perdition. He has sinned the sin "unto death" (I John 5:16; see also Heb. 6:4–8).

For anyone who is truly penitent, no matter how shameful his transgressions may have been, there is no reason to despair (Ps. 103:12; Isa. 1:18; 44:22; 55:6, 7; Mic. 7:18–20; I John 1:9).

On the other hand, there is no excuse for being indifferent, as if the subject of the unpardonable sin is of no concern to the average church member. The blasphemy against the Spirit is the result of gradual progress in sin. Grieving the Spirit (Eph. 4:30), if unrepented of, leads to resisting the Spirit (Acts 7:51), which, if persisted in, develops into quenching the Spirit (I Thess. 5:19). The true solution is found in Ps. 95:7b, 8a, *"Today* O that y o u would listen to his voice. Harden not y o u r hearts!" Cf. Heb. 3:7, 8a.

This warning regarding the blasphemy against the Holy Spirit does not mean that he is someone to be avoided at all cost. On the contrary, not only does the Father tenderly care for his own (verses 4-7), and the Son assure them that he will acknowledge them as his very own (verse 8), but also the Holy Spirit will help them in their hour of need:

11, 12. And when they are bringing y o u before synagogues, rulers, and authorities, do not worry about how y o u will defend yourselves or what y o u will say, for in that very hour the Holy Spirit will teach y o u what y o u should say.

On the *synagogue,* its history, functions, importance, see N.T.C. on Mark, pp. 74-76. Being brought to trial before synagogues could be a frightening experience. But not only does Jesus mention synagogues, he also speaks of "rulers and authorities." These might be either Jewish or Gentile. How to conduct oneself before such judges, not excluding governors and kings, how to address them and what to say to them in defense, might well fill the minds and hearts of unlearned disciples of Jesus with apprehension and horror.

Nevertheless, Jesus tells his followers, "Do not worry," that is, "Whenever worry raises its head, knock it down at once." Reason: in that very hour the Holy Spirit will teach y o u what to say.

As is clear from 21:14, 15 and from Matt. 10:19, 20, what Jesus means is: at the very moment when y o u need to know what to say, then and not before, the Holy Spirit will work within y o u in such an effective manner, illumining the mind and sharpening the power of speech, that y o u will know exactly what to say.

That this prophecy too was gloriously fulfilled is evident from the speeches of Peter, or Peter and John (Acts 4:8-12, 19, 20, with the effect upon the audience described in 4:13, 14), and from those of Paul (Acts 21:39—22:21; 23:1, 6; 24:10-21; 26:1-23).[400]

Practical Lessons Derived from 12:1-12

The Lesson Summary is: be sincere, wise, strong, reverent, fearless, trusting, outspoken.

Verse 2

"Nothing is concealed that will not be revealed." "You can fool some of the people all of the time, and all of the people some of the time, but you cannot fool all of the people all the time." Attributed to A. Lincoln. See chart on page 658.

Verses 6, 7

"Are not five sparrows sold for two cents? . . . Have no fear; y o u are of more value than any number of sparrows."

---

400. Notes on Greek words, phrases, and constructions in 12:1-12 begin on page 658.

Biblical Examples of Hypocrisy and Its Results

Name(s) of the Person(s) Guilty of Hypocrisy	Description of the Deed Read:	Result Read:
Jacob	Gen. 27:1–33	Gen. 27:41
Absalom	II Sam. 15:1–3	II Sam. 18:9, 14
Jeroboam	I Kings 14:1–4	I Kings 14:5–17
Gehazi	II Kings 5:20–25	II Kings 5:26, 27
Judas Iscariot	Matt. 26:49	Matt. 27:3–5
Ananias and Sapphira	Acts 5:1, 2, 7, 8	Acts 2:3–6, 9, 10

> Said the robin to the sparrow,
> I should really like to know
> Why those anxious human beings
> Rush about and worry so.
>
> Said the sparrow to the robin,
> Well, I think that it must be
> That they have no heavenly Father
> Such as cares for you and me.
>
> *The Prairie Pastor*

Verse 10

"But anyone who blasphemes against the Holy Spirit will not be forgiven."

The essence of the sin against the Holy Spirit can be condensed into just one word—*i m p e n i t e n c e.*

If anyone is truly sorry for his sins, he cannot at the same time be guilty of "the sin against the Holy Spirit," "the unpardonable sin," for true sorrow is the work and fruit of the Holy Spirit, and shows that this Spirit is dwelling in the heart of that penitent.

Notes on Greek Words, Phrases, and Constructions in 12:1–12

Verse 1

Ἐν οἷς, in the midst of which; that is, in the meantime. To begin a new paragraph with a relative was in harmony with classical usage. Note gen. absolute construction: "a crowd of so many thousands having gathered," etc.

ἐπισυναχθεισῶν, gen. pl. aor. pass. participle of ἐπισυνάγω, to gather, assemble.

μυριάδων, gen. pl. of μυριάς, basically *ten thousand.* The word is used in that sense in Acts 19:19, where "five ten thousands" means "fifty thousand." Secondary meaning: innumerable multitude, pl. "thousands" or even "thousands upon thousands." Cf. *myriad.*

Greijdanus constructs πρῶτον with προσέχετε, "be on y o u r guard." His argument is that "later on in the chapter we do not read that Jesus subsequently began to speak to others" (*Korte Verklaring,* Vol. I, p. 328). Geldenhuys agrees, *op. cit.,* p. 350.

Well, that construction makes sense, and these authors may be right in favoring it. Nevertheless, is it correct to say that in the entire chapter Jesus is not represented as addressing another group? What of verse 54? That verse has convinced me that the more generally accepted rendering "he began to say first of all to his disciples" has a slight edge.

προσέχετε . . . ἀπό, put y o u r mind (supply τὸν νοῦν) on avoiding, etc.; that is, be on y o u r guard against, etc.

Verse 2

συγκεκαλυμμένον ἐστιν, third per. s. perf. pass. periphrastic of συγκαλύπτω*, to cover up completely, conceal.

ἀποκαλυφθήσεται, third per. s. fut. indicat. pass. of ἀποκαλύπτω, to uncover, reveal. See also 2:35; 10:21, 22; 17:30.

Verse 3

ἀνθ' ὧν. Robertson (*Translation,* pp. 75, 195) offers "because" as English equivalent. It is difficult, however, to understand how the statement "Whatever y o u have said in the dark will be heard in the light" can indicate the cause of the far more general truth "Nothing is concealed that will not be revealed." But, as I have shown in my dissertation "The Meaning of the Preposition ἀντί in the New Testament," pp. 26, 27, 40, the solution is that ἀντί does *not always* mean *because.* It can also mean *wherefore.* An interesting example is the one from the Rosetta Stone: ". . . *wherefore* the gods gave you health, victory, strength, and all other good things."

Of course, one is not limited to the word *wherefore.* Any true synonym will do; e.g., *therefore, accordingly, so, so then,* etc. Among those translations that show that the authors have correctly grasped the connection between verses 2 and 3, and the true meaning here of ἀνθ' ὧν, are the following: A.V., A.R.V., N.A.S., N.E.B., Berkeley Version, Moffatt, Weymouth, Norlie, Jerusalem Bible, Good News for Modern Man, Lenski, Dutch (both Statenvertaling and Nieuwe Vertaling). Even the omission in English of any connecting word, such as *wherefore,* cannot be considered incorrect, since the omission at this point will almost certainly convey to the reader the same idea as *wherefore.* In the group of correct translations the following must therefore also be included: R.S.V., Beck, Phillips, Amplified, N.I.V.

Now everything runs smoothly: because the *general* proposition holds, namely, that nothing is concealed that will not be revealed, it follows that the *far more restricted* proposition is also true: "Whatever y o u have said in the dark will be heard in the light."

ταμείοις, dat. pl. of ταμεῖον; here: inner room; in verse 24: storeroom. For an obvious reason (see Matt. 6:19, 20) a storeroom for precious commodities was generally an *inner* room.

Verses 4–7

We should distinguish carefully between the various forms of the verb φοβέω here used:

φοβηθῆτε (verses 4a, 5a), sec. per. pl. aor. subjunct. middle (verse 4a, in a prohibition).

φοβήθητε (twice in verse 5), sec. per. pl. aor. imperat. middle, in a command.

φοβεῖσθε (verse 7), sec. per. pl. pres. imperat. middle, in a prohibition; durative: have no fear.

Note also in verse 6 the nom. pl., and in verse 7 the gen. pl. (because of διαφέρετε) of the noun στρουθίον, sparrow.

A few more words—two in verse 6, three in verse 7—merit comment:

πωλοῦνται, third per. pl. indicat. pass. of πωλέω, to sell. Note also the sec. per. pl. aor. imperat. act. form of this verb in verse 33. Cf. *monopoly.*

ἔστιν ἐπιλελησμένον, periphrastic third per. s. perf. indicat. pass. of ἐπιλανθάνομαι, to forget; pass., as here: to be forgotten, to escape notice.

ἀλλά (see also the note on 1:60 on page 119) is not always an adversative particle; it can also be ascensive. When this is true the meaning will vary according to context. The following translations have been suggested: "in fact" (here in 12:7), "why" (16:21), "in addition [or besides]" (24:22), "yes" (Phil. 1:18).

ἠρίθμηνται, third per. pl. indicat. pass. of ἀριθμέω, to number.

διαφέρετε, sec. per. pl. pres. indicat. of διαφέρω; lit. to carry in different directions, or: to carry through (Mark 11:16); to *differ* (I Cor. 15:41); and here in Luke 12:7 to differ favorably; that is, to *excel;* so also in verse 24.

Verses 8–10

For ὁμολογήσῃ, third per. s. aor. subjunct. act. of ὁμολογέω, to confess, acknowledge; see also N.T.C. on Matthew, footnote 477 on pp. 497, 498. The phrase ὁμολογέω ἐν can be regarded as an Aramaism.

πᾶς ὅς ... ἐν αὐτῷ. There is an anacoluthon here, for αὐτῷ refers to πᾶς ὅς, which, however, the Greek allows to remain in the nominative, πᾶς ὅς ... ἀνθρώπων being a nominative absolute. Note somewhat similar anacolutha in verses 9 and 10.

ἀρνησάμενος, nom. aor. (timeless) s. participle of ἀρνέομαι, to deny, disown. A compound form of the same verb is ἀπαρνηθήσεται, third per. s. fut. pass. of ἀπαρνέομαι.

ἀφεθήσεται (twice in verse 10), third per. s. fut. indicat. pass. of ἀφίημι, here meaning: to forgive (impersonal use of verb in both cases). For various meanings of this verb see the note on 4:39 on page 271, and the note on 6:42 on page 364.

βλασφημήσαντι, dat. s. masc. aor. act. participle of βλασφημέω. When, as here, this verb is used with the Deity as its object, the meaning is: to blaspheme; when men are the objects, the sense is: to revile, insult.

Verse 11

εἰσφέρωσιν, third per. pl. pres. subjunct. (after ὅταν, when or whenever) act. of εἰσφέρω, to bring in.

μεριμνήσητε, sec. per. pl. aor. subjunct. (in a prohibition) of μεριμνάω (lit., to divide the mind), to be anxious, to worry.

We have already met this verb in 10:41; see the note on that verse on page 603. And now in chapter 12 forms of this verb are found also in verse 22 (μεριμνᾶτε), sec. per. pl. pres. *imperat.*; in verse 26, same form but now pres. *indicat.*; and in verse 25 (μεριμνῶν), pres. participle.

Aside from these occurrences in Luke, the New Testament use of this verb is confined to Matt. 6:25–34 (6 times); 10:19; I Cor. 7:32–34 (4 times); 12:25; and Phil. 2:20; 4:6.

ἀπολογήσησθε, sec. per. pl. aor. subjunct. (deliberative) middle of ἀπολογέομαι, to defend oneself. Cf. *apology*.

---

13 Someone from the crowd said to him, "Teacher, tell my brother to share the inheritance with me." 14 He answered, "Man, who appointed me judge or arbitrator in y o u r case?" 15 Then he said to them, "Watch out! Be on y o u r guard against greed of every description, for a man's life does not consist in the abundance of his possessions."

16 And he told them a parable, saying:

"The ground of a certain rich man produced bumper crops. 17 So he carried on a dialogue within himself, saying, 'What shall I do, for I have no space where I can store my crops?' 18 Then he said, 'This is what I'll do: I will tear down my barns[401] and I will build bigger ones, and there I will store all my grain and goods. 19 And I will say to my soul, Soul, you have ample goods laid up for many years. Take it easy; eat, drink, and have a good time.' 20 But God said to him, 'You fool! This very night your soul is being demanded of you, and the things you have prepared (for yourself), whose shall they be?' 21 So it goes with one who hoards up riches for himself but is not rich in God's sight."[402]

12:13-21 *The Parable of*
(The Notorious One)
The Rich Fool

Jesus has been emphasizing the folly of worry. He has been saying, "Are not five sparrows sold for two cents? Yet not one of them is forgotten in God's sight. . . . Have no fear; y o u are of more value than any number of sparrows."

One would think that in view of such words of encouragement the reaction of everyone would be, "How rich we are!"

Upon one listener, however, the words of Jesus seem to have made no impression whatever. Someone has said, "When there is an inheritance 99 percent of the people become wolves."

13. Someone from the crowd said to him, Teacher, tell my brother to share the inheritance with me.

The person who made this request could think of only one thing: the inheritance! He was convinced that he was being cheated. To be sure, regulations concerning the division of an inheritance could be found in Deut. 21:15-17; see also Num. 27:8-11 and ch. 36. But it is possible that in the present case justice was not being done. So, at least, it seemed to the complainant. Was he, perhaps, the younger of two brothers, and was his brother totally unwilling to share the inheritance with him?

But why did he urge *Jesus* to intervene in this dispute? The reason may have been that he took this Teacher to be a rabbi, and, knowing that rabbis at times settled matters of this nature, therefore asked him to bring this quarrel to a conclusion favorable to himself, the younger brother.

---

401. Or: granaries.
402. Literally: is not rich toward God.

14. He answered, Man, who appointed me judge or arbitrator in y o u r case?

Jesus definitely refuses to comply with the request; this probably for two reasons: (a) he did not wish to ignore the authorities who were supposed to take care of such matters; and (b) he himself had been appointed to shoulder a task far more important and sublime, namely, to seek and to save the lost (19:10).

The Master knew very well that the petitioner's preoccupation with strictly mundane affairs had its root in cupidity. Therefore he now issues a warning, addressed not only to this man but to the entire multitude: **15. Then he said to them, Watch out! Be on y o u r guard against greed of every description.**

This is a most earnest warning. Let every listener take it to heart. Let him begin to take inventory. Let him make it his serious business to ask himself again and again, "Am I perhaps a greedy individual? Do I experience joy in giving, in helping along good causes? Or am I, perhaps, a selfish person? Do I have an inordinate yearning for material possessions? For honor, prestige? For power and position? Briefly, am I greedy?"

The Greek word for *greed* is very descriptive. Literally it means: the thirst for *having more,* always having more and more and still more. It is as if a man in order to quench his thirst takes a drink of salt water, which happens to be the only water that is available. This makes him still more thirsty. So he drinks again and again, until his thirst kills him. In this connection think also of one of the German words for greed: die *Habgier;* cf. the Dutch: *hebzucht,* the uncontrolled *yearning* to *have ... have ... have ...* more ... and ... more ... and still more.

Jesus tells these people—and is telling us today—not to become enslaved to this demon of greed, and he adds: **for a man's life** [the life that really matters] **does not consist in the abundance of his possessions,** his earthly goods.

In order to drive home this point, there follows:

16. And he told them a parable, saying: The ground of a certain rich man produced bumper crops.

What was wrong with this farmer? The fact that he was successful? Of course not. Nowhere does Scripture condemn success or riches as such. God never rebuked the following because they were rich: Abraham, Solomon, Job, Joseph of Arimathea (see Gen. 13:2; I Kings 3:10-13; Job 42:12; Matt. 27:57).

What then? Had he acquired his wealth by dishonest means? There is nothing in the text that points in that direction. On the contrary, we are given the distinct impression that this man had become rich because God had blessed the labors of his hands and had caused his soil to be so fertile that it produced bumper crops.

What was really wrong becomes clear from the following verses: **17-19. So he carried on a dialogue within himself, saying, What shall I** do, for I have no space where I can store my crops? Then he said, This is what I'll do: I will tear down my barns and I will build bigger ones, and there I will store all my grain and goods. And I will say to my soul, Soul, you have ample goods laid up for many years. Take it easy; eat, drink, and have a good time.

Note the following:

First of all, the rich man shows that he does not know *himself.* He fails to realize that his *body* is mortal and will not necessarily live on "for many years:" Also, he does not take account of the fact that the "ample goods" in which he rejoices cannot satisfy the *soul.* His soul has nothing!

Secondly, he does not figure with the needs of *others.* He is thoroughly selfish. Both in the Greek original and in my translation the words *I* and *my* occur an even dozen times. There are 8 *I*'s and 4 *my*'s. He should have realized that there were other people who were in need of some of his grain. He missed the joy of generous giving. All he could think of was tearing down the old barns or granaries in order to build bigger ones, in which to store for *himself his* grain, etc.

Applying this to the present-day situation, we may well ask ourselves whether we are doing all we should for the hungry and poverty-stricken. Consider the population explosion. It is estimated that at the time when this parable was spoken there were about one-fourth of a billion people living on earth. Not until the year A.D. 1830 did the number reach one billion, a century later two billion. Today (1978) the estimated world population is over four billion.

These people need food. They need healthy bodies. In certain regions of the earth there are hundreds of thousands of children with bloated abdomens, toothpick arms, and bulging eyes! Indeed, the outline of their ribs is visible on their chests!

In addition to the population explosion there are other reasons for this deplorable situation. Some of them are: unfavorable climatic and/or soil conditions, lack of sanitation, crude farm implements, lack of technical skills, and, let us not forget, superstition. Thus, to a Hindu the cow is the most sacred of animals. It is not an article of food.

What the hungry people of the earth need, therefore, is technical skill, knowledge and application of the rules of hygiene, of crop-raising and soil cultivation and irrigation, in some instances better seed, and a sufficient number of good doctors. All these needs are urgent. They must not be underestimated. But what they need above all else is the gospel of the saving grace of God in Jesus Christ!

> Shall we, whose souls are lighted
>   With wisdom from on high,
> Shall we to men benighted
>   The lamp of life deny?
> Salvation! O salvation!
>   The joyful sound proclaim

Till earth's remotest nation
Has learned Messiah's Name.

R. Heber,
third stanza of
"From Greenland's Icy Mountains"

Thirdly, the rich man does not thank and glorify *God.* For all practical purposes this man is an atheist. In view of his abundant harvest we were justified in expecting him to exclaim, "Bless Jehovah, O my soul, and forget not all his benefits! Who am I that thou hast brought me so far? What shall I render to the Lord for all his benefits toward me?" But no, he says nothing of the kind. What he does say in his soliloquy is, "Take it easy; eat, drink, and have a good time"!

The grim awakening follows:

20. But God said to him, You fool! This very night your soul is being demanded of you, and the things you have prepared (for yourself), whose shall they be?

God calls this man "Fool," and a fool he was indeed, for he seemed to think that he had no need of God whatever, that he himself was in control of his life, soul and body both, that he was "the master of his fate and the captain of his soul." Now God tells him that his soul will be required of him not after "many years" but "this very night." God himself will demand it of him. Note that the fool was wrong not only in thinking that he was *in control* of life's ending. He was also wrong in forgetting that *he did not even know* when it would be terminated. He should have reminded himself of the words of Ps. 39:4-6 (in part), "Jehovah, let me know how frail I am.... Surely every man is mere breath.... He heaps up riches, and knows not who shall gather them." See also Ps. 90:10 and 103:15, 16.

How the heirs must have laughed as they were dividing the things he had so studiously heaped up ... *for himself!* And while they were doing this, *where was he?* Read Ps. 73:19, 20.

Jesus sums up the parable's main lesson as follows:

21. So it goes with one who hoards up riches for himself but is not rich in God's sight. Jesus has reference to the man who lives only for himself and does not figure with God.

To be sure, a man should, in thorough consciousness of his dependence on God, and in gratitude to him, try to supply his own needs and those of his family. Prov. 6:6 ("Go to the ant, you sluggard," etc.) was not written in vain; neither was the advice Joseph gave to Pharaoh (Gen. 41:25-36). Just so one does not forget the principle laid down so clearly here in Luke 12:21. And is not this the same, in essence, as that which the Lord also established in Matt. 6:33, "But seek first his kingdom and his righteousness, and all these things will be granted to y o u as an extra gift"? It's a matter of selecting the right item to be placed *first* on our list of priorities. It should be *"his* kingdom and *his* righteousness." "Delight yourself in Jehovah, and he will give you the desires of your heart" (Ps. 37:4). See also I Cor. 10:31.

For *Practical Lessons* and *Greek Words,* etc., see pp. 671–675.

---

22 And he said to his disciples, "Therefore I say to y o u, Do not be anxious about y o u r life, what y o u are going to eat; or about y o u r body, what y o u are going to wear. 23 Life is worth more than food, and the body than clothes. 24 Consider the ravens: they neither sow nor reap; they have neither storeroom nor granary;[403] yet God feeds them. How much more valuable y o u are than the birds! 25 And who among y o u is able, by worrying, to add even one cubit to his life-span? 26 Since, then, y o u cannot do this very little thing, why are y o u anxious about the rest?

27 "Consider the lilies, how they grow. They neither toil nor spin; yet I tell y o u that even Solomon in all his splendor did not dress himself like one of these. 28 Now if God so clothes the grass in the field, which today is alive and tomorrow is thrown into the furnace, how much more will he clothe y o u, O men of little faith! 29 Y o u surely must not set y o u r heart on what y o u will eat or what y o u will drink, nor must y o u live in a state of constant worry. 30 For all of these matters are the very things worldly people[404] are constantly craving. Besides, y o u r heavenly Father knows that y o u need them. 31 But seek his kingdom, and these things will be granted to y o u as an extra gift.

32 "Fear not, little flock, for y o u r Father takes pleasure in giving y o u the kingdom. 33 Sell y o u r possessions and give to charity. Provide for yourselves purses that will never wear out, a treasure in heaven that will never give out, where no thief can reach and no moth ravage. 34 For where y o u r treasure is, there will y o u r heart be also."

12:22–34 *Warning Against Earthly Anxiety*
Cf. Matt. 6:19–21, 25–34; 19:21; Mark 10:21; Luke 11:41; 18:22

22, 23. And he said to his disciples, Therefore I say to y o u, Do not be anxious about y o u r life, what y o u are going to eat; or about y o u r body, what y o u are going to wear. Life is worth more than food, and the body than clothes.

At this point it is clear that Jesus addresses himself again particularly to his disciples. He starts out by saying, "Therefore," etc.

In other words, worry about what to eat and what to wear ill befits the person who realizes that his life and his body are under God's constant care, and that it is God, he alone, who determines the length of anyone's life-span (see verses 6, 7, 20). Moreover, he who has provided the greater, namely, life and the body, will he not also furnish the lesser, namely, food and clothes?

To anyone who is acquainted with The Sermon on the Mount (Matt. 5–7; Luke 6) it is immediately clear that the part of the discourse recorded here in Luke 12:22–34 is a repetition, with variations, omissions, and additions, of a section of that famous sermon, namely, of Matt. 6:25–34. And would it not have been a great loss if these precious passages had been spoken only once during Christ's earthly ministry?

Continuing, then, with passages from The Sermon on the Mount, Jesus says (he may have been pointing upward to a flock of ravens or—as others

---

403. Or: barn.
404. Or: the nations of the world.

Similarities Between Luke 12 and Matthew 6

Verse in Luke 12	*Key to Content*	*Verse(s) in Matthew 6*
22	Do not be anxious about y o u r life . . . y o u r body	25a
23	Life is worth more than food, and the body than clothes	25b
24	Consider the ravens [the birds of the air]	26
25	Who is able, by worrying, to add one cubit to his life-span?	27
27	Consider the lilies, how they grow	28b, 29
28	If God so clothes the grass, etc.	30
29	Y o u . . . must not live in . . . constant worry, etc.	cf. 31, 34
30	All these things worldly people are craving	cf. 32
31	Seek his kingdom [Seek first his kingdom]	33
33b	. . . where no thief can reach and no moth ravage	cf. 19, 20
34	Where y o u r treasure is, etc.	21

interpret the word—crows): **24. Consider the ravens; they neither sow nor reap; they have neither storeroom nor granary; yet God feeds them. How much more valuable y o u are than the birds.**

These ravens were merely birds. Besides, they knew nothing about farming; that is, they neither sowed nor reaped. Also, they neither owned nor had at their disposal storerooms or barns to which they could bring their goods. To top it all, they were even counted among the unclean birds (see the list in Lev. 11:13–19). Nevertheless, they were well taken care of, for God himself fed them. Jesus implies: then why should *y o u* worry? How much more valuable y o u are than the birds!

The senselessness of worry is evident also from the following:

25, 26. And who among y o u is able, by worrying, to add even one cubit to his life-span? Since, then, y o u cannot do this very little thing, why are y o u anxious about the rest?

The word I have translated "life-span" may refer either to *age* or to *height* or *stature*. Thus Zacchaeus was small in *stature* (Luke 19:3), but Sarah was long past the *age* of conceiving (Heb. 11:11). The man born blind, healed by Jesus, had reached the *age* of legal maturity (John 9:21, 23). Here in Luke 12:25 A.V. has "stature." But in the present context this meaning is improbable, and this for two reasons: (a) adding this amount is here represented as being "a very little thing." Adding a cubit to a life-span of seventy or eighty years would not amount to much, but actually becoming taller by forty-six centimeters can hardly be considered an altogether insignificant accomplishment; and (b) who, except perhaps a dwarf or a midget, would impatiently desire to add that amount to his height? A man may worry himself to death; he cannot worry himself into a longer span of life. See also Ps. 39:4-6.

The Lord now turns to another example from nature. Paralleling what he has said about the ravens (verse 24), he now turns to the lilies (verses 27, 28). In line with his teaching regarding the divine provision of food so that a person may keep alive (verse 24), he now shows that God will also provide clothes so that this person's body may be covered. Jesus says: **27. Consider the lilies, how they grow. They neither toil nor spin; yet I tell y o u that even Solomon in all his splendor did not dress himself like one of these.**

"Consider"—that is, notice carefully, study closely—the "lilies." Exactly what kind of flower the Lord had in mind when he said "lilies" cannot be determined. Some guesses are: irises, narcissi, Turk's cap lilies, and gladioli. In the light of the context (note "the grass in the field") it is very well possible that Jesus, instead of referring to any particular kind of flower, was thinking of all the beautiful flowers that were adding their splendor to the landscape at that time of the year.

"How they grow" must mean, as the context indicates: without any toil whatever on their part, nor any care being bestowed on them by any human individual, "how *easily* and *freely,* and yet how *gorgeously.*" Though the "lilies" do not spin a single thread, yet even Solomon in all his splendor did not dress himself like one of these. Is not this true in at least this respect, namely, that Solomon's finest apparel was at best but a mimicry and derivative of that which in nature comes fresh from the hand of God? *Pristine beauty cannot be matched!*

Yet the simultaneous outburst of flowers in the spring of the year just as suddenly vanishes: today these flowers are fully alive and adorn the fields; tomorrow this "grass in the field," that is, this sum total of uncultivated (in contrast with cultivated) plants, serves as fuel for the domestic oven, in a land where fuel was not plentiful.

28. Now if God so clothes the grass in the field, which today is alive and tomorrow is thrown into the furnace, how much more will he clothe y o u, O men of little faith!

There is a double argument here, as follows:

a. from the less to the greater: If God provides for the short-lived *grass,* he will surely provide for *his children,* destined for eternal glory.

b. from the greater to the less: If God decks the wild flowers with such *very beautiful garments,* then he will certainly clothe his children with the *ordinary garments* which they need.

Jesus calls his worrying followers "men of little faith." The various passages and the contexts in which he makes use of this description are as follows:

Matt. 6:30 and its parallel here in Luke 12:28 (worry about clothes)
Matt. 8:26 (the disciples' fear of drowning during a storm at sea)
Matt. 14:31 (Peter's similar fear)

Matt. 16:8 (the disciples' failure to remember the lesson they had received in connection with Christ's miracle-working power).

Based upon these passages, it would seem that the description refers to the fact that those so characterized were not sufficiently taking to heart the comfort they should have derived from the presence, promises, power, and love of Christ.

So far in this section Jesus has shown that worry or earthly anxiety is inconsistent with his disciples' position as *the crown of God's creation* (verses 22–24, 28, 29), and that it is also thoroughly useless (verses 25, 26). In verses 29, 30 he adds as a further argument against worry the fact that it is inconsistent with the disciples' position as *believers* over against *unbelievers,* worldlings. Are not Christ's followers the children of the heavenly Father, that is, of him who knows their needs and will therefore supply them? Jesus says: **29, 30. Y o u surely must not set y o u r heart on what y o u will eat or what y o u will drink, nor must y o u live in a state of constant worry. For all of these matters are the very things worldly people are constantly craving. Besides, y o u r heavenly Father knows that y o u need them.**

Note the marked emphasis on *y o u* over against others!

What Jesus is stressing is that God's children must not behave like "the nations of the world." They must be distinctive in their thinking, speaking, acting.

It would be difficult to exaggerate the significance of the passage before us. What Jesus is saying is that believers must differ in their inner yearnings, must set their hearts on different things, must be controlled by different ideals, and must be motivated by a different love.

When church members hardly differ at all from "outsiders" in the ambitions they cherish, in the goals they try to achieve, in the manner in which they react to the disappointments and adversities of life, in the way they conduct their social events and parties, in the kind of literature they prefer to read, in the songs they prefer to sing, in their choice of friends with whom they feel at home, etc., there is something very wrong. What Jesus here teaches is entirely in line with the rest of Scripture. A few passages must suffice:

"It is a people that dwells alone and shall not be reckoned among the nations" (Num. 23:9).

"If Jehovah be God, follow him; but if Baal, then follow him" (I Kings 18:21).

"Be not unequally yoked with unbelievers" (II Cor. 6:14).

To be *real,* religion must be *vital.* It is easy to "recite" the Apostles' Creed, and in doing so to say, "I believe in God the Father, Almighty, Maker of heaven and earth," but to realize in one's heart of hearts that this "heavenly Father" actually knows that we need food and drink, and will take care that we have it, to be convinced of this even though we may be unemployed . . . that is another matter. But that is exactly what Jesus here teaches.

Note also that Jesus refers not only to eating but also to drinking. The reason for this may well be that he knew and figured with the fact that there and then water—especially water fit to drink—was not always and everywhere easily obtainable.

Jesus has been speaking in negative terms. He has been saying, "Do *not* be anxious about y o u r life" (verse 22) and "Do *not* set y o u r heart on what y o u will eat or what y o u will drink." He now changes to the positive approach and says, **31. But seek his kingdom, and these things will be granted to y o u as an extra gift.**

For the meaning of the term *the kingdom of God* see on 4:43. Christ's disciples are being urged, therefore, to see to it that the rule of God is being established more and more in their own lives and in the lives of others. The reward of grace is this, that while they are concentrating all their attention on establishing God's kingdom everywhere, their heavenly Father sees to it that they do not only have an abundance of spiritual blessings, but also, in addition, food and clothing. The necessities of daily living will not be lacking to them. For further elucidation see I Kings 3:10–14; Mark 10:29, 30; Luke 22:35; and I Tim. 4:8.

Very tenderly Jesus now adds, **32. Fear not, little flock** [a form of address found nowhere else in the New Testament], **for y o u r Father takes pleasure in giving y o u the kingdom.** Though *small* in number, the flock is *dear* to the Father!

Jesus a moment ago (verse 31) told his disciples that they must *seek* the kingdom, making it an object of continuous search. Now he calls the kingdom a *gift*. Nevertheless, these two ideas are not contradictory. An example from nature will clarify this. Of itself a tree has no power to maintain itself. Its roots are, as it were, empty hands stretched out to the environment. It is dependent on the sun, the air, the clouds, and the soil. It does not even have the strength to absorb the nourishment it requires. The sun is the source of its energy. But does this mean that the tree is therefore inactive? Not at all; its roots and leaves, though completely receptive, are enormously active. For example, it has been estimated that the amount of work performed by a certain large tree in a single day to raise water and minerals from the soil to the leaves is equal to the amount of energy expended by a person who carries three hundred buckets full of water, two at a time, up a ten-foot flight of stairs. The leaves too are virtual factories. They too are tremendously active.

The same holds also with respect to the citizens of the kingdom. They receive the kingdom as a gift. Yet, after the new principle of life has been received, the recipients become very active. They work very hard, not by means of anything in themselves but by the power that is being constantly supplied to them by the Lord's Spirit. They "work out their own salvation," and are able to do this because "it is God who works in them both to will and to work for his good pleasure" (Phil. 2:12, 13. See also Matt. 7:13; cf. Luke

13:24; 16:16b). They trust in God's promises, pray, spread the message of salvation, and out of gratitude perform good works to benefit men and to glorify God. And the *gift* increases with the search!

A second thought on which the emphasis also falls is this: the One whom Jesus tenderly calls "y o u r Father" does not bestow the kingdom upon the disciples grudgingly. On the contrary. It is his *good pleasure* to do so. It is with keen delight that he does it.

Because of the past tense of the verb *to take pleasure* there are those who insist on the rendering, "It *did* please the Father," etc., or "The Father *has been* pleased to give y o u," etc. This may be correct. On the other hand, in connection with this particular verb the past tense can be used even to indicate present action. See, for example, 3:22. The difference is minor. God is from everlasting to everlasting, and he is unchangeable. So, when he *took* pleasure he also *takes* pleasure and *will take* pleasure. What *was* his delight *is still* his delight and *will ever remain* so. It is therefore possible to say that the rendering "Y o u r Father has been pleased to give y o u the kingdom" is correct, and so is the translation "Y o u r Father is pleased to give y o u the kingdom." The main fact on which the passage rivets our attention is that when the Father gives, he gives unstintingly, a marvelous truth confirmed also by such passages as Isa. 55:6, 7; Ezek. 18:23, 32; 33:11; Hos. 11:8; Matt. 23:37; Luke 2:14; 13:34, 35; Eph. 1:5, 9, etc.

The Father gives. His children should do the same, in their own limited way, but from the heart and generously: **33a. Sell y o u r possessions and give to charity.** Verses 32, 33a are not duplicated in Matt. 6. Nevertheless, broadly speaking, the "philosophy" of the contents of 12:33a can be found in The Sermon on the Mount (e.g., Matt. 5:7; 6:3). For a somewhat closer parallel one would have to turn to such passages as Luke 11:41; and see also 18:22 (cf. Matt. 19:21; Mark 10:21: Christ's command to "the rich young ruler").

As to the meaning of the passage, it has at times been grossly misinterpreted, as if Jesus said to *all* his followers, "Sell *all* y o u r possessions and give *the entire proceeds* to the poor." The result would be that very soon the church would become a burden to society. A text must be explained in the light of its context. A moment ago Jesus told the parable of that notorious individual, The Rich Fool (verses 16–21). That man kept everything for himself. It is that selfish spirit which Jesus is here combating. The true interpretation of what the Master says here in Luke 12:33a can be found in such passages as I Cor. 16:2, 3; II Cor. 8:1–9; and Gal. 6:10.

Broadly parallel with a passage from Matt. 6 is Luke 12:**33b. Provide for yourselves purses that will never wear out, a treasure in heaven that will never give out, where no thief can reach and no moth ravage.**

For the nature of that treasure in heaven see such passages as Matt. 10:41, 42; 25:34–46; and cf. Luke 16:9; 19:17–19. That treasure can indeed be symbolized by "purses that never wear out." Moreover, it never gives out. There is always more and more and still more. And, to top it all, the riches of the heavenly life, in principle begun already on earth but in fulness reserved for heaven, will be completely out of reach for thieves and moths.

That the heavenly treasures are moth-proof and burglar-proof, in other words, that they endure forever in all their sparkling luster, as the irremovable possession of the children of the heavenly Father, is the teaching of Scripture throughout, for it tells us about:

a faithfulness that will never be removed (Ps. 89:33; 138:8),

a life that will never end (John 3:16),

a spring of water that will never cease to bubble up within the one who drinks of it (John 4:14),

a gift that will never be lost (John 6:37, 39),

a hand out of which the Good Shepherd's sheep will never be snatched (John 10:28),

a chain that will never be broken (Rom. 8:29, 30),

a love from which we shall never be separated (Rom. 8:39),

a calling that will never be revoked (Rom. 11:29),

a foundation that will never be destroyed (II Tim. 2:19),

and an inheritance that will never fade out (I Peter 1:4, 5).

34. For where y o u r treasure is, there will y o u r heart be also.
The sentence introduced by "For" states the reason why the exhortations of verses 32, 33 should be obeyed. Naturally, if a person's real treasure, his ultimate aim in all his striving, is something pertaining to this earth—the acquisition of money, fame, popularity, prestige, power—then his heart, the very center of his life (Prov. 4:23), will be completely absorbed in that mundane object. All of his activities, including even the so-called religious, will be subservient to this one goal. On the other hand, if, out of sincere and humble gratitude to God, he has made God's kingdom, that is, the joyful recognition of God's sovereignty in his own life and in every sphere, his treasure, then *there* is also where his heart will be. Money, in that case, will be a help, not a hindrance. The "heart" cannot be in both of these places at the same time. It is an either-or proposition! See 16:13.[405]

Practical Lessons Derived from 12:13–34

Verses 13, 15

"Tell my brother to share the inheritance with me." "Be on y o u r guard against greed."

Let us say that, in connection with an inheritance, you received "a bum deal." The trouble is that you make so much fuss about it that it begins to look as if all your happiness depends upon the solution, in your favor, of this injustice. You are not putting first things first. Better examine yourself and repent.

---

405. Notes on Greek words, phrases, and constructions in 12:13–34 begin on page 672.

Verse 20

"This very night your soul is being demanded of you." Does not this parable imply that our real riches consists in that which is stated so beautifully in Rom. 8:31–39?

Verses 24, 27

"Consider the ravens ... the lilies." What Jesus says about them does not mean that we too should not work for a living. Rather, it means that if even these creatures are the objects of God's concern, then surely we, whom God has endowed with gifts and talents enabling us to plan and to work, will be provided for.

Verse 29

"Y o u surely must not set y o u r heart on what y o u will eat or what y o u will drink." Making such things our chief aim in life is what is wrong with us. Our chief aim should be obedience to I Cor. 10:31.

Verse 32

"Y o u r Father takes pleasure in giving y o u the kingdom." Does not this passage reveal the very heart of God? See also John 3:16; Rom. 5:6–11; 8:32. When we make obedience to God's will our chief joy, God is so happy that he sings! You don't believe it? Read Zeph. 3:17.

Notes on Greek Words, Phrases, and Constructions in 12:13–34

Verses 13, 14

μερίσασθαι, aor. middle infinitive of μερίζω, to divide; middle, to share.
μεριστήν, acc. s. of μεριστής, divider, arbitrator.

Verse 15

πλεονεξίας (πλέον plus ἔχω), eagerness *to have more,* covetousness, greed.
ὅτι οὐκ ... τῶν ὑπαρχόντων αὐτῷ; lit. for not in the abounding to anyone of the things belonging to him does his life consist; i.e., for a man's life does not consist in the abundance of his possessions.

Verse 16

εὐφόρησεν, third per. s. aor. indicat. of εὐφορέω* (εὖ plus φέρω), to bear well; to bring forth plentifully, bumper crops.

Verses 17, 18

συνάξω (twice), first per. fut. indicat. act. of συνάγω, to bring together, to store, a verb especially frequent in Matthew and in the writings of Luke.
καθελῶ, first per. s. fut. indicat. act. of καθαιρέω, to tear down, demolish. See 1:52, "He has brought down rulers from their thrones."

For ἀποθήκας, acc. pl. of ἀποθήκη (ἀπό plus τίθημι), the place where grain is stored away, granary, barn; see 3:17.

Verses 19, 20

In verses 19, 20 the word ψυχή is used three times, first, the dat. form occurs, as indirect object of the verb ἐρῶ; immediately after that the vocative, both of these at the beginning of verse 19; hence, "And I will say to my soul, Soul, you have," etc. Finally, in verse 20 the same word is used once more, this time in the accusative, as the direct object of a verb.

How should these three instances of the word ψυχή be translated? I have found that the great majority of the translators use as English equivalent the word *soul*, and this in all three cases. This is done by A.V., A.R.V., R.S.V., N.A.S., Moffatt, Goodspeed, Weymouth, Williams, Phillips, Robertson, Lenski, Amplified, Berkeley, Norlie, Jerusalem Bible, Dutch (both Statenvertaling and Nieuwe Vertaling: ziel), etc., etc. I too believe that this is the best procedure. On the other hand, here in Luke 12:19, 20 N.I.V.—all in all an excellent translation; by all means purchase a copy!—leaves out entirely the word *soul*. One should be careful in criticizing this. It is true that the clause, "And I will say to my soul," can probably also be correctly rendered, "And I will say to myself," for this use of a form of ψυχή may well be influenced by Hebrew style, so that the reflexive relationship is here conveyed. Hence, N.I.V. cannot be taken to task for its translation, "And I'll say to myself" (instead of "to my soul"). See L.N.T. (A. and G.), p. 902. It is also true that ψυχή can at times be correctly rendered "life." See verses 22, 23. Therefore, N.I.V.'s rendering "This very night your life will be demanded of you" is again a tenable rendering. What, as far as I see, is an error, is N.I.V.'s complete omission of the second of the three instances of ψυχή, the vocative. Here N.I.V. offers "You have plenty of good things," etc. But the original has, "Soul, you have," etc. As L.N.T. (A. and G.), p. 901, points out, here the ψυχή is viewed as the seat and center of the inner life of man. I can see no good reason for omitting *this* ψυχή in translation, just as I can see no justification for omitting it in the translation of Rev. 6:9 and 20:4, where N.I.V. is certainly correct. On ψυχή see also N.T.C. on Mark, p. 315, footnote 370.

Note that while φάγε and πίε are *aor.*, ἀναπαύου and εὐφραίνου are *pres.* imperatives, and see the translation. On the verb εὐφραίνω, to be merry, etc., see also the note on 15:23, 24 on page 762.

"You fool! This very night your soul is being demanded of you." Robertson (*Word Pictures, Luke,* p. 176) points out that the rabbis used "they" to avoid saying "God." Without denying this, is not what we have here another instance of Luke's frequent use of Semitic style? Cf. Dan. 4:25 where "They shall make thee eat" (A.V., retaining the grammatical structure of the original) sounds better to us when transposed to "you shall be made to eat" (R.S.V.).

ἀπαιτοῦσιν, third per. pl. pres. indicat. act. of ἀπαιτέω*, to ask for, demand, require.

Verse 21

θησαυρίζων, nom. s. masc. pres. participle of θησαυρίζω, to treasure up, hoard. For the noun θησαυρός see verse 34. Cf. *thesaurus.* The verb is found also in Matt. 6:19, 20; Rom. 2:5; I Cor. 16:2; II Cor. 12:14; James 5:3; II Peter 3:7.

Verse 22

For forms of the verb μεριμνᾶτε in verses 22, 25, 26, see on verse 11. The aor. subjunctives φάγητε and ἐνδύσησθε are retained in the indirect question.

Verses 23, 24

Both the noun τροφή (here gen. -ῆς) and the verb τρέφω are represented here. The noun means food, nourishment; the cognate verb, to feed, rear, cause to grow. Cf. *atrophy* (a wasting away because of insufficient nutrition).

κόρακας, acc. pl. of κόραξ, crow, raven.

ὅτι, probably declarative here. Either a colon or "that" can serve as the English equivalent.

Verse 25

ἡλικίαν, acc. of ἡλικία, life-span, *not* (with Robertson, *Translation*, p. 77) stature. See the commentary.

πῆχυν, acc. of πῆχυς, cubit; so also in Matt. 6:27; John 21:8; Rev. 21:17, basically the distance between the bend in the elbow and the tip of the middle finger. For more on biblical measurements see N.T.C. on John, Vol. II, pp. 482, 483, footnote 299.

Verse 26

ἐλάχιστον, acc. s. neut. superlative of μικρός (small). This form is here used in the elative sense: very little.

Verse 27

κατανοήσατε, sec. per. pl. aor. imperat. act. of κατανοέω (κατά perfective plus νοῦς), carefully fix y o u r mind on, observe, consider.

κρίνα, acc. pl. of κρίνον, lily. Cf. *crinoid* (lily-like). A beautiful and very colorful tree is the *crinodendron*.

νήθει, third per. s. pres. indicat. of νήθω, to spin. Though to sew is not the same as to spin, yet the two are related. Accordingly cf. *needle*, German *Nähen*, Dutch *naaien*.

περιεβάλετο, third per. s. 2nd aor. indicat. middle of περιβάλλω, to cast around, clothe; in middle, to dress oneself.

Verse 28

This is a simple or first class conditional sentence, generally with εἰ and any tense of the indicat. (in this case the present) in the protasis, and here (as also, e.g., in John 5:47) a question in the apodosis. In the present passage the question is incompletely expressed, but the verb ἀμφιάζει is easily supplied from the preceding clause.

κλίβανον, acc. s. of κλίβανος, in the New Testament occurring only here and in the parallel passage Matt. 6:30, means oven, furnace.

Verse 29

Note the fully expressed (not merely implied in a verb) ὑμεῖς, and its forward position. This emphasis should be retained in translation. Among the well-known translations there are very few that have retained this emphasis. Among the favorable exceptions are Lenski, Robertson, A.V., A.R.V., Jerusalem Bible, and the Dutch versions (both Statenvertaling and Nieuwe Vertaling).

Verse 32

τὸ ... ποίμνιον (= ἡ ποίμνη), flock. Note preceding article. Though such an article preceding a noun in the vocative is not unusual even in Greek, it can be expected in Hebrew and Aramaic, and is not strange here, since, as has been shown, Semitisms abound in Luke's Gospel.

εὐδόκησεν, third per. s. aor. (probably timeless here) indicat. of εὐδοκέω. See the note on 3:22 on page 220.

Verse 33

For πωλήσατε see the note on 12:6 on page 660.
For ἐλεημοσύνη see the note on 11:41 on page 646.
For βαλλάντια see the note on 10:4 on page 587.
σής, moth, as in Matt. 6:19, 20.
διαφθείρει, third per. s. pres. indicat. act. of διαφθείρω. See also II Cor. 4:16; I Tim. 6:5; Rev. 8:9; 11:18, to destroy thoroughly, to corrupt.

Verse 34

Use of the word θησαυρός can be distributed under the following four categories:

A. General Sense

man's treasure viewed as the object of his chief interest and devotion, whatever that object may be (Matt. 6:21 and also here in Luke 12:34).

B. Man's Heart and Mind

viewed as a source of good (Matt. 12:35a; Luke 6:45) or of evil (Matt. 12:35b); or (in favorable sense) of things new and old (Matt. 13:52).

C. Emphasis on the Physical or Earthly

treasure chest (Matt. 2:11); treasures on earth (Matt. 6:19); "treasure hidden in the field" (Matt. 13:44); "treasures of Egypt" (Heb. 11:26).

D. Emphasis on the Spiritual or Heavenly

treasures of wisdom and knowledge (Col. 2:3); "the light of the knowledge of the glory of God," etc., viewed as "a treasure in jars of clay" (II Cor. 4:7); a treasure (or treasures) in heaven (or: in the heavens), see Matt. 6:20; 19:21; Mark 10:21; Luke 12:33; 18:22.

---

35 "Always be dressed so that y o u are ready for action,[406] and keep y o u r lamps burning, 36 like men who, when their master is about to return from the marriage feast, are waiting for him; so that when he comes and knocks they can immediately open the door for him. 37 Blessed are those servants whom the master at his coming will find on the alert. I solemnly declare to y o u that he will dress himself to serve, will have them recline at table, and

---

406. Lit., Let y o u r loins be well-girt [or: girded about].

will go ahead and wait on them. 38 Whether he comes in the second or in the third watch and finds them so, blessed are they!

39 "But of this be assured, that if the owner of the house had known at what hour the burglar was coming, he would not have permitted his house to be broken into. 40 Y o u also must be ever ready, for at an hour when y o u do not expect him, the Son of man arrives."

41 Peter asked him, "Lord, are you addressing this parable to us or to all alike?" 42 The Lord answered, "Who then is the faithful and sensible manager, whom the master will put in charge of his servants, to give them their food allowance at the proper time? 43 Blessed is that servant whom his master at his coming will find so doing. 44 Truly I tell y o u, he will set him over all his possessions. 45 But if that servant shall say in his heart, 'My master is taking his time in coming,' and shall begin to beat up the men and the women servants, and to eat and drink and get drunk, 46 the master of that servant shall arrive on a day he does not expect him and at an hour he does not figure on, and shall cut him to pieces and assign him a place with the unfaithful.

47 "And that servant who knew his master's will but did not get ready or act in accordance with that will shall receive many blows of the lash. 48 But he who did not know and did things that call for a beating shall receive few blows. From every one who has been given much, much will be required; and from the one who has been entrusted with much, all the more will be demanded."

12:35–48 *The Parable of*
(The Noble Ones)
The Watchful Servants
Interruption by Peter
Jesus' Answer
including
The Parable of The Faithful versus the Unfaithful Servant
Cf. Matt. 24:42, 43, 45–51; 25:1 ff.; Mark 13:32–37; Luke 22:27;
John 13:1–17

It will be recalled that in 12:13–21 Jesus told the parable of The Rich Fool. This was followed by a warning against earthly anxiety (verses 22–34), which may be considered an elaboration of the lesson taught by that parable. It is therefore easy to remember that Jesus now calls attention to people who form a contrast to the fool. The fool had his heart and mind centered on the earth, the watchful servants on heaven.

For the sake of simplicity verses 35–48 can be divided into two parables, that of The Watchful Servants (verses 35–40) and that of The Faithful versus the Unfaithful Servant (verses 41–48). In this arrangement Peter's question is included in the second parable, since it led to the telling of that parable. With the exception of a few verses the first of these two parables is peculiar to Luke, the second is common to Luke and Matthew.

A. *The Parable of The Watchful Servants*

35, 36. Always be dressed so that y o u are ready for action, and keep y o u r lamps burning, like men who, when their master is about to return from the marriage feast, are waiting for him; so that when he comes and knocks they can immediately open the door for him.

The meaning of the expression used in the original, namely, "Let y o u r loins be girded about," is that the long, flowing robes of the servants must not be left hanging loose, making work difficult or even impossible (cf. Acts 7:58). These robes must be tucked into the belt, so that the servants can work with ease and are ready to wait on their master.

Applied spiritually, the resultant sense is always be ready (a) to welcome the Master at his return from the marriage feast of heavenly glory, and (b) to render to him any service he desires. "Keep y o u r lamps burning" also points to the necessity of preparation. What we have here is essentially the same lesson as is found in the parable of The Five Foolish and The Five Sensible Girls ("The Ten Virgins"). See N.T.C. on Matt. 25:1–13.

37. Blessed are those servants whom the master at his coming will find on the alert. I solemnly declare to y o u that he will dress himself to serve, will have them recline at table, and will go ahead and wait on them.

The underlying figure seems strange. Must we imagine, then, that an earthly master would actually wait on his servants? Probably not, but *this* Master, the One here symbolized, did that very thing when he was on earth. Note, "I am among y o u as one who serves" (Luke 22:27), and cf. John 13:1–15, picturing Jesus washing the feet of his disciples. What is promised here, therefore, is that our Lord, at his second coming will, in a manner consonant with his glory and majesty, "wait on" his faithful servants!

No wonder these servants are called "blessed." This almost unbelievable promise is introduced by the formula, "Amen, I say to y o u" (or: "I solemnly declare to y o u").

Continued: **38. Whether he comes in the second or in the third watch and finds them so, blessed are they!**

As Plummer (*op. cit.,* p. 331) and many after him see it, Luke is here following the Jewish division of the night into three watches (cf. Judg. 7:19), not the Roman division into four watches. This *may* be correct, but we cannot be sure. That Mark divided the night into *four* watches is clear from 13:35; that Matthew did also follows from 14:25. I can see no compelling reason to conclude that Luke, whose report, in these few verses, in other respects follows Matthew's, adopted a different time computation. That not all translators and interpreters agree with Plummer on this point is clear from (to mention but two examples) (a) the footnote on verse 38 in N.A.S., and (b) Lenski's comment (*op. cit.,* p. 444).

However, this is a minor point. The reason why Jesus did not say "in the first watch" is probably that then the wedding feast would still be in progress. For the rest, the main thought is this: the believers' superlative blessedness at Christ's return.

Because the truth here revealed, namely, that at his return Jesus will himself wait on the redeemed, is so exceedingly precious, the benediction of verse 37 is repeated in verse 38: *"blessed are they."*

39, 40. But of this be assured, that if the owner of the house had known at what hour the burglar was coming, he would not have permitted his house to be broken into. Y o u also must be ever ready, for at an hour when y o u do not expect him, the Son of man arrives.

For the term *Son of man* see on 5:24. When will he return? Jesus states that just as the owner of a house does not know when the burglar is coming but must be at all times ready to protect his property, so also believers do not know when their Master will return, and should, accordingly, always be prepared in mind and heart. When least expected, he arrives. For other passages that stress this same truth see Matt. 24:36; 42–44; Luke 21:34; I Thess. 5:2–4; II Peter 3:10; Rev. 3:3; 16:15.

B. *The Parable of The Faithful versus The Unfaithful Servant*

41. Peter asked him, Lord, are you addressing this parable to us or to all alike?

Though this parable is also found in Matthew (24:45–51), it is not there preceded by Peter's question. What moved this apostle to ask the question? The answer is not given. One guess might well be the following:

Peter's curiosity had been aroused. Jesus had been speaking about those who at his coming would be "ready" (verse 37), but he had implied that some would not be ready. An understandable inference would be that The Twelve and some other constant followers would be the ready ones; the rest of the people, the unready ones. Yet, from verse 22 on the Master had been directing his attention to his disciples, and not nearly as directly to the vast multitude. Did the Master mean, then, that even among his disciples there would be those not ready to welcome him? To whom was Jesus telling the parable?

42–44. The Lord answered, Who then is the faithful and sensible manager, whom the master will put in charge of his servants, to give them their food allowance at the proper time? Blessed is that servant whom his master at his coming will find so doing. Truly I tell y o u, he will set him over all his possessions.[407]

---

407. The resemblance between Matt. 24:45–51 and its parallel in Luke 12:42–46 is striking. The slight differences are noted in the following chart.

Matthew 24:45–51 Compared with Luke 12:42–46

Matthew	*Luke*
servant	manager
has put in charge	will put in charge
household employees	servants
food	food allowance or food ration
wicked	omitted in Luke
is taking his time	is taking his time in coming
his fellow servants	the men and women servants
shall eat and drink with drunkards	to eat and drink and get drunk
with the hypocrites	with the unfaithful

Note that what happens here may be compared to what takes place at another occasion (13:23). See on that passage. There too the question of curiosity does not receive a direct answer. What Jesus seems to be saying, then, is this, "Never mind asking questions stemming from curiosity pure and simple. What you should do is try very hard to be a faithful and sensible manager."

To illustrate what he means Jesus now tells another parable, that of *the faithful* over against *the unfaithful* servant. As to the meaning of this parable, a safe presupposition is that a master of a number of "servants" or, if one prefers, "slaves," is about to leave on a journey. Before he leaves he places his most trusted underling in charge of the other employees. In this capacity this newly appointed manager not only supervises the work of the other servants but also and specifically takes care that they are well provided for. Some are of the opinion that Jesus was thinking especially of his disciples, considered as office-bearers, and so, by extension, of all *ministers* and *pastors* of the churches to be organized during the entire new dispensation. They may well be right. But we cannot be certain about this. After all, the duty of faithfulness applies not only to pastors but also to elders, deacons, teachers, parents; in fact, to all believers. Doing the will of the Master and caring for those in need is certainly the task assigned to all.

Now upon the faithful and sensible manager a special beatitude is pronounced. He is called *blessed*. He is the object of his master's special favor. Moreover, the clause "whom his master shall find *so doing*" shows that the proper attitude on the part of the one who awaits the master's return is eagerness to render active service in the interest of those entrusted to the servant.

When the figure is interpreted, this means that the proper spirit in which believers should await as Savior the Lord Jesus Christ (Phil. 3:20) is not the feverish nervousness of certain Thessalonians (II Thess. 2:1, 2; 3:6–12), nor the nauseating lukewarmness of the Laodiceans (Rev. 3:14–22), but the active faithfulness of the Smyrniots (Rev. 2:8–11). Just as in the parable the master, upon his return, rewards his faithful servant by setting him over all his possessions, so also Jesus himself at his glorious coming will bestow on all his faithful ones a high degree of glory and honor. See Luke 19:17, 19. Does not Christ's promise also imply the assignment of certain specific tasks in the life hereafter, each task a matter of pure delight and satisfaction, and each in harmony with the individuality of the person for whom it is marked out?

Having revealed what will happen to the faithful servant, Jesus now shows what will be the lot of the unfaithful one. In reality the two, the faithful and the unfaithful, are here represented as one and the same person. Note verse 45, "But if *that servant* shall say in his heart," etc. But in the parable this man has how changed so radically that he may not incorrectly be viewed as a different individual.

45, 46. But if that servant shall say in his heart, My master is taking his time in coming, and shall begin to beat up the men and the women

servants, and to eat and drink and get drunk, the master of that servant shall arrive on a day he does not expect him and at an hour he does not figure on, and shall cut him to pieces and assign him a place with the unfaithful.

Note that this servant is saying something "in his heart," that is, to himself. Now what a man says to himself is often even more important than what he says openly. See Prov. 23:7; Matt. 9:3, 21; Luke 12:17; 15:17-19. But within the secret precincts of his own being this particular man is conversing wickedly, irresponsibly. We are reminded of II Peter 3:4. He is saying, "It will be a long, long time before the master returns. In the meantime let me have some fun."

He is not thinking of innocent fun. No, this man is a sadist. Just for fun he begins to beat up the male and female slaves that have been entrusted to his care. He begins to throw his weight around. "Let those slaves cower. Let them cringe." Meantime he revels in eating, drinking, and getting drunk.

Suddenly and unexpectedly the master returns! Convinced by the evidence that this servant, whom he had elevated to a high position, has abused the trust reposed in him and is a thoroughly unreliable person, he issues orders that the culprit be cut to pieces.

Anyone who has made a thorough study of Church History—not only ancient and medieval but also modern—will have discovered, if he has not experienced it in his own person, that what Jesus here presents was a true picture of events to come. To be sure, there have been and there are many faithful servants, who will one day hear the welcome words, "Well done!" But are there not also many of the opposite type, men filled with envy, lust to rule, selfishness? The tribe of Korah, Dathan, and Abiram, who rebelled against Moses (Num. 16:1 ff.), of Diotrephes, who made life difficult for the apostle John (III John 9), and of scribes and chief priests, who brought about the death of Jesus, has not yet died out.

In telling this parable Jesus' aim may well have been: (a) to open the eyes of the true church, and (b) to warn the deceivers in order that they may even now repent. If they do not, the Lord will assign to them a place with the unfaithful. They will be "cut to pieces."

Does this mean, then, that the Master is cruel? Not at all. That he is just and reasonable appears from the closing passage of this section:

47, 48. And that servant who knew his master's will but did not get ready or act in accordance with that will shall receive many blows of the lash. But he who did not know and did things that call for a beating shall receive few blows. From every one who has been given much, much will be required; and from the one who has been entrusted with much, all the more will be demanded.

Note the following:

a. The parable has ended. Nevertheless, verses 47, 48 are perhaps not as loosely related to the preceding verses as some maintain. Do not these verses make clear that "the master" to whom reference is made in verses 47,

48 is the same as the one in the immediately preceding verses, and that in both cases he is—at least symbolizes—Jesus Christ?

Also, do not verses 47, 48 shed light on the reason why the punishment described in verse 46 ("he shall cut him to pieces") was so severe? Is not the answer: "because the servant who received this punishment *knew his master's will* but did not obey it" (see verse 47)?

b. Among those who at the master's return are punished there is indeed a difference: some are punished severely, others lightly. This shows that not only are there degrees of glory in the new heaven and earth (I Cor. 15:41, 42), but there are also degrees of suffering in hell.

c. Responsibility varies with gifts; it is commensurate with knowledge and opportunity. But see also *Practical Lessons* on verse 48.

d. The New Testament teaches this not only here but also in such passages as Matt. 10:15; 11:22, 24; Luke 10:12-14; 23:34; Acts 3:17; I Tim. 1:13.

e. Even the Old Testament teaches this (Lev. 26:28; Num. 15:22-31; Ps. 19:12, 13; and, last but not least, Amos 3:2).

f. Why should the servant who did not know his master's will be punished at all? Answer: ignorance is never absolute. See Rom. 1:20, 21; 2:14-16.

g. The entire passage—see especially verse 48b—makes clear that the talents with which God has endowed men must be used, the time must be "redeemed," the opportunities improved. No one has the right to be lazy. Also, no one has the right to live for himself alone. A person must live for others (I Cor. 9:22), and for God (I Cor. 10:31).

For *Practical Lessons* and *Greek Words,* etc., see pp. 686-690.

---

49 "I have come to cast fire on the earth, and how I wish it were already kindled! 50 I have a baptism with which to be baptized, and how overwhelmed with anguish I am until it is accomplished! 51 Do y o u think that I have come to give peace on earth? No, I tell y o u, but rather division. 52 For from now on in one family there will be five divided against each other: three against two, and two against three. 53 They will be divided: father against son, and son against father; mother against daughter, and daughter against mother; mother-in-law against daughter-in-law, and daughter-in-law against mother-in-law."

12:49-53 *Jesus the Divider*
Cf. Matt. 10:34-36; Mark 10:38

49. I have come to cast fire on the earth, and how I wish it were already kindled!

For a possible topical connection between this verse and the immediately preceding passage see p. 536. The *fire* of which Jesus speaks in all probability refers to the judgment of God upon the sins of his people. That judgment would be rendered at Calvary. It is Jesus himself who will satisfy God's justice and bear the punishment.

That there is a connection between *fire* and *judgment* is very clear. See the following passages: Isa. 66:15; Joel 2:30; Amos 1:7, 10–14; 2:2, 5; Mal. 3:2, 5; I Cor. 3:13; II Thess. 1:7, 8. Jesus is thinking of his fast approaching passion and death.

He realizes that his suffering will be intense. It is not surprising therefore that he says, "and how I wish it were already kindled." Besides, he knows that the firm foundation for the salvation of his people will not have been completed until at Calvary the sacrifice will have been brought.

In line with this is also verse **50. I have a baptism with which to be baptized, and how overwhelmed with anguish I am until it is accomplished!**

The words *baptism* and *to be baptized* are here probably used in a figurative sense: Jesus is going to be "overwhelmed" by agony. He will be plunged into the flood of horrible distress. Note the somewhat similar use of this verb in Isa. 21:4 (LXX) and in Josephus, *Jewish War* IV.137. See also Ps. 42:7, "All thy waves and thy billows have gone over me"; and Ps. 124:4, "Then would the waters have overwhelmed us; the torrent would have passed over our soul." Cf. Mark 10:38.

But Jesus is not complaining. The opposite is true: the opening words of verses 49, 50 are "I have come to [or: in order to]." Jesus knew what awaited him on earth. Other children are passive in their birth. Jesus was active: he came *in order to* take upon himself the burden of God's wrath resulting from the sin of his people, and to suffer the agonies of hell—the hell of Calvary—in their stead. But when he now reflects on the agony that lies ahead, is it any wonder that he says, "How overwhelmed with anguish I am until it is accomplished"? Cf. 22:44.

51–53. Do y o u think that I have come to give peace on earth! No, I tell y o u, but rather division. For from now on in one family there will be five divided against each other: three against two, and two against three. They will be divided: father against son, and son against father; mother against daughter, and daughter against mother; mother-in-law against daughter-in-law, and daughter-in-law against mother-in-law.

We have here a *mashal;* that is, a paradoxical saying, one that sounds unbelievable! That it is contrary to prevailing opinion is indicated by the question, "Do y o u think that I have come to give peace on earth?" and the answer, "No, I tell y o u, but rather division." What Jesus says here causes the one who hears or reads it to startle in shocked disbelief. The natural reaction to the surprising statement would be: "How can this saying be true? Is not Christ 'the Prince of Peace' (Isa. 9:6)? Is he not the One who pronounces a blessing on those who make peace (Matt. 5:9)? If he did not come in order to bring peace how can the following passages be true: Ps. 72:3, 7; Luke 1:79; 2:14; 7:50; 8:48; John 14:27; 16:33; 20:19, 21; Rom. 5:1; 10:15; 14:17; Eph. 2:14; Col. 1:20; Heb. 6:20—7:2? Do not all of them in the strongest terms proclaim Jesus as the Bringer of peace?"

We should remember, however, that it is the characteristic of many a *mashal* to place emphasis on one aspect of the truth rather than on a proposition that is universally valid. See on Matt. 5:34, "Do not take any oath at all." The merit of such aphorisms is that they stop a person short and make him think. So here also. A little reflection will soon convince the earnest student of Scripture that there is a sense in which the coming of Christ into this world not only brought division but was even intended to do so. If that had not been its immediate purpose would not *all* men have been lost (John 3:3, 5; Rom. 3:9–18)? Would they not *all* have rushed onward toward their doom? Besides, even in the lives of those who are ultimately saved is it not true that *through many tribulations* they must enter into the kingdom of God (Acts 14:22)? Is not the life of the believer one of Sturm und Drang (storm and stress)? To be sure, *in the end all is peace,* but the same Paul who exclaims, "I thank God through Jesus Christ our Lord," also complains, "Wretched man that I am!" (Rom. 7:24, 25).

In addition, there will be bitter opponents. Here "on earth," that is, during this present dispensation, the followers of Christ must expect division. It is thus that it will become evident who is on the Lord's side and who is not. It is thus that "the thoughts of many hearts will be revealed" (Josh. 5:13, 14; Matt. 21:44; Luke 2:34, 35; 20:18). The entrance of Christ into this world divides in two, splits apart, *cleaves asunder,* and in so doing turns one person *against* another.

Faith not only creates division between one race and another, one people and another, one church and another; it even brings about division in the family, in fact often the sharpest division of all. In this connection Luke here mentions "five" family members all living under the same roof; father, mother, unmarried daughter, married son and his wife (the parents' daughter-in-law). Because of the relation which these various members assume toward Christ there is intense friction between them: "three against two, and two against three."

For *Practical Lessons* and *Greek Words,* etc., see pp. 686–690.

---

54 He also said to the crowds, "When y o u see a cloud rising in the west, at once y o u say, 'It is going to rain.' And so it does. 55 And when a south wind is blowing, y o u say, 'Scorching heat is on the way.' And it comes. 56 Hypocrites! The look of earth and sky y o u know how to interpret. Then how is it that y o u do not know how to interpret this present critical hour?"

12:54–56 *Knowing How to Interpret the Weather*
versus
Knowing How to Interpret the Time
Cf. Matt. 16:2, 3

For a possible connection between this section and the immediately preceding one see p. 537.

Again, as once before (verses 14–21), Jesus turns to the crowds.

54, 55. He also said to the crowds, When y o u see a cloud rising in the west, at once y o u say, It is going to rain. And so it does. And when a south wind is blowing, y o u say, Scorching heat is on the way. And it comes.

Israel's rain comes from the west, from the Mediterranean Sea. So

> When in the west the sky turns grey,
> One can expect a rainy day.

The sirocco wind blows into the country from the south and east, that is, from the desert. Hence,

> When blows the south wind, y o u will say,
> "Some scorching heat is on the way."

Jesus continues:

56. Hypocrites! The look of earth and sky y o u know how to interpret. Then how is it that y o u do not know how to interpret this present critical hour?

Jesus rebukes these people because they pay far more attention to constantly changing weather conditions than to events that usher in epoch-making historical changes. Did not the coming into this world of the Son of man, with his emphasis on the power, grace, and love of God, rather than on man-made regulations, and with his exhibition of power over everything, including even disease, death, demons, and destructive storms, foretell the downfall of legalistic Judaism? Did it not spell the rise of a church gathered out of both Jews and Gentiles and consisting of all those who believed in salvation by grace through faith and in a life of gratitude to God and of service to man? Were not this coming and that manifestation of power and grace a clear prediction both of the doom of Satan and of the significant strengthening of the kingdom that can never be destroyed? Were these critics utterly blind? Could they not read the handwriting on the wall? Did they not understand that their days, including their quibbling about nonessentials, were numbered, and that the gospel that was being proclaimed by the Prophet from Galilee, even the Son of God, would begin to spread and spread until it covered the earth? But no, the present critical hour does not seem to interest them. *They* prefer to concentrate on the weather! Jesus calls these people *hypocrites,* for, though they pretended to be religious, they were showing far more interest in the weather than in the mighty work God was doing on earth just now. They were better weather forecasters than crisis interpreters.

For *Practical Lessons* and *Greek Words,* etc., see pp. 686–690.

---

57 "Why do y o u not judge for yourselves what is right?   58 For instance, when you are going with your opponent before a magistrate, on the way make every effort to settle with him, lest he drag you before the judge, and the judge turn you over to the constable, and the

constable throw you into prison.   59 I tell you, never will you get out of that place until you
have paid the last mite."

12:57-59 *Becoming Reconciled with the Accuser*
Cf. Matt. 5:25, 26

57. Why do y o u not judge for yourselves what is right?
For the interpretation see also p. 537. Opinions with respect to the meaning of this passage vary widely. Among those I have come across are the
following (not quoted literally but reproduced here in abbreviated form):
   a. Why do y o u not judge *what is right,* that is, why not concentrate on
ethics, instead of on the weather?
   b. Why not judge yourselves instead of judging and condemning other
people?
   c. Why not judge for yourselves instead of allowing others—scribes,
Pharisees—to do y o u r thinking for y o u?
   d. Why not let conscience be y o u r guide?
   e. Why not learn to think for yourselves (implying that up to this time
they had not done so)? One author opines that what Jesus said amounted to
a rebuke to the listeners for not using their common sense in the sphere of
religious matters.
   When opinions differ so widely, it is not always easy to make the right
choice. For myself, I see little merit in opinions (a) and (b). On the other
hand, (c), (d), and (e) are not far apart and may well lead us in the right
direction. One thing must not be ignored, namely, that verses 58, 59 certainly picture a situation in which each person has to make his own individual decision, and what an important decision it is:
   **58, 59. For instance, when you are going with your opponent before a
magistrate, on the way make every effort to settle with him, lest he drag
you before the judge, and the judge turn you over to the constable, and
the constable throw you into prison. I tell you, never will you get out of
that place until you have paid the last mite.**
   The preceding context has driven home the following truths: It is necessary for everyone to ask himself the question, "Am I a faithful or unfaithful
servant" (verses 41–46)? The hour of crisis has arrived (verse 49). You must
choose sides (verses 52, 53). God is speaking to you in the present critical
hour (verses 54–56).
   In harmony with all this, Jesus is winding up his address with a dramatic
appeal to every listener, urging him to make his peace with God; to do so
now, before it is too late. Note change of y o u (pl.) to you (s.). To each
person Jesus is saying, "Be reconciled to God."
   To impress this truth on the heart of every individual Jesus uses an
allegory or "parable" (in the broader sense of the term). He is saying that in
ordinary life, when you are involved in a legal dispute in which you are the
accused, the best thing to do is to try to settle the case "out of court"; in

other words, to become reconciled with the opponent or accuser. By doing this you can avoid being dragged before the judge and being put in prison, with no chance of escape.

Thus also in the religious sphere what each person should do is to become reconciled to God.

Once a person enters hell, he will never get out, "not until you have paid the last *lepton*," says Jesus; i.e., the last fraction of a penny.[408]

Implication: The heavenly Father will be glad to welcome his penitent child back to his loving heart.[409]

Practical Lessons Derived from 12:35–59

Verse 35

"Always be . . . ready for action . . . keep y o u r lamps burning." Whatever we do here and now has significance for all eternity.

Verse 37

"He will dress himself to . . . wait on them." Could anything be more wonderful?

Verse 48

"And from the one who has been entrusted with much, all the more will be demanded." Does this mean "the greater the trust, the higher the bracket"? Cf. graduated income tax. Does Matt. 25:20–23 shed any light on this?

Cf. 9:51 "Jesus resolutely set out for [stedfastly set his face to go to] Jerusalem" and 12:49, 50, "How I wish it [the fire] were already kindled"; "How overwhelmed with anguish I am until it is accomplished." Does not the Savior's anguish, his sensitivity to suffering, make his determination to lay down his life all the more wonderful?

Verse 56

"How is it that y o u do not know how to interpret this present critical hour?"

People may be divided into two groups: (a) some regard time only as *chronos,* the stream of moments flying by with incredible speed. They sigh *tempus fugit,* and do nothing positive about it. (b) Others have an eye for the *kairos,* the critical and often favorable moment to do something for God and his kingdom. Putting it differently, we might say some interpret *carpe diem* to mean "snatch the opportunity to have fun, never mind the future"; others explain it to mean "snatch the opportunity to promote the kingdom of God and its causes."

---

408. According to Mark 12:42 two *lepta* equals a quarter of an *as* or *assarius.* And an assarius was worth only *one sixteenth of a denarius!* The denarius was a laborer's average daily wage (Matt. 18:28; 20:2, 9, 13; 22:19). Due to constantly varying monetary values it is impossible to indicate with any degree of accuracy what such coins would be worth today in American or in English money. *If* the denarius be viewed as the equivalent of 16 or 18 American cents, then the assarius would be worth about a cent, the "quarter" or "quadrant" only about ¼ cent, and the "lepton" merely ⅛ cent.

409. Notes on Greek words, phrases, and constructions in 12:35–59 begin on page 687.

Verse 59

"Never will you get out of that place until you have paid the last mite." This sounds terrible. It *is* terrible. But it should be read in conjunction with Isa. 1:18, "Though y o u r sins be as scarlet," etc.

Notes on Greek Words, Phrases, and Constructions in 12:35-59

Verses 35-37

ἔστωσαν... περιεζωσμέναι, third per. pl. periphrastic perf. imperat. pass. of περιζώννυμι, to gird around. "Let your loins be girded about" (A.V.) correctly reproduces the meaning of the original, though "Keep y o u r belts fastened" or even better, "Always be dressed so that y o u are ready for action," or "ready to serve," is probably what we would say today. The same verb, but now third per. s. future indicat. middle, occurs in verse 37.

ἀναλύσῃ, third per. s. intrans. aor. subjunct. (here deliberative) of ἀναλύω, to depart, return. Tense and mood are retained in the indirect question. The only other use of this verb in the New Testament is Phil. 1:23, where Paul speaks about his desire "to depart and be with Christ." See N.T.C. on that passage.

Note ἐκ τῶν γάμων, and with this compare 14:8 and Matt. 22:2. This plural may have arisen from the fact that a wedding feast frequently lasted several days and included many festive activities. Cf. *nuptials* (also plural).

In the final clause of verse 36 ("so that they may open for him") "him" is modified by "coming and knocking." Yet, the *genitive* absolute, consisting of the aor. act. participles ἐλθόντος καὶ κρούσαντος, remains unchanged in spite of "to him" (αὐτῷ) in the *dative*. Note also that it is the master that is coming and knocking; yet the pronoun αὐτοῦ, though definitely implied, is not written out as part of the genitive absolute. But are not such peculiarities, which basically fall under the heading of "abbreviated expression" (see N.T.C. on John, Vol. I, p. 206), part and parcel of every language? Would it not be a sad situation if everything had to be spelled out in full?

For ἀνοίξωσιν, third per. pl. aor. subjunct. act. of ἀνοίγω, see the note on 1:64 on page 120.

γρηγοροῦντας, masc. acc. pl. pres. act. participle of γρηγορέω. Cf. *Gregory*.

Verses 38, 39

In verse 38 note third class (or future more vivid) conditional sentence, with repeated κἄν (= καὶ ἐάν) and 2nd aor. subjunct. for both verbs in the protasis, and pres. indicat. in the apodosis; and in verse 39 note second class (or contrary to fact) conditional sentence, with εἰ and pluperf. indicat. (followed by present) in the protasis, and οὐκ ἄν and aor. indicat. (followed by aor. pass. infinitive) in the apodosis. This is all very regular. See N.T.C. on John, Vol. I, pp. 40-45.

Verse 42

For θεραπεία (here gen. -ς) see the note on 9:11 on page 484.

σιτομέτριον*, food ration (or food allowance), from σῖτος and μετρέω. The word σιτομέτριον, formerly thought to be confined to the New Testament, has been discovered also in secular Greek. See A. Deissmann, *op. cit.*, pp. 76, 104.

Verses 45, 46

These two verses clearly belong together, forming one third class or future more vivid conditional sentence, with ἐάν followed by two aor. subjunct. verbs ("shall say" and "shall begin"), the second of which is followed by four pres. infinitives, in the protasis; and with three future tense verbs ("will arrive, cut to pieces, assign") in the apodosis.

With διχοτομήσει (third per. s. fut. indicat. act. of διχοτομέω), compare the English word *dichotomize*, but note that while the latter generally has a very innocent meaning, the Greek in the present context means *to cut in two, cut to pieces, dismember*, and this *here applied to persons*.

μετὰ τῶν ἀπίστων, with the unfaithful, unreliable; or, as Matt. 24:51 has it, "with the hypocrites." It is clear, therefore, that at least in the present instance the rendering "with the unbelievers" is not the best.

Verses 47, 48a

ὁ γνούς, 2nd aor. act. participle of γινώσκω.

δαρήσεται, third per. s. fut. indicat. pass. of δέρω, to skin, flay, beat. According to Robertson (*Word Pictures, Luke*, p. 182), the aor. participles—γνούς, ἑτοιμάσας, ποιήσας—must be considered "timeless." Accordingly he translates as follows, "But that slave who knows . . . while the one who does not know," etc. (*Translation*, p. 79). Among modern translations several agree with this position. The possibility that this view is correct cannot be denied. There can be no question of the fact that, whether directly or by implication, a general principle is here announced. On the other hand, whether this principle is here *directly* expressed is open to some doubt. The picture of the final judgment drawn in such passages as Matt. 25:31-46; II Cor. 5:10; Rev. 20:11-15 shows that rewards and punishments are rendered in accordance with that which men *have done*. Accordingly the rendering, "And that servant who *knew*. . . . But he who *did not know*," etc., cannot be considered incorrect. Among those who favor it are A.V., N.A.S., R.S.V., N.E.B., Beck, and Dutch (both Staten-vertaling and Nieuwe Vertaling). To be supplied in both verse 47 (end of verse, after πολλάς) and verse 48 (after ὀλίγας) is πληγάς; cf. 10:30.

Verse 48b

Note inverse attraction from ᾧ to παντί; also παρ' αὐτοῦ regardless of παντί. For παρέθεντο, third per. pl. 2nd aor. indicat. middle of παρατίθημι, here to *entrust,* see the note on 9:16 on page 485.

περισσότερον αἰτήσουσιν, literally "They will ask [or demand] all the more." This may be another Semitism; see on 12:20; also the note on 6:38 on page 359.

Verses 49, 50

In the light of the context it would seem that τί in verse 49 is equivalent to πῶς in verse 50. As to εἰ, after a verb of emotion—such as, being surprised, amazed, longing, agonizing—this little word at times approaches ὅτι in meaning. For other examples see Mark 15:44; II Cor. 11:15; I John 3:13.

ἀνήφθη, third per. s. aor. indicat. pass. of ἀνάπτω, to kindle. Cf. James 3:5.

For συνέχομαι, first per. s. pres. indicat. pass. of συνέχω; in pass.: to be hemmed in, held tight, seized (for example, with great fear), and here: to be overwhelmed (with anguish), see the note on 8:37 on page 453. Cf. Phil. 1:23, "I am hard pressed between the two."

τελεσθῇ (after ἕως ὅτου), third per. s. aor. subjunct. passive of τελέω, to bring to an end, finish, accomplish, fulfil. Among other examples see also 2:39; 18:31; 22:37; and John 19:30 ("It is finished.").

Verses 51-53

διαμερισμόν, acc. s. of διαμερισμός (διά plus μερίζω), division, dissension.

ἔσονται... διαμεμερισμένοι, third per. pl. fut. perf. pass. periphrastic of διαμερίζω; in the pass.: to be split into dissenting parties, to be divided. See the note on 11:17 on page 633.

διαμερισθήσονται, third per. pl. fut. indicat. pass. of the same verb.

πενθερά, mother-in-law.

In the New Testament the word νύμφη has three distinct meanings:

a. *bride.* This, or closely related *marriageable young woman, young wife,* is the basic meaning of the term, so used in Greek from the time of Homer. In the New Testament the meaning *bride* must be ascribed to the word as used in John 3:29; Rev. 18:23; 21:2.

b. *Bride,* figurative sense: the church viewed as wedded to Christ, the Lamb (Rev. 21:9; 22:17).

c. Not found in Greek outside of biblical sources and writings based on these sources is the meaning *daughter-in-law,* as here in Luke 12:53 and its parallel Matt. 10:35. This is also the meaning in LXX Gen. 11:31; 38:11, 16, 24, etc. This extension of meaning can be explained by the fact that the underlying Hebrew word, and also the closely related Aramaic word, have two distinct meanings: *bride* and *daughter-in-law.* For more on this see the article by J. Jeremias, "νύμφη, νυμφίος," Th.D.N.T., Vol. IV, p. 1099.

Though the fact that this Greek word has three meanings, and that two of these, referring to earthly family relationships, have connotations that differ rather widely, may seem somewhat confusing, it should be borne in mind that this peculiarity is characteristic of language in general. It does not pertain only to Greek. English, too, is full of examples. When a mother asks the teacher, "How is my child doing in school?" the answer "Johnnie is trying" may mean "He is doing his best." It may also mean, "He makes life miserable for me." When a Netherlander introduces a young lady as being his *nicht,* this can mean that she is his niece. It can also mean that she is his cousin. If the American or the Britisher is becoming impatient with the Dutchman because of such ambiguities, the latter can answer that at least with respect to the second personal pronoun ("you") the inhabitant of the low country is way ahead. The pronoun *you* may refer to a president or to a pauper. It may be used in addressing one person or a thousand. Were it not for the context in which it is used, it would indeed be very ambiguous. Compare this with the rich variety of pronouns the Netherlander has at his disposal in addressing a person or persons: *jij, gij, u, jelui, jullie, gijlieden, ulieden.*

Verse 54

ἀνατέλλουσαν, acc. s. fem. pres. participle (here intransit.) of ἀνατέλλω, to rise. Cf. Matt. 5:45, transit., to cause to rise. Also note ἀνατολή, the Rising Sun (see explanation of Luke 1:78).

ἐπὶ δυσμῶν, in the west. In the New Testament δυσμή, west, always occurs in the gen. pl. form. See Matt. 8:11; 24:27; Luke 13:29; Rev. 21:13.

ὄμβρος*, a shower, rain. Cf. *to imbrue* (drench, soak).

Verse 55

Καύσων (see also Matt. 20:12; James 1:11), a heat wave, scorching heat. Cf. *holocaust, caustic.*

Verse 56

πρόσωπον, here used in the sense of appearance, look. See also 9:29, 51-53; 10:1; 20:21; 21:35.

καιρόν, acc. s. of καιρός. The distinction between χρόνος and καιρός should be observed: χρόνος is the more inclusive term. It is "time" considered as duration, succession of moments. καιρός, on the other hand, is an era, epoch, hour, or moment within this χρόνος. *The correct translation varies with the specific context in which the word is used.* "Right or proper or opportune time," "favorable season," "critical hour," "time of crisis," "opportunity" are some of the words that can be used in translation. See R. C. Trench, *Synonyms of the New Testament,* par. lvii.

Earlier instances of this word in Luke's Gospel: 1:20; 4:13; 8:13; 12:42. This evangelist is going to use it again in 13:1; 18:30; 19:44; 20:10; 21:8, 24, 36. In fact, no New Testament writer uses this word as often as do Luke (Gospel and Acts) and Paul. It occurs in all except two of Paul's epistles; also in Matthew, Mark, John, Hebrews, I Peter, and Revelation.

Verse 57

τὸ δίκαιον, what is right, or the right thing.

Verse 58

This verse contains several terms that merit brief comment:

ἀντιδίκου, gen. s. (after μετὰ τοῦ) of ἀντίδικος, opponent.

ἄρχοντα, acc. s. (after ἐπ') of ἄρχων, magistrate.

δὸς ἐργάσιαν, Lat. *da operam,* to take pains, put forth effort.

ἀπηλλάχθαι, perf. pass. infinitive of ἀπαλλάσσω, here: to get rid of, come to terms with.

κατασύρῃ, third per. s. aor. (probably), subjunct. (after μήποτε) act. of κατασύρω*, to drag down or away.

πράκτωρ, constable or bailiff, the man who carries out (or: into *practice*) the orders of the judge. Note also the dat. s. πράκτορι.

Verse 59

Note double negative οὐ μή, not at all, never . . . until, etc.

Summary of Chapter 12

See p. 535.

Outline of Chapter 13

Theme: *The Work Thou Gavest Him to Do*

CHAPTER XIII

13   1 Now at that very time there arrived[410] some people who informed Jesus about the Galileans whose blood Pilate had mingled with their sacrifices. 2 He answered, "Do y o u think that because these Galileans suffered like this they were greater sinners than all (the other) Galileans? 3 I tell y o u, No; but unless y o u are converted, y o u will all likewise perish. 4 Or those eighteen people on whom the tower at Siloam fell, killing them, do y o u think that they were more guilty than all (other people) living in Jerusalem? 5 I tell y o u, No; but unless y o u are converted, y o u will similarly perish."

13:1-5 *Be Converted or Perish*

1. Now at that very time there arrived some people who informed Jesus about the Galileans whose blood Pilate had mingled with their sacrifices.

Between the close of chapter 12 and the beginning of chapter 13 there is a twofold connection: (a) *topical:* the necessity of conversion is stressed both here and there; (b) *temporal;* note "at that very time," therefore probably during Christ's final trip to Jerusalem.

It is impossible to be more specific. Neither Josephus nor any other writer, sacred or secular, relates this incident. All we really know is what Luke tells us here, namely, that while some people who lived in Galilee and had made a pilgrimage to Jerusalem were busily engaged in offering their sacrifices in the temple, they were suddenly cut down, upon orders of Pilate. Consequently, in some sense, the blood of these Galileans was mingled with their sacrifices. That Pilate was cruel we know. See on 3:1 and on 23:1.

Exactly when this gruesome event had taken place and *why* the governor had caused them to be murdered is not stated. To be sure, all kinds of elaborations have been attempted. We are told, for example, that the reported incident must have occurred in connection with the Feast of Dedication, and that the reason Pilate had done this was that these men from Galilee were zealots, members of a nationalistic party that was openly and aggressively opposed to Roman rule. But all this is theory.

What is clearly implied is only this: the informers and/or the people who were crowding around Jesus did not interpret this incident as an illustration of Pilate's cruelty—such, at least, was not their main purpose—but

---

410. Or: were present.

rather as an evidence of the divine displeasure with the slaughtered Galileans. Their reasoning was: the victims of Pilate's wrath must have been very wicked, indeed; otherwise God would not have allowed them to be put to death in this fashion.

Thus interpreted, the next two verses become understandable:

2, 3. He answered, Do y o u think that because these Galileans suffered like this they were greater sinners than all (the other) Galileans? I tell y o u, No; but unless y o u are converted, y o u will all likewise perish.

The notion that personal disaster is the result of personal sin was deeply rooted in the consciousness of the Jew; see, for example, Job 4:7; 8:20; 11:6; 22:5–10; John 9:2. Jesus not only refuted it but also emphasized that without genuine conversion no one is saved; *all* perish.

Note especially the word *likewise* and in verse 5 *similarly*. These words can be regarded as accurate English equivalents of the original. In both cases (original and English) they are somewhat ambiguous. The meaning could conceivably be either: (a) *in the same manner,* or (b) *also.* If (a) is correct, Jesus would be saying, "If y o u are not converted, y o u will perish *in the same horrible manner,*" or perhaps *"just as suddenly."* Some of those who accept that interpretation link the Master's words with the terrible massacre of the Jews in the year A.D. 70. More reasonable, however, it would seem to me, is (b), according to which Jesus is simply telling the people that unless they experience a complete and radical change they *also* will perish. Not for a moment should they imagine that they can escape the judgment of God just because they happen to be the seed of Abraham. See Luke 3:7, 8.

Jesus makes very plain that what he has just now affirmed applies not only to Galileans but also to everybody else, including even the inhabitants of Jerusalem: **4, 5. Or those eighteen people on whom the tower at Siloam fell, killing them, do y o u think that they were more guilty than all (other people) living in Jerusalem? I tell y o u, No; but unless y o u are converted, y o u will similarly perish.**

The tower of Siloam was the one built inside the southeast portion of Jerusalem's wall. It was located near the pool of Siloam. The water from the spring Gihon was carried to the pool within the city. See L. H. Grollenberg, *op. cit.,* map 33, plate 327 (pp. 114, 115). See also N.T.C. on John 9:7, Vol. II, pp. 75, 76. Further: Neh. 3:15, 26; Isa. 8:6; Josephus, *Jewish War* V.145.

Evidently there had been an accident. The tower of Siloam had fallen, crushing eighteen people to death. Jesus points out, however, that these eighteen people were not more *guilty*—more highly *indebted* to God—than the rest of the Jerusalemites.

Every man in the audience should examine his own heart and life, and should ask himself the question, "Has the basic change, from Satan to God, from darkness to light, from sin to holiness, taken place in my own life? Have I truly repented and do I really place all my confidence in God, serving him alone? In other words, Am I converted?" If not, let him ask God to enable him to take that important step. Says Jesus, "Unless y o u are converted, y o u, too, will perish."

For *Practical Lessons* and *Greek Words,* etc., see pp. 697–698.

---

6 And he told this parable: "A man had a fig tree, planted in his vineyard; and he came looking for fruit on it, but did not find any. 7 So he said to the vineyard-keeper, 'Look here! For three years now I've been coming, constantly looking for fruit for this fig tree, but I do not find any. Cut it down! Why should it use up the soil?'

8 "But he replied, 'Sir, leave it alone this year also, while I dig around it and put on manure. 9 Then if it bears fruit afterward—; but if not, you may cut it down.'"

13:6–9 *The Parable of The Barren Fig Tree*
and
The Magnanimous Vineyard-Keeper

If the central lesson of verses 1–5 is "Be converted," then that of verses 6–9 is "Be converted NOW." Do not delay!

The parable, as such, is as follows:

6. And he told this parable: A man had a fig tree, planted in his vineyard; and he came looking for fruit on it, but did not find any.

It generally takes a long time for a fig tree to bear fruit.[411] This tree had been planted in the owner's vineyard, as was not unusual, for that generally meant that the tree would be given the best care.

Finally the time arrived when it was reasonable to expect fruit on this tree. On this kind of tree fruit is not visible from a long distance. It is generally hidden beneath the foliage, so that one must come and look for it. This the owner did, but he did not find any. The following year he kept looking again, with the same result. So also the third year.

7. So he said to the vineyard-keeper, Look here! For three years now I've been coming, constantly looking for fruit on this fig tree, but I do not find any. Cut it down! Why should it use up the soil?

As the owner saw it, this tree was worse than useless: not only did it fail to produce fruit but it also occupied space that could be put to better use, and by means of its strong roots it was drawing from the soil moisture and minerals needed by other plants. Therefore the owner said to the vinedresser or vineyard-keeper, "Cut it down," etc.

8, 9. But he replied, Sir, leave it alone this year also, while I dig around it and put on manure. Then if it bears fruit afterward—; but if not, you may cut it down.

The vinedresser was visibly disturbed when he heard these words. It would appear that this fig tree had become an object of his special interest. And now the owner had ordered him to cut it down! Everything within him rebelled at the thought. He therefore begged for permission to dig around the tree, thereby loosening the soil so that both the sun and the clouds

---

411. Dr. H. Mulder, who spent many years in the region where figs are grown, states this fact in his very interesting description of the tree and its growth. See his book *Spoorzoeker in Bijbelse Landen,* p. 92.

could perform their separate tasks more effectively with respect to this tree. Also, he wanted to enrich the soil by spreading manure around the tree.

The man became emotional, as appears from the words, "Then if it bears fruit afterward. . . ." At this point there was, as it were, a lump in his throat, so that he could not even finish the sentence. Finally, a few additional words issued from his lips: "but if not, you may cut it down."

At this point of the commentary you are reading the author must put in a remark that has nothing to do with exegesis. This particular "story" is of special interest to me. When we (my wife and I) settled in Boca Raton, Florida, we planted several fruit trees around our house, one of them being a very small tangelo tree. Not long after planting it, it was doing so poorly that "everybody" told us the tree had died and should be pulled out of the ground and replaced by something more promising. Though we are certainly no arborists, we could not think of accepting the advice of our well-meaning friends. So we did something similar to what the vinedresser of this parable received permission to do. We dug around the tree and applied fertilizer. The result? Ever since that time the tree has been doing very well. In fact, this past fall we picked no less than four hundred large delicious tangelos from that tree!

Purposely the Lord does not state whether the fig tree of this parable ever bore fruit. The answer is left to the hearers . . . and readers. Let each supply the answer in his own life, and may that answer be favorable!

The one main lesson has already been stated: Turn to the Lord without delay! Since the role of the magnanimous vineyard-keeper is very significant, a subsidiary truth can now be added: God is very patient. However, his patience does not last forever. One day—God alone knows when that day will arrive—the opportunity to be saved will be withdrawn. The procrastinator will die in his sins and be lost forevermore.

If the fig tree, planted in a vineyard, has symbolical significance (and it probably does—see N.T.C. on Matthew, pp. 773-775), it would refer to highly privileged Israel.[412] As a nation it did not turn to the Lord. Result? Read Luke 20:16; 21:20-24. The challenge presented to everyone is clear:

"Seek Jehovah while he may be found; call upon him while he is near: let the wicked forsake his way, and the unrighteous man his thoughts; and let him return to Jehovah, and he will have mercy on him, and to our God, for he will abundantly pardon."[413]

---

412. The attempt to discover a symbolical meaning for each or for most of the items mentioned in the parable leads to confusion. Thus, according to one expositor the "three years" represent "the whole course of the history of Israel"; according to another, "the three years of Christ's ministry"; and according to still another, "the period beginning with the ministry of John the Baptist." Similarly, the fig tree that was planted *in a vineyard* indicates "Jerusalem located *in Israel*," but according to several others, "Israel *in the midst of the world*," etc.

In my own interpretation I have tried to remain true to the principles of parable interpretation set forth on pp. 550-555.

413. Notes on Greek words, phrases, and constructions in 13:1-9 begin on page 697.

Practical Lessons Derived from Luke 13:1–9

Verses 2-4

"Do y o u think ... they were greater sinners ... more guilty? Unless y o u are converted, y o u will all likewise perish." Jesus teaches that when calamity strikes we should ask, "What lesson is there in this for me?"

Verse 5

"Unless y o u are converted, y o u will similarly perish." The doctrine of salvation by grace through faith by no means cancels human responsibility.

Verse 8

"Sir, leave it alone this year also." It is good to derive comfort from the doctrine of God's patience with us, but are we "imitators of God" in this respect? See Eph. 5:1.

Verse 9

"But if not, you may cut it down." Someone wrote:

There is a line by us unseen
That crosses every path,
The hidden boundary between
God's patience and his wrath.

O where is that mysterious bourne
By which our path is crossed,
Beyond which God himself has sworn
That he who goes is lost?

How far can one go on in sin?
How long will mercy spare?
Where does grace end and where begin
The confines of despair?

An answer from the sky is sent:
Ye who from God depart,
While it is called today repent,
And harden not your heart.

Notes on Greek Words, Phrases, and Constructions in 13:1–9

Verse 1

ἐν αὐτῷ τῷ καιρῷ, at that very time. For καιρός see the note on 12:56 on page 690.

ἔμιξεν, third per. s. aor. indicat. of μίγνυμι, to mingle. Cf. *mix*.

Verse 2

πεπόνθασιν, third per. pl. 2nd perf. indicat. of πάσχω, to suffer. Cf. *passion*.

Verses 3–5

Note third class (future more vivid) conditional sentence in verses 3 and 5, with (in both cases) ἐάν followed by sec. per. pl. pres. subjunct. of μετανοέω in the protasis, and sec. per. pl. fut. indicat. middle of ἀπόλλυμι in the apodosis.

For the verb μετανοέω see the note on 10:13 on page 588; also the detailed discussion in N.T.C. on Matthew, pp. 196, 197, and on Mark, pp. 57, 58.

In verse 4 note ὀφειλέται, nom. pl. of ὀφειλέτης, debtor, guilty person, sinner. Cf. ὀφείλω, to owe, be indebted, deserve.

Verse 6

συκῆν, acc. s. of συκῆ, fig tree. Cf. *sycamore.*

εἶχεν, third per. s. imperf. of ἔχω, to have.

πεφυτευμένην, acc. s. fem. perf. pass. participle of φυτεύω, to plant, modifies συκῆν. Cf. *neophyte, spermatophyte.*

ἀμπελῶνι, dat. s. of ἀμπελών, vineyard.

Verse 7

ἀμπελουργόν, acc. s. of ἀμπελουργός* (ἄμπελος plus ἔργον), vineyard-worker or -keeper, vinedresser.

τρία ἔτη ἀφ' οὗ, for three years since the time when = for three years now.

ἔρχομαι ζητῶν. Note progressive action emphasis: I've been coming, constantly looking for.

ἔκκοψον, sec. per. aor. imperat. act. of ἐκκόπτω; literally, to cut *out,* where we say: to cut *down.* Note sec. per. s. fut. (volitive) indicat. act. of the same verb in verse 9.

ἱνατί = ἵνα τί, in order that what; or: for what reason; even more briefly: *why.*

καταργεῖ, third per. s. pres. indicat. act. of καταργέω, here in the sense of *to wear down,* to render useless, to use up. In the New Testament this verb is used 25 times by Paul; for the rest, only here and in Heb. 2:14. For the meaning of this verb in Paul's epistles see N.T.C. on Galatians, pp. 137, 139; and on I and II Thessalonians, p. 183.

Verse 8

Note the first per. s. aor. act. subjunctives (after ἕως ὅτου) σκάψω, from σκάπτω*, to dig (cf. *scoop*), and βάλω, from βάλλω, to throw, put (cf. *hyperbole*).

κόπρια, acc. pl. of κόπριον*, manure, dung.

Verse 9

κἂν (= καὶ ἐάν) μὲν . . . μέλλον. Here note the sudden breaking off of a statement, allowing the listener or reader to complete it. For other examples of "aposiopesis" see Mark 11:32; Luke 22:42; Acts 23:9.

---

10 Now he was teaching in one of the synagogues on the sabbath.　11 And look, a woman who had an evil spirit in her that had kept her in a state of infirmity for eighteen years![414] She was bent double and could not straighten up at all.　12 When Jesus saw her, he called her to

---

414. Literally: a woman having a spirit of infirmity for eighteen years.

him and said to her, "Woman, you are released from your infirmity." 13 Then he put his hands on her, and immediately she was raised upright and began to glorify God.[415]

14 But the ruler of the synagogue, indignant because on the sabbath Jesus had performed an act of healing, responded by saying to the crowd, "There are six days on which work must be done. So come on those days and be healed, and not on the sabbath."

15 The Lord answered him, saying, "Y o u hypocrites! Does not each of y o u on the sabbath untie his ox or his donkey from the stall and lead it away to water it? 16 Then should not this woman, a daughter of Abraham, whom Satan has bound for no less than eighteen years, be released from this bond on the sabbath day?"

17 As he said this, all his opponents were being put to shame,[416] but all the people were rejoicing over all the glorious deeds that were being done by him.

13:10-17 *The Healing of a Crippled Woman on the Sabbath*

A. *The Miracle*

The previous section ended with "But if not, you may cut it down"; that is, if genuine conversion does not result, doom follows. The present section indicates that Christ's opponents, instead of turning to the Lord in sorrow for their sins (i.e., in true repentance) and in faith, became all the more hardened.

The scene is that of Jesus teaching in a synagogue, probably for the last time during his earthly ministry. At least this is the last recorded instance of such synagogue teaching by our Lord.

10. Now he was teaching in one of the synagogues on the sabbath. Just where this was is not stated, nor when the incident occurred. A reasonable assumption is that *the place* was somewhere in Perea, and *the time* on some sabbath during the last few months of Christ's earthly ministry; hence, not long before his death by crucifixion.

As the story develops it becomes clear that particular emphasis is placed on the fact that it was *on the sabbath* that this miracle took place.

11. And look, a woman who had an evil spirit in her that had kept her in a state of infirmity for eighteen years! She was bent double and could not straighten up at all.

The vividness of the original is retained by omitting a verb in the first part of this sentence; hence, "And look, a woman . . . !" It would seem, therefore, that this woman entered the synagogue while Jesus was teaching. Poor woman! Her condition was pitiable. If she was not actually demon-possessed—the expression "having a spirit of infirmity" would seem to favor the suggestion that she was—at the very least, she was demon-influenced. And this to such an extent that during a period of no less than eighteen years (repeated in verse 16) she had suffered from an infirmity which was apparently *spondylitis deformans*.[417] This, as the same authority

---

415. Or simply: and glorified God.
416. Or: were humiliated.
417. Thus A. Rendle Short, *Modern Discovery and the Bible*, p. 91. But cf. Index, *Women*, f.

informs us, implies that "the bones of her spine were fused into a rigid mass" and that "she was bent double and could not straighten up at all." Her ailment must also have been very painful, as such conditions affecting the spine generally are.

We are told that this affliction had already lasted for eighteen years. This period of *eighteen years* should be taken literally. This must be emphasized in view of the fact that there are those who claim that the note of time is merely Luke's rhetorical device to aid the memory. They reach that conclusion because in the same chapter the evangelist also tells us that the tower of Siloam fell on *eighteen* people (verse 4). Well, rhetorical devices and memory aids are fine, but they do not cancel historical accuracy. There is no reason to doubt Luke's word (verse 11) and that of the Lord himself (verse 16).

12, 13. When Jesus saw her, he called her to him and said to her, Woman, you are released from your infirmity. —Then he put his hands on her, and immediately she was raised upright and began to glorify God.

Though Jesus was busily engaged in teaching, the entrance of this woman did not bother him. On the contrary, he saw in it an opportunity to make happy, to heal, to save. And we may well add, also an opportunity to show what kind of activities were right and proper on the sabbath!

Picture the scene. The woman, upon hearing that Jesus was going to be teaching in the synagogue, went there. Perhaps the news that Jesus was going to be teaching there that day had reached her late. Having arrived, she takes her place in the back of the auditorium, and, of course, on the side where the women sat. Jesus, busily engaged in speaking the words of life, sees what is taking place. His heart goes out to this woman. Gently he calls her to the front. Then, in accents firm and tender he addresses her, uttering the most wonderful words she had ever heard, "Woman, you are released from your infirmity." Simultaneously, putting his hands on her, he exerts his divine power and heals her immediately, completely, and permanently. In full view of the entire assembled congregation she is now standing upright and is glorifying . . . *God,* fully realizing that it was by the power of *God*—and not of Satan or any of his underlings—power working through Jesus, that she had been cured. She had been delivered not only from her physical affliction but also from Satan (see verse 16).

In a situation such as this one would expect that at once every eye would fill with tears of joy and that the entire assembly, at the suggestion of the leader, would rise to sing or shout a doxology. But what actually happens?

B. *The Criticism*

14. But the ruler of the synagogue, indignant because on the sabbath Jesus had performed an act of healing, responded by saying to the crowd, There are six days on which work must be done. So come on those days and be healed, and not on the sabbath.

The following items require attention:

1. This man was responsible for the maintenance of order at the service and for the selection of those who would perform its various functions; such as, leading in prayer, Scripture reading, and preaching. He was probably the head of the local board of elders in charge of the synagogue. See on 8:41.

2. He was indignant. Why? Perhaps because his "authority" had been bypassed? Judging only by what he actually *said*, we might conclude that his anger resulted from the fact that, as he saw it, the sabbath had been desecrated. He must have thought that "man was made for the sabbath" (cf. Mark 2:27, 28).

3. The ruler *responded;* that is, he reacted to the situation.

4. He was a hypocrite, for though he was angry with Jesus, he criticized the crowd. He probably lacked the nerve to attack Jesus personally.

5. He misinterpreted the divine sabbath commandment. To be sure, he was literally correct when he said, "There are six days on which work must be done." See Exod. 20:9, 10; Deut. 5:13. But he evidently ignored such interpretative passages as Gen. 2:1–3; Isa. 58; and Micah 6:8.

C. *The Answer to the Criticism*

15, 16. The Lord answered him, saying, Y o u hypocrites! Does not each of y o u on the sabbath untie his ox or his donkey from the stall and lead it away to water it? Then should not this woman, a daughter of Abraham, whom Satan has bound for no less than eighteen years, be released from this bond on the sabbath day?

Note the plural: *hypocrites,* "you and all those in agreement with you." For the essence of this hypocrisy see point (4) above. Besides, though this ruler professed to be so thoroughly concerned about keeping the law, his real concern was to discredit the Great Benefactor!

Next, Jesus points out how very inconsistent his opponents are. They hold that on the sabbath it is entirely proper to lead an animal away from its stall in order to water it ... provided, however, that the animal carry no burden on the sabbath![418] If, then, the needs of *animals may* be supplied even on the sabbath, *must* not *human* needs be met, on every day of the week, including certainly the sabbath? Is this "daughter of Abraham" of less importance than an ox or a donkey? Besides, is it really true that Satan must be allowed to keep this woman in bondage for still another day—on top of the eighteen years during which he has already held her a captive— just because it happens to be the sabbath? Is not the sabbath the very day when more than ever one should exert himself to the utmost to destroy the works of the devil?

---

418. See *Shabbath* 5:1.

D. *Result*

17. As he said this, all his opponents were being put to shame, but all the people were rejoicing over all the glorious deeds that were being done by him.

So crushing had been Christ's argument, and so effective his rebuke, that all the adversaries—this ruler of the synagogue and those who had sided with him—were silenced and were hanging their heads for very shame.

At the same time the people in general continued to rejoice, and this not only because of this one striking miracle but because of all the glorious deeds that were being done by the Savior.

For *Practical Lessons* and *Greek Words,* etc., see pp. 711–716.

---

18 He said therefore, "What is the kingdom of God like, and to what shall I compare it? 19 It is like a mustard seed which a man took and planted in his garden; and it grew to be a tree, and the birds of the air lodged in its branches."

20 Again he said, "To what shall I compare the kingdom of God? 21 It is like yeast which a woman took and put into[419] three measures of wheat flour, until the whole batch had risen."[420]

13:18–21 *The Parable of The Mustard Seed*
and
The Parable of The Yeast
Cf. Matt. 13:31–33; Mark 4:30–32

A. *The Mustard Seed*

18. He said therefore, What is the kingdom of God like, and to what shall I compare it?

As the very phrase "He said *therefore*" indicates, there is a connection between the immediately preceding section and this one. The nature of that connection has been indicated. See p. 537. To this it might be added that not only did *the healed woman* glorify God, but "*all the people* were rejoicing over all the glorious deeds that were done by Jesus" (13:17). Even though some of that rejoicing may have been of a superficial nature, it is not necessary to suppose that all of it was. The kingdom was growing . . . like a mustard seed.

What we have in verse 18 is an oratorical question to arouse interest. Note the striking resemblance in form to the similarly double question found in Isa. 40:18 and to the one in Luke 7:31. Such a question was a device to sharpen the interest of the audience.

Speaking, then, about the growth of the kingdom, Jesus continues:

---

419. Or: hid in, mixed into.
420. Literally: was leavened.

19. It is like a mustard seed which a man took and planted in his garden; and it grew to be a tree, and the birds of the air lodged in its branches.

Though the same parable occurs also in Matthew (13:31, 32) and in Mark (4:30–32), the emphasis is different. In these other Gospels there is a much stronger emphasis on the contrast between the tiny seed and the huge shrub than there is in Luke. To be sure, even here in Luke that contrast is implied, but now the attention is focused more definitely on the size of the full-grown plant. In fact, in Luke the diminutive size of the seed is not even mentioned. The plant resulting from the mustard seed grows and grows until it becomes as tall as a tree.

In actual life the mustard plant reaches ten feet, sometimes even fifteen (hence, may reach as high as from three to four and one-half meters). In the fall of the year when the branches have become rigid, birds of many species find here a shelter from the storm, rest from weariness, and shade from the heat of the sun. Similarly the kingdom of God, once established, expands and keeps on expanding. As to the birds finding shelter in the shade of the "tree" (cf. Ezek. 17:22–24; Dan. 4:20, 21), does not this indicate that the kingdom becomes a blessing for men of every clime, race, and nation?

Within forty years of Christ's death the gospel had reached all the great centers of the Roman world, and ever so many out-of-the-way places besides. Since that time it has been spreading, gaining people of every race. It is doing this today. "From vict'ry unto vict'ry his army shall be lead." Cf. Matt. 24:14.

B. *The Yeast*

20. Again he said, To what shall I compare the kingdom of God?

For explanation see on verse 18. The similar manner in which these two little parables—the one of the mustard seed and the one of the yeast—are introduced points to the fact that Jesus considered them to be a pair. This conclusion would tend to support the theory according to which the first of the pair symbolizes the outward growth of the kingdom; the second, its inner expansion.

21. It is like yeast which a woman took and put into three measures of wheat flour, until the whole batch had risen.

With respect to this parable there is wide diversity of interpretation. R. W. Funk, *op. cit.*, pp. 56, 64, 68, believes that the theory according to which each parable has one main point must be scrapped. The right way in parable interpretation, as he sees it, is "away-from-here." He interprets the three measures of meal (verse 21) to mean "the sacramental power of the kingdom, the festive occasion of an epiphany." By all means read his interesting book.

Lenski, *op. cit.,* p. 468, is of the opinion that the woman in this parable symbolizes the church.

And G. C. Morgan, in *The Parables and Metaphors of Our Lord,* pp. 59–65, reasons that the yeast is something evil, "the principle of disintegration."

I, the author of this commentary, disagree, though I appreciate the many fine things all these three authors have written. I again urge the readers to study Funk's, Lenski's, and Morgan's books. One should never depend merely on what someone else writes about the ideas of such stimulating and thought-provoking writers. Besides, along the way one can pick up many fine ideas even in the writings with which one cannot fully agree.

As to Funk, it is my belief that the restoration of the allegorical method of parable interpretation will open a Pandora's Box of fanciful interpretations. Besides, what is so strange about the three measures of flour? To be sure, it is a large batch, but not unusual. See Gen. 18:6; Judg. 6:19; I Sam. 1:24. And is it not true that the very size of the batch serves to bring out the tremendously effective penetrating and transforming power of the rule of God in hearts and lives?

As to Lenski, is it not altogether natural that the person who produces homemade bread is a woman? There is no need to introduce *the church* at this point.

And as to Morgan, nowhere does Scripture even hint that when yeast is used as a leaven in baking bread it is evil!

What we should do is practice economy in interpretation. The point Jesus is making in this parable is this: the reign of God, introduced into human hearts and lives *from without,* once having entered, exerts a wholesome, penetrating, and transforming influence *within and from within outward,* upon hearts and lives. It leads men onward toward the goal of perfection God has set for them. In doing so, it favorably affects every sphere of life in which they move.

For the meaning of the word *measures* (original *sata,* pl. of *saton*) see the note on 13:21 on page 714.

The believer's purpose is not merely to get to heaven when he dies, or only to be an instrument in God's hand to bring others there, but everywhere to bring every thought of whatever kind into submission to, and therefore harmony with, the mind and will of Christ (see II Cor. 10:5); that is, to demand that not only every tongue but also every "domain of life" shall exalt him. Therefore Christ's true follower actively promotes such causes as the abolition of slavery, the restoration of women's rights, the alleviation of poverty, the repatriation, if practicable, of the displaced (if not practicable then help of some other kind), the education of the illiterate, the reorientation of fine arts along Christian lines, etc. He promotes honesty among those who govern and those who are governed, as well as in business, industry, and commerce. He does all this not apart from but in connection with, in fact as part and parcel of, the evangelization of the world. That this "yeast" of the rule of Christ in human hearts, lives, *and spheres* has already exerted a wholesome influence in thousands of ways, and that this influence is still continuing, is clear to all who have eyes to see. All one has to do is to compare conditions—for example, the treatment of prisoners of war, of women, of workmen, of the underprivileged—in countries where Christ's rule has not yet become acknowledged to any great extent with those existing in nations where this principle has already been operative for some time on a generous scale.

For *Practical Lessons* and *Greek Words*, etc., see pp. 711–716.

---

22 Now he was traveling through cities and villages, teaching and making his way to Jerusalem. 23 Someone asked him, "Lord, will the saved be few in number?" He said to them, 24 "Strive to enter through the narrow door; for many, I tell y o u, will seek to enter and will not be able. 25 When once the owner of the house gets up and closes the door, and y o u begin to stand outside and to knock[421] on the door, saying, 'Lord, open (the door) for us,' he will answer and say to y o u, 'I do not know where y o u come from.' 26 Then y o u will begin to say,[422] 'We ate and drank in your presence, and you taught in our streets.' 27 But he will reply, 'I do not know where y o u come from. Depart from me, all y o u wrongdoers.' 28 There shall be weeping and grinding of teeth, when y o u see Abraham and Isaac and Jacob and all the prophets in the kingdom of God, but y o u yourselves thrown out. 29 And they will come from east and west, and from north and south, and will recline at table in the kingdom of God. 30 Moreover, note well, there are some (now) last who will (then) be first, and there are some (now) first who will (then) be last."

13:22–30 *"Strive to Enter by the Narrow Door"*
Cf. Matt. 7:13, 14, 21–23; 8:11, 12; 19:30; 25:10–12, 41

22. Now he was traveling through cities and villages, teaching and making his way to Jerusalem.

The beginning of this journey was indicated in 9:51. It would seem that Jesus was not in a hurry. He stopped at the cities and villages along the way. In fact, he lingered long enough at these places to be able to teach there.

For a possible connection between verses 22–30 and the immediately preceding section see p. 537.

23a. Someone asked him, Lord, will the saved be few in number?

According to a widely-held Jewish opinion, endorsed by the rabbis, Israel as a whole would be saved.[423] On the other hand, according to the teaching of Jesus the line of demarcation between saved and unsaved was not nationalistic but distinctly spiritual. See Luke 4:25–27; 6:20–38, 46–49; 7:9; 8:4–15; 11:29–52. It is not surprising that someone asked Jesus whether the saved were few in number. Is it not true that wherever Jesus went he proclaimed that only those whose hearts were comparable to good soil, only those who were willing to deny themselves, only those who not only heard his teaching but also were putting it into practice, would be saved? That left

---

421. Or: and y o u stand outside and knock.
422. Or: Then y o u will say.
423. *Sanhedrin* 10:1.

out a great many. Was not the inference legitimate, then, that only a few would enter the gate to the palace of salvation?

23b, 24. He said to them, Strive to enter through the narrow door; for many, I tell y o u, will seek to enter and will not be able.

Jesus handled this question as he had handled Peter's (12:41, 42). He did not give a direct answer, but did something far more important and necessary: he told the inquirer, and also the entire assembled multitude—note plural "y o u"—that everyone should strive to enter through the narrow door.

The verb *to strive*, as it occurs in the original, has given rise to our English verb *to agonize*. It places us not on the battlefield but in the *arena* or in the *wrestling-ring*. The struggle is fierce. Our opponents are Satan, sin, self (the old, sinful nature).

To strive means to exert oneself to the full, to strain every nerve in our struggle with these opponents.

The narrow entrance door mentioned here reminds one of Matt. 7:13, 14: "Enter by the narrow gate; for wide is the gate and broad the way that leads to destruction, and many are those that enter by it. For narrow is the gate and constricted the way that leads to life, and few are those who find it."

The words, "Many . . . will seek to enter and will not be able," are an earnest warning to all to leave the ways of wickedness and unconcern at once and to accept the Savior and the salvation he offers as a free gift. On the other hand, these words were not meant to scare God's children. They do not mean that entrance into the palace of salvation is only for those who are without sin. All those who *struggle*—in obedience to the command, "Strive to enter"—will enter.

Another misconception must be removed. The command, "Strive to enter," does not imply that salvation is, after all, the product of human exertion and not of grace. It is all of grace, *enabling* grace. The true situation is described in Phil. 2:12, 13, "With fear and trembling continue to work out y o u r own salvation, for it is God who is working in y o u both to will and to work for his good pleasure."

25. When once the owner of the house gets up and closes the door, and y o u begin to stand outside and to knock on the door [or: and y o u stand outside and knock on the door], saying, Lord, open (the door) for us, he will answer and say to y o u, I do not know where y o u come from.

There comes a time when the owner—Jesus himself; see verse 26b—of the palace of salvation will shut the door. Those who have refused to strive will then be standing outside, furiously knocking on the door in order to get in. The scene here pictured reminds us of Matt. 25:1–13; see especially verses 10b, 11 of that parable.

26, 27. Then y o u will begin to say [or: Then y o u will say], We ate and drank in your presence, and you taught in our streets. But he will reply, I do not know where y o u come from. Depart from me, all y o u wrongdoers.

The Final Judgment Dialogue
Between Jesus and The Lost

The Dialogue	*Explanatory Remarks*
The Lost	
Lord, open the door for us.	Those who during their life on earth never acknowledged him as their Lord call him "Lord" now ... but in vain.
Jesus	
I do not know where y o u come from.	Where were they when the door was still open? They were always "elsewhere," not where they should have been.
The Lost	
We ate and drank in your presence, and you taught in our streets.	Did some of these people perhaps eat of the miraculously multiplied bread-cakes? As if the presence and teaching of Jesus in their streets would be sufficient for salvation! Did they even go out of their way to hear Jesus? But if they did, at least they did not believe and act on his message. Merely outward contact with Jesus has never saved anybody. A vital change is needed.
Jesus	
I do not know where y o u come from. Depart from me, all y o u wrongdoers.	Wrongdoers: Literally "workers of unrighteousness." Even at this very moment they are proving that they are indeed "workers of unrighteousness," for they are urging Jesus to break his own word by opening the door for them. For the terrible word *Depart* see also Ps. 6:8; 119:115; 139:19; Matt. 7:23; 25:41.

What we have in verses 25b through 27 is a description of the final judgment as it affects the lost.

In immediate connection with the thought of verse 27, Jesus now tells *his audience* **28, 29. There shall be weeping and grinding of teeth, when y o u see Abraham and Isaac and Jacob and all the prophets in the kingdom of God, but y o u yourselves thrown out. And they will come from east and west, and from north and south, and will recline at table in the kingdom of God.**

For the expression "weeping and grinding of teeth" see also Matt. 8:12; 13:42, 50; 22:13; 24:51; 25:30. In Luke it occurs only in this one passage. Somewhat similar is Rev. 18:19.

The weeping is that of inconsolable, never-ending wretchedness, and utter, everlasting hopelessness. The accompanying grinding or gnashing of teeth is that of frenzied anger, unmitigated rage. For this weeping and grinding of teeth there are three causes:

a. They "see" (are made aware of the presence of) Abraham, Isaac, Jacob, and all the prophets in the kingdom of God; that is, the kingdom in its final consummation.

b. They also take note of the fact that ever so many others, including (converted) Gentiles, from every region of the earth—east, west, north, and south—are participating in the Messianic banquet (cf. Matt. 8:11, 12).

c. They themselves are "thrown out"; that is, not only was admission refused, but also they were forcefully expelled.

30. Moreover, note well, there are some (now) last who will (then) be first, and there are some (now) first who will (then) be last.

In connection with the immediate context, referring to the contrasted conditions of the saved and the lost, the "last" who will then be "first" may refer to those people who at first lacked the means of grace, but when they received them, joyfully accepted them. Similarly, the "first" who will then be "last" may indicate those who from the very first had these means of grace but ignored them. In line with this interpretation, among the "last" who will then be "first" there will be many a Gentile. Among the "first" who will then be "last" there will be many a Jew.

We must, however, be careful. In view of the fact that Scripture clearly teaches that there are not only degrees of suffering in hell (Luke 12:47, 48) but also degrees of glory in the restored universe (I Cor. 15:42), the possibility must not be excluded that Jesus means that even among those ultimately saved there will be those who were "first" in honor, prestige, etc., here, but who will be "last" in degree of glory there. Similarly that among those ultimately saved there will be those "last" in reputation here, who will be "first" there.

Note should also be taken of the fact that Jesus does not say that *all* those who are "first" *now* will be "last" *then;* only "some." The same applies to those who are "last" now.

For *Practical Lessons* and *Greek Words*, etc., see pp. 711–716.

---

31 At that very time some Pharisees came and said to Jesus, "Get out and move on from here, for Herod wants to kill you!" 32 He replied, "Go and tell that fox, 'Look, I am casting out demons and performing cures today and tomorrow, and on the third day I reach my goal. 33 But I must continue on my way today, tomorrow, and the next day, because it would never do for a prophet to meet his death outside Jerusalem!'

34 "Jerusalem, Jerusalem, who kills the prophets and stones those that are sent to her! How often would I have gathered your children together as a hen gathers her brood under her wings, but y o u would not! 35 Behold, y o u r house is abandoned to y o u. And I tell y o u, Y o u will certainly not see me until the time arrives when y o u will say, 'Blessed is he who comes in the name of the Lord.' "

13:31–35 *Jerusalem Characterized and Lamented*
Cf. Matt. 23:37–39

A. *Characterized*

In spite of the earnest and well-meant words of warning Jesus had uttered (see verses 24–30) there were those who wanted, above everything else, to do away with him, as again becomes evident:

31. At that very time some Pharisees came and said to Jesus, Get out and move on from here, for Herod wants to kill you!

Herod Antipas was the tetrarch who held sway over Galilee and Perea, the very region through which Jesus had been and was still traveling. It will be recalled (see on 3:1) that this ruler started his reign in the year 4 B.C., and was going to continue in that capacity until A.D. 39. Now some Pharisees inform Jesus that Herod wants to kill him and that he therefore should depart from the Galilee-Perea region. An obvious way for Jesus to do this would be to go to Judea as quickly as possible.

Was it not friendly and considerate of these Pharisees to issue this warning? Nevertheless, Jesus does not thank them. Why not? This will become clear as the story proceeds:

32. He replied, Go and tell that fox, Look, I am casting out demons and performing cures today and tomorrow, and on the third day I reach my goal.

The very fact that Jesus sends these Pharisees to Herod with a message would seem to indicate that he knew that there was a close relationship between his informers and the tetrarch. To be sure, basically Herod and the Pharisees were opposed to each other. Religiously they stood far apart; that is, outwardly. Also, did not Herod represent Rome, the hated oppressor? Nevertheless, in their attitude to Jesus, Herod and the Pharisees were friends. For evidence read Mark 3:6; 12:13. And, of course, Jesus knew this.

Both wanted Jesus to go to Judea. Herod, perhaps because he was afraid that the Jesus movement might cause political trouble for him. Perhaps also because Jesus reminded him too much of John the Baptist. It would seem that the presence of Jesus in Galilee or in Perea bothered Herod's conscience. See Luke 9:7–9. By his "wife"(?) Herod had been tricked into murdering the Baptist. He probably did not care to become responsible for another murder of this kind. But if he could get rid of Jesus by threatening him, all might work out well. So he seems to have thought.

As for the Pharisees, they also wanted Jesus in Judea, specifically in Jerusalem; and the sooner the better. Reason: they realized that in Judea their influence was far more potent than anywhere else.

Jesus told the Pharisees, "Go and tell that fox," etc. Why did he call Herod a fox? According to some, to indicate Herod's insignificance. That is possible. The more commonly held view that it was because of the tetrarch's slyness or craftiness agrees better with the context. Jesus saw through Herod's trick: making use of others to try to scare him away from the territory under Herod's control, and suggesting that they give him a "friendly" warning, while, all the time, Herod himself remained in the background!

Further, by informing Herod, via these Pharisees, that he, Jesus, is casting out demons and performing cures, Jesus is reminding the "fox" of the fact that from Jesus he really has nothing to fear. Jesus is *helping* Herod's subjects. He certainly is not hurting them in any way.

But Jesus reminds Herod also that not the tetrarch's timetable but God's will be carried out. On the third day—that is, on the divinely appointed day, not a day earlier nor a day later—"I will reach my goal," says Jesus. What a glorious way of describing his death. By means of that death he would be reaching his goal, that goal being the redemption of his people. See Matt. 20:28; Mark 10:45.

33. But I must continue on my way today, tomorrow, and the next day, because it would never do for a prophet to meet his death outside Jerusalem!

How ironic this statement, yet how true! In Jerusalem the Sanhedrin gathered, deliberated, made decisions, and was going to condemn Jesus to death. It was Jerusalem that killed the prophets. So Jesus must continue on his way today, tomorrow, and the next day; every day in exact accordance with God's plan from eternity, until he reached Jerusalem, also according to the divine counsel; and until he was crucified . . . in fulfilment of prophecy. Jerusalem, the holy city? Rather, Jerusalem "who kills the prophets."

B. *Lamented*

Did Jesus utter this lament twice: *now,* on his way toward Jerusalem, and *a little later,* during the week of the Passion (Matt. 23:37–39)? Or is Luke incorporating some material from Matthew (or from some other source) into his Gospel, since it fits into the present context so very neatly?

I accept the latter alternative. If these words were spoken earlier than the almost exactly similar ones found in Matt. 23:37–39, I do not understand how at this earlier time Jesus would have been able to say, "Y o u will certainly not see me until," etc.

But note how beautifully inspiration operates. The same evangelist, namely, Luke, who has been inserting notes of time ever so often (10:21; 11:27, 37, 53; 13:31) omits every indication of time at the beginning of 13:34. Therefore, there is no problem at all.

34. Jerusalem, Jerusalem, who kills the prophets and stones those that are sent to her! How often would I have gathered your children together as a hen gathers her brood under her wings, but y o u would not!

This outpouring of grief is addressed to "Jerusalem" because this city, being the capital, Israel's very heart and center, symbolizes the spirit or attitude of the nation as a whole. Intense emotion, unfathomable pathos, finds its expression in the repetition of the word *Jerusalem.* Cf. "altar, altar" (I Kings 13:2), "Martha, Martha" (Luke 10:41), "Simon, Simon" (Luke 22:31), and such multiple repetitions as "O my son Absalom, my son, my son Absalom! if only I had died for you, O Absalom, my son, my son!" (II Sam. 18:33); and "Land, land, land, hear the word of the Lord" (Jer. 22:29; cf. 7:4). That the nation was indeed guilty of killing and stoning God's official ambassadors is clear from Matt. 5:12. See N.T.C. on that passage. Proof for "How often would I have gathered your children together" is found first of all in the Gospel of John (2:14; 5:14; 7:14, 28, 37; [8:2]; 10:22, 23).

Incidentally, this statement of Jesus also shows that even the Synoptics, though stressing Christ's work in and around Galilee, do bear testimony to the extensive labor which Jesus had performed in Jerusalem and vicinity. Bearing in mind, however, that Jerusalem represented the nation, it should be pointed out that Christ's sympathy and yearning love had by no means been confined to the inhabitants of this city or even of Judea. It had been abundantly evident also in the northern regions. See Matt. 9:36; 11:25–30; 15:32; Luke 15; etc.

The simile Jesus uses is unforgettable. A chicken hawk suddenly appears, its wings folded, its eyes concentrated on the farmyard, its ominous claws ready to grasp a chick. Or, to change the figure, a storm is approaching. Lightning flashes become more frequent, the rumbling of the thunder grows louder and follows the electrical discharges more and more closely. Raindrops develop into a shower, the shower into a cloudburst. In either case what happens is that with an anxious and commanding "cluck, cluck, cluck!" the hen calls her chicks, conceals them under her protecting wings, and rushes off to a place of shelter. "How frequently," says Jesus, "I have similarly yearned to gather y o u. But y o u refused to come." Did they really think that his threats were empty, his predictions of approaching woe ridiculous?

The result of these constant refusals, this hardening of heart, is described in verse **35. Behold, y o u r house is abandoned to y o u. And I tell y o u, Y o u will certainly not see me until the time arrives when y o u will say, Blessed is he who comes in the name of the Lord.**

"Y o u r house" does not merely indicate "y o u r temple," but "y o u r city." Nevertheless, the temple is certainly included. For fulfilment see on 21:20, 24, 28. The meaning of "Y o u will certainly not see me," etc., is that after the week of the passion Jesus will not again publicly reveal himself to the Jews until the day of his second coming. Except for a brief transition period (Acts 13:46), the day of *special* opportunity for the Jews is past. At Christ's return upon the clouds of glory "every eye shall see him" (Rev. 1:7). "Blessed is he who comes in the name of the Lord" (see on Luke 19:38) will then be on every lip. Those who repented before they died will then, at that glorious coming, proclaim Christ joyfully; the others ruefully, remorsefully, *not* penitently. But so majestic and radiant will be Christ's glory that all will feel impelled to render homage to him. Cf. Isa. 45:23; Rom. 14:11; Phil. 2:10, 11.[424]

Practical Lessons Derived from Luke 13:10–35

Verses 15, 16

"Does not each of y o u on the sabbath untie his ox. . . . Should not this woman . . . bound for no less than eighteen years, be released . . .?" The sabbath must be observed, to be sure. Jesus never advocated sabbath laxity. On the other hand, when

---

424. Notes on Greek words, phrases, and constructions in 13:10–35 begin on page 713.

sabbath rules and regulations become so rigid that the dictates of both mind (verse 15) and heart (verse 16) are left unheeded, we are on the wrong track. Works of charity and works of necessity are not only allowed; they are required. Study Isa. 58; John 5:17.

Verse 19

"It [the kingdom of God] is like a mustard seed which . . . grew to be a tree." Real growth or progress is the product not of evolution but of the reign of God in human hearts and lives. And such progress is not limited to one nation—for example, the Jews—but affects Jew and Gentile alike. There is no other hope for the world.

Verse 21

"It [the kingdom of God] is like yeast which a woman took and put into three measures of wheat flour, until the whole batch had risen." The difference between "the social gospel" and the teaching of this parable is that the former focuses its attention solely on society as a whole, neglecting the needs of individual hearts and lives, while the latter, by first of all radically changing hearts and lives, works from within outward, thus creating better conditions all around. Contrast the effectiveness of Rome's spurts of philanthropic endeavor with the effects of Paul's conversion!

Verse 23

"Lord, will the saved be few in number?" Much time wasted in vain speculation could be put to better use in gospel proclamation.

Verse 24

"The narrow door." Yes, the door is narrow, but it is wide enough to admit "the chief of sinners." See Eph. 3:8; I Tim. 1:15.

> Chief of sinners though I be,
> Jesus shed his blood for me;
> Died that I might live on high,
> Lives that I may never die.
>
> —William McComb

Verse 32

"And on the third day I reach my goal," that is, I will have accomplished my mission. We, too, are in this life to reach a goal, to accomplish a mission. What is that goal or mission? See I Cor. 9:22; 10:31; Phil. 1:19–21.

Verse 34

"Jerusalem, Jerusalem, who kills the prophets." The holy city . . . a prophet-killer! At last it killed the greatest Prophet of all. And he, symbolized by a hen gathering her brood under her wings, reveals his tender compassion. Hallelujah, what a Savior!

However, if even now Jerusalem does *not* repent, then doom comes at last, for it cannot be denied that verse 35 reveals "the wrath of the Lamb." Cf. Rev. 6:16. By and large, Jerusalem did not repent. It killed Jesus. The wrath was poured out (A.D. 70), and on the day of the final judgment will descend on all impenitents (II Thess. 1:8, 9).

Notes on Greek Words, Phrases, and Constructions in 13:10–35

Verse 11

ἦν συγκύπτουσα, third per. s. periphrastic imperf. of συγκύπτω*, to be bent double. ἀνακύψαι, aor. act. infinitive of ἀνακύπτω, to raise oneself, bend back, straighten up. In 21:28 to look up.

εἰς τὸ παντελές, at all; in Heb. 7:25 "to the uttermost" (A.V.).

Verse 12

ἀπολέλυσαι, sec. per. s. perf. indicat. pass. of ἀπολύω (ἀπό plus λύω), to release; in pass., to be released. See the note on 2:29 on page 176.

Verse 13

ἀνωρθώθη, third per. s. aor. indicat. pass. of ἀνορθόω (ἀνά plus ὀρθόω); in the pass., as here, to be straightened out, raised upright, set straight.

Verse 14

ἀγανακτῶν, nom. s. masc. pres. participle of ἀγανακτέω, to be indignant. Cf. Matt. 20:24; 21:15; 26:8; Mark 10:14, 41; 14:4; II Cor. 7:11.

ἐθεράπευσεν, third per. s. aor. indicat. act. of θεραπεύω, to heal. Derived from the same verb is θεραπεύεσθε, sec. per. pl. pres. imperat. pass. See the note on 4:23 on page 261.

Verses 15, 16

From the very common verb λύω, to loosen, release, untie, are derived λύει, third per. s. pres. indicat. act., to untie (verse 15); and λυθῆναι, aor. pass. infinitive, in the passive (verse 16) to be released.

Verse 17

κατῃσχύνοντο, third per. pl. imperf. pass. of καταισχύνω; in pass. to be put to shame. Luke uses this verb only here, but it occurs 10 times in Paul's epistles, beginning with Rom. 5:5; also in I Peter 2:6; 3:16.

ἐπὶ πᾶσιν τοῖς ἐνδόξοις, over all *the glorious deeds*. Cf. 7:25, "in *gorgeous* apparel" (or: "*gorgeously* appareled"); I Cor. 4:10, "y o u are *honored!*"; "the church *radiant* (in purity)."

Verse 19

κόκκῳ, dat. of κόκκος, seed. In all the Synoptic passages in which this word occurs (Matt. 13:31; 17:20; Mark 4:31; Luke 13:19; 17:6) the reference is to the κόκκος σινάπεως, mustard seed. John 12:24 mentions a grain or kernel of wheat; I Cor. 15:37, a grain of wheat "or of something else."

κῆπον, acc. s. of κῆπος, garden. By some this word is held to be related to σκάπτω, to dig (a garden). Elsewhere in the New Testament this word is found only in John's Gospel, 4 times: 18:1, 26; 19:41 (twice).

κλάδοις, dat. pl. of κλάδος, branch; from κλάω, to break in pieces. This is the only Lucan passage in which the word occurs. But it is found also in Matthew (13:32; 21:8; 24:32), Mark (4:32; 13:28); and Romans 11 (verses 16–21, 5 times in these few lines).

Verse 21

ἐνέκρυψεν, third per. s. aor. indicat. act. of ἐγκρύπτω, to hide in, or put into, mix into.

ἀλεύρου, gen. of ἄλευρον, wheat flour; cf. ἀλέω, to grind. By some this word is connected with the stem μαλ (μάλευρον = ἄλευρον); cf. English *mill;* German *mahlen;* Dutch *malen,* to grind.

σάτα, acc. pl. of σάτον, derived from Hebrew *s^eah*, about one and one-half peck. Cf. Hag. 2:16; Josephus, *Antiquities* IX.85. "Three measures of wheat flour" is by N.E.B. considered the equivalent of "half a hundredweight of flour."

Verse 22

Note descriptive and continuative (durative) tenses: the imperfect, "he was traveling," and the present, "teaching and making his way. . . ."

κατά, distributive, as in 8:1; 9:6, 23; 11:3, etc.

πορείαν, acc. s. of πορεία, journey, in the New Testament occurring only here and in James 1:11, where the meaning of the pl. of this noun is in dispute, being variously rendered: "ways," "undertakings," "pursuits," "business," etc. The connection between the noun πορεία and the verb πορεύω is obvious.

Verse 23

εἰ, interrogative particle; here, as often, particularly in the kind of Greek that is influenced by Hebrew and Aramaic, introducing a direct question.

οἱ σωζόμενοι: nom. pl. masc. pres. pass. participle of σώζω, to save. Is the reference to "those who are being saved" or to "those destined to be saved"? According to Robertson, *Translation,* Luke, pp. 83, 301, the latter. But see also commentaries on Luke 13:23 and on Acts 2:47. And see L.N.T. (A. and G.), and it will become clear that "those who are to be saved" and "those who are being saved" are both possible. Perhaps, in view of the present context, here in Luke 13:23 the questioner was thinking of the total number of those who would ultimately be saved.

Verse 24

ἀγωνίζεσθε, sec. per. pl. pres. imperat. of ἀγωνίζομαι, to fight, struggle, strive, strain every nerve. Cf. *agonize.*

ἰσχύσουσιν, third per. pl. fut. indicat. of ἰσχύω, a verb of which Luke is fond. He uses it 8 times in his Gospel, 6 times in Acts; hence 14 times in all, as often as all the rest of the New Testament together (4 times each in Matthew and Mark, once each in John, Galatians, Philippians, Hebrews, James, and Revelation). The meaning is basically: to be strong; hence, to be in good health, to have value, be valid; and, as here, to be able.

Verses 25, 26

ἀφ' οὖ, supply χρόνου; hence, "from the moment when," or "when once."

In verse 25 note the aor. subjunct. middle, and in verse 26 the future indicat. middle, of the verb ἄρχω, to begin. But this verb may be redundant. See the note on 11:53 on page 647, and see L.N.T. (A. and G.), p. 113.

Verse 27

ἀπόστητε, sec. per. pl. 2nd aor. imperat. intransit. of ἀφίστημι, to depart.

Verse 28

κλαυθμός, weeping. Cf. κλαίω, to weep. It is probable that our English verbs *to claim, exclaim,* and also *to cry,* as well as the Dutch and German *klagen* (to lament, complain), are derived from the same stem.

βρυγμός, gnashing, grinding; cf. βρύχω, to gnash the teeth (Acts 7:54). The combination "weeping and grinding of teeth" is found also in Matt. 8:12; 13:42, 50; 22:13; 24:51; 25:30.

Verse 29

ἀνακλιθήσονται, third per. pl. fut. indicat. pass. of ἀνακλίνω; in the pass. as here, to recline. For use of this verb in the active voice see 2:7 and 12:37.

Verse 32

ἀλώπεκι, dat. s. of ἀλώπηξ, fox. See the note on 9:58 on page 565.

ἰάσεις ἀποτελῶ: I am performing cures.

ἰάσεις, acc. pl. of ἴασις, cure; see also Acts 4:22, 30, and the note on 4:23 on page 261.

τελειοῦμαι, first per. s. pres. (here prophetic or futuristic) indicat. pass. of τελ-ειόω, to bring to the goal, or: to completion. Hence, the passive τελειοῦμαι means "I am being brought to the goal"; in other words, "I reach my goal."

Verse 33

δεῖ με . . . πορεύεσθαι; lit.: "It is necessary for me to be journeying." Somewhat freer translation: "I must continue on my way."

οὐκ ἐνδέχεται, *it is not accepted* or *permitted.* This rendering does justice to the basic verb δέχομαι, to accept, receive. The rendering "It would not do" (Berkeley), "It would never do" (Phillips), "It will not do" (Dutch, Nieuwe Vertaling; note original: "het gaat niet aan") is not only technically correct but also retains the cutting irony in this exclamation. This holds also for "It is unthinkable" (N.E.B.).

Verse 34

Note sharp contrast between ἠθέλησα, first per. s. aor. indicat. in the middle of verse 34, and οὐκ ἠθελήσατε, sec. per. pl. aor. indicat. at the close of the verse. Both are forms of ἐθέλω or θέλω, to be willing, wishing, desiring.

ὄρνις, in the New Testament only here and in Matt. 23:37, bird; specifically *hen*.

νοσσιάν, acc. s. of νοσσιά, brood of young birds; classical νεοσσιά, literally "new ones." Cf. *new, novice*.

πτέρυγας, acc. pl. of πτέρυξ, wing. See also Matt. 23:37; Rev. 4:8; 9:9; 12:14; and for the related πτερύγιον see the note on 4:9 on page 242.

Verse 35

ἀφίεται, third per. s. pres. (linear) indicat. pass. of ἀφίημι; here, to abandon. For more on this verb see the note on 4:39 on page 271.

Summary of Chapter 13

See p. 537.

Outline of Chapter 14

Theme: *The Work Thou Gavest Him to Do*

CHAPTER XIV

14   1 Now it happened on a sabbath, as Jesus went to eat in the house of one of the leading Pharisees, that they were watching him closely. 2 And right there in front of him was a man afflicted with dropsy. 3 Jesus reacted by asking the law-experts and Pharisees, "Is it lawful to heal on the sabbath or not?" 4 But they were silent. And he took hold of the man, healed him, and let him go.[425]

5 Then he asked them, "Who of y o u, if his son[426] or his ox falls into a well on the sabbath day, will not immediately pull him out?" 6 And they could not return an answer.

14:1-6 The Healing, on a Sabbath, of a Man Afflicted with Dropsy

1. Now it happened on a sabbath, as Jesus went to eat in the house of one of the leading Pharisees, that they were watching him closely.

If there is any topical connection between this and the preceding chapter, it could be one of the following:

a. The hostility of Christ's adversaries and their followers (13:14, 17, 31-35) is continued in chapter 14:1 f.

b. The healings to which Jesus refers in 13:32, an example of which is recorded in 13:10-17, are continued in 14:1-6. Chapter 13 records the cure of a woman; chapter 14 that of a man.

c. The sabbath controversy between Jesus and his adversaries (13:10-17) is continued in 14:1-6.

A prominent Pharisee invites Jesus for dinner. For earlier occasions when an invitation to eat with a Pharisee was extended to Jesus see 7:36; 11:37. But the invitation now recorded was different: it was a request to recline at table with the Pharisee and the other guests for the important *sabbath day dinner*. All preparations had been made the day before, of course. The important Pharisee at whose home the festive meal was given seems to have been well supplied with earthly goods (read verse 12).

We feel inclined to say, "How kind of this prominent Pharisee to extend such an invitation to Jesus!" However, the evangelist adds, "They were watching him closely." The purpose of inviting Jesus was that *they*—the host plus the fellow Pharisees and law-experts he had invited—by closely watching Jesus, might discover a ground for an accusation against him.

---

425. Or: sent him away.
426. Some manuscripts read *donkey*.

2. And right there in front of him was a man afflicted with dropsy. Had this man been "planted" there? Had they brought him in to serve as a trap into which, they hoped, Jesus would fall? Some interpreters favor this view. The possibility cannot be excluded, but it is by no means certain. In these regions and at that time it was not at all unusual for people to walk in uninvited. See on 7:37, 38.

The poor man was afflicted with dropsy. This abnormal accumulation of fluid is not only serious in itself but is also a sign of illness affecting the kidneys, liver, blood, and/or heart. Moreover, the rabbis were of the opinion that the person so afflicted had committed a grievous sin.[427]

It would seem that up to this point the guests had not yet reclined at table. Since we already know that the heart of Jesus was ever filled with sympathy and that he had power to heal, we can predict what is about to happen.

3. Jesus reacted by asking the law-experts and Pharisees, Is it lawful to heal on the sabbath or not?

It is becoming clear that another sabbath controversy is in the making. For earlier clashes of this nature see on 6:1–5; 6:6–11; and 13:10–17, the final two dealing with *healings* on the sabbath (the withered hand and the crippled woman). When Jesus now asks his critics whether a work of healing is permitted on the sabbath day, he is repeating in essence what he had asked in connection with the healing of the man with the withered hand (6:9). In both cases he asked the question before effecting the cure. The prevailing opinion among the rabbis was that healing of the sick and/or handicapped is not allowed on the sabbath unless there is a distinct probability that delay will be fatal.

As had happened in the case recorded in chapter 6 so also now Christ's critics remained silent: **4. But they were silent.** Since they did not avail themselves of the opportunity to object, they had no ground to stand on if they would later try to accuse Jesus before the authorities. **And he took hold of the man, healed him, and let him go.**

The passage reads as if for Jesus healing this sorely afflicted man was the easiest thing in the world. In a sense it was. He did not have to overexert himself. He had power enough and to spare. In another sense, however, it was not easy. See Matt. 8:17 and N.T.C. on that passage.

5. Then he asked them, Who of y o u, if his son or his ox falls into a well on the sabbath day, will not immediately pull him out?

Even in all the massive Jewish sabbath regulations I have not been able to discover any that forbids a sabbath day rescue of a son or of an ox[428] that had fallen into a well.

With respect to the Qumran people the situation was different. The following regulation is found in The Damascus Document XIII, "Let not a

---

427. S.BK., Vol. II, pp. 203, 204.

428. For the variant "donkey or ox" see the note on this verse on page 727.

man help an animal to give birth on the sabbath day, and if she lets her young fall into a cistern or ditch, let him not lift it out on the sabbath." Among the Jews in general, however, no one would hesitate to hurry to the rescue. Note especially the word *immediately;* that is (in this case) without waiting until the end of the sabbath.

6. And they could not return an answer. Compare:
"But they were silent" (verse 4)
.with
"And they could not return an answer" (verse 6)
In the first instance they did not want to answer; in the second they were not able to do so. They could not because they were unwilling to admit that they were wrong. The majesty of Christ and his triumph over his enemies stands out clearly.

For *Practical Lessons* and *Greek Words,* etc., see pp. 726–729.

---

7 Noticing how the guests were picking out the places of honor at the table, he spoke this parable to them: 8 "When you are invited by anyone to a wedding feast, do not recline in the place of honor, for a person more distinguished than you may have been invited by him.   9 If so, the one who invited both you and him will come and say to you, 'Make room for this man.' Then with embarrassment you will be taking and keeping the lowest place.   10 Instead, when you are invited, go and recline in the lowest place, so that when your host comes he will say to you, 'Friend, move up higher.' Then you will be honored in the eyes of all your fellow guests. 11 For everyone who exalts himself will be humbled, and the one who humbles himself will be exalted."

12 Then, also (addressing) his host, he said, "When you give a luncheon or a dinner, do not habitually invite your friends or your brothers or your relatives or your rich neighbors, lest they invite you back and you receive a return payment.   13 On the contrary, when you give a reception,[429] make it a practice to invite poor people, crippled, lame, blind,   14 and you will be blessed, since they cannot repay you; for you will be repaid at the resurrection of the righteous."

14:7–14   A Lesson for Guests (The Parable of The Reserved Seats)
and
A Lesson for the Host

A.   A Lesson for Guests: The Parable of The Reserved Seats

And now the invited guests are beginning to take their places at table:
7. Noticing how the guests were picking out the places of honor at the table, he spoke this parable to them:
If rabbinic sources written somewhat later furnish a true description of dinner habits that prevailed during Christ's sojourn on earth, as they probably do, then in the room where the festive dinner was to be held the "couches for three" were arranged each in the shape of a U around a low table.

---

429. Or: banquet.

The central position (think of the U's curved base) of table No. 1 was considered the place of highest honor. To the left of the most highly honored person the one second in honor would be reclining; to the right of the most highly honored one the third in honor would take his place. On the three-person couch (the triclinium) to the left of the first couch the order of reclining would continue as follows: central, fourth; left of central, fifth; right of central, sixth; and so also for the third couch (the one to the right of the first couch); central position, seventh; left of central, eighth; right of central, ninth, etc.[430]

What Jesus noticed was this, that when the moment arrived for the guests to recline at table there was an unseemly scramble for the places of honor. This was definitely a violation of proper table etiquette. The person in charge—let us call him the host—acting on orders of the owner of the house, though often owner and host were the same person, had *reserved* the select seats. Not in the sense that he had placed a huge sign on them, reading R E S E R V E D, but in the sense that he wanted these places to be occupied by certain definite guests, and not by other people. The fact that, in the sense indicated, these places were indeed *reserved* and not meant for just "anybody" is clear from verse 9.

But to the mind and heart of Jesus what was happening was not merely a violation of table etiquette but a manifestation of *lack of humility,* as verse 11 proves. It is for this reason that the contents of 14:8-11 are called, and actually are, a *parable.*

8, 9. When you are invited by anyone to a wedding feast, do not recline in the place of honor, for a person more distinguished than you may have been invited by him. If so, the one who invited both you and him will come and say to you, Make room for this man. Then with embarrassment you will be taking and keeping the lowest place.

Jesus now shows what can be expected to happen when *at a wedding feast* (in connection with which rules were rather stringent) someone rushes to occupy a place not intended for him. The host, seeing what has happened, will come and, accompanied by another invited guest, will tell the usurper, "Give your seat to this man," a man who, as the host regards him, is more distinguished. The result will be that the bold and presumptuous guest will then, in painful embarrassment, have to vacate his seat and take and keep the lowest place.

But why the lowest? Probably for one of two reasons: (a) because by this time all the other places are occupied; or (b) because even if there are still several vacant places, the humiliated individual will wisely take the very lowest seat, for he will not wish to experience a second humiliation.

10. Instead, when you are invited, go and recline in the lowest place, so that when your host comes he will say to you, Friend, move up higher. Then you will be honored in the eyes of all your fellow guests.

---

430. S.BK., Vol. IV., p. 618.

The meaning is clear enough. What is somewhat surprising is that the Pharisees and the experts in the law were in need of hearing these truths. They should have known better. After all, what Jesus was saying came close to being a repetition of what Prov. 25:6, 7 had taught long ago (freely translated): "Do not give yourself airs in the presence of a king. Do not occupy the place *reserved* for important people. It is better to have someone say to you, 'Come up here,' than to be forced to a lower place in the presence of a prince."

And now the key sentence, the one that shows that the words of verses 8–10, though certainly descriptive of that which actually took place, constitute a parable:

11. For everyone who exalts himself will be humbled, and the one who humbles himself will be exalted. Very appropriately these same words are also found in the conclusion of the parable of The Pharisee and The Tax Collector (18:14) and in Matt. 23:12. See also Job 22:29; Prov. 29:23; James 4:6; I Peter 5:5.

The meaning is clear. It will probably stand out even more clearly when some biblical examples are given.

What happened to those who exalted themselves?

Do y o u remember *Nabal?*

> "This bread and water are my own.
> They are not David's, mine alone."
> His heart then died. 'Twas like a stone.

Read that man's story in I Sam. 25:3, 10, 11, 36–38.

Do y o u recall *Jezebel?*

> Her boastful words, her lying tongue?
> How she was out the window flung,
> Her body then reduced to dung?

For the report on her, turn to I Kings 21:7, 23; II Kings 9:30–37.

And *Nebuchadnezzar?*

> He said, "This is the place *I* built."
> His heart with ugly pride was filled.
> God intervened: his pride was killed.

Be sure to study Dan. 4:30–33, but do not stop there. In fairness to Nebuchadnezzar read also verses 34–37.

And *Herod Agrippa I*

> Now look at him, so richly groomed,
> And listen to him ... but he's doomed:
> His body by the worms consumed.

723

Acts 12:20-23 contains the story.

But now the other side of the picture: what happened to those who humbled themselves?

First of all, *Hannah*

> In sorrow she did not rebel.
> Humbly she prayed, as *God* could tell.
> He gave her little Samuel.

Read I Sam. 1:12-20.

Next, *Mary,* the mother of Jesus

> "My soul doth magnify the Lord,"
> She said, her heart in full accord
> With God, by heaven and earth adored.

For the full story read Luke 1:26-56.

Then *the tax collector* or publican, in the parable of The Pharisee and The Tax Collector

> "O God be merciful to me,"
> He said, "the sinner though I be."
> And fully *justified* went he.

Be sure to study Luke 18:9-14.

Last of all, there was *Paul.*

> His life was Christ. 'Twas not a dream.
> "We're saved by grace," that was his theme:
> "God sent his Son us to redeem."

Among the many passages that could be cited to prove Paul's humility and how the grace of God was magnified in his life some of the most important are the following: I Cor. 15:9; II Cor. 12:9; Gal. 2:20; 6:14; I Tim. 1:15.

Moreover, Scripture is full of passages in which the necessity of humility is held before us: Ps. 10:17; 69:32; Prov. 26:12; Isa. 14:12-15; 57:15; Matt. 18:4; 20:25-28; 23:12; Luke 22:27; John 13:1-15; Phil. 2:5-8; and the already mentioned James 4:6; I Peter 5:5 (to which can now be added verse 6).

Christ's teaching on humility is one of the most important and constantly recurring subjects in the entire New Testament. *Does it not harmonize beautifully with the doctrine of salvation by grace alone?* Without fear of successful contradiction one can state that humble trust in God and grateful eagerness to carry out his will are stressed throughout Scripture. "Where then is the glorying [or boasting]? It is excluded!" (Rom. 3:27).

724

B. *A Lesson for the Host*

12-14. Then, also (addressing) his host, he said, When you give a luncheon or a dinner, do not habitually invite your friends or your brothers or your relatives or your rich neighbors, lest they invite you back and you receive a return payment. On the contrary, when you give a reception, make it a practice to invite poor people, crippled, lame, blind, and you will be blessed, since they cannot repay you; for you will be repaid at the resurrection of the righteous.

The parable has ended. But Jesus still has a word for the host. The Master had undoubtedly observed that most of the guests were important people. But if the rich socialize only with the rich, the learned only with the learned, the influential only with the influential, what happens to the rest of society?

Jesus does not forbid normal social life. Birds of a feather will indeed flock together. That is natural and good. But rigid restrictions along those lines are not in keeping with the spirit of the gospel. The words of Jesus were and are very wise indeed. His order should be obeyed. Note the following:

a. By constantly inviting only those who are able to invite you in return, where is there any room for putting into practice the biblical requirement that hospitality be shown to those in need? See Rom. 12:13; I Tim. 3:2; Titus 1:8; I Peter 4:9.

b. If such selfishness is practiced, where is the reward "at the resurrection of the righteous," for which see the beautiful words of Matt. 25:34–40? "The righteous" not as they are in themselves but as pronounced by God, on the basis of Christ's atonement.

c. Even in the present life those who associate only with the people of their own "set" miss the thrill resulting from generous sharing, the joy beaming from the eyes of those who have been blessed.

> Somehow, not only for Christmas
> But all the long year through,
> The joy that you give to others
> Is the joy that comes back to you.
> And the more you spend in blessing
> The poor and the lonely and sad,
> The more of your heart's possessions
> Return to make you glad.

> John Greenleaf Whittier

d. Selfish people are cheating themselves also in other ways. To give an example: What minister cannot bear testimony to the fact that some of the finest lessons he ever learned were given to him by the poor, the dull, the small, the sick, the handicapped, the dying?

Therefore, by failing to heed Christ's command one is not only cheating others but even himself . . . and dishonoring God, the God who loves those who without that love would have perished everlastingly (John 3:16; II Cor. 8:9).[431]

Practical Lessons Derived from Luke 14:1-14

Verse 5

"Who of y o u, if his son or his ox falls into a well on the sabbath day, will not immediately pull him out?" Evidently, then, there are certain things that may not be left undone on the sabbath.

"Who . . . will not immediately pull him out?" But are we as concerned about the spiritual welfare of our children as we are about their physical safety? If we are, we should insist on providing a thorough *Christian* education for them.

Verse 10

"Go and recline in the lowest place." The glory of taking the lowest place is that from there the only direction one can go is "up."

Verse 13

"Invite poor people." To be sure, this advice was revolutionary. But the revolution here advocated permits no violence. It does not amount to "taking from the rich to give to the poor." Those who have are admonished *of their own accord* to share with the have-nots.

Notes on Greek Words, Phrases, and Constructions in 14:1-14

Verse 1

Note ἐγένετο . . . καί: it happened . . . *that*. The style here is based on Hebrew.

αὐτοὶ ἦσαν παρατηρούμενοι, third per. pl. periphrastic imperf. middle indicat. of παρατηρέω, to watch closely; in the present case with evil intent. Whether the pronoun is emphatic here is by no means certain. In Koine Greek αὐτός does not always indicate special emphasis.

Verse 2

ὑδρωπικός* (from ὕδρωψ, dropsy; cf. ὕδωρ, water), afflicted with dropsy. Etymologically related are *water, dropsy, hydrant, hydrangea*. Dropsy consists of excessive accumulation of fluid in body tissues.

Verse 3

ἀποκριθείς, nom. s. masc. aor. participle of ἀποκρίνομαι. Although in very many cases this Greek verb corresponds to English *answer, reply*, indicating an answer to a

---

431. Notes on Greek words, phrases, and constructions in 14:1-14 begin on this page.

question that was asked, this is by no means always the case. Frequently the Greek verb introduces *a response or reaction to a situation.* See the following passages: Luke 1:60; 5:5; 7:40; 8:21, 50; 9:41, 49; 11:45, etc. So also here.

ἔξεστιν, here occurring in a question and meaning, "Is it proper or lawful?"

Verse 4

ἡσύχασαν, third per. pl. aor. indicat. of ἡσυχάζω, to be quiet. In accordance with the specific context in which this verb occurs it acquires the following meanings: They were quiet; i.e., offered no further objection (Acts 11:18; 21:14). Paul instructs certain excitable individuals "to be ambitious about *living calmly*"; i.e., leading a quiet life (I Thess. 4:11). The women who saw the tomb and how the body was laid in it were quiet—that is, they *rested*—on the sabbath (Luke 23:56).

ἐπιλαβόμενος, nom. s. masc. 2nd aor. middle participle of ἐπιλαμβάνω, to take hold of; so also in I Tim. 6:12. Further, to lay hold on (Luke 20:20); to seize (23:26, etc.); and to take to oneself, be concerned about, help (Heb. 2:16).

Verse 5

τίνος. That this is an anacoluthon is clear, for we have to look ahead all the way to the subject of ἀνασπάσει to find the antecedent on which this pronoun depends. Literally the sentence reads, "Whose son or ox of y o u shall fall into a well, and he [the father of the son, and owner of the ox] will not immediately pull him up (even) on the sabbath day?" It makes little difference whether "on the sabbath day" is combined with "fall into a well" or with "pull him up," since obviously both actions take place on that day and in immediate succession. In *thought,* at least, "on the sabbath day" belongs to the entire question.

Although there is some degree of doubt regarding the reading "*son* or ox" instead of the variant "*donkey* or ox," the textual evidence would seem to favor the former. In an early copy did a scribe unwittingly write "donkey," because he was reminded of the somewhat similar passage, Luke 13:15? And was his error also partly due to the close resemblance between the two words υἱός, son, and ὄνος, donkey, when written in abbreviated uncials?

φρέαρ, well. Cf. "The well is deep" and "Jacob . . . gave us this well" (John 4:11, 12). In Rev. 9:1, 2 the reference is to "the shaft of the abyss."

πεσεῖται, third per. s. future indicat. middle of πίπτω, to fall.

ἀνασπάσει, third per. s. future indicat. act. of ἀνασπάω**, in the New Testament used only here and in Acts 11:10, to pull or draw up. Cf. *space.*

Verse 6

ἀνταποκριθῆναι. Note double compound (ἀντί and ἀπό), aor. infinitive of ἀνταποκρίνομαι. The only other New Testament instance of this compound is Rom. 9:20, to talk back. In my thesis I have shown that in Luke 14:6 ἀντί has the meaning "in return" ("They could not return an answer"). Cf. Matt. 22:34 and Syriac rendering of Luke 14:6, "They were not able to give answer." In Rom. 9:20, on the other hand, the prefix ἀντί indicates opposition, *to argue against,* as is clear from the entire context there.

Forms of καλέω in verses 7–24

Verses 7–14 contain *a lesson for guests* (the parable of *The Reserved or Best Seats*) and *a lesson for the host.* Verses 15–24 present the parable of *The Slighted,* and therefore in a sense *Rejected Invitation* (also called that of *The Great Supper* or *The Great Banquet*). It is understandable that material of this kind would contain several references to invitations. In fact, in verses 7-24 forms of the verb καλέω, *to call,* but here especially in the sense *to invite,* occur no less than 12 times. It may be helpful to treat these twelve as a group, beginning with the most simple or basic form.

1. ἐκάλεσαν (verse 16), third per. s. aor. indicat. act.: "A man... *invited* many guests."

2. ὁ... καλέσας (verse 9), nom. s. aor. act. participle: "the one having invited" or "the one who invited." Compare this with No. 8.

3. κάλει (verse 13), sec. per. s. pres. imperat. act., "invite," meaning, "you must invite."

4. τοὺς κεκλημένους (verse 7), *acc.* pl. of οἱ κεκλημένοι, perf. pass. participle: those who had been invited; in the present context "the guests," for it is clear that the individuals to whom reference is made here had accepted the invitation that had been extended to them, and were actually present.

5. τοῖς κεκλημένοις (verse 17), same form as the immediately preceding except that (a) here we have the *dat.* pl.: "(to tell) those who had been invited," and (b) the invited individuals had responded negatively to the invitation; hence, were not "guests."

6. τῶν κεκλημένων (verse 24), again the same but now *gen.* pl.: "of those... invited."

7. ᾖ κεκλημένος (verse 8), third per. s. perf. pass. subjunct. periphrastic: "a... person may have been invited."

8. ὁ κεκληκώς (verse 10), *nom.* s. masc. perf. act. participle: the man who has extended the invitation, the host. Compare this with No. 2.

9. τῷ κεκληκότι (verse 12), same as the immediately preceding, but now in the *dat.*: "... he said... to the one who had invited him," or simply, "to the host."

10, 11. κληθῇς, sec. per. s. aor. subjunct. (after ὅταν) pass.: "when you are invited" (thus both in verse 8 and verse 10).

12. ἀντικαλέσωσιν (verse 12), third per. pl. aor. subjunct. (after μήποτε) of ἀντικαλέω: "lest they invite you back."

Verses 7-9
(from here on minus καλέω forms)

ἐπέχων, pres. act. participle of ἐπέχω, to hold toward, fix attention (with νοῦν understood) on, notice.

πρωτοκλισία, place of honor; acc. pl. -ς in verse 7; acc. s. -ν in verse 8. See also Luke 20:46; Matt. 23:6; Mark 12:39.

ἐξελέγοντο, third per. pl. imperfect (descriptive or progressive) middle of ἐκλέγω, to choose. Cf. *elect,* and see the note on 6:13 on page 333.

μὴ κατακλιθῇς, sec. per. s. aor. subjunct. (in a prohibition) pass. of κατακλίνω, to recline at table. See the note on 7:36 on page 411; and for this verb and its synonyms see the note on 11:37 on page 645.

In order to understand the grammatical construction of verses 8, 9 it is probably best first of all, without regard to what sounds best in modern English, to translate the original literally. The result would be as follows: "When [or: whenever] you are invited by anyone to a wedding feast, do not recline in the place of honor, lest [μήποτε] one more distinguished than you may have been invited by him, and (lest) the one who invited both you and him come and say to you," etc.

The question then arises, since both ἢ κεκλημένος and ἐρεῖ are dependent on μήποτε, how is it that the first is in the subjunctive, the second in the future indicative? The answer is that there is, and always has been, a very close relation between the future indicative and the subjunctive. Both may express contingency, relative uncertainty, possibility rather than certainty. See A. T. Robertson's excellent discussion in Gram. N.T., p. 846 and especially pp. 926–928. For another illustration of this interchange between subjunctive and future indicative see 12:58.

Δὸς ... τόπον. This aorist has been called "punctiliar," "impressive," "authoritative." It surely is all that. It indicates a brusque command, one that anticipates immediate compliance.

While ἄρξῃ (sec. per. s. aor. subjunct. middle of ἄρχω) may simply indicate a change of action, the pres. continuative infinitive κατέχειν indicates that the embarrassed person takes and keeps the lowest place.

Verse 10

ἀνάπεσε, sec. per. s. 2nd aor. imperat. of ἀναπίπτω; see the note on 11:37 on page 645.

ἐρεῖ most naturally goes with ἵνα: "so that he will say to you."

προσανάβηθι, sec. per. s. 2nd aor. imperat. of προσαναβαίνω*, to move up.

Verse 11

ὑψῶν and ταπεινῶν are nom. s. masc. pres. act. participles; and ὑψωθήσεται and ταπεινωθήσεται are third per. s. fut. indicat. passive verbs. Meaning: "For everyone who exalts himself will be humbled, and the one who humbles himself will be exalted."

Verse 12

ποιῇς, sec. per. s. pres. (durative) subjunct. act. of ποιέω, to do, make, produce, but in connection with meals, such as breakfasts, luncheons, etc., to give, arrange.

ἄριστον, luncheon. See also the note on 11:37 on page 645.

δεῖπνον, dinner, supper, the day's principal meal; sometimes banquet. See M.M., p. 139.

μὴ φώνει, note pres. tense; hence, do not keep inviting, do not habitually invite. Similarly in verse 13 κάλει is pres. tense, make a practice of inviting.

γείτονας, acc. pl. of γείτων, neighbor; from γῆ, in the sense of *land;* hence, a person from the same land or region and thus a neighbor.

μήποτε ... ἀνταπόδομά σοι, lest they invite you back and you receive a return payment (lit. and a return payment—or repayment—come to you). Acceptable also is the somewhat freer rendering, "if you do, they may invite you back," etc. For a different construction and translation, one I cannot accept, see Robertson, *Translation,* Luke, p. 86. Jesus is not explicitly warning against a wrongly motivated invitation, but against a wrong social attitude, the ignoring of the underprivileged.

Verse 13

For δοχήν, s. acc. of δοχή, see the note on 5:29 on page 306.

ἀναπείρους, acc. pl. m. of ἀνάπειρος* (also spelled -ηρος), here and in verse 21, maimed or crippled. According to some the prefix ἀνά means "all the way up." This is possible.

15 Now when one of those reclining at table with him heard this, he said to Jesus, "Blessed is the man who will partake of the feast[432] in the kingdom of God." 16 Jesus said to him: "A certain man was arranging a big dinner and invited many guests. 17 At the time fixed for the dinner he sent out his servant to tell those who had been invited, 'Come, for everything is now ready.' 18 But they all alike began to make excuses.

"The first one said to him, 'I have just bought a piece of land,[433] and I must go out and look it over; consider me excused.' 19 Another said, 'I just bought five teams of oxen, and I'm on my way to try them out; consider me excused.' 20 And still another said, 'I just got married; that's why I can't come.'

21 "So the servant came and reported these answers to his master. Then the owner of the house became angry and said to his servant, 'Hurry out into the streets and alleys of the town, and bring in the poor, crippled, blind, and lame.'

22 "The servant answered, 'Sir, what you ordered has been done, but there is still room.'

23 "Then the master told his servant, 'Go out into the highways and hedgerows and compel people to come in, that my house may be full; 24 for I tell y o u that not one of those men who were invited shall taste my dinner.'"

14:15-24 *The Parable of The Rejected Invitation*
or of
The Great Supper[434]

The reference Jesus made to "the resurrection of the righteous" and the blessedness connected with it produced an enthusiastic comment by one of the guests:

15. Now when one of those reclining at table with him heard this, he said to Jesus, Blessed is the man who will partake of the feast in the kingdom of God.

Some commentators view this exclamation as the expression of commendable yearning for the kingdom of God in its final stage. Others interpret it to have been a superficial ejaculation from a self-righteous Pharisee. It is not necessary to choose sides in this dispute.

As to describing the eschatological blessedness pertaining to the kingdom of God under the symbolism of a heavenly banquet, this representation is not at all unbiblical. In fact, Scripture often pictures the joy of the new heaven and earth as that of guests reclining together on couches at a table loaded with food and drink (wine, for example), and communicating with each other and with the host in a spacious banqueting hall flooded with light. Elements of this representation can be found in such passages as Ps. 23:5; Isa. 25:6; Matt. 8:11, 12; 22:1 ff.; 26:29; Mark 14:25; Rev. 3:20; 19:9.

The question is always: to what extent should these elements be interpreted literally, to what extent figuratively? When we answer, "Symbolism

---

432. Literally, who will eat bread, etc.

433. Or: a field, a farm.

434. This parable is peculiar to Luke. Matt. 22:1-14 is not a true parallel. See N.T.C. on Matthew, pp. 21-23.

probably predominates," this should not be interpreted to mean that the blessedness and the joys will be unreal. They will be very real indeed, but it is useless to speculate, and it is unjustifiable to be positive where Scripture sheds little or no light.

As Jesus saw it, the far more important question for everyone to answer is this, "Have I really accepted the invitation to enter this house of feasting? Does *my life* show that I have accepted it and am on the way to this blessed experience, enjoying a foretaste of it even now?" This may well be considered the introduction to the parable Jesus now tells:

16, 17. Jesus said to him: A certain man was arranging a big dinner and invited many guests. At the time fixed for the dinner he sent out his servant to tell those who had been invited, Come, for everything is now ready.

First there was the preparatory invitation. It would seem that in the present case all who were invited accepted. There is no mention of any who declined. Then, shortly before the beginning of the feast, the host sent a servant to tell the invited people, "Come, for everything is now ready."

The custom of double invitation, as here, was not at all unusual among the Jews. This appears not only from Esther 5:8; 6:14 but also from "the boast of the men of Jerusalem that none of them went to a banquet unless he were invited twice."[435]

18–20. But they all alike began to make excuses. The first one said to him, I have just bought a piece of land, and I must go out and look it over; consider me excused. —Another said, I just bought five teams of oxen, and I'm on my way to try them out; consider me excused. —And still another said, I just got married; that's why I can't come.

It should be stressed that all these people had already promised to come. However, now all go back on their earlier promises. In view of the huge amount of work involved in getting everything ready for the guests, that cancellation of commitments was an offense. It proved that they had been insincere. They had said "Yes," when they meant "No."

Besides, how shallow were the excuses offered! The man who said, "I have just bought a piece of land, and I must go out and look it over," and who, on that ground, begged to be excused, knew very well that he had not bought that field "sight unseen." Also, if he wanted to examine it more carefully, he would have every opportunity to do so afterward. Similarly, the fellow who had bought the five yoke of oxen knew he was stretching the truth when he said that on that account he would not be able to attend the banquet. "I'm on my way to try them out," he said. Well, if he had entertained any serious doubts about the excellence of these animals he would not have paid out his money for them. And as to trying them out, that could easily be done at a later time. The third fellow's excuse was as lame as were the others. Even Deut. 24:5, which during the first year of his married

---

435. P. A. Micklem, *St. Matthew, with Introduction and Notes,* London, 1917, p. 210.

life exempted a man from military service and from being charged with any public business, did not at all deprive him of the right to attend a banquet. In fact, it rather encouraged the exercise of this right; note the words at the end of that passage: "he shall cheer up his wife whom he has taken." Taking her along to the feast would have cheered her up, indeed! And if, before doing so, he had told the host about his marriage, that warmhearted person would have said, "By all means take her along!"

What we have here, therefore, is a series of trifling subterfuges, empty pretexts.

Thus also, from the beginning until now, ever so many people had offered alibis for refusing to accept from the heart and hand of God salvation full and free. The prophets had spoken. The people had said "No!" (Isa. 53:1; 65:2). And now, during Christ's ministry, they were saying "No!" once more (Luke 13:34).

21. So the servant came and reported these answers to his master. Then the owner of the house became angry and said to his servant, Hurry out into the streets and alleys of the town, and bring in the poor, crippled, blind, and lame.

When the master heard his servant's report he was angry. Was the banquet to be called off now? No indeed! It was going to be held, and at the time previously determined. So, in order that guests might not be lacking, the servant is now sent into that part of the city where the underprivileged people were living: the poor, crippled, blind, and lame, the very people already mentioned in verse 13. They must now be invited; rather, they must be taken by the hand and brought in. This was probably necessary, not so much because, for example, the blind would not have been able to find the banqueting hall unless they were taken by the hand and led, but rather because all of the groups here mentioned might well entertain serious doubts with respect to the question whether a sumptuous banquet could really be for *them.*

22, 23. The servant answered, Sir, what you ordered has been done, but there is still room. Then the master told his servant, Go out into the highways and hedgerows and compel people to come in, that my house may be full...

Not only has the owner of the house definitely decided that there shall be a banquet and that it shall be held on the date originally planned, but also he wants his house *filled* with guests. He is that kind of person, very big-hearted and generous. He loves to make people happy, especially those down and out. So into the major roads *outside the city* he now sends his servant. Along the outside highways here and there some people are living, foreigners perhaps. The very poor people and the kind of folks who, were they living in another part of the world, would be called "untouchables" had constructed some kind of shelters for themselves amid the rows of shrubs and bushes lining those highways. These highway and these hedgerow people must now be "compelled" to come to the banquet; "compelled" not physically but by the force of powerful and loving persuasion.

And what about those people who had been invited first of all, had first accepted the invitation but at the last moment had refused, advancing all kinds of shallow excuses? The answer is found in verse **24. for I tell y o u that not one of those men who were invited shall taste my dinner.**

The little word *for* should not be left untranslated. There is indeed a causal connection here. The meaning is: since I want my house to be full, and since none of those first invited shall taste of my dinner, therefore people must be gathered from the highways and the hedgerows.

Who is meant by the pronoun *I* in "I tell y o u"? The master? But when the master speaks to his servant he uses the second person singular. What we have here is the plural: y o u.

Probable, therefore, is that here the parable stops. Its central lesson surfaces. Jesus himself is saying to all present at that dinner, including the man who uttered the exclamation (verse 15), and further to everyone who reads or hears this parable down through the ages, that refusal to accept God's gracious invitation of salvation by grace through faith will result in being excluded from the blessings and joys of the new heaven and earth, the kingdom in its consummation, the church triumphant.

When Israel, as a whole, rejects Christ (verses 18–20), God's plan is not abandoned. Even among the Jews in the old dispensation and during the period of Christ's earthly ministry there were genuine believers (verse 21). There was always that little remnant (I Kings 19:18; Isa. 14:32; 29:19; Luke 6:20; Rom. 9:27; 11:5).

But now something very wonderful happens, already predicted, to be sure, in the Old Testament (Isa. 54:2, 3; 60:1–3; cf. Ps. 72:8 f.; 87): the church, present even during the old dispensation, now begins to *expand* among the Gentiles. It now becomes universal, international (see above, verses 22, 23), the body of Christ consisting of both Jew and Gentile. Cf. Eph. 2:14, 18.

The old Israel, that is, those who rejected God's gracious invitation, extended first by the old dispensation prophets and afterward by Jesus himself and his apostles (see verses 16, 17), perishes. Not one of the rejecters is saved (verse 24). The new Israel, consisting of both Jew and Gentile (Gal. 6:16), lives on. "There can be neither Jew nor Greek; there can be neither slave nor freeman; there can be no male and female; for y o u are all one in Christ Jesus," says Paul (Gal. 3:28). In all this the bountiful character of God's love is revealed:

> There's a wideness in God's mercy,
> Like the wideness of the sea;
> There's a kindness in his justice
> That is more than liberty.
>
> For the love of God is broader
> Than the measure of man's mind;
> And the heart of the eternal
> Is most wonderfully kind.
>
>   F. W. Faber

Positively stated, then, the one central lesson of the parable is: ACCEPT GOD'S GRACIOUS INVITATION. DO IT NOW!

For *Practical Lessons* and *Greek Words*, etc., see pp. 738–740.

---

25 Now huge crowds were traveling with Jesus; and he suddenly turned and said to them, 26 "If anyone comes to me and does not hate his father and mother and wife and children and brothers and sisters—yes, and even his own life—he cannot be my disciple. 27 Anyone who does not carry his cross and follow me[436] cannot be my disciple.

28 "For who of y o u, wishing to erect a tower,[437] does not first sit down and figure out the cost, (to see) whether he has enough money to complete it? 29 Lest perhaps, when he has laid a foundation but is unable to complete the building, all the onlookers poke fun of[438] him, 30 saying, 'This fellow began to build but was not able to finish.'

31 "Or what king, setting out to wage war with another king, does not first sit down and consider whether he is able with ten thousand to meet in battle the one coming against him with twenty thousand? 32 And if he is not able, then, while the other king is still a long way off, he sends a delegation and asks for terms of peace. 33 Similarly, therefore, no one of y o u who does not give up all that belongs to him can be my disciple."

14:25–33 *The Cost of Discipleship. The Parable of*
The Rash Builder
and
The Reasonable King
For 14:26, 27 cf. Matt. 10:37, 38

A. *The Cost of Discipleship*

25, 26. Now huge crowds were traveling with Jesus; and he suddenly turned and said to them, If anyone comes to me and does not hate his father and mother and wife and children and brothers and sisters—yes, and even his own life—he cannot be my disciple.

The topical connection between this and the preceding section is close; see pp. 538, 539.

On his way toward Jerusalem, through Perea, huge crowds are following Jesus. All at once he turns to them and addresses them in words which in substance, though not exactly, are found also in Matt. 10:37. He tells the people that devotion to himself must be so wholehearted that even attachment to parents and to the other members of one's family must not be allowed to stand in the way.

What has bothered many people is the word *hate* which Jesus uses here. Does the Master really mean that a true disciple must dislike, detest, abhor, loathe his father and mother, wife and children, brothers and sisters?

A good rule to follow is always this one: "Let Scripture be its own interpreter." The two parallel passages should be placed side by side.

---

436. Or: and come behind me.
437. Or: farm building.
438. Or: begin to poke fun of.

Matthew 10:37 Compared with Luke 14:26

Matt. 10:37	*Luke 14:26*
He who loves father or mother more than me is not worthy of me; he who loves son or daughter more than me is not worthy of me.	If anyone comes to me and does not hate his father and mother and wife and children and brothers and sisters . . . he cannot be my disciple.

Clearly, then, the meaning of *hate* in the Lucan passage is *to love less*. In all things Christ must always have the pre-eminence (Col. 1:18).

Other arguments in support of this view:

a. The word *hate* has the same meaning—to love less—in Gen. 29:31, "Jehovah saw that Leah was hated." The explanation of "hated" is given in the immediate context, verse 30, "Jacob . . . loved Rachel more than Leah." In other words, he loved Leah less than Rachel. It was in that sense that he "hated" Leah.

b. That the word *hate* in Luke 14:26 cannot have the meaning which we generally attach to it is clear also from the fact that Jesus tells us to love even our enemies (Matt. 5:44). Then we should certainly love and not hate members of our immediate family.

What the Savior demands in Luke 14:26 and other passages is complete devotion, the type of loyalty that is so true and unswerving that every other attachment, even that to one's own life, must be subjected to it.

When an alien wishes to become a citizen of the United States of America he must renounce allegiance to his native land and take an oath of loyalty to the country of his choice. This does not mean that he cannot continue to think highly of the nation to which he has said Farewell, but it does mean that from now on he must serve "the land of the free and the home of the brave." Even far more absolute and unconditional must be the loyalty which citizens of the kingdom of God sustain toward their heavenly country and its "Lord of lords and King of kings." If a person is unwilling to tender that unconditional devotion, then, says Jesus, "he cannot be my disciple." That same expression is found also in the next verse:

27. Anyone who does not carry his cross and follow me cannot be my disciple. Cf. Matt. 10:38. This negative statement is implied in its positive parallel, found in 9:23. For the meaning see on that passage.

B. *The Parable of The Rash Builder*

One might also call this "The Parable of The Reasonable Builder," for that reasonable or sensible man is certainly *implied* in the words, "Who of y o u does not first sit down and figure out the cost," etc. But though that title must be allowed, it remains true that in this little illustration more is said about the *rash* builder than about his opposite.

28–30. For who of y o u, wishing to erect a tower [or farm building] does not first sit down and figure out the cost, (to see) whether he has

**enough money to complete it? Lest perhaps, when he has laid a founda-
tion but is unable to complete the building, all the onlookers poke fun of
him, saying, This fellow began to build but was not able to finish.**

The lesson is *Look Before You Leap.*

Here is a man who is thinking about building a "tower." What kind of
tower? The original does not make this clear. Perhaps a watchtower for his
vineyard, so that he can be protected against pillagers, etc., and will have a
place—or an extra place—for storage, and even for temporary residence.
Or the "tower" of which the text speaks may have meant an entire farm
building. Whatever it be, the point is that before a man starts to erect the
structure he should count the cost. If he does not, he will become a
laughingstock, an object of ridicule.

Similarly, before one decides to be Christ's follower, he should realize
that being a Christian is not "a bed of roses." Did not Jesus make this very
clear? See Matt. 7:14; Luke 13:24; cf. John 16:33; II Tim. 3:12. To be sure,
a true believer is never lost (John 10:27, 28; I John 2:19), but there are
many people who *seem* to have cast their lot with Christ and then . . . fall
away. Think of Demas and of Judas.

What, then, is the solution? Perhaps I can remain neutral? Read on:

C. *The Parable of The Reasonable King*

**31, 32. Or what king, setting out to wage war with another king, does
not first sit down and consider whether he is able with ten thousand to
meet in battle the one coming against him with twenty thousand? And if
he is not able, then, while the other king is still a long way off, he sends a
delegation and asks for terms of peace.**

No, you cannot remain neutral. *You must leap.*

The title *The Parable of The Reckless King* is based upon the fact that such a
king is indeed implied, one who does *not* first sit down and consider, etc.
But, again, though that title is applicable, the emphasis is on the *reasonable,*
sensible king.

This king is not in the same position as the builder of the preceding
parable. That man was free to act or not to act, to build or not to build. The
king, however, is being attacked. Someone is coming against him with
twenty thousand soldiers, but he himself has only ten thousand. So he must
make a decision. That decision will probably be to send a delegation and
make peace with the attacker.

The illustration is apt. The foe is formidable. See I Peter 5:8; I John
2:16. The sinner too must act. Neutrality is impossible. What, then, should
he do? He should become reconciled with God. That is the wise, sensible,
reasonable thing to do. And is not that exactly what Jesus has been saying
all along? See 12:57-59; 13:3, 5, 24, 34. Cf. II Cor. 5:20, 21.

The two little parables form a unit. "Look before you leap." "But be sure
to leap . . . in the right direction!" Jesus is nearing the cross. *Now* is the
critical hour. "Today, O that y o u would hear his voice!" (Ps. 95:7).

Jesus sums it all up in these words:

33. Similarly, therefore, no one of y o u who does not give up all that belongs to him can be my disciple.

Wholehearted devotion, all-out loyalty, complete self-denial, so that one places himself, his time, his earthly possessions, his talents, etc., at the disposal of Christ, is what Jesus asks.

> But we never can prove the delights of his love
> Until all on the altar we lay;
> For the favor he shows, and the joy he bestows,
> Are for them who will trust and obey.
>
> Trust and obey, for there's no other way
> To be happy in Jesus, but to trust and obey.
>
> —Rev. J. H. Sammis

For *Practical Lessons* and *Greek Words,* etc., see pp. 738–740.

---

34 "Salt, indeed, is good; but if even the salt becomes tasteless, what will restore it?[439]   35 It is fit neither for soil nor for the manure pile; it is thrown out. He who has ears to hear, let him hear."

14:34, 35 *Useless Salt*
Cf. Matt. 5:13; Mark 9:50

Jesus has been emphasizing that his followers must be wholeheartedly devoted to him. They must not be merely nominal disciples. They should be genuine salt, salt that has not lost its flavor:

34, 35. Salt, indeed, is good; but if even the salt becomes tasteless, what will restore it? It is fit neither for soil nor for the manure pile; it is thrown out.

As to the underlying figure, it is easy to understand that salt is good. It is good because it preserves (combats deterioration) and imparts flavor. However, salt may lose its flavor and become tasteless. The salt from the marshes and lagoons or from the rocks in the neighborhood of the Dead Sea easily acquires a stale or alkaline taste, because of its mixture with gypsum, etc. It is then literally useless. It cannot fertilize the soil, and throwing it on the manure pile will not help any.

Jesus, as he walked on earth, saw many Pharisees and scribes, people who advocated a formal, legalistic religion in the place of the true religion proclaimed by the ancient prophets in the name of the Lord. Thus by and large the salt had lost its flavor in the religious life of Israel. Many "sons of the kingdom" would be cast out (Matt. 8:12).

The implication is clear. Just as salt having lost its saltiness cannot be

---

439. Literally: wherewith shall it be seasoned? (A.V. and A.R.V.).

restored, so also those who were trained in the knowledge of the truth but who then resolutely set themselves against the exhortation of the Holy Spirit and become hardened in their opposition are not renewed unto repentance (Matt. 12:32; Heb. 6:4-6).

Because unswerving loyalty to Jesus Christ, and thus to God Triune, is not at all in harmony with the natural cravings of sinful human nature, and yet is absolutely necessary, Jesus concludes with the words **He who has ears to hear, let him hear.** For explanation see on 8:8b.[440]

Practical Lessons Derived from Luke 14:15-35

Verses 18, 24

"But they all alike began to make excuses." "Not one of those men who were invited shall taste my dinner."

Not for a moment was the host fooled by the excuses.

Here are some modern alibis:

"I always have a headache on Sunday."

"Did you know that many more babies are born on Sunday than on any other day of the week?" (an excuse by an M.D. for skipping so many services).

"There are too many hypocrites in church."

Verse 33

"No one ... who does not give up all that belongs to him can be my disciple."

If this sacrifice seems too great, compare it with Christ's sacrifice for us (II Cor. 8:9; and cf. Rom. 8:32).

Though what was demanded of the rich young ruler is not required of everyone, in one way or another God wants each of us to surrender himself with body and soul to him, serving him wholeheartedly according to the talents he has given us.

Notes on Greek Words, Phrases, and Constructions in 14:15-35

Verses 18, 19

It is uncertain which word to supply after μιᾶς. The following have been suggested: γνώμης (hence, "with one mind" or "with one consent"), ψυχῆς ("with one soul"), φωνῆς ("with one voice"). Probably safe would be "all alike."

Note παραιτεῖσθαι in verse 18, παρῃτημένον in verses 18 and 19. These are forms of the verb παραιτέομαι (= παρά plus αἰτέομαι), to beg off, to make excuses. The first is the pres. infinitive; the second is the acc. s. masc. perf. pass. participle. The various shades of meaning of this verb may be classified as follows:

to make excuses, to excuse oneself (Luke 14:18a);

consider me excused, or: please excuse me (Luke 14:18b, 19);

to shun or have nothing to do with (I Tim. 4:7; Titus 3:10);

to refuse (Acts 25:11; Heb. 12:25);

---

440. Notes on Greek words, phrases, and constructions in 14:15-35 begin on this page.

to refuse to place on the list (I Tim. 5:11);
to reject (II Tim. 2:23).
In Heb. 12:19 the meaning of the entire clause seems to be, "They begged that no
further message be given them."

Verse 20

ἔγημα, first per. s. aor. indicat. of γαμέω, to marry. Cf. *bigamy*.

Verse 21

ὀργισθείς, nom. s. masc. aor. pass. participle of ὀργίζω; in the pass. to become
angry. Cf. *orgy*.
ῥύμας, acc. pl. of ῥύμη, found also in Matt. 6:2; Acts 9:11; 12:10, alley. More than
one attempt has been made to explain the origin of this Greek word. By some it is
traced to the flow or *rush* (cf. ῥέω, ῥύσις) of an object, leaving a *trail* or *lane* behind it,
and this easily leads to the meaning *narrow street, alley*. But the very fact that
etymologists do not agree would seem to indicate that this is no more than a guess.

Verse 24

ἀνδρῶν, gen. pl. of ἀνήρ. This shows that, as far as the parable is concerned, the
invitation had been extended to, and refused by, the *men* (males), as those held
responsible for attendance.

Verse 28

πύργον, acc. s. of πύργος. This word reminds one of German *Burg* and of Dutch
burcht. The meaning is stronghold, citadel, fortress, farm building, tower. See also
13:4; Matt. 21:33; Mark 12:1.
ψηφίζει, third per. s. pres. indicat. of ψηφίζω, used here and in Rev. 13:18 (there
third per. s. aor. imperat. is used). A ψῆφος is a pebble. At one time pebbles were
used in counting. So, the verb means: to count, calculate.
δαπάνην, acc. s. of δαπάνη*, cost, expense; probably from δαπανάω, to consume,
devour, tear. What we spend *devours* what we have. For this verb see also on 15:14.
εἰς ἀπαρτισμόν, acc. s. of ἀπαρτισμός*, for completion.

Verses 29, 30

ἐκτελέσαι (occurs once in each verse), aor. infinitive act. of ἐκτελέω* (ἐκ perfective, plus τελέω), to carry out to the very end; hence, to finish.
ἄρξωνται, third per. pl. aor. subjunct. middle (after μήποτε) of ἄρχω.
ἐμπαίζειν, pres. infinitive of ἐμπαίζω, to play like a child (παῖς); hence, to make
sport of, poke fun of.
ἄρξωνται αὐτῷ ἐμπαίζειν. Either "(all the onlookers) poke fun of him," or "begin
to poke fun of him" is possible. In other words, ἄρξωνται may be redundant here,
but this is not certain.

Verse 31

συμβαλεῖν, aor. infinitive (here ingressive), with perfective prefix σύν, of συμβάλλω**. This verb may have the following meanings. The precise sense depends in
each case on the context:

a. to mull over (Luke 2:19; see the note on that passage on page 162).

b. to throw words together (with someone); hence, to converse (Acts 4:15; 17:18).

c. to co-operate, be of assistance, help (Acts 18:27).

d. to fall in with, meet (Acts 20:14).

e. here in Luke 14:31 (with εἰς πόλεμον), to engage in battle, wage war.

ὑπαντῆσαι. Note the two prefixes: ὑπό and ἀντί. As to the first, if any of its former force is left, it probably indicates that the verb it here introduces describes a motion toward a certain goal; cf. our expression "to *under*take something." As to the second, namely, ἀντί, in the present passage (unlike Matt. 8:28; 28:9; Mark 5:2; Luke 8:27, etc., where this prefix indicates local oppositeness; such as coming face to face with someone, *meeting* that person) the reference is definitely to spiritual *opposition, hostility*, as the context indicates. The two kings are confronting each other with the purpose of destroying each other. The form here used is the aor. infinitive of ὑπαντάω, to meet in battle.

Verse 32

πρεσβείαν, acc. s. of πρεσβεία*; in the New Testament occurring only here and in 19:14, delegation, embassy.

Verse 33

ἀποτάσσεται, third per. s. pres. indicat. of ἀποτάσσω, to lay aside, give up, take leave of, say good-bye to. With but little variation in meaning it occurs here and also in Mark 6:46; II Cor. 2:13; for the rest, only in Luke's writings (Luke 9:61; Acts 18:18, 21).

Verse 34

μωρανθῇ, third per. s. aor. subjunct. pass. of μωραίνω, to show to be foolish (I Cor. 1:20), to become fools (Rom. 1:22). Cf. *moron, sophomore*. But here in Luke 14:34 (cf. Matt. 5:13) in the pass., to become tasteless.

ἀρτυθήσεται, third per. s. fut. indicat. pass. of ἀρτύω, to season.

Verse 35

κοπρίαν, acc. s. of κοπρία*, manure pile.

βάλλουσιν. This pl. is probably simply a Semitism. See the note on 12:20 on page 673. For a different explanation see Robertson, *Translation*, Luke, pp. 88, 204.

Summary of Chapter 14

See pp. 538, 539.

Outline of Chapter 15

Theme: *The Work Thou Gavest Him to Do*

CHAPTER XV

15 1 Now the tax-collectors and the sinners were all in the habit of gathering[441] around Jesus in order to hear him. 2 But the Pharisees and the scribes were constantly grumbling, saying, "This fellow welcomes sinners and eats with them!" 3 So he told them this parable:

4 "What man among y o u, if he has a hundred sheep and has lost one of them, does not leave the ninety-nine in the open country and go after the lost sheep until he finds it? 5 And when he has found it, he joyfully puts it on his shoulders, 6 and on reaching home calls together his friends and his neighbors, saying to them, 'Rejoice with me, for I have found my sheep that was lost.' 7 I tell y o u that similarly there will be joy in heaven over one sinner who is converted (more)[442] than over ninety-nine righteous persons who do not need conversion."

15:1-7 *The Parable of The Lost Sheep*
Cf. Matt. 18:12-14

With respect to the connection between this and the preceding chapter see p. 539.

To many people Luke's Gospel is a closed book. But that does not apply in equal measure to such portions as chapter 2; 10:30-37; and chapter 15. Even children will ask to have these sections read to them, or will themselves read them. In the realm of literature there is nothing finer.

The present chapter contains three closely related parables, that of The Lost Sheep, The Lost Coin, and The Lost Son. The second and the third are peculiar to Luke. Of the first Matt. 18:12-14 gives an abbreviated parallel.

The three have one central theme, namely, *The Father's Yearning Love for the Lost.* It is that theme on which the emphasis is placed throughout. The shepherd seeks the one lost sheep. The woman searches carefully until she has found the one lost coin. The father's heart goes out to his lost son. When he sees him, he welcomes him back to his heart and home. We do not need to investigate diligently in order to find the one leading thought. It is there for all to see in verses 7, 10, 20b-24, 32.

Why did Jesus tell these parables in the order: lost sheep, lost coin, lost

---

441. Or: were all gathering.
442. Or: (rather).

son? It has been suggested that the sequence is one of proportion—from the smallest to the largest—as follows:

first parable: one sheep out of a hundred is lost;
second parable: one coin out of ten is lost;
third parable: one son out of two is lost.

But whether this has any significance is not clear. It must be admitted, however, that the parable of The Lost (or Prodigal) Son, being the longest of the three and also the most touching, forms a fitting climax.

1. Now the tax-collectors and the sinners were all in the habit of gathering [or: were all gathering] around Jesus in order to hear him.

As the Pharisees and the scribes saw it, tax-collectors were extortioners and traitors, as has been explained in connection with 3:12. But here and in 5:30; 7:34 these "publicans" are mentioned in one breath with "sinners," that is, all other people of bad reputation, people who did not even try to live in accordance with the standards established by the rabbis. To *associate* with people of this class was considered contaminating; to *eat* with them, outrageous!

Yet Jesus was often seen in their company. He had even selected a tax-collector to be one of The Twelve, and did not hesitate to dine with publicans (5:27–29). Was not this in accordance with his own instructions? See 14:12–14. He associated with publicans and sinners, meeting them on their own level, in order to deliver them from their sinful ways and to raise them to the level of genuine holiness, the holiness required by *God's* law (Lev. 19:2). In reality, therefore, it was Jesus, rather than the rabbis, who was honoring the law.

Tax-collectors and sinners, in turn, were not slow to recognize the contrast between Christ's attitude toward them and that of the Pharisees and scribes. So they regarded Jesus as their Friend and were in the habit of gathering around him *to hear* him, which was exactly what, according to 14:35, they were supposed to do.

2. But the Pharisees and the scribes were constantly grumbling, saying, This fellow welcomes sinners and eats with them.

On a previous occasion these opponents of Jesus had found fault with *his disciples* for eating and drinking with publicans and sinners (5:30). Now, having grown bolder, they criticize Jesus himself for doing this. Contemptuously they refer to him as "this fellow." Clearly they had not taken to heart the lesson Jesus had taught them (5:31, 32). They refused to believe that it was for the very purpose of seeking and saving the lost that he had come into the world (19:10).

3, 4. So he told them this parable: What man among y o u, if he has a hundred sheep and has lost one of them, does not leave the ninety-nine in the open country and go after the lost sheep until he finds it?

In order to expose the terrible mistake the Pharisees, etc., were making and the horrible wrong they were committing, and at the same time to convince them of this, that even now they might turn from their wicked attitude toward those who were in need of compassion and help, Jesus tells this parable.

Since the country through which Jesus was passing was a region where the shepherd tending his sheep was not an unfamiliar sight, Jesus made use of this fact in order to illustrate what, according to God's will, must be done with a lost sheep. Must it be ignored, neglected, despised, as was the attitude of Pharisees toward the people whom they regarded as wayward and lost? Was that the way a good shepherd dealt with a lost sheep?

Besides, many people in the audience—and presumably especially the Pharisees and scribes—were familiar with precious Old Testament passages concerning the shepherd and his sheep; for example: "Jehovah is my shepherd; I shall not lack" (Ps. 23:1); "He will feed his flock like a shepherd; he will gather the lambs in his arms, carry them in his bosom, and will gently lead those that have their young" (Isa. 40:11); "I myself will be the shepherd of my sheep . . . *I will seek that which was lost*" (Ezek. 34:15, 16).

So Jesus says, "What man of y o u, if he has a hundred sheep and has lost one of them, does not . . . go after the lost sheep?" He means, "Every good shepherd would do this." Moreover, his search would not be halfhearted, not merely a token search. No, he would leave behind the ninety-nine and look for that one lost sheep *until he finds it!*

5, 6. And when he has found it, he joyfully puts it on his shoulders, and on reaching home calls together his friends and his neighbors, saying to them, Rejoice with me, for I have found my sheep that was lost.

Even though the search was time-consuming and physically exhausting, once having found his sheep, the shepherd, in typically Mid-Eastern fashion, places it over his two shoulders, with its stomach against the back of his neck, and with its four feet tied together in front of his face.[443] Loaded down thus heavily, he returns to his home in the village. The shepherd rejoices, and this not simply because of the recovery of a physical loss. No, he loves that sheep. His shepherd's heart rejoices because the sheep was not devoured or did not perish in some other way. The shepherd even invites his male friends and neighbors to rejoice with him. Result: a joyous stag party.

And now Jesus makes the application, drives home the parable's one main lesson: **7. I tell y o u that similarly there will be joy in heaven over one sinner who is converted (more) than [or: rather than] over ninety-nine righteous persons who do not need conversion.**

What kind of people did Jesus have in mind when he spoke of those

---

443. K. E. Bailey, *The Cross,* p. 23.

"ninety-nine righteous persons"? See the footnote for views I reject.[444] Several commentators skip the problem entirely.

There can be no question about the fact that the ninety-nine sheep have symbolical significance. They do not merely belong to the fringes of the parable. The words of Jesus, clearly identifying the ninety-nine sheep with the ninety-nine righteous persons (cf. verse 4 with verse 7), cannot be ignored.

In harmony with several other interpreters[445] I am convinced that the meaning of verse 7 is, "I tell y o u that similarly *God* [perhaps also angels— see verse 10—and the redeemed?] will rejoice over one sinner who becomes converted, *and not* over ninety-nine self-righteous people." Undoubtedly, in mentioning the ninety-nine, Jesus was thinking of the Pharisees, scribes, and their followers.

This explanation does justice to the introduction of this parable (verses 1, 2). The ninety-nine sheep represent the grumblers. They were the ones who were erecting the palace of their hope and security on the frail foundation of their own vaunted righteousness (18:9).

The two main objections to this interpretation are easy to answer. The answers will also show why the other interpretations, those summarized in footnote 444, are incorrect.

Objection No. 1. The passage states that there will be *more* joy over one sinner who is converted than over ninety-nine righteous persons, etc. This implies that there must be *some* joy also over the ninety-nine. But this could not be true with reference to Pharisees and scribes. Therefore it must apply to others; such as faithful covenant members, sincere Israelites, or angels.

Answer. The original says no more than this: "There will be joy in heaven over one sinner who becomes converted [or, if one prefers, who repents] than over ninety-nine righteous persons," etc. The word to be supplied

---

444. (a) They are faithful covenant members who have not wandered away from God; e.g., Timothy. These people have already begun to regulate their lives by the standards of the divine law. They need no repentance because they already have it. With respect to them there is "constant, steady joy," while over the others, represented by the one lost sheep that was found, there is a sudden shout of joy; hence "more joy." For this opinion, with minor variations, see Lenski, *op. cit.,* pp. 504, 505; John Calvin, *Harmony,* Vol. II, pp. 341, 342; F. Godet ("sincere Israelites"), *op. cit.,* Vol. II, p. 147; W. P. Van Wyk, *My Sermon Notes on Parables and Metaphors,* Grand Rapids, 1947, p. 79.

(b) They indicate the good angels. Thus W. M. Taylor, *op. cit.,* p. 313.

445. Among them, with minor variations, are the following. All of them either accept the view which I share or lean in this direction:

C. R. Erdman, *op. cit.,* p. 143;

A. Fahling, *op. cit.,* p. 469;

S. Greijdanus, *Korte Verklaring,* Vol. II, p. 56;

A. Plummer, *op. cit.,* p. 369;

A. T. Robertson, *Word Pictures,* Vol. II, p. 206;

J. W. Shepherd, *The Christ of the Gospels,* Grand Rapids, 1946, p. 417;

J. Van Oosterzee, volume on Luke (in *Lang's Commentary on the Holy Scriptures*), Grand Rapids, no date, p. 235.

before "than" can be either "rather" or "more." See also the note on this verse on page 751. If the implied word is "rather," the meaning is that there will be joy in heaven over the convert, *but not* over the ninety-nine. See the explanation of 18:14. But even if here in 15:7 we allow the rendering "more than" to stand, the result is still the same. What we are dealing with here is the same ironic language that is still being used by ourselves and by others. When a teacher tells her pupils, "I am *more* pleased with students who study diligently than with those who have all the answers," she means, "I am pleased with students who study diligently, *but not* with those who refuse to study because they think they know it all."

Jesus used human language just as we do today, with all its nuances and figures of speech. The difference is that what *he* said was always important and always true, a statement which cannot be predicated of our speech.

If we fail to accept this fact, we introduce into our explanation of Christ's words all kinds of strange elements; such as, that heaven is far happier about a sudden convert than about those who serve God all their lives, and also rejoices far more over that sudden convert than it does over the good angels, etc. Is it not strange that, according to Taylor's explanation, of the one hundred sheep, ninety-nine would symbolize angels, and one would refer to a human being? What a mixture, that flock!

Objection No. 2. "Jesus refers to *righteous* persons. The phrase *in their own estimation* is not in the text."

Answer. It does not need to be. In John 9:39 Jesus calls his opponents "those who see." Verses 40, 41 make clear that he had in mind those who think they see, namely, the Pharisees. Similarly, in Luke 5:31 Jesus describes the Pharisees and scribes as "those who are healthy," and in verse 32 he calls them "righteous people." However, the context shows that he was thinking of those who *thought* they were healthy and righteous. They were righteous "in their own estimation." Something very similar happens in Matt. 9:13; Mark 2:17. Jesus had reference to those people who "trusted in themselves that they were righteous and looked down on everybody else" (Luke 18:9).

We have spent sufficient time explaining the ninety-nine. Christ's emphasis, however, was on *the one* that was lost, searched for, found, and cheered. Even more emphatically, what Jesus is saying is this: if even a human shepherd will leave the ninety-nine to find the one sheep that was lost, how much more will the Great Shepherd do *to seek and reclaim* the lost sinner! And how much greater will be his joy!

Implied in all this is the thought: should not y o u, Pharisees and scribes, imitate God in this respect and try to find and restore the lost? Would not that course of action be much better than to keep yourselves at a distance from "publicans and sinners" and to despise them? For The Twelve too this was a valuable lesson. And for the people of low reputation it was an encouragement. Besides, the illustration is unforgettable.

For *Practical Lessons* and *Greek Words*, etc., see pp. 749-751.

---

8 "Or what woman, if she has ten silver coins[446] and loses one coin, does not light a lamp and sweep the house and search carefully until she finds it? 9 And when she has found it, she calls in the other women: her friends and neighbors, and says, 'Celebrate with me, for I have found the coin I lost.' 10 Similarly, I tell y o u, there is joy in the presence of the angels of God over one sinner who is converted."

15:8-10 *The Parable of The Lost Coin*

Here we are introduced to peasant life: **8. Or what woman, if she has ten silver coins and loses one coin, does not light a lamp and sweep the house and search carefully until she finds it?**

The silver coin here mentioned, like the Roman denarius, amounted to a day's wages for a common laborer (Matt. 20:2). The woman may have worn the ten drachmas on a chain around her neck, or, more likely, she may have tied them up in a little rag. The chain may have broken or the knot may have worked loose, with the result in either case that she lost one of her coins.

The home of a person of the poorer classes, such as this woman, was generally small. It had a dirt floor and either no windows or very small ones. Therefore, once the coin had slipped out and fallen to the floor it was not easy to find.

So, because the house was rather dark she lights a lamp and starts sweeping. She sweeps every nook and cranny of the house and . . . there it is! She finds it. What a joy!

9. And when she has found it, she calls in the other women: her friends and neighbors, and says, Celebrate with me, for I have found the coin I lost.

How these women celebrate! Over and over again the woman who lost the coin and found it again recounts all the details of what actually happened. In the preceding parable the *men* were celebrating; here the *women*.

What is the meaning of all this? I have come across the following "explanations":

a. The woman symbolizes the Holy Spirit. A process of logical elimination leads some expositors to this conclusion. There are three Persons in the Trinity. The *second* Person, the Son, has already been symbolized, namely, in the parable of The Lost Sheep. Is not Jesus the Good Shepherd? The *first* Person is clearly represented by "the father" in the parable of The Lost (or Prodigal) Son (verses 11-32). Only the Holy Spirit, the *third* Person, is left. Therefore the woman in the second of the three parables of chapter 15 must symbolize the Holy Spirit.

---

446. Literally: ten drachmas.

Not all agree, however. For example, Lenski (*op. cit.,* p. 506) does not hesitate a moment to make the woman a symbol of the Church.

b. The lamp indicates the gospel.

c. The broom—yes, even the broom is not spared!—signifies the law, so we are told.

As to myself, I cannot find any of this in the parable. I believe that the one and only point, the central lesson, of the parable is indicated by Jesus himself when he brings the parable to a beautiful and very comforting conclusion with these words:

10. Similarly, I tell y o u, there is joy in the presence of the angels of God over one sinner who is converted.

Does this passage mean that the angels rejoice when a sinner is converted? There can be no question about the fact that God's holy angels take a deep interest in our salvation. See Matt. 18:10; 25:31; Luke 2:10–14; I Cor. 13:1; I Peter 1:12; Rev. 3:5; 5:11; 14:10. They may know more about it than we imagine, for they dwell in God's immediate presence. Hence, their rejoicing over a sinner's conversion must not be ruled out.

But that is not exactly the teaching of our passage; at least, that is not its main point. That main point is this: God, who has his dwelling in the presence of the angels, *seeks sinners,* and *rejoices* over even *one* of them who repents or is converted. So, should not y o u, Pharisees and scribes, be concerned about those people y o u now despise? Should y o u not do all in y o u r power to help them?

On the subject of God's deep interest in sinners and his joy in their conversion and salvation see also the following beautiful passages: Isa. 62:5; Jer. 7:13 (and its many parallels in that book); 32:41; Ezek. 18:23, 32; 33:11; Hos. 11:8; Zeph. 3:17; John 3:16; Rom. 5:6–11; 8:32; II Peter 3:9.[447]

Practical Lessons Derived from Luke 15:1–10

Verse 2

"This fellow welcomes sinners and eats with them." From the point of view of the Pharisees the situation was even worse; and from the point of view of faith, even better, as will become clear. There are at least four different attitudes one can assume toward the lost:

a. hating them

b. regarding them with indifference

c. welcoming them when they come to you

d. seeking them.

The Pharisees were accusing Jesus of being "guilty" (as they saw it) of (c). Actu-

---

447. Notes on Greek words, phrases, and constructions in 15:1–10 begin on page 750.

ally Jesus not only *welcomed* sinners (c) but even *sought* them (19:10; cf. 19:5; Matt. 14:14; 18:12-14; John 4:4 f.; 10:16).

> I sought the Lord, and afterward I knew
> He moved my soul to seek him, seeking me;
> It was not I that found, O Savior true,
> No, I was found, was found of thee.

> Anonymous

Verse 4

"Until he finds it."

Many years ago someone signed up for a correspondence course. He had to pay in advance. Upon completing the course and receiving his diploma, he asked those who gave the course, "How is it that you are able to charge so little for this course? You must have lost money on it." The answer came back, "Because so few complete it." It is comforting to know that our Great Shepherd never stops seeking his sheep *until he finds it* (Phil. 1:6).

Verses 6, 9, 32

In each case the one who finds shares his joy with others. There is a fellowship of rejoicing. Cf. Phil. 2:17; II Tim. 4:7, 8.

Notes on Greek Words, Phrases, and Constructions in 15:1-10

Verse 1

Ἦσαν ... ἐγγίζοντες, third per. pl. periphrastic imperf. indicat. of ἐγγίζω, to draw near to, come to, gather around. The tense here employed may mean either: (a) that the tax-collectors and the sinners were *at a particular occasion* coming to Jesus, or (b) that they were *in the habit* of doing this. With A. B. Bruce (*Expositor's Greek Testament,* Vol. I, p. 577) I leave room for both views, though with Calvin (*Harmony,* Vol. II, p. 340) and Godet (*op. cit.,* Vol. II, p. 143) I agree that the second theory probably deserves the preference.

Forms of ἀπόλλυμι in verses 4–32

The verb ἀπόλλυμι, which in various forms occurs repeatedly in this chapter, is derived from ἀπό plus ὄλλυμι; hence, basically means: to destroy completely. As is true of prefixes generally, the full force of ἀπό is not always in evidence. In the New Testament ἀπόλλυμι, *act.,* has such meanings as: to destroy, put to death, kill, ruin, lose; *middle:* to be destroyed, to be killed, to perish, die, be lost, pass away. Etymological relationship between ἀπόλλυμι and the English word *abolish* has not been firmly established. On the other hand, *Apollyon* (Rev. 9:11) is definitely related, and means *Destroyer.*

1. ἀπολέσας (verse 4a), nom. s. masc. aor. act. participle: "having lost."

2, 3. τὸ ἀπολωλός (verses 4b, 6), acc. s. neut. 2nd perf. participle: the lost (sheep), the sheep that was lost.

4. ἀπολέσῃ (verse 8), third per. s. aor. subjunct. act. (after ἐάν): "if she loses."

5. ἀπώλεσα (verse 9), first per. aor. indicat. act.: "I lost."

6. ἀπόλλυμαι (verse 17), first per. s. pres. (linear) indicat. middle: "I am perishing."

7, 8. ἦν ἀπολωλώς (verses 24, 32), third per. s. periphrastic (intensive) past perf., expressing existing state in the past: "he was lost." Cf. Gram. N.T., p. 904.

Verses 4–32 (from here on minus ἀπόλλυμι forms)

For εὑρίσκω see the note on 1:30 on page 92. Note the following forms of this verb in chapter 15:

εὕρῃ, third per. s. aor. subjunct. act. (after ἕως), verses 4, 8.

εὑρών, nom. masc. s. 2nd aor. act. participle, verse 5.

εὑροῦσα, same, except fem., verse 9.

εὗρον, first per. s. aor. indicat. act., verses 6, 9.

εὑρέθη, third per. aor. indicat. pass., verses 24, 32.

ὤμους, acc. pl. of ὦμος, shoulder, in the New Testament occurring only here and in Matt. 23:4. Cf. *humerus*.

Verse 6

Note both in verse 6 and verse 9 συγκαλεῖ (*he or she calls together*, except for Mark 15:16 in the New Testament confined to Luke's writings), and συγχάρητέ μοι (*rejoice with me*, found also in Luke 1:58; I Cor. 12:26; 13:6; Phil. 2:17, 18).

Verse 7

ἤ, a particle indicating comparison, but here (and also in 17:2 and I Cor. 14:19) occurring without preceding comparative. Meaning "more than" or perhaps "rather than."

Verses 8, 9

δραχμάς, acc. pl. of δραχμή*, drachma, a Greek silver coin, about equal in value to the Roman denarius, a common laborer's daily wage. Note acc. pl. in verse 8, and acc. s. in both verses. See Matt. 17:24 for "double drachma."

σαροῖ, third per. s. pres. indicat. act. of σαρόω (for earlier σαίρω), to sweep. See also the note on 11:25 on page 634.

---

11 And he said, "A certain man had two sons. 12 Now the younger of them said to his father, 'Father, give me my share of the estate.' So he divided his property between them. 13 "Not many days afterward the younger son gathered all he had and went away to a distant country, and there he squandered his wealth by living extravagantly. 14 When he had spent everything, a severe famine arose throughout that country, and he began to be in need. 15 So he went and hired himself out to[448] a citizen of that country, who sent him into his fields to feed pigs. 16 And he was longing to fill his stomach with the carob pods which the pigs were eating, but no one was giving anything to him. 17 "But when he came to his senses he said, 'How many of my father's hired men have more than they can eat, and here I am dying of hunger! 18 I will arise and go to my father, and I

---

448. Or: attached himself to.

will say to him, Father, I have sinned against heaven and in your sight. 19 I am no longer worthy to be called your son; make me as one of your hired men.' 20 So he arose and went to his father.

"But while he was still a long way off, his father saw him, and his heart went out to him. The father ran, threw his arms around his son's neck, and kissed him fervently. 21 And the son said to him, 'Father, I have sinned against heaven and in your sight; I am no longer worthy to be called your son.'[449]

22 "But the father said to his servants, 'Quickly bring a robe, the best one, and put it on him. Put a ring on his hand and sandals on his feet. 23 Bring on the fattened calf and kill it, and let's eat and celebrate, 24 because this son of mine was dead and is alive again; he was lost, and is found.' And they began to celebrate.

25 "Meanwhile his older son was in the field. And as he was returning and approaching the house, he heard music and dancing. 26 And having called one of the servant boys to him, he began to inquire what this could be. 27 So he told him, 'Your brother has arrived, and your father has killed the fattened calf because he has received him back safe and sound.'

28 "But the older brother became angry and refused to go inside. Then his father came outside and began to plead with him.[450] 29 However, he answered and said to his father, 'Look, these many years I've been slaving for you, and never did I disobey your command; yet to me you never gave (even) a young goat, so I could celebrate with my friends. 30 But when this son of yours, who devoured your property with prostitutes, came home, for him you killed the fattened calf.'

31 "'My child,' the father answered, 'you're always with me, and all that is mine is yours. 32 But we just had to celebrate and rejoice, because this brother of yours was dead and is alive; he was lost, and is found.'"

15:11-32 *The Parable of The Lost Son*

A. *His Departure from Home*

The general theme "The Father's Yearning Love for the Lost," a theme which, as has been pointed out, covers all three parables, continues; in fact, now more conspicuously than ever.

11, 12. And he said, A certain man had two sons. Now the younger of them said to his father, Father, give me my share of the estate. So he divided his property between them.

The younger of the two sons became tired of staying at home. As has been the case with certain young people ever since (and the situation is deplorable even today), this young man desired to be free from parental restraint. He was convinced that being by himself, away from the eyes of his parents (though the mother is never mentioned in this parable), he would be able to do whatever he wanted, and this "freedom" would make him happy.

Of course, to carry out his plan he needed money. He probably knew that according to the law of Deut. 21:17 one-third of the parental estate would be his when his father died. But he wanted that portion *now*. He could not wait.

---

449. 'Make me like one of your hired men' is found in some manuscripts; a few of them early. It is probably unauthentic, merely copied from verse 19.

450. Or: kept urging him.

Now it must be granted that a father did at times make "gifts" to his children while he was still alive (Gen. 25:6), but this young man was not satisfied with a mere gift. He wanted his entire portion, and he wanted it here and now.

Entirely aside from the fact that in all probability this meant that the entire estate had to be broken up—a considerable portion of the holdings sold and converted into cash—and that as a result whatever was left would be seriously affected, did he at all consider how what he was doing would grieve his father? What an insult it was to him? As if the young man's "freedom" would actually be better for him than the loving care and advice he was constantly receiving from his father at home!

But, sorely as the unreasonable request must have grieved the father, he gave in, so that one-third of the property, converted into cash, was given to the younger son, leaving two-thirds for the older one, who, however, did not take actual possession until the father's death.

13. Not many days afterward the younger son gathered all he had and went away to a distant country . . .

We are told at times that what this young man did was not at all unusual. Is it not true that ever so many Jews were moving away from their own country, so that, while only about half a million remained in Palestine, four million were living in the Diaspora? Granted, but what we have in our parable is not the case of a *family* moving away but of a conceited young man moving away from his family. Note also "into a *distant* country!" Apparently as far away from his home as he dared to go. Does not this folly remind one of the prophet Jonah who seems to have thought that by boarding a ship for Tarshish he could get away from God?

B. *His Life Abroad*

Continued: **and there he squandered his wealth by living extravagantly.** How utterly foolish this conduct of his! First he gathered "all he had," leaving nothing behind in case his plan should not work out and he should wish to return home; and now, in addition, he spent money right and left until in no time there was nothing left.

But things went from bad to worse: **14. When he had spent everything, a severe famine arose throughout that country, and he began to be in need.**

His money is gone; the famine arrives. Moreover, this new disaster has struck not only the *place* where he happened to be living at that time, but the entire *country!* He himself had nothing left and he could not expect help from anyone else.

15. So he went and hired himself out to a citizen of that country, who sent him into his fields to feed pigs.

A *Jew* feeding *pigs*, unclean animals (Lev. 11:7), how degrading! How *humiliating!* Was not this saying current among the Jews: "May a curse come upon the man who cares for swine"?

16. And he was longing to fill his stomach with the carob pods which the pigs were eating, but no one was giving anything to him.

Hunger was added to *humiliation*. He was hungry all the time, as the original implies, so hungry that his stomach was aching for something, just anything, to eat. Hornlike pods of the carob tree were being devoured by the pigs. He yearned to eat some of this food himself. We ask, "Well, why did he not take it?" We do not know. It has been suggested[451] that though he himself *tended* the animals while they were in the field (see verse 15), they *were fed* by others after returning from the field. However that may be, we are definitely told that no one gave anything to him. Did he steal enough to keep alive?

And now to *humiliation* and *hunger* there is added *homesickness:*

17. But when he came to his senses he said, How many of my father's hired men have more than they can eat, and here I am dying of hunger!

In the midst of his misery this young man begins to think of the home he left. Literally the original says, "When he came to *himself*," that is, when he began to reflect on all that had happened since he left home, and on the question whether he *himself* was not, perhaps, to blame for what he was undergoing. Serious and perhaps prolonged meditation resulted in his awakening to the fact that even the condition of his father's "hired men" was far better than his own condition.

Note this term *hired men*. In the Near East one does not *hire* a teacher or an engineer. In fact, one does not even *hire* a regular full-time servant. One hires a day-laborer.[452] Well, even these hired men have plenty to eat and to spare. He himself is starving to death. And all this owing to his own foolish and sinful departure from home!

Continued: **18, 19. I will arise and go to my father, and I will say to him, Father, I have sinned against heaven and in your sight. I am no longer worthy to be called your son; make me as one of your hired men.**

Though I respect K. E. Bailey's works, I differ with him here. I believe that the prodigal's confession was not shallow, and that it meant more than an expression of sorrow for money lost, and a request that he might be accepted as a hired servant, so as not to be eating his brother's bread. See his *The Cross*, pp. 46–50; *P & P.*, pp. 174–180.

My own interpretation of the prodigal's confession is as follows:

He arrives at the conclusion that his decision to leave home was what? Simply unwise? A practical error? No, definitely a *sin*, nothing less. A sin committed against whom? Against his father? Well, first and most of all against "heaven," that is, "against God" (Hebrews often substituted the word *heaven* for God). It was God who had given him a wonderful, kind, and loving father; hence "against heaven" and "in your sight" (or: against you).

He now realizes how ungrateful and selfish he has been. No longer has

---

451. By S. Greijdanus, *Korte Verklaring*, Vol. II, p. 61.
452. See K. E. Bailey, *The Cross*, pp. 46, 47.

he a right to be called a son. He will go to his father and tell him, "I have sinned . . . make me as one of your hired men."

What a *change* in this young man. How penitent he has become.

C. *His Return*

1. *Warmly welcomed by his father*

20. So he arose and went to his father.

Many pious resolutions are never carried out. This young man did what he had resolved to do. He started out and kept going. It must have been a long journey, for he had gone to a distant country (verse 13). Moreover, in his weakened condition the return trip must have been difficult. But he persevered.

Continued: **But while he was still a long way off, his father saw him, and his heart went out to him. The father ran, threw his arms around his son's neck, and kissed him fervently.**

It is clear that the father had never lost interest in his wayward son. Again and again he must have been on the lookout for him. And now . . . there he sees him in the distance. What does the father do? Each of his four actions deserves comment: he sympathizes deeply, runs, embraces, and kisses. And all this before the son has even said a word! Such marvelous love!

a. He sympathizes. I can think of no better rendering than "his heart went out to him." As the distance between father and son diminishes, the former sees more and more clearly how tired and wretched his son is looking. He pities him. He interprets the return of "his boy" in the most favorable sense: the lad has repented. He is sorry for what he has done. How intensely this father loves his son. Shall we say, "Now, more than ever"?

b. He runs. The father cannot have been very young anymore; yet, he runs. In that part of the world it was generally not considered dignified for an elderly man to run; yet, he runs. Nothing can keep him from doing so.

c. He throws his arms around his son's neck. Passionately he embraces his son. Does not this very fact indicate that the father has already in his heart granted forgiveness to his son?

d. He kisses him again and again, tenderly, fervently.

21. And the son said to him, Father, I have sinned against heaven and in your sight; I am no longer worthy to be called your son.

That is what the son had intended to say. But he had also intended to say even more, namely, "Make me as one of your hired men" (verse 19). He never said it. The father never gave him a chance to say it. Marvelous!

22-24. But the father said to his servants, Quickly bring a robe, the best one, and put it on him. Put a ring on his hand and sandals on his feet. Bring on the fattened calf and kill it, and let's eat and celebrate . . .

Note these brisk commands. So boundless is the father's joy and so all-out his forgiveness that he wishes to have his son treated as an important person. Therefore his servants must bring the *best* robe, a status symbol, and they must put it on him. On his hand they must put a ring, probably a signet ring (Gen. 41:42), an indication of authority. Sandals must be tied on his feet, for he is not a slave but a freeman. There was also a fattened calf, intended to be slaughtered for some special occasion when important guests were expected. Well, could there be a more appropriate occasion for the use of this calf than right now? Of course not. So the father orders it killed that there may be a jubilant celebration.

The father states the reason for the celebration in these words: **because this son of mine was dead and is alive again; he was lost, and is found.** The four words: dead, alive; lost, found—note the sharp double contrast—must be interpreted in a spiritual sense, of course. See Eph. 2:1 and Luke 19:10 (in that order).

The father's orders were obeyed, with the result: **and they began to celebrate.**

2. *Petulantly rejected by his brother*

25–27. Meanwhile his older son was in the field. And as he was returning and approaching the house, he heard music and dancing. And having called one of the servant boys to him, he began to inquire what this could be. So he told him, Your brother has arrived, and your father has killed the fattened calf because he has received him back safe and sound.

For the theory according to which verses 25–32 did not originally belong to this parable there is no evidence whatever. Nor is there the least bit of proof for the notion that a second parable begins at this point. Anyone who reflects for a moment on the reason for this parable (see verses 1, 2, 7, 10) will understand why these closing verses were necessary. To bring out the meaning of his story illustration Jesus wanted to make clear that the penitent son, though warmly welcomed back by his father, was rejected by his brother. How terrible such a rejection!

While the party is in progress, the older son comes in from his work on the farm. He hears music and the rhythmic sound of dancing feet. The noise is coming from the house. And *he* does not know anything about it! His suspicion is aroused. He asks a servant, "What's happening?" Undoubtedly the servant congratulates himself on the fact that to him has been accorded the privilege of being the one who can impart the electrifying news to the inquirer. Full of enthusiasm he shouts, "Your brother has arrived, and your father has killed the fattened calf because he has received him back safe and sound."

Note "your brother." That was correct; cf. verse 32. However, as will appear in a moment, the older brother does not at all appreciate hearing these two words. Even less does he appreciate the news in general.

28–30. But the older brother became angry and refused to go inside. Then his father came outside and began to plead with him. However, he

answered and said to his father, Look, these many years I've been slaving for you, and never did I disobey your command; yet to me you never gave (even) a young goat, so I could celebrate with my friends. But when this son of yours, who devoured your property with prostitutes, came home, for him you killed the fattened calf!

Several items require attention:

a. Note forward position of "to me" and "for him," for emphasis.

b. Though in his anger the older brother refused to enter the house, his father graciously leaves the house to talk to him. Cf. Gen. 4:6, 7.

c. "I've been slaving for you." That was the spirit in which this grouch had been doing his work all these years. No wonder he was unhappy.

d. "Never did I disobey your command." He is self-righteous through and through, and apparently does not realize that more than merely outward obedience is expected of a son.

e. "Yet to me you never gave," etc. Not only had two-thirds of the estate already been assigned to him, but also his father would have been happy to grant him anything reasonable.

f. Note the derisive epithet "this son of yours," instead of "my brother."

g. "who devoured your property." That was untrue, for the money had been given to him as his share of the inheritance.

h. "with prostitutes [or harlots]." This was slander.

31, 32. My child, the father answered, you're always with me, and all that is mine is yours. But we just had to celebrate and rejoice, because this brother of yours was dead and is alive; he was lost, and is found.

Note how tenderly the father treats also *this* son. He addresses him as "My child." By saying, "All that is mine is yours," he confirms the division of the estate agreed on earlier (verse 12). All the same, he does not end the celebration. Instead of admitting that it was wrong or unwise, he does the very opposite. He tells his son, "We just had to celebrate." In other words, to celebrate was a must. It was the only right and proper thing to do.

Over against "this son of yours," the expression used by the older son (verse 30), the father places "this brother of yours," thus reminding the self-righteous son that the one who returned was still his brother and should be treated as such. And he repeats what he had said earlier to the servants, namely, that the one who had been dead was now alive, and that the one who had been lost was now found.

Beautifully Jesus does not tell us what became of these two sons. He wants us to see them reflected in our own lives, so that we will all draw the proper lesson from this parable.

What, then, is the central lesson? Clearly the father symbolizes the heavenly Father, representing the Holy Trinity, God in all his yearning love. The lost son in his penitent return indicates the penitent sinner; hence, certainly also "the publicans and sinners" who had found in Jesus their Savior and Friend, and were now eagerly listening to him. And the older son clearly points to the self-righteous Pharisees and scribes, just as did also the ninety-nine sheep of the first parable. The central theme is, therefore, "The Father's Yearning Love for the Lost." The Father seeks them, brings them back and rejoices in their Spirit-wrought conversion. That is the thrust of all three parables.

How marvelously they describe who God really is, and also what he wants us to be and to do. And it should ever be borne in mind that if Jesus had not himself been the very image of the Father, he could never have composed this unforgettably touching series of parables. They should make it easier for every sinner to surrender his heart to God. Also, they should make it easier for everyone to see what should be done about those lost in sin.[453]

Practical Lessons Derived from Luke 15:11-32

Verses 20-24

"Quickly bring a robe, the best one," etc. Note the intensity of the joy resulting from the successful search. Add similar passages such as Isa. 5:1-4; 55:6, 7; Ezek. 18:23, 32; 33:11; Hos. 11:8; Matt. 11:28-30; John 7:37; 13:1. Is not the material found in Luke 15, as well as that contained in the references mentioned just now, very suitable for meditation during the week previous to the celebration of the Lord's Supper, or on the very Sunday of communion?

One of the lessons taught in this chapter is surely this, that without conversion there is no salvation.

But *the main* point is surely:

> In tenderness he sought me, weary and sick with sin,
> And on his shoulders brought me back to his fold again,
> While angels in his presence sang
> Until the courts of heaven rang.
> Oh, tbe love that sought me! Oh, the blood that bought me!
> Oh, the grace that brought me to the fold,
> Wondrous grace that brought me to the fold!

> W. Spencer Walton

Notes on Greek Words, Phrases, and Constructions in 15:11-32

Verse 12

ἐπιβάλλον, acc. s. neut. pres. (futuristic) participle of ἐπιβάλλω: "the portion of the estate *that is falling* to me," or less literally, "my share of the estate."

This is perhaps as good a place as any to show how verbs, while always retaining at least a trace of their original or basic sense, will branch out into various shades of meaning. Various meanings of the verb ἐπιβάλλω are shown in the chart on the opposite page.

---

453. Notes on Greek words, phrases, and constructions in 15:11-32 begin on this page.

Classification of the Meaning of the Verb ἐπιβάλλω in the New Testament

	lay [hands] on, seize	put a patch on	dash into	lay [their garments] on	reflect on (?)	fall to	put [one's hand] to	throw [a noose] over	throw [dust] on
Matt.	26:50	9:16							
Mark	14:46		4:37	11:7	14:72 (uncertain) See N.T.C. on Mark				
Luke	20:19 21:12	5:36				15:12	9:62		
John	7:30 7:44								
Acts	4:3 5:18 12:1 21:27								
1 Cor.								7:35	
Rev.									18:19

διεῖλεν, third per. s. 2nd aor. indicat. act. of διαιρέω, to divide; so also in I Cor. 12:11.

βίον, acc. s. of βίος, life; but here and in verse 30 *means of living, substance, property.* For the distinction between βίος and ζωή see R. C. Trench, *Synonyms of the New Testament,* par. xxvii; also N.T.C. on Mark, footnote 612 on pp. 507, 508.

Verse 13

For "not many days afterward" see also Acts 1:5.

ἀπεδήμησεν, third per. s. aor. indicat. of ἀποδημέω, to travel away from one's δῆμος, people, country. Cf. 20:9; also Matt. 21:33; 25:14, 15; Mark 12:1.

διεσκόρπισεν, same construction as the preceding verb; basically *to scatter* (here: his property), and to do so διά, all around; hence, to squander, waste. This verb also occurs in Luke 1:51; 16:1; and in Matt. 25:24, 26; 26:31; Mark 14:27; John 11:52; Acts 5:37, though not always in exactly the same sense.

ἀσώτως*. Perhaps basically this adverb marks the action of someone who, if he so continues, *cannot be saved* (ἀ plus σώζω). Another interpretation that has been suggested is that it characterizes the person who *cannot save.* It should be borne in mind, however, that although derivations and word histories are helpful since they shed some light on meanings, *actual use of a word in a given context* is far more important. The context in the present case proves that the younger son was living *extravagantly.* He squandered his wealth. In a dissolute, unrestrained manner he allowed his impulses to exercise control over himself. Good translations of the adverb are: extravagantly, recklessly, dissolutely.

Verse 14

Note gen. absolute δαπανήσαντος αὐτοῦ. The aor. participle is from δαπανάω, to spend; cf. Mark 5:26; Acts 21:24; II Cor. 12:15; James 4:3; and for the cognate noun δαπάνη see the note on 14:28 on page 739.

ὑστερεῖσθαι, pres. middle and pass. infinitive of ὑστερέω, to be or fall behind, be in need, to lack (Matt. 19:20; Mark 10:21; Luke 22:35; Phil. 4:12).

Verse 15

ἐκολλήθη, third per. s. aor. indicat. pass. of κολλάω, for which see the note on 10:11 on page 587. Meaning: he "glued" or attached himself to, hired himself out to.

πολιτῶν, gen. pl. of πολίτης, citizen. See also 19:14; Acts 21:39; Heb. 8:11. The word is derived from πόλις, city, town. Cf. *political.*

βόσκειν, pres. (continuative) infinitive: day in, day out he was feeding the swine.

Verse 16

ἐπεθύμει. Some call this imperf. (of ἐπιθυμέω) inchoative or ingressive: he began to crave. But another possibility is *he was craving* or *longing.* In fact, the *descriptive* or *progressive* imperfect fits beautifully into this context. This verb is used by *Luke* (in addition to the present passage see also 16:21; 17:22; 22:15; Acts 20:33); by his companion *Paul* (Rom. 7:7; 13:9; I Cor. 10:6; Gal. 5:17; I Tim. 3:1); and, for the rest of the New Testament, only twice by *Matthew* (5:28; 13:17) and once each by *the author of Hebrews* (6:11), and by *James* (4:2), *Peter* (I Peter 1:12), and *John* (Rev. 9:6). For a word study of the cognate noun ἐπιθυμία see N.T.C. on I and II Timothy and Titus, pp. 271, 272, footnote 147.

For χορτασθῆναι, aor. pass. infinitive of χορτάζω see the note on 6:21 on page 345.

κερατίων, gen. pl. of κεράτιον*, little horn; hence pod (resembling a little horn) of the carob tree.

οὐδεὶς ἐδίδου. Note imperf. tense: no one was giving.

Verse 17

μίσθιοι, nom. pl. masc. of μίσθιος*, hired servant; cf. μισθός, pay, wages. For gen. pl. of μίσθιος see verse 19.

περισσεύονται, lit. "they abound in bread [or bread-cakes]." They are, as it were, surrounded and engulfed by this commodity. They have bread enough and to spare, far more than they can eat.

Verse 20

Note gen. absolute αὐτοῦ μακρὰν ἀπέχοντος, "while he [the son] was . . . a long way off."

ἐσπλαγχνίσθη, third per. s. aor. indicat. pass. of σπλαγχνίζομαι; see the note on 7:13 on page 390, and N.T.C. on Philippians, footnote 39 on p. 58. The father "was filled with compassion"; or, perhaps even better, "the father's heart went out to him."

δραμών, used as nom. s. masc. 2nd aor. participle of τρέχω, to run. Cf. *dromedary.*

τράχηλον, acc. s. of τράχηλος, neck. Cf. *trachea,* the (rough, cf. Luke 3:5) windpipe.

κατεφίλησεν, kissed (him) fervently, eagerly, tenderly, repeatedly; perfective force of κατά.

Verse 21

The words, "Make me like one of your hired men," are probably not authentic here. Did a scribe mistakenly insert them, wishing to create complete harmony between the proposed speech (verses 18, 19) and the actual one (here in verse 21)?

Verse 22

στολήν, acc. s. of στολή, robe. This noun also occurs in 20:46; in Mark 12:38; 16:5, and in several passages of the book of Revelation. Basically such a robe is a long flowing outer garment, going down all the way to the feet. Though the English rendering "stole" would not be wrong, this word is rather ambiguous, since it can also denote the narrow cloth band which priests and bishops wear around their neck, and which descends from their shoulder. In fact, the English word can even mean an article of feminine apparel: a long wide scarf.

τὴν πρώτην, the first, here *in quality;* hence, the best.

δακτύλιον, acc. s. of δακτύλιος*, ring. Cf. δάκτυλος, finger. See the note on 11:20 on page 633.

Verses 23, 24

μόσχον, acc. s. of μόσχος (see also verses 27 and 30; Heb. 9:12, 19; Rev. 4:7). The etymological derivation of this word is disputed. It seems to refer basically to a young shoot or twig, and so also to the young or offspring of men, and, as here, of animals; hence, calf, heifer, bullock.

σιτευτόν*, verbal adj. of σιτεύω, to feed with wheat; hence, to fatten. We have already met σῖτος in 3:17; 12:18; and will meet it again in 16:7; 22:31.

τὸν μόσχον τὸν σιτευτόν, accordingly, means "the fattened calf."

θύσατε, sec. per. pl. imperat. act. of θύω, *not* here in the more usual sense *to sacrifice* (Mark 14:12; Luke 22:7; Acts 14:13, 18) but in the sense *to kill.* So also in verse 27.

Note the following words, all based on the verb εὐφραίνω: pass. to be merry, rejoice in, celebrate (derived from εὖ, well, and φρήν, mind). It is a verb which in this Gospel we have met first in 12:19, and will meet again in 16:19, and which also occurs in Acts 2:26; 7:41; Rom. 15:10; II Cor. 2:2; Gal. 4:27; Rev. 11:10; 12:12; 18:20:

εὐφρανθῶμεν, first per. pl. aor. subjunct. pass., verse 23, "let's celebrate."

εὐφραίνεσθαι, pres. middle infinitive after ἤρξαντο, verse 24, "to celebrate."

εὐφρανθῶ, first per. s. aor. subjunct. (after ἵνα) pass., verse 29, "(so) I could celebrate."

εὐφρανθῆναι, aor. pass. infinitive (in thought after ἔδει), verse 32, "to celebrate."

ἀνέζησεν, third per. s. aor. indicat. of ἀναζάω, to come to life, be alive again, "and is alive again," verse 24.

Verse 25

συμφωνίας, gen. of συμφωνία (σύν, together or in harmony with, plus φωνή, sound; hence, sound-harmony), music. Cf. *symphony.*

χορῶν, gen. pl. of χορός*, dancing (accompanied by music). Cf. *chorus, choir.*

Verse 26

ἐπυνθάνετο, third per. s. imperf. (probably inchoative) of πυνθάνομαι, to inquire, investigate; in Acts 23:34 to ascertain in answer to inquiry, to understand.

τί ἂν εἴη, third per. s. pres. optat. of εἰμί, the form of the direct question retained in the indirect. On Luke's use of the optative, an indication of his "deferential style" (Moulton), and on the optative in general, see Robertson's excellent discussion (Gram. N.T., pp. 320, 325–327, 935–940, 1044).

Verse 27

Although ἥκει, strictly speaking, is in the pres. tense (third per. s. indicat. act.), it has the meaning of a perfect and must be rendered "has arrived" or "has come."

Note the third per. s. aor. indicat. actives ἔθυσεν and ἀπέλαβεν, in English probably best rendered "has killed" and "has received (him) back."

ὑγιαίνοντα, acc. s. masc. pres. act. participle of ὑγιαίνω, to be in health, safe and sound, hale and hearty. Cf. *hygiene.*

Verse 28

Note the ingressive imperfect ὠργίσθη, he became angry, and see the note on 14:21 on page 739. Note the three vivid imperfects: the older brother *became angry, was not willing* (hence, *refused*) to enter, and his father . . . either *began to plead* with him, or *kept urging* him.

Verse 29

δουλεύω, first per. s. pres. (continuative or progressive; cf. δοῦλος, slave), to work like a slave, to slave.

παρῆλθον, first per. s. 2nd aor. indicat. of παρέρχομαι, basically *to come to the side of;* hence, simply *to come, pass by,* and so *disappear;* also, in a more figurative sense: *to bypass,* ignore, neglect, disregard, and so (as here) *disobey.* All these meanings are closely related. But one never really understands a word without taking time to live with it for a little while. Then, how interesting it becomes! Note how this Greek verb develops from one meaning to another:

For the basic sense, "to arrive by the side of" or simply "to come," see Luke 12:37, *having come,* or: *at his coming.* Here also belongs Luke 17:7, "Come at once."

True to this etymological sense are also such passages as Matt. 8:28, "No one could pass by along that road"; Mark 6:48, "He was about to pass them by"; Luke 18:37, "Jesus of Nazareth is passing by"; and perhaps even the controversial Acts 16:8. By L.N.T. (A. and G.), p. 631, the verb, as used in that passage, is interpreted as meaning "through." Reason given for this view is that "passing by" is impossible in this case. But is it really? Does not the theory merit consideration that here, as frequently, we are dealing with "abbreviated expression" (see N.T.C. on John, Vol. I, p. 206), the meaning fully spelled out being "in going through they passed by (Mysia)"; i.e., without stopping to do evangelistic work there they headed straight for Troas?

The line of demarcation between the literal and the figurative sense is at times almost invisible. We speak of *people* passing by. Can we not also think of *things* passing by? For example *time?* It may be conceived as coming to us out of the past, stopping for a very brief moment and then departing again until it seems to have vanished. Luke mentions the Fast—that is, the Day of Atonement—as having *gone by* (Acts 27:9). The disciples tell Jesus, "The time has gone by; that is, it is already late in the day" (Matt. 14:15). Peter also speaks of time that has gone by (I Peter 4:3).

So also *suffering* can be conceived of as an entity that passes by, preferably without touching us. Such passages as Matt. 26:39, 42; Mark 14:35, "Let this cup pass me by"; i.e., "Let it be spared me," fall under this category.

When a vehicle has passed by, it finally becomes a mere speck, has no longer any significance for us. So also a *word* or *message* may be conceived of as losing significance, *becoming invalid.* That this will *not* happen in the case of God's law or in the case of the words of Jesus is clearly stated in Matt. 5:18b; 24:35b; Mark 13:31b; and Luke 21:33b. On the other hand, the universe, *in its present form,* will indeed pass by and away, vanish (Matt. 5:18a; 24:35a; Mark 13:31a; Luke 16:17; 21:33a; II Peter 3:10; Rev. 21:1). So also the old order of things has passed by and away for the person who has become "a new creature" (II Cor. 5:17). And "the rich man" should bear in mind that he too will pass by and away like a wild flower (James 1:10).

Jesus, however, assures his disciples that "this generation"—the Jews as a nation?—*will not pass away* until "all these things," such as the preaching of the gospel to all the nations, have taken place (Matt. 24:34; Mark 13:30; Luke 21:32).

Finally, one may *bypass* someone's word or command by ignoring and thus disobeying it, a sin which the elder brother in the well-known parable had never committed, *if* you can believe his assertion (our present passage, Luke 15:29; and cf. 11:42).

ἔριφον, acc. s. of ἔριφος, kid; Matt. 25:32: goat.

Verse 30

καταφαγών, nom. s. masc. 2nd aor. participle of κατεσθίω, to devour. See explanation of 8:5.

πορνῶν, gen. pl. of πόρνη, prostitute, harlot. Cf. *fornication, pornography.*

Verse 31

Note σύ, separately expressed and placed forward for emphasis.

Verse 32

Note the two aor. pass. infinitives εὐφρανθῆναι and χαρῆναι. For the first see on verses 23, 24. As to the second, to rejoice, this can be traced back to the basic word χάρις, not only indicating *grace* but also *joyful thanksgiving.* For more on this see the note on 2:40 on pp. 181, 182.

Summary of Chapter 15

See p. 539.

Outline of Chapter 16

Theme: *The Work Thou Gavest Him to Do*

16:1-13   The Parable of The Shrewd Manager
16:14-18   Pharisaic Errors Rebuked
16:19-31   The Parable of The Show-off: A Rich man;
        and
      The Beggar: Lazarus

CHAPTER XVI

16 1 He continued to speak, now to his disciples, "There was a rich man who employed a manager. This manager was accused to him of squandering his possessions. 2 So he called him in and asked him, 'What is this I am hearing about you? Surrender the account books, for you can no longer be manager.'

3 "The manager said within himself, 'What am I going to do, since my master is taking away from me my position as manager? I'm not strong enough to dig; I'm ashamed to beg. —4 I know what I'll do, so that when I'm discharged from my position, people will welcome me into their homes.'

5 "So one by one he called in his master's debtors. He asked the first, 'How much do you owe my master?' 6 'A hundred measures of oil,' he replied. The manager told him, 'Take your account, sit down quickly, and write fifty.' 7 Then he said to another, 'And how much do you owe?' 'A hundred measures of wheat,' he replied. The manager told him, 'Take your account and write eighty.'

8 "The master praised the dishonest manager because he had acted shrewdly. For the people of this world, in dealing with their own kind, are more shrewd than the people who have the light.[454] 9 And I say to y o u, make friends for yourselves by means of the mammon of unrighteousness,[455] so that when it is gone, they may welcome y o u into everlasting habitations.

10 "He who is trustworthy in a very small matter is also trustworthy in an important one; and he who is untrustworthy in a very small matter is also untrustworthy in an important one. 11 So if y o u have not been trustworthy in (the use of) the unrighteous mammon, who will entrust the true riches to y o u? 12 And if y o u have not been trustworthy with respect to someone else's property, who will give y o u what is y o u r own?

13 "No servant can serve two masters; for either he will hate the one and love the other, or he will be devoted to one and look down on the other. Y o u cannot serve God and mammon."

16:1-13 *The Parable of The Shrewd Manager*
For 16:13 cf. Matt. 6:24

For possible connection between chapters 15 and 16 see p. 539. To this may be added the following:

a. Chapters 15 and 16 may be viewed as forming a pair: the first exposes the wrong attitude toward *people;* the second opens with a section on the sinful use of *wealth*. But note "squander" both in 15:13 and 16:1.

b. Chapter 15 was meant especially for the Pharisees and the scribes (see

---

454. Literally: the sons of this world . . . the sons of the light.
455. Or: worldly wealth; so also in verse 11.

15:2, 3); 16:1–13 was addressed to Christ's disciples (16:1), though also heard by and meant for the Pharisees (16:14).

As shown in the Outline, chapter 16 consists of three easily recognized parts (as did also chapter 15), two of them being parables.

The parable of The Shrewd Manager begins as follows:

1, 2. He continued to speak, now to his disciples, There was a rich man who employed a manager. This manager was accused to him of squandering his possessions. So he called him in and asked him, What is this I am hearing about you? Surrender the account books, for you can no longer be manager.

The word *disciples* probably indicates the wider circle of followers, more than just The Twelve. See 6:13; 10:1.

The rich man of this parable was probably the owner of a landed estate. He had a manager to take care of the estate's business affairs. The debtors were probably renters. They paid their rent by giving the owner a fixed amount of the yearly produce. We must assume that the rich man or owner was a man of integrity.

The manager appointed by him was not a slave but a freeman. Accordingly, when this man loses his job the punishment he receives is not that which would be meted out to a slave. Contrast "You can no longer be manager" with "and shall cut him to pieces" (12:46).

The rich man's manager was accused of squandering or wasting his employer's holdings. This points to mismanagement, not necessarily to fraud. The verb is the one used in connection with the parable of The Lost Son (15:13).

So the owner calls him in and demands an explanation. When it is evident that the manager cannot clear himself, the owner fires him and naturally demands that he surrender the account books, so that a successor will be able to take over. This leaves the impression that at this point in the story the manager had not been guilty of fraud or embezzlement, for in that case legal action would probably have been instituted against him. Also, the fired manager is given an opportunity to make the necessary arrangements for his departure. He does not have to leave immediately. He may get his books in order before he hands them to his master.

3, 4. The manager said within himself, What am I going to do, since my master is taking away from me my position as manager? I'm not strong enough to dig; I'm ashamed to beg. —I know what I'll do, so that when I'm discharged from my position, people will welcome me into their homes.

Note that the manager remains silent when the owner charges him with being guilty of mismanagement. He does not loudly assert his innocence. He must have been guilty, as charged.

The man realizes, however, that he is in a terrible predicament. He is not strong enough to dig, meaning perhaps to undertake manual labor of any kind, and he has too much self-respect to go begging. He thinks and thinks.... All of a sudden we hear him saying, "I've got it! I know exactly how to feather my nest for the time when I'll be out of a job."

5–7. So one by one he called in his master's debtors. He asked the first, How much do you owe my master? A hundred measures of oil, he replied. The manager told him, Take your account, sit down quickly, and write fifty. Then he said to another, And how much do you owe? A hundred measures of wheat, he replied. The manager told him, Take your account and write eighty.

This was clearly a scheme to make these renters personally indebted to him, and to achieve his purpose in such a manner that they would not complain or refuse hospitality to him after he has lost his position as manager.

One by one he calls in those who owed debts. Only two examples are given of that which happened next, but these two represent all the others he must have called in.

When the first man arrives, the manager asks him, "How much do you owe my master?" Note "my master," as if he had not been fired. The answer is, "A hundred measures of oil," amounting in all to somewhat less than 1000—probably about 875—gallons. The manager then takes from a drawer, strongbox or whatever, the document which the debtor had himself drawn up and in which he had promised to pay that amount of oil. He hands that "account" or "promissory note" to the renter and tells him to sit down quickly and to change the figure, so that, instead of owing a hundred measures of oil, he will now be owing only fifty measures. Why did he order the renter to sit down *quickly*, etc.? Could it be because he was afraid that the owner might suddenly enter and see what was going on? However that may be, the debtor quickly complied and handed the manager the new account. With the next debtor, who owed a hundred measures of wheat, that is, about a thousand bushels of that commodity, and who was told to change his account to eighty measures, he deals similarly.

Did the debtors realize that the manager was dishonest, and was asking them to co-operate in a shady business transaction? Probably not. As K. E. Bailey has convincingly shown—see his *P. & P.*, p. 100—the debtors assumed that the note-changing was legitimate. They probably thought that the manager had talked the owner into reducing the amounts. Reducing such account figures—sometimes because of unfavorable weather conditions affecting the crops—was not at all unusual.

The manager, the books now "in order," hands them back to the owner.

What is the owner's reaction? He realizes, of course, that the renters, and the people of the village in general, are already celebrating, *praising both the manager and the owner.* If the owner should now tell these people what has really happened and should change the figures back to where they were originally, his reputation will go down to zero. This he cannot risk. So, he makes the best of the situation. He must have said to himself, "What a clever crook!"

8, 9. The master praised the dishonest manager because he had acted shrewdly.

It should be stressed that the master praised the (now discharged) manager not for being so dishonest but *for being so clever, so astute, so shrewd.* In other words, for "feathering his nest," seeing to it that his physical needs would be supplied for a long time to come, perhaps for the rest of his life.

At this point a question arises. In verse 8, to whom does the expression *kurios* (master, lord) refer? Is the reference to the owner or to the Lord Jesus Christ? The answer must be "to the owner" of this huge landed estate. The Greek word *kurios* occurs also in verses 3 (once) and 5 (twice). In all three cases the reference is to the human owner, the master, not to Jesus. There is, accordingly, no reason to assume that a different meaning must be assigned to the identical word here in verse 8. *Jesus* is telling this parable. It is he who is saying that the master or owner praised the dishonest manager. The owner praised him not because he had been so crooked but because he had planned ahead. Jesus agrees that looking ahead is the thing to do, and adds, **For the people of this world, in dealing with their own kind, are more shrewd than the people who have the light. And I say to y o u , make friends for yourselves by means of the mammon of unrighteousness, so that when it is gone, they may welcome y o u into everlasting habitations.**

I am in agreement with Danker[456] when he expresses surprise that this comment "caused so much perplexity." He regards this as "one of the curiosities in the history of interpretation." And so it is. Jesus is not telling us that we should become worldly-minded or crooked. He is stating the obvious fact that in worldly matters worldly people often show more astuteness or shrewdness than God's children do in matters affecting their everlasting salvation. For the term *sons of light* (people who have the light) see the note on 10:6 on page 587, and the diagram on p. 588, No. 10.

Jesus wants his people similarly to look ahead and by means of "the mammon of unrighteousness" so to support all good causes and needy people that when the givers die, there will be a grand welcome for them. Those heavenly inhabitants who, while still on earth, benefited by the kindness of these big-hearted ones will then be welcoming the new arrivals. They will with gladness usher them into their heavenly habitations. For the term *mammon of unrighteousness* see the note on 16:9 on page 779.

With respect to this interpretation, accepted by most commentators, where is there a problem? There is none, unless we ourselves create it. The objection is raised, at times, "Surely, no honest individual would ever praise a crook; yet, here the owner is actually doing this. Worse even, Jesus joins in bestowing praise on this fellow."

We ask, "And why not?" Neither the owner (or master) nor Jesus is praising the crook *for his crookedness,* only for his *shrewdness,* for the fact that he looks ahead and makes provision for his future needs. What is wrong with that? Nothing, of course.

When, in spite of ever so many precautions and burglar protection de-

---

456. *Op. cit.,* p. 173.

vices, a bank is robbed, and the newspapers describe how it was done, people will remark, "How clever!" This surely does not mean that they are recommending the burglars for a Distinguished Service Medal! Far from it. They want those criminals to receive the sentence they deserve. But it is, nevertheless, consistent to say, "Would that all true believers were as clever in spiritual matters as are these crooks in plying their trade."

There are two other explanations of 16:4–8 that deserve brief consideration. One is described by W. J. Harrington, *op. cit.*, pp. 198–200, who, however, does not accept it; and by L. Morris, *The Gospel According to St. Luke*, Grand Rapids, 1974, pp. 245, 246, who seems to favor it. Briefly it amounts to this: Jews were not permitted to take interest of fellow Jews (Exod. 22:25; Lev. 25:36; Deut. 23:19). But there was a way to evade this law, namely, by reasoning that it was intended to protect only the poor. Therefore, if it could be shown that the debtor was not really poor, the law would not apply. So in many cases, including the one of this parable, the owner would add a considerable amount of interest (really usury) to the sale price of his goods. Hence, what the action of the "steward" in the present parable amounts to is this: he returns the promissory notes to the debtors, and requests that they write new ones which would show that they owed the principal minus the illegally added interest. In gratitude to him the debtors would welcome him into their homes. The owner, learning what had happened, could not very well repudiate the steward's action without exposing himself as being a man who accepted usury.

Evaluation. One would think that if the transaction was so complicated, there would at least have been a hint of this in the text. Also, in that case would not the steward deserve the name *the honest steward* instead of *the dishonest or unjust steward*? On the basis of this theory, was he not honest in forcing the amounts of the bills back to what they should have been in the first place (principal with no interest added)? He seems to have been honest, unless the previously mentioned squandering of his master's goods implies that he had been guilty of fraud, embezzlement. But it has already been shown that this is improbable; at least, that it cannot be proved. Also, if this theory were correct, would not *the owner* have been the dishonest fellow?

The other theory is that proposed by E. Trueblood. See his very interesting book *The Humor of Christ*, New York, 1964, pp. 98–110. He reasons that when Jesus exhorts his listeners to make friends by means of the unrighteous mammon, he means the very opposite of what he actually says. In other words, Trueblood regards the words of Jesus as a bit of humerous banter.

Evaluation. The author has not shown to my satisfaction that the usual explanation—the one I share with very many others—is unreasonable. We should be very careful before we interpret some of the words of Jesus as bits of humorous banter.

Probably to prevent the very misunderstanding that still persists, as if Jesus were praising dishonesty, he now continues: **10. He who is trustwor-**

thy in a very small matter is also trustworthy in an important one; and he who is untrustworthy in a very small matter is also untrustworthy in an important one.

It is clear from these words that Jesus did not approve of, did not even excuse, dishonesty, unfaithfulness. If a person can be trusted in handling a matter of small importance, he can also be trusted with important matters; if he cannot be depended on in connection with the first, it would not be safe either to entrust to him the second. Everything depends on the quality of the person's invisible being, call it his soul or whatever you wish. That soul is not divided.

What is meant becomes even more clear in what follows in verses **11, 12. So if y o u have not been trustworthy in (the use of) the unrighteous mammon, who will entrust the true riches to y o u? And if y o u have not been trustworthy with respect to someone else's property, who will give y o u what is y o u r own?**

In this parallelism *the unrighteous mammon* = *someone else's property; the true riches* = *y o u r own.* The meaning, then, is this: if y o u have not been trustworthy in the use of material wealth, which, after all, is not really y o u r s but belongs to Someone Else, namely, to God, then who will entrust to y o u the true, heavenly riches, y o u r own possession, the kingdom prepared for y o u from the foundation of the world (Matt. 25:34)?

What is stressed here, therefore, is that what we fondly call *our* money, *our* house, *our* bonds, *our* stocks, *our* bank certificates, etc., is not really our own. It is a trust handed to us to use in such a manner that God can be pleased. Nabal, who said, "Shall I then take *my* bread and *my* water and *my* meat that I have killed for *my* shearers, and give it," etc. (I Sam. 25:11), forgot this. So did the rich fool (Luke 12:16–21), and so did also the manager of our present parable. To be sure, he wisely had an eye for the future. So far, so good. But only for his *earthly* future. The believers' rule is expressed beautifully by Paul in these words: "We fix our eyes not on what is seen, but on what is not seen. For what is seen is temporary, but what is not seen is everlasting" (II Cor. 4:18).

The person who experiences a difficulty in connection with the parable of The Shrewd Manager, erroneously thinking that either the "master" in the parable, or Jesus himself, or both, is (are) commending dishonesty, should read on, also studying verses 10–12. Then his difficulty will vanish; his problem will be solved.

Entirely in line with what immediately precedes is also verse **13. No servant can serve two masters; for either he will hate the one and love the other, or he will be devoted to one and look down on the other. Y o u cannot serve God and mammon.**

It is immediately evident that Jesus is here repeating the words he used in The Sermon on the Mount (Matt. 6:24). And why not? Such a precious saying is certainly worthy of being repeated. Besides, the passage fits very neatly into the context in both places. It simply means that it is psychologically impossible for anyone to give his wholehearted devotion to two masters. The object of devotion will be *either* God *or* mammon. It cannot be both.

The psychological tension that is built up in the soul of a person who imagines for a while that he will be able to love and serve both masters becomes so severe and unendurable that in attitude, word, and deed he will sooner or later begin to show where his real allegiance lies. Either the one master or the other will win out, actually has been "on top" all the while; though, perhaps, the individual in question was not fully aware of this. In the crisis the agitated soul, out of love for the one master, will begin to show that he hates the other, perhaps even to the point of being willing to betray him. Think of Judas Iscariot. Was it not mammon that led him to deliver Christ into the hands of the enemy? See Luke 22:3–6; John 12:6. And on the other hand, think of Paul. There came a time in the life of this former persecutor when he began to look down on whatever of personal merit, earthly possessions, and prestige he at one time had prized so highly. Whatever used to be gain had now become loss (Phil. 3:7 ff.). His slogan became "that in all things Christ might have the pre-eminence."

For *Practical Lessons* and *Greek Words*, etc., see pp. 776–781.

---

14 Now the Pharisees, who were lovers of money, had been listening[457] to all this, and began to sneer at him.   15 So he said to them, "Y o u are the people who justify[458] yourselves before men, but God knows y o u r hearts; for that which before men is highly regarded is disgusting in God's sight.

16 "The law and the prophets (were proclaimed) until John. Since that time the gospel of the kingdom of God is being preached,[459] and everybody is vigorously pressing forward into it.   17 It is easier for heaven and earth to disappear than for the tiniest hook on a letter of the law to lose its force.

18 "Whoever divorces his wife and marries another woman commits adultery, and the man who marries the woman who is divorced from her husband (also) commits adultery."

16:14–18 *Pharisaic Errors Rebuked*
With 16:16 cf. Matt. 11:12, 13; with verse 17 cf. Matt. 5:18;
and with verse 18 cf. Matt. 5:32; 19:9; Mark 10:11, 12.

14. Now the Pharisees, who were lovers of money, had been listening to all this, and began to sneer at him.

Even though the Lord had directed his message especially to his disciples, others too had been listening. Among them were the Pharisees. They had heard whatever Jesus had said about a person's attitude toward, and use of, material possessions, and about the impossibility of being devoted to both God and goods. They had, however, not appreciated this teaching, for

---

457. Or: were listening.
458. Or: try to justify.
459. Literally: the kingdom of God is being gospeled.

they were lovers of money. So, their pride had been injured. Jesus had touched their sore spot. Yet, they did not dare to contradict the Master openly. Had they done so, they would have exposed themselves as money-grubbers. So what they did was this: they turned up their noses—that is, they sneered—at him. **15. So he said to them, Y o u are the people who justify yourselves before men, but God knows y o u r hearts; for that which before men is highly regarded is disgusting in God's sight.**

Knowing exactly what was happening, Jesus unmasked these hypocrites. What he told them amounted to this: Y o u are the people who pass your-selves off before men as if y o u were living in harmony with God's holy law. But y o u r righteousness is only a façade. On the inside y o u are the very opposite of what y o u want people to believe y o u are. However, God has y o u r number. He knows that y o u r religion is sham. For, what *men* see of y o u and admire is an abomination in *God's* sight.

Jesus continued: **16. The law and the prophets (were proclaimed) until John. Since that time the gospel of the kingdom of God is being preached, and everybody is vigorously pressing forward into it.**

The Pharisees seemed to have been of the opinion that they could enter the kingdom of God by circumventing the law. The most glaring examples of this are found in Matt. 15:1–9; 23:16–26. But what is necessary is that men vigorously press forward into the kingdom, and this is exactly what since the days of John the Baptist courageous men had been doing. Entrance into the kingdom requires genuine self-denial, earnest endeavor, untiring energy, utmost exertion.

What is the meaning of the statement that this has been going on *since the days of John?* Before that time God had revealed himself in the law and the prophets; that is, in what we now call the Old Testament. That revelation was *preparatory.* With John the Baptist the new dispensation, that of *fulfilment,* arrived, as is clear from the fact that John pointed to the Christ as being actually present (John 1:29, 36). With John, therefore, a new stage in the history of God's kingdom had arrived (cf. Mark 1:1–4; Acts 1:22; 10:37), and the gospel of the reign of God in hearts and lives was being proclaimed by message and confirmatory signs. Everyone who wishes to belong to this sphere of light and love will have to enter that kingdom in the manner indicated; that is, by vigorously entering into it. There is no other way. And was not that also exactly what Jesus had previously stated, using different words, namely. "*Strive* to enter through the narrow door" (13:24)? The energy to do this comes from God, of course, but that does not remove the factor of human responsibility (Phil. 2:12, 13).

Over against the Pharisaic method of circumventing the law Jesus now declares **17. It is easier for heaven and earth to disappear than for the tiniest hook on a letter of the law to lose its force.**

Regardless of Pharisaic attempts at circumvention and evasion, the moral law (cf. verse 18) retains its force. It would be easier for heaven and earth to cease to exist than for even one little letter-hook of the law to become devoid of authority.

The Old Testament was originally written in Hebrew letters. The "hook" or *keraia* is a very small projection that distinguishes one Hebrew letter from another. Thus the second letter of the Hebrew alphabet, the one called *beth,* in English corresponding to "b" or "bh," has a slight extension at the lower right hand corner, to distinguish it from the letter *kaph,* corresponding to English "k" or "kh." *Beth* is written ב, *kaph* is כ. In the present context the meaning, then, is this, that not even in the slightest respect will the moral law be invalidated. In fact, the gospel, by showing how marvelously, by means of the work of Christ, God has blessed men, makes the believer all the more eager to obey God's law *out of gratitude.* Hence, instead of weakening the demands of the law, it strengthens them.

Jesus now gives us an example of the abiding character of the moral law, over against Pharisaic attempts at evasion:

18. Whoever divorces his wife and marries another woman commits adultery, and the man who marries the woman who is divorced from her husband (also) commits adultery.

These words are clear. However, Pharisees made light of God's marriage ordinance (Gen. 1:27; 2:24). See N.T.C. on Matt. 5:31, 32 (pp. 304–306), and on Matt. 19:1–9 (pp. 713–717). So, for example, the famous rabbi Hillel, who flourished during the last half century B.C., hence during the reign of King Herod I, taught that a husband had the right to divorce his wife if she served him food that had been slightly burned, and rabbi Akiba (fl. about A.D. 110) even permitted a husband to divorce his wife if he found someone prettier.

Over against the attempts to circumvent God's law (including that of Deut. 24) Jesus declares that whoever divorces his wife and marries another commits adultery, and that the man who marries a divorcée also commits adultery. In Matt. 5:32 the Lord mentions the one exception to this rule, namely, infidelity on the part of one of the contracting parties (literally, on the part of the wife, but the principal applies, of course, to both of the contracting parties; see N.T.C. on Matthew, p. 305, footnote 295).

In our own day the error of the Pharisees, their attempt to get out from under the implications of God's marriage ordinance, is being repeated. All kinds of excuses are being offered in order to show:

a. that the evangelists were mistaken when they wrote that Jesus taught this;

b. that the word occurring in the exceptive clause of Matt. 5:32 and signifying "fornication," and in this case "marital infidelity," is broad enough to cover all manner of unpleasant traits in a spouse; and

c. that Jesus did not mean that this rule should hold for society in general.

Thus *eisegesis* (reading one's own ideas into a text) is being substituted for *exegesis.* But God's Word does not change.[460]

---

460. Notes on Greek words, phrases, and constructions in 16:1–18 begin on page 777.

Practical Lessons Derived from Luke 16:1–18

Verse 8

"The people of this world ... are more shrewd, more forward looking" with respect to making provision for their physical needs than some church people are in providing for their spiritual needs. For example, some who have made profession of their faith in the Lord Jesus Christ will go *all out* for sports but are lukewarm with respect to kingdom causes. This parable is a warning for them.

Verse 10a

"He who is trustworthy in a very small matter is also trustworthy in an important one." The sum total of things pertaining to this earthly life can be considered the "very small matter"; the "important matter" would then be whatever pertains to the life hereafter. But even with respect to so-called earthly things a distinction can be made between less important and more important. Also in this area those who are trustworthy in "a very small matter" can be depended upon to discharge their important duties faithfully. Examples: (a) the child who never forgets to say "Thank you" for favors received; (b) the young lady (or any other family member) who, in making use of the telephone, is considerate of others who may also wish to use the line, and of the person "on the other end" for whom time is precious; (c) the family that is always in church "on time," etc. All things being equal, these are the people upon whom one can depend when something very important has to be decided or has to be done.

Verse 10b

"And he who is untrustworthy in a very small matter is also untrustworthy in an important one."

The Dutch have a proverb which reads: "Wie het kleine niet eert/Is het grote niet weerd." A rather free translation would be: "If you don't have respect for whatever is small,/You're not worthy to handle the big things at all."

Verse 13

"Y o u cannot serve God and mammon." Not "Y o u *must* not" but "Y o u *cannot.*" No more than y o u can turn right and left at the same time. Some have tried it: Ananias and Sapphira, Demas, Judas. It never works.

> Give me *the single eye*
> Thy name to glorify,
> O Lord, my God Most High,
> With heart sincere.

> *Psalter Hymnal* of the Christian
> Reformed Church (Centennial Edition),
> No. 164, last 4 lines of stanza 5;
> based on Ps. 86:11.

Verse 15

"That which before men is highly regarded is disgusting in God's sight." With this compare I Sam. 16:7; 17:42–51; Luke 18:10–14; 21:1–4; Acts 12:22, 23.

Notes on Greek Words, Phrases, and Constructions in 16:1–18

Verse 1

ἔλεγεν, imperf. tense: he continued to speak, but this time especially: πρὸς τοὺς μαθητάς, to the disciples, instead of to the Pharisees and the scribes (mentioned in 15:2).

οἰκονόμον, acc. s. of οἰκονόμος (from οἶκος, house, household, plus νέμω, to manage), household manager, or simply *manager*. Cf. *economist*.

διεβλήθη, third per. s. aor. indicat. pass. of διαβάλλω*, to accuse, whether slanderously (see Josephus, *Antiquities* VII.267) or justly, as presumably in the present case. In connection with the use of this verb in the unfavorable sense note *diabolic, devil*. The root idea is that of throwing words back and forth.

For διασκορπίζων, nom. s. masc. pres. participle of διασκορπίζω, to squander, see the note on 15:13 on page 760.

For τὰ ὑπάρχοντα αὐτοῦ, his possessions, see the note on 8:3 on page 421.

Verse 2

As to τί τοῦτο, here one must choose between:
a. *What* is this, etc.? and
b. *Why* do I hear this, etc.? Cf. Acts 14:15.
Since indignant surprise is more natural here than innocent request for information, theory (a) is probably correct.

ἀπόδος, sec. per. s. 2nd aor. imperat. act. of ἀποδίδωμι, to give, surrender. Hence ἀπόδος τὸν λόγον probably means: surrender the account book. Cf. "give account" or something similar, in Matt. 12:36; Acts 19:40; Rom. 14:12; Heb. 13:17; I Peter 4:5. In I Peter 3:15 the preferred rendering is "reason" ("Always be ready to give an answer to anyone who asks y o u to give a reason," etc.).

Verse 3

ἀφαιρεῖται, third per. s. pres. (linear) indicat. middle of ἀφαιρέω, to take away, remove; as in 1:25; 10:42. See the note on 10:42 on page 604.

σκάπτειν, pres. (linear) infinitive of σκάπτω*; in the New Testament only here and in 6:48; 13:8; see the note on 13:8 on page 698.

ἐπαιτεῖν, pres. (linear) infinitive of ἐπαιτέω* = ἐπί plus αἰτέω; hence, to ask favor upon favor, or: to ask again and again, more and more; and so: to beg. In the New Testament only here and in 18:35.

Verse 4

ἔγνων, first per. s. 2nd aor. indicat. act of γινώσκω, here probably in the sense of suddenly arriving at a solution, suddenly getting to know what to do. Cf. vernacular, "I've got it." Such an aor. may truly be called "timeless." (In a broader sense that is true, of course, of every aorist, as the very name indicates.) It has also been called "ingressive" and "dramatic."

ποιήσω is first per. s. For the rest, it is either aor. subjunct. or fut. indicat. In this case the forms are the same. The very close relation between the subjunctive and the future indicative has been discussed earlier. See the note on 14:7–9 on page 729.

μετασταθῶ, first per. s. aor. subjunct. pass. of μεθίστημι = μετά plus ἵστημι; hence, to bring about a change of position; in the present context: to remove (from office), to discharge; here, in the passive, "when I'm discharged."

As always, in such cases, the exact rendering varies with the context. Thus in Acts 13:22; I Cor. 13:2, to remove; in Acts 19:26, to turn away or astray; and in Col. 1:13, to transplant. Cf. *metastasis*.

Verse 5

χρεοφειλετῶν*, gen. pl. of debtor, on which see the note on 7:41 on page 412. In the New Testament the word occurs only in these two passages (Luke 7:41; 16:5).

Verses 6, 7

βάτους, acc. pl. of βάτος, a transliteration of the Hebrew word בַּת (*bath*), a measure of fluids (e.g., oil or wine). It corresponds to an *ephah* of dry measure. A bath (1/10 of a homer, Ezek. 45:11, 14) has been variously estimated as amounting to anywhere from 8½ to 10 gallons, liquid measure, to which verse 5 refers.

δέξαι, sec. per. s. aor. imperat. of δέχομαι, here meaning *to take into one's hand*. Note that this brief word of command occurs twice, once in verse 6, and once in verse 7.

On γράμματα, lit. "writings," or somewhat less literally "papers," see J. D. M. Derret, "'Take Thy Bond . . . And Write Fifty' (Luke 16:6): The Nature of the Bond," *JTS*, 18 (1972), pp. 438–440. Attempts at translation of this term have resulted in: promissory note, note, acknowledgment, obligation, bill, account, statement of indebtedness; all this in addition to "writings" and "papers." These renderings are correct at least to some extent. The reference is to a written promise to pay the stipulated amount. Therefore such a rendering as "account" may well be among the best. The rendering "bond" in the sense of "written obligation to pay a specified sum" is certainly correct. However, since today the term *bond* is often immediately interpreted as referring to an interest-bearing certificate, it may be best to avoid it in the present connection.

κόρους, acc. pl. of κόρος, transliteration of Hebrew כֹּר (*kor*), in the present instance clearly a unit of dry measure, about 10 bushels. "*Bath*, (a little less than) ten gallons; *kor*, ten bushels" is easy to remember.

Verse 8

For the descriptive genitives τῆς ἀδικίας, τοῦ φωτός, etc., see the diagram and the discussion on pp. 587 and 588. A "manager of unrighteousness" or "of dishonesty" is an unrighteous or dishonest manager.

φρονίμως*, shrewdly; here in the sense of providently, exercising foresight. With this adverb compare the adjective φρόνιμος, which in the New Testament occurs no less than 14 times, beginning with Matt. 7:24.

The second ὅτι in verse 8 can be rendered "for," meaning, "this is true as is clear from the fact that," or simply "showing that."

Verse 9

μαμωνά, gen. s. of μαμωνᾶς, wealth, riches, here personified. Cf. El Dorado, Plutus, Fortuna. The term used here in Luke 16:9, 11, 13 and in Matt. 6:24 is of uncertain derivation. Its meaning is, however, not uncertain. Note that the same descriptive genitive modifier τῆς ἀδικίας that was used in verse 8 with respect to this manager occurs in verse 9 with reference to mammon.

ἐκλίπῃ, third per. s. 2nd aor. subjunct. (after ὅταν) act. of ἐκλείπω, lit. to leave off; hence, to run out, fail. Aside from Heb. 1:12 (in a quotation from the Old Testament), this verb is in the New Testament used only by Luke (16:9; 22:32; 23:45).

δέξωνται, third per. pl. aor. subjunct. (after ἵνα) of δέχομαι, to receive, welcome.

Verse 10

ἐλαχίστῳ, dat. s. neut. elative superlative (the nom. being ἐλάχιστον) of μικρός, small. Hence, ἐλαχίστῳ means "in a very small matter."

Verse 11

τὸ ἀληθινόν refers here to "the true riches," as the context clearly indicates.

What we have here is a simple or first class conditional sentence; with εἰ and sec. per. pl. 2nd aor. indicat. middle of γίνομαι in the protasis; and a question, third per. s. fut. indicat., in the apodosis.

Verse 12

On the basis of the data supplied in the textual apparatus of Grk. N.T. (A-B-M-W) the reading ὑμέτερον is to be preferred to ἡμέτερον. Besides, the second per. pl. implied in the verb ἐγένεσθε and expressed in the pronoun ὑμῖν harmonizes best with ὑμέτερον, y o u r own.

Verse 13

οἰκέτης, cf. Acts 10:7; Rom. 14:4; I Peter 2:18, is derived from οἰκία, house, household. The reference is accordingly to a "household servant," or simply "servant."

ἀνθέξεται, third per. s. fut. indicat. middle of ἀντέχομαι, to cling or adhere to, be devoted to. As is clear from the chiastic parallelism of the synoptic passages (Matt. 6:24; Luke 16:13), in which this verb is explained by ἀγαπήσει, and is contrasted with μισήσει and καταφρονήσει, the meaning of ἀντέχομαι is *to be devoted to.* Here the ἀντί or face-to-face relationship is one of love.

καταφρονήσει, third per. s. fut. indicat. of καταφρονέω, lit. to think (or look) *down* on; hence, to hate, scorn, despise.

FIRST MEMBER

SECOND MEMBER

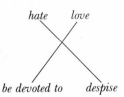

hate   love

be devoted to   despise

Verse 14

Note (progressive) imperfect ἤκουον, probably best rendered "were listening" (with N.A.S.) or "had been listening" (with Robertson and Williams).

φιλάργυροι, pl. of φιλάργυρος, lovers of money, is found also in II Tim. 3:2; while φιλαργυρία occurs in I Tim. 6:10.

ἐξεμυκτήριζον, third per. pl. imperf. indicat. act. of ἐκμυκτηρίζω*, derived from ἐκ plus μυκτήρ, the nose; hence lit., to turn *out* (where we would say *up*) the nose at, to sneer at, mock. Cf. *mucus*. In the New Testament this compound is found only here and in 23:35. The simple verb occurs in Gal. 6:7, "God is not mocked."

Verse 15

δικαιοῦντες, nom. pl. masc. act. participle of δικαιόω, to justify. It is possible that in the present instance the verb must be considered conative. If this be true, the proper rendering would be "try to justify." For more on this verb see the note on 18:14 on pp. 824, 825.

ὑψηλός, high, lofty, exalted, highly regarded. Luke also uses this word in Acts 13:17, "a high arm," that is, mighty power. Elsewhere in the New Testament the word occurs in Matt. 4:8; 17:1; Mark 9:2; Rev. 21:10, in all these instances in connection with a *mountain*, describing it as being *high*. A high *wall* is mentioned in Rev. 21:12. Christ's exaltation to his position of majesty in the heavens—hence "on high"—is described in Heb. 1:3; 7:26. Finally, in Rom. 11:20 (see also 12:16) and I Tim. 6:17 Paul warns his readers not to be "highminded" (A.V.). It is to be regretted that, in the sense of arrogant, proud, haughty, this word *highminded* is becoming, or perhaps has already become, obsolete. The Germans still use *hochmütig;* the Dutch *hoogmoedig.*

βδέλυγμα, a detestable thing; hence *disgusting, abominable.* Cf. Prov. 11:1. Disgusting, loathsome, abominable things are mentioned also in Rev. 17:4, 5; 21:27. Think of scandals, shameful things and actions. For an explanation of the term *the abomination of desolation* or *the desolating sacrilege* see N.T.C. on Matt., pp. 857, 858; and on Mark, pp. 524–528.

Verse 16

εὐαγγελίζεται, third per. s. pres. (continuative and progressive) indicat. pass. of εὐαγγελίζω, to bring, proclaim, or announce *good news,* to preach the gospel. In the New Testament this verb is used especially by Luke—10 times in his Gospel, 15 times in Acts—and by Paul, about 20 times. It occurs once in Matthew (11:5), twice in Hebrews (4:2, 6), also twice in Revelation (10:7; 14:6), and 3 times in I Peter (1:12, 25; 4:6). Cf. *evangelize.*

βιάζεται, third per. s. pres. indicat. middle of βιάζω, a verb which in the New Testament occurs only here and in Matt. 11:12. See the discussion of this verb in N.T.C. on Matthew, footnote 469, p. 489. In harmony with its meaning in the Matthew passage the sense *to press forward vigorously* (into it; that is, into the kingdom of God) seems to be required here.

Verse 17

εὐκοπώτερον, comparative of εὔκοπος; hence *easier.* In the New Testament this adjective is always used in the comparative degree. It also occurs in 5:23; 18:25; Matt. 9:5; 19:24; Mark 2:9; 10:25.

κεραίαν, acc. s. of κεραία. In the New Testament this word occurs only here and in Matt. 5:18. It probably indicates the little hook that distinguishes one Hebrew letter from another. See further explanation in the commentary.

Verse 18

μοιχεύει, occurring twice in this verse, is third per. s. pres. indicat. of μοιχεύω, to commit adultery; cf. μοιχεύομαι. The New Testament use of this verb (and of the very similar μοιχάω, μοιχάομαι) may be briefly summarized as follows:

a. *literal sense* in a quotation from the Ten Commandments (Exod. 20:14; Deut. 5:18): Matt. 5:27; 19:18; Mark 10:19; Luke 18:20; Rom. 13:9; James 2:11a.

b. *other uses of this verb in its literal sense:* Matt. 5:32 (twice); 19:9 (twice); Mark 10:11, 12; the present passage (Luke 16:18 twice); John 8:4; Rom. 2:22 (twice); James 2:11b.

c. *other than strictly literal sense:* adultery of the heart and eye (Matt. 5:28); unfaithfulness to God: Rev. 2:22.

From this last passage, viewed in its context (hence, from Rev. 2:20-22), it appears that there is a very close relationship between πορνεία, fornication, and μοιχεία, adultery. Though originally μοιχεία may have been limited to adultery involving a married person, while πορνεία indicated all unlawful sexual intercourse outside of the bond of marriage, the term πορνεία gradually expanded in meaning, so that in the New Testament it may refer to any and all illicit sexual relationships. So, for example, in Matt. 5:32; 19:9 a wife's marital unfaithfulness, surely μοιχεία, adultery, is called πορνεία. In the New Testament, then, the verb πορνεύω and its cognate noun πορνεία may refer to immorality in general, any phase of it, whether inside or outside of marriage. Thus μοιχεία, adultery, is always πορνεία, fornication, immorality; but not all πορνεία is μοιχεία.

---

19 "Once there was a rich man who was in the habit of dressing up in purple and fine linen and living in dazzling splendor day in, day out. 20 And a certain beggar named Lazarus, covered with sores, had been laid at his gate. 21 He was eager to be fed with the scraps that fell from the rich man's table. Yes, even the dogs used to come and lick his sores.

22 "In course of time the beggar died and was carried away by the angels to Abraham's bosom. The rich man also died, and he was buried. 23 And in Hades,[461] being in torment, he lifted up his eyes. He sees Abraham afar off, and Lazarus by his side.[462] 24 And he cried out and said, 'Father Abraham, take pity on me and send Lazarus, that he may dip the tip of his finger in water and cool my tongue, for I am in agony in this flame.'

25 "But Abraham answered, 'Son, remember that during your lifetime you received in full your good things, and similarly Lazarus (received) the bad things. Now he is being comforted here, and you are in agony. 26 And besides all this, between us and you a vast chasm has been fixed, in order that those who want to cross from this side to y o u would not be able to do so, and that those who would pass over from there to us would (also) not be able.'

27 "He answered, 'Then I beg you, father, that you send Lazarus to my father's house, 28 for I have five brothers, lest they too come into this place of torment.'

29 "But Abraham said, 'They have Moses and the Prophets; let them listen to them.'

30 "'No, father Abraham,' he replied, 'but if someone from the dead goes to them, they will be converted.'

---

461. Or: hell.
462. Literally: in his bosom.

31 "He said to him, 'If they do not listen to Moses and the Prophets, neither will they be convinced even if someone rises from the dead.'"

16:19-31 *The Parable of The Show-off: A Rich Man;*
and
The Beggar: Lazarus

First a few introductory remarks. Is there any connection between 16:1-18 and this parable? It might seem at first that there is none. Careful examination reveals, however, that there is indeed a connection, a rather close one. As has been pointed out, chapter 15 exposes the wrong attitude toward *people;* chapter 16 opens by showing us the sinful use of *material possessions.* The parable found in verses 19-31 is as it were a climax, combining these two. It describes the terrible result of the wicked handling of people and wealth. The "rich man" of this parable completely neglected to make friends for himself by means of "the mammon of unrighteousness" (16:9). He was the kind of person who, because of his wealth, must have been "highly regarded" by men, but because of his selfishness was "disgusting in God's sight" (16:15). He was, moreover, the very opposite of The Samaritan Who Cared (10:30-37). For the connection see also pp. 539, 540.

The section (verses 19-31) can be conveniently divided into two very unequal parts. In the first part (verses 19-22) we are shown "the rich man" and "the poor beggar" *in this life;* in the second (verses 23-31) we see them again, but now *in the hereafter.*

A. *In This Life*

19. Once there was a rich man who was in the habit of dressing up in purple and fine linen and living in dazzling splendor day in, day out.
He was rich. Well, so was Abraham and so was Joseph of Arimathea. Nowhere does the Bible blame them for being rich. But with reference to Abraham and Joseph we do not read what is said further in the description of the rich man of this parable, namely, that he was in the habit of dressing up in purple and fine linen. Obtaining purple dye from the shellfish was an expensive process. It is not surprising, therefore, that a purple outer garment, such as worn by the rich man of this parable, was often reserved for royalty. Think of the expression *royal purple.* In addition to this purple outer garment or robe, this man wore a fine linen undergarment. Add to this the fact that he was "living in dazzling splendor day in, day out," and it becomes apparent that what is stressed here is not so much that he was rich but something else.

He was not just rich. He belonged to that class of people to whom the epithet *filthy rich* is often applied, and not without reason. His living day by day in dazzling splendor marks him as a *show-off,* a strutting peacock. He wanted everybody to know that he was rich. He was in love . . . with himself. That he was utterly selfish will become clear as the parable moves along:

20, 21. And a certain beggar named Lazarus, covered with sores, had been laid at his gate. He was eager to be fed with the scraps that fell from the rich man's table. Yes, even the dogs used to come and lick his sores.

Here is the test, the opportunity for the opulent swaggerer to show whether, after all, he has a heart. A very, very poor man, one in need of everything, is lying at the gateway (cf. Matt. 26:71; Acts 10:17) of the rich man's mansion, having been laid there, this evidently indicating that he was unable to walk.

He was a beggar, and his name was Lazarus (cf. John 11:2 f.). This name is Latin and is derived from the Greek Lazaros (from Eleazaros), which, in turn, represents the Hebrew name Eleazar, meaning "God has helped." There is a difference of opinion with respect to the question whether this name was given to him simply because, as the story develops (see especially verse 24), this man needed a name, or whether Jesus purposely gave the man this name in order to indicate that the beggar, in all his distress, placed his trust in God. Cannot both be true?

Not only was Lazarus a begger, totally unable to provide for his own needs, he was also covered with sores.

Here, then, was an opportunity for the rich fop to show pity, for whenever he went into or out of the gateway, he could not help seeing Lazarus. Besides, the beggar was eager to be fed with the scraps that fell from the rich man's table. The parable does not say that he received these scraps. Does not that omission leave the impression that he must have received very little? One thing is certain: the rich exhibitionist paid no attention to the beggar, did not himself help him in any way, lived only for himself.

What must have made the poor man's condition even worse was that the big, unclean, pesky pariah dogs were in the habit of coming to him and licking his sores!

22. In course of time the beggar died and was carried away by the angels to Abraham's bosom. The rich man also died, and he was buried.

The beggar's misery ended at last. He died. Whether he was also buried is not even mentioned. If there was a real burial, it must have been so obscure and dismal that it better be passed by in silence. On the other hand, what happened to the *soul* of Lazarus is all-important. *He*—for man's soul or spirit is the real *person*—was carried away by the angels to Abraham's bosom.

Two expressions here merit special attention:

First of all *the angels.* According to Scripture

ANGELS ARE:

Attendants of Christ (II Thess. 1:7), their exalted Head (Eph. 1:21, 22; Col. 2:10).

Bringers of good tidings concerning our salvation (see on Luke 2:14; 24:4–7; Acts 1:11; I Tim. 3:16).

Choristers of heaven (Luke 15:10; I Cor. 13:1; Rev. 5:11, 12).

Defenders of God's children (Ps. 34:7; 91:11; Dan. 6:22; 10:10, 13, 20;

Matt. 18:10; Acts 5:19; II Thess. 1:7–10; Rev. 12:7), though the latter
outrank them and will judge them (I Cor. 6:3; Heb. 1:14).

Examples in obedience (Matt. 6:10; I Cor. 11:10).

Friends of the redeemed, constantly watching over them, deeply interested in their salvation, and rendering service to them in every way,
including executing the judgment of God upon the enemy (Matt.
13:41; 25:31, 32; Luke 15:10; 16:22; I Cor. 4:9; Gal. 3:19; II Thess. 1:7;
Heb. 1:14; I Peter 1:12; Rev. 20:1–3).

Next, *Abraham's bosom.* The fact that Lazarus was by the angels carried to
Abraham's bosom certainly proves that he had been true to his name.
While on earth he had placed his trust in God as his Helper, and now God
had ordered the angels to take his soul to Paradise. He who had yearned to
receive crumbs and scraps is now reclining at heaven's table, where a banquet is being held. Moreover, to recline in Abraham's bosom, as the apostle
John was going to recline in the bosom of Jesus, indicates special favor, as
has been shown in connection with Luke 14:7; see on that verse. See also
John 1:18. We should not forget, in this connection, that Abraham is regarded in Scripture as being not only the great patriarch (Heb. 7:4) but also
the father of all believers (Rom. 4:11).

The rich man also died *and was buried.* It must have been a splendid
burial. Note the meaningful contrast: nothing is said about the beggar's
burial; on the other hand, nothing is here said about the rich man's soul, as
to what happened to it at the moment of death.

B. *In the Hereafter*

**23, 24. And in Hades, being in torment, he lifted up his eyes. He sees
Abraham afar off, and Lazarus by his side. And he cried out and said,
Father Abraham, take pity on me and send Lazarus, that he may dip the
tip of his finger in water and cool my tongue, for I am in agony in this
flame.**

A few matters stand out:

a. The rich show-off is pictured as being in Hades. The popular view,
according to which the term *Hades* in the entire New Testament is the
abode of all the dead, believers and unbelievers, is certainly incorrect. As
far as *the Gospels* are concerned[463] the following is true:

In the present parable Hades is clearly the place of torments and of the
flame. It is *hell.* So also *hell* may well be the correct rendering of Hades in
Matt. 11:23 and in Luke 10:15, for there *Hades* is sharply contrasted with
heaven, and should probably be understood in the figurative sense of
thorough ruin. In Matt. 16:18 the thought may well be that not even all the
demons streaming forth out of the gates of *hell* will ever be able to destroy
Christ's true church.

---

463. For more on *Sheol* and *Hades* see my book *The Bible on the Life Hereafter,* Grand Rapids,
1971, pp. 83–86.

b. The condition of the dead and the communication between them is represented here in very literal, earthly terms, so that a vivid impression is created. It should be clear, nevertheless, that much of what is here conveyed cannot be interpreted literally. For example, we read about the lifting up of the eyes, of seeing people afar off, of a finger and of a tongue, even though we have been told that the rich man had been buried.

This does not take away the fact, however, that certain definite truths concerning the life hereafter are conveyed here, one of them being that the departed ones are not asleep but fully awake; another, that some are saved, others are suffering.

c. If all this is understood, it will have become clear that the one great truth here emphasized is that once a person has died, his soul having been separated from his body, *his condition,* whether blessed or doomed, *is fixed forever.* There is no such thing as a "second" chance. Therefore opportunities to help those in need and, in general, to live a fruitful life to the glory of God should be seized *now.*

These preliminary remarks should guard us against taking literally what was never meant to be so interpreted.

With all this in mind, note that the rich man of the parable is here represented as being in torment, a condition which is not relieved by the fact that in the distance he sees Abraham and Lazarus by his side. Very respectfully he now addresses the arch-patriarch as "Father Abraham," and asks him to take pity on him. Such pity he, the rich man himself, had never shown when he had the opportunity to do so. He requests that Abraham dispatch Lazarus, so that the latter, having dipped the tip of his finger in water, might cool the sufferer's tongue. "I am in agony in this flame," he adds.

Note the word *flame.* That hell is a place of *fire* or of the flame is the language of Scripture throughout (Isa. 33:14; 66:24; Matt. 3:12; 5:22; 13:40, 42, 50; 18:8, 9; 25:41; Mark 9:43–48; Luke 3:17; Jude 7; Rev. 14:10; 19:20; 20:10, 14, 15; 21:8). This fire is unquenchable. It devours forever and ever.

Yet, hell is also the abode where *darkness* dwells. For some it is the place of "outer darkness" (Matt. 8:12; 22:13; 25:30). It is the region where the evil spirits are kept "in everlasting chains under darkness" (Jude 6; cf. Jude 13).

But if hell is a place of *fire,* how can it also be a place of *darkness?* Are not these two concepts mutually exclusive? Well, not always necessarily. For example, by means of a certain form of radiation people have been seriously burned even though when it happened they were in a dark room. Nevertheless, it is advisable not to speculate. *Everlasting fire* has been prepared "for the devil and his angels," yet these are *spirits.* It should be sufficient to conclude from all this that such terms as *fire* and *darkness* should not be taken too literally. Each in its own way indicates the terrors of the lost in the place from which there is no return.

Note that the rich man's character has not changed any. He still views

Lazarus as his servant, and is not a bit ashamed to ask for a favor from the very person who never received a favor from him! Also, he expects Abraham to send Lazarus, even though he, the show-off, never tried, during his life on earth, to imitate Abraham's faith.

25, 26. But Abraham answered, Son, remember that during your lifetime you received in full your good things, and similarly Lazarus (received) the bad things. Now he is being comforted here, and you are in agony. And besides all this, between us and you a vast chasm has been fixed, in order that those who want to cross from this side to y o u would not be able to do so, and that those who would pass over from there to us would (also) not be able.

Abraham answers in a friendly manner, even calls him "son," for the rich man has called Abraham "father." Besides, is not the sufferer a child of Abraham, biologically speaking?

In his answer Abraham intends to indicate that for two reasons the request cannot be honored: to grant it would be (a) improper and (b) impossible.

It would be *improper,* contrary to the requirements of justice—"During your lifetime you received . . . *your* good things; that is, those things you considered good, namely, being dressed in purple and fine linen, and living in dazzling splendor day in, day out. Those matters were first on the list of your priorities." Implied is: to help poor Lazarus and, in general, to live a life of being useful to your fellow men and of glorifying God was not at all your aim. Now, then, you receive what is coming to you. On the other hand, Lazarus received *the bad things,* not *his* bad things. He did not bring them upon himself. (On the contrary, he was true to his name.) Now he is being comforted and this, again, is as it should be.

It would also be *impossible.* Abraham tells the doomed man that there is a vast chasm, a yawning gorge—a typically Palestinian figure, for the country where this parable was spoken has many of these ravines (see the note on 16:26 on page 789)—separating the lost from the redeemed. Crossing over from one side to the other is, therefore, forever and absolutely impossible. This is a very graphic and unforgettable symbolical representation of the *irreversibility* of a person's lot after death. The chasm *was intended* for rendering crossing over impossible.

27, 28. He answered, Then I beg you, father, that you send Lazarus to my father's house, for I have five brothers, lest they too come into this place of torment.

Here, for the first time in this parable, the man who used to be rich reveals a bit of sympathy. But even this interest in others may have been mixed with selfishness. He wants his five brothers to be warned so that they may stay out of hell. The most favorable construction one can put on this request is that it issued from love for his brothers. Other possibilities that have been suggested by commentators are: (a) He is trying to say, "If I myself had only been warned, I would not be here today," and (b) He does not want his brothers to join him for fear they will blame him for the bad example he gave them.

However that may be, note that even now he is not asking that anything be done for people in general, only for *his* five brothers. And even now he seems not to be able to get rid of the notion that Lazarus is his messenger boy!

29. But Abraham said, They have Moses and the Prophets; let them listen to them.

This passage does not always receive the attention it deserves. Why did Jesus insert it in the parable? The obvious reason is that if the doomed man himself had only read and taken to heart Moses and the Prophets, and if his brothers would only do the same, they would not be lost. Why not? What is the point? Is it not this, that it is precisely in the books of Moses and in the writings of Isaiah, etc., that the life which is the exact opposite of that which the rich man had lived is commended? Trust in God, self-denial in the interest of others, kindness, help for the needy, for widows and orphans, the humble, etc., is constantly being urged. To give but a few examples:

MOSES: Gen. 50:21; Exod. 2:17; 22:22, 25; 32:32; Lev. 19:10; 25:25–47; Deut. 10:18; 14:29; 15:4; 16:11, 14; etc.

THE PROPHETS: Isa. 14:32; 25:4; 29:19; 57:15; Dan. 4:27; Amos 2:6, 7; 4:1; 5:11, 12; Jon. 4:11; Mic. 6:8; Zeph. 3:12; Zech. 7:10, 11.

Besides, did not both Moses (Deut. 18:15, 18) and the Prophets (Isa. 42:3; ch. 53) point forward to him who would give himself as a ransom for many?

30. No, father Abraham, he replied, but if someone from the dead goes to them, they will be converted.

How wrong he was! Someone from the dead did actually appear to the people. And his name was Lazarus (though not the Lazarus of the parable). The story is found in John 11. Was the result that everybody was converted? Not at all. The result was that Christ's enemies planned to put to death the risen Lazarus (John 12:10), and were more determined than ever to destroy Jesus (John 11:47–50).

31. He said to him, If they do not listen to Moses and the Prophets, neither will they be convinced even if someone rises from the dead.

Jesus rose from the dead. But those who refused to believe Moses and the Prophets were not convinced, and certainly not converted. Read Matt. 28:11–15. The important lesson is: Accept Scripture as the Word of God and, by God's grace, live the kind of life it demands and which, in the person of Jesus Christ, it illustrates. Cf. Eph. 4:32—5:2.[464]

---

464. Notes on Greek words, phrases, and constructions in 16:19–31 begin on page 788.

Practical Lesson Derived from Luke 16:19-31

Verses 19, 23

"A rich man . . . living in dazzling splendor . . . in torment, he lifted up his eyes."
One great lesson to be learned from this parable: no sin, whether of omission or
of commission, ever stands alone: the chord one touches here vibrates there. You
dial a number in New York, the phone rings in San Francisco.

Notes on Greek Words, Phrases, and Constructions in 16:19-31

Verse 19

ἐνεδιδύσκετο, third per. s. imperf. middle of ἐνδιδύσκω, to dress. Cf. Mark 15:17,
"They dressed him in a purple robe." In middle, as here in Luke 16:19, to dress
oneself.

πορφύραν, acc. s. of πορφύρα, purple garment or robe. Cf. Rev. 17:4; 18:12.

βύσσον, acc. s. of βύσσος*; cf. Hebrew בּוּץ, butz, byssus, fine yellow flax and the
linen cloth and undergarment made from it. The outer robe was of purple; the
inner garment, of fine linen.

εὐφραινόμενος, nom. s. masc. pres. middle participle of εὐφραίνω. See the note
on 15:23 on page 762. Here, in Luke 16:19, the meaning *to make merry* fits the
context. Add λαμπρῶς*, brilliantly (cf. *lamp*), and the result is: he made merry
brilliantly; that is, he was living in dazzling, ostentatious splendor. He was a rich
show-off, a dandy or coxcomb.

Verse 20

ἐβέβλητο, third per. s. pluperf. indicat. pass. of βάλλω, to throw, put, lay. There
are those who think that the verb here used implies that Lazarus had been "flung"
there. But it is a well-known fact that the verb βάλλω also has weakened meanings,
as indicated.

εἱλκωμένος, perf. pass. participle of ἑλκόω*, to make sore, to cause ulcers; hence,
in the pass. as here: "covered with ulcers." The acc. pl. of the noun ἕλκος is used in
verse 21. The English word *ulcer* is related to the Greek ἕλκος.

Verse 21

For χορτασθῆναι, as also in 15:16, aor. pass. infinitive of χορτάζω, see the note on
6:21 on page 345. The meaning is *to feed;* in the pass., as here, to be fed.

ἐπέλειχον, third per. pl. imperf. of ἐπιλείχω*, to lick.

Verses 22, 23

ἀπενεχθῆναι, aor. pass. infinitive (after ἐγένετο) of ἀποφέρω (see also Mark 15:1;
Acts 19:12; I Cor. 16:3; Rev. 17:3; 21:10), to carry away.

κόλπον, acc. s. of κόλπος, bosom, breast, place of closest friendship and fellowship. In verse 23 note dat. *pl.*, with perhaps no essential difference in meaning,
unless it be that of placing even greater emphasis on the striking contrast between

the blessedness of Lazarus and the wretched condition of the rich man. For the meaning *bosom* see also John 1:18; 13:23. A related meaning is *lap*, formed by the fold of a garment and providing room for things to be stored and carried (Luke 6:38). There is also the connotation *bay* (Acts 27:39), with its bosom-resembling shape. With κόλπος cf. *gulf.*

ἐτάφη, third per. s. 2nd aor. indicat. pass. of θάπτω, to bury; in pass., as here, to be buried. See the note on 9:59, 60 on page 566.

ᾅδῃ, dat. s. of ᾅδης, Hades. See also 10:15; then Matt. 11:23; 16:18; Acts 2:27, 31; Rev. 1:18; 6:8; 20:13, 14.

ἐπάρας, nom. s. masc. aor. act. participle of ἐπαίρω (ἐπί plus αἴρω), to lift up, raise.

βασάνοις, lit. "in torments," dat. pl. of βάσανος; cf. gen. s. in verse 28, agony, torment, torture. Cf. *basanite* and see the note on 8:28 on page 452; and N.T.C. on Mark, footnote 288 on p. 260.

ὁρᾷ, third per. s. pres. (dramatic) indicat. act. of ὁράω, to see.

Verse 24

βάψῃ, sec. per. s. aor. subjunct. (after ἵνα) act. of βάπτω, to dip; so also in John 13:26 and in Rev. 19:13, where *dyed* (in blood) has been suggested.

ἄκρον, top, tip; also in Heb. 11:21. In Matt. 24:31 and Mark 13:27 the meaning is *end, extremity, farthest reach.* Cf. *acropolis.*

For δακτύλου, gen. s. of δάκτυλος, see the note on 11:20 on page 633, and on 15:22 on page 761.

καταψύξῃ, third per. s. aor. subjunct. act. (after ἵνα) of καταψύχω** = κατά plus ψύχω, to blow; hence, *to cool off by blowing;* and so simply *to cool.* The Greek literally says *to cool down,* where our idiom is *to cool off;* or, again, simply *to cool.*

For ὀδυνῶμαι, first per. s. pres. indicat. pass. of ὀδυνάω, to pain; in pass., as here, to be in pain or agony; see the note on 2:48 on page 188. See also Acts 20:38.

Verse 25

μνήσθητι, sec. per. s. aor. imperat. pass. of μιμνήσκω, to remember; in pass. *to be reminded of,* which, when used in the imperative, is about the same as *to remember.*

ἀπέλαβες, sec. per. s. 2nd aor. indicat. act. of ἀπολαμβάνω, to receive in full. Note also 15:27; 18:30; 23:41; and see the note on 6:34 on page 359.

παρακαλεῖται, third per. s. pres. indicat. pass. of παρακαλέω (lit. to call to one's side), to invite, comfort, console, encourage, cheer up, etc.; and here, in the pass., *to be comforted.* When we bear in mind that this verb occurs about a hundred times in the New Testament, we see more clearly that this book is indeed a source of comfort and encouragement. And back of the book is God Triune, "the God of all comfort."

Verse 26

χάσμα*, chasm. The Greek word is derived from χαίνω, to gape, yawn. Very informative is the article by E. F. F. Bishop, "A Yawning Chasm, an Exegesis of Luke 16:19–31," *EQ* (1973), pp. 3–5. What is meant is a ravine, vast in depth, length, and breadth; a wadi, gorge.

ἐστήρικται, third per. s. perf. indicat. pass. of στηρίζω, to set fast, fix; in pass., as here, "has been fixed and so stands firmly and permanently."

ὅπως... μὴ δύνωνται (third per. pl. pres. subjunct. of δύναμαι), "in order that they be not able (to cross over)." Differently expressed, the sense is: *to prevent them from crossing over,* etc. Not merely result but purpose is expressed here.

διαπερῶσιν, third per. pl. pres. subjunct. of διαπεράω, to pass over. See also Matt. 9:1; 14:34; Mark 5:21; 6:53; Acts 21:2.

Verse 29

ἀκουσάτωσαν, third per. pl. aor. imperat. act. of ἀκούω, to hear.

Verse 30

μετανοήσουσιν, third per. pl. fut. indicat. of μετανοέω, to be converted. For more on the meaning of this verb see N.T.C. on Matthew, pp. 196, 197.

Verse 31

ἀναστῇ, third per. s. 2nd aor. subjunct. of ἀνίστημι, to raise up. But the 2nd aor. and all middle forms are intransit.; hence here: to rise.

Summary of Chapter 16

See pp. 539, 540.

Outline of Chapter 17

Theme: *The Work Thou Gavest Him to Do*

CHAPTER XVII

17   1 He said to his disciples, "Temptations are bound to come, but woe to him through whom they come. 2 Better is it for him if, with a millstone hung around his neck,[465] he has been hurled into the sea, than that he should cause one of these little ones to sin.

3 "Constantly be looking out for one another.[466] If your brother commits a sin, reprove him; and if he repents, forgive him. 4 Even if he sins against you seven times in a day, and seven times comes back to you, saying, 'I'm sorry,' you must forgive him."

5 The apostles said to the Lord, "Increase our faith." 6 The Lord replied, "If y o u have faith as (small as) a mustard seed, y o u would say to this mulberry tree, 'Be uprooted and planted in the sea,' and it would have obeyed y o u.

7 "Who among y o u, if he has a servant plowing or tending sheep, will say to him when he comes in from the field, 'Come at once and recline at table'?[467] 8 Will he not rather say to him, 'Prepare my supper, dress up properly so you can wait on me[468] until I finish eating and drinking, and after that you may eat and drink'? 9 Does he thank the servant because the latter did what he had been ordered to do?[469] 10 So y o u also, when y o u have done everything y o u were ordered to do, say, 'We are unprofitable servants; we have (merely) done our duty.' "[470]

17:1-10 *A Warning Issuing in The Parable of The Coldly Calculating*
Servant
For 17:1, 2 cf. Matt. 18:6, 7; Mark 9:42;
For 17:3b, 4 cf. Matt. 18:21, 22;
and for 17:5, 6 cf. Matt. 17:20; 21:21.

A. *The Warning*

For a possible connection between chapters 16 and 17 see p. 540. Another possible link is as follows: Hell (16:23, 24) is terrible. Once there, escape is impossible (16:26–31). The disciples of Jesus should be on their guard, therefore, lest through their words or actions others are led astray and perish everlastingly (see 17:1).

As was true with respect to chapters 15 and 16, so also chapter 17 can be

---

465. Literally, "if a millstone is hung around his neck," etc.
466. Or: Be constantly watching yourselves.
467. Or: and sit down to eat.
468. Or: fasten your belt and wait on me.
469. Or: He does not thank the servant . . . does he?
470. Or: what we were obliged to do.

conveniently divided into three parts. See the Outline. Part I contains an earnest *warning* and ends with a *parable* (verses 1–10). Part II reports a *miracle* (verses 11–19). Part III is, to a large extent, a *prophecy* (verses 20–37).

1. He said to his disciples, Temptations are bound to come, but woe to him through whom they come.

Though in the opinion of many exegetes there is no topical or any other connection between the various parts of chapter 17, this verdict is not necessarily true. There are connections, though the one which this or that interpreter sees may not have been the one which the evangelist had in mind. The notion that the sayings are wholly disconnected flies in the face of 1:3. Luke has given us "an orderly account." His thoroughly inspired report is not a hodgepodge.

The Pharisees had been treating with disdain the tax-collectors and sinners who crowded around Jesus (15:1, 2). The rich show-off of the parable had treated Lazarus similarly (16:19–21). By means of this attitude spiritual harm could easily be done to the neglected and/or despised people. Jesus now warns his *disciples* not to commit a similar sin; that is, in their case, not to be an occasion of stumbling for the outcasts who had turned to the Savior for refuge.

It is, however, impossible in this present realm of sin to put an end to every temptation, every enticement to sin. "Temptations are bound to come." Cf. Matt. 18:7; I Cor. 11:19; I Tim. 4:1. It is of the very nature of sin that it spreads. It would be easier to stop water hyacinths from clogging the waterways of Florida than to prevent temptations from clogging the tracks of the human race, including even the church. But though it is impossible to eradicate temptations, by God's grace it is possible to prevent oneself from belonging to the company of the tempters. And a wrong attitude on the part of a disciple could easily tempt the despised one to sin by returning evil for evil. It is understandable that Jesus continues:

2. Better is it for him if, with a millstone hung around his neck, he has been hurled into the sea, than that he should cause one of these little ones to sin.

What a terrible thing it is to place in the path of even the least of Christ's disciples a temptation; that is, an enticement to sin, a beguiling allurement, a *trap*.

The millstone of which Jesus speaks is the top stone of the two between which the grain is crushed. The reference is not to the handmill but to the much heavier stone drawn by a donkey. In the middle of the topstone there is a hole through which grain can be fed so as to be crushed between the two stones. The presence of this hole explains the phrase "a millstone hung around his neck." With such a stone around the neck to have been hurled into the sea makes drowning doubly sure. Note "these little ones." How dear they are to the Savior!

Because the sin of leading others astray is so terrible, Jesus may have added the admonition, "Be constantly watching yourselves," so as not to

794

become involved in this sin. This interpretation makes the connection with the immediately preceding clear. However, the original can also be rendered: **3. Constantly be looking out for one another.** Thus construed these words easily link with what immediately follows: **if your brother commits a sin reprove him; and if he repents forgive him.** Jesus continues: **4. Even if he sins against you seven times in a day, and seven times comes back to you, saying, I'm sorry, you must forgive him.**

Just as it is wrong for disciples to entice others into sin, so also it would be wrong for them not to be forgiving when others sin against them. They should reprove the offender, and if he repents they should be quick to forgive him. Moreover, as in his answer to Peter's question, recorded in Matt. 18:21, 22, so also here Jesus emphasizes that the spirit of forgiving love recognizes no boundaries or limitations. What Jesus means, therefore, is "Forgive *the penitent* without ever stopping."

This double requirement, namely, on the one hand, to steer clear from causing others to stumble, and on the other, always to be ready to forgive, requires strength from above. And believing that such strength will be given to them in answer to their prayers requires more faith than the disciples feel they now have. This situation explains verse **5. The apostles said to the Lord, Increase our faith.**

Note the encouraging reply: **6. The Lord replied, If y o u have faith as (small as) a mustard seed, y o u would say to this mulberry tree, Be uprooted and planted in the sea, and it would have obeyed y o u.**

As the note on 17:6 on pp. 801, 802 shows, this probably means, "If y o u have faith as small as a mustard seed, and if y o u would constantly put it into practice, y o u would say to this mulberry tree," etc. In other words, no task assigned by the Lord, including even causing a mulberry tree to be uprooted and planted in the sea, would be impossible for y o u to accomplish, *as long as y o u remain in trustful contact with God.*

Thus also a mustard seed, be it ever so small, *because of its vital and uninterrupted contact with its nourishing environment,* grows and grows until it becomes a tree so tall that the birds of the air come and lodge in its branches. Cf. Matt. 17:20.

The apostles, strengthened by this assurance, will now supposedly begin to perform marvelous works. But in what spirit? With what attitude of mind and heart? That this makes a difference is clear from 10:17, 20, and from the paragraph which now follows:

B. *A Parable*

7–10. Who among y o u, if he has a servant plowing or tending sheep, will say to him when he comes in from the field, Come at once and recline at table? Will he not rather say to him, Prepare my supper, dress up properly so you can wait on me until I finish eating and drinking, and after that you may eat and drink? Does he thank the servant because the latter did what he had been ordered to do? So y o u also, when y o u have

done everything y o u were ordered to do, say, We are unprofitable servants; we have (merely) done our duty.

Wrong interpretations of this parable have led to various difficulties. Questions such as the following have been asked:

a. Does not Jesus contradict himself when he says that no master would ever tell his servant, when he comes in from the field, to recline at table, with the implication that he, the master, would wait on him; while in 12:37 Jesus promises to do that very thing?

b. Why would servants, who have done everything they had been ordered to do, be called unprofitable?

c. What moved Luke, immediately after reporting this parable, to go all the way back to the beginning of the journey he is describing, and thus picture Jesus as traveling "along the border between Samaria and Galilee"? See 17:11.

With the right interpretation of this parable everything falls into line and the difficulties vanish.

It is clear that we are dealing here with the owner of a small farm. This farmer has only one servant. Some insist that the word used in the original—namely *doulos*—a word which sometimes means slave, sometimes servant, must here be rendered *slave*. We should remember, however, that Jesus is addressing his message primarily to "his disciples" (verse 1). He is saying, "Who among y o u ...?" Is it not probable that some of these disciples had *servants* rather than *slaves*? See Mark 1:20. Further, we should understand that what the parable is picturing is that which does *not* happen in the realm in which God is consistently recognized as King. In fact, the very opposite takes place here.

The servant pictured in this parable does only what he has been ordered to do, and *the spirit* of a *slave* has taken possession of him. All day long he has been plowing or tending sheep. When he comes in from the field, his boss orders him to wait on him while he, the master, is eating and drinking. The servant is told, "When I'm finished, you can eat." The servant obeys. He does exactly what he was told to do, no less but also certainly no more. Why does he do it at all? Probably because he does not want to lose his job. After all, he has to eat. So, grudgingly he finishes his chores. Are we becoming guilty of exaggeration when we picture this coldly calculating servant as looking out of the corner of his eye every once in a while to see how the farmer is doing, whether he is not almost finished with his meal?

However that may be, we believe that Robertson, *Word Pictures*, Vol. II, p. 227, has interpreted the parable correctly when he states, "The slavish spirit gains no promotion in business life or in the kingdom of God." Naturally the master of this coldly calculating servant would not even think of "waiting on" such a servant.

What the parable means, therefore, is this:

a. In the kingdom of God—the realm in which God's sovereignty is gladly recognized—matters are entirely different. To be sure, here, too,

God's children aim to do his will, but they do it with gladness of heart, in the spirit of love and gratitude.

b. In *their* case the promise of Luke 12:37 (the Lord waiting on them) will be realized. See the explanation of that passage.

c. And now, too, we begin to understand what may well have been the reason why the evangelist, after reporting this parable, immediately proceeds to tell the story about the ten lepers who were cured by Jesus. All ten were ordered to "show themselves to the priests." All ten, in obedience to the command, go on their way. *One*, however, returns. He is *the exact opposite* of the coldly calculating servant. He *praises* God and *thanks* Jesus. He does *more* than he had been ordered to do. And he does it *exuberantly*. Luke has indeed given us *"an orderly account."*

For *Practical Lessons* and *Greek Words*, etc., see pp. 799–803.

---

11 Now as Jesus was going on to Jerusalem, he was traveling along the border between Samaria and Galilee. 12 And as he was entering a certain village, there met him ten leprous men, who stood at a distance 13 and lifted up their voices, saying, "Jesus, Master, take pity on us."[471] 14 When he saw them he said to them, "Go and show yourselves to the priests." And as they were going they were cleansed.

15 Then one of them, upon seeing that he was cured, turned back and in a loud voice praised God, 16 and fell on his face before Jesus' feet, thanking him. —And he was a Samaritan!

17 Jesus asked, "Were not all ten cleansed? Where, then, (are) the nine? 18 Were none found to return and give praise to God except this foreigner?" 19 And he said to him, "Get up and go on your way; your faith has made you well."

17:11–19 *A Miracle: The Cleansing of Ten Lepers, Only One of Whom Returned to Give Thanks*

11. Now as Jesus was going on to Jerusalem, he was traveling along the border between Samaria and Galilee.

The probable reason why Luke turns back in his story to what happened earlier, that is, at the very beginning of the journey to Jerusalem by way of Perea, has already been given. See on verses 7–10. For the translation "along the border between Samaria and Galilee" see the note on 17:11 on page 803.

As we see it, then, Jesus, in the company of his disciples, was traveling along the border between Samaria and Galilee, probably taking the road which near Bethshean crosses the Jordan into Perea. See map, p. 854.

12, 13. And as he was entering a certain village, there met him ten leprous men, who stood at a distance and lifted up their voices, saying, Jesus, Master, take pity on us.

The exact place where the miracle took place is not indicated, and is of little importance. The ten lepers were of mixed nationality (verses 16, 18);

---

471. Or: have mercy on us.

this is not a strange phenomenon where two provinces meet. Besides, misery loves company, and when one is afflicted with leprosy nationality ceases to be a barrier to fellowship: Jew and Samaritan unite. For more on leprosy see on 5:12–16. In view of Lev. 13:45, 46; Num. 5:2–4; 12:14, 15; II Kings 7:3 it is not surprising that these ten leprous men stood *at a distance*. When Jesus was entering the unnamed village the ten cry out—their voices still enabling them to do so—"Jesus, Master, take pity on us."

14. When he saw them he said to them, Go and show yourselves to the priests.

How different this act of healing leprosy from the one described in 5:13. In the present case Jesus does not touch the ten. In fact, he does not even say, "Be cleansed," or anything similar. He simply tells them to go and show themselves to the priests. This was required by the law (Lev. 14:1 f.). Besides, once the priests had pronounced them healed, they would be restored to full social and religious fellowship with the rest of the people. **And as they were going they were cleansed.**

Note in how many respects these ten men were alike: (a) all were afflicted with the dreadful disease; (b) all were determined to do something about it; (c) all had heard about Jesus, and believed that he might be able to cure them, at the very least would take pity on them; (d) all appeal to Jesus, acknowledging him as Master or Rabbi; (e) all, in obedience to Christ's command, proceed on their way to the priests; and (f) all are healed.

But at this point the similarity ends. The evangelist must have been happy to be able to record that not all the ten were like the unprofitable servant of the immediately preceding parable, who did only what he had been commanded to do. It must have grieved the beloved physician that he was unable to report that what was true of the *one* was also, in every respect, true of the nine. Here is Luke's report:

15, 16. Then one of them, upon seeing that he was cured, turned back and in a loud voice praised God, and fell on his face before Jesus' feet, thanking him. —And he was a Samaritan!

While the ten had started on their way to the priests, a current of health and vigor was rushing through every tissue of their bodies. They were completely cured and they knew it. But suddenly one of the ten—only *one*—turned around and walked back to Jesus. It may be assumed that he had not as yet arrived at the headquarters of the priests. The account leaves the impression that the ten had not walked very far away from their Healer before this one man returned. Nothing prevented him from seeing the priests a little later.

As he returned he praised God, thereby publicly acknowledging him as the One to whom he owed the great blessing he had just now received. Also, he fell on his face and thanked Jesus, for in the Master he recognized God's Representative, God's power and love operating through Jesus. That at least! How this man loved Jesus! Was not his humble gratitude born of love?

It is with marked emphasis that the evangelist adds, "and he was a

Samaritan!" As if to say, "Think of it, a Samaritan!" A man belonging to a race hated by the Jews. Were not Jews and Samaritans enemies? See 9:52, 53; cf. John 4:9. Did not the Jews look down on the Samaritans because this mixed race was not "sound" in its theology? But *this* Samaritan is different; by God's grace, of course. He thanks . . . a Jew! When the present passage is added to such other Lucan references as 4:25-27; 7:9 (cf. Matt. 8:10-12); 11:30-32, does it not become clear that what Luke is saying is this: an international church, consisting not only of Jews but certainly also of non-Jews, is gradually being established?

17-19. Jesus asked, Were not all ten cleansed? Where, then, (are) the nine? Were none found to return and give praise to God except this foreigner? And he said to him, Get up and go on your way; your faith has made you well.

It is clear that Jesus was grieved because only one of the ten cleansed lepers returned to give praise to God. Think of it: only one out of ten, and that one not a Jew but a Samaritan! This shows that although the Jews, as a nation, had been blessed far above any other nation (Ps. 147:20; Isa. 5:1-4; Amos 3:2), yet here a group of Jews allow a Samaritan to surpass them in praising God and giving thanks.

There must have been an argument. It is hard to believe that without revealing his intentions the Samaritan had suddenly left the group to return to Jesus. The probability—almost certainty—is that he had urged the others to return with him. But no, they refused.

Yes, the refusal of the nine pained Jesus. What is often overlooked is the humility revealed in his double question, "Where, then, are the nine? Were none found . . .?" Jesus asks, "Were none found to return *and give praise to God* . . . ?" He does not even add, "and to thank me." He is deeply concerned about the fact that his Father in heaven did not receive the praise due to him. He says nothing about himself.

"The Most High . . . is kind to the ungrateful and wicked" (6:35). "He causes his sun to rise on evil (people) and good, and sends rain on righteous and unrighteous" (Matt. 5:45). Common blessings, to be sure. But no common gratitude!

Jesus, having received the offering of a thankful heart and thankful lips, dismisses the Samaritan with the familiar words—they occur also in 7:50; 8:48; 18:42; and cf. Matt. 9:22; Mark 5:34; 10:52—"Your faith has made you well." See on 7:50 for explanation.[472]

Practical Lessons Derived from Luke 17:1-19

Verse 2

"These little ones." The same Savior who, when he himself was afflicted, "opened not his mouth" was filled with indignation when anyone tried to hurt "his little ones."

---

472. Notes on Greek words, phrases, and constructions in 17:1-19 begin on page 800.

Verse 4

"Even if he sins against you seven times . . . you must forgive him." The way of the world is entirely different. Gen. 4:24 places the world's sevenfold vengeance over against the Savior's sevenfold forgiveness.

Verse 10

"When y o u have done everything y o u were ordered to do, say, 'We are unprofitable servants.'"
Not how much we do but in what spirit we do it is what counts:
Cain and Abel both brought an offering.
The Pharisee and the publican both entered the temple to pray.
In each case, what a difference!

Verse 18

"Were none found to return and give praise to God except this foreigner?"
It is not how much light we have received that is the most important, but what we have done with the light we received. In the present case the Samaritan, though less enlightened than the Jews, used what he received to better advantage.

Notes on Greek Words, Phrases, and Constructions in 17:1–19

Verses 1, 2

ἀνένδεκτόν* ἐστιν . . . μὴ ἐλθεῖν: lit., it is impossible (that temptations) should not come; i.e., they are bound to come. The idea that they will not arrive is (lit.) inadmissible, unacceptable. Note ἀ-privative plus δέχομαι.
σκάνδαλα, acc. pl. of σκάνδαλον. See the note on 7:23 on page 403.
Note the verb σκανδαλίσῃ, third per. s. aor. subjunct. act. of σκανδαλίζω, to cause to sin, to lead astray.
λυσιτελεῖ, third per. s. pres. indicat. of λυσιτελέω* = λύω, to pay, plus τέλη, taxes (cf. *toll*); hence, in general this verb came to mean: to pay; imperson., it pays; it is profitable; followed by ἤ, it is more profitable . . . *than;* or simply, as here, *it is better . . . than.*
For τράχηλον, s. acc. of τράχηλος, neck, see the note on 15:20 on page 761.
ἔρριπται, third per. s. perf. indicat. pass. of ῥίπτω, to hurl. Some see a connection between this Greek verb and English "rip." A connection with Germ. *werfen* and Dutch *werpen* (both meaning: to throw, hurl) has also been suggested.
Note graphic change from pres. to perf. tense: "if a millstone is hung around his neck and he has been hurled" (thus literally).

Verse 3a

προσέχετε ἑαυτοῖς. Some prefer the translation "Watch yourselves." The preceding context harmonizes well with this rendering, and with "Be constantly watching yourselves." It is a well-known fact, however, that the Greek reflexive pronoun is used at times with reciprocal sense. In the present case this reciprocal meaning suits the immediately following conditional sentences (verses 3b, 4). It is best, therefore, to leave room for both possibilities, reciprocal and reflexive: "Constantly be looking out for one another" and "Be constantly watching yourselves."

Verses 3b, 4

The three clauses introduced by ἐάν are third class (or future more vivid) conditional directives. In each case the ἐάν protasis is followed by an aor. subjunct.

As to the apodoses in the first and second cases—reprove him, forgive him—the verb is sec. per. s. aor. imperat. The action must be immediate, definite, incisive. In the third case—you must forgive him—the verb is sec. per. s. fut. (volitive) indicat. act., again very definite and positive: you must forgive him!

Verse 5

As some see it, the words πρόσθες ἡμῖν πίστιν mean, "Add faith to us," that is, "Give us faith in addition to other things." So, for example, Robertson, Translation, pp. 97, 210. Similar is the rendering suggested in L.N.T. (A. and G.), p. 726, "Grant us faith." And so also Maurer in his article on προστίθημι, Th.D.N.T., Vol. VIII, pp. 167, 168, "Lord confer faith on us."

On the whole, however, translators and commentators are not in agreement with this view. They favor the translation, "Increase our faith." They do so for good reasons:

a. The verb used in the original, πρόσθες, sec. per. s. 2nd aor. imperat. act. of προστίθημι, does not necessarily have to refer to the addition of things different in character from those already possessed. It can also indicate an increase in that which one already has. See II Chron. 28:13; LXX Psalm 70:14; and in the New Testament see Matt. 6:27; Luke 12:25.

b. Nowhere does Jesus state that his disciples, considered as a group, had no faith. He affirms the very opposite (John 17:6-8, 25). They had faith, but it was "little faith" (Matt. 6:30; 8:26; 14:31; 16:8; Luke 12:28), faith in need of being increased. The prayer of the father of the epileptic boy—"I do believe; help my unbelief"—would have befitted the little group of Christ's constant and immediate followers also.

c. The present context, according to which the Master requires of the disciples a sincere manifestation of the loving and forgiving attitude (see verses 3, 4), may well have alerted them to the realization of the fact that much was still lacking in their faith.

In view of all this, the rendering "Increase our faith," or something similar—e.g., "Give us more faith"—is undoubtedly the best.

Before proceeding any farther it should be pointed out that in the New Testament the verb προστίθημι occurs in still another sense, in harmony with Hebrew usage. In that case its English equivalent may be an adverb. So, for example, προσθεὶς εἶπεν. παραβολήν means, "Again he told a parable." This can also be rendered, "He proceeded to tell a parable" (19:11). Similar is, "He proceeded to send" (20:11, 12).

Verse 6

After the introductory words εἶπεν δὲ ὁ κύριος, there follows a mixed conditional sentence, with a simple or first class protasis, indicating reality—in this case with εἰ followed by pres. indicat. ἔχετε—and a compound apodosis. This apodosis or conclusion consists of:

   a. the imperf. indicat. ἐλέγχετε with ἄν in its first member, implying *present unreality;* and

   b. the aor. indicat. ὑπήκουσεν with ἄν in its second member, implying *past unreality.*

The correct translation is therefore, "If y o u have faith as (small as) a mustard seed, y o u would say to this mulberry tree, 'Be uprooted and planted in the sea,' and it would have obeyed y o u."

However, this rendering, accepted in substance also by Robertson (*Translation,* p. 97), may not sound right to some. What is probably expected, in English, is something like, "If y o u had faith . . . y o u would say," or "If y o u have faith, y o u will [or can] say." Several translators have adopted one of these alternatives. But the first of these attempts ignores the fact that in the original the protasis indicates reality; the second attempt overlooks the fact that the compound apodosis is one of unreality.

The solution is probably this: what we have here is another instance of *abbreviated discourse.* See N.T.C. on John, Vol. I, p. 206, a type of idiom that is far more frequent, both in literature and in daily conversation, than we sometimes realize. The complete thought, including what is expressed and what is implied (as the context indicates), is probably this, "If y o u have faith as (small as) a mustard seed, and if y o u would constantly put it into practice, y o u would say to this mulberry tree," etc.

Jesus did not deny that these men had faith. He reprimanded them because of their *little* faith. It should be noted that also in the parallel passage (Matt. 17:20) Jesus did not use a protasis of unreality. The protasis there is that of a future more vivid or third class conditional sentence. As was noted in the explanation of that passage, "No task assigned by the Lord is going to be impossible to perform when the person who receives the mandate *is and remains in trustful contact with God.*"

For κόκκος (here acc. s. κόκκον) σινάπεως, mustard seed, see the note on 13:19 on page 713.

συκαμίνῳ, dat. s. of συκάμινος*, the sycamine or black mulberry tree, not to be confused with the συκομορέα, sycamore tree, or with the συκῆ, fig tree.

The two verbs in verse 6 that have not yet been mentioned are sec. per. s. aor. imperat. pass. forms, respectively of ἐκριζόω, to uproot, and φυτεύω, to plant.

Verse 7

ἀροτριῶντα, acc. s. masc. pres. participle of ἀροτριάω, to plow. See I Cor. 9:10. Cf. *arable.*

For ἀνάπεσε—sec. per. s. 2nd aor. imperat. of ἀναπίπτω, to fall backward to recline for a meal—and its synonyms, see the note on 11:37 on page 645.

Verse 8

τί δειπνήσω, first per. s. fut. indicat. of δειπνέω, to eat, sup. Lit. "Get ready what I shall eat," i.e., in the present context, "Prepare my supper." See also the note on 14:12 on page 729.

περιζωσάμενος, nom. s. masc. aor. middle (causative) participle of περιζώννυμι, to fasten one's belt by binding it around oneself; hence, to dress up properly.

φάγω καὶ πίω, first per. s. 2nd aor. subjunctives (after ἕως), respectively of ἐσθίω, to eat, and πίνω, to drink.

φάγεσαι καὶ πίεσαι, both sec. per. s. fut. (here volitive) indicat. middle forms, respectively of ἐσθίω and πίνω; Koine for classical Greek φάγῃ and πίῃ; lit. "and afterward you may eat and drink."

Verses 9, 10

μή expects a negative answer. It can be translated correctly in more than one way. See the translation and suggested alternative on p. 793.

ἔχει χάριν . . . ; = does he thank . . . ? χάριν ἔχειν τινί = to be thankful to someone; also: to express this gratitude, to thank.

διαταχθέντα (twice), acc. pl. neut. aor. pass. participle of διατάσσω, to assign, order, charge.

ἀχρεῖοι (ἀ plus χρεία), useless, unprofitable, unworthy.

Verse 11

διὰ μέσον; lit. "through the middle of," and so probably "along the border between," that border being indeed "in the middle," with Galilee to the north, and Samaria to the south. Jesus was traveling through this middle line. For a different view see Robertson, *Word Pictures*, pp. 227, 228. Was that author's view influenced by his theory discussed above, on p. 542, according to which what he considers Luke's *three* journeys must be identified with John's three?

Verse 13

ἦραν, third per. pl. aor. indicat. act. of αἴρω, to lift up, raise. Related meanings in Luke's Gospel:

to take, carry (9:3)
to take along (22:36)
to take out, withdraw (19:21, 22)
to bear up (4:11)
to pick up (9:17)
to take up (9:23)
to get (17:31)
to take away, remove (6:29, 30; 8:12, 18; 11:22, 52; 19:24, 26; 23:18).

Verse 14

ἐκαθαρίσθησαν, third per. pl. aor. indicat. pass. of καθαρίζω, to cleanse; pass., as here, to be cleansed; same form in verse 17. See also 4:27; 5:12, 13; 7:22; 11:39.

Verse 18

ἀλλογενής* (ἄλλος plus γένος), "man of another nation" (or race), foreigner. In the temple at Jerusalem this word was included in a warning, addressed to non-Israelites, to proceed no farther toward the interior than the Court of the Gentiles. The inscription in Greek and Latin reads:
"Let no man of another nation enter inside the barrier and the fence around the temple. Whoever is caught will have himself to blame that his death follows."

803

20 Asked by the Pharisees when the kingdom of God would come, Jesus replied by saying, "The kingdom of God does not come with outward display; 21 nor will people say, 'Look, here (it is)!' or 'There (it is)!' for, note well, the kingdom of God is within y o u."

22 And he said to the disciples, "The days shall come when y o u will long to see one of the days of the Son of man, but will not see it. 23 And they will say to y o u, 'Look, here!' or 'Look, there!' Do not go running off after them. 24 For as the lightning lights up the sky from one end to the other, so will the Son of man be in his day.[473] 25 But first he must suffer many things and be rejected by this generation.

26 "And just as it was in the days of Noah, so also will it be in the days of the Son of man: 27 People were eating, they were drinking, they were marrying, they were being given in marriage, right up to the day Noah entered the ark. Then the flood came and destroyed them all. 28 So also it was in the days of Lot: People were eating, they were drinking, they were buying, they were selling, they were planting, they were building. 29 But on the day Lot went out of Sodom, fire and sulfur rained down from heaven and destroyed them all. 30 So it will be on the day the Son of man is revealed.

31 "On that day let him who happens to be on the housetop, with his goods in the house, not go down to get them. Similarly, let not the person who is in the field turn back. 32 Remember Lot's wife! 33 Whoever tries to keep his life shall lose it, but whoever loses (his life) shall preserve it. 34 I tell y o u, in that night there will be two people in one bed; one will be taken, the other left behind. 35 Two women will be grinding together; one will be taken, the other left behind."[474]

37 They asked him, "Where, Lord?" He told them, "Wherever (there is) a corpse, there also the vultures will gather."

17:20–37 A Prophecy: The Coming of the Kingdom
Cf. Matt. 24:23–28, 37–41

Such qualities as gratitude and faith, with love implied (17:15–19), are not man-made but result from the dynamic operation of the rule or kingship of God in human hearts and lives. Very logically, therefore, the evangelist, by the inspiration of the Holy Spirit, proceeds now to the discussion of this very basic theme: the kingship or kingdom of God.

In order to understand what follows it should be borne in mind that in the Greek original the word *basileia* sometimes means *kingdom,* sometimes *kingship* (rule, reign, sovereignty). Unless this fact is kept in mind, one will experience some difficulty in understanding verses

20, 21. Asked by the Pharisees when the kingdom of God would come, Jesus replied by saying, The kingdom of God does not come with outward display; nor will people say, Look, here (it is)! or There (it is)! for, note well, the kingdom of God is within y o u.

The Pharisees and their many followers were looking forward to the arrival of an outward, earthly, visible kingdom, one in which the Jews would occupy a very prominent place. They were hardly able to wait for its

473. Some manuscripts leave out "in his day."
474. There is insufficient manuscript support for verse 36, "Two men will be in the field; one will be taken, the other left behind." But see Matt. 24:40.

arrival. So anxious were they to know when it would be established that they were willing to obtain information with respect to this subject from any source whatever . . . even from Jesus.

Jesus, however, in his answer indicates that they harbor a misconception concerning the nature of the kingdom, as if it would arrive with loud proclamations, prancing horses, marching armies, martial music; briefly, with "outward show." If that were true, people would be greeting its arrival by shouting, "Here it is," "There it is." Over against all this, Jesus declares that the kingdom—or here preferably kingship, reign, rule—of God is basically *spiritual* in its essence. It is *within,* or, if one prefers, *inside* a person. Wherever God is truly recognized and honored as King, there one finds his kingdom or kingship.

Note that little word *within* or *inside.* See the defense of this translation in the note on 17:20, 21 on page 810. Either "within" or "inside (of)" is also favored by A.V., Williams, A.R.V. (in the text), N.I.V. (in the text), Phillips, Norlie, Weymouth, Goodspeed, Good News for Modern Man, Lenski, Robertson (very strongly), etc. *The context certainly favors it:* the kingdom-kingship Jesus has in mind here is not an outward, visible entity, so that people would be able to point to it and exclaim, "There it is," but consists of inner qualities, such as "righteousness and peace and joy in the Holy Spirit" (Rom. 14:17), qualities that exist wherever God is recognized as King.

An objection has been advanced against this interpretation, however. We are told that Jesus is answering the *Pharisees* (verse 20), and that he certainly could not have told these people, his bitter opponents, "The kingdom of God is *within y o u.*" He must, therefore, have meant, "The kingdom of God is *among* y o u, for I am here and my disciples are scattered here and there among y o u."

The answer to that objection lies ready at hand. The pronoun *you* (whether s. or pl.) has more than one meaning. The most common meaning is "the person(s) addressed." But another and not at all uncommon meaning, both in Greek and in English (and other languages), is "a person" or "one." For example, *"You* don't know what love is unless *you* have experienced and practiced it," meaning "A person does not know," etc.

The contextual interpretation stands, therefore.

Although Jesus has been speaking about his spiritual entrance into hearts, lives, and spheres, that is, about God's spiritual kingdom or kingship, he never denies that there will also be a glorious visible manifestation of God's kingdom at the close of the new dispensation:

22-25. And he said to the disciples, The days shall come when y o u will long to see one of the days of the Son of man, but will not see it. And they will say to y o u, Look, here! or Look, there! Do not go running off after them. For as the lightning lights up the sky from one end to the other, so will the Son of man be in his day. But first he must suffer many things and be rejected by this generation.

The Pharisees are out of the picture now. These words are spoken to Christ's followers, both then and down through the ages. Note the following:

a. The expression *The days shall come* means, "The time will arrive."

b. The word *one* in "one of the days" may be a Semitism for "the first" (of the days). See John 20:1.

c. The phrase *the days of the Son of man* probably signifies "the Messianic era" at the close of the world's history. See S.BK., Vol. II, p. 237.

d. For the expression *the Son of man* see the explanation of 5:24. He is "the Son of man" in his character as the One who through suffering attains to glory, but, in a sense, was glorious all the while, even from eternity. For his ultimate manifestation in glory see also Dan. 7:13, 14; Matt. 26:64.

e. Believers will long to see the beginning of this Messianic era. Today we would say, "They will yearn for the second coming of Christ," because the days immediately preceding that time of fulfilment will be days of severe oppression and persecution.

f. The words, ". . . but will not see it. And they will say to y o u, 'Look, here!'" etc., indicate that there will be people who, in their nervous excitement, will believe that the Son of man has already arrived but is hiding somewhere. Jesus warns his followers not to go running after them. The time of arrival will not be known in advance (Matt. 24:36; Mark 13:32); and the actual return, when it occurs, will be visible all over the world. It will be as lightning which, flashing suddenly and brilliantly, lights up *the entire sky,* from one end to the other.

g. However, long before the second coming takes place the Son of man *must* suffer. It is a must, for the decree of God from eternity must be carried out, prophecy must be fulfilled, those chosen from eternity must be ransomed. He must suffer "many things." The gruesome details of this suffering are here lovingly withheld.

h. The words "and must be rejected *by this generation*" show that Jesus was pointing to Calvary.

Having spoken about his second coming and about his suffering that was to occur much earlier, Jesus now pictures how people will be living during the days just before his return:

26, 27. And just as it was in the days of Noah, so also will it be in the days of the Son of man: People were eating, they were drinking, they were marrying, they were being given in marriage, right up to the day Noah entered the ark. Then the flood came and destroyed them all.

The very suddenness of the coming points up the necessity to guard against unpreparedness and carelessness. During the days of Noah—that is, when this "preacher of righteousness" was building the ark (Gen. 5:32—7:5) and warning the people (II Peter 2:5)—they refused to take to heart what he was doing and saying. They were unconcerned. They continued to live "as always," eating and drinking, marrying and giving in marriage.

The question might be asked, "What is wrong with these activities?" The answer is, "Nothing at all." In fact, by means of them men are able to glorify God (I Cor. 10:31). But when the soul becomes entirely wrapped up in them, so that matters such as these become ends in themselves, and spiritual tasks are neglected, they are no longer a blessing but have become a curse. They have become evidences of gross materialism, false security, and often cold selfishness.

The men of Noah's day failed to realize their perilous situation until it was too late. Suddenly the *cataclysm*—the word used in the original—came. For them it was indeed a "washing down," which is the basic meaning of the word. The flood destroyed them all. Cf. I Thess. 5:3.

Continued, with another example from history:

28-30. So also it was in the days of Lot: People were eating, they were drinking, they were buying, they were selling, they were planting, they were building. But on the day Lot went out of Sodom, fire and sulfur rained down from heaven and destroyed them all. So it will be on the day the Son of man is revealed.

The people of Lot's day were also engaged in the ordinary affairs of life: eating and drinking, buying and selling, planting and building. Again, there was nothing wrong with that. What was definitely wrong, though, was the fact that their minds and hearts were entirely absorbed in these matters. They took no time to satisfy their souls' needs. They were utterly self-centered. Lot lived among them, as a righteous man who was distressed by their filthy lives (II Peter 2:7, 8). Sodom's inhabitants paid no attention to him. Even when, at God's command, Lot left Sodom, the people in general went right ahead in their "business as usual" manner. Then fire and sulfur rained down from heaven and destroyed them all.

The question occurs, "Why did Jesus select Noah and Lot as examples of men who took heed?" Certainly, in view of Gen. 9:20, 21, with reference to Noah, and of Gen. 19:30-38, with reference to Lot, these two Old Testament characters were not exactly paragons of virtue.

The point is, however, that both heeded God's warning. Noah built an ark—an action which must have seemed to many to be the most foolish thing he could possibly do. Cf. Gen. 6:14; 7:5. And as to Lot, when God ordered him to leave Sodom, he did, though with a degree of hesitancy. Cf. Gen. 19:14-16. While these two made the necessary preparations in obedience to God's commands, the indifferent multitudes perished. In both cases sudden destruction overtook them. The water drowned them. The fire (and sulfur) consumed them.

So, says Jesus, it will be also on the day "the Son of man" at his coming is revealed in all his glory.

31. On that day let him who happens to be on the housetop, with his goods in the house, not go down to get them. Similarly, let not the person who is in the field turn back.

In Matt. 24:17, 18 and its parallel Mark 13:15, 16, this warning is applied to the days just previous to Jerusalem's fall (A.D. 70). The meaning of these passages is that the man who is on the flat roof of his house—from which by means of an outside ladder he can descend in order as quickly as possible to flee to the hills—must not, after descending, enter his house in order to rescue any of his goods. Similarly, the laborer, dressed only in his tunic and thus working in the field, must not before his flight to the hills go back into his house to get his coat. Both of these men *should flee at once*, without trying to rescue any possessions, whether a coat or anything else.

In connection with the present passage any thought of *fleeing* is, of course, out of the question. Nevertheless, the passage as such is entirely appropriate. It means that in connection with Christ's return the only proper attitude both then and now is wholehearted surrender to him and his word. Such complete devotion should be placed *above all worldly interests*.

To this admonition Jesus adds an illustration, showing what is the tragic result of looking back with yearning to possessions that have been left behind:

32. Remember Lot's wife! The story is told in Gen. 19:17, 26: "And when they [two angels] had brought them [Lot, his wife, and two daughters] out, they said, 'Flee for your life; do not look back or stop anywhere in the valley. Flee to the hills, lest you be consumed.' . . . But Lot's wife looked back from behind him, and she became a pillar of salt."

The sad thing about Lot's wife was, however, not what many think it was. It was not, at least *not primarily*, that she turned into a pillar of salt (however one may wish to interpret this), but that in her scale of values she placed earth above heaven, material things above spiritual.

What Jesus holds before his followers, then, is that they should be so prepared for his return that in their thoughts, words, and deeds, they always assign the pre-eminence to him, doing everything out of love for him, and thus for God Triune.

In complete harmony with this interpretation is what follows in verse **33. Whoever tries to keep his life shall lose it, but whoever loses (his life) shall preserve it.**

For explanation see on 9:24 which, in slightly different phraseology, conveys the same meaning. In the present context those who are represented as trying to hang on to their life, and losing it, are the earth-bound people of Noah's day and of Lot's day, including definitely also Lot's wife, and all those similarly minded. That they are indeed losers will become apparent especially on the day of Christ's return. On that day the preservation and victory of the people who have shown the opposite attitude, that of self-denial and self-sacrifice, out of love for their Savior, will also become publicly manifest.

At Christ's return mankind splits in two, in line with the *spiritual* division that had occurred earlier. Cf. Matt. 25:31–46. This thought is emphasized in verses

34, 35. I tell y o u, in that night there will be two people in one bed; one will be taken; the other left behind. Two women will be grinding together; one will be taken, the other left behind.

Physical nearness will neither save nor damn anyone. Also, once the final day arrives, every opportunity to be saved is gone forever. The door is shut for those who have not taken advantage of the opportunity to be saved. See Matt. 25:10.

Of two people in one bed—either two men, or perhaps husband and wife; the original permits either view—one will be taken; the other left behind. Similarly, of two women grinding together, one will be taken, the other left behind.

Verse 34 pictures what happens during the night; verse 35 what takes place during the day. This is very logical, for if the Son of man arrives in the air above a place where it is night, it will be day on the other side of the globe; and vice versa. What does "taken" mean? The answer is found in I Thess. 4:17, "They shall be caught up in clouds to meet the Lord in the air." See also Rev. 14:14-16.

And what does "left behind" signify? It signifies "left to their doom." For further details see Matt. 13:41, 42; II Thess. 1:7-9; Rev. 14:17-20.

37. They asked him, Where, Lord? He told them, Wherever (there is) a corpse, there also the vultures will gather.

Meaning: wherever there are those who are spiritually dead, there the final judgment will overtake them. Cf. Matt. 24:28.

Vultures (not eagles) swoop down upon *a carcass.*[475]

Practical Lessons Derived from Luke 17:20-37

Verse 21

"The kingdom of God is within y o u."

Throughout the Gospels Jesus is emphasizing the importance of that which is *within* the heart (Matt. 12:34; 13:52; 15:18; Luke 6:45). Those who maintain that it was Paul (Rom. 14:17) but never Jesus who viewed God's kingdom as being spiritual in nature seem never to have read such passages as Matt. 5:3; 6:10; 13:33; Mark 10:15; Luke 10:9; 11:2; John 18:36.

Recognition of the important truth that what is within man's heart is what matters, not what man is on the outside, would do much to relieve interracial (and also many other) tensions.

Verses 27, 29

"Then the flood came and destroyed them all ... fire and sulfur rained down from heaven and destroyed them all."

---

475. Notes on Greek words, phrases, and constructions in 17:20-37 begin on page 810.

Life is short. Therefore opportunities to make our lives "shine for Jesus" should be grasped. In this connection there is a Dutch hymn which stresses this very thought. I refer to "Grijp toch de kansen door God u gegeven." My free translation of the first stanza—in which for the Dutch word *kansen,* meaning *opportunities,* I have selected the English equivalent *doors* (cf. Rev. 3:8)—is as follows:

> Enter the doors which to you God is giving;
> Few are your days and the time rushes on.
> What, would you say, will be left of your living?
> Only whate'er *out of love* you have done.
> Nothing abideth, nothing abideth.
> Life and its beauty, 'twill wither away,
> But what was done out of love for the Savior—
> That lasts forever; its mem'ry will stay.

Notes on Greek Words, Phrases, and Constructions in 17:20–37

Verses 20, 21

ἐπερωτηθείς, nom. s. masc. aor. pass. participle of ἐπερωτάω, to ask; here, in pass., being asked.

παρατηρήσεως, gen. s. of παρατήρησις* (cf. παρατηρέω, to observe closely), "with outward observation" or "display."

ἐντός, within, inside (of). There is no justification for the rendering "among." See the following sources on which this conclusion is based: the use of the word in Matt. 23:26 ("the inside of the cup") and in such passages as LXX Isa. 16:11, where the word in question appears as a synonym of "my heart," and I Macc. 4:48, "the inner parts of the house." See also A. Deissmann, *op. cit.,* pp. 426–428, and L. E. Wright, "The Oxyrhynchus Sayings of Jesus," *JBL* (1946), p. 177.

Verse 23

Note sec. per. pl. aor. subjunctives ἀπέλθητε, διώξητε, respectively from ἀπέρχομαι and διώκω. Lit.: "Do not go (away) after nor follow (them)"; that is, "Do not go running off after them."

Verse 24

ἀστραπή, lightning. See the note on 10:18 on page 589.

ἀστράπτουσα, nom. s. fem. pres. participle of ἀστράπτω*, to flash.

After ἐκ τῆς the word χώρας, *region* or *part,* should be mentally inserted, since it is clearly implied. A rather literal translation would be, "For as the lightning, flashing from one part under the heaven, shines to the other part under heaven, so will be the Son of man in his day." Less literal but probably better: "For as the lightning lights up the sky from one end to the other, so," etc.

Verse 25

παθεῖν, sec. aor. infinitive of πάσχω, to suffer.

ἀποδοκιμασθῆναι, aor. pass. infinitive of ἀποδοκιμάζω, to reject (after examination). The prefix ἀπό of the Greek verbal compound is reflected in the German prefix *ab;* for example, in *abweisen,* and in the Dutch prefix *af,* as in *afkeuren.* In English the prefix *re* in *reject,* to throw away or back, as not being wanted, has the same significance.

Verse 27

κιβωτόν, acc. s. of κιβωτός, ark; *of Noah* here and in Matt. 24:38; Heb. 11:7; I Peter 3:20; *of the covenant,* (a) in the Holy of Holies on earth, Heb. 9:4; (b) in the sanctuary of heaven, Rev. 11:19.

Very effectively the four imperfects—they were eating, etc.—are followed by three aorists: Noah entered, the flood came, destroyed all.

Verses 28, 29

A similar dramatic contrast is pictured here: the six imperfects of verse 28— people were eating, were drinking, were marrying, etc.—are climaxed by the three aorists of verse 29: Lot left Sodom, it rained fire and sulfur . . . (which) destroyed all.

For ἔβρεξεν see the note on 7:38, 44 on page 411.

Verse 30

ἀποκαλύπτεται, third per. s. pres. (prophetic and futuristic) indicat. pass. of ἀποκαλύπτω, to reveal; in pass., as here, to be revealed.

Verse 31

καταβάτω, third per. s. 2nd aor. imperat. (in a prohibition) of καταβαίνω, to go down. This verb occurs with great frequency in the four Gospels, Acts, and Revelation; but in all of Paul's epistles only four times, and once in James.

Verse 32

μνημονεύετε, sec. per. pl. pres. imperat. act. of μνημονεύω, to remember. Though in Luke's Gospel this verb occurs only here—for a synonym see Luke 1:54, 72; 16:25, etc.—it is also found in Matthew, Mark, John, Acts, Paul's epistles, etc. On the other hand, the little sentence, "Remember Lot's wife," is found only in Luke 17:32.

Verse 33

See the commentary on 9:24, since the present passage (17:33) is, to some extent, a repetition of the earlier one. Here, in 17:33 "tries to keep" is substituted for "would save" of 9:24; and "shall preserve" for "shall save." There is no essential difference.

περιποιήσασθαι, aor. middle infinitive of περιποιέω, cf. Acts 20:28; I Tim. 3:13, to acquire or use for oneself, to keep.

ζῳογονήσει, third per. s. fut. indicat. act. of ζῳογονέω; cf. Acts 7:19; I Tim. 6:13, to endue with life, preserve alive, preserve.

811

Verses 34, 35

Here are two third per. s. fut. indicat. passives, each occurring twice, once in each verse. The first, παραλημφθήσεται, is a form of παραλαμβάνω; in the pass. "to be taken"; the second, ἀφεθήσεται, is a form of ἀφίημι, here in the sense of "to be left behind." See the note on 6:42 on page 364.

ἔσονται ἀλήθουσαι, third per. pl. periphrastic fut. act. indicat. of ἀλήθω, in the New Testament occurring only here and in Matt. 24:41, to grind.

Verse 37

ἀετοί, nom. pl. of ἀετός, here and in Matt. 24:28 probably *vulture;* elsewhere (Rev. 4:7; 8:13; 12:14) *eagle.*

ἐπισυναχθήσονται, third per. pl. fut. indicat. pass. of ἐπισυνάγω, to gather; in pass., as here, to be gathered. But there is little or no essential difference between "there the vultures will be gathered" or ". . . will gather." Either translation can be considered correct. For the verb used by Luke see the note on 12:1 on page 658.

Summary of Chapter 17

See p. 540.

Outline of Chapter 18:1-14

Theme: *The Work Thou Gavest Him to Do*

CHAPTER
XVIII:1-14

18 1 Moreover, Jesus told them a parable to show that they should always pray and not lose heart. 2 He said, "In a certain city there was a judge who had no reverence for God nor respect for people. 3 There was also a widow in that city. She kept coming to him, saying, 'Grant me justice against my opponent.' 4 For a while he was unwilling but at last he said to himself, 'Though I have no reverence for God nor respect for people, 5 yet, because this widow keeps on bothering me, I'll grant her justice, lest she finally wears me out by her continual coming.' "

6 Then the Lord said, "Listen to what the unrighteous judge said. 7 And will not God see to it that justice is done for his elect, who continue to cry to him day and night? Will he be slow to help them?[476] 8 I assure y o u that he will see to it that justice is done for them, and quickly. But still, when the Son of man comes, will he find that faith[477] on the earth?"

18:1-8 *The Parable of The Widow Who Persevered*

For the obvious link between chapters 17 and 18 see p. 541.

The two parables of 18:1-14 are closely related. Prayer should be both persevering (verses 1-8) and humble (verses 9-14). The first parable can be divided into two parts, as will be indicated:

A. *The Parable*

1. Moreover, Jesus told them a parable to show that they should always pray and not lose heart.

We may assume that Jesus is still addressing his disciples, in the broader sense of that term (17:22). He tells them that during the lengthy and increasingly difficult period of time before the Son of man returns (see 17:22, 23), his followers down through the ages, instead of losing heart, should persevere in prayer.

But will their prayers avail? Will the supplicants be vindicated? To answer this question Jesus tells a parable. Its purpose is to show that if even a worldly judge, a very wicked man, finally gives a persevering widow her due, *how much more* will not the just, holy, and loving Father vindicate his elect who continue to cry to him day and night?

---

476. Or: Will he keep putting them off? Or: Will he postpone helping them?
477. Or: will he find faith, etc.

815

2. He said, In a certain city there was a judge who had no reverence for God nor respect for people.

Jesus links this judge with a *city* probably because that is where the audience expected a judge to function. This judge was anti-God and anti-people. He did whatever he pleased, never asking himself, "What does God want me to do?" or even "What do the people in general approve or disapprove?" He was nothing but a hateful egotist. Here, then, is a *judge* without any love for *justice*. And as to sympathy for the oppressed and satisfaction because, in his capacity as judge, he might be able to help them, he did not know what sympathy was. Tender feelings were completely foreign to him.

3. There was also a widow in that city.

Strikingly beautiful is what Scripture teaches with reference to widows, how God protects them, how he urges people to show kindness to them, blessing those who help them and punishing those who hurt them. See such passages as Exod. 22:22, 23; Deut. 10:18; Ps. 68:5. For a longer list of references see N.T.C. on I and II Timothy and Titus, pp. 167, 168. Moreover, it has been pointed out that it is especially Luke who pictures Jesus as being filled with love for the underprivileged, including widows. See *Introduction,* point V D.

The judge and the widow are living in the same city. This leads to a confrontation: **She kept coming to him, saying, Grant me justice against my opponent.**

This widow had been unjustly treated. Someone may have deprived her of the little she had, or may have prevented her from receiving that to which she was entitled. So she went to the judge, hoping that he would confirm her claim and give her whatever justice demanded. This would probably also imply punishment for the opponent, but the emphasis is rather on the urgent request by the wronged widow that she receive her due.

The rude judge flatly refused to have anything to do with her. She went home disappointed, for she knew that her cause was just. So a little later she tried again . . . with the same result. And again . . . and then again . . . and so on. At last the judge was "sick and tired" of her:

4, 5. For a while he was unwilling, but at last he said to himself, Though I have no reverence for God nor respect for people, yet, because this widow keeps on bothering me, I'll grant her justice, lest she finally wears me out by her continual coming.

Evidently the judge knew that the widow's claim was just. But he probably also knew that she was not able to bribe him and had little or no influence in the city. However, her persistence was what finally toppled him. So he said to himself, "I'll grant her justice, lest she finally wears me out," etc. Was he afraid, perhaps, that the widow would become so furious that she would fly at him and give him a black eye? Well, probably not, but see the note on 18:5 on page 823. At any rate, the widow's request was finally granted and she received whatever was due her.

B. *The Lesson*

6, 7a. Then the Lord said, Listen to what the unrighteous judge said. And will not God see to it that justice is done for his elect, who continue to cry to him day and night?

See what has already been said about this in connection with verse 1. In addition, note that Jesus uses the significant title *his elect* to describe believers. Certainly God will not let his chosen ones down. From before the foundation of the world he has, of his sovereign will, elected them unto service and salvation, for his glory. He has loved them with an everlasting love (Jer. 31:3). Therefore he will surely see to it that they are fully vindicated. *God and the wicked judge are opposites.*

What God demands is that his people persevere in opening their hearts to him. He answers the supplications of those who "continue to cry to him day and night."

Moreover, the wicked judge *finally* granted the needed help: the holy God will do so *quickly:* **7b, 8a. Will he be slow to help them? I assure y o u that he will see to it that justice is done for them, and quickly.**

The question may be asked, "Does not this word *quickly* clash with the fact that the return of the Son of man to judge has not yet occurred?" The answer must be, "The Lord is not slow in fulfilling his promise, as some understand slowness, but is patient [or long-suffering] with y o u, not wishing that any should perish, but that all should be converted" (II Peter 3:9).

Once the proper time has arrived, the Lord will move very quickly. It is interesting to observe with what speed the various eschatological events will take place. Believers who have not yet died will be changed "in a moment, *in the twinkling of an eye*" (I Cor. 15:51, 52). The entire company of the saved will be "caught up [or *snatched* away] . . . in clouds, to meet the Lord in the air" (I Thess. 4:17). Earth and sky *flee* from his presence (Rev. 20:11; cf. 6:14). Certainly the present passage (Luke 18:8a)—note especially "and quickly"—is in harmony with all this.

When the question is asked, "Why will the Son of man see to it that justice is done for his own *quickly?*" the answer must be that he loves so very deeply those who, by sovereign grace, have placed their trust in him. The contrast between him and the unrighteous judge of the parable is indescribably sharp. And does not the depth of that love guarantee that in the lives of all those children of God who throughout the centuries *before* the Son of man's return suffer persecution all those precious promises described in such passages as Ps. 34:19; Isa. 43:2; Rom. 8:28; I Cor. 10:13; II Cor. 4:17, will be fulfilled?

8b. But still, when the Son of man comes, will he find that faith on the earth? For this rendering see the note on this verse on page 823. There can be no question of the fact that there will still be believers on earth when the Son of man returns (see Matt. 24:44-46; Luke 12:37; 17:34, 35; I Thess. 4:13-18). But will there be *that* faith, the faith that perseveres, as did that of this widow? The question is asked for the purpose not of speculation but of self-examination. Let each answer for himself.

For *Practical Lessons* and *Greek Words*, etc., see pp. 821-825.

---

9 Now to some self-righteous persons, those who trusted in themselves[478] and looked down on everybody else, Jesus told this parable:

10 "Two men went up to the temple to pray; one a Pharisee, and the other a tax-collector.

11 The Pharisee stood and was directing a prayer to himself, as follows:

"'O God, I thank thee that I am not like the rest of the people—robbers, cheats,[479] adulterers—or even like this tax-collector. 12 I fast twice a week; I pay the tithe on all my income.'

13 "But the tax-collector, standing at a distance, did not even venture to lift up his eyes to heaven, but kept beating his breast, saying:

"'O God, be merciful to me, the sinner.'

14 "I say to y o u, this man, and not the other,[480] went home justified;[481] for everyone who exalts himself will be humbled, while he who humbles himself will be exalted."

18:9-14 *The Parable of The Pharisee and The Tax-Collector*

A person should pray and not give up (Luke 18:1-8). Also, he should pray with the right attitude of mind and heart:

9. Now to some self-righteous persons, those who trusted in themselves and looked down on everybody else, Jesus told this parable.

There is no reason to doubt that Jesus addressed this parable to a group of Pharisees. That is the plain meaning of Luke's statement. See the note on this verse on pp. 823, 824. Exactly when it was spoken, whether immediately after the parable of The Widow Who Persevered, or at another time, has not been revealed and is not very important. What is clear is that the two parables belong together.

Jesus addressed this story-illustration to those who trusted in themselves and were of the opinion that everybody else amounted to nothing. That this description was not an exaggeration but a true picture of what was wrong with the Pharisees of that day cannot be doubted. The parable presents two men, two prayers, two results.

A. *Two Men*

10. Two men went up to the temple to pray; one a Pharisee, and the other a tax-collector.

The temple was used not only for public religious transactions, for the

---

478. Literally: Now to some who trusted in themselves that they were righteous, etc.
479. Or: unjust, dishonest.
480. Literally: rather than the other.
481. Or: forgiven and accepted by God.

bringing of sacrifices, and for teaching, but also for private devotions. It is not strange, therefore, that we see a Pharisee entering the temple for that purpose. Whether or not this took place at one of the regular hours of prayer, as seems probable, or at some other time, is not certain. At any rate, we more or less expect to see a Pharisee entering the temple to pray, for those belonging to this sect were—at least were looked upon as being, and also considered themselves to be—very pious. Praying at places where they could be seen was one of their hobbies (20:47).

What *is* striking, however, is that a tax-collector also enters, and for the same purpose, namely, to pray. See what has been said about these "publicans" in connection with 3:12, and cf. 5:27–30; 7:29, 34; 15:1.

B. *Two Prayers*

11, 12. The Pharisee stood and was directing a prayer to himself, as follows: O God, I thank thee that I am not like the rest of the people— robbers, cheats, adulterers—or even like this tax-collector. I fast twice a week; I pay the tithe on all my income.

Note the following:

a. Boldly the Pharisee takes his stand. Praying in a standing position, with hands and eyes uplifted, was not at all unusual. In the case of a Pharisee we would even expect this. See N.T.C. on I and II Timothy and Titus, pp. 103, 104, for a description of the various prayer postures mentioned in Scripture.

Just where, in this temple complex, does the Pharisee stand? We are not told, but a comparison with verse 13 may indicate that he stands as close as possible to the actual sanctuary, with its Holy Place and the Holy of Holies.

b. Whom does he address? Outwardly he addresses God, for he says, "O God." But inwardly and actually the man is talking about himself *to* himself. See the note on 18:11 on page 824. Moreover, having mentioned God once, he never refers to him again. Throughout his prayer the Pharisee is congratulating himself.

That this is the true state of affairs follows also from the fact that nowhere in his prayer does the man confess his sins. Nowhere does he ask God to forgive him what he has done amiss. Now if he had had any sense of the divine presence, would he not also have had a sense of guilt? See Isa. 6:1–5; Luke 5:8.

c. He begins by comparing himself with other people. Not, however, with truly devout men like Samuel (I Sam. 1:20, 28; 2:18, 26) or Simeon (Luke 2:25–32), but with those of bad reputation. He says that he is *not a robber* . . . as if he were not at that very moment robbing God of the honor due to him. He is *not a cheat* or dishonest person . . . as if he were not cheating himself out of a blessing. And he is *not an adulterer*. Well, probably not literally, but was not this proud Pharisee departing from the true God, and thereby making himself guilty of the worst adultery of all (Hos. 1:2; 5:3)?

d. Of a sudden the attention of the Pharisee is drawn to the tax-collector, who is pounding his breast and crying to God for mercy. So he includes also this "publican" in his prayer, by adding "or even like this tax-collector." Little did he realize that the man he so despised was on his way to heaven, a place the Pharisee would never see unless a very basic inner change would take place in his heart, a total transformation.

e. A Pharisaic prayer, dating from about the time Jesus told this parable, runs as follows:

"I thank thee, Jehovah my God, that thou hast assigned my lot with those who sit in the house of learning, and not with those who sit at street corners. For I rise early and they rise early: I rise early to study the words of the Torah, and they rise early to attend to things of no importance. I weary myself and they weary themselves: I weary myself and gain thereby, while they weary themselves without gaining anything. I run and they run: I run toward the life of the age to come, while they run toward the pit of destruction."[482] Another typical example of the same Pharisaic self-righteousness.

f. On the positive side, the Pharisee in his prayer mentions some works of supererogation he is performing. Is he not doing even more than the law requires? "I fast twice a week," he says. See on 5:33. This man does not fast only once a year, as Lev. 16:29 suggests, or only in certain months; no, he fasts twice a week (probably on Monday and Thursday). And when it comes to tithing, also in this respect he goes all out, way beyond the law's requirements (see Deut. 14:22, 23). *He* tithes even garden herbs (Luke 11:42). —Do y o u remember the nursery rhyme ending with ". . . And he said, 'What a good boy am I' "?

13. But the tax-collector, standing at a distance, did not even venture to lift up his eyes to heaven, but kept beating his breast, saying, O God, be merciful to me, the sinner.

a. He stands "at a distance." To be sure, he must be in the temple, for it is there that, in a special sense, God dwells. He desperately needs God, the God of pardoning love! But having arrived in the temple, he stands away, far away from the sanctuary.

b. He is ashamed of his sins; hence, ashamed of himself, and therefore stands with downcast eyes.

c. He keeps beating his breast, in self-accusation and near-despair.

d. Being deeply conscious of God's presence, he takes hold of God in prayer (cf. Isa. 64:7), and from the very depths of his being cries out, "O God, be merciful to me, the sinner." He is earnestly and fervently begging God to be propitiated. He is hungering and thirsting for the one great blessing, namely, that God's anger may be removed and his favor obtained. His prayer is entirely in the spirit of:

---

482. S.BK., Vol. II, p. 240.

Nothing in my hand I bring,
Simply to thy cross I cling.

Lines from "Rock of Ages"
by A. M. Toplady

e. Was the Pharisee thinking only of himself? The tax-collector, too, singles himself out from all of mankind, but in an entirely different way. He does not place himself above others. He does not say, for example, "O God, I thank thee that I am at least better than most other tax-collectors." Nothing of the kind. He singles himself out as . . . THE sinner! A little later the great apostle to the Gentiles was going to do the same thing. He was going to say, "Christ Jesus came into the world sinners to save, *foremost of whom am I*" (I Tim. 1:15).

C. *Two Results*

14. I say to y o u, this man, and not the other, went home justified . . .

It is with great emphasis that Jesus continues, "I say to y o u," etc. He asserts, "this man rather than the other," clearly meaning "and not the other."

The tax-collector went home *justified.* Here the word is used in the forensic sense. God himself has pronounced this "publican" to be righteous. Yes, he is righteous in the eyes of the Almighty. The man's sins have been blotted out. See Ps. 51:1, 2. His transgressions have been removed "as far as the east is from the west" (Ps. 103:12). They have been cast into the depths of the sea (Mic. 7:19). And the penitent has himself been adopted into the family of God.

He goes home now. From his heart the storm has been removed. All is peace now, for he is deeply convinced that God's approval rests upon him.

The Pharisee also goes home, but he has . . . nothing! He might as well have stayed home that day, and never gone to the temple. In fact, this might have been better for him.

To all this the very appropriate words of Luke 14:11 are added: **for everyone who exalts himself will be humbled, while he who humbles himself will be exalted.** See on 14:11; also on 1:52, 53. And do not forget Isa. 57:15.

Thus, very touchingly, ends Luke's Central Section.[483]

Practical Lessons Derived from Luke 18:1–14

Verse 1

"Always pray and do not lose heart." Possible reasons why prayers are not always answered at once:

---

483. Notes on Greek words, phrases, and constructions in 18:1–14 begin on page 822.

a. To teach us patience and other virtues.

b. To increase our thanksgiving when we finally receive the blessing.

c. Because God has a greater blessing in store for us. See John 11:5, 6.

d. For reasons that lie (or lie partly) outside the sphere of human experience. See Job 1:6-12.

e. For other reasons known to God but not to us. God does not owe us an explanation for the riddles of life.

Verse 7

"And will not God see to it that justice is done for his elect...?"

The comforting doctrine of election was not invented by Paul. Is it not encouraging to know that at the root of our salvation lies *God's* election, not *our* innate (?) goodness?

Verse 8

"When the Son of man comes, will he find that faith on the earth?" Self-examination is good for the soul.

When the answers to our riddles are not readily available, we still should trust.

> Careless seems the great Avenger; history's pages but record
> One death-grapple in the darkness 'twixt old systems and the Word;
> Truth forever on the scaffold, Wrong forever on the throne,—
> Yet that scaffold sways the future, and, behind the dim unknown,
> Standeth God within the shadow, keeping watch above his own.
>
> J. R. Lowell, *The Present Crisis*

Verse 13

"O God, be merciful to me, the sinner."

Old Testament, New Testament; David, the tax-collector, Paul; all unite here, in ascribing salvation, from start to finish, to the mercy (God's love revealed to those in misery) and grace (God's love shown to the undeserving) of God. See Ps. 51:1; Luke 18:13; Eph. 2:8; Titus 3:5.

The despised "publican's" theology was sound; his attitude of heart was the best, all of this originating in God himself. *Soli Deo Gloria.*

Notes on Greek Words, Phrases, and Constructions in 18:1-14

Verse 1

ἐγκακεῖν, pres. infinitive of ἐγκακέω, to lose heart, to become weary. See also II Cor. 4:1, 16; Gal. 6:9; Eph. 3:13; II Thess. 3:13.

Verses 2-5

From the verb ἐντρέπω, to turn oneself to another person with respect or deference, here middle voice, are derived ἐντρεπόμενος (verse 2), nom. s. masc. pres. participle; and ἐντρέπομαι (verse 4), first per. s. pres. indicat.

And from ἐκδικέω, to avenge someone; i.e., to procure *justice* for a person by protecting him *from* his opponent, are derived ἐκδίκησον (verse 3), sec. per. s. aor. imperat. act.; and ἐκδικήσω (verse 5), first per. s. fut. indicat. act. ἤρχετο (verse 3), third per. s. imperf. (iterative) indicat. of ἔρχομαι. γε (verse 5), yet. τὸ παρέχειν . . . κόπον (verse 5), articular pres. act. infinitive, to furnish trouble, to bother. τὴν χήραν ταύτην (verse 5), acc. of general reference. ὑπωπιάζῃ (verse 5), third per. s. pres. subjunct. (after ἵνα μή), lit. to strike (a person) under the eye; here, because of the tense, probably: to wear (a person) out; in I Cor. 9:27, to buffet or beat ("I beat my body").

Verse 6

κριτὴς τῆς ἀδικίας, judge of unrighteousness, unrighteous judge. For similar forms and their explanation see the note on 10:6 on page 587, also the diagram there; and see the note on 16:8, 9 on pp. 778, 779.

Verse 7

μακροθυμεῖ, third per. s. pres. indicat. of μακροθυμέω, generally *to have patience* (Matt. 18:26, 29; I Cor. 13:4; I Thess. 5:14). But in Heb. 6:15 *to wait patiently*. See also James 5:7. It is clear, therefore, that the connotation *to be patient* has its ramifications; probably such as: to wait, postpone, delay, put off, be slow (to do something). Here in Luke 18:7b the contexts, both preceding—the unrighteous judge was *very slow* to act; *contrast God*—and following—"and this quickly"—require a rendering on the order of "Will he be slow to help them?" or "Will he keep putting them off?" or "Will he postpone helping them?" The difficulty of the passage must be admitted.

Verse 8

πλὴν . . . ἆρα; probably "But still." τὴν πίστιν. Since it is a known fact that in Greek the article often precedes the name of a virtue—such as faith or hope or love—where in English the article would generally be omitted, the rendering, "Will he *find faith* on the earth?"—or even simply "*on earth?*"—is not necessarily wrong. However, it may well be questioned whether *in the present context* this rendering is the best. Even many of the very commentators who allow it to stand hasten to add that Jesus was not referring to faith in general but to the kind of faith exercised by this widow. Others, in keeping with the context, give the Greek article its full due, and translate "the faith" or even "that faith." The context would seem to justify this rendering.

Verse 9

Εἶπεν . . . πρός. I can see no good reason, with Ridderbos, to translate πρός "with respect to." The phrase εἶπεν πρός occurs very frequently in Luke, and means "He said to." See 1:13, 18, 28, 34; 2:34, 48, 49; 17:1, 22; 19:5, 8, etc. The fact that in 18:1 πρός is used in a different sense has nothing to do with its meaning here in 18:9, since the construction in verse 1 (πρός followed by the art. infinitive) is entirely different.

πεποιθότας, acc. pl. masc. 2nd perf. participle of πείθω, to persuade; in the perfect, as here, to be confident, to trust.

ἐξουθενοῦντας, acc. pl. masc. pres. act. participle of ἐξουθενέω, lit. to treat as amounting to nothing (οὐθέν = οὐδέν), to look down on, scorn, despise, treat with contempt. See also 23:11, and elsewhere: Mark 9:12; Acts 4:11; Rom. 14:3, 10, etc.

Verse 11

On the reasonable assumption that the phrase πρὸς ἑαυτόν is authentic—there is a variant that omits it—and that it modifies the verb προσηύχετο, and not the participle σταθείς, the question remains "Just what does it mean?" The following renderings can all be found: *with, to, about, by, and for* (himself). I favor *to*, since, after verbs of asking and praying, πρός followed by the acc. generally has that meaning. See L.N.T. (A. and G.), pp. 717, 718. So also Goodspeed, Godet, Greijdanus; also B. Reicke, art. πρός, Th.D.N.T., Vol. VI, p. 723. Robertson has *to* in *Translation*, p. 102 (not in *Word Pictures*). Though the Pharisee's prayer was indeed addressed to God—note "O God, I thank thee," etc.—it never reached God. The man was actually talking *to himself*, congratulating himself. A possibility worthy of consideration (my second choice) is "with" (A.V., A.R.V., R.S.V., etc.).

Verse 12

κτῶμαι, first per. s. pres. indicat. of κτάομαι, to get; not (with A.V.) to possess, which would be perf. tense κέκτημαι.

Verse 13

ἑστώς, nom. s. masc. perf. participle of ἵστημι, having taken his stand, and thus *standing*.

οὐκ . . . οὐδέ, two negatives; was *not* willing *even*, etc.

Note the imperfects that make the story very graphic: the progressive and descriptive ἤθελεν, he was not willing, did not venture; and the iterative ἔτυπτε, he kept beating.

ἐπᾶραι, aor. act. infinitive of ἐπαίρω, to lift up, raise; see the note on 16:23 on page 789.

στῆθος, breast, chest. Cf. *stethoscope* (= chest-viewer).

ἱλάσθητι, sec. per. s. aor. imperat. pass. of ἱλάσκομαι, to render propitious, gracious; to appease, to cause to become favorably inclined; in pass., as here, to be merciful. In Heb. 2:17 this verb means: to make atonement for, to expiate. When God is appeased, man's sins are expiated. The two go together. See also on this verb L. Berkhof, *Systematic Theology*, Grand Rapids, 1949, p. 374; and Büchsel on ἱλάσκομαι, ἱλασμός, Th.D.N.T., Vol. III, pp. 314–318.

τῷ ἁμαρτωλῷ, (to me) *the* sinner.

Verse 14

δεδικαιωμένος, nom. s. masc. perf. pass. participle of δικαιόω, to declare or adjudge righteous. The verb ending οω generally expresses causation. See W. D.

Chamberlain, *An Exegetical Grammar of the Greek New Testament,* New York, 1941, p. 14.

παρ' ἐκεῖνον, alongside of; i.e., compared to; here: rather (than), the idea being that the Pharisee had *not* received the grace of justification, the publican had.

Summary of Chapter 18:1 –14

See p. 541.

The Perean Ministry

(continued)

18:15—19:27

Outline of Chapter 18:15-43

Theme: *The Work Thou Gavest Him to Do*

18:15-17 Jesus and the Children
18:18-30 The Peril of Riches
           and
           The Reward of Sacrifice
18:31-34 The Third Prediction of the Passion and the Resurrection
18:35-43 The Healing of a Blind Beggar near Jericho

CHAPTER
XVIII:15-43

---

15 Now they were bringing even infants to him, for him to touch. When the disciples saw this they began to rebuke (those who brought) them.   16 But Jesus called them to himself, saying, "Let the little children come to me, and stop hindering them, for to such belongs the kingdom of God.   17 I solemnly declare to y o u, whoever shall not receive the kingdom of God as a little child shall never enter it."

18:15-17 *Jesus and the Children*
Cf. Matt. 19:13-15; Mark 10:13-16

Beginning with 18:15 Luke and Mark run parallel again. Now in Mark Jesus' sayings regarding marriage (10:1-12), children (verses 13-16), and property (verses 17-31) follow each other in that order. Matthew 19 has the same sequence. Luke, however, here omits the first subject, probably because he has already reported Christ's teaching on marriage (16:18). So he starts at once with *Jesus and the children.*

Besides, Luke may well have had in mind a thematic connection between the present section (verses 15-17) and the immediately preceding one (verses 9-14). If so, he is reporting that, according to the mind of Christ, it is not by means of boasting about one's good works, as did the Pharisee, but by trustfully committing oneself to God and his love, as did the tax-collector, thereby revealing the attitude of a humble, trustful little child, that the kingdom is entered.

15. Now they were bringing even infants to him, for him to touch.
Note complete absence of time or place indications. On the basis of Luke 9:51; 13:22; 17:11, a reasonable assumption is that the incident here reported took place in a house in Perea while Jesus and The Twelve were traveling south toward Jerusalem.

Little children were brought to Jesus. Even *infants,* says Luke, were included. They were brought presumably by their parents or other close relatives, perhaps including bigger children. The purpose was that Jesus might "touch" the little ones, meaning: might place his hands on them while asking the Father to bless them. Cf. Matt. 19:13; Mark 10:13, 16. There was nothing magical about Christ's touch. It should be considered part of the blessing the little ones received.

When the disciples saw this they began to rebuke (those who brought) them.

Were the disciples standing in the doorway of the house and with angry gestures shooing away those who approached holding little ones by the hand or carrying infants in their arms? The reaction of the disciples was rather characteristic of them. They did not want the Master to be bothered by such unimportant (?) creatures as infants! For somewhat similar man- ifestations of unkindness on the part of the disciples see 9:49, 50; Matt. 15:23. But this certainly was not Christ's attitude, or God's. See Matt. 5:43–48; 11:25–30; Luke 6:27–38; John 3:16.

16. But Jesus called them to himself, saying, Let the little children come to me, and stop hindering them, for to such belongs the kingdom of God.

The reason Jesus gives for ordering the disciples to allow the little ones to come to him and to stop hindering them is "to such belongs the kingdom of God." For the meaning of "kingdom of God" see on 4:43. In the present case the verse means that *in principle* all the blessings of salvation belong even now to these little ones, a fact that was to be realized progressively here on earth and perfectly in the hereafter.

17. I solemnly declare to y o u, whoever shall not receive the kingdom of God as a little child shall never enter it.

The meaning is: the only possible way to enter the kingdom is by receiv- ing it readily and trustfully as a child accepts a gift. A child is not too proud to accept *a gift!*

For *Practical Lessons* and *Greek Words,* etc., see pp. 845–849.

---

18 And a certain ruler asked him, "Good Teacher, what shall I do that I may inherit everlasting life?"

19 Jesus said to him, "Why do you call me good? No one is good except One—God. 20 You know the commandments: 'You shall not commit adultery, you shall not kill, you shall not steal, you shall not bear false witness, honor your father and mother.'"

21 He said, "All these things have I observed ever since I was a child."

22 When Jesus heard this, he said to him, "One thing you still lack; sell all you have and distribute (the proceeds) to the poor, and you will have treasure in heaven, and come, follow me."

23 When he heard this, he became very sad, for he was extremely rich.

24 Jesus looked at him and said, "How hard it is for those who possess wealth to enter the kingdom of God. 25 Indeed, it is easier for a camel to go through the eye of a needle than for a rich man to enter the kingdom of God."

26 Those who heard (this) asked, "Then who can be saved?"

27 Jesus replied, "What is impossible with men is possible with God."[484]

28 Peter said, "Look, we have left all we had and followed you."

---

484. Or: The things that are impossible with men are possible with God.

29 He said to them, "I solemnly declare to y o u, there is no one who has given up house or wife or brothers or parents or children, for the sake of the kingdom of God, 30 who shall not surely receive many times as much now in this time, and in the age to come everlasting life."

18:18–30 *The Peril of Riches*
and
The Reward of Sacrifice
Cf. Matt. 19:16–30; Mark 10:17–31

According to the teaching of Jesus entrance into the kingdom of God (see on 4:43) or obtaining possession of everlasting life is God's free gift. It cannot be earned by human exertion. That truth was made very clear in the preceding section (see 18:17). This was a lesson which many of Jesus' contemporaries had to learn, as is emphasized here in 18:18 ff.

For the slight differences between the three reports (Matthew 19, Mark 10, Luke 18) see N.T.C. on Mark, pp. 386–389. Though there are these variations, there are no conflicts.

18. And a certain ruler asked him, Good Teacher, what shall I do that I may inherit everlasting life?

The stranger here introduced is by Matthew called a *young man* (19:20), by Luke a *ruler* (here in 18:18), and is by all three synoptists described as a *very rich person*, one who owned much property (Matt. 19:22; Mark 10:22; Luke 18:23). Therefore the composite title *rich young ruler* is generally applied to him. He was probably one of the officials in charge of the local synagogue.

Mark's description of this ruler's action is the most vivid of the three accounts. As he tells it, not only did this young man run up to Jesus, he also dropped to his knees in front of him. Luke, as often, abbreviates, and simply states that a certain ruler asked Jesus a question. In view of his highly emotional state, shown by his running and dropping to his knees, he may well have been gasping out the question that was disturbing his heart and mind. He addresses Jesus as "Good Teacher." Since his manner of addressing Jesus is intimately linked with the latter's reply (verse 19), I shall for the moment reserve any further comments on it. The young man continues: ". . . what shall I do that I may inherit everlasting life [or, according to the order of the words in the original, life everlasting]?"

Exactly what the anxious inquirer meant by "everlasting life" we do not know. In order to discover what it may have meant to him it should be borne in mind that he had undoubtedly been instructed by the Pharisaic scribes. The best informed among them knew that the concept *life everlasting* had its origin in what we now call the Old Testament. Dan. 12:2 mentions it in connection with the resurrection of God's faithful children: "And many that shall sleep in the dust of the earth shall awaken, some to everlasting life, and some to shame and everlasting contempt." And, to give but one example from apocryphal literature, II Macc. 7:9 states, "The King of the world shall raise us up . . . unto an everlasting renewal of life." It may be taken for granted, therefore, that by those who were well acquainted with Jewish religious literature the term *life everlasting* was associated with the resurrection. The rich young ruler's question can therefore perhaps be paraphrased as follows, "What must I do in order to become a partaker of salvation at the close of the age?" Coupled with this was undoubtedly the yearning to gain assurance in the here and now that he was indeed headed in the right direction toward that ultimate destiny. For the moment at least he *seemed* to be willing to do most anything that was necessary to reach this goal. He wanted peace of mind for the present and never-ending blessedness for the future.[485]

It is time now to return to the manner in which this rich young ruler opens the conversation. It has been mentioned that he addresses Jesus as "Good Teacher." The designation *Teacher* or *Master* was entirely proper. Jesus was—and is—indeed The Teacher (Matt. 26:55; Mark 14:49; Luke 11:1; John 3:2; 7:35; Acts 1:1). To a certain extent this fact was even acknowledged by his opponents (Matt. 22:16). He was indeed The Prophet sent from God. See also N.T.C. on Matthew, pp. 82, 83.

According to Luke's report, however, the enthusiastic inquirer attaches an adjective to the noun: he addresses Jesus as "*Good* Teacher." Of course, this too was true, but evidently not in the sense meant by the young man. At least, as will now be shown, Jesus is not at all satisfied with the manner in which the man addressed him.

19. Jesus said to him, Why do you call me good? No one is good except One—God. Does Jesus by means of this statement disclaim goodness and deity? Does he mean, "You should not have called me *good*, for God alone is good. I am not God; therefore I am not good"? Many have so interpreted Christ's answer. They have concluded—with variations in minor details— that Jesus is here drawing a tacit contrast between the absolute goodness of God and his own goodness. My own view is this:

Jesus knew that the rich young ruler, in addressing him as "Good Teacher," was being very superficial. If this young man had really believed with all his heart that Jesus was good in the highest sense of the term, he would have obeyed the command the Lord was about to give him (see verse 22). That same shallowness is evident also from the praise he bestows on himself (verse 21). The Master knew very well that if this inquirer was going to be saved, he must be confronted with the absolute standard of goodness, namely, the *perfect* law enacted by *The Perfect One*, God.

So Jesus continues as follows: **20. You know the commandments: You**

---

485. Since Matt. 19:16 has ". . . that I may possess," it is clear that the synonym *inherit* here in Luke 18:18 does not have the fulness of meaning that it sometimes has. In the present instance, as also in several other places, it simply means *have, come into possession of, become a partaker of.*

shall not commit adultery, you shall not kill, you shall not steal, you shall not bear false witness, honor your father and mother.

Just why it was that in all three accounts "Honor your father and your mother" is made the last of the regular Decalog commandments we do not know. Was there a special reason why in this particular case Jesus placed this commandment at the very close (except for the summary in Matthew)? Neither do we know why Jesus mentioned only the commandments of the second table. To the many guesses I wish to add one more: It was not necessary for Jesus to include the commandments relating to man's duty with respect to God, for failure to observe the second table implies failure to observe the first: "He who does not love his brother whom he has seen cannot love God whom he has not seen" (I John 4:20).

Another question to which we do not know the answer is, "Why does 'You shall not commit adultery' here precede 'You shall not kill,' and why is 'You shall not covet' omitted?" There may well be some truth in Lenski's position, namely, that Jesus shows that he is not bound either by the exact wording of the commandments or by their order in the Decalog, and simply indicates how very much the law requires before it grants life everlasting.[486]

It is understandable that in answering the young man's question Jesus starts out by referring him to the law of God, for "through the law comes the knowledge of sin" (Rom. 3:20; cf. Gal. 3:24). We have met with a similar situation before; see on 10:25-28.

However, the law does not make us conscious of our sins if we fail to discern its real meaning, its depth, as set forth by Jesus in Matt. 5:21-48. That the young man's attitude to God's holy law was of a superficial character is clear from his answer: **21. He said: All these things have I observed ever since I was a child.** One can also translate: "from my youth." According to some he means, "since I became a *bar mitzvah*," that is, "a son of the law," the name given to a Jewish boy who has reached the age of religious responsibility. Others interpret the expression in a more general sense, "from childhood on."

We might ask, "But if the rich young ruler is convinced that he has kept the whole law, why is he still so perturbed?" It is clear that he is trying hard to make himself believe that he had indeed been living in harmony with all God's commandments. He may have been encouraged in this attempt by rabbis who had deceived themselves into thinking that spiritual perfection was indeed attainable in this life.[487]

But has this young man really loved his neighbor as himself? Living among people some of whom must have been desperately poor, has he

---

486. *Op. cit.,* p. 576.
487. See S.BK., Vol. I, p. 814.

performed his full duty? Why, then, this lack of peace of heart and mind that made him rush to Jesus with a question born of anxiety?

We can somewhat appreciate the young man's struggle, especially in the light of what we know about someone else who was going to experience a similar agony, but found the right answer (Rom. 7:7—8:1; Phil. 3:1-16).

What this young man needs to learn is to surrender himself completely to the mercy of God and to accept from him *as a free gift* that which he cannot earn. Jesus will show him the way:

22. When Jesus heard this, he said to him, One thing you still lack; sell all you have and distribute (the proceeds) to the poor, and you will have treasure in heaven...

The question may be asked, "But by thus instructing the young man was not Jesus endorsing the 'salvation by good works' doctrine?" Should he not rather have told him, "Trust in me"? The answer is that "Trust completely in me" was exactly what the Lord was telling him, for certainly without complete confidence in and self-surrender to the One who was issuing the order, the rich young ruler could not be expected to sell all he had and give the proceeds to the poor. This was the test. If he sustains it he will have "treasure in heaven." The reference is to all those blessings that are heavenly in character, are in full measure reserved for God's child in heaven, and of which we experience a foretaste even now. For more about this concept see N.T.C. on Matt. 6:19, 20. It is important to note that Jesus adds **and come, follow me.** Jesus implies that in following him, to be accompanied by and to prepare for active witness-bearing, the young man must learn to "deny himself and take up his cross," in complete self-surrender.

The young man's response was tragic. It showed that Christ's command had been the arrow that wounded his Achilles' heel, his most vulnerable spot: love of earthly possessions:

23. When he heard this, he became very sad, for he was extremely rich.

The young man was bitterly disappointed. His countenance fell (see Mark 10:22). As enthusiastic as he had been at first, so sad he was now that he departed sorrowful and aggrieved, probably thinking, "This requirement is not fair. None of the other rabbis would have demanded this much of me."

The demand which Jesus had made on this bewildered man was suited to his particular circumstances and state of mind. The Lord does not ask every rich person—for example, Abraham (Gen. 13:2), or Joseph of Arimathea (Matt. 27:57)—to do exactly this same thing. There are those opulent individuals who, by and large, are living for themselves. What they contribute to the cause of others is wholly out of proportion to what they keep for themselves. There are other wealthy persons, however, who are willing to go all out in helping others, including even the ungenerous (Gen. 13:7-11; 14:14); and who, motivated by gratitude, are constantly building altars and bringing offerings to God (Gen. 12:8; 13:18; 15:9, 10; 22:13).

The young man "was extremely rich." He owned much property. He had it; it had him, holding him tightly in its grasp. It is clear that this young man needed exactly the treatment Jesus gave him.

Did the rich young ruler persist forever in his deplorable refusal? The answer has not been revealed. Some reason as follows: Scripture tells us that Jesus loved him (Mark 10:21). God loves the elect, no one else. Conclusion: this young man must have become converted.

But this amounts to superimposing an erroneous theological idea upon the text. If those who cling to it would be satisfied with the proposition that God loves *in a peculiar way* all those who place their trust in him (Ps. 103:13; I John 3:1), their teaching would be on firm ground. But when they go beyond this and deny that there is a love of God which extends beyond the sum total of the elect, we must part company with them. See Ps. 145:9, 17; Matt. 5:45; Luke 6:35, 36. And since this is true, there is no basis whatever for believing that the rich young ruler must have become a believer before he died. Instead of speculating about what may or may not have happened, the lesson of Luke 13:23, 24 should be taken to heart. It is in that vein that Luke's account now continues:

24. Jesus looked at him and said, How hard it is for those who possess wealth to enter the kingdom of God.

Jesus looked at the deeply disappointed young man. He saw him leaving (Matt. 19:22; Mark 10:22).

Now picture the scene. The rich young ruler has left. Jesus and The Twelve are by themselves once more. Turning to them (Mark 10:23) he impresses upon them the fact that it is indeed hard for the rich to enter the kingdom of God. Attachment to God requires detachment from the world, and that is not easy.

25. Indeed, it is easier for a camel to go through the eye of a needle than for a rich man to enter the kingdom of God.

It is, of course, entirely impossible for a camel, hump and all, to pass through the eye of a needle. Think of it: a camel, Palestine's largest animal, passing through the very tiny opening of a needle! Ridiculous! It cannot be done.

The reason Jesus expressed himself in such a dramatic fashion was that he wanted the disciples to take notice. He wanted the truth of human total inability to sink in.[488]

To explain what Jesus means it is useless and unwarranted to try to change "camel" into "cable"—see Matt. 23:24, where a real camel must have been meant—or to define the "needle's eye" as the narrow gate in a city wall, a gate, so the reasoning goes, through which a camel can pass only on its knees and after its burden has been removed. Such "explanations" (?), aside from being objectionable from a linguistic point of view, strive to make possible what Jesus specifically declared to be impossible. The Lord

---

488. E. Trueblood's remarks about this "violent metaphor" are excellent: *op. cit.*, pp. 47, 48.

means that for a rich man in his own power to try to work or worm his way into the kingdom of God is impossible. So powerful is the hold which wealth has on the heart of the natural man! He is held fast by its bewitching charm, and is thereby prevented from obtaining the attitude of heart and mind necessary for entrance into God's kingdom. See Luke 16:13; cf. I Tim. 6:10. It should be noted that Jesus purposely speaks in absolute terms. A moment ago we used the phrase *in his own power*. Though in view of verse 27 this qualification does not need to be retracted, yet it should be pointed out that here in verse 25 Jesus does not thus qualify his assertion. He speaks in absolute terms in order all the more to impress upon the minds of the disciples that salvation, from start to finish, is not a human "achievement." The fact that "man's extremity is God's opportunity" is reserved for later (see verse 27).

26. Those who heard (this) asked, Then who can be saved?

Jesus' startling remark had the desired effect. It shocked those who heard him, so that they cried out, "Then who can be saved?" They probably reasoned as follows: what Jesus said about rich men he said about all, for though not all are rich, even the poor yearn to become rich.

In this connection also notice that the rich man had inquired about *inheriting everlasting life* (verse 18). Jesus had answered in terms of *entering the kingdom of God* (verse 25). And the hearers—probably mostly disciples (see verses 15, 28)—had interpreted their Master's remark as indicating that no one could *be saved* (verse 26). It is clear, therefore, these three designations are synonymous, all describing the same blessing, but each viewing it from a different angle.

27. Jesus replied, What is impossible with men is possible with God.

In this dramatic moment the eyes of Jesus, as he fixed them on his disciples (Mark 10:27), must have been filled with deep earnestness and tender love. When he now tells them, "What is impossible with men," he means exactly that. At every point, beginning, middle, end, man is completely dependent on God for salvation. Of himself man can do nothing. If he is to be saved at all he must be born again or "from above" (John 3:3, 5). In order to reach out to God by faith—God-given faith! (Eph. 2:8)—man must be enabled and supported every day, hour, minute, and second by God's omnipotent grace. For the religion of the rich young ruler (see verses 18 and 21), which was the religion current among the Jews of that day and age, there is no room here. Whatever detracts from the sovereignty of God in the salvation of men stands condemned.

Glory be to God, however: there is a way out. What is impossible with men is possible with God. It is he who, through Christ, is able to save to the uttermost (Heb. 7:25). His grace extends even to the determined and relentless persecutor Saul of Tarsus (Acts 9:1; 26:9–11; I Cor. 15:8–10; Gal. 1:15, 16; I Tim. 1:15). Just how, through the Mediator, this salvation is brought about, Jesus has already begun to reveal (Luke 9:22–27; 9:43, 44). He will continue to do so with increasing clarity (see 18:31, 34; especially 22:19, 20; cf. Matt. 20:28; Mark 10:45).

Peter is still thinking about the words Jesus had addressed to the rich young ruler (see verse 22). Jesus had asked him to sell all he had and to distribute the proceeds among the poor, promising that if he did this he would have treasure in heaven.

So the story continues: **28. Peter said, Look, we have left all we had and followed you.**

According to Matt. 19:27 Peter added, "What then shall we have?" Had The Twelve not done exactly what Jesus had asked the young man to do? Had they not "left everything" and followed Jesus? See especially Luke 5:2-11, 27-38; cf. Matt. 9:9; Mark 2:14; and to a lesser degree Matt. 4:18-22; Mark 1:16-20. The answer, then, would seem to be obvious, namely, that The Twelve would have treasure in heaven. Nevertheless, Peter seems not to have been entirely certain about this, for the Master had also declared that with men it is impossible to be saved, and that it is God, he alone, who imparts salvation (verses 24-27).

In all probability Peter was speaking not only for himself but as the representative of The Twelve. He says *We* have left all," etc. He often was their spokesman. See especially Matt. 16:13-16; 26:35; John 6:67-69; Acts 1:15; 2:14, 37, 38; 5:29; and perhaps also Matt. 15:15, 16; 17:4 (cf. Mark 9:5; Luke 9:32, 33). And so, we may well believe, also here in Luke 18:28 (cf. Matt. 19:27; Mark 10:28).

Confirmation of this theory, namely, that Peter was speaking representatively, is also found in the fact that Jesus, in answering Peter, addresses the entire group. He uses the plural:

29, 30. He said to them, I solemnly declare to y o u, there is no one who has given up house or wife or brothers or parents or children, for the sake of the kingdom of God, who shall not surely receive many times as much now in this time, and in the age to come everlasting life.

It is clear that this promise is for all true followers of the Lord, not just for The Twelve or for the larger circle of believers living at the time of Jesus' sojourn on earth. It is for all who have chosen Christ above all else, even above their dearest relatives and choicest earthly possessions. They made the sacrifice "for the sake of the kingdom of God," or, as Mark reproduces the thought of Jesus, "for my sake and for the gospel's sake."

These loyal disciples of the Lord are promised that they will be reimbursed many times over.

Even in the present time, that is, before the great day of judgment, and for each believer before his death, these loyal followers receive the blessings indicated in such passages as Prov. 15:16; 16:8; Matt. 7:7; John 17:3; Rom. 8:26-39; Phil. 4:7; I Tim. 6:6; Heb. 6:19, 20; 10:34; I Peter 1:8. In spite of the persecutions which they will have to endure, they will be able to enjoy even their material possessions far more than the ungodly enjoy theirs. Reason? See Isa. 26:3; contrast 48:22.

For the sake of the kingdom has it become necessary to forsake close relatives? New "relatives" will now be theirs (Luke 8:19-21; see also Matt. 12:46-50; Mark 3:31-35; and cf. John 19:27; Rom. 16:13; I Cor. 4:15; Gal.

4:19; I Tim. 1:2; 5:2; II Tim. 2:1; Philem. 10; I Peter 5:13), relatives that belong to "the household of the faith" (Gal. 6:10), "the Father's family" (Eph. 2:19; 3:15).

In "the age to come" believers are going to receive life everlasting. In principle they have it here and now, for in a very real sense "the *age* or *eon* to come" has already arrived; that is, believers have "tasted the powers of the age to come" (Heb. 6:5).[489]

Do they not even now possess "the peace of God that surpasses all understanding" (Phil. 4:7), "joy unspeakable and full of glory" (I Peter 1:8), "the light of the knowledge of the glory of God in the face of Christ" (II Cor. 4:6), and "the love of God poured out into our hearts through the Holy Spirit" (Rom. 5:5)?

In "the age to come" all these blessings that constitute life everlasting will become the believers' treasure in an even much fuller sense.

For *Practical Lessons* and *Greek Words,* etc., see pp. 845-849.

---

31 Jesus took the twelve aside and said to them, "Listen, we are now going up to Jerusalem, and everything (that is) written through the prophets about the Son of man will be fulfilled.
32 For he shall be handed over to the Gentiles and mocked and insulted and spit upon.
33 They shall scourge him and kill him, but on the third day he shall rise again."
34 But they understood none of this; in fact, the (meaning of this) statement had been concealed from them, and they did not (even) begin to grasp what was said.

18:31-34 *The Third Prediction of the Passion and the Resurrection* Cf. Matt. 20:17-19; Mark 10:32-34

Peter had called the attention of Jesus to the sacrifice he and the other disciples had made (verse 28). Jesus now rivets the attention of the group on the infinitely greater sacrifice he is about to make:

31. Jesus took the twelve aside and said to them, Listen, we are now going up to Jerusalem, and everything (that is) written through the prophets about the Son of man will be fulfilled.

Though the time and place are indefinite, it is becoming clear that the long journey from Galilee through Perea is nearing its end. Jericho is almost in sight (see verse 35; 19:1). Jerusalem (and its environs) is next (19:11, 28, 41). Matters are becoming more and more serious now. So, in order to impress upon the disciples the gravity of the events that are about to take place, Jesus takes The Twelve aside. He tells them, "We are going up to Jerusalem."

"Going up to Jerusalem" (John 2:13; 5:1; 11:55; Acts 11:2; 25:1, 9; Gal. 2:1) must be understood as having reference not only to physical ascent, Jerusalem being situated on higher ground, so that from whatever side one approaches it, that approach is always an ascent; it is far more than that. It

---

489. In this connection see the instructive article on αἰών in Th.D.N.T., Vol. I, pp. 202-209, by H. Sasse.

must be interpreted as a matter not just pertaining to the feet (Ps. 122:2), but also—in fact especially—to the heart (Ps. 84:5). In Jerusalem was God's temple! When in connection with the great feasts pilgrims wended their way to Jerusalem, they were going there to worship, and this included the bringing of an offering. Jesus, too, is now "going up to Jerusalem," to bring *himself* as an offering for "the sin of the world." See Isa. 53:10; John 1:29.

Having taken The Twelve aside, Jesus makes a very important announcement. To indicate its importance he prefaces it by saying "Behold," or, in the present case because of the context, "Listen." He then directs their mind to the fact that they are now "going up to Jerusalem," this time not from some distant place or region, but from nearby. In other words, he tells them that this is the beginning of the end of the road. This is it!

He adds that everything that was written in ancient days and now therefore *stands* written, with reference to "the Son of man" (see on 5:24), will be fulfilled. Cf. 24:26, 27. See also Luke 22:22, 37; John 2:4; 7:6; 19:30, and it will become evident that Jesus definitely looked upon his life as part of the realization of the divine plan; that is, of God's eternal counsel.

The things concerning the Son of man were written *by* the Lord, *through* the prophets (Matt. 1:22), though here in Luke 18:31 only the agent is mentioned.

32, 33. For he shall be handed over to the Gentiles and mocked and insulted and spit upon. They shall scourge him and kill him, but on the third day he shall rise again.

We generally speak of three *main* predictions of Christ's suffering, death, and resurrection: (a) Luke 9:21–27; cf. Matt. 16:21–28; Mark 8:31—9:1; (b) Luke 9:43b–45; cf. Matt. 17:22, 23; Mark 9:30–32; and (c) Luke 18:31–34; cf. Matt. 20:17–19; Mark 10:32–34. Of these three, this is the third or last. If one wishes to include in the count every veiled or figurative reference to the approaching passion, etc., the number of predictions would be substantially increased. In Luke, for example, see also 5:35; 12:50; 13:32, 33; 17:25.

Limiting ourselves to the three *main* ones, we note that *Mark* lists seven items for the third prediction. These seven are:

1. The Son of man will be betrayed into the hands of chief priests and scribes,
2. They will condemn him to death,
3. And will hand him over to the Gentiles,
4. Who will mock him, spit upon him,
5. Scourge him,
6. And kill him.
7. Three days later he will rise again.

Matthew has a similar arrangement. There are minor differences; e.g., Matthew has "crucify" for "kill." *Luke,* who often abbreviates, here mentions only the last five; hence items 3–7.

Since the Romans did not allow the Jews to carry out the death sentence, the Jewish authorities were going to hand Jesus over to the Gentiles, that is, in the present case to Pilate and those who carried out his commands.

Jesus predicted that these Gentiles would mock him and spit upon him.

The *scourging* of which Jesus speaks was a prelude to the *killing* by *crucifixion.*

This prediction, as well as previous ones, ends on a note of triumph: he shall rise again.

The question now arises, "How must we conceive of this very detailed passion announcement?" Was it really a "prediction"? Or was it rather, at least to a certain extent, a *vaticinium ex eventu,* that is, "a prophecy arising out of—and therefore made after—the event" to which it refers? That it was the latter is the opinion of many. In one way or another, the suggestion is offered that although Jesus in a very general way did indeed predict his suffering, death, and resurrection, he did not predict them in this detailed form.

The question arises, "Why not?" He who knew beforehand exactly where a certain fish would be swimming at a definite moment of time and what it would have in its mouth (Matt. 17:27), how often a strange woman whom he had never met before had been married (John 4:17, 18), where a colt would be and what its owners would say to those who tried to untie it (Luke 19:29–33), and what kind of pitcher-bearer two disciples would meet as they entered the city of Jerusalem (22:10); he who was able to forecast the very manner of Jerusalem's fall (Matt. 21:40–43; 22:7; 23:37, 38; 24:1, 2, 15; Mark 13:1, 2; Luke 19:41–44), and the victorious march of the gospel along the path of the centuries (Matt. 24:14), would he not have been able to predict the details of his own imminent passion, especially after two messengers from heaven had discussed these matters with him (Luke 9:31)? I take it that what is here presented as prediction was exactly that. "A prophecy that grows out of an event" is no prophecy at all!

It would be inexcusable to close the treatment of this precious passage (18:31–34) without showing what it implies with respect to the majesty of Christ's love. The prediction is far more detailed than the previous ones. The *gradual* revelation of the approaching events had a pedagogical purpose. But the possibility must also be granted that even in the human consciousness of our Lord the "feel" of the approaching horror was little by little becoming more real. There was nothing static about the mind of Jesus. See Luke 2:52; Heb. 5:8. Even this third prediction, though indeed very comprehensive and detailed, does not necessarily prove that in the mind of Jesus the image of impending distress was already as vivid as it would be in Gethsemane.

Nevertheless, even now the horror must have been very real and very terrifying. See Luke 12:50. The man of sorrows sees it coming toward him. He already senses something of the perfidy, the hypocrisy, the calumny, the mockery, the pain, and the shame which like an avalanche threatens to overwhelm him. Yet, he does not retreat or even stand still. With unflinching determination he walks right into it, for he knows that this is necessary in order that his people may be saved. "Having loved his own . . . he loved them to the uttermost" (John 13:1).

34. But they understood none of this; in fact, the (meaning of this) statement had been concealed from them, and they did not (even) begin to grasp what was said.

The Twelve understood neither the prediction as a whole, nor its separate items. The reason for this dullness on their part may well have been that they cherished other ideas with respect to the Messiah and his course of life on earth. This appears clearly from such passages as Matt. 16:22; 17:10; John 20:25; Acts 1:6.

That did not make these predictions useless. By means of their fulfilment these predictions would come back to their minds, and their faith would be strengthened. Cf. John 16:4.

For *Practical Lessons* and *Greek Words*, etc., see pp. 845-849.

---

35 Now it came about that as Jesus was approaching Jericho,[490] a blind man was sitting by the roadside, begging. 36 When he heard a crowd going by, he began to inquire what this was. 37 They told him, "Jesus of Nazareth is passing by." 38 So he shouted, "Jesus, Son of David, take pity[491] on me."

39 Those in front started to warn him to be quiet, but he cried out all the more, "Son of David, take pity on me."

40 So Jesus stopped and ordered the man to be brought to him. When he came near, Jesus asked him, 41 "What do you want me to do for you?" He said, "Lord, I want to regain my sight."[492]

42 Jesus said to him, "Regain your sight; your faith has made you well."

43 Immediately he regained his sight and began to follow Jesus, glorifying God. When all the people saw it, they also gave praise to God.

18:35-43 *The Healing of a Blind Beggar near Jericho*
Cf. Matt. 20:29-34; Mark 10:46-52

If the disciples had listened carefully and had been thoroughly versed in the Old Testament—for example, in the Hebrew Psalter, the prophecies of Isaiah, and the contents of the book of Daniel—they would have understood, at least to some extent, that by means of the third prediction of the passion and the resurrection (verses 31-34) Jesus not only identified himself as the Messiah but also indicated in what sense he was indeed the Promised One.

This identification and this characterization are also set forth in the story of the blind beggar, by Mark called Bartimaeus.

Jesus was now approaching Jericho. The road from the fords of the Jordan to Jerusalem passed through this city. One might say that the ascent

---

490. Or simply: As Jesus was approaching Jericho, etc.
491. Or: have mercy on me. So also in the next verse.
492. Or: Lord, (grant) that I may recover my sight.

to Jerusalem began here. Since many Galilean pilgrims on their way to Jerusalem to attend the Passover would travel through Perea in order to avoid Samaria, it is understandable that at Jericho, a very important stopping place, Jesus and The Twelve would be surrounded by a large crowd. Beggars would take advantage of the favorable opportunity thus afforded them.

35a. Now it came about that as Jesus was approaching Jericho...

The Roman Jericho of Jesus' day and its present-day ruins lie somewhat to the south of Old Testament or Jewish Jericho. Now according to Matthew and Mark the miracle about to be related occurred as Jesus and his disciples were leaving Jericho; but according to Luke, as he was approaching Jericho. Some have argued, therefore, that Matthew and Mark are speaking of the Jewish city which Jesus had left, whereas Luke is speaking of the Roman, at which Jesus had not yet arrived.[493] Also, Matthew speaks of *two* blind men, while Mark and Luke make mention of *one*. This is not really a contradiction, for neither Mark nor Luke tells us that Jesus restored sight to the eyes of *only* one blind man. There are many attempts at solving these problems. See N.T.C. on Mark, pp. 417, 418. The best answer is, There is a solution, for this "Scripture," too, is inspired. However, *we do not now have the solution to these problems.*[494]

In connection with the blind man, note:

A. His Wretched Condition

35b–38.... a blind man was sitting by the roadside, begging. When he heard a crowd going by, he began to inquire what this was. They told him, Jesus of Nazareth is passing by. So he shouted, Jesus, Son of David, take pity on me.

It is at this point of time and place that the blind man enters the picture. He is sitting by the roadside, begging. Although he cannot see Jesus, he can hear the bustle of the crowd. Upon inquiry he learns that Jesus of Nazareth is passing by. He must have heard about Jesus before, for upon receiving the news, he immediately cries out, "Jesus, Son of David, take pity [or, have mercy] on me."

In the Psalter—see Ps. 4:1; 6:2; 9:13; 25:16; 27:7; 30:10; 31:9; 41:4; 51:1; 86:16—this ("take pity") is a cry addressed to God by an afflicted person, or (Ps. 123:3) by afflicted persons.

As far as is known, in pre-Christian literature the designation *Son of David* as a title for the Messiah occurs only in the pseudepigraphical Psalms of Solomon 17:21.[495] Though there are those who deny that Bartimaeus

---

493. So, for example, J. P. Free, *Archaeology and Bible History,* Wheaton, 1950, p. 295.

494. On Jericho, etc., see also G. Dalman, *Orte und Wege Jesu,* Leipzig, 1924, pp. 257–259; P. Ketter, "Zur Lokalisierung der Blindenheilung bei Jericho," *Biblica* 15 (1934), pp. 411–418; M. F. Unger, *op. cit.,* pp. 114, 115; and see on 10:30.

495. S.BK., Vol. I, p. 525.

was using the term in the messianic sense, the probability is that he did so intend it, for on the basis of Mark 11:9, 10; 12:35-37 (see on those verses) it is clear that during Christ's ministry on earth "Son of David" and "Messiah" had become synonyms. Otherwise how can one satisfactorily explain the indignation of the chief priests and the scribes when the children were honoring Jesus with the title *Son of David* (Matt. 21:15, 16)?

It is argued that since, when the blind man finally stands before Jesus, he, according to Mark 10:51, merely (?) calls Jesus "Rabboni," that is, "Master,".it must be that also when he previously addressed Jesus as "Son of David," this title did not have any messianic implications. But this argument is weak; for: (a) Does Jesus cease to be "Master" because he is the Messiah? (b) Has it been proved that when Mark was writing his Gospel "Rabboni" had already lost the meaning "Great Rabbi"? Is it not true that at least for some time the Jews recognized three ranks of "teachers," called, in ascending order of prominence, *rab, rabbi,* and *rabboni,* and that the title *Rabboni* was given to only a few rabbis (for example, to Gamaliel I and Gamaliel II), and was frequently used with reference to God? (c) Both Matthew (20:33) and Luke (18:41) state that Bartimaeus addressed Jesus as Lord *(kurie).* Is it really possible *to deny* that when Luke, in his report, represents the blind man as calling Jesus "Lord," that author is referring to the One to whom the Father had committed all authority?[496]

B. *His Added Difficulty*

39a. Those in front started to warn him to be quiet . . . Just why these people in the van of the crowd did this we do not know. Possible answers: (a) The people were in a hurry to get to Jerusalem and did not want Jesus to be stopped by this blind beggar; (b) they deemed this yelling to be out of harmony with the dignity of the person addressed; (c) they were not ready to hear Jesus publicly proclaimed as "the Son of David"; (d) they knew that their religious leaders would not appreciate this; and (e) while walking, Jesus was also teaching, and these people did not want this teaching to be interrupted.

C. *His Commendable Persistence*

39b. but he cried out all the more, Son of David, take pity on me. That was to his credit. He realized that if help was going to come from any source, it would have to come from the Son of David.

D. *The Marvelous Blessing Jesus Bestowed on Him*

40, 41a. So Jesus stopped and ordered the man to be brought to him. When he came near, Jesus asked him, What do you want me to do for you? For a fuller account see Mark 10:49-51. Luke abbreviates.

---

496. See W. Foerster's article χύριος (and related words) in Th.D.N.T., Vol. III, especially p. 1094.

Jesus reveals himself throughout the Gospels to be not only very powerful but also very merciful. His heart is constantly going out to people in need. So also here, *though he himself is approaching the cross!* He stands still and orders the people—probably those very people who have been telling the man to keep still—to bring the man to him. Very tenderly Jesus asks him what he wants. Is it alms this beggar wants? Let him concentrate for a moment on that which he wants most of all, so that the satisfaction of his desire will be appreciated all the more. To be sure, Jesus already knew what Bartimaeus wanted, but he wants him to ask for it. So also it is true in general that even though the heavenly Father is well acquainted with the needs of his children, he nevertheless tells them to "open their mouth wide" (Ps. 81:10), so he may fill it. What Jesus wants is not only to cure this man but *to enter into personal fellowship* with him, so that, as a result, his "faith" (verse 42) may be more than merely "miraculous" (the conviction that Jesus is able to perform miracles), and so that he may "glorify God," as is actually going to happen.

41b. He said, Lord, I want to regain my sight.

As has been indicated, the word *Lord* in Matthew's and Luke's accounts is the equivalent of Mark's "Rabboni," which must not be downgraded. The man's answer was as plain and simple, as direct and honest, as the question had been.

42. Jesus said to him, Regain your sight; your faith has made you well.

The response of Jesus was immediate. The Master (Rabboni, Lord) ordered that the very thing the man was eager to receive be granted to him. Moreover, in view of the fact that faith is itself God's gift (see N.T.C. on Eph. 2:8), it is nothing less than astounding that Jesus here and elsewhere praises the recipient of the gift for exercising it! This proves the generous character of his love. Undoubtedly Eph. 2:8 refers to what is often called "saving faith." However, even in the present case it may well be doubted that the faith of which Jesus speaks is merely miraculous. In view of what this man is about to do, it would appear that when Jesus makes him well by promptly restoring to him his vision, he blesses him not only physically but also spiritually. A. T. Robertson, *Word Pictures,* I, p. 356, may therefore indeed be correct when he states that the expression *made thee whole* may well have the meaning here: *saved* thee. And is not more than physical restoration implied also in the other cases where the identical expression is used in the Gospels—the woman who suffered hemorrhages (Matt. 9:22; Mark 5:34; Luke 8:48); the great sinner (Luke 7:50); and the *one* cured leper who praised God and returned to thank Jesus (Luke 17:19)?

43a. Immediately he regained his sight...

One moment total blindness... the next unimpaired vision. How astounding!

43b. and began to follow Jesus, glorifying God.

Just what does this mean? That Bartimaeus joined the caravan of pilgrims who surrounded Jesus on the way to Jerusalem and the feast? It certainly means that. But in view of "Your faith has made you well" and "glorifying God," and also in view of the man's previous ascription of the title *Son of David* to Jesus, can we not also conclude that he joined the company of Christ's "disciples," as that term is interpreted in its broader sense?

43c. When all the people saw it, they also gave praise to God.

Was not that exactly what Jesus wanted them to do? See John 17:4. No doubt among those people there were some whose praise was genuine and upon whom Christ's words and deeds had made a saving impression. See also on 5:26.[497]

Practical Lessons Derived from Luke 18:15–43

Verse 17

"Whoever shall not receive the kingdom of God as a little child shall never enter it."

> Make me, O Lord, a child again,
> So tender, frail, and small,
> In self possessing nothing, and
> In thee possessing all.
>
> O Savior, make me small once more,
> That downward I may grow,
> And in this heart of mine restore
> The faith of long ago.
>
> With thee may I be crucified—
> No longer *I* that lives—
> O Savior, crush my sinful pride
> By grace which pardon gives.
>
> Make me, O Lord, a child again,
> Obedient to thy call,
> In self possessing nothing, and
> In thee possessing all.

Verse 21

"All these things have I observed ever since I was a child." The rich young ruler must not have taken to heart the words of Jer. 17:9, "Deceitful is the heart above all things . . . who can know it?"

And he must not have prayed the prayer of Ps. 139:23, 24,

> Search me, O God, and know my heart;
> Try me, and know my thoughts;
> And see if there be any wicked way in me,
> And lead me in the way everlasting.

---

497. Notes on Greek words, phrases, and constructions in 18:15–43 begin on page 846.

Verse 23

"When he heard this, he became very sad, for he was extremely rich."
Note how one sin can outweigh several virtues. Cf. Eccles. 10:1; Song of Sol. 2:15.

> Take my silver and my gold;
> Not a mite would I withhold.

Really?

Verse 34

"But they [The Twelve] understood none of this." Note that this lack of under-standing is stated three times in this verse. This ignorance or dullness was due, in part, to the fact that Jesus had not yet risen from the dead. Those who reject the truth of Christ's resurrection deprive themselves of *knowledge* (Luke 18:34) and of *joy* (I Cor. 15:19); in fact, of everything!

Verse 38

"So he [the blind man] shouted, 'Jesus, Son of David, take pity on me.'"

> There is a tide in the affairs of men,
> Which, taken at the flood, leads on to fortune;
> Omitted, all the voyage of their life
> Is bound in shallows and in miseries.

> Shakespeare, *Julius Caesar*

Notes on Greek Words, Phrases, and Constructions in 18:15–43

Verses 15, 16

βρέφη, acc. pl. of βρέφος, infant; see the note on 1:41 on page 99.

ἅπτηται, third per. s. pres. subjunct. (after ἵνα) middle of ἅπτω, to touch; see the note on 7:14 on page 390.

ἐπετίμων, third per. pl. imperf. indicat. of ἐπιτιμάω. The same form also appears in verse 39. In both cases the imperf. is probably ingressive. There is a difference in meaning, however. In verse 15 the meaning is to *rebuke;* in verse 39, *to warn.* See the note on 4:35 on page 267.

Note αὐτοῖς at the end of verse 15, but αὐτά (twice) in verse 16. The disciples started to rebuke those who brought the infants, but Jesus called the little ones to himself and ordered the disciples to stop hindering them.

Verse 17

οὐ μή, certainly not, never.

Verse 20

ψευδομαρτυρήσῃς, sec. per. s. aor. subjunct. of ψευδομαρτυρέω, to bear false witness. Cf. Matt. 19:18; Mark 10:19; 14:56, 57. For the cognate noun—false testimony—see Matt. 15:19; 26:59, and for the person guilty of this sin see Matt. 26:60; I Cor. 15:15, false witness.

Verse 21

νεότητος, gen. of νεότης, youth, childhood. ἐκ νεότητος, "since I was a child." See also Mark 10:20; Acts 26:4; I Tim. 4:12.

Verse 22

ἔτι ἕν σοι λείπει; lit. "one thing is still lacking [or wanting] to you." Cf. parallel in Mark 10:21; and see N.T.C. on Mark, p. 396, footnote 477.

διάδος, sec. per. s. 2nd aor. imperat. of διαδίδωμι, to distribute. See the note on 11:22 on page 634.

Verses 23, 24

περίλυπος, note intensive περί; hence, very sad. See also Matt. 26:38; Mark 6:26; 14:34.

δυσκόλως, adv., with difficulty, hardly. The prefix δυς has a meaning opposite to εὖ; and κόλον—cf. *colon, colic*—means *food*. Originally the meaning was probably: hard to please with food; then, in general, hard to please, difficult, hard. For the adverb, as here in Luke 18:24, see also Matt. 19:23; Mark 10:23.

Verse 25

For εὐκοπώτερον, easier, see the note on 16:17 on page 780.

κάμηλον, acc. s. of κάμηλος, camel; see also Matt. 3:4; 19:24; 23:24; Mark 1:6; 10:25.

τρήματος, gen. s. of τρῆμα, perforation, aperture, eye (cf. τιτράω, to bore). See also Matt. 19:24.

βελόνης, gen. s. of βελόνη*, point of a spear, here *needle*. The word is related to βέλος, a sharply pointed dart or missile that is thrown. Cf. βάλλω, to throw. Dr. Luke's needle was the surgical kind.

Verses 28, 29

From ἀφίημι, on which see the note on 4:39 on page 271, are derived both ἀφέντες, verse 28, nom. pl. masc. aor. participle, and ἀφῆκεν, third per. s. aor. indicat. act. It is clear that in these verses the verb has the meaning *to leave, to give up*.

Verse 30

ὃς οὐχὶ μὴ ἀπολάβῃ, note double negative, and third per. s. aor. subjunct. of ἀπολαμβάνω, "who shall not surely receive," etc.

πολλαπλασίονα*(?), acc. pl. neut. of πολλαπλασίων, many times as much. The preferred reading in Matt. 19:29 is ἑκατονταπλασίονα, a hundredfold. However, a variant has πολλαπλασίονα. If this variant should represent the authentic text in the Matthew passage, then the asterisk would have to be removed from the word as used here in Luke 18:30.

The Five Third Person Singular Future Indicative Passives in Luke 18:31, 32

The Five Verbs	Base	Meaning	Passages in Luke's Gospel Where This Verb Has a Broadly Similar Meaning	Remarks on Grammatical Construction
τελεσθήσεται	τελέω	to fulfill	22:37	Unless there is good reason to do otherwise, of two possible antecedents choose the closer. Therefore, τῷ υἱῷ τοῦ ἀνθρώπου should be viewed as modifying γεγραμμένα, and not τελεσθήσεται.
παραδοθήσεται	παραδίδωμι	to hand over	9:44; 12:58; 20:20; 21:12, 16; 22:4, 6, 21, 22, 48; 23:25; 24:7, 20	The combination of ten words πάντα ... ἀνθρώπου has τελεσθήσεται as its predicate.
ἐμπαιχθήσεται	ἐμπαίζω	to mock	14:29; 22:63; 23:11, 36	The subject of the next four verbs, beginning with παραδοθήσεται, is ὁ υἱὸς τοῦ ἀνθρώπου. It is implied in the dat. τῷ υἱῷ τοῦ ἀνθρώπου.
ὑβρισθήσεται	ὑβρίζω	to insult	11:45	
ἐμπτυσθήσεται	ἐμπτύω	to spit upon		

Verse 33

μαστιγώσαντες, nom. pl. masc. aor. participle of μαστιγόω, to scourge. In Luke's Gospel this verb occurs only here; but see also Matt. 10:17; 20:19; 23:34; Mark 10:34; John 19:1; Heb. 12:6.

ἀποκτενοῦσιν, third per. pl. fut. indicat. act. of ἀποκτείνω, to kill.

ἀναστήσεται, he shall rise again. See note on 16:31 on page 790.

Verse 34

συνῆκαν, third per. pl. aor. indicat. of συνίημι, to send together ("to put two and two together"), to understand. See also 2:50; 8:10; 24:45, etc.

ἦν κεκρυμμένον, third per. periphrastic pluperf. pass. of κρύπτω, to hide, conceal.

Verse 36

ἐπυνθάνετο, third per. s. imperf. (ingressive) of πυνθάνω, as in 15:26; see the note on that passage on page 762; to inquire.

Verse 37

ἀπήγγειλαν, third per. pl. aor. indicat. of ἀπαγγέλλω, to announce, inform, tell. See the note on 8:20 on page 437.

Verses 38, 39

ἐλέησον (once in each verse), sec. per. s. aor. imperat. act. of ἐλεέω, to take pity, to have mercy. Cf. ἔλεος, mercy, compassion, pity. See also Luke 16:24; 17:13. For a synonym see 18:13.

σιγήσῃ, third per. s. aor. subjunct. (after ἵνα) of σιγάω, to be quiet. See also 9:36; 20:26; Acts 12:17; 15:12, 13; Rom. 16:25; I Cor. 14:28, 30, 34. The word probably stems from imitation of a sound intended to hush. Cf. *sh!*

Verse 40

ἀχθῆναι, aor. pass. infinitive of ἄγω, to bring, lead.

Verses 41–43

Note the three forms of the verb ἀναβλέπω, here, and also in 7:22 (cf. Matt. 11:5; 20:34; Mark 10:51, 52) in the sense of *to regain* or *recover sight:*

ἀναβλέψω (verse 41), first per. s. aor. subjunct. (after ἵνα);

ἀνάβλεψον (verse 42), sec. per. s. aor. imperat.; and

ἀνέβλεψεν (verse 43), third per. s. aor. indicat.

At times this verb has the meaning *to look up* (9:16; 19:5; 21:1; cf. Matt. 14:19; Mark 6:41; 7:34; 16:4).

Summary of Chapter 18:15–43

In Luke's Gospel the parallel to Mark's account of Christ's Perean Ministry is resumed at this point. The report of that ministry continues through 19:27, though 19:1–27 is peculiar to Luke.

The four parts into which Luke 18:15–43 can be divided may be summarized as follows:

In the first paragraph (verses 15–17) Luke describes the attempt of the disciples to keep infants away from Jesus. But Jesus orders the little ones to be brought to him, "for," he says, "to such belongs the kingdom of God." He adds, "Whoever shall not receive the kingdom of God as a little child shall never enter it."

Next (verses 18–30) Luke tells the story of the ruler who approached Jesus with the question, "Good Teacher, what shall I do that I may inherit everlasting life?" Jesus answered, "Why do you call me good? No one is good except One—God." The Master spoke thus because the ruler had used the word *good* thoughtlessly. Jesus then referred him to God's perfect law, for "through the law comes the knowledge of sin." By saying, "All these things have I observed ever since I was a child," the inquirer once more revealed how shallow he was. Jesus answered, "One thing you still lack; sell all you have and distribute (the proceeds) to the poor, and you will have treasure in heaven, and come, follow me." Sadly the young man left.

As Jesus saw him leaving, he said to The Twelve, "How hard it is for those who possess wealth to enter the kingdom of God. Indeed, it is easier for a camel to go through the eye of a needle than for a rich man to enter the kingdom of God." Those who heard this remark said, "Then who can be saved?" Jesus replied, "What is impossible with men is possible with God."

In response to Peter's observation, "We have left all we had and followed you," Jesus promised blessings for the present and for the age to come.

The third paragraph covers verses 31–34. Peter had called Jesus' attention to the sacrifices this disciple and the others had made (verse 28). Jesus, in his third main passion-and-resurrection prediction, focused the attention of the group on the infinitely greater sacrifice he was about to make. For the five items that belong to this prediction see p. 839. The disciples failed completely to grasp its meaning.

The fourth or final paragraph (verses 35–43) reports that Jesus (and The Twelve) arrived at last at Jericho. He was surrounded by a large crowd of Passover pilgrims. When Jesus entered the city, a blind beggar, having been informed that Jesus of Nazareth was passing by, began to cry out, "Jesus, Son of David, take pity on me." When the people told him to be quiet, he cried all the more, "Son of David, take pity on me." Jesus did exactly that. He ordered the blind man to be brought to him, asked him, "What do you want me to do for you?" and healed him. Result: the happy man began to follow Jesus and glorified God. When all the people saw it, they also gave praise to God.

Outline of Chapter 19:1-27

Theme: *The Work Thou Gavest Him to Do*

CHAPTER XIX: 1-27

19 1 Then he entered Jericho and was passing through. 2 Here there was a man named Zacchaeus. He was a chief tax-collector and was wealthy.

3 He was trying to see who Jesus was, but being small in stature was unable to see him on account of the crowd.

4 So he ran ahead and climbed a sycamore tree to see him, since Jesus was about to pass through that way.

5 When Jesus reached the spot, he looked up and said to him, "Zacchaeus, hurry down, for today I must stay at your home."   6 So he hurried down and welcomed him joyfully.

7 But on seeing (this), all the people began to grumble, "He has gone to be the guest of[498] a sinner."

8 But Zacchaeus stood up and said to the Lord, "Listen, Lord! Here and now I'm giving half of my possessions to the poor, and if I've cheated anybody out of anything, I'm giving back four times as much."

9 So Jesus told him, "Today salvation has come to this home, because even this man[499] is a son of Abraham.   10 For the Son of man came to seek and to save what was lost."

19:1-10 *Jesus and Zacchaeus*

The connection between the closing paragraph of chapter 18 and the opening paragraph of chapter 19 is almost unforgettable; for (a) both events took place in Jericho land, and (b) in the first instance a *poor* man became a follower of Jesus; in the second, a *rich* man did.

1. Then he entered Jericho and was passing through.

Even before the reign of Herod I Jericho was already "a little paradise," with its palm trees, rose gardens, etc. Herod the Great and his son Archelaus had made it even more beautiful. A grand winter palace had been built there, also a theater and a hippodrome. Some of the streets were lined with sycamore trees. The climate was delightful. Had not Mark Antony given the city to the Egyptian Queen (Cleopatra) as a token of his affection?

2. Here there was a man named Zacchaeus. He was a chief tax-collector and was wealthy.

This is the only place in the New Testament where a "chief tax-collector" is mentioned. The system of collecting taxes has been explained in connection with 3:12; see on that passage and also on 5:27. Zacchaeus, then, must

---

498. Or: to lodge with.
499. Or: this man, too.

PALESTINE IN THE TIME OF CHRIST, SHOWING TRADE AND TRAVEL ROUTES:

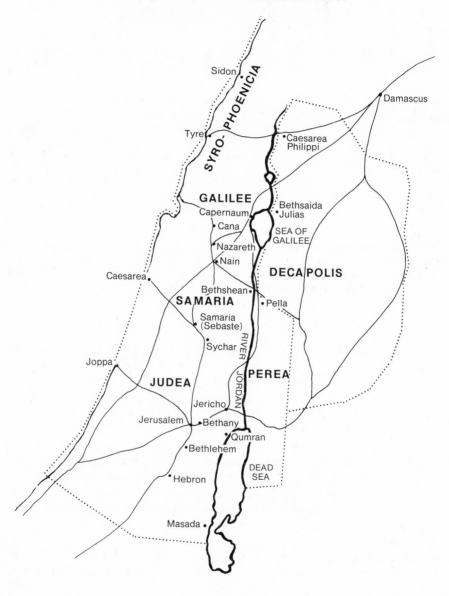

Sidon

SYRO-PHOENICIA

Damascus

Tyre

Caesarea
Philippi

GALILEE

Bethsaida
Julias

Capernaum

Cana

SEA OF
GALILEE

Nazareth

Nain

DECAPOLIS

Caesarea

Bethshean

SAMARIA

Pella

Samaria
(Sebaste)

Sychar

RIVER JORDAN

Joppa

JUDEA

PEREA

Jericho

Jerusalem

Bethany

Qumran

Bethlehem

DEAD
SEA

Hebron

Masada

have been considered a very prominent individual. He had been placed at the head of the entire tax district of Jericho and vicinity, one of the three main Palestinian tax offices, the other two being located at Caesarea and Capernaum.

Now one of the things for which Jericho was famous was the balm derived from the balsam tree. Josephus (*Antiquities* XV.96) calls balsam "the most precious thing there is." It was fragrant, soothing, and highly regarded for its healing qualities. The trade in this commodity—and in other commodities abounding in the Jericho region—yielded high taxes for the Roman government. Besides, Jericho was at the heart and center of a vast trade route network, as is clear from the map on p. 854. The city had trade connections with Damascus, Tyre, and Sidon to the north, Caesarea and Joppa to the west, and Egypt to the south, as well as with many other cities and countries in every direction. An important man, therefore, this Zacchaeus! However, by the Jews "publicans" (certainly including chief publicans) were regarded as traitors and crooks. This man's name, however, means "the righteous one."[500]

3, 4. He was trying to see who Jesus was, but being small in stature was unable to see him on account of the crowd. So he ran ahead and climbed a sycamore tree to see him, since Jesus was about to pass through that way.

Being small he was unable to catch a view of Jesus. Nevertheless, so deep was his interest in the Master that he was willing to do almost anything to see him. So, knowing where Jesus was going, he quickly ran ahead of the crowd and then, important man though he was, climbed into a sycamore tree, one of those that had been planted by the roadside. It is also called "sycamore fig tree," and is highly prized for the shade it provides. Moreover, since some of its branches extend from the trunk close to the ground, even a man like Zacchaeus, small in stature, could easily climb it.

5, 6. When Jesus reached the spot, he looked up and said to him, Zacchaeus, hurry down, for today I must stay at your home. —So he hurried down and welcomed him joyfully.

It is especially significant to note that although Zacchaeus was certainly very eager to see Jesus, it was Jesus, not the chief tax-collector, who took the initiative in arranging a personal contact between the two. It was Jesus who was seeking and saving (see verse 10).

It is also significant that Jesus does not say to the man in the tree, "Will it be convenient for you to have me visit you?" He says, "Zacchaeus, hurry down, for today I *must* stay at your home." And the Lord knew very well that the huge surrounding crowd would be less than pleased by these words. Jesus *must* stay at the chief publican's home because that was in keeping with the Savior's calling, in line with the purpose for which he had become incarnate.

---

500. See S.BK., Vol. II, p. 249.

Never had Zacchaeus descended from a tree more quickly than now, and never with greater joy.

7. But on seeing (this), all the people began to grumble, He has gone to be the guest of a sinner.

It is clear that the people—note "all" the people (that is, the people in general)—hate Zacchaeus. In view of what has been pointed out earlier—namely, that they regarded publicans as being extortionists and traitors—that is understandable, though not excusable. What, however, makes their grumbling all the more wicked is the fact that again and again during his ministry, which by now has almost ended, Jesus had explained why such a hateful attitude toward publicans was so thoroughly reprehensible (Matt. 9:11, cf. Mark 2:16; Luke 5:30; Matt. 11:19, cf. Luke 7:34; Luke 15). Nevertheless, the people continue in their loveless way! They are in the process of hardening their hearts.

8. But Zacchaeus stood up and said to the Lord, Listen, Lord. Here and now I'm giving half of my possessions to the poor, and if I've cheated anybody out of anything, I'm giving back four times as much.

We must assume that Jesus has now entered the home of the chief publican. Is it not natural to believe also that to all those gathered there he spoke the words of life? The loving concern Jesus had shown for Zacchaeus made the latter a changed man.

So deeply impressed is he that, in response, he rises, and states that here and now he is giving half of his possessions to the poor. That is his thank-offering.

Has he at times been guilty of (directly or indirectly) exacting too much money from anybody? He has. See the note on this verse on page 864. So, in the presence of all he now declares that he is returning whatever he has unlawfully taken away. Not only that, he is going to add something to it. The law (Lev. 6:1–5; Num. 5:7) required that in certain cases one-fifth of the unjustly obtained amount—in the present case one-fifth of the overcharge—had to be added when making restitution. In other cases double restitution had to be made (Exod. 22:4, 7, 9).[501] Zacchaeus, however, has just now decided to restore not double but fourfold the amount overcharged. Incidentally, does not that fourfold amount plus "half of my possessions" (the latter for the poor) tend to prove that Zacchaeus cannot have been grossly dishonest? Otherwise would he have been able to make such a generous restitution?

9. So Jesus told him, Today salvation has come to this home, because even this man is a son of Abraham.

Note *salvation*, nothing less. Does this not mean emancipation from the

---

501. In cases where an animal was not only stolen but was afterward killed or sold, four-fold or even fivefold restitution was required (Exod. 22:1; cf. II Sam. 12:6). In all probability, however, this rule was not applicable in the present case, which was of a completely different character.

greatest evil and being placed in possession of the greatest good? Does it not mean "everlasting life"? *Today* Jesus had called the chief publican out of that tree and had with blessing entered his home. *Today,* therefore, the great spiritual miracle had taken place. The Great Shepherd had found his sheep.

Note also "to this home," apparently not just to one individual in that home. The covenant is still in effect. See Gen. 17:7, 9; 18:19; Ps. 103:17, 18; Luke 1:72–75; Acts 2:38, 39. As is clear from all these passages, this by no means excludes the necessity of living faith on the part of the children. It very definitely requires such faith on the part of all who have reached the years of discretion.

When Jesus now declares that Zacchaeus is indeed a son of Abraham, he is, of course, not merely declaring that the chief publican is a physical descendant of the arch-patriarch. He is using "son of Abraham" in a spiritual sense. Cf. Gal. 3:9, 29. The chief publican was a "son of Abraham" in the same sense in which the Syrophoenician woman was a true Israelite. See N.T.C. on Matthew, p. 625.

Very appropriately Jesus adds: **10. For the Son of man came to seek and to save what was lost.** Zacchaeus had not sought Jesus. Jesus had sought . . . and found Zacchaeus. Cf. Luke 15:1–7. In a few days the Good Shepherd was going to lay down his life for the sheep, including Zacchaeus.

For *Practical Lessons* and *Greek Words,* etc., see pp. 863–866.

---

11 Now while they were listening to these things, he proceeded to tell a parable, because he was near Jerusalem, and because the people thought that the kingdom of God was going to appear at once. 12 He said:

"A certain nobleman went to a distant country to receive a kingdom for himself and (then) to return. 13 So he called in ten of his servants, gave them a pound apiece, and said to them, 'Do business with these[502] until I come (back).'

14 "But his subjects hated him, and sent a delegation on his heels, saying, 'We don't want this man to become king over us.'

15 "But he was made king and returned home. Then he ordered these servants, to whom he had given the money, to be summoned before him,[503] that he might learn what each had gained by doing business.

16 "The first one came and said, 'Sir, your pound has earned ten more.'

17 "His master said to him, 'Splendid, my good servant! Because in a very small matter you have been faithful, be in authority over ten cities.'

18 "The second came and said, 'Your pound, Sir, has made five pounds.'

19 "So he said similarly to him, 'Be in charge of five cities.'

20 "Then another servant came and said, 'Sir, here is your pound, which I have been keeping wrapped up in a napkin. 21 For I lived in constant fear of you, because you are a stern man: you withdraw what you did not deposit, and you reap what you did not sow.'

22 "His master said to him, 'Out of your own mouth do I judge you, you wicked servant! You knew, did you, that I am a stern man, withdrawing what I did not deposit, and reaping

---

502. Or: Trade with these.

503. Literally: And it came about that when he returned home, having received the kingdom, he ordered, etc.

what I did not sow?   23 Then why didn't you put my money in a bank, so that on my return I could have collected it with interest?'

24 "Then he said to the bystanders, 'Take his pound away from him and give it to him who has the ten pounds.'

25 "But they said to him, 'Sir, he (already) has ten pounds!'

26 "(He replied), 'I tell y o u that to everyone who has, (more) will be given, but from him who does not have, even what he has will be taken away.   27 But as for these enemies of mine, who did not want me to be king over them, bring them here and cut them down in my presence.'"

19:11–27 *The Parable of The Pounds*
Resemblances and Differences Between Two Parables:
that of The Talents (Matt. 25:14–30)
and that of The Pounds (Luke 19:11–27).

Resemblances: In each case the chief character, before leaving on a journey, entrusts a certain sum of money to his servants. When he returns, he calls them to account. Also in each case the first two servants who report are rewarded for their diligence, the third is punished for his negligence.

Differences: In the parable of The Talents the entrusted amount is huge, and the servants receive different amounts. In that of The Pounds the entrusted amount is relatively small, and each receives the same amount. Also, in the parable of The Talents there are only two "parties," a businessman and his servants. In that of The Pounds there are three: the nobleman-king, the servants, and the citizens. The idea of a nobleman going abroad in quest of a kingdom is absent from the parable of The Talents. Proof for the proposition that at one time these two parables were one and the same is lacking.

In the parable of *The Pounds* four "movements" are clearly in evidence:

A. *A nobleman, in quest of a kingdom,*
entrusts a pound apiece to ten servants, and then leaves.

11. Now while they were listening to these things, he proceeded to tell a parable, because he was near Jerusalem, and because the people thought that the kingdom of God was going to appear at once.

While those present in the home of Zacchaeus were listening to Jesus describing himself as the One who had come to seek and to save the lost, he proceeded to tell a parable. He did this in order to correct certain harmful ideas that were being spread; especially the notion that now the kingdom of God was immediately going to appear, the kingdom of outward, earthly, Jewish splendor.

That the people in general were constantly looking for such a kingdom is clear from John 6:15. That even the minds of The Twelve continued for a long time to be filled with such expectations can be learned from Mark 10:35–45 (the request of the sons of Zebedee) and Acts 1:6.

It was especially the Passover Festival, with its many reminders of the glorious deliverance from Egypt, that fanned the embers of the revolutionary spirit. Moreover, the closer these pilgrims drew to Jerusalem, from which leadership in any such upheaval was expected, the more also the hope of instant deliverance rose. And now that they had arrived at Jericho, Jerusalem was just around the corner. The distance from Jericho to Jerusalem was only 27 kilometers (17 miles); in fact, only 24 kilometers (15 miles) when Bethany is figured in with Jerusalem, as is sometimes done.

To counteract these harmful views Jesus is going to show that:

a. the kingdom he proclaims is not confined to one particular nation: nowhere in the parable is there even a hint of obtaining political freedom;

b. its outward manifestation is not a matter of the immediate future (see verse 12); and

c. everyone should be faithful in the performance of his God-given duties. On the day of the final judgment it is faithfulness that will be rewarded, unfaithfulness punished (verses 15–27).

12. He said: A certain nobleman went to a distant country to receive a kingdom for himself and (then) to return.

There are those who think that Jesus was referring first of all to Archelaus, the cruel son of a cruel father, who more than thirty years earlier had gone to Rome to have his claim to the throne confirmed. However, it is not at all certain that the Master was referring especially or exclusively to him. It was not at all unusual for someone to go to Rome in order to obtain a kingdom. See N.T.C. on Matthew, pp. 158, 164.

What Jesus was really telling his audience, in symbolical phraseology, was probably this, that he himself, at the conclusion of his suffering, would ascend to the Father in heaven; that the Father, as a reward upon the Son's accomplished mediatorial work, would cause him to sit at his right hand, thereby bestowing on him rulership over the entire universe in the interest of his church (Eph. 1:20–23); and that from heaven he would return to earth after a *long* (but indefinite) time, symbolized by "the far country" to which the nobleman of the parable was wending his way.

The idea that the Son of man will not return at once is stressed also in certain other passages, two of the clearest being Matt. 25:5 ("While the bridegroom tarried," A.V.), and Matt. 25:19 ("A long while afterward the master . . . came"). See also Matt. 24:14; II Thess. 2:2, 3; II Peter 3:4–9; Rev. 20:1–3, 7–11.

13. So he called in ten of his servants, gave them a pound apiece, and said to them, Do business with these until I come (back).

Literally the passage reads, "Having called his [or: his own] servants, he gave them ten minas," etc. A *mina* was a Greek coin worth 100 drachmas, the drachma being a laborer's daily wage. This could well be the best description of the value of the mina. Among other attempts at expressing the value of *one mina* in English terms are the following:

a. "about three months' wages." By working and earning wages also on the sabbath?

b. "five pounds." At today's currency value?

c. "$10," "$17," "$20," "$100." Each of these has been suggested.

But the exact value, expressed in British pounds or in American dollars, is of no importance to the understanding of the parable. Far more important is the fact that in this parable each of the servants receives *the same* amount, namely, *one mina.* If, with many translators—e.g., A.V., A.R.V., R.S.V., N.E.B., Weymouth, Jerusalem Bible, A. T. Robertson, Dutch (both Statenvertaling and Nieuwe Vertaling: *pond*), etc.—we call this mina a *pound,* and stress the fact that this was a *pound* of very high value (not a deflated one), a pound so high in value that it amounted to the standard earnings which the ordinary laborer would receive for 100 days of actual work, we need say no more.

With that "pound" each of these servants *must do business.* That is the point of the parable. *Those who have heard the gospel must proclaim it!* They must conduct themselves in such a manner that through their word and example sinners are brought to the Lord, believers are strengthened in the faith, they themselves grow in every Christian virtue, and every sphere (social, economic, political, educational, etc.) is brought under the influence of the gospel, all this to the glory of God.

That is the one important task for each and every one.

Having entrusted a pound apiece to each of ten servants, the nobleman then goes on his way to secure a kingdom for himself.

B. *The citizens try to prevent him from achieving his purpose.*

14. But his subjects hated him, and sent a delegation on his heels, saying, We don't want this man to become king over us.

As applied to earthly rulers, this too was happening again and again; for example, when the attempts of Alexandra's sons (Hyrcanus II and Aristobulus) were frustrated; again, when, on account of a citizen's embassy to Rome, Archelaus became ethnarch instead of king, and later, as a result of still another embassy, was deposed (A.D. 6). And something similar was going to happen in the case of Herod Antipas. His attempt to receive the royal title and authority was frustrated by Herod Agrippa I. For more details read N.T.C. on Matthew, pp. 158, 187, 188, 590, and the literature on p. 159, footnote 163 in that commentary.

But Jesus is ultimately speaking about an attempt at frustration which was *not* successful. Ultimately he is pointing to "the stone which the builders rejected but which became the cornerstone" (Ps. 118:22, 23; Matt. 21:42). He is speaking about himself!

C. *Having succeeded, he returns and calls his servants to account.*

15–19. But he was made king and returned home. Then he ordered these servants, to whom he had given the money, to be summoned before him, that he might learn what each had gained by doing business. The first one came and said, Sir, your pound has earned ten more. His master

said to him, Splendid, my good servant! Because in a very small matter you have been faithful, be in authority over ten cities. The second came and said, Your pound, Sir, has made five pounds. So he said similarly to him, Be in charge of five cities.

The attempt to prevent the nobleman from receiving his kingdom failed. So also every attempt to frustrate the Son of man's plans will fail. He ascends to heaven and receives his kingdom, as has already been indicated. The nobleman's return and session with his servants symbolizes Christ's glorious second coming, when he will demand of his servants that they render an account of the manner in which they have dealt with *the gospel;* and, in this connection, with the gifts and opportunities for service that were placed at their disposal.

In the parable the first servant reports that he has turned his pound into ten pounds. Nevertheless, he does not thus express himself. With becoming humility he says, "Your pound has gained ten more." So also the second servant, whose pound has gained five pounds.

The nobleman, now king, praises both servants and assigns control over cities to both, to each in exact proportion to the profit made. Similarly, the Lord Jesus Christ, at his glorious return will praise his faithful servants and will reward them in proportion to the degree of faithfulness they have shown. They will be given an opportunity to render even greater service in the new heaven and earth.

Note (verse 17) "in a very small matter," for how small are our tasks here and now compared to our responsibilities in the new heaven and earth!

20, 21. Then another servant came and said, Sir, here is your pound, which I have been keeping wrapped up in a napkin. For I lived in constant fear of you, because you are a stern man: you withdraw what you did not deposit, and you reap what you did not sow.

Though one fine commentator calls this lazy fellow "a believer," I disagree. He was a Christian only in a nominal sense; that is, in reality he was not a believer at all.

When he says, "Sir, here is your pound," is he not implying, "I kept your property intact. You should be thankful for that"?

Even rabbinical law frowned upon keeping a deposit wrapped up merely in a napkin. And the proverbial saying he uses—"you withdraw what you did not deposit," etc., in other words, "you are a grossly unfair, *austere* man, who is, as it were, trying 'to squeeze blood out of a turnip' "—shows how wicked he is.

22, 23. His master said to him, Out of your own mouth do I judge you, you wicked servant! You knew, did you, that I am a stern man, withdrawing what I did not deposit, and reaping what I did not sow? Then why didn't you put my money in a bank, so that on my return I could have collected it with interest?

His master is, as it were, saying to him, "Your own words convict you; for if you were so sure that I was austere, you should have exerted yourself all

the more. The least you could have done would have been to put my money
in a bank, so that, on my return, I could have received it back with interest."

Literally, what the nobleman, now king, said to him was, "Why didn't you
put my money *on the (moneylender's) bench?*" Since moneylenders paid interest on money deposited with them, which in turn they would lend out at a
higher rate of interest, it follows that our modern banking system had its
origin here, the very word *bank* being derived from this word *bench.*

Here again we should not lose sight of the real or ultimate meaning of
the parable, namely, that we must put forth every effort to make the best
possible use of the good tidings of salvation proclaimed to us. When Christ
returns, he will severely punish those who have not done so:

**24–26. Then he said to the bystanders, Take his pound away from him
and give it to him who has the ten pounds. But they said to him, Sir, he
(already) has ten pounds! (He replied), I tell y o u that to everyone who
has, (more) will be given, but from him who does not have, even what he
has will be taken away.**[504]

It cannot very well be questioned that the bystanders who are ordered to
take the pound away from the wicked servant and who interject, "Sir, he
(already) has ten pounds," are persons present *in the parable* and not people
who are listening to the parable. Also, it should not be open to doubt that
the one who states, "I tell y o u that," etc., is the nobleman-king.

It should be added, however, that since this exalted individual represents
the Son of man coming to judge, this last item is of minor importance, for
whichever way these words are taken, in the final analysis they indicate the
mind of Jesus.

A superficial glance at the rule here expressed might cause sharp disagreement and perhaps even resentment. One might ask, "What? Does
Jesus actually justify taking from the poor in order to give to the rich?"
However, in the light of the entire context and of other passages, such as
Luke 9:23, 24; 17:33; cf. Matt. 10:39; 16:26; Mark 8:34–38; and John
12:25, 26, one soon discovers the true meaning. It is this: the man who
through diligent use of the gospel has enriched himself and others, will, by
continuing in this course, become richer and richer. On the other hand,
from the person who has become poor because he has neglected his duty in
this respect, even whatever little he once had shall be taken away. For the
rest, see the explanation of the almost identical passage, Luke 8:18.

D. *He orders the destruction of his opponents.*

**27. But as for these enemies of mine, who did not want me to be king
over them, bring them here and cut them down in my presence.**

As concerns the parable itself, those who receive the punishment here

---

504. Only three of the ten servants are introduced in the parable: two good men, one wicked
person. The other seven need not be discussed, since each of them belongs to one of the two
groups, the good or the bad.

described are the "haters" of verse 14. For the severe treatment they receive there are numerous examples in ancient history.[505]

As to the parable's ultimate meaning, the reference is to what will happen to Christ rejectors when he returns. If one is filled with revulsion at the thought that such vengeance is ascribed to a Savior whose love and tenderness are beyond all imagination and description, might not the solution be that these very attributes make hating and rejecting *such* a Savior worthy of supreme retribution?[506]

Practical Lessons Derived from Luke 19:1–27

Verses 8, 9

"Zacchaeus said, 'Here and now I'm giving half of my possessions to the poor...' Jesus told him, 'Today salvation has come to this home.'" Good works do not earn salvation, but a saved man does not want to do without them. A converted person is a changed person, "a new creation" (II Cor. 5:17). He is the kind of individual who likes to sing F. R. Havergal's songs: "Lord, speak to me" and "Take my life, and let it be."

Verse 10

"The Son of man came to seek and to save what was lost." That description is, indeed, very general. It includes people of each sex, race, nationality, age group, vocation, degree of education, rank, etc. For snobbery there is no room in the Christian religion.

Verse 14

"We don't want this man to become king over us." Whoever wants Jesus to be his Savior must first of all recognize him as his Lord and King. He must ardently desire that all his aspirations, thoughts, words, and deeds, shall be under the control of Christ's will.

Verse 17

"His master said to him, 'Splendid, my good servant!'" The Lord takes delight in rewarding his children, not in punishing the wicked. Cf. Ezek. 18:23, 32.

Notes on Greek Words, Phrases, and Constructions in 19:1–27

Verse 1

διήρχετο, third per. s. imperf. (progressive) of διέρχομαι, to pass through. In verse 4 note pres. infinitive of the same verb.

---

505. In this connection see also T. W. Manson, *The Sayings of Jesus*, London, 1949, p. 317.
506. Notes on Greek words, phrases, and constructions in 19:1–27 begin on this page.

Verse 3

ἡλικίᾳ, dat. s. of ἡλικία, here physical stature, height; in 12:25 life-span, age.

Verse 4

συκομορέαν, acc. s. of συκομορέα*, sycamore tree.

Verses 5, 6

ἀναβλέψας, nom. s. masc. aor. participle of ἀναβλέπω. See the note on 18:41–43 on page 849.

σπεύσας (once in each verse), nom. s. masc. aor. participle of σπεύδω, to make haste, hurry. Cf. *speed.*

κατάβηθι (verse 5), sec. per. s. 2nd aor. imperat.; and κατέβη (verse 6), third per. s. aor. indicat., are forms of καταβαίνω, to come down.

Verse 7

διεγόγγυζον, third per. pl. imperf. (descriptive and progressive) of διαγογγύζω*, to mutter, grumble, is clearly an onomatopoeia (sound-imitation). In the New Testament this compound verb is found only here and in 15:2. For the simple form see Matt. 20:11; Luke 5:30; John 6:41, 43, 61; 7:32; I Cor. 10:10.

καταλῦσαι, aor. act. infinitive of καταλύω, to unloose; hence, to lodge. For more on this verb see the note on 9:12 on page 485.

Verse 8

"If I've cheated anybody," etc., is a first class or simple conditional sentence (statement assumed to be true). Its protasis has εἰ with aor. act. indicat., followed by pres. infinitive; its apodosis, the pres. indicative act.

For ἐσυκοφάντησα, first per. s. aor. indicat. act. of συκοφαντέω*, here in the sense of *to cheat,* see the note on 3:14 on page 215.

τετραπλοῦν, acc. s. neut. of τετραπλόος*, fourfold, four times as much.

Verse 9

ὅτι, used here to introduce a direct quotation; so also in verse 42.

Verse 10

τὸ ἀπολωλός, the lost; i.e., what was lost. See the note on 15:4b, 6 on page 750.

Verse 11

γπροσθεὶς εἶπεν, he proceeded to tell (a parable). The Greek idiom has been explained in the note on 17:5 on page 801.

ἀναφαίνεσθαι, pres. middle or pass. infinitive of ἀναφαίνω**, to bring to light; in middle or pass., as here, to appear; in Acts 21:3, to come in sight of.

Verse 12

εὐγενής, lit. wellborn (I Cor. 1:26); here in Luke 19:12 and also in Acts 17:11, noble.

Verse 13

μνᾶς, acc. pl. of μνᾶ, mina. For details see the commentary.

πραγματεύσασθε, sec. per. pl. aor. imperat. of πραγματεύομαι*, to transact business, to trade. Cf. πρᾶγμα, thing, matter, affair, transaction.

ἐν ᾧ ἔρχομαι, lit. "while I am coming"; hence, "during my absence and until I return."

Verse 14

πολῖται, nom. pl. of πολίτης, subject. See also the note on 15:15 on page 760.

πρεσβείαν, acc. s. of πρεσβεία*, delegation, as in 14:32.

Verses 15, 16

ἐν τῷ ἐπανελθεῖν αὐτόν, upon his return. Note articular (2nd aor.) infinitive of ἐπανέρχομαι (for which see the note on 10:35 on page 602), followed by the acc. of general reference αὐτόν, the entire expression meaning literally "on the return as to him," i.e., "on his return."

δεδώκει, for ἐδεδώκει, third per. s. pluperf. act. of δίδωμι, to give.

διεπραγματεύσαντο, third per. pl. aor. indicat. of διαπραγματεύομαι*, to gain by doing business.

προσηργάσατο, third per. s. aor. indicat. act. of προσεργάζομαι*, to work up in addition, to earn.

Verse 17

Εὖγε*, note γε. To bring out the full emotional force of this exclamation "Splendid . . . !" is probably even better than "Well done . . . !"

ἴσθι . . . ἔχων, sec. per. s. periphrastic pres. imperat. of εἰμί; hence, "be having," i.e., "have and keep on having (authority)," "be (in authority)."

Verse 19

γίνου, sec. per. s. pres. (durative) middle imperat. of γίνομαι, "Be and remain (in charge)."

Verse 20

εἶχον, here *first* per. s. imperf. indicat. of ἔχω, to have, hold, keep; "I have been keeping."

ἀποκειμένην, acc. s. fem. (agreeing with ἥν) pres. pass. participle of ἀπόκειμαι, with sense of perf. pass. of τίθημι, to be laid up; elsewhere in somewhat similar sense, laid up, stored up (Col. 1:5; II Tim. 4:8), "appointed" (Heb. 9:27).

σουδαρίῳ, dat. of σουδάριον, from Lat. *sudarium;* here napkin; cf. Acts 19:12 handkerchief; John 11:44; 20:7 sweatband.

Verses 21, 22

The word αὐστηρός*, stern; cf. *austere,* is found in both verses. This holds too for the four verbs: to withdraw, deposit, reap, sow.

αἴρω, to withdraw (for this sense and other meanings see the note on 17:13 on page 803); in verse 21 sec. per. s. pres. indicat. act.: *you withdraw;* in verse 22 nom. s. masc. pres. participle: *withdrawing.*

τίθημι, to deposit; in verse 21 sec. per. s. aor. indicat. act., preceded by οὐκ: *you did not deposit;* in verse 22 first per. s. aor. indicat. act., preceded by οὐκ: *I did not deposit.*

θερίζω, to reap; in verse 21, sec. per. s. pres. indicat. act.: *you reap;* in verse 22 nom. s. masc. pres. participle: *reaping.*

σπείρω, to sow; in verse 21 sec. per. s. aor. indicat. act. preceded by οὐκ: *you did not sow;* in verse 22 first per. s. aor. indicat. act., preceded by οὐκ: *I did not sow.*

Verse 23

ἐπὶ τράπεζαν, lit. on the bench (of the moneylender); hence, in the bank.

τόκῳ, dat. of τόκος, from τίκτω, to bear; hence, offspring, interest.

ἂν ... ἔπραξα, "I could have collected," first per. s. aor. indicat. of πράσσω, in the apodosis of a second class (contrary to fact) conditional sentence, with "If you had put my money in a bank" in the *implied* protasis.

Verse 24

παρεστῶσιν, dat. pl. masc. 2nd perf. act. participle of παρίστημι, to stand by; hence, "to the bystanders."

Verse 27

κατασφάξατε, sec. per. pl. aor. imperat. of κατασφάζω*, to cut down, slay, slaughter.

Summary of Chapter 19:1-27

The story as Luke tells it (in verses 1–10) turns from poor Bartimaeus (see Mark 10:46), whose sight Jesus restored (Luke 18:35–43), to rich Zacchaeus, chief tax-collector, who, being a small man, had climbed into a sycamore tree so as to be able to see Jesus. Jesus told him, "Zacchaeus, hurry down, for today I must stay at your home." When the Lord entered the home of the chief publican, the latter, by his words and actions—the gift of half of all his property to the poor, fourfold restitution of overcharges—proved that he had become a saved man. Luke's report ends with a striking quotation from the lips of Jesus, "Today salvation has come to this home, because even this man is a son of Abraham. For the Son of man came to seek and to save what was lost."

In the parable of The Pounds (verses 11–27) Jesus teaches that not only Zacchaeus but everyone should prove the sincerity of his convictions and the genuine character of his faith by his actions. He should use to the best advantage the precious gift of the good tidings of salvation. He can do this by striving to win others for Christ, etc. He has no right to allow that gospel to remain unused. On the day of the final judgment Jesus, as King of kings and Lord of lords, will recompense each person according to the faithfulness he has shown, or the lack of it.

The Work Thou Gavest Him to Do

Its Climax

or

Culmination

Chapters 19:28—24:53

Outline of Chapter 19:28–48

Theme: *The Work Thou Gavest Him to Do*

A. *The Week of The Passion*

19:28–44 The Triumphal Entry into Jerusalem
19:45–48 The Cleansing of the Temple

CHAPTER XIX:28-48

28 After Jesus had said these things, he went on ahead, going up to Jerusalem.   29 As he approached Bethphage and Bethany near the mount[507] that is called Olivet, he sent two of his disciples,   30 and said, "Go into the village opposite (y o u), and as y o u enter it, y o u will find a colt tied, on which no one ever sat. Untie it and bring it here.   31 And if anyone asks y o u, 'Why are y o u untying it?' y o u must say,[508] 'The Lord needs it.'"

32 So those who had been sent went away and found it just as he had told them.   33 As they were untying the colt, its owners said to them, "Why are y o u untying the colt?"   34 They said, "The Lord needs it."   35 And they brought it to Jesus, threw their cloaks on the colt, and set Jesus on it.   36 And as he went along, people were constantly spreading their cloaks under him on the road.

37 As he was now approaching the descent of the Mount of Olives, the entire multitude of the disciples began to praise God joyfully with a loud voice for all the miracles they had seen,   38 saying:

"Blessed (is) the Coming One,
The King, in the name of the Lord![509]
In heaven peace,
And glory in the highest."

39 Then some of the Pharisees from the throng said to Jesus, "Teacher, rebuke your disciples."   40 He answered, "I tell y o u, if these become silent, the stones will cry out."

41 Now when he approached (Jerusalem), he came in sight of the city and burst into tears over it,   42 saying, "Would that on this day you, even you, had known the things that pertain to peace! But now they are hidden from your eyes.   43 For days will come upon you when your enemies will throw up a palisade[510] against you, encircle you, and hem you in from all directions.   44 They will dash to the ground you and your children along with you, and will not leave in you one stone on another,[511] because you did not recognize the season when God (in his grace) visited you."[512]

PALM SUNDAY
19:28-44 *The Triumphal Entry into Jerusalem*
Cf. Matt. 21:1-11; Mark 11:1-11; John 12:12-19

The account of The Perean Ministry has ended, and so has the entire second division of Luke's story concerning the work the Father gave the

---

507. Or: hill; so also in verse 37.
508. Literally: y o u must speak thus. . . .
509. Or: Blessed (is) the King who comes in the name of the Lord.
510. Or: siege works, earthworks.
511. Literally: stone upon stone.
512. Literally: the season [time or moment] of your visitation.

Mediator to do. The evangelist has told us all he, guided by the Holy Spirit, wanted to relate concerning the Progress or Continuation of Christ's work. At this point, therefore, the narrative of The Week of the Passion begins. It covers Luke 19:28—23:56, and is followed by the story of The Resurrection and Ascension, chapter 24.

Luke 18:35-19:27 described what Jesus did when he was in the Jericho region. From Jericho the little party continued on its way toward Jerusalem (19:28). On reasonable grounds it may be assumed that Bethany, about two miles from Jerusalem (John 11:18), was reached before sunset on Friday, that on the sabbath (Friday sunset to Saturday sunset) Jesus enjoyed the sabbath rest with his friends, that on Saturday evening a supper was given in his honor at the home of "Simon the leper" (Mark 14:3-9), and that the next day, being Sunday, the triumphal entry into Jerusalem occurred. From this point on the day by day events recorded in Luke's Gospel are found in the following passages:

Sunday	19:28-44
Monday	19:45-48
Tuesday & Wednesday	20:1—22:6
Thursday	(including the night from Thursday to very early Friday) 22:7-71
Friday	Chapter 23
Saturday	No events reported in Luke, but see Matt. 27:62-66
Sunday	24:1-49
"forty days later"	24:50-53 (cf. Acts 1:1-5)

In the preceding section (19:11-27) there has been constant reference to "the kingdom" and "the king" (verses 11, 12, 14, 15, and 27). And now "the king"—not, however, the kind of king the people wanted, but the very opposite (see Matt. 21:5)—comes riding into Jerusalem.

28. After Jesus had said these things, he went on ahead, going up to Jerusalem.

The triumphal entry of Jesus into Jerusalem was an event of outstanding significance. Note the following:

1. By means of it Jesus deliberately evokes a demonstration. He fully realizes that, as a result, the enthusiasm of the masses will enrage the hostile leaders at Jerusalem, so that they will desire more than ever to carry out their plot against him.

2. Jesus forces the members of the Sanhedrin to change their timetable, so that it will harmonize with his (and the Father's) timetable. The enthusiasm of the crowds with respect to Jesus will hasten the crisis.

3. By means of this triumphal entry Jesus fulfils the Messianic prophecy of Zech. 9:9. See Matt. 21:4, 5. When the people hail him as the Son of David, i.e., the Messiah, he does not try to restrain them.

4. However, he also shows the crowds what kind of Messiah he is, namely, not the earthly Messiah of Israel's dreams, the One who wages war against an earthly oppressor, but the One who came to promote and establish "the things that make for peace" (Luke 19:42), lasting peace: reconciliation between God and man, and between a man and his fellow man. Accordingly, Jesus enters Jerusalem mounted on a colt, the foal of an ass, an animal associated not with the rigors of war but with the pursuits of peace, for he is the Prince of Peace (Isa. 9:6). But the people in general, their minds filled with earthly ideas concerning the Coming One, do not understand or appreciate this. In hailing him as the Messiah, the people are right; the Pharisees, chief priests, and scribes (Matt. 21:15, 16; Luke 19:39, 40) are wrong. But in expecting this Messiah to reveal himself as a political, earthly Messiah the Hosanna shouters are as wrong as are their leaders. Those who in every way reject Jesus are committing a crime, but those who outwardly "accept" and cheer him are also doing him a gross injustice, for they do not accept him for what he really is. Their tragic mistake is committed with dire results for themselves. It is not surprising therefore that Luke pictures a weeping King in the midst of a shouting multitude (19:39-44), nor is it strange that, a little later, when the crowds begin to understand that Jesus is not the kind of Messiah they had expected, they, at the urging of their leaders, are shouting, "Crucify (him)!"

It is clear from verse 28 that Jesus was taking the lead, in proceeding with his little band of disciples, from Jericho to Jerusalem. Cf. Mark 10:32. After a while they have reached a point from which Jesus is going to issue a command:

29, 30. As he approached Bethphage and Bethany near the mount that is called Olivet, he sent two of his disciples, and said, Go into the village opposite (y o u), and as y o u enter it, y o u will find a colt tied, on which no one ever sat. Untie it and bring it here.

Bethany is situated on the eastern slope of Mt. Olivet, and Bethphage—exact location unknown—has by tradition been located northwest of Bethany.

It would seem that from Bethany—or, if one prefers, from Mt. Olivet's eastern slope—Jesus this Sunday morning sends two of his disciples to Bethphage. His instruction is, "Go into the village opposite [or: over against] y o u," hence, "just ahead of y o u." He assures them that upon entering the village they will find a colt tied up.

What kind of colt? Of a camel, a horse, a donkey? It is natural to expect "of a donkey." Cf. Gen. 49:11; Judg. 10:4; 12:14. Besides, from Matt. 21:5 we know that this answer is correct and in harmony with the prophecy of Zech. 9:9 (according to the Hebrew). See N.T.C. on Matthew, p. 764, footnote 722. And for a discussion of the problem that arises from the fact that Matthew mentions two animals, Mark and Luke only one, see the same commentary, pp. 763, 765.

It will be a colt "upon which no one ever sat," hence, an unbroken or unbacked colt, by God reserved for sacred use. Cf. Num. 19:2; Deut. 21:3;

I Sam. 6:7. Is not this in line with the fact that Mary too was still "unused" (cf. Rom. 1:26, 27), still a virgin, when Jesus was conceived within her womb and even at his birth? See Matt. 1:25; Luke 1:34. The tomb too in which the body of the dead Jesus was laid had never been used (Luke 23:53). We notice, therefore, that there is nothing haphazard about the triumphal entry. Everything has been carefully planned and is orderly and appropriate, exactly as it should be.

How did Jesus know that the two disciples would find everything as he had predicted? The possibility that this knowledge had come to him in a very natural way, the owners of the colt having conveyed it to him whether directly or indirectly, cannot be entirely ruled out. Nevertheless, in view of the somewhat similar prediction recorded in 22:10, the theory that this bit of information had reached Christ's human consciousness in a super- natural manner may well be preferable. Note also that verse 33 can be interpreted as meaning that there had been no previous understanding with respect to this incident between Jesus and the owners of the colt. However that may be, the fact as such that Jesus did at times receive information in ways which surpass human comprehension is clear from such passages as Matt. 17:27; John 1:48; 2:4, 25. See also on Mark 10:33, 34.

The two disciples are told to untie the colt and bring it to Jesus.

31. And if anyone asks y o u, Why are y o u untying it? y o u must say, The Lord needs it.

From this we are able to conclude that the owners (verse 33) were friends of Jesus. They must have been people who recognized Jesus as their Lord. Therefore, by giving the two disciples these instructions Jesus has taken care that they will not experience any difficulty in obtaining the colt. For a discussion of the problem in connection with the use of the title *Lord* in Mark 11:3 see N.T.C. on Mark, pp. 433–435.

32–34. So those who had been sent went away and found it just as he had told them. As they were untying the colt, its owners said to them, Why are y o u untying the colt? They said, The Lord needs it.

The two men found everything exactly as Jesus had predicted (see verse 30). As they started to unhitch the colt, the owners understandably pro- tested. They asked, "Why are y o u untying the colt?" But when, in accord- ance with Christ's instruction (verse 31), the disciples were heard to say, "The Lord needs it," objections quickly vanished. The mere mention of the fact that Jesus needed the colt was enough to secure immediate and unqual- ified assent.

A very important practical application must not escape our attention. It is clear from this passage—and from many others; e.g., Luke 6:13; 10:1; cf. Mark 15:40—16:1; John 12:19; 19:38—20:1—that in addition to The Twelve Jesus had many other disciples, men and women who stood ready to serve him in various ways. There must have been a large number of supporters in Judea, Galilee, Perea, and wherever the Lord went. Whether it was a place of lodging, a colt, a room in which to celebrate the Passover, or even at last a tomb, whatever it was that he needed, if they had it these friends were ready to provide it. That one word, "The Lord needs it," was all that was required.

Today, too, a broad body of true followers of the Lord and supporters of his causes is urgently needed, and this not only to follow directions that are handed down to them from "the top," the ecclesiastical authorities, but also to act independently: to pray, to study, to guide, to support the poor by word and deed, to encourage the fearful, to bear testimony concerning the goodness of God in providing salvation for sinners, etc., etc. These tasks should be performed willingly and eagerly.

35, 36. And they brought it to Jesus, threw their cloaks on the colt, and set Jesus on it. And as he went along, people were constantly spreading their cloaks under him on the road.

The two disciples now (a) brought the colt to Jesus; (b)—in conjunction perhaps with the other ten disciples—placed their long, thin, quadrangular robes on the colt so as to provide as comfortable a seat as possible for Jesus; and (c) mounted him on the colt.

By this time a large crowd, accompanying Jesus from Bethany, not wishing to be outdone by The Twelve, began to carpet the road with their outer garments.

37, 38. As he was now approaching the descent of the Mount of Olives, the entire multitude of the disciples began to praise God joyfully with a loud voice for all the miracles they had seen, saying:

Blessed (is) the Coming One,
The King, in the name of the Lord!
In heaven peace,
And glory in the highest.

At this point it is important to take note of the fact that the crowd that accompanied Jesus as he started out from Bethany does not remain the only one that participates in the activities pertaining to the triumphal entry. A caravan of pilgrims had arrived at Jerusalem previously. Having heard that Jesus had raised Lazarus from the dead and was now on his way toward the city, these people came pouring out of the eastern gate to meet him. With fronds cut from palm trees they go forth to welcome Jesus (John 12:1, 12, 13a, 18). Having done so they turn around and, as it were, lead Jesus down the western slope of the mount of Olives and so into the city. The crowd from Bethany continues to follow.

As this huge crowd is descending toward the city they are praising God joyfully and with a loud voice. What an excitement! What exuberance! Not only did the people shout praises to God; they were also busily talking to each other. There was one topic which especially absorbed the interest of everybody, namely, those miracles Jesus had performed. What a wide variety to choose from: (a) those mentioned in Luke (4:23, 31–41; 5:1–26; 6:6–11; 7:1–17; 8:22–56; 11:14; 13:10–17; 14:1–6); (b) those reported in the other Gospels but not in Luke; (c) specifically, the very recent restoration of sight to Bartimaeus (Luke 18:35-43); and (d) last but by no means least, the (also rather recent) resurrection of Lazarus (John 11). It was this sign which, as John 12:17 shows, especially excited the masses. Surely one who was able to raise the dead would also be able to deliver the Jews from all their enemies and restore them as a great and independent nation!

As reported by Luke, the anthem of praise consisted of these lines:

a. "Blessed (is) the Coming One."

This is a quotation from Ps. 118:26. All the four Gospels include this line in their report of the triumphal entry (besides Luke 19:38 see also Matt. 21:9; Mark 11:9; John 12:13). It is a quotation from one of the Hallel Psalms sung during Passover. It is also one of the Psalms most often referred to in the New Testament. The others are Psalms 2, 22, 69, 89, and 110. It is a distinctly Messianic Psalm, which speaks about the stone which the builders rejected and which became the cornerstone. As the combination (in Matt. 21:9) with "the Son of David" shows, "Blessed (is) the Coming One" should be regarded as a reference to the Messiah.[513]

This Messianic implication is also clear from the next line:

b. "The King, in the name of the Lord."

Clearly what the seething multitudes were proclaiming was the restoration at this time of the kingdom of David, implying deliverance from the yoke of Rome and Israel's re-establishment as a great and independent nation.

Of course, all this would also mean:

c. "In heaven peace."

It meant, as these people saw it, that God was at peace with the human race, particularly with Israel, which, in turn, would redound to his glory; hence:

d. "And glory in the highest."

What joy, elation, exuberance, unity . . . well, not without exception, however. There was "a fly in the ointment":

39, 40. Then some of the Pharisees from the throng said to Jesus, Teacher, rebuke your disciples. —He answered, I tell y o u, if these become silent, the stones will cry out.

It is not difficult to understand why the Pharisees, most of whom were enemies of Jesus, were disgruntled. Not that they loved the Romans or had ceased to yearn for independence from Rome. But they disapproved of any abortive attempt to cast off the yoke, realizing what such an unsuccessful move would mean for the nation as a whole and for the security of their own position. Besides, they hated Jesus and resented this outpouring of praise in which he shared honors with God.

---

513. On this see also J. Sickenberger, "Das in die Welt Kommende Licht," *ThG* 33 (1941), pp. 129-134; and the article on ἔρχομαι by J. Schneider, Th.D.N.T., Vol. II, pp. 669, 670.

But for the moment Jesus was so popular that the Pharisees did not dare to silence the people directly. So they asked Jesus to do it for them!

It is Luke, he alone, who reports this incident. It is also he who reports Christ's answer. In the full realization that he is indeed the Messiah, and that the time has finally arrived for everybody to know this, Jesus answers that if his disciples would become silent, the very stones would cry out. For a somewhat similar saying see Hab. 2:11.[514] This seems to have been a proverbial saying.

Does this mean, then, that Jesus approved of that which was taking place? He approved of it only to the extent to which one great truth was being proclaimed, namely, that of his messiahship. But he was terribly displeased with the people's inexcusable misunderstanding of that messiahship. And he wept when he thought of the punishment in store for Jerusalem for the great sin of actually rejecting him. This becomes clear from the next four verses, beginning with

41, 42. Now when he approached (Jerusalem), he came in sight of the city and burst into tears over it, saying, Would that on this day you, even you, had known the things that pertain to peace! But now they are hidden from your eyes.

Jesus has reached a spot from which the city, its magnificent temple, many peaceful dwellings, etc., are clearly visible. At one time Jerusalem had been "the joy of the whole earth" (Ps. 48:2, 12–14; 137:6).

As the city lies there, stretched out before his view, the Master's prophetic eye beholds a sharp contrast: on the one hand, Jerusalem as it is, to a certain extent, even now; on the other, a smoldering, hideous ruin, thousands upon thousands of the city's inhabitants and visitors doomed to meet death in a gruesome manner; other thousands assigned to a lot in many cases deemed even worse than death.

Bursting into tears Jesus laments, "Would that on this day you, even you, had known the things that pertain to peace!" Cf. 11:47–51; 13:33–35.

But up to now the opposite course had been followed. Instead of penitence there had been hardening; instead of conversion, apostasy. And, as always, when sinners harden themselves, God, in turn, hardens them; note, "But now they are hidden from your eyes." To be sure, even now the door of grace is not entirely closed, but it is rapidly closing.

In Jesus, on that day, Israel recognized its Messiah. No doubt in that huge crowd there were some truly converted people: those who had, by God's grace, accepted Jesus as their Messiah *in the spiritual, biblical sense.* Also, Matt. 21:15, 16 tells us about "children shouting in the temple." Undoubtedly *their* hosannas were far more pure in spirit than those of most of the older people. (It is hard to imagine that the hearts and minds of children were as filled with chauvinistic dreams as were those of the

---

514. S.BK., Vol. II, p. 253.

middle-aged and the elderly.) All this was wonderful. But by and large. what Israel wanted was *its own kind of Messiah,* a Messiah of the earth, a political deliverer. And that was deplorable. No wonder Jesus was weeping. He saw very clearly how wicked these people were, and what would be the result.

For this materialistic attitude there was no excuse whatever. Even in the Old Testament—the only "Bible" these people knew—the Messianic prophecies had placed the emphasis on spiritual rescue. See Isa. 53:10, 12; Jer. 23:6; 31:34; Mic. 5:2; 7:18–20; Zech. 13:1; Mal. 3:1–6. And when the Savior himself arrived, even though he was indeed a *perfect* Redeemer, with blessings for both soul and body, *his* emphasis too had been very strongly on the spiritual. A few examples will prove this. Even when we limit ourselves entirely to Luke's Gospel note the following passages: 4:4, 8; 5:20, 32; 6:20–49; 7:47–50; 8:4–15; 9:23–26; 10:20–24, 38–42; 11:1–4, 40–42, etc., etc. The stress had been on salvation *from sin,* conversion *to holiness of life,* spiritual fruitfulness.

Unless even now Jerusalem repents, dreadful punishment will be inflicted upon it. God's wrath will be poured out.

This, sad to say, is what actually happened. Think of A.D. 70, Jerusalem's fall, with all its attendant horrors. And for each impenitent the moment of vengeance arrived at the close of his earthly life; in a sense even before, for "There is no peace, says my God, for the wicked" (Isa. 57:21).

43, 44. For days will come upon you when your enemies will throw up a palisade against you, encircle you, and hem you in from all directions. They will dash to the ground you and your children along with you, and will not leave in you one stone on another, because you did not recognize the season when God (in his grace) visited you.

See *Introduction,* point IV A on this passage. For the rest, note the following:

a. a *palisade* or *embankment.* This was for the purpose of protecting oneself and launching an attack.

b. *encirclement.* This left no room for any escape. Many of those who tried to flee were crucified.

c. *annihilation of population* (dashing to the ground). A horrible blood bath!

d. *not one stone on another.* The demolition was complete.

The meaning is made clear by the manner in which this prophecy was fulfilled. See Josephus, *History of the Jewish War,* books IV–VI. Here are two quotations:

"While the sanctuary was burning . . . neither pity for age nor respect for rank was shown. On the contrary, children and old people, laity and priests alike were massacred" (VI.271).

"The emperor ordered the entire city and the temple to be razed to the ground, leaving only the loftiest of the towers . . . and the portion of the wall enclosing the city on the west. . . . All the rest of the wall that surrounded the city was so completely razed to the ground as to leave future visitors to the spot no reason to believe that the city had ever been inhabited" (VII.1–3).

See also the note on 19:43, 44 on pp. 883, 884 for the meaning of separate words.

The inspired writer also reports Christ's concluding words, indicating that this severe retribution would be reaped by the city and its inhabitants because, by and large, a favorable response to the manner in which God in his compassion had "visited" Israel, by sending his Son into the world, had been lacking.

For *Practical Lessons* and *Greek Words,* etc., see pp. 881–884.

---

45 And having entered the temple area, Jesus began to drive out those who were selling. 46 He said to them, "It is written:
'My house shall be a house of prayer.'
but y o u made it 'a robbers' den.'"

47 And he was daily teaching in the temple. The chief priests, the scribes, and the leading men among the people were trying to destroy him. 48 But they could not find anything they might do, for all the people were hanging on his words.[515]

MONDAY
19:45–48 *The Cleansing of the Temple*
Cf. Matt. 21:12–17; Mark 11:15–19

The New Testament reports two temple cleansings. The one here reported cannot be identified with that described in John 2:13–17. That one occurred at the beginning of Christ's public ministry, this one at the close. Moreover, the words spoken in connection with the second cleansing bear no resemblance to those spoken at the first.

Of the second cleansing Luke presents a very abbreviated account. For the far more detailed report one should read Mark 11:15–19, and N.T.C. on that paragraph. See also the description of the temple, together with the diagram on pp. 446–452 of that volume.

Luke does not even state when this cleansing occurred. However, Mark 11:11, 12, 15 makes clear that it took place on Monday of the week of the passion.

45. And having entered the temple area, Jesus began to drive out those who were selling.

Jesus, then, has entered the temple area; that is, the Court of the Gentiles. What a sorry spectacle greets his eyes, ears, and even nostrils! He notices that the court is being desecrated. It resembles a market place. Business is booming, lucrative too. Some men are selling oxen and sheep. At this time of the year, with Passover so close at hand and pilgrims crowding into the court from everywhere, there are many buyers. They pay high

---

515. Or: were eager to hear him.

prices for these sacrificial animals. True, a worshiper can bring in an animal of his own choice. But if he does that he is taking a chance that it will not be approved. The temple merchants have paid the priests generously for their concession. Some of this money finally reaches the coffers of sly, wealthy Annas and of clever Caiaphas. It is therefore understandable that the tradesmen and the priestly caste are partners in this business. As Jesus enters he notices the hustle and bustle of all these buyers and sellers; also the noise, filth, and stench produced by all the animals. Could this, in any sense whatever, be called *worship*?

It is not difficult to picture the righteous indignation that must have flashed from the eyes of Jesus when he drove out all who were engaged in this nefarious business. Whether also at this time, as in the first temple cleansing, he made a whip out of cords that were lying around and then let fly with that scourge, we do not know. One thing is certain: Jesus revealed himself as being indeed Lord of the temple (cf. Matt. 12:6).

46. He said to them, It is written: My house shall be a house of prayer, but y o u made it a robbers' den.

Mark's more complete report has: ". . . a house of prayer *for all the nations.*" The words in italics are not in Luke.

The quoted words are found in Isa. 56:7b, and signify that "for all the nations [or peoples]" the temple was intended to be a sanctuary for quiet spiritual devotion, prayer, and meditation. See also I Kings 8:29, 30, 33; Ps. 27:4; 65:4; cf. I Sam. 1:9–18; Luke 18:10; Acts 3:1.

The second part of the statement, "But y o u made it 'a robbers' den' " is Christ's comment, in which he contrasts the divine ideal for worship as described in Isa. 56:7b with the present situation, a condition that reminded Jesus of Jer. 7:11, which he quotes.

In the days of Jeremiah, too, as is proved by that prophet's famous Temple Discourse, the Jews were oppressing aliens, stealing, murdering, etc. Nevertheless, they continued to offer their sacrifices in the temple; as if such merely formalistic worship of Jehovah would do any good, and as if the very presence of the temple would protect them from the outpouring of God's wrath. It was then that Jeremiah had said, "Do not trust in lying words, saying, 'The temple of Jehovah, the temple of Jehovah, the temple of Jehovah, is this.' . . . Has this house that is called by my name become a den of robbers in y o u r eyes?" In the days of Christ's sojourn history was repeating itself: the temple had again become "a cave of thieves," an allusion, perhaps, to the rocky caves in the hills of Judea, where thieves and robbers would often assemble. The thieves were crowding out the Gentiles or "nations."

The lessons taught by this cleansing of the temple can be summarized as follows:

a. Jesus punished degradation of religion and insisted on reverence.

b. He rebuked fraud, in the present connection especially "religious" (?) racketeering, and demanded honesty.

c. By declaring that the temple must be a house of prayer *for all the nations,* he gave his endorsement to the wonderful cause of Christian missions. Cf. I Kings 8:41–43; Matt. 28:19.

d. By means of all this he glorified his heavenly Father. Was not the temple his Father's house?

If it be true that even in general vastness inspires *awe,* and beauty is conducive to *worship,* the conditions for awakening both of these feelings being amply present in the temple complex as has been shown, then all the more, in view of the fact that by the Lord this area had been specifically set aside for the purpose of *prayer and devotion,* it was not at all the proper place to conduct a business enterprise, a fraudulent one at that. So Jesus cleansed it.

47, 48. And he was daily teaching in the temple. The chief priests, the scribes and the leading men among the people were trying to destroy him. But they could not find anything they might do, for all the people were hanging on his words.

In spite of the fact that by means of the temple cleansing Jesus had made the temple authorities very unhappy, in fact, so thoroughly upset that they were trying to kill him, he calmly continued his day by day teaching in those very precincts. So eagerly did the people listen to Jesus that for the time being, in spite of the fact that the decision to do away with him had already been reached (John 11:53), the authorities did not dare to lay hands on him.[516]

Practical Lessons Derived from Luke 19:28–48

Verse 31

"The Lord needs it." Cf. "(needs) . . . you . . . me," etc. This expression is at times used rather carelessly, as if God cannot do without us. In this connection it is well always also to read Esther 4:14. That should make us humble. It remains true, however, that *we need God.*

Verse 41

"When he came in sight of the city, he burst into tears over it." The philosophy that would deprive God of any emotional life, or at least something akin to it, may sound reasonable, but one should be very, very careful here. What about passages such as the following: Hos. 11:8; Mic. 7:18; Zeph. 3:17; Rom. 8:26, 32 (to which others could easily be added)? Should we really try to neutralize their force by calling them anthropomorphisms? And, in the light of such passages as Eph. 5:1 f., is there a "practical lesson" for us here?

Verse 42

"Would that on this day you, even you, had known . . . but now they are hidden

---

516. Notes on Greek words, phrases, and constructions in 19:28–48 begin on page 882.

from your eyes." Does not this passage place tremendous stress on the question,
"What am I (or: are you) doing with the opportunities placed before me (or: you)?"
How often do we not hear people say, "If I had only known this or that . . . it would
never have happened." In some cases the sad event that could have been avoided
can still serve us. However, the lost in hell can never regain the opportunity of
which they did not take advantage. Therefore the lesson is "Today, O that y o u
would hear his voice!"

Notes on Greek Words, Phrases, and Constructions in 19:28-48

Verses 30-33

κατέναντι, opposite or over against (y o u); hence, just ahead of y o u.

Note the following forms of the verb λύω, to loosen, to untie: λύσαντες (verse 30),
nom. masc. pl. aor. act. participle, here with imperative force; λύετε (verses 31, 33b),
sec. per. pl. pres. indicat. act.; λυόντων (verse 33a), gen. pl. masc. pres. act. participle, in a gen. absolute construction. See also 19:7.

Note also: ἀγάγετε (verse 30), sec. per. pl. 2nd aor. (effective) imperat. of ἄγω, to
bring.

Verse 31 is a third class, or future more vivid, conditional sentence, with ἐάν and
pres. subjunct. (ἐρωτᾷ) in the protasis, and sec. per. pl. fut. indicat. (ἐρεῖτε) in the
apodosis.

Verse 35

ἤγαγον, third per. pl. 2nd aor. indicat. act of ἄγω, they brought; cf. verse 30:
bring it.

ἐπιρίψαντες, nom. pl. masc. aor. participle of ἐπιρίπτω, to cast or throw on. See
also I Peter 5:7 (in a quotation).

ἐπεβίβασαν, third per. pl. aor. indicat. act. of ἐπιβιβάζω**, to cause to ascend on,
to set on, mount. In the New Testament this verb occurs only three times: 10:34;
19:35; Acts 23:24.

Verse 36

ὑπεστρώννυον, third per. pl. imperf. (probably iterative) indicat. of ὑποστρωννύω
= ὑποστρώννυμι*, to spread under or underneath.

Verse 37

καταβάσει, dat. s. of κατάβασις*, descent.

περὶ πασῶν ὧν εἶδον, note here the attraction of the relative to the case of the
incorporated antecedent. See Gram. N.T., p. 719.

Verse 40

As the fut. *indicative* (σιωπήσουσιν) shows, what we have here, after "He answered, I tell y o u," is a first class or simple conditional sentence, even though, by
way of exception, the protasis has ἐάν instead of εἰ. This is still another illustration
of the close connection between the fut. indicat. and the subjunctive, commented on

earlier. See the note on 14:7-9 on page 729, and the note on 16:4 on page 778. The apodosis also has the third per. pl. fut. indicative, namely, κράξουσιν, will cry out.

Verse 41

In the present context it is natural to regard both ἰδών and ἔκλαυσεν as *ingressive* aorists; hence, "He came in sight of the city and burst into tears over it."

Verse 42

εἰ ἔγνως, sec. per. s. 2nd aor. indicat. act. of γινώσκω. This is the protasis of a second class, or contrary to fact, conditional sentence, relating to the past. For conditional sentences see N.T.C. on John, Vol. I, pp. 40-45; in the present connection especially p. 41. So the translation, "If you had known, even you, the things that make for peace!" (with minor variations favored by many) must be considered correct. In that case the aposiopesis (on this see footnote 413 on 13:9) is clear, effective, and dramatic.

The possibility must be granted that the "if" clause is in line with a Hebrew **אם** clause. See, for example, Ps. 81:8 (Heb. 81:9). This points to the meaning, "O that ... !" or "Would that ... !" See R.S.V. on Luke 19:42. To be considered also is "If you had only ... !"

ἐκρύβη, third per. s. 2nd aor. (effective) indicat. pass. of κρύπτω, to hide. See 11:52; 18:34.

Verses 43, 44

A. *Construction*

This is a prophecy of woe. Unsurprisingly it contains six *future* (third person plural) indicatives distributed over two clauses, with the first of the six in the first clause, the remaining five in the second. Verse 44b is a concluding clause which states the reason for the coming of the predicted woe. Its verb is a (negative) aor. indicative.

The first of these three clauses refers very indefinitely to the time within which the prophecy will be fulfilled. All it says is "For days will come upon you." The second clause is "your enemies will throw up a palisade against you," etc. A peculiarity is the manner in which clause 1 and clause 2 are connected. The connecting word is simply καί. Luke says *and* where we would say *when*. Such parataxis or co-ordination instead of hypotaxis or subordination of clauses, occurring when an expression of time is joined to a statement showing what happens within that time, is in all probability due to Hebrew background and/or colloquial speech. There are several instances of this peculiarity in the New Testament and, of course, in the Old.

B. *Notes on Individual Words*

ἥξουσιν, from ἥκω, to have come to, to be present.
παρεμβαλοῦσιν, from παρεμβάλλω, to throw up.
χάρακα, acc. s. of χάραξ, stake, palisade (fence of stakes), siege works.
περικυκλώσουσιν, from περικυκλόω* (περί, around, plus κύκλος, circle), to encircle, surround.

συνέξουσιν, from συνέχω, lit. to hold together; here, to hem in. See also the note on 4:38 on page 271.

πάντοθεν, from all directions. Elsewhere: from everywhere (Mark 1:45); on all sides, roundabout, entirely (Heb. 9:4).

ἐδαφιοῦσιν, from ἐδαφίζω*, to dash to the ground.

ἀφήσουσιν, from ἀφίημι, here: to leave. For more on this verb see the note on 4:39 on page 271.

ἀνθ' ὧν. Here the rendering *because* is obviously correct. But see the note on 12:3 on page 659.

ἐπισκοπῆς, gen. s. of ἐπισκοπή, visit (of God in Christ with tender concern for his people). Cf. Acts 1:20; I Tim. 3:1; I Peter 2:12. For a related verb see the note on 1:68 on page 131. Other related words are ἐπίσκοπος and ἐπισκοπέω.

Verse 45

πωλοῦντας, acc. pl. masc. pres. act. participle of πωλέω, to sell. See the note on 12:6 on page 660.

Verse 46

σπήλαιον, cave; here (robbers') den. In John 11:38 a cave-tomb; and in Rev. 6:15 a cave considered as a shelter in time of danger. Cf. the English word *spelunker,* a person whose hobby is the study of caves; the German *Spelunke,* den, low tavern; and the Dutch *spelonk,* cave, grotto, cavern.

λῃστῶν, gen. pl. of λῃστής, robber. More about this in the note on 10:30 on page 602.

Verse 47

ἦν διδάσκων, third per. s. periphrastic imperf. of διδάσκω, to teach. Cf. *didactic.*
οἱ πρῶτοι, the most prominent ones among the people.

Verse 48

οὐχ εὕρισκον, another very graphic, descriptive, and progressive imperfect; this time from εὑρίσκω, to discover, find. "They were constantly unable to find."

τὸ τί ποιήσωσιν, articular indirect question with deliberative third per. pl. aor. act. subjunctive retained in indirect discourse.

ἐξεκρέματο, third per. s. imperf. of ἐκκρέμαμαι*; in middle, as here, to hang on a speaker's lips. Note ἐκ. As it were with necks *out*stretched, and heads forward in order to listen better, they were attending Christ's discourses. For related words see 8:33 and 23:39.

Summary of Chapter 19:28-48

As appears from verses 28-44, The Week of the Passion begins on Sunday with Christ's triumphal entry into Jerusalem. Jesus sends two of his disciples to a little village (Bethphage) to fetch a colt. His predictions regarding this animal and its owners are literally fulfilled. Having been permitted by the owners to bring this colt to Jesus, the disciples throw their cloaks on the animal and set Jesus on it. As he is riding along toward Jerusalem, people are constantly carpeting with their outer garments the road over which he is about to pass. The minds of the multitudes are filled with anticipation of earthly glory, as is clear from their shouts in praise of "the Coming One, the King."

To the extent to which the people recognize in Jesus the long-awaited Messiah, they are right. That is why he refuses to grant the request of the Pharisees that he should rebuke his disciples. On the other hand, to the extent to which the shouters misinterpret the nature of Christ's messiahship, they are wrong. It is therefore not strange that when Jesus comes in sight of Jerusalem he bursts into tears. He knows, and at this time even openly predicts, what will happen to the city, its temple, and its population because his spiritual message has not been accepted.

In a final stirring appeal he addresses Jerusalem in these words, "Your enemies ... will dash to the ground you and your children within you ... because you did not recognize the season when God (in his grace) visited you."

On the next day (Monday) Jesus, on entering the temple, notices that its great outer court, that "of the Gentiles," has been turned into a market place. So he drives out those who are selling animals for sacrifices. He says, "It is written, 'My house shall be a house of prayer.'" He adds, "But y o u have made it 'a robbers' den.'"

One of the reasons why Jesus did this was that the temple authorities by using this great outer court as a market place were depriving the Gentiles of its use for religious purposes. This was all the more deplorable because the Gentiles, from whom the court derived its name, were not permitted to serve God in any other quarter of the temple.

Having cleared the temple, Jesus now used its facilities for teaching, as he had done in former days. Though the chief priests and scribes resented this, they were not able, for the time being, to do anything about it, because all the people were eagerly listening to the Savior.

Outline of Chapter 20

Theme: *The Work Thou Gavest Him to Do*

CHAPTER XX

20   1 One day, while Jesus was teaching the people in the temple and preaching the good news,[517] the chief priests and the scribes, together with the elders, came up to him   2 and said, "Tell us by what authority you are doing these things, or who it is that gave you this authority."

3 He replied, "I will also ask y o u a question. Tell me: 4 John's baptism, was it from heaven or from men?"

5 They reasoned among themselves, "If we say, 'From heaven,' he will say, 'Why, then, didn't you believe him?'   6 But if we say, 'From men,' all the people will stone us to death, for they are persuaded that John was a prophet."

7 So they answered that they did not know where John's baptism came from.[518]

8 Jesus said to them, "Neither do I tell y o u by what authority I am doing these things."

TUESDAY AND WEDNESDAY
The exact point (before 22:7) where one day ends and the other
begins is uncertain
20:1–8 *Christ's Authority: Question and Counter-Question*
Cf. Matt. 21:23–27; Mark 11:27–33

1, 2. One day, while Jesus was teaching the people in the temple and preaching the good news, the chief priests and the scribes, together with the elders, came up to him and said, Tell us by what authority you are doing these things, or who it is that gave you this authority.

On Sunday evening after the triumphal entry Jesus had entered the temple (Mark 11:11). He entered it again on Monday and cleansed it (Mark 11:15; cf. Luke 19:45, 46). And now, probably on Tuesday morning, though Luke is very indefinite ("one day"), Jesus enters it once more.

We find him perhaps in the Stoa Basilica or (as in John 10:23) in Solomon's Porch. He is surrounded by a group of people and is teaching them. While this teaching is going on his opponents are approaching. Do they wait until he is through teaching? We don't know. One thing is certain, however: these men are in an angry mood.

Who are they? Three groups are mentioned: the chief priests and the scribes and the elders, the three component parts of the Sanhedrin. *The*

---

517. Or: the gospel.
518. Literally: that they did not know whence.

chief priests constituted a group or order consisting of the present ruling highpriest, those who had formerly occupied this high office, and other dignitaries from whose ranks the highpriest was generally selected. The custody of the temple had been entrusted to these people, mostly Sadducees. It is not strange that *the scribes,* mostly Pharisees, are also mentioned, for these were the men who studied, interpreted, and taught the law. Their teaching was done in both temple and synagogue. *The elders,* too, were present. In ancient Israel an elder was the head of a tribe or of a tribal division. In fact, every city or town of any importance soon had its ruling elders. With the establishment of the Sanhedrin the more prominent local elders became members of this august body. We might call them the Sanhedrin's "lay members."

It is possible that in approaching Jesus, all these men acted independently and unofficially. Far more reasonable, however, is the assumption that they acted in an official capacity, having been delegated by the Sanhedrin.

Their question is clear. They want to know by what authority Jesus was doing these things, that is, who had given him the right. They were saying, "Show us your credentials!" It was an attempt to embarrass Jesus. If he admitted that he had no credentials the people could be expected to lose respect for him. On the other hand, if he considered himself authorized to do the things he had been doing, was he not arrogating to himself rights that belonged only to God? Could he not then be accused of being guilty of blasphemous behavior? By not assaulting him directly, for example, by having him arrested, they reveal that they are afraid of him because of his following.

But what do they mean by "these things"? They must have been referring to recent or present activities, that is, to things he had done on Sunday or on Monday, or to what he was doing now. Among commentators there is general agreement that the cleansing of the temple was included in "these things." This opinion is undoubtedly correct (cf. John 2:18). That action was in all probability uppermost in their minds. But was this the only thing to which these enemies of Jesus referred? There is a wide difference of opinion among commentators. Some would include Sunday's royal entry into Jerusalem. And if we bear in mind the fact that Christ's enemies ascribed his miracles to the power of Beelzebul, even the deeds of kindness to the blind and the lame (Matt. 21:14) may have been included, and also Christ's present teaching and gospel preaching in the temple.

3, 4. He replied, I will also ask y o u a question. Tell me: John's baptism, was it from heaven or from men?

When a person is verbally attacked—whether directly, or, as in verse 2, by implication—he often denies the charge, downgrades the crime, starts arguing, or produces an accusation. There are times when the best thing to do would be to admit the wrong, ask forgiveness, and make amends. For Jesus this was, of course, entirely out of the question, for he had committed no wrong.

What then? At times a charge can be effectively met by complete silence, or perhaps by a counter-charge, or, as in the present case, by a counter-question.

It has been pointed out by several interpreters that the method of answering a question by means of a counter-question was rather common in rabbinical discussions. *True, but when Jesus employs this method he in every instance vanquishes his opponents,* and *this* certainly was not true with respect to rabbis in general.

To see for himself that the statement just made is true, let the reader view the following Lucan accounts. In each of them Christ's opponents attack him, sometimes directly, then again in a veiled manner, by half-concealing their disgust inside the wrapper of a question. In each case Jesus crushes their attack. Also, his answer, *in each of these cases,* begins with, or contains, a counter-question.

The opponents' attack	Jesus' answer
5:21	5:22–24
5:33	5:34–39
6:2	6:3–5
11:15	11:17–22
20:27–33	20:34–38 (for the question see Mark 12:24)
20:1, 2	20:3–8

Now by means of the counter-question—"The baptism of John, was it from heaven or from men?"—Jesus was by no means evading the question that had been asked him, for an honest and correct answer to *his* question would unmistakably have pointed to himself as the Greater One whom John had proclaimed, and would therefore have meant that Jesus' right or authority to do these things had come from God. It was by God that Jesus had been commissioned (Luke 9:48; cf. Matt. 10:40; Mark 9:37). It was while John was baptizing that he had proclaimed Jesus as being his superior (Luke 3:16 f.; cf. John 1:26, 27), and it was soon after the Lord's baptism by John that the latter had described Jesus as "the Lamb of God who is taking away the sin of the world" (John 1:29).

By means of Christ's question his enemies had been driven into a corner. Obviously they did not want to answer, "The baptism of John had a heavenly source," for they knew very well that the reply would be, "Why, then, did y o u not believe him?" On the other hand, were they to give a response which reflected what most of them probably believed, or at least wanted to believe, namely, that the baptism of John was from men, the general public—perhaps especially the crowds of pilgrims that had come from Galilee—would become definitely hostile toward them, and, as here indicated, might even stone them. Did not these people consider John a prophet? So these dignitaries start reasoning among themselves as to what to answer. Their decision was dishonest, though not surprising. They do not say, "We don't want to answer that question," a response which would at least have been honest, but "We do not know."

Given this background, verses 5-8 require little further explanation.

5-8. They reasoned among themselves, If we say, From heaven, he will say, Why, then, didn't y o u believe him? But if we say, From men, all the people will stone us to death, for they are persuaded that John was a prophet. So they answered that they did not know where John's baptism came from. Jesus said to them, Neither do I tell y o u by what authority I am doing these things.

An important practical lesson is taught here. Christ's opponents failed to see the truth because they hardened themselves against it. The reason why many people know so little about Jesus and about the joy of living the Christian life is that they refuse to submit themselves to his will. The prayer of everyone should be: "Teach me to do thy will, for thou art my God" (Ps. 143:10).

For *Practical Lessons* and *Greek Words,* etc., see pp. 896-898.

---

9 Then he proceeded to tell the people this parable: "A man planted a vineyard, leasing it to sharecroppers,[519] and went abroad for a considerable period. 10 At the proper time he sent a servant to the sharecroppers, that they might give him a share of the vintage. But the sharecroppers beat him up,[520] and sent him back empty-handed. 11 Then he sent another servant; but him also they beat up and treated disgracefully and sent back empty-handed. 12 He sent still a third, and this one they wounded and flung out.

13 "Then the owner of the vineyard said, 'What shall I do? I will send my son, my beloved. Perhaps they will respect him.'

14 "But on seeing him the sharecroppers began to carry on a dialogue with one another,[521] saying: 'This is the heir; let's kill him, that the inheritance may become ours.' 15 So they threw him out of the vineyard and killed him. What then will the owner of the vineyard do to them? 16 He will come and kill those sharecroppers and give the vineyard to others."

When the people heard this, they said, "May this never be!"

17 But Jesus looked straight at them and said, "What then is this that is written:

'The stone the builders rejected,

This became the cornerstone'?

18 Everyone who falls on that stone will be smashed to pieces; and he on whom it falls—it will crush him."

19 The scribes and the chief priests tried to lay hands on him that very hour, because they knew he had spoken this parable against them, but they were afraid of the people.

20:9-19 *The Parable of The Wicked Tenants, and Its Sequel*[522]
Cf. Matt. 21:33-46; Mark 12:1-12

A. *Agreement Between Owner and Tenants; Owner's Departure*

9. Then he proceeded to tell the people this parable: A man planted a vineyard, leasing it to sharecroppers, and went abroad for a considerable period.

---

519. Or: tenants; literally "workers of the soil."

520. Other translations: thrashed him, beat him, beat him unmercifully.

521. Or: began to talk the matter over with one another.

522. For slight variations between the three Gospel accounts of this parable see N.T.C. on Mark, pp. 171, 172.

By wicked leaders Jesus had been attacked (verses 1, 2). He now proceeds, by means of a parable, to warn the people against these very men (see verse 19).

To understand this parable it must be borne in mind that the upper Jordan Valley, the western and northern shores of the Sea of Galilee, and even a considerable portion of Galilee itself, contained vast estates owned by foreigners, men who lived far away from their holdings. They had given the care of their farms and vineyards into the hands of local people. The absence of the landlords implied that those who ran the estates enjoyed a considerable measure of independence. However, this was not an unmixed blessing for either party. For the vinedressers it meant that when there were problems—unexpected expenses, bad harvests, marauders, etc.—the owner could not be consulted. For the owner it meant that for his share of the yield of the soil he was dependent not only on natural conditions (weather, soil) but also on the honesty and co-operation of the tenants or sharecroppers.

In this parable Jesus introduces an owner who has planted a vineyard (cf. Isa. 5:1–7), has made a contract with the sharecroppers, stipulating that at the time of the vintage he shall receive a specified share of the harvest, and typically has gone away to some distant place, with the intention of remaining absent for a considerable period of time.

B. *Mistreatment of Owner's Servants*

10–12. At the proper time he sent a servant to the sharecroppers, that they might give him a share of the vintage. But the sharecroppers beat him up, and sent him back empty-handed. Then he sent another servant; but him also they beat up and treated disgracefully and sent back empty-handed. He sent still a third, and this one they wounded and flung out.

When the proper time arrived, not any sooner, the owner commissioned one of his servants to collect and carry back to the owner's home the portion of the vintage which, according to contract, belonged to him. But not only did the tenants refuse to carry out the terms of their contract, they even maltreated the servant. When another servant was sent, he received similar treatment. And a third one was treated worse. Not only did he return empty-handed; he had even been grievously wounded, having been thrown out of the vineyard.

For the explanation of the parable see especially the following:

M. Hengel, "Das Gleichnis von den Weingärtnern Mc 12,1–12 im Lichte der Zenonpapyri und der rabbinischen Gleichnisse," *ZNW* 59 (1968), pp. 9–31.

J. D. M. Derret, "Fresh Light on the Parable of the Wicked Vinedressers," *RIDA*, 3rd series 10 (1963), pp. 11–41.

N. Geldenhuys, *op. cit.*, p. 500.

S. F. H. J. Berkelbach van der Sprenkel, *op. cit.*, p. 338.

W. J. Harrington, *op. cit.*, p. 231.

A. Stöger, *op. cit.*, Vol. II, pp. 126, 127.

E. E. Ellis, *op. cit.*, pp. 232, 233.

C. *Killing of Owner's Son*

13–15a. Then the owner of the vineyard said, What shall I do? I will send my son, my beloved. Perhaps they will respect him. —But on seeing him the sharecroppers began to carry on a dialogue with one another, saying, This is the heir; let's kill him, that the inheritance may become ours. So they threw him out of the vineyard and killed him.

The parable now reaches its dramatic climax. The owner says, "I will send my son, my beloved." What intense feeling, love, pathos is implied in this decision! Is it even possible to read this passage without thinking immediately of such passages as John 3:16; Rom. 8:32; Gal. 4:4; II Cor. 9:15?

But what happens? When the wicked tenants see the son approaching they begin to plot. They reason, This is the . . . what? The son? No, what they actually say is, "This is the *heir*." They seem to take for granted that the owner has died, and that, accordingly, the person who is approaching, being "the heir," is now the owner. According to a then existing law, under certain conditions if the owner died, leaving no heir, whoever were the first to claim the estate, particularly the occupants, were allowed to have it. Therefore, by killing the heir, they will be able to lay claim to the inheritance. So they think.

The fallacy in this line of argumentation was, of course, that they had no reason to think that the owner had died!

The villains carry out their wicked plan. When the son arrives, they take him, cast him out of the vineyard, and kill him.

D. *Punishment Awaiting the Murderers*

15b, 16a. What then will the owner of the vineyard do to them? He will come and kill those sharecroppers and give the vineyard to others.

Note that in Matt. 21:41 the question here asked is answered by the audience, Jesus himself—as the subsequent context shows—being in thorough agreement with that answer. In Mark and Luke the answer is represented as having been given by Jesus himself. There is no essential difference.

It is clear that not the sharecroppers but the owner of the vineyard triumphs in the end. And so does his son. Here the meaning of the parable is surfacing. The "owner" is God, and his Son is Jesus, the Christ.

The remainder of the parable now also becomes clear. Note the following:

God did indeed send his "servants"—often called by this very name—to his people Israel. In various ways these prophets were scorned, wounded, and rejected (Matt. 23:29–37; Luke 6:23; 11:49–51; 13:31–35; Acts 7:52). See also N.T.C. on Matt. 5:12. But even then did God actually send his only-begotten, beloved Son (John 3:16; Rom. 8:32; etc.). He sent him first of all to Israel (Matt. 10:5, 6; 15:24). He too was rejected by the Jews (Mark

15:12, 13; John 1:11; 12:37–41; Acts 2:23; 4:10); exception: the believing remnant destined for everlasting glory (John 1:12; Rom. 11:5).

The threatened destruction of the wicked sharecroppers points not only to A.D. 70 but also to everlasting punishment for *every* rejector.

The vineyard, i.e., the privileged position, once granted to Israel, was subsequently transferred to the church universal (Matt. 21:41; 28:19; Acts 13:46), a truth whose realization was already foreshadowed when Jesus walked on earth (Matt. 8:11, 12; 15:28; John 3:16; 4:41, 42; 10:16; 17:20, 21). The parable, accordingly, is not an abstraction. It pictures reality.

E. *The People's Reaction to the Parable*

16b. When the people heard this, they said, May this never be!

So certain are the people, however, that the privileges of the Jews will never be given to "others" that when they sense that this is what Jesus means, they cry out in horror, "May this never be," or, in their own idiom, "God forbid." See also the note on this expression on page 898.

F. *The Manner in Which Jesus Applies This Parable*

17. But Jesus looked straight at them and said, What then is this that is written:
The Stone the builders rejected,
This became the cornerstone?

Here, again, for the linguistic aspects of these lines see the note on page 898.

The underlying figure is that of a huge building block, one of those that were used in the building of Solomon's temple. When the builders examined this particular "stone," they rejected it. In doing this they erred. Subsequently this rejected stone became "the cornerstone."

The words quoted are taken from Ps. 118 (LXX 117):22. The quotation as here reproduced is from the Septuagint, which, in turn, for this passage faithfully reproduces the Hebrew original. It will be recalled that the parable reached its climax when the wicked tenants were described as casting the owner's son out of the vineyard and killing him. They had utterly *rejected* not only the servants but even the son! They had done this in order to enrich themselves. The son was gone now, so they thought, so his inheritance would be theirs. Jesus now surprises them by reminding them about this passage from the psalms. Here a very similar transaction had been described: builders had *rejected* a stone; ultimately meaning: prominent men had rejected, despised, scoffed Israel. Nevertheless, Israel had become in a very true sense the head of the nations (Ps. 147:20). This, moreover, had not happened because of Israel's own intrinsic moral and spiritual excellence or because of its own power. On the contrary, by the Lord this wonderful thing had been accomplished. Jesus now shows that the words of Ps. 118 reach their ultimate fulfilment in "the owner's son," that is, in himself, the *true* Israel. He is that stone that was being rejected by the chief priests, scribes,[523] elders, and at Calvary, by the nation as a whole ("Crucify, crucify!"). See John 1:11.

But something marvelous was going to happen: *the rejected stone would become the cornerstone:* Christ crucified would rise again triumphantly. And what about the nation, namely, the old unconverted Israel, the rejectors of the Messiah? "From y o u," says Jesus, the "kingdom of God," that is, the special kingdom privileges—the special standing in the eyes of God which this people had enjoyed during the old dispensation, to which had now been added the blessed words and works of Jesus—"will be taken away." Why? Because they had not lived up to their obligations. They had been like the sharecroppers who at the time of the vintage had refused to render to the owner that portion of the vintage that was his due. So, in the place of the old covenant people there would arise—was it not already beginning to happen?—"a nation producing its fruit," a church international gathered from both Jews and Gentiles.

Briefly, therefore, the thrust—the one main lesson—of the parable can be expressed in the words of Ps. 2:12: "Kiss [or: pay homage to] the Son, lest he be angry, and y o u perish in the way; for soon shall his wrath be kindled. Blessed are all those who take refuge in him."

As to the separate items in this parable, it has now become clear that:

a. *The vineyard* reminds us immediately of Israel. See Isa. 5:1–7, on which the parable is clearly based. Also cf. Deut. 32:32; Ps. 80:8–16; Isa. 27:2, 3; Jer. 2:21; Ezek. 15:1–6; 19:10; Hos. 10:1. Nevertheless, not the nation as such but "the special advantages and opportunities which were given to the people as the chosen seed, and in virtue of God's covenant with them" (W. M. Taylor, *op. cit.,* p. 140) is what is signified, for we are told that the vineyard "will be given to a nation producing its fruit" (Matt. 21:43).

b. *The one who planted and owns the vineyard* is God.

c. *The wicked sharecroppers or tenants* are especially Israel's *leaders:* chief priests, scribes, elders, though their followers (hence, the nation as a whole) need not be entirely excluded.

d. *The servants* who were sent to collect the portion of the vintage that could be rightfully claimed by the owner, and who were treated shamefully, are the prophets, as has been shown.

e. As already indicated, *the owner's son* is Jesus Christ himself.

An additional word, in conclusion, should be said about Jesus as "the stone which the builders rejected."[524] Other references to this stone (in addition to Ps. 118:22, 23 and the present passage [Luke 19:17, 18]) are Isa. 28:16; Acts 4:11; Rom. 9:33; Eph. 2:20; and I Peter 2:6.

---

523. The expression *builders* for scribes or law-doctors is not unusual in Jewish literature. See S.BK., Vol. I, pp. 875 f.

524. See the following: F. F. Bruce, *The Book of Acts (N.I.C.),* pp. 99, 100; G. H. Whitaker, "The Chief Cornerstone," *Exp,* Eighth Series (1921), pp. 470–472; and E. G. Selwyn, *The First Epistle of St. Peter,* London, 1946, pp. 286 ff.

The cornerstone of a building, in addition to being part of the foundation and therefore *supporting* the superstructure, *finalizes* its shape, for, being placed at the corner formed by the junction of two primary walls, it determines the lay of the walls and crosswalls throughout. All the other stones must adjust themselves to this cornerstone. Such is the relation of Christ to his church. By his glorious resurrection, ascension, and coronation he has become highly exalted, and from his place at the Father's right hand sends out the Spirit to dwell in the hearts of his followers and to rule over the entire universe in the interest of the church, to the glory of God Triune.

18. Everyone who falls on that stone will be smashed to pieces; and he on whom it falls—it will crush him.

Meaning: Anyone who persists in opposing Christ is going to be "pulverized" (cf. Luke 3:17). If Christ strikes him with his judgment, the person so stricken will be crushed. In other words, if people reject Christ, not he but they will be the losers, both now and especially in the day of the final judgment. Cf. Isa. 8:14, 15; Dan. 2:34, 35.

G. *The Reaction on the Part of the Scribes and the Chief Priests*

19. The scribes and the chief priests tried to lay hands on him that very hour, because they knew he had spoken this parable against them, but they were afraid of the people.

As has been pointed out, the parable was based on Isa. 5:1–7, which states in so many words, "The vineyard of Jehovah of hosts is the house of Israel."

Also, it was not difficult to believe that when Jesus quoted Ps. 118, he was equating "the builders" there mentioned with the religious leaders among his own contemporaries.

And, of course, the scribes and chief priests who were among those who heard Jesus speak this parable knew very well that in his mind *they* were the ones who had been, and still were engaged in, rejecting him. There had been too many clashes to doubt this.

Result: so filled with hatred were they that they tried to lay hands on Jesus that very hour.

What prevented them from carrying out their plan at this particular moment is stated in these words: But they were afraid of the people. That is not very surprising, for:

a. these people held Jesus to be a prophet (Luke 7:16; cf. 24:19);

b. on the preceding Sunday they had been shouting in his honor (19:37, 38);

c. on a previous occasion they had tried to make him their king (John 6:15);

d. for many, Passover Week was a period during which political enthusiasm ran high, and hero worship would be difficult to control; and·

e. very recently many "believers"—whether their faith was genuine or whimsical—had been added to the ranks of those who sided with the Prophet of Galilee, for he had brought back to life Lazarus, who had been dead four days (John 11:39, 43, 44; 12:10, 17–19).[525]

Practical Lessons Derived from Luke 20:1–19

Verses 6, 7

" 'All the people ... are persuaded that John was a prophet.' ... [The chief priests, etc.] answered that they did not know." Does not this passage show that at times the judgment of the laity is better than that of the clergy? The lesson is this: Though it is indeed wrong for a congregation to indulge, without very good reason, in the habit of being adversely critical of their minister(s), in the final analysis every member, with the help of God's Spirit, should make up his own mind. *Heresy often begins at the top!* An excellent example to follow is that of the Bereans (Acts 17:11).

Verses 10–15

"The sharecroppers beat him up and sent him back empty-handed. ... This one they wounded and flung out. ... They threw him [the son] out of the vineyard and killed him." Note how, step by step, the cruelty of these tenants increases. That is not at all unusual, except when grace intervenes. See this increase in wickedness exemplified in Cain, Herod I, Herod Antipas, etc. The lesson is: *Principiis obsta:* "Resist the beginnings!" Watch out for the first misstep. Every further advance into sin will be easier than the previous step.

Verse 16

"He will come and kill these sharecroppers and ..." what? take it back? ... destroy it? ... forget about it? No, "and give the vineyard to others!" Isn't that wonderful? The blessings are not completely withdrawn. They are simply removed from the Jews as a nation and given to the church universal *consisting of both Jew and Gentile.* In other words God substitutes a greater blessing for the one that is withdrawn. The river bed of God's grace is widened! "How great thou art!" Think of Lam. 3:23; John 1:16; Eph. 3:14–19; James 4:6.

Notes on Greek Words, Phrases, and Constructions in 20:1–19

Verse 1

ἐπέστησαν, third per. pl. aor. (ingressive) indicat. act. of ἐφίστημι; here: to confront; i.e., to come up to a person boldly, defiantly. For more on this verb see the note on 10:40 on page 603.

Verse 3

λόγον, acc. s. of λόγος, a word with a great variety of meanings; such as, word, Word (the Christ), message, prayer, prophecy, account, reason, motive, etc. In each

---

525. Notes on Greek words, phrases, and constructions in 20:1–19 begin on this page.

case the exact sense is determined by the context. Here and in the parallel passages the meaning is obviously *question*.

Verses 5, 6

συνελογίσαντο, third per. pl. aor. indicat. of συλλογίζομαι, to reason (together). The reciprocal idea, already present in the verb, is expressed also by πρὸς ἑαυτούς.

The clauses introduced by ἐάν are conditions of the third class (future more vivid). In each verse ἐάν is followed by εἴπωμεν, first per. pl. subjunct. of εἶπον, used as 2nd aor. of λέγω, in the protasis; and a third per. s. future indicat. (respectively ἐρεῖ and καταλιθάσει [from καταλιθάζω*, to stone down, stone to death]) in the apodosis.

πεπεισμένος . . . ἐστιν, (having been and therefore) being persuaded, periphrastic perfect of πείθω, to persuade.

Note indirect discourse: 'Ιωάννην προφήτην εἶναι: John to be a prophet; that is, that John was a prophet.

Verse 9

ἤρξατο . . . λέγειν, he proceeded (or: went on) . . . to tell.

ἐφύτευσεν, third per. s. aor. indicat. act. of φυτεύω, to plant. See also 17:6, 28, and the note on 13:6 on page 698.

ἀμπελῶνα, acc. s. of ἀμπελών, vineyard, as in 13:6 and I Cor. 9:7.

ἐξέδετο, third per. s. 2nd aor. (ingressive) middle of ἐκδίδωμι, to lease, let out.

γεωργός (from γῆ plus ἔργον), lit. worker of the soil; specifically:

John 15:1, vinedresser
II Tim. 2:6 and James 5:7, farmer.

In the present parable the γεωργός is clearly a tenant farmer, one who works the land— in this case a vineyard—for a share of the crop. He is therefore a sharecropper.

For ἀπεδήμησεν, he went abroad, see the note on 15:13 on page 760.

χρόνους ἱκανούς, for a considerable period of time, for a long time. Here pl.; in 8:27 s. but with little, if any, difference in meaning.

Verse 10

καιρῷ, at the proper time. For the distinction between χρόνος (verse 9) and καιρός (verse 10) see the note on 12:56 on page 690.

δώσουσιν, third per. pl. fut. indicat., where aor. subjunct. would be more usual. This can be explained either as showing the close relationship between the subjunctive and the future indicative, or as being a means to add to the vividness of the story.

δείραντες, nom. pl. masc. aor. participle of δέρω, basically meaning: to skin, flay, but here: to beat (up). See also the note on 12:47, 48 on page 688.

Verses 11, 12

For the idiom (in both verses) προσέθετο, here followed by πέμψαι, see the note on 17:5 on page 801.

Verse 13

ἐντραπήσονται, third per. pl. fut. indicat. pass. of ἐντρέπω; act. meaning: to make someone turn in on himself; i.e., to make him ashamed; pass., as here, with middle sense: they will turn in on themselves, will be ashamed out of respect for someone; in the present context: they will respect him. German: "Vielleicht, wenn sie den sehen, werden sie sich scheuen." Dutch: "Dien zullen zij wel ontzien."

Verses 14, 15

διελογίζοντο πρὸς ἀλλήλους means about the same thing as συνελογίσαντο πρὸς ἑαυτούς in verse 5.

ἀποκτείνωμεν, first per. pl. subjunct. (volitive) act. of ἀποκτείνω, to kill; hence, "Let us kill."

ἀπέκτειναν, third per. pl. aor. indicat. act. of the same verb. Beginning at 9:22 this verb appears frequently in this Gospel.

γένηται, third per. s. 2nd aor. subjunct. after ἵνα, indicating purpose: "that the inheritance may become ours."

Verse 16

μὴ γένοιτο, third per. s. 2nd aor. optat. of γίνομαι. May it never be! In view of the fact that the people spoke Aramaic, what they actually said may well have been, "God forbid!" Cf. Gen. 44:7, 17; Josh. 22:29; 24:16; I Sam. 12:23; 14:45; 20:2; Job 27:5.

Verse 17

ἐμβλέψας, nom. s. masc. aor. (ingressive) participle of ἐμβλέπω, to look straight at, fix one's gaze on. The antecedent λίθον, which, being the subject of "became the cornerstone," would normally be in the nom., has been attracted to the case of ὅν, the relative. This is not what happens normally. It is called inverse attraction. See Gram. N.T., pp. 717, 718. For quotation of the same Old Testament passage but with λίθος instead of λίθον see I Peter 2:7.

Note εἰς; as if "This became *for* a cornerstone." *The New Testament in Modern Greek* omits this εἰς. Its inclusion may be considered a Hebraism (cf. לְ in Ps. 118:22), though it is not entirely absent even from Greek secular literature. This εἰς shows that something (here the stone) passes from one state (that of being rejected) to another (that of being honored as cornerstone). In English εἰς in such a context is generally omitted. German, however, has "... ist *zum* Eckstein geworden"; Dutch, "... is *tot* een hoeksteen geworden." Frisian also has retained the little word (*ta*), and so has Danish (*til*), but South African and also Swedish omit it.

Verse 18

συνθλασθήσεται, third per. s. fut. indicat. pass. of συνθλάω*(?). In the New Testament this word occurs in this one passage, unless Matt. 21:44 should be authentic (an improbability). Meaning: to dash to pieces. The same is true with respect to λικμήσει, to crush.

Verse 19

ἐπιβαλεῖν, aor. (ingressive) act. infinitive of ἐπιβάλλω; here: to lay hands on, seize. For a complete summary of the meaning of this word in the New Testament see the note on 15:12 on page 759.

20 Now they watched (him) closely and sent spies, who pretended to be honorable men. Their purpose was to lay hold on something he might say, so as to hand him over to the control and authority of the governor.

21 So the spies questioned him, saying, "Teacher, we know that you speak and teach what is right and show no partiality but truthfully teach God's way. 22 Is it lawful for us to pay taxes to Caesar or is it not?"

23 But he saw through their craftiness and said to them, 24 "Show me a denarius! Whose image[526] and inscription does it bear?"

25 "Caesar's," they told him. He said to them, "Well then, what is due to Caesar render to Caesar, and what is due to God render to God."

26 So they were unable to get a handle on him[527] because of what he had said in the presence of the people, and amazed by his answer they became silent.

27 Next, some of the Sadducees, who say that there is no resurrection, came up and asked Jesus, 28 "Teacher, Moses wrote for us that if a man's brother dies, leaving a wife but no child, that man should take the widow and raise up children for his brother. 29 Now there were seven brothers. The first took a wife and died childless. 30 The second 31 and then the third took her, and similarly all seven, and they died leaving no children. 32 Last of all the woman herself died. 33 Now then, at the resurrection whose wife will the woman be, since all seven had her as wife?"

34 Then Jesus said to them, "The sons of this age marry and are given in marriage, 35 but those who are accounted worthy to attain to that age, even to the resurrection from the dead, neither marry nor are given in marriage: 36 for they can no longer die, because they are like the angels and are sons of God, being sons of the resurrection.

37 "But that the dead are raised up even Moses disclosed in the passage about the bush, when he calls the Lord:
'the God of Abraham and the God of Isaac and the God of Jacob.'
38 He is not the God of the dead but of the living, for all are alive to him."

39 Some of the scribes answered, "Well said, Teacher." 40 For they no longer dared to ask him any more questions.

41 Then Jesus said to them, "How can people say that the Christ is the Son of David? 42 For David himself in the book of Psalms declares:
'The Lord said to my Lord,
Sit at my right hand
43 Until I make your enemies your footstool.'[528]
44 "David therefore calls him 'Lord.' How then can he be his son?"

20:20–44 *Captious Questions and Authoritative Answers*
also
Christ's Own Question
verses 20–26 Cf. Matt. 22:15–22; Mark 12:13–17
verses 27–40 Cf. Matt. 22:23–33; Mark 12:18–27
verses 41–44 Cf. Matt. 22:41–46; Mark 12:35–37

Without any indication as to time or place Luke here begins to present his report with respect to captious questions put to Jesus during the week of The Passion. The place, however, must have been the temple (cf. Mark

---

526. Or: likeness.
527. Or: to take advantage of him.
528. Literally: a footstool for your feet.

12:35). As to the time, note that even when we reach Luke 22:1 (= Mark 14:1) the story has not advanced beyond Tuesday. This does not mean, however, that some of what Luke 20:21 ff. relates may not have taken place a little later, say on Wednesday.[529] Subsuming the events here recorded under the caption TUESDAY-WEDNESDAY, as we have done, should suffice. We now proceed at once to the first of the two captious questions reported by Luke.

A. *Is it lawful for us to pay taxes to Caesar or is it not?*

20. Now they watched (him) closely and sent spies, who pretended to be honorable men. Their purpose was to lay hold on something he might say, so as to hand him over to the control and authority of the governor.

It is necessary to keep the context in mind. The Sanhedrists had bluntly questioned Jesus' authority. This attack had failed. By means of a counter-question ("The baptism of John, was it from heaven or from men?") Jesus had silenced them. Not only that, but by means of the parable of The Wicked Tenants he had predicted their doom. So, more than ever they were determined to kill him. But "they were afraid of the people" (20:19).

So they now decided to use the opposite method. For implied accusation they substituted adulation, flattery. At the same time they probably figured that their clever device would result in discrediting their enemy in the estimation of the people, at least of a large group.

Therefore the enemies of Jesus sent a committee to him. The committee consisted of Pharisees and Herodians (Mark 12:13). These men pretended to be *honorable*. They, especially the Pharisees, acted as if they were deeply troubled by a question of conscience, and were seeking his advice. Meanwhile their real purpose was to see whether they could make him say something that could serve as a reason for accusing him before the Roman governor. With the Herodians going along as witnesses, the governor, so they hoped, might be willing to take Jesus off their hands, condemning him. Very clever... and wicked! The "honorable men" were in reality tricky, prying spies.

21. So the spies questioned him, saying, Teacher, we know that you speak and teach what is right and show no partiality but truthfully teach God's way.

As to "Teacher," this form of address was certainly correct. Not only do the evangelists constantly describe Jesus as such, but so do also many others (see Mark 4:38; 5:35; 9:17, 38; 10:17, 20, 35; John 3:2; etc.). In fact, Jesus himself stated that teaching was one of his main activities (Mark 14:49; cf.

---

529. Neither, on the other hand, is it necessary to accept the theory according to which the sequence of the questions as reported in the synoptic accounts was influenced by the traditional structure of the Passover eve liturgy. For that theory see D. Daube, "Evangelisten und Rabbinen," *ZNW* 48 (1957), pp. 119–126. Luke at this point presents only two of the three captious questions reported in Matthew and Mark.

Matt. 26:55; Luke 21:37; John 18:20). He was the greatest Teacher ever to walk the earth. Being God's true Prophet he taught men as the Father had taught him (John 1:18; 3:34; 8:28; 12:49). It was a pity that those who now addressed him as "Teacher" did not accept his teaching.

And now the flattery. These men tell Jesus that he speaks and teaches "what is right," that is, he truthfully teaches God's way. The word *way,* as here used, indicates the manner in which God wants people to think and to live. It is his will for man's heart, mind, and behavior. They are saying, therefore, "You are a teacher on whom people can depend; you faithfully declare the will of God for doctrine and life."

In further explication of what they have in mind they say, "You are not partial to anyone"; literally, "You do not look on anyone's countenance." They mean, "No matter to whom you speak, what you say is still the same. You do not allow yourself to be swayed by rich or poor, learned or unlearned, master or slave...."[530]

Thinking, perhaps, that by means of their kind (?) words they have completely disarmed Jesus, having dispelled any suspicion which he might otherwise have entertained with respect to their motives, they now spring their question, **22. Is it lawful for us to pay taxes to Caesar or is it not?** The tribute to which the present passage refers was a poll tax which, after the deposition of Archelaus (A.D. 6), was collected by the procurator from every adult male in Judea, and was paid directly into the imperial treasury. Since this coinage bore the image of the emperor, who ascribed divinity to himself and claimed to possess supreme authority not only in political but even in spiritual affairs (as "the highest priest"), and since, in addition to this, it reminded the Jews that they were a subject nation, it is understandable that payment of this personal tax was very distasteful to many freedom-loving, devout Jews. It was in connection with the introduction of this imposition that Judas of Galilee had vehemently proclaimed, "Taxation is no better than downright slavery." He had blasted it as being no less than high treason against God. See Acts 5:37; Josephus, *Jewish War* II.117, 118; *Jewish Antiquities* XVIII.1–10.

The question put to Jesus was therefore a very clever scheme. If he answered affirmatively, he would be alienating ever so many devout, patriotic Jews; but a negative reply would be exposing himself to the charge of rebellion against the Roman government (cf. Luke 20:20; 23:2).

23–25. But he saw through their craftiness and said to them, Show me a denarius! Whose image and inscription does it bear? —Caesar's, they told him.

Jesus was fully aware of their "wickedness" (Matt. 22:18), "unscrupu-

---

530. The phraseology here used is probably typically Hebraic. For "way," as here used, see also Gen. 6:12; Ps. 1:1; Jer. 21:8. Cf. Acts 9:2; 19:9, 23; 24:14, 22. So also "looking on a person's countenance" immediately reminds one of Lev. 19:15; I Sam. 16:7; Ps. 82:2; Mal. 2:9. Cf. Acts 10:34; Eph. 6:9; Col. 3:25; James 2:1, 9. It must be admitted, however, that idioms such as these may develop in more than one language; for example, Greek as well as Hebrew.

lousness," or "craftiness," their *readiness to do anything,* no matter how wicked, to attain their purpose. Their question, after an introduction of honeyed words, sounded like a pious request for direction in deciding what to do in a difficult matter of ethics, but their real intention was the destruction of Jesus. Their action was diabolical. While feigning innocence, they thought they had lured their enemy into a trap from which, as they saw it, he would not be able to escape.

So Jesus asked them to show him a denarius. This was a small silver coin equal to a laborer's average wages for one day's work. It was the amount fixed by law for the payment of the poll tax. It is held by many that Christ's asking for this coin implied that he himself was so poor that he did not possess that much. To this observation some add that it showed that even his disciples did not have a denarius. But perhaps this is reading into the account something that is not really there. One could, for example, advance an entirely different explanation for this request, namely, that Jesus wanted the coin to come from the pockets of his opponents, so as to impress upon them the fact that they themselves were using this coinage, were benefiting from its use, and had accordingly accepted the resulting obligations. That explanation has in its favor that it fits into the succeeding context. But this point need not be pressed.

Jesus' question, "Whose image and inscription does it bear?" was easily answered. "Caesar's," of course.

A denarius from the reign of the then ruling emperor Tiberius pictures on its *obverse side* the head of that ruler. On the *reverse side* he is shown seated on a throne. He is wearing a diadem and is clothed as a highpriest.

The inscriptions, with abbreviations as indicated and with V representing our present U, are as follows:

Obverse
TICAESARDIVI AVGFAVGVSTVS
Translated:
TIBERIUS CAESAR AUGUSTUS
SON OF THE DIVINE AUGUSTUS
Reverse
PONTIF MAXIM
Translated:
HIGHEST PRIEST

The tension must have been very high when **He said to them, Well then, what is due to Caesar render to Caesar, and what is due to God render to God.** Explanation:

a. Jesus was not evading the issue, but was clearly saying, "Yes, pay the tax." Honoring God does not mean dishonoring the emperor by refusing to pay for the privileges—a relatively orderly society, police protection, good roads, courts, etc., etc.—one enjoys. At this particular time the Roman Empire had brought peace and tranquility to the people under its sway, and this to a degree seldom if ever experienced either before or afterward. Such a blessing implies a responsibility. Cf. I Tim. 2:2; I Peter 2:17. Thus, no truthful charge of sedition could be made against Jesus.

b. He was qualifying his "yes" answer by stating that the emperor should be paid (given back) only what was *his due*. Hence, the divine honor which the emperor claimed but which is due to God alone must be refused. How could the Pharisees find any fault with that? Besides, this word was a warning to all—from the most exalted emperor to the subject lowest in rank—not to claim undue honors. Cf. II Kings 18:19—19:37 (II Chron. 32:9-23; Isa. 36, 37); Dan. 4:28-32; 5; Acts 12:20-23.

c. By adding "and what is due to God render to God" Jesus was stressing the fact that all the service, gratitude, glory, etc., due to God should be constantly and gladly accorded to him. Nothing must be withheld. See, for example, Ps. 29; 95; 96; 103-105; 116; John 17:4; Rom. 11:33-36; I Cor. 6:20; 10:31; 16:1, 2; II Cor. 9:15. One does not give God what is his due by plotting to destroy his beloved Son! But this was exactly what these spies and their teachers were trying to do.

d. By drawing a distinction between "what is due to Caesar" and "what is due to God" Jesus was rejecting the very claim of Caesar, a claim made on the coin and elsewhere, to the effect that his was not only a physical kingdom but also a spiritual one (note: "Pontifex Maximus," i.e., "Highest Priest"). Cf. John 18:36. Naturally God is Sovereign *over all* (Dan. 4:34, 35), even over the emperor. Cf. John 19:11. The emperor, to be sure, should be respected and obeyed whenever his will does not clash with the divine will. See Rom. 13:1-7. But when there is a clash the rule laid down in Acts 5:29 must be followed.

By means of this answer Jesus had discomfited his enemies. We are not surprised to read: **26. So they were unable to get a handle on him because of what he had said in the presence of the people, and amazed by his answer they became silent.**

The spies had not expected this kind of answer. Jesus had frankly and courageously answered their question. The answer implied, Yes, the tax must be paid. There must be an adequate response to privileges enjoyed. But though the emperor must receive his due, he must not receive more than that; that is, he must not receive the divine honor he claims. At the same time, God must receive *all* glory and honor.

Who could find fault with this answer? Certainly no one. So the spies were reduced to silence. They left (Matt. 22:22).

B. *At the resurrection whose wife will the woman be?*

27, 28. Next, some of the Sadducees, who say that there is no resurrection, came up and asked Jesus, Teacher, Moses wrote for us that if a man's brother dies, leaving a wife but no child, that man should take the widow and raise up children for his brother.

Who were these Sadducees?[531] How this party originated we do not know. They loved to trace their name and origin back to Zadok, the man who during David's reign shared the highpriestly office with Abiathar (II Sam. 8:17; 15:24; I Kings 1:34), and was made sole highpriest by Solomon (I Kings 2:35). Whether they were right in so doing cannot be proved, but they may well have been.

That there was indeed, even during the days of Christ's sojourn on earth, a close relationship between *priesthood, temple,* and *Sadducees* is not open to doubt. It is clearly implied in Acts 4:1; 5:17. Let the reader see for himself.

As to doctrinal beliefs, the Sadducees accepted only the written word; not, like the Pharisees, also oral tradition. So much is clear from Josephus, *Antiquities* XIII.297. Also, they denied the soul's immortality. As they saw it, the soul perishes along with the body (*Antiquities* XVIII.16, 17). They said, "There is no resurrection, neither angel nor spirit" (Acts 23:6-8). They rejected the eternal divine decree—or as they called it "fate"—and accepted the freedom of the will (*Antiquities* XIII.171-173).

Politically they supported the *status quo,* were satisfied to have matters remain as they were. They were not a popular party, as were the Pharisees, but were in favor with the wealthy (*Antiquities* XIII.298).

In so many respects did they differ from the Pharisees that, at first glance, it may seem strange that at times Pharisees and Sadducees co-operated (Matt. 16:1), and that Jesus warned against the teaching of both, mentioning them in one breath (Matt. 16:6, 11). But this co-operation was, after all, not so strange. In the final analysis both of these parties tried to obtain their feeling of security by their own efforts—whether this sense of ease and salvation was based on material possessions on this side of the grave, as with the Sadducees, or on imagined spiritual possessions on the

---

531. See the following sources:

a. Matt. 3:7; 16:1, 6, 11, 12; 22:23, 34; Mark 12:18; our present passage (Luke 20:27); Acts 4:1; 5:17; 23:6-8.

b. The Jerusalem Talmud, Hagigah IV.77b.

c. Josephus, *Jewish War* II.164-166; *Antiquities* XIII.171-173, 297, 298; XVIII.16, 17.

Also see R. Meyer, art. Σαδδουκαῖος in Th.D.N.T., Vol. VII, pp. 35-54.

What may well come to be regarded as one of the best recent works on the Sadducees is that by H. Mulder, namely, *De Sadduceeën,* Amsterdam, 1973. Among other things he points out that uncritical references to Jewish sources, such as the Talmud (Jer. and Bab.), are of little value because they are not impartial, pp. 8, 9. He also repeatedly emphasizes the importance of the priesthood for the Sadducean party, since "a significant proportion of the Sadducean party consisted of priestly families," p. 61. Very vividly he portrays what happened to the Sadducees after the Fall of Jerusalem, A.D. 70, and what accounted for the rapid dissolution of this party.

No less than twenty-five pages (pp. 16-40) are devoted to a thorough investigation of the derivation of the name *Sadducees*. After discussing several theories advanced by others, Mulder finally reaches the conclusion that the word is actually a nickname—the Jews were con-stantly changing names into nicknames—indicating that these Zadokites had departed from the way of *righteousness,* had gone *aside* from it, so that now they should be thought of as only half-righteous. As their opponents, including the Pharisees, saw it, they had become com-promisers, the kind of people who were willing to do almost anything for money and prestige.

This well-documented Dutch work merits translation into English.

other side, as with the Pharisees, who were striving with all their might to work their way into heaven.

It should not be a surprise, therefore, that when Jesus, with his emphasis on the sincere religion of the heart and on God as the sole Author of salvation, appeared upon the scene of human history, he was rejected by both groups: by the Pharisees, who resented his exposure of their hypocrisy, and by the Sadducees, who considered him a threat to their *status quo*. Besides, both parties *envied* Jesus (Matt. 27:18) because of his miracles and the crowds he attracted.

When the Sadducees now come up to Jesus they probably intend to strike a double blow. By exposing to ridicule Christ's belief in a bodily resurrection would they not also triumph over the Pharisees who likewise accepted the doctrine of a life after death? If we are permitted to assume that news of the victory of Jesus over the Pharisees (and their allies) soon reached the ears of the Sadducees—in view of Matt. 22:34 not an unreasonable assumption—may we not also assume that the latter were already saying to each other, "We'll show the Pharisees that we can do better"? Were they perhaps already chuckling over the prospect of "killing two birds with one stone," that is, of exposing to ridicule both Jesus and the Pharisees?

For their word of address, "Teacher," see on verse 21. They continue with an appeal to the great lawgiver Moses ("Moses wrote for us"). It should be borne in mind that the Sadducees regarded the Pentateuch as being higher in value than the other books of the Old Testament. They now make Deut. 25:5, 6 the springboard of their question. In that passage the law of "levirate[532] marriage" is given to Israel. According to this law, if a wife loses her husband before any male child has been born, the brother of that husband—or else the nearest of kin—must marry the widow, so that the first child born of this marriage may be counted as a child of the deceased, and the latter's line may not die out. Disobedience to this command was frowned upon (Deut. 25:7-10). The halfhearted obedience of Onan, who was willing to marry the widow but not to raise offspring by her since such a child could not be counted as his own, was punished with death (Gen. 38:8-10). For an interesting application of the law of levirate marriage see Ruth 4:1-8. To what extent this law was still being obeyed during Christ's sojourn on earth is not clear.

The Sadducees, then, make use of this commandment in order to show how thoroughly absurd, as they see it, is belief in the resurrection of the body. Whether the story which they are about to relate was a report on an actual event, as some commentators believe; or whether it was suggested by the apocryphal book of Tobit (3:8, 15; 6:13; 7:11); or finally, whether from start to finish it was their own fabrication; let the reader judge for himself.

Continued: **29-33. Now there were seven brothers. The first took a wife**

---

532. *Levirate* is from the Latin *levir* (for *devir*; cf. Greek δαήρ), a husband's brother; hence, brother-in-law.

and died childless. The second and then the third took her, and similarly
all seven, and they died leaving no children. Last of all the woman herself
died. Now then, at the resurrection whose wife will the woman be, since
all seven had her as wife?

Provided that their opponent (in this case, Jesus) accepted the basic assumption that married life continues in the hereafter, two husbands would
have been sufficient to prove the Sadducees' point. But seven makes the
story more interesting and might also make belief in the resurrection seem
even more absurd. Think of it: when the dead arise, this woman—
husband-killer?—will have seven husbands! Of course, that cannot, must
not, be. She is allowed to have only one, but which one?

It is clear, of course, that the entire representation was absurd. It was
atrociously unfair; for Jesus, though believing in the doctrine of the physical resurrection, did not believe that the state of marriage would continue
after the resurrection. What the opponents were doing, therefore, was
setting up a man of straw, to be bowled down very readily. Not the doctrine
of the resurrection but the assumption from which the Sadducees were
proceeding was false. In fact, it was grotesquely fictitious.

And now Christ's answer: **34–36. Then Jesus said to them, The sons of
this age marry and are given in marriage, but those who are accounted
worthy to attain to that age, even to the resurrection from the dead,
neither marry nor are given in marriage; for they can no longer die,
because they are like the angels and are sons of God, being sons of the
resurrection.**

Meaning: Those who live in this world marry and are given in marriage.
But those who, apart from any merit of theirs but only by virtue of God's
sovereign grace, are considered worthy of partaking in the glories of the
coming age, the new heaven and earth, so as to be sharers in the resurrection of the righteous (cf. John 5:29a), neither marry nor are given in
marriage. Reason: they do not die; therefore marriage with a view to the
perpetuation of the race will not be necessary. With respect to marriage
they are like the angels, who also do not marry. The redeemed in glory are
sons of God, being born of God and being, in a sense, like him (John 1:13;
I John 3:2), and thus also sharers in the resurrection "unto life."

For the "sons of" expressions see the note on 10:6 on page 587 and the
diagram (of some of these forms) on page 588.

Continued: **37, 38. But that the dead are raised up even Moses disclosed in the passage about the bush, when he calls the Lord: the God of
Abraham and the God of Isaac and the God of Jacob. —He is not the God of
the dead but of the living, for all are alive to him.**

It is true that the Sadducees did not have the New Testament, which
mentions or implies the resurrection (whether of Jesus himself or of his
people, or even of all the dead) again and again.

But even the Old Testament is not lacking in references to the bodily
resurrection. Clearest, perhaps, are Ps. 16:9–11 (interpreted by Peter in

Acts 2:27, 31) and Dan. 12:2. Worthy of consideration are also Job 14:14; 19:25-27; Ps. 17:15; 73:24-26; Isa. 26:19; Ezek. 37:1-14; Hos. 6:2; 13:14 (cf. I Cor. 15:55); these are passages which, though not always directly teaching the resurrection of the body, may well imply belief in this truth. Take, for example, Ps. 73:24-26, which clearly teaches the blessed after-death existence of the believer's soul in heaven. Does not this very existence of the soul in the intermediate state demand the resurrection of the body? Two facts certainly point in that direction: (a) the creation of man as "body and soul" (Gen. 2:7), and (b) this very passage, "He is not the God of the dead but of the living." Note also that Abraham surely believed in the possibility of a physical resurrection (Heb. 11:19).

Jesus, however, refers to another passage, "I am the God of Abraham . . .," and implies that since God is not the God of the dead but of the living, the conclusion is that Abraham, Isaac, and Jacob are still alive, and are awaiting a glorious resurrection.

Luke (cf. Mark 12:26) represents Jesus as tracing the saying to Moses, that is, to the Pentateuch, the very book which by the Sadducees was esteemed above all others. More precisely, Jesus points out the very place in the Pentateuch where the quoted words are found, namely, "in the passage about the bush," that is, "the burning bush that was not consumed." The reference is, of course, to Exod. 3:1 ff.; see verse 6 and cf. verses 15, 16.

Attempts have been made to rob Christ's argument of its value. It has been said, for example, that the expression *the God of Abraham* simply means that while Abraham was on earth he worshiped Jehovah. However, a study of the context in which Exod. 3:6 and all similar passages occur quickly proves that the One who reveals himself as "the God of Abraham . . ." is the unchangeable, eternal covenant God who blesses, loves, encourages, protects, etc., his people, and whose favors do not suddenly stop when a person dies but go with that person beyond death (Ps. 16:10, 11; 17:15; 73:23-26).

Another fact must be mentioned in this connection. The men with whom the immutable Jehovah (Exod. 3:6, 14; Mal. 3:6) established an everlasting covenant (Gen. 17:7) were Israelites, not Greeks. According to the Greek (and afterward also the Roman) conception, the body is merely the prison house of the soul. See N.T.C. on I and II Thessalonians, pp. 110, 111. The Hebrew conception, product of special revelation, is entirely different. Here God deals with man as a whole, not only with his soul or merely with his body. On the contrary, when God blesses his child he enriches him with physical as well as spiritual benefits (Deut. 28:1-14; Neh. 9:21-25; Ps. 104:14, 15; 107; 136; and many similar passages). He loves him *body and soul.* He is going to send his beloved Son in order to ransom him *completely.* The body, accordingly, shares with the soul the honor of being "the sanctuary of the Holy Spirit" (I Cor. 6:19, 20). The body is "for the Lord, and the Lord for the body" (I Cor. 6:13). God loves the entire person, and the declaration, "I am the God of Abraham and the God of Isaac and the God of Jacob" (note the triple occurrence of the word *God,* mentioned separately in connection with each of the three to stress personal relationship with each), certainly implies that their bodies will not be left to the worms but will one day be gloriously resurrected. The God of the covenant is not the God of dead bodies but of living people! Those dear ones who have exchanged this life for the life hereafter may seem "dead" to us, but to God they are very much alive. The vital and glorious relationship between himself and them cannot be broken. See Rom. 8:35–39. Hence, he will not forget their bodies!

The burden of proof is entirely on the person who denies this. See also H. W. Robinson, *The People and the Book,* Oxford, 1925, p. 353 f.

39, 40. Some of the scribes answered, Well said, Teacher. —For they no longer dared to ask him any more questions.

These scribes were probably Pharisees, and believed in a bodily resurrection. On this particular question they, accordingly, stood with Jesus, and were happy that their enemies, the Sadducees, had been defeated. The Sadducees, realizing that they had been worsted, did not again venture to ask Jesus a question.

C. *Jesus' own question: Whose Son is the Christ?*

41. Then Jesus said to them, How can people say that the Christ is the Son of David?

The blind beggar had called Jesus "the Son of David" (18:38). The multitudes had shouted "Hosanna to the Son of David" (Matt. 21:9). Jesus, by accepting these praises without protest, and by fulfilling the prophecy of Zech. 9:9, had indicated, though indirectly, that he was indeed the very Son of David that was to come. The direct and open affirmation would follow a little later (Luke 22:69, 70).

However, in what sense was he the Son of David? For the sake of man's salvation unto God's glory that question must be answered. Especially *now,* with the cross so very, very near, and deadly error prevailing on every side.

We might say, therefore, that there were three propositions Jesus wanted everyone to accept, and this with heart and mind:

a. David's Son is not merely David's descendant; he is David's Lord.

b. Being David's Lord, he is the Son of *God.*

c. Since he is the Son of *God,* everyone should place his trust in him.

It is for this reason that Jesus now asks the all-important question, "How can people [the scribes, Mark 12:35, and their followers, people in general] say that the Christ is the Son of David?" Jesus is asking as it were, "Is he *merely* David's *descendant?* In which sense is he *Son?* How does David himself answer that question?"

42–44. For David himself in the book of Psalms declares: The Lord said to my Lord, Sit at my right hand until I make your enemies your footstool. David therefore calls him Lord. How then can he be his son?

We return, then, to proposition (a): David's Son is not merely David's descendant; he is David's *Lord.*

Jesus ascribes this Psalm (110) to David, and is saying that it is a Messianic Psalm. Note "that the Christ," etc. (verse 41). It was so regarded also by Peter (Acts 2:34, 35), by Paul (I Cor. 15:25), by the author of the Epistle to the Hebrews (1:13; cf. 10:13), and, during New Testament times, by the rabbis.[533]

The words, "David himself in the book of Psalms . . . calls him Lord. How then can he be his son?" cannot mean, "The Messiah is not David's son." They must mean, "He cannot be David's son *merely in the sense of his descendant.*" He is far more than that. He is the root as well as the offspring of David (Rev. 22:16; cf. Isa. 11:1, 10). He is David's *Lord.*

The figure "Sit at my right hand until I make your enemies your footstool" is that of an enemy lying in the dust so that the conqueror's feet can be placed on his neck. Cf. Josh. 10:24. Complete triumph over every foe is assured to David's *Lord.*

This brings us to proposition (b): Being David's Lord, he is the Son of *God.*

In this psalm David is making a distinction between YHWH (Jehovah) and 'Adonai. YHWH is addressing David's 'Adonai; that is, God is addressing the Mediator. He is promising that Mediator such pre-eminence, power, authority, majesty as would be proper only for One who, as to his person, from all eternity was, is now, and forever will be GOD. See Eph. 1:20–23; Phil. 2:5–11; Heb. 2:9; Rev. 5:1–10; 12:5.

The clear implication is surely proposition (c): Since he is the Son of *God,* hence also himself *God,* everyone should place his trust in him.

For *Practical Lessons* and *Greek Words,* etc., see pp. 911–915.

---

45 Now while all the people were listening, Jesus said to his disciples:

46 "Beware of the scribes, who relish parading about in long, flowing robes, and who love formal salutations in the market places, chief seats in the synagogues, and places of honor at the banquets. 47 They devour widows' houses, and for a show[534] offer lengthy prayers. Such men will receive a heavier sentence."

20:45–47 *Denunciation of the Scribes*
Cf. Matt. 23:1–36; Mark 12:38–40; Luke 11:37–54

45. Now while all the people were listening, Jesus said to his disciples:
Having now attacked the *doctrine* of the scribes and their allies, Jesus next exposes their corrupt *practice.*

From the Woes against the Scribes, as recorded at length in Matt. 23 (and cf. Mark 12:38–40), Luke selects a representative few. Note that the scribes are not addressed directly. Any reference to them is in the third person. If

---

533. Read the very interesting and detailed discussion of this point in S.BK., Vol. IV, pp. 452–465.

534. Or: to attract attention.

from this fact someone wishes to draw the conclusion that they were no longer present, or, if present, then only sparsely, he can hardly be blamed.

What must not escape us is the fact that the Master, fully realizing that the scribes had a large following, warns his audience against them, *out of love for all who were prone to be easily led astray*. To be sure, the descriptions of the enemies of the truth are not mild, but underneath throbs a loving heart!

46, 47a. Beware of the scribes, who relish parading about in long, flowing robes, and who love formal salutations in the market places, chief seats in the synagogues, and places of honor at the banquets. They devour widows' houses, and for a show offer lengthy prayers.

Note the six items of criticism, followed by the statement of condemnation:

A. *Items of Criticism*

a. "who relish parading about in long, flowing robes." These men were putting on airs; they walked around attired like kings or priests about to perform official functions.

b. "formal salutations in the market places." Cf. 11:43b. Though the word for "salutation" that is here used can indicate a friendly spoken greeting, or a written message of regards (I Cor. 16:21; Col. 4:18; II Thess. 3:17), here it has a more formidable connotation, as the immediate context in the parallel passage, Matt. 23:7, indicates (". . . the formal salutations in the market places, and to have the people address them as 'rabbi.'"). What the men who are here described were always longing for was not a mere token of friendliness but rather a demonstration of respect, a public recognition of their prominence.

c. "chief seats in the synagogues." Cf. 11:43a. Those were the seats in front of the raised platform on which stood the prayer leader and the reader of the Scriptures. Thus seated, a man had the double advantage of being near the person reading or leading in prayer, and of facing the congregation and thus being able to see everybody. Besides, being ushered to such a seat was regarded as a mark of honor.

d. "places of honor at the banquets." Jesus had issued a warning against this very sin of seeking the best seat at a banquet or dinner (Luke 14:8). James condemned the sin of assigning the best seat to the rich, while telling the poor man to stand or else to sit on the floor near someone's footstool (2:2-4).

e. "widows' houses." The scribes are described as devouring—fattening themselves on—the houses of these lonely women.

The question, "Just how did these men do this?" has been answered differently. Some of the answers that have been suggested are: to funds under their control and from which they, these scribes, could draw, they asked widows to contribute more than could reasonably have been expected of them; or, they offered their help in settling estates that fell to widows, meanwhile taking for themselves more than was coming to them;

or, they took unfair advantage of material support which initially had been volunteered by widows. Whatever may have been the method used, it is clear that Jesus is here condemning the crime of extortion practiced on widows, according to Scripture a most heinous wrong indeed. The history of the church supplies many examples of this evil. Read C. Chiniquy's chapter, "The Priest, Purgatory, and the Poor Widow's Cow."[535]

f. praise from men. ". . . and for a show offer lengthy prayers." It was for the purpose of drawing attention to themselves that the scribes offered these almost endless prayers. Cf. I Thess. 2:5, 6. All they were seeking was honor from men. . . . Or, was this really all? The close grammatical juxtaposition of "devouring widows' houses" and "offering lengthy prayers" has led some to suggest that between these two activities there was a very close connection, the meaning being: they devour widows' houses and *to cover up their wickedness* they make long prayers. The longer they pray for the widows (or at least in their presence), the more they can prey upon them! Whether there is sufficient evidence for this interpretation let everyone decide for himself. Even apart from it, the evil here condemned was scandalous. For "lengthy prayers" see N.T.C. on Matthew, pp. 323–325.

B. *Judgment Pronounced*

As with a crash of thunder doom is pronounced upon these hypocrites:
47b. Such men will receive a heavier sentence.

For the men described here in such detail—not necessarily for every scribe, but for those here described—the punishment is going to be heavier, since they were the very people who were constantly studying, teaching, and interpreting God's law. *They* had every opportunity to know that God required humility, sincerity, and love. Accordingly, when, by means of their hypocrisy, they revealed the absence of these qualities, though they were pretending to be very holy indeed, their sentence would be all the more severe.[536]

Practical Lessons Derived from Luke 20:20–47

Verse 21

"Teacher, we know that you . . . truthfully teach God's way." So truthful is Christ that even his enemies admit it. Therefore, heed him!

Verses 24, 25

"Caesar's, they told him." . . . "Well then, what is due to Caesar render to Caesar." Jesus defeats his enemies by using their own words! This happens also in 19:22. So great is he!

---

535. *Fifty Years in the Church of Rome*, New York, Chicago, Toronto, 1886, pp. 41–48.
536. Notes on Greek words, phrases, and constructions in 20:20–47 begin on page 912.

Verse 39

"Well said, Teacher." Even his enemies admit Christ's greatness . . . a foretaste of what will happen on the day of the final judgment (Phil. 2:10) and a comfort for all his true disciples.

Verse 44

"How then can he be [merely] his son?" Any doctrine that falls short of confessing Christ's deity dishonors him and does not help to save anyone.

A certain poet has said:

> I sought Thee, weeping, high and low,
> I found Thee not; I did not know
> I was a sinner—even so,
> I missed Thee for my Savior.
>
> I saw Thee sweetly condescend,
> Of humble men to be the Friend,
> I chose Thee for my Way, my End,
> But found Thee not my Savior.
>
> Until upon the cross I saw
> *My God,* who died to meet the law
> That man had broken; then I saw
> My sin, and then my Savior.
>
> What seek I longer? let me be
> A sinner all my days to Thee,
> Yet more and more, and Thee to me,
> Yet more and more my Savior.
>
> Be Thou to me my Lord, my Guide,
> My Friend, yea, everything beside;
> But first, last, best, whate'er betide,
> Be Thou to me my Savior.

Verse 47

"They devour widows' houses, and for a show offer lengthy prayers." Contrast Christ's simplicity, honesty, and generosity with the duplicity, mendacity, and cupidity of his opponents. On which side would you rather be?

Notes on Greek Words, Phrases, and Constructions in 20:20-47

Verse 20

παρατηρήσαντες, nom. pl. masc. aor. participle of παρατηρέω, to watch closely; as it were, standing by a person's side or looking over his shoulder. See also the note on 6:7 on page 324, and the note on 14:1 on page 726.

ἐγκαθέτους, pl. acc. of the verbal ἐγκάθετος*, referring to one who lit. has been "let down into" a place for the purpose of spying; hence, a spy.

ὑποκρινομένους, acc. pl. masc. pres. participle of ὑποκρίνομαι, to pretend. Cf. ὑποκριτής, hypocrite, pretender.

ἐπιλάβωνται, third per. pl. 2nd aor. (ingressive) subjunct. (after ἵνα) middle of ἐπιλαμβάνω, here: to lay hold on.

Verse 21

οὐ λαμβάνεις πρόσωπον, lit. you do not lift up (someone's) face, clearly a Hebraism for "you show no partiality or special favor." See N.T.C. on Galatians, p. 82. On Hebraisms involving the concept *face* see also the note on 9:51 on p. 564, and the note on 10:1 on page 586; and cf. N.T.C. on Mark, p. 481, footnote 579.

Verse 22

φόρον, acc. s. of φόρος (see also 23:2; Rom. 13:6, 7), related to φέρω, to bear, bring up, produce; hence, tribute, tax.

Verse 23

κατανοήσας, nom. s. masc. aor. participle of κατανοέω; lit. to know to the bottom; to know thoroughly, perceive, see through. See also 6:41; 12:24, 27; Acts 7:31, 32; 11:6; 27:39; Rom. 4:19; Heb. 3:1; 10:24; James 1:23, 24.

πανουργίαν, acc. s. of πανουργία; lit. doing anything; hence, craftiness, wickedness, duplicity. Those guilty of the sin here indicated will "do most anything" to achieve their purpose.

Verse 24

εἰκόνα, acc. s. of εἰκών, figure, image, likeness, portrait, picture. Cf. *iconoclast.* See also parallels in Matthew and Mark; further: Rom. 1:23; 8:29; I Cor. 11:7; 15:49; II Cor. 3:18; 4:4; Col. 1:15; 3:10; Heb. 10:1 and 10 references in Rev., beginning with 13:14, 15.

ἐπιγραφήν, acc. s. of ἐπιγραφή, inscription. Cf. *epigraphy.* See also parallels in Matthew and Mark, to which add Luke 23:38.

Verses 28, 29

Literally the verse reads, "Moses wrote for us, If a man's brother die, having a wife, and he be childless, that his brother should take the wife and raise up seed for his brother." Here the first and third "brother" is the man who dies, and the second is his surviving "brother." To the average reader such a rendering—and also that of A.V.—is probably somewhat confusing. See, therefore, my translation. In fact, one can find several excellent renderings of this passage in modern translations. The essential meaning of the passage remains the same in all of them. They faithfully reflect the original.

ἐξαναστήσῃ, third per. s. aor. subjunct. (after ἵνα) act. of ἐξανίστημι, in a third class conditional sentence. See also Mark 12:19; Acts 15:5.

ἄτεκνος*, childless, occurring once in each verse.

Verse 31

κατέλιπον, third per. pl. 2nd aor. (normal or constative) indicat. act. of καταλείπω, to leave behind (at death).

Other meanings of this verb in Luke's Gospel: to leave in the lurch (10:40); to leave behind the ninety-nine (15:4); to leave or give up everything in order to follow Jesus (5:28).

Verse 32

ὕστερον, used here as adverb in the (superlative) sense of *finally*.

Verse 33

γίνεται, third per. s. pres. (here futuristic) indicat. of γίνομαι, to become, to be. ἔσχον, here. *third* per. pl. 2nd aor. indicat. of ἔχω, to have.

Verses 34, 35

γαμοῦσιν, once in each verse, third per. pl. pres. indicat. act. of γαμέω, to marry; γαμίσκονται, third per. pl. pass. of γαμίσκω*; in the act., to give in marriage; in the pass., to be given in marriage. A synonym of γαμίσκω is γαμίζω. In meaning and construction the form here used matches its mate.

καταξιωθέντες, nom. pl. masc. aor. pass. participle of καταξιόω, to account worthy of; in pass., as here, to be accounted worthy of. See also Acts 5:41; II Thess. 1:5.

τυχεῖν, 2nd aor. infinitive of τυγχάνω, to hit, attain, obtain, enjoy, experience, etc., in such passages as Acts 24:2; 26:22; 27:3; II Tim. 2:10; Heb. 8:6; 11:35. There is also the intransit.: to happen (Luke 10:30), to fall out, turn out; to which is related εἰ τύχοι, if it turns out, hence *perhaps* (I Cor. 15:37); and τυχόν, *perhaps, for example* (I Cor. 16:6). Finally, οὐχ ὁ τυχών means "not generally happening"; hence, not common, exceptional (Acts 19:11; 28:2).

Verse 36

ἰσάγγελοι, nom. pl. masc. of ἰσάγγελος, lit. equal to angels; hence, like (the) angels. Cf. *isosceles.*

υἱοί, here *children,* not just *sons.*

Verse 37

ἐμήνυσεν, third per. s. aor. indicat. act. of μηνύω, to disclose, reveal, report, point out. See also John 11:57; Acts 23:30; I Cor. 10:28.

"In the passage about" is one of the normal meanings of ἐπί followed by the genitive.

βάτου, gen. s. of βάτος, bush. See also Mark 12:26; Luke 6:44; Acts 7:30, 35.

Verse 40

ἐτόλμων, third per. pl. imperf. (descriptive) of τολμάω, to dare, venture; here only in Luke; also in Matthew's and Mark's parallel passages; and see Mark 15:43; John 21:12; Acts 5:13; 7:32; Romans, I and II Corinthians, Philippians, and Jude.

Verse 42

κάθου, sec. per. s. imperat. of κάθημαι, to sit, sit down (cf. 1:79), to live (21:35), to be enthroned (Rev. 18:7). ,

Verse 43

θῶ, first per. s. 2nd aor. subjunct. (after ἕως ἂν) of τίθημι, to set, establish, put, place; and here: to make.

Some of the Words Used in Verse 46

Form here used	Relation to Basic Form	Meaning of Form here used	Footnote Reference
προσέχετε (ἀπό)	sec. per. pl. pres. imperat. of προσέχω	Beware (of)	on 12:1
(ἐν) στολαῖς	dat. pl. of στολή	in long, flowing robes	on 15:22
ἀσπασμούς	acc. pl. of ἀσπασμός	formal salutations	on 11:43
πρωτοκαθεδρίας	acc. pl. of πρωτοκαθεδρία	chief seats	on 11:43
πρωτοκλισίας	acc. pl. of πρωτοκλισία	places of honor	on 14:7, 8
(ἐν) τοῖς δείπνοις	dat. pl. of δεῖπνον	at the banquets	on 14:12

Verse 47

προφάσει, dat. s. of πρόφασις (πρό plus φαίνω), that which is put *forward* to make wrong conduct *appear* right, a show, pretext.

περισσότερον, acc. s. neut. adj. in comparative degree of περισσός (over and above), modifies κρίμα; hence, a heavier sentence, implying more severe punishment.

Summary of Chapter 20

On Monday of Passion Week Jesus had cleansed the temple. And now, probably on Tuesday morning—though Luke is very indefinite ("One day")—Jesus entered it once more. While he was teaching the people, or immediately afterward, his opponents—chief priests, scribes, elders—angered by the things Jesus had been doing, especially by the temple cleansing, addressed him as follows, "Tell us by what authority you are doing these things, or who it is that gave you this authority." In return, Jesus asks them, "John's baptism, was it from heaven or from men?" This question embarrassed Christ's opponents. They realized that the very One whom they were trying to destroy had been enthusiastically acclaimed by John. So, if they now answered "from heaven," the rejoinder would be, "Why, then, did y o u not believe him?" If they answered "from men," they feared that the people might stone them. So they answered, "We do not know." Jesus told them, "Neither do I tell y o u by what authority I am doing these things" (verses 1–8).

In order to expose these wicked leaders and at the same time to warn them, Jesus told the parable of The Wicked Sharecroppers (or Tenants). These men not only refused to give the owner his due but even, with increasing cruelty, maltreated the servants who had been sent to them to fetch the portion of the harvest he had a right to demand. Finally they did not shrink from killing the owner's son, with dire consequences for themselves. Christ's enemies understood that when Jesus mentioned those wicked tenants he was referring, among others, to *them.* They wanted to arrest him, but were afraid of the crowd (verses 9–19).

They then try to catch him in his "words," his teaching. After a flattering introduction they ask him, "Is it lawful for us to pay taxes to Caesar or is it not?" Jesus answers, "What is due to Caesar render to Caesar, and what is due to God render to God" (verses 20–26).

The Sadducees, who rejected the doctrine of bodily resurrection, in order to expose that doctrine to ridicule now ask Jesus this question (in summary): "One by one marrying and then dying, seven brothers successively married the same wife; in the resurrection whose wife will she be?" Jesus answers, "Those who are accounted worthy to attain . . . to the resurrection . . . neither marry nor are given in marriage." He adds that when Moses called God "the God of Abraham and the God of Isaac and the God of Jacob" this implied that God was still their God and would therefore not suffer their bodies to remain in their graves but would raise them gloriously (verses 27–40).

Jesus now asks them a question, namely, "How can people say that the Christ is [merely] the *son* of David, since in Psalm 110 David calls him *Lord?*" Implication: the Son of David is David's Lord; hence, is really the Son of *God,* whom they should worship as such (verses 41–44).

Having just now attacked the *doctrine* of the scribes, Jesus next exposes their corrupt *practice.* His criticism is not directed against every scribe but against the group in general. He brands them as being ostentatious, greedy, and hypocritical. He states, "They devour widows' houses and for a show offer lengthy prayers." He announces that those who know God's law but disobey it will receive a heavier sentence (verses 45–47).

Outline of Chapter 21

Theme: *The Work Thou Gavest Him to Do*

CHAPTER XXI

21 1 Looking up, Jesus saw the rich dropping their gifts into the temple treasury. 2 He also saw a poor widow drop in two very small coins, 3 and he said, "Truly I say to y o u, this poor widow dropped in more than all the others. 4 For all these people out of their abundance dropped in (something) among the gifts, but she out of her poverty dropped in all she had, her whole living."

21:1–4 *A Widow's Offering*
Cf. Mark 12:41–44

1. Looking up, Jesus saw the rich dropping their gifts into the temple treasury.

The connection between the present paragraph and the preceding is twofold. First of all, it is temporal. It seems reasonable to infer that after Jesus had delivered his Fifth Great Discourse, the Seven Woes (Matt. 23), briefly summarized in Luke 20:45–47, he would take a brief rest. It was during that rest that, looking up from the bench on which he was probably sitting, he saw the rich dropping their gifts into the temple treasury. It is clear, therefore, that we must picture Jesus as being seated somewhere in the Women's Court, with its thirteen trumpet-shaped chests, that is, receptacles for gifts and dues. See map of the Temple on p. 924.

Secondly, the connection is *topical,* and this in a twofold sense: (a) Having just now exposed the *hypocrisy* of the scribes (20:45–47), Jesus proceeds to reveal the *sincerity* of a certain widow. He places her *genuine* religion over against the *sham* religion of the law-interpreters. (b) Just as important: Jesus has just now denounced the scribes for "devouring widows' houses" (20:47). So now, by his own example, he shows how widows should be treated. The connection "widows' "—"poor widow" (20:47; 21:2) must not be missed. It must have been intentional. One should help and encourage widows and, wherever this can be done, one should hold them up as examples.

As Jesus was looking he noticed that the rich were dropping their gifts into the temple treasury, that is, into its receptacles, separately marked for different purposes. Some of these rich people were dropping in large amounts (Mark 12:41). Of course, there was nothing wrong with that. Nevertheless, as Jesus saw it, it was not the amount of the gift that mattered most but the heart of the giver. This becomes clear from the following verses:

2. He also saw a poor widow drop in two very small coins.

The original says *two lepta.* How much was this? It took two lepta to make one *quadrant* (Mark 12:42); four quadrants or eight *lepta* to equal one *as* or *assarion;* and sixteen of the latter to reach the value of one *denarius.* It will be recalled that the denarius was a common laborer's daily wage (Matt. 20:9, 10). So if a denarius was worth sixteen American pennies, then an assarion would be worth one penny, and a lepton one-eighth of a penny; hence the two lepta the widow contributed would amount to one-quarter of a cent.

However, we cannot really figure this way, for the purchasing power of money is constantly changing. All we can safely say, therefore, is that, by human standards, what the widow gave did not seem to amount to much. Far more important, however, was the value *Jesus* placed on her gift: **3, 4. and he said, Truly I say to y o u, this poor widow dropped in more than all the others. For all these people out of their abundance dropped in (something) among the gifts, but she out of her poverty dropped in all she had, her whole living.**[537]

By human calculation what this widow gave was insignificant. Measured by the divine standard, however, her contribution was priceless. Note the following:

a. What this widow did was so important in the eyes of Jesus that, according to Mark 12:43, he summoned his disciples, in order to rivet their attention upon it. This calling to himself of The Twelve had happened before, that is, on very important occasions, and this was another.

b. In line with this is the fact that the Master introduced his teaching by saying, "Truly I say to y o u," showing that what he was about to say was of great significance and should be taken to heart by them.

c. "This poor widow dropped in more than all the others," said Jesus. In his estimation the two copper coins were sparkling diamonds. One might even say: they resembled talents which over a period of time doubled in value (Matt. 25:20, 22); yes, doubled and redoubled, for her deed and Jesus' comment have inspired thousands of people to follow her example.

d. When the question is asked, "What was it that made her gift so precious?" the answer is that all the others had given "out of their abundance," she "out of her poverty," her want or lack.

---

537. For additional information with respect to coins used in Palestine during the days of Christ's earthly sojourn see the following:

L. M. Petersen, art. "Money," *Zondervan Pictorial Bible Dictionary,* pp. 551–555, with picture of a *lepton* (obverse and reverse) on p. 553.

A. Sizoo, *De Antieke Wereld en Het Nieuwe Testament,* pp. 70–76.

C. Seltmann, *Greek Coins,* London, 1933.

D. Sperber, "Mark 12:42 and Its Metrological Background. A Study in Ancient Syriac Versions," *NT* 9 (1967), pp. 178–190.

Shall we say that she might at least have kept *one* of these small, thin copper coins for herself? But no, she gave both. In fact, she, knowing that God would not fail her, sacrificed everything. These two coins represented all she had to live on.

Total commitment to God and his cause is the lesson she has taught us. For *Practical Lessons* and *Greek Words,* etc., see pp. 933–936.

---

5 Now while some were talking about the temple, how it was adorned with goodly stones and votive offerings,[538] he said:

6 "As for these things y o u are admiring, days will come when there will not be left one stone upon another that will not be thrown down."

7 "Teacher," they asked him, "when then will this happen, and what will be the sign when this is about to take place?"

21:5 ff. *Christ's Discourse on The Last Things*

21:5-7 *The Occasion. The Temple's Destruction Foretold*

Cf. Matt. 24:1-3; Mark 13:1-4

A. *The Temple Admired*

5. Now while some were talking about the temple, how it was adorned with goodly stones and votive offerings...

Matthew (24:1) and Mark (13:1) point out that Jesus left the temple, and that it was while the little band—Jesus and The Twelve—was in the process of walking away from that magnificent building complex that the remarks recorded here in Luke 21:5 and parallels were made.

"One of Christ's disciples" (Mark 13:1), deeply impressed with the size and beauty of the temple, was unable to suppress an exclamation. Others followed until probably all joined in (Matt. 24:1; Luke 21:5). They made remarks to Jesus about its huge stones and magnificent buildings. Luke's report has "goodly stones and votive offerings."

In order that we may be able to enter somewhat into their thoughts and emotions a brief description of the temple and its history is in order.

It was David who conceived in his heart to build a temple for the Lord. But for the reason stated in I Chron. 28:3 not to David but to his son Solomon was given the privilege to build it. He began to do so in the fourth year of his reign, hence in or about the year 969 B.C. See I Kings 6:1. It was finished seven years later (I Kings 6:38). Cedar and cypress wood from Lebanon, and white hard limestone were used in its construction. Because the level area of Moriah, on which it was built, was too small, the foundation had to be laid very deep and the space between hilltop and outer wall filled in. For an account of the furniture of this temple and of the manner in which it was dedicated see I Kings 6–8. This temple experienced stress and

---

538. Or: gifts consecrated to God.

strain. In the course of the centuries it was plundered, renovated, desecrated, purged. See I Kings 14:26; 15:18; II Kings 14:14; 15:35; 16:17 f.;
23:4 f. Its treasures were carried to Babylon (II Kings 24:13). Finally, about
the year 586 B.C. the Chaldean army destroyed Jerusalem, including Solomon's beautiful temple.

About fifty years later, at the return of a remnant from Babylonian
captivity, an altar for a new temple was immediately built (Ezra 3:3). Sometime later work was begun in earnest on the building itself. It was completed about twenty years after the return. However, since it became clear
that it would not be nearly as imposing and beautiful a structure as that of
Solomon, the older people, who had known that first building, wept (Ezra
3:12, 13). It was this temple that was plundered and desecrated by An-
tiochus Epiphanes in 168 B.C. Approximately three years later it was
cleansed and rededicated by Judas Maccabaeus. Pompey captured and entered this temple but did not destroy it. However, Crassus deprived it of its
treasures in 54–53 B.C.

Herod the Great altered and enlarged the temple complex. He expanded and beautified it to such an extent that the result could be called a
new temple, though devout Jews probably refused to consider it such. In an
eloquent address to the people the king, if we can trust Josephus, divulged
his plan "to make a thankful return, after the most pious manner, to God,
for the blessings I have received from him, who has given me this kingdom,
and to do this by making his temple as complete as I am able." He began to
build it about the year 19 B.C. Long after his death it had not yet been
entirely completed. See John 2:20. The grandeur and beauty of the temple
which Herod started to build and on which he had made very considerable
progress is evident from Luke 21:5, 6; cf. Matt. 24:1, 2; Mark 13:1, 2. See
also Matt. 4:5; Luke 4:9. It is interesting to note that this elaborate structure was not finished until . . . just a few years before it was destroyed by the
Romans, A.D. 70.

Here follows a brief description of Herod's temple complex. It should be
studied in connection with the diagram. The entire huge area on which it
stood—a square measuring not much less than a thousand feet on each
side—was enclosed by a massive outer wall. Those coming from the
north—for example, from the suburb of Bethesda—could enter by the
north gate. The east wall overlooked the Kidron Valley. By way of what in
later years was called the Golden Gate one was able from the temple area to
cross the brook, and thus go to the Garden of Gethsemane, Bethany, and
the Mount of Olives; or vice versa. See Mark 11:1, 11; John 18:1. See also
on Mark 11:16. Coming from the south—for example, from the Lower
City—it was possible to reach the Court of the Gentiles by means of the two
Gates of Huldah. One of these was a double, the other a triple gate. Of all
the gates that led from or to the outside these were the most widely used.
Finally, from the Upper City one was able, by means of the four western
gates, to enter the temple area. Very useful also were the two bridges with

which two of these western gates were linked. Their remnants have been preserved to this very day.

Lining the outer wall were rows of high pillars. Each consisted of a single block of pure white polished marble. On the east, west, and north there were three parallel rows of columns, on the south four. This meant that three sides had two parallel halls, while the Royal Porch, where according to tradition the palace of Solomon used to be, had three.

John 10:23 states, "It was winter, and Jesus was walking inside the temple, in Solomon's Porch [Portico or Colonnade]." This covered "porch" probably derived its name from the fact that of the temple which that king had built, this was in the days of Jesus the only remaining part. Cf. Acts 3:11; 5:12. It is understandable that the various ample and beautiful colonnades provided every opportunity for teaching (Mark 12:41-44 and parallels; Luke 19:47, etc.).

Beyond these colonnades—that is, farther away from the outside wall—there was the very spacious Court of the Gentiles, also extending all around. It was paved with variegated marble of the finest quality. This court was given its name because, though both Jews and Gentiles were welcome here, the latter were not allowed to proceed any farther toward the interior. In order to remind them of that restriction, the smaller area immediately enclosed by the Court of the Gentiles was surrounded by a 4½ ft. high balustrade furnished with slabs on which was written, both in Greek and in Latin, this warning:

"Let no man of another nation enter inside the barrier and the fence around the temple. Whoever is caught will have himself to blame that his death follows."

For a picture of part of a slab with Greek lettering see Kollek and Pearlman, *Jerusalem, A History of Forty Centuries*, New York, 1968, p. 124.

Proceeding westward from Solomon's Porch the person privileged to do so would, after crossing a portion of the Court of the Gentiles, via the Beautiful Gate enter the Women's Court. Men as well as women were allowed here. Just as "Court of the Gentiles" meant that Gentiles were not permitted any closer to the interior, so "Women's Court" was thus named in order to indicate that this was as far as women were allowed to go. It was equipped with large chambers and gave access to treasure vaults. Against the walls stood thirteen trumpet-shaped chests for gifts and dues. Luke 21:1-4 (cf. Mark 12:41-44) and John 8:20 come to mind at once.

Male Israelites were allowed to proceed even farther, namely, into "Israel's Court," a relatively narrow one. Between that and the "Priests' Court" there was only a low partition, so that by some authors these two are considered one.

It was the Priests' Court that encompassed the inner sanctuary with its Holy Place and Holy of Holies. To the east of it stood the very large altar of burnt-offering. Nearer to the sanctuary and a little farther to the south could be seen the laver, a colossal brazen reservoir that rested on the back of

GROUND PLAN OF THE TEMPLE
IN THE DAYS OF JESUS [539]

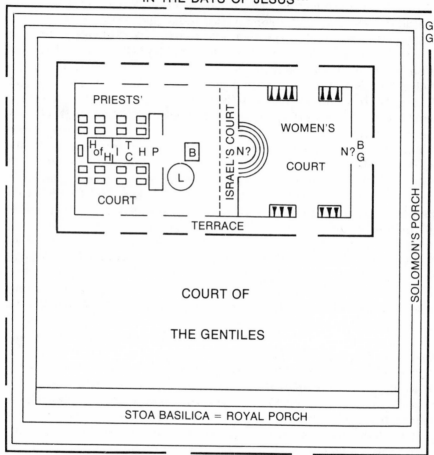

LOOKING NORTH

H = Holy Place with Table of
   Showbread, Incense Altar,
   and Candelabrum
H of H = Holy of Holies
B = Burntoffering Altar
L = Laver (Washbasin)

P = Porch
N? = Nicanor's Gate
   (location disputed)
B G = Beautiful Gate
G G = Golden Gate

twelve big lions. Finally, there was the sanctuary itself. As to measurements, Josephus states that its ground floor "was sixty cubits in height, the same in length, and twenty cubits in breadth. But the sixty cubits of its length were again divided. The first portion [the Holy Place] was partitioned off at forty cubits . . . the innermost recess [Holy of Holies] measured twenty cubits."

This magnificent sanctuary must have been a marvelous sight to behold, since it was built of white marble, richly set off with gold on its front and sides. It was entered by means of a huge double-winged porch or vestibule, as indicated on the diagram. In front of the doorway to the Holy Place hung a beautifully colored Babylonian veil or curtain. There was also "the second veil," the one that separated the Holy Place from the Holy of Holies. See Matt. 27:51; Heb. 6:19; cf. 9:3; 10:20.

As it was during the old dispensation so also now, the Holy Place contained "A lampstand, a table, and an altar of incense," thus again Josephus, who adds, "But in this [that is, in the Holy of Holies] stood nothing at all. . . ." The candelabrum or seven-branched lampstand was among the temple treasures which by Titus and Vespasian were displayed in the triumphal procession which they conducted in Rome after the fall of Jerusalem, A.D. 70. See the picture in the aforementioned book, *Jerusalem, A History of Forty Centuries*, p. 131, and in many other sources.

I have purposely left to the last for special emphasis one very important point, namely, *the height* of the various parts. Now before proceeding any further it is only proper to call attention to the fact that we cannot be entirely certain about the dimensions—mostly *length* and *breadth*—given thus far. The Bible furnishes no information on this point. Josephus and the Mishnaic tractate by no means always agree. It is not surprising, therefore, that the secondary sources—even our best textbooks—disagree among themselves on several points. See W. S. Caldecott and James Orr, *The Temple of Herod*, I.S.B.E., Vol. V, 2937–2940. The general picture is clear enough; conjecture—sometimes probable, sometimes improbable or at least fruitless—enters into the determination of many details. This holds also with respect to the *height* of the various parts.

With that reservation, it can now be pointed out that there were especially three features that made this temple unforgettable:

---

539. The diagram gives *only the main features* of Herod's temple. No attempt has been made to picture the rooms lining the walls of the outer court, the additional equipment pertaining to the Priests' Court— such as the place of slaughter north of the altar, tables for preparing the sacrifices, drainage canal conducting the blood to the Kidron—and several other details. Also, there is no certainty with respect to the identity of each gate. This is especially true with respect to Nicanor's Gate, which by Edersheim and by Halberthal is placed west of the Women's Court, but which by many others is placed east of that court and identified with the Beautiful Gate.

The chief sources for our knowledge of Herod's temple, in addition to the New Testament references to it, are the Mishnaic tractate *Middoth* ("Measurements"); and Josephus, *Jewish War* V.184–247, and *Jewish Antiquities* XV.380–425. Also consulted were A. Edersheim, *The Temple*; L. Halberthal, *The Plan of the Holy Temple of Jerusalem*, Montreal, 1967; T. Kollek & M. Pearlman, *op. cit.;* A. Parrot, *The Temple of Jerusalem*, London, 1957; and several archaeological books and articles.

a. *Its vastness.*

From east to west or northwest the temple complex increased in height. From the Court of the Gentiles to that of Women there was an ascent of fourteen steps; from there to the Court of Israel a rise of fifteen steps. A few more upward steps would bring one to the Priests' Court; and twelve more, to the entrance of the sanctuary. Accordingly, highest of any of the buildings of this entire complex was "the temple" or "sanctuary." It soared high above the vast Court of the Gentiles. "Some of the stones in the building were forty-five cubits [67¼ feet] in length, five [7½] in height, and six [9] in breadth" (Josephus). The sanctuary, moreover, occupied the most elevated ground, and was buttressed by very formidable substructures. Its height was no less than sixty feet, compared to forty-five for the temple of Solomon (I Kings 6:2). To this should be added another sixty feet for the upper chamber that covered the entire sanctuary. The whole temple, with the exception of the porch, was covered with a gabled roof of cedar wood. "From its summit protruded sharp golden spikes to prevent birds from settling upon and polluting the roof" (Josephus).

From all this it follows that the best pictorial map of Herod's vast temple complex is the three-dimensional. See, for example, the reconstruction by the Conte de Vogue (*Jerusalem,* p. 100) or the Schick model, reproduced in several English and other language encyclopedias and archaeological texts, or Lazar Halberthal's colorful drawing.

Vastness, by reminding man of his littleness, inspires awe.

b. *Its beauty.*

Says Josephus, "The exterior of the building lacked nothing that could astonish either the soul or the eyes. For, [the exterior] being covered on every side with massive plates of gold, the sun had no sooner risen than it radiated so fiery a flash that those straining to look at it were forced to avert their eyes as from the solar rays. To approaching strangers it appeared from a distance like a snow-clad mountain, the reason being that whatever was not overlain with gold was purest white" (*Jewish War* V.222). Though the rabbis were not at all in love with Herod I, nor with those who followed him, they had to admit, "He who has not seen Jerusalem in her splendor has never in his life seen a desirable city. He who has not seen the temple in its full construction has never in his life seen a glorious building."[540]

Beauty is conducive to worship.

c. *Its purpose.*

That purpose is clearly stated in I Kings 8:13, 31–61; 9:3; and especially in Isa. 56:7, for even though these passages pertain to the temple of *Solomon,* they clearly have meaning also with respect to the temple as it existed in the days of Jesus. Even the child Jesus called it "my Father's house" (Luke 2:49). And during his earthly ministry *Jesus, quoting from Isaiah, de-*

---

540. *The Babylonian Talmud Sukkah* 41 b (Baraitha); *Baba Baththra* 4a (Baraitha).

clared the temple to be a house of worship. He said, "Is it not written: 'My house shall be called a house of prayer for all the nations...'?"

The reason why just at this particular moment these men were thinking of the temple may well have been that Jesus had just said, "Behold, y o u r house is left to y o u a deserted place" (Matt. 23:38; cf. Luke 13:35). Though it is probable that the expression *y o u r house* meant Jerusalem, its temple was certainly included. It is as if the disciples were saying, "Is it true that also this glorious structure is going to be entirely deserted?" In substance Jesus answers, "Not only *deserted* but totally *destroyed.*"

After what has already been said about the temple's huge and goodly stones, no more need be added. The (votive) offerings were in the form of presents, probably on top of the walls and decorating them. Such offerings were, for example, the golden vines which Herod had donated, "with grapeclusters as tall as a man" (Josephus, *Jewish War* V.210). There must have been several such gifts, all very beautiful and clearly visible from the outside.

B. *The Temple To Be Destroyed*

Continued: **he said, 6. As for these things y o u are admiring, days will come when there will not be left one stone upon another that will not be thrown down.**

As to the fulfilment, when the Jews rebelled against the Romans, Jerusalem was taken by Titus, son of the emperor Vespasian (A.D. 69–79). The temple was destroyed. It is believed that more than a million Jews, who had crowded into the city, perished. As a political unit Israel ceased to exist. As a nation specially favored by the Lord it had reached the end of the road even long before the beginning of the Jewish War.

An ex-combatant and eyewitness, Josephus, almost immediately after the struggle between the Jews and the Romans had ended, began to write his *History of the Jewish War.* On the whole his narrative may be described as trustworthy, although a definitely pro-Roman bias cannot be denied.

An excerpt from Josephus may illumine the fulfilment of 21:6:

"That building [the temple at Jerusalem], however, God long ago had sentenced to the flames; but now in the revolution of the time periods the fateful day had arrived, the tenth of the month Lous, the very day on which previously it had been burned by the king of Babylon.... One of the soldiers, neither awaiting orders nor filled with horror of so dread an undertaking, but moved by some supernatural impulse, snatched a brand from the blazing timber and, hoisted up by one of his fellow soldiers, flung the fiery missile through a golden window.... When the flame rose, a scream, as poignant as the tragedy, went up from the Jews... now that the object which before they had guarded so closely was going to ruin" (VI.250–253).

The words, "There will not be left one stone on another that will not be thrown down," are probably to be interpreted as a hyperbolic prophecy of the thorough character of the destruction that would take place. See also on verse 24.

When the *cleansing* of the temple did not bring about genuine repentance, its *destruction* must follow.

Nevertheless, in his wrath the Lord "remembered mercy" (Hab. 3:2). Over the ruins of the earthly temple another "temple" was being established, that of Christ's body (John 2:20), the church consisting of both Jew and Gentile. Doom came at last, but even that sentence of doom opened the door to blessing, and this for both Jew and Gentile. And throughout the ages the ancient prophecies would be going into fulfilment: Gen. 12:3; Ps. 87; Isa. 54:2, 3; 60:3; 65:1; Jer. 31:31 f.; Mal. 1:11, all this "unto God's glory."

C. When Will This Happen?

7. Teacher, they asked him, when then will this happen, and what will be the sign when this is about to take place?

A little later, when Jesus and The Twelve had arrived on the Mount of Olives, four disciples—namely, Peter, James, John, and Andrew (Mark 13:3)—stepped up to the Master and voiced the question which undoubtedly was in the minds of the entire little company, namely, "When will this happen, and what will be the sign when this is about to take place?" In a parallel passage (Matt. 24:3), this question is framed somewhat differently, "Tell us, when will this happen, and what (will be) the sign of thy coming and of the end of the age?"

It is clear that, as these men interpreted the Master's words, Jerusalem's fall, particularly the destruction of the temple, would mean the end of the world. In this opinion they were partly mistaken, for a lengthy period of time would intervene between Jerusalem's fall and the culmination of the age, the second coming. Nevertheless, they were not entirely wrong: there was indeed a connection between the judgment to be executed upon nation and temple, on the one hand; and on the other hand, the final judgment on the day of the consummation of all things. The first was a type of the second.

Jesus, in a very general way, answered their question, and told them about "the sign" to look for. He did this in his *Discourse on The Last Things,* which begins at this point.

For *Practical Lessons* and *Greek Words,* etc., see pp. 933-936.

---

8 He said to them, "Take care that y o u are not deceived. For many will come in my name, saying, 'I am he,' and 'The time is near.' Do not follow them. 9 And when y o u hear of wars and insurrections, do not panic,[541] for these things must happen first, but (that is) not immediately the end."

10 Then he said to them, "Nation will rise up in arms against nation, and kingdom against

---

541. Or: do not become terrified.

kingdom. 11 There will be great earthquakes, and in various places famines and pestilences, and there will be dreadful portents and great signs from heaven.[542]

12 "But before all this they will lay their hands on y o u and will persecute y o u, handing y o u over to the synagogues and prisons, bringing y o u before kings and governors for my name's sake. 13 This will furnish y o u with an opportunity to testify.[543] 14 So fix it in y o u r hearts not to plan y o u r defense beforehand, 15 for I will give y o u such wisdom of speech as all y o u r adversaries combined will be unable to withstand or contradict. 16 Indeed, y o u will be betrayed even by parents and brothers and relatives and friends, and they will put some of y o u to death. 17 And y o u will be hated by everybody for my name's sake. 18 But not a hair of y o u r head will perish. 19 By means of y o u r endurance y o u will win y o u r souls."

21:8-19 *The Beginning of Woes or Birth Pains*
Cf. Matt. 24:4-14; Mark 13:5-13

8-11. He said to them, Take care that y o u are not deceived. For many will come in my name, saying, I am he, and The time is near. Do not follow them. And when y o u hear of wars and insurrections, do not panic, for these things must happen first, but (that is) not immediately the end.

Then he said to them, Nation will rise up in arms against nation, and kingdom against kingdom. There will be great earthquakes, and in various places famines and pestilences, and there will be dreadful portents and great signs from heaven.

Jesus now proceeds to correct his disciples' mistaken inference. He shows them that "not everything that seems to be a sign of the end of the world is in reality such a sign." In other words, there are also signs which only in a very general sense are deserving of that name. Whenever these separate happenings are interpreted as being infallible indications that the end of the age is immediately in sight, they deserve the name *mistaken signs*. Thus Jesus predicts the coming of those who will say, "I am he," and "The time is near." Jesus adds, "Do not follow them."

This also holds true with respect to "wars and insurrections." When Jesus speaks these words, the Roman empire has been enjoying a long era of peace. But about four decades later political turmoil will upset the great realm from one end to the other, so that Rome will see four emperors in one year: Galba, Otho, Vitellus, and Vespasian. But these violent revolts and insurrections cannot by any stretch of the imagination constitute definite indications that the Lord will return immediately. So Jesus adds, "Do not panic, for these things must happen first, but (that is) not immediately the end." This is evident at once when one considers the fact that wars and insurrections did not cease with Jerusalem's fall. Throughout the centuries the prophecy attains fulfilment: "nation will rise up in arms against nation, and kingdom against kingdom" (verse 10). One author counted three

---

542. Or: from the sky.
543. Literally: It will turn out to y o u for a testimony. Cf. A.V.

hundred wars in Europe during the last three hundred years. And these wars are increasing in intensity. It is perfectly clear that when any particular war is singled out as a help for "date-fixers," another "mistaken sign" has been produced.

Jesus also speaks about great earthquakes, and in various places famines and pestilences (verse 11). As was true with respect to other predicted events, so it is here. These disturbances in the physical realm are indeed foreshadowings and portrayals of that which, on a much more extensive and intensive scale, will take place in the realm of nature at the end of the age; but except in that very general sense they cannot be correctly termed signs. Not any single one of them could ever give anyone the right to make predictions with reference either to the date of Jerusalem's fall or to the time of the Parousia (Christ's second coming). It is true that during the period A.D. 60–80 famine, pestilence, fire, hurricane, and earthquake ravaged the empire, as Renan points out in *l'Antichrist*. Vesuvius erupted violently in the summer of 79, destroying Pompeii and its surroundings. But, as is already clear from the preceding sentence, these catastrophes were not limited to the decade preceding the fall of Jerusalem in the year 70. Moreover, throughout the centuries there have been violent earthquakes. Ancient historians, geographers, and philosophers—such as Thucydides, Aristotle, Strabo, Seneca, Livy, and Pliny—describe similar seismic phenomena in their days. And as early as the year 1668 Robert Hooke wrote his work bearing the title, *Discourse on Earthquakes*. A certain author counted no less than seven hundred disturbances of this nature, great and small, which had occurred in the nineteenth century! Famines and pestilences, too, occur constantly. So do "dreadful portents and great signs from heaven." Such things as comets, meteors, and even eclipses have always terrified people. But Jesus includes all such "signs" under the general caption of things that do not indicate that the time is near.

In spite of this clear warning which our Lord gave to his disciples, many present-day church members are filled with admiration for the minister or evangelist who speaks learnedly about "The Signs of the Times," and strives to show his audience that this or that terrible battle, serious earthquake, devastating famine, or threatening comet "on the basis of prophecy" is the infallible "sign" of Christ's imminent return.

To be sure, the events here indicated have significance. They are steppingstones leading to the final goal. By means of them the end of the age is both foreshadowed and brought closer, and God's eternal plan is being carried forward. Moreover, when we realize that toward the end of the present dispensation the indicated disturbances will occur together (Matt. 24:33), will probably be more numerous, extensive, and fearful than ever before (Luke 21:11, 25, 26), and are going to take place in connection with the great tribulation that will usher in the Parousia, we may conclude that it would not be unreasonable to call *the final outbreak* of these terrors "concurrent or accompanying signs."

**12. But before all this they will lay their hands on y o u and will perse-
cute y o u, handing y o u over to the synagogues and prisons, bringing
y o u before kings and governors for my name's sake.**

Note *"before* all this." Predictions mentioned in the preceding lines, such
as "Nation will rise up in arms against nation, kingdom against kingdom,
great earthquakes," etc., would be fulfilled throughout the entire new dispensation. On the other hand, being handed over to *synagogues* would
occur only at the very beginning of this period, for after A.D. 70
(Jerusalem's fall) the synagogue would lose most of its persecuting power
against Christians.

Substantiation for the fulfilment of this prophecy, as concerns persecution by the synagogue, during these very early days of the church, is found
in such passages as Acts 9:1; 22:19. The latter passage shows that these
early believers were flogged, and that one of those persecuters who caused
believers in Christ to receive this horrible punishment was Saul (= Paul) of
Tarsus. After his conversion he himself was going to be similarly tortured.
He was going to write, "From the Jews five times I received forty lashes less
one" (II Cor. 11:24).

This also implied *"imprisonment* of Christians," as that same apostle shows
by writing, "I went from one synagogue to another *to imprison* and flog,"
etc. (Acts 22:19).

As to "kings and governors" who figured in the persecution of the early
church, think of such "kings" as (a) Herod Agrippa I, who killed James (son
of Zebedee), brother of the apostle John (Acts 12:1), and (b) Herod Agrippa II before whom Paul made his defense. Even (c) Herod Antipas, who
technically was not a king, is given this title at times (Mark 6:14, 22, 25–27;
Luke 23:6–12).

And as to "governors" who took an active part in the persecution of
Christ and/or his disciples, think of such procurators as Pontius Pilate,
Felix, and Festus.

What is important is that Jesus says that this persecution will take place
"for my name's sake." When anyone persecutes Christ's disciples he is
persecuting Christ himself, a fact that was stamped so indelibly on the mind
and heart of Paul that, however much the accounts of that apostle's conversion may vary, the words, "Saul, Saul, why do you persecute *me?"* are found
in all three (Acts 9:4, 5; 22:7, 8; 26:14, 15). The persecuted one was maltreated *because of his loyalty to Jesus.* And no one was ever able to separate
him from Christ's love and from the comfort imparted to him by that
knowledge.

Jesus continued: **13. This will furnish y o u with an opportunity to testify.** How richly this prophecy was fulfilled. Christ's disciples testified by
word of mouth (Acts 4:5–12, 19, 20; 9:15, 16; 22:1–21; 23:1, 6, 11; 24:10–
21; 26:1–29; 27:21–26; 28:23–28); by personal conduct (II Cor. 6:1–10;
11:22–32; Phil. 1:12 ff.); and even by means of their songs (Acts 16:25; cf.
Eph. 5:19; Col. 3:16).

In days of sore trial and persecution, lying in dungeons perhaps, having been unmercifully beaten, etc., the followers of Jesus might be wondering what they should say when they are brought to trial. So Jesus here essentially repeats the promise of 12:11, 12. He says: **14, 15. So fix it in y o u r hearts not to plan y o u r defense beforehand, for I will give y o u such wisdom of speech as all y o u r adversaries combined will be unable to withstand or contradict.**

Comparison with the earlier promise (12:11, 12) shows that what the Holy Spirit does Jesus does also. From his position at the Father's right hand in glory he will, through his Spirit, impart to his dear ones the ability to say the right thing at the right time. In fact, by stating "all y o u r adversaries combined will not be able to withstand or contradict y o u" he is even strengthening the promise of 12:11, 12. That this prediction was gloriously fulfilled is clear from the book of Acts. See the references mentioned in the explanation of verse 13.

So frightful will be the hatred against believers because of their faith in the Lord Jesus Christ that even some of their relatives will join the opposition:

16, 17. Indeed, y o u will be betrayed even by parents and brothers and relatives and friends, and they will put some of y o u to death. And y o u will be hated by everybody for my name's sake.

In a passage reminding one of Matt. 10:21, 22 and Mark 13:12 Jesus predicts that hatred against himself and his cause will in some cases overcome ties of blood and of friendship.

That because of fundamental religious difference—note "for my name's sake"—hostility not infrequently arises between members of the same family is clear not only from such general statements as are found in Ezek. 38:21 and Mal. 4:6 but also from such actual examples as are recorded in Gen. 4:8 (cf. Heb. 11:4) and Gen. 27:41. Does not this fact help to explain the stern demand Jesus makes in Luke 14:26, 27? Some believers would even be put to death through the mediation of nearest relatives and/or former friends.

The expression "Y o u will be hated by everybody" or "by all" means "by men in general, regardless of rank, station, race, nationality, sex, or age." Is not the same true also with respect to the use of "all" in such passages as Mark 1:37; 5:20; 11:32; Luke 3:15; John 3:26; I Tim. 2:1; and Titus 2:11? Because the world hates Christ it also hates his representatives, the Christians.

The paragraph ends on a note of comfort: **18, 19. But not a hair of y o u r head will perish. By means of y o u r endurance y o u will win y o u r souls.**

But is not this a contradiction? After saying "They will put some of y o u to death" (verse 16), how can Jesus almost immediately add, "But not a hair of y o u r head will perish" (verse 18)? But certainly Jesus would not, in one and the same breath, utter two violently conflicting sayings! And Luke did not think it necessary to offer an explanation. The solution, it would seem to me, is rather easy for anyone acquainted with the teaching of Jesus. All one has to do is to turn back to Matt. 10:29, 30. He will then see that what Jesus meant was that nothing, not even our hairs, is excluded from the domain of God's tender care, so that we may be assured that if any hair perishes it is by his will and for his purpose. And that purpose is always the promotion of our salvation, to God's glory. See such passages as Rom. 8:28; Phil. 1:19; I Peter 4:11; 5:10.

What is necessary, however, is that God's children persevere. They must never lose courage, but should remain faithful no matter how fierce the persecution may get to be. Their endurance—by God's strength-imparting grace, of course—is the instrument the Lord uses to give them the ultimate victory. Cf. Luke 18:1, 8.[544]

Practical Lessons Derived from Luke 21:1–19

Verse 4

"She out of her poverty dropped in all she had, her whole living."
The deed was beautiful because it was Christlike. Cf. II Cor. 8:9.
Appropriate songs, in this connection, are:
H. B. Grose, "Give of your best to the Master."
F. R. Havergal, "I gave my life for thee."
There are different varieties of giving:
a. The flint gives off sparks when struck hard.
b. A lemon yields juice when it is squeezed.
c. The rose, orange blossom, jasmine, gardenia, and mint (to mention only a few) release fragrance "of their own accord."
Should not every person ask himself, "To which of these groups do I belong?"

Verses 5, 6

"The temple ... adorned with goodly stones. ... There will not be left one stone upon another that will not be thrown down."
Herod's temple was very beautiful and costly ... but not destined to last. God's temple, the church universal, is destined to last and last and last. See Matt. 16:18; II Cor. 4:18.
Someone wrote:
"All things that are on earth shall surely pass away
Except the love of God, which shall live and last for aye."

Verse 13

"This will furnish y o u with an opportunity to testify." What a refreshing way to regard trial and persecution!
Moreover, that was exactly what the leaders—and many of the followers too, of

---

544. Notes on Greek words, phrases, and constructions in 21:1–19 begin on page 934.

course—in the early church did with these experiences. Note, for example, what Stephen did when he was being stoned (Acts 7:54-60); what Peter did (Acts 4:1-12); and Paul (Phil. 1:12-18).

Verse 19

"By means of y o u r endurance y o u will win y o u r souls." Endurance is pertinacity, stick-to-itiveness. An old illustration: A man drives a tunnel a mile long through strata he is sure contain gold. Not finding it, he gives up. He then sells his property, including the tunnel, for a very modest sum. The buyer extends the tunnel a yard farther... and finds gold!

"He that endures to the end, he will be saved" (Matt. 10:22). It can be done through God's grace (I Cor. 15:10).

Notes on Greek Words, Phrases, and Constructions in 21:1-19

Verse 1

The term γαζοφυλακεῖον (or -κιον) consists of two parts: γάζα, Persian for *treasure,* and φυλακή, guard, safeguard; hence a chest into which treasures or gifts could be dropped and guarded; i.e., safely kept.

Verse 2

πενιχράν, fem. acc. s. of πενιχρός*, needy, poor. Cf. *penury.*

λεπτά, acc. pl. of λεπτός, peeled, small, light, thin; hence, a very thin (leafy) copper coin. The value of "⅛ of a penny" is at times ascribed to it, but whether or not this is correct depends on the buying power (at a particular time) of the coins that are being compared.

Verse 3

πτωχή, begging, depending on others for support, poor. See Trench, *Synonyms* par. xxxvi.

Verse 4

ἐκ τοῦ περισσεύοντος αὐτοῖς, lit. of what was overflowing to them; hence, of their abundance. See also N.T.C. on Ephesians, p. 84, footnote 25.

ὑστερήματος, gen. s. of ὑστέρημα, lack, need, deficiency, poverty.

βίον, acc. s. of βίος, here: (means of) living. See the note on 15:12 on page 760.

εἶχεν, third per. s. imperf. (descriptive) of ἔχω, to have.

εἰς τὰ δῶρα, probably (they dropped it) *among* the gifts; so Beck, and cf. Dutch (Nieuwe Vertaling), "bij de gaven."

Verse 5

Note gen. absolute: while some were talking.

ὅτι, *that,* where we say "how."

ἀναθήμασιν, dat. pl. of ἀνάθημα, votive offering.

According to S.BK., Vol. III, p. 260, in the terminology of the Septuagint the word ἀνάθεμα indicates anything which by God or in God's name has been devoted to destruction and ruin. The rabbinical *"herem"* is a broader concept, inasmuch as it comprises *whatever* is devoted to God, not only that which is devoted to him for destruction. The same distinction is carried over into the New Testament, where the noun ἀνάθημα (here in Luke 21:5, according to the best reading) means "that which has been devoted to God as a votive offering," naturally with no curse implications; while ἀνάθεμα (used in Acts 23:14; Rom. 9:3; I Cor. 12:3; 16:22; Gal. 1:8, 9) refers to that which is devoted to God without hope of being redeemed; hence, that which, or he who, is doomed to destruction, accursed.

κεκόσμηται, third per. s. perf. pass. indicat. of κοσμέω, to adorn.

Verse 6

Note acc. of general reference: "As for these things y o u are admiring."

θεωρεῖτε, sec. per. pl. pres. indicat. act. of θεωρέω, observe, contemplate, admire. For synonyms see N.T.C. on John, Vol. I, footnote 33 on p. 85.

οὐκ ἀφεθήσεται, third per. s. fut. indicat. pass. of ἀφίημι; see the note on 4:39 on page 271.

καταλυθήσεται, third per. s. fut. indicat. pass. of καταλύω; here: to throw down. For related meanings see the note on 9:12 on page 485.

Verses 8, 9

πλανηθῆτε, sec. per. pl. aor. subjunct. pass. of πλανάω, to deceive, lead astray, cause to wander; here pass.: to be deceived. Cf. *planet,* a "wandering star." The verb occurs very frequently in the New Testament, especially in Matthew and Revelation; in Luke only here.

ἤγγικεν, third per. s. perf. indicat. of ἐγγίζω, to come near. See the note on 10:9 on page 587.

μὴ πορευθῆτε . . . μὴ πτοηθῆτε, sec. per. pl. aor. subjunctives (ingressive and volitive), respectively of πορεύομαι, to go, and of πτοέω*, to terrify; in the New Testament only here and in 24:37.

Verse 11

λιμοὶ καὶ λοιμοί, a play on words, famines and pestilences; cf. paucity and plague.

φόβητρα, nom. pl. of φόβητρον*, in the New Testament only here, something that produces fright, terror (cf. φόβος, fear; φοβέω, to frighten).

ἀπαγομένους, acc. pl. masc. pres. pass. participle of ἀπάγω, to lead away. Though the tense of the participle is pres., the time indicated is that of the principal verb, hence future.

Verse 13

ἀποβήσεται, third per. fut. indicat. middle of ἀποβαίνω, to step off, disembark (Luke 5:2), and here: to result, turn out, lead (to). Cf. Phil. 1:19.

Verse 14

θέτε, sec. per. pl. aor. act. imperat. of τίθημι; here: to put, place, fix.

προμελετᾶν, pres. act. infinitive of προμελετάω*, to plan beforehand.

ἀπολογηθῆναι, aor. pass. (ingressive) infinitive of ἀπολογέομαι, to defend oneself (against an accusation); see also the note on 12:11 on page 661. In Acts 19:33—26:24 Luke uses this verb six times. Paul uses it in Rom. 2:15; II Cor. 12:19. The cognate noun ἀπολογία occurs in Acts 22:1; 25:16, while Paul uses it five times (I Cor. 9:3, etc.), Peter once (I Peter 3:15). Cf. *apology*.

Verse 15

στόμα καὶ σοφίαν, "a mouth and wisdom." Here "mouth" is metonomy for "what the mouth utters," hence eloquence, speech. The entire expression is probably hendiadys for "wisdom of speech." Cf. Deut. 19:15; Luke 19:22.

Note the three ἀντί-compounds: withstand, contradict, adversaries. As I have shown in my dissertation, all three belong to that subdivision of ἀντί-compounds which may be considered *o*(pposition, oppositeness) *m*(etaphorical).

ἀντιστῆναι, 2nd aor. act. infinitive of ἀνθίστημι; ἀντειπεῖν is used as 2nd aor. act. infinitive of ἀντιλέγω; and ἀντικείμενοι, nom. pl. masc. pres. participle of ἀντίκειμαι, lit. to be lying (situated) against. The participle indicates opponents, adversaries.

Verse 16

θανατώσουσιν, third per. pl. fut. indicat. of θανατόω, to put to death. In Luke this verb is used only here. It is used also by Matt. (10:21, etc.), Mark (13:12; 14:55), Paul (Rom. 7:4, etc.), and Peter (I Peter 3:18). Cf. *euthanasia, thanatopsis*.

Verse 17

ἔσεσθε μισούμενοι, sec. per. pl. periphrastic (durative) fut. pass. infinitive: y o u will be hated.

Verse 19

κτήσασθε, sec. per. pl. fut. (ingressive) indicat. middle of κτάομαι, to get, gain. For this verb see also the note on 18:12 on page 824.

---

20 "When y o u see Jerusalem being surrounded by armies, then understand that its desolation is near. 21 Then let those (who are) in Judea flee to the hills. And let those inside the city get out, and let not those in the country enter the city. 22 For these are days of retribution, that whatever is written may be fulfilled. 23 Woe to those who are pregnant and to those who nurse babies in those days, for there will be great distress upon the land and wrath against this people. 24 And they will fall by the edge of the sword and will be carried off as captives into all the nations; and Jerusalem will be trodden down[545] by the Gentiles until the times of the Gentiles are fulfilled."

---

545. Or: trampled underfoot.

21:20-24 *The Destruction of Jerusalem Foretold*
Cf. Matt. 24:15-21; Mark 13:14-19

20, 21. When y o u see Jerusalem being surrounded by armies, then understand that its desolation is near. Then let those (who are) in Judea flee to the hills. And let those inside the city get out, and let not those in the country enter the city.

To a large extent the problems that confront anyone who tries to explain Matthew's or Mark's parallel accounts, with their highly symbolic language and manifestations of prophetic foreshortening, are absent from Luke's report. The latter could almost be called a commentary on that of Matthew and Mark.

Having summarized what, according to Christ's prediction, would happen primarily and emphatically *before* Jerusalem's fall—although verses 8-19 also have their implications for the post A.D. 70 period—Luke now in clear language reports what Jesus predicted concerning that fall.

He predicts that Jerusalem is going to be surrounded by armies. When that happens, says Jesus, then y o u should recognize it as the "sign" for which y o u have been asking (verse 7), the sign of Jerusalem's impending destruction and desolation. For more on "the sign" see on verse 27. Concerned about the welfare of the people he loves, Jesus issues three succinct orders: (a) Those who are in Judea must flee to the hills; (b) those within the city must get out; and (c) those outside the city must stay out.

According to many commentators the people who heeded Christ's command finally found refuge in Perean Pella. See map on p. 854. To substantiate their opinion these commentators appeal to the statement of Eusebius, "On the other hand, the people of the Jerusalem church were commanded by an oracle, given by revelation before the war to those in the city who were worthy of it, to depart and dwell in one of the cities of Perea which is called Pella" (*Eccl. Hist.* III.v.3). And according to Epiphanius the exit from Jerusalem and the flight to Pella began just before the Romans laid siege to Jerusalem (*Ag. Her.* XXIX.7). But other commentators have raised doubts about the historicity of this flight to Pella. The debate has by no means ended. See the footnote.[546]

What is important, in this connection, is that Jesus never told the endangered ones to flee to *Pella.* He ordered them "to flee to the hills."

---

546. The arguments that aim to undermine the report of Eusebius can be found in N.T.C. on Matthew, p. 858. Supporting Eusebius and the view that there was indeed a flight to Pella is S. Sowers, "The Circumstances and Recollection of the Pella Flight," *ThZ* 26 (1970), pp. 305-320. Dr. H. Mulder, who has given years of study to the subject of the early Palestinian Church is even now preparing an article in which he will restate and amplify his reasons for believing that the flight to Pella never took place. How this debate will finally turn out I do not know. What stands out in these lines is Christ's knowledge of the future and his concern for his people.

Besides, what we are—at least should be—most interested in is not how this order was carried out but that it was issued at all. Think of it, just a few days before he suffered the agonies of hell, Jesus is thinking about the safety not of himself but of his disciples, including even of those who would not be living in these parts until many years later. What marvelous love!

For hardened unbelievers, however, the days to come would be days of wrath: **22. For these are days of retribution, that whatever is written may be fulfilled.** The expression *days of retribution* reminds us immediately of Luke 11:50, 51. Jesus had been sent from heaven to earth, with a message of God's grace. But by ever so many, especially by the leaders, he and his message had been rejected. See 19:44; 20:17. As a result, prophecies of vengeance, predictions of woe, were going to be fulfilled. We think especially of Jer. 18:9-11; Dan. 9:27; Zech. 11:6; Mal. 3:1, 2. Some of these prophecies were destined to have more than one fulfilment. To be sure, God is love, but he is also "a consuming fire" (Heb. 12:29), namely, for those who consistently reject that love.

23. Woe to those who are pregnant and to those who nurse babies in those days, for there will be great distress upon the land and wrath against this people.

What shines through very clearly in this passage is that even though Jesus *predicts* the outpouring of wrath, *he does not take delight* in it. The fact that he is thinking about pregnant women and nursing mothers reveals this.

What a vast difference between Menahem and the Messiah! The former was the cruel monster who, after seizing Israel's vacant throne, razed a city that refused to acknowledge him as the new ruler, and ripped open all its pregnant women (II Kings 15:16; cf. 8:12; Amos 1:13). Jesus, on the other hand, carried the burdens of women in such and similar conditions on his heart. He still does!

24. And they will fall by the edge of the sword and will be carried off as captives into all the nations...

What happened, in fulfilment of this prophecy, was as follows: Even several years before the outbreak of the Jewish War the Roman yoke was becoming more oppressive than ever. Action produced reaction, with the result that Jewish hatred of their heathen oppressors rose to the point of organized rebellion. By no means every Jew was in sympathy with this movement, but after a while the warnings of the moderates were drowned out by the voices of the Zealots. Emperor Nero sent his famous general Vespasian to Galilee, which was soon overrun. But, due to the forced return to Rome of this general and Nero's suicide, the conquest of Galilee was short-lived. A period of confusion followed in Rome, with four emperors in one year. See on verses 8-11. The Jews took advantage of this situation, so that the rebellion began to make some headway again. But then Vespasian, now emperor, having restored order, sent his son Titus (who himself later on became emperor, A.D. 79-81) to Jerusalem with a large army.

The siege began in April of the year A.D. 70, while Jerusalem was still filled with Passover pilgrims. For the terror that ensued one should read Josephus, *Jewish War,* especially Books IV to VII. After a siege of about five months the Romans finally overwhelmed the entire city. According to Josephus the total number of prisoners taken throughout the entire war was 97,000, while 1,100,000 perished during the siege (*Jewish War* VI.420). Even though these figures may be exaggerated, the number must have been enormous.

The war was inexcusably cruel. Not only was the temple given up to the flames but the entire city—except three towers and a portion of the western wall—was razed. By the thousands aged men, women, regardless of their physical condition, and even little children were murdered. Some of the prisoners were subsequently thrown to the wild beasts, others were sold into slavery "into all the nations," while a select number of the strongest and best-looking captives figured in the triumphal procession which Rome gave to the conquerors, and which Josephus describes in such elaborate detail, as if the terrible slaughter were really something to be proud of.

For many, many years no Jew was allowed to reside in or even to visit Jerusalem, which was made a pagan city. But enough has been said to show in what manner Christ's prediction, recorded in Luke 21:24a, was fulfilled.

Continued: **and Jerusalem will be trodden down by the Gentiles until the times of the Gentiles are fulfilled.**

S. Greijdanus explains this passage as probably meaning that the time of oppression for Jerusalem will last "to the end of the centuries, the coming of the final judgment and the return of Christ in glory, the very theme to which the Lord now [in verses 25–28] turns."

Lenski similarly states that "the seasons here meant continue from the destruction of Jerusalem to the time of the Parousia."[547]

With this judgment I am in agreement. The claim that "the time of the Gentiles ended May 14, 1948, when Israel became an independent state," and that "the Jews have returned to their country in fulfilment of prophecy" is contradicted by the following facts:

a. Even today only about one out of every five Jews is living in Israel.

b. Even today the very existence of Israel—and of Jerusalem as an independent Jewish city—is still being threatened.

c. The great majority of Jews do not regard Jesus as their Lord and Savior.

For much more on this see my book *Israel in Prophecy,* Grand Rapids, 1972.

For *Practical Lessons* and *Greek Words,* etc., see pp. 945–948.

---

25 "And there will be signs in sun and moon and stars, and upon the earth distress of nations in perplexity at the roaring of the surging sea. 26 People will be fainting from fear

---

547. See Greijdanus, *Korte Verklaring,* Vol. II, p. 194; and Lenski, *op. cit.,* p. 642.

and apprehension of the things that will happen to the world, for the powers of the heavens will be shaken.

27 "And then they will see the Son of man coming in a cloud, with power and great glory. 28 Now when these things are beginning to occur, look up and lift up y o u r heads, because y o u r redemption is drawing near."

21:25-28 *The Coming of the Son of Man*
Cf. Matt. 24:29-31; Mark 13:24-27

25, 26. And there will be signs in sun and moon and stars, and upon the earth distress of nations in perplexity at the roaring of the surging sea. People will be fainting from fear and apprehension of the things that will happen to the world, for the powers of the heavens will be shaken.

In connection, then, with Christ's return (see verse 27) there will be signs in the heavenly bodies, etc. The parallel passage (Matt. 24:29; cf. Mark 13:24) states, "The sun will be darkened, the moon will not give her light, and the stars will fall from the sky." Luke also mentions "the roaring of the surging sea," and indicates that, as a result of the *shaking* of "the powers of the heavens," people will be fainting from fear and apprehension.

That, at least with respect to sun, moon, and stars, this picture is deeply rooted in Old Testament prophecy has been shown in N.T.C. on Matthew, p. 862.

The total picture is indeed very vivid. All at once the sun becomes darkened. Naturally the moon now also ceases to impart its light. And since sun and moon exert a potent influence on our planet—think, for example, about the moon and the tides—it is not surprising that the sea also is deeply disturbed. Terrifying sounds are heard. Result of all this: People are frightened. They are fainting from fear.

Until this prophetic panorama becomes history we shall probably not know how much of this description must be taken literally and how much figuratively. That at least some of it must be taken literally is clear from II Peter 3:10. There will indeed be "a new heaven and earth" (Rev. 21:1). For the fourfold change that will take place—conflagration, rejuvenation, self-realization, and harmonization—see N.T.C. on Matthew, pp. 863, 864.

And now the second coming itself: **27. And then they will see the Son of man coming in a cloud, with power and great glory.**

This "they" must mean "all mankind," cf. Rev. 1:7. Matt. 24:30 states, "And then the sign of the Son of man will appear in the sky," but both Mark and Luke leave out the word *sign*. They simply represent Jesus as declaring that men will see "the Son of man coming" majestically. Probable solution: the very appearance of the Son of man upon clouds of glory is itself the sign, the one great final sign from the point of view of the earth. Christ's brilliant self-manifestation will be the sign or signal that *he* is about to go forth to meet his people, while *they* ascend to meet him in the air. He comes *to deliver* the oppressed elect people (see verse 28). In fact, he will gather *all* the elect—both the survivors and those who have previously fallen asleep—to himself, to be with him forever.

This appearance of the Son of man in majesty is a sign in still another respect: the glorious manner of his appearance corresponds exactly with the prediction of Dan. 7:13, 14; cf. Mark 14:62. The glory that marks the Son of man's sudden and brilliant manifestation is a definite proof of the Father's delight in his Son and of the justice of the cause of him who was once "a man of sorrows and acquainted with grief" (Isa. 53:3).

Note "the Son of man"—see on Luke 5:24; and note also "with power and great glory." That "power" is evident from what happens at his coming; see verses 25, 26; add Rev. 14:14–16; also 20:11. "And great glory," for at his coming all his attributes—power, wisdom, holiness, love, etc.—shine forth brilliantly.

As to "coming with a cloud," in Scripture the presence of God is often indicated by the mention of a cloud (Exod. 13:21; 16:10; 40:35; I Kings 8:10; Neh. 9:19; Ps. 78:14; Rev. 14:14, 16). And since Jesus is himself fully divine (John 1:1; Col. 2:9; Heb. 1:3), his coming "in a cloud" is altogether proper.

It is Luke alone who has preserved the very comforting word of Jesus: **28. Now when these things are beginning to occur, look up and lift up y o u r heads, because y o u r redemption is drawing near.**

"These things," that is, those mentioned in verses 25, 26, are the very things that will fill the hearts and minds of the rest of mankind with alarm. But for the followers of Christ who will then be living on earth these very things will be foreshadowings of imminent deliverance. For them the coming of these terrifying disturbances in the heavenly bodies and in the waters will mean that the days of their suffering will soon be over and gone. To be sure, no human being will ever know beforehand exactly when Jesus will return (Matt. 24:36), but God's children will know that the final tribulation will be of very brief duration (Matt. 24:22; Rev. 11:9–11; 20:3b), to be followed immediately by Christ's glorious return.

Together with this return will come their redemption. That redemption, which will already have been merited for them on the cross, and which they have already experienced in their souls, will then also be imparted to their bodies. Together with those children of God who have died earlier and whose souls will then be reunited with their wonderfully transformed bodies, they will ascend to meet Jesus in the air, to remain with him forevermore, now in the *full* possession of their salvation, to God's glory (I Thess. 4:17).

For *Practical Lessons* and *Greek Words,* etc., see pp. 945–948.

---

29 And he gave them this illustration:[548]
"Look at the fig tree and all the trees. 30 As soon as they sprout leaves, seeing (it) y o u

---

548. Literally: told them this parable.

know for yourselves that now the summer is near. 31 Similarly, when y o u see these things taking place, know then[549] that the kingdom[550] of God is near.

32 "I solemnly declare to y o u, this generation will certainly not pass away until all has taken place. 33 Heaven and earth will pass away, but my words will never pass away."

21:29-33 *The Lesson from the Fig Tree and All the Trees*
Cf. Matt. 24:32-35; Mark 13:28-31

The three synoptic accounts of this lesson are almost identical. The differences that should be briefly noted are as follows:

a. Luke reads, "Look at the fig tree *and all the trees*," as if to say, "What holds with respect to the fig tree is basically true also with respect to other fruit trees."

b. Instead of ". . . know then that *it* is near, at the very gates," Luke offers ". . . know then that the kingdom [or kingship, rule] of God is near."

c. When Luke writes "these things" (verse 31), this expression should be understood in the light of Luke's own context; that is, in the light of verses 25, 26, which, as has been indicated, relate to what is going to happen in connection with Christ's second coming.

To state it differently, Luke makes things a bit easier for us. He clearly differentiates between Jerusalem's fall and the final judgment. Contrast Matthew. In 24:15 f. that evangelist clearly refers to woes in connection with Jerusalem's fall. Note "then let those in Judea flee to the hills" (verse 16). In this connection he also mentions "great tribulation" (verse 21). But in verse 29 he writes, "Immediately after the tribulation of those days the sun shall be darkened," etc. This indicates that in Matthew's account the term *great tribulation* has a double reference, namely, to what happened at the time of Jerusalem's fall, and also to what will happen in connection with the Parousia. In Luke, however, we do not encounter that same difficulty. In verses 21-24 the destruction of Jerusalem is foretold. At the close of verse 24 the evangelist quotes Jesus' prediction that "Jerusalem will be trodden down by the Gentiles until the times of the Gentiles are fulfilled." That brings us to the end of the age, that is, to the second coming, including the signs accompanying it. So there is not really any great difficulty in explaining the words *these things* in verse 31. They naturally refer to the things mentioned in verses 25, 26.

29-31. And he gave them this illustration:

Look at the fig tree and all the trees. As soon as they sprout leaves, seeing (it) y o u know for yourselves that now the summer is near. Similarly, when y o u see these things taking place, know then that the kingdom of God is near.

---

549. Or: recognize.
550. Or: kingship, rule.

For the use of the word *parable*—here meaning "illustration"—in the original ("he told them this parable") see on 4:23-27, pp. 256-257.

The branch of a fig tree becomes soft and tender because of the sap that is swelling within it. It is not surprising, therefore, that soon this branch is generating leaves, and still more leaves. Now when this happens to a fig tree—or, for that matter, to fruit trees in general[551]—the disciples realize that the summer is near. Similarly when the things mentioned in the present context (verses 25, 26, signs in sun, moon, and stars, etc.) take place, believers then living must recognize that "the kingdom of God" in its final manifestation is at the very door. Christ's royal reign in the new heaven and earth is at hand. And no longer will "the dragon and his allies" (Rev. 12:3; 13:1, 11) be able to do any damage.

In close connection with this, Jesus now makes the declaration: **32. I solemnly declare to y o u, this generation will certainly not pass away until all has taken place.**

Probable meaning of this passage: "This generation, namely, the Jewish people [see Deut. 32:5, 20; Ps. 12:7; 78:8, etc.] will not cease to exist until all those things which I [Jesus] predicted have happened." The expression *all* or *all things* covers the events predicted for the entire dispensation (see verses 6-31), including even the Lord's glorious return. For the detailed argument in defense of this interpretation and for refutation of other theories see N.T.C. on the parallel passage, Matt. 24 (pp. 867-869 of that commentary).

The section ends with the majestic statement **33. Heaven and earth will pass away, but my words will never pass away.** The abiding character of Christ's message, over against the transient nature even of "heaven and earth" in their present condition, is the foundation on which faith can build. See also Isa. 40:8; John 15:7; Col. 3:16; I Peter 1:24, 25.

For *Practical Lessons* and *Greek Words,* etc., see pp. 945-948.

---

34 "Ever be on y o u r guard, lest y o u r hearts be loaded down with dissipation, drunkenness, and the anxieties of life, and that day close on y o u unexpectedly, like a trap.   35 For it will come upon all those who live on the face of the entire earth.   36 Keep watch at all times, praying that y o u may have strength to escape all these things that are going to take place, and to take y o u r stand before the Son of man."

37 Now during the days Jesus was teaching in the temple, but during the nights he would go out and lodge on the hill called the Mount of Olives.   38 And all the people would rise early to go to him in the temple and hear him.

---

551. H. Mulder, *Spoorzocker in Bijbelse Landen,* p. 93, is of the opinion that the fig tree is singled out here because it generally produces leaves later than other fruit trees; for example, much later than the almond tree. See also N.T.C. on Matthew, p. 866. The great popularity and abundance of fig trees should also be taken into account.

21:34-38 *Exhortation to Watch*
Summary of Final
Days in the Temple
and
Nights on the Mountain

34-36. Ever be on y o u r guard, lest y o u r hearts be loaded down with dissipation, drunkenness, and the anxieties of life, and that day close on y o u unexpectedly, like a trap. For it will come upon all those who live on the face of the entire earth. Keep watch at all times, praying that y o u may have strength to escape all these things that are going to take place, and to take y o u r stand before the Son of man.

In the preceding verses Jesus has provided much food for *thought.* In answer to the disciples' question (21:7) he has furnished information. He has predicted the destruction of the temple, imminent persecution, political upheavals, fear-inspiring happenings in the realm of nature, family divisions, the fall of Jerusalem, and finally, his own glorious return and the signs accompanying it.

He knows, however, that these men, and also those who would follow them down the lane of the centuries, stand in need of more than information. As a tenderly loving Shepherd he wishes to give them something for the heart, the inner self, as well as for the mind. He knows that often a person's inner drives, his emotions, or else perhaps his friends or associates, may bring him to a fall. So he admonishes them to be on their guard, and this always.

Are we shocked to read that he even issued a warning against such evils as *dissipation,* that is, excessive indulgence in pleasures, and *drunkenness?* But is it not true that when we today look back or even look round about us, we see a good many church members, or perhaps former church members, who have ruined or are ruining their lives by yielding to these very temptations? And is anyone free from the temptation of giving in to worrying about the cares of day by day living? By leaning on one's own imagined resources, and by neglecting prayer, one can easily fall into a trap. Against this the Savior issues a badly needed warning.

All the more urgent is this warning because "it," that is, the final day, including the judgment, will come for everybody, without exception. Cf. 17:26-30. Only by being watchful at all times, through fervent prayer and consecrated living, can one escape the terrors of that day, and thus, by God's sovereign grace, take his stand, without fear, before the Son of man (see on 5:24).

37. Now during the days Jesus was teaching in the temple, but during the nights he would go out and lodge on the hill called the Mount of Olives.

Luke closes this chapter by informing us where Jesus spent these last few days and nights before his crucifixion. See also 19:47, 48. During these

944

days he was busily engaged teaching in the temple. Cf. 22:53. For the contents of some of this temple teaching see on 20:1 ff.; 21:1 ff. We have noted before that Luke places special emphasis on the relation of Jesus to his Father's house, the temple. See *Introduction,* point V D; also on 4:2a.

The nights, however, he would spend on Mt. Olivet. Or, according to Mark's phraseology (11:19), "And whenever evening arrived, they went out of the city." The verb used by Luke for *to lodge* or *to pass the night* may mean either (a) that Jesus (in the company of his disciples) camped out in the open somewhere on one of the slopes of this hill, or (b) that he lodged there, perhaps at the home of friends, for there were clusters of homes in that vicinity.

38. And all the people would rise early to go to him in the temple and hear him.

There must have been thousands upon thousands of people in Jerusalem just then. In addition to those who had their residence in the city, pilgrims had come from all over to attend the Passover. Cf. Acts 2:5-11. They wanted by all means to hear Jesus. It was for that very reason that the Jewish leaders did not dare to arrest him. They were afraid of the people (Luke 22:2).

The crucifixion, accordingly, would be timed according to *God's* timetable, not that of the priests.

What mainly interests us, however, is the fact that so close to the day of his indescribable suffering Jesus was still engaged in "the work the Father gave him to do." He was still thinking not just about himself but definitely also about others, people whom he wanted to save. Luke pictures him therefore as being throughout "a merciful and faithful highpriest in service to God" (Heb. 2:17).[552]

Practical Lessons Derived from Luke 21:20-38

Verse 24

"And Jerusalem will be trampled underfoot by the Gentiles until the times of the Gentiles are fulfilled." God fulfils his threats. Therefore we know that he will also fulfil his promises, for God is holy and he is love. He will fulfil his promises with respect to both Jew and Gentile, for "there is no distinction" (Rom. 10:12).

Verses 26, 27

"The powers of the heavens will be shaken. And then they will see the Son of man coming in a *cloud."*

The universe is shaking violently. Nevertheless, nothing prevents a *cloud* from serving as a means of conveyance for Christ! Does not this indicate that whatever happens to the realm of nature at Christ's return is firmly in God's hand, and is

---

552. Notes on Greek words, phrases, and constructions in 21:20-38 begin on page 946.

therefore not the product of physical forces and of circumstances over which God has no control?

Hence, one has a right to sing:

> Though the earth be shaking,
> Every heart be quaking,
> Jesus calms my fear.
> Fires may flash and thunder crash,
> Yea, and sin and hell assail me,
> Jesus shall not fail me.

Lines from "Jesus Precious Treasure"
by Johann Franck; tr. by Catherine Winkworth.

Verses 33, 34

"Heaven and earth will pass away, but my words will never pass away.... Ever be on y o u r guard, lest y o u r hearts be loaded [or weighed] down with dissipation," etc.

Is there any connection between these two lines?

A minister announced as his text, "Thanks be to God, who gives us the victory through our Lord Jesus Christ.... Now concerning the collection" (I Cor. 15:57; 16:1). No connection? Does not the outburst of thanksgiving, and this for a very good reason, call for a generous offering?

So also here in Luke 21:33, 34. Does not the certainty—note, "My words will never pass away"—of Christ's return unto judgment point to the necessity of consecrated living? Especially in view of Matt. 25:31–46?

Verse 38

"And all the people would rise early to go to him." If this is done in the proper spirit, is it not a fitting response to (figuratively speaking) God's *rising early* in order to call sinners to repentance? See Jer. 7:13, 25; 25:3, 4; 26:5; 29:19; 32:33; 35:14, 15; 44:4?

Notes on Greek Words, Phrases, and Constructions in 21:20–38

Verse 20

κυκλουμένην, fem. acc. s. pres. pass. participle of κυκλόω, to encircle. Though in Luke's Gospel this verb is found only here, it occurs also in Acts 14:20 and in John 10:24; Heb. 11:30. See the note on 9:12 on page 484 for a related form.

Verse 21

Note the three third per. pl. pres. (inchoative) imperatives; let them flee, get out, not enter.

Verse 22

ἐκδικήσεως, gen. s. of ἐκδίκησις, retribution, satisfaction, vengeance, punishment, justice (cf. 18:7, 8).

τοῦ πληθῆναι, articular aor. pass. infinitive of πίμπλημι, "that . . . may be ful-filled." See also the note on 1:15 on page 80.

Verse 24

αἰχμαλωτισθήσονται, third per. pl. fut. pass. indicat. of αἰχμαλωτίζω—from αἰχμή, spear, and ἁλίσκομαι, to capture—hence, originally: to capture with the spear; and so simply: to capture, to carry off as captives. See also the note on 4:18 on page 260. The verb also occurs in Rom. 7:23; II Cor. 10:5; II Tim. 3:6.

ἔσται πατουμένη, third per. s. periphrastic fut. pass. of πατέω, to tread, trample. See the note on 10:19 on page 589. In the New Testament this verb is found only in Luke and in the book of Revelation (11:2; 14:20; 19:15).

πληρωθῶσιν, third per. pl. aor. (effective) subjunct. pass. (after ἄχρι) of πληρόω, and thus futuristic in meaning. See what was said in the explanation of 1:1, as to Luke's conviction that history is a fulfilment of prophecy, a realization of God's eternal plan; and see the note on 1:1 on page 61 for the synonym πληροφορέω.

Verses 25, 26

συνοχή, from συνέχω, to hold together; here in the sense of to compress, con-strain. The noun, accordingly, acquires the meaning constraint, distress, anguish.

ἀπορία, basically the condition of being without (ἀ) a πόρος, way or means, resource; hence, being at a loss as to what to do, perplexity.

ἤχους, gen. s. of ἦχος, sound; here in the sense of roaring.

σάλου, gen. s. of σάλος*, surging, rolling; used only here in the New Testament. However, note also σαλευθήσονται at the close of verse 26, third per. pl. fut. indicat. pass. of the cognate verb σαλεύω, to shake.

Literally verse 25 reads, "And there will be signs in sun and moon and stars, and upon the earth distress of nations, in perplexity at roaring and surging [or swelling] of sea."

Note also (at beginning of verse 26) gen. absolute "people fainting."

ἀποψυχόντων (from ἀπό and ψύχω), to breathe away from, breathe out, faint.

προσδοκίας, gen. s. of προσδοκία**, here apprehension, dread; in Acts 12:11 anticipation, expectation.

Verse 28

ἀνακύψατε and ἐπάρατε, sec. per. pl. aor. imperatives. Here the meaning is look up (but see also the note on 13:11 on page 713) and lift up (see the note on 16:23 on page 789).

ἀπολύτρωσις (ἀπό plus λύτρον), basically, the act of delivering a person from bondage by the payment of a ransom; hence here redemption. The word also occurs in Rom. 3:24; 8:23; I Cor. 1:30; Eph. 1:7, 14; 4:30; Col. 1:14; Heb. 9:15; 11:35. Cf. German Erlösung; Dutch verlossing.

Verses 30, 31

προβάλωσιν, third per. pl. 2nd aor. act. (ingressive) subjunct. (after ὅταν) of προβάλλω** (πρό and βάλλω), to thrust forward, project; here: sprout leaves; in Acts 19:33, to push to the front. In the New Testament these are the only occur-rences of this verb.

γινώσκετε, in verse 30: sec. per. pl. pres. indicat., but in all probability in verse 31 sec. per. pl. pres. *imperat.*

Verse 33

Note double negative for emphasis: will *certainly not*, will *never.*

παρελεύσονται, third per. pl. fut. indicat. of παρέρχομαι. See comprehensive discussion of this verb in the note on 15:29 on page 763.

Verse 34

προσέχετε, sec. per. pl. pres. imperat. of προσέχω, to turn (one's mind) to, and be on one's guard against, look out for, give heed to, be concerned about, etc. The exact translation, in any given case, depends on the specific context.

βαρηθῶσιν, third per. pl. aor. subjunct. pass. of βαρέω, to weigh down, burden; in pass. to be weighed down, be heavy. See the note on 9:32 on page 511.

κραιπάλῃ, dat. of κραιπάλη*, drunken headache, dissipation. In the New Testament only here. Cf. *crapulence.*

βιωτικαῖς, fem. dat. pl. of βιωτικός, pertaining to (or: of) this life.

ἐπιστῇ, third per. s. 2nd aor. (ingressive) subjunct. of ἐφίστημι; here: to spring (or: close suddenly) upon. See also the note on 2:9 on page 160, and the note on 10:40 on page 603.

αἰφνίδιος, sudden. This is an *adjective* agreeing with ἡμέρα: "and that day spring upon y o u (as something) sudden, like a trap." English idiom, however, requires "and that day spring [or close] upon y o u suddenly, like a trap," or something similar.

παγίς, a trap; "like a trap" = "suddenly," "unexpectedly." See also Rom. 11:9; I Tim. 3:7; 6:9; II Tim. 2:26.

Verse 36

ἀγρυπνεῖτε, sec. per. pres. imperat. of ἀγρυπνέω, to keep awake, keep watch. An interesting etymology is:

ἀγρυπνέω = ἄγρα, a catch, chase; plus ὕπνος, sleep; hence, "chase sleep away," and so: keep watch. But this etymology is uncertain.

κατισχύσητε, sec. per. pl. aor. subjunct. (after ἵνα) of κατισχύω, to have strength, be able, prevail.

σταθῆναι, aor. pass. infinitive of ἵστημι; here: to stand, take a stand.

Verses 37, 38

ἦν διδάσκων, periphrastic imperfect act. of διδάσκω, to teach.

ηὐλίζετο, third per. s. imperf. (iterative) of αὐλίζομαι, in the New Testament only here and in Matt. 21:17; basically, to spend the night in the αὐλή, on which see the note on 22:55 on pp. 1000, 1001; and so: to spend the night, lodge. Cf. N.T.C. on Matthew, footnote 732 on p. 772.

ὤρθριζεν, third per. s. imperf. (iterative) of ὀρθρίζω*, to get up early in the morning; cf. ὄρθρος, daybreak, dawn.

Summary of Chapter 21

Having exposed the hypocrisy of the scribes (20:45-47), Jesus, in commending the total commitment of a widow who dropped into the temple treasury two very small coins, which was all she had, not only contrasted hypocrisy with sincerity but also showed how widows should be treated (verses 1-4).

While Jesus and The Twelve were walking away from the temple, his disciples made remarks about its "goodly stones and votive offerings." Jesus answered, "Days will come when there will not be left one stone upon another that will not be thrown down." The astonished men wanted to know when this would happen and what would be the sign whereby they could know that it was about to take place. As the parallel passage, Matt. 24:3, shows, they thought that the destruction of the temple would mean the end of the world. So they wanted to know what would be the sign that both of these events were about to occur. Jesus is, therefore, going to show that these two things (destruction of Jerusalem and end of the world) will not coincide, and that there will be two signs, two visible spectacles instead of only one. One of these signs will be the encirclement of Jerusalem by invading armies, the other the appearance of Jesus in the sky, about to descend. However, the second "sign" is not so designated by Mark and Luke, only by Matthew (verses 5-7).

Jesus then pointed out that such things as wars, insurrections, earthquakes, famines, pestilences, portents in the sky would not be indications of the end. He predicted that before any of these would take place the persecution of the disciples would start. They would be betrayed even by members of their immediate families. But they must regard all such happenings as "opportunities to testify," Jesus himself promising to provide them with "words of wisdom" to speak. He added, "By means of y o u r endurance y o u will win y o u r souls" (verses 8-19).

"When y o u see Jerusalem being surrounded by armies, then understand that its desolation is near," says Jesus. He tells them that when these armies begin their encirclement the people in Judea should flee to the hills, those in the city should get out, and those in the country should stay out. In the fall of Jerusalem Old Testament prophecies would go into fulfilment. He expresses deep concern over pregnant and over nursing women. He predicts that many people will be killed or taken captive, and states, "Jerusalem will be trampled underfoot by the Gentiles until the times of the Gentiles are fulfilled" (verses 20-24).

As do Matthew and Mark, so also Luke represents Jesus as predicting that certain astonishing phenomena will accompany his return: "the powers of the heavens will be shaken." Luke adds, "and upon the earth distress of nations in perplexity at the roaring of the surging sea."

"And then," continues Luke, "they will see the Son of man coming in a cloud, with power and great glory" (Matthew's second *sign*). Luke has preserved Christ's very comforting words, "Now when these things are beginning to occur, look up and lift up y o u r heads, because y o u r redemption is drawing near" (verses 25–28).

"The lesson from the fig tree and all the trees" may be summarized as follows: "Just as leaves appearing on trees announce that summer is near, so also when y o u see these things taking place y o u should realize that the kingdom of God (in its final manifestation) is near." Jesus further solemnly predicts that the Jews as a people will continue to live on earth "until all has taken place," that is, "until the very end of the world" (verses 29–33).

In conclusion Jesus, according to Luke's report, adds that the contemplation of all these predictions should lead to an attitude of watchfulness, a life of sanctification.

Having finished reporting Christ's discourse, Luke adds that during his final very brief stay in Jerusalem Jesus was in the habit of teaching in the temple during the daytime and lodging on Mt. Olivet at night. He concludes his account as follows, "And all the people would rise early to go to him in the temple and hear him" (verses 34–38).

Outline of Chapter 22

Theme: *The Work Thou Gavest Him to Do*

---

553. 22:63–71 can also be considered *one* section, indicating what happened in connection with The Trial Before the Sanhedrin. In reality that section is already introduced in verse 54. Though Luke describes a mockery of Jesus in verses 63–65, he omits a later mockery (Matt. 27:27–31; Mark 15:16–20; John 19:2, 3).

CHAPTER XXII

22 1 Now the feast of Unleavened Bread, called the Passover, was approaching. 2 So the chief priests and the scribes were looking for a way to do away with Jesus, for they were afraid of the people. 3 Then Satan entered Judas, called Iscariot, one of the twelve. 4 He went off and discussed with the chief priests and the captains of the temple guards how he might betray Jesus to them. 5 They were delighted and agreed to give him money. 6 He, in turn, consented, and began to look for a good opportunity to hand him over to them in the absence of a crowd.

22:1-6 *The Plot of the Chief Priests and Scribes to Kill Jesus*
and
The Agreement Between Judas and the Plotters
Cf. Matt. 26:1-5, 14-16; Mark 14:1, 2, 10, 11; John 11:45-53

1. Now the feast of Unleavened Bread, called the Passover, was approaching.

For the manner in which the three final chapters of the Synoptics parallel each other see N.T.C. on Mark, pp. 549-552.

A reasonable assumption is that Jesus was crucified in the year A.D. 30, when the fourteenth day of Nisan fell on Thursday, and the fifteenth on Friday. In Israel the first appearance of the new moon marked the beginning of the new month. It was marked by the blowing of trumpets, sacrifices, celebrations, suspension of ordinary business, and wherever necessary by signal fires (Num. 10:10; 28:11-14; Ps. 81:3-5; Amos 8:5, 6). The important days of the month—for example, the tenth of the month Nisan, when the Passover lamb was selected, the killing of the lamb on the fourteenth, etc.—were figured from the first day, or day of the new moon, as a base. See the detailed regulations in Exod. 12:1-14; Num. 9:2-14; Deut. 16:1; cf. Esther 3:7.

There is no good reason to believe that Jesus and his disciples ate the lamb and celebrated Passover either earlier or later than on the appointed day. The fourteenth of Nisan was the day when the lamb "had to be sacrificed" (Luke 22:7). It is also clear that immediately after the eating of the lamb and the institution of what has come to be known as "the Lord's Supper" Jesus and his disciples (with the exception of Judas, who had left earlier for his own destination, John 13:30) went to Gethsemane (Mark 14:32; Luke 22:39; John 18:1). Here, during what we would call the night from Thursday to Friday Jesus was taken into custody. Early Friday morning the Sanhedrin "took counsel against Jesus to put him to death" (Matt. 27:1; Luke 22:66–71). He was led to Pilate that same morning and crucified that same day (Mark 15:1, 25; Luke 23:1, 33). It is clear, therefore, that Jesus was crucified on Friday, the day before the sabbath (Mark 15:42, 43; Luke 23:46, 54; John 19:14, 30, 42). It was early in the morning of the day "after the sabbath"—hence on Sunday, the first day of the week— that some women went to the tomb and heard the startling news, "He is risen" (Matt. 28:1, 6; Mark 16:2, 6; Luke 24:1, 6; John 20:1).

Therefore, the theory according to which Jesus was crucified on Thursday is opposed by the evidence of the Gospels.[554]

The day on which the lamb was killed was followed by the seven-day feast of the Unleavened Bread,[555] celebrated from the fifteenth to the twenty-first of Nisan. So close was the connection between the Passover meal proper and the festival of the Unleavened Bread which followed immediately that the term *Passover* is sometimes used to cover both, as clearly here in Luke 22:1.[556]

Since the feast of the Passover, etc., was "approaching" (Luke 22:1), "two days off" (Mark 14:1), it must have been Tuesday when Christ's enemies held their meeting for the purpose of plotting how to bring about the arrest and death of Jesus.

Such a meeting, for which see Matt. 26:3, is not mentioned in Mark and Luke, only in Matthew, but is probably implied in verse

2. So the chief priests and the scribes were looking for a way to do away with Jesus, for they were afraid of the people.

The plotters were "the chief priests and the scribes"; according to Matt. 26:3 also "the elders of the people." A description of the three groups has been given in the explanation of Luke 20:1, 2.

The plan to kill Jesus was of long standing, as is clear from such passages as Mark 3:6; 11:18; 12:7, 12; John 5:18; 7:1, 19, 25; 8:37, 40; 11:53. In Luke see especially 19:47; 20:19. In fact the present passage (22:2) is virtually a repetition of 19:47, 48 and 20:19, for in all three passages it is

---

554. On this question see also N.T.C. on Matthew, p. 534. The "crucifixion on Thursday" theory was revived by Roger Rusk, in the March 29, 1974 issue of *Christianity Today*, pp. 720–722. It was refuted by Harold W. Hoehner in the April 26, 1974 issue, pp. 878, 881. As Hoehner points out, if Jesus had died on Thursday instead of on Friday, Pilate would have secured the sepulcher until the fourth day, not the third (Matt. 27:62–66). As to the computer which established the exact times of all the new and full moons from 1001 B.C. to A.D. 1651, and confirmed the fact that in the year A.D. 30 the fourteenth of Nisan occurred on Thursday, the fifteenth on Friday, though this information is interesting and helpful, yet as far as the date A.D. 30 is concerned it is not exactly new. See, for example, P. Schaff, *History of the Christian Church*, New York, 1916, Vol. I, p. 135.

555. Note the plural τὰ ἄζυμα, probably referring to the unleavened cakes of bread, and based on the Hebrew plural *matzoth*. Besides, it must be borne in mind that this was a feast lasting *several* days and including *many* festive activities. That fact too may account for the plural. See N.T.C. on Matthew, pp. 792, 793.

556. See also S.BK., Vol. IV, pp. 41–76.

either stated or implied that the plotters "were afraid of the people." It must be borne in mind that Jesus had many followers, especially among the Galileans who had come to the feast. Add to this the fact that especially during Passover the thought of deliverance from the Roman yoke was uppermost in the minds of many, and it will be evident that there was sound basis for the fear in the hearts of Christ's opponents. According to Matt. 26:57 the plotters met in the palace of Caiaphas the highpriest. Does this mean, then, that it was Caiaphas who was mainly responsible for the plot against Jesus? Well, John 11:47–53 may seem to point in that direction, and undoubtedly that conclusion may well be correct, at least to some extent. Caiaphas must have played a very important role. On the other hand, is not the theory justified that back of Caiaphas stood Annas? See N.T.C. on John, Vol. II, pp. 385–388.

3, 4. Then Satan entered Judas, called Iscariot, one of the twelve. He went off and discussed with the chief priests and the captains of the temple guards how he might betray Jesus to them.

The connection with the immediately preceding context is very close. Christ's enemies were looking for an opportunity to arrest him without creating a riot. See also John 11:57. Judas makes matters easier for them by volunteering to deliver their enemy to them secretly; that is, without public disturbance.

Why did Judas do this? Answer: because Satan had entered his heart. Full justice must be done to this fact, mentioned also by John (13:27). The active part played by Satan in the events of Passion Week must not be ignored. See also Gen. 3:15; Luke 4:13; 22:31, 32.

All this, however, does not clear Judas from blame. See Luke 22:22. Judas was guilty because he failed to resist the devil (I Peter 5:8, 9). For more on the reasons which may have prompted Judas to yield to the influence of Satan and to betray Jesus, see above, on 6:16, under the heading *Judas Iscariot.*

For his shockingly loathsome deed there was no excuse whatever. Judas was, after all, a specially privileged person. He was "one of the twelve," as all four evangelists take the trouble to point out (Matt. 26:14; Mark 14:10; Luke 22:3; John 6:70, 71). For many months Judas had been living in Christ's immediate presence, had been eating, drinking, and traveling with him. He had noticed the strength in the Master's voice when he stilled the storm, cursed the barren fig tree, and rebuked those who devoured widows' houses. But Judas had also become aware of the tenderness of that same voice when it pleaded with sinners, including Judas(!), to come to him and rest. He had listened to the Savior's marvelous discourses and to the decisive and authoritative answers he had given to the many questions that had been hurled at him, sometimes with the intention of ensnaring him. Judas had watched the Great Physician in the act of tenderly restoring the handicapped, or bending down mercifully over the sick and healing them ... and then even adding (at times), *"Your* faith has made you well."

Yes, Judas had witnessed all this and much more. Cf. Matt. 13:17. And then he decided to deliver this unsurpassably powerful, wise, and compassionate Benefactor into the hands of cruel men . . . "for thirty pieces of silver."

We are not at all surprised to read:

5, 6. They were delighted and agreed to give him money. He, in turn, consented, and began to look for a good opportunity to hand him over to them in the absence of a crowd.

The chief priests and captains of the temple guard were delighted. Their problem was solved. So the price was agreed on and paid. It is Matthew alone who mentions the amount of money the traitor received (26:15). This too was fulfilment of prophecy. See N.T.C. on that passage in Matthew's Gospel.

For *Practical Lessons* and *Greek Words,* etc., see pp. 965–969.

---

7 Then came the day of Unleavened Bread, on which the Passover lamb had to be sacrificed. 8 So Jesus sent Peter and John, saying (to them), "Go and make preparations for us to eat the Passover."

9 They asked him, "Where do you want us to prepare it?" 10 He replied, "Just after y o u enter the city a man carrying a jar of water will meet y o u. Follow him into the house to which he is going, 11 and say to the owner of the house, 'The Teacher asks, Where is my guest room in which I may eat the Passover with my disciples?' 12 And he will show y o u a large upper room, furnished. There make ready."

13 So they went away and found (everything) just as Jesus had told them; and they prepared the Passover.

THURSDAY AND FRIDAY
22:7–13 *The Preparation of the Passover*
Cf. Matt. 26:17–19; Mark 14:12–16; or,
including the Passover itself,
Cf. Matt. 26:17–25; Mark 14:12–21; John 13:1–30

7, 8. Then came the day of Unleavened Bread, on which the Passover lamb had to be sacrificed. So Jesus sent Peter and John, saying (to them), Go and make preparations for us to eat the Passover.

Finally the first day of the festival arrived, Thursday, the fourteenth of Nisan. It was the day when the Passover lamb had to be sacrificed. Cf. Exod. 12:6; Lev. 23:5, 6.

Luke does not say anything about the purchase of the lamb. We may assume that this had been attended to a few days earlier. See Exod. 12:3. Further preparations had to be made, however. During the afternoon the lamb must be killed in the forecourt of the temple (Exod. 12:6). A room of sufficient size must be obtained, and everything in connection with this room and its furniture must be arranged. Besides, purchases must be made: unleavened bread, bitter herbs, wine, etc. The lamb must be made ready for use, the sauce must be prepared. Since by now it was probably Thursday morning, there could be no delay.

The words "the day . . . on which the Passover lamb had to be sacrificed" are probably added by Luke for the sake of his Gentile readers.

So, in answer to the question of his disciples, "Where do you want us to go and prepare the Passover Supper?" (Mark 14:12), Jesus gives instructions to two disciples, namely, to Peter and John, as Luke alone informs us. He orders them to go and make preparations for the feast.

9-12. They asked him, Where do you want us to prepare it? He replied, Just after y o u enter the city a man carrying a jar of water will meet y o u. Follow him into the house to which he is going, and say to the owner of the house, The Teacher asks, Where is my guest room in which I may eat the Passover with my disciples? And he will show y o u a large upper room, furnished. There make ready.

It is clear that the directions given are in a sense very definite; in another sense very indefinite. They are definite enough so that the two men will experience no difficulty in finding the place where the supper is to be held. Yet, they are indefinite enough for the present to conceal the name of the owner of the house and the location of his home. The indefiniteness may very well have been due to the fact that not until evening must Judas know where the Passover is kept. Jesus must be able before his arrest to observe the feast with his disciples, must have time to institute what has come to be known as "the Lord's Supper," to deliver his touchingly beautiful "Supper Room Discourses" (John 14-16), and to pray his Highpriestly Prayer (John 17). If early in the day Judas had known where Jesus would be in the evening, he could have informed the chief priests, etc., who could then have arrested Jesus without any crowd being present, since the people in general would be eating the supper at that time, group by group in ever so many separate homes. Cf. Exod. 12:3, 4.

The two disciples will have no difficulty in locating the place. What they will see upon entering the city will be something rather strange: a *man* carrying a jar or jug of water. *Men* usually carried water in a skin; *women* in a jar. Peter and John are directed to enter the house where this man is going.

The man who carries this jar must not be confused with the owner of the house which he enters. The exact relation of the water carrier and the owner is not known. He may have been the owner's servant, relative, or friend.

It is reasonable to assume that at least the owner—the other man also?—was a disciple of Jesus, ready to serve the Master in every possible way. In answer to their question this owner will show Peter and John a large upper room, "furnished." The original uses a word that has the basic sense "spread." When this is taken literally, it is sometimes interpreted to indicate such things as couches "with coverings *spread* over them." Thus Moffatt offers the translation "a large room upstairs with couches spread." Others accept the rendering "paved with tile." But an *unfurnished*, merely *paved*, room would not serve the purpose for which Jesus wanted to use it. And since, in the process of time, words often acquire meanings other than (but often related to) their original sense, it is entirely possible that the interpretation given to this word by most English translators, namely, "furnished (perhaps with carpets, couches, and table)" is correct.

It was in that room that Peter and John must prepare the Passover.

13. So they went away and found (everything) just as Jesus had told them; and they prepared the Passover.

In this connection the question has been asked, "How did Jesus know that the two disciples would, upon entering the city, have exactly these experiences?" A previous detailed agreement between Jesus and the owner of the house has been suggested.[557] Others, however, mention "supernatural knowledge" on the part of Jesus.[558] And does not the very fact that Luke includes verse 13, as if he is recording something wonderful, something that must not escape the attention of the reader, confirm the second theory? What we have here should probably be regarded as in a class with such other passages as Matt. 17:27; John 1:47-50; 2:24, 25; 21:17; and perhaps also Luke 19:29 f., all of them either stating or at least implying that Jesus would at times draw upon the omniscience which he, as the Son of God, shared with the Father and the Holy Spirit.

In connection with "and they prepared the Passover" it is probably necessary to assert once again that Jesus partook of the Passover and instituted the Lord's Supper *at the regular time,* namely, on what we would call Thursday. It was on that day, the fourteenth of Nisan, that the lamb had to be slaughtered and the preparations for the feast had to be made. It is true that by Jewish time reckoning the new day began at sunset, so that when the feast was proceeding it was already the fifteenth of Nisan.

All four Gospels support the theory: Passover and institution of the Lord's Supper, Thursday; crucifixion, Friday (still the fifteenth of Nisan).

The question may be asked, however, "Is not this theory in conflict with John 18:28, according to which early Friday morning Christ's bitter enemies—they hated Jesus—'in order that they might not be defiled but might eat the Passover, did not enter the governor's residence'?" Answer: there is no conflict. For what may well be the solution of this problem see N.T.C. on John, Vol. II, pp. 401-404.

For *Practical Lessons* and *Greek Words,* etc., see pp. 965-969.

---

14 Now when the hour had come Jesus reclined at table, and the apostles with him.　15 He said to them, "I have eagerly desired to eat this Passover with y o u before I suffer.　16 For I tell y o u that I shall never eat it again until it is fulfilled in the kingdom of God."

17 Then he received a cup, gave thanks, and said, "Take this and divide it among yourselves;　18 for I assure y o u that from now on I will not drink from the fruit of the vine until the kingdom of God comes."

---

557. So, for example, Geldenhuys, *op. cit.,* p. 552.
558. Lenski, *op. cit.,* p. 652; cf. Greijdanus, *Korte Verklaring,* p. 213.

19 Then he took (some) bread, gave thanks, broke it, and gave it to them, saying, "This is my body given for y o u. This do in remembrance of me."

20 And in the same way after supper (he took) the cup, saying, "This cup (is) the new covenant in my blood, poured out for y o u.[559]

21 "But look! The hand of the man who is betraying[560] me is with me on the table. 22 For the Son of man is going as it has been decreed, but woe to that man by whom he is being[561] betrayed!"

23 Then they began to discuss among themselves which of them it might be who was going to do this.

22:14-23 *Passover and the Institution of the Lord's Supper*
For 22:14-20 cf. Matt. 26:26-30; Mark 14:22-26;
John 13:31—18:1; I Cor. 11:23-25
For 22:21-23 cf. Matt. 26:21-25; Mark 14:18-21;
John 13:21-30

A few preliminary matters require our attention first of all:

a. Much has been written about the question whether verses 19b through 20 (beginning with "given for y o u," verse 19, and ending with "poured out for y o u," verse 20) are genuine. Did Luke write them or did he not? This question is discussed in the note on verses 19-21 on pp. 968, 969. My answer is that the verses are indeed authentic, part of God's inspired Word. The reasons for taking this position are given in that note.

b. It is well-nigh impossible to enter into the meaning of the present section without some knowledge of the nature of the Jewish Passover Feast, especially the manner in which the various elements of the Passover meal followed each other. So here is a brief description, based on the best available sources:

The Order of The Passover Feast[562]

The main elements were as follows:

1. A prayer of thanksgiving by the head of the house; drinking the first cup of (diluted) wine.

2. The eating of bitter herbs, as a reminder of the bitter slavery in Egypt.

3. The son's inquiry, "Why is this night distinguished from all other nights?" and the father's appropriate reply, either narrated or read.

---

559. For the textual question with respect to verses 19b, 20 ("given for y o u . . . poured out for y o u") see the note on this passage on pp. 968, 969.

560. Or: is going to betray.

561. Or: is to be.

562. See the following sources:
Mishnah Pesaḥim X. 2-10.
S.BK. on Matt. 26.
A. Edersheim, *The Temple*, pp. 208-248 (especially pp. 238-246).
S. Greijdanus, *Korte Verklaring*, Vol. II, p. 218.
J. B. Segal, *The Jewish Passover from the Earliest Times to A.D. 70*, London, 1963.

4. The singing of the first part of the Hallel (Psalms 113, 114), and the washing of hands. The second cup.

5. The carving and eating of the lamb, together with unleavened bread. The lamb was eaten in commemoration of what the ancestors had been commanded to do in the night when the Lord smote all the first-born of Egypt and delivered his people (Exod. 12 and 13). The unleavened bread was in commemoration of "the bread of haste" eaten by the ancestors.

6. Continuation of the meal, each eating as much as he liked, but always last of the lamb. The third cup.

7. Singing of the last part of the Hallel (Psalms 115-118). Fourth cup.

c. Luke's account, though not strictly chronological, is certainly orderly. Verses 14-38 can be divided as follows:

(1) Jesus addresses The Twelve, informing them that this is his final Passover "until it is fulfilled in the kingdom of God" (verses 14-16).

(2) He partakes of the Passover with his disciples (verses 17, 18).

(3) In connection with the conclusion of the Passover meal he institutes the Lord's Supper (verses 19, 20).

(4) Having briefly indicated what Jesus, during this evening and night, did for his disciples and (by means of the institution of the Lord's Supper) for the Church at large, Luke now shows how they, in turn, are reacting to Jesus and his teaching. He shows this in connection with Judas (verses 21-23), The Twelve (verses 24-30), Simon (verses 31-34), and again, the little group as a whole (verses 35-38). And in each case they—Judas, etc.— are not in control of the situation. *He, the Lord,* is. *His* word is final!

14-16. Now when the hour had come Jesus reclined at table, and the apostles with him. He said to them, I have eagerly desired to eat this Passover with y o u before I suffer. For I tell y o u that I shall never eat it again until it is fulfilled in the kingdom of God.

Reclining at table with The Twelve the soul of Jesus is surcharged with deep emotion, to which he gives utterance in words preserved by Luke alone. Note the following:

a. "I have eagerly desired." Cf. "I am overwhelmed" (12:50).

b. Not only "to eat this Passover," but to do so "*with y o u.*" Does not this remind us of John 13:1, "having loved his own, he loved them to the uttermost"? Jesus knew what his death, within a matter of hours, would do for them (taken as a group), and of course for millions of others also. He loved them with a love inexpressible in words.

c. "... before I suffer." But the Lord realized that this suffering would not be the end. It would be the means of achieving glory for his disciples and for himself. It is for this reason that he immediately adds:

d. "... I shall never eat it again until it is fulfilled in the kingdom of God," that is, "I shall never eat it again until its typical and symbolical meaning has become fully realized in the new heaven and earth." It is there that the deliverance of his people, not from Egypt, but from all sin and evil, will have been fully accomplished. It is there that they will at last have been fully redeemed. It is there also that the fellowship between himself and all the redeemed will have been perfected (cf. Rev. 3:21).

17, 18. Then he received a cup, gave thanks, and said, Take this and divide it among yourselves; for I assure y o u that from now on I will not drink from the fruit of the vine until the kingdom of God comes.

It is natural to assume that the cup here mentioned was the very first one, the one that followed the opening prayer. See No. 1 under *The Order of The Passover Feast.* The drinking of this cup was definitely a part of the *Passover* meal. Note the giving of thanks that preceded the drinking of the wine. By ordering the contents of the cup to be divided among all those present, Jesus, acting as the Host, emphasizes the unity which, when conditions are as they should be, exists among and is experienced by all the partakers. Cf. Ps. 133. As the cup is being passed around Jesus repeats the prediction of verse 16b.

We should be sure, however, to interpret these words correctly, that is, optimistically. Jesus is not really saying, "This is the end. After tonight we'll never see each other again." What he is saying is rather this, "Though our continued fellowship here is about to end, it will be renewed gloriously in the kingdom to come, a kingdom of light and love, of triumph and praise, and this throughout all eternity." What a fulfilment, what a reunion that will be, when the meaning of this Passover will be experienced in all its fulness, when the wicked cease from troubling and the weary are at rest, and when the earth shall be full of the knowledge of Jehovah, as the waters cover the sea (Job 3:17; Isa. 11:9)!

It was probably in connection with point 6 of *The Order of The Passover Feast* (see pp. 959, 960) that the Lord's Supper was instituted. Here Passover passes over into the Lord's Supper. It was while, toward the close of the Passover meal, the men were all eating freely that Jesus instituted the new sacrament that was to replace the old. This also explains why both Luke (verse 20) and Paul (I Cor. 11:25) speak of "the cup *after* supper."

19, 20. Then he took (some) bread, gave thanks, broke it, and gave it to them, saying, This is my body given for y o u. This do in remembrance of me. And in the same way after supper (he took) the cup, saying, This cup (is) the new covenant in my blood, poured out for y o u. For the authenticity of 19b, 20 see the note on this passage on pp. 968, 969.

A few more hours and the old symbol, being bloody—for it required the slaying of the lamb—will have served its purpose forever, having reached its fulfilment in the blood shed on Calvary. It was time, therefore, that a new and unbloody symbol replace the old. Nevertheless, by historically linking Passover and the Lord's Supper so closely together Jesus also made clear that what was essential in the first was not lost in the second. Both point to *him,* the only and all-sufficient sacrifice for the sins of his people. Passover pointed forward to this; the Lord's Supper points back to it.

Having taken from the table a thin slice or sheet of unleavened bread,

Jesus "gave thanks" and then started to break up the slice. The words which the Lord used in this thanksgiving have not been revealed. To try to reconstruct them from Jewish formula prayers would serve no useful purpose. How do we even know that our Lord availed himself of these prayers?

The *breaking* of the bread, to which reference is made in all four accounts, must be considered as belonging to the very essence of the sacrament. This becomes clear in the light of that which immediately follows, namely, "This is my body given for y o u."

To interpret this to mean that Jesus was actually saying that these portions of bread which he handed to the disciples were identical with his physical body, or were at that moment being changed into his body, is to ignore (a) the fact that *in his body* Jesus was standing there in front of his disciples, for all to see. He was holding in his hand the bread, and giving them the portions as he broke them off. *Body and bread* were clearly distinct and remained so. Neither changed into the other, or took on the physical properties or characteristics of the other. Besides, such an interpretation also ignores (b) the fact that during his earthly ministry the Master very frequently used symbolical language (Mark 8:15; John 2:19; 3:3; 4:14, 32; 6:51, 53–56; 11:11). It is striking that in *all* of the instances indicated by *these* references the symbolical or figurative character of our Lord's language was disregarded by those who first heard it! In *each* case also, the context makes clear that those who interpreted Christ's words literally were mistaken! Is it not high time that the implied lesson be taken to heart? Finally, there is (c): when Jesus spoke of himself as being "the vine" (John 15:1, 5), is it not clear that he meant that what a natural vine is in relation to its branches, which find their unity, life, and fruit-bearing capacity in this plant, *that,* in a far more exalted sense, Christ is to his people? Is it not clear, therefore, that the vine *represents* or *symbolizes* Jesus, the genuine Vine? Thus also he calls himself—or is called—the door, the morning star, the cornerstone, the lamb, the fountain, the rock, etc. He also refers to himself as "the bread of life" (John 6:35, 48), "the bread that came down out of heaven" (John 6:58). So, why should he not be, and be represented and symbolized by, "the broken bread"? Accordingly, the meaning of "the broken bread" and the poured-out wine is correctly indicated in a Communion Form which represents Christ as saying: "Whereas otherwise you should have suffered eternal death, I give my body in death on the tree of the cross and shed my blood for you, and nourish and refresh your hungry and thirsty souls with my crucified body and shed blood to everlasting life, as certainly as this bread is broken before your eyes and this cup is given to you, and you eat and drink with your mouth in remembrance of Me."[563]

---

563. *Form for The Lord's Supper,* from the Liturgy of the Christian Reformed Church. See *Psalter Hymnal* (Centennial Edition), "Doctrinal Standards and Liturgy of the Christian Reformed Church," Grand Rapids, 1959, p. 94 of the Liturgical Forms.

Jesus adds, "This do in remembrance of me." It was the desire of our Lord that by means of the supper, here instituted, the church should *remember* his sacrifice and *love* him, should reflect on that sacrifice and embrace him by *faith*, and should look forward in living *hope* to his glorious return. Surely, the proper celebration of communion is a loving remembrance. It is, however, more than that. Jesus Christ is most certainly, and through his Spirit most actively, present at this genuine feast! Cf. Matt. 18:20. His followers "take" and "eat." They appropriate Christ by means of living faith, and are strengthened in this faith.

With respect to "And in the same way after supper (he took) the cup," etc., note the following:

Jesus says, "This cup (is) the new covenant in my blood."

But why does he speak of a *new* covenant? Do not such passages as Rom. 4:16; Gal. 3:8, 9, 29 clearly teach that the old covenant, the one made with Abraham, "the father of us all," is still in force? They certainly do. Nevertheless, there has been a tremendous change, a change so significant that even Jeremiah (31:31), looking into the future, could speak of a new covenant. That newness consists in this, (a) that for believers in the new dispensation the law is no longer written on tables of stone but on their hearts, the Holy Spirit having been poured out into these hearts; and (b) that the covenant is no longer almost exclusively between God and Israel but between God and all believers, regardless of race or nationality (Rom. 10:12, 13).

Note also "the new covenant *in my blood, poured out for y o u.*"

In all four accounts (Matthew, Mark, Luke, I Cor. 11) a relation is established between Christ's *blood* and his *covenant.* As reported by Matthew and Mark, Jesus said, "my blood of the covenant"; here in Luke—with little if any difference in meaning—"the new covenant in my blood." The expression goes back to such passages as Exod. 24:8; Jer. 31:31–34. See also the significant passage Lev. 17:11. And note: "Apart from the shedding of blood there is no *remission*" (Heb. 9:22; cf. Eph. 1:7); therefore also no *covenant,* no *special relation of friendship* between God and his people. Reconciliation with God always requires blood, an atoning sacrifice. And since man himself is unable to render such a sacrifice, a *substitutionary* offering, accepted by faith, is required (Isa. 53:6, 8, 10, 12; Matt. 20:28; Mark 10:45; John 3:16; 6:51; Rom. 5:19; 8:32; II Cor. 5:20, 21; Gal. 2:20; 3:13; I Peter 2:24).

As Luke reports it, Jesus said, ". . . my blood, poured out for y o u." Both Matthew (26:28) and Mark (14:24) read "poured out for many." There is no conflict. Christ's true disciples (The Eleven) were included in the "many."

As was shown in our little summary on p. 960, having briefly indicated what Jesus, during this evening and this night, did for his disciples (while still in the upper room), Luke now describes how they, in turn, reacted to

Jesus and his teaching. In this connection the evangelist returns to what happened *before* the institution of the Lord's Supper; in other words, to what took place while the Passover meal was still in progress:

21. But look! The hand of the man who is betraying me is with me on the table.

That in all probability what is here recorded took place *before* the institution of the Lord's Supper is confirmed by the following facts:

a. In the somewhat more chronologically arranged Synoptics, Matthew and Mark, the institution of the Lord's Supper *follows* the announcement concerning the betrayer. Cf. Matt. 26:26–29 with 26:20–25; and Mark 14:22–25 with 14:17–21.

b. In John's parallel report concerning the exposure of the traitor, Judas leaves the upper room immediately after Jesus told him, "What you are doing, do it faster" (John 13:21–30).

Think of it: "The hand of the man who is betraying me is with me on the table," or as Mark has it, "I solemnly declare to y o u, one of y o u will betray me: one who eats with me" (14:18), and, even more sharply and dramatically, "one of the twelve, one who is dipping (his hand) into the bowl with me" (verse 20).

Jesus continues: **22. For the Son of man is going as it has been decreed, but woe to that man by whom he is being betrayed.**

For "the Son of man" see on 5:24 and on Matt. 8:20. Jesus, the One who via the path of humiliation attains to glorification, and in fact was glorious from the very beginning, *goes,* that is, lives on earth, suffers, dies, all this not as a victim of circumstances, but "as it has been decreed," hence as predicted by the prophets (Isa. 53, etc.) and established in God's eternal decree. It was necessary for the Master to emphasize this truth once again, for it was so very difficult for the disciples to reconcile themselves with the idea of a Messiah who would die. Besides, when, on the day of tomorrow—by Jewish reckoning "today"—he dies on the cross, let the disciples reflect on this solemn statement, that they may know that this death does not mean the triumph of his enemies but rather the realization of God's gracious, sovereign, and ever victorious plan.

However, nowhere in Scripture do predestination and prophecy cancel human responsibility. So also here: the cry of sorrow and pity, "Woe to that man by whom he is being betrayed," fully maintains the guilt and establishes the doom of the traitor. We know that he did not truly repent. Hence he faces everlasting damnation (see Matt. 25:46). What makes his guilt all the heavier is the fact that he not only planned the treachery and took the next step—volunteering to deliver Jesus to the enemy—and the next—accepting the thirty pieces of silver—but even now, in spite of Christ's impressive warnings, goes right ahead.

Continued: **23. Then they began to discuss among themselves which of them it might be who was going to do this.**

It is clear that here, as so often, Luke summarizes. For a more detailed

964

account one should consult the parallels in the other Gospels. Very briefly: Christ's shocking announcement evoked three responses, in the form of questions, as follows: (a) a question of *wholesome self-distrust,* "Surely not I?" That was the reaction on the part of all the disciples with the exception of Judas Iscariot. In Mark's Gospel the question in this form is found in 14:19; Christ's answer in verses 20, 21. There was also (b) a question of *loathsome hypocrisy,* "Surely, not I, Rabbi?" That, probably after considerable hesitation, was Judas' reaction. For both his question and Christ's answer see Matt. 26:25. Finally, there was (c) a question of *childlike confidence,* "Lord, who is it?" That was the way in which John, prompted by Peter, expressed himself. The question in this form, the events relating to it, Christ's response, and the disciples' reaction to that response are recorded only in John 13:23–30, which also (in verse 30) mentions the traitor's departure.

One more fact should be stressed. As has been indicated, Jesus was himself the Host. All the others were eating *his* food. That very fact, especially in the Near East, a region where *accepting someone's hospitality and then injuring him* was considered most reprehensible, should have tied the hands of all. It should have made it impossible for any of The Twelve to take any action against their Host. Think of Ps. 41:9. And in addition to what Jesus did for The Twelve *this night,* how many (in fact very many) other favors had not the Lord bestowed upon them, including Judas, during all these months of their association with him?

Nevertheless, we should not rivet our attention solely on *Judas.* We should fix it on Jesus! In a treacherous and humiliating manner he, the Lord of glory, is being handed over to his enemies. It is very important that we see this. Our reflection on the story of Christ's Passion should not become lost in all kinds of details regarding Judas and Peter and Annas and Pilate. It is, after all, the story of *his* suffering. It centers in *him,* and we should never forget to see *him* at the very center of the developing events.

The present little paragraph (verses 21–23) shows again that Jesus was in full control of the situation. He was not taken by surprise. He knew exactly what was happening and what was going to happen, the very details. And the fact that he reveals this to his disciples will prove to be a support to them when they subsequently discover that everything actually develops exactly as he had foreseen! What a wonderful Savior![564]

Practical Lessons Derived from Luke 22:1–23

Verse 3

"Then Satan entered Judas." Scripture emphasizes the role of Satan in the affairs of men. See, for example, Gen. 3:15; Job 1:6; 2:1; Zech. 3:1 f.; Matt. 16:23; Luke 4:1 f.; 10:18; 13:16; 22:31, 32; John 13:27; Acts 5:3; 26:18; Rom. 16:20; I Cor. 5:5;

---

564. Notes on Greek words, phrases, and constructions in 22:1–23 begin on page 966.

7:5; Eph. 6:12, 13; I Peter 5:8, 9; Rev. 20:2, 7. To make our children more keenly aware of the activity of Satan, and of their duty to resist him and his temptations, would it not be advisable to teach them, when they pray the Lord's Prayer, to say, "And deliver us from *the evil one*" (instead of "from evil")? Especially since that is probably what Jesus meant when he taught his disciples this prayer. See N.T.C. on Matt. 6:13.

Verse 5

"They were delighted." This was not the only time in the history of the world when religious leaders, such as priests and scribes, have with relish endorsed wicked plans. The fact that a meeting is opened and closed with prayer, that Scripture is read, and hymns are sung, does not necessarily mean that God places the stamp of his approval on such a meeting. It is the heart that counts.

Verse 13

"So they . . . found everything just as Jesus had told them." Divine omniscience, how comprehensive (Ps. 139), and how comforting (John 21:17).

Verses 19, 20

"My body given for you . . . my blood, poured out for y o u." "*This do in remembrance of me.*" Therefore:

> According to thy gracious word,
>   In meek humility
> This will I do, my dying Lord:
>   I will remember thee.
>
> When to the cross I turn mine eyes,
>   And rest on Calvary,
> O Lamb of God, my sacrifice,
>   I must remember thee.
>
> Stanzas from
> "According to Thy Gracious Word"
> by J. Montgomery

Notes on Greek Words, Phrases, and Constructions in 22:1-23

Verse 1
(see also verses 7, 8)

ἀζύμων, gen. pl. of ἄζυμος (= ἀ plus ζύμη), without leaven, unleavened. Hence, here the entire expression is "the feast of Unleavened Bread." τὰ ἄζυμα means "unleavened bread." The reference is to the unleavened, flat bread-cakes; see verse 7.

πάσχα, from Aramaic פַּסְחָא, is related to a verb meaning *to pass over*. See Exod. 12:13, 27. The word πάσχα occurs in the following senses:

a. the Passover festival on the fourteenth of Nisan, but in popular usage covering also the festival of Unleavened Bread from the fifteenth to the twenty-first of that month. That is the meaning here in 22:1.

966

b. the paschal lamb (22:7; Mark 14:12a).

c. Christ, the Lamb (I Cor. 5:7).

d. the Passover meal (22:8, 13; cf. Matt. 26:19; Mark 14:12b; 14:16).

Verse 2

ἐζήτουν, third per. pl. imperf. (either descriptive or iterative) of ζητέω, to seek, look for.

τὸ πῶς introduces indirect question; cf. verse 4.

ἀνέλωσιν, third per. pl. 2nd aor. (effective) subjunct. (deliberat.) of ἀναιρέω, to take up, destroy. See also 23:32.

Verse 4

συνελάλησεν, third per. s. aor. indicat. of συλλαλέω, to talk or discuss with. See 9:30; Matt. 17:3; Mark 9:4.

στρατηγοῖς, dat. pl. of στρατηγός**; also in 22:52; Acts 4:1; 5:24, 26, captain of the temple guard.

παραδῷ, third per. s. aor. subjunct. (deliberat.) act. of παραδίδωμι, to give or hand over, deliver up, betray. So also in verses 6, 21, 22, 48. Other meanings: to commit, yield (up), hazard, etc. See also the note on 1:2 on page 61: to hand down.

Verse 5

ἐχάρησαν, third per. pl. 2nd aor. (ingressive) indicat. pass. of χαίρω, to be glad, delighted. This verb is related to χάρις, on which see the note on 2:40 on pp. 181, 182.

συνέθεντο, third per. pl. 2nd aor. (ingress.) middle of συντίθημι, to place together, agree. Cf. John 9:22; Acts 23:20.

Verse 6

ἐξωμολόγησεν, third per. s. aor. indicat. of ἐξομολογέω, to say the same thing, agree, consent. See the note on 10:21 on page 589; also N.T.C. on Matthew, footnote 477 on pp. 497, 498.

ἄτερ*, from, without, in the absence of; in the New Testament only here and in verse 35.

Verse 7
(see also verse 1)

θύεσθαι, pres. pass. infinitive of θύω, to sacrifice. See the note on 15:23 on page 762.

Verse 8

See verse 1.

Verse 9

ἑτοιμάσωμεν, first per. pl. aor. subjunct. (deliberat.) act. of ἑτοιμάζω, to prepare. Note absence of ἵνα before the subjunct.

Verse 10

Note gen. absolute "y o u having entered" = "after y o u enter."
κεράμιον, diminutive of κέραμος, pitcher, jar. Cf. *ceramics.*

Verse 11

οἰκοδεσπότῃ, dat. s. of οἰκοδεσπότης, owner of the house. The modifier τῆς οἰκίας has been called "pleonastic" since this idea is already implied in the noun it modifies. Is it possible that it was added because the sense "of the house" as part of the compound noun had faded?
κατάλυμα, here guest room, but see also the note on 2:7 on page 148.
φάγω, first per. s. 2nd aor. subjunct. (futuristic after ὅπου). See also verse 16. The present uses ἐσθίω, to eat.

Verse 12

ἀνάγαιον, upper room; so also in Mark 14:15, the only New Testament instances of its use.
ἐστρωμένον, acc. s. neut. perf. pass. participle of στρώννυμι, to spread; here probably: to furnish.

Verse 15

Note Hebraism "With desire I have desired" (A.V.), meaning "I have eagerly desired."
Also note "before the suffering with respect to me," meaning "before my suffering" or "before I suffer." In this one verse Hebrew and Greek style are combined, Luke being well-versed in both.
παθεῖν, 2nd aor. infinitive of πάσχω, to suffer. Cf. *passion.*

Verse 16

οὐ μή, strong negative: certainly not; never.
As in verse 11 φάγω is futuristic.
Note ἕως followed by the gen. of a neut. relat. pronoun = *until.* Therefore: *Futuristic aor. subjunctive* is also *this* φάγω. And so is third per. s. pass. πληρωθῇ, from πληρόω, to make full, fulfil.

Verse 17

διαμερίσατε, sec. per. pl. aor. imperat. act. of διαμερίζω, to divide into parts (διά plus μερίζω; cf. μέρος, part), to distribute. See also the note on 11:17 on page 633.

Verse 18

With οὐ μὴ πίω cf. οὐ μὴ φάγω in verse 16; and with ἔλθῃ cf. πληρωθῇ in that same verse.

Verses 19–21

The words beginning with τὸ ὑπέρ and ending with ἐκχυννόμενον are rejected by many. Reasons for rejection:

a. They are lacking in Codex Bezae and certain Latin and Syriac witnesses.

b. If the longer text was the original, how can the shorter text be explained? Is it not easier to explain how a short text would be unjustifiably expanded than how a long text would be shortened?

c. The shorter text, which fails to ascribe any redemptive significance to the outpouring of Christ's blood, makes it easier to understand why Luke did not include in his Gospel the ransom passage found in Mark 10:45 (cf. Matt. 20:28).

The answer might be as follows:

a. The type of text which includes the disputed words (verse 19b and all of verse 20) is more often than not regarded as being superior to the other or Western text, with its many additions and (sometimes) subtractions.

b. Explaining the rise of the shorter text may not be so difficult after all. It may have arisen because a second-century copyist failed to understand why, after the mention of a "cup" in verse 17, there would be mention of still another cup in verse 20. Neither Matt. 26:27 nor Mark 14:23 makes mention of more than one cup. So it is possible that this scribe was not well acquainted with the complicated ritual of the Jewish Passover, with its many—at least four—cups. See S.BK., Vol. IV, p. 75.

c. Referring to Luke's omission of Mark 10:45 and its parallel, without also taking note of Acts 20:28 ("the church of the Lord, which he *purchased with his own blood*") and of Acts 8:32 (with its emphasis on the slaughtered lamb of Isa. 53), is hardly fair.

d. Adopting the shorter text leads us into the following dilemma: (a) if *the cup* (verse 17) *is regarded as part of the Lord's Supper,* we must accept a sequence (cup-bread) that is in conflict with Matt. 26:26, 27; Mark 14:22, 23; (b) *if the cup is regarded as part of the Passover* (probably correct), we must conclude that in the Lord's Supper only bread was used. Neither position is tenable. See also B. M. Metzger, *The Text of the New Testament,* p. 50.

I have found no sound reason, therefore, to reject the longer text.

ἐκχυννόμενον, nom. s. neut. pres. (futuristic) pass. participle of ἐκχύννομαι; cf. the basic form ἐκχέω, to shed, pour out. See also the note on 5:37 on page 313, and the note on 11:50 on page 647. The pres. act. participle παραδιδόντος in verse 21 is also futuristic.

Verse 22

ὡρισμένον, acc. s. neut. perf. pass. participle of ὁρίζω, to set limits to, determine, decree, appoint. This verb is found also in Acts 2:23; 10:42; 11:29; 17:26, 31; Rom. 1:4; Heb. 4:7. For the related προορίζω see N.T.C. on Eph. 1:5. Cf. *horizon.*

παραδίδοται, third per. s. pres. (futuristic) indicat. of παραδίδωμι, for which see on verse 4 above.

Verse 23

συζητεῖν, pres. infinitive of συζητέω, to seek, discuss, talk with someone else; to discuss (together); sometimes, as in Mark 8:11; 9:14, 16, to argue, dispute.

Here in Luke 22:23 the subordinate clause, including an indirect question, is introduced by τό.

εἴη, third per. s. pres. optat. of εἰμί.

24 There also arose a dispute among them as to which one of them was considered to be the greatest. 25 So Jesus said to them, "The kings of the Gentiles lord it over them, and those who exercise authority over them are styled 'Benefactors.' 26 But y o u (are) not (to do)[565] so. On the contrary, let the greatest among y o u become like the youngest, and the leader like the servant. 27 For who is greater, the one who reclines at table or the one who serves? Is it not the one who reclines at table? However, I am among y o u as one who serves. 28 But y o u are those who have stood by me in my trials. 29 Moreover, I on my part am assigning to y o u, even as my Father assigned to me, a kingdom, 30 that y o u may eat and drink at my table in my kingdom, and may sit on thrones judging the twelve tribes of Israel."

22:24-30 *The Dispute About Greatness*

Though this section, considered as a unit, has no parallel, its individual passages or combinations of certain passages do have parallels; some close, some not so close:

With verse 24 cf. Matt. 18:1; Mark 9:34; Luke 9:46.

With the combined verses 25-27 cf. Matt. 20:25-28; Mark 10:42-45.

With verse 26 (considered by itself) cf. Matt. 23:11; Mark 9:35.

With verse 27, similarly, cf. John 13:1-17.

With verse 28 cf. John 6:66-69; 17:6c, 8, 12, 14.

With verse 29 cf. Luke 12:32; Rev. 3:21; 5:10; 17:14; 20:4.

With verse 30 cf. Matt. 19:28.

24. There also arose a dispute among them as to which one of them was considered to be the greatest.

The little summary on p. 960 shows that from Judas Luke now turns to The Twelve (verses 24-30). The evangelist does not indicate just when, during that memorable night, the dispute about greatness occurred. Nevertheless, the other Gospels strongly suggest a background for it. It probably took place at the very beginning of the feast. The occasion may well have been the question, "Just how will the thirteen be arranged around the table? Who will occupy the positions of honor, and in what order of rank?" See what has been said about this in connection with 14:7 f. Or again, "Which disciple should wash the feet of the other disciples and of the Master?" See John 13:1 f. We observe therefore that even though the other Gospels do not parallel this Lucan account, they certainly suggest a background for it.

Picture the scene. Here was Jesus, about to lay down his life for these men, centering his attention on *their* needs, loving *them* very tenderly and intensely. For proof that this was indeed the situation that very night read such passages as John 13:1; 17:6-19. And do not the following passages *imply* as much: Rom. 5:6-11; 8:31-39; Gal. 2:20? Yet, while his heart goes out to them, they are quarreling about the question, "Who of us is the greatest?" What made their attitude even more reprehensible was that they

---

565. Or: (to be).

had been reprimanded before with respect to this selfish attitude. See Matt. 18:1-5; Mark 9:34-37; Luke 9:46-48. Had they forgotten so quickly?

25. So Jesus said to them, The kings of the Gentiles lord it over them, and those who exercise authority over them are styled Benefactors.

Jesus again showed these men that their egotism was a worldly, pagan trait. It reminded one of the self-centeredness of "the kings of the Gentiles." These men, while exercising their authority ruthlessly, nevertheless took delight in being called *Benefactors!*

How very true! On a denarius was not Augustus called "god"? On a copper coin was not Tiberius described as "one who deserved to be adored"? But, more to the point, had not the very title *Benefactor* (or Well-doer), *Euergetes,* been ascribed to both Ptolemy I and Ptolemy II?

Continued: **26, 27. But y o u (are) not (to do) so. On the contrary, let the greatest among y o u become like the youngest, and the leader like the servant. For who is greater, the one who reclines at table or the one who serves? Is it not the one who reclines at table? However, I am among y o u as one who serves.**

Jesus wants his disciples to be of an opposite mind, and therefore also to show the opposite disposition. Therefore he tells them that the greatest among them—the one who so regards himself or is so regarded by others—should become like the . . . *youngest;* that is, like the one least in honor.

This mention of "the youngest," where we might have expected "the least," is in line with the fact that under normal conditions the Bible, as these men knew it (our Old Testament), regarded old age as honorable and to be held in respect. See Lev. 19:32; Job 32:6, 7; Prov. 16:31; 20:29. What happened to Rehoboam when he rejected the counsel of the aged and followed that of the young (I Kings 12) had not been effaced from their memory.

Jesus, then, wants the greatest to become like the youngest, the one least in honor. He wants the leader to serve.

Appealing to something these men know very well, so that from the known he may proceed to the unknown or less well known and appreciated, he asks his disciples, "Who is greater, the one who is dining or the one who is waiting on him?" Of course, the former is generally regarded as the greater. Yet, does true greatness really consist in having someone wait on you? Jesus answers this question by stating, "But I am among y o u as one who serves."

Was he not literally serving them, perhaps even at this very moment, or at least close to this moment, in a manner never to be forgotten? Read the story in John 13:1-11 (Jesus washing the feet of his disciples). In fact was not his entire earthly sojourn a life of rendering service to others in ever so many ways? Was not this the essence of his purpose in coming to earth? Who, in this connection, can forget Matt. 20:28; Mark 10:45?

28-30. But y o u are those who have stood by me in my trials. More-

971

over, I on my part am assigning to y o u, even as my Father assigned to me, a kingdom, that y o u may eat and drink at my table in my kingdom, and may sit on thrones judging the twelve tribes of Israel.

And now, ignoring the many character defects these men have exhibited, in fact even this very night, the Merciful Highpriest praises them for the faithfulness they have shown throughout his many trials. It was true that while others, by the score and perhaps even at times by the hundreds, had left the Savior (John 6:66), these men—Judas excepted—had remained loyal to him. Had not this loyalty been expressed beautifully by Peter as their spokesman (John 6:67–69), and by Thomas (John 11:16)?

So Jesus assigns to them a kingdom. The word *kingdom* should probably be interpreted here in the sense of "royal rule," though the idea of "domain" cannot be entirely excluded, as the phrase *in my kingdom* indicates.

Jesus reminds his disciples that to him, too, a kingdom had been assigned, namely, by his Father. For proof see Luke 1:32, 33. Therefore, when he now assigns a kingdom to them, he means that they will share in his royal rule. Cf. Rev. 3:21; 20:4. He is referring to the kingdom in its final manifestation.

As has been pointed out several times, such expressions as *eating and drinking in my kingdom* (see N.T.C. on Matt. 8:11 and on 22:2) are part of the symbolism of the joys which God's children will experience in the new heaven and earth.

As to "judging the twelve tribes of Israel," a repetition of the promise Jesus had made earlier (see Matt. 19:28), in all probability he was thinking of the restored new Israel. Whether, as such, the term *Israel* indicates the total number of the elect gathered out of the twelve tribes of the Jews from the beginning to the end of the world's history (cf. Rom. 11:26), or even *all* the chosen ones of both the Jews and the Gentiles (cf. Gal. 6:16), in either case it must refer to those who have been regenerated, for into the reborn universe to which Matt. 19:28 refers nothing unclean will ever enter (Rev. 21:27). The Twelve, who have followed Jesus here, having remained loyal to him in his trials (Luke 22:28), are going to receive the special reward that among all the members belonging to the new Israel they will be preeminent in reflecting the glory of their Lord and Savior. Those who have been closest to Jesus here will also be closest to him there. See also II Tim. 2:11, 12; Rev. 3:21; 20:4.

For *Practical Lessons* and *Greek Words,* etc., see pp. 977–980.

---

31 "Simon, Simon, watch out! Satan has asked to sift y o u as wheat. 32 But I have prayed for you, that your faith may not utterly fail; and you, once you have returned (to me), strengthen your brothers."

33 But he replied, "Lord, with you I am ready to go even to prison and to death."

34 But Jesus answered, "I tell you, Peter, a rooster will not crow today before you deny three times that you know me."

22:31–34 *Peter's Denial Foretold*
Cf. Matt. 26:31–35; Mark 14:27–31; John 13:36–38

**31, 32. Simon, Simon, watch out! Satan has asked to sift y o u as wheat.
But I have prayed for you, that your faith may not utterly fail; and you,
once you have returned (to me), strengthen your brothers.**

As shown in the summary on p. 960, from The Twelve Luke now turns
to Simon Peter. There are commentators who believe that this discussion
between Jesus and Simon must have taken place after the group had left
the upper room. They base this conclusion on Matt. 26:30–33 and on John
13:31–38. Others, however, hold that it is entirely possible that the Master
started to warn Peter even while the group was still in the upper room, and
that the discussion between that disciple and Jesus was continued afterward.

Note the following:

a. Jesus calls this disciple Simon, not (that is, not until verse 34) Peter,
the Rock. If any significance can be attached to this fact, it may well be that
the Master wishes to fix the attention of this leader upon the fact that in
himself he is a weak creature, not at all a man of stability, no rock.

b. The repetition ("Simon, Simon") indicates emphasis and deep concern. For other instances of this stylistic form see on 10:41.

c. Jesus says, "Behold" or "Take note," "Pay attention," "Watch out,"
whichever rendering one may prefer. Simon will never be able to say that
he was not warned.

d. Satan.

We seldom realize that beyond the struggle that goes on within the heart,
and the conflict between opposing forces on earth, there is the probably
even more intense encounter in the spiritual world. In the present case the
ardent desire of Satan, his insistent demand, had been counteracted by the
Savior's prayer for Simon's salvation. For other instances of this superter-
restrial warfare see Job 1:6–12; 2:1–6; Zech. 3:1–5.

e. "Satan has desired to sift . . . as wheat."

This sifting of wheat basically refers to the repeated, swift, and violent
shaking of the wheat in a sieve. Someone—often a woman—grasps a sieve
in both hands, and begins to shake it vigorously from side to side so that the
chaff will rise to the surface. This is then thrown away. Next, she puts that
sieve through a teeter-totter motion, raising now this and then that side,
and blowing over it, so that what still remains of the chaff gathers in an
easily removable pile. The purpose is, of course, to save the wheat, now
separated from chaff and other unwanted materials.

What Jesus is saying, then, is this: the disciples too will be subjected to a
severe trial. That trial is going to happen this very night, and probably
often afterward in their lives. But the emphasis is upon the events of this
night.

f. Although Jesus is here addressing *one* individual, namely, Simon, he is predicting what is going to happen to *the entire group:* note "Satan has desired to sift y o u" (not "you").

g. Satan has desired . . . that is, has asked to have for himself. We are again reminded of the story of Job, how Satan demanded that he be given a free hand with respect to that eminent child of God.

h. But I have prayed for you. Note *here* the singular *you,* namely Simon. Not as if Jesus did not also pray for the other disciples. He prayed for them this very night (John 17:6–19), and must have prayed for them many times previously. But in the present passage the reference is to the intercession of Jesus for Simon, for him alone. Why this was we do not know. Was it perhaps because Simon was the recognized leader, a man who could be expected to exert influence on the others? Other suggestions that have been made are: because Simon was very headstrong, impetuous, a hard case therefore.

i. The substance of Christ's prayer was "that your faith may not utterly fail," in other words, that in the end your faith may prevail.

j. This interpretation also harmonizes with the words "and you, once you have returned [or: have retraced your steps], strengthen your brothers." To be sure, considered in and by itself, Simon's fall was bad, very bad, tragic. Yet, once it had occurred, Simon must make good use of this bad fall. He must use it to strengthen his fellow disciples.

33. But he replied, Lord, with you I am ready to go even to prison and to death.

It is clear from this that Simon did not know himself. "The heart is deceitful above all things; it is exceedingly corrupt; who can know it?" Simon should have prayed the prayer of Ps. 139:23, 24.

34. But Jesus answered, I tell you, Peter, a rooster will not crow today before you deny three times that you know me.

Cf. Matt. 26:34; Mark 14:30; John 13:38.

The threefold denial will accordingly take place before the early morning hours.

The reference to the crowing of the rooster does double duty: (a) It indicates the shallow character of Simon's boast. Within just a few hours, yes, even before dawn, Peter will publicly disown his Master! Yet, (b) this very rooster-crowing will also serve as a means of bringing Peter back to repentance, for Christ's reference to it becomes firmly embedded in that disciple's mind, so that at the appropriate moment this hidden memory will suddenly pull the rope that will ring the bell of Peter's conscience. See 22:60–62.

Note that here, in verse 34, Jesus, by exception—it never happened before or afterward—calls this disciple *Peter,* as if to remind him of his duty, namely, to be a *rock,* a duty which he was about to neglect so shamefully.

For *Practical Lessons* and *Greek Words,* etc., see pp. 977–980.

35 Then Jesus asked them, "When I sent y o u out without purse or bag or sandals, y o u did not lack anything, did y o u?" They replied, "No, nothing."

36 He said to them, "But now let him who has a purse take it along, and also a bag. And let him who has no sword sell his coat[566] and buy one. 37 For I tell y o u, what has been written must be fulfilled in me:

'And he was numbered with the transgressors.'

Yes, that (passage) about me is reaching its fulfilment."

38 They said, "Lord, look, here are two swords!"

He said to them, "Enough of that!"[567]

22:35-38 *"Y o u did not lack anything, did y o u?"*

The discussion between Jesus and his disciples is resumed at this point. See the summary on p. 960. In all probability by now Judas has already left. See on verse 39 and cf. John 13:30. It is Jesus himself who starts the conversation with the remaining Eleven (verse 35a). It is he also who brings it to a conclusion (verse 38b). And throughout it is he who is in control.

Yet, they are not merely listeners. Twice their reactions are recorded (verses 35b and 38a).

Jesus opens the discussion by informing The Eleven that they are about to be confronted with a situation totally different than heretofore. Up to now he had fully assumed the responsibility of caring for them. And the enemies had aimed their poisoned arrows mainly at *him*. From now on things would be different. For this change they must prepare themselves.

The contrast between the two situations is brought out sharply in verses 35, 36. Note the wide gap between these two verses. Jesus had been providing for them (verse 35). From now on they must provide for themselves (verse 36). Of course, that is not true in an absolute sense. The disciples had not been entirely passive until now, and from now on Jesus, from his position on the Father's right hand in heaven, would certainly still bless and keep them. But in a relative sense it is definitely true, for in just a little while Jesus will be taken away from these men and they will no longer be able to walk by his side, asking him questions and listening to his answers. Also, once Jesus has been crucified, the wrath of the opponents will be directed against Christ's disciples. It is they who will then be persecuted.

35. Then Jesus asked them, When I sent y o u out without purse or bag or sandals, y o u did not lack anything, did y o u? They replied, No, nothing.

Though it is true that the terminology—purse, bag, sandals—corresponds more precisely with the charge to the seventy (or seventy-two) than with that to The Twelve (cf. 10:4 with 9:3), yet, as Matt. 10:10; Mark

---

566. Or: outer garment, or robe.

567. Or: It is enough.

6:8, 9 make clear, there is no essential difference. In both cases precautionary measures with a view to what might happen on the journey had been ruled out. So now the Lord asks the disciples whether under these circumstances they had suffered lack of anything. When they answer that they had not,

36. He said to them, But now let him who has a purse take it along, and also a bag. And let him who has no sword sell his coat [or robe] and buy one.

That the situation in which Christ's apostles would find themselves after his departure would indeed be different from what it was before follows also from the words found in the highpriestly prayer (John 17:11-13). From now on these men will have to take the initiative. They will need to cultivate courage to a degree not expected of them before. Making provision for missionary travels, such as taking along a purse and a traveling bag, will now be necessary.

Up to this point the reader experiences no great difficulty. But the puzzling statement "Let him who has no sword sell his coat and buy one" has led to all kinds of interpretations. Chief among them are the following:

a. Jesus was speaking of a literal sword, for protection against robbers, brigands, etc.

Objection: In that case why would he have rebuked Peter when he wielded his sword? See verses 49-51; cf. Matt. 26:51, 52; John 18:10, 11.

b. The reference is to a knife (butcher knife, carving knife). Before this time the needs of the disciples had been supplied by others. Their hosts would do the cutting and carving of the meat. Now they will have to do this themselves.

Objection: We can hardly imagine that in this very connection Jesus, using the same word for the instrument in question, would have said, "All who take the knife shall perish with the knife." See Matt. 26:52.

c. The term *sword* must be interpreted figuratively. The meaning is that in the circumstances that are about to arise The Eleven will need all the courage they can muster.

In view of the context (see especially verse 38) and of the fact that again and again Jesus used figurative language (Matt. 16:6; Luke 8:52; John 2:19; 3:3; 4:13, 14, 32; 6:51; 11:11; etc.), this is probably the correct explanation.

It is not difficult to understand that the constant reference Jesus made to his imminent suffering and death, even his reference to it this very night (see verses 15, 20, and what is implied in verses 35, 36), filled the hearts of the disciples with dismay and their minds with bewilderment. Cf. 18:34. Was he, their Master, about to *die?* But in view of what they had confessed him to be (9:20), a confession with which he had apparently agreed, how was this even possible? So again, as on more than one previous occasion (see especially 9:21, 22; 18:31-33), Jesus emphasizes this very fact (his imminent death), a fact apart from which verses 35, 36 cannot be explained.

**37. For I tell y o u, what has been written must be fulfilled in me:
And he was numbered with the transgressors.
Yes, that (passage) about me is reaching its fulfilment.**

A few thoughts stand out here:

a. This is one of the New Testament passages in which Isaiah 53 is definitely applied to Jesus. For the prominence of Isa. 53 in the New Testament see N.T.C. on Philippians, pp. 82, 83.

b. Not only that, but it is Jesus himself who informs us that Isa. 53 refers to him!

c. The statement is by no means pessimistic. It is the very opposite. The words *must be fulfilled* indicate that the Savior regarded not only his life but also his death as the fulfilment of God's plan.

d. Moreover, by mentioning the fact that he, though conscious of his innocence, in fact of his holiness, will, in fulfilment of prophecy, be numbered with the transgressors, does he not clearly imply that his death is substitutionary in character? Would Jesus have quoted these words from Isa. 53:12 if he had not also believed the words which immediately follow: "yet he bare the sin of many and made intercession for the transgressors"?

How tragic that, once again, the disciples do not understand the meaning of Christ's words. Besides, they are still thinking of the immediately preceding passage (verse 36b), "And let him who has no sword sell his coat and buy one." So **38. They said, Lord, look, here are two swords!** As if Jesus had been talking about the necessity of having and using literal swords!

No wonder that his answer is curt and decisive: **He said to them, Enough of that!** This reply prevents any further conversation about that subject.

One important element in Christ's suffering was certainly this, that even his most intimate disciples failed to understand him.[568]

Practical Lessons Derived from Luke 22:24–38

Verses 24, 27, 28

"There . . . arose a dispute among them as to which one of them was considered to be the greatest." . . . "I am among y o u as one who serves. . . . But y o u are those who have stood by me in my trials." What a sharp contrast between self-centered disciples and the self-sacrificing Savior! Nevertheless, even now he praises these men for having stood by him in his trials. What a lesson he gives us in "humans relations"!

Verses 31, 32

"Satan has asked . . . I have prayed." Christ's prayers are effective because they are based on his merits, his self-sacrifice.

---

568. Notes on Greek words, phrases, and constructions in 22:24–38 begin on page 978.

Verse 32

"Strengthen your brothers." Bringing the gospel of salvation full and free to those who have never heard it is surely to be encouraged in every way. See Prov. 11:30; Matt. 28:19, 20; I Cor. 9:22. But are we probably forgetting that the strengthening of the "brothers" is also necessary?

Paul addressed his letters to "the saints," "the faithful in Christ Jesus," "the church," etc. He realized that *edification* of those already in the fold was just as necessary as *evangelization* of those still outside. We sometimes forget this! The church should pray not only for its missionaries; it should also pray for and co-operate with its ministers. In certain situations the task assigned to the latter is as difficult as is that placed upon the shoulders of the former.

Verse 33

"Peter replied, . . . 'I am ready.' " Well, he was *not.*
God's command is "Be ready" (Matt. 24:44).
The believer's prayer should be "Make me ready." See Ps. 119:36.

> Open my eyes that I may see
> Glimpses of truth thou hast for me.
> Place in my hands the wonderful key
> That shall unclasp and set me free.
>
> Open my ears, that I may hear
> Voices of truth thou sendest clear,
> And while the wave-notes fall on my ear
> Everything false will disappear.
>
> Silently now I wait for thee,
> Ready, my God, thy will to see.
> Open my eyes, illumine me,
> Spirit divine.
>
> Stanzas from
> "Open My Eyes"
> by C. H. Scott

Notes on Greek Words, Phrases, and Constructions in 22:24–38

Verse 24

φιλονεικία* (φίλος plus νεῖκος = loving strife), strife, dispute; cf. φιλόνεικος, contentious (I Cor. 11:16).

Here again, as in the preceding verse, the article introduces the indirect question. Mood and tense of the direct question are retained.

Degrees of comparison in verses 24, 26, and 27

In verses 24 and 26 the comparative μείζων is used in the sense of a superlative "greatest." See the note on 7:28 on page 403, and the note on 7:42 on page 412. In verse 27, however, the comparative "greater" makes good sense. And in verse 26 the comparative νεώτερος should probably also be interpreted as a superlative.

Verse 25

κυριεύουσιν, third per. pl. pres. indicat. of κυριεύω, to be κύριος (lord) over, to lord it over. In Luke's writings here only, but the word occurs also in Rom. 6:9, 14; 7:1; 14:9; II Cor. 1:24; and I Tim. 6:15.

εὐεργέται, nom. pl. of εὐεργέτης, well-doer, benefactor.

Verse 26

γινέσθω, third per. s. pres. imperat. middle of γίνομαι, hence here: let him become; or, if full force of pres. has been retained: let him continue to be.

ὁ ἡγούμενος, the one leading, the leader.

Verse 28

διαμεμενηκότες, nom. pl. masc. perf. act. participle of διαμένω, with intensive or perfective use of διά, to remain continually (with someone), to stand by (him).

πειρασμοῖς, dat. pl. of πειρασμός, trial, proof, temptation.

Verse 29

διατίθεμαι, to decree, ordain, dispose of property by διαθήκη, will (cf. Heb. 9:16 f.), but here in Luke 22:29 probably: "I confer, bestow." Note also the third per. s. 2nd aor. indicat. middle of the same verb: (the Father) has bestowed.

Verse 30

Note here the second per. pl. pres. subjunct. (after ἵνα, futuristic) act., "that y o u may eat and drink," followed by the fut. indicat., "and may sit," etc. As has been indicated previously, the relation between the subjunct. and the future indicat. is very close.

Verses 31, 32

ἐξῃτήσατο, third per. s. aor. middle indicat. of ἐξαιτέω*, in the middle: to ask something or someone of (ἐκ) someone, for oneself (sense of middle voice). In the New Testament this verb occurs only here, though the base αἰτέω, to ask, is very common, especially in the Gospels and Acts.

σινιάσαι, aor. infinitive of σινιάζω*, to sift; cf. σινίον, a sieve or strainer.

Important: note distinction between y o u in verse 31, and *you* in verse 32. See explanation.

ἐδεήθην, first per. s. aor. indicat. pass. of δέομαι, to make request, ask, pray.

ἐκλίπῃ, third per. s. aor. (effective) subjunct. (after ἵνα μὴ) of ἐκλείπω. The prefix probably has perfective force; hence "that your faith may not run out," "may not utterly fail." See also on 16:9 and on 23:45.

ἐπιστρέψας, nom. s. masc. aor. act. participle of ἐπιστρέφω, to turn around, return, turn back.

στήρισον, sec. per. s. aor. imperat. act. of στηρίζω, to render stedfast, strengthen.

Verse 34

ἀπαρνήσῃ, sec. per. s. aor. subjunct. middle, or fut. indicat. middle (same form) of ἀπαρνέομαι, to deny, disown. See the note on 12:9 on page 660.

εἰδέναι, 2nd perf. act. infinitive of οἶδα, to know, related to an assumed εἴδω, to see.

Verse 35

ἀπέστειλα, first per. s. aor. indicat. of ἀποστέλλω, to send out. Cf. *apostle.* This verb occurs very frequently in the New Testament, especially in the Gospels and Acts.

After ἄτερ this verse uses the gen. (or "ablative" if one prefers) of βαλλάντιον, purse; πήρα, traveler's bag; and ὑποδήματα, sandals. For all three, mentioned in the same order but as accusatives, see the note on 10:4 on page 587.

ὑστερήσατε, sec. per. pl. aor. indicat. of ὑστερέω, to fall short, lack; see the note on 15:14 on page 760.

οὐθενός, gen. s. of οὐδείς, no one; here (neuter) nothing. To account for the genitive one might render the question and answer as follows, "Did y o u experience lack of anything?" They said, "No, of nothing."

Verse 36

The three verbs "let him take (it) along, let him sell, let him buy," are third per. s. aor. imperatives. For a summary of the meanings of αἴρω see the note on 17:13 on page 803.

Verse 37

τελεσθῆναι, aor. pass. infinitive of τελέω, to bring to an end, finish; pass. to be brought to an end, be finished, be fulfilled; see the note on 12:50 on page 689.

---

39 Then Jesus came outside and, as usual, went to the Mount of Olives. His disciples followed him.   40 When he arrived at the place, he said to them, "Keep praying that y o u may not enter at all into temptation."   41 And he withdrew about a stone's throw beyond them, knelt down, and continued in prayer, saying,   42 "Father, if thou art willing, remove this cup from me; nevertheless, not my will but thine be done."

43[569] There appeared to him an angel from heaven, strengthening him.   44 And being in anguish, he prayed very fervently;[570] and his sweat became like thick drops of blood falling down upon the ground.

45 When he rose from prayer and came to the disciples, he found them sleeping from sorrow,   46 and he asked them, "Why are y o u asleep? Get up and pray, that y o u may not enter into temptation."

---

569. Are verses 43 and 44 authentic? See the note on these verses on pages 990-991.
570. Or: more intensely.

22:39–46 *On the Mount of Olives*
The Prayer of Jesus
and
His Exhortation to Pray
Cf. (Gethsemane) Matt. 26:36–46; Mark 14:32–42;
(a garden) John 18:1

Gethsemane can I forget?
Or there thy conflict see,
Thine agony and bloody sweat,
And not remember thee?

J. Montgomery, lines from
"According to Thy Gracious Word"

The beloved physician must have been deeply moved when he described what occurred in Gethsemane, or, as he simply calls the place, "the Mount of Olives." He abbreviates, making no mention of the eight disciples who were left at the garden's gate, and of the three (Peter, James, and John) who accompanied Jesus into the grove; nor of the three separate prayers and the Savior's return, each time, to the three disciples, always finding them sleeping. On the other hand it is Luke alone who mentions the angel who came to strengthen Jesus. It is he alone who refers to the sweat that became like thick drops of blood falling down upon the ground. It is Luke who, even more emphatically than Matthew and Mark, rivets our attention on the appalling horror to which the Savior was exposed, the frightful, soul-piercing anguish he experienced.

39. Then Jesus came outside and, as usual, went to the Mount of Olives. His disciples followed him.

The very fact that Jesus did the usual thing (cf. 21:37) makes this action of Jesus most unusual, most unlike what other people generally do when they are confronted with danger. When *they* know that going to the usual place is dangerous, they go somewhere else or stay where they are. Jesus, however, knowing that if tonight, as on previous nights, he should go to the Mount of Olives, he will be captured, with determination moves right ahead to that very place! He is fully aware of the fact that Judas the traitor knows this place and will have informed his bosses and co-conspirators about it (John 18:2). So that's where Jesus goes. We can see him wending his way, followed by eleven—and after entering the grove by three—disciples. The Shepherd is in the process of laying down his life for his sheep. He must make, and wants to make, a voluntary sacrifice, the only kind of sacrifice that will suffice as an atonement for the sins of all those who repose their trust in him.

40. When he arrived at the place, he said to them, Keep praying that y o u may not enter at all into temptation.

How wonderfully considerate is the Master. How big is his heart. So big

981

that even during this night of bitter woe there is room in it for "others." His heart goes out to them, for he fully realizes that the wrath of the Sanhedrin will not be appeased when he himself, the Leader, is caught. That wrath will be vented next upon those who have been following him. As a result, these disciples will be tempted to disown their Leader. Should that happen, it would be the worst evil that could overtake them.

If someone should raise the objection, "But this cannot happen, for *once a believer, always a believer*," the answer would be that Jesus knew very well that this favorable result is brought about through the use of means, one of them being prayer: his own prayer for them ("Holy Father, keep them in thy name," John 17:11), and their prayers for themselves. So he urges them to pray and to keep on praying that they may not enter at all into this insidious temptation.

41, 42. And he withdrew about a stone's throw beyond them, knelt down, and continued in prayer, saying, Father, if thou art willing, remove this cup from me; nevertheless, not my will but thine be done.

Note the following:

a. "A stone's throw" probably from the eight disciples near the garden's entrance. The three disciples would still be close enough to Jesus to see what he did and to hear what he said. To be sure, as the Savior kept on praying and agonizing these men fell asleep. But nothing prevents us from believing that they had kept awake long enough to preserve for that and later generations of believers a record of what happened here.

b. As to Christ's prayer as here recorded, careful study of the three separate petitions as reported by Matthew (26:39, 42, 44), the second and third being identical, shows that the *one* prayer of Luke 22:42 faithfully reproduces the essence of the three petitions of which Matthew makes mention.

Though it will never be possible for our minds to penetrate into the mystery of the horror Jesus experienced in Gethsemane, we cannot be far amiss if we state that it probably included at least this, that he was given a preview of the agonies of the fast approaching crucifixion. He had a foretaste of what it meant to be "forsaken" by his heavenly Father. And is it not reasonable to assume that during these dreadful periods of anguish Satan and his demons assaulted him, with the intention of causing him to turn aside from the path of obedience to God? Cf. Ps. 22:12, 13.

The best commentary on what Jesus experienced in Gethsemane is surely the inspired statement of Heb. 5:7, "He offered up prayers and supplications with loud crying and tears. . . ."

c. He prayed that "this cup," this terrible impending experience climaxed by the cross and the sense of complete abandonment, might be spared him. As with his entire human nature he recoiled before this terror, he "knelt down" (so Luke), "fell on his face" (so Matthew). He was, as it were, being torn apart by agony.

d. To be noted especially, and this in all the reports, hence also here in Luke, is the Sufferer's complete and unqualified submission to the will of his heavenly Father: "nevertheless, not my will but thine be done."

In a passage that must be regarded as authentic—see the note on pp. 990, 991—Luke adds: **43, 44. There appeared to him an angel from heaven, strengthening him. And being in anguish, he prayed very fervently [or: more intensely] and his sweat became like thick drops of blood falling down upon the ground.**

There are those who say that for Jesus to realize that an angel had to descend from heaven to strengthen him must have added to his feeling of deep humiliation. Granted, but should we not immediately add that in this dark hour the ministry of an angel must also have reconfirmed him in the belief that at this moment the Father had not completely forsaken him? Was it not, after all, the Father who sent the angel?

The opinion has been expressed by several that this strengthening affected only Christ's body, not his soul. Now it must be granted immediately that throughout this fiery ordeal Jesus never, even for a moment, crossed the boundary line between fear and sin. Nevertheless, to say that the strengthening he received was entirely limited to his body and in no sense whatever affected his soul is more than is probably warranted by such a passage as "He learned obedience from the things which he suffered" (Heb. 5:8).

In connection with Christ's sweat becoming like thick drops of blood, it is natural that Luke as a physician would inquire into and record this occurrence of *hematidrosis*. It took place while Jesus, suffering intensely, was engaged in fervent prayer. It must be borne in mind that the human nature of Jesus was sinless, and therefore very sensitive. When these factors—extreme anguish, earnest supplication, unparalleled sensitivity—are combined, the resulting strain can easily cause subcutaneous capillaries to dilate to such an extent that they will burst. And when this happens, as it is almost bound to do, in the vicinity of sweat glands, blood and sweat will be exuded together. This can happen over a large part of the body. The thick drops or clots of blood, imparting a reddish color to the beads of perspiration, will then trickle down to the ground.

The main point to bear in mind is certainly this, that the anguish which brought about this phenomenon was "for us." It was an indication of the Savior's undying love for the poor, lost sinners he had come to save.

45, 46. When he rose from prayer and came to the disciples, he found them sleeping from sorrow, and he asked them, Why are y o u asleep? Get up and pray, that y o u may not enter into temptation.

When Jesus returned to the three disciples he asked them, "Why are y o u asleep?" It was late, very late, midnight or perhaps even a little later. Peter, James, and John were filled with sorrow, as Luke does not forget to mention. To be sure, they should have kept awake, and they could have done so had they only continued in earnest prayer. Jesus was willing to forgive. As he stood watching over his own he said very tenderly, "Sleep on now and take y o u r rest" (Mark 14:41).

Then, perhaps after but a short period of time, he addressed the sleepers again, saying, "Get up and pray, that y o u may not enter into temptation." See above, on verse 40.

For *Practical Lessons* and *Greek Words,* etc., see pp. 989–992.

---

47 While he was still speaking, look a crowd! The one called Judas, one of the twelve, was leading them, and he approached Jesus to kiss him.

48 But Jesus said to him, "Judas, (is it) with a kiss that you are betraying the Son of man?"

49 Now when those around Jesus saw what was going to happen, they said, "Lord, shall we strike with a sword?" 50 And one of them slashed at the servant of the highpriest and severed his right ear.

51 But Jesus said, "No more of this!" And he touched the man's ear and healed him.

52 Then to the chief priests, captains of the temple guard, and elders, who had come out against him, Jesus said, "As against a robber [or rebel] did y o u come out with swords and clubs? 53 When day by day I was with y o u in the temple y o u did not lay hands on me. But this is y o u r hour and the rule of darkness."

22:47-53 *The Betrayal of Jesus and His Reaction*
Cf. Matt. 26:47-56; Mark 14:43-50; John 18:3-11

47. While he was still speaking, look, a crowd! The one called Judas, one of the twelve, was leading them, and he approached Jesus to kiss him.

"So, having taken the morsel, Judas went out immediately, and it was night." So reads John 13:30. Where did he go? He must have hurried off to the chief priests, etc., the men who had hired him. Was he afraid that once his treachery became known the alarm would spread and from everywhere friends of Jesus—think especially of the many from Galilee now in the city—would gather in his defense? "Act quickly," he must have told the Jewish authorities, "preferably by night, when no crowds are around. Act tonight." The authorities had been waiting for him. So busy were they with this plot to destroy Jesus that, as explained in N.T.C. on John, Vol. II, pp. 401-404 (on John 18:28), they had not yet partaken of the Passover meal. The probable whereabouts of Jesus had to be ascertained; a posse had to be organized; the temple police must be notified; permission must be obtained, whether from Pilate (which in view of Matt. 27:62-65 seems probable) or from the Roman "chiliarch," so that a group of soldiers could accompany the temple police; all the members of the Sanhedrin must be alerted; Annas must not be left in the dark; lanterns, swords, and clubs must be collected; the need of secrecy must be emphasized to all those who are "in" on this; etc., etc.

Finally, then, all is in readiness. Now to find Jesus. Judas did not know for certain where the group might have gone after leaving the upper room, but since he knew that Gethsemane was a place often visited by the Master and his disciples (John 18:2), the traitor was able to make a good guess, one that proved to be correct. So, while Jesus was still talking to the three disciples, Judas was seen entering the grove. "Judas, one of the twelve," says the text, to emphasize the terrible character of the crime this man was committing. Since he was "one of the twelve," it would be impossible to mention all the privileges that had been bestowed upon him during the many days, weeks, and months he had spent in Christ's immediate company. Such confidence had the other eleven reposed in this same Judas that they had even made him their treasurer. And now he was proving himself totally unworthy of all these honors and advantages, of all this trust. A shameless, disgusting quisling he had become, a wretched turncoat, one who for the paltry sum of thirty pieces of silver was delivering over to the enemy the greatest Benefactor whose feet ever trod this earth, even the Mediator, both God and man, the Lord Jesus Christ.

No one knows exactly how the crowd that accompanied Judas was arranged, if it even be correct to speak about any order of arrangement. If a guess be permissible it would be as follows:

In front Judas. Luke calls him the leader. He is the one who is going to approach Jesus, to kiss him, and thereby to point him out to the others. The highpriest's personal servant, Malchus, must also have been near to the front (verse 50; John 18:10) and so were also probably the temple police, Levites (verse 52; John 18:3). The detachment of soldiers, together with their commander, cannot have been far behind (John 18:3, 12). John 18:3 mentions a "cohort," probably obtained from the tower of Antonia, situated at the northwest corner of the temple area. Though a cohort at full strength consisted of six hundred men (one-tenth of a legion), the Roman authorities would probably not have depleted their garrison to that extent. At any rate, the band must have been rather large.

But why Roman legionaries at all? Would not the temple police have sufficed? The answer is that the Sanhedrin had learned that these officers could not always be relied on. Who knows, they might even side with Jesus, as had happened once before. See John 7:32, 45. Hence, it was felt that a detachment of soldiers was also needed. And because the Roman authorities themselves were very desirous of preventing trouble in Jerusalem, especially during Passover, when there was always danger of Jewish rebellion, the requested legionaries were quickly obtained.

Perhaps somewhat farther toward the back were members of the Sanhedrin (Luke 22:52). Whether any others were present we cannot be certain.

The force that had been commissioned to capture Jesus was well-equipped. The men carried swords and clubs (verse 52). As to the first, these were probably the short swords carried by the heavily-armed Roman soldier. See N.T.C. on Ephesians, p. 279, including footnote 177. The clubs or cudgels, we may assume, were in the hands of the temple police. Absolute certainty in such matters is not possible. Words have histories—in the present case this means that the term used in the original for "swords" may at times have had a more general meaning. It was not always used to distinguish these weapons from the broadswords. Also, we cannot be entirely certain that none but soldiers carried swords. Did not even Peter have a sword (John 18:10)? All we really know is that those who came to arrest Jesus carried swords and clubs. Their distribution is not definitely indicated, though it is natural to think of soldiers equipped with swords. The Gospel of John also mentions "torches and lanterns." Torches and lanterns—to search for the Light of the world. And it was full moon! Swords and cudgels—to subdue the Prince of Peace. For the Man of Sorrows the very sight of this band of ruffians, who considered him their quarry, meant indescribable suffering. —And to think that the men who were supposed to be leaders in Israel, highly religious and devout, chief priests and scribes and elders, together composing the Sanhedrin, had sent this force. Instead of welcoming Jesus as the long-expected Messiah, they were sending a posse to capture him, with the ultimate purpose of having him brought before the authorities that he might be sentenced to death.

48. But Jesus said to him, Judas, (is it) with a kiss that you are betraying the Son of man?

There are those who say that a kiss was the customary way of greeting a rabbi. However that may be, we may be sure that then as well as today—though more so in certain regions of the globe than in others—a kiss was the symbol of friendship and affection. As used by Judas, however, it is the prearranged signal for the arresting band to grab Jesus and, as Mark 14:44 adds, to lead him away "safely" or "under guard" (cf. Acts 16:23). To be sure, Judas already has his money (Matt. 26:15), but he also knows that he will not be able to keep it until he has made sure that the one he is betraying is actually in the hands of the Sanhedrin.

So, having arrived in Gethsemane, in front of the posse that had been dispatched to arrest Jesus, Judas, on seeing Jesus, steps forward. He then greets Jesus by saying "Rabbi" (Mark 14:45) or, as Matthew has it, "Hello, Rabbi." And what he does next has caused all later generations to recoil with horror at the mere mention of his name. Embracing Jesus he kisses him—probably fervently or repeatedly. See on Mark 14:45.

From the response of Jesus—"Judas, (is it) with a kiss that you are betraying the Son of man?"—it is clear that even at this very late moment Jesus is earnestly warning Judas. For his everlasting perdition he has only himself to blame. On the term *Son of man* see 5:24.

49. Now when those around Jesus saw what was going to happen, they said, Lord, shall we strike with a sword?

By this time the other eight disciples had probably also joined Jesus. See Matt. 26:56, "Then *all the disciples* deserted him and fled." If a little later they all fled, they must all have been with Jesus at this time. So when The Eleven saw what was about to happen, namely, that their Master was about to be captured, they asked him whether they should use force ("the sword"). Note that again, as so often previously, they had failed to grasp the meaning of the words of Jesus (verses 36, 38).

One of the men did not even wait for an answer but went into action at once: **50. And one of them slashed at the servant of the highpriest and severed his right ear.**

Although the incident is related in all four Gospels, only John (18:10) mentions the names of the two persons who (in addition to Jesus himself) figured most prominently in it. These two were Peter and Malchus, the highpriest's servant. The reason why John alone mentions these two names may well have been that when he published his Gospel it was no longer possible to punish the assailant.

That assailant was Simon Peter. Emboldened perhaps by the marvelous triumph of Jesus over the men who had come to capture him—at first the would-be captors, at the word of Jesus, had lurched backward and fallen to the ground (John 18:6)—and impelled by his own previous boasts (Matt. 26:33, 35; Mark 14:29, 31; Luke 22:33; John 13:37), Simon drew his short sword from its scabbard. Then he sprang at Malchus and, probably because the servant saw what was coming and quickly jumped aside, cut off his ear. Among the synoptists it is Luke alone who makes mention of the fact that it was the *right* ear. As a doctor his interest in the anatomy of the human body was keener than that of the other synoptists. But see also John 18:10.

51. But Jesus said, No more of this! —And he touched the man's ear and healed him.

Although the rendering "No more of this" is not certain, it is possible and would bring the words in line with those used by the Lord in verse 38. It is clear at any rate that Jesus was forbidding the use of force. An expanded version of what he said is found in John 18:11, and an even more detailed account in Matt. 26:52–54.

But not only what Jesus *said* is significant, also what he *did*. Had the ear been slashed off and was it hanging by a shred of skin (Lenski)? However one conceives of this, Luke, himself a healer, reports that Jesus touched the man's ear and healed him. It must not be possible for anyone to report truthfully that Jesus has either himself done anything wrong or has permitted it to remain uncorrected when done by someone else. Besides we once more see Jesus as the Great Sympathizer and Healer, the Savior, and this not only for the soul (in the case of all who place their trust in him) but even for the body. See Matt. 4:23; Luke 4:40; 7:21; Acts 2:22; 10:38.

52, 53. Then to the chief priests, captains of the temple guard, and elders, who had come out against him, Jesus said, As against a robber [or rebel] did y o u come out with swords and clubs? When day by day I was with y o u in the temple y o u did not lay hands on me.

Right then and there Jesus addressed the crowd; particularly, as Luke points out, "the chief priests, captains of the temple guard, and elders."

Probably some scribes were also being addressed. See Mark 14:43. All three groups that composed the Sanhedrin were represented here. For more on them see above, on 20:1, 2.

Of course, these people had no business being here during this sacred night, but they were so anxious to see whether their sinister plot against the enemy would succeed that they were actually to be seen among this crowd, probably in the rear. See N.T.C. on John, Vol. II, pp. 403, 404. Jesus then pointed out to the crowd—to all those who had come to arrest him and all those who gloated over his capture—how cowardly and perfidiously they were behaving. They had come out against him with an army, equipped with swords and clubs, as if he were a highwayman or, as the text can also be rendered, an insurrectionist, rebel, or revolutionary. In reality he was and had been a quiet, peaceful Prophet, sitting day by day in the temple, teaching the people. His life had been an open book. Had he been guilty of any crimes, those in charge of law and order would have had every chance to seize him.

If anyone wishes to know what kind of person this Jesus had proved himself to be during the slightly more than three years of his public ministry, let him read such passages as Mark 1:39; 10:13-16; and see also Matt. 4:23-25; 11:25-30; 12:18-21; Luke 22:49-51; 24:19; John 6:15; 18:11, 36, 37; Acts 2:22. To say, as some have done, that Jesus was "harmless" is putting it too mildly. He was and is "the Savior of the world" (John 4:42; I John 4:14), the world's greatest Benefactor. How absurd and hypocritical it was for the foe in the hour of darkness to pounce upon this Good Shepherd, from whom no one who heeded his message had anything to fear, and who even taught people to love their enemies! See Matt. 5:44.

By addressing the crowds in this manner Jesus was in reality doing them a favor. He was exposing their guilt. Is it not true that it takes confession of guilt to bring about salvation? Though it is a fact that the great majority of those who heard Jesus speak these words hardened themselves in sin, we have no right to conclude that the message, together with other messages that followed (for example, the seven words from the cross, Peter's Pentecost address, etc.), was completely ineffective. See, for example, Acts 6:7. The impression left upon us by these words of our Lord is that they were spoken in a calm and earnest manner. To be sure, Jesus rebukes, but at the same time he is even now seeking the lost, that he may save them.

Luke reports that Jesus added: **But this is y o u r hour and the rule of darkness.**

This was the hour—that is, the predestined hour (see above on verse 22)—in which the powers of darkness had their own way with Jesus, always, however, subject to God's overruling providence![571]

---

571. Notes on Greek words, phrases, and constructions in 22:39-53 begin on page 990.

Practical Lessons Derived from Luke 22:39–53

Verse 42

"Father, if thou art willing, remove this cup from me; nevertheless, not my will but thine be done."

This prayer should serve as a model for our prayers, in the sense that we, too, should always submit our will to his.

Verse 43

"There appeared to him an angel from heaven, strengthening him." Is not this in line with Lam. 3:33, "He does not afflict from the heart [thus the original] nor grieve the children of men"? What a comfort to know this!

Verse 49

"Lord, shall we strike with a sword?" Simon's rashness, reminding us of Jehu (II Kings 10:18–28), is here contrasted with Christ's calmness (see verses 48, 51–53), a lesson for us all.

Verse 51

"He touched the man's ear and healed him." Cf. verse 54, "Then, seizing him, they led him away." Cf. Mark 14:46, "They laid their hands on Jesus and arrested him." John 18:12, "Then the cohort and its commander and the officers of the Jews seized Jesus *and bound* him."

From these passages it becomes clear that when Jesus extended his hand to touch and heal the ear of Malchus, this was the last service he rendered *with his hand* before he was bound. Therefore, the last action of that hand, while it was still free, was one of love, one of rendering service to men. How it reminds us of his other similar deeds! Again and again he had placed his hand on people to heal and to bless them. He had even taken the little ones into his arm to bless them. Here, again, what a lesson for us all!

> And lo, thy touch brought life and health,
> Gave speech and strength and sight;
> Lo, youth renewed and frenzy calmed,
> Owned thee, the Lord of light.
> And now, O Lord, be near to bless,
> Almighty as of yore,
> In crowded streets, by restless couch,
> As by Gennesareth's shore.

> From "Thine Arm, O Lord"
> by E. H. Plumptre

Notes on Greek Words, Phrases, and Constructions in 22:39-53

Verse 40

προσεύχεσθε, sec. per. pl. pres. (durative) imperat. of προσεύχομαι, to pray. See the note on 9:18 on page 509.

εἰσελθεῖν, aor. (ingressive) infinitive of εἰσέρχομαι, to enter.

Verse 41

ἀπεσπάσθη, third per. s. aor. indicat. pass. of ἀποσπάω, to draw away from; in pass. (here probably with middle meaning), to separate oneself from, draw away from, withdraw. In Luke's writings this verb occurs only here and in Acts 20:30; 21:1. It is also found in Matt. 26:51, there in the sense of *to draw* (a sword).

θείς (nom. s. masc. 2nd aor. act. participle of τίθημι) τὰ γόνατα, knelt down.

προσηύχετο, third per. s. imperf. middle indicat. of προσεύχομαι, to pray. What kind of imperfect? Some say *ingressive:* began to pray; some, *descriptive:* was praying; some, *progressive:* continued to pray. Which of these is correct is hard to say.

Verse 42

βούλει, Attic form of Koine βούλῃ, *sec.* per. s. of βούλομαι. In Attic Greek the ending of the sec. per. middle or pass. is generally ει instead of η; thus always in the verbs βούλομαι, I will; οἴομαι, I think; and ὄψομαι, I shall see.

γινέσθω, third per. s. pres. imperat. middle of γίνομαι, here with the sense of: to be done; hence "(Thy will) be (constantly) done."

Verses 43, 44

Those who reject verses 43, 44 present the following reasons for this rejection: (a) this passage is missing from Codex Vaticanus and from other important manuscripts; (b) it looks like a scribal embellishment of Luke's text; (c) it may be considered a Western interpolation; and (d) it is out of harmony with the contents of the immediately preceding verse.

On the other hand, those who take the opposite view answer: (a) the passage is present in Codex Sinaiticus and is supported by several other witnesses, some of them early; (b) it is especially Luke who throughout his Gospel and book of Acts mentions angels again and again (see any good concordance and note the frequency of the word *angel* in Luke's writings as compared with its frequency in the other Gospels); (c) Luke also shows that Jesus himself was very conscious of the presence and work of angels; (d) the question is legitimate whether the omission of verses 43, 44 from several important manuscripts, etc., may not be ascribed to a theological bias, namely, the *mistaken* belief that what is reported here, being supposedly out of harmony with the doctrine of Christ's deity, was a legitimate basis of appeal for the Arians; and (e) the passage is entirely in line with Heb. 5:7, 8. In both passages the fact that, in a sense, Christ's human nature, though entirely without sin, needed strengthening is held before us. Besides, as to the reasoning of those who reject the passage, are not some of their arguments of a purely subjective character? I believe the passage should be retained.

All this can be found in my N.T.C. on Mark, pp. 583, 584, footnote 722. After that commentary had been published, an article appeared by G. Schneider, "Engel und Blutschweiss (Lk 22, 43-44). 'Redaktionsgeschichte' im Dienste der Textkritik," *BibZ* 20 (1976), pp. 112-116. In defense of the authenticity of Luke 22:43, 44 that author presents some of the same arguments I had advanced. He adds that the pattern in Luke 22:39-46 corresponds to the scheme in the Lucan transfiguration narrative (9:28-32), and that the deletion of these verses may be traced, among other things, to an aversion to the miraculous. Schneider credits Redaction Criticism with the result he has reached.

Undoubtedly Redaction Criticism should be given all the credit to which it can properly lay claim, but is it not true that, without any recourse to that discipline, I, for one—and probably many others along with me—had already reached the same conclusion with respect to the genuine character of Luke 22:43, 44? To reach the right conclusion Redaction Criticism was not needed.

ὤφθη, third per. s. aor. indicat. pass. of ὁράω, to see; in pass., as here, to be seen, to appear. The first time Luke, in his Gospel, uses this form (ὤφθη in 1:11) he similarly ascribes this appearance to an *angel*.

ἐνισχύων, nom. s. masc. pres. participle of ἐνισχύω**, to strengthen (ἰσχύς = strength); in the New Testament only here and in Acts 9:19.

ἐκτενέστερον (ἐκ plus τείνω; hence, to stretch out), adv. (comparative degree), more intensely; or (if elative) very intensely, very fervently. For the adverb ἐκτενῶς see also Acts 12:5; I Peter 1:22. For the related verb ἐκτείνω see on verse 53.

ἱδρώς*, sweat, perspiration; in the New Testament found only here. Cf. *sudatorium.*

Another hapax legomenon is θρόμβοι, nom. pl. of θρόμβος*, clot, thick drop. Cf. *thrombosis.*

Verse 45

λύπης, gen. s. of λύπη, pain, grief, sorrow; in Luke only here; but four times in John 16, three times in II Cor. 2, twice in II Cor. 7, and once each in II Cor. 9, Phil. 2, Heb. 12, and I Peter 2.

Verse 46

εἰσέλθητε, sec. per. pl. aor. (ingress.) subjunct. (after ἵνα μὴ), to enter. This verb is very common in all four Gospels, also in Acts and Hebrews. It occurs five times in Rev.; elsewhere in the New Testament its use is scattered.

Verse 47

φιλῆσαι, aor. infinitive of φιλέω, to kiss. In the New Testament this verb is used in a threefold sense: (a) as a synonym of ἀγαπάω, to have affection for; see N.T.C. on John, Vol. II, pp. 494-500; (b) to like something or to like to do something, as in Luke 20:46; and (c), as here in 22:47, to kiss.

Verse 48

φιλήματι, dat. s. of φίλημα, kiss. Note the following:
a. the unholiest kiss of all, that of Judas, as here.
b. the holy kiss (Rom. 16:16; I Cor. 16:20; II Cor. 13:12; I Thess. 5:26).

c. the kiss of love (I Peter 5:14).

d. the welcoming kiss, the one Simon the Pharisee neglected to give Jesus (Luke 7:45).

Verse 49

τὸ ἐσόμενον, acc. s. neut. fut. participle of εἰμί; therefore: what was going to be; i.e., what was going to happen.

εἰ, in a direct question, reminding one of Hebrew style, not to be translated.

ἐν, instrumental.

μαχαίρῃ, dat. s. of μάχαιρα, sword; to be distinguished from ῥομφαία, broadsword, or simply *sword,* when this distinction is not clear.

Verse 50

ἀφεῖλεν, third per. s. 2nd aor. act. indicat. of ἀφαιρέω, to take away, remove, cut off, sever.

Verse 51

ἐᾶτε, sec. per. pl. pres. imperat. act. of ἐάω, to allow, let be; hence here, "let be until this," probably meaning, "No more of this," or simply "Stop."

Verse 52

παραγενομένους, acc. pl. masc. 2nd aor. participle of παραγίνομαι, here: to come out (against). See the note on 7:4 on page 380.

For στρατηγός (captain of the temple guard) see the note on 22:4 on page 967.

λῃστήν, acc. s. of λῃστής, here perhaps *robber,* but *rebel* is also definitely possible. More about this word in the note on 10:30 on page 602.

Verse 53

ἐξετείνατε, sec. per. pl. aor. indicat. act. of ἐκτείνω, to stretch out; here: to lay (hands) on. See verse 44 for related adverb.

ἐξουσία, here perhaps domain, reign, rule. See W. Foerster, the article on this word in Th.D.N.T., Vol. II, p. 568, where that author points out that such *power* or *rule* is subject to God's overruling providence.

---

54 Then, seizing him, they led him away and took him to the house of the highpriest. And Peter was following at a distance. 55 Now when they had kindled a fire in the middle of the courtyard and had sat down together, Peter was sitting in the midst of them. 56 Then a servant girl saw him as he sat in the light (of the fire), and looking intently at him said, "This fellow was also with him." 57 But he denied it, saying, "I don't know him, woman."

58 A little later someone else saw him and said, "You're one of them too." But Peter replied, "Man, I'm not!"

59 About an hour later another man began to insist emphatically, "Certainly this fellow was with him, for he's indeed a Galilean." 60 Peter replied, "Man, I don't know what you're talking about." All at once, while he [Peter] was still speaking, a rooster crowed.

61 The Lord turned and looked straight at Peter.

And Peter was reminded of the word of the Lord, how he had said to him, "Before a rooster crows today, you will deny me three times." 62 And he went outside and wept bitterly.

22:54-62 *Peter's Threefold Denial*
Cf. Matt. 26:57, 58, 69-75; Mark 14:53, 54, 66-72;
John 18:15-18, 25-27

54-57. Then, seizing him, they led him away and took him to the house of the highpriest. And Peter was following at a distance. Now when they had kindled a fire in the middle of the courtyard and had sat down together, Peter was sitting in the midst of them. Then a servant girl saw him as he sat in the light (of the fire), and looking intently at him said, This fellow was also with him. But he denied it, saying, I don't know him, woman.

Having seized Jesus, his captors brought him to the highpriest's house or palace. Such a house looks into its own interior: that is, its rooms are built around an *open* courtyard. An arched passage leads from the heavy outside *door* or (better) *gate* into this inner court. In this passage there is a place (in some houses a little room) for the gate-keeper. Sometimes, as also in the present instance, the court was *lower* than the rooms which ranged around it. It is not entirely impossible that the room to which Jesus had been led was a kind of gallery, from which what happened in the court could be seen and heard.

That the house here mentioned was the residence of Caiaphas is clearly implied in Matt. 26:57, 58. That it was, nevertheless, also occupied by Annas, the father-in-law of Caiaphas, becomes clear by comparing the passage from Matthew with John 18:13, 15, 24. Besides, is it not very natural to assume that these two close relatives, in mind and heart two of a kind, would be living in the same spacious mansion? Probably one wing was occupied by Annas, another by Caiaphas.[572]

Though all the disciples had fled, two—Peter and "another disciple"—soon rallied and began to follow the band that was leading Jesus to the highpriest's palace. In the case of Peter, "following Jesus" was probably prompted, in part, by the loud boasts he had uttered, as recorded in verse 33; cf. Mark 14:29, 31; in part also, by sheer curiosity, as Matt. 26:58 states, and perhaps we should add, in part by love for his Master. Note, however, that he was following "at a distance," probably through fear. How this disciple secured admission to the palace is described in John 18:15, 16. Peter, then, having been allowed to enter the palace by its outer gate, walked through the archway that led to the unroofed courtyard, where he sat down with the palace servants and the temple guards (policemen), warming himself near the fire. By this time most of the soldiers, having delivered their prisoner, had probably returned to the fortress of Antonia.

At this point Luke tells the story of Peter's three denials. These denials are reported in all four Gospels. For the manner in which the accounts are related to each other and for the interesting variations see N.T.C. on John, Vol. II, pp. 388-390; and on Mark, pp. 615, 616.

---

572. For this conclusion see also A. Sizoo, *Uit De Wereld van het Nieuwe Testament*, Kampen, 1946, pp. 81, 82.

It would seem that the very moment when Peter had entered the palace, the portress, viewing him from her nook in the vestibule, had her suspicions. The fact that she had admitted him at the request of John seemed to indicate that Peter too was a disciple of Jesus. The uneasiness that could be read on his face confirmed her suspicions. So, about to be relieved by another gate-keeper, she walks toward Peter, who has already entered the open courtyard, and who in the light of the fire by which he is warming himself is clearly visible. She fixes her eyes on him. Then, stepping even closer, she exclaims, "This fellow was also with him." That the words she uses are reported somewhat differently in the other Gospels presents no difficulty. It must not be taken for granted that any Gospel, all by itself, reports all the words spoken by this girl.

Peter evidently has been floored. The suddenness and boldness of the servant girl's incriminating remark catch him off guard. In spite of all his loud and repeated promises of unswerving loyalty to Jesus, promises made only a few hours earlier, he is now thoroughly frightened. One might say: he panics. Evidently he has failed to take to heart Christ's admonition recorded in 22:40. So he tells the girl, "I don't know him, woman."

58. A little later someone else saw him and said, You're one of them too. —But Peter replied, Man, I'm not!

The second denial follows closely upon the first. In his frustration resulting from the first embarrassment Peter tries to get out of the building. However, the portresses are unwilling to let him out. So he gets no farther than the entrance way or vestibule which via the gate leads to the outside. Several people are standing around. It seems that the portress who is about to go off duty has already told the news about Peter to the girl who has come to relieve her. So this second girl (cf. Matt. 26:71 and Mark 14:69) now says to those standing around, "This fellow is one of them" (as Mark has it); "This fellow was with Jesus the Nazarene" (Matthew's way of stating the same thing).

The fact that, according to our present passage (Luke 22:58), at least one male bystander now chimes in with what the two girls are saying does not make matters any easier for Peter. Again Peter denies his Lord. He says, "I'm not." According to Matthew this time his denial is accompanied by an oath.

59, 60a. About an hour later another man began to insist emphatically, Certainly this fellow was with him, for he's indeed a Galilean. —Peter replied, Man, I don't know what you're talking about.

We have noticed that even during the second denial interest in Peter's case was no longer confined to the portresses. And now the bystanders *again* express themselves. The reason for this is as follows: Having been refused exit, Peter returns to the open courtyard. An hour elapses. It would seem, therefore, that the first two denials took place during Christ's appearance before Annas. Now the situation changes somewhat: Jesus has been brought before Caiaphas and the entire Sanhedrin. Christ's first trial before this body is almost over.

During the interval of an hour the news about Peter has been spreading. Now the palace servants and the officers, the men who are standing around the fire with Peter, begin to tell him that he is one of Christ's disciples, and that his very accent or brogue identifies him as a Galilean. Cf. Matt. 26:73. One man, as Luke shows, asserts emphatically, "Certainly this fellow was with him, for he is indeed a Galilean." A comparison of the Gospel accounts shows that some people are talking *to* Peter, others *about* him. Accusations are flying in from every direction. This was enough to get anyone excited, especially excitable Simon! He answers, "I don't know what you're talking about."

But as if all this were not enough, a relative of Malchus bursts out, "Did I not see you in the garden with Jesus?" For this story see N.T.C. on John, Vol. II, pp. 399, 400.

Angry and excited Peter now begins to call down curses on himself and to swear that he doesn't even know Jesus. He must have said something like, "May God do this or that to me if it be true that I am or ever was a disciple of Jesus." He stands there invoking on himself one curse after another. And the louder this Galilean talks, the more, without realizing it, he is saying to all those standing around, "I'm a liar."

What happened next was probably this: Jesus, his night trial ended, was being led across the court to his prison cell, from which within a few hours he would be led once more before the Sanhedrin.

60b, 61. All at once while he [Peter] was still speaking, a rooster crowed. The Lord turned and looked straight at Peter. And Peter was reminded of the word of the Lord, how he had said to him, Before a rooster crows today, you will deny me three times.

When Peter heard the crowing of the rooster, and saw Jesus looking at him, with eyes full of pain, yet also of pardon, his memory of Christ's warning prediction was suddenly awakened. —In this connection we must not forget that "the look of Jesus would have been wasted on Peter if it had not been that Peter was looking at Jesus."[573]

62. And he went outside and wept bitterly.

How it came about that Peter is at last permitted to leave the palace is not stated. Can it have been because now everybody's attention is fixed on *Jesus*? However that may be, Peter goes out and weeps as only he can weep: bitterly, profusely, sorrowfully, his heart being filled with genuine regret for what he has done.

How deceitful is man's heart. It is "exceedingly corrupt. Who can know it?" (Jer. 17:9). See also II Kings 8:13; cf. verse 15. Think of it: "Thou art the Christ, the Son of the living God."—"I don't know what you're talking about."

How Jesus must have suffered! No doubt much more because of these base denials by a highly favored disciple and friend than because of the

---

573. G. Campbell Morgan, *op. cit.,* p. 312.

blows and the mockery inflicted on him by his avowed enemies. See Ps. 55:12–14.

Finally, how God's pardoning grace and the Savior's forgiving love are here revealed! See Isa. 1:18; 53:6; 55:6, 7; I John 1:7b.

For *Practical Lessons* and *Greek Words,* etc., see pp. 999–1002.

---

63 Meanwhile the men who were holding Jesus in custody began to mock and to beat him. 64 And having blindfolded him, they were demanding, "Prophesy! Who is it that struck you?" 65 And they were saying many other insulting things to him.

22:63–65 *The Mocking and Beating of Jesus*
Cf. Matt. 26:67, 68; Mark 14:65

The story now turns from Peter to Jesus. Having been captured and led to the highpriest's palace, he was informally condemned to death by the Sanhedrin in a night session. Luke does not report that incident. See, however, Matt. 26:57–66; Mark 14:53–64.

Luke relates what immediately followed (cf. Matt. 26:67, 68; Mark 14:65). He writes:

63, 64. Meanwhile the men who were holding Jesus in custody began to mock and to beat him. And having blindfolded him, they were demanding, Prophesy! Who is it that struck you?

The venerable (?) members of the Sanhedrin now show their cruel, vengeful, sadistic character. Utterly mean are they, inhuman, base, contemptible! Even if we allow that the cruelty to which Jesus was now subjected was the action of the "underlings," and not directly of the priests, etc., it remains true that it was carried out with the wholehearted permission and co-operation of the members of the Sanhedrin. Think of it, he who throughout his earthly sojourn went about doing good was now made the object of cruelty inflicted upon body and soul. They struck him heavy blows. And cruelty plus mockery reached its climax when with their fists these wicked men struck the blindfolded prisoner in the face, and then shouted, "Prophesy! Who is it that struck you?"

Filled with such horror is the evangelist when he reflects on this that he refuses to go into more detail but simply states:

65. And they were saying many other insulting things to him.

For *Practical Lessons* and *Greek Words,* etc., see pp. 999–1002.

---

66 As soon as it was day the council of the elders of the people, both chief priests and scribes, assembled, and they brought him back to[574] their Sanhedrin. 67 They said to him, "If you are the Christ, tell us."

He answered, "If I tell y o u, y o u will certainly not believe; 68 and if I question y o u, y o u will certainly not answer. 69 But from now on the Son of man will be seated at the right hand of the power of God."

---

574. Or: and they led him away to, etc.

70 Then they all asked, "So you are the Son of God?"

He replied, "Y o u are right; I am."

71 They said, "What further need do we have of testimony? For we have heard it ourselves from his own mouth."

22:66-71 *The Early Morning Trial Before the Sanhedrin*
Cf. Matt. 27:1; Mark 15:1a

As to *substance* also cf. Luke 22:66-71 with Matt. 26:63-66 and with Mark 14:61-64. And for the preliminary hearing before Annas see John 18:12-14, 19-23 (note N.T.C. on the Gospel of John, Vol. II, pp. 385-388).

66. As soon as it was day the council of the elders of the people, both chief priests and scribes, assembled, and they brought him back to their Sanhedrin.

The reason this meeting was called was in all probability to give a semblance of legality to the proceedings against Jesus. With respect to the question "Were the trials of Jesus (before the Sanhedrin and before Pilate) legal or illegal?" a vast literature has sprung up.[575]

From the Jewish side an attempt has been made to prove that the Sanhedrin tried its level best to rescue Jesus, not being at all anxious to condemn him to death. Needless to say there is nothing in Scripture that supports this theory in any way. When an official body like the Jewish Sanhedrin, by the unofficial and illegal action of its members, *goes in search of witnesses* against Jesus, when it brings Jesus before Annas, a man who no

---

575. To mention but a few of the many books and articles that can be consulted:

Amram, D. W., *Leading Cases in the Bible,* Philadelphia, 1905.

Baldensperger, G., "Il a rendu témoignage devant Ponce Pilate," *RHPR,* 2 (1922), pp. 1-25, 95-117.

Barton, G. A., "On the Trial of Jesus Before the Sanhedrin," *JBL,* 41 (1922), pp. 205-211.

Bentfort, J. A. D., "Enige beknopte beschouwingen met betrekking tot de processen van de Here Jezus Christus en van de Apostel Paulus," *GTT,* 55 (1955), pp. 33-68.

Blinzler, J., "Der Entschied des Pilatus—Exekutionsbefehl oder Todesurteil?" *MTZ,* 5 (1954), pp. 171-184.

. . . . . , *Der Prozess Jesu,* Ratisbonne, 1960.

Cheever, H. M., "The Legal Aspects of the Trial of Christ," *BS,* 60 (1903), pp. 495-509.

Cohen, B., "Evidence in Jewish Law," *Recueils de la Société J. Bodin* 16 (1965).

Dalmann, G., *Jesus-Jeshua,* New York, 1929, especially p. 98.

Danby, H., "The Bearing of the Rabbinical Criminal Code on the Jewish Trial Narratives in the Gospels," *JTS,* 21 (1920), pp. 51-76.

Derret, J. D. M., *An Oriental Lawyer Looks at the Trial of Jesus and the Doctrine of Redemption,* London, 1966.

Easton, B. S., "The Trial of Jesus," *AJT,* 19 (1915), pp. 430-452.

Goguel, M., "A propos du procès de Jésus," *ZNW,* 31 (1929-30), pp. 289-301.

Hendriksen, W., *Israel in Prophecy,* Grand Rapids, 1972, especially pp. 10-15.

Jeremias, J., "Zur Geschichtlichkeit des Verhörs Jesu vor dem Hohen Rat," *ZNW,* 43 (1950-51), pp. 145-150.

Price, O. J., "Jesus' Arrest and Trial," *BW,* 36 (1919), pp. 345-353.

Tubbs, R. S., "Local Attorney Eyes Legal Maneuvering Which Led to Death of Jesus," article in *The Grand Rapids Press,* April 6, 1963.

Winter, P., "Marginal Notes on the Trial of Jesus," *ZNW,* 50 (1959), pp. 14-33, 221-251.

longer had any judicial authority (though he probably still exercised a tremendous amount of influence), when the highpriest attempts to force the prisoner to testify against himself, etc., etc., the only fair conclusion is that we are dealing here with a case not of justice but of the perversion or miscarriage of justice.

Note in this passage the mention of all three groups that entered into the composition of the Sanhedrin.[576]

67a. They said to him, If you are the Christ, tell us.

As Mark 14:55-59 makes clear, the witnesses that had been "sought" could not agree and consequently were of no help. So in sheer desperation the judges begin to assume the role of prosecuting attorneys or of accusers. This is not an exaggeration. That the leaders hated Jesus and were determined to destroy him must be accepted by anyone who claims to believe the testimony of Scripture. And this sinister desire had not taken possession of them just "yesterday." See above, on verse 2.

So now this august body, with Caiaphas in charge, is asking Jesus to make a statement which can be used by them for the formulation of a charge sufficient to have him put to death! If he will now only co-operate and tell them that he is the Christ—with all the political overtones they could read into this confession—he could be accused before the Roman authorities and destroyed.

67b-69. He answered, If I tell y o u, y o u will certainly not believe; and if I question y o u, y o u will certainly not answer. But from now on the Son of man will be seated at the right hand of the power of God.

What Jesus is saying, therefore, amounts to this, "No matter what I say, y o u will certainly not believe me, for y o u are prejudiced. And if I put a question to y o u regarding this matter, in order that by this method y o u might be led to the right answer, y o u will certainly not answer." As to the latter, was not that exactly what had already occurred? See Luke 20:3-7.

The great saying "But from now on," etc. (cf. Matt. 26:64; Mark 14:62), is a commentary on Ps. 110:1 and Dan. 7:13, 14. The idea that the Messiah would be seated at the right hand of God, etc., was accepted even in Jewish circles.[577] For the term *Son of man* see above, on 5:24. As to the expression *the power of God* here the reference is to God in all his majesty and greatness.[578]

Jesus is looking down history's lane. He sees the miracles of Calvary, the resurrection, the ascension, the coronation at the Father's right hand ("the right hand of the Power," that is, "of the Almighty"). He sees Pentecost, the glorious return on the clouds of heaven, the judgment day, all rolled into

---

576. See M. Wolff, "De samenstelling en het karaktervan het grote *synedrion* te Jeruzalem voor het jaar 70 na Christus," *TT* 51 (1917), pp. 299-320.

577. See the *Midrash on Psalms* (on Ps. 2:7 and Ps. 18).

578. See A. M. Goldberg, "Sitzend zur Rechten der Kraft. Zur Gottesbezechnung *Gebura* in der frühen rabbinischen Literatur," *BibZ* 8 (1964), pp. 284-293.

one, manifesting his power and glory. On the final day of judgment he, even Jesus, will be the Judge, and these very men—Caiaphas and his partners—will have to answer for the crime they are now committing. Christ's prophecy is also a warning!

The members of the Sanhedrin did not doubt at all that Jesus by saying "the Son of man" was referring to himself. They also knew that the One so indicated in Dan. 7:13 was indeed divine. This explains their question: **70. Then they all asked, So you are the Son of God?** Now note the unqualified, solemn answer: **He replied, Y o u are right; I am.** The fact that the original, which, literally rendered, is "Y o u say that I am," can have no other meaning than "Y o u are right; I am" is clear from what immediately follows, namely: **71. They said, What further need do we have of testimony? For we have heard it ourselves from his own mouth.**

The highpriest and the others present regarded this claim as usurpation of divine honor by a mere man; in other words, as *blasphemy*. So the highpriest tore his garment (Matt. 26:65; Mark 14:63), and all agreed that further testimony was unnecessary.[579]

Practical Lessons Derived from Luke 22:54-71

Note the following items in the story of Peter's fall and restoration:

a. "Simon, Simon, watch out! Satan has asked to sift y o u as wheat. But I have prayed for you . . . and you, once you have returned to me, strengthen your brothers" (Luke 22:31, 32).

b. "Lord, with you I am ready to go even to prison and to death" (22:33).

c. "A rooster will not crow today before you deny three times that you know me" (22:34).

d. The three denials, ending with "Man, I don't know what you're talking about" (22:57-60a).

e. "All at once . . . a rooster crowed. The Lord turned and looked straight at Peter" (22:60b, 61a).

f. "Peter remembered. . . . He went outside and wept bitterly" (22:61b, 62).

g. Peter's rehabilitation (John 21:15 f.).

h. Now note how Peter, having by God's grace retraced his steps and having been restored, strengthened, and is still strengthening, his "brothers":

(1) his Pentecost address (Acts 2:14-42).

(2) "Silver and gold have I none," etc. (Acts 3:1-26).

(3) "And in no one else is there salvation," etc. (4:5-12).

(4) Other testimonies by Peter, or, as in point (2), by Peter and one or more others: Acts 5:1-11; 5:17-32; 8:14-24; 9:36-43; ch. 10; 11:1-18; 12:1-19.

i. The testimony found in Peter's epistles, an example being:

"Be clothed with *humility*. . . . Be sober, be watchful, y o u r adversary, the devil, as a roaring lion, is prowling around, seeking someone to devour. But resist him by

---

579. Notes on Greek words, phrases, and constructions in 22:54-71 begin on page 1000.

standing firm in (y o u r) faith" (I Peter 5:5, 8, 9). When Peter wrote these words he was speaking "from experience."

See also on Luke 22:65, "And they were saying many other insulting things to him." Peter reflects on this in I Peter 2:23, 24, "While he was reviled, he did not revile in return; while suffering, he made no threats, but constantly entrusted himself to him who judges righteously. . . . He himself bore our sins in his body on the cross. . . . By his wounds we are healed."

All this does not mean that while still on earth Peter became "perfect," that is, "sinless." On the contrary, read the story of his temporary lapse (Gal. 2:11-21). But, by and large, the grace of God was certainly magnified in his labors, so that, by means of it, he became a Rock of strength.

Verse 70

"So you are the Son of God?" Jesus replied, "Y o u are right. I am." This, too, as well as the one before Pilate (I Tim. 6:13), can justly be termed "a good confession." Its significance stands out all the more sharply because of Christ's many *silences* (Matt. 26:63; 27:12, 14; Mark 15:5; Luke 23:9; John 19:9). Jesus knew when to speak, and when not, a lesson for us to take to heart.

Notes on Greek Words, Phrases, and Constructions in 22:54-71

Verse 54

συλλαβόντες, nom. pl. masc. 2nd aor. act. participle of συλλαμβάνω, to seize, arrest. For a summary of the various meanings of this verb see the note on 1:24 on pp. 81, 82.

Note: they *led* him away and *brought* him *to,* etc., two third per. pl. 2nd aor. (effective) indicat. act. verbs, the first *simple,* the second *compound,* both based on ἄγω, to lead, bring.

ἠκολούθει, third per. s. imperfect of ἀκολουθέω, to follow. This imperfect has been called *graphic, vivid, progressive, descriptive,* and even *picturesque!* The author is picturing, very vividly describing, what was happening. Luke has already used this verb many times, beginning at 5:11, and is going to use it once more in his Gospel (23:27), and a few times in Acts. It abounds also in the other three Gospels and occurs six times in the book of Revelation. For the rest, in the entire New Testament it is found only once (I Cor. 10:4, ". . . the Rock that followed [or: accompanied] them"). The meaning is *to follow, accompany.* Cf. *acolyte.*

Verse 55

Note the two gen. absolutes: *they having kindled* and *they having sat down together.* The περί in περιαψάντων may basically indicate that they had kindled the fire "all around," hence *thoroughly.* How much of the perfective sense still remained is hard to say.

αὐλῆς, gen. s. of αὐλή, courtyard. This is a word about which there has been much dispute. Because of the context in each individual case, the following meanings are probably correct:

a. *sheepfold:* John 10:1, 16. The context has reference to shepherds and their sheep. The meaning *sheepfold* is therefore natural.

b. *court, courtyard:* Matt. 26:58, 69; Mark 14:54, 66; Luke 22:55; John 18:15. In all these cases Peter is represented as being with the temple police and the palace servants, warming himself near the fire in an "open" or "roofless" place, one that is represented as being "lower" than the rest of the house or palace. Hence, the natural meaning is "court" or "courtyard." Rev. 11:1, 2 makes a distinction between the inner temple and naturally the "outer court."

c. *house, palace:* Matt. 26:3; Mark 15:16; Luke 11:21. Respectively, the argument for "house" or "palace" is as follows: A courtyard, with servants passing in and out, would not have suited the context of Matt. 26:3. The expressed synonym *praetorium* indicates that more than a courtyard is meant in Mark 15:16. And the owner of a house or palace (Luke 11:21) would guard more than his courtyard; besides, his "possessions" would not be confined to that area.

Verse 56

πρὸς τὸ φῶς, in front of (or facing) the light; or, as we would say, "in the light." ἀτενίσασα, nom. s. fem. aor. participle of ἀτενίζω, to look intently, gaze.

Verse 59

Note gen. absolute: *about an hour having intervened.*

διαστάσης, gen. s. fem. 2nd aor. participle of διΐστημι, to intervene. A time interval is indicated. In 24:51 the interval is one of space; some interpret the interval in Acts 27:28 as one of space, others as one of time.

καὶ γάρ; cf. Latin *etenim*, in fact, indeed!

Verse 60

Again a gen. absolute: *he still speaking.*

Verse 61

ἐνέβλεψεν, third per. s. aor. indicat. of ἐμβλέπω; cf. 20:17; Acts 22:11; also in Matt. 6:26; 19:26; Mark 8:25; 10:21, 27; 14:67; John 1:36, 42; to look straight at, fix one's gaze upon. See the note on 20:17 on page 898.

ὑπεμνήσθη, third per. s. aor. indicat. pass. of ὑπομιμνήσκω, to remind, bring up; in pass., as here: to be reminded, to remember. The verb occurs also in John 14:26; II Tim. 2:14; Titus 3:1; II Peter 1:12; III John 10; Jude 5. The related form μνήσθητί μου (from μιμνήσκω) is found in 23:42.

Verse 62

ἔκλαυσεν, third per. s. aor. indicat. of κλαίω, to weep; same form as in 19:41, he burst into tears.

Verse 63

ἐνέπαιζον, third per. pl. imperf. act. of ἐμπαίζω, to mock, scoff, make sport of. See the note on 14:29 on page 739.

δέροντες, nom. pl. masc. pres. act. participle of δέρω, to beat, strike, flay. See the note on 12:47, 48 on page 688.

Verse 64

περικαλύψαντες, nom. pl. masc. aor. participle of περικαλύπτω, lit. to put a veil around; hence, to cover, and (since the veil is put around the face) to blindfold.

ἐπηρώτων, third per. pl. imperf. act. of ἐπερωτάω, to question, demand.

παίσας, nom. s. masc. aor. participle of παίω, to strike.

Verse 65

βλασφημοῦντες, masc. pl. pres. act. participle of βλασφημέω, to insult, blaspheme. See the note on 12:10 on page 660. The word also occurs in 23:39.

ἔλεγον, third per. pl. imperf. (iterative) of λέγω.

Verse 66

συνήχθη, third per. s. aor. indicat. pass. of συνάγω, to bring together, gather; pass. (here), "was gathered" or simply "assembled," "met." See the note on 12:17, 18 on page 672.

πρεσβυτέριον, the council of elders. See also Acts 22:5; I Tim. 4:14. Cf. *presbytery*.

συνέδριον, the Sanhedrin.

Verses 67, 68

εἰπὸν ἡμῖν, tell us; sec. per. s. imperat., a late substitute for εἰπέ. Note how in these two verses a first class condition is followed by two third class (future more vivid) conditions.

εἴπω, first per. s. subjunct. of εἶπον, which is used as a sec. aor. of λέγω.

πιστεύσητε, sec. per. pl. aor. subjunct. of πιστεύω; note strong negation (οὐ μή) y o u will certainly not believe.

ἐρωτήσω, first per. sing. fut. indicat. or aor. subjunct. (same form) of ἐρωτάω, to question.

ἀποκριθῆτε, sec. per. pl. aor. subjunct. pass. of ἀποκρίνομαι, to answer.

Verse 69

ἔσται... καθήμενος, third per. s. periphrastic fut. of κάθημαι, to sit, be seated.

Verse 70

Lit. "Y o u say that I am," meaning "Y o u are right. I am."

Summary of Chapter 22

It is understandable that the popularity of Jesus, so that "all the people would rise early to go to him in the temple and hear him" (21:38), angered the leaders. So they were looking for a way to do away with him without creating a riot.

In this difficult situation they received unexpected help from a man who belonged to the inner circle of Christ's disciples. His name was Judas Iscariot, one of The Twelve. He agreed to deliver Jesus into their hands. The price? Thirty pieces of silver (Matt. 26:15). This was paid (verses 1–6).

Since Passover was at hand, Jesus sent *Peter* and *John* to Jerusalem to secure a room and to make the necessary preparations. His predictions with respect to the experiences of the two in the city were fulfilled in every detail (verses 7–13).

At the Passover Jesus told his disciples, "From now on I will not drink from the fruit of the vine with y o u until the kingdom of God has arrived." Cf. Matt. 26:29. He shocked them by declaring, "The hand of the traitor is with me on the table."

Judas having left (cf. John 13:21–30), Jesus instituted the Lord's Supper, to be observed ever after, "in remembrance of" him, that is, of his body, given for those who place their trust in him, and of his blood, poured out for them (verses 14–23).

Perhaps almost immediately after entering the upper room (cf. John 13:1 f.) the disciples had been arguing with each other about the question, "Who is the greatest?" In substance Jesus answered that the greatest is the one who is willing to be the servant of all. In this connection he declared, "I am among y o u as one who serves." He promised that because of their loyalty to him his disciples would be richly rewarded in his Father's kingdom, where they would feast and reign in close association with their Lord (verses 24–30).

He told Simon that he and his fellow disciples would be "sifted as wheat"; that is, they would be terribly shaken up and tempted by Satan. *All* would be, but *especially Simon*. He, however, received the comforting assurance, "I have prayed for you." And he was told, "Once you have returned (to me), strengthen your brothers." When that disciple boasted, "Lord, with you I am ready to go even to prison and to death," Jesus predicted, "A rooster will not crow today before you deny three times that you know me" (verses 31–34).

In answer to a question asked by Jesus, The Eleven assure him that when they had been sent out on their mission tour they had lacked nothing. Jesus told them that from now on they would be "on their own," in the sense that he would no longer be physically with them, providing for them. "Let him who has no sword sell his coat and buy one," he said. The fact that one would not readily sell his all-purpose coat, cloak, or robe should have prevented them from interpreting this saying literally. When they nevertheless do so—note "Lord, look, here are two swords"—Jesus ends the discussion by saying, "Enough of that!" (verses 35–38).

On the Mount of Olives Jesus instructs his disciples to pray that they may not enter into temptation. At the distance of a stone's throw away from them he himself, being in agony, offered this prayer: "Father, if thou art willing, remove this cup [probably the descent into the hell of Calvary] from me." However, in complete submission to the Father he added, "Not my will but thine be done."

While his sweat became like thick drops of blood trickling down upon the ground, an angel, sent from heaven, strengthened him. Returning to the disciples he found them asleep. At the proper moment he told them, "Get up and pray, that y o u may not enter into temptation" (verses 39–46).

The band, with Judas in the lead, now arrived. By means of a kiss Judas identified Jesus and thus delivered him into the hands of those who had come to capture him. The disciples asked Jesus, "Shall we strike with a sword?" Without even waiting for an answer one of the disciples—it was Peter (John 18:10)—with his sword slashed at the servant of the highpriest, severing his right ear. Jesus said, "No more of this!" and healed the man. Then the Lord exposed the hypocrisy of his captors, who had never dared to lay hands on him when he had been daily with them in the temple (verses 47–53).

Jesus was now led to the house or palace of the highpriest. While the authorities were busy with their captive, Peter, in three separate situations, denied that he even knew Jesus at all. All at once a rooster crowed, and at the same moment Jesus, who after his midnight trial was probably being led across the court to his cell, turned and looked at Peter. "And Peter was reminded of the word of the Lord, how he had said to him, 'Before a rooster crows today, you will deny me three times.' And he went outside and wept bitterly" (verses 54–62).

Returning now to what happened to Jesus after he had been led into the highpriest's palace, Luke relates how the Savior had been mocked and physically abused by his captors (verses 63–65).

At a hastily gathered meeting, held very early in the day, Jesus was asked, "So you are the Son of God?" He replied, "Y o u are right; I am." They said, "What further need do we have of testimony? For we have heard it ourselves from his own mouth" (verses 66–71).

Outline of Chapter 23

Theme:• *The Work Thou Gavest Him to Do*

CHAPTER XXIII

23 1 Then the entire assembly rose and brought him to Pilate. 2 And they began to accuse him, saying, "We have found this man misleading our nation, forbidding us to pay taxes to Caesar, and saying that he himself is Christ, a king."

3 So Pilate asked Jesus, "*You* are the king of the Jews?" Answering, he said to him, "It is as you say."

4 Then Pilate said to the chief priests and the crowds, "No crime[580] whatever do I find in this man."

5 But they kept on insisting, "He stirs up the people, teaching throughout the entire country of the Jews, starting from Galilee and (continuing) even to this place."

23:1–5 *Jesus Brought Before Pilate and Questioned by Him*
Cf. Matt. 27:2, 11–14; Mark 15:1b–5; John 18:28–38

1. Then the entire assembly rose and brought him to Pilate.

"The entire assembly" means the Sanhedrin (cf. Acts 23:7). The reason the assembly did this was that for the Jews to carry out the sentence of execution would have been a violation of Roman law.[581]

Pontius Pilate[582] was the fifth procurator of Samaria and Judea. He was under the authority of Syria's legate. Many reports have come down to us about him. Estimates of his character range all the way from that of Philo who, quoting a letter from Agrippa I to Caligula, calls him "inflexible, merciless, and obstinate," a man who repeatedly inflicted punishment without previous trial and committed ever so many acts of cruelty; to that of the Copts and Abyssinians who rank him among the saints! One thing is certain: he exercised little common sense in handling the delicate problem

---

580. Or: basis for a charge.

581. Many sources can be quoted to prove this point; e.g., Babylonian Talmud, *Sanhedrin*, 41a; *Abodah Zarah*, 8b (the Jer. Talmud contains similar proof); A. N. Sherwin-White, *Roman Society and Roman Law in the New Testament*, Oxford, 1963, pp. 1–47; E. Lohse, art. in Th.D.N.T., Vol. VII, p. 865, etc. But in the present connection none of these are really necessary. All that is needed for anyone who still accepts Scripture as the Word of God is John 18:31b, "The Jews said to Pilate, 'We have no right to execute anyone.'" In fact, in order to prove his point, namely, that the Jews did not have this right, *Lohse appeals to this passage!*

582. Sources on Pilate are, first of all, *The Gospels;* then Philo, *De legationem ad Caium* XXXVIII; Josephus, *Antiquities* XVIII.55–64; 85–89; Josephus, *The Jewish War* II.169–177; Tacitus, *Annals* XV.xliv; and Eusebius, *Ecclesiastical History* I.ix, x; II.ii, vii. See also G. A. Müller, *Pontius Pilatus der fünfte Prokurator von Judäa*, Stuttgart, 1888; and P. L. Maier, *Pontius Pilate*, Garden City, New York, 1968.

of the strained relations between the Jews and their Roman conquerors. In fact, it would almost seem as if he enjoyed annoying the Jews: using the temple treasure to pay for an aqueduct, bringing Roman standards into Jerusalem, and even defiling the temple with golden shields inscribed with the images and names of Roman deities. Add the incident recorded in Luke 13:1 f.

The occasion which led to Pilate's removal from office was his interference with a mob of fanatics who, under the leadership of a false prophet, were at the point of ascending Mt. Gerizim in order to find the sacred vessels which, as they thought, Moses had hidden there. Pilate's cavalry attacked them, killing many of them. Upon complaint by the Samaritans, Pilate was then removed from office. He started out for Rome in order to answer the charges that had been leveled against him. Before he reached Rome, the emperor (Tiberius) had died. An unconfirmed story, related by Eusebius, states that Pilate "was forced to become his own slayer."

From the Gospels we gather that he was *proud* (see N.T.C. on John 19:10), and *cruel* (Luke 13:1). He was probably just as *superstitious* as his wife (Matt. 27:19). Above all, as all the accounts of the trial of Jesus before him indicate, he was a *self-seeker,* wishing to stand well with the emperor. He thoroughly hated the Jews who, as he saw it, were always causing him trouble upon trouble. That he was *utterly* devoid of any remnant of human sympathy and any sense of justice cannot be proved. In fact, there are passages which seem to point in the opposite direction. At any rate, though his guilt was great, it was not as great as that of Annas and Caiaphas; cf. John 19:11.

By combining the Gospel accounts one gains the impression that from start almost to finish Pilate did everything in his power to get rid of the case respecting Jesus. He had no love for the Jews. He hated to please them and to grant their request. Yet, on the other hand, deep down in his heart he was afraid of them and of the possibility that they might use their influence to hurt him. Up to a point he was willing to do what justice demanded, but only up to a point. When his *position* was threatened, he surrendered.

In harmony with this attitude on the part of Pilate the story begins to unfold as follows:

Pilate asks those who have brought Jesus to him, "What charges do y o u prefer against this man?" They answer, "If this man were not an evildoer, we would not have handed him over to you." In other words, "Don't ask any questions, just confirm the sentence we have passed." But Pilate refuses to bestow this favor on them. When they fail to bring any charges, he tries to return the prisoner to them: "Take him yourselves, and judge him according to y o u r own law" (John 18:29–31a). However, the Jews then make clear that they desire nothing short of the prisoner's *death.*

The Jews now understand that they will have to present a formal bill of indictment. They will have to make definite charges. So they quickly advance three of them:

2. And they began to accuse him, saying, We have found this man misleading our nation, forbidding us to pay taxes to Caesar, and saying that he himself is Christ, a king.

It is clear that though the Sanhedrin had accused Jesus of blasphemy, before Pilate the Jewish leaders do not immediately press this charge. They must have been of the opinion—and rightly—that a more definitely political accusation would have a better chance to be considered legally valid from the aspect of Roman jurisprudence. Besides, they may have felt that a strictly religious charge would make little impression on a pagan. This does not mean, however, that the religious charge played no part in the trial. It did play a part, but not immediately. It was reserved for later (John 19:7).

The first item in what may be regarded as a threefold charge was rather vague. It may perhaps be viewed as the introduction to the next two items. So construed, the total charge would be, "We have found Jesus to be a man who has been misleading our nation by forbidding people to pay taxes to Caesar and by claiming that he himself is the Messiah, and, as such, a king."

As to "forbidding us to pay taxes to Caesar," this was a downright lie, as is clear from Luke 20:21-26 (see especially verse 25).

And as to "saying that he himself is Christ, a king," meaning "in the political sense," another lie, for that Jesus never wanted to be king or Messiah in that sense is clear from John 6:15, as well as from his entire ministry with its strong emphasis on such qualities as humility, service, self-denial.

Besides, Pilate knew very well that the Jews were not so deeply in love with Rome and with Roman rule that they would have been hankering for the execution of someone who uttered anti-Roman sentiments. He was well aware of the fact that the real reason for the demand that he confirm the death sentence which the Sanhedrin had already passed was *envy* (Matt. 27:18).

3. So Pilate asked Jesus, *You* are the king of the Jews?

Pilate asked this question for his own protection, not because he believed the charge. The pronoun *You* is not only spelled out but heads the question. Great emphasis is placed on it, as if the procurator were saying, *"You . . . king of the Jews? How ridiculous!"* **Answering he said to him, It is as you say.** As Matt. 26:25; John 18:36, 37 clearly show, the answer Jesus gave was an affirmation.

Luke abbreviates. According to John 18:33-38 Jesus explained to Pilate in what sense he was indeed a king, namely, not in any political sense but in a very real spiritual sense, king over all those who pay homage to the truth.

At this point Pilate steps outside and from the porch of the praetorium addresses the rapidly gathering crowds and their leaders:

4. Then Pilate said to the chief priests and the crowds, No crime whatever do I find in this man.

This should have ended the matter. Jesus should now have been acquitted and released; that is, as far as human justice was concerned. We know, of course, that in a deeper sense this was not to be, for Jesus had to die for our sins. But that fact does not at all remove the guilt of the Sanhedrin and of Pilate (Acts 2:23). The story continues as follows:

5. But they kept on insisting, He stirs up the people, teaching throughout the entire country of the Jews, starting from Galilee and (continuing) even to this place.

As these words were being spoken Pilate listened very carefully. "Teaching throughout the entire country of the Jews." To be sure, the original says "throughout Judea," but, as has been shown earlier—see the note on 4:44 on page 275—at times "Judea" means Palestine, "the country of the Jews." The present passage is one of these instances, for "Galilee" seems to be included in "Judea" here.

But what must have especially aroused the interest of Pilate was something else. According to the charge that was now being made, Jesus hailed from Galilee. Galilee's "king"—not really; he was merely a tetrarch, but the term *king* was popularly ascribed to him—was Herod Antipas. And right at this moment that ruler was staying in Jerusalem! As Pilate saw it, this was surely a marvelous coincidence and possibly . . . a way out for the procurator!

For *Practical Lessons* and *Greek Words*, etc., see pp. 1013–1015.

---

6 Now when Pilate heard this, he asked if the man was a Galilean.   7 And when he learned that Jesus belonged to Herod's jurisdiction, he sent him up to Herod, who also was in Jerusalem at that time.

8 Now Herod was highly pleased when he saw Jesus, because, having heard about him, he for a long time had been eager to see him, and now he was hoping to see him perform some sign.   9 So he questioned him at some length, but Jesus gave him no reply whatever.

10 Meanwhile the chief priests and the scribes were standing there, vehemently accusing him.

11 Then Herod, together with his soldiers, having treated Jesus with contempt and having mocked him, put a gorgeous robe around him[583] and sent him back to Pilate.   12 On that very day Herod and Pilate became friends, for before this they had been enemies.

23:6-12 *Jesus Before Herod*

6, 7. Now when Pilate heard this, he asked if the man was a Galilean. And when he learned that Jesus belonged to Herod's jurisdiction, he sent him up to Herod, who also was in Jerusalem at that time.

The accusers must have regarded their remark that Jesus was a man *from Galilee* as being a *coup de maître* (master stroke). Was not Galilee always the very hotbed of revolution? Think of Herod the Great's battle against the guerrillas (N.T.C. on Matthew, p. 159), and of the "Zealots" and the "patriots" who since that time were always making trouble for the Roman government. Well, that was the region to which Jesus belonged, and he himself was one of the troublemakers!

---

583. Or: dressed him in a bright robe.

Little did they realize that exactly when they thought they had scored a point against Jesus and had probably persuaded Pilate to take the necessary action, they, at least for the time being, were being defeated. For Pilate, consistent with his purpose almost to the very end of the trial, saw in this link between Jesus and Galilee the very opportunity he was looking for to get rid of this annoying case. We can, as it were, hear him say, "Well, since this man is from Galilee, and since Roman law allows an accused person to be tried either in the province where his crime is said to have been committed [which in the present case could be anywhere from Galilee to Jerusalem] or in the province to which he belongs, and finally since the ruler of this Galilean is right now in Jerusalem, I remand his case to the ruler of Galilee, namely, Herod (Antipas), for adjudication."

8. Now Herod was highly pleased when he saw Jesus, because, having heard about him, he for a long time had been eager to see him, and now he was hoping to see him perform some sign.

To understand what now takes place it is necessary to give a brief review of the story of Herod Antipas up to this point.

It will be recalled that in the year 4 B.C., upon the death of his father, Herod Antipas had been made tetrarch of Galilee and Perea (Luke 3:1). Later on, while visiting his half-brother, Herod Philip, he had become infatuated with the latter's wife, Herodias. The two illicit lovers had eloped. For the sin of having "his brother's wife" he was sternly and repeatedly rebuked by John the Baptist (3:19, 20). But instead of repenting, the tetrarch imprisoned John. At the occasion of his birthday celebration Herod Antipas foolishly promised to give the daughter of Herodias whatever she might ask, so fascinated was he with her dancing exhibition. Instructed by her mother she asked for and received "the head of John the Baptist on a platter" (Matt. 14:6–12; Mark 6:21–29; Luke 9:7–9).

Afterward, when Herod heard about the marvelous deeds of Jesus, he exclaimed, "This is John the Baptist, risen from the dead" (Matt. 14:1, 2). He was eager to see Jesus (Luke 9:9).

Toward the close of Christ's ministry certain Pharisees warned Jesus, "Get out and move on from here, for Herod wants to kill you!" Did the presence of Jesus anywhere within the realm of the tetrarch bother his conscience?

Whatever may be the answer, now Jesus, as a prisoner, is being brought before this same impenitent, restless, inquisitive, superstitious Herod Antipas. The latter is still as wicked as he was before. Though he had been repeatedly warned, there is no evidence whatever of even an inkling of repentance. He simply wants to be entertained by Jesus. He is hoping to see him perform a miracle.

9, 10. So he questioned him at some length, but Jesus gave him no reply whatever. Meanwhile the chief priests and the scribes were standing there, vehemently accusing him.

Though Jesus did not perform any miracle in the presence of Herod, the latter seems to have thought that the captive would at least talk to him,

1011

would certainly answer his questions. But he did not, not at all. This is significant. To be sure, other silences on the part of the Savior are also reported. There was a time when he was silent before Caiaphas (Mark 14:60, 61), before Pilate (Mark 15:4, 5), and again before Pilate (John 19:9b). But these silences were balanced by testimonies. In the case of Herod it was different. *He* never heard Jesus say anything at all! This man had had his full opportunity. He had been talked to and reasoned with again and again and again (Mark 6:20). But he had ignored all these warnings. And even now his only interest in Jesus was that born of perverse, contemptuous curiosity. He received no answer and deserved none.

But when Jesus refused to speak, his enemies, the chief priests and the scribes, talked all the louder and the more incessantly, vehemently accusing him before Herod. Were they afraid that Herod might pronounce Jesus innocent and might even release him? They need not have feared, for although Herod, too, could find no basis for any charge against Jesus, he did not set him free. On the contrary, being utterly disgusted with him, he made him the object of ridicule:

11. Then Herod, together with his soldiers, having treated Jesus with contempt and having mocked him, put a gorgeous robe around him and sent him back to Pilate.

Herod was probably *too scared* to condemn Jesus to death. His conscience had not allowed him to forget what he had done to another innocent person, John the Baptist. He was filled with haunting superstitition. But also, he was probably *too angry* with Jesus to acquit him, for his curiosity had not been gratified. Jesus had refused to perform a miracle or even to answer any of his questions. So he and his bodyguard started to treat the manacled prisoner with contempt and ridicule. They dressed him in a brilliant robe, as if he were already an earthly king, and sent him thus arrayed back to Pilate. From the Hasmonean Palace, where Herod was probably staying,[584] the procession returned to Pilate and the Praetorium.

12. On that very day Herod and Pilate became friends, for before this they had been enemies.

From this brief note we learn that Herod and Pilate had been mutual enemies. The reason for this is not stated. Some point to Luke 13:1, which reports that in a very gruesome manner Pilate had ordered some of Herod's subjects (Galileans) killed. For another theory see P. L. Maier, *op. cit.*, pp. 171–177. But all we know is what is stated here in Luke 23:12: the former enemies had become friends. Pilate had honored Herod by sending Jesus to him for adjudication. Herod had reciprocated in kind. The fact that both treated Jesus, and caused or permitted him to be treated, in a most shameful manner indicates that this type of reconciliation of former

---

584. For the location of this palace see G. A. Turner, *Historical Geography of the Holy Land,* Grand Rapids, 1973, pp. 27, 28.

enemies contrasts sharply with the laudable one to which Paul refers in Eph. 2:14-18.[585]

Practical Lessons Derived from Luke 23:1-12

Verse 2 (cf. verse 5)

"And they began to accuse him, saying, 'We have found this man misleading our nation,'" etc.

You have not intentionally been hurting anybody. Yet you are being slandered. Remember, then, that this happened, too, to Jesus. Derive comfort from this and from such passages as Matt. 5:10-12; John 16:33.

Verse 7

"And when Pilate learned that Jesus belonged to Herod's jurisdiction, he sent him up to Herod." Why did Pilate do this? Because he did not wish "to become involved." Where have we heard this before? What do you think of it?

Verse 8

"Now Herod . . . for a long time had been eager to see Jesus." At another occasion the Greeks, too, were eager to see Jesus (John 12:21). But what a difference! God looks at the heart. He discerns the motive. Two people are eager to do kingdom work. Wonderful. But the question is *Why?*

Verse 11

"Herod . . . treated Jesus with contempt and . . . sent him back to Pilate."

Herod as well as Pilate did not find any justification for the charge that had been advanced against Jesus. Pilate declared, several times, "Not guilty." Herod said this too. So did even the penitent robber. Yet Jesus was condemned to death. *And God Almighty allowed this to happen.* Is it not logical to conclude that what Luke is bringing out is that, as far as God was concerned, Jesus was being punished for the sins of others? See Isa. 53.

Verse 12

"On that very day Herod and Pilate became friends, for before this they had been enemies."

Friendship based on evil is worthless.

Notes on Greek Words, Phrases, and Constructions in 23:1-12

Verse 1

ἀναστάν, nom. s. neut. 2nd aor. participle of ἀνίστημι, to raise; in middle and, as here, 2nd aor., to rise.

---

585. Notes on Greek words, phrases, and constructions in 23:1-12 begin on this page.

Verse 2

κατηγορεῖν, pres. infinitive of κατηγορέω, to accuse (also in verses 10, 14); and see 6:7; 11:54.

διαστρέφοντα, acc. s. masc. pres. act. participle of διαστρέφω, to turn away, pervert, mislead; and see 9:41; Acts 13:8, 10; 20:30; Phil. 2:15.

φόρους διδόναι, to pay taxes, as in 20:22.

Verse 3

Σὺ λέγεις, you said (it); or: it is as you say.

Verse 4

αἴτιον, acc. s. neut. of αἴτιος**, cause, reason, reason for punishment, crime, guilt, basis for a charge. See also verses 14, 22; cf. Acts 19:40.

Verse 5

ἐπίσχυον, third per. pl. imperf. (iterative) of ἐπισχύω*, to grow strong, urge, insist.

ἀνασείει, third per. s. indicat. act. of ἀνασείω, to shake or stir up, instigate.

Verse 7

ἐπιγνούς, nom. s. masc. 2nd aor. (effective) act. participle of ἐπιγινώσκω, to come upon (or arrive at) the knowledge concerning a matter, to learn, perceive, recognize.

ἐξουσίας, gen. s. of ἐξουσία; here, jurisdiction.

ἀνέπεμψεν, third per. s. aor. indicat. act. of ἀναπέμπω, to send up to a higher authority; or, as here, to send up to the proper authority; in verses 11 and 15: to send back. See also Acts 25:21 and Philem. 12.

Verse 8

ἐχάρη, third per. s. 2nd aor. indicat. pass. of χαίρω, to rejoice, be pleased; see on 19:37.

λίαν, highly, exceedingly.

For ἐξ ἱκανῶν χρόνων see the note on 8:27 on page 452.

ἤλπιζεν, third per. s. imperf. (progress.) indicat. of ἐλπίζω, to hope.

Verse 9

ἐπηρώτα, the construction is the same as for ἤλπιζεν.

ἐν λόγοις ἱκανοῖς, in a considerable number of words; hence, at some length.

Verse 10

εἱστήκεισαν, third per. pl. pluperf., with sense of imperf., of ἵστημι, which in perf. and pluperf. is intransitive, to stand; hence here: were standing.

εὐτόνως** (εὖ plus τείνω), lit. stretching themselves well or strenuously; hence simply *strenuously*, vigorously, vehemently.

Verse 11

ἐξουθενήσας, nom. s. masc. aor. act. participle of ἐξουθενέω, to regard as amounting to nothing, to treat with contempt; see also on 18:9.

στρατεύμασιν, dat. pl. of στράτευμα, armed force; in pl. troops, soldiers.

ἐμπαίξας (same construction as the preceding verbal form), to mock. See also 14:29; 18:32; 22:63; 23:36.

ἐσθῆτα, acc. s. of ἐσθής, clothing, robe. Cf. *vestment.*

λαμπρός, -ά, -ον, bright, shining, gorgeous; here fem. acc. s. Cf. *lamp.*

Verse 12

προϋπῆρχον, third per. pl. periphrastic imperf. of προϋπάρχω**, to be formerly; in the New Testament only here and in Acts 8:9.

---

13 Then Pilate called together the chief priests, the rulers, and the people, 14 and said to them, "Y o u have brought this man to me as one who incites the people to rebellion. But look, having examined him in y o u r presence I have found nothing in this man to substantiate the charges y o u bring against him. 15 Neither has Herod, for he sent him back to us. And, indeed, nothing that deserves the death penalty was done by him. 16 I will therefore punish and (then) release him."586

18 But all together they cried back,587 "Away with this man! Release Barabbas for us!" 19 Now Barabbas was a man who had been thrown into prison because of an insurrection that had occurred in the city, and for murder.

20 Then Pilate, wishing to release Jesus, once more appealed to them. 21 But they kept yelling, "Crucify, crucify him!"

22 For the third time he spoke to them: "Why? What wrong has he done? No basis whatever for the death penalty have I found in him. I will therefore punish and (then) release him."

23 But they continued to press upon him with loud voices, demanding that he be crucified, and their voices prevailed.588 24 So Pilate pronounced sentence that their demand should be granted. 25 He released the man they were asking for, the one who because of insurrection and murder had been thrown into prison, but Jesus he surrendered to their will.

23:13–25 *Jesus Sentenced to Die*
Cf. Matt. 27:15–26; Mark 15:6–15; John 18:39—19:16

13–16. Then Pilate called together the chief priests, the rulers, and the people, and said to them, Y o u have brought this man to me as one who incites the people to rebellion. But look, having examined him in y o u r presence I have found nothing in this man to substantiate the charges y o u bring against him. Neither has Herod, for he sent him back to us. And, indeed, nothing that deserves the death penalty was done by him. I will therefore punish and (then) release him.

When Jesus had been returned to Pilate, the latter summoned not only the members of the Sanhedrin but also the people in general, for he wished

---

586. Sufficient textual support is lacking for verse 17 ("for of necessity he must release one unto them at the feast," A.V.). But for the thought see Matt. 27:15; Mark 15:6; John 18:39.

587. Or: cried out.

588. Or: began to prevail.

to make a public announcement. The suggestion that "he included the people because he thought that in their presence the Sanhedrin would not have the courage to insist on crucifixion" is hard to prove or disprove.

In connection with the charge that Jesus was a revolutionary, Pilate declares, "I have examined him in y o u r presence." This would indicate that Luke has been giving us only a summary of what had taken place, for in his account we read little (at the most verse 3) about such a public examination. Even Matt. 27:11-14; Mark 15:2-5 are probably mere summaries of that which had already occurred.

Then Pilate makes the startling announcements:

"I have found nothing in this man to substantiate the charges y o u bring against him."

"And, indeed, nothing that deserves the death penalty was done by him."

Two very remarkable statements. Add to them those found in verses 4 and 22 of the present chapter and those recorded in John 18:38; 19:6, and it will be clear that on no less than five occasions did Pilate publicly declare Christ's innocence!

In the present speech he even added the implied testimony of Herod. That ruler, by having returned Jesus to Pilate, and having done this without condemning the prisoner, had clearly reached the same conclusion, namely, "Jesus is innocent with respect to the charges that were brought against him."

We have a right to expect that Pilate will now say, "I will therefore release him." Why did he not say this? In all probability, as his later conduct shows (see John 19:12-16), because he was afraid of what the Sanhedrin and the crowds that had allowed themselves to be persuaded by that body might do to him. He was being motivated not by principle but by political expedience.

So what Pilate actually says is, "I will therefore *punish* him and release him."

The word used in the original and here rendered "punish" can mean "scourge." It may have that meaning here. It has been suggested, however,[589] that in this particular case the reference is to a punishment lighter than scourging. Even so, how thoroughly unfair!

As to verse 17 see above, p. 1015, footnote 586.

18, 19. But all together they cried back, Away with this man! Release Barabbas for us! —Now Barabbas was a man who had been thrown into prison because of an insurrection that had occurred in the city, and for murder.

Pilate was beginning to become desperate. He was eager, very eager, to get rid of this case, to shake it off. First he had tried to return Jesus to the Sanhedrin, but that did not work. Next he had endeavored to let Herod make the decision. Again, no success. Now he had made an attempt to

---

589. See A. N. Sherwin-White, *op. cit.,* p. 27.

compromise the issue: first punish Jesus and then release him. That too did not satisfy the crowd.

A new opportunity for the solution of Pilate's problem now seemed to present itself. Since here, once more, Luke abbreviates, let us turn, for elucidation, to Mark's parallel:

"Now at a feast it was customary to release to the people any one prisoner whom they asked for. And among the rebels in prison, who had committed murder in the insurrection, there was a man called Barabbas [meaning 'son of the father']. So the crowd came up and asked (Pilate) to do as he had been accustomed to do for them. Pilate asked them, 'Do y o u want me to release to y o u the king of the Jews?' For he was aware that because of envy the chief priests had handed him over (to him). But the chief priests stirred up the mob (to get) him to release to them Barabbas instead (of Jesus)" (15:6-11).

The release of a prisoner as the result of a shouted request of the populace was not unknown in the Roman world of that day, as a papyrus document has shown.[590]

For information about the particular form which this request for, and granting of, release took among the Jews we are dependent upon the Gospels. As was indicated, Mark spells this out in some detail: the request had to be made at a feast. The Passover feast only or *any* of the great religious festivals? This is not clear. At this particular occasion it was the crowd that took the initiative. They asked Pilate to do as he had been accustomed to do for them. Pilate, anxious to get rid of the case regarding Jesus, immediately saw an opportunity to reach his goal. He already knew that it was because of envy that the chief priests had delivered Jesus to him, envy aroused by the Nazarene's popularity. So he probably reasoned as follows: "I will give the people a choice between Jesus and a dangerous criminal, namely, Barabbas. Surely, they will choose to have Jesus released. Why, even the leaders cannot with any consistency ask for the release of a violent, murderous insurrectionist, since just a little while ago they were accusing Jesus of insurrection! And as to the crowd, I *know* how they will vote. With them Jesus is very popular, as was shown even a few days ago (in connection with the triumphal entry)."

Nevertheless, Pilate was wrong. The people chose not Jesus but Barabbas: "Away with this man! Release Barabbas for us!" was their response.

What was it that prompted the people to make this choice? Among the reasons may well have been the following:

a. The triumphal entry had not turned out the way many of the Jews had hoped. They wanted a political Messiah, a Strong Man who would deliver them from the Roman yoke, not one who was meek and lowly, who wept and predicted punishment for them.

b. As the people saw it, the choice was not so much between Jesus and

---

590. See J. Blinzler, *Der Prozess Jesu*, pp. 301-303.

Barabbas as it was between *the will of Pilate* and *the will of their own Sanhedrin.* They knew that Pilate hated them. He had already proved it in many ways. So they were not about to please Pilate. The fact that he wanted the release of Jesus was one big reason why they did not want it.

c. The temporary absence of Pilate to study the message he had received from his wife (Matt. 27:19, 20) gave the members of the Sanhedrin the opportunity to move among the people in order to influence them to ask for the release of Barabbas and the destruction of Jesus.

20, 21. Then Pilate, wishing to release Jesus, once more appealed to them. But they kept yelling, Crucify, crucify him!

Why was Pilate so determined on releasing Jesus? Was it because even in the heart of this Gentile there was a remnant of a sense of justice, perhaps even justice and sympathy? Was it because he realized that Jesus was at least a far more noble person than were his accusers? Was it because he hated the Jews so thoroughly that it was almost impossible to yield to their wishes? Was it because he had become filled with superstitious fear because of Christ's claim to divinity? See John 19:7, 8. Or was his reluctance due to a combination of some or all of these factors?

The mob, constantly being prompted by the leaders—this must be borne in mind!—screamed back, "Crucify, crucify him!" What these people demanded was nothing less than torture. They refused to be satisfied with mild punishment for Jesus. *Crucifixion* is what they insisted on, nothing less.

"Crucify, crucify him!" Over and over again these terrible words were being yelled until they became a monotonous refrain, an eerie, ominous chant. The crowd was becoming a riotous mob, an emotion-charged, screaming rabble.

22. For the third time he spoke to them: Why? What wrong has he done? No basis whatever for the death penalty have I found in him. I will therefore punish and (then) release him.

There are those who experience some difficulty with the phrase *For the third time.* They argue that even if the report found in John's Gospel is left out of consideration, is not this *the fourth* appeal to the people? Count these appeals and declarations of innocence: verses 4, 15, 20, and now 22. Were there not four of them, not just three?

It has been suggested that the four can be reduced to three by regarding verse 15 as being a reference to Herod's view. To me it seems more natural to interpret the phrase *For the third time* as meaning "three times in succession," namely, the three appeals that were made by Pilate *after* the return of Jesus from Herod. The reference then would be to what is found in verses 15 (really 13–16), 20, and now 22.

Since the rest of verse 22 is virtually a repetition of what Pilate said earlier, no further comment is needed. This is true with one slight exception: this time Pilate frankly asks the audience, "What wrong has he done?" He implies, "He has committed no wrong; at least, no wrong that would require the death penalty."

The words, "I will therefore punish and release him," show that Pilate is again violating the demands of justice, for surely Jesus deserved no punishment at all, not even mild punishment. By this time, however, the people have become fully aware of the fact that if they but persist in their demand they can bend and break obstinate Pilate:

23. But they continued to press upon him with loud voices, demanding that he be crucified, and their voices prevailed.

As a translation "their voices *began* to prevail" is also possible. The meaning then might be that, due to constant prompting by the chief priests, scribes, and elders, the screams of the mob demanding that Jesus be crucified became louder and louder until at last they drowned out whatever opposition there may have been. But in connection with either translation the end result is the same: victory for the screamers, for the Sanhedrin, for cruel injustice . . . but also for the overruling providence of God and *his* people's salvation!

24, 25. So Pilate pronounced sentence that their demand should be granted. He released the man they were asking for, the one who because of insurrection and murder had been thrown into prison, but Jesus he surrendered to their will.

The stubborn insistence of the fanatical mob, louder and louder in its demand that Jesus be crucified, coupled with the implied threat, "If you release this man, you are no friend of Caesar" (John 19:12), brought about the surrender of weak-kneed Pilate, so that he pronounced sentence that Jesus was to be crucified. This pronouncement, made by a judge who again and again had declared that Jesus was innocent, was the most shocking travesty of justice history has ever recorded.

In order to make this injustice stand out all the more glaringly the evangelist here highlights the contrast between *the release* of *the rebel-murderer* and *the sentence of death* pronounced upon *the Savior*. Luke omits the story of the scourging and mockery to which Jesus was now subjected. For that report we must turn to Matt. 27:27–31; Mark 15:16–20; and John 19:1–3.

What Luke does say is this, "But Jesus he surrendered [or *delivered up*] to their will." How significant this formulation! We cannot help thinking of Isa. 53:6, 12 (LXX), "And the Lord [i.e. Jehovah] *delivered him up* for our sins"; "his soul *was delivered up* to death." We should never forget that Luke was writing under the inspiration of the Holy Spirit. That very Spirit is therefore telling us that the One who was delivered up is the fulfilment of prophecy, the Messiah, the Savior from sin. Hallelujah![591]

Practical Lessons Derived from Luke 23:13–25

Verses 14–16

"I have found nothing in this man to substantiate the charges. . . . I will therefore punish and (then) release him."

---

591. Notes on Greek words, phrases, and constructions in 23:13–25 begin on page 1020.

Is it ever right to do what is morally wrong (in this case punishing the Innocent) in order to avoid committing a greater wrong (sentencing him to death)?

Could this be compared with the decision to try to shorten a war by dropping atom bombs on millions of civilians without giving them previous warning? Does the end justify the means?

Verses 18, 19

"But all together they cried back, 'Away with this man! Release Barabbas for us.' Now Barabbas was a man who had been thrown into prison because of an insurrection that had occurred in the city, and for murder."

If we could believe the reasoning of the rulers, we would have to conclude that they wanted Jesus destroyed because they regarded him to be an insurrectionist. But this charge had not been proved. Yet they wanted a proved and convicted insurrectionist and murderer to be released. Does not this inconsistency show that they were deceivers and that their real motive was indeed *envy* (Matt. 27:18)?

Children and young people should be warned against giving in to this evil. Tell them the oft-repeated story of the two athletes. A huge statue had been erected for the winner. That made the loser so envious that evening after evening he would go out and chisel away at the statue, to cause it to fall. And it did ... on top of him, crushing him to death.

On the positive side, we should encourage our children and young people to congratulate all who accomplish things worthy of praise, and to do this from the heart.

In fact, everyone, both old and young, should pray to be delivered from the demon of envy and to receive grace and energy to accomplish great things for his family, his country, his church and/or school, and for God!

Notes on Greek Words, Phrases, and Constructions in 23:13-25

Verse 14

ἀποστρέφοντα, acc. s. masc. pres. act. participle of ἀποστρέφω, to turn away (people from their loyalty to the emperor), to incite to rebellion. See synonym in verse 2: the sense is similar, not the same.

ἀνακρίνας, nom. s. masc. aor. (effective) act. participle of ἀνακρίνω, to examine closely ("up and down").

ὦν, for τούτων ὦν, the relative attracted to the case of the implied antecedent.

Verse 15

ἐστὶν πεπραγμένον, third per. s. periphrastic perfect pass. indicat. of πράσσω, to do, commit; cf. *practice.*

Verse 16

παιδεύσας, nom. s. masc. aor. act. participle of παιδεύω, from παῖς, child; hence, to instruct and discipline a child; and, in connection with criminals, to punish; so also in verse 22.

Verse 18

ἀνέκραγον, third per. pl. 2nd aor. indicat. act. of ἀνακράζω; see also on 4:33; 8:28 (= ἀνά plus κράζω), to cry back or out.

παμπληθεί*, all together.

αἶρε, sec. per. s. pres. imperat. act. of αἴρω, to take away (by killing). For summary of meanings of this verb see the note on 17:13 on page 803.

ἀπόλυσον, sec. per. s. aor. imperat. act. of ἀπολύω, here in the basic sense of *to release*. Other meanings: to divorce, forgive, send away, dismiss, permit, etc.

Verse 19

ἦν βληθείς, third per. s. periphrastic aor. (effective) indicat. pass. of βάλλω, to throw.

στάσιν, acc. s. of στάσις, an uprising, insurrection. Cf. German *Aufstand,* Dutch *opstand.*

Verse 20

προσεφώνησεν, third per. s. aor. indicat. of προσφωνέω, to call out (to), to appeal (to); cf. 7:32; Acts 22:2. Sometimes this verb has the meaning *to call to oneself* (6:13).

Verse 21

ἐπεφώνουν, third per. pl. imperf. (iterat.) of ἐπιφωνέω** (only here and in Acts 12:22; 21:34; 22:24), to cry out loudly, to yell, scream, shout.

σταύρου, sec. per. s. pres. imperat. act. of σταυρόω, to crucify.

Verse 22

The language of verses 14-16 is substantially repeated here.

αἴτιον θανάτου, reason for the death penalty; see above, on verse 4.

Verse 23

ἐπέκειντο, third per. pl. imperf. indicat. of ἐπίκειμαι (cf. 5:1), to lie upon, press upon.

σταυρωθῆναι, aor. (ingressive) pass. infinitive of σταυρόω, see on verse 21.

κατίσχυον, third per. pl. imperf. indicat. of κατισχύω (κατά, down; plus ἰσχύω, to be strong, have power), to bear *down* on with strength, to prevail. In the New Testament this verb is found only here and in 21:36; Matt. 16:18. If the imperf. here is ingressive, the meaning is *began to prevail,* but this is not certain.

Verse 24

ἐπέκρινεν, third per. s. aor. (effective) act. of ἐπικρίνω*, to pronounce or give sentence. It would seem that the contextual meaning, supported by the parallel passage John 19:13-16, is not merely "decided" but *decreed, passed judgment on.* I agree here with Robertson, *Word Pictures,* Vol. II, p. 283, as against several translators and some lexicons.

αἴτημα, request, demand. Cf. the cognate verb (αἰτέω) in the immediately preceding and in the immediately following verse.

Verse 25

φόνον, acc. s. of φόνος, murder.

βεβλημένον, acc. s. masc. perf. pass. participle of βάλλω.

ᾐτοῦντο, third per. pl. imperf. middle (iterat. or progress.) of αἰτέω, to ask (for themselves).

παρέδωκε, third per. s. aor. (effect.) act. of παραδίδωμι, to hand over or deliver up; to surrender. Cf. 9:44; 18:32; 20:20; etc.

---

26 Now as they led him away, they caught hold of a certain Cyrenian named Simon, who was coming in from the country. On him they placed the cross, to carry it (as he walked) behind Jesus. 27 There was following him a huge crowd of people, and of women who were beating their breasts[592] and lamenting him.

28 Jesus turned to them and said, "Daughters of Jerusalem, do not weep for me but weep for yourselves and for y o u r children. 29 For—note well—days are coming when people will say: 'Blessed are the barren women, the wombs that never bore and the breasts that never nursed!' 30 Then they will begin to say[593] to the mountains, 'Fall on us,' and to the hills, 'Cover us.' 31 For if men do this to the green wood, what will happen to the dry?"

32 Along with Jesus two others, criminals, were being led away to be executed. 33 And when they came to the place called Skull, there they crucified him, along with the criminals, one on his right, the other on his left.

34 Then Jesus said, "Father, forgive them, for they do not know what they are doing."[594] And they cast lots to divide his clothes among them. 35 Meanwhile the people were standing by, looking on. And even the rulers were sneering at him, saying, "Others he saved; let him save himself if he is the Christ of God, his Chosen One."

36 The soldiers also, coming up, mocked him, offering him sour wine, 37 and saying, "If you are the king of the Jews, save yourself."

38 And there was also a superscription over him:

THIS IS THE KING OF THE JEWS

39 One of the crucified criminals began to hurl abuse at[595] him, saying, "Aren't you the Christ? Save yourself and us." 40 But the other one, rebuking him, replied, "Don't you even fear God, since you're under the same sentence of condemnation? 41 And we indeed justly, for we are getting what we deserve.[596] But this man has done nothing out of place."[597] 42 Then he said, "Jesus, remember me when you come in your kingdom."

43 Jesus said to him, "I solemnly declare to you, today you will be with me in Paradise."

23:26–43 *Calvary: The Crucifixion of Jesus*
Cf. Matt. 27:32–44; Mark 15:21–32; John 19:17–27

26. Now as they led him away, they caught hold of a certain Cyrenian named Simon, who was coming in from the country. On him they placed the cross, to carry it (as he walked) behind Jesus.

As was customary and according to law, the execution was carried out

---

592. Or: were mourning.

593. Or: Then they will say.

594. This prayer is omitted by certain ancient manuscripts.

595. Or: was hurling abuse at; or: began to blaspheme; or: was blaspheming.

596. Literally: we are getting (a penalty) worthy of [or: corresponding to] the things we have done.

597. Or: improper.

outside the city (Lev. 24:14; Num. 15:35, 36; 19:3; I Kings 21:13; cf. John 19:20; Heb. 13:12, 13). Those condemned to be crucified had to carry their own cross. Commentators are divided on the question whether this refers to the crossbeam alone, the upright having already been set in place on Golgotha, or the entire cross.

Jesus too carried his own cross (John 19:16, 17), but not for long. Sheer physical exhaustion made it impossible for him to carry it very far. Consider what he had already endured within the last fifteen hours: the tense atmosphere of the upper room, the betrayal by Judas, the agonies of Gethsemane, the desertion by his disciples, the torture of a totally hypocritical trial before the Sanhedrin, the mockery in the palace of Caiaphas, the denial by his most prominent disciple, the trial before an unjust judge, the pronunciation of the death sentence upon him, the terrible ordeal of being scourged, and the seven-itemed abuse by the soldiers in the praetorium! Humanly speaking, is it not a wonder that he was able to carry the cross any distance at all?

When Jesus succumbed beneath his load, the legionaries, exercising their right of "requisitioning" or "making demands on" people, forced Simon, a Cyrenian or man from Cyrene—located on a plateau, ten miles from the Mediterranean Sea, in what is now Libya (west of Egypt)—to carry Christ's cross for the rest of the distance. The theory that Simon could not have been a Jew, because he gave his sons Greek names (Mark 15:21), is without merit, since many Jews followed that practice. Besides, in Cyrene there was a large colony of Jews (Acts 2:10; 6:9; 11:20; 13:1). The further speculation that the man must have been a farmer, because on this particular Friday morning he came "from the country," is also without any basis. Even today many people besides farmers have business or social connections in the country. Some even live there!

The following reconstruction, though not certain, is, however, probable. Simon, a Jew, has come to Jerusalem to attend one of the great festivals (in this case Passover), as was the custom of many Jews, including those from Cyrene (Acts 2:10). There was even a Cyrenian synagogue in Jerusalem (Acts 6:9).

Now on this particular Friday, returning to the city from a visit to the country, Simon is pressed into service by the soldiers who are leading Jesus to Calvary, perhaps (but this is by no means certain) along the Via Dolorosa (Sorrowful Way), and are just now coming through the gate out of the city. So—reluctantly at first?—Simon carries Christ's cross, arrives at Calvary, and witnesses what happens there. The behavior of Jesus and his words from the cross leave such an impression on Simon that he becomes a Christian. Subsequently he and his family are living in Rome. He may have been living there before, but in any event he was a Cyrenian by birth. (Among the early Christians there were many Cyrenians, Acts 11:20; 13:1.)

Mark, writing to the Romans, mentions "Simon, the father of Alexander and Rufus," as if to say, "people with whom y o u, in Rome, are well acquainted." Paul, in his letter to the Romans (16:13), writes, "Greet Rufus, outstanding in the Lord, and his mother and mine." Evidently the mother of Rufus—hence, the wife of Simon—had rendered some motherly service to Paul.

If this reconstruction is factual, then the service which Simon rendered, though initially "forced," turned out to be a genuine blessing for himself, his family, and many others.

27. There was following him a huge crowd of people, and of women who were beating their breasts and lamenting him.

The preceding verses—see especially verse 23—may have left the impression that just about everybody in Jerusalem was opposed to Jesus. We now discover that this was not at all the case. There continued to be those who were his loyal followers. And then there were those who at least sympathized with him. In that huge crowd that was following Jesus there were women who felt very sorry for the Master. They may have been members of a Jerusalem society of charitable women. As with great difficulty Jesus was moving on, and they noticed his bruised features, his utterly tired appearance, they wept. Their hearts were going out to him in genuine sympathy. In fact, they were beating their breasts and lamenting him.

It is not surprising that Luke—he alone—records this incident. We have come to expect this of him. See *Introduction,* point V D.

These "daughters of Jerusalem" must not be confused with women such as Mary Magdalene, Joanna, Susanna, etc., who out of their own substance had helped to support Jesus and The Twelve. Those women were disciples of Jesus; the daughters of Jerusalem were not. This fact also explains what immediately follows:

28. Jesus turned to them and said, Daughters of Jerusalem, do not weep for me but weep for yourselves and for y o u r children.

As to Jesus, though right now he is agonizing and though during the next several hours he will be suffering the torments of hell, his future is secure. But unless these women repent, theirs is not. Neither is that of their children. By and large Jerusalem's population consisted of unregenerate people (Luke 13:34, 35; cf. Matt. 23:37, 38). Moreover, God does not permit impenitence to go unpunished, and this both now and in the hereafter.

The troubles in connection with the fall of Jerusalem would be a terrible *prelude* to everlasting woe:

29. For—note well—days are coming when people will say: Blessed are the barren women, the wombs that never bore and the breasts that never nursed!

Such terrible woes would befall the city that women would be considered blessed if they were childless. The enemy would destroy Jerusalem's inhabitants without showing any regard for sex or age. See above, on 21:24.

30. Then they will begin to say to the mountains, Fall on us, and to the hills, Cover us.

With variations this saying occurs three times in Scripture. It is found first of all in Hos. 10:8. So appalling would be the divine judgment against

Samaria that in deathly agony people would yearn—but in vain—to be covered by toppling mountains and overturning hills.

In our present passage (Luke 23:30) the scene is, if possible, even more horrible, as anyone who has studied the writings of Josephus knows. This time it is the fall not of Samaria but of Jerusalem, in the year A.D. 70, that is in view. For "Mountains, cover us, and hills, fall on us," the reverse, namely, "Mountains, fall on us, and hills, cover us," is now substituted. This is probably merely a stylistic change.

But for the impenitents the *final* cry of anguish will be the most hopeless of all. It will be uttered on the great day of judgment. In that connection the wording is, "Mountains and rocks, fall on us and hide us from the face of him who sits on the throne and from the wrath of the Lamb, for the day of their wrath is come, and who is able to stand?" (Rev. 6:16, 17).

Continued: **31. For if men do this to the green wood, what will happen to the dry?**

Jesus is making use of a rather common proverb.[598] He is drawing a contrast between "green" (that is, *moist*) wood and "dry" wood. Dry wood burns and is consumed readily; when the wood is still green and wet this is not the case. Therefore if even green wood is made to burn, then surely dry wood will burn and be consumed.

The green wood represents Jesus; the dry wood, his impenitent opponents; one might say *the Jews in their impenitent state*. J. Schneider, in his excellent article on this word (Th.D.N.T., Vol. V., pp. 37–41), points out that if God has not spared Jesus, then the divine judgment will fall in full and undiminished severity on the Jewish people if they persist in unbelief and disobedience.

This is a very logical explanation and in harmony with the context, for, as has been explained, in the immediately preceding verse Jesus has predicted the punishment that would be inflicted upon Jerusalem.

John Calvin was right when he interpreted verse 31 as follows, "We know that dry wood is generally thrown into the fire first; but if what is moist and green be burned, much less shall the dry be ultimately spared.... *The lamentation of the women* is foolish, if they do not likewise expect and dread the awful judgment of God which hangs over the wicked" (*Harmony*, Vol. III, pp. 294, 295).

This explanation makes good sense and also shows that the rendering "tree" in Luke 23:31 must be considered an error. The passage has nothing to do with any tree; it has to do with *wood* in its green (moist) condition contrasted with *wood* in its dry state. To be sure, Jesus suffered the agonies of hell especially on Calvary, but when that suffering was finished he sat down at the right hand of the Father, full of glory, honor, and power. But for the impenitents the suffering will never end: Jerusalem's fall will be only a foretaste of their everlasting damnation. Or, to quote Greijdanus,

---

598. The popularity of this proverb, in its various forms, as summarized in S.BK., Vol. II, p. 263, is very interesting.

"Jesus was innocent. Now if he, the Innocent One, was made the object of such ill treatment and plunged into suffering, what will happen to those who are guilty?" (*Korte Verklaring*, Vol. II, p. 264). See also Geldenhuys, *op. cit.*, p. 604.

Justice is not done to this passage unless it is added that the entire address of Jesus to "the daughters of Jerusalem" (verses 28–31; note especially, "Weep not for me but weep for yourselves and for y o u r children") is an unforgettable manifestation of the Savior's complete lack of self-pity and of his ardent desire, even now, that the impenitent may repent and be saved.

32, 33. Along with Jesus two others, criminals, were being led away to be executed. And when they came to the place called Skull, there they crucified him, along with the criminals, one on his right, the other on his left.

The Greek word for *Skull* is *Kranion* (cf. *cranium*). In the Vulgate (Jerome's Latin version of the Bible) *Kranion* was rendered *Calvaria;* cf. *Calvary.*

Why was this name given to the place? Because it looked like a skull? Because a skull was found there? We can only guess. Precisely where was Calvary? Is it possible to point out its exact location today? All we really know is that Jesus was crucified outside the city wall. This is definitely stated in Heb. 13:12, and probably implied also in such passages as Luke 20:15; 23:26. But which wall? The first wall, that built by David and Solomon, would no longer be applicable. The third wall, that begun by Herod Agrippa I, was not built until after the time of Christ. The reference must therefore be to the second or northern wall. The Church of the Holy Sepulchre, or somewhere very near to it, is favored as the site by tradition. It has become clear by now that the spot it occupies was at that time just outside this wall. Calvary was "near the city," and in its immediate vicinity there was a garden (John 19:20, 41).[599]

Note how few words—in the original only three: ". . . there they crucified him"—are used to indicate this enormously significant event! With this marvelous restraint we might compare the manner in which Scripture tells the story of the creation of the billions of stars: "and the stars" (Gen. 1:16b).

The pronoun *they* (in ". . . there they crucified him") refers to *the soldiers,* as is clear from the parallel passages in Mark 15:16, 24. The mode of execution to which reference is made existed in many nations, including the Roman Empire. Rome generally (not always!) reserved this form of punishment for slaves and those who had been convicted of the grossest crimes.

It has been well said that the person who was crucified "died a thousand

---

599. For more on this see the following: L. H. Grollenberg, *op. cit.*, p. 115; G. A. Turner, *op. cit.*, p. 336; H. Mulder, *Spoorzoeker*, p. 157; and C. Kopp, *The Holy Places of the Gospels*, New York, 1963, pp. 374–388.

deaths." Large nails were driven through hands and feet (John 20:25; cf. Luke 24:40). Among the horrors which one suffered while thus suspended (with the feet resting upon a little tablet, not very far away from the ground) were the following: severe inflammation, the swelling of the wounds in the region of the nails, unbearable pain from torn tendons, fearful discomfort from the strained position of the body, throbbing headache, and burning thirst (John 19:28).

In the case of Jesus the emphasis, however, should not be placed on this physical torture which he endured. It has been said that only the damned in hell know what Jesus suffered when he died on the cross. In a sense this is true, for they too suffer eternal death. One should add, however, that *they* have never been in heaven. The Son of God, on the other hand, descended from the regions of infinite delight in the closest possible fellowship with his Father (John 1:1; 17:5) to the abysmal depths of hell. On the cross he cried out, "My God, my God, why hast thou forsaken me?" (Mark 15:34).

It was a gross injustice that Jesus was crucified between two criminals, as if he too were a criminal. Nevertheless, viewed in the light of God's providence, it was also an honor. Is it not true that Jesus came to earth in order to seek and save the lost (19:10)? Was he not "the Friend of publicans and sinners" (Matt. 11:19)? See also N.T.C. on John 3:16 and on I Tim. 1:15.

By causing Jesus to be crucified between these two culprits did Pilate intend to insult the Jews even more? Did he intend to say, "Such is y o u r king, O Jews, one who is not any better than a bandit, and therefore deserves to be crucified between two of them"? However that may have been, one thing is certain, the prophecy of Isa. 53:12—"He was reckoned with the transgressors"—was here being fulfilled. And, in view of Luke 23:39-43, fulfilled gloriously.

34a. Then Jesus said, Father, forgive them, for they do not know what they are doing.

On the omission of these words from certain manuscripts see the note on this passage on page 1040.

In all probability what we have here is the first of

The Seven Words of the Cross:

a. *From 9 o'clock until noon:*

(1) "Father, forgive them: for they do not know what they are doing" (Luke 23:34).

(2) "I solemnly declare to you, Today you shall be with me in Paradise" (Luke 23:43).

(3) "Woman, look, your son! . . . Look, your mother!" (John 19:27).

b. *The three hours of darkness: from noon until 3 o'clock; no words reported.*

c. *About 3 o'clock:*

(4) "My God, my God, why hast thou forsaken me?" (Mark 15:34).

(5) "I am thirsty" (John 19:28).

(6) "It is finished" (John 19:30).

(7) "Father, into thy hands I commend my spirit" (Luke 23:46).

It is certainly in keeping with the spirit of Luke's Gospel that the three "words" in which the love of God as reflected in the Son is most emphatically set forth are found here (*words 1, 2, and 7*).

It is deplorable that so much opposition has arisen against this first saying. Some would exclude it entirely, and others try to tone it down.

The reasoning of some is as follows: those who killed Jesus were reprobates. God does not in any sense bless reprobates. Therefore Jesus cannot have asked that they be forgiven. Besides, the verb here used has a very wide meaning (this, by the way, is true). Conclusion: Jesus must have meant, "Father, hold back thy wrath; do not immediately pour out the full measure of thy fury."

The true meaning of the earnest supplication is probably as follows:

a. "Forgive them" means exactly that. It means "Blot out their transgression completely. In thy sovereign grace cause them to repent truly, so that they can be and will be pardoned fully."

b. That this is the meaning is clear from the fact that the grammatical construction is exactly the same as in 11:4, "And forgive us our sins," and as in 17:3, "If he repents, forgive him."

c. Is it even conceivable that he who insists so strongly that his followers must forgive *every* debtor, and that they must even love their enemies, should not exemplify this virtue himself?

d. When Stephen, at death's portal, clearly in imitation of the dying Christ, prayed, "Lord, *lay not this sin to their charge*," was he not giving us the truest interpretation of Christ's supplication, "Father, *forgive* them"?

e. Take special note of the word *Father*. What trust, what love! We are reminded of "Though he slay me, yet will I trust him" (Job 13:15, A.V.).

f. Is it not marvelous beyond words that Jesus, in his earnest intercession for his torturers, even presents to the Father a special plea, an argument, as it were, for the granting of his petition, namely, "for they do not know what they are doing"?

It was true: the soldiers certainly did not know. But even the members of the Sanhedrin, though they must have known that what they were doing was wicked, did not comprehend the extent of that wickedness.

Did the Father hear and answer this prayer? Part of the answer may well be the fact that Jerusalem's fall did not occur immediately. For a period of about forty years the gospel of salvation full and free was still being proclaimed to the Jews. Not only that but also: *many were actually led to the Lord.* On the day of Pentecost three thousand were converted (Acts 2:31, 42); a little later thousands more (Acts 4:4). Even "a large number of priests became obedient to the faith" (Acts 6:7). Not the people as a whole, but many families and individuals were converted.

g. By offering this prayer Jesus fulfilled the prophecy of Isa. 53: "Yet he bore the sin of many, *and made intercession for the transgressors.*" See also on Luke 22:37.

34b. And they cast lots to divide his clothes among them.

Having crucified Jesus, the legionaries, as was their custom, divided his garments by casting lots. In all probability by means of throwing of dice the four pieces—headgear, sandals, belt, and outer garment—were divided among the four (John 19:23) soldiers. The seamless tunic, all of one piece, woven all the way from top to bottom, was also put into the lottery, all of this in accordance with the prophecy of Ps. 22:18 (LXX Ps. 21:19), which Luke may well have had in mind.

Poor, poor soldiers! How much did they take home from Calvary? A few pieces of clothing! No truly penitent hearts, no renewed visions, no changed lives, no Savior? Even today, how much—or how little—do some people carry home with them from the church service, the Bible class, the hymn sing, the revival meeting? Each individual should answer this question for himself.

35a. Meanwhile the people were standing by, looking on.

Thousands upon thousands of people must have gathered in and around Jerusalem for the feast. And now here they stand, looking on. What a contrast between Jesus and his tormentors. He was not even angry, though he suffered indescribable agonies. In fact, he even prayed for those who had brought these woes upon him. Are some of the people even now beginning to have second thoughts about the propriety of their shouts, "Crucify him"? Are they starting to recall his words of majesty, his earnest pleadings, and his deeds of power and compassion? But see also N.T.C. on Matt. 27:39, 40.

35b. And even the rulers were sneering at him, saying, Others he saved; let him save himself if he is the Christ of God, his Chosen One.

The rulers or Jewish leaders—chief priests, scribes, and elders (Matt. 27:41)—were not satisfied with the mere fact that they had triumphed over Pilate and, as they thought, over Jesus. They also *reveled* in their victim's misery. They *gloated* over his apparently helpless condition. Casting overboard all decency and decorum that is generally associated with men of their rank, they were actually sneering at their enemy. They were shouting that he who saved others should save himself if he were indeed the Messiah (Luke 22:67–70), God's Chosen One (Isa. 42:1; Matt. 12:18).

Note also that in their hatred of him they did not even deign to address him. They considered that beneath their dignity. Not once, in the narrative of Christ's crucifixion, do the leaders address Jesus directly. Each time they talk *about* him, never *to* him.

When according to Luke they *implied,* and according to Matthew and Mark they actually *said,* "He cannot save himself," they were right; that is, in a sense. They were also terribly wrong. They thought that it was weakness that kept him nailed to the cross. Actually it was power, the power of his love, love for others, that he might save them, sacrificing himself as their Substitute, voluntarily surrendering himself to fathomless agonies in order that all who repose their trust in him might be saved (John 3:16).

36, 37. The soldiers also, coming up, mocked him, offering him sour wine, and saying, If you are the king of the Jews, save yourself.

The incident here recorded cannot very well refer to the drugged wine offered to Jesus when he arrived at Golgotha, and which he refused (Matt. 27:34; Mark 15:23). It must refer either to an incident reported only by Luke, or otherwise to that found also in John 19:28, 29. Closely connected with the latter is what is found in Matt. 27:47-49. It will be recalled that when the end was fast approaching Jesus cried out, "I am thirsty." One of the soldiers, having dipped a sponge into a vinegar vessel, brought the liquid to the mouth of Jesus, so that it might bring some relief to his lips and throat. As Matthew reports, this happened while other soldiers, the heartless ones, were mocking.

If this was what Luke had in mind, he would once again be departing from the chronological order of events. But how can there be any objection to that? The evangelist is still writing in an orderly fashion. After reporting what *the people* did, and *the rulers*, he now turns to *the soldiers* to describe what *they* did, without in any way stating exactly when it was that they did it.

The essence of the mockery was, "If you are the king of the Jews, save yourself." Had the soldiers heard about: (a) the charge advanced against Jesus by his accusers (Luke 23:2); (b) his own claim to true spiritual kingship (23:3; John 18:37); or (c) the taunting exclamation of Pilate (John 19:14)? However that may be, they use whatever information they may have gathered with reference to this subject, in order with it to ridicule the Crucified One.

Entirely aside from the possible sources of information already mentioned there was, of course, one very obvious source from which the soldiers derived their incentive to ridicule. It was *the superscription* over Jesus' head:

38. And there was also a superscription over him:
THIS IS THE KING OF THE JEWS

Pilate had caused a notice or label to be attached to the cross above Jesus' head. In John's Gospel (19:19, 20) this notice is called a "title," in Matthew's (27:37), a "charge," "accusation" or "indictment," and in Mark's (15:26) and Luke's (23:38) a "superscription." With respect to this written notice critics have discovered another contradiction in the Bible. They point to the fact that the words of which it was composed differ in all four Gospels. But there is more than one possible way in which this attack upon Scripture can be refuted. First, it must be considered possible that each Gospel writer gives the gist of the superscription as he sees it. The full wording may have been "This is Jesus of Nazareth the King of the Jews." So Matthew says that the charge read: "This is Jesus the King of the Jews"; Mark states the superscription was "the King of the Jews"; Luke's version is: "This is the King of the Jews"; and John, who was himself present and must have seen it, says that the title was: "Jesus of Nazareth the King of the Jews." It certainly was not necessary for each evangelist to write down all the words.

Another possibility is this: since the superscription was written in three languages, Aramaic, Latin, and Greek, in one, two, or even all three of these—but differently in each case—it may have been abbreviated.

The four agree in informing the reader that on this superscription Pilate called Jesus "the King of the Jews." Why did the governor word it thus? *Negatively,* because he did *not* want to write, "Jesus *who claimed* to be the King of the Jews," for he had proclaimed again and again that Jesus was innocent of this charge which the Jews had preferred against him. Therefore the governor absolutely refused to yield to the subsequent demand of the chief priests that he change the wording of the superscription. See John 19:21, 22. It is impossible to state *positively* why Pilate worded the superscription as he did. Did he do it to bestow honor on Jesus? One would like to think so. Yet, honoring Jesus, on the one hand, and on the other, allowing him to be mocked, and ordering him to be scourged and crucified, hardly go hand in hand. What then? Although we cannot be sure, perhaps the true answer is as follows: Pilate hated the Jews, especially their leaders. He was keenly aware that just now they had won a victory over him; for, as he probably saw it, they had forced him to sentence Jesus to be crucified. So, now he is mocking them. By means of the superscription he is saying, "Here is Jesus, the King of the Jews, the only king they have been able to produce, a king crucified at their own urgent request!"

All this does not take away the fact that although Pilate may have purposely worded the superscription as he did in order, negatively, to tell the Jews, "I do not at all believe the charge you brought against him," and positively, to mock them, God Almighty is also speaking in and through this same superscription. He is making a proclamation to one and all. Bear in mind the three languages in which the notice was written. He is saying, "This is Jesus, King of the Jews indeed; and not only this, but by means of this very cross he is King of kings and Lord of lords."

39-41. One of the crucified criminals began to hurl abuse at him, saying, Aren't you the Christ? Save yourself and us. —But the other one, rebuking him, replied, Don't you even fear God, since you're under the same sentence of condemnation? And we indeed justly, for we are getting what we deserve. But this man has done nothing out of place.

The following points should be noted:

1. This story is peculiar to Luke. And what a story, how full of comfort for every sinner who truly repents!

2. At first both robbers scoffed. They *blasphemed* the Holy One. They repeated the words and sentiments of the rulers. See Matt. 27:44; Mark 15:32.

3. At last one of the two criminals grew silent and repented. In his little speech he:

a. rebuked his partner.

b. admitted his own guilt. In fact, he even admitted that he and his partner fully deserved the terrible death by crucifixion.

c. confessed Jesus, adding his own testimony with respect to Christ's innocence to all the other similar testimonies that had already been made (by Pilate and by Herod).

4. What led to his conversion? We do not know, but the following items may well have been involved, certainly the last one:

a. fear of falling unprepared into the hands of the living God (Heb. 10:31). Note his words, "Don't you even fear God?"

b. the first word of the cross, in which Jesus asked the Father to forgive his tormentors, etc.

c. the calm and majestic behavior of Jesus.

d. things he may have heard about Jesus.

e. the Holy Spirit working in his heart.

The penitent robber not only rebuked his partner, admitted his guilt, and confessed Jesus as the Innocent One. He did one more thing, for which he will always be remembered:

42. Then he said, Jesus, remember me when you come in your kingdom.

He addresses the One to whom he has now surrendered his heart as Jesus, that is, Savior. See Luke 1:31; 2:21. And, as Gabriel had done (Luke 1:31–33), with that name *Jesus* the penitent immediately associates *royal rule*. The angel had said to Mary, "You shall give him the name Jesus. . . . And the Lord God will give him the throne of his father David. He will reign over the house of Jacob forever, and his kingdom [or royal rule] will never end."

Just what did the penitent mean? Did he think of Jesus as coming *into* his kingdom at death? Probably not. What he was asking for was that when, at the end of the age, Jesus would return in royal glory, he would remember this now converted supplicant.

About that eschatological coming Jesus had spoken again and again. See, for example, the following passages: Matt. 16:27; 19:28; 24:27, 30; 25:31–46; 26:64; Luke 17:22–37; 21:27, 36; 22:29, 30. If the penitent had heard anything about Jesus at all—and his prayer is hard to explain if he had not—he must have heard about his predictions in connection with the glorious Return at the end of the age.

The man is asking Jesus, therefore, to be remembered by him at that time. He does not ask for any place of honor. He knows very well that such a place is not for him. But he casts himself entirely upon the Savior's grace, asking only *to be remembered;* that is, of course, to be remembered *for good.*

43. Jesus said to him, I solemnly declare to you, today you will be with me in Paradise.

Eph. 3:20, 21 contains a most touchingly beautiful doxology, namely, "Now to him who is able to do infinitely more than all we ask or imagine, according to the power that is at work within us, to him be the glory in the church and in Christ Jesus to all generations forever and ever; Amen." Note especially these words *infinitely more than all we ask.*

That too was what the penitent supplicant received: far more than he has asked for. Note the beauty and the comfort of Christ's answer:

1. The man had asked for a blessing . . . in the remote future. He receives a promise pertaining to *this very day.* Jesus says, "Today."

2. He had asked "to be remembered." That was all he had dared to request. He receives the assurance, "Not only will I remember you; *you will be with me;* that is, in my immediate presence."

3. "With me" where? Not in some mystical region of phantoms, nor in purgatory, but *in Paradise.* But what is meant by Paradise? Paradise is heaven. It is as simple as that. From my book *The Bible on the Life Hereafter* I quote the following:

"The fact that 'heaven' and 'Paradise' are simply different words that indicate the same place is clear from II Cor. 12; compare verses 2 and 4. Here we read that someone was caught up to 'the third heaven.' It may be assumed that the first heaven was that of the clouds, the second that of the stars, the third that of the redeemed. But we immediately notice that the man who, according to verse 2, was said to have been caught up to *heaven,* was caught up to *paradise* according to verse 4. This certainly indicates that heaven and paradise are the same place and not two different places."

Rev. 2:7 ("the tree of life which is in the paradise of God") leads to the same conclusion, for also in the book of Revelation *paradise* is definitely another term for *heaven.* We read that "the tree of life" is in the paradise of God (Rev. 2:7), and that tree of life is in chapter 22 associated with "the holy city" (see verses 14, 19; also Rev. 21:1, 2).

For *Practical Lessons* and *Greek Words,* etc., see pp. 1038–1042.

---

44 It was already about the sixth hour,[600] and darkness enveloped the whole land until the ninth hour,[601]   45 the sun failing. And the curtain of the sanctuary was torn in two.   46 And with a loud voice Jesus cried out, "Father, into thy hands I commend my spirit." And when he had said this, he breathed his last.

47 Now when the centurion saw what had happened, he began to praise God, saying, "Surely, this was a righteous man." 48 And all the crowds that had come together to witness this spectacle, after observing what had occurred, began to return, beating their breasts. 49 But all his acquaintances, including the women who had followed him from Galilee, were standing afar off, watching these things.

23:44–49 *Calvary: The Death of Jesus*
Cf. Matt. 27:45–56; Mark 15:33–41; John 19:28–30

The people had been standing there, looking on. Rulers had been sneering. Robbers had been hurling abuse. One of them had repented and had

---

600. Or: 12 noon.
601. Or: 3 P.M.

received a wonderful assurance of *salvation this very day*. Jesus had uttered his first three words, the first two of which are reported by Luke.

Then, at twelve o'clock noon, something of a very dramatic character took place:

44, 45a. It was already about the sixth hour, and darkness enveloped the whole land until the ninth hour, the sun failing.

Suddenly the land became dark. Cf. Amos 8:9. The very fact that this darkness is mentioned shows that it must have been intense and unforgettable. Moreover, it occurred when least expected, at high noon, and lasted three hours.

Much has been written about this darkness. What caused it? How extensive was it? Did it have any meaning? As to the first question, very little information is given. We are safe in saying, "God brought it about." That is far better than to say that either the devil or Nature caused it. But when the further question is asked, "By what means did God bring it about?" a completely satisfactory answer cannot be given. A sudden thunderstorm, even if it lasted three hours, would not have covered the entire country and would probably not have been singled out for special mention. A black sirocco storm from the desert is not generally known to cause such darkness. To be sure, Luke here in 23:44, 45 may seem to supply the answer for which we are looking. Does it not say, "the sun being eclipsed"? But, first of all, the reading is not entirely certain. There are several variants. Secondly, granted that "eclipsed" is the right word, this cannot refer to an eclipse in the technical, astronomical sense, for that is impossible at the time of Passover (full moon). Besides, such an eclipse would hardly last three hours! But if the term be taken in a broader sense, namely, "darkened," we are back to where we were: darkened by what? The best answer may well be to regard what happened here as a special act of God, a miracle, and to inquire no further as to any secondary means.

How extensive was it? Here too we must abstain from giving a definite answer. It will not do to say that when the light of the sun is shut off half of the globe must be darkened. The light of the sun could be shut off for a certain country or region. See Exod. 10:22, 23. Luther, Calvin, Zahn, Ridderbos, etc., prefer the translation "land" for Mark 15:33. Cf. Matt. 27:45 and here in Luke 23:44. Even if the translation "land" instead of "earth" should be correct, as may well be the case, the fact must not be ignored that the darkness "enveloped *the whole* land," and was therefore very extensive.

As to the third question, "Did it have any meaning?" here a positive answer is certainly in order. Yes, it did have a very important meaning. The darkness meant judgment, the judgment of God upon our sins. This punishment was borne by Jesus, so that he, as our Substitute, suffered most intense agony, indescribable woe, terrible isolation or forsakenness. Hell came to Calvary that day, and the Savior descended into it and bore its horrors in our stead. How do we know that this answer is correct? Note the following:

a. Darkness in Scripture is very often a symbol of judgment. See Isa.
5:30; 60:2; Joel 2:30, 31; Amos 5:18, 20; Zeph. 1:14-18; Matt. 24:29, 30;
Acts 2:20; II Peter 2:17; Rev. 6:12-17.

b. With a view to his impending death the Savior had himself stated that
he was giving and was about to give his life as "a ransom for many" (Mark
10:45; cf. Matt. 20:28; 26:28).

c. The agony suffered by our Lord during these three hours was such
that he finally uttered the explanatory words found in Matt. 27:46 and
Mark 15:34, but not recorded by Luke, the words, "My God, my God, why
hast thou forsaken me?"

45b. And the curtain of the sanctuary was torn in two.

Does this have reference to the outer veil—the one between the
sanctuary and the rest of the temple—or to the inner, the one between the
Holy Place and the Holy of Holies? On the basis of Heb. 6:19; 9:3; and
10:20, all of which refer to the inner veil, it is natural to think of this second
or inner curtain. As Godet points out,[602] this veil alone "had a typical sense,
and alone bore, strictly speaking, the name *katapetasma* [the word used in
the original]." Similarly C. Schneider states,[603] "The evangelists are almost
certainly thinking of the inner curtain, since the other had no great significance." That the rent veil of the Synoptics is the one to which Heb. 9:3
refers is also the view of F. F. Bruce.[604]

As often, so also now, Luke is not arranging his material chronologically
when he mentions the tearing of this curtain before reporting the actual
death of Christ. Matthew and Mark make clear that the rending of the veil
followed immediately upon Christ's death; one might even say, "occurred
at the moment of that death." *Through that death the way into the heavenly
sanctuary was opened.*

But something can be said also in favor of Luke's arrangement. It is
again, as often, topical. He first mentions the material signs (the darkness
and the rending of the veil), then the death, and then, without interruption, the effect of that death *upon people:* (a) upon the centurion, (b) upon
the crowds, (c) upon the women from Galilee.

At the moment of Christ's death this curtain was suddenly sliced in two
from top to bottom, as Matthew and Mark relate. This happened at three
o'clock, when priests must have been busy in the temple. How did it come
about? Not through natural wear, for in that case there would probably
have been rents all over, and the tearing would more likely have been from
the bottom up. Nor is it at all probable that Matthew, who immediately
afterward mentions an earthquake (27:51), is trying to convey the idea that
this splitting in two of the curtain was caused by the earthquake. Had that
been his intention, would he not have mentioned the earthquake before the

602. *Op. cit.,* Vol. II, p. 336.
603. Th.D.N.T., Vol. III, p. 629.
604. *The Epistle to the Hebrews (N.I.C.),* p. 246.

tearing of the curtain? What happened must be regarded as a miracle. Any secondary means that may have been used to effect it are not mentioned, and it would be futile to speculate. As to the symbolic significance, this is made clear by two considerations: first, it occurred at the moment when Jesus died; secondly, it is explained in Heb. 10:19, 20: through the death of Christ, symbolized by the tearing of the curtain, the way into "the Holy of Holies," that is, heaven, is opened to all those who take refuge in him. For the practical lesson see Heb. 4:16. More may be implied, but by limiting the interpretation to this we are on safe ground.

46. And with a loud voice Jesus cried out, Father, into thy hands I commend my spirit.

The third, fourth, fifth, and sixth words of the cross (see above, pp. 1027, 1028) are not reported by Luke. He does, however, report the first, second, and seventh. What a beautiful relation between the first and the last of these seven words. Do they not show that from first to last the Son of God never rejects his Father? He keeps clinging to him throughout; yes, even when he utters the fourth word. Even then Jesus calls the One who had sent him *"my God."*

The final word, by means of which the Savior, making use of the phraseology of Ps. 31:5, entrusts his soul to the care of his Father is beautiful because of: (a) what it retains of Ps. 31:5; (b) what it adds; and (c) what it omits.

a. It *retains* "I commend my spirit." This is significant, for it indicates that the Savior died the only kind of death that was able to satisfy the justice of God and to save man. It had to be *a voluntary sacrifice.* The very fact that Jesus uttered this word *with a loud voice* also shows that he willingly, voluntarily laid down his life (John 10:11, 15).

b. It *adds* the significant word *Father,* not found in the psalm. The importance of this word at this point has already been indicated.

c. It *omits* the clause that immediately follows in the psalm, namely, "Thou hast redeemed me." In the case of Christ, the Sinless One, no such redemption was necessary nor even possible.

The closing words of Luke 23:46, namely, **And when he had said this, he breathed his last,** show the "calm restfulness" (Geldenhuys) in the mind and heart of Jesus at the moment when his soul parted from this earth. Having fully accomplished *the work the Father gave him to do* (John 17:4), he enjoyed to the full "the peace of God that surpasses all understanding" (Phil. 4:7).

47. Now when the centurion saw what had happened, he began to praise God, saying, Surely, this was a righteous man.

The centurion had seen how Jesus had been conducting himself in the midst of all the wicked taunts and mockeries and all the pain he suffered. And now there was that loud cry of restful resignation; rather, of *voluntary surrender.* It was a cry of confidence, a cry which once it was heard could never be forgotten.

This legionary was in all likelihood not a Jew. His heart had not been hardened against Jesus, as had the hearts of many of the Jews, especially those of their leaders. Besides, he had seen and must have felt how even nature reacted to the death of Jesus. Think of the earthquake, the splitting of the rocks, and the opening of the tombs (Matt. 27:51-54).

So, he began to praise or glorify God, saying, "Surely, this was a righteous man." This probably means that he glorified God by acknowledging the righteousness of Jesus. Matt. 27:54 and Mark 15:39 state that he said, "Surely, this (man) was God's Son." Undoubtedly he said both, proclaiming Jesus to be both God's Son and a righteous man. There is no conflict.

48. And all the crowds that had come together to witness this spectacle, after observing what had occurred, began to return, beating their breasts.

This is not difficult to understand. Think of what these people had heard and seen and experienced. There had been the three hours of darkness, the earthquake, the splitting of the rocks, the opening of graves. Add to this the behavior of Jesus, including his words of trust in the heavenly Father and forgiveness toward men. Besides, many of these people must have been filled with a feeling of guilt. They must have said to themselves over and over again, "*We* did this." In saying this they were right (Acts 2:36; I Thess. 2:14, 15).

So, returning to the city, they began to beat their breasts in self-reproach. In this connection see also Luke 18:13; 23:27. Lenski states their feelings admirably, "They came to witness a show; they left with feelings of woe."

This explains, at least to some extent, why on the Day of Pentecost there were no less than three thousand conversions. It may also go far to explain the temporary hesitancy on the part of the Jewish authorities to persecute the followers of Jesus.

49. But all his acquaintances, including the women who had followed him from Galilee, were standing afar off, watching these things.

Who were these acquaintances that stood afar off? As far as the *men* are concerned, from the Gospel of John we learn that "the disciple whom Jesus loved" was standing close enough to the cross so that he could hear what Jesus said to him (John 19:26, 27). Were any of the other Eleven also present? Were Joseph of Arimathea and Nicodemus?

Our passage states that the acquaintances, men and women, were standing "afar off," perhaps from fear that harm might befall them if they tried to come closer. On the other hand, John 19:25 seems to place these acquaintances *near* the cross. Did they perhaps stand afar off at first, and did they draw closer later on when they had become convinced that the soldiers would not harm them? Something like this may well have happened.

As to the identity of the women, this group included *some,* and *may* have included *all* of the following: (a) Mary the mother of Jesus—Not for very long did she stand near the cross (John 19:26, 27); (b) Mary's sister Salome, who was the mother of the sons of Zebedee; (c) Mary the wife of Clopas = the mother of James the Less and of Joses, and (d) Mary Magdalene. This suggested grouping results from a comparison of Matt. 27:56; Mark 15:40, 41; and John 19:25. Luke 24:10 also mentions Joanna. And note also Luke 8:3, where a lady by that name is called "the wife of Chuza, manager of Herod's household," and where Susanna's name is added. For more on this subject see N.T.C. on John, Vol. II, pp. 431, 432 and see above, on 8:2, 3. No doubt there were other women who are not named; note the phrase *among others* in Luke 24:10.

Notable women were these, and this for at least three reasons:

a. With the exception of John none of the other disciples who belonged to the group of eleven is reported to have been present at Calvary, but these women were present! They displayed rare courage.

b. We are distinctly told that they were women who had followed Jesus from Galilee to Jerusalem and had been in the habit of ministering to his needs. Cf. Luke 8:2, 3. They had given evidence of hearts filled with love and sympathy.

c. Being witnesses of Christ's death, burial, and resurrection appearance, they were qualified witnesses of facts of redemption on which, under God, the church depends for its faith.[605]

Practical Lessons Derived from Luke 23:26–49

Verse 28

"Daughters of Jerusalem, do not weep for me," etc.

When someone wrongs us we tend to exaggerate the wrong and to pity ourselves. Jesus did the opposite: in the midst of the agonies he suffered as the Innocent, in fact, the Righteous One, his heart went out to others. He was seeking to save them.

Verse 34

"Father, forgive them, for they do not know what they are doing." This was true *then*. But as the centuries roll along and the gospel continues to spread, the words "for they do *not* know," etc., lose a bit of their relevance. Therefore, "Today, O that y o u would hear his voice!"

Since Jesus prayed even for his tormentors he certainly is *our* Intercessor now.

IN ONE SENSE HOW FALSE IN ANOTHER HOW TRUE

Matt. 27:42; cf. Luke 23:35: "Others he saved; he cannot save himself."
John 11:50; 18:14: "It is expedient that one man die for the people."
Luke 23:5: "He stirs up the people."

Verse 46

"And with a loud voice Jesus cried out, 'Father, into thy hands I commend my spirit.' And when he had said this, he breathed his last."

In "the theology of Luke" what was the significance of Christ's death?

---

605. Notes on Greek words, phrases, and constructions in 23:26–49 begin on page 1039.

That Luke viewed it as a divine *must* and as a ransom for sin, resulting in the salvation of all who trust in the Savior, is clear from such passages as Luke 9:22; 12:49, 50; 22:19, 20; 23:25 (cf. Isa. 53:6, 12); 24:25-27, 44-49; Acts 8:32-35; 20:28 (what beautiful harmony between Matt. 20:28 and Acts 20:28!). Luke and Paul were close friends and frequently were travel companions. When these two describe the Lord's Supper, in which the meaning of Christ's death is set forth, they do so in language that is almost identical (cf. Luke 22:19, 20 with I Cor. 11:23-25). And Paul's doctrine of redemption through the payment of a ransom, effective for all who place their trust in Christ, is well known (Rom. 3:24; 5:8, 18; 8:1; II Cor. 5:20, 21).

Notes on Greek Words, Phrases, and Constructions in 23:26–49

Verse 26

ἐπιλαβόμενοι, nom. pl. masc. 2nd aor. middle participle of ἐπιλαμβάνω, to catch, lay hold of.

ἐπέθηκαν, third per. pl. aor. indicat. act. of ἐπιτίθημι, to place or lay upon.

Verse 27

ἐκόπτοντο, third per. pl. imperf. indicat. middle of κόπτω, to beat oneself while mourning, to mourn, lament. See the note on 8:52 on page 467.

Verse 29

Though ἔρχονται is pres. tense, this pres. is clearly futuristic, as is our English "Days are coming."

Verse 30

πέσετε, sec. per. pl. 2nd aor. imperat. of πίπτω, to fall.

βουνοῖς, dat. pl. of βουνός*, a hill; cf. 3:5.

καλύψατε, sec. per. pl. aor. imperat. act. of καλύπτω. to cover.

Verse 31

ὑγρῷ, dat. s. neut. of ὑγρός*, only here in the New Testament, wet, moist, humid, fresh, green.

ξύλῳ, dat. s. of ξύλον. Cf. *xylophone.* The following meanings of this word in the New Testament can be distinguished:

a. wood (I Cor. 3:12; Rev. 18:12, twice).

b. things made of wood: club, cudgel (Matt. 26:47, 55; Mark 14:43, 48; Luke 22:52); pl. stocks (Acts 16:24).

c. "tree" of the cross (Acts 5:30; 10:39; 13:29; Gal. 3:13; I Peter 2:24).

d. "tree" of life (Rev. 2:7; 22:2, 14, 19).

The question, then, is, "To which group does the word ξύλον as used here in Luke 23:31 belong?"

Among those who favor the rendering "tree"—though here obviously neither "tree of the cross" nor "tree of life"—are L.N.T. (A. and G.), A.V., A.R.V., N.A.S.,

Beck, N.I.V. But, for the reason stated in the commentary, this view is hard to defend. All things considered, the rendering "wood" must be considered the best. So also J. Schneider, art. on this word in Th.D.N.T., Vol. V, p. 38, R.S.V., N.E.B., Berkeley, Lenski, Phillips, Williams, Robertson, Weymouth, Goodspeed, Greijdanus, Moffatt, Jerusalem Bible, Dutch (both old and new), Schlatter, Frisian, South African, etc. The references to Talmud and Midrash in S.BK., Vol. II, p. 263, are also in line with this translation. Since the underlying figure in Ezek. 17:24 is entirely different, that passage too fails to support the sense *tree* here in Luke 23:31, as Schlatter (*Das Evangelium des Lukas*, Stuttgart, 1960, p. 449) and Schneider have pointed out.

γένηται, third per. s. 2nd aor. subjunct. (deliberat.) of γίνομαι, to become, happen to, be done to.

Verse 32

ἤγοντο, third per. pl. imperf. (descriptive) pass. of ἄγω, to lead, bring.

κακοῦργοι, nom. pl. masc. of κακοῦργος (κακός plus ἔργον), evildoer, criminal.

ἀναιρεθῆναι, aor. pass. infinitive of ἀναιρέω, to lift up from the ground, to put to death, execute. See on 22:2.

Verse 33

Κρανίον, Skull (cf. Matt. 27:33; Mark 15:22; John 19:17). Cf. *cranium*.

Verse 34

Although the words, "Father, forgive them, for they do not know what they are doing," are omitted in some of the best manuscripts, who would be bold enough to ascribe them to anyone but Jesus? Besides, the textual support for their retention cannot be regarded as weak.

ἄφες, sec. per. s. 2nd aor. imperat. of ἀφίημι; here in the sense of *to forgive*. For a summary of meanings of this verb see the note on 4:39 on page 271.

Verses 35, 36

εἰστήκει, third per. s. past perf. of ἵστημι, with sense of imperf.; hence, "they were standing (by)."

ἐξεμυκτήριζον, third per. pl. imperf. (iterat. or progress.) of ἐκμυκτηρίζω; see on 16:14, to sneer, mock, scoff. Note first class (simple) conditional sentence in verse 35 and again in verse 37.

σωσάτω, third per. s. imperat. (effect.) act. of σώζω, to save.

Verse 37

From the same verb is also σῶσον, here and in verse 39, sec. per. s. aor. imperat. act.

Verse 38

ἐπιγραφή, superscription. Cf. *epigraph*.

Verse 39

κρεμασθέντων, gen. pl. masc. aor. pass. participle of κρεμάννυμι, to hang; pass. to be hanged; here: on a cross; hence, to be crucified; said of the crucified criminals. For a related word see the note on 8:33 on page 452.

Verse 40

ἐπιτιμῶν, nom. s. masc. pres. participle of ἐπιτιμάω, here *to rebuke;* but see also the note on 4:35 on page 267.

φοβῇ, sec. per. s. pres. indicat. middle of φοβέω, to fear.

κρίματι, dat. s. of κρίμα, judicial verdict, judgment, sentence. In I Cor. 6:7, lawsuit.

Verse 41

ἄτοπον, acc. s. of ἄτοπος, out of place, improper. In the New Testament this word occurs four times: Luke 23:41; Acts 25:5; Acts 28:6; and II Thess. 3:2.

Verse 42

μνήσθητί μου, remember me. The verbal form is sec. per. s. aor. imperat. pass. of the simple verb μιμνήσκω. The compound form is found in 22:61.

ἔλθῃς, sec. per. s. 2nd aor. subjunct. of ἔρχομαι, to come.

Verse 44

Note: "about the sixth hour . . . until the ninth hour"; i.e., by Jewish time reckoning: from noon until 3 P.M.

Verse 45

Note gen. absolute "the sun failing." The reading τοῦ ἡλίου ἐκλιπόντος is probably the best. The verbal form is gen. s. of the pres. act. participle of ἐκλείπω, to fail, run out; see the note on 16:9 on page 779; cf. 22:32; Heb. 1:12. Cf. *eclipse,* though what happened at Calvary cannot have been a "solar eclipse" in the technical sense. See the explanation.

ἐσχίσθη, third per. s. aor. indicat. pass. of σχίζω, to tear. See the note on 5:36 on page 312.

Verse 46

παρατίθεμαι, first per. s. pres. indicat. middle of παρατίθημι, to place by the side of, to set before, commit, commend, entrust. See also 9:16; 10:8; 11:6; 12:48. In Luke's Gospel-Acts this verb occurs almost as often as in all the rest of the New Testament.

ἐξέπνευσεν, third per. s. aor. indicat. of ἐκπνέω, to breathe out, expire; cf. Mark 15:37, 39.

Verse 47

ὄντως, really, without any doubt, certainly; cf. 24:34.

1041

Verse 48

συμπαραγενόμενοι, nom. pl. masc. 2nd aor. participle of συνπαραγίνομαι*, to come to the side of together, to gather; only here in the New Testament.

θεωρίαν, acc. of θεωρία*, sight, spectacle; only here in the New Testament.

θεωρήσαντες, nom. pl. masc. aor. participle of θεωρέω, to see, observe, contemplate. Cf. *theorize*. See also N.T.C. on John, Vol. I, p. 85.

ὑπέστρεφον, third per. pl. imperf. (probably inchoative) indicat. of ὑποστρέφω, to return. This verb, in the New Testament occurring once each in Mark, Galatians, Hebrews, and II Peter, is found about thirty times in the writings of Luke!

Verse 49

For εἱστήκεισαν, third per. pl. past. perf., see above, on verse 35 (s. there).

ὁρῶσαι, nom. pl. fem. pres. act. participle of ὁράω, to see.

---

50 And behold, a man named Joseph, a member of the council, a good and upright man—
51 he had not consented to their decision and action—(a man) of Arimathea, a town of the Jews, who was constantly waiting for the kingdom of God, 52 this man went to Pilate and asked for the body of Jesus. 53 Then he took it down, wrapped it in a linen cloth, and laid it in a rock-hewn tomb, in which no one had yet been laid. 54 It was Preparation Day, and the sabbath was about to begin.

55 Now the women who had come with Jesus from Galilee followed closely and saw the tomb and how his body was laid. 56 Then they went home and prepared spices and perfumes. But during the sabbath they rested in obedience to the commandment.

23:50–56 *The Burial of Jesus*
Cf. Matt. 27:57–61; Mark 15:42–47; John 19:38–42

50–52. And behold, a man named Joseph, a member of the council, a good and upright man—he had not consented to their decision and action—(a man) of Arimathea, a town of the Jews, who was constantly waiting for the kingdom of God, this man went to Pilate and asked for the body of Jesus.

With reference to this man note the following:

a. Joseph was a member of the council, that is, of the Jewish Supreme Court, the Sanhedrin. According to Mark 15:43 he was a distinguished, highly respected member, a prominent one, a person whose counsel must have been eagerly sought, one whose word carried weight.

b. He is called "a good and upright man," one who reminds us of Barnabas (Acts 11:24).

c. He proved his goodness of heart, his fairness and honesty, by not consenting to the decision and action of the Sanhedrin against Jesus. He had probably purposely remained absent from the meeting where the wicked deeds were perpetrated. See Mark 14:64; 15:1. According to these passages the action against Jesus was unanimous. That is why we say that Joseph had probably been absent.

d. He was a man from Arimathea, a town of the Jews. This probably

1042

means that he came from Ramah (= "height"), the city of Samuel. In ancient times it was located in the tribe of Ephraim and was known also as Ramathaimzophim (I Sam. 1:1). It was located about 32 kilometers (20 miles) northwest of Jerusalem.

e. He is said to have been "constantly waiting for the kingdom of God." This probably means that, in harmony with Christ's own message (Matt. 11:4-6, 12), Joseph believed that the reign of God in human hearts and lives was being established and that he ardently hoped for it to be established more and more. *In a sense* this man had already become a disciple of Jesus (Matt. 27:57b). The work of God had begun in him. That is why he wanted to do what was right.

Now this man went to Pilate to ask for the body of Jesus, that it might receive an honorable interment. It took courage to do this (Mark 15:43), and for more than one reason. First, it should be borne in mind that according to Roman law those condemned to death had lost the right to be buried.[606]

Add to this the fact that Pilate hated the Jews and had but a little while ago refused their request to change the wording of the superscription (John 19:20-22). But more than that, by means of what Joseph of Arimathea was now doing he was openly professing before the entire world, including the Sanhedrin, that he was a believer in Jesus Christ.

Yes, it took real courage. He had been *a secret disciple,* one who for fear of the Jews did not dare to stand up openly for Jesus (John 19:38). Terrible were the threats of the Sanhedrin against the followers of Jesus. Read John 9:22; 12:42.

But now, because of God's sovereign grace, there was a change, a significant change in the heart and life of Joseph. By his action he shows that he now insists on being openly counted on the side of the disciples of Jesus. He will no longer be merely a *secret* disciple.

How did Pilate answer his request? Here Luke, as often, abbreviates. Details omitted by Luke are found in Mark 15:44, 45:

"Pilate was surprised to hear that Jesus was already dead. So, summoning the centurion, he asked whether Jesus had already died. When he was so informed by the centurion, he granted the body to Joseph."

Now back to Luke again:

53, 54. Then he took it down, wrapped it in a linen cloth, and laid it in a rock-hewn tomb, in which no one had yet been laid. It was Preparation Day, and the sabbath was about to begin.

The words, "He took it down," cannot mean that Joseph did this all by himself. He had helpers. One of them was Nicodemus. See John 19:39-42. And there were probably others, servants perhaps. It must be borne in mind that Joseph of Arimathea was a rich man (Matt. 27:57).

Having taken the body down Joseph treated it in accordance with "the

---

606. See Tacitus, *Annals* VI.29.

burial custom of the Jews" (John 19:40). This probably includes that it was washed. All three Synoptics state that the body was wrapped in linen. As the linen was wound tightly around the body limb by limb, the mixture of myrrh and aloes supplied by Nicodemus was strewn in.

Then the body was carried to Joseph's tomb. The distance was probably very short, for, since it was the Day of Preparation, that is, Friday, and since sunset, that is, the sabbath, was approaching, the body of Jesus could not be buried in a distant tomb. Time would not allow. With reference to this tomb note also the following:

a. It was new, in the sense that it had never been used. Decay and decomposition had never entered it. It was therefore a fit resting place for the body of the Lord. In this connection see the remarks on 19:30, "a colt on which no one ever sat."

b. It was Joseph's own tomb. Moreover, he himself had hewn it (or caused it to be hewn) out of bedrock (Matt. 27:60). Isa. 53:9 comes to mind, "He was with a rich man in his death."

c. From 24:2 it becomes clear that a stone had been placed against the tomb's entrance. With respect to this stone see also Matt. 27:60; 28:2; Mark 15:46; 16:3, 4; John 20:1. It was huge and heavy, resembling a great millstone.

For the probable location of the tomb, just outside the city wall, probably at or very close to the place assigned to it in the Church of the Holy Sepulchre, see above, on verses 32, 33. More details about the placing of the body of Jesus in this tomb Luke does not supply. See, however, footnote 610 on p. 1052; also Mark 16:5; John 20:5-7.

55, 56. Now the women who had come with Jesus from Galilee followed closely and saw the tomb and how his body was laid. Then they went home and prepared spices and perfumes. But during the sabbath they rested in obedience to the commandment.

Although there is nothing to show that the women (see verse 49) assisted in any way with the taking down of the body and the interment, they remained keenly interested in what was going on. They followed *closely* so that they saw exactly where the tomb was and how the body was laid. Then they went home and prepared spices and perfumes. But so close was the beginning of the sabbath that they were unable to make all the necessary preparations before the beginning of the day of rest. During that day, in strict obedience to the commandment, they rested.

And now the sabbath was ended. Accordingly it was now Saturday after 6 P.M. The bazaars were open again. So, as we learn from Mark 16:1, Mary Magdalene, and Mary the mother of James, and Salome purchased spices in order that without any further delay they might go to the tomb the very next morning and anoint Jesus' body. It is true that Joseph of Arimathea and Nicodemus had already wound linen bandages around the body, strewing in a mixture of myrrh and aloes. But the corpse had not yet been anointed. The *living* body had been anointed (John 12:1-8) but not the *dead* one. Besides, a week had gone by since the other anointing had taken place.[607]

Practical Lessons Derived from Luke 23:50-56

Verses 50-53, 55, 56

"*Joseph* asked for the body of Jesus, took it down, wrapped it in a linen cloth, and laid it in a rock-hewn tomb."
"*Women* . . . from Galilee . . . prepared spices and perfumes."
In Christ there is neither male nor female (Gal. 3:28).

With respect to Christ's body

a. The enemies fear that the disciples of Jesus will steal it (Matt. 27:62-66).
b. Joseph of Arimathea provides an honorable interment for it (Luke 23:50-54).
c. Women disciples come to anoint it (24:1 and parallels).
d. God raises it (24:6 and parallels; Rom. 1:3, 4; I Cor. 15:4, 50-58).
e. Paul describes Christ's raised body as being a prototype of the glorious resurrection body believers will one day receive from God (Rom. 8:23; Phil. 3:20, 21).

Notes on Greek Words, Phrases, and Constructions in 23:50-56

There is a kind of poetic cadence, a rhythmic beauty, about the manner in which Luke, led by the Spirit, expresses himself in the lengthy sentence (verses 50-53). It may well be questioned whether something of this beauty is not lost when in translation this sentence is broken up into several little pieces.

Verse 50

καὶ ἰδού. Luke has been reporting so many terrible things *men* did to Jesus that he calls special attention to the deed of a man who was of the opposite disposition. Note, therefore, "And behold!" Among several translators who have tried to preserve this special emphasis are the following: Lenski, A.R.V., N.A.S., Dutch (both new and old).

βουλευτής, both here and in Mark 15:43 a member of the council or Sanhedrin. Cf. βουλεύω, to impart counsel.

Verse 51

ἦν συγκατατεθειμένος, third per. s. periphrastic perf. middle of συγκατατίθημι*, lit. to set down together, to assent, agree.

προσεδέχετο, third per. s. imperf. (descript. and progress.) of προσδέχομαι, to look forward to, wait for. The word is also used in the sense of *to welcome* (15:2).

---

607. Notes on Greek words, phrases, and constructions in 23:50-56 begin on this page.

Verse 53

καθελών, nom. s. masc. 2nd aor. participle of καθαιρέω, here: to take down. But see also 1:52 and 12:18. However, the verbs "took it down," "wrapped" and "laid" are probably causative: he caused it to be taken down, etc. He did not do it all by himself.

ἐνετύλιξεν, third per. s. aor. indicat. act. of ἐντυλίσσω, to wrap up in. The word has the same meaning in Matt. 27:59. In John 20:7 it means *to fold up*.

σινδόνι, dat. s. of σινδών, linen cloth. See also Matt. 27:59; Mark 14:51, 52; 15:46.

λαξευτῷ, dat. s. neut. of λαξευτός* (λᾶς, rock, stone, plus ξέω, to hew), rock-hewn, in the New Testament a hapax legomenon.

ἦν κείμενος, third per. s. periphrastic imperf. of κεῖμαι, to lie, to be laid; hence here "had been laid" (as if the verbal form were a pluperf. passive).

Verse 54

Even the modern Greek word for Friday is Παρασκευή. It is the day of *preparation* for the sabbath.

ἐπέφωσκεν, third per. s. imperf. indicat. of ἐπιφώσκω, basically: to dawn; more generally: to begin. The expression refers here to the time of sunset when, according to Jewish time reckoning, a new day *begins*.

Verse 55

κατακολουθήσασαι, nom. pl. fem. aor. participle of κατακολουθέω**, to follow closely, in the New Testament only here and in Acts 16:17.

ἦσαν συνεληλυθυῖαι, third per. pl. periphrastic past perf. act. of συνέρχομαι, to come with, accompany.

ἐθεάσαντο, third per. pl. aor. indicat. of θεάομαι, to see, behold. See N.T.C. on John, Vol. I, p. 85.

ἐτέθη, third per. s. aor. indicat. pass. of τίθημι, to lay, place.

Verse 56

τὸ σάββατον, acc. of extent of time, (all) during the sabbath, throughout the sabbath.

ἡσύχασαν, third per. pl. aor. indicat. of ἡσυχάζω, to rest; in 14:4, to be silent. This verb also occurs in Acts 11:18; 21:14; and I Thess. 4:11 ("Be ambitious about living calmly").

Summary of Chapter 23

When Jesus had openly confessed before the Sanhedrin that he was indeed the Messiah, the very Son of God, that body had condemned him to death. But Roman law did not permit the Jews to carry out that sentence. So now the entire assembly brought Jesus to Pilate, the procurator ("governor"), who at that time was staying in the praetorium or the governor's Jerusalem residence.

The Jewish authorities, having been compelled by Pilate to present a formal bill of indictment, advanced several charges, amounting to the accusation, "Jesus is guilty of high treason. He considers himself a king." When Pilate asked Jesus whether he was indeed the king of the Jews, he answered, "It is as you say." From John 18:33–38 we learn that Jesus explained to Pilate that the implied kingdom was spiritual, not political. At the close of the interview Pilate told the chief priests and the crowds, "No crime whatever do I find in this man." But the enemies of Jesus answered, "He stirs up the people, teaching throughout the entire country of the Jews, starting from Galilee and continuing even to this place" (verses 1–5).

When Pilate heard that Jesus hailed from Galilee, he, anxious to get rid of the case, decided to bind the defendant over to Herod, Galilee's tetrarch (ruler, popularly called "king"). The chief priests and scribes, who had come along, vehemently accused Jesus before Herod. It will be recalled that Herod (Antipas) was the ruler who had caused John the Baptist to be beheaded. Afterward, when miracles performed by Jesus were reported to him, he had exclaimed, "This is John the Baptist, risen from the dead." Now he was anxious to see Jesus and especially to witness some of his miracles. However, Jesus refused to satisfy the wicked ruler. Before Herod he did not even open his mouth, since that ruler had hardened himself in sin. The result of Christ's refusal to answer was that Herod, having treated Jesus with contempt, dressed him in a bright robe and returned him to Pilate (verses 6–12).

Pilate now thought of another way of shaking off his own responsibility. He told the crowds (in substance), "Since neither I nor Herod have found Jesus guilty of the charges y o u have brought against him, I will punish him and then release him." He thought that merely "punishing" Jesus would satisfy the accusers. But the shouted answer came back, "Away with this man. Release Barabbas to us." Barabbas was an insurrectionist and murderer. Yet, the Jews, given the opportunity to ask for the release of any one prisoner at Passover time, as was the custom, demanded that Barabbas be released and Jesus crucified. And though Pilate repeatedly asserted Christ's innocence and wanted him to be released (Acts 3:13), the Jews, urged on by their leaders, continued to demand the crucifixion of Jesus. At last Pilate, intimidated by the threat recorded in John 19:12, yielded, and sentenced Jesus to be crucified (verses 13–25).

At first Jesus carried the cross himself. When he could no longer carry it, the soldiers forced Simon of Cyrene to do so. Mark's parallel (15:21) calls Simon "the father of Alexander and Rufus." Paul writes, "Greet Rufus, the chosen in the Lord, and his mother and mine" (Rom. 16:13). Was the mother of Rufus the wife of the Simon who carried Christ's cross? We cannot be sure.

To certain women of Jerusalem who were lamenting Jesus, he said, "Do not weep for me but for yourselves and for y o u r children . . . for if men do this to the green wood, what will happen to the dry?"

Two criminals were crucified with Jesus, one on his right, the other on his left. With reference to all who had brought these agonies upon him, the

Savior prayed, "Father, forgive them, for they do not know what they are doing." His clothes were divided by lot among the soldiers. Cf. Ps. 22:18; John 19:23, 24. The people were looking on; the rulers were scoffing. They said, "Others he saved; let him save himself," etc. The soldiers offered him sour wine and said, "If you are the king of the Jews, save yourself." The superscription above Jesus' head read, "This is the king of the Jews."

At first both crucified criminals hurled abuse at Jesus. Finally one repented and asked the Savior to remember him. Jesus answered, "I solemnly declare to you, today you will be with me in Paradise" (verses 26–43).

From noon until 3 P.M. darkness covered the land. In connection with Jesus' death the curtain of the sanctuary was sliced in two, indicating that by his substitutionary sufferings Jesus had opened the way to heaven for all believers. It was with a loud voice that he cried out, "Father, into thy hands I commend my spirit." Cf. Ps. 31:5.

When the centurion saw what had happened he cried out, "Surely, this was a righteous man." Cf. Mark 15:39. The crowds returned to the city beating their breasts in self-reproach. Cf. Acts 2:37. "But all his acquaintances, including the women who had followed him from Galilee, were standing afar off, watching these things" (verses 44–49).

Before sunset (i.e., before the sabbath) Joseph of Arimathea, a member of the council and according to Matt. 27:57 a rich man, having secured permission from Pilate, took down Christ's body, wrapped it in linen, and laid it in his own rock-hewn tomb (cf. Matt. 27:60), fulfilling the prophecy of Isa. 53:9.

The women who had come with Jesus from Galilee followed and saw where the body was laid. They went home and prepared spices and perfumes, so that, having rested throughout the sabbath and having afterward made further preparations (Mark 16:1), they might be ready to come and anoint the body of Jesus on Sunday morning. Such was their intention (verses 50–56).

Outline of Chapter 24

Theme: *The Work Thou Gavest Him to Do*

B. *The Resurrection and Ascension*

CHAPTER XXIV

24 1 But on the first day of the week at early dawn the women, taking with them the aromatic spices they had prepared, went to the tomb. 2 They found the stone rolled away from the tomb, 3 but on entering they did not find the body of the Lord Jesus. 4 While they were perplexed about this, two men, dressed in garments that flashed like lightning, stood beside them. 5 But as the women were frightened and bowed their faces to the ground, the men said to them, "Why are y o u seeking the living among the dead? 6 He is not here but is risen.[608] Remember how he told y o u while he was still in Galilee 7 that the Son of man must be delivered into the hands of sinful men, must be crucified, and on the third day rise again." 8 Then they remembered his words.

9 Now when they returned from the tomb, they reported all these things to the eleven and to all the rest. 10 Those who told these things to the apostles were, among other women companions, Mary Magdalene, Joanna, and Mary the mother of James. 11 But these words seemed to the apostles to be nonsense, and so they continued to disbelieve the women. 12 Peter, however, got up and ran to the tomb. Stooping down, he saw[609] the strips of linen (lying) by themselves, and he went home wondering about what had happened.

EASTER SUNDAY AND AFTERWARD
24:1-12 *Christ's Resurrection Revealed to Women Disciples*
Cf. Matt. 28:1-10; Mark 16:1-8; John 20:1-10

1. But on the first day of the week at early dawn the women, taking with them the aromatic spices they had prepared, went to the tomb.

Finally the day of all the best had arrived. But for the women (see verse 10; also 23:49) this day did not start out as one of special joy. There was deep sorrow and there was work to do. In this particular climate decomposition of the body was rapid. So these women went to the tomb in order to anoint the body of Jesus with the "aromatics," that is the spices and perfumes, they had prepared (see 23:56).

What they did certainly demonstrated their love and devotion, but also their lack of faith. They should have reminded themselves of the Savior's repeated promises of his resurrection "on the third day." But would we have done any better?

As to the time when these women came, much has been written about this. Mark says "when the sun was risen" (16:2); Matthew "at dawn" (28:1);

---

608. The readings vary. Some even omit 6a entirely; but see Matt. 28:6; Mark 16:16.
609. The original uses the historical present here: he sees.

Luke "at early dawn" (here in 24:1); and John "while it was still dark" (20:1). Possible solution: although it was still dark when the women started out, the sun had risen when they arrived at the tomb.

2, 3. They found the stone rolled away from the tomb, but on entering they did not find the body of the Lord Jesus.

Apparently the women had not heard about the sealing of the tomb and the posting of a guard (Matt. 27:62–66). The evangelist Mark reports that on the way to the tomb the women had been worried about the stone. We read, "And they were saying to each other, 'Who will roll away the stone for us from the entrance of the tomb?'"

However, they need not have worried. As Mark and Luke both report, they suddenly noticed that the stone had already been removed. John 20:1, 2 relates the reaction of Mary Magdalene when she saw that the stone had been taken away. And Matthew tells us *how* this had been accomplished: "Suddenly there was a violent earthquake, for an angel of the Lord came down from heaven, stepped forward, rolled away the stone and was sitting on it" (28:2).

Though Mary Magdalene hurried away to blurt out her story to Peter, the rest of the women entered the tomb, but did not find the body of Jesus. Very little information about the sepulchre, in addition to what has already been supplied (see above, on 23:53, 54), can be added. The New Testament nowhere furnishes a detailed description. It has been suggested that it had an antechamber which by means of a *low* doorway at the rear—note "and as he stooped down" (John 20:5)—gave access to an inner chamber in which the body had been placed.[610] But whether this particular tomb actually had two chambers has not been revealed. Not every first-century tomb followed this precise pattern. The same holds with respect to the exact appearance of the spot where the body of Jesus had been placed. It has been suggested that there was a declivity in the floor, and that at the foot-end and at the head-end the rock was left somewhat elevated, to provide seats. This would explain Mark 16:5 and John 20:12. But see footnote 610 on Smith's article.

The really important fact, however, far outweighing any detail regarding the construction and appearance of the tomb, was that upon entering, *the women did not find the body of the Lord Jesus!* The tomb was empty.

---

610. For interesting literature on this subject see the following:

L. H. Grollenberg, *op. cit.*, p. 132, with photographs and diagrams.

G. E. Wright, *op. cit.*, p. 381, picture of a first-century sepulchre near Jerusalem. According to the author it resembles the one in which Jesus was buried.

Lenski, *op. cit.*, pp. 730, 731, gives a description of the Garden Tomb. Though this may not have been the tomb or even the site where the body of Jesus had been interred, is it not possible that it resembled that tomb?

Very interesting and informative is R. H. Smith, "The Tomb of Jesus," *BA* 30 (1967), pp. 74–89. This author favors the two-chamber theory (cf. Luke 24:12; John 20:5, 11) and makes John 20:12 comprehensible (pp. 87, 89). It is an excellent article.

For the "discovery" of the tomb and what happened to the sacred places subsequently see T. Kollek and M. Pearlman, *op. cit.*, pp. 145–148; also R. H. Smith, *op. cit.*, pp. 76–80.

4. While they were perplexed about this, two men, dressed in garments that flashed like lightning, stood beside them.

Suddenly *two men*, dressed in robes that were absolutely dazzling, were standing beside the women. Matthew mentions *one angel* (28:3, 5); Mark, *a young man* dressed in a white robe (16:5); and John, *two angels* (20:12). Sometimes those addressing the women are represented as *standing*, then again as *sitting*. Sometimes they are reported as saying one thing; then, as saying something else.

Though we do not know exactly how all of these facts dovetail, this should not be a hindrance to faith. Rather the very opposite. The variation indicates that one evangelist was not simply copying what another had said or written. There were different sources, but all were reliable. It should also be borne in mind that if one angel was spokesman for both, a reporter could truthfully use either the singular or the plural in referring to the speaker(s). Again, as to *angel* or *young man*, this is not the only instance in Scripture in which angels appear in the form of men (and see Heb. 13:2). As to sitting or standing, is it impossible that at one moment these heavenly visitors were sitting, at another moment standing? And as to difference in the messages that were spoken, why should it be regarded as impossible that the messengers spoke more than once?

That the garments of these "men" flashed like lightning is not strange, for they belonged to and had descended from the realm of beauty, splendor, and purity. Cf. 9:29.

5-7. But as the women were frightened and bowed their faces to the ground, the men said to them, Why are y o u seeking the living one among the dead? He is not here but is risen. Remember how he told y o u while he was still in Galilee that the Son of man must be delivered into the hands of sinful men, must be crucified, and on the third day rise again.

It is not surprising that these women, who after all were sinful human beings, were frightened, and that out of fear and respect they inclined their faces to the ground. Besides, they really had no business to be here for the purpose of anointing a corpse. They meant well but were badly in error. The heavenly messengers therefore asked them why they were seeking the living among the dead. They followed this up by gently but firmly reminding them of the predictions which the Savior, while still in Galilee, had made to them, namely, that he would (a) be delivered into the hands of sinful men; (b) be crucified; and (c) on the third day rise again. For these predictions see Matt. 16:21; 17:22, 23; 20:17-19; Mark 8:31; 9:31; 10:33, 34; Luke 9:22, 44; 18:31-34.

8. Then they remembered his words.

What a wonderful thing is memory! We generally take it—or at times its absence—for granted. But no one as yet has been able to show exactly how it operates and what makes it possible. Generally the most celebrated specialists are also the first to admit its unsolved mysteries.

In the case of these women there were especially two things that aided the memory: (a) the fact that they had been emotionally involved in the happenings of the last several days. How they, friends and followers of Jesus as they were, active supporters, indeed, had suffered when their Master had been surrendered into the hands of sinful men! And as to his crucifixion, having been present at Calvary, never would they be able to forget what they had seen and what, consequently, they themselves had undergone. And (b) the fact that Jesus had told the disciples not only once but at least three times—in fact, if one adds all the figuratively phrased language, far more often—what was going to happen to him and how he of his own accord would lay down his life for his sheep. And since we know that these women could often be seen in the very company of the disciples, the conclusion that from the start they were also in on the Lord's important predictions follows naturally.

And now the messengers from heaven link these two things together— the dramatic *events* that had transpired and of which, to a large extent, the women too had been the witnesses, and the *words*, the predictions. Yes, the women knew that Jesus had not only referred to his approaching cross but also to his resurrection on the third day. They now remember. They now realize that the Master had not been speaking about the resurrection at the last day but about that which by now had actually occurred. If they needed any additional memory aid, *the empty tomb* and *the confirming message* proceeding from the lips of these heavenly visitors supplied that need, and fully.

9. Now when they returned from the tomb, they reported all these things to the eleven and to all the rest.

Note how Luke abbreviates. Such interesting Easter stories as are related in Matt. 28:8–10, 11–15; John 20:10–18, 24–29; ch. 21 cannot be found in his Gospel. But, on the other hand, who would want to miss the material contained in Luke 24:13–53, which, to a large extent, is peculiar to the evangelist?

The women reported to The Eleven, and even to as many of the other disciples of Jesus as they could reach, what had happened. They did what they had been told to do (Matt. 28:7; Mark 16:7). And they were rewarded by meeting the risen Lord himself (Matt. 28:9, 10).

10. Those who told these things to the apostles were, among other women companions, Mary Magdalene, Joanna, and Mary the mother of James.

The first two have been discussed in connection with 8:2, 3. And as to Mary the mother of James (the Less), she was probably the wife of Clopas, as a comparison between Matt. 27:56; Mark 15:40; and John 19:25 would seem to indicate. See N.T.C. on John, Vol. II, p. 431.

Of course, these women were not the only ones who had found the tomb to be empty, and who were addressed by the two men dressed in garments that flashed like lightning. Verse 10 reads "among other women companions" or even more literally, "and the other women with them."

These women, then, reported their experiences to the apostles.

How was their exciting news received? The answer is found in verse 11:

11. But these words seemed to the apostles to be nonsense, and so they continued to disbelieve the women.

What makes the Easter story so convincing is that the disciples of Jesus did not at all expect Jesus to arise from the grave. In fact they considered the reports of the women to be sheer nonsense. Yet, after a while, these very men—all of them but especially Peter and John—are proclaiming the startling news to all and sundry and are willing to face any opposition they may encounter. For more on 24:11 see on verse 24.

12. Peter, however, got up and ran to the tomb. Stooping down, he saw the strips of linen (lying) by themselves, and he went home wondering about what had happened.

Some translations—e.g., R.S.V. and N.E.B. in their texts—omit this passage. It should be retained. On this question see the note on this verse on page 1058.

For the full story see John 20:1-10, and for comments consult N.T.C. on John, Vol. II, pp. 447-451.

Alerted by Mary Magdalene, Peter ran to the tomb. When he entered it he noticed that everything was orderly. Though the body of the Lord was no longer present, it was clear that no disciple had been there to remove it, nor had any enemy pillaged it. In either case no bandages or strips of linen would have remained in the sepulchre. Could it be that the Lord had himself removed these wrappings, had in a very orderly fashion placed the linen strips here and the sweatband there, after having neatly folded it (John 20:7); that next he had provided for himself a garment such as is worn by the living, and had then departed from the tomb gloriously alive? Luke does not say that Peter immediately drew that conclusion. Neither can we find this in the story as reported by John. All we know is that Peter went home wondering about these things.[611]

Practical Lessons Derived from Luke 24:1-12

Verses 3 and 6

"They did not find the body of the Lord Jesus."

"He is not here but is risen."

The comfort of Christ's resurrection includes the following items:

a. The believer knows that his sins are forgiven, for if the Father had not been satisfied with the atonement rendered by his Son for our sins he would not have raised him from the dead.

b. He knows that he has a Savior who lives evermore to intercede for him, watches over him, governs him by his Spirit, and will one day return to him.

---

611. Notes on Greek words, phrases, and constructions in 24:1-12 begin on page 1056.

c. He knows that his body, too, will one day rise gloriously, or else will be changed "in a moment, in the twinkling of an eye."

Verse 7

"The Son of man must be . . . crucified, and on the third day rise again."
Some people make it a habit to come to church once a year, namely, on Easter. Are they forgetting that Christ's resurrection has no value apart from his crucifixion? Only he who, by God's grace, has learned to glory in Christ's death can truly glory in his resurrection. The cross and the crown must not be separated.

> Now cheerful to the house of prayer
> Your early footsteps bend;
> The Savior will himself be there,
> Your Advocate and Friend.
> Once by the law your hopes were slain,
> But now in Christ ye live again.
>
> Lines from a hymn,
> "How Calm and Beautiful"
> by T. Hastings

Notes on Greek Words, Phrases, and Constructions in 24:1-12

Verse 1

ὄρθρου (cf. John 8:2 and related forms in Luke 21:38; 24:22), gen. of ὄρθρος, dawn. Cf. *origin*.

βαθέως, gen. of βαθύς, deep. The entire expression ὄρθρου βαθέως means "at deep [= early] dawn." For βαθύς see also John 4:11; Acts 20:9; Rev. 2:24; and for the related verb Luke 6:48.

μνῆμα, synonym of μνημεῖον; see next verse.

Verse 2

ἀποκεκυλισμένον, acc. s. masc. perf. pass. participle of ἀποκυλίω, to roll away. Cf. Matt. 28:2; Mark 16:3. Cf. *cylinder*. See also N.T.C. on Mark, p. 679, including footnote 844.

μνημείου, gen. s. of μνημεῖον, tomb, considered as a memorial; related to μιμνήσκω, to remind. For the noun (tomb) see also verse 9; 11:44, 47; 23:55; 24:2, 12, 22, 24. It occurs several times in each of the other Gospels and once in Acts (13:29). See also N.T.C. on Mark, p. 671, footnote 836.

Verse 3

With this verse a lengthy list of so-called "Western non-interpolations" in Luke 24 begins. First is the phrase *of the Lord Jesus*, which is omitted by the Western text (Codex Bezae = D, and including also certain Old Latin Version manuscripts). Other similar Western omissions—which those who originally called them "Western non-interpolations" really considered "Neutral interpolations"—are found in verses 6, 9, 12, 36, 40, 52, 53. On this entire subject one should consult A. T. Robertson, *An Introduction to The Textual Criticism of The New Testament*, New York, 1925, pp.

225–237; and also B. M. Metzger, *The Text of the New Testament*, pp. 132 f., 162, 213 f. Robertson's final verdict (p. 236) was that when the Western text is compared with the Neutral, the Western is right perhaps one time in ten, the Neutral is right nine times in ten. Metzger informs us that the Western text "is usually considered to be the result of an undisciplined and 'wild' growth of manuscript tradition and translational activity" (p. 213). He states that today extreme positions regarding the Western text find little favor and that "most scholars recognize that all of the pre-Koine forms of text deserve a hearing" (p. 214).

As will become clear, as far as faith in the inspired Word of God is concerned, there is no real problem here, for most if not all of these Western omissions relate to words or phrases which, as to essence, are found in the undisputed passages of one or more of the other Gospels or of the book of Acts.

I have not been able to find any solid reasons to exclude from the text of 24:3 the phrase *of the Lord Jesus*.

Verse 4

For the stylistic form ἐν τῷ followed by an infinitive, a mode of expression that reminds one of Hebrew writing, see also verses 15 and 30.

ἀπορεῖσθαι, pres. pass. infinitive of ἀπορέω (ἀπό plus πόρος), literally: to be without a way, means, or resource, to be at a loss what to do, to be perplexed. Cf. ἀπορία in 21:25.

ἐπέστησαν, third per. pl. aor. (ingress.) indicat. of ἐφίστημι, suddenly to stand by or come upon. See the note on 2:9 on page 160, and the note on 10:40 on page 603. This verb occurs very frequently in Luke-Acts.

ἐσθῆτι, dat. s. of ἐσθής, robe, garment, clothing. Cf. 23:11.

ἀστραπτούσῃ, dat. s. fem. pres. participle of ἀστράπτω*, to flash like lightning. The entire expression means "in flashing [or dazzling] apparel." See also 17:24.

Verse 5

Note genitive absolute: "the women being frightened and bowing their faces to the ground." Here γενομένων is gen. pl. 2nd aor. middle participle of γίνομαι; and ἐμφόβων is gen. pl. of ἔμφοβος, terrified, frightened. Cf. verse 37; also Acts 10:4; 24:25; Rev. 11:13.

Verses 6 and 8

Whatever opinion may prevail with respect to "He is not here but is risen," another so-called Western non-interpolation, note the same expression in undoubtedly genuine Matt. 28:6; Mark 16:6.

ἠγέρθη, third per. s. aor. pass. of ἐγείρω; in the pass., to be risen.

μνήσθητε, sec. per. pl. aor. (ingress.) imperat. pass. of μιμνήσκω, to be reminded of, to remember. For this verb see also on 1:54, 72; 16:25; 23:42. Here, in ch. 24, the third per. pl. aor. indicat. pass. of this verb occurs in verse 8.

Verse 7

ἀναστῆναι, 2nd aor. act. infinitive of ἀνίστημι, trans. to raise; intrans., as here, to rise.

Verse 9

ὑποστϱέψασαι, nom. pl. fem. aor. participle of ὑποστϱέφω, to return, a verb occurring very often in Luke's writings, very seldom in the rest of the New Testament.

For μνημεῖον see above, on verse 2.

ἀπήγγειλαν, third per. pl. aor. indicat. of ἀπαγγέλλω, to announce, proclaim, report, tell.

Verse 11

ἐφάνησαν, third per. pl. 2nd aor. pass. indicat. of φαίνω, to cause to appear, bring to light; in pass. as here: to appear, seem.

λῆϱος*, nonsense. Cf. Dutch *larie* (same meaning).

ἠπίστουν, third per. pl. imperf. indicat. of ἀπιστέω, to disbelieve. See also verse 41. The same word occurs also in Mark's disputed section (16:11, 16), and in Acts 28:24; Rom. 3:3; II Tim. 2:13; and I Peter 2:7.

Verse 12

This verse is another Western omission or "non-interpolation." It is by some regarded to be a later addition, formulated after John 20:2 f. But in that case why is not *John's* name also mentioned here in Luke 24:12? Is it not more likely that the omission of John's name caused some copyists to reject the passage? But, again, whatever be the truth with respect to Luke 24:12, in any case what is here reported actually took place, as John 20:2 f. shows. Besides, the textual attestation in favor of the retention of Luke 24:12 is by no means weak, as the textual apparatus shows.

παϱακύψας, nom. s. masc. aor. participle of παϱακύπτω, to stoop beside or down. See also John 20:5, 11; James 1:25 (to look intently); I Peter 1:12 (to look into).

βλέπει, third per. s. *pres.* indicat. act., to see.

ὀθόνια, acc. pl. of ὀθόνιον, linen cloth, bandage. Cf. John 19:40; 20:5-7. μόνα, alone; i.e., by themselves.

πϱὸς ἑαυτόν (probably modifies ἀπῆλθεν), to himself = to his home.

---

13 Now it so happened that on that very day two of them were going to a village called Emmaus, about eleven kilometers[612] from Jerusalem. 14 They were conversing with each other concerning all these things that had taken place. 15 While they were conversing and discussing together, Jesus also himself drew near and began to walk along with them, 16 but their eyes were being kept from recognizing him. 17 He asked them, "What are these words that y o u are exchanging with each other as y o u are walking along?" They stood still, looking glum. 18 Finally one of them, named Cleopas, asked him, "Are you the only one so strange in Jerusalem that you did not get to know the things that have occurred there these days?" 19 "What things?" he asked. They told him, "The things concerning Jesus of Nazareth, who was a prophet mighty in word and deed, 20 and how our chief priests and rulers delivered him up to be sentenced to death, and crucified him. 21 But we were hoping that he was the one who was going to redeem Israel. Moreover, besides all this, it is now the third day since these things took place. 22 Some of our women, though, startled us.[613] They went to the tomb early this morning, 23 and not finding his body, they came and were saying that they

---

612. Or: about seven miles; literally: sixty stadia.
613. Literally: knocked us out of our senses.

had even seen a vision of angels, who affirmed that he was alive. 24 Then some of those who were with us went to the tomb, and found it exactly as the women had said, but him they did not see."

25 Jesus said to them, "O foolish men, and slow of heart to believe everything that the prophets have spoken! 26 Was it not necessary for the Christ to suffer these things and to enter into his glory?" 27 And beginning with Moses and with all the prophets he interpreted to them in all the Scriptures the things concerning himself.

28 Then they drew near to the village to which they were going, and he acted as though he would go farther. 29 But they strongly urged him, saying, "Stay with us, for it is (getting) toward evening, and the day is almost over." So he went in to stay with them.

30 Now as he was reclining at table with them, he took the bread,[614] blessed it, broke it, and began to give it to them. 31 Then their eyes were instantly opened, and they recognized him, but he vanished from their sight.[615] 32 And they said to each other, "Were not our hearts burning within us while he was talking to us on the way, while he was opening the Scripture to us?"

33 At once they got up and went back to Jerusalem, and they found the eleven and those with them gathered together, 34 saying, "The Lord has risen indeed and has appeared to Simon." 35 Then the two themselves began to relate what had happened on the way, and how Jesus had been made known to them in the breaking of the bread.

24:13-35 *The Appearance of the Risen Christ to Cleopas and His Companion*

Did the Resurrected Savior appear in Jerusalem, in Galilee, or in both places?

The problem arises from the circumstance that while Matt. (see 28:7, 10, 16-20), Mark (see 16:7), and John 21 (see verses 1-23) picture Christ's appearances as having occurred in Galilee, on the other hand Luke (24:13-43 or even 24:13-53), John 20 (see verses 11-29), and Acts (see 1:4-9) mention only Jerusalem and its vicinity as the place where the appearances occurred.

The conclusion has been drawn that these "conflicting" (?) accounts are based on two irreconcilable traditions. If the one is chosen, the other must be rejected. The Galilee theory has been endorsed by C. H. Weisse, T. Keim, C. von Weizsäcker, W. Brandt, P. Rohrach, A. von Harnack, P. W. Schmiedel, A. Meyer, K. Lake, etc.; the Jerusalem theory by A. Hilgenfeld, F. Loofs, F. Spitta, Joh. Weiss, A. Schweitzer, F. C. Burkitt, etc.

However, as has been pointed out by several authors, the theory of conflict is open to serious objections, including the following:

a. Matt. 28:9 shows that this Gospel recognizes at least one appearance that occurred in the Jerusalem region.

b. The early church allowed both John 20 and 21 to stand, without seeing any conflict.

c. Luke, as so often, abbreviates. Besides, limitation of space may have prevented him from writing more than he did. There was, after all, a limit to the length of a papyrus roll. So he *may have* restricted himself to appear-

---

614. Or: the bread-cake.
615. Literally: he became invisible.

ances in the Jerusalem region. But is it certain that *all* of 24:13–53 refers to Jerusalem? Could not some of 24:44–48 have been spoken in Galilee?

d. Neither Acts 1:3 nor I Cor. 15:1–8 forces us to believe that the appearances of the Risen Lord were confined to any one particular city or region. They rather confirm the view that he appeared to a very wide circle and perhaps even in more than one place.

Though several articles have been written on this controversy, I shall mention just one treatise, the best of them all, as far as I can judge. It is the doctoral dissertation on this very question by H. Holtrop, *De Verschijningen Onzes Heeren Te Jeruzalem En in Galilea*, Amsterdam, 1947. See especially pp. 22, 65, 71, 137, 138, 143, 194, 231, and 234. Holtrop, too, sees no real conflict.

A. *Easter Tragedy*

13, 14. Now it so happened that on that very day two of them were going to a village called Emmaus, about eleven kilometers [about seven miles] from Jerusalem. They were conversing with each other concerning all these things that had taken place.

Up to this point Luke has reported the empty tomb, the message of the two men in dazzling robes ("He is risen"), and Peter's visit to the tomb. He has not yet reported any *appearance* of the Risen Christ. Such an account follows now. It is a stirring and vivid report of the appearance of the Risen Savior to two men who belonged to the wider circle of disciples.

On the day of the resurrection these two were walking from Jerusalem (see verse 33) to their home in Emmaus. Although it is not specifically stated that they lived there, this can be considered a reasonable inference from verses 28, 29.

Except for the statement in the text that Emmaus was located sixty stadia from Jerusalem, the location of this place is unknown. The identification of Emmaus with Anwas, more than thirty kilometers (about nineteen miles) WNW of Jerusalem is highly improbable, since it is hard to imagine that the two men covered twice that distance on foot that afternoon-evening.

As they were walking, they were talking to each other about all the things that had taken place; that is, about Jesus' crucifixion and the report of some women that had been to the tomb, had found it empty, and had received a message from "angels, who affirmed that he was alive" (verse 23).

15, 16. While they were conversing and discussing together, Jesus also himself drew near and began to walk along with them, but their eyes were being kept from recognizing him.

Suddenly footsteps were heard behind them, those of Jesus. He was catching up with them and presently was walking alongside of them. In a manner not here explained—Jesus appearing in another form? (Mark 16:12); divine restraining action?—the two men were being kept from recognizing the "stranger." Cf. Matt. 28:17; John 20:14; 21:4.

17. He asked them, What are these words that y o u are exchanging with each other as y o u are walking along? —They stood still, looking glum.

The unrecognized "intruder" now asked them a question. During his public ministry Jesus had often used this method of approach (6:3, 9; 8:30; 9:18; 18:40, 41; 20:3, 4, 41–44; 22:35, etc.). He did not ask because he lacked knowledge. He asked to arouse interest, so that he would have an opportunity to explain what those questioned needed to know.

When the two men heard this question, they stood still, as if the question, if not even highly improper, certainly was very unexpected. They looked sad, for the happenings of the last few days had filled their hearts and minds with sorrow and a feeling of disappointment.

18. Finally, one of them, named Cleopas, asked him, Are you the only one so strange in Jerusalem that you did not get to know the things that have occurred there these days?

Probably after an embarrassing pause one of the two men started to answer. His name was Cleopas, but there is not any good reason to identify him with the Clopas of John 19:25. His answer was in the form of a counter-question. He wanted to know whether the intruder was the only stranger in, or visitor to, Jerusalem who had managed to remain completely uninformed about matters that were on everybody's lips.

19, 20. What things? he asked.

With marvelous psychological tact Jesus gives Cleopas a full opportunity to unburden himself.

Continued: **They told him, The things concerning Jesus of Nazareth, who was a prophet mighty in word and deed, and how our chief priests and rulers delivered him up to be sentenced to death, and crucified him.**

Here note the following:

a. Jesus *of Nazareth.*

Cleopas and his companion were convinced that the stranger who had joined them was very uninformed. So, the mere answer "Jesus" would not do. After all, there must have been several people by that name, living at that very time, earlier or later. There was, for example, "Jesus Barabbas" (according to a Matt. 27:16 reading), Jesus the son of Sirach, etc. In certain ethnic communities even today not a few boys are called Jesus. So, they deemed it necessary to add "of Nazareth."

b. a prophet mighty in word and deed.

They were certainly right in so describing Jesus. See Deut. 18:15, 18; Luke 7:16; John 4:19, 44; 9:17; Acts 3:22; 7:37.

c. how our chief priests and rulers delivered him up.

Not how Pilate and the Romans did this. The two men placed the main blame exactly where it belonged, namely, on the chief priests and rulers of *the Jews.* This is not anti-Semitism. It is simply a true reflection of historical fact. To be sure, both the Jewish leaders and the Romans were guilty, but the chief responsibility and therefore also the heavier guilt rested on the Jews (see John 19:11).

The speech continued as follows: **21. But we were hoping that he was the one who was going to redeem Israel.**

There are those who interpret this to mean: "We were hoping that he was the one who would bring about the redemption of Israel by the payment of a ransom of blood; that is, by his death." It may well be doubted, however, that these men—note how Jesus describes them in verse 25—were so far advanced in their theology. Besides, words have histories. The basic meaning "deliverance through the payment of a ransom" does not necessarily remain the only meaning. Probably the most favorable construction we can place on the words of Cleopas and his companion is this: "We were hoping that he was the one who, in some way, would deliver Israel from its woes, both spiritual and political." Cf. 1:74.

They were hoping, but the flame of hope had almost been extinguished, as is clear from the continuation: **Moreover, besides all this, it is now the third day since these things took place.** As if to say, "Even after Jesus was crucified we entertained some hope that God might suddenly intervene and send deliverance. But it did not happen, not on the first day, nor on the second, and now it is already the third day, and still no change for the better . . . and yet, and yet"—here a tiny flicker of hope begins to drive away the night of total darkness and despair:

22–24. Some of our women, though, startled us. They went to the tomb early this morning, and, not finding his body, they came and were saying that they had even seen a vision of angels, who affirmed that he was alive.

This shows that the report of the women to The Eleven had already been spreading. There must have been a rather close relationship between the inner and the wider circle of disciples. And no wonder, when the news was so startling. It was too exciting not to be told.

Continued: **Then some of those who were with us went to the tomb, and found it exactly as the women had said, but him they did not see.**

The two men were probably thinking of Peter and John, for they were the ones who had gone to the tomb and had found everything exactly as the women had reported, but had not seen the Risen Savior. See above, on verse 12 and see also John 20:1–10. Cf. N.T.C. on John, Vol. II, pp. 468–470. So now Cleopas and his companion are bewildered. They don't know what to make of it.

When we now briefly review the situation that existed very early on Easter morning and continued well into the day, we notice that despair had taken over; yes, despair and bewilderment.

1. *The Women.*

See these women trudging sorrowfully through the streets of Jerusalem very early Sunday morning. While The Eleven are in deep mourning and despair, Thomas resembling a man who is caught in the midst of an earth-quake, the very ground under his feet caving in; Peter overwhelmed with remorse; John tenderly caring for the woman with the tempest-tossed soul (Mary); while night was settled upon these eleven men, what are these women going to do? Is it their design to welcome the Risen Lord? Not in the least. The cross has blasted their hopes. The grave has buried them forever. They come ... to anoint a dead body, the corpse of Jesus of Nazareth, their Friend and Helper.

Never was there a more dejected, disappointed, crushed group of women! Their experience is, perhaps, best described in that well-known poem:

> Now he is dead, far hence he lies
> In that lorn Syrian town;
> And on his grave with shining eyes
> The Syrian stars look down.

2. *Mary, the Mother of the Lord.*

She too was in the grip of cold winter. A sword was piercing through her soul (Luke 2:35) as she saw her own son, her first-born, dying the death of a condemned criminal. A feeling of overwhelming sadness takes possession of a person whenever he reads the lines of that ancient hymn describing Mary's tears, *Stabat Mater.* See pp. 170, 171. For her, too, the Cross was the Farewell to Hope, and this in more ways than one.

3. *The Eleven.*

Their Master ... gone. Their friend—and what a Friend!—departed. Their plans wrecked. Their hopes shattered. They are perplexed, baffled. They despair. Like men whose none too sturdy vessel is frozen solid in the Arctic ice pack, with ice, ice, ice, cold, bleak, barren, stretching in every direction for hundreds of miles. Ice, screeching, roaring, grinding. Will they ever see their dear ones again? Abandon hope, all ye who enter here! Or—to change the figure—they resemble individuals who have been con-demned to die and are pining away in some gloomy, dreadful prison hole, knowing that the "best" they can expect is the arrival of the executioner. See John 20:19, their "doors were shut for fear of the Jews." Jesus of Nazareth ... Crucified ... that was the Farewell to Hope!

Am I exaggerating? Was there not so much as a ray of hope shining through the clouds of gloom and despair? A half-conscious expectation that somehow light would arise out of darkness, that the night would make room for the dawn, that ... perhaps ... the Master might even ... rise again? Read the account for yourself:

"And the ... women ... told these things to the apostles. But these words seemed to the apostles to be nonsense, and so they continued to disbelieve the women."

"The other disciples therefore said to Thomas, 'We have seen the Lord.'

1063

But he said unto them, 'Except I shall see in his hands the print of the nails, and put my finger into the print of the nails and put my hand into his side, I will not believe.'"

Not one of The Eleven expected Jesus to arise from the grave. That thought was farthest removed from their minds. Jesus was *dead.* He was *gone!* Those happy days of close fellowship and intimate association with the Great Prophet of Nazareth would never return.

4. *Cleopas and His Companion.*

These two friends of Jesus are returning to Emmaus. It is springtime. Yet they hear not the singing of birds. They see not the awakening of Nature. With lagging feet, under leaden skies, they continue on their way home . . . home from a funeral! A dear one has been buried. Jesus of Nazareth. "Yes, stranger, we hoped that he was the One who would redeem Israel." "We hoped [past tense] but now all hope is gone."

B. *Easter Triumph*

25, 26. Jesus said to them, O foolish men, and slow of heart to believe everything that the prophets have spoken! Was it not necessary for the Christ to suffer these things and to enter into his glory?

The emphasis is on two words: *everything* and *necessary.*

The trouble with the Jewish religious leaders of Jesus' day was that, on the whole, in reading the Old Testament they saw only the glory and victory of the Messiah, not the fact that the path to these blessings was one of suffering.[616] At times they would even go so far as to apply to *the Messiah* the references (in Isa. 52:13—53:12) to the Servant's *glory,* but to apply to *Israel* the references to the Servant's *suffering.*[617]

Now there was no excuse for this. It must be borne in mind that the people of Jesus' day not only had the Old Testament. They also had in their midst the Lord Jesus Christ, who was constantly interpreting it for them, by what he *was,* what he *did,* and what he *taught.*

That for the Messiah it is the way of suffering that leads to glory is basically already pointed out in Gen. 3:15 (in the process of bruising Satan's head, Messiah's own heel will be bruised). Did not Jesus interpret this prophecy, for example, in John 12:31, 32, where he teaches that when he himself is lifted up from the earth (see also John 3:14; 8:28), the prince of this world is cast out and all men are drawn to himself? This "being lifted up" certainly includes the cross.

Another Old Testament passage clearly teaching the same lesson—that for the Messiah it is the path of suffering that leads to glory—is Ps. 118; see especially verse 22, with reference to *the rejected stone,* which becomes the cornerstone. And did not Jesus also interpret this figure as having reference to himself? See Matt. 21:42; Mark 12:10; Luke 20:17.

---

616. See S.BK., Vol. II, pp. 273–299; also S.BK., Vol. I, pp. 481 ff.

617. See R. H. Gundry, *op. cit.,* p. 230; N. Geldenhuys, *op. cit.,* pp. 636, 637.

Then there is Isa. 53 (or 52:13—53:12). Jesus himself stated in so many words that this prophecy referred to him (Luke 22:37).[618]

In fact, even some of the words spoken from the cross were quotations (sometimes modified) and interpretations of phrases taken from the Old Testament.

Moreover, we may be sure that the teaching of Jesus recorded in the Gospels is only a fraction of all he actually taught, just as the recorded miracles are only a fraction of those performed (John 20:30; 21:25).

All this should suffice to prove that the two men who were on their way to Emmaus deserved to be called "foolish" or "dull" for failing to believe that for Christ the way to glory was and had to be through suffering.

27. And beginning with Moses and with all the prophets he interpreted to them in all the Scriptures the things concerning himself.

Jesus may have interpreted such passages as Gen. 3:15; 9:26; 12:3; 22:18; 49:10; Exod. 12:13; Num. 24:17; Deut. 18:15, 18; II Sam. 7:12, 13; Ps. 2:2; 22:1, 18; 45:11; 68:18; 69:20, 21; 72:8, 9; 110:1; 118:22; 132:11; Isa. 2:4; 7:14; 8:8, 10; 9:1, 2, 6, 7; 11:10; 25:8; 28:16; 35:5, 6; 42:1; 49:6; 52:14; ch. 53; 55:4; 59:16; Jer. 23:5; Ezek. 17:22; Dan. 2:24, 35, 44; 7:13, 14; 9:25; Mic. 5:2; Hag. 2:6-9; Zech. 3:8; 6:12 f.; 9:9; 11:12; 12:10; 13:7; Mal. 3:1.

But the Old Testament picture of the Messiah is not confined to a number of specific passages. As I have shown earlier (see above on 1:70), there are, as it were, four lines, which, running through the Old Testament from beginning to end, converge at Bethlehem and Calvary: the historical, typological, psychological, and prophetical. It is reasonable to believe that our Lord, in interpreting in all the Scriptures the things concerning himself, showed how the entire Old Testament, in various ways, pointed to himself. See also Acts 10:43.

28, 29. Then they drew near to the village to which they were going, and he acted as though he would go farther. But they strongly urged him, saying, Stay with us, for it is (getting) toward evening, and the day is almost over. —So he went in to stay with them.

When the three neared Emmaus Jesus acted as though he would go farther. And he would have done so, had they not prevailed upon him to stay with them. The plan of God for our lives does not cancel decision-making on our part.

Traveling late in the evening involved danger from various sources: robbers, obstacles upon the path, perhaps even wild animals. Moreover, the darkness was no help. But undoubtedly the main reason why the two men urged Jesus to stay with them was that they had become enamored of him. At the moment when the Savior had first joined them, they were probably not at all pleased to have this stranger intrude on them. But by now, for a

618. On Isa. 53 as fulfilled in Christ see also N.T.C. on Philippians, pp. 82, 83; A. M. Hodgkin, *Christ in All the Scriptures*, London, 1945, pp. 151-153.

very understandable reason, they could not think of letting him go. So, he allowed himself to be persuaded. And having entered their home, the two even honored their unknown but very remarkable guest by asking him to perform the duties of a host.

30, 31. Now as he was reclining at table with them, he took the bread, blessed it, broke it, and began to give it to them. Then their eyes were instantly opened, and they recognized him, but he vanished from their sight.

How was it that in the breaking of the bread they suddenly recognized him? Did they see the marks of the nails in his hands? Was it the manner in which he broke the bread and gave it to them that opened their eyes? Or was it the way he spoke to his Father that refreshed their memories? Whatever may be the answer, the body of his resurrection now possessed qualities enabling him to appear at will and also, as here, to vanish at will. So, almost before they fully realized what had happened, he was gone.

32. And they said to each other, Were not our hearts burning within us while he was talking to us on the way, while he was opening the Scriptures to us?

Their exclamation is understandable. They reflect on the manner in which their hearts had been warmed, their spirits illumined, their hope revived when the man who was now no longer a stranger had explained to them that which before they had never understood. Also, now they know that the women had been right after all. Far from talking nonsense, they had spoken the truth. And how kind, how absolutely wonderful was it that the Christ had singled them out for receiving the privilege of having the Scriptures opened to them, so that they now understood as they had never understood before. So filled are these two men with joy that they must needs tell others. Have they already walked seven miles? Then seven more miles. Was it dark and dangerous? All of that means nothing now. This news is so electrifying and reassuring that the other disciples must know about it. Not tomorrow but *tonight*.

33–35. At once they got up and went back to Jerusalem, and they found the eleven and those with them gathered together, saying, The Lord has risen indeed and has appeared to Simon. —Then the two themselves began to relate what had happened on the way, and how Jesus had been made known to them in the breaking of the bread.

Note the following:

a. The resolution to start out at once on their seven-mile return trip to Jerusalem, because the news they wished to share with others was so astounding, reminds us of the four lepers of Samaria who said, "We are not doing right. This day is a day of good news... now therefore let us go and tell..." (II Kings 7:9).

b. "And they found *the eleven*." The expression *the eleven* is a technical term for the group. It does not mean that all eleven were actually present. We know that one, namely Thomas, was not (John 20:24).

c. What had brought the inner circle of disciples together was probably the report of the women and Christ's appearance to Peter.

d. It is remarkable that the two men of Emmaus knew exactly where they could find The Eleven. That confirms our opinion, expressed earlier, that there was a very close relation between the inner and the wider circle of disciples.

e. Note the drama of the situation. We picture it as follows: The two men, having completed their seven-mile trip—was it about 9 o'clock by now?—arrive at the door of the room in which The Eleven (and probably others with them) are gathered. When the door opens, they are ready to shout the news. But before they even get a chance they hear the blessed tiding, "The Lord has risen indeed and has appeared to Simon." Cf. I Cor. 15:5.

f. Finally, they too get a chance to tell their story. What an asking and answering of questions! What ecstasy! What a foretaste of "joy unspeakable and full of glory"!

A new beginning! Light in the darkness! Life conquering death! The Lord is risen indeed! Here all changes. The Cross, the very instrument of despair, becomes an object of glory. The resurrection of Jesus Christ from the dead is the source of a living hope. Listen to the message of exuberant joy, praise, and thanksgiving. Hear it from the lips of one who experienced the deepest darkness of despair and remorse. Says Peter:

"Blessed be the God and Father of our Lord Jesus Christ, who according to his great mercy gave us new birth into a living hope through the resurrection of Jesus Christ from the dead" (I Peter 1:3).

"Gave us new birth into a living hope." Now Peter can smile again. We can all be happy once more. A living hope, living, real, a desire plus expectation plus conviction that our lives here are not in vain. A hope not based upon legend or fancy but upon the immovable Rock of Christ's resurrection from the grave. The apostles proclaim the resurrection because they cannot do anything else. The proof was too clear!

He *lives*. Hence, life is worth living. Hence, all things work together for good to them that love God. Hence, we too shall live. Hence, the curse is going to be removed from the universe and we expect a new heaven and a new earth. All the darkness is dispelled. Hope lives again.

A stream of light descends from veiled skies: an angel mighty and terrible arrives. His appearance is as lightning and his garments white as snow. And the angel says:

"Don't y o u be afraid, for I know that y o u are looking for Jesus, who was crucified. He is not here, for he has been raised just as he said" (Matt. 28:5, 6). *He is risen . . . and hope is revived.*

The bodily resurrection of Jesus is a historical fact. How absurd are the theories of those who deny it:

a. "The disciples stole the body." See Matt. 28:11-15. That this attempt to solve the problem of the empty tomb is indeed absurd has been shown in N.T.C. on Matthew, pp. 995–996.

b. "An enemy removed it." But in that case it would have been easy to disprove the claim of the Christians. The opponents of Christ and of the Christian religion could then have produced the body, to show that Jesus had not risen from the grave.

c. "The first so-called 'witnesses' were afflicted with mass hallucinations." The question is whether such mass hallucinations are even possible. Besides, it should be emphasized that none of the disciples expected Jesus to rise from the grave. Therefore, they were not psychologically prepared for hallucinations of this nature. They did not expect a resurrection. When they heard that it had occurred, they refused to believe it ... until the evidence became so strong that they were willing to sacrifice their very lives in the defense of this great truth. Many actually did.

There is only one "solution" which satisfies, being in accord with all the other known facts and circumstances, and which also helps to explain the strength and rapid growth of the church. That solution is: the Gospels are telling the truth. Hallelujah, Christ arose![619]

Practical Lessons Derived from Luke 24:13-35

Verses 17 and 25

"They stood still, looking glum."
"O foolish men, and slow of heart to believe everything that the prophets have spoken."
These men missed the *joy* of salvation because they failed to pay enough attention to, and to believe, the word of prophecy in its entirety. Those who neglect the study of God's Word do not realize how much they miss. No wonder they look glum. See Ps. 119:77, 103, 119.

Verses 27 and 32

"He interpreted to them in all the Scriptures the things concerning himself."
"Were not our hearts burning within us while he was talking to us on the way, while he was opening the Scriptures to us?"
Only when we see how all the Scriptures are centered in Christ, as the revelation of the Triune God, so that in the Old Testament everything points forward to him, and in the New everything proceeds from him, will we be able to understand the Bible.

Verse 33

"They found the eleven and those with them gathered together."
The fellowship of God's children should be encouraged.

---

619. Notes on Greek words, phrases, and constructions in 24:13-35 begin on page 1069.

Verse 34

"The Lord has risen indeed!"

Spiritual appropriation of the comfort imparted by the doctrine of the resurrection leads to exclamations, doxologies, and songs of praise. It is by means of such expressions that the church grows inwardly and outwardly.

Notes on Greek Words, Phrases, and Constructions in 24:13-35

Verses 14, 15

ὡμίλουν, third per. pl. imperf. (vivid, progress.) indicat. of ὁμιλέω**, to be associated with, converse with; only here in verses 14, 15; and in Acts 20:11; 24:26. Cf. *homiletics.*

συμβεβηκότων, gen. pl. neut. perf. participle of συμβαίνω, to step together; hence, to occur, happen.

For συζητεῖν see the note on 22:23 on page 969.

συνεπορεύετο, third per. s. imperf. (here inchoat.) of συμπορεύομαι, to come, go, or walk along with. See also 7:11; 14:25; Mark 10:1.

Verse 16

ἐκρατοῦντο, third per. pl. imperf. (iterat. or progress.) indic. pass. of κρατέω, to be strong, lay hold on, hold, hold back, restrain; pass., as here, to be held back, be restrained, be kept (from).

μή may be considered a redundant negative, after a verb of hindering.

ἐπιγνῶναι, 2nd aor. act. infinitive of ἐπιγινώσκω, here in the sense of *to recognize;* so also in verse 31, where the third per. pl. aor. (effect.) indicat. act. is used.

Verse 17

ἀντιβάλλετε, sec. per. pl. pres. indicat. of ἀντιβάλλω*, to throw in turn, throw back and forth, to exchange (words). There is no good reason to interpret ἀντί here as meaning *against.* The verb belongs to that group of ἀντί-compounds in which the prefix indicates *substitution* in its most comprehensive sense; here with submeaning of *reciprocity:* they are throwing words back and forth like a ball.

ἐστάθησαν, third per. pl. aor. indicat. pass. of ἵστημι, to cause to stand, place; in pass., as here, to stand.

σκυθρωποί, nom. pl. masc. adj. of σκυθρωπός*, gloomy, glum. See also Matt. 6:16. The word is derived from σκυθρός plus ὤψ; hence: of a gloomy countenance, or, as we would say: looking glum.

Verse 18

μόνος, alone, pred. adject. here; as if "Are you dwelling alone...?"

παροικεῖς, sec. per. s. pres. indicat. of παροικέω (= παρά plus οἶκος), to occupy a house by the side of, to reside as a stranger or alien, to sojourn. In the New Testament this verb is found only here and in Heb. 11:9. Abraham sojourned. He lived as an alien, a stranger in a strange land. For a cognate noun see Acts 7:6; Eph. 2:19; I Peter 2:11; and for still another see Acts 13:17; I Peter 1:17.

ἔγνως, sec. per. s. 2nd aor. indicat. act. of γινώσκω, to know. The aor. may be accounted for as follows: "Have you not heard, ascertained, found out, discovered?" Hence, "Did you not get to know?"

Verse 20

κρίμα, sentence; see the note on 23:40 on page 1041.

Verse 21

Note emphatic ἡμεῖς: we ourselves, we on our part.

ἠλπίζομεν, first per. pl. imperf. (progress.) indicat. of ἐλπίζω, to hope.

λυτροῦσθαι, pres. middle infinitive of λυτρόω, to redeem (by or for oneself).

ἀλλά . . . πᾶσιν, note heavy use of particles: "moreover, besides all this." For a somewhat similar heaping up of particles see N.T.C. on Phil. 3:8 (p. 162, footnote 140 in that volume).

Note idiomatic use of impersonal ἄγει; perhaps in the sense of *to spend* or *to keep*. The exact meaning here is difficult to determine; perhaps: "One is keeping this, the third day." The resultant meaning must be something on the order of "This is now the third day."

Verse 22

ἐξέστησαν, third per. pl. aor. act. of ἐξίστημι, to knock out (of their senses), to astonish, amaze, startle.

γενόμεναι ὀρθριναί, lit. "having been early ones (at the tomb)." We would say, "They went to the tomb early this morning." Cf. 24:1.

Verse 23

εὑροῦσαι, nom. pl. fem. 2nd aor. act. participle of εὑρίσκω, to find. λέγουσαι, same, except pres. instead of 2nd aor., to say.

ἑωρακέναι, perf. infinitive of ὁράω, to see.

ζῆν, pres. infinitive of ζάω, to live. Hence, literally: "The women, not having found his body, came saying that they had also seen a vision of angels, who are saying that he is alive."

Verse 25

ἀνόητοι, not knowing, unintelligent, foolish. Cf. Gal. 3:1, "O foolish Galatians."

βραδεῖς, nom. pl. masc. of βραδύς, slow, stupid.

Verse 26

ἔδει, third per. s. imperf. of δεῖ, it is necessary (that), one must, has to. So here, preceded by οὐχί, "Was it not necessary . . . ?"

Note the two 2nd aor. infinitives: παθεῖν (from πάσχω, to suffer) and εἰσελθεῖν (from εἰσέρχομαι, to enter); the first progressive, the second ingressive.

Verse 27

διερμήνευσεν, third per. aor. (effect.) act. indicat. of διερμηνεύω, to interpret, explain. Cf. *hermeneutics, Hermes* (Acts 14:12).

Verse 28

ἤγγισαν, third per. pl. aor. indicat. of ἐγγίζω, intrans., to approach.

προσεποιήσατο, third per. s. aor. indicat. middle of προσποιέω*, to make or act as though.

Verse 29

παρεβιάσαντο, third per. pl. aor. indicat. of παραβιάζομαι**; in the New Testament only here and in Acts 16:15 (cf. βία, force), to strongly urge, constrain, prevail upon.

μεῖνον, sec. per. s. aor. imperat. of μένω, to stay, remain, abide. This is a word of frequent occurrence in the New Testament, especially in the writings of Luke and John.

ἑσπέραν, acc. s. of ἑσπέρα**, evening. Cf. *vesper*. It is also found in Acts 4:3; 28:23.

κέκλικεν, third per. s. perf. indicat. act. of κλίνω, trans., to bend, bow, lay down; intrans., to be far spent, be almost over (of the day), the sun having nearly gone down. Cf. *incline, decline*.

Verse 30

For the idiom ἐν τῷ followed by infinitive see above, on verse 4.

For synonyms of the verb κατακλίνω* see the note on 11:37 on page 645; also see the note on 9:12 on page 484.

ἐπεδίδου, third per. s. imperf. (inchoative) indicat. act. of ἐπιδίδωμι, to give (something to someone). In Acts 27:15 to give up or surrender to (the wind), to allow oneself to be driven (by the wind).

Verses 31, 32

Note the two forms of the verb διανοίγω: in verse 31 the third per. pl. aor. indicat. pass.; in verse 32 the third per. s. imperf. indicat. act. "Their eyes were opened ... he was opening the Scriptures." Perhaps basically the verb meant: to open *up through and through* (note prefixes διά and ἀνά). But in the course of time such prefixes began to lose some of their force. In the New Testament, with one exception (Mark 7:34), this verb is confined to Luke-Acts.

καιομένη ἦν, third per. s. periphrastic imperf. indicat. middle of καίω; here and in 12:35, to burn; in Matt. 5:15, to kindle. In the remaining New Testament passages the idea of burning or consuming something with fire predominates. Cf. *caustic, holocaust*.

ἐλάλει, third per. s. imperf. indicat. act. of λαλέω, a sound-imitation (onomatopoeia) resembling the inarticulate attempt of babies to communicate and the chirping of birds; hence, basically *to chatter;* then, in general, *to talk, speak.* Cf. *lullaby*. The word occurs in every New Testament book except Galatians, II Thessalonians, II Timothy, and Philemon.

Verse 33

ἠθροισμένους, acc. pl. masc. perf. (here predicate) pass. participle of ἀθροίζω*, to collect, gather; realted to θρόος, noise. Cf. *drone, threnody*.

Verse 34

ὄντως, really, indeed, surely. See the note on 23:47 on page 1041.

ὤφθη, third per. s. aor. pass. indicat. of the very common verb ὁράω, to see; in pass. to be seen, to appear, seem. The same form occurs here in 24:34 as in 1:11 and in 22:43. Here, in 24:34, it is the Risen Lord who appears; in the other two passages it is an angel.

Verse 35

ἐξηγοῦντο, third per. pl. imperf. (probably inchoat.) indicat. middle of ἐξηγέομαι. This verb is composed of ἐκ plus ἡγέομαι; therefore basically: to lead out or lead off (the conversation or the narrative), to relate, recount, narrate, tell. Cf. *exegesis*.

κλάσει, dat. of κλάσις, breaking; cf. κλάω, to break.

---

36 Then, while they were saying these things, he himself stood among them and said to them, "Peace (be) with y o u."[620]

37 Startled and frightened, they thought they were seeing a ghost.

38 But he said to them, "Why are y o u troubled, and why are doubts arising in y o u r hearts?   39 See my hands and my feet, that it is I myself. Handle me and see, for a ghost does not have flesh and bones as y o u see me having."

40 After he had said this he showed them his hands and his feet.[621]   41 And while they continued in a state of disbelief for joy, and were filled with amazement, he said to them, "Do y o u have anything here to eat?"   42 So they gave him a piece of broiled fish,   43 and he took it and ate it in their presence.

44 And he said to them:

"These (are) my words that I spoke to y o u while I was still with y o u, that all that is written about me in the law of Moses and the prophets and the psalms must be fulfilled."   45 Then he opened their minds to (enable them to) understand the Scriptures.   46 He told them, "Thus it is written that the Christ should suffer and rise again from the dead on the third day,   47 and that conversion and forgiveness of sins should be preached in his name to all the nations, beginning from Jerusalem.   48 Y o u are witnesses of these things.   49 Moreover, note well, I am sending upon y o u what my Father promised; but remain in the city until y o u are clothed with power from on high."

24:36–49 *The Appearance of the Risen Christ to the Apostles, etc.* Cf. Mark 16:14 (part of The Ending); John 20:19–23[622]

Does what is found in Luke 24:36–49 pertain to one appearance, namely, on Easter evening, or must this section be divided (perhaps at verse 44), with the resulting conclusion that what is found in verses 36–43 pertains to that Sunday evening, but what is found in verses 44–49 pertains to a later appearance, or later appearances?

Opinions are rather sharply divided, Geldenhuys being among those who favor the division of the section at verse 44. According to this view,

---

620. Some documents omit "Peace (be) with y o u."

621. Some ancient authorities omit verse 40.

622. Matt. 28:16–20 is not wholly parallel, since it belongs to an appearance of Jesus in Galilee. But with Matt. 28:19 cf. Luke 24:47.

from that verse on Luke records "a number of important announcements made by the Risen Lord to his disciples during the forty days before his ascension" (*op. cit.,* p. 641). Lenski, on the other hand, favors the opposite view, on the basis of what he considers the "correspondence of John 20:21-23 with this passage [verses 44-49] in Luke" (*op. cit.,* p. 755).

I find it rather difficult to decide this question. The reason I incline toward the view of Geldenhuys is that I cannot see that there is such a close correspondence between *these* particular verses (44-49) in Luke and John 20:21-23. Also I *do* see a very close resemblance between Luke 24:49 ("Remain in the city until y o u are clothed with power from on high") and Acts 1:4, which reports that moments before Jesus ascended to heaven, "He commanded them not to leave Jerusalem, but to wait for what the Father had promised." If this be correct, we could indeed with Geldenhuys view verses 44-49 as containing various sayings of our Lord to be ascribed indefinitely to the forty days before the ascension, and then possibly assign the last of these verses (verse 49) to the final day, the very day of the ascension.

But, interpreted either way, verses 44-49, as well as those immediately preceding, must be considered as being very precious sayings of our Lord, worthy of diligent study.

Luke has arranged his account climactically. In verses 1-12 he has reported the empty tomb and the message of the "angels," "He is risen." In verses 13-35 he has related the appearance of Jesus himself to the men who were walking from Jerusalem to Emmaus, and (separately) to Simon Peter. Now, here in verses 36-49 he describes the appearance of the Risen Lord to an entire group.

36. Then, while they were saying these things, he himself stood among them and said to them, Peace (be) with y o u.

It is Easter Sunday, late in the evening. Ten of the apostles, the men from Emmaus, and perhaps others, are gathered in a house somewhere in Jerusalem. For fear of the Jews the doors are locked (John 20:19). All of a sudden Jesus is standing right in their midst. How he entered we do not know. All we know is that the resurrection body must have certain properties which do not pertain to "the body of humiliation." On this see also I Cor. 15:35-38.

Not only is the Risen Lord standing here, right among them, but he also, to put them at rest, says, "Peace (be) with y o u." When these words flow from his lips they must not be interpreted as a mere "How do y o u do?" The reference is to the peace which Jesus had obtained for all his people by his death on the cross. See Eph. 2:14-18; Phil. 4:7.

37. Startled and frightened, they thought they were seeing a ghost.

One might ask, "But how can it be explained that the men from Emmaus were so startled and frightened, since only a few hours ago they had been conversing with Jesus? And how was it that Peter, to whom the Lord had also already appeared this very day, was so surprised and so filled with fear?"

The *sudden* character of the appearance, and the fact that no one had seen Jesus enter the room—all at once, there he was, as if he had materialized out of thin air—may well account for these reactions on the part of the disciples.

38–40. But he said to them, Why are y o u troubled, and why are doubts arising in y o u r hearts? See my hands and my feet, that it is I myself. Handle me and see, for a ghost does not have flesh and bones as y o u see me having. —After he had said this he showed them his hands and his feet.

When Jesus notices that these men are still filled with fear and doubt, he directs their attention to his hands and feet. He *shows* them these bodily members. John has "his hands and his side." What Jesus wants them to see is undoubtedly *the stigmata,* the marks of his crucifixion. It is, of course, impossible for us, who do not as yet possess the resurrection body, to understand how it was possible for the body of Jesus to be, on the one hand, so unlike our present bodies that he was able to enter a room without opening either a door or a window; yet, on the other hand, so similar to our present bodies that the very scars resulting from his crucifixion were still showing.

We receive comfort from the fact that the Resurrected Christ is as sympathetic and loving as was this same Savior before his crucifixion. With marvelous condescension he "showed them his hands and his feet" probably with the twofold purpose of proving to them: (a) "I am not a ghost," and (b) "I am indeed y o u r Lord and Savior."

41–43. And while they continued in a state of disbelief for joy, and were filled with amazement, he said to them, Do y o u have anything here to eat? —So they gave him a piece of broiled fish, and he took it and ate it in their presence.

The disciples disbelieved for joy and continued for a while in this state. Psychologically this is understandable. We should bear in mind that only (what we would call) "day before yesterday" their hearts had been pierced with a feeling of utter hopelessness. When Jesus breathed his last the situation seemed to be irreparably desperate. It was the end. Jesus was gone. He was dead. And now to believe that he was standing here in their very midst, alive and well, was almost impossible. Was what they were looking at *a ghost?* One moment they would say to themselves, "This must be Jesus. How wonderful." The next moment they would say, "It is just too good to be true. It must be a ghost."

It was for this reason that the Lord, as patient as ever, ate a piece of broiled fish in their presence, so as to convince them that they were not looking at a ghost but at their own Lord and Savior Jesus Christ.

44. And he said to them: These (are) my words that I spoke to y o u while I was still with y o u, that all that is written about me in the law of Moses and the prophets and the psalms must be fulfilled.

The words of Jesus from here on were not necessarily spoken on Easter evening. They may have been, but may also have been spoken at later appearances. Whenever and wherever they were spoken, one thing is certain: the One who is addressing the audience wants everyone to know that what had happened to him was the necessary fulfilment of the plan of God as previously revealed in the sacred writings.

Note that Jesus says that each of the three large divisions of the Old Testament—nowhere in the New Testament so fully indicated—had borne witness to him. Moreover, what he is now saying he has said before. See, for example, 18:31-33.

Note also the words "while I was still with y o u." Jesus wants his disciples to realize that his former mode of association with them has ceased and will not be resumed.

45-47. Then he opened their minds to (enable them to) understand the Scriptures. He told them, Thus it is written that the Christ should suffer and rise again from the dead on the third day, and that conversion and forgiveness of sins should be preached in his name to all the nations, beginning from Jerusalem.

Note the following:

a. Jesus now does for the entire group he addresses what he had already done for the men of Emmaus: he gives them the key to the Scriptures. He illumines their minds so that in all the Scriptures they will see Christ: his suffering (Ps. 22, 69; Isa. 53) and resurrection (Ps. 118; Isa. 53).

b. He causes them to see that he *had to* suffer, and to rise on the third day, in order that the good news of salvation through conversion and forgiveness of sins might be proclaimed to all the nations.

c. "In his name," that is, on the basis of his self-revelation.

d. This proclamation, though beginning from Jerusalem, must fan outward from there to "all the nations."

e. The fact that the proclamation of the gospel must reach all the nations shows that Old and New Testament are in reality *one* book. That worldwide proclamation of the gospel is one of the main themes of the *New* Testament is clear not only from the present passage but also from Matt. 28:19; Acts 1:8; 28:28; Eph. 2:14-18; etc.

That basically the same thing holds for the *Old* Testament is clear from Gen. 22:18; I Kings 8:41-43; Ps. 72:8-11; 87; Isa. 2:3; 45:14, 22-25; 49:23; 54:1-3; 60:1-3; 65:1; Mal. 1:11. To be sure there is a difference between the Old and the New Testament in this respect. For this see N.T.C. on Eph. 3:5, 6 (pp. 154, 155), but that difference does not cancel the fact that both Old and New Testament proclaim a *Christ for all the nations.*

48. Y o u are witnesses of these things.

Since Christ's disciples—first of all the inner circle, but to a certain extent also the wider circle of believers—have seen the works of the Lord, have heard his words, and have experienced in their hearts the meaning and value of the good news, they should bear testimony concerning it. They are and must be Christ's witnesses.

49. Moreover, note well, I am sending upon y o u what my Father

promised; but remain in the city until y o u are clothed with power from on high.

Although what is here recorded concerned especially The Eleven (soon again to become The Twelve, Acts 1:26), it had and has significance for every believer.

Jesus is telling the apostles that he is about to send upon them that which the Father promised, namely, the Holy Spirit. See John 14:16, 17, 26; Acts 1:8. That Spirit will qualify them to be true and effective witnesses. Until they receive this great gift they must remain quietly in Jerusalem. Cf. Acts 1:4.

This promise was fulfilled on the day of Pentecost; that is, on the fiftieth day after Christ's resurrection, the tenth after his ascension. That by means of the words of Jesus when he opened their minds and by means of the outpouring upon them of the Holy Spirit these men indeed became effective witnesses is clear from the book of Acts. One illustration of this increased power and effectiveness is certainly Peter's address on the day of Pentecost (Acts 2:14-36).

For *Practical Lessons* and *Greek Words,* etc., see pp. 1077-1081.

---

50 Then he led them out as far as Bethany, and lifting up his hands he blessed them.
51 Now while he was blessing them he departed from them and was carried up into heaven.
52 They worshiped him and returned to Jerusalem with great joy. 53 And they were continually in the temple, praising God.

24:50-53 *Christ's Ascension*
Cf. Mark 16:19, 20 (part of The Ending); Acts 1:9-11

50. Then he led them out as far as Bethany, and lifting up his hands he blessed them.

If our interpretation of verse 49 is correct, so that this passage and Acts 1:4 run parallel, then (in Luke) verse 50 follows very naturally. The erroneous view, aired by some, according to which Luke would be saying that Christ's ascension took place on the day of Easter will then no longer bother us.

Jesus is here pictured as leading his disciples, The Eleven (see Acts 1:13), out to Bethany, on the eastern slopes of Mt. Olivet. Having arrived there he is busily engaged in conversation with them. He corrects one of their errors. He repeats the promise that they will receive the energizing Holy Spirit who will qualify them for their task (Acts 1:6-8). Then he lifts up his hands over them in blessing.

This act of blessing is more than mere well-wishing. It is an effective impartation of welfare, peace, and power. To be sure, there is nothing mechanical or magical about it, but it is effective for all those whose minds and hearts are truly receptive. For more on this subject see N.T.C. on Matt. 10:12, 13 (pp. 459, 460) and on I Thess. 1:1 (pp. 43-45).

51. Now while he was blessing them he departed from them and was carried up into heaven.

For the authenticity of the final clause see the note on this passage on pp. 1080, 1081.

In full view of the disciples the Lord is lifted up into the sky. They see him ascend until a cloud hides him from their sight (Acts 1:9).

The view according to which from that point on the body of our Lord became diffused or assumed divine properties, so that it became omnipresent, does not rest on any scriptural basis. What Scripture does teach is that Jesus "was caught up to God and to his throne" (Rev. 12:5), that he "sat down at the right hand of God" (Rom. 8:34; Eph. 1:20; Col. 3:1; Heb. 1:3; 8:1; 10:12; 12:2; I Peter 3:22), and that he will come back in the same manner in which the disciples saw him go into heaven (Acts 1:11). All the rest is mere speculation.

52. They worshiped him and returned to Jerusalem with great joy.

The eleven men did as they had been told. They returned to Jerusalem, there to await the outpouring upon them of the Holy Spirit. However, they returned *with great joy*. Why this great joy? Should they not rather have mourned the loss of a true Friend?

They knew better. They had lost nothing and had gained much. Among the reasons for their great joy may well have been the following:

a. They had had Jesus with them *for a while*. They were going to have him with them *forever*, namely, in the Spirit. That was, in fact, the promise he had made to them (Matt. 28:20).

b. They knew, therefore, that they had been commissioned to carry out a great task, the spread of the gospel, and that they were about to receive the power to shoulder it.

c. They had received the promise of his glorious return at the end of the age (Acts 1:11).

d. Should we not also add this reason for their great joy, namely, that they rejoiced in *his* joy, in *his* exaltation?

53. And they were continually in the temple, praising God.

Apart from praise to God joy is incomplete. See Rom. 11:36; I Cor. 10:31; II Cor. 3:18.

Luke began his book with a temple scene (1:5–23). He ends it similarly. He began with songs: of Elizabeth, of Mary, of Zechariah, of angels, of Simeon. So he ends, most appropriately, with praises to God, for "of him and through him, and to him are all things. To him be the glory forever."[623]

Practical Lessons Derived from Luke 24:36–53

Verse 38

"Why are y o u troubled, and why are doubts arising in y o u r hearts?"

---

623. Notes on Greek words, phrases, and constructions in 24:36–53 begin on page 1078.

Compare this with John 14:1, and note that the Risen Christ is as tenderhearted and loving as was the Christ before his death and resurrection.

Verse 47

"Conversion and forgiveness of sins should be preached in his name to all the nations." Is this Luke's version of The Great Commission (cf. Matt. 28:19, 20)? Note that Christ's mission mandate was the last one he issued before ascending to heaven. Does not that make it very important?

Verse 50

"Lifting up his hands he blessed them."
Acts 1:11 "This same Jesus will come back in the same way."
If, then, he departed while blessing his disciples, and if he is coming again with blessing for his church, does it not follow that even now, during the intervening period, he, as representative of the Triune God, Father, Son, and Holy Spirit, delights in being for his people a source of blessing? Also, that he wants us, in a derived or secondary manner, to be a blessing to everyone with whom we come into contact?

Verse 51

"He departed from them."
Matt. 28:20 "I am with y o u always."
He departed in order to remain with his church; in fact, now more than ever. When he was still on earth he was not able physically to be everywhere at the same time. But now that he is in heaven he is able, in and through the Holy Spirit, to be everywhere (not bodily, to be sure, but spiritually). Also, while he was still on earth he was present *with* the church. Now he is present *in* the church. In other words, he has departed from us in order to draw closer to us.

Notes on Greek Words, Phrases, and Constructions in 24:36–53

Verse 36

ἔστη, third per. s. 2nd aor. indicat. of ἵστημι, to set; here, in 2nd aor., probably simply *to stand;* hence, he stood.

λέγει, third per. s. pres. indicat. of λέγω, to say. The change in the tense indicates that what we have here is a dramatic or historical present. Some, therefore, translate "(he) says." Others, realizing that it would never do to retain the present in the translation of all such cases, prefer the rendering "(he) said." Have your choice! The Western omission of the words "and (he) said to them, 'Peace (be) with y o u'" may be in a class with the omission of 22:19b, 20. But even if these words are omitted here, they are found in John 20:19.

Verse 37

πτοηθέντες, nom. pl. aor. pass. participle of πτοέω*, to terrify, frighten, startle; pass. to be frightened, etc. See also the note on 21:9 on page 935, the only other New Testament occurrence.

By some the imperf. tense in ἐδόκουν is regarded as inchoative, resulting in the translation "They began to think." But "They were thinking" (progressive imperf.) or even "They thought" is also possible and may even be preferable.

Verse 38

For τεταραγμένοι ἐστέ, sec. per. pl. periphrastic perf. indicat. pass. of ταράσσω, to trouble, stir up, shake; pass. to be troubled, etc., see the note on 1:12 on page 80. It is this verb that is used in the well-known passage, "Let not y o u r hearts any longer be troubled" (John 14:1).

διαλογισμοί, pl. of διαλογισμός, deliberation, thought; here: divided thought, doubt. See also the note on 9:46 on page 525. Cf. *dialog.*

As often, in such cases, the original uses the sing. *heart,* where we would say *hearts;* so also in verse 45 *mind* becomes *minds* in translation.

Verse 39

ἐγώ ... αὐτός, I myself.

ψηλαφήσατε, sec. per. pl. aor. (ingress.) imperat. of ψηλαφάω, to touch, handle. Cf. ψάλλω, to strike (a musical instrument). Cf. *Psalm.* See also Acts 17:27; Heb. 12:18; and especially in the present connection I John 1:1.

Verse 40

The textual support for this verse is considerable. There are those, however, who—again with the Western text—regard this passage to be unauthentic here, an interpolation from John 20:20. The question then remains, "Why was 'and his side' left out?" There is insufficient reason to omit this verse.

Verse 41

Note genitive absolute "They disbelieving ... and being filled with amazement." βρώσιμον, acc. s. neut. of βρώσιμος*, edible, fit to eat, from βρῶμα, food. Cf. *Ambrose, ambrosial.*

Verse 42

ὀπτοῦ, gen. s. masc. of ὀπτός*, broiled; cf. ὀπτάω, to bake, broil.

Verse 44

ὅτι, either "that," or simply recitative, equivalent to our quotation marks. So also in verse 46.

πληρωθῆναι, aor. (effect.) pass. infinitive of πληρόω, to fill, fulfil. See the note on 1:1 on page 61.

Verse 45

τοῦ συνιέναι, articular pres. infinitive of συνίημι, expressing purpose, *to understand.* See also the note on 18:34 on page 849.

Verse 46

As the context (see verses 26 and 44) clearly indicates, the thought expressed here is not "the Christ will suffer," etc., but "Thus it is written that the Christ *should* suffer," etc.

Verse 47

The reading "conversion εἰς *for* (or *with a view to*) forgiveness of sins," may indicate conflation with the text of 3:3.

Verse 48

With the majority of interpreters I combine "beginning from Jerusalem" with "should be preached ... to all the nations." Reason: see Matt. 10:5, 6; Acts 1:8; 13:46.

Verse 49

ἀποστέλλω, I am sending; i.e., I will send, first per. s. futuristic indicat.

ἐπαγγελίαν, acc. s. of ἐπαγγελία, promise, or, as here: the thing promised. This is the only instance of this word in the Gospels. It occurs frequently in Acts (beginning with 1:4), Romans, Galatians, Ephesians, and Hebrews. Elsewhere in the New Testament its use is scattered. Cf. ἐπαγγέλλω, to announce, promise.

καθίσατε, sec. per. pl. aor. imperat. of καθίζω, here intransit., to sit, keep sitting, remain.

ἕως οὗ, until the time when.

ἐνδύσησθε, sec. per. pl. aor. (futuristic) subjunct. of ἐνδύω, here probably pass. rather than middle, and used in the figurative sense of: to be clothed or invested with (this or that endowment), in the present case, with δύναμιν, acc. s. of δύναμις, power. Cf. *dynamite.*

Verse 50

ἔξω ἕως πρὸς Β., out as far as (Bethany).

Verses 51, 52

ἐν τῷ εὐλογεῖν. Note similar idiom in verses 4, 15, 30; here: while he was blessing them.

For διέστη, third per. s. 2nd aor. (effect.) indicat. act. of διΐστημι, intransit., to part or go away (from), see the note on 22:59 on page 1001.

ἀνεφέρετο, third per. s. imperf. (descript.) indicat. pass. of ἀναφέρω: he was carried up (to heaven). In Luke only here, but found also in Matt. 17:1; Mark 9:2 in the sense of *to lead up* (a mountain); and in several other passages—Heb. 7:27 (twice); 13:15; James 2:21; I Peter 2:5, 24—in the sense of *to offer* (whether sacrifice or prayer or praise or oneself). The use of this verb in Heb. 9:28 has given rise to some difficulty. That passage probably reflects Isa. 53:12, so that the verb in question would have the meaning *to bear, to take away.*

With respect to the words "and was carried into heaven" and "they worshiped him," omitted by the Western text, see the fully attested passage in Acts 1:6–11. And even in connection with the present passage, Luke 24:51, 52, we may well ask, "Would there have been a return 'with great joy' if there had been no glorious ascension?" The disputed words should be retained.

Verse 53

εὐλογοῦντες, nom. pl. masc. pres. act. participle of εὐλογέω, to praise, glorify, bless. This verb is used more often by Luke than by any other New Testament author.

Summary of Chapter 24

When, very early Sunday morning, the women went to the tomb to anoint the body of Jesus, they discovered that the stone had already been rolled away. However, on entering they did not find the body. Two men in bright apparel ("angels," verse 23) told them, "He is not here but is risen, as he told you he would be." The women reported their experience to The Eleven. Their response: "Nonsense!" Peter, however, ran to the tomb. Stooping, he saw the strips of linen lying there, neatly arranged, but did not see the body. He went home, wondering (verses 1–12).

In the afternoon Cleopas and his companion, admirers of Jesus, were on their way from Jerusalem to their home in Emmaus. They were rehearsing the sad events of the last few days. Someone was catching up with them. The stranger asked the two what they were so busily discussing. After expressing surprise about the inquirer's ignorance they answered his question. They ended with, "Some of our women went to the tomb and returned saying that they had seen a vision of angels who affirmed that he was alive. Some of our friends found it exactly as the women had said, but him they did not see."

The stranger then explained to the two that according to the entire Old Testament it was the path of suffering that would bring the Messiah to glory.

Arriving at their destination the two urged the one who had joined them to stay and eat with them. While he was breaking bread they suddenly noticed that the stranger was Jesus himself, risen from the dead. He then vanished.

In spite of the lateness of the hour the two walked the eleven kilometers (seven miles) back to Jerusalem to tell the apostles the marvelous news. On arrival they were greeted with the shout, "The Lord has risen indeed and has appeared to Simon." Then they, too, told their story (verses 13–35).

In the midst of the lively discussion Jesus himself stood among them and said, "Peace (be) with y o u." To dispel the fear that they were looking at a ghost he showed them his hands and feet and in their presence ate a piece of broiled fish.

After relating this part of the story Luke reports sayings of Jesus probably spoken at one time or another during the forty days between his resurrection and ascension. He states that the Risen Savior opened the Scripture to his audience so that they might understand that whatever was written concerning him must be fulfilled. The narrative of his suffering and resurrection must be made known to all the nations so that all who turn to him may have their sins forgiven and be saved. The last recorded saying in this section is, "I am sending upon y o u what my Father promised; but remain in the city until y o u are clothed with power from on high" (verses 36–49).

At the appropriate moment he led The Eleven to Bethany. While lifting up his hands and blessing them he was carried up to heaven. "They worshiped him and returned to Jerusalem with great joy. And they were continually in the temple, praising God" (verses 50–53).

SELECT BIBLIOGRAPHY

Calvin, J., *Commentary on a Harmony of the Evangelists, Matthew, Mark, and Luke* (tr. of *Commentarius in Harmoniam Evangelicam, Opera Omnia*), three volumes, Grand Rapids, 1949 ff.

Erdman, C. R., *Exposition of the Gospel of Luke*, Philadelphia, 1929.

Geldenhuys, N., *Commentary on the Gospel of Luke (The New International Commentary on the New Testament)*, Grand Rapids, 1951.

Lenski, R. C. H., *Interpretation of St. Luke's Gospel*, Columbus, 1934.

Plummer, A., *The Gospel According to St. Luke (The International Critical Commentary)*, New York, 1910.

Stonehouse, N. B., *The Witness of Luke to Christ*, Grand Rapids, 1951.

GENERAL BIBLIOGRAPHY

Aalders, G. J. D., *Het Romeinsche Imperium En Het Nieuwe Testament,* Kampen, 1938.

Amram, D. W., *Leading Cases in the Bible,* Philadelphia, 1905.

Ante-Nicene Fathers, ten volumes, reprint, Grand Rapids, 1950, for references to Clement of Alexandria, Irenaeus, Justin Martyr, Origen, Tertullian, etc.

Ash, A. L., *The Gospel According to Luke (The Living Word Commentary),* Austin, 1972.

Bailey, A. E., *The Gospel in Art,* Boston, 1946.

Bailey, J. A., *The Traditions Common to the Gospels of Luke and John,* Leiden, 1963.

Bailey, K. E., *The Cross and the Prodigal, the Fifteenth Chapter of Luke, Seen Through the Eyes of Middle Eastern Peasants,* St. Louis, London, 1973.

———, *Poet and Peasant,* Grand Rapids, 1976.

Balljon, J., *Commentaar op het Evangelie van Lukas,* Utrecht, 1908.

Barclay, W., *Jesus Christ for Today,* Nashville, n.d.

Barker, G. W., Lane, W. L., and Michaels, J. R., *The New Testament Speaks,* New York, 1969.

Barrett, C. K., *Luke the Historian in Recent Study,* London, 1961.

Bavinck, H., *Gereformeerde Dogmatiek,* four volumes, third edition, Kampen, 1918.

———, *The Doctrine of God* (tr. of *Gereformeerde Dogmatiek,* Vol. II, *Over God*), Grand Rapids, 1977.

Berkhof, L., *Systematic Theology,* Grand Rapids, 1949.

———, *New Testament Introduction,* Grand Rapids, 1915.

———, *Principles of Biblical Interpretation,* Grand Rapids, 1950.

———, *Vicarious Atonement Through Christ,* Grand Rapids, 1936.

Berkouwer, G. C., *Dogmatische Studiën* (the series), Kampen, 1949, etc.

Bisek, A. S., *The Trial of Jesus Christ,* Chicago, 1925.

Bishop, J., *The Day Christ Died,* New York and Evanston, 1957.

Blinzler, J., *Der Prozess Jesu,* Ratisbonne, 1960.

Bornkamm, G., *Jesus of Nazareth* (tr. of *Jesus von Nazareth*), London and New York, 1961.

Bornkamm, G., Barth, G., Held, H. J., *Tradition and Interpretation in Matthew,* Philadelphia, 1963.

Brouwer, A. M., *De Gelijkenissen,* Leiden, 1946.

Brown, A. I., *God and You: Wonders of the Human Body,* Findlay, n.d.

Brown, Driver, Briggs, *A Hebrew and English Lexicon of the Old Testament,* Boston, New York, 1906.

Brown, R. E., *New Testament Essays,* Milwaukee, 1965.

Brown, S., *Apostasy and Perseverance in the Theology of Luke,* Rome, 1969.

Brownlee, W. H., "John the Baptist in the New Light of Ancient Scrolls" in K. Stendahl, *The Scrolls and the New Testament,* New York, 1957.

Bruce, A. B., *The Parabolic Teaching of Christ,* London, 1882.

———, *The Synoptic Gospels (The Expositor's Greek Testament,* Vol. I), Grand Rapids, n.d.

Bruce, F. F., *Commentary on the Book of the Acts (The New International Commentary on the New Testament),* Grand Rapids, 1964.

———, *The Epistle to the Hebrews (The New International Commentary on the New Testament)*, Grand Rapids, 1964.

Bultmann, R., *From Tradition to Gospel* (tr. of *Die Formgeschichte des Evangeliums*), New York, 1935.

Burrows, M., *The Dead Sea Scrolls*, New York, 1956.

———, *More Light on the Dead Sea Scrolls*, New York, 1958.

Burton, E. D., *Syntax of the Moods and Tenses in New Testament Greek*, Chicago, 1923.

Burton, H., *The Gospel According to St. Luke (The Expositor's Bible)*, Grand Rapids, 1943.

Buttrick, G. A., *The Parables of Jesus*, New York, 1928.

Cadbury, H. J., *The Style and Literary Method of Luke*, Cambridge, 1920.

———, *The Beginnings of Christianity*, five volumes, London, 1920–1933.

———, *The Making of Luke-Acts*, New York, 1927.

Cadoux, A. T., *The Parables of Jesus*, London, n.d.

Caird, G. B., *Saint Luke (Pelican Gospel Commentaries)*, London, 1963.

Calvin, J., *Commentary on a Harmony of the Evangelists, Matthew, Mark, and Luke* (tr. of *Commentarius in Harmoniam Evangelicam, Opera Omnia*), three volumes, Grand Rapids, 1949 ff.

Chamberlain, W. D., *An Exegetical Grammar of the Greek New Testament*, New York, 1941.

———, *The Manner of Prayer*, Philadelphia, 1943.

———, *The Meaning of Repentance*, Philadelphia, 1943.

Chapman, J., *Matthew, Mark, and Luke*, London, 1937.

Chappell, C. C., *Sermons from the Parables*, Nashville, 1933.

Childs, A. T., *Parables to the Point*, Philadelphia, 1963.

Chiniquy, C., *Fifty Years in the Church of Rome*, New York, Chicago, Toronto, 1886.

Clark, R. E. D., *The New International Dictionary of the Christian Church*, Grand Rapids, 1974.

Coates, T., *The Parables for Today*, St. Louis, 1971.

Conzelmann, H., *Die Mitte der Zeit, Studien zur Theologie des Lukas*, Tübingen, 1954 (tr. *The Theology of Luke*, New York, Evanston, San Francisco, London, 1957).

Cowell, F. R., *Everyday Life in Ancient Rome*, Edinburgh, 1961.

Creed, J. M., *The Gospel According to St. Luke*, New York, 1942.

Crossan, J. D., *In Parables*, New York, etc., 1973.

Dabney, R. L., *Systematic and Polemic Theology*, Richmond, 1927.

Dalman, G., *Aramäisch-neuhebräisches Wörterbuch zu Targum, Talmud, und Midrasch*, Frankfort, 1897–1901.

———, *Christianity and Judaism* (tr. of *Christentum und Judentum*), Oxford, 1901.

———, *Orte und Wege Jesu*, Leipzig, 1924.

———, *Jesus-Jeshua, Studies in the Gospels*, New York, 1929.

Dana, H. E., and Mantey, J. R., *A Manual Grammar of the Greek New Testament*, New York, 1950.

Daniélou, J., *Les Manuscripts de la Mer Mort et les origines du Christianisme*, Paris, 1957.

Danker, F. W., *Jesus and the New Age, a Commentary on the Third Gospel*, St. Louis, 1972.

Deissmann, A., *Light from the Ancient East*, New York, 1927.

De Jong, A. C., *The Well-Meant Gospel Offer* (doctoral dissertation), Franeker, n.d.

Derritt, J. D. M., *An Oriental Lawyer Looks at the Trial of Jesus and the Doctrine of Redemption*, London, 1966.

De Zwaan, J., *Het Evangelie van Lucas, Tekst en Uitleg*, Groningen, Den Haag, 1917.

Dibelius, M., *From Tradition to Gospel* (tr. of *Die Formgeschichte des Evangeliums*), New York, 1935.

Dobler, L., *Customs and Holidays Around the World*, New York, 1962.

Dodd, C. H., *The Parables of the Kingdom*, London, 1935.

Dungan, D. L., and Cartlidge, D. R., *Sourcebook of Texts for the Comparative Study of the Gospels*, Missoula, 1971.

Dupont-Sommer, *The Jewish Sect of Qumran and the Essenes, New Studies on the Dead Sea Scrolls*, London, 1954.

LUKE

Easton, B. S., *The Gospel According to St. Luke,* Edinburgh, 1926.

Edersheim, A., *The Life and Times of Jesus the Messiah,* two volumes, New York, 1897.

Ellis, E. E., *The Gospel of Luke (The Century Bible),* London, etc., 1966.

Erdman, C. R., *Exposition of the Gospel of Luke,* Philadelphia, 1929.

Evans, W., *From the Upper Room to the Empty Tomb,* Grand Rapids, 1934.

Fahling, A., *The Life of Christ,* St. Louis, 1936.

Farrar, F. W., *The Life of Christ,* New York, 1875.

———, *St. Luke,* Cambridge, 1912.

Finkelstein, L., *The Jews, Their History, Culture, and Religion,* two volumes, New York, 1949.

Flood, E., *Parables of Jesus,* New York, 1971.

Fonck, L., *Die Parabeln des Herrn,* Innsbruck, 1902.

Foster, R. C., *Studies in the Life of Christ,* three volumes, Grand Rapids, 1966.

Free, J. P., *Archaeology and Bible History,* Wheaton, 1950.

Funk, R. B., *Jesus as Precursor,* Philadelphia, 1975.

Furst, B., *How to Remember,* 1948 (place of publication not indicated).

Geldenhuys, N., *Commentary on the Gospel of Luke (The New International Commentary on the New Testament),* Grand Rapids, 1951.

Gilmour, S. M., *The Gospel According to St. Luke (The Interpreter's Bible,* Vol. VIII), New York and Nashville, 1952.

Gispen, W. H., *Exodus (Korte Verklaring),* Kampen, 1932.

———, *Het Boek Leviticus (Commentaar op het Oude Testament),* Kampen, 1950.

Glen, J. W., *The Parables of Conflict in Luke,* Philadelphia, 1962.

Godet, F., *A Commentary on the Gospel of St. Luke,* two volumes, Edinburgh, 1890.

Goodspeed, E. J., *New Solutions of New Testament Problems,* Chicago, 1927.

———, *New Chapters in New Testament Study,* New York, 1937.

———, *Problems of New Testament Translation,* Chicago, 1945.

Greijdanus, S., *Het Evangelie naar Lucas (Korte Verklaring),* Kampen, 1941.

———, *Het Heilig Evangelie naar de Beschrijving van Lucas (Kommentaar op het Nieuwe Testament),* two volumes, Amsterdam, 1940–41.

Grollenberg, L. H., *Atlas of the Bible,* New York, etc., 1956.

Grundmann, W., *Das Evangelium nach Lukas,* Berlin, 1959.

Guignebert, C., *The Jewish World in the Time of Jesus,* London, 1939.

Gundry, R. H., *The Use of the Old Testament in St. Matthew's Gospel,* Leiden, 1967.

———, *A Survey of the New Testament,* Grand Rapids, 1970.

Halberthal, L., *The Plan of the Holy Temple of Jerusalem,* Montreal, 1967.

Harnack, A., *Luke the Physician, the Author of the Third Gospel and the Acts of the Apostles,* London, 1907.

———, *Sayings of Jesus,* London, 1908.

———, *The Acts of the Apostles,* London, 1908.

———, *The Date of the Acts and of the Synoptics,* London, 1911.

Harrington, W. J., *The Gospel According to St. Luke,* London, etc., 1968.

———, *Parables Told by Jesus,* New York, 1974.

Hauch, F., *Das Evangelium des Lukas,* Leipzig, 1934.

Hawkins, J. C., *Horae Synopticae,* Oxford, 1911.

Hayes, D. A., *The Most Beautiful Book Ever Written, the Gospel According to Luke,* New York, etc., 1913.

Heichelheim, F. M., *An Economic Survey of Ancient Rome,* edited by T. Frank, Vol. IV, Baltimore, 1938.

Hendriksen, W., *New Testament Commentary,* Grand Rapids and Edinburgh, 1953 f. (Completed so far: a volume on each of the four Gospels, and volumes on Paul's epistles, except Romans and I and II Corinthians).

1087

LUKE

_____, *The Meaning of the Preposition* ἀντί *in the New Testament* (unpublished doctoral dissertation), Princeton, 1948.

_____, *More Than Conquerors, An Interpretation of the Book of Revelation*, Grand Rapids, 22nd ed., 1977.

_____, *The Covenant of Grace*, Grand Rapids, 1932.

_____, *The Bible on the Life Hereafter*, Grand Rapids, 1971.

_____, *Israel in Prophecy*, Grand Rapids, 1972.

_____, *Survey of the Bible*, Grand Rapids, 1976.

Hertzberg, A. (editor), *Judaism*, New York, 1962.

Higgins, A. J. B., *The Lord's Supper in the New Testament*, London, 1952.

Hobart, W. K., *The Medical Language of St. Luke*, Dublin, 1882 (reprint, Grand Rapids, 1954).

Hodgkin, A. M., *Christ in All the Scriptures*, London, 1945.

Hoekstra, H., *De opgang uit de hoogte (15 leerredenen over Lucas 1, 2)*, Utrecht, n.d.

Holtrop, H., *De Verschijningen Onzes Heeren Te Jeruzalem En in Galilea*, Amsterdam, 1947 (doctoral dissertation).

Howard, W. F., *The Fourth Gospel in Recent Criticism*, London, etc., 1955.

Howley, C. D., Bruce, F. F., and Ellison, H. L., eds., *A New Testament Commentary*, Grand Rapids, 1969.

Hughes, P. E., *Paul's Second Epistle to the Corinthians (The New International Commentary on the New Testament)*, Grand Rapids, 1962.

Hurlbut, J. L., and Vincent, J. H., *A Bible Atlas*, New York, etc., 1940.

Hyma, A., and Stach, J. F., *World History, A Christian Interpretation*, Grand Rapids, 1942.

Jeremias, J., *Rediscovering the Parables*, New York, 1966.

Johnson, M. C., *The Purpose of the Biblical Genealogies*, Cambridge, 1969.

Jülicher, A., *Die Gleichnisreden Jesu*, two volumes, Zweiter Teil, Darmstadt, 1963.

Keck, L. E. (ed.), *Studies in Luke-Acts*, Nashville, 1966.

Keil, C. F., *Commentar über die Evangelien des Markus und Lucas*, Leipzig, 1879.

Kenyon, F. G., and Bell, H. I., *Greek Papyri in the British Museum*, London, 1907.

Knap, J., *Gelijkenissen des Heeren*, Nijkerk, 1921–1922.

Kollek, T., and Pearlman, M., *Jerusalem, A History of Forty Centuries*, New York, 1968.

Kopp, C., *The Holy Places of the Gospels*, New York, 1963.

Kraeling, E. G., *Rand-McNally Bible Atlas*, New York, etc., 1966.

Krämer, M., *Das Rätsel der parabel vom Ungerechten Verwalter, Lk. 16, 1–13*, Zurich, 1972.

Kuyper, A., Sr., *De Engelen Gods*, Kampen, 1923.

Lagrange, M. J., *Évangile selon Saint Luc*, Paris, 1921.

Lang, G. H., *The Parabolic Teaching of Scripture*, Grand Rapids, 1955.

Leaney, A. R. C., *A Commentary on the Gospel According to St. Luke (Harper's New Testament Commentary)*, New York, 1958.

Lenski, R. C. H., *The Interpretation of St. Mark's and St. Luke's Gospels*, Columbus, 1934.

Lloyd, R., *The Private Letters of Luke*, New York, 1958.

Lloyd-Jones, D. M., *Studies in the Sermon on the Mount*, Grand Rapids, 1959.

Loeb Classical Library, New York (various dates), for The Apostolic Fathers, Eusebius, Josephus, Philo, Pliny, Plutarch, Strabo, etc.

Loisy, A., *L'Évangile selon Luc*, Paris, 1924.

Luce, H. K., *St. Luke*, Cambridge, 1933.

Macartney, C. E., *Of Them He Chose Twelve*, Philadelphia, 1927.

Machen, J. G., *The Virgin Birth of Christ*, New York and London, 1930.

Maier, P. L., *Pontius Pilate*, Garden City, N.Y., 1968.

Manson, T. W., *The Sayings of Jesus*, London, 1949.

_____, *The Teaching of Jesus*, Cambridge, 1951.

LUKE

Manson, W., *Jesus the Messiah*, Philadelphia, 1946.

———, *The Gospel of Luke (The Moffatt New Testament Commentary)*, London, 1948.

Martin, H., *The Parables of the Gospels*, London, 1962.

Marxsen, W., *Der Evangelist Markus*, Göttingen, 1959.

Maus, C. P., *Christ and the Fine Arts*, New York, 1959.

McMillen, S. E., *None of These Diseases*, Westwood, N.J., 1963.

Metzger, B. M., compiler, *Index to Periodical Literature on Christ and the Gospels*, Grand Rapids, 1962.

———, *The Text of the New Testament*, Oxford, 1964.

———, *The New Testament, Its Background, Growth, and Content*, New York and Nashville, 1965.

———, *An Introduction to the Apocrypha*, New York and Oxford, 1957.

Micklem, P. A., *St. Matthew, with Introduction and Notes*, London, 1917.

Miller, D. G., *The Gospel of Luke*, Richmond, 1959.

Mishna, The, English translation by H. Danby, London, 1933.

Moldenke, H. N., and A. L., *Plants of the Bible*, Waltham, 1952.

Montefiore, C. F., *Rabbinic Literature and Gospel Teaching*, New York, 1970.

Moore, G. F., *Judaism in the First Five Centuries of the Christian Era*, Cambridge, 1927–1930.

Morgan, G. C., *The Gospel According to Luke*, London, 1931.

———, *The Parables and Metaphors of Our Lord*, New York, London, 1943.

Morgenthaler, R., *Die Lukanische Geschichtsachreibung als Zeugnis*, two volumes, Zürich, 1949.

Morison, F., *Who Moved the Stone?*, New York, London, 1930.

Morris, L., *The Gospel According to St. Luke* (Tyndale Series), Grand Rapids, 1974.

Mulder, H., *De Sadduceeën*, Amsterdam, 1973.

———, *De Eerste Hoofdstukken van het Evangelie naar Lukas in hun Structurele Samenhang* (doctoral dissertation), Delft, 1948.

———, *Hoofdlijnen van Lucas 2*, The Hague, 1959.

———, *De Synagoge in de Nieuwtestamentische Tijd*, Kampen, 1969.

———, *De Minim*, Kampen, 1971.

———, *Spoorzoeker in Bijbelse Landen*, Amsterdam, 1973.

———, *Geschiedenis van de Palestijnse Kerk*, Kampen, n.d.

———, *Dienaren van de Koning*, Kampen, 1956.

Müller, G. A., *Pontius Pilatus der fünfte Prokurator von Judäa*, Stuttgart, 1888.

Murray, J., *The Epistle to the Romans*, two volumes (*The New International Commentary on the New Testament*), Grand Rapids, 1965.

Navone, J., *Themes of St. Luke*, Rome, n.d.

Neirynck, F., *L'Évangile de Luc*, Gembloux, 1973.

Oesterley, W. O. E., *The Gospel Parables in the Light of Their Jewish Background*, London, 1938.

Orr, J., *The Virgin Birth of Christ*, New York, 1924.

Paddock, W., and P., *Hungry Nations*, Boston and Toronto, 1964.

Parmelee, A., *All the Birds of the Bible*, New York, 1959.

Parrot, A., *The Temple of Jerusalem*, London, 1957.

Perrin, N., *What Is Redaction Criticism?*, Philadelphia, 1969.

Pick, B., *The Talmud, What It Is*, New York, 1887.

Plummer, A., *The Gospel According to St. Luke (The International Critical Commentary)*, New York, 1910.

Ramsay, W., *Was Christ Born at Bethlehem?*, 1898.

———, *The Bearing of Recent Discovery on the Trustworthiness of the New Testament*, reprint, Grand Rapids, 1953.

Reicke, B., *The Gospel of Luke*, Richmond, 1964.

Reiling, J., and Swellengrebel, J. L., *A Translator's Handbook on the Gospel of Luke*, Leiden, 1971.

LUKE

Rengstorf, K. H., *Das Evangelium nach Lukas*, Göttingen, 1949.

Renkema, W., *De Gelijkenissen onzes Heeren Jezus Christus voor de Gemeente Verklaard*, Doesburg, 1905.

Ridderbos, H. N., *Zelfopenbaring en Zelfverberging*, Kampen, 1950.

———, *De Komst van het Koninkrijk*, Kampen, 1950.

Ridderbos, J., *De Kleine Profeten*, three volumes (Korte Verklaring), Kampen, 1935.

Rienecker, F., *Das Evangelium des Lukas*, Wuppertal, 1959.

Robertson, A. T., *A Translation of Luke's Gospel*, New York, 1923.

———, *Word Pictures in the New Testament*, Vol. II, Nashville, 1930.

———, *A Harmony of the Gospels for Students of the Life of Christ*, New York, 1922.

———, *Luke the Historian in the Light of Research*, New York, 1923.

———, *An Introduction to the Textual Criticism of the New Testament*, New York, 1925.

———, *The Pharisees and Jesus*, New York, 1920.

Robinson, H. W., *The People and the Book*, Oxford, 1925.

Roth, D. M., *The Famous Roth Memory Course*, Cleveland, 1934.

Sahlin, H., *Der Messias und das Gottesvolk*, Uppsala, 1945.

Schaff, P., *History of the Christian Church*, seven volumes, New York, 1916.

Schippers, R., *Gelijkenissen van Jezus*, Kampen, 1962.

Schlatter, A., *Das Evangelium des Lukas*, Stuttgart, 1960.

Schürer, E., *A History of the Jewish People in the Time of Jesus Christ* (tr. of *Geschichte des jüdischen Volkes im Zeitalter Jesu Christi*), Edinburgh, 1890, 1891.

Schürmann, H., *Das Lukasevangelium (Herders Theologischer Kommentar zum Neuen Testament*, three volumes), Freiburg, etc., 1969 f.

Scobie, C. H. H., *John the Baptist*, Philadelphia, 1964.

Segal, J. B., *The Jewish Passover from the Earliest Times to A.D. 70*, London, 1963.

Seltmann, C., *Greek Coins*, London, 1933.

Selwyn, E. C., *St. Luke the Prophet*, London, 1901.

Selwyn, E. G., *The First Epistle of St. Peter*, London, 1946.

Sense, P. C., *A Critical and Historical Enquiry into the Origin of the Third Gospel*, London, etc., 1901.

Shepherd, J. W., *The Christ of the Gospels*, Grand Rapids, 1946.

Sherwin-White, A. N., *Roman Society and Roman Law in the New Testament*, Oxford, 1963.

Sizoo, A., *Uit De Wereld van het Nieuwe Testament*, Kampen, 1946.

———, *De Antieke Wereld en het Nieuwe Testament*, Kampen, 1948.

Smith, B. I. D., *The Parables of the Synoptic Gospels*, Cambridge, England, 1937.

Stagg, F., σημεῖον *in the Fourth Gospel* (unpublished dissertation), Louisville, 1943.

Stalker, J., *The Trial and Death of Jesus Christ*, New York, 1894.

Stevens, G. B., *The Theology of the New Testament*, New York, 1925.

Stöger, A., *Das Evangelium nach Lukas*, Düsseldorf, 1964; English tr., *The Gospel According to St. Luke*, two volumes, Dublin, 1969.

Stonehouse, N. B., *The Witness of Luke to Christ*, Grand Rapids, 1951.

Strack, H. L., *Jesus, die Häretiker und die Christen nach den ältesten jüdischen Angaben*, Munich, 1910.

Swete, H. B., *The Parables of the Kingdom*, London, 1921.

Talmud, The Babylonian (English tr.), Boston, 1918.

Tannehill, R. C., *The Sword of His Mouth*, Philadelphia, 1975.

Tasker, R. V. G., *The Gospel According to St. Matthew* (Tyndale series), Grand Rapids, 1961.

Taylor, V., *Behind the Third Gospel*, Oxford, 1926.

———, *The First Draft of St. Luke's Gospel*, London, 1927.

Taylor, W. M., *The Parables of Our Savior*, New York, 1886.

Te Selle, S. M., *Speaking in Parables*, Philadelphia, 1973.

Trench, R. C., *Notes on the Parables of Our Lord*, Philadelphia, 1878.

LUKE

_____, *Synonyms of the New Testament,* Grand Rapids, 1948.

Trueblood, E., *The Humor of Christ,* New York, 1964.

Turner, G. A., *Historical Geography of the Holy Land,* Grand Rapids, 1973.

Unger, M. F., *Archaeology and the New Testament,* Grand Rapids, 1962.

Van Der Sprenkel, S. F. H. J., *Het Evangelie van Lukas,* 'S-Gravenhage (The Hague), 1964.

Van Oosterzee, J. J., *Luke (Lange's Commentary on the Holy Scriptures),* Grand Rapids, n.d.

Van Wyk, W. P., *My Sermon Notes on Parables and Metaphors,* Grand Rapids, 1944.

Veldhóen, N. G., *Het Process van den Apostel Paulus,* Leiden, 1924.

Walker, T., *Jewish Views of Jesus,* New York, 1951.

Warfield, B. B., *Christology and Criticism,* New York, 1929.

_____, *The Inspiration and Authority of the Bible,* Philadelphia, 1948.

_____, *Biblical and Theological Studies,* Philadelphia, 1953.

Weiss, C. P. B., *Die Quellen des Lukas-Evangeliums,* Stuttgart, 1907.

Winter, P., *On the Trial of Jesus,* Berlin, 1961.

Wright, G. E. (ed.), *Great People of the Bible and How They Lived,* Pleasantville, Montreal, etc., 1974.

Zahn, Th., *Introduction to the New Testament,* three volumes, Grand Rapids, 1953.

Zondervan Pictorial Bible Dictionary, Grand Rapids, 1963.

INDEX OF NOTES ON GREEK WORDS, PHRASES, AND CONSTRUCTIONS IN LUKE'S GOSPEL

SUBJECT INDEX
of
THE SYNOPTICS

This Index covers only the main commentary, not (in Luke) the Practical Lessons and the Greek Sections. Neither is this necessary, for once the *subject* has been located in *the main commentary,* possible references to it in those two other Sections are readily found.

Words which, in this Index, are listed in the plural include also those which in the commentary text occur in the singular.

	Matthew	Mark	Luke
Abba		13,588	
Abel	837–839		642, 643
Abijah			64, 65
Abraham	105–114, 129, 204, 205, 396, 397, 806, 807	488	108, 109, 126, 204, 205, 220–223, 701, 707, 783–787, 856–857, 906, 907
Adultery	302–306	379, 380, 393	775, 832, 833
Advent, Second. *See also* Judgment Day	843, 862–892, 932, 933	524–544, 611, 612	676–681, 858–863, 940–944, 998, 999
Alexander and Rufus		14, 648, 649	
Amen	290, 291. *This word occurs in Matt. 5:18, 26 and at least once in every following chapter in Matthew except chapters 7, 9, 12, 14, 15, 20, 22, 27, and 28.*	137. *Occurs in Mark 3:28; 8:12, and at least once in every chapter thereafter except chapter 15 and chapter 16:1–8.*	256, 257, 677, 830, 837, 943, 1032
Andrew	245–248, 450–452	58–61, 126, 513	328

	Matthew	Mark	Luke
Beatitudes	264–282		337–343
Beelzebul. *See also* Devil; Evil One; Satan	468, 524, 525	134–137	617–621
Bethsaida	494, 495	256–258, 321	475, 476, 576, 577
Birth of Jesus in Bethlehem	130–146, 166–174, 179–185		135–159
Blind, Healing the, and being kind to them	434, 435, 753, 754	321–323, 416–422	252–255, 360, 361, 393, 394, 725, 726, 732, 841–845
Blind Guides	616, 617, 829, 830, 832–834		360, 361
Boanerges		13, 125, 126	
Brothers and Sisters of Jesus	144, 145, 541–543, 581	140–143, 222, 223	143, 435–437
Caesarea Philippi	641, 642	323, 324	489–495
Caiaphas	896, 897, 927, 928	604, 609–613	195, 197, 198, 993, 994
Calling Four Disciples	245–249	58–62	*See* Catch of Fishes
Calvary. *See* Crucifixion of Jesus			
Canaanite Woman, The, whose daughter Jesus healed	621–628	293–301	
Capernaum	239–242, 394, 496, 677	63, 86, 295, 355, 356	256, 257, 262, 263, 373, 374, 578, 579
Catch of Fishes (Miraculous) and Call to Discipleship	245, 246		279–286
Centurion, Commended	394–398		373–379
Centurion (at Calvary)	976–977	666, 667, 671	1036, 1037
Ceremonial Defilement	607–618	269–289	
Charge to the Seventy-two (or Seventy)			569–576

	Matthew	Mark	Luke
ginal see N.T.C. on Matthew, p. 504, footnote 488.	*ence to disciples of Jesus in every chapter except 22 and 25.*	*chapter except 15.*	*chapter except 13, 15, 21, 23, and 24.*
Disciples of John the Baptist	429, 481, 482–484, 591	98–100	307, 308, 392–395, 608
Disciples of the Pharisees	800, 801	98–100	307, 308
Double-drachma	677, 678		
Drachma			748
Dragnet, The, Parable of	577–579		
Dreams, Dreaming	174–176		
Dropsy, Cure of the Man Afflicted with			719–721
Dumb. *See* Speech, Taking Away and/or Restoring the Power of			
Egypt, Flight to, and Return from, including Slaughter of Bethlehem's Infants	176–188		177, 178
Elders	608–612, 653, 654, 776, 896, 921, 927, 928, 941, 943, 948, 951, 966, 967, 993, 994	272–274, 327, 463–465, 591–595, 627	374–376, 496, 887, 888, 987, 988, 997–999
Elijah	490, 491, 642, 666–672, 972, 973	234, 235, 324, 339, 340, 342, 343, 663, 664	256, 258, 474, 494, 504–507, 558
Elisha			256, 258
Elizabeth			65–67, 69, 70, 77, 89, 93–98
Emmanuel. *See* Immanuel			
Emmaus			1060
Encouragement: Jesus the Great Encourager		496, 497	
Envy	952	636	1017

	Matthew	Mark	Luke
Genealogy of Herod I	189		
Genealogy of Mariamne I	161		
Gennesaret	603, 604	15, 264	279, 280
Gethsemane	916–921	582–591	
Glory, (splendor, brilliance, honor), glorying, glorify, glorifying, glorious	231, 320, 338, 339, 352, 420, 421, 627, 658, 659, 729, 862, 865	92, 332, 333, 410, 536	151, 155, 158, 168, 235, 298, 299, 501, 504, 505, 667, 702, 799, 845, 875, 876, 940, 941, 1064, 1065
God. Some of His (or Christ's) Attributes:			
a. Covenant Faithfulness			108–110, 123–126
b. Goodness (including Mercy, Grace, Love)	312–318, 424, 425	391, 400, 401	75, 76, 105–110, 126, 179, 180, 354, 355, 695, 696, 835
c. Holiness	327–331		264, 265
d. Omnipotence	327, 412, 413, 728, 729	400, 487	441, 442, 652, 653, 836, 837
e. Omniscience	324, 353, 354, 472, 473		774
f. Patience	839, 840		696, 710, 711
g. Sovereignty	249, 250	56, 57, 166, 167	401, 836
h. Wisdom	493, 581	219, 221	179, 180, 186, 187, 401, 642
Golden Rule, The	363–366		351, 352
Golgotha. See Crucifixion			
Good Samaritan, The, Parable of. See Samaritan Who Cared.			
Gospel, The, and Its Proclamation	3–5, 249, 438, 439, 484, 901	32–34, 55–57, 520, 560	249, 252–254, 393, 394, 471–473, 887, 888, 1075

	Matthew	Mark	Luke
	519, 523, 555, 556, 593, 603, 604, 625–628, 713, 771	416–422	418, 419, 444–450, 456–460, 471, 473, 477, 478, 515, 516, 575, 699–702, 719–721, 797–799, 987
Healing Many People and Raising the Dead	248–252, 400, 401, 457, 484, 485, 603, 604, 625–628	70, 74, 223, 224, 231–234, 264–266, 306	269, 334–336, 381–395, 453–456, 460–464
Heart	276–278, 346, 530, 533, 555 f., 558, 559, 614, 615, 617, 618, 809, 873	263, 274, 282–289, 319, 320, 377, 459, 492–495	158, 186, 363, 364, 429, 519, 592, 671, 679–680, 1064, 1066
Herod I (The Great)	158–168, 177–193	236	64, 65
Herod Antipas ("The Tetrarch")	187, 189, 585–591	233–242, 317–319	195, 212, 213, 474, 475, 708–710, 1010–1013, 1015, 1016
Herod Philip	189, 587	236	213, 1011
Herod Agrippa I	189		195
Herod Agrippa II	189		
Herodias and Her Daughter (Salome)	189, 585, 586	236–241	212, 213, 1011
Hidden Treasure, The, Parable of	575, 576		
Holy Spirit (Spirit of God, Spirit of the Father, etc.)	130, 131, 208, 214, 215, 222, 520, 521, 526–529, 811, 812, 1000, 1001	42–44, 46, 137–139, 500, 521	70, 71, 88, 94, 121, 165, 166, 209, 210, 216–219, 229, 230, 614, 655–657
Holy Trinity	215, 998–1001	42, 43	219, 656, 657
Hope	522	495	67, 128, 129, 1067
Hyrcanus I	161, 162		
Hyrcanus II	161, 163		
Imitation (of God or of Christ). See Example.			
Immanuel or Emmanuel	133–141		
Impenitent Cities, Woes Pronounced upon	494–496		576–579

	Matthew	Mark	Luke
	201, 251, 711, 712, 857, 858		387, 388, 937, 1010
Judges, Judging, Judicial Bench	300, 301, 356–358, 525, 729, 730, 836, 953		355, 356, 620, 621, 662, 685, 686, 816, 817, 861, 972
Judgment Day, The Final. *See also* Advent, Second	460, 496, 531, 535–539, 729, 730, 885–892	535–537	575, 576, 628–630, 676–681, 706, 707, 804–809, 815–821, 838
Julius Caesar	163		137, 138
Justice	520, 521, 831		75, 76, 638, 639, 816, 817
Kindness. *See also* Mercy			354, 355
Kingdom (earthly)	525, 851, 852	135, 136, 239, 437, 438, 515, 516	620, 621, 858, 859, 929
Kingdom (heavenly in essence)	*Beginning with 3:2 (p. 195) Matthew uses the term "kingdom" (usually "of heaven") in every chapter except chapters 14, 15, 17, 27, and 28. For explanation of the term see pp. 87, 249, 250.*	*55–57, 151, 152, 165–174, 333, 365, 366, 383, 384, 398, 399, 496, 670. For explanation of the term see pp. 56, 57.*	*Beginning with 1:33 (p. 86) Luke uses the word "kingdom" (usually "of God") in every chapter except chapters 2, 3, 15, 20, and 24. For explanation of the term see on 1:33 (p. 86); on 4:43f. (pp. 272–274); and on 17:21 (pp. 804, 805).*
Knowledge			59, 60, 127, 643, 644
Laborers in the Vineyard, The, Parable of	735–740		
Lamp	285, 286, 346, 347, 875–877	161, 162	430, 630–632, 676, 677, 748
Law Experts	808		399, 590–592, 595, 640–644, 720, 721
Law of God ("the law," "the law of Moses," "the law of the Lord")	288f., 366, 490, 513, 514, 613, 614, 807–810, 831–836		163–166, 177, 293, 294, 592, 774, 775, 1074, 1075
Lazarus (of the parable)			782–787
Leaven. *See* Yeast.			

	Matthew	Mark	Luke
Leaven, The, Parable of	567, 568		703–705
Lepers, Cleansing of	388–394, 457, 484, 898	77–81, 83, 556–558	256, 258, 288–290, 393, 797–799
Lepton		506, 507	920
Levi. *See* Matthew.			
Life, Everlasting	370, 371, 691, 692, 723, 724, 730, 731, 891, 892	115, 116, 331, 332, 365, 366, 389, 390, 401, 402, 414–416	126, 127, 322, 323, 428, 499, 591, 662, 665, 735, 808, 830–832, 837, 838, 944
Light	242–244, 284–286, 346, 347, 465, 466, 862, 863	536	129, 168, 430, 630–632, 650, 651, 770
Lord	*Beginning with 1:20 this word occurs in every chapter of Matthew except 6 and 19. It occurs more than 70 times in all. See especially on 7:21–23; pp. 375–378.*	*Beginning with 1:3 this word is found in every chapter of Mark except 6, 8, 14, and 15; in all, 18 times. See especially on 11:3; pp. 433–435.*	*Beginning with 1:6 this word occurs in every chapter of Luke except 8, 15, and 21; in all more than 100 times. See especially on 3:4–6; pp. 201–203, and on 20:41–44; pp. 908, 909.*
Lord's Prayer, The. *See* Prayer, The Lord's.			
Lord's Supper, The, Institution of	908–912	571–576	961–964
Lost Coin, The, Parable of			748–749
Lost Sheep, The, Parable of	695–697		743–747
Lost Son, The, Parable of			752–758
Lot			807–808
Love	312–316, 321, 322, 347, 348, 475, 476, 725, 809, 810, 823, 824, 852	395, 492–495	346–349, 352–355, 407–409, 592, 638, 639, 772, 773
Luke, the Gospel Writer			3–15
Lysanias			195, 197
Maccabees	127, 156f.		

	Matthew	Mark	Luke
Pontius Pilate	188, 941, 942, 949	627–641, 668–671	195, 693, 694, 1007–1013, 1018, 1019, 1042, 1043
Prayer, Praying	321–324, 360–363, 675, 676, 769, 775, 916–921	451, 452, 454, 460–462, 502–504, 582–590	69–70, 173, 216–218, 291, 307–309, 325, 326, 493, 503, 607–614, 818–821, 880, 881, 911, 973, 974, 981–984
Prayer, The Lord's	324–340		608–610
Predestination, Divine	798, 862, 865, 907, 926	532–534, 571	155, 156, 582, 669, 670, 817, 964, 977, 1029, 1064, 1065, 1074, 1075
Predictions of the Lord's Passion and Resurrection, The Three	9, 653, 654, 676, 741–743	326, 327, 352–354, 403–407	496, 497, 516–518, 838–841
Preservation, Divine	343–346		669, 670, 974, 981, 982
Priests, Chief Priests, and High Priests	166, 512–514, 653, 654, 742, 743, 771, 776, 777, 787	549, 562, 593–597, 602–606, 609–615	64, 65, 67, 68, 195, 197, 290, 291, 319, 497, 594, 798, 881, 887, 888, 895, 954, 955, 987, 988, 997–999, 1009, 1011, 1012, 1015, 1018
Prologue, Luke's			53–60
Prophetess. *See* Anna.			
Prophets and Prophecy. *See also* False Prophets.	280, 288f., 478, 486, 490f., 557, 582, 587f., 642, 767f., 777f., 787, 809, 835–839, 926f.	223, 234, 235, 324, 467, 532–534	124, 125, 127, 172, 201–203, 249–255, 258, 342, 343, 387, 388, 396, 397, 407, 475, 494, 584, 585, 625–630, 642, 643, 707–711, 787, 805–809, 838–841, 921–944, 977, 998, 999, 1064, 1065, 1074, 1075
Prophets, What was spoken (or written) through the prophets, or something similar.	133, 166, 178, 188, 197, 198, 242, 400, 519, 520, 554, 555, 568, 569, 614, 764	31, 34, 274, 343, 454, 571, 578	124, 125, 201, 234, 237, 239, 251, 396, 397, 838, 880, 881, 893, 938, 977, 1074, 1075

	Matthew	Mark	Luke
Prophetic Fore-shortening	205, 206, 467, 468, 659, 660	526	937
Prostitutes	779		757
Publicans. *See* Tax Collectors.			
"Q"	47–49		22, 23, 26, 27
Quadrant		506	920
Queen of the South (=Queen of Sheba)	536–541		628
Quirinius			139, 140
Qumran. *See also* W. Hendriksen, *Survey of the Bible,* pp. 24–30.	47, 154, 506	15, 38, 242	419, 593
Rash Builder, The, Parable of			735, 736
Reaper, Reaping. *See* Harvest and Reaping.			
Reasonable (and implied Reckless) King, The, Para-of			736, 737
Rejected (or Slighted) Invitation, The, Parable of			730–734
Reserved (or Chief) Seats, The, Parable of			721–723
Resurrection of Jesus	653, 654, 669, 677, 742, 743, 786, 913, 914, 980–996	327, 328, 341, 342, 352–354, 405, 406, 475, 579, 677f.	517, 839, 840, 895, 1051–1076
Resurrection of Others a. The Ruler's Daughter	429, 430, 432–434	202, 203, 211–216	453–456, 460–464
b. The Dead (in general)	484, 485		725
c. Whose Wife?	804–807	484–489	903–908
d. Calvary Saints	975, 976		

	Matthew	Mark	Luke
Signs of the Times, Signs and Wonders	636, 637, 843–864	511–536	684, 805–809
Simeon			165–171
Simon of Cyrene	962–964	647–649	1022–1024
Simon Peter	245, 248, 398, 450–452, 601–603, 642–656, 677–679, 703, 704, 729–732, 914–925, 935–937	58–61, 67–69, 72, 73, 124, 125, 212, 213, 324, 325, 328, 337, 338, 340, 341, 401, 402, 577–582, 585, 588, 589, 602, 615–622, 681	268, 279–286, 328, 458, 494, 495, 503–506, 837, 838, 956, 973, 974, 993–996
Simon, Son of Mattathias	161, 162		
Simon the Cananaean (or: the Zealot)	450, 452, 454	127	330
Simon the Leper	898	556, 558	
Simon the Pharisee			405–410
Solomon	116, 117, 118, 119, 173, 352, 537, 538		628, 667
Son of David (=Jesus)	105–111, 434, 435, 523, 524, 621, 622, 753, 754, 766, 771, 772, 810–812	419, 420, 498–501	841–845, 908, 909
Son of God, Son of the Living God, God's Son, "my (beloved) Son" (= Jesus, according to his divine nature)	215, 216, 225, 226, 228, 229, 414, 603, 643, 931, 932, 965–968, 976, 977	17, 31–34, 121, 122, 190, 191, 610–613, 666, 667	86–88, 233, 237, 238, 269, 507, 584, 999
Son of Man (=Jesus). *The list of passages for Matthew, Mark, and Luke is found on p. 406 of N.T.C. on Matthew.*	403–407		
Sower, The, Parable of	550–552, 557–562	147–151, 154–161	421–423, 426–429
Sparrows	472, 473		653, 654
Speech, Taking away and/or Re-	436–438, 523–525, 626–628	301–306, 344–352	74–77, 117, 617

	Matthew	Mark	Luke
Thomas (Didymus)	450, 451, 453	124, 127	330, 1066
Tiberius Emperor	803		195, 197–199
Transfiguration, Christ's	660, 663–672	337–344	503–508
Treasure, The, Parable of the Hidden	575, 576		
Treasure, Treasury	171f., 343, 344, 346, 530, 575, 576, 579, 726, 944, 945	396, 505–507	363, 364, 664, 670, 671, 834, 919
Triumphal Entry, Christ's	759–768	429–440	871–879
Troubled (or Embarrassed) Host, The, Parable of			610–614
Trust. *See* Faith.			
Two Builders, The, Parable of	379–382		365–368
Two Debtors, The, Parable of			407–410
Two Sons, The, Parable of	778–780		
Tyre and Sidon	494–496, 621	119, 293f., 302	334, 577
Unclean Spirit, uncleanness	449, 539, 540, 834	64–67, 121, 139, 140, 188, 189, 191, 192, 193, 194, 225–227, 298	264, 265, 335, 445, 446, 511–516, 622–624
Unjust Steward, The, Parable of. *See* Shrewd Manager			
Unleavened Bread, Feast of	903, 904	553, 566	953–958
Unmerciful Servant, The, Parable of	703–709		
Unpardonable Sin, The	527–529	134–140	655, 656
Unprofitable Servant. *See* Coldly Calculating Ser-			

	Matthew	Mark	Luke
vant, The, Parable of			
Vine, Vineyard. *See also* Laborers in the Vineyard, The, Parable of	778–780, 781–785	471–478, 575, 576	890–895, 961
Virgin Birth, Christ's	130–146		82–90, 135–146, 220–225
Watchful Servants, The, Parable of			676–678
Wicked Sharecrop-pers (or Tenants), The, Parable of	781–788	471–478	890–895
Widow Who Perse-vered, The, Para-ble of			815–818
Widows			
a. Anna			171–174
b. W. of Zar-ephath			256, 258
c. W. of Nain			381–388
d. The Persever-ing W.			815–818
e. Their Houses Devoured		502–504	910, 911
f. The W. Who Gave All		505–508	919–921
Wisdom	493, 537, 538, 581	219, 222	179, 180, 186, 187, 401, 642
Wise Men from the East	149–176		
Withered Fig Tree, The	773–775	440–443, 456–461	
Withered Hand, Healing of the Man with	516–518	113–118	320–324
Woes	494–496, 691, 817–839, 859, 907	502–505, 528, 529, 571	343, 344, 576–579, 638–644, 794, 938, 964
Women. For Wid-	302, 303, 430–432,	204–211, 298–302,	43, 95, 96, 397, 417–

	Matthew	Mark	Luke
ows *see separate entry.*	567, 568, 621–626, 804–807, 898–901	379–381, 484–489, 556–562, 667, 668	421, 808, 809, 1024–1026, 1037, 1038, 1044, 1045, 1062, 1063
a. Sinful *(actually penitent)* Woman			405–410
b. W. Who touched Christ's Garment	430–432	204–211	456–460
c. W. Who Pronounced a Blessing on Jesus' Mother			624, 625
d. W. of Canaan (Syrophoenician W.). *See* Canaanite W.			
e. W. Who Successively Married 7 Husbands	804–807	484–489	903–908
f. Crippled or Bent W., victim of spondylitis deformans or sp. ankylopoeietica. *See* J. Wilkinson, *EQ,* 49 (1977), pp. 195–205.			699–702
g. W. Who Lost a Piece of Silver. *See* Lost Coin. *Also see separate entries; for example, on* Mary, Martha, *etc.*			
h. Ministering Women	977–979	667, 668	417–421, 1037, 1038
i. Simon's Mother-in-law			268, 269
Worry	348–355, 464, 470–473, 602, 668, 669	209–211, 211–216, 679, 680	599, 652–654, 657, 665–671, 932, 933, 941, 944
Xerxes' Queen	588		

	Matthew	Mark	Luke
Vashti compared with Queen Herodias			
Yeast of the Pharisees and Sadducees (or: and of Herod).	638–640	317–320	
"Yes"	306–309, 436, 486, 579, 772		396, 625, 653
YHWH	327, 328		609, 907
Yodh. *See* Iota and Keraia.			
Zaccheus			853–857
Zarephath			256, 258
Zebedee, His Wife and Their Sons. *See also* James, Son of Z.; John, Son of Z.	248, 450–452, 663, 664, 744, 745, 916	61, 62, 124–126, 338, 407–413, 585, 586	283
Zechariah (husband of Elizabeth and father of John the Baptist)			64, 65, 67–77, 93, 114, 121, 122, 195
Zechariah (who was murdered)	837–839		642, 643